DECISION SUPPORT SYSTEMS

A KNOWLEDGE-BASED APPROACH

DECISION SUPPORT SYSTEMS

A KNOWLEDGE-BASED APPROACH

CLYDE W. HOLSAPPLE
The University of Kentucky

ANDREW B. WHINSTON
The University of Texas at Austin

COURSE
TECHNOLOGY

ONE MAIN STREET, CAMBRIDGE, MA 02142

an International Thomson Publishing company I(T)P®

Cambridge • Albany • Bonn • Boston • Cincinnati • London • Madrid • Melbourne • Mexico City
New York • Paris • San Francisco • Singapore • Tokyo • Toronto • Washington

PRODUCTION CREDITS

Copyeditor: Linda Thompson
Cover & Text Design: Lois Stanfield, LightSource Images
Artist: Randy Miyake/Miyake Illustration
Index: Northwind Editorial Services
Composition: Parkwood Composition
Text credits follow the Index

A NOTE ON THE TYPE

Decision Support Systems: A Knowledge-Based Approach is set in ten-point Garamond. Various weights of ITC Kabel are used for heads and other display elements. The computer code is set in Courier Bold.

For more information contact:

Course Technology
One Main Street
Cambridge, MA 02142

International Thomson Publishing Europe
Berkshire House 168-173
High Holborn
London WCIV 7AA
England

Thomas Nelson Australia
102 Dodds Street
South Melbourne, 3205
Victoria, Australia

Nelson Canada
1120 Birchmount Road
Scarborough, Ontario
Canada M1K 5G4

International Thomson Editores
Campos Eliseos 385, Piso 7
Col. Polanco
11560 Mexico D.F. Mexico

International Thomson Publishing GmbH
Königswinterer Strasse 418
53227 Bonn
Germany

International Thomson Publishing Asia
211 Henderson Road
#05-10 Henderson Building
Singapore 0315

International Thomson Publishing Japan
Hirakawacho Kyowa Building, 3F
2-2-1 Hirakawacho
Chiyoda-ku, Tokyo 102
Japan

Printed in the United States of America

ISBN 0-314-06510-5

10 9 8 7 6 5 4 3 2

Dedicated with love and
gratitude to our families
Carol, Christiana, and Claire
and Veronika, Juliet, and Stephen

CONTENTS

*Denotes sections that may be skipped in an accelerated coverage of Part One.

PREFACE

OVERVIEW

In the course of their decision activities, managers work with many pieces of knowledge. Some of this knowledge is descriptive, characterizing the state of past, present, future, or hypothetical worlds. Such knowledge is commonly called information, or data. Other pieces of knowledge are procedural in nature, specifying how to accomplish various tasks. In addition to "know what" (information) and "know how" (procedures), a manager may work with reasoning knowledge on the way toward reaching a decision. This third kind of knowledge indicates that certain conclusions are valid under particular circumstances. Two other kinds of knowledge are involved in communication. One is linguistic knowledge, which enables a manager to understand incoming messages. Conversely, a manager works with presentation knowledge when constructing outgoing messages.

Managers are first and foremost knowledge workers who are involved in the making of decisions. Sometimes a manager makes decisions individually. In other cases, decision making may be distributed, involving the combined and coordinated efforts of many knowledge workers. Both individual and distributed decision making are susceptible to support by systems that facilitate, expand, or enhance a manager's ability to work with one or more kinds of knowledge. Such knowledge-based systems are called decision support systems (DSSs).

This book focuses on computerized decision support systems, emphasizing a knowledge-based perspective. With the relentless advances in the technology and economics of computers, we are rapidly reaching the point where a manager's success depends on his or her understanding of DSS possibilities and skill in DSS application. This book is designed to foster a comprehensive understanding of DSS possibilities and, used with workbook supplements of an instructor's choosing, impart practical DSS development and usage skills.

Many DSSs are oriented toward individual decision support. There is growing interest in DSSs that directly support distributed decision making at the group, organization, and interorganization levels. Both individual and multiparticipant DSS orientations are examined in this book.

Decision support systems also differ with respect to the kinds of knowledge they help manage. The majority of conventional DSSs have been devised to help manage primarily descriptive and procedural knowledge. In contrast, there is a class of artificially intelligent DSSs concerned mainly with the representation and processing of reasoning knowledge. We examine both conventional and artificially intelligent DSSs in this book. Indeed, we explore computer-assisted management of every major type of knowledge relevant to supporting decision activities.

AUDIENCE

Although this book is designed especially for students in management and business schools, we expect that many practicing decision makers will also find its fresh perspective of interest. We assume that the reader has some basic familiarity with computers (e.g., the distinction between secondary and primary memory, the role of an operating system). This knowledge can be attained through prior coursework or experience. Alternatively, selected workbook supplements used with the book may begin with an examination of salient computer basics.

The text is appropriate for an advanced undergraduate course in decision support systems. We envision it as the backbone for such a course, furnishing a unified view of DSS concepts and possibilities. Most likely, the course instructor will also want to give students hands-on experiences in developing or using DSSs. Recognizing the diversity of instructor needs and tastes in providing such experiences, we have deliberately avoided tying the book to any particular software packages. As such, it can readily be used in tandem with any of the many presently available workbooks that offer tutorials on the use of various popular software tools for managing knowledge. Examples includes the West *Understanding and Using* Series of software tutorials. Thus, it is straightforward for an instructor to give students a firsthand understanding of selected knowledge management techniques to be used in developing their own prototype DSSs during the course.

The book is also appropriate for graduate courses on decision support systems. At the master's level, workbook supplements may also be used to complement the text. We have found it valuable to form master's students into teams, where each team is responsible for identifying a DSS need (based on team members' experiences), developing a DSS to meet that need (using tools covered in prior courses or supplemental workbooks), and demonstrating the DSS to the rest of the class. At the doctoral level, we have used the text as a basis for discussion of research directions and for organizing readings assignments from journals. At this level, individual projects of DSS development have been used successfully, plus the assignment of writing and presenting tutorial or critique papers on DSS-related topics.

ORGANIZATION AND LEARNING AIDS

Decision Support Systems: A Knowledge-Based Approach is organized into five major parts. Part One, "Decision Making and Knowledge" (Chapters 1–4), furnishes a contextual knowledge-oriented platform for understanding the issues and possibilities of computer-based decision support. Part Two, "Foundations of Decision Support Systems" (Chapters 5–8), examines the nature of decision support systems and how they are developed. Part Three, "Knowledge-Management Techniques for Decision Support" (Chapters 9–11), surveys the important objects and processing methods for 13 knowledge-management techniques used in decision support systems.

Part Four, "Artificially Intelligent Decision Support Systems" (Chapters 12–15), provides a thorough introduction to decision support systems that embody concepts from the field of artificial intelligence, focusing especially on DSSs that represent and process knowledge in the form of rules. Part Five, "Multiparticipant and Executive Decision Support Systems" (Chapters 16–19), explores the nature of DSSs intended to support multiple participants engaged in decision making plus those specifically oriented toward supporting the decisions of top-level executives.

Each chapter begins with the description of a DSS. These real-world application cases offer practical illustrations of concepts covered in the chapters that they introduce. They can also be used as suggestive starting points for students in developing their own prototype decision support systems. Further guidelines for student projects, along with detailed examples, are given in the case studies that conclude Parts Two through Four. In addition to application descriptions, relevant news items are placed throughout the book to emphasize the practical and topical importance of the material covered.

We have carefully designed the text to promote a unified understanding of important concepts. We have made a concerted effort to avoid producing a book that reads like a collection of lists, consists of a loosely related collection of essays on various topics, or attempts to be a DSS encyclopedia. Aside from the unique knowledge-based perspective that forms the book's unifying theme, a variety of special learning aids are incorporated into each part and each chapter.

For each part, the learning aids include the following:

- *Keynote:* A brief keynote quotation kicks off each part, setting the tone and establishing the significance of its chapters' contents.
- *Preview:* A short preview helps orient readers by indicating the scope of the part and highlighting the contents of each of its chapters.
- *Case study:* Each of the first four parts concludes with a case study that illustrates and integrates topics covered in its chapters. These can be used to stimulate class discussion about those topics and to guide student projects that involve hands-on development of decision support systems.

For each chapter, the learning aids include these:

- *Outline:* An initial chapter outline helps orient readers by showing the flow of concepts to be covered.
- *DSS Insights:* An opening description of a computer system that has been developed to support decision makers gives a practical, real-world context for appreciating the chapter's contents. It introduces and illustrates some of the main ideas covered in the chapter. It also gives insights into actual DSS features and usage in a particular organizational setting.
- *Learning objectives:* Objectives that readers should meet upon completing a chapter are briefly and explicitly stated at the beginning.
- *Special-interest boxes:* Boxes are sprinkled throughout a chapter's main body of text to highlight presented ideas or point out issues of special interest that are related to presented ideas.
- *DSS in the News:* Most chapters contain news items from newspapers and magazines. These news items show that presented ideas are relevant to what is happening in the workplace.
- *Summary:* The summary at the end of a chapter reminds readers of the main concepts that have been presented.
- *Important terms:* There is a list of important terms that should be understood upon completing the chapter. Definitions of these terms appear in the glossary.
- *Application to the DSS Insights:* A set of exercises asks the reader to apply what was learned in the chapter to an analysis of the real-world application that opened the chapter.
- *Review questions:* Review questions at the end of a chapter can help in a self-evaluation of what a reader has learned or can be used for student testing. The

reader can find answers to these questions through a careful reading of the chapter.

- *Discussion topics:* Each chapter's discussion topics are designed to stimulate thinking beyond what we explicitly covered in the chapter. You can use them as a basis for class discussion or as essay questions for student testing. Although the text provides a basic background for addressing the discussion topics, considerable thought and insight are also required. In many cases, there is no single correct position. Consideration of these topics encourages students to develop, express, and justify viewpoints.
- *References:* A set of references includes citations to all publications that served as source material for the chapter. These provide a starting point for further investigation of writings about specific issues. To stay abreast of advances in the DSS field, information about periodicals to monitor on a continuing basis is provided in the directory of publications that follows the glossary.

ANCILLARY MATERIALS

The instructor's manual includes answers to review questions, thoughts on the discussion topics, and responses to the application exercises.

We furnish a large test bank of multiple choice, short essay, and true-false problems. In preparing exams, these can supplement the review questions (which can be readily transformed into problems of the short-answer or fill-in-the-blank variety) and the discussion topics (which can serve as essay problems).

An extensive set of transparency masters for selected figures, tables, and boxes is available. Additional masters furnishing an outline of text topics have been prepared using Microsoft PowerPoint.

We produced a videotape for adopters of the text. It contains demonstrations of prototype DSSs implemented by students who took courses centered around earlier manuscript versions of this book. As such, it shows current students the kinds of systems they could expect to develop as course projects. You could use this tape at the outset of the DSS course to give a visual orientation to what a student will have accomplished by the end of the term. You could also use it at a later point when the student projects are assigned, giving a visual sense of project expectations.

Other ancillary materials include whatever software tools and associated workbook tutorials an instructor may choose to use in the course. Because the possibilities are so varied and we have no intention of forcing all instructors into using a single tool, no such ancillaries accompany the book. They are readily available from a variety of software vendors and book publishers. In many cases, these supplements are already in place at an institution.

In all, the ancillaries are valuable aids in helping the instructor teach a course based on *Decision Support Systems: A Knowledge-Based Approach*.

USING THIS TEXT IN YOUR CURRICULUM

The content of *Decision Support Systems: A Knowledge-Based Approach* is fairly modular and sufficiently flexible to support a wide variety of course needs. These needs are influenced by the backgrounds of students, the course length, the course's position in a business computing curriculum, and the instructor's objectives. For instance, for students whose backgrounds include thorough grounding in the nature of decision making and managerial work, you may skip the first three chapters of Part One. For a quarter-length DSS course, you may omit Part Four and perhaps cover it in a subsequent quarter-length course focusing on business expert systems. If a curriculum's DSS course follows a course that surveys knowledge management techniques, then Part Three may be omitted or merely skimmed. If an instructor's course objectives do not include in-depth coverage of artificially intelligent DSSs, then Part Four may be omitted (with the possible exception of Chapter 12); if examination of executive information systems is not an objective, then Chapter 18 can be skipped; and so forth.

We designed the book to give instructors considerable discretion in the choice of reading assignments to meet their particular courses' needs.

A sample course schedule for undergraduate MIS majors or MBA students is shown in Exhibit A. As indicated before, many adjustments can be made to this schedule, depending on student backgrounds, instructor inclinations, and so on. In the first 6 weeks, for instance, the fraction of class time devoted to the text (as opposed to selected supplements on specific software tools) might range from two-thirds to one-third. In the former case, students would be fairly well versed in software tools but in need of considerable coverage and synthesis regarding basics of management and decision making. In the latter case, students would need only a review of the highlights of Part One (e.g., omitting sections marked with asterisks) but would require more extensive treatment of software tools. This schedule assumes that students (either individually or in groups) will prepare proposals for

EXHIBIT A   Sample Schedule for Undergraduate MIS Majors or MBA Students

Instructor Activities	Week	Student Activities
Cover Chapters 1–6 and software tool basics from supplement.	1	
	2	Do assigned software tool exercises.
	3	
	4	
	5	
Cover Chapters 7–8.	6	
	7	Prepare DSS project proposal.
Cover Chapters 9–11 and advanced tool features from supplement.	8	
	9	Develop DSS prototype.
	10	
Cover Chapters 12–15	11	
and/or	12	
Cover Chapters 16–19.	13	
	14	
View prototype demonstrations.	15	Demonstrate DSS prototype.

EXHIBIT B   Sample Doctoral Course Schedule

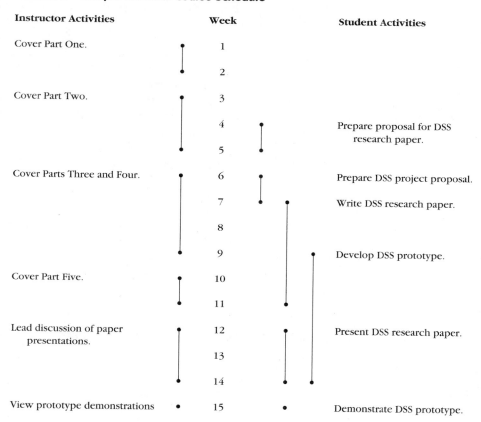

Instructor Activities	Week	Student Activities
Cover Part One.	1	
	2	
Cover Part Two.	3	
	4	Prepare proposal for DSS research paper.
	5	
Cover Parts Three and Four.	6	Prepare DSS project proposal.
	7	Write DSS research paper.
	8	
	9	Develop DSS prototype.
Cover Part Five.	10	
	11	
Lead discussion of paper presentations.	12	Present DSS research paper.
	13	
	14	
View prototype demonstrations	15	Demonstrate DSS prototype.

DSS development projects to be undertaken with selected software tools. Ideally, Chapter 7 should have been covered by the time such proposals are due.

All or portions of Part Three may be considered optional, based on the degree of student grounding in basic knowledge-management techniques. In a curriculum where expert systems are treated in a separate course, an instructor can omit all or portions of Part Four from Exhibit A. The chapters in this part are arranged so that Chapter 15 has the most advanced material and can be omitted if desired. The coverage of Parts Four and Five could be readily interchanged in the schedule.

A sample course schedule for a doctoral course in decision support systems is shown in Exhibit B. It assumes that students are already well versed in the use of specific software tools or that they can become so through their own independent efforts during the course. Research paper topics would probably be chosen from a list of DSS issues that are more advanced that those treated in the book, but for which the book gives a foundation on which to build.

Yet another way to use this book is as the backbone for the core business computing course in a management curriculum. If a management student takes only one business computing course, what should be its content? There are several ways to answer this question. It could be a survey of business computing topics, a study of what information systems professionals do, or coverage of bits, bytes, baud rates, and other technical building blocks. There are many fine books available to address these topics. However, there is another compelling way to answer the question. Because every management student aspires to be a knowledge worker engaged in some kind of decision making, at the minimum he or she should appreciate the concepts and techniques of knowledge management as a foundation for decision making. That is, the core business computing course could well be an exploration of computer-based knowledge management.

This book furnishes a strong and unique conceptual backbone for a knowledge-management course—with software-specific supplements being used to flesh out the applied side. Thus, the student is learning not only about the current features of some software tool for managing knowledge, but also learning about 1) the nature and significance of managing knowledge (Part One), 2) the role of knowledge management in devising computer systems that support decision making of managers (Part Two), 3) the main traits of major computer-based techniques for managing knowledge (Part Three), and 4) the growing importance of knowledge management from an organizational perspective (Part Five). (Part Four is too advanced for an introductory knowledge management course, and more advanced portions of the other Parts can be skipped as well.)

Exhibit C shows one way to organize a knowledge management course that is a core business computing component of a management curriculum. It assumes that

EXHIBIT C   Sample Schedule for a Knowledge-Management Core Course

Instructor Activities	Week	Student Activities
Cover Chapters 1–4 and text management tutorial	1	
	2	Do text management exercises.
	3	
Cover Chapters 5 and 6 and data management tutorial.	4	
	5	Do data management exercises.
	6	
Cover Chapters 9–11 and spreadsheet tutorial.	7	
	8	Do spreadsheet exercises.
	9	
Cover Chapter 7 and graphics tutorial.	10	
	11	Do graphics exercises.
Cover Chapters 8 and 16 and message management tutorial.	12	
	13	Do message management exercises.
	14	
Cover Chapter 19.	15	

EXHIBIT D   Sample Schedule for a Business Expert System Course

Instructor Activities	Week	Student Activities
Introduction and background.	1	
Cover Chapters 12 and 13 in detail.	2	
	3	
	4	
	5	Identify ES opportunity.
Cover Chapter 14 in detail and present tutorial on the tool(s) to be used.	6	
	7	Prepare ES project proposal.
	8	
	9	Develop ES prototype.
	10	
Cover Chapter 15 in detail.	11	
	12	
	13	
Cover Appendices E and F.	14	
View prototype.	15	Demonstrate ES prototype.

the instructor will select a specific software tool or tools that permit students to do hands-on exercises with five knowledge management techniques: text management, data management, spreadsheet management, graphics management, and message management. Of course, the choice and number of knowledge-management techniques as well as the order of their coverage and the supplemental product-specific tutorials used, are at the discretion of the instructor.

The book can also form the heart of a course in business expert systems in a curriculum that treats this subject matter separately from decision support systems. Complementing the text, the instructor would select a specific expert system development tool (e.g., VP-Expert, M.1) and associated tutorial (e.g., *VP-Expert for Business Applications* by Hicks and Lee from Holden-Day, *Developing Knowledge-Based Systems Using an Expert System Shell* by Mockler from Macmillan). Exhibit D illustrates a sample course structure based on the book. The introduction and background could use early parts of the book to provide a context for the detailed study of Part Four (e.g., sections 4.1, 4.3, 4.4, 8.1, 8.2, 8.3, 8.5, 11.5, 11.7, and perhaps other sections from Part Three).

ACKNOWLEDGMENTS

We thank the many students who have taken our decision support system and business expert system courses over the past several years. Their feedback has been instrumental in clarifying and organizing the ideas presented in the text. We also appreciate the feedback from faculty colleagues who have used earlier manuscript versions of the text in their courses.

We are especially grateful to the individuals who have directly contributed portions of the text: Skip Benamati, David Cook, Mary Curtis, Bopana Ganapathy, Dan Jacovitch, Linda Johnson, Doug Maxwell, Ram Pakath, and Meenu Singh. Their contributions underwent a review and revision process and are explicitly identified where they occur in the text.

We would like to acknowledge that portions of Chapters 3, 4, 5, 12, 17, and 19 have been borrowed from the contents of a few of our previously published articles:

"Decision Support in Multiparticipant Decision Makers," *Journal of Computer Information Systems* 31, no. 4, (1991): 37–45.

"Knowledge Management in Decision Making and Decision Support," *Knowledge and Policy* 8, no. 1 (1995): 5–22.

"A Human Metaphor for DSS Research," *Journal of Computer Information Systems* 34, no. 2 (1994): 16–20.

"Business Expert Systems—Gaining a Competitive Edge," *Proceedings of Hawaiian International Conference on Systems Sciences,* Kona, Hawaii (January 1990).

"Implications of Negotiation Theory for Research and Development of Negotiation Support Systems," *Group Decision and Negotiation,* forthcoming 1995 (with H. Lai).

"Knowledge-Based Organizations," *The Information Society* 5, no. 2 (1987): 77–90.

The editorial assistance essential to this project was furnished by our Editor, John Szilagyi, whose guidance and encouragement were indispensable; Susanna Smart, our Developmental Editor, who coordinated and organized input from anonymous reviewers; and Steven Yaeger, our Production Editor, who directed the many operational details that resulted in the final, physical text. We are thankful for all their efforts. We also appreciate the diligent and tireless efforts of Carol Holsapple in preparing our original manuscript and Karen Rivera in handling some of our revisions to it.

Finally, we thank the following reviewers for carefully reading and constructively critiquing our work. Their input resulted in significant improvements to the quality of the final output.

James Buffington
Indiana State University

Joey F. George
Florida State University

Charles K. Davis
University of Houston–Downtown

Amit Gupta
University of Wisconsin–Madison

James H. Gerlach
University of Colorado–Denver

Jack T. Hogue
University of North Carolina–Charlotte

Leonard M. Jessup
University of Idaho

Fred Lupone
Salve Regina College

Fred S. Patterson
St. Edwards University

Stephen R. Ruth
George Mason University

Thomas E. Sandman
California State University–Sacramento

Jung P. Shim
Mississippi State University

Sanjay Singh
University of Alabama–Birmingham

Randall R. Smith
University of Virginia

Edward J. Szcwczak
Canisius College

Jacqueline Wyatt
Middle Tennessee State University

David C. Yen
Miami University–Ohio

Ilze Zigurs
University of Colorado–Boulder

Clyde W. Holsapple, University of Kentucky
Andrew B. Whinston, University of Texas–Austin

Part One

DECISION MAKING AND KNOWLEDGE

. . .[T]rying to define what is unique about DSS technology is not a very useful exercise. The technological building blocks—the hardware and the software components—in isolation distinguish only to a very limited extent DSS from other computer-based systems. The key characteristics of DSS are linked to the context where such systems are to be used, to why and how the systems are developed, and to how the systems are intended to be used. . . . The point is not that technology is of no importance. Rather, it is an argument for keeping our attention focused on the central theme: Better decisions and decision support. *A viable DSS-school should provide a perspective on how we might apply any technology, existing and future, as a means to achieve these ends.*

— DR. CHARLES STABELL, Professor of Administrative and Cognitive
Sciences, Norwegian School of Management, Oslo, Norway

"Decision Support Systems: Alternative Perspectives and Schools," *Decision Support Systems, 3, no. 3: 1987 243, 250*

The study of decision support systems (DSS) has many technical aspects. But before delving into these, it is important to appreciate the setting in which they are used. The setting is a competitive, knowledge-rich world in which managers make decisions about what to do with their organizations' resources. Many decisions, ranging from simple to complex, are made every day. Each decision involves the use of knowledge of varying kinds and amounts, and many can benefit from (or even require) the use of technology known as decision support systems.

Part One establishes the context for understanding decision support systems from a knowledge-based viewpoint. This context emphasizes the place of managers in organizations, of decision making in management, and of knowledge in decision making.

Chapter 1 introduces a seven-point perspective of managerial work as a basis for subsequent chapters' treatments of decision making and knowledge. This perspective considers the manager's task of structuring an organization's resources to fulfill specified purposes in the face of a dynamic environment. Traditional characterizations of the functions managers perform and the roles they play also contribute to the seven-point perspective.

Chapter 2 examines the notion of decision making in more detail. It presents the classical view of decision making as an activity of choosing from among alternatives and the complementary knowledge-oriented view of manufacturing a piece of knowledge about what to do. The chapter examines the setting in which decisions are made from several angles, because the setting can influence the kind of decision support that is warranted. Similarly, it looks at ways of classifying decisions, because the type of decision can influence what decision support features are appropriate.

Chapter 3 continues the survey of decision making by focusing on decision makers and decision processes. Different kinds of decision makers are identified as a basis for understanding decision support variations. The process of making a decision is characterized as a flow of various problem-solving episodes, typically involving three phases and guided by some strategy. Decision support systems differ in terms of the kinds of episodes, phases, and strategies they support.

Chapter 4 explores the major flows of knowledge involved in manufacturing a decision and draws an important distinction between acquiring knowledge and deriving it. A number of computer-based techniques for managing knowledge are cited, and their value in being incorporated into decision support systems is considered. Knowledge management is concerned with more than specific computer-based techniques. It also encompasses an appreciation of the distinctions among various types of knowledge, because some techniques are better at handling one type of knowledge than another. The developer of a DSS must be aware of such distinctions.

The case study that concludes Part One pulls together much of the content from the first four chapters to synthesize a unified view of the main ideas in an applied setting. The case exercises give a way to apply what has been learned from the four chapters, to draw on prior knowledge of technology, and to anticipate some of the topics of the remainder of the book.

Chapter 1

MANAGING TO EXCEL

*Denotes sections that may be skipped in an accelerated coverage of this chapter.

DSS INSIGHTS

MONSANTO: A DSS FOR SHIP-SCHEDULING DECISIONS

Overview

Monsanto has one ocean-going chemical tanker vessel, the S.S. Edgar Queeny, transporting chemicals up and down the east coast of the United States and in the Gulf of Mexico. The vessel's main purpose is to deliver chemicals from Monsanto plants to customers, but it also carries chemicals for outside clients on a contract basis or when space is available. Annual contracts with other companies are on a take-or-pay basis, meaning that the customer pays for their contract space whether they use it or not.

The schedule alternative that will best maximize ship usage and minimize operations cost must be selected. This schedule consists of the ports of call and the dates and times of arrival and departure for each port. The different alternatives available result from selecting steaming speed, which determines how many trips can be made per year.

Maximizing the number of trips per year will provide the most outside income but will also increase costs. Also, management frequently needs to determine the impact of taking on the additional loads that are available from outside sources because they may require additional stops.

To help management at Monsanto to select the best schedule, a decision support system (DSS) was developed. The users of the DSS are the management staff of the distribution department. . . .

. . . [T]he DSS allowed management to evaluate a large number of alternatives rapidly. . . . Because the decision makers required a quick response, the DSS was developed in an interactive computing environment.

Example

. . . [S]uppose the vessel manager wishes to evaluate the impact on the schedule and on costs of an additional load he has the opportunity to obtain. This additional load will require an extra stop for loading and one for unloading. The manager would first use the DSS to simulate his current trip plan without the additional stop. He may analyze the current trip plan at different steaming speeds to evaluate the effect on time and cost.

After completing this analysis he inserts the data for the additional load and simulates different voyages at different steaming speeds, including the additional ports. One of the first questions would be, Can the steaming speed for the voyage be increased so that the additional stops cause little or no increase in total voyage trip time? The manager would also examine the effects this faster steaming speed would have on fuel consumption and operating expenses. He would then compare the increase in costs with the added revenue to determine whether the load would be profitable or not. In some cases, the amount the potential customer should be charged for the additional load could be calculated using this approach. By using the DSS the manager can make this evaluation in minutes instead of hours.

Benefits

Currently, the main use of the DSS is planning voyage itineraries. The DSS saves an estimated $20,000 per year by reducing the management and clerical time needed. . . .

continued

The DSS is also used to analyze steaming speed, to evaluate potential additional loads, and to estimate the effects of changes in costs. . .on vessel operations. Because these applications are performed as needed, evaluating potential savings from these applications is difficult.

The DSS was developed for an internal company cost of $2,500, in several days. . . .

Condensed quotation from R.F. Boykin and R. R. Levary, "An Interactive Decision Support System for Analyzing Ship Voyage Alternatives," in *Interfaces*, 15, no. 2 (1985): 81–84.

LEARNING OBJECTIVES

The Monsanto case illustrates the role of decision making in managerial work. It shows that there can be many considerations involved in making a decision and that the decisions made can impact the organization in which managers work. The decision support system (DSS) helped managers excel by storing and processing large amounts of knowledge relevant to the decisions being made. Keep the Monsanto case in mind as you study this chapter.

After studying this chapter, you should be able to

1. Explain what managers do and describe what you would do as a manager.
2. Describe the general nature of organizations that you may someday manage.
3. Cite the four major resources of organizations and explain what managers do with them.
4. Identify the various functions or roles that describe the work a manager performs.
5. Explain relationships that exist among management, knowledge, decision making, and technology.

To check on your progress and reinforce what you have learned, three kinds of exercises are provided at the end of the chapter. Some allow you to apply what you have learned by analyzing the Monsanto case with respect to the learning objectives. Review questions can be used to sharpen your understanding. Discussion topics are intended to stimulate your thinking to build on what is presented.

1.1 INTRODUCTION

In its 65th anniversary issue, *Business Week* presents a special report on rethinking the nature of work—arguing that economic and technological forces are producing a radical redefinition of work and the workplace. "Better technology, better processes, and fewer better workers. The ideal: Technology that actually helps workers make decisions, in organizations that encourage them to do so. That's the promise of computers, just now starting the be realized" (Hammonds, Kelly, and Thurston 1994, 81). Known as decision support systems, this technology is what we are about to explore from several vantage points. What is the organizational setting in which such systems exist? What are their major features? How are these systems created? How can they be made to exhibit artificial intelligence? How can they support the decision making of individuals (from line workers to executives), groups, teams, and entire organizations? This book provides answers to such questions about a technology of fundamental importance to individuals, organizations, and nations.

THE IMPORTANCE OF KNOWLEDGE

For centuries, managers have used the **knowledge** available to them to make **decisions** shaping the world in which they lived. The impacts of managers' decisions have ranged from those affecting the world in some small or fleeting way to those of global and lasting proportions. Over the centuries, the number of decisions being made per time period has tended to increase. The complexity of decision activities has grown. The amount of knowledge used in making decisions has exploded (Toffler 1970; Drucker 1994). There is no sign that these trends are about to stop. If anything, they appear to be accelerating. At the same time, many devices—from the abacus to modern computers—have been invented that support decision making in various ways.

THE IMPORTANCE OF DECISION MAKING

Decisions made by today's managers in business, government, and other organizations play an important part in determining the landscape of tomorrow's world. In seeking to join in the **decision-making** process, students in schools of business administration, public administration, and management need to acquire a practical understanding of the decision support possibilities afforded by **computers.** Failure to do so leaves the prospective manager at a severe disadvantage, because others are using computer systems to handle large volumes of complex data involved in making decisions. We call these computer systems **decision support systems.** They allow managers to be more productive in the sense of facilitating more effective and more efficient decision making.

DSS IN THE NEWS

Information Technology Drives Productivity

. . . Productivity numbers probably far understate the critical role of information technology and services in driving growth.

. . . Just as the U.S. economy today would be unthinkable without electricity, so will tomorrow's economy be spurred by . . . free flow of information. Judging by the explosive growth of information technology so far, the juice is only starting to flow.

M. J. Mandel, "The Digital Juggernaut," *Business Week,* Special 1994 Bonus Issue, pp. 26, 31.

THE RISE OF THE KNOWLEDGE WORKER AND TECHNOLOGICAL SUPPORT

"By the end of this century knowledge workers will make up a third or more of the work force in the United States—as large a proportion as manufacturing workers ever made up, except in wartime. The majority of them will be paid at least as well as, or better than, manufacturing workers ever were. And the new jobs offer much greater opportunities.

"But—and this is a big but—the great majority of the new jobs require qualifications the industrial worker does not possess and is poorly equipped to acquire. They require a great deal of formal education and the ability to acquire and apply theoretical knowledge. They require a different approach to work and a different mind-set. Above all, they require a habit of continuous learning." —**Peter F. Drucker,** Professor of Social Sciences and Management, Claremont Graduate School in "The Age of Social Transformation," p. 62

"Managers who fail to understand the potential that modern technology offers will fall by the wayside in this highly competitive world. The requirement is not to convert people into technologists, but rather to have a sense of awareness of what these devices can and cannot do.

"We are finally reaching a stage in our society when computer technology in the hands of truly creative people is being used as it's meant to be: to amplify man's intelligence and provide a business life-style that is more rewarding and productive."
—**Buck Rodgers,** IBM Vice President of Marketing (retired) in *The IBM Way,* p. 121

PRELIMINARIES FOR STUDYING DECISION SUPPORT SYSTEMS

Before we can clearly consider the characteristics of decision support systems that exist today and those that might exist tomorrow, we need to examine three preliminaries: management, decision making, and knowledge. In the present chapter, the focus is on management, as the context for studying decision making in Chapters 2 and 3. Understanding what it means to make a decision provides a useful basis for exploring decision support possibilities. The topic of knowledge is examined in detail in Chapter 4. Understanding the nature of knowledge gives a starting point for appreciating various ways in which computers might support a manager's use of knowledge during the making of a decision.

The examination of managerial activity leads through a consideration of organizations. **Managers** both exist in organizations and shape them. One way to characterize a manager's work is in terms of functions that he or she performs. Another view is based on the roles a manager plays. Drawing on these two viewpoints, we establish the working perspective of managerial activity that will guide our exploration of decision making, knowledge handling, and decision support.

1.2 MANAGERIAL WORK

An appreciation of what managers do allows us to see where decision support systems can fit in the overall scheme of managerial work. The coursework typically offered to students of management usually gives many glimpses of what managers do. Courses in finance, accounting, marketing, production, purchasing, personnel, economics, and computer systems have traditionally concentrated on imparting specific knowledge and developing certain skills that a manager might employ in the course of his or her work (Farmer 1984). Although this is essential, it does not give the "big picture" of what management is all about. Capstone courses dealing with policy and strategy often attempt to provide that picture by requiring students to exercise the specialized knowledge gleaned from various courses in the context of making a decision.

Here, we complement traditional coursework by taking an organized look at the big picture first, reviewing and synthesizing ideas that may have been encountered in a variety of preparatory courses. The result is a background that allows study of decision support systems in perspective. Against this background, succeeding chapters sketch out what every student should understand about the nature, development, and use of decision support systems. In other words, decision support systems do not exist in a vacuum. Rather than examining them in isolation, the text seeks to identify those aspects of managerial work that can benefit from decision support systems.

1.3 AN ORGANIZATION*

The existence of managers implies there is something to be managed. In broadest terms, that something is an **organization** (Miner 1978). As Figure 1.1 suggests, organizations differ in terms of such features as orientation, size, and duration. These variations give rise to a broad range of organizations in which management, decision making, and decision support can occur.

DSS IN THE NEWS

Technoid and Strategist

. . . In the early 1980s, the chief information officer was often a technoid, caught up in the wonderful and ultimately pointless things that could be done with technology. . . .

By the latter part of the decade, attention had shifted to aligning systems with business goals, and chief information officers suddenly began presenting themselves as business strategists. Some companies went so far as to hire CIOs with no technology training whatsoever.

Now the pendulum is starting to swing back to a more technologically oriented information executive. . . .

. . . It's not enough for the new generation of CIOs to understand technology. They also must understand the value of information within their businesses and how systems can be deployed to improve competitiveness. . . .

M. Mehler, "CEO Briefing on Information Technology," *Investor's Business Daily,* 16 December 1993, p. 4.

WHAT DOES A MANAGER DO?

In trying to appreciate what a manager does, it is useful to keep the following questions in mind (Mintzberg 1973). After reading this chapter, you should be better able to answer them.

- What activities does a manager perform?
- What kinds of knowledge does a manager process?
- What characteristics of managerial work distinguish it from other types of work?
- What is of interest about the tools a manager uses, the activities in which he or she prefers to engage, the flow of these activities, the use of time, and the pressures experienced?
- What roles does a manager play in accomplishing his or her work?
- What variations exist among managerial jobs and why?
- To what extent is management a science and manager's work repetitive, systematic, or predictable?

ORIENTATION*

A spectrum of orientation from private organizations, such as limited partnerships, to public organizations, such as governmental agencies, exists. Strictly private organizations are not generally open to widespread participation, their behavior is not readily observable, and their actions are devoted to a particular group or class. On the other hand, purely public organizations are open to universal participation, permit their behaviors to be easily observed, and devote their actions toward achieving universal impacts. There are, of course, various kinds of participation, such as financial participation, electoral participation, and employment.

Most organizations probably lie between these two extremes, having some private and some public aspects. Coursework in public administration is concerned with the management of organizations near the public end of the spectrum.

FIGURE 1.1   Some Dimensions of Organization

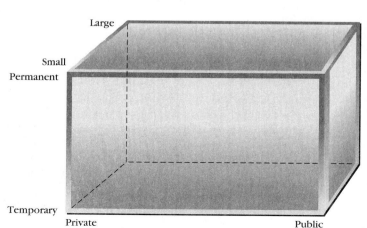

> ## THE CHANGING NATURE OF WORK
>
> "Computer-based technologies are not neutral; they embody essential characteristics that are bound to alter the nature of work within our factories and offices, and among workers, professionals, and managers. New choices are laid open by these technologies, and these choices are being confronted in the daily lives of men and women across the landscape of modern organizations." — **Shoshan Zuboff**, in *In the Age of the Smart Machine*, p. 7

Business administration coursework is more concerned with management of organizations in the middle or toward the private end of the range. A decision support systems course belongs in both curricula, because both can benefit from computer-based support of decision making.

SIZE*

The size of organizations ranges from small to large. One way to measure organization size is in terms of the number of people who participate in it: from only one person to millions. A very different measure of organization size involves such monetary terms as assets or revenues. Yet another measure of size is the material an organization possesses, including the land, buildings, machines, and natural resources it has or controls. A fourth way of looking at size is in terms of the knowledge an organization possesses. Decision support systems can allow organizations to grow by enlarging their pools of knowledge and can help an organization's managers make better use of available knowledge.

DURATION*

Some organizations have persisted for more than a thousand years. Others do not last long. In some cases, the dissolution of an organization may have been planned from its inception: it ceases to exist once its ordained purpose has been fulfilled. In

DSS IN THE NEWS

Cashing In

Chief information officers are cashing in on the growing importance of technology in corporate America, according to a survey released recently by Edward Perlin Associates, a management consulting firm based in New York.

In the last 10 years, total cash compensation of data processing heads and chief information officers has risen to an average of $407,400 from $159,000. . . .

The survey gathered information on technology executives' salaries at some of America's largest corporations. . . .

K. Doler, "CEO Briefing on Information Technology," *Investor's Business Daily*, 1 July 1993, p. 4.

other cases, dissolution is unanticipated and perhaps not desired by the organization's participants. Each year in the United States there are thousands of business failures, many of which can be traced to the decisions made by their managers. We can speculate that with better support, the managers' decisions may have been different, perhaps leading to organizations that would have survived by better adapting to the changing world in which they operated. Even in the case of a persisting organization, technical support of a manager's decision activities may very well enhance the organization's performance. Rather than just getting by, management is able to excel.

1.4 ASPECTS OF AN ORGANIZATION

To this point we have used the term *organization* without defining it. Precisely what is an organization? Regardless of orientation, size, or duration, what do organizations have in common? Definitions in textbooks on organization behavior often define organizations in terms of systematic patterns of interaction among social entities (e.g., Katz and Kahn 1978; Daft 1986). Although not precluding this view, the following definition admits other elements in addition to social (i.e., human) entities. For purposes of this book we shall think of an organization as

> a *system*
>   of *resources*
>   *structured* by
>   *power centers* to
>   achieve some *purposes*
>   within some *environment*

The ensuing discussion elaborates on each of these six notions. This conception of an organization is consistent with general systems theory (Laszlo 1972).

DEFINITION OF A SYSTEM

In general terms, a **system** is an interdependent collection of elements that interact with each other in regular, nonrandom ways and form a unified whole. This

DSS IN THE NEWS

Digital Juggernaut

. . . [C]omputers and other information technology now make up nearly half of all business spending on equipment [not including billions spent annually on programmers and software]. . . .

[M.I.T. researchers] Erik Brynjolfsson and Lorin Hitt . . . surveyed 400 large companies to gauge the effect of technology on output per employee. They found . . . return on investment in information systems exceeded 50%.

M. J. Mandel, "The Digital Juggernaut," *Business Week*, Special 1994 Bonus Issue, pp. 23, 26.

unified whole can be studied from either of two perspectives. We can explore it internally to understand the kinds of elements of which it is made, how the elements are configured, and the patterns of their interactions. Alternatively, we can study a system from the outside, looking at the outputs it produces and the inputs it accepts. In other words, we can examine how it affects and is affected by its surroundings. When this is possible, the system is called an *open system*. In contrast, a *closed system* is one that does not interact with its surroundings. Such systems are not of concern here. Indeed, textbooks devoted to organization behavior commonly assert that all organizations are open systems.

We are surrounded by open systems. In fact, each of us is an open system. Examples of open systems include a person (a living system), an automobile (a mechanical system), a pond (an ecological system), a language (a symbolic system), and a decision support system (a computer system). Every day we deal with weather systems, transportation systems, telephone systems, educational systems, and digestive systems. We can examine each of these from either an internal or external perspective. But here we concentrate on another kind of open system: the organization (Miller 1972; Katz and Kahn 1978).

An organization differs from other open systems in terms of the elements of which it is composed, the way in which they interact, the inputs to which it is sensitive, and the outputs it generates. There can be great variation among organizations themselves. Research into organizational behavior focuses on these variations (Katz and Kahn 1978; Vecchio 1988). Here, we consider the commonalities suggested by our six-fold definition of an organization. For instance, regardless of what organization we consider, that organizations' elements fall into four categories: monetary, material, human, and knowledge. These elements can be thought of as an organization's basic resources. How they are structured by managers in an effort to attain the organization's aim is a source of organizational variations.

FOUR MAJOR RESOURCES

Many of the elements that constitute an organizational system are acquired from the organization's surroundings. In addition, some elements may be produced or derived through the activities of other elements. Traditionally, the elements that can be input to an organization have been put into the three categories shown in Figure 1.2 (Miner 1978). Monetary inputs (e.g., proceeds from issuing stock) become monetary elements in the organization. Material inputs (e.g., new computers) become material elements in the organization. Human inputs (e.g., new employees) add to the organization's human elements. We conclude that monetary, material, and human resources are three important categories for classifying the elements that make up an organizational system.

Figure 1.2 suggests certain organization outputs corresponding to the three resource categories. For instance, profits are distributed to shareholders and goods or services are provided to customers. But, there are a couple of difficulties with the conventional view portrayed in Figure 1.2. First, it implies that each kind of organization output is dependent on only one type of input or resource, which is too simplistic. For example, the goods produced by an organization typically depend not only on the application of material resources, but also on the use of monetary and human resources. Second, and most important, is the omission of an extremely important resource from the conventional view of organizations.

FIGURE 1.2   Conventional Categories of Organization Inputs

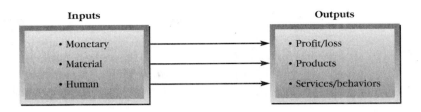

A fourth type of element essential to understanding organizational systems is knowledge. An organization's knowledge resources are one of its most important assets. Organizations routinely accept knowledge **inputs** and emit knowledge **outputs**. Knowledge can be added to an organization without necessarily adding money, material, or people. For some organizations (e.g., a news organization), the output of knowledge is more important than any other output. This expanded view of organizational systems is illustrated in Figure 1.3. Although the first three kinds of resources are very important, they are amply treated in other books. This text focuses on knowledge, which has rarely received direct, in-depth coverage in management books and courses.

Perhaps knowledge is frequently taken for granted because its use is so routine. Or, perhaps it is taken for granted because human and material resources routinely store and process knowledge. But even though they may carry and convey knowledge, neither people nor materials (e.g., computers) are themselves knowledge. This text does not take knowledge for granted but instead views it as a distinct type of resource. It is just as capable and deserving of being studied as monetary resources (in accounting and financial management courses), material resources (in production and operations management courses), and human resources (in organizational behavior and personnel courses).

STRUCTURING THE RESOURCES

At any moment, an organization's resources are configured in some nonrandom manner. This configuration is called the **current state** of the organization. Over

FIGURE 1.3   Four Types of Organization Resources

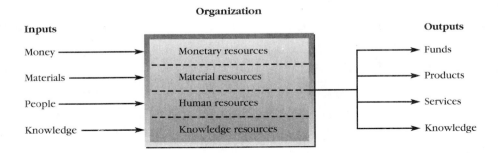

time, an organization undergoes many changes, which take it through a series of different states. For instance, every time a new input (e.g., piece of knowledge) is accepted into the organization, the state of the organization has changed. A new current state can also result from internal activities that alter the relationships among the system's elements or generate new elements. For instance, a person might be promoted to a different position, a piece of knowledge might be sent by one person to another, a product might be added to inventory after being assembled from several pieces of material, or several pieces of knowledge might be combined to derive some new piece of knowledge, such as a forecast. Each of these involves a change in the structure of an **organization's resources**, or **resource structuring**.

The study of financial management is concerned with alternatives for arranging and using monetary resources (Johnson 1971; Brigham 1986). Should a given quantity of money be held as cash, invested in some mix of securities (e.g., bonds, stocks), devoted to accounts receivable, traded for a different kind of resource (e.g., purchase of a factory or a piece of knowledge), or employed in some other way? A picture, at any moment, of the deployment of all money possessed by an organization would give its current financial state or monetary structure. An important function of accountants is to construct such pictures. In most organizations the structuring of monetary resources is a never-ending task, resulting in a continually changing picture of the current financial state.

DSS IN THE NEWS

Knowing What Technology Can Do For You

A new report by General Accounting Office . . . summarizes a 2½-year effort by the GAO on a subject that some claim hits to the core of American democracy in the electronic age. . . .

The federal government is the single-largest producer, collector, consumer and disseminator of information in the U.S. The way information resources . . . are acquired and managed "is critical to nearly every government program's mission, from exploring space, to collecting taxes, to providing Social Security benefits," wrote Jack Brock, director of government information and financial management, in a letter prefacing the new 16-page report. . . .

A key finding in the new study is that there is a lack of well-defined IRM [information resources management] concepts. In addition, government staff at all levels often lack the training, background or education needed to successfully implement and use information technology.

The report noted, "Until you have a work force that knows what technology can do for them, you cannot expect them to help you find a way to improve what they are now doing. . . ."

"The lack of a well-defined IRM concept is a common problem between industry and government,". . . [the] vice president of information technology consulting at SRI International . . . said after reading the report. "Many managers do not really understand the potential or scope of information technology."

B. Deagon, "Lack of Staff Expertise Often Dooms Government's Information Systems," *Investor's Business Daily*, 14 October 1992, p.4.

The study of operations management is concerned with alternatives for arranging and using material resources (Marshall et al. 1975). Where should plants, offices, stores, and other facilities be located? How should machines and fixtures be positioned in a facility to allow for smooth operations? How many and what kinds of machines and fixtures are needed? What parts and materials are necessary for production or sales operations? Where do they come from, when are they needed, in what quantities should they be ordered, and where are they stored? How should the work (i.e., the operations) be arranged and scheduled in the interest of efficient, high-quality products and distribution? A view, at any moment, of how all an organization's material resources are deployed would give a snapshot of its current material structure. As with monetary resources, an organization's material state can change rapidly and incessantly.

Human resources management is concerned with alternatives for arranging and using an organization's people (Beer 1985). What tasks do people carry out in an organization? How is the human labor to be divided in order not to overburden or underburden any individual? This structuring of human resources involves the specification of distinct roles that people can fill and the specification of patterns for communication among the roles (Biddle and Thomas 1966; Katz and Kahn 1978). The issues of which persons to assign to which roles, procuring and retaining qualified persons for the various roles, determining whether materials (e.g., machines) can help a person fill a role or even substitute for the human labor involved in a

DSS IN THE NEWS

Reengineering—The Holy Grail?

Business process reengineering, a management concept that uses information technology to achieve radical productivity improvements, has burst into the corporate consciousness. . . .

Reengineering involves a fundamental change in the way companies manage their business processes, such as order processing or customer service. . . .

Reengineering efforts are under way at more than 70% of companies, according to various surveys in the past year. . . .

While mainframe computers still play a significant role in most companies' information system strategies, the trend is toward using small networks of computers.

Deloitte & Touche notes that most reengineering projects are focused on customer service. In descending order, projects are also under way in systems development, accounting and finance, order processing, distribution, inventory and warehousing, sales and marketing, product development, manufacturing, and research and development. . . .

Other popular technologies used in reengineering are hand-held computing devices, bar code systems, imaging, voice response, neural networks used in forecasting and text retrieval, and expert systems. . . .

B. Deagon, "Reengineering Hailed as Holy Grail But, Predictably, Can Lag Projections," *Investor's Business Daily,* 25 March 1993, p.4.

role, evaluating a person's performance in filling a role, and rearranging the organization's role structure over time to improve the productivity of available human resources are also important (Mintzberg 1979). Organizations vary widely in terms of how often or quickly the configurations of human resources (i.e., their human structures) change.

Alternatives for arranging and using knowledge in an organization are topics for study in courses dealing with knowledge management (Holsapple and Whinston 1988). What types of knowledge should an organization have? How should the organization position and distribute this knowledge? Can the organization computerize a given piece of knowledge, such as last year's sales figures or knowledge about how to forecast next year's sales or rules for reasoning about the setting of sales quotas? If so, what computer-based techniques are appropriate? What is the best way to represent a piece of knowledge so that its relationships to other pieces of knowledge are clear and usable? How might alternative structures of knowledge influence an organization's productivity and survivability? An organization's knowledge state is subject to rapid, ongoing change. In the remainder of this book, we shall see how decision support systems can supplement a person's innate knowledge-handling abilities in the interest of efficient, high-quality decision making.

POWER CENTERS

The structuring of an organization's resources does not just happen. Structuring is directed, controlled, and enforced by certain **power centers** within the organization. These power centers cause ongoing changes in the organization's current state. In simplest terms, power is the ability to get things done with regularity and relative ease (Vecchio 1988). A center that has the formal right to exercise power can

DSS IN THE NEWS

Getting Serious about Knowledge Management

. . . General Motors Corp., Fidelity, Inc., Ford Motor Co., Monsanto Corp., Dow Chemical Corp., Hallmark, G.E. Lighting, Hewlett-Packard Co., AT&T Corp., IBM and a growing number of other leading firms are taking the infant discipline of knowledge management very seriously. Each is working to improve how they acquire, share and use knowledge in their organizations. . . .

The basic idea is this: Companies must gather, cultivate and manage intellectual capital as carefully as they do financial capital. Leverage knowledge, the thinking goes, and you can reduce time to market, cut research and development costs and boost productivity.

But that can only happen if a company's intellectual assets—for information, know-how and understanding about customers, competitors, markets, processes and people—is freed from the computers, brains, libraries and file cabinets where it's now trapped.

J. Maglitta, "Smarten up!" *Computerworld*, 5 June 1995, p. 85.

also be thought of as a *center of authority*. Some power centers in an organization may not be authority centers but instead exercise power by informal means (e.g., through coalitions) or by influence (e.g., in an advisory capacity).

The exercise of power can cause changes in the monetary, material, human, or knowledge elements existing in an organization. But who or what is it that wields power in an organization? Literature in the field of organizational behavior observes that every person in an organization possesses power, even though the potency of some of these power centers may be quite limited. It goes on to point out that power "is an essential feature of a manager's role" (Vecchio 1988). Put in another way, a major task of managers is to "attract, select, and allocate resources" (Miner 1978).

The extent of a manger's ability to structure resources is a reflection of that manager's power. In other words, we can differentiate managers based on the scope or magnitude of power they possess. We can also differentiate managers with respect to the kinds of resources that are most subject to their power. It should be clear that alternative distributions of power are possible in an organization, giving rise to alternative organization cultures and designs (Sathe 1983). Regardless of these distinctions, the central issue is how to ensure that each power center adequately structures the resources in its purview. Decision support systems can be instrumental in accomplishing this purpose.

ORGANIZATIONAL PURPOSE

It is a common purpose or goal that guides the activities of an organization's managers. In a way, this purpose can be thought of as the "glue" that holds the organization together. Without it, the power centers have little basis for cooperative action and the organization may well disintegrate amid a tangle of uncoordinated, conflicting arrangements and uses of its resources. An organization's managers work to bring the system to a state that is consistent with its purpose or goal. In other words, they exercise their differing powers to structure the organization's resources in a way that allows the common purpose to be fulfilled or the common goal to be met.

DSS IN THE NEWS

Systems Vision

. . . Often, complex corporate organizational structures impede communication between top executives and information system managers, leading to confusion over expected results from a system or its capabilities.

Senior management frequently fails to provide any information systems vision or strategy, leaving technology specialists ill-equipped to devise a system that complements the company's business goals.

B. Deagon, "How Companies Can Pry Productivity Gains from Investments in Technology," *Investor's Business Daily,* 22 April 1992, p.4.

A single organization often has several **purposes** simultaneously. For instance, a corporation's purposes might include offering value to its customers, providing excellent working conditions for its employees, inventing new products, generating high near-term returns for its shareholders, and maintaining or expanding its share of a market. Each such purpose could translate into several specific goals, which if met mean that the purpose has been fulfilled within some time period. Similar or different goals might be devised for continuing to fulfill the same purpose in a different time frame. When there are multiple purposes or goals, they may conflict. In the foregoing example, the purpose of generating high near-term returns could be at odds with the purpose of capturing a larger market share. Even when multiple purposes have been prioritized (e.g., near-term returns have a higher priority than market share), the managers' work of harnessing the organization's resources to meet the common purposes is challenging.

Managers' work to fulfill organizational purpose can also become entangled with personal purposes. Organizational and personal purposes do not always coincide (Katz and Kahn 1978). For example, there may be a power center that is not also an authority center. If this power center is a manager who regards personal purposes or goals as more important than those of the organization, the other managers' attempts to structure the organization may suffer. They will have to contend with conflicts between organization and personal purposes via such activities as negotiation, political maneuvering, or outright restructuring of human resources (Vecchio 1988).

ORGANIZATION ENVIRONMENT

Open systems exist in **environments**. An organization has a physical environment (geographic and ecological surroundings), a social environment (cultural climate), a political environment (legal statutes and governing rules), an economic environment (markets for exchanging resources), and a technological environment (Katz and Kahn 1978). An organization exists and operates in each of these environmental sectors. At the same time, the conditions in a sector can limit or influence the organization's activities in various ways. Environmental conditions may vary in their turbulence, diversity, orderliness, and richness in resources (Emery and Trist 1965, 1973).

From another viewpoint, an organization's environment may be another organization. As Figure 1.4 illustrates, organizations often exist inside of larger organiza-

NO ORGANIZATION IS AN ISLAND

". . . [T]he study of organizations should include the study of organization-environment relations. We must examine the ways in which an organization is tied to other structures, not only those that furnish economic inputs and support but also structures that can provide political influence and societal legitimation. The open-system emphasis on such relationships implies an interest in properties of the environment itself. Its turbulence or placidity, for example, limits the kinds of relationships that an organization can form with systems in the environment and indicates also the kinds of relationships that an organization will require to assure its own survival." —**Daniel Katz** and **Robert L. Kahn** in *The Social Psychology of Organizations*, p. 31

FIGURE 1.4   An Organization's Environment

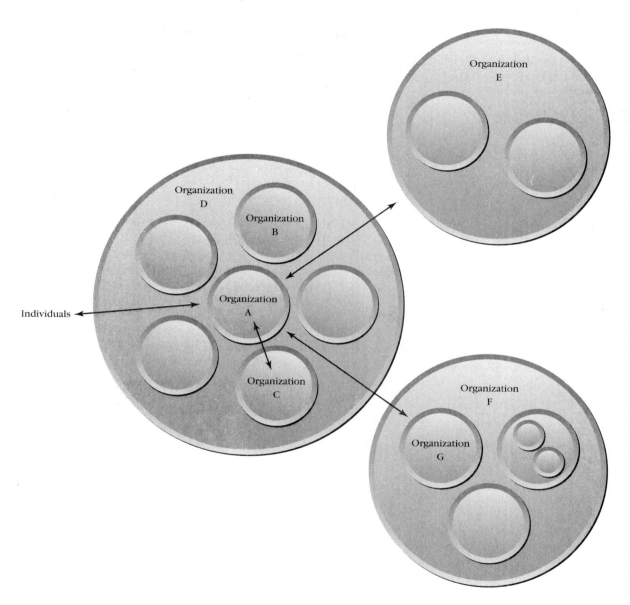

tions. For instance, organization A exists in organization D. Organization A could be the sales division of a corporation. Its purposes are subservient to those of the larger organization. Its resources are part of the larger organization's resources. Notice that there are other organizations in D (e.g., a manufacturing division, an accounting department) and that any of these could comprise smaller organizations.

The arrows in Figure 1.4 indicate a pattern of interactions for organization A. They involve the transferral of money, material, human effort, and knowledge (recall Figure 1.3). The transferral of knowledge is often simply called **communication**.

NESTED ENVIRONMENTS

". . . [T]he environment of organizations tends to be other organizations. . .organizations more often deal with a clustered environment of other organizations than is generally realized." —**Daniel Katz** and **Robert L. Kahn** in *The Social Psychology of Organizations,* p. 127

Aside from being conditioned by the organization of which it is a part, organization A directly affects and is affected by organizations B, C, E, and G and various individuals (e.g., customers). Together, these make up the immediate environment for organization A. Conversely, organization A is part of the immediate environment of organization G. Whenever an organization can be involved in a transferral to or from something, that something forms part of the organization's environment.

Some of organization A's activities may arise internally, without regard to what is happening in its environment. They do not involve an interchange of money, material, human effort, or knowledge with the organization's environment. But many, if not most, changes in the current state of organization A are reactions to changes in the state of its environment. For instance, an individual decides to place an order, organization B has a production shortfall, or organization G predicts strong demand over the next quarter. In what ways will organization A react to these environment changes? In general, a changing environment instigates changes in an organization's current state. These changes are the results of power center

DSS IN THE NEWS

Tough Questions about Technology

Corporate information officers need to confront the tough societal questions regarding the consequences of information technology use. . . .

One bank executive was asked to supply the company's marketing department with information culled from customer mortgage application forms. Marketing officials wanted data on household incomes, debt histories and other personal information so they could target customers for new bank services.

The executive agreed, believing that following orders took priority over the propriety of information use. The media caught wind of it and created a public relations disaster for the bank.

Mistakes in ethical analysis often occur when executives take a narrow view of their role in information technology, typically restricted to serving the needs of system users or the corporate political engine. A broader vision is needed. . . .

Information technology executives should think about the effects of their programs on employees, suppliers, customers, regulators and local communities. . . .

B. Deagon, "CEO Briefing on Information Technology," *Investor's Business Daily,* 15 April 1993, p. 30.

activities aimed at maintaining consistency with the organization's purposes and goals.

An organization senses changes in its environment or, as part of an environment, makes another organization aware of changes in itself using communication: the interchange of knowledge between an organization and its environment. An environment can transfer knowledge describing its state to an organization. In turn, this organization can transfer knowledge describing its own state to the environment. An organization's state is determined at any given moment by decision making: the manufacture of knowledge about what to do in a given environmental setting. As we shall see in the remainder of this chapter, these two notions of communication and decision making underlie nearly all managerial activity.

1.5 MANAGERIAL FUNCTIONS*

Managers are vital power centers in organizations. By now, it should be clear that their ongoing efforts at structuring organization resources to achieve various purposes in the face of a constantly changing environment are by no means a trivial undertaking. To help understand managerial activity in more detail, we can try to break it down into specific functions a manager might perform in the course of structuring an organization's resources. A well-known, early effort at identifying **managerial functions** was the work of Fayol (1949, first published in 1916). His ideas were later extended by other observers through the middle part of the century. Subsequently, Barnard (1968, first published in 1938) provided an alternative conception of managerial functions.

FIVE COMMON FUNCTIONS*

Fayol identified five functions of a manager: planning, organizing, commanding, coordinating, and controlling. This is sometimes called the POCCC view of management. It regards **planning** as the making of forecasts, the formulation of an outline of things to do, and the identification of methods to accomplish these things. Planning is carried out with respect to an organization's resources and in light of the organization's purposes. The **organizing** function, as described by Fayol, is especially concerned with the structuring of human resources. It includes the selection, education, and evaluation of workers as well as assigning workers to roles.

The function of **commanding** involves issuing specific or general instructions that cause things to happen (e.g., according to plans formulated by the manager). Command implies a transferral of knowledge from the manager to other elements (human or machine) in the organization. The **coordinating** function is concerned with a manager's efforts at interrelating and harmonizing activities in an organization. The function of **controlling** occurs when a manager seeks to assure that plans are carried out properly.

ADDITIONAL FUNCTIONS*

To these five managerial functions, Urwick (1943) added two more. He views forecasting as a separate function, rather than treating it as part of planning. Although forecasting can be a useful basis for planning, it can also be conducted separately from a planning episode. Another extension is to view investigation as an important function of managers. Managers investigate in the sense of conducting research (Davis and Cosenza 1993). For our purposes, investigation can be regarded as the effort to acquire knowledge. Managers who do not frequently seek to increase their knowledge are likely to be left behind (Grove 1983)—that is, their abilities to forecast, plan, organize, command, coordinate, and control can benefit from the new knowledge that results from investigation.

There have been other contributions to the functional view of what a manager does. For instance, Miner (1978) added three other functions to POCCC: staffing the organization, being its representative to the outside world, and engaging in bargaining activities. As another example, Barnard (1968) offered an alternative characterization to the POCCC-based views. He identified three managerial functions: establish and staff managerial roles to provide a system of communication within the organization, secure appropriate efforts from persons staffing the various roles, and formulate purpose, including specification of the work to do.

CRITIQUING THE FUNCTIONAL VIEW*

The foregoing functional approaches to characterizing what a manager does are based on Fayol's and Barnard's interpretations of their own personal experiences as industrialists. They have been quite influential in shaping much that has been written about managerial work (e.g., Drucker 1954; Strong 1965; Mackenzie 1969; Miner 1978). They may also give us a starting point for thinking about ways in which computers might be able to support managerial work. The extent to which a computer can help a manager plan, organize, command, coordinate, or control depends on reaching a more detailed and precise understanding of the functions and their interrelationships.

Critics of the functional view of management maintain that the functions are but indications of what we need to be explaining (Braybrooke 1964), vague objectives of managerial work (Mintzberg 1980), or difficult to study in isolation from each other (Carlson 1951). Moreover, it is interesting that the notions of decision making and knowledge are not prominent in the classic functional views of management.

If a manager is a power center who structures resources on a continuing basis, he or she is continually making decisions about what resources to acquire, select,

---

MANAGERIAL FUNCTIONS

Fayol	Urwick	Miner
Planning	POCCC	POCCC
Organizing	Forecasting	Staffing
Commanding	Investigation	Representing
Coordinating		Bargaining
Controlling		

Barnard

Establish and staff managerial roles to provide a system of communication

Secure appropriate efforts from those staffing roles

Formulate purpose, including specifications of the work to do

and allocate to fulfill specific purposes. Presumably, these decisions are based on knowledge. The knowledge available to and used by a manager affects the decisions that are made. Thus a characterization of managerial work must recognize decision making and knowledge handling. There is an alternative way of looking at managers' activities that explicitly accounts for these phenomena.

1.6 MANAGERIAL ROLES

Instead of considering a manager's work in terms of functions, we might ask what **roles** a manager typically plays in the course of a day's activity. Based on empirical studies of managerial work, Mintzberg (1980) has derived ten interrelated **managerial roles**. He points out that these roles fall into three categories:

- Interpersonal roles
- Informational roles
- Decisional roles

The latter two categories begin to address our concerns of accounting for knowledge handling and decision making.

INTERPERSONAL ROLES

Interpersonal roles are concerned with a manager's interactions with other persons. The scope of a manager's interpersonal roles depends on the manager's authority or status in an organization. According to Mintzberg, a manager can interact as either a figurehead, a leader, or a liaison.

As a figurehead, the manager performs routine social, ceremonial, or legal duties. For instance, a manager may be obliged to attend an awards ceremony, give a speech to a college class, or sign various documents. As a leader, the manager motivates and activates subordinates, including staffing, training, promoting, and encouraging. As a liaison, the manager is concerned with building and maintaining a network of contacts in the organization's environment. This network allows direct communication with persons outside the organization.

To these three interpersonal roles, we might add follower and peer. Sometimes a manager interacts as a subordinate to higher-level managers. Also, a manager may communicate with other managers who are neither subordinates nor leaders.

MANAGERIAL ROLES

Interpersonal	Informational	Decisional
Figurehead	Monitor	Entrepreneur
Leader	Disseminator	Disturbance
Liaison	Spokesperson	handler
Follower	Storer	Resource
Peer	Deriver	allocator
		Negotiator

INFORMATIONAL ROLES

In playing an interpersonal role, the manager is opening a channel of communication. **Informational roles** grow out of the resultant information access that is provided by interpersonal roles. Mintzberg identifies three informational roles: monitor, disseminator, and spokesperson.

When playing the monitor role, the manager seeks and acquires **information** in order to have a knowledge of the organization and its environment. Acting as a disseminator, the manager transmits information to others in the organization. This information may have been acquired from others inside or outside the organization. Alternatively, it may have been created by the disseminating manager. The spokesperson role involves transmitting information into the organization's environment. For instance, the manager sometimes serves in a public relations capacity.

The three informational roles are concerned with acquiring and distributing information. But what happens to a piece of information between the time it is acquired and the time it is distributed? This suggests another informational role, which could be called *storage*. When playing the storage role, a manager is concerned with representing information (e.g., in memory, on paper) in such a way that it can later be recalled or used as desired. But how is a piece of stored information used when it is recalled? Is it merely sent along to someone else? Perhaps, but very often a manager will manipulate information in various ways before transmission, or the manipulated information may not be transmitted at all.

The manager may create new information by manipulating stored information. For instance, a manager may use acquired information about the organization and its environment to create a sales forecast. This forecast is a new piece of information that may be disseminated or retained for subsequent personal use. Thus, we can say that there is yet another informational role, which might be called the *derivation role* (to indicate that managers can derive new information by processing existing information).

DECISIONAL ROLES

According to Mintzberg, there are four **decisional roles**, each of which depends on a manager's authority and information: the roles of entrepreneur, disturbance handler, resource allocator, and negotiator. When playing the entrepreneur role, the manager searches the organization or its environment for opportunities to steer the organization in a new direction within its field of purpose. If such an opportunity is discovered, the manager initiates and devises controlled change in the organization in an effort to seize the opportunity. As a disturbance handler, the manager initiates and devises corrective action when the organization faces an unexpected disturbance. For example, the supplier of a critical part for an organization's manufacturing process may fail to deliver the needed quantity on time.

As a resource allocator, the manager is engaged in determining where the organization will expend its efforts to decide, for instance, how much of which resources should be devoted to manufacturing product X as opposed to product Y. This decision can be thought of as determining the organization's strategy for structuring its resources. When playing the negotiator role, the manager represents the organization in bargaining with others. These others may be inside the organization or may be in its environment. The four decisional roles might be regarded as the pinnacles of managerial activity, for they most clearly tend to distinguish managers from other persons in an organization.

> **INFORMATION: THE BASIS OF DECISION MAKING**
>
> "It's obvious that your decision-making depends finally on how well you comprehend the facts and issues facing your business. This is why information-gathering is so important in a manager's life. Other activities—conveying information, making decisions, and being a role model for your subordinates—are all governed by the *base of information* that you, the manager, have about the tasks, the issues, the needs and the problems facing your organization. In short, information-gathering is the basis of all other managerial work, which is why I choose to spend so much of my day doing it." —**Andrew S. Grove**, President, Intel Corporation, in *High Output Management*, p.51

1.7 A WORKING PERSPECTIVE OF WHAT MANAGERS DO

The role view of managerial activity emphasizes interpersonal communications, information handling, and decision making as three intertwined strands in a manager's line of work. These can be tied together with the functional view of management by recognizing that they run through each function. Planning, for instance, typically involves interacting with others, handling information, and making decisions about what is to be included in the plan. Miner (1978) points out that each of these functions is concerned with decision making and communication. He states that these two "permeate all important components of the management process." Although this statement does not comment on information handling, we contend that it also pervades all major components of a management process (Grove 1983).

KNOWLEDGE HANDLING—THE FOUNDATION OF MANAGERIAL WORK

In fact, we shall view knowledge handling as being an even more basic capability than either communication or decision making. Knowledge is the stuff of which both decisions and communications are made. As Figure 1.5 suggests, the ability to

FIGURE 1.5   Knowledge Handling as the Basis for Decision Making and Communication

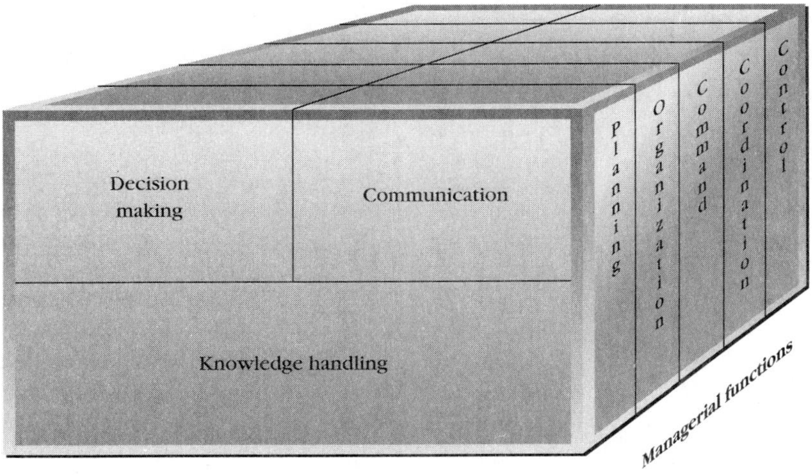

handle (acquire, store, use, maintain) knowledge is the basis for decision making and communication capabilities. Notice that we have replaced the term *information* with *knowledge*. Although the two terms are often used interchangeably in casual conversation, we shall make a distinction between them.

Information is commonly used to refer to descriptions of the state of an organization or its environment. For example, sales figures, inventory levels, personnel records, and production information all contribute to describing the situation a manager faces. Aside from such descriptive knowledge, there are other types of knowledge that managers routinely use. For instance, there is knowledge about how to do something, such as how to calculate the quantity of material to order from a supplier. This is called procedural knowledge, because it is a step-by-step characterization of a procedure for accomplishing something. Chapter 4 explores distinctions between these and other types of knowledge in more detail.

A SEVEN-POINT PROFILE

For the present, we are concerned with establishing a simple, clear, realistic perspective of what managers do. This working perspective should furnish a useful background for sketching out the nature and significance of decision making in Chapter 2. Within those outlines of decision making, we can then begin to fill in the issues of knowledge management. Shapes of computer-based possibilities for decision support can then begin to be seen. The working perspective that leads us toward decision support systems involves the seven points that follow:

1. A manager is an entity having the power to structure some monetary, material, human, and knowledge resources existing in an organization, with the intent of pursuing some purpose of the organization with respect to its environment.
2. An organization's managers transform its resources from one state to another in the interest of conforming to its purpose within a changing environment.
3. An organization's managers can acquire resources from the environment and release resources into the environment. Often, an output is traded for an input.

TWO TYPES OF KNOWLEDGE

Descriptive Knowledge

- Characterizes a situation
- Examples:
    Sales figures
    Inventory records
    Personnel records
- Also called information or data

Procedural Knowledge

- Characterizes how to do something
- Example: steps to follow when determining how much to order
- Also called algorithms

KNOWLEDGE—THE KEY RESOURCE

"Knowledge as the key resource is fundamentally different from the traditional key resources of the economist—land, labor, and even capital. . . .Every country, every industry, and every business will be in an increasingly competitive environment. Every country, every industry, and every business will, in its decisions, have to consider its competitive standing in the world economy and the competitiveness of its knowledge competencies." —**Peter F. Drucker** in "The Age of Social Transformation," p. 76

4. A manager's activities that lead to the acquisition, transformation, and release of resources can be characterized as roles that a manager plays or functions that a manager performs. These activities involve communication and decision making.
5. Both communication and decision making are based on a manager's ability to handle knowledge, in the sense of acquiring it (i.e., learning), storing it, recalling it, using it, deriving new knowledge, and distributing it.
6. In communicating, a manager transmits and receives knowledge. This process includes knowledge about what is observed, predicted, recalled, desired, necessary, recommended, accepted, or decided.
7. In making a decision, a manager draws on available knowledge about the organization and its environment to produce a new piece of knowledge. Called a decision, this new piece of knowledge tells us what will be done with the organization's resources.

THE ROLE OF COMPUTER TECHNOLOGY

Considering the seventh point, we might ask how computers can support a manager's decision-making efforts. How can they increase a manager's leverage to allow more to be done with less effort? Computers may increase the amount of knowledge available to draw on or make it easier to draw on whatever knowledge is available. They may help the manager in producing the new knowledge about what is to be done. Clearly, the manager will need to communicate with the computer so that knowledge can pass between them during a decision process. Perhaps computers are better suited for supporting some kinds of decisions than they are for others. Or, perhaps they can support different decisions or decision makers in different ways. To better appreciate such support possibilities, the next chapter takes a look at the phenomenon of decision making.

HIGH OUTPUT MANAGEMENT

"A manager must keep many balls in the air at the same time and shift his energy and attention to activities that will most increase the output of his organization. In other words, he should move to the point where his leverage will be the greatest."
—**Andrew S. Grove**, President, Intel Corporation, in *High Output Management*, p. 47

1.8 SUMMARY

For today's aspiring managers, a practical grasp of computer-based decision support is essential (Zuboff 1988). Try to imagine an organization in which managers are unable to use computers to aid any of their decisional activities. Contrast this vision with one of an organization whose managers routinely employ computers to get at and process knowledge that has a bearing on the decisions being made. These decision support systems store and process certain kinds of knowledge at much higher speeds than the human mind. In addition to such efficiency advantages, they can also be more effective in certain kinds of knowledge handling because they are not subject to such common human conditions as oversight, forgetfulness, miscalculation, bias, and stress. Failure to appreciate or exploit such decision support possibilities can put managers and their organizations at a major disadvantage.

This chapter has laid the foundation for understanding where decision support systems can fit into a manager's activities. We have seen that decision making pervades managerial activities. Thus, aids to decision making can have far-reaching impacts on a manager's efforts to excel. We have seen that, as a decision maker, the manager is very much concerned with handling knowledge. This is exactly where decision support systems can help. They automate various knowledge management tasks. Decision support systems are fundamentally concerned with improving the effectiveness and efficiency of knowledge management activities that occur in the course of decision making.

▲ IMPORTANT TERMS

commanding	environment	organization resources
communication	information	organizing
computer	informational role	output
controlling	input	planning
coordinating	interpersonal role	power center
current state	knowledge	purpose
decision	manager	resource structuring
decision making	managerial functions	role
decision support system	managerial roles	system
decisional role	organization	

▲ APPLICATION TO THE MONSANTO CASE

1. What kind of decision(s) needed support?
2. What managers used the DSS?
3. What knowledge can the DSS provide to its users? How does this knowledge support the decision making of managers?
4. Explain why the Monsanto distribution department is an open system.
5. Explain how the DSS affects each of the four kinds of resources possessed by the distribution department.
6. Give specific examples of knowledge that might be structured within the DSS.

7. How does the DSS help managers structure resources under their control?
8. What organizational goal or purpose does the DSS help distribution department managers achieve?
9. What conditions in the distribution department's environment make its task of managing especially challenging? How does the DSS help meet this challenge?
10. Which managerial function(s) does the DSS support?
11. What informational role(s) does the DSS help managers play?
12. What decisional role(s) does the DSS help managers play?
13. How does the DSS help a manager draw on existing knowledge to produce a new piece of knowledge? What new knowledge does the DSS produce? What new knowledge does the manager produce?
14. What would be the impact on the managers and their organization if the DSS were not available?

▲ REVIEW QUESTIONS

1. Why is an appreciation of computer-based decision support possibilities important to modern managers?
2. In what two ways can decision support systems help managers to be more productive?
3. What relationships exist among management, decision making, and knowledge?
4. In what major way do organizations differ from each other?
5. How can the size of an organization be measured?
6. Is it possible to offer a definition of organizations that applies to all organizations? If so, what is that definition?
7. What is a system?
8. How does an open system differ from a closed system?
9. What are the major resources that make up an organization?
10. What is meant by the *current state* of an organization?
11. Explain in your own words what it means to structure an organization's resources.
12. Which field of study is primarily concerned with the structuring of (a) monetary resources, (b) material resources, and (c) human resources?
13. With what issues is the field of knowledge management concerned?
14. Explain what it means for a manager to have power. Over what does a manager exercise power?
15. In what sense is purpose the "glue" of an organization?
16. When personal and organizational purposes are inconsistent, what difficulties arise?
17. When an organization interacts with its environment, what is being transferred?
18. Distinguish between the two types of triggers for organization activity.
19. Which functions are involved in the POCCC view of management?
20. In addition to POCCC, what other functions have been proposed to characterize a manager's work?
21. On what grounds have functional views of management been criticized?
22. What are the three categories of managerial roles?
23. What roles exist in each category?
24. How are the three role categories interrelated?

25. Identify two phenomena that seem to pervade all management functions.
26. In what sense is knowledge the basis for communication and decision making?
27. How does procedural knowledge differ from information?
28. From an organizational point of view, what does a manager do?
29. From a functional point of view, what does a manager do?
30. From a role point of view, what does a manager do?
31. In what way might a computer help knowledge handling in a decision process to be more efficient?
32. In what way might a computer help knowledge handling in a decision process to be more effective?

▲ DISCUSSION TOPICS

1. Why is an appreciation of managerial activity relevant to the study of decision support systems?
2. Explain ways in which a corporation such as IBM can be regarded as a public organization. In what ways is it private?
3. Which measure of organization size is most relevant to a consideration of decision support systems?
4. Discuss how organization outputs can trigger organization inputs, and vice versa.
5. Can a power center be made of a nonhuman element? Give an example.
6. Are there other managerial functions in addition to those cited in this chapter?
7. Can you identify additional decisional, informational, or interpersonal roles that managers play?
8. Based on your own experiences give examples of both descriptive and procedural knowledge.
9. In addition to information and procedural knowledge, identify other types of knowledge and give examples of each.
10. In what ways might you want or expect decision support systems to aid your managerial work?
11. Discuss ways in which a system to support decision making might differ from a system to support communication.
12. In what sense can a computer system that supports the planning function be regarded as a decision support system?
13. How does a living system differ from a symbolic system or a computer system? In what respects are they the same or similar?
14. Can one organization resource be considered to be more important than the other three? Why?
15. Describe a power center that is not also an authority center.
16. Discuss the relationships among power, authority, and knowledge.
17. How would you extend the notion of interpersonal roles to account for a manager's ability to interact with nonpersons such as computers?
18. Discuss the difference between efficiency and effectiveness with respect to knowledge management.

▲ REFERENCES

Barnard, C.I. 1968. *The functions of the executive*. Cambridge, Mass.: Harvard University Press (first published in 1938).

Beer, M. 1985. *Human resource management: A general manager's perspective*. New York: Free Press.

Biddle, B. J., and E. G. Thomas. 1966. Basic concepts for classifying the phenomena of role. In *Role theory: Concepts and research* edited by B. Biddle and E. Thomas. New York: John Wiley.

Boykin, R. F., and R. R. Levary. 1985. "An interactive decision support system for analyzing ship voyage alternatives. *Interfaces* 15, no. 2.

Braybrooke, D. 1964. The mystery of executive success re-examined, *Administrative Science Quarterly* 8.

Brigham, E. F. 1986. *Fundamentals of financial management*. Chicago: Dryden.

Carlson, S. 1951. *Executive behavior*. Stockholm: Strombergs.

Daft, Richard L. 1986. *Organization theory and design,* 2nd ed. St. Paul, Minn.: West Publishing.

Davis, D., and R. M. Cosenza. 1993. *Business research for decision making,* 3rd ed. Belmont, Calif.: Wadsworth.

Drucker, P. F. 1954. *The practice of management*. New York: Harper and Row.

———. 1994. The age of social transformation, *Atlantic Monthly,* 274, no. 5.

Emery, F. E., and Trist, E. L. 1965. The causal texture of organizational environments. *Human Relations,* 18, no. 1.

———. 1973. *Toward a social ecology*. New York: Plenum.

Farmer, R. N. 1984. *Business: A novel approach,* Berkeley, Calif.: Ten-Speed Press.

Fayol, H. 1949. *General and industrial management*. London: Pitman (first published in 1916).

Grove, A. S. 1983. *High output management*. New York: Random House.

Hammonds, K. H., K. Kelly, and K. Thurston. 1994. The new world of work. *Business Week* 17 October.

Holsapple, C. W., and A. B. Whinston. 1988. *The information jungle*. Homewood, Ill.: Dow Jones-Irwin.

Johnson, R. W. 1971. *Financial management*. Boston: Allyn Bacon,

Katz, D., and R. L. Kahn. 1978. *The social psychology of organizations,* 2nd ed., New York: John Wiley.

Laszlo, E. 1972. *Introduction to systems philosophy*. New York: Gordon and Breach,

Marshall, P. W., W. J. Abernathy, J. G. Miller, R. P. Olsen, R. S. Rosenbloom, and D. D. Wycoff. 1975. *Operations management*. Homewood, Ill.: Irwin.

Mackenzie, R. A. 1969. The management process in 3-D. *Harvard Business Review* 47, no. 6.

Miller, J. 1972. Living systems: The organization. *Behavioral Science,* 17, no. 1,

Miner, J. B. 1978. *The management process: Theory, research, and practice,* 2nd ed. New York: Macmillian.

Mintzberg, H. 1979. *The structuring of organizations,* Englewood Cliffs, N.J.: Prentice Hall,

———. 1980. *The nature of managerial work*. Englewood Cliffs, N.J.: Prentice Hall (first published in 1973).

Rodgers, F. G. 1986. *The IBM way*. New York: Harper & Row,

Sathe, V. 1983. Implication of corporate culture: A manager's guide to action. *Organization Dynamics* (Autumn).

Strong, E. P. 1965. *The management of business: An introduction*. New York: Harper & Row.

Toffler, A. 1970. *Future shock*. New York: Random House.

Urwick, L. F. 1943. *The elements of administration*. New York: Harper,

Vecchio, R. P. 1988. *Organizational behavior*. Chicago: Dryden.

Zuboff, S. 1988. *In the age of the smart machine*. New York: Basic Books.

Chapter 2

DECISIONS, DECISIONS, DECISIONS

*Denotes sections that may be skipped
in an accelerated coverage of this chapter.

INSIGHTS

IDAHO TRANSPORTATION DEPARTMENT: A DSS FOR TAXATION DECISIONS

Overview

Idaho currently has both a weight-distance tax and a registration fee system for collecting money for highway maintenance and construction. The registration fee is relatively low, but the weight-distance tax is quite high. . . . Proposals are regularly made to the Idaho legislature to change the truck tax system. . . . Proposed legislation has called for eliminating (or reducing) the weight-distance tax and offsetting the loss in revenue with a higher registration fee.

The primary issues in making substantive changes in tax policy center on the impact these changes will have on tax revenues and the state's economic system. Before it can make an informed decision, the legislature needs answers to such questions as: How much revenue will be lost (or gained) from the proposal? What changes in registration fees will be needed to offset changes in weight-distance taxes and remain revenue-neutral? Which classes of trucks will pay more taxes and which will pay less? What behavioral changes might occur if the tax changes are made, and what will the economic impact of these changes be?

Idaho Transportation Department officials recognized that informed answers to these questions would require a careful analysis of Idaho's current and proposed truck taxation systems . . . [N]eed for answers would occur frequently over time . . . [We set out to] develop a decision support system (DSS) to deal with the problem.

System Features

In practice, implemented DSSs often have to sacrifice a certain degree of conceptual elegance to provide the necessary decision-supporting features in a timely and cost-effective manner. The motor carrier taxation DSS (MCTDSS). . . . exhibits some of these trade-offs . . . [It was] designed . . . to support policy-making decisions and writing legislation governing the taxation of motor carriers in the state of Idaho. This is obviously not a well-structured task as various constituencies, criteria, objectives, and measurement problems enter into the decision.

In the MCTDSS, judgment and decision-making effectiveness are enhanced through the use of statistical models and data bases that help to evaluate the economic impact of various taxation structures. The system can be used to answer what-if questions . . . and may be modified to incorporate future changes in motor vehicle registration procedures, reporting requirements, and so forth. While the amount of data and processing required often makes real-time operation impractical, a fairly short response time to most queries is possible.

The MCTDSS comprises over 200 distinct programs and several dozen data sets. Each program may be thought of as essentially a data transformation—that is, a program accepts data from a data set as input and produces either another data set or a printed report as output. These programs and data sets must be managed to ensure that programs are executed in the proper order, and that when data or programs change, programs are selected and ordered properly for re-execution to maintain the validity of the ultimate outputs.

continued

System Usage

When state officials consider modifying a tax structure . . . they . . . want to know what impact the changes will have on current total revenues and what impact the changes will have on revenues over time. . . .

. . . The MCTDSS was employed . . . to answer several what-if questions . . . Among these was what would have been the impact on revenues . . . if the tax system of a flat 22.45 mill rate and $941 vehicle registration fee . . . had been in place. . . .

. . . [R]evenues would have decreased by more than $1.3 million. This type of information is critical to state officials and legislative committee members in assessing the merits of proposed tax changes.

In the months prior to the . . . legislative session, the MCTDSS was used to respond to a series of other what-if questions posed by members of the ton-mile subcommittee of the Idaho Legislature. For example, three different tax scenarios were proposed, all of which eliminated the weight-distance tax altogether. One scenario proposed that the limited class registration fee be raised from $120 to $560 and the regular class fee be raised from $120 to $1,496 per vehicle. This proposal would have resulted in a $3.7 million shortfall. . . . A second scenario proposed that registration fees would be raised to $730 and regular class registration fees to $1,947. This plan would have generated $785,000 more in total revenue. . . . A third alternative proposed a limited class registration fee of $647 and a regular class fee of $1,721 . . . [and] would have resulted in about $1.5 million less in revenues. . . .

The MCTDSS was also used to analyze behavior changes that could result from changes in the tax system. For example, each year in Idaho, a number of "convenience registrations" occur. Trucks are registered at the $120 per truck fee, but they are driven few or no miles in Idaho. Idaho officials suspect that some or all of these convenience registrations would be eliminated if the registration fee were increased substantially. The MCTDSS was used to determine the effect on revenue if all zero-mileage vehicles had not registered. . . . In another analysis, all vehicles that traveled less than 1,800 miles were assumed to not register.

Benefits

For any proposed tax structure, the MCTDSS can very clearly show its impact on revenue. It also can show what tax shifts will occur—what groups will benefit and what groups will pay higher taxes. Based on the MCTDSS results in 1987, proponents of one particular tax structure reconsidered their position and did not propose legislation to support that tax structure. The system was used again in 1989/90 when a group composed of members of the ton-mile subcommittee of the Idaho Legislature and the Idaho Transportation Department assessed the truck tax issue. The MCTDSS was used to analyze a variety of tax proposals from this group. Ultimately, this group elected not to revise the current truck tax system. . . .

The MCTDSS is an example of how decision support system concepts can be applied in complex and imperfect decision-making environments. . . . Without the MCTDSS, legislators might have changed the tax policy without completely considering the serious impacts of those changes.

Condensed quotation from P. W. Shannon and R. P. Minch, "A Decision Support System for Motor Vehicle Taxation Evaluation," *Interfaces,* 22, no. 2 (1992): 52–56, 58–63.

LEARNING OBJECTIVES

The Idaho case portrays a very different decision context than the Monsanto case in Chapter 1. Although it is clear the taxation decision can be seen as the choice of one out of many alternatives, it can also be seen as a chunk of knowledge specifying an action. This chunk of knowledge is determined only after many questions are answered, and those answers are themselves pieces of knowledge. The overall decision is far from routine. The DSS in this case provides support by generating responses to a wide assortment of what-if queries that happen to strike state officials as important in the course of their deliberations. Keep the Idaho case in mind as you read the rest of this chapter.

After studying this chapter, you should be able to

1. Explain what a decision is and what it means to make a decision.
2. Distinguish among various decision contexts that you might encounter as a manager.
3. Recognize the different types of decisions that managers make.
4. Classify a given decision as either structured, semistructured, or unstructured.
5. Converse about decision support needs and characteristics for various decision contexts and decision types that managers face.

Various exercises provided at the end of the chapter allow you to apply what you have learned to the Idaho case, review your understanding of presented concepts, and think about related topics for discussion.

2.1 INTRODUCTION

Decision making is a common thread running through all managerial functions. It denotes an important category of managerial roles and is the essential mechanism that causes an organization's resources to be structured as they are at any given moment. But, just what is a decision? In what settings are decisions produced? Can we identify distinct types of decisions? This chapter answers such questions in order to give a more solid basis for understanding decision support opportunities and challenges.

We first consider the notion of decision making from two complementary perspectives: the classical viewpoint and the knowledge-oriented angle. Next we look at various settings in which decisions are made. For instance, a decision produced in the context of a crashing stock market occurs in a different kind of setting than a decision made in the context of normal market activity. After exploring decision settings, we turn to the question of decision types, which is concerned with alternative ways to classify decisions. For example, one classification approach distinguishes among structured, unstructured, and semistructured types of decisions. An examination of decisions, decision settings, and decision types furnishes a solid background for the examination of the makers of decisions and the process of decision making in Chapter 3.

2.2 MAKING A DECISION

There is general agreement in the management literature that a **decision** is a choice. Some say that it is a choice about a "course of action" (Simon 1960; Costello and

THE WORLD OF DECISIONS

"Making decisions—or more properly, participating in the process by which they are made—is an important and essential part of every manager's work from one day to the next. Decisions range from the profound to the trivial, from the complex to the very simple: Should we buy a building or should we lease it? Issue debt or equity? Should we hire this person or that one? Should we give someone a 7 percent or a 12 percent raise? Can we deposit phosphosilicate glass with 9 percent phosphorus content without jeopardizing its stability in a plastic package? Can we appeal this case on the basis of Regulation 939 of the Internal Revenue Code? Should we serve free drinks at our departmental Christmas party?" —**Andrew S. Grove**, President, Intel Corporation, in *High Output Management*, p. 88

Zalkind 1963). Similarly, a decision has been defined as the choice of a "strategy for action" (Fishburn 1964). Others say that a decision is a choice leading "to a certain desired objective" (Churchman 1968). These definitions suggest that we can think of decision making as an activity culminating in the selection of one from among multiple alternative courses of action. It follows that a **decision support system** (**DSS**) is a system that somehow assists in such an activity.

A CLASSIC VIEW

This classic view of decision making is depicted in Figure 2.1. In the illustrated example, the decision-making activity has resulted in the identification of 12 alternative courses of action and will select one of them as the decision. In general, the number of alternatives identified and considered in decision making could be very large. The work involved in becoming aware of alternatives often makes up a major share of a decision making episode. It is concerned with such questions as

Where do alternatives come from?

How many alternatives are enough?

Should more effort be devoted to uncovering alternatives?

How can large numbers of alternatives be managed so none is forgotten or garbled?

A computer-based system can help a decision maker cope with such issues.

Ultimately, one of the alternatives is selected. But, which one? This depends on what we might call a *study of the alternatives*. It is an effort to understand the implications of the alternatives. For instance, the rental alternative (alternative 1) in Figure 2.1 would have certain impacts on the organization if it were selected to be the decision. The expected impacts of purchasing a used machine (alternative 2) might be very different. They may in some ways seem more favorable than those of the rental alternative 1 (e.g., costing less than a year's rent), but in other ways seem less desirable (e.g., not quickly replaced in the event of a breakdown).

The work involved in selecting one of the alternatives usually makes up a major share of a decision-making episode. It is concerned with such questions as these:

FIGURE 2.1   Classic View of Decision Making

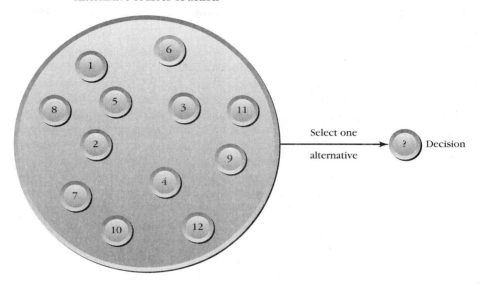

Alternative courses of action

Example: Deciding about the source for a machine needed in a factory.
Alternative 1.   Rent the machine from Industrial Rentals Company.
Alternative 2.   Buy the machine in used condition from a local liquidation sale.
Alternative 3.   Buy the machine new from XYZ Corporation.
Alternative 4.   Buy the machine new from Tool Supply, Inc.

.
.
.

Alternative 12. Manufacture the machine.

- To what extent should each alternative be studied?
- How reliable is our expectation about an alternative's impacts?
- Are an alternative's expected impacts compatible with the organization's purposes?
- What basis should be used to compare alternatives to each other?
- What strategy will be followed in arriving at a choice?

Computer-based systems can be very beneficial in supporting the study of alternatives. Some may even recommend the selection of a particular alternative and explain the rationale underlying that advice.

A KNOWLEDGE-BASED VIEW

Aside from the classic view of decisions and decision making, there is another useful way of looking at the issue, which we call the *knowledge-based view* (Holsapple and Whinston 1988). This view holds that a decision is a piece of **knowledge** indicating the nature of an action commitment. A decision could be a piece of descrip-

A CLASSIC DEFINITION

"What is a "decision"? It may be defined as a *commitment to action*, usually a commitment of resources. In other words, a decision signals an explicit intention to act."
—**Henry Mintzberg** in *The Structuring of Organizations,* p. 58

tive knowledge. For instance, "spend $10,000 on advertising in the next quarter" describes a future change to an organization's monetary state involving a commitment of $10,000. This decision is one of many alternative descriptions (e.g., spend $5,000 advertising in the next quarter) that could have been chosen.

A decision could be a piece of procedural knowledge, involving a step-by-step specification of how to accomplish something (Katz and Kahn 1978). For instance, "determine the country with the most favorable tax structure, identify the sites within that country having sufficient qualified work forces, then visit those sites to assess their respective qualities of life, and, from among those that are acceptable, locate the new factory at the site with the best transportation infrastructure" is a chunk of procedural knowledge committing an organization to a certain sequence of actions. It is one of many alternative procedures that could have been chosen.

Clearly, the knowledge-based view is compatible with the classic view of decisions. In addition, it leads to an extra insight into the nature of decision making. When we regard a decision as a piece of knowledge, making a decision means we are making a new piece of knowledge that did not exist before. We are manufacturing new knowledge by transforming or assembling existing pieces of knowledge. As Figure 2.2 shows, decision making can be viewed as the activity of manufacturing a new piece of knowledge expressing commitment to some course of action. A decision support system is a system that aids the manufacturing process, just as machines aid in the manufacturing of material goods.

FIGURE 2.2   Knowledge-Based View of Decision Making

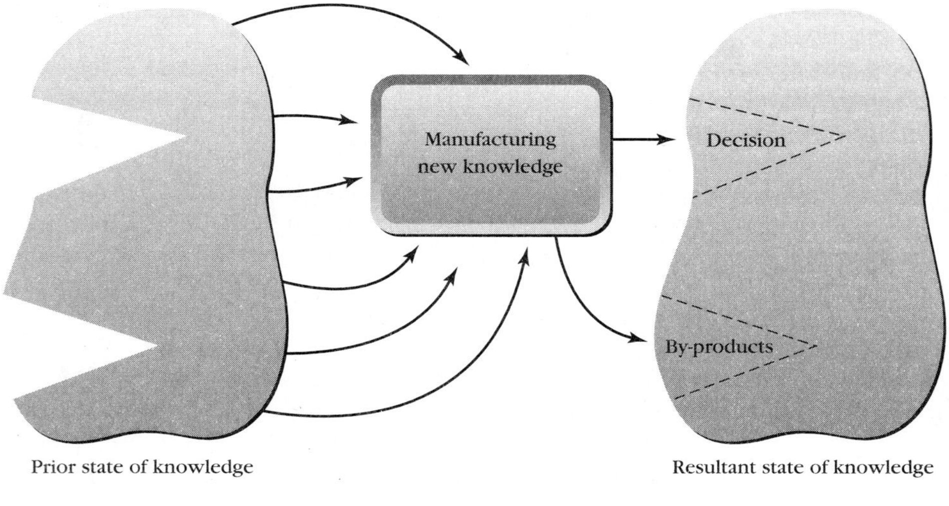

Prior state of knowledge   Resultant state of knowledge

Decision making is a knowledge-intensive activity that alters an organization's state of knowledge. More is known after a decision is made than before. Not only is there the new piece of knowledge, called a decision, but the manufacturing process itself may have resulted in additional new knowledge as by-products (see Figure 2.2). For instance, in manufacturing a decision, we may have derived other knowledge as evidence to justify our decision. We may have produced knowledge about alternatives that were not chosen, including expectations about their possible impacts. More fundamentally, we may have developed knowledge about improving the decision manufacturing process itself. Such by-products can be useful later in making other decisions.

Having established a working perspective on what decisions are and why they are important, we are now in a position to consider more carefully how they come into being. A solid appreciation of the process of manufacturing decisions is essential for grasping the decision support possibilities offered by computers. It has been observed that this process is influenced by (1) the organizational context in which a decision is produced, (2) the nature or type of decision being produced, (3) the basic constitution of the decision maker, and (4) cognitive limitations (Katz and Kahn 1978). The remainder of this chapter explores the factors of decision contexts and decision types. The other two factors, along with various decision-making strategies, are examined in Chapter 3, which culminates in an identification of decision support possibilities.

2.3   DECISION CONTEXTS*

The contexts in which decisions are manufactured can influence the nature of decision making. For this reason, decision-making contexts can also influence what we might expect of decision support systems. A **decision context** is simply the setting in which a decision is made. It can be examined from several angles, such as those portrayed in Figure 2.3. Does the decision making occur at the top, lower, or middle level of management? Does it occur in a newly emerging situation or in a well-established setting? Does the decision making occupy the full attention of the decision maker or is it occurring in the context of many other simultaneous decision-making ventures? What is the design of the **organization** wherein a decision is being made?

MANAGEMENT LEVEL*

It is common for organizations to have several levels of management. These are often referred to as top, middle, and lower management. Decisions are made and need to be supported at each level. Each provides a different setting for decision making. These settings are often called strategic planning, management control, and operational control (Anthony 1965).

Strategic planning refers to establishing organization purposes, determining overall objectives in light of organization purposes, changing objectives as needed, and settling on policies to guide the acquisition, use, and release of resources. **Management control** is concerned with ensuring that resources are acquired, used, and released to meet objectives within policy guidelines. In contrast, **operational control** seeks to assure that specific tasks are carried out effectively and efficiently by the organization's operating personnel.

FIGURE 2.3   Four Contexts of Decision Making

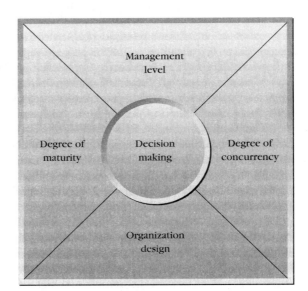

Top management tends to be most concerned with strategic planning issues, middle management with management control issues, and lower management with operational control issues. Thus, within an organization, we make some decisions in the context of strategic planning, some in the context of management control, and others in operational control contexts. As we move from decisions made in strategic planning contexts toward those at the operational control end of the spectrum, the following tendencies can be observed:

MANAGEMENT LEVELS AS DECISION CONTEXTS

To appreciate the different decision-making contexts that arise from management levels, think about the analogy between running an organization and building a house (Bonczek, Holsapple, and Whinston 1981). Top-management decisions are akin to those of an architect. Middle-management's decisions resemble those of the builder contracted for construction. A lower-management decision-making context is similar to that of the supervisor who directly oversees construction work. Operating personnel typically are not called managers. Nevertheless, they too make decisions that affect an organization's performance, just as a carpenter has some discretion over minute-to-minute operations.

Top management	→	Strategic planning	→	Architect
Middle management	→	Management control	→	Builder
Lower management	→	Operational control	→	Supervisor
Operating personnel	→	Operational performance	→	Carpenter

Obviously, the facilities for supporting an architect differ from those useful to a builder, supervisor, or carpenter. Similarly, decision support facilities in top management contexts can differ markedly from those used at other levels.

- Shorter time horizons for deciding
- Greater need for very precise and detailed knowledge
- Less need for wide-ranging knowledge
- Greater rhythm to decision-making activities
- Not as much creativity or qualitative judgment required
- More amenity to formal specification of activities

Each factor influences the nature of decision making and the kinds of decision support features that would be helpful. For instance, an important class of decision support systems, called *executive support systems*, is designed specifically for support of top executives (see Chapter 18).

EMERGENT VERSUS ESTABLISHED SETTINGS*

Another way of assessing decision-making contexts is to look at the maturity of the situation in which a decision is to be made. Some decisions are made in the context of an **established situation**. As an example, consider an assembly line that has produced hundreds of thousands of electric blenders. The decision about the quantity of chopping blades to order to allow blender assembly to continue smoothly occurs in an established situation. This is very different than a decision about how to respond to a new technology that makes electric blenders obsolete. Here, the decision is being made in an **emergent situation** rather than in a highly mature setting.

Well-established situations imply considerable experience in having made similar kinds of decisions. A relatively high level of knowledge exists about the current state of affairs and the history of previous decisions of a similar nature. In contrast, emergent situations are characterized not only by some surprising new knowledge, but often by a scarcity of relevant knowledge as well. Decisions need to be made in a new context, in unfamiliar territory, with an intense effort to acquire needed knowledge. Of course, decision settings exist in a continuum extending from highly established to extremely emergent situations. The types of support likely to be most useful at one extreme could be quite different than what is most useful at the other extreme.

DEGREE OF CONCURRENCY*

A third way of looking at the issue of decision-making contexts is concerned with the degree of **concurrency**. Figure 2.4 illustrates some of the possibilities. The first two decision-making episodes are strictly serial. Decision 1 is made before the manufacture of decision 2 begins. Similarly, the second decision-making episode is completed before the third one begins. However, before decision 3 is made, another decision-making effort is underway. Thus, the making of decision 3 occurs (partially, at least) in the context of making decision 4, and vice versa. Notice that the entire effort involved in reaching decision 5 occurs in the context of making decision 4.

Several complications can arise when a decision is made in a concurrent context. For instance, the concurrency between times f and g may mean that it takes longer to produce either or both of decisions 3 and 4. One decision process can distract the decision maker from another that is happening simultaneously, causing one or both to take more time than would be required in a serial context.

FIGURE 2.4   Serial Versus Concurrent Decision Making

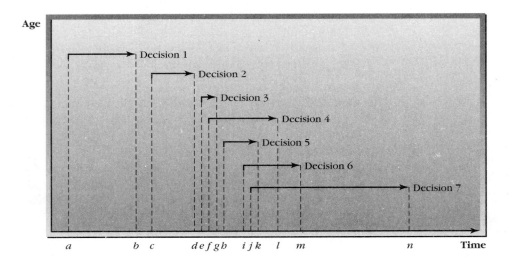

On the other hand, it may be that the time from f to g is mainly a lull in the action of producing decision 3. The decision maker might be awaiting the arrival of some piece of knowledge before proceeding to decision 3. During the lull, the decision maker might make a good start toward decision 4. So the time from e to l could be less than what would be required if decisions 3 and 4 had been manufactured in a serial fashion. It is even possible that initial work toward decision 4 yields certain insights or pieces of knowledge that impact the other decision process, actually reducing the amount of time that would otherwise be required to reach decision 3.

Thus, some degree of concurrency can result in improved decision-making efficiency. Too much concurrency will be counterproductive. It is unlikely that a decision maker who is involved in making 100 decisions simultaneously will do a very good job. The degree of concurrency in a decision-making context can affect not only the efficiency with which decisions are reached, but the very nature of the decisions as well. Referring again to Figure 2.4, the fact that decision 3 is made in a concurrent context may have caused it to be different than it would have been in a serial context. The concurrency may have distracted or stressed the decision maker, resulting in a poorer or at least different decision. On the other hand, concurrency may stimulate the decision maker to identify alternatives that would otherwise remain hidden, resulting in a better or at least different decision.

Sometimes a decision maker has limited control over the degree of concurrency in a decision-making context. Where there is some control, the foregoing points should be considered in coordinating the timing of multiple decision-making episodes. It becomes a matter of recognizing dependencies and potential synergies among an assortment of decision-making challenges. For instance, at some point, further progress toward decision 4 could very well depend on decision 3 having been made. Or, we might expect that by working simultaneously on decisions 4 and 5 we can increase our output. The synergy that comes from considering them at the same time allows us to accomplish more than manufacturing the decisions at separate times.

It seems reasonable that computer-based systems that support decision making in a concurrent context might be more elaborate than those intended for a serial context. They may aid the decision maker's efforts to gain the benefits of concurrency or avoid its drawbacks by assisting in coordination and promoting synergy.

ORGANIZATION DESIGN*

Beyond the concurrent decision-making episodes a particular manager faces, we should realize that in the organization as a whole there are many more decision-making processes concurrently underway. The ways of coordinating concurrent decision-making efforts by an organization's many managers are strongly influenced by the organization's design. **Organization design** is concerned with interrelationships that exist between managers. It therefore forms a context in which the manager's decisions are manufactured, one in which a manager's decision making is influenced by activities of other related managers.

Many organization designs are possible. A particular design causes a decision maker's activities to be more or less dependent on, constrained by, and monitored by other managers. Organization designs differ along such dimensions as centralization, authority levels, command unity, and command chains (Vecchio 1988).

Centralization* Decisions made in the context of high **centralization** tend to be concentrated in a relatively small number of power centers. Any decision-making authority that exists beyond these tends to be highly constrained and closely monitored by the centers where power is concentrated. **Decentralization** results in an organization in which there are more power centers. Decision making in such a context tends to be less tightly constrained and monitored. Decision support systems are likely to be in more widespread use.

Authority Levels* Along another dimension, organization designs can range from only a few to a very large number of **authority levels**. The former are called *flat*

FROM CENTRALIZED TO DECENTRALIZED DECISION CONTEXTS

"When all the power of decision making rests at a single point in the organization—ultimately in the hands of a single individual—we shall call the structure centralized; to the extent that the power is dispersed among many individuals, we shall call the structure decentralized. . . . [H]aving the power to make a decision gives one neither the information nor the cognitive capacity to make it. In fact, because so many organizations face complex conditions, decentralization is a very widespread phenomenon. One individual can hardly make all the important decisions for a ten-person social work agency, let alone a General Electric. Decision-making powers are shared so that the individuals who are able to understand the specifics can respond intelligently to them. Power is placed where the knowledge is. . . . [C]entralization and decentralization should not be treated as absolutes, but rather as two ends of a continuum." —**Henry Mintzberg** in *The Structuring of Organizations*, pp. 181, 183, 185

organizations and the latter are referred to as *tall organizations*. In a flat organization, a decision maker is more likely to be a generalist, capable of handling a wide variety of knowledge in the course of making diverse decisions. For example, a manger decides about such diverse issues as hiring new employees, starting a major new product line, where to advertise, and what quantities of parts to stock.

In tall organizations, a decision maker tends to be more of a specialist, dealing with only a small class of decisions. For instance, a manager may specialize in deciding how much of various parts to order at various times. Another manager would specialize in hiring decisions, another in advertising decisions, and so forth. The type of system to support specialized decision making could be less ambitious in scope (i.e., more specialized) than what a generalist would find helpful.

Command Unity*   Another dimension of organization design is concerned with **command unity**. Where there is complete unity of command, a decision maker is the direct subordinate of one and only one supervisor, thus avoiding the introduction of conflict and confusion into decision-making contexts. On the other hand, there are organizations in which a manager serves two (or more) masters. For instance, in organizations that adhere to the *matrix design*, a decision maker might report to both a functional manager (e.g., vice president of marketing) and product manager (e.g., manager of the electrical appliance product line) (Davis and Lawrence 1977). This situation introduces more flexibility into the use of an organization's human resources. Decision making in such a context is apt to be more time consuming, involving a larger amount of communication and greater attempts at resolving conflicts arising from multiple bosses. It is interesting to speculate whether this could be mitigated by incorporating some special traits into decision support systems used in a matrix context.

Command Chain*   A fourth dimension of organization design involves the kind of **command chain** that exists. Where there is a strict chain of command, knowledge is allowed to flow to a decision maker only from the next-higher and next-lower levels in the organization. Moreover, the decision maker accepts instructions only from the next-higher level and issues instructions only to the next-lower level. The

DSS IN THE NEWS

Virtual Business

. . . [V]irtualization of business [enabled by technology] is well underway. . . . Today, virtualization is eliminating slack at every level . . . from the internal routines of single companies to the organization of industries and marketplaces. It's removing intermediaries, speeding transactions, rebalancing power relationships, and slashing costly fat—all of which is intensifying competition. . . . .

J. W. Verity, "The Information Revolution," *Business Week*, Special 1994 Bonus Issue, p. 14.

decision maker is a captive of the two levels between which he or she is sandwiched.

In organizations that do not adhere strictly to the chain-of-command principle, there is a potential for freer flows of knowledge. This situation may be accompanied by a less disciplined approach to knowledge transferral or situations in which a decision maker is overwhelmed by a mass of available knowledge, of which only a small percentage is relevant to the decision at hand. Clearly, we would like our decision support system to help us manage incoming and outgoing knowledge in either context. However, when making decisions in a context lacking a strict command chain, we are more likely to need even more help in scouting for knowledge and separating the wheat from the chaff.

CONTEXT IMPLICATIONS FOR DECISION SUPPORT*

Several researchers in the DSS field have explored the implications of different decision-making contexts for decision support systems (e.g., Huber 1981, 1984; Watabe, Holsapple, and Whinston 1992; Kersten 1985; Alter 1980; Keen and Scott Morton 1978). Much research remains before achieving a full appreciation of the implications that various decision-making contexts have for computer-based support systems.

Our purpose here has been to point out that there are different decision-making contexts, identify some of those contexts, and convey a sense of their relevance to the study of computer-based systems. The kind of decision support system that works well in one context may be inappropriate or inadequate in a different context. As a final point about contexts, we could say that the decision support system available to a decision maker is itself another kind of context. As with the managerial level, maturity degree, concurrency degree, and organization design, it can strongly influence the kinds of things that happen during the manufacture of a decision.

DSS IN THE NEWS

All in a Day's Work

. . .Charles Chaser scanned the inventory reports from his company's distribution centers . . . . [He saw that] stocks of Rose Awakening Cutex nail polish were down to three days' supply. . . . So Chaser turned to his terminal . . . [to request that] 400 dozen more bottles [be produced the next day]. . . .

All in a day's work for a scheduling manager, right? Except for one detail: Chaser isn't management [but one of hundreds of line workers who use the] . . . plant's computer network to track shipments, schedule their own workloads, . . . [doing what] used to be the province of management.

J. B. Treece, "Breaking the Chains of Command," *Business Week*, Special 1994 Bonus Issue, p. 112.

2.4 DECISION TYPES

Context is not the only factor influencing the nature of decision making and, hence, the range of decision-support needs and possibilities. Another major influence is the **decision type**. There are many ways to classify decisions. One way to classify decisions is by the contexts in which they are made. For instance, we could talk about strategic decisions versus management control (also called administrative) decisions versus operating control decisions (Mintzberg 1979).

In Chapter 1, we saw that decision making pervades each of the managerial functions. Therefore, we can categorize decisions into those made in the course of planning, those made while organizing, those made when commanding, and so on. Although the practical dividing lines among POCCC functions may not always be clear, it may still be helpful to distinguish between a decision to adopt a certain plan, a decision to issue a certain command, a decision to organize resources in a certain way, and so forth. For instance, the kind of support that would aid in the determination of a plan conceivably has some differences from the kind of support that would help in deciding on what command to issue. At the very least, they would be based on different types of knowledge.

Figure 2.5 shows three other ways to classify decisions: based on the notions of functional area distinctions, structuredness, and negotiation. We shall focus on these three approaches. They should not be regarded as competing approaches, but rather as complementary ways of grasping distinctions that exist among decisions.

FIGURE 2.5   Five Ways of Classifying Decisions

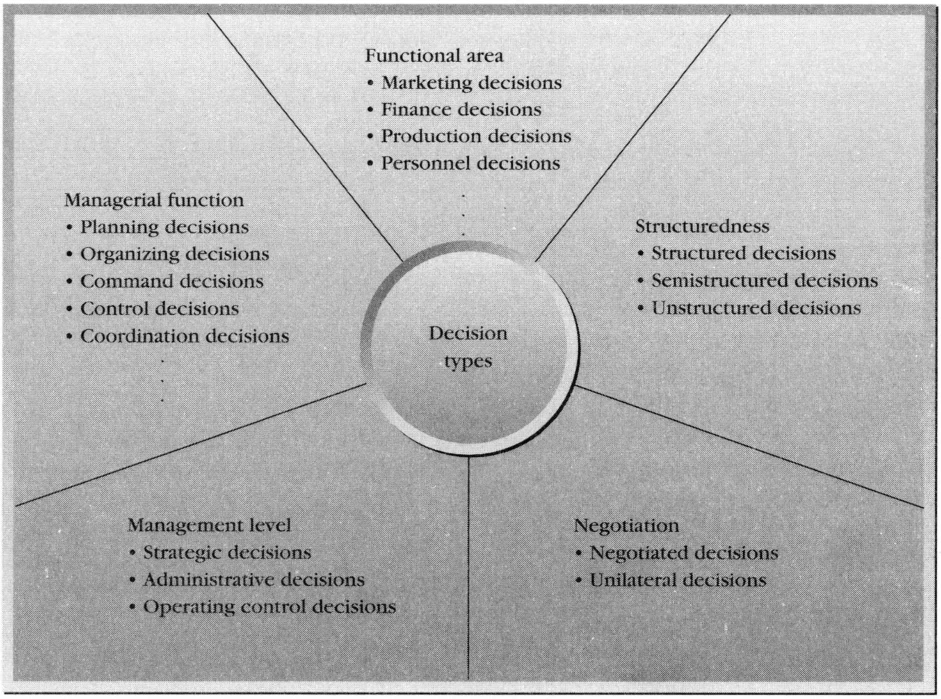

Functional area
• Marketing decisions
• Finance decisions
• Production decisions
• Personnel decisions

Managerial function
• Planning decisions
• Organizing decisions
• Command decisions
• Control decisions
• Coordination decisions

Structuredness
• Structured decisions
• Semistructured decisions
• Unstructured decisions

Decision types

Management level
• Strategic decisions
• Administrative decisions
• Operating control decisions

Negotiation
• Negotiated decisions
• Unilateral decisions

FUNCTIONAL AREA DISTINCTIONS*

A very common way to classify decisions is in terms of the functional areas of management. These areas include finance, marketing, business law, and operations management (also called production). The curriculum of a management school is typically designed with such areas in mind. In marketing courses we learn about marketing decisions, in finance courses we learn about financial decisions, in operations management courses we learn about production decisions, and so on.

From a decision support perspective, this classification scheme is fairly useful. It is not difficult to imagine a decision support system specially equipped to aid with marketing decisions. Such a system would likely be very different from one designed strictly for supporting financial decisions (see the Part Two Case Study for contrasting examples). Neither would be particularly valuable in supporting the types of decisions for which the other is well suited, because the marketing system holds knowledge about marketing, whereas the financial system holds knowledge about finance. So, decision support systems can be tailored to assist with certain types of decisions by controlling the kinds of knowledge they have.

STRUCTURED VERSUS UNSTRUCTURED DECISIONS

A fourth approach to classifying decisions involves placing them on a continuum that ranges from **structured** to **unstructured** (Simon 1957, 1960). The structuredness of a decision is concerned with how routine and repetitive the manufacturing process that produced it is. A highly structured decision is one that has been manufactured in an established context, whereas unstructured decisions tend to be produced in emergent contexts. Structured decisions can be thought of as being ordinary and commonplace. In contrast, unstructured decisions are novel or in some way remarkable. For instance, decisions made by a typical pension fund manager on October 19, 1987 (the day of a major market crash) were much more unstructured than decisions made by that same manager a year before or a year later.

Unlike the repetitive nature of structured decisions, an unstructured decision may be a one-shot proposition. A similar type of decision may never again be manufactured. The residential loan manager at a bank in Muncie, Indiana, repeatedly makes decisions about mortgage applications in a price range of $10,000 to

FROM STRUCTURED TO UNSTRUCTURED DECISIONS

Structured Decisions	Semistructured Decisions	Unstructured Decisions
Established situation		Emergent situation
Ordinary		Novel, unique
Repetitive		One-shot
Issues understood		Issues elusive
Knowledge readily available		Knowledge difficult to get
Programmable		Creative
Specialized manufacturing strategy		General manufacturing strategies

$300,000. Such decisions are structured compared to a mortgage request for $1,000,000, which might occur only once in a career. The decision about a request of this rare or unprecedented magnitude is less structured, involving special attention and a consideration of issues not usually addressed. Exactly what additional issues to consider or what special treatment to give the manufacture of this decision may well be unclear to the manager.

When issues relevant to making a decision are well understood, the decision tends to be structured. The alternatives from which the choice is made are clear-cut, and each can be readily evaluated in light of the organization's purposes and goals. Put another way, all the knowledge required to make the decision is available in a form that makes it straightforward to use. Often times, however, the issues pertinent to producing a decision are not well understood. Some issues may be entirely unknown to the decision maker, which is a hallmark of unstructured decisions. The alternatives from which a choice will be made are vague, are difficult to compare and contrast, or cannot be easily evaluated with respect to the organization's purposes and goals. It may even be that there is great difficulty in attempting to discover what the alternatives are. In other words, the knowledge required to produce a decision is unavailable, difficult to acquire, incomplete, suspect, or in a form that cannot be readily used by the decision maker.

Programmed Decisions   Structured decisions are often called *programmed decisions*, and unstructured decisions are similarly referred to as *nonprogrammed decisions* (e.g., Vecchio 1988). Actions leading to a fully structured decision can be programmed; that is, we can state a complete, unambiguous sequence of instructions to be followed in making the decision. Such an instruction sequence is called a *program*. It is procedural knowledge, telling how to accomplish some task. In the case of a structured decision, that task is one of reaching a decision.

For example, the following program is a piece of procedural knowledge telling us how to decide on what quantity of an item to order:

1. Determine the number of items to be used annually.
2. Determine the cost of placing an order.
3. Multiply these two numbers and double the result.
4. Divide this by the product of the cost of procuring a unit of the item and the annual cost of holding a unit of the item in inventory.
5. Use the square root of the quotient as the order quantity.

This particular program produces a structured decision that management scientists call the *economic order quantity* (Lapin 1975). It is one of many programs that management scientists have invented for deciding what quantity of an item to order.

Semi-structured Decisions   Some aspects of the decision-manufacturing activity may be able to be programmed, whereas others cannot. The result is a semistructured decision. For instance, it may be that knowledge about the number of items to be used annually is not known, cannot be simply looked up in a report, and cannot be produced from some other program concerned with forecasting demand. Thus, the first step in the economic order quantity program is ambiguous, and we do not have a complete program. Part of the decision making is not programmed. In more extreme cases, little or none of the activity leading to a decision is programmed. Clearly, this is to be expected for highly unstructured decisions, where we have an emergent context, novelty, rareness, elusive issues, and a lack of knowledge.

Governing Strategies   When a decision maker is in a situation where a program does not exist to specify all details about how to make a decision, he or she exercises ingenuity, creativity, imagination, intuition, and an exploratory attitude. The use of such faculties is likely to be guided by some general reasoning strategies for unstructured decisions (Simon 1960). In contrast, a fully structured decision is manufactured by following a very specialized procedural strategy which we have called a program.

General strategies that might be employed in making unstructured decisions include such elements as the following:

- Lateral thinking, or making a conscious effort to see issues from unconventional perspectives (deBono 1973)
- Analogy, or studying past decision-making episodes to stimulate the identification of analogous ways of dealing with making the present decision (Holsapple and Whinston 1988)
- Exploration, or acquiring more knowledge in an effort to better understand issues involved in making the present decision (Holsapple and Whinston 1988)
- Synthesis, or combining known specialized methods to build a new method for decision making (Bonczek, Holsapple, and Whinston 1981)
- Creativity, or using the imagination to create new knowledge needed for manufacturing the unstructured decision (Koestler 1969)
- Brainstorming, or producing a large quantity of ideas (often by interacting with others) that could have a bearing on the decision (Taylor, Berry, and Black 1958);

We can imagine many ways to combine or sequence such elements in the course of making an unstructured decision.

Shifts in Decision Type   Over time, what was once regarded as an unstructured decision may tend to be viewed as much more structured. Contexts that were once emergent can become established. Through repeated experience in coping with a given kind of decision, decision makers can develop increasingly programmatic means of handling the next encounter with such a decision. The field of management science (also called operations research) is devoted to inventing programs that allow unstructured decisions to be more structured (Bonczek, Holsapple, and Whinston 1981). Although it has had some significant successes (e.g., Lapin 1975), semistructured and unstructured decisions remain a fact of life for today's managers. Management is every bit as much an art as it is a science.

Decision Support Systems   Decision support systems can be valuable aids in the manufacture of semistructured and unstructured decisions (Keen and Scott Morton 1978). They can be designed to facilitate the exploration of knowledge, help synthesize methods for reaching decisions, catalog and examine the results of brainstorming, provide multiple perspectives on issues, or stimulate a decision-maker's creative capabilities.

Such traits are unnecessary in a decision support system intended for structured decisions. Instead, the system automatically carries out some portion of the program used to produce a decision. For example, a decision maker might perform the first two steps of the economic order quantity program, leaving the remaining steps for a decision support system. The chief benefits of this sort of system are more efficiency and less likelihood of human error in the decision process. Of course, if the system were to perform all steps of a program for decision making, we would call it a decision-making system (not a decision support system).

NEGOTIATED VERSUS UNILATERAL DECISIONS

Another approach to classifying decisions distinguishes between those that are negotiated and those that are unilateral. Recall from Chapter 1 that negotiation is one of a manager's decisional roles. Thus, there are negotiated (also called bargained) decisions and those that are not negotiated. Both are commonplace in organizations (Miner 1978). When a manager works to produce a negotiated decision, there is a give-and-take interchange with other persons until all agree on a particular alternative (Lax and Sebenius 1986). That manager is not really the decision maker but rather a participant in the decision making.

Participants   Negotiated decisions always involve multiple participants who must agree. They may not all agree with the same degree of enthusiasm, and some may

---

DSS IN THE NEWS

More Power to the Branches

. . . Some of the nation's top banks are spending heavily on technology to keep their branches up-to-date. One of these is Winston-Salem, N.C.-based Wachovia Corp., which is plowing $30 million into its 505 branches in the Carolinas and Georgia. Its main goal: improved decision-support for branch officers.

. . . With the new system, a routine task—say, handling a request for a loan on a new fishing boat—will work like this: A consumer loan officer will go to an Intel 486-based PC and punch up a comprehensive client profile. The software then will take the officer through a range of financing scenarios. These might include a home equity loan and personal loan secured by the boat. "Before, the lending official had to remember to ask the right questions and gather all the relevant data," said Walter Leonard, Wachovia executive vice president and information systems chief. "Now, the system asks the questions, runs through all the available options, goes off and gets the customer's credit report and automatically 'scores' the loan," or rates its worthiness. On the back end, says Leonard, the system will spit out all disclosure documents, compliance forms and other paperwork needed. "We believe the system will cut the total (loan) process at least in half," he said.

. . . Next year, the bank will add decision-support tools to handle more complex products like annuities and life insurance. "If a customer comes in to do retirement planning, we'll be able to run sophisticated 'what-if' simulations," Leonard explained. "The officer will help the customer determine his tolerance for risk and create an appropriate financial plan.". . . As deregulation pushes banks into new spheres, they must learn to compete on their intellectual assets. . . .

Mark Mehler, "More Power to the Branches: Wachovia's New Loan System," *Investor's Business Daily*, 13 July 1995, p. A6.

agree only with reluctance, arm-twisting, or strong reservations. For instance, a production manager and a marketing manager may negotiate the date for announcing a new product. Neither individually makes the decision. Together, they work to find a mutually agreeable date.

Nonnegotiated, or unilateral, decisions may also have multiple participants. Consider the inventory manager who is deciding on an order quantity for some item. This manager may ask someone else (e.g., a staff assistant or product manager) for a determination of the annual usage of the item. This other person becomes a participant in the decision making but does not need to agree with or even know about the inventory manager's decision.

Thus, unilateral decisions can be influenced by others who actively participate in the manufacturing process. They can even be influenced by persons who do not directly participate. For example, a manager's superior may have instituted a policy that constrains the alternatives this manager can legitimately study during decision making.

Decision Support Systems   Systems supporting the production of unilateral decisions are likely to be more elaborate in the case of multiparticipant decision making than where there is just one participant. Systems supporting the making of negotiated decisions have a potential to be even more elaborate. In some negotiated decisions, the multiple participants compose a group or committee that meets to produce a group decision. So-called group decision support systems (GDSS) or electronic meeting systems have been devised to aid in such efforts (Huber 1981; Kersten 1985; Nunamaker, Applegate, and Konsynski 1987; Bui and Jarke 1986). These systems receive detailed consideration in Chapter 17.

A very different kind of multiparticipant negotiated decision making occurs in Japanese organizations, involving behind-the-scenes consensus building across managers on diverse organization levels. The result is a very different kind of decision support system than those for groups (Watabe, Holsapple, and Whinston 1992). Recent research into negotiation support systems indicates a multitude of possibilities for supporting the manufacture of negotiated decisions (Lai 1989). As discussed in Chapter 17, there is a class of decision support systems (called negotiation support systems) specifically oriented toward facilitating negotiation activities.

2.5   SUMMARY

This chapter has provided a perspective of decision making that is both wide-ranging and fairly detailed. Experiences as a student of management and later as an active manager will serve to enrich and reinforce this perspective. We have seen that decision making is an activity culminating in the choice of a course of action. It can also be seen as a manufacturing activity that produces a new piece of knowledge committing us to a course of action. This knowledge-based view of decision making is further developed in Chapter 4.

Decisions are not manufactured in a vacuum. They are made within some setting or context. We can consider contextual differences in terms of such factors as management level, situation maturity, decision concurrency, and organization design. All decisions are not of the same type. They can be classified according to such factors as managerial levels, managerial functions, functional area distinctions, degree of structuredness, and presence of negotiation. An appreciation of decision contexts and types can help us understand what features would be useful to have in a decision support system. The same can be said for an appreciation of decision makers and decision processes. These are explored in the next chapter.

▲ IMPORTANT TERMS

authority level
centralization
command chain
command unity
concurrency
decentralization
decision
decision context
decision making
decision support system
decision type

DSS
emergent situation
established situation
knowledge
management control
operational control
organization
organization design
strategic planning
structured decision
unstructured decision

▲ APPLICATION TO THE IDAHO TRANSPORTATION DEPARTMENT CASE

1. Give an example of one of the taxation decision alternatives.
2. Who uses this DSS? Can you distinguish between direct users and those who indirectly use it by examining its results?
3. How does this DSS help decision makers cope with alternatives?
4. Give an example of a what-if question that might be asked of this DSS.
5. Explain how the DSS's ability to solve problems contributes to the decision-making process.
6. How has this DSS aided the process of manufacturing decisions?
7. What knowledge by-products may have resulted during the process of manufacturing decisions with the support of this DSS?
8. Describe the procedural and descriptive knowledge possessed by this DSS.
9. What management level or levels are supported by this DSS?
10. Has this DSS been used in an emergent or well-established setting? Explain.
11. Has this DSS been used to support concurrent decisions or serial decisions? Explain.
12. Does the DSS support structured or unstructured decisions? Explain.
13. Is the type of decision being supported negotiated or unilateral? Explain.
14. What benefits were realized from using the DSS?

▲ REVIEW QUESTIONS

1. Can you define a decision from the (a) classical viewpoint and (b) knowledge-oriented perspective?
2. Can you give an example of a decision that is (a) descriptive and (b) procedural?
3. What is decision making from the (a) classical viewpoint and (b) knowledge-oriented perspective?

4. Why is it important to study alternatives in the course of making a decision? What are the results of such study?
5. How do strategic planning, management control, and operational control differ from each other?
6. In what sense does decision making in an established situation differ from making decisions in emerging situations?
7. How does a concurrent decision making context differ from a serial decision making context?
8. Referring to Figure 2.4, identify three distinct time periods in which decision making is not occurring in a concurrent context.
9. Can you distinguish between the unity of command and the matrix contexts of decision making?
10. Why is an understanding of decision contexts important for the study of decision support systems?
11. With respect to purpose, how does a personal decision differ from an organizational decision?
12. How does a structured decision differ from an unstructured one?
13. What can be said about the alternatives from which a structured decision is made? What about alternatives from which an unstructured decision is made?
14. What can be said about the knowledge from which a structured decision is manufactured? What about the knowledge on which an unstructured decision is based?
15. Give an example of a structured decision. What is it that makes that decision structured?
16. Give an example of an unstructured decision. What is it that makes that decision unstructured?
17. Can an unstructured type of decision become more structured? How?
18. In what ways can a computer-based system help support a structured decision?
19. In what ways might a computer-based system help support decisions that are not structured?
20. Explain how unilateral and negotiated decisions differ.
21. Can unilateral decisions involve multiple participants? If so, how?

▲ DISCUSSION TOPICS

1. If insufficient attention is paid to the identification of alternatives, what is likely to be the effect?
2. Discuss the relationships between the classic and knowledge-oriented views of decision making.
3. Describe the key elements of a process that manufactures boxes containing cereal. In what respects is the manufacture of decisions about selling that cereal similar? How is it different?
4. Explain the relationships between strategic planning, management control, and operational control. Which constrains the others and which furnish vehicles for carrying out the will of another?
5. Speculate about the different decision support needs (if any) of managers at different organizational levels.
6. In which of the three management levels is the highest percentage of decision making likely to occur in emergent situations?

7. What differences would you expect between a system that supports decisions in an established situation and one intended for emergent situations?
8. Under what circumstance would it be impossible to reschedule efforts leading to decisions 1 and 2 in Figure 2.4 to make them concurrent?
9. Beyond the properties useful for supporting decision making in a serial context, what decision support traits could be especially useful in concurrent contexts?
10. Would you expect flat structures to encourage centralization or decentralization?
11. Speculate about special decision support needs of a decision maker operating in the context of a matrix organization design.
12. Give an example of personal decision making that affects organizational decision making.
13. What happens when a decision maker confuses personal and organizational decision making?
14. Give an example of knowledge about knowledge.
15. For each of the four organization resources, identify a decision that is concerned exclusively with that resource.
16. What would be the major differences between a system to support marketing decisions and one to support financial decisions? In what respects could the two systems be similar or even identical?
17. Would you expect a top-level manager to be more involved in making unstructured decisions than lower levels of management? Why?
18. Would decisions tend to be more structured in a tall or flat organization? Why?
19. Discuss ways in which what were once unstructured decisions could become structured decisions.
20. Are unstructured decisions always more complex than structured ones?
21. Can a structured type of decision become more unstructured as time goes by? How?
22. What do negotiated decisions have in common and how can they differ?

▲ REFERENCES

Anthony, R. N. 1965. Planning and control systems: A framework for analysis. Boston: Harvard University Graduate School of Business Administration.

Alter, S. L. 1980. *Decision support systems: Current practice and continuing challenges.* Reading Mass: Addison-Wesley.

Bonczek, R. H., C. W. Holsapple, and A. B. Whinston. 1981. *Foundations of decision support systems.* New York: Academic Press.

Bui, T. X., and M. Jarke. 1986. Communications design for co-op: A group decision support system. *ACM Transactions on Office Information Systems,* 2. no. 4.

Churchman, C. W. 1968. *Challenge to reason.* New York: McGraw-Hill.

Costello, T. W., and S. S. Zalkind. 1963. *Psychology in administration: A research orientation.* Englewood Cliffs, N.J.: Prentice Hall.

Davis, S. M., and P. R. Lawrence. 1977. *Matrix.* Reading, Mass.: Addison-Wesley.

de Bono, E. 1973. *Lateral thinking.* New York, Harper & Row.

Fishburn, P. C. 1964. *Decision and value theory.* New York: John Wiley.

Grove, A. S. 1983. *High output management.* New York: Random House.

Holsapple, C. W. and A. B. Whinston. 1988. *The information jungle.* Homewood, Ill.: Dow Jones–Irwin.

Huber, G. P. 1981. The nature of organizational decision making and the design of decision support systems. *MIS Quarterly,* (June).

_____. 1984. Issues in the design of group decision support systems. *MIS Quarterly* (Sept.).

Katz, D., and R. L. Kahn. 1978. *The social psychology of organizations,* 2nd ed. New York: John Wiley.

Keen, P. G. W., and M. S. Scott Morton. 1978. *Decision support systems: An organizational perspective.* Reading, Mass.: Addison-Wesley.

Kersten, G. E. 1985. NEGO-group decision support systems. *Information and Management,* 8.

Koestler, A. 1969. *The act of creation.* London: Hutchinson.

Lai, H. 1989. A theoretical basis for negotiation support systems. Ph. D. dissertation, Purdue University.

Lapin, L. L. 1975. *Quantitative methods for business decisions.* New York: Harcourt Brace Jovanovich.

Lax, D. A., and J. K. Sebenius. 1986. *The manager as negotiator.* New York: The Free Press.

Miner, J. B. 1978. *The management process: Theory, research, and practice.* 2nd ed. New York: Macmillian.

Mintzberg, H. 1979. *The structuring of organizations.* Englewood Cliffs, N.J.: Prentice Hall.

Nunamaker, J. F., L. M. Applegate, and B. R. Konsynski. 1987. Facilitating group creativity: Experience with a group decision support system. *Journal of Management Information Systems* 3, no. 4.

Russo, J. E., and P. J. H. Schoemaker. 1989. *Decision traps.* New York: Simon and Schuster.

Shannon, P. W., and R. P. Minch. 1992. A decision support system for motor vehicle taxation evaluation. *Interfaces,* 22, no. 2.

Simon, H. A. 1957. *Models of man.* New York: John Wiley.

_____. 1960. *The new science of management decision.* New York: Harper & Row.

Taylor, D. W., R. C. Berry, and C. H. Black. 1958. Does group participation when using brainstorming techniques facilitate or inhibit creative thinking? *Administrative Science Quarterly,* 3, no. 1.

Vecchio, R. P. 1988. *Organizational Behavior.* Chicago: Dryden.

Watabe, K., C. W. Holsapple, and A. B. Whinston. 1992. Coordinator support in a nemawashi decision process. *Decision Support Systems,* 8, no. 2.

Chapter 3

DECISION MAKERS AND PROCESSES

*Denotes sections that may be skipped
in an accelerated coverage of this chapter.

DSS INSIGHTS

QUEBEC: A DSS FOR VEHICLE FLEET-PLANNING DECISIONS

Overview

Following gradual deregulation of the trucking industry in the province of Quebec in Canada, productivity improvement has become a major concern for many trucking companies. It was felt that vehicle fleet productivity could further be improved by better adjusting fleet size to demand. . . .

Fleet planning is a complex management process which aims at adjusting fleet size and composition to meet the demand in a cost-effective way. It affects both short term and long term operations. For example, enough vehicles should be available daily to meet the demand. In the long run, if vehicle replacement is not carefully planned, substantial costs could be incurred later to update a fleet that is getting too old and obsolete. Uncertainty of demand, future maintenance cost, vehicle residual values, and new vehicle availability are important issues. . . .

In order to help managers with fleet planning, a decision support system (DSS) was developed. The DSS was designed to assist the manager in every step of the fleet planning process: (i) to forecast demand; (ii) to determine relevant criteria; (iii) to generate alternative plans; (iv) to evaluate alternative plans with respect to the criteria determined in ii); and (v) to choose "the best" plan. . . .

. . . In demand forecasting, . . . two sources of data can be used: past sales (ton-miles of merchandise carried) and future service needs, expressed by actual and potential customers. . . . [A] second activity aims at generating alternative plans to meet the forecasted demand subject to budget constraints and new vehicle availability. A plan is defined for each period by the number of vehicles kept or sold in each different group to meet the demand. A group is composed of vehicles of same make and age at a given period.

. . . [The] selection of relevant criteria is a third activity. . . . Criteria are chosen according to corporate objectives: profitability, productivity, customer satisfaction, driver satisfaction, etc. The plans are then evaluated with respect to the criteria selected . . . presented in an evaluation grid, a matrix in which lines represent alternatives, columns, criteria, and elements are evaluations. . . [T]he fifth activity is the selection of the 'best' plan from the evaluation grid. . . .

System Features

The DSS . . . takes into account tax allowances, non homogeneous fleet, the demand as a non stationary stochastic seasonal process, vehicle rental or leasing, replacement/expansion policy . . . [It] generates a minimal discounted cost plan covering the purchase, replacement, sale and/or rental of the vehicles necessary to deal with a seasonal stochastic demand . . . using basic information from the user and/or a data base. . . .

. . . [The DSS will] print the solution of the model in a way that could easily be understood by managers who do not necessarily have knowledge of mathematical programming. Because managers are often reluctant to use the solution of a model they do not understand . . . [the] system allows users to input alternative plans that would be validated by the system and then compared to the optimal solution of the model.

Continued

. . . [The] system for vehicle fleet planning is composed of five modules: FORECASTING; CRITERIA; PLANS; EVALUATION; and SELECTION . . . and a data base management system. . . . A menu-based approach gives access to the modules. Each module includes a secondary menu of procedures. All procedures are independent and can be used in any order. All data can easily be stored for further processing. . . .

The FORECASTING module helps to forecast the number of ton-miles of merchandise to be carried in each of the planning periods and to determine the number of vehicles required to carry the forecasted volume of merchandise. The module contains five procedures: SUBJECTIVE allows the manager to input subjective forecasts. . . . OBJECTIVE generates objective forecasts from past data. . . . COMBINE does a weighted linear combination of the objective and subjective forecast. . . . TRANSFORM transforms the forecasted volume (ton-miles) of merchandise to be carried into the number of vehicles required to carry it. . . .

The CRITERIA module assists the user in defining a set of relevant criteria. Two procedures are available: LIST allows the manager to choose the most frequently used criteria set, the criteria deemed relevant to the problem on hand. . . . INPUT allows the user to define any other criteria. . . .

The Plan module, which helps the manager to determine alternative plans, is composed of six procedures: FLEET allows the manager to input data on the existing fleet (type of vehicles, number, costs, etc.). . . . NEW allows the manager to input data on new vehicles . . . PLAN helps the manager to develop alternative plans; the manager first chooses the different vehicle groups to include in the plan and then specifies the number of vehicles in each group kept and sold at each period. . . . GENERATE . . . generates a . . . fleet planning model. . . . MODIFY modifies any data of a plan. . . . CONSTRAINT allows for the introduction of additional constraints such as capital availability or vehicle availability.

The EVALUATION module assists the manager in evaluating each alternative plan with respect to the criteria selected. The three procedures of this module are: INPUT allows the user to directly input evaluations. . . . CALCULATION . . . performs all calculations (estimated ownership costs, estimated maintenance cost, interest, fleet productivity, net present value, mean cost per mile, etc.) . . . MODIFY [is used] to modify any data of the evaluation grid.

. . . [The] SELECTION module helps the manager to choose the "best" plan. . . [where] TOTAL does the sum of all costs and the weighted average of quantitative criteria. . . . WEIGHT does a weighted sum of quantitative and qualitative criteria. . . .

System Usage

. . . To illustrate the utilization of the DSS . . . suppose that quarterly forecasts of the number of tractors required for the next two years, beginning as of January 1988, were obtained. . . .

Three plans . . . are analyzed. According to the first plan, vehicles are replaced when they reach their economic life (the economic life of a vehicle is obtained by minimizing the maintenance and ownership costs functions). . . .

Plan 2 minimizes the maintenance and ownership costs over the two years

Continued

period, and the last plan was generated by the stochastic model.

. . . For the given situation, replacing vehicles when they reach their economic life (Plan 1) not only increases total operating cost, but also the average fleet age. Plan 2 yields the lowest total operating cost but the average fleet age is significantly higher than in Plan 3, postponing more expenses for a later date. The choice between Plan 2 and Plan 3 then becomes a matter of long-term and short-term objectives.

Because cost estimates are rapidly generated by the DSS, a wide variety of 'what if' questions can be dealt with. For example, what happens if residual value goes down 10% (i.e., the depreciation rate goes from 30% to 40%). . . .

All estimates and parameters can be modified, one or many at a time, for sensitivity analysis. This is a very important feature of the DSS, making it a useful tool for this rapidly changing environment.

Condensed quotation from J. Couillard, "A Decision Support System for Vehicle Fleet Planning," *Decision Support Systems* 9, no. 2 (1993): 149–52, 157–58.

LEARNING OBJECTIVES

The Quebec case illustrates a DSS that is used for multiple problem-solving steps in a complex decision-making process. The system is designed to support a particular kind of decision maker and to conform to a particular kind of decision-making strategy. As we shall see in this chapter, other kinds of decision makers and decision-making strategies exist. The DSS in this case is designed to help relax certain limitations that exist for the human decision maker. It exhibits some of the main decision support traits identified in this chapter.

After studying this chapter, you should be able to

1. Compare and contrast major kinds of decision makers that you are likely to encounter in an organization.
2. Describe the phases you would go through in a decision-making process.
3. Explain the relationship between problem solving and decision making.
4. Identify common strategies that are used in guiding decision-making processes.
5. Describe limitations that managers encounter in making decisions.
6. Discuss decision support needs and characteristics for various kinds of decision makers and decision-making strategies.

To check on your progress in meeting these objectives, three kinds of exercises are provided at the end of the chapter. They allow you to apply the concepts learned to the Quebec case, to review specific points that are presented, and to speculate about a variety of related discussion topics.

3.1 INTRODUCTION

To this point we have seen what a decision is, looked at contexts in which decisions are made, and discussed various types of decisions. The context and the type of a particular decision are important factors in determining who will decide. But we have yet to characterize directly a decision maker. What is the nature of an entity who manufactures a decision? What types of decision makers exist? The answers to these questions strongly influence the manufacturing process whereby decisions are produced.

That manufacturing process has many variants. But, there are also common traits that appear repeatedly as decisions are made. For instance, a decision process typically involves three phases; it usually consists of a sequence of problem-solving episodes; and there is usually some strategy to guide the quest for a decision. Understanding such traits gives a good basis for appreciating ways in which computers can provide support. To what degree is each phase susceptible to computerized support? What is the nature of that support? What problem-solving episodes can be aided by a decision support system? What strategies are conducive to what kinds of support?

In this chapter we consider the characteristics of entities that make decisions: from individual persons to groups and teams to elaborate organizations. Next, the process of making a decision is examined, including decision-making phases, flows of problem recognition and problem solving, and strategies for guiding the process. All this provides a helpful background for closing the chapter with a discussion of the need for decision support and the nature of that support.

3.2 THE DECISION MAKER

To understand what is desirable in a decision support system, it is important to know who it is that is being supported. As we saw in the previous chapter, **decision making** may involve an individual participant or multiple participants. In the individual case, the **decision maker** is a person or a computer system. In the multiparticipant case, we have either a unilateral decision or a negotiated decision, which suggest different kinds of decision makers. These possibilities are summarized in Figure 3.1. Before considering them in detail, let's briefly survey some of the main traits of each kind of multiparticipant decision maker.

UNILATERAL DECISIONS

In making a **unilateral** decision, one of the multiple participants is vested with the power to decide. Although the others do not have the power to decide, they can

---

DECISION-MAKING LINKAGES

"More important than a typology of decisions is an understanding of how decision processes flow through an organization. Specifically, we need to understand how operating, administrative, and strategic decisions link together and what roles the different participants—operators, top and middle-line managers, technocratic and staff supporters—play in the phases of different decision processes. We need to know who recognizes the need to make a given kind of decision, who diagnoses the situation, who develops the solution, who authorizes it, and so on." —**Henry Mintzberg** in *The Structuring of Organizations*, p. 61.

FIGURE 3.1   Types of Decision Makers

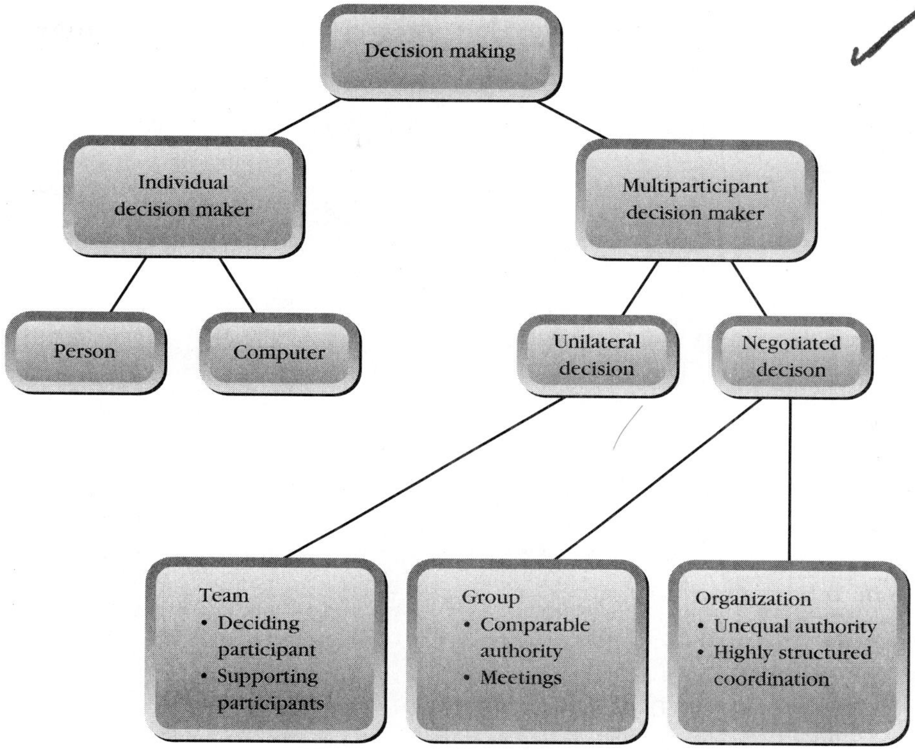

strongly influence what the decision will be and how efficiently it will be manu-factured. They do so by carrying out tasks that the deciding participant assigns to them during the course of making the decision. We can think of them as being sup-porting participants, who serve as extensions to the deciding participant's own capabilities. For brevity, we call this kind of multiparticipant decision maker a **team** (Holsapple 1991; Applegate et al. 1991).

NEGOTIATED DECISIONS

In making a negotiated decision, multiple participants share decision-making authority. One common decision maker of this type is a **group,** wherein the par-ticipants have comparable authority with respect to the decision. The group typi-cally has meetings in which the participants air their views. They conduct discus-sions that lead to eventual agreement about committing to a course of action. In contrast to a group decision maker, it can happen that participants do not have equal authority with respect to making the decision, they do not meet as a group, or there are not open discussions among all participants. Instead, there are highly structured patterns of communication among participants, clear acknowledgment of distinct authority levels, and established policies for coordinating participant activi-ties. Instead of a mere group of participants, we have an organization of partici-pants who act as the decision maker.

MULTIPARTICIPANT DECISION MAKERS: SOME EXAMPLES

Type of Multiparticipant Decision Maker	Other Related Terms
Team (with deciding participant)	Crew (with supervisor)
	Squad (with commander)
	Cast (with director)
	Hierarchy (with head)
	Bureau (with chief)
	Tall organization
Group	Committee
	Council
	Panel
	Clan
	Flat organization
Organization	Agency
	Corporation
	Institution
	Network
	Matrix organization

MULTIPARTICIPANT DECISION MAKERS

The various **multiparticipant** decision makers differ primarily in terms of how the participants are deployed, what the participants can do, how they interact, and for what reason they interact. Each participant's activities as part of the decision maker can involve individual decision making. As an individual decision maker, the participant decides what actions it will take within the multiparticipant decision maker. For instance, a participant may decide on a negotiating strategy or problem-solving approach that it will use in contributing to the larger multiparticipant decision. In addition, any of the multiple participants could itself be an individual with a support staff. A participant could even be a group or an **organization.**

THE INDIVIDUAL DECISION MAKER

The individual decision maker of greatest interest is a person. These decision makers vary in terms of intelligence, knowledge, training, experience, personality, and cognitive styles (Miner 1978). **Intelligence** refers to innate mental skills. Some of these skills may lie dormant due to lack of use, stimulation, or recognition. The remainder make up a person's active intelligence. Using these mental skills, a person is able to acquire, retain, manipulate, create, and disseminate **knowledge.**

An individual's **cognitive style** is concerned with the way in which he or she tends to use mental skills in working with knowledge. For instance, a decision maker that pays great attention to detail and precision is employing a different cognitive style than one concerned mainly with broad, sweeping principles, themes, or ideas. Differing personalities or cognitive styles may benefit from **alternative** kinds of decision support systems (Huber 1983).

INDIVIDUAL DIFFERENCES

". . . [O]rganizational decisions are affected by deep-seated orientations of personality, those attributes that individual decision makers bring with them because they are what they are. . . . Among the more important personality dimensions. . .that may affect their decisions are: (1) their orientation to power versus their ideological orientation, (2) their emotionality versus their objectivity, (3) their creativity versus their conventional common sense, and (4) their action orientation versus their contemplative qualities. . . .

"Few organizational leaders are pure types, either crusading warriors for their ideas or power-actuated political manipulators. Most decision makers represent combinations of these. . . .

". . . [E]motionality may affect organizational leaders and the objectivity of their judgments. . . ."

"Some individuals are gifted in originality; they are able to see new relationships and to impose new structure on old facts. Others may have marked ability in making common-sense judgements requiring the assessment of many relevant factors and accurate prediction of likely outcomes. . . . [T]hese abilities do not often occur in the same person. . . .

"Many people have excellent ideas; not nearly as many translate their ideas or even their decisions into the required implementing actions." —**Daniel Katz** and **R. L. Kahn** in *The Social Psychology of Organizations,* pp. 509–513

In spite of such differences among individual decision makers, we can identify some common traits. Any individual decision maker

1. Can accept messages stated in some language,
2. Possess a reservoir of knowledge, and
3. Can process incoming messages and stored knowledge to manufacture a decision.

A **message** is simply a communicated piece of knowledge. It may be stated in ordinary English. Or, it may be stated in a specialized language, such as the one used by accountants, which results in messages such as balance sheets and income statements. A message can be conveyed via a visual language such as a graph, drawing, table of data, or gesture. Messages are a significant means for acquiring knowledge, and they give the decision maker a basis for recognizing a decision opportunity.

The acceptance of such an opportunity marks the start of a decision-making episode. From this point until the end of the episode, an individual decision maker is preoccupied with drawing on the contents of his or her knowledge storehouse and exercising his or her innate capabilities in working with that knowledge. Because the person's knowledge storehouse may be inadequate for addressing an accepted decision opportunity, he or she should be able to collect additional knowledge as needed during the decision-making episode.

The individual must be able to recognize problems during a decision episode. For instance, in making a decision about the quantity of an item to order, the person might recognize that this depends on solving problems such as how much of the item is expected to be used and what the holding and order costs are expected to be. They may be solved by simply scrutinizing the knowledge storehouse to find the desired values. If the values are not there, the individual may need to formulate an approach to solving a problem and then implement it to reach a solution.

Problem solving often involves the use of analysis to produce expectations, forecasts, or beliefs. For instance, using analytical ability may be part of an approach invented for predicting the demand for an item. Analysis is particularly important in an individual's efforts to understand the implications of each alternative. An individual's ability to evaluate is crucial in choosing among alternatives. Because it is concerned with assessing the value of each alternative's implications, it allows a person to compare and rank them in order of preference.

Instead of a person, an individual decision maker could be a computer. Such decision makers can be found in automated factories. Robots that decide what movements to make in response to changing surroundings are individual decision makers. In spite of decades of impressive technological advances, the capacity of present-day computers to function as decision makers is limited compared to ordinary managers. Although research in the field known as *artificial intelligence* (AI) aims to give computers greater capacity for intelligent behavior, computerized decision makers are still limited mainly to structured decisions. On the other hand, there are many things a computer can do to assist actively the efforts of human decision makers. Exploring these support possibilities is our mission.

THE TEAM DECISION MAKER

It is not unusual for a manager to have one or more **staff assistants.** In the course of making a decision, the manager can assign various tasks to these assistants. Each task is, in essence, a problem that the assistant is requested to solve. The solution is communicated back to the manager. Some assistants might be specialists in solving certain kinds of problems that the manager has recognized but is unable to personally solve. Other assistants may be assigned to do tasks that the manager could do. By farming out these tasks, the manager is able to concentrate on the most difficult and crucial aspects of making the decision. Moreover, the assistants may be able to do their work in parallel, thereby speeding up the decision process.

Working together, the manager and staff assistants are a team that manufactures decisions. In other words, the team is a multiparticipant decision maker, having one deciding participant (i.e., the manager) and one or more supporting participants

DSS IN THE NEWS

The New Catbird Seat

". . . Technology . . . will cause management in the future to be quite different from the past," says James I. Cash [who chairs the Harvard MBA program]. . . . .

"There's no better catbird seat than the information view of an organization," says Bernard Mathaise [who directs the Center for Busienss Innovation at Ernst & Young]. . . .

J. B. Truce, "Breaking the Chains of Command—The New 'Catbird Seat,'" *Business Week,* Special 1994 Bonus Issue, p. 114.

HIERARCHIES AND TEAMS

What we are calling a team is also known as a hierarchy, or hierarchical team. It is analogous to the everyday notion of a sports team, whose coach or manager corresponds to the deciding participant and whose players and assistant coaches correspond to supporting participants. The players and assistant coaches tend to be specialists in terms of the functions they perform. Their activities are governed by certain regulations and the authority of the coach. The same holds for a team decision maker.

(i.e., the staff). The decisions produced are unilateral, not involving **negotiation** and agreement among participants.

Figure 3.2 illustrates three different team scenarios. Circles denote participants with decision-making authority. Squares denote participants who have no authority with respect to making the team's decision. They are strictly problem solvers whose efforts support that decision. Each of these problem solvers can make decisions about ways of attacking the problem it faces and can, therefore, be regarded

FIGURE 3.2   Examples of Team Players

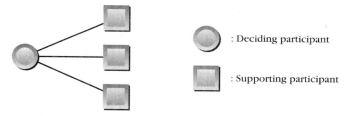

(a) Team of one deciding and three supporting participants

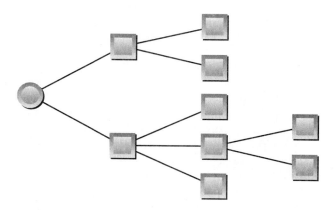

(b) Team with three levels of supporting participants

(c) Team of a manager and a decision support system

as an individual decision maker operating within the team. That person's individual decisions can affect the team decision, but he or she has no authority in making the team's decision. That power resides in the deciding participant.

The lines connecting participants in Figure 3.2 indicate flows of knowledge. The deciding participant's messages to a supporting participant let that assistant know what problem(s) to solve. Messages flowing back from the supporting participants let the deciding participant know what the solutions are. These are factored into the deciding participant's deliberations. Notice in Figure 3.2(b) that supporting participants can themselves receive support from other assistants.

In Figure 3.2(c), we see that a team can consist of a manager and one supporting participant. When that assistant is a computer, we call it a **decision support system (DSS).** The DSS carries out problem-solving tasks assigned to it by the manager. There are flows of knowledge between this team's two participants. Generalizing, a manager may use multiple DSSs when manufacturing a decision (Figure 3.2(a)), and it can happen that one DSS receives assistance from other DSSs by farming out subproblems for them to solve (Figure 3.2(b)).

THE GROUP DECISION MAKER

When a group is the decision maker, there are multiple deciding participants having comparable authority. This is illustrated in Figure 3.3 by the large circle enclosing the smaller uniformly sized circles. Notice that there is no formal structure of authority, such as we had in a team or as we shall see in an organization decision maker. The group may or may not have a leader (e.g., chairperson or facilitator) who enforces some protocols or rituals of interaction among participants. This participant has no more authority in reaching the decision than other participants but does have the extra duty of trying to shape the meeting so it does not get bogged down into talking in circles (Grove 1983). Common examples of group decision makers are committees, panels, boards, and juries.

Any participant in the group may be supported by other entities who are not themselves part of the group. Figure 3.3(b) shows one participant having three levels of support. These supporting entities can be some mix of persons and computers who respond to the participant's problem-solving requests by supplying knowledge he or she needs for deciding what actions to take as a group member. For instance, they may support a decision about what negotiation strategy to use. This group member could be regarded as being a team. In fact, every participant in a group might be a team composed of a person and his or her own DSS.

As Figure 3.3(c) suggests, support can be provided to the group decision maker as a whole. This support can be in addition to possible private support of various participants. If the square in Figure 3.3(c) is a computer, then it is known as a **group decision support system (GDSS).** It might, for example, be a system to facilitate brainstorming among group members. Group brainstorming is an activity wherein participants produce and circulate ideas without criticism (Summers and White 1976). A GDSS could support the group by cataloging participants' ideas, electronically circulating them, and protecting anonymity of each idea's author. In general, the objective of a GDSS is to emphasize the possible advantages and remedy the possible disadvantages of a group decision maker.

Compared to an individual decision maker, a group has several potential advantages. Foremost among these are the greater pool of knowledge that can be brought to bear on the decision and the stimulatory effects of open interchange among par-

FIGURE 3.3 Examples of Group Decision Makers

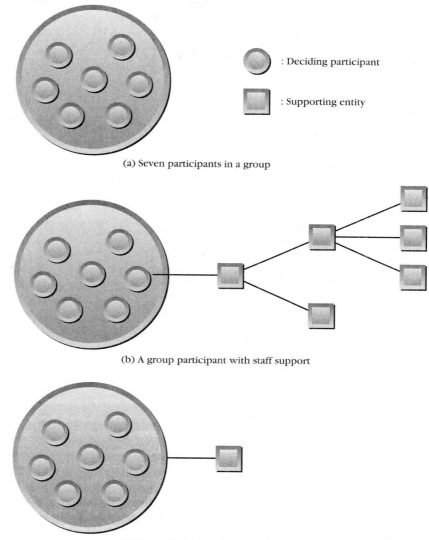

: Deciding participant

: Supporting entity

(a) Seven participants in a group

(b) A group participant with staff support

(c) Group decision maker receiving support

ticipants. There can also be significant drawbacks to group decision making, including the "too many cooks spoil the broth" syndrome, greater consumption of time and effort, and a tendency to make extreme decisions. Researchers call this latter phenomenon *risky shift* or *cautious shift,* depending on the extreme.

A team decision maker partakes of some of the advantages of both a group and an individual while avoiding some of their disadvantages. But it is not feasible to require all decision makers to be teams. Because agreement among equal-authority participants is absolutely necessary for some types of decisions, group decision makers cannot be replaced by teams. Because of insufficient resources to give

BENEFITS AND DRAWBACKS OF GROUP DECISION MAKING

Observers have identified a number of potential advantages and potential disadvantages of a group decision maker (Vecchio 1988).

Potential Advantages	Potential Disadvantages
Participants' knowledge is pooled.	Conflicts in participants' knowledge and motives can produce confusion or "us-versus-them" situations.
Participants stimulate and inspire each other.	Groups have a tendency to consider few alternatives and develop blind spots.
Participants are encouraged to expend greater effort to attain social approval.	Face-to-face meetings can inhibit participant effort or engender hostility.
Higher-quality decisions are made.	Extreme decisions (ultracautious or ultrarisky) may be endorsed. More time and energy are needed to reach a decision.

Which of these potentials become real for a group decision maker depends on such factors as the decision context, the decision type, and the compatibility of group participants.

everyone team support for every decision, some decisions will continue to be made by individuals. However, to the extent that the cost of readily usable decision support systems continues to decrease, the scope of their **knowledge-management** capabilities continues to increase, and managers' awareness of DSS possibilities expands, we will see continued growth in the human-computer teams. They will operate both independently of and as participants in group decision makers.

DSS IN THE NEWS

Groupware

. . . The future of corporate computing in flattened, nonhierarchical organizations could be defined by a category of software known as groupware.
. . . [It] enable[s] people across a far-flung enterprise to work together. . . . While electronic mail allows one-to-one communication, groupware facilitates "many-to-many" communication. . . .

M. Mehler, "CEO Briefing on Information Technology," *Investor's Business Daily,* 16 December, 1993, p. 4.

MULTIPARTICIPANT DECISION MAKERS: DISTINGUISHING TRAITS

DISTINGUISHING TRAITS	DECISION MAKERS			
	Individual	**Team**	**Group**	**Organization**
Participants	One	Multiple	Multiple	Multiple
Authority	Vested in one person	Vested in one person (deciding participant)	More or less equally shared by all participants	Can be distributed unequally among participants
Formal communication among participations	None	Relatively structured	Relatively few restrictions	Can be quite structured
Division of decision-making labor	No division of labor	Division of labor among specialists (supporting participants)	Relatively little division of labor	Can be extensive division of labor and specialization
Duration	Ongoing	Often ongoing, but can be limited	Often limited (e.g., to scope of one decision) but can be ongoing	Ongoing

THE ORGANIZATION DECISION MAKER

Teams and groups are special cases of the organization concept introduced in Chapter 1. Because these special kinds of organizations are so commonplace (e.g., within other organizations) as multiparticipant decision makers, we single them out for special comment and give them brief descriptive labels. However, there are many other kinds of organizations that resemble teams in some respects and groups in other respects. For instance, like teams, they may accommodate specialization and division of labor. At the same time, like groups, authority may be shared by participants. Here, we shall refer to these other kinds of multiparticipant decision makers as organizations, continuing to use the terms *team* and *group* to refer to the special cases.

A manager can share the making of a decision with his or her subordinates (Heller 1976). This gives us a multiparticipant decision maker in which the subordinates are not just supporting participants who solve problems (as in Figure 3.2). Instead, they are given varying degrees of authority with respect to the decision being made. Negotiation is employed to reach a decision to which all agree to commit themselves. This kind of decision maker often appears as an organization (e.g., a department) within an organization. It possesses a structure of multiple power centers who are united in the intention of making a decision consistent with its (e.g., the department's) purpose. Each of these participating power centers may be supported by problem-solving entities.

A manager should consider forming an organization decision maker with his or her subordinate managers when the following conditions exist: (1) the decision is unstructured, (2) a high-quality decision is needed, (3) the manager lacks the knowledge to act as an individual decision maker, or (4) carrying out the commitment made in the decision will recquire or benefit from acceptance by the manager's subordinates (Collins and Guetzkow 1964).

If there is some doubt about securing subordinates' acceptance of a decision, it is more appropriate to get them involved in negotiating toward the decision than to make the decision unilaterally via a team. For an organization decision maker to be effective, it is important that the subordinates are devoted to the organization's purpose and that there be little conflict among them. A team decision maker tends to be more insulated from difficulties that arise when these last two conditions are not met.

The central question is what pattern or mechanism exists for distributing decision-making power across multiple authority levels. The answer is very much related to the issue of organization design. Thus, there are many possibilities for determining how a participant is allowed to use his or her authority, how conflicts are resolved in light of different authority levels, and how the participation of managers is coordinated.

One possibility is suggested by Figure 3.4. The sizes of circles reflect differing degrees of authority possessed by the participants. The small triangle enclosing a circle denotes a special participant called the coordinator. Serving as a sort of focal point of the organization decision maker, the coordinator works with other participants to form a concensus about what the decision should be. In Japanese organizations, for instance, this effort proceeds according to certain conventions that are collectively called *nemawashi*[1] (Watanabe 1987; Yang 1984). As Figure 3.4 indi-

FIGURE 3.4   Example of an Organization Decision Maker

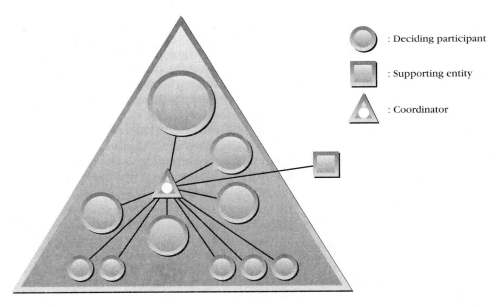

---

1. Pronounced ne-mah'-wash.

cates, this distributed decision making can be facilitated by a system that supports the coordinator's work (Watabe, Holsapple, and Whinston 1992).

3.3   THE DECISION-MAKING PROCESS

Armed with a basic understanding of what decisions and decision makers are, let's take a closer look at the process of making a decision. The action a decision maker follows to produce a decision depends on the decision context and decision type. It also depends on the nature of the decision maker. But there are some common threads that can be found in nearly any decision-making process regardless of the decision's context, type, and maker. A decision-making process involves three

DSS IN THE NEWS

Taking Advantage of Technology

Many are finding they must rethink how tasks are performed to gain benefits from technology. . . .

"Reengineering is about radical change in your processes," said Michael Hammer . . . author of a seminal 1990 paper on the subject published in the Harvard Business Review.

"By and large, the only way you can achieve radical change in your process-es is by exploiting technology," Hammer said . . . But, technology, he cautioned, is merely a facilitator of change. . . .

For some, reengineering is a remedial action or outgrowth of corporate restructuring.

At Caterpillar Inc., in Peoria, Ill., a revamped corporate structure designed to break down functional barriers required . . . a new system . . . that will let man-agers obtain and assess information from multiple geographic areas, product lines and functional groups.

For others, like PepsiCo Inc.'s Frito-Lay unit, reengineering is driven by tech-nology. Recently, the company made organizational changes that should put more authority in the hands of lower-level managers. These managers had gained access to huge pools of market data after distributors were equipped with portable data collection computers but needed the power to act on this new infor-mation.

. . . Interest in reengineering has spawned growing demand for the services of computer systems integrators and software writers. It also has hatched a mar-ket for computer programs designed to model business operations. . . .

More and more . . . managers recognize the need to rearrange their operations to use available technologies to their greatest advantage. . . .

Increasingly, the emphasis is expected to shift to networks of smaller machines that can get at and process data available from throughout the organization, includ-ing the largest computers run by the data processing professionals. . . .

"T. Bunker, "Why Firms are 'Reengineering' Information Systems," *Investor's Business Daily,* 3 April, 1992, p. 3.

important phases, known as intelligence, design, and choice (Simon 1960). In any decision-making process, the decision maker is concerned with solving some problems in some sequence (Bonczek, Holsapple, and Whinston 1981). Any decision-making process is governed by the decision maker's strategy for reaching a choice (Janis and Mann 1977).

DECISION-MAKING PHASES

The three **decision-making phases** we just noted are intelligence, design, and choice. The **intelligence** phase is a period when the decision maker is alert for occasions to make decisions, preoccupied with collecting knowledge, and concerned with evaluating it in light of the organization's purpose. For example, a newly acquired piece of knowledge may suggest that an assembly line is not running as smoothly as it should, alerting the decision maker that a decision will need to be made about what corrective action to take.

The **design** phase is a period when the decision maker formulates alternative courses of action, analyzes those alternatives to arrive at expectations about the likely outcomes of choosing each, and evaluates those expectations with respect to the organization's purpose. During the design phase, the decision maker could find that additional knowledge is needed. This would trigger a return to the intelligence phase to satisfy that need before continuing with the design activity.

Continuing our example, the decision maker formulates several alternative actions and thinks through the implications of each. The results of these analyses are assessed in light of the organization's ideal for assembly-line performance. Evaluations of the alternatives are carried forward into the choice phase of the decision process, where they are compared and one is chosen.

In a **choice** phase, the decision maker exercises authority to select an alternative. This is done in the face of internal and external pressures related to the nature of the decision maker and the decision context. It can happen that none of the alternatives are palatable, that several competing alternatives yield very positive evaluations, or that the state of the world has changed significantly since the alternatives were formulated and analyzed. Nevertheless, there comes a time when one must be selected for implementation. If that time has not yet been reached, the decision maker may return to one of the two earlier phases to collect more up-to-date knowledge, formulate new alternatives, reanalyze alternatives, reevaluate them, and so forth. Then, upon returning to the choice phase, some of the conflicts and pressures may have subsided, allowing the selection to be made more easily.

Figure 3.5 summarizes the three phases of a decision process. It shows that a decision maker can loop back to earlier phases as needed and as allowed by the decision-making time frame. In effect, this means that phases can overlap. We can begin the design phase before all intelligence activity is finished. Knowledge collection is rarely instantaneous. While waiting on the arrival of some piece of knowledge, we can work on the design of alternatives that do not depend on it. Similarly, the choice phase can begin before we have completed our analysis and evaluation of all alternatives. This completion could be awaiting further progress in the intelligence phase. The subset of alternatives considered in the choice phase may contain one that the decision maker can select immediately, without waiting to develop the full set of alternatives in the design phase. Any of the phases is susceptible to computer-based support.

FIGURE 3.5   Three Phases in a Decision Process

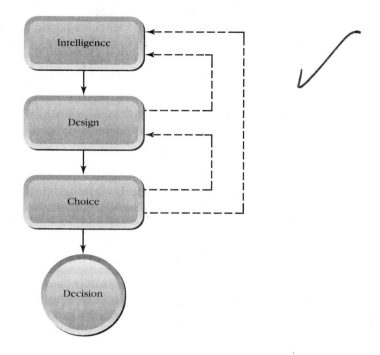

PROBLEM-SOLVING FLOWS

Within each phase of a decision-making process, the decision maker initiates various subactivities. Each of these activities is intended to solve some problem. The decision maker might need to solve such problems as acquiring a competitor's sales figures, predicting the demand for a product, assessing the benefits and costs of a new law, inventing a feasible way of packaging a product into a smaller box, or finding out the cultural difficulties of attempting to market a certain product in foreign countries. Solutions to such problems not only influence decisions but are typically worked out in the course of a decision process. They are not separate from the process.

Solving problems is the essence of the decision-making activity. It permeates the intelligence, design, and choice phases. We might say that a decision-making process is fundamentally one of both recognizing and solving problems along the way toward the objective of producing a decision (Bonczek, Holsapple, and Whinston 1981; Thierauf 1988). For structured decisions, the path toward the objective is well charted. The problems to be surmounted are recognized easily, and the means for solving them are readily available. Unstructured decisions take us into uncharted territory. The problems that will be encountered along the way are not known in advance. Even when stumbled across, they may be difficult to recognize and subsequently solve. Ingenuity and an exploratory attitude are vital for coping with these types of decisions.

Thus, a decision-making process can be thought of as a flow of problem-recognition and -solution exercises. In the case of a multiparticipant decision maker,

STEPS IN A DECISION PROCESS

"A decision process encompasses all those steps taken from the time a stimulus for an action is perceived until the time the commitment to the action is made. . . . Those steps draw on seven fundamentally different kinds of activities or routines. Two take place in the *identification* phase of decision making: the *recognition* routine, wherein the need to initiate a decision process is perceived, and the *diagnosis* routine, where the decision situation is assessed. Two routines are associated with the phase of *development* of solutions: the *search* routine, to find ready-made solutions, and the *design* routine, to develop custom-made ones. The *selection* phase includes three routines: the *screening* of ready-made solutions, the *evaluation-choice* of one solution, and the *authorization* of this. . . ." —**Henry Mintzberg** in *The Structuring of Organizations,* p. 58

Notice that what Mintzberg calls identification, development, and selection correspond to Simon's phases of intelligence, design, and choice. Each of the seven routines can be thought of as a kind of problem-solving activity. That is, there are recognition problems, diagnosis problems, search problems, and so forth. A DSS may help a decision maker handle one or more of these kinds of problems.

this flow has many tributaries, made up of different participants working on various problems simultaneously, in parallel, or in some necessary sequence. From this viewpoint, the overall task of reaching a decision is a superproblem. Only if we solve its subproblems can we solve the overall decision problem. Notice that some problems a manager faces are decision problems. Their solutions are decisions. However, not all problems are decision problems. None of the sample problems just cited is a decision problem. Solving the problem of acquiring a competitor's sales figures does not involve making a decision, although it may be a subproblem within the scope of making a decision about next year's marketing strategy.

It is important not to confuse the notions of problem solving and decision making. Problem solving is an activity directed toward satisfying some sensed need (Costello and Zalkind 1963). That need may or may not be to reach a decision. Interestingly, problem solving itself can involve decision making (Ebert and Mitchell 1975). For instance, in solving the problem of acquiring sales figures, a decision

WHAT IS IMPORTANT IN MAKING DECISIONS?

A survey of more than 450 managers in the United States and Europe asked them to rank the considerations they feel are important in making decisions (Rowe and Boulgardes 1992). Results showed that the top three considerations are

1. Perception, including problem awareness and understanding of data;
2. Commitment, involving the willingness and ability to see that decisions are implemented;
3. Integrity, exhibiting consistent behavior resulting in greater credibility and confidence.

maker may need to decide what degree of accuracy is necessary or how much can be paid for the information. However, we shall be concerned mainly with the problem recognition and solving that occurs during the process of making a decision. Decision support systems can help decision makers in both recognizing and solving problems (Thierauf 1988).

STRATEGIES TO GUIDE DECISION MAKING*

Within a decision-making process, there are various strategies that a decision maker can use to organize his or her efforts. The process is strongly colored by the strategy being used to choose an alternative. Among the well-known **decision-making strategies** are optimizing, satisficing, elimination-by-aspects, incrementalism, mixed scanning, and the analytic hierarchy process. A particular decision maker in a particular decision process may be using one of these, some hybrid of them, or some entirely different strategy. Here, we briefly discuss these six strategies. A decision support system designed to support the use of optimizing may be of little help when a satisficing strategy is being used and vice versa.

Optimization* Using an **optimization** strategy, a decision maker will select the alternative that gives the best overall value. Suppose we need to decide where to locate a warehouse. The warehouse will serve retail outlets in several midwestern states. If we begin to list all the possible sites, it quickly becomes clear that the number of alternatives is enormous. Nevertheless, assume that we have such a list. Employing an optimization strategy, we pick the "best" site from the list of alternatives. In so doing, we are making an optimal decision. The big question here concerns which alternative is best (i.e., optimal). To answer this question, we need to identify the **criteria** by which we will judge the alternatives.

Examples of criteria that could be relevant include distances of a site from current retail outlets that it would service, work-force availability at the site, local property tax rates, local construction costs, cost of land for a building site, proximity of railroad and air transport terminals, government incentives for building the plant at a site, and availability of adjacent land for potential warehouse expansion. Such criteria can play two roles in an optimization strategy.

First, they can help us identify which alternatives on our list are really feasible. For instance, we might impose a constraint that says we are uninterested in any site where the local property tax rate exceeds 2%. Another constraint, combining multiple criteria, might be that the sum of construction and land costs cannot exceed our budget of $6,000,000. Thus, criteria can be used to specify a set of constraints that all alternatives must obey. This allows us to prune down the original list to a smaller (albeit still quite large) group of feasible alternatives.

Secondly, criteria give us a basis for comparing the value of one alternative against others. We can look at the property tax rate for each alternative and see which is best (i.e., lowest). Using a different criterion, such as the average distance to retail outlets, we might find that a different alternative gives us the best (i.e., shortest) result. In effect, an alternative yields a certain score for each criterion. The idea in an optimization strategy is to combine (e.g., add or multiply) the various scores an alternative yields for the criteria into one overall measure of the alternative's goodness. In the course of combining scores we may want to weight them. For instance, we might double the tax rate score if we consider it to be twice as important.

If a weighted combination were produced for each alternative, we would then select the alternative with the best overall score as our decision. In some cases, our objective would be to find the alternative with the lowest score. We would be seeking to minimize a combination of costs, travel distances, production times, and so forth. In other cases, optimization seeks to maximize a combination of factors such as profits, production rates, speed, and so on. When we want to maximize with respect to such criteria, the overall score of an alternative is typically called its payoff, or **utility.** In any event, a decision-making process based on an optimization strategy, involves the recognition and solution of optimization problems.

Much of the field known as **management science** is concerned with expressing optimization problems in mathematical terms and inventing formal procedures to solve such problems (Lapin 1975). Such a procedure is then implemented as a computer program that can accept the statement of an optimization problem and respond with the optimal alternative. In making a problem statement to the computer, we need to specify what criteria are of interest, what constraints must be satisfied by feasible alternatives, how an alternative's scores on the various criteria are to be weighted and combined, and whether the objective is to maximize or minimize. Computer programs that solve optimization problems are important elements of some decision support systems, especially those intended to support decision makers opting for an optimization strategy. Once the decision maker has formulated an optimization problem statement, the DSS solves that problem for the decision maker.

Although the optimizing strategy has proven to be invaluable for many decisions, its practical application is severely limited by a number of factors. First, it becomes difficult to solve optimization problems when the criteria are qualitative. In locating a warehouse one important criterion might be the quality of life that a site affords for employees. It is difficult to combine such a factor mathematically with a tax rate. When criteria cannot be readily quantified, the solution methods that management scientists have worked out for optimization problems are of little help. The optimizing decision maker must find and rely on some less formal way of recognizing, analyzing, and evaluating alternatives.

Second, the task of estimating the cost or benefits of every viable alternative can be formidable. Third, the amount of knowledge on which an optimizing strategy depends can be enormous. It can be very costly in terms of time and effort to collect and examine the volumes of necessary knowledge. This cost might be unbearable or could outweigh the savings achieved by picking the best alternative rather than a very good alternative. A fourth, and very fundamental, criticism of optimization is that there is often no adequate way to combine all scores for an alternative into a single overall measure of goodness or utility (Miller and Starr 1967). In summary, making an optimal decision is a noble notion, but it can be difficult or impractical to achieve in many situations.

Satisficing*   A strategy that does not suffer from the practical difficulties of optimizing is to select the first alternative discovered to be good enough with respect to some minimal criteria. This strategy is known as **satisficing** (Simon 1957, 1976; March and Simon 1958). The idea is to find any needle in the haystack rather than seeking the sharpest of all needles. In the decision about a warehouse site, using the satisficing strategy would mean selecting the first alternative that is satisfactory with respect to every one of the relevant criteria. In other words, it satisfies all the specified constraints. It may or may not be the best. In fact, we would be unconcerned with trying to define *best*.

With this strategy, each alternative is considered as it is identified. It is either rejected because it does not meet the cutoff level for some constraint (e.g., total land and construction cost is too high) or it is accepted as the decision because it passes all cutoff levels. An interesting issue is the sequence in which alternatives are identified and considered. Simon says that decision makers tend to develop and use "rules of thumb" to govern this sequencing (1957). Also called *heuristics,* these rules could arise from a wide variety of factors, such as experience, formal training, ingenuity, or inspiration. For instance, we might "feel" that sites in central Indiana should be considered before others, and among these we might want to begin with the sites in the largest cities. A DSS tailored to support satisficing facilitates the decision maker's need to explore. It aids in the analysis and evaluation of alternatives, and it may even recommend a sequence of alternatives.

Elimination-by-Aspects* A third strategy used in decision-making processes is known as **elimination-by-aspects** (Tversky 1972). Here, decision making becomes a narrowing process, eliminating all alternatives that fail with respect to one aspect, then those that fail with respect to another, and so forth. An aspect is like a constraint involving one or more criteria. In deciding on a warehouse location, we might first eliminate all alternatives not having a low-enough property tax rate. Among those that remain, we might then eliminate all that have a total land and construction cost in excess of some cutoff. We would continue in this fashion until one alternative remains, which becomes our decision.

If we run out of aspects before eliminating all but one alternative, then additional aspects need to be invented to allow the narrowing process to continue. Another difficulty is that we could run out of alternatives or eliminate one that is superior overall to the remaining alternatives. An alternative may barely fail on the

CONTRASTING STRATEGIES

Satisficing	Optimizing
• Small set of criteria exists, all of which must be met by chosen alternative.	• Possibly many criteria; the alternative that overall does the best in meeting them is chosen.
• As each alternative is formulated, test it against the criteria.	• Formulate and consider as many good alternatives as possible.
• Each alternative is tested once.	• Repeatedly reexamine the best alternatives.
• Test for each criterion is with respect to a cutoff point.	• Evaluate overall goodness of an alternative across all criteria.
• Criteria are of equal importance.	• Some criteria are weighted more heavily than others in determining overall goodness of the alternative.

first aspect and be eliminated, even though it is vastly superior for all other aspects. Thus the order of aspects can strongly influence the result. So, we might want to apply the most important aspect first, then the second most important aspect, and so forth. A DSS to support elimination-by-aspects would have less of the exploratory character than one supporting satisficing. It could be expected to offer strong support in solving analysis and evaluation problems.

Incrementalism*   A fourth strategy is called **incrementalism,** or simply *muddling through* (Lindbolm 1959, 1965; Braybrooke and Lindbolm 1963). Here, the decision maker successfully compares alternative courses of action to the current course of action. In this comparison activity, the decision maker is looking for an alternative that can overcome shortcomings that have been observed in the current course of

DSS IN THE NEWS

Refocused Decision Making: Changing the Criteria

In the mid-1980's, Colgate-Palmolive Co. executives knew something had to be done about the company's performance.

Corporate raiders stood ready to bag big, old, slow-moving companies whenever management stumbled and share prices sank. At Colgate, earnings growth was sluggish, capital expenditures weren't paying off, and product development took too long. . . .

Company accountants work closely with . . . systems specialists, using computers to quantify the principal elements of the business and to build up databases that make it easier to evaluate the profitability of all activities and capital investments.

New investments and other business plans now must clear specific financial hurdles, based on estimated returns and projected cash-flow impact.

By working smarter and making better use of technology, Colgate has achieved the results it set for itself. . . .

. . . Colgate management refocused decision-making through the shareholder value prism, calling the new assessment technique BASICS, for Building Added Strength in Cashflow Streams.

"One of the driving points of BASICS when we first initiated it was to have the same criteria for measuring a decision . . . used within the company (as) would be used externally, by the investment community. And that criteria is future cash flows," Agate said. . . .

Colgate managers from all parts of the company now use the approach to evaluate every key business decision, from capital spending and acquisitions to new-product development and marketing campaigns. . . .

Agate says this would not have been possible without using computers and the databases they can manipulate. . . .

T. Bunker, "How Information Systems Helped Colgate-Palmolive Clean Up Results," *Investor's Business Daily,* 24 June, 1993, p. 4.

action. If such an alternative does not itself have shortcomings relative to the current course of action, it becomes the selected alternative.

Each decision is very much a reaction to observed results of the prior decision. The main idea is to make a series of decisions that result in incremental improvements based on growing experience. A DSS designed to support such decision making could be expected to monitor closely current situations resulting from prior decisions, recognize shortcomings in those results, and aid in the analyses that compare an alternative with the current practice.

DSS IN THE NEWS

Decision Criteria

. . .Capital budgeting for information technology forces managers to make their decisions in a haze of unquantifiable benefits and only slightly more identifiable costs.

So for a decision maker, it becomes a choice between two evils: making the investment and taking it on faith that it's paying off, or not making the investment and running the risk of conceding a technical advantage to less risk-averse competitors. . . .

What's a decision maker to do?

Recognize the limitations of the traditional capital budgeting model as it applies to investments in information technology—standard cost/benefit analyses won't work.

Don't get preoccupied with trying to account for the "soft" benefits. Understand that those benefits—while almost impossible to quantify—provide some of the most persuasive arguments for making the investment.

You may not be able to accurately measure the increase in customer satisfaction, or the improvements in your firm's ability to deliver products to market. But if your investment decision was a well-reasoned one, you'll realize the benefits whether you can measure them or not. . . .

Recognize that the decision is not easier for your competitors, and that many of them will take the leap of faith necessary to make a substantial investment in information technology. . . .

When confronted with that reality, more often than not management will take the plunge—sometimes without anything resembling an analysis of return on investment.

"One of the reasons for that," explained Boston Consulting Group's Gary A. Curtis, "is that a lot of information technology capital projects started without a strategic or major tactical direction."

Which brings up a point: Before concerning yourself with making sure the technology investment is consistent with your firm's strategic objectives, make sure you have a clearly stated set of objectives and goals.

W. B. Yanes, "Benefits of Information Technology Hard to Figure," *Investor's Business Daily,* 31 January, 1991, p. 8.

USING THE ANALYTIC HIERARCHY PROCESS

In using the AHP to govern a decision about a new warehouse site, we might structure our analysis in terms of the following hierarchy:

At the top of this hierarchy is the overall objective of choosing a warehouse site. At the next level, there are five main criteria that have a bearing on meeting this objective. A third level consists of subcriteria related to the main criteria. Additional levels of more detailed subcriteria could exist but are not shown. Ultimately, the lowest level consists of four alternative sites. Although not shown in this diagram, each site can be considered to be linked to all of the prior level's subcriteria.

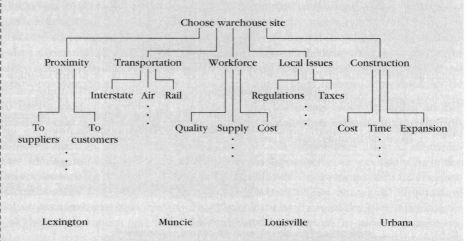

An example of a pairwise comparison matrix for the main criteria is shown in the following table.

IMPORTANCE OF	versus PROXIMITY	TRANSPORTATION	WORK FORCE	REGULATION	CONSTRUCTION
Proximity	1	1	5	6	6
Transportation	⅓	1	3	3	4
Work force	⅕	⅓	1	3	3
Regulation	⅙	⅓	⅓	1	½
Construction	⅙	¼	⅓	2	1

Here, a decision maker judged the proximity criterion to be moderately more important (3) than the transportation criterion, strongly more important (5) than the workforce criterion, and of even stronger importance (6) relative to the other two criteria. Similarly, construction issues are of very little importance (⅙) compared to proximity, little importance (¼) relative to transportation issues, modestly less importance (⅓) than work force, and somewhat greater importance (2) than local issues.

At the next level, five pairwise comparison matrices would be constructed, one for the subcriteria of each main criterion. For instance, there would be a 3-by-3 matrix

Continued

involving the quality, supply, and cost subcriteria of the work-force criterion. For the lowest level in the hierarchy, there is a 4-by-4 matrix for each of the prior level's subcriteria. Suppose one of the subcriteria is the cost of land under the construction-cost branch of the hierarchy. The pairwise comparison matrix of alternatives relative to land cost might be as follows.

PREFERENCE OF VERSUS	LEXINGTON	MUNCIE	LOUISVILLE	URBANA
Lexington	1	½	⅓	1
Muncie	2	1	4	⅕
Louisville	3	¼	1	¼
Urbana	1	5	4	1

Following the AHP, all the matrices are mathematically processed to yield relative weights of criteria and subcriteria. The weights are then used to mathematically synthesize a score for each alternative. These scores form a basis for selecting an alternative.

Mixed Scanning*   Another decision strategy is called **mixed scanning** (Etzioni 1967). Scanning refers to the search for, collection, processing, evaluating, and weighing of information. With this strategy, the importance of a decision determines the degree of scanning and the choice approach. For major decisions, we list all alternatives. Each is briefly considered. Those for which we can find a crippling objection are rejected. We examine and analyze remaining alternatives in greater detail. Again, those for which we detect strong objections are rejected. This approach is repeated, scrutinizing remaining alternatives with increasing detail until only one remains, which becomes the decision. For ensuing minor decisions, we would use an incremental satisficing approach. A DSS customized for mixed scanning is expected to solve knowledge collection and analysis problems at many different levels of detail.

Analytic Hierarchy Process*   The final strategy that we consider here is the **analytic hierarchy process** (Saaty 1987, 1990b, 1994). When applied to decision making, the analytic hierarchy process (AHP) decomposes the overall decision objective into a hierarchic structure of criteria, subcriteria, and alternatives. Using the AHP, a decision maker then compares each pair of criteria by answering the question, with respect to meeting the overall decision objective, which of the two criteria is more important and by how much? Each such judgment is represented by a number in the range ⅑ to 9, where ⅑ means that the first criterion in a pair is of only very minor importance compared to the second criterion, 1 means that the two criteria are equally important, and 9 means that the first criterion is of maximal importance relative to the second. The result is a matrix of pairwise comparisons with respect to the overall objective.

The decision maker proceeds to the first level of subcriteria beneath the level of main criteria and repeats the process. He or she compares each pair of subcriteria by answering the question: With respect to satisfying a certain criterion in the prior level, which of these two subcriteria is more important and by how much? Then the decision maker uses the numeric scale noted earlier to represent these judgments. The result is a matrix of pairwise subcriteria comparisons for each criterion in the prior level. The decision maker repeats this process for succeeding levels of subcriteria. Upon reaching the lowest level of the hierarchy, which consists of specific alternatives for meeting the overall objective, the decision maker does a pairwise comparison of the alternative with respect to subcriteria in the prior level. For each of these subcriteria, a matrix of pairwise comparisons results from answering the question; With respect to a certain subcriterion, which alternative is preferred and by how much?

For each matrix of pairwise comparisons, the AHP mathematically derives a ratio scale of relative magnitudes expressed in terms of priority units (Saaty 1987). These serve as estimates of relative weights for each element in the hierarchy. These relative weights are then aggregated to synthesize a ranking of alternatives, as a basis for choosing one of them. There are variants of the AHP described here (e.g., alternatives are not pairwise compared but rated as to categories into which they fall for each subcriteria (Saaty 1990b)). A decision support system oriented toward the analytic hierarchy process can assist decision makers in constructing or modifying hierarchies, building pairwise comparison matrices, deriving relative weights, and/or synthesizing rankings of alternatives.

A debate among scholars has challenged and defended the AHP on theoretical grounds (e.g., Dyer 1990; Saaty 1990a). However, from a practical standpoint, numerous situations in which AHP has been used are documented (e.g., Zahedi 1986). These tend to involve at least some qualitative criteria as important factors in the decision to be made. The AHP gives a way to quantify such factors. Applicability of the AHP is constrained by the task of constructing the pairwise comparison matrix, which becomes formidable as the number of hierarchy levels, criteria, and alternatives increase. Reported AHP applications tend to involve three to seven levels and a limited number of alternatives.

Other Strategies*   The strategies surveyed here are by no means the only ones possible in a decision-making process. They are symptomatic of a diverse assortment of strategies. Each has variations, and hybrid strategies involving two or more strategies are certainly conceivable. The main point is that the strategy employed can color what a decision maker would like to see in a DSS. Every DSS will not be ideally suited to supporting every strategy. Nevertheless, it would be a big plus for a decision maker to have a DSS sufficiently flexible and adaptable to aid in pursuing whatever the current strategy happens to be.

3.4   DECISION SUPPORT

To this point we have spoken of decision support quite informally. We have seen that there are various kinds of decision makers operating in a range of decision contexts and working toward diverse types of decisions. In their decision-making processes, they tend to go through common phases, identify and solve problems, and use some strategy to guide their efforts. Throughout this discussion, we have repeatedly hinted that computer-based systems could help decision makers. It is now time to ask two important questions in this connection. Why does a decision maker need support? What is the nature of the needed support?

THE NEED FOR SUPPORT

Computer systems to support decision makers are not free. Not only is there the cost of purchasing or developing a DSS, there are also costs associated with learning about, using, and maintaining a DSS. It is only reasonable that the benefits of a DSS should be required to outweigh its costs (Marsden and Pingry 1993). Although some DSS benefits can be difficult to measure in precise quantitative terms, all the benefits are the result of a decision maker's need for support. When a decision maker needs support it is because of cognitive, economic, or time limits.

Cognitive Limits* **Cognitive limits** refer to limits in the human mind's ability to store and process knowledge. A person does not know everything all the time. In fact, a person's memory contents are typically quite modest relative to the world's constantly growing volumes of knowledge. Even the knowledge that has been stored away cannot always be recalled in an instantaneous, error-free fashion. All the knowledge existing in what psychologists call long-term memory cannot be summoned simultaneously into a person's immediate field of awareness.

Because decision making is a knowledge-intensive activity, cognitive limits substantially restrict an individual's decision-making efficiency and effectiveness. They may even make it impossible for the individual to reach some decisions. If these limits are relaxed, decision-maker productivity should improve. The main reason team decision makers exist is due to this situation. Rather than having an individual who must solve all problems leading to a decision, additional participants serve as extensions to the deciding participant's own knowledge-handling skills. They allow problems to be solved more reliably or rapidly. Recall from figure 3.2(c) that a DSS can be a supporting participant. As such, it is regarded as extending a person's cognitive capabilities.

Economic Limits* To relax cognitive limits as much as possible, we could consider forming a very large team. But as a team incorporates more and more participants, the tasks of communicating and coordinating their efforts also grow. The proportion of activity spent in solving communication and coordination problems rises relative to the problem solving directly concerned with making the decision.

HUMAN KNOWLEDGE-PROCESSING LIMITS

Studies suggest that a person's capacity for processing the contents of his or her immediate field of awareness is limited to manipulating up to about seven pieces of knowledge at any one time (Miller 1956). The stress, errors, and oversights that can result from being overloaded with knowledge can be just as detrimental as not having enough knowledge (Miller 1960; Miller and Starr 1967). In addition, a person may not be especially skilled at some kinds of knowledge manipulations (e.g., mathematical ones).

Increasing a team's size can be expensive not only in terms of paying and equipping staff assistants, but also with respect to increased communication and coordination costs. At some point, the benefits of increased cognitive abilities may be outweighed by the costs of more participants.

Even before that point is reached, a decision maker may run into other economic barriers. The monetary resources available may not permit the addition of another staff assistant, even if it were deemed to be beneficial. The **economic limits** on a decision maker are every bit as real as the cognitive limits. Decision support systems can soften the effects of economic limits when they are admitted as team participants. If properly conceived and used, added DSSs increase the productivity of human participants and allow the team decision maker to solve problems more efficiently and effectively.

DSS IN THE NEWS

Technology's Competitive Impacts

Technology has changed competition by decreasing the time it takes to enter new markets while expanding the variety of products and services available.

Change has become so pervasive and persistent that it's now the norm. . . .

IBM Credit Corp. . . . used to take six to 14 days to approve or deny a request for financing. During this period, the potential customer could find another source of financing for IBM products or be seduced by another equipment supplier.

By empowering workers to make more decisions and developing a sophisticated new computer system, IBM slashed credit approval turnaround time to just four hours.

Information technology plays a crucial role in enabling companies to reengineer business processes. Here's how information technology can facilitate reengineering concepts. . . .

- Information can appear simultaneously in as many places as needed. In an insurance business, for instance, one clerk can calculate an applicant's premium rate while another checks the applicant's credit rating, both using the same application form.
- Computer systems can turn employees from generalists into experts. As illustrated by the IBM credit example, a caseworker can handle all steps in an order process, eliminating the need to hand off files, which can create errors and delays.
- Field workers can send and receive information wherever they are. When a customer returns a rental car, an attendant equipped with a portable computer can meet the car, electronically pull up a copy of the rental transaction and enter the charge. The customer never has to visit the office.
- Plans can be revised instantaneously. A computer supplied with up-to-the-minute data can be monitored to constantly adjust, say, manufacturing schedules or product delivery.

B. Deagon, "The Reengineering Revolution: Right Cause for U.S. Business Today?" *Investor's Business Daily,* 24 March 1993, p. 4.

Time Limits* A third limit that decision makers commonly encounter is a **time limit.** A decision maker may be blessed with extraordinary cognitive abilities and vast monetary resources but very little time. Time limits can put severe pressure on the decision maker, increasing the likelihood of errors and poor-quality decisions. There may not be sufficient time to consider relevant knowledge, to solve relevant problems, or to employ a desirable decision-making strategy. Because computers can process some kinds of knowledge much faster than humans, are not error-prone, work tirelessly, and are immune to stresses from looming deadlines, decision support systems can help lessen the impacts of time limits.

Competitive Demands* Aside from relaxing limits on a decision maker, DSSs are needed for another important reason. Decision makers, staff assistants, and organizations often find themselves in competitive situations. Their continued success— or even their outright survival—depends on being competitive. If one competitor successfully uses DSSs for better decision making and another does not, then the second competitor will be at a competitive disadvantage. All else being equal, the first competitor will be able to make decisions more efficiently or effectively. Thus, it is prudent to consider using DSSs to keep pace. Taking an even more aggressive stance, we might actively seek out opportunities for using DSSs in innovative ways in order to achieve a competitive advantage (Holsapple and Whinston 1990).

KINDS OF SUPPORT THAT CAN BE PROVIDED

In closing it is worthwhile to summarize some of the ways in which computers can support decision makers. As we have seen, a DSS and the person who uses it form a team. This team may produce unilateral decisions, be a participant in a group decision maker, or participate in an organization decision maker. In addition, there are cases where the DSS user possesses no decision-making authority, such as when a staff assistant in a team uses the DSS.

Finally, the DSS user may not be an individual but a group or organization as a whole. Thus, it is conceivable that a single DSS could simultaneously support multiple decision-making participants. Carrying this to the extreme, a single DSS could even support multiple decision makers at the same time. These support possibilities are illustrated in Figure 3.6. The focus in Parts Two through Four is mainly on DSSs that support a single deciding or supporting participant (Figure 3.6(a) through (d)). Part Five considers the other possibilities.

The nature of support a DSS can offer to its user will normally includes at least one of the following:

1. It alerts the user to a decision-making opportunity or challenge.
2. It recognizes problems that need to be solved as part of the decision-making process.
3. It solves problems recognized by itself or by the user.
4. It facilitates or extends the user's ability to process (e.g., acquire, transform, explore) knowledge.
5. It offers advice, expectations, evaluations, facts, analyses, and designs to the user.
6. It stimulates the user's perception, imagination, or creative insight.
7. It coordinates or facilitates interactions among participants in multiparticipant decision makers.

FIGURE 3.6   Some Ways a DSS Can Help

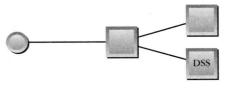

(a) DSS for single deciding participant

(b) DSS for single deciding supporting participant

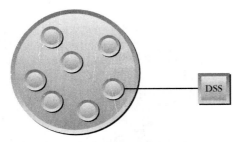

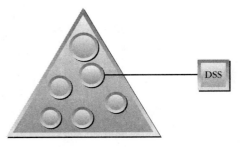

(c) DSS for single deciding participant in group
     decision maker

(d) DSS for single deciding participant in organization
     decision maker

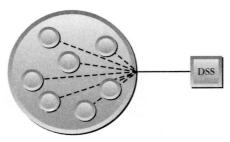

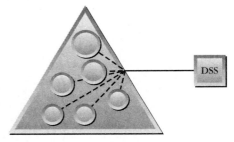

(e) DSS for group of deciding participants

(f) DSS for organization of deciding participants

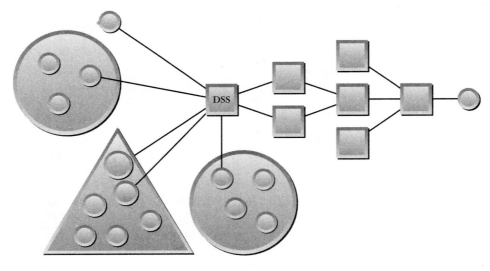

(h) DSS for multiple participants in multiple decision makers

As we have seen, some of these traits are likely to be more valuable than others, depending on the decision context, decision type, and decision maker. Part Two examines the internal nature of systems that exhibit these decision support traits.

3.5 SUMMARY

We have seen that all decision makers are not alike. Some are individuals. Others have multiple participants. Some multiparticipant decision makers are teams, others are groups, and yet others are organizations. Differences in decision contexts, types, and makers suggest that there may also be differences in decision support systems.

There are certain common traits that decision-making processes tend to exhibit. They typically involve the phases of intelligence, design, and choice. They are very much concerned with the recognition and subsequent solution of problems. A decision-making episode is a flow of problem-solving episodes. Decision-making processes are based on strategies to guide the flow. Some common strategies include optimizing, satisficing, and incrementalism. Decision support systems can help in any of the phases, in problem recognition and solution efforts, and in the implementation of various strategies.

The need for decision support systems stems from the realities of cognitive, economic, and time limits. The capacity for having decision support systems stems from ongoing technological advances that put inexpensive, yet powerful, computers on our desktops, in our vehicles, and even in our pockets. It also stems from conceptual and software advances made by decision support researchers and practitioners. The nature of support that can be furnished by a DSS has progressed rapidly over the past decade and is likely to make continued advances. Because knowledge forms the fabric of decision making, all the various kinds of support that a DSS can provide are essentially exercises in knowledge management. Thus, we now take a closer look at the matter of knowledge.

▲ IMPORTANT TERMS

alternative	DSS	mixed scanning
analytic hierarchy	economic limit	multiparticipant
process	elimination-by-aspects	negotiation
choice	GDSS	optimization
cognitive limit	group	organization
cognitive style	group decision support	problem solving
criteria	system	satisfice
decision maker	incrementalism	staff assistant
decision making	intelligence	team
decision-making phase	knowledge	time limit
decision-making strategy	knowledge management	unilateral
decision support system	management science	utility
design	message	

▲ APPLICATION TO THE QUEBEC CASE

1. What decision(s) need to be made by a manager who does fleet planning?
2. Is the decision in this case more or less structured than the one in the Idaho case?
3. What steps are used in deciding on a fleet plan?
4. What is the nature of the DSS user in this case? Does it appear to be a unilateral or negotiated decision (or could the DSS support both)?
5. Which of the three phases of decision making is (are) supported by the DSS? What is the nature of that support?
6. Trace the flow of problem solving that occurs in deciding on a fleet plan. Which problem-solving episodes are accomplished by the DSS and which are done by humans?
7. Describe the kinds of procedural and descriptive knowledge incorporated into the DSS.
8. What is the purpose of each of the DSS's five major problem-solving modules?
9. What decision-making strategy has this DSS been designed to support? Explain.
10. What limit(s) on the decision maker has the DSS been designed to overcome? Explain.
11. Which of the seven decision support traits (recall Section 3.4) has this DSS been designed to include? Give an example for each.
12. Give an example of a what-if question that could be posed to this DSS.

▲ REVIEW QUESTIONS

1. How does a negotiated decision differ from a unilateral decision?
2. Do all multiparticipant decision making episodes result in negotiated decisions? Why?
3. Are all negotiated decisions produced by groups? If not, give an example of a negotiated decision made by multiple participants who are not merely a group?
4. What factors determine who will be the maker of a particular decision?
5. In the making of a decision, how does a group of participants differ from an organization of participants?
6. What are the three main types of multiparticipant decision makers?
7. How does a team decision maker differ from a group decision maker?
8. How does a GDSS differ from a DSS?
9. What are the two kinds of unilateral decision making?
10. Under what circumstances is each of the four kinds of decision makers appropriate?
11. What are three major phases of a decision-making process?
12. What is meant by the term *problem solving?*
13. Describe the relationship between decision making and problem solving.
14. What is satisficing? How does it differ from optimizing?
15. As a practical decision-making strategy, what are the drawbacks of optimizing?
16. Identify five strategies that could guide decision-making efforts.
17. In what ways do AHP and satisficing differ?
18. How does satisficing differ from elimination-by-aspects.
19. What are three major limits on a decision maker that a decision support system might help overcome?

20. What are some of the cognitive limits on an individual decision maker and how are these limits lessened for a team decision maker?
21. Can you cite several ways in which a computer-based system might provide support to a decision maker?

▲ DISCUSSION TOPICS

1. Give an example of multiparticipant decision making that does not involve negotiation.
2. Discuss the ways in which a particular decision's context (e.g., organization design, degree of concurrency) determines who the decision maker will be.
3. Discuss the way in which a particular decision's type (e.g., structuredness, impact, functional area) determines who the decision maker will be.
4. What kind of decision maker produces each of the following decisions?
   a. A jury verdict
   b. Response to a national security threat
   c. A legislative resolution
   d. The introductory price to charge for a new automobile line
   e. The features to be incorporated into next year's version of an established product line
   f. The play to call in the final 5 seconds of a close basketball game
   g. How much to allocate as an IRA contribution in the current tax year
5. Discuss the value of brainstorming as a part of group negotiation.
6. Comment on the relationships between (a) a group decision maker and a flat organization and (b) an organization decision maker and a tall organization.
7. Relate the three phases of decision making to the seven capabilities present in an individual decision maker. Would you expect to find the same capabilities in multiparticipant decision makers?
8. Explain how a group and a team can be regarded as two special cases of an organization.
9. Organization decision makers exist on a continuum that stretches from a team at one end to a group at the other extreme. What team traits and what group traits would you expect to see in organization decision makers that lie between the extremes?
10. Identify and analyze advantages and drawbacks of allowing the three phases of decision making to overlap.

▲ REFERENCES

Applegate, L., C. Ellis, C. Holsapple, F. Radermacher, and A. Whinston. 1991. Organizational computing: Definition and issues. *Organizational Computing* 1, no. 1.

Bonczek, R. H., C. W. Holsapple, and A. B. Whinston. 1981. *Foundations of decision support systems.* New York: Academic Press.

Braybrooke, D., and C. E. Lindblom. 1963. *A strategy for decision.* New York: Free Press.

Collins, B. E., and H. Guetzkow. 1964. *A social psychology of group process for decision making.* New York: John Wiley.

Costello, T. W., and S. S. Zalkind. 1963. *Psychology in administration: A research orientation,* Englewood Cliffs, N.J.: Prentice Hall.

Couillard, J. 1993. A decision support system for vehicle fleet planning," *Decision Support Systems* 9, no. 2.

Dyer, J. S. 1990. Remarks on the analytic hierarchy process. *Management Science* 36, no. 3.

Ebert, R. J., and T. R. Mitchell. 1975. *Organizational decision processes: Concepts and analysis.* New York: Crane, Russak & Co.

Etzioni, A. 1967. Mixed scanning: A third approach to decision making. *Public Administration Review* 27.

Grove, A. S. 1983. *High output management.* New York: Random House.

Heller, F. A. 1976. Decision processes: An analysis of power sharing at senior organizational levels. In *Handbook of work, organization, and society,* edited by R. Durbin. New York: Rand McNally.

Holsapple, C. W. 1991. Decision support in multiparticipant decision makers. *Journal of Computer Information Systems* 31, no. 4.

Holsapple, C. W., and A. B. Whinston. 1990. "Business expert systems: Gaining a competitive edge. *Proceedings of the Hawaiian International Conference on Systems Sciences,* Kona, Hawaii, January.

Huber, G. P. 1983. Cognitive style as a basis for MIS and DSS designs: Much ado about nothing? *Management Science* 29, no. 5.

Janis, I. L., and Mann, L. 1977. *Decision making: A psychological analysis of conflict, choice, and commitment.* New York: The Free Press.

Katz, D., and R. L. Kahn. 1978. *The social psychology of organizations,* 2nd ed., New York: John Wiley.

Lapin, L. L. 1975. *Quantitative methods for business decisions.* New York: Harcourt Brace Jovanovich.

Lindblom, C. E. 1959. The science of muddling through. *Public Administration Review* 19, no. 1.

_____. 1965. *The intelligence of democracy.* New York: The Free Press.

March, J. G., and H. A. Simon. 1958. *Organizations.* New York: John Wiley.

Marsden, J. R., and D. Pingry. 1993. A theory of decision support systems design evaluation. *Decision Support Systems* 9, no. 2.

Miller, D. W., and M. K. Starr. 1967. *The structure of human decisions.* Englewood Cliffs, N.J.: Prentice-Hall.

Miller, G. A. 1956. The magical number seven, plus or minus two. *Psychological Review* 63, no. 1.

Miller, J. G. 1960. Information input, overload, and psychopathology. *American Journal of Psychiatry* 116 (February).

Miner, J. B. 1978. *The management process: Theory, research, and practice,* 2nd ed. New York: Macmillian.

Mintzberg, H. 1979. *The structuring of organizations.* Englewood Cliffs, N.J.: Prentice-Hall.

Rowe, A. J., and J. D. Boulgardes. 1992. *Managerial decision making,* New York: Macmillan. 1992.

Saaty, T. L. 1987. The analytical hierarchy process—What it is and how it is used. *Mathematical Modelling* 9 no. 3–5.

_____. 1990a. An exposition of the AHP in reply to the paper "Remarks on the analytical hierarchy process." *Management Science* 36, no. 3.

_____. 1990b. How to make a decision: The analytic hierarchy process. *European Journal of Operational Research* 48, no. 1.

_____. 1994. How to make a decision: The analytic hierarchy process. *Interfaces* 24, no. 6.

Simon, H. A. 1957. *Models of man.* New York: John Wiley.

_____. 1960. *The new science of management decision.* New York: Harper & Row.

_____. 1976. *Administrative behavior: A study of decision-making process in administrative organization.* New York: The Free Press.

Summers, I., and D. B. White. 1976. Creativity techniques: Toward improvement of the decision process. *Academy of Management Review* 1.

Thierauf, R. J. 1988. *User-oriented decision support systems*. Englewood Cliffs, N. J. Prentice-Hall.

Tversky, A. 1972. Elimination by aspects: A theory of choice. *Psychological Review* 79.

Vecchio, P. 1988. *Organizational behavior*. Chicago: Dryden.

Watabe, K., C. W. Holsapple, and A. B. Whinston. 1992. Coordinator support in a nemawashi decision process. *Decision Support Systems* 8, no. 2.

Watanabe, T. 1987. *Demystifying Japanese management*. Tokyo: Gakuseisha.

Yang, C. Y. 1984. Demystifying Japanese management practices. *Harvard Business Review* November–December.

Zahedi, F. 1986. The analytic hierarchy process—A survey of the method and its applications. *Interfaces* 16, no. 4.

Chapter 4

KNOWLEDGE MATTERS

*Denotes sections that may be skipped
in an accelerated coverage of this chapter.

INSIGHTS

GEM: A DSS FOR WORKLOAD-PLANNING DECISIONS

Overview

The Graan Elevator Maatschappij (GEM) is a large stevedoring company situated in the port of Rotterdam. Some 1000 sea-going vessels, varying from dry cargo ships to bulkcarriers up to 200,000 ton DWT are handled annually. The cargo of these ships consists of agricultural products destined for the West-European hinterland, Great Britain and the East-European countries.

Transhipment involves some 45,000 river vessels and 1,500 coasters which are loaded either directly. . . or indirectly via interim storage. For this purpose some 125,000 tons of storage capacity is available.

Terminals equipped in the main with pneumatic elevators have been established at three different locations in the port of Rotterdam. Part of the equipment is situated on shore while in addition some 20 floating pneumatic elevators are available. The unloading capacity of the elevators at each location varies and amounts to 1,000 tons/hour per elevator.

Each ship is scheduled according to a plan set up by the central planning section in close cooperation with the local planning authorities at each location. . . . GEM publishes a weekly schedule in which for each ship which is expected to arrive within ten days, the planned location, berth and expected time of departure is given. These data are the result of a careful planning process involving a large number of parameters. . . . Two planning-levels are to be considered: location and berth allocation, equipment allocation on the locations. . . .

. . . Every time an unexpected change takes place as a result of bad weather, incorrect cargo specification, extra arrivals, etc., the planning or a part of it has to be reconsidered. Especially in busy periods, this is a time-consuming practice and the consequent lack of time prevents the planner from taking into account—possibly better—alternative schedules.

Use of a computer may improve planning results, because the bulk of the planning routine can be performed in a relatively short time, giving the planner the opportunity to use his skill and experience to compare several alternative plans. For this purpose a computer-aided planning system . . . is in use by the GEM and has been fully accepted and is integrated in the planning section of the company.

System Description

Two important elements are considered in the system:

- the ships;
- the location with equipment.

A location can be considered to be composed of a number of single berths and a common set of elevators which are used for these berths. Both ship and berths possess characteristic features. The planning has to match these features in such a way that certain objectives are achieved. . . .

The main characteristic features of ships and berths are:

SHIP
- Expected Time of Arrival (ETA);

Continued

- Cargo information;
- Ship's workload per location;
- Type of the ship;
- DWT;
- Permitted berths;
- Maximum number of elevators;
- Expected Time of Departure (ETD).

BERTH
- Equipment information;
- Availability of equipment;
- Maximum permitted length;
- Maximum permitted draught;
- Maximum permitted DWT.

The ETA and the cargo information are generally known some ten days before the actual arrival. . . . Workload is calculated from the cargo information, particularly from the plan of stowage. For the same ship the workload may differ according to the location, because each location may have its own standard elevator capacity. Furthermore, the ship's workload depends on the type of the ship, the type of cargo and the number of separations between the layers of different materials in the same hold. . . .

For each location a scheme must be available giving the effective unloading capacity of the elevators as a function of the type of cargo and type of vessel.

Type, length draught and DWT determine in the first instance whether or not a ship may be handled on a certain berth. However, the planner may have his own reasons for preferring or excluding certain berths. Therefore, he must be free to further reduce the set of permitted berths.

Each ship has a maximum number of elevators. This is an arbitrary number, which may be set by the planner. It depends, for instance, on physical restrictions like the number of holds and whether or not there are barges aside to be loaded directly.

. . . [The] availability of equipment depends on the availability of elevator crews and . . . delays resulting from stoppages for maintenance and equipment failure. For each planning period an "availability scheme" must be set up in which the crew's work schedules, weekends, public holidays, etc., are taken into account. . . .

A very important variable is the ETD. In most cases a contractual ETD will exist. . . . In general it will be profitable for a client to have his ETD as early as possible. On the other hand, it may happen that, for commercial reasons a client may wish the unloading to be delayed for some time. The planner has to take account of this. The planner must further ensure that different clients, who may be competitors, are treated fairly. . . . To cope with these problems, the planner must have the possibility to manipulate the ETD data and to survey the consequences of this in his planning. A computer aided planning system is preeminently suitable to meet these requirements. . . .

Continued

The system is built for use by people who are not experienced computer users. . . . The method normally used is as follows:

- Run a planning [scenario] with no penalties and all berths allowed;
- Study the results;
- If there are ships in an unfavorable position try to improve this planning by manipulation of penalties and excluding berths;
- Repeat until the planning is satisfactory.

As seen from this description, the computer system is a support system for the planner. In all cases the planner retains his responsibility.

Condensed quotation from W.P.A. van der Heyden and J.A. Ottjes, "A Decision Support System for the Planning of the Workload on a Grain Terminal," *Decision Support Systems*, 1, 4 (1985): 293–296.

LEARNING OBJECTIVES

The GEM case illustrates the diversity, complexity, and volume of knowledge that can be relevant to making a decision. Efficient and effective management of this knowledge is critical for quality workload-planning decisions. The computer-based system to support these planning decisions helps the planner by keeping track of knowledge about ships, berths, and equipment—and then using that knowledge quickly to assess implications of alternative plans. This frees the planner to have more time for dealing with exceptions (disturbance handling, in Mintzberg's terms) and incrementally improving plans. In manufacturing a decision about a weekly schedule, the planner–DSS team uses descriptive knowledge from various sources, procedural knowledge, and reasoning knowledge. The DSS itself is implemented using various computer-based techniques for handling such knowledge. Keep the GEM case in mind as you study this chapter.

After studying this chapter, you should be able to

1. Explain the significance that efficient and effective knowledge management has for decision-making efforts.
2. Describe the major flows of knowledge that are involved in manufacturing decisions.
3. Characterize the nature of knowledge, identify its sources, and discuss its qualities.
4. Cite several computer-based techniques you might use for knowledge management and explain their relevance to decision support system.
5. Identify, describe, compare, contrast, and give examples of six types of knowledge that you are likely to manage as a decision maker.
6. Clearly differentiate between knowledge representation and processing, knowledge validity and utility, knowledge acquisition and derivation, a knowledge-management technique, and a knowledge type.

To apply what you learn in this chapter, exercises are provided to analyze the GEM case in terms of these objectives. The end of the chapter also provides specific review questions and discussion topics related to the general objectives.

4.1 INTRODUCTION

In preceding chapters we have used the term **knowledge** frequently, without pausing to scrutinize it. Most people have a commonsense understanding of the term, and, even though it is often taken for granted, most will agree that knowledge is an indispensable basis for coping in the modern world. Nevertheless, it is worthwhile to pause now to consider the notion of knowledge in more detail. In particular, we shall be especially interested in better understanding those aspects of knowledge related to decision making and having a bearing on decision support systems. Although knowledge is a major foundation of decision making, there has been comparatively "little attention paid to how it is marshalled and managed in its various forms, both within and related to" decision-making processes (van Lohuizen 1986).

With few exceptions (e.g., Holsapple and Whinston 1988), introductory books on business computing pay scant attention to the notion of knowledge. The same is true of most books specializing in decision support systems. In contrast, knowledge is a central theme of this book. We are interested in how computers can help us manage not just information, but all the knowledge that we use in the course of manufacturing decisions. The "question of knowledge and representation is central to the design of computer-based devices intended as tools for knowledge amplification" (Winograd and Flores 1987). Because knowledge matters so much, we devote this chapter to examining significant knowledge matters.

First, the knowledge-oriented view of decision making introduced in Chapter 2 is expanded. Decision making is very much a knowledge-intensive, knowledge-amplification activity. We then turn to an exploration of the nature of knowledge. What is knowledge, from where does it come, and what are its qualities? Finally, we take an introductory look at the field of inquiry called *knowledge management*. This includes (1) an overview of knowledge-management techniques that can be incorporated into DSSs and (2) a useful classification scheme for distinguishing among various types of knowledge that a DSS can help us manage.

THE IMPORTANCE OF KNOWLEDGE

"The knowledge society will inevitably be far more competitive than any society we have yet known—for the simple reason that with knowledge being universally accessible, there will be no excuses for nonperformance. There will be no 'poor' countries. There will only be ignorant countries. And the same will be true for companies, industries, and organizations of all kinds. It will be true for individuals, too." (Drucker 1994, 68).

". . . The most crucial variable in economic development is the knowledge embedded in the minds of the people of a nation. . . . In the final analysis, it is a country's ability to mobilize its knowledge in product design, in manufacturing techniques, and in management to increase productivity that determines its economic power" (Cyert 1991, 5).

Organizations that are successful innovators are those that build and manage knowledge effectively through such activities as developing shared problem-solving skills, experimentation, integrating knowledge across functional boundaries, and importing expertise from external sources (Leonard-Barton 1995).

As we argue in this chapter, knowledge can also be embedded in computer systems in the interest of increased managerial productivity and performance.

4.2 THE KNOWLEDGE-BASED VIEW OF DECISION MAKING

Recall that from a knowledge-based perspective, decision making is the activity of manufacturing knowledge about what to do. As Figure 4.1 indicates, a decision maker possesses a storehouse of knowledge, plus abilities to both alter and draw on the contents of that storehouse (Holsapple 1995). This characterization holds for all types of decision makers—individuals, teams, groups, and organizations. In the multiparticipant cases, both the knowledge and the abilities are distributed among participants. Let's take a more detailed look at a decision maker's knowledge processing.

ACCEPTING MESSAGES

Again referring to Figure 4.1, we see that the decision maker is able to accept stimuli from its surroundings. These stimuli are **messages** that carry knowledge with them. Some incoming messages have direct and immediate impacts on decisions being manufactured and may either trigger new decision processes or alter the outcome of a decision process that is already well underway. For example, knowledge of a large new order may trigger decisions about how to meet that order in a timely fashion or influence a decision being made about expanding production facilities.

Other incoming messages have no immediate impact on decisions currently being manufactured. The knowledge they convey may be discarded, may be passed along to some other entity, or may be deposited in the decision maker's storehouse of knowledge in anticipation of use in later decision-making episodes. For instance, the decision maker may observe that a certain advertising approach does not seem to work well. This knowledge is stored, because it may be relevant to upcoming advertising decisions.

DSS IN THE NEWS

The Challenge of Knowledge Management

Consider Monsanto Corp. Its new 20-member Knowledge Management Architecture team faces a Herculean task, says Bipin Junarkar, director of the 3-month-old effort. "We must understand the business and . . . [knowledge] needs of 15 strategic business units 2½ years from now," he says.

The St. Louis based manufacturer will look at everything from internal accounting data and point-of-sale data to information on distributors, regulations and joint ventures. Filtering such mountains of [knowledge] . . . is an "overwhelming" task . . . [The] solution, Junnarkar says: "Take one bit at a time."

J Maglitta, *Computerworld*, 5 June 1995, p. 86.

FIGURE 4.1   Birds-Eye View of a Decision Maker

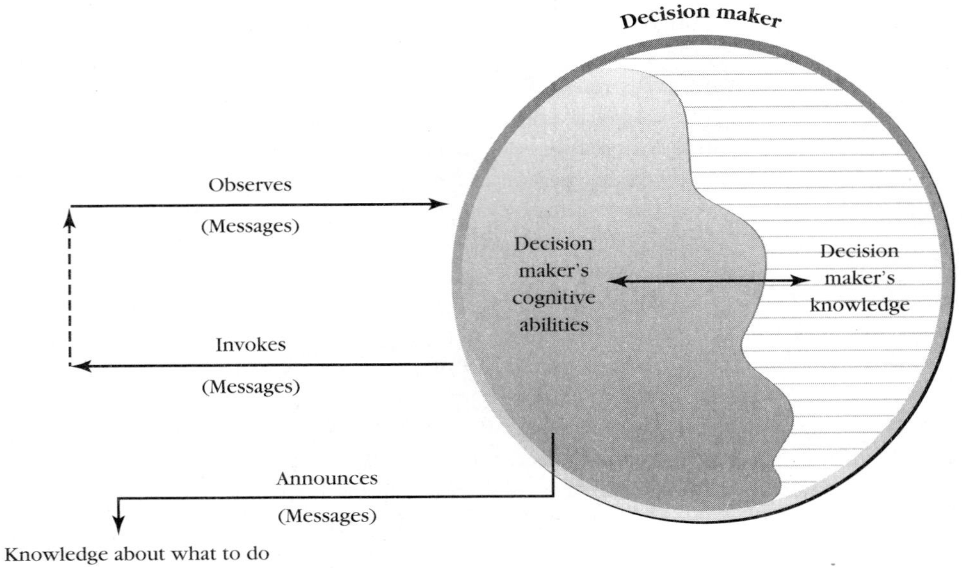

ISSUING MESSAGES

Figure 4.1 also suggests that a decision maker can issue messages conveying knowl-edge to its surroundings. Some of these are attempts by the decision maker to invoke desired stimuli. For instance, in the course of making a decision about pro-duction facility expansion, the decision maker might broadcast messages describing the nature of the envisioned expansion to various contractors. Along with this descriptive knowledge, the message would carry invitations to submit bids. The elicited bids become new stimuli for the decision maker. A different kind of mes-sage emanating from decision makers is the announcement of the decision, con-veying the manufactured knowledge to those who will carry out the actions to which it commits the organization. In some cases, the decision maker may also be the decision implementor.

ASSIMILATING KNOWLEDGE

The relationship between a decision maker's cognitive abilities and that decision-maker's knowledge is illustrated in more detail in Figure 4.2. Observed stimuli are interpreted in the light of existing knowledge. Once the decision maker has estab-lished the meaning of an incoming message, it can be assimilated into the decision maker's store of knowledge. On the other hand, knowledge interpreted from the incoming message may be rejected as not being useful to the decision maker.

When a piece of knowledge is assimilated, it alters the knowledge store in some way. It may simply be added to the existing body of knowledge, or it may cause some existing knowledge to be altered, discarded, or marked as being obsolete. In some cases, the new piece of knowledge may be so extraordinary that its assimila-

FIGURE 4.2   Manufacturing Knowledge about What to Do

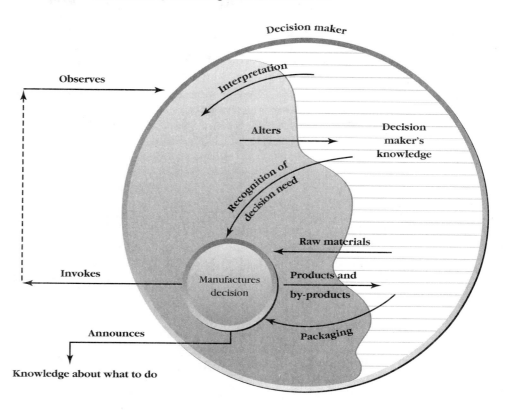

tion causes some fundamental alteration of large portions of the knowledge store-house. Imagine what happens to a marketing manager's body of knowledge when a product previously thought to be safe is realized to be harmful.

RECOGNIZING THE NEED FOR A DECISION

When an interpreted message is examined in light of knowledge about the environment and the organization's purposes, goals, and resources, the decision maker may recognize the opportunity or need for a decision. In perhaps the simplest case, the message explicitly tells the decision maker to make a decision about some issue. For instance, a supervisor tells workers to decide on a budget for the upcoming year, or a breakdown on an assembly line tells workers that a decision about corrective action is demanded.

In other cases, the need or opportunity for decision making may not be obvious from a single incoming message. It may be recognized only after many messages have been received and their impacts on the knowledge store have been actively pondered. By observing economic conditions, competitor's activities, and marketing effectiveness over some period of time, we may come to recognize that a decision about plant expansion is warranted.

MANUFACTURING A DECISION

As Figure 4.2 shows, using knowledge to recognize the need for a decision initiates the cognitive activities that manufacture a decision. The manufacturing process produces knowledge from knowledge. The source of raw materials used in the manufacturing process is the decision maker's storehouse of knowledge. We might think of this as a knowledge **inventory** from which various pieces of knowledge can be extracted for use in the manufacturing process (Holsapple and Whinston 1987, 1988; Ronen and Spiegler 1991).

Knowledge is extracted on an as-needed basis and manipulated by cognitive abilities to produce solutions for the flow of problems that constitutes the manufacturing process. When a decision maker detects that the inventory is inadequate for solving some problem, outgoing messages are used in an effort to acquire the additional pieces of knowledge. One important difference between an inventory of knowledge and an inventory of material goods is that the knowledge used in manufacturing one decision can be used again in making other decisions.

The solution to each problem arising during the manufacturing process is itself a piece of knowledge. In turn, it may be used in solving other problems, whose solutions are knowledge allowing still other problems to be solved, and so forth, until the overall problem of producing a decision is solved (Bonczek, Holsapple, and Whinston 1981).

A MANUFACTURING ANALOGY

Making decisions is, in many ways, analogous to manufacturing finished material products.

Material Product	Decision
The process begins in reaction to a customer order or anticipated order.	The process begins in reaction to a recognized need or opportunity.
The process draws on an inventory of raw materials	The process draws on an inventory of knowledge.
Items entering inventory are subject to quality testing controls.	Knowledge is assimilated into inventory only if it is expected to be usable.
Abilities for manipulating materials transform/assemble raw materials into final products.	Abilities for manipulating knowledge transform/assemble existing knowledge into new knowledge about what to do.
During the process there are intermediate products called work-in-process.	During the process there are intermediate pieces of knowledge called problem solutions.
The process may yield material by-products that are stored in inventory or discarded.	The process may yield knowledge by-products that are stored in inventory or discarded.
The manufacturer may be an individual or have multiple participants.	The manufacturer may be an individual or have multiple participants.
The finished product is packaged for distribution.	The decision is packaged for distribution.

The many intermediate solutions derived along the way toward a decision are **by-products** of the manufacturing process. Like the decision itself, they may be deposited in the decision maker's knowledge storehouse. When it comes to announcing a decision, the decision maker uses additional knowledge to determine how to present the decision. In fact, all outgoing messages are subject to packaging considerations, just as all incoming messages are subject to **interpretation**.

The knowledge-manufacturing view expressed in Figure 4.2 has very wide applicability. It is unaffected by decision context, decision type, decision maker, or decision process. These factors affect the details of what happens inside the "manufactures decision" circle far more than what happens outside it. For instance, the structuredness of a decision is related to how routine or novel the flow of problem solving happens to be. It does not determine whether a decision maker **observes**, interprets, alters, **recognizes**, **invokes**, uses raw materials, produces by-products, packages, or **announces**. These traits are common to all types of decisions. Similarly, they are common to all kinds of decision makers.

For multiparticipant decision makers, both the cognitive abilities and knowledge storehouse are distributed among the participants. For instance, each participant contributes knowledge from its part of the collective storehouse as raw materials for the manufacturing process. This process, of course, involves communication among the participants via message passing. As we saw in Chapter 3, the patterns and objectives of such knowledge transferrals depend on whether the decision maker is a team, group, organization, or some hybrid of these.

TEAMING WITH A DSS

Looking at Figure 4.2, think about a team decision maker comprising a person as the deciding participant and a DSS as a supporting participant. The person's knowledge forms a large part of the decision maker's storehouse. The rest, which may itself be sizable, comprises knowledge held in the computer. Some of the decision maker's cognitive abilities are provided by the person. These abilities allow the person to manipulate his or her part of the decision maker's knowledge inventory. These human cognitive abilities are supplemented by the computer's ability to manipulate its part of the knowledge inventory.

Communication Because the DSS serves as a problem solver for the person during the decision-making process, the two must be able to communicate. The person must know what problem-solving requests the DSS can accept. The DSS must have knowledge that allows it to interpret what the person presents to it. Conversely, the person must have knowledge allowing him or her to interpret what the DSS presents. The DSS must know what responses the person can accept. If these communication requirements are lacking, the computer will not be able to serve as a DSS, no matter how vast its knowledge or how extensive its capabilities for manipulating that knowledge.

Assimilation Both the person and the DSS control the assimilation of knowledge into their respective parts of the decision maker's knowledge inventory. The person may instruct the DSS about what it can or should accept. That is, the person can be in control of the DSS's filtering of incoming messages and its discarding of obsolete knowledge. Because of the communication that happens between the person and DSS while manufacturing a decision, a piece of knowledge may be copied or moved from the DSS to the person, or vice versa. This movement of knowledge is subjected to each participant's assimilation controls.

Problem Recognition   Either the person or the DSS may recognize the need for a decision. A DSS may have sufficient intelligence to monitor the state of its own knowledge, looking for discrepancies between its knowledge about the world and its knowledge about the organization's purposes. For instance, it may detect that the current sales trend for a product is not in line with expectations for that product, recognizing that a decision needs to be made about what corrective action to take. The DSS alerts the person about this decision need. On the other hand, the person often recognizes that a decision is needed. This recognition might be assisted by the DSS. For example, the person might ask the DSS to produce a graph comparing the current and expected sales trends.

Problem Solving   Within the "manufactures decision" circle of Figure 4.2, the person poses problems to the DSS. The person might ask to seek last year's sales figures, the current production schedule, a forecast of interest rates, a recommendation about where to set next year's sales quotas, and so forth. By drawing on its knowledge, the DSS solves those problems and presents their solutions to the person. The knowledge embodied in these messages from the DSS is used at the person's discretion. It may trigger some insight in the person or stimulate an unanticipated flow of **problem solving**.

The kinds of problems that can be posed to a DSS depend on what the DSS knows and what skills it has for manipulating its knowledge. As we shall see in Chapter 6, all DSSs are not the same in terms of the types of knowledge they can handle. In other words, they differ in terms of what problems they can solve. As it is working to solve a problem, the DSS may ask the person for some additional knowledge in the sense of a clarification, advice, facts, and so forth. Thus, the person may need to solve some problem and pass the solution along to the DSS before it can proceed in solving its problem for the person.

While a decision is being manufactured, knowledge by-products can be assimilated into both the human and the DSS portions of the decision maker's knowledge storehouse. They may be used later in the same process or in altogether different decision-making episodes that occur either later or concurrently.

Packaging   **Packaging** the decision reached by the person is often done by the person instead of the DSS. Nevertheless, a DSS can support the packaging efforts. For instance, the person may ask the DSS to produce customized reports, letters, or graphs. The DSS may be able to do so more effectively or efficiently than the decision maker. A DSS's abilities and knowledge for making presentations also come into play when it needs to send messages to the deciding participant (e.g., about problem solutions) or to entities outside the team (e.g., involving an inflow of additional knowledge).

The Capabilities of the DSSs   To summarize, knowledge serves as the raw material, work-in-process, and finished good of decision making. Regardless of decision context, type, maker, or process, there are certain common knowledge-handling activities in which decision makers engage. These include interpreting observations, assimilating knowledge to alter the inventory, recognizing decision needs, invoking additional knowledge from external sources, posing problems to itself, solving problems with available knowledge, storing problem-solving and decision-making results, and packaging the knowledge about what to do. Every one of these knowledge-handling activities can be supported by decision support systems.

4.3 DEFINING KNOWLEDGE*

Exactly what is the nature of the contents of a decision maker's knowledge storehouse? Exactly how is it manipulated? We all have some commonsense notions about knowledge, but given the importance of knowledge as a foundation of decision making and decision support, it is worthwhile to explore knowledge in more detail. In the branch of philosophy known as *epistemology*, people have spent lifetimes trying to characterize knowledge. Our efforts here are much more modest. Nevertheless, they are useful for appreciating decision support possibilities.

We begin by briefly considering three views of what knowledge is: the representation, states, and production views. These views complement each other, and all three recognize that knowledge is intangible. Second, alternative sources of knowledge are considered. The distinction between acquiring and deriving knowledge is highlighted. Third, we take a look at various qualities of knowledge in terms of its validity and its utility.

THREE VIEWS OF KNOWLEDGE*

Knowledge Representations* If a system has and can use a representation of "something (an object, a procedure, . . . whatever), then the system itself can also

DSS IN THE NEWS

Competing in a Knowledge Economy

. . . Rather than using information technology to do more in less time, the primary focus needs to be on how technology can be used to organize, manage and link information sources and users.

. . . The 10 contributing authors to "The Knowledge Economy" affirm a recent perception that information is fast becoming the most sought-after commodity, replacing capital and energy as the primary wealth-creating asset, just as capital and energy replaced land and labor 200 years ago.

. . . Organizations no longer will be distinguished by how they manage physical material or product flows but by how they manage their information resources.

. . . Successful organizations will empower their employees with more decision-making authority and provide them with the information to respond to unpredictable opportunities arising from their relationships with customers, suppliers and business partners.

B. Deagon, "Has Your Firm Changed Ways to Compete in a 'Knowledge Economy,?'" *Investor's Business Daily,* 6 January 1994, p. 3.

be said to have knowledge, namely, the knowledge embodied in that representation about that thing" (Newell 1982). This view holds that knowledge is embodied in usable representations. It draws a distinction between a representation and the knowledge conveyed by that representation. For instance, this book is not itself knowledge. To someone unfamiliar with English, it is not even a usable representation of knowledge. However, to someone who is able to use the patterns of symbols on these pages, the book embodies knowledge.

A **representation** is some pattern of **symbols**. To the extent that we can make use of that representation, it embodies knowledge. Consider what this means for a decision maker's storehouse of knowledge. It suggests that we might consider the storehouse to be filled with representations that the decision maker can use. Of particular interest to our study of DSSs are the representations that a computer is able to use. A DSS must be concerned with at least one approach (and possibly several approaches) for representing knowledge in computer memory. As we shall see in ensuing chapters, a variety of ways exist to represent knowledge in a computer's memory.

The representation view holds that "knowledge cannot so easily be seen, only imagined as the result of interpretive processes operating on symbolic expressions" (Newell 1982). Thus, we need to be clear about the distinction between the knowledge required for solving a problem and the processing required to apply that knowledge. In the case of a DSS, we should expect it to have a **knowledge-processing** ability corresponding to each of the **knowledge representation** approaches permitted in its portion of the knowledge storehouse. Each such processing ability consists of the operations the computer can perform in manipulating the pieces of knowledge represented according to a particular approach.

In considering the treatment of knowledge, the two issues of representation and processing go hand in hand. A DSS cannot process knowledge that it cannot represent. Conversely, a DSS cannot know what is represented by some pattern of symbols that it is unable to process.

DSS IN THE NEWS

The Most Powerful Knowledge Management Tool

. . . The world has never seen anything like the computer. It is by far the most powerful tool ever for recording and communicating representations of human knowledge. . . .

. . . [S]oftware can turn a computer into a television, record player, or paint box and canvas—or make it transmit telephone conversations, edit and replay video images and music, snap family photos, synthesize human speech, imitate a 16th century harpsichord, organize databases and libraries full of books, and coordinate activities across space and time.

J.W. Verity, "The Information Revolution," *Business Week*, Special 1994 Bonus Issue, p. 14.

Knowledge States* From a different perspective, we can regard knowledge as denoting a "complete set of knowledge states" (van Lohuizen 1986).

This view identifies six states of knowledge called **data, information**, structured information, insight, judgment, and decision. In the states view, one state of knowledge can be used to generate a different state of knowledge. This generation is accomplished by various activities, such as gathering, selecting, analyzing, synthesizing, weighing, and evaluating.

As we progress from one state to another, there is an increased relevance of the knowledge with respect to some objective, the possibilities of knowledge overload are lessened, and there may be a gain in the quality of knowledge. Ultimately, there is the generation of a piece of knowledge belonging to the highest state: a decision (i.e., new knowledge indicating a commitment to act). The states view of knowledge is consistent with the knowledge-based view of the decision making. Both regard decisions as knowledge attained by manipulating other knowledge.

With respect to decision support, the states view offers two other key ideas. First, states of knowledge do exist and are subject to change. The generating activities that produce these changes are kinds of knowledge processing, concerned with manipulating representations of knowledge. A DSS can help a decision maker by keeping track of knowledge states and engaging in some of the generating activities. Second, there is a basic distinction between knowledge that is acquired and knowledge that is derived. Some of the generating activities (e.g., gathering data) involve the acquisition of knowledge, whereas other activities (e.g., analyzing) involve deriving new knowledge from existing knowledge. To help decision makers, DSSs must be able to acquire knowledge, and they can be of enormous value in quickly deriving knowledge.

Knowledge Production* A third relevant perspective on knowledge, the production view, involves flows and stocks of knowledge (Machlup 1980). A stock is like an inventory. As Figure 4.3 illustrates, a flow is a transferral from one inventory to another (i.e., it is akin to a message) or from an inventory into itself (i.e., entailing the use of existing knowledge to produce new knowledge). The production view equates learning with knowledge production.

DSS IN THE NEWS

Cornerstones of Wealth

. . . Comparative advantage stems less from what a country can grow, or extract from its soil. Instead it depends on what a country can extract from its workers.

Countries that see strong backs and low wages as their comparative advantages have little hope of generating long-term wealth. The most valuable workers are the most highly skilled and specialized. The countries that provide the best-trained, best-educated workers create their own comparative advantage.

Education and knowledge provide two advantages to nations: productivity and efficiency, which are the cornerstones of wealth. . . .

"Perspective: Wealth and Specialization," *Investor's Business Daily*, 30 November 1994, p. B1.

FIGURE 4.3   A Production View of Knowledge

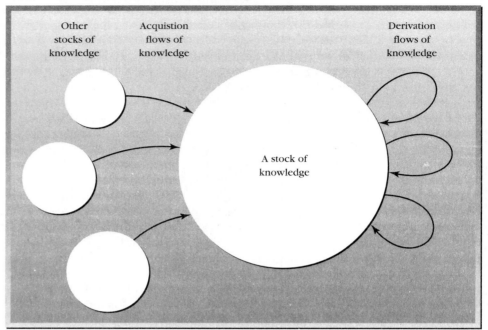

The production view of knowledge reinforces our characterization of decision making as a manufacturing process. It confirms the distinction between acquired and derived knowledge. It suggests that the phenomenon of learning (via either acquisition or derivation of knowledge) is crucial for decision making. In considering DSS possibilities, we are basically concerned with the flows and stocks of knowledge that a computer can handle and the extent to which computers can learn.

KNOWLEDGE SOURCES

The contents of a decision maker's knowledge storehouse can come from external sources and internal sources. When knowledge production is due solely to interaction of a decision maker with his or her (or its) surroundings, the source is external. The decision maker may be active or passive in acquiring knowledge from external sources. In the active case, messages are emitted by the decision maker to

---

THREE VIEWS OF KNOWLEDGE

Knowledge is:

- A usable representation of something;
- A set of states ranging from raw data to decisions;
- The result of a production activity (i.e., learning) involving acquisition and/or derivation.

invoke some desired reaction by others in the organization or in the environment. In the passive case, the decision maker simply observes without invoking reactions.

The Decision to Acquire or Derive Knowledge   When knowledge production proceeds without any interaction with a decision maker's surroundings, the knowledge source is internal. The new knowledge is either derived from existing knowledge or, in multiparticipant decision makers, passed from one participant to another. In actual practice, decision making often relies on a mixture of knowledge sources, interspersing acquisition and derivation of knowledge.

Thus, when a decision maker needs a piece of knowledge not already in his or her possession, there are two options: acquire it (actively or passively) from an external source or produce it internally. Cognitive, time, and economic limits on the decision maker will usually determine which option makes more sense. Each taxes the cognitive abilities, takes time to complete, and has some cost. There are trade-offs among these factors. For instance, knowledge acquisition may be less of a burden on the cognitive abilities, relying mainly on invocation, observation, and interpretation. On the other hand, it may well take more time or cost more than internally producing the same knowledge. By relaxing a decision maker's limits, a DSS tends to promote greater reliance on internal production of knowledge.

Reliability of Knowledge   Another important issue is reliability. Do we really get the same piece of knowledge from an external source that we would get from internal

DSS IN THE NEWS

Knowledge: Appetite and Nutrition

The job of corporate information officers is expanding to include the gathering of external information that will help companies create new markets and attract new customers. . . .

The traditional role of information officers is to manage data created internally by company operations. But this effort fails to address problems spawned by changes in markets, companies, and nations.

Hence, information officers are being asked to access and filter information that helps managers understand business. An example might be tapping into weather databases to help a retailer determine the right moment to stock stores with snow shovels, or monitoring financial news to alert customers about a hostile business takeover attempt.

. . . Many bank failures could have been prevented had managers accurately foreseen the growing number of delinquent debtors. Banks lacked the information to understand the extent of their own activities with commercial customers. . . .

Sophisticated software is emerging that helps a company scan a variety of information media—including on-line databases, CD-ROMs and computer tapes—and then route the information to the people who need it.

B. Deagon, "Appetite for Information," *Investor's Business Daily*, 1 April 1993, p. 4.

KNOWLEDGE QUALITIES

Knowledge Validity
- Accuracy
- Consistency
- Certainty

Knowledge Utility
- Clarity
- Meaning
- Relevance
- Importance

production? If there are multiple external sources, do all yield the same piece of knowledge? A decision maker's sense of the reliability of internal versus external knowledge sources can outweigh the trade-offs noted before. It may be very easy, fast, and cheap to acquire a piece of knowledge. But if we are suspicious of its reliability, we may prefer to derive the knowledge. Here again, a DSS can be helpful. Without a DSS it may be infeasible to produce the needed knowledge internally. We may also use a DSS in parallel with knowledge acquisition to check on the reliability of what comes from an external source.

KNOWLEDGE QUALITIES

The quality of knowledge is a significant issue for problem solving and decision making. Good-quality knowledge is essential for establishing accountability, easing controversies, and implementing checks and controls (Weiss 1980). The quality of knowledge depends on its source and on the way in which it is processed. As input

KNOWLEDGE RELIABILITY

From the scientific perspective, something is not called knowledge until it has passed some test of reliability. Although much of the modern world has grown out of the scientific perspective, we need to realize that management is as much an art as it is a science. This art depends just as much on knowledge as do the scientific aspects of managing. The scientific perspective does not—and perhaps cannot—address many aspects of experience. As a practical matter, the time and cost requirements of scientific testing for knowledge validity may be very large relative to the importance or time horizon of a decision.

For instance, a decision about purchasing a new machine today may depend, in part, on knowledge about what its price is now and what it will be in the future. How can we scientifically test our knowledge of its future prices? Do we repeatedly ask the vendor to tell us what the future price will be, look for consistency in the answers received, and conduct a study of the vendor's past accuracy in giving price quotes? All this may cost as much as the machine itself and may be impossible to accomplish today. Another problem in applying the scientific perspective is failure to realize that situations can change, sometimes in very subtle ways. Is our study that shows high historical accuracy in price quotes still applicable when the vendor has undergone some personnel changes of which we may be unaware?

to a decision-making process, knowledge "has to meet two requirements: It must be valid and useful" (van Louhuizen 1986). **Validity** is concerned with such factors as accuracy, consistency, and certainty. Usefulness, also known as **utility**, is concerned with such factors as clarity, meaning, relevance, and importance.

Validity of Knowledge* Is the knowledge that goes into a decision-making process sufficiently valid? Answering this question depends on assessing the accuracy of the knowledge, its consistency with other knowledge, and our certainty or confidence in the knowledge. It might be nice if all knowledge involved in decision making were scientifically validated as being entirely correct and consistent. It might also be nice if all knowledge involved in decision making could be philosophically certified as being absolutely trustworthy and certain. As a practical matter, however, it is often not feasible to validate scientifically all **raw materials** of decision making and demonstrate absolutely their trustworthiness with philosophical certitude.

Within the scope of this book, we regard a belief as a piece of knowledge about which there is some degree of uncertainty. A decision-maker's beliefs are important raw materials for the decision-making processes. For instance, a decision maker typically is not equally certain about all the knowledge factored into a decision-making process. A decision maker may believe that a recession will occur next year. For that decision maker, this belief serves as a piece of knowledge that is factored into decision making. The degree of confidence in this piece of knowledge is also taken into account.

If we consider knowledge to encompass beliefs about which there are varying degrees of certainty, who is it that determines the degree of certainty in a particular piece of knowledge? Two persons might ascribe very different levels of confidence to the same economic forecast. Even one person might be more or less certain about that forecast tomorrow than he or she is today. The relativistic perspective on knowledge validity holds that knowledge is relative to the knower and the world being known (Eckhardt 1981).

An accounting principle that is valid in the United States may not be valid in Japan or Great Britain. A law that was valid yesterday may not be so today. A forecast made last week may be less valid than one we could make today. We may be very sure that our market share will be at least 20% if there is an increase in general economic activity. However, we might regard a 20% market share with much less confidence in the current economic climate.

A decision maker may need knowledge about multiple worlds. For instance, in deciding whether to launch a new product, we need to know about the world of consumer tastes, the world of manufacturing technology, the world of labor relations, future economic environs, hypothetical marketing scenarios, and so on. Clearly, a piece of knowledge that is valid in one world may be much less valid in a different world. Knowledge about one world can even conflict with knowledge about another world, yet the various worlds need to be reconciled in the course of making a decision. This process becomes increasingly apparent and difficult as we move from structured to very unstructured decisions. Nevertheless, it must be done.

Decision support systems can contribute to improving the validity of knowledge involved in decision processes in a variety of ways: accurately retaining knowledge, flagging inconsistencies in knowledge, analyzing uncertainties, or tracking multiple sets of knowledge for different persons and diverse worlds.

Utility of Knowledge*   The quality of knowledge can be examined not only from the standpoint of its validity, but also from the angle of its utility. Knowledge utility is concerned with the question of the usefulness of a piece of knowledge. Just as there are degrees of validity, there are degrees of utility. The utility of a particular piece of knowledge can be assessed only relative to who the knower is and what problems are being faced. A piece of knowledge may be very useful to one decision maker and, at the same time, useless to another. It may have a high utility for a decision maker with respect to some problems but not with respect to other problems.

As Figure 4.4 suggests, the utility of knowledge depends on such factors as clarity, meaning, relevance, and importance. Clarity is concerned with how much effort the knower must expend in the interpretation of some knowledge representation. If knowledge is represented in an incomprehensible manner, then a knower is unlikely to find it useful. Of course, what is clear to one knower may be murky to another. Suppose two knowers have succeeded in interpreting the same piece of knowledge. One may be able to process it further, whereas the other cannot. For instance, we may be able to spot a trend in some sales figures, but someone else who knows those same figures cannot. In other words, the sales knowledge is more meaningful to us than to someone else. Because of this greater usability, the sales knowledge has a greater utility for us.

Suppose a piece of knowledge is both clear and meaningful. It may or may not be pertinent to the problem currently at hand. The sales knowledge has high utili-

FIGURE 4.4   Factors Influencing the Usefulness of Knowledge

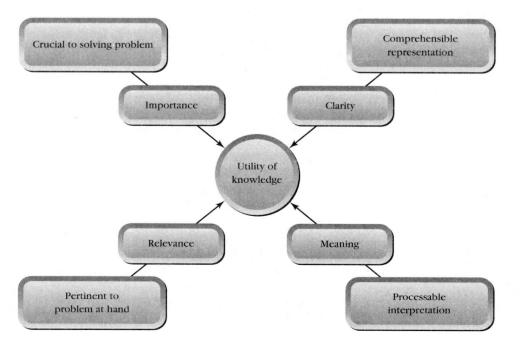

ty if we are trying to solve a problem about setting sales quotas. On the other hand, it is largely irrelevant to the problem of figuring a depreciation schedule for a machine and thus has little utility for such a problem. Ultimately, it is the knower who assesses the value of a piece of knowledge for a specific problem or across a portfolio of problems.

Interestingly, the qualities of validity and utility are interrelated. Generally, as our confidence in a piece of knowledge falls, its utility for us also tends to decrease. Conversely, as our use of some piece of knowledge increases, we tend to have greater confidence about it. Obviously, we would like our DSSs to work with high-quality knowledge or enhance the quality of knowledge with which we work. To the extent possible, a DSS should improve decision making by increasing the degree of knowledge validity, utility, or both.

4.4 KNOWLEDGE MANAGEMENT

It has been remarked that "the knowledge management concept may serve both as a framework and as a structuring device. . . to inject intelligence into decision making" (van Lohuizen and Kochen 1986). As a field of inquiry, **knowledge management** is concerned with representing knowledge and processing knowledge (Holsapple and Whinston 1986). It is particularly interested in identifying and harnessing computers' potential for representing and processing knowledge. Because such topics are so crucial to the support of decision making, they give us a solid basis for studying decision support systems. When designing or encountering a particular DSS, we should examine it in terms of the possibilities it presents for representing and processing knowledge—that is, the knowledge-management abilities it has to supplement human cognitive abilities.

TECHNIQUES FOR MANAGING KNOWLEDGE

Decision support systems are concerned primarily with using **knowledge-management techniques** to solve problems. Viewed another way, decision support depends on solving knowledge-management problems. If making a decision is

DSS IN THE NEWS

New Challenges

Most organizations have a ton of decision support information available. . . . Availability and quantity of data are no longer limiting factors. . . . Now, information from multiple, possibly conflicting sources, can be made readily available to anyone in an organization. Quality, credibility and accountability are the new challenges.

"How IS Can Answer Corporate Needs With Client/Server Computing," *Datamation*, 15 June 1993, p. S26.

REASONS FOR UNDERSTANDING KNOWLEDGE MANAGEMENT

Researchers contend there are four functions of knowledge management (van Lohuizen and Kochen 1986):

1. Position or integrate knowledge into a decision-making process.
2. Extend the role of supporting participants "from mere production to the processing, storage, retrieval, dissemination, utilization, and general management of knowledge."
3. Facilitate and develop a philosophy and methodologies for handling knowledge.
4. Shift the role of supporting participants "from producing certainty and complete knowledge to structuring ignorance and managing uncertainty."

The twin issues of knowledge representation and processing lie at the root of each of these functions.

---

the manufacturing of knowledge, then effective and efficient knowledge management is essential for productivity and high-quality results.

Over the years, a number of computer-based techniques for managing knowledge have been successfully applied to support decision makers, including the following:

Text management	Database management
Forms management	Report generation
Business graphics	Spreadsheet analysis
Solver management	Programming
Rule management	Message management

In Chapter 6, we shall see that these techniques can be incorporated in decision support systems to support different knowledge management needs that arise during decision making. In Chapter 9, each technique is examined from the standpoints of its conventions for knowledge representation and its methods of knowledge processing.

The diverse knowledge-management techniques have arisen largely as practical responses to various sensed needs. Text management has grown out of the need to handle knowledge rapidly in text form. Database management emerged from the

DSS IN THE NEWS

Digital Streams

Today, a stream of digital bits can be engineered to represent a complex expression of text, calculations, sound, moving pictures, real-time simulations, a menu of interactive programs, and even connections to "live" data off a network. . . .

J.W. Verity, "The Information Revolution," *Business Week*, Special 1994 Bonus Issue, p. 18.

need to cope with large amounts of intricately interrelated data. Spreadsheet analysis arose from the need to alter financial worksheets quickly. Forms management grew from the benefit of having electronic visualization of paper forms.

For the most part, each specialized technique has tended to evolve in isolation, independent of other techniques. Advances in database management have, for instance, had little impact on developments in spreadsheet analysis, and vice versa. As a result, the knowledge-management landscape can present a fragmented or even confusing picture at first glance. When seen from the decision support vantage point developed in this book, however, the techniques not only complement each other, but can be integrated to the extent that dividing lines between them begin to disappear.

Today's knowledge-management techniques have not been based explicitly on fundamental principles of decision making, problem solving, knowledge management, or decision support, yet such principles offer a unifying basis for orderly study of today's popular knowledge-management techniques. Prior chapters introduced important principles of decision making and its cohort, problem solving. This chapter develops the theme of knowledge management, which underlies all problem-solving and decision making efforts. Part Two details key principles of decision support that let us exploit knowledge-management techniques in solving problems encountered during decision making. Figure 4.5 indicates the relationship among these four topics.

Knowledge management (by whatever technique it is accomplished) lies at the foundation of problem solving, which in turn is the basis of decision making. The study of decision support necessarily involves all three of these activities. Thus, understanding these activities is necessary for appreciating decision support. Conversely, building an understanding of decision support should yield insights into the relationship among decision making, problem solving, and knowledge management.

TYPES OF KNOWLEDGE TO BE MANAGED

The realm of knowledge management can be considered not only in terms of techniques, but also in terms of the types of knowledge being managed. Some techniques are better for managing one type of knowledge than for others. Thus, an

FIGURE 4.5   The Knowledge-Management Foundation

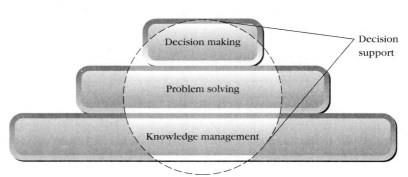

appreciation of distinctions among different types of knowledge is important to our knowledge-based study of decision support systems.

A bit of introspection and common sense tells us that all pieces of knowledge are not the same. But how might we go about classifying pieces of knowledge into a few useful categories or types? Machlup (1980) suggests that knowledge can be classified into five types: practical, intellectual, pastime, spiritual, and unwanted.

DSS IN THE NEWS

Knowledge Management in Practice

. . . [S]ystematic thinking, technology know-how and experience working with many departments can be the perfect background for knowledge management. Visions vary, but most agree that duties include the following:

- Mapping knowledge and information resources both on-line and off-line.
- Serving as a "knowledge champion" who obtains funding and sets policies.
- Training, guiding and equipping users with knowledge access tools.
- Building "knowledge networks" and "knowledge infrastructures."
- Monitoring outside news and information.

It's more than theory. Take Stockholm-based Skandia Corp., a multinational financial services and insurance company. Four years ago, Skandia used its knowledge about how to set up and manage its offices to create a system that slashes the time needed to create a branch office from 24 months to six. The prototype contains all the information, business processes and technology required to open and run an office . . .

Four years ago, General Motors began looking at new ways to ensure that new models reflected what buyers wanted, says Vincent Barabba, GM's CIO and knowledge guru based in Warren, Mich.

"If you spend $500 million to develop and introduce a new vehicle only to find out it doesn't meet customer requirements, that's a very expensive lesson," Barabba says.

So starting with the 1993 Chevrolet Camaro and Pontiac Firebird models, GM began seeking ways to provide engineers and designers with as much high quality intelligence on buyers as possible. A major goal: get cars out the door quickly, before buying tastes change.

Among other things, GM created a dynamic computer model that simulates customer reactions to various vehicle concepts and alternatives.

Barabba credits the huge success of the Chevy Blazer and GMC Jimmy in part to the application of underused knowledge about customer's buying habits. Ultimately, he says, better management and use of knowledge have helped GM avoid costly mistakes.

"If you sat down with a vehicle program team just starting a product launch today, you'd find they are provided with significantly more understanding on how to meet customer requirements and get to market faster than two years ago," Barabba says.

Joseph Maglitta, "Smarten Up!" *Computerworld*, 5 June 1995, p. 85.

This classification is not particularly productive for our purposes. An alternative would be to have subdivisions based on functional areas of management: marketing knowledge, financial knowledge, operations knowledge, and so on. Students in business and management schools are preoccupied with acquiring knowledge of these kinds. However, this classification does not take us very far in trying to understand the knowledge-management capabilities of DSSs. About all it could allow us to do is distinguish between a marketing DSS (one that manages marketing knowledge) and a financial DSS (one that manages financial knowledge).

A Decision-Oriented Classification   Instead we opt for a decision-oriented classification of knowledge, consistent with the picture painted by Figure 4.2. It differentiates among types of knowledge based on their roles in the problem-solving flows that make up decision making. It identifies types of knowledge that decision makers will likely have in their knowledge storehouses, regardless of whether they are making marketing, financial, operations, or some other decisions. It lets us consider the types of knowledge that a DSS could possess regardless of whether it is a marketing DSS, financial DSS, or a DSS for some other decision domain. The result is a general-purpose way for thinking about the knowledge-management possibilities of decision support systems.

The following six **knowledge types** are important for a study of decision support systems: descriptive, procedural, reasoning, linguistic, assimilative, and presentation (Holsapple 1983, 1995; Holsapple and Whinston 1986, 1987, 1988). In theory, a particular DSS could acquire any or all of these types of knowledge, use any or all of them in the course of solving a problem, and derive any or all from its existing knowledge. In practice, most DSSs today are limited to managing only some subset of these knowledge types or to dealing with some types of knowledge in very restrictive ways. We close our overview of knowledge management with an examination of the six knowledge types.

Three Primary Types of Knowledge   Knowledge about the state of some world is called **descriptive knowledge**. It includes descriptions of past, present, future, and

KNOWLEDGE MANAGEMENT

Techniques	Types
Text management	Descriptive
Database management	Procedural
Forms management	Reasoning
Report generation	Linguistic
Business graphics	Assimilative
Spreadsheet analysis	Presentation
Solvers	
Programming	
Rule management	

INFORMATION?

"All information is knowledge, not all knowledge is information" (Machlup 1980). It happens, however, that people sometimes use the term *information* in the same broad sense as we have been using the term *knowledge*. In this book the two terms are not used interchangeably. *Webster's Dictionary* defines information as "knowledge of a special event, situation, or the like." Thus, it is equivalent to the notion of descriptive knowledge. Moreover, management information systems are concerned with the storage and retrieval of descriptive knowledge. Thus, the *I* in MIS typically denotes descriptive knowledge. In keeping with this tradition, we shall use information to refer only to that particular kind of knowledge. Accordingly, knowledge management encompasses a much broader realm than information management.

hypothetical situations. Sometimes called *environmental knowledge*, it is more commonly referred to as *data,* or *information.*

Data about last year's exports, information about the present dividend for a particular stock, forecasts of economic conditions, and speculations about the effects of a proposed merchandise return policy are all examples of descriptive knowledge. A decision maker can acquire descriptive knowledge via observation and can produce it by transforming or assembling existing pieces of knowledge. As a decision maker comes into possession of more or better descriptive knowledge, we say that decision maker is more informed.

Bertrand Russell (1948) states "there is knowledge which may be described as 'mirroring,' and knowledge which consists in capacity to handle." The former is descriptive knowledge, mirroring a state of some world of interest. The latter is knowledge about how to do something and is quite different from knowledge of a state (Ryle 1949). Because it is concerned with a step-by-step procedure for accomplishing some task, we call it **procedural knowledge** (Scheffler 1965).

Like descriptive knowledge, procedures can be acquired or derived. The steps used to compute an economic order quantity, a procedure for calculating an expected demand for some product, the sequence of actions to be followed in a marketing plan, and the strategy that a negotiator follows in a bargaining session are all examples of procedural knowledge. As a decision maker comes into possession of more or better procedural knowledge, we say that decision maker is more skilled.

A third major type of knowledge is **reasoning knowledge**. A piece of reasoning knowledge specifies the conclusion that can be drawn when a specified situation exists. A code of conduct, a set of regulations, a customer service policy, rules that prescribe forecasting approaches, and rules used to diagnose causes of situations are all examples of reasoning knowledge.

Whereas procedural knowledge is "know how" and descriptive knowledge is "know what," reasoning knowledge is "know why." By putting together pieces of reasoning knowledge, we can reach logical conclusions and justify them by citing other reasons. This activity is known as *drawing inferences.* The reasoning knowledge that fuels an inference may be acquired or derived by a decision maker. Either way, as a decision maker comes to possess more or better reasoning knowledge, we say that decision maker is more of an expert.

In Figure 4.2 the raw materials that can go into a manufacturing process are pieces of descriptive, procedural, and reasoning knowledge. These are common ingredients in decision-making recipes. During the process, varying amounts of descriptive, procedural, and reasoning knowledge may be added at different times in different combinations. That is, pieces of different types of knowledge can be made to interact, and the value of one piece may depend on having another available at the proper time.

For example, we have said that we can derive (e.g., from past data) descriptive knowledge (e.g., a forecast) as the solution to a problem. How might we accomplish the derivation? Perhaps there is a piece of procedural knowledge indicating how to derive the new knowledge (e.g., how to calculate a forecast from historical observations). Solving a problem by carrying out some procedure on some data is typically called *analysis*.

If there are many available procedures for solving a forecasting problem, reasoning knowledge becomes valuable. With rules about the procedures valid under different circumstances, we can infer which procedure is appropriate for solving a specific forecasting problem. If there is no available procedure for solving our problem, we may have procedural knowledge that tells us, step by step, how to construct a new procedure that would apply. Or, we may have reasoning knowledge that can be used to infer a valid sequence of existing procedures that, when carried out, would yield a solution. Lacking such reasoning knowledge we might seek advice from an external expert on how to proceed.

Three types of knowledge discussed so far not only serve as raw materials to decision-manufacturing activities, but are also instrumental in recognizing the need or opportunity for a decision (refer to Figure 4.2). Decision makers with no knowledge describing the worlds in which they exist will be unable to recognize effectively when a decision is warranted. When descriptive knowledge does exist, procedural knowledge may be used to analyze it in search of a decision need or opportunity. In addition, reasoning knowledge may govern the use of procedural and descriptive knowledge during recognition efforts. The same relationships among the three knowledge types also holds when it comes to recognizing problems that need to be solved in the course of the manufacturing process itself.

Three Secondary Types of Knowledge   Aside from the three core types already discussed, Figure 4.2 implies three ancillary types of knowledge. *Linguistic* knowledge is required to interpret incoming observations. *Assimilation knowledge* is required to alter the contents of a knowledge storehouse properly in reaction to either interpreted observations or manufacturing products and by-products. *Presentation knowledge* is required to package outgoing messages, be they invocations or announcements. Although these three types of knowledge are somewhat secondary to the three primary types of knowledge, they are nevertheless essential to a decision maker.

Linguistic knowledge is the basis for acquiring every other type of knowledge as well as for acquiring greater linguistic knowledge. It enables the decision maker to make sense out of what is observed. As a decision maker comes to possess more or better linguistic knowledge, there is a better chance of acquiring valid knowledge of high utility. A vocabulary, grammar, knowledge of the meanings of gestures (i.e., body language), and an understanding of graphing conventions are all examples of linguistic knowledge.

Assimilative knowledge is the basis for controlling the changes permitted to a knowledge storehouse. It can be thought of as a filter to keep out low-quality knowledge and prevent knowledge overloads. It also serves to govern the arrangement, configuration, or placement of knowledge in the storehouse. In a very real sense, it is housekeeping knowledge governing the permissible contents, orderliness, and efficiency of a knowledge storehouse. Examples of this kind of knowledge include knowledge about how long to retain some historical observations or derived data, what to regard as irrelevant or lacking in sufficient validity, and the impact of new additions on existing pieces of knowledge.

As with other kinds of knowledge, the assimilative variety can be acquired or derived. As a decision maker's assimilative knowledge improves, there is a better chance of acquiring valid knowledge of high utility and properly retaining derived knowledge that is high in quality. This improvement could just as easily involve less stringent assimilation standards as a tightening of standards. Assimilation knowledge that causes a decision maker to be too restrictive about the housekeeping could be just as debilitating as that causing the decision maker to be overly lax.

Presentation knowledge is the inverse of linguistic knowledge. It is the basis for packaging outgoing messages, which may be announcements (e.g., of decisions) or invocations for knowledge acquisition. Customized and standard forms, templates, vocabularies, grammars, and knowledge about preparing graphs are all examples of presentation knowledge.

Some entity or entities exist to receive a decision maker's message. What a receiver does with a message depends not only on the message content, but also on the manner in which it is packaged. To interpret the message, a receiver draws on its own linguistic knowledge. When different receivers have different linguistic knowledge, it follows that different presentations of a message are warranted. The greater a decision maker's presentation knowledge is, the more effective he or she is likely to be in achieving desired results from emitted messages.

Putting the Knowledge Types in Perspective

The six types of knowledge can be visualized as shown in Figure 4.6. The three primary types are the raw materials used in the process of manufacturing decisions. The lines connecting them suggest the previously discussed interplays among reasoning, procedural, and descriptive knowledge. The three secondary types are used on the periphery of the manufacturing effort. They have strong influences on the decision produced. Even though they might not directly be raw materials, they are usually essential in allowing the manufacturing activity to precede smoothly. Thus, a typical decision maker must be able to manage each of the six types of knowledge.

It should not be surprising if approaches that work in representing one type of knowledge are less workable or even unworkable in representing another type of knowledge. Nor should it be surprising if the processing methods appropriate in managing one type of knowledge are inappropriate for others. Furthermore, there is no reason to suspect that there is one best approach to representing all pieces of a given type of knowledge. Similarly, it may well be that there is not one best method for processing all pieces of a given type of knowledge.

Let's say that a DSS is part of a team decision maker. As we have seen, this means that part of the decision maker's knowledge storehouse is possessed by the DSS and the DSS's knowledge processing abilities supplement human cognitive abilities. Which types of knowledge should we expect a DSS to be capable of managing? Which of the computer-based techniques for managing knowledge could a

FIGURE 4.6   Six Types of Knowledge

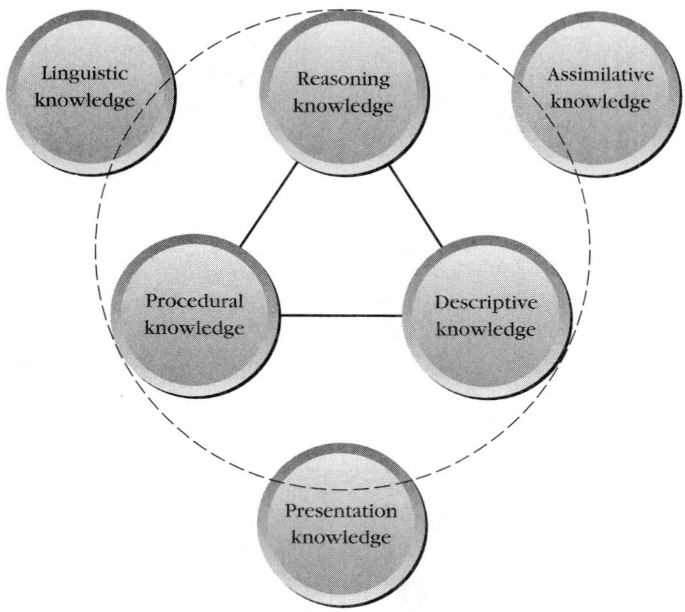

ALTERNATIVE CLASSIFICATIONS OF KNOWLEDGE TYPES

There are other ways of classifying knowledge types that are complementary to the six-fold classification. One holds that the contents of a knowledge storehouse fall into three categories: domain knowledge, knowledge of others with whom communications can occur, and self-knowledge (Dos Santos and Holsapple 1989).

The first is concerned with what is known about solving problems related to some decision domain. For instance, domain knowledge for making decisions about investments might include information on investment alternatives, procedures for forecasting economic conditions, and rules of thumb for timing the purchase of securities. Knowledge of others, also called relative knowledge, is the basis for effectively communicating: the more that is known of another, the more facile message passing will be. Self-knowledge enables a decision maker to know what knowledge it has or could potentially have, plus what cognitive abilities it possesses.

To date, most DSSs have been developed to handle domain knowledge, with little attention being given to the treatment of relative or self-knowledge. It has been argued that the latter two are essential for creating DSSs with flexible, adaptable user interfaces (Dos Santos and Holsapple 1989).

Another alternative classification distinguishes between professional knowledge and improvement knowledge (Batalden and Stolz 1993). The former refers to knowledge of professions, disciplines, and crafts. The latter refers to knowledge that can be applied to improve the quality of work (e.g., of decision making).

DSS usefully employ in handling a particular type of knowledge? Which techniques might be useful for managing more than one type of knowledge? How might multiple techniques be integrated into a DSS that is able to accommodate multiple knowledge types?

The answers to such knowledge-management questions are pivotal to an understanding of possibilities for computerized support of managerial decision making. Part Two lays the groundwork for answering them by taking a detailed look at the architecture and development of decision support systems.

4.5 SUMMARY

The topic of knowledge is often taken for granted in discussions of decision making, problem solving, decision support, and computer systems. It is sometimes vaguely equated with the notion of information, masking important distinctions between information and other types of knowledge. Given that knowledge is the object of decision making and problem solving, it is only reasonable that students interested in computer-based decision support should pay attention to how knowledge "is marshalled and managed in its various forms, both within and related to" decision-making processes (van Lohuizen 1986). The purpose of this chapter has been to highlight a number of significant knowledge matters.

We began with a characterization of basic knowledge flows related to the manufacture of decisions. Summarized in Figure 4.2, these emphasize the fact that decision making is a knowledge-intensive activity. We then grappled with the question, What is knowledge? This led to several insights about knowledge. It is embodied in representations that are usable (i.e., processable). There are various states of knowledge that result from acquisition and derivation. Knowledge production involves stocks and flows of knowledge. The flows are concerned with acquiring knowledge and deriving knowledge. Both are typically interspersed in a decision-making process, and there can be trade-offs between acquiring and deriving needed knowledge. The source of knowledge can influence its quality. Validity and utility are two major aspects of knowledge quality.

Finally, we turned to the topic of knowledge management. As a field of study, it is concerned with the representation and processing of knowledge. It is related to investigations in the field known as cognitive science (Simon 1980; Gardner 1985; Minsky 1985). Here, we focused on knowledge management from two angles. First, there are a number of computerized techniques that have arisen with their own distinctive approaches to representing and processing knowledge. A good grounding in decision making and problem solving principles is essential for appreciating the roles of each technique. Second, we examined six important types of knowledge that decision makers need to manage. In ensuing chapters, we shall see how a DSS can aid in the management of each.

▲ IMPORTANT TERMS

announces
assimilative knowledge

by-products
data

descriptive knowledge   observes
information   packaging
interpretation   presentation knowledge
invokes   problem solving
knowledge   procedural knowledge
knowledge management   raw materials
knowledge processing   reasoning knowledge
knowledge representation   recognize
knowledge-management technique   representations
knowledge type   symbols
linguitic knowledge   utility
message   validity

▲ APPLICATION TO THE GEM CASE

1. What is the nature of the decisions being made in the GEM case?
2. What strategy is used to guide the decision-making process?
3. Why is computer-based support desirable for the decisions being made?
4. Is the decision maker an individual, team, or group? Explain.
5. Give an example of each of the following:
   a. A message the decision maker accepts from the environment
   b. A message issued by the decision maker
   c. Knowledge that is assimilated by the decision maker
6. How is the need for a decision recognized in this case?
7. What part does the computer-based system play in manufacturing a workload decision?
8. Give examples of raw materials, work-in-process, by-products, and finished goods for manufacturing decisions in this case.
9. Give an example of a specific problem solved by the DSS.
10. Give an example of knowledge represented in the DSS.
11. Give an example of (a) knowledge acquired by the DSS from an external source and (b) knowledge derived by the DSS from the knowledge it possesses.
12. What knowledge management technique(s) would be most appropriate to employ in the implementation of this DSS? Why?
13. Give an example of each of the following:
    a. The descriptive knowledge represented in the DSS
    b. Procedural knowledge incorporated into the DSS
    c. Reasoning knowledge used by the decision maker

▲ REVIEW QUESTIONS

1. In what ways can messages emitted by a decision maker differ?
2. How are a decision maker's cognitive abilities related to that decision maker's knowledge?
3. What happens between the time a decision maker observes a stimulus and the time a decision is announced?
4. In what different ways might assimilation alter a decision-maker's storehouse of knowledge?

5. How does the manufacture of a decision resemble and differ from the manufacture of a finished material product?
6. Both decision making and problem solving produce new knowledge from existing knowledge. What is it that differentiates a decision from problem solutions that are not decisions?
7. What contributions do the representation, states, and production views of knowledge make to an understanding of decision support systems?
8. How does knowledge acquisition differ from knowledge derivation?
9. In what sense does a DSS promote internal knowledge sources?
10. What trade-offs exist between acquiring and deriving knowledge?
11. What two qualities should knowledge possess if it is to serve as input to decision processes?
12. What are the main aspects of knowledge validity?
13. What is meant by knowledge utility?
14. How can we assess the utility of a piece of knowledge?
15. As a field of inquiry, knowledge management is concerned with what central issues?
16. What is a knowledge-management technique?
17. Identify three commonly used knowledge-management techniques.
18. Why are the knowledge-management techniques relevant to a study of decision support systems?
19. What six types of knowledge are important to a decision maker?
20. How does descriptive knowledge differ from procedural knowledge? Give an example of each.
21. How might descriptive and procedural knowledge both be used in solving some problem faced by a decision maker? Give an example.
22. What is reasoning knowledge and how does it differ from procedural knowledge?
23. Give an example of all three primary types of knowledge being used to solve a problem.
24. What are some important uses of procedural knowledge? Of reasoning knowledge?
25. In what sense are linguistic, presentation, and assimilative knowledge secondary to the other three types of knowledge?
26. What is linguistic knowledge? What is assimilative knowledge? What is presentation knowledge? Give an example of each.
27. How are linguistic and assimilative knowledge related in the cognitive activity of a decision maker.
28. What is presentation knowledge? Explain how it differs from linguistic knowledge.
29. Why are knowledge types relevant to a study of decision support systems?

▲ DISCUSSION TOPICS

1. Describe some cognitive activities of a decision maker that are not directly concerned with manufacturing a decision.
2. Give an example of knowledge in an interpreted message being rejected. What are some reasons for such rejection?
3. Discuss the applicability of Figure 4.2 to both individual and multiparticipant decision makers.
4. Adapt Figure 4.2 to characterize a problem solver rather than a decision maker.

5. Discuss the advantages and disadvantages of a piece of knowledge existing twice in a multiparticipant decision maker's storehouse.
6. Give two usable representations for the same piece of knowledge. What are the relative advantages and disadvantages of each representation?
7. In what ways can knowing too many details be counterproductive for decision making?
8. Discuss the relationship between limits on knowing and limits on decision making.
9. Explain how knowledge representation depends on knowledge processing, and vice versa.
10. Identify difficulties that can arise in trying to use multiple knowledge-management techniques in the scope of solving a single problem.
11. Why might it be helpful to use multiple knowledge-management techniques in working on a single problem?
12. Why is it useful to categorize knowledge into types?
13. What types of knowledge might be produced by carrying out the steps in a procedure?
14. Explain how procedural knowledge can operate on reasoning knowledge. (*Hint*: What is inference?)
15. Why is reasoning knowledge at the pinnacle of the triangle in Figure 4.6?
16. Does an ability to make inferences rely on types of knowledge other than reasoning knowledge? How so?
17. Discuss the idea that linguistic knowledge could be descriptive, procedural, or reasoning. Do the same for the other two secondary types of knowledge.
18. Is one type of knowledge more important for inclusion in a DSS than other types of knowledge? If so, why?

▲ REFERENCES

Batalden, P.B., and P.K. Stoltz. 1993. Å framework for the continual improvement of health care: building and applying professional and improvement knowledge to test changes in daily work. *Journal of Quality Improvement* 19, no. 10.

Bonczek, R.H., C.W. Holsapple, and A.B. Whinston. 1981. *Foundations of decision support systems.* New York: Academic Press.

Cyert, R.M. 1991. Knowledge and economic development. *Operations Research*, 39 1.

Dos Santos, B., and C.W. Holsapple. 1989. A framework for designing adaptive DSS interfaces. *Decision Support Systems* 5, 1.

Drucker, P.F. 1994. The age of social transformation. *Atlantic Monthly* 274, no. 5.

Eckhardt, W. 1981. Limits to knowledge. *Knowledge: Creation Diffusion, Utilization* 3, no. 1.

Gardner, H. 1985. *The mind's new science.* New York: Basic Books.

Holsapple, C.W. 1983. The knowledge system for generalized problem processor. *Krannert Institute Paper*, no. 827, Purdue University.

———. 1995. Knowledge management in decision making and decision support. *Knowledge and Policy: The International Journal of Knowledge Transfer and Utilization* 8, no. 1.

Holsapple, C.W. and A.B. Whinston. 1986. Knowledge representation and processing in economics and management. *Conference on Integrated Modeling Systems*, Austin (October).

———. 1987. Knowledge-based organizations. *Information Society* 5, no. 2.

———. 1988. *The information jungle*, Homewood, Ill.: Dow Jones–Irwin.

Leonard-Barton, D. 1995. *Wellsprings of knowledge: building and sustaining the sources of innovation.* Boston: Harvard Business School Press.

Machlup, F. 1980. *Knowledge: Its creation, distribution, and economic significance*, vol. 1. Princeton, N.J.: Princeton University Press.

Minsky, M. 1985. *The society of mind.* New York: Simon and Schuster.

Newell, A. 1982. The knowledge level. *Artificial Intelligence* 18, no. 1.

Polanyi, M. 1958. *Personal knowledge.* London: Routledge & Kegan Paul.

Ronen, B., and I. Spiegler. 1991. Information as inventory. *Information and Management* 21, no. 4.

Russell, B. 1948. *Human knowledge.* New York: Simon and Schuster.

Ryle, G. 1949. *The concept of mind.* London: Hutchinson.

Scheffler, I. 1965. *Conditions of knowledge.* Chicago: Scott, Foresman.

Simon, H.A. 1980. Cognitive science: The newest science of the artificial. *Cognitive Science* 4, no. 1.

van der Heyden, W.P.A., and J.A. Ottjes. 1985. A decision support system for the planning of the workload on a grain terminal. *Decision Support Systems* 1, no. 4.

van Lohuizen, C.W.W. 1986. Knowledge management and policymaking. *Knowledge : Creation, Diffusion, Utilization* 8, no. 1.

van Lohuizen, C.W.W., and M. Kochen. 1986. Managing knowledge in policymaking. *Knowledge: Creation, Diffusion, Utilization* 8, no. 1.

Weiss, C.H. 1980. Knowledge creep and decision accretion. *Knowledge: Creation, Diffusion, Utilization* 1, no. 3.

Winograd, T., and F. Flores. 1987. *Understanding Computers and Cognition.* Reading, Mass.: Addison-Wesley.

CASE STUDY

Christopher Warren is the manager of technical services for AI Tools Incorporated, a company that specializes in the creation and sale of artificial intelligence (AI) software. Founded in the late 1970s, AI Tools has about 140 employees at its main site in a small midwestern city. It also has sales offices in four major U.S. cities and London. Last year, the company's revenues exceeded $10,000,000.

Mr. Warren joined the company in the early 1980s as a customer support specialist, helping AI Tools customers overcome various problems they encountered when using the company's software. He had earned a B.S. in management, with a business computing concentration, from a nearby university. Gradually, as his experience grew and his performance remained solid, Mr. Warren worked his way to head of the customer support staff and then became manager of the technical services division.

Technical services is one of several divisions within AI Tools. Others include sales and marketing, research and development, production, accounting, and corporate administration. Managers of these divisions are major power centers in the organization. They are concerned with how to use the company's limited human, material, financial, and knowledge resources for the purpose of serving its customers and increasing its value to shareholders in an environment of growing customer demand, widespread unfamiliarity with AI techniques, intense competition with other software vendors, and legal uncertainty over software copyright protections.

As an organization within the larger AI Tools organization, the technical services (TS) division has its own purpose and resources. Its aim is to make the company's existing and future products as usable as possible to a growing customer base. Mr. Warren knows that when there are difficulties in a customer's ability to use the company's products, the company will experience difficulties in its earnings. To help avoid this prospect, the TS division's efforts are organized into customer support and education departments.

The customer support department deals with inquiries and complaints from customers who use the AI products. Many of these are handled over the telephone or via electronic mail. Some problems are sufficiently complex or vexing that parts of customers' systems need to be sent to the customer support staff for detailed study on its own computers. Often, these turn out to be obscure errors made by customers, and the customers are informed about corrective actions to take. Sometimes, however, a customer's problem is due to a bug (error) in the company's product. The customer is informed about evasive action to take (if any is possible), and the research and development division is alerted to the bug's existence.

The education department is responsible for educating customers about each product's features and uses. In so doing, it helps reduce the workload of the customer service department. The education department works to fulfill its purposes through periodic 2-day training seminars (in major cities and at major customers' sites), preparing tutorial books and videos that illustrate a product's uses, and using the product to build sample systems for distribution to customers (i.e., educate by example).

A NEWS DECISION

During his tenure in the customer service department, Mr. Warren had observed that considerable time was spent passing along news to customers. Typical examples included news about upcoming product releases, hints about how to use a product more efficiently or in novel ways, information on how to evade known bugs in a product, training seminar schedules, announcements of new educational materials, and sharing of customer insights or experiences in using this product. Mr. Warren was convinced there must be another way of distributing the news, which would better serve both the customer and company.

He asked one of his assistants, Bobby Johnson, to prepare a list of alternatives. In so doing, Mr. Johnson acquired knowledge about customer attitudes on the matter, support specialist's desires, sources and patterns of news, and various dissemination approaches. For each alternative, he derived cost information and noted its relative advantages and disadvantages (e.g., with respect to timeliness of distribution).

Mr. Johnson presented Mr. Warren with three basic alternatives. First, he could decide not to alter the present way of doing things. Second, the TS division could prepare and publish a periodic newsletter for distribution to customers. As a third alternative, an electronic bulletin board, consisting of a computer connected to a phone line at the company's headquarters, could be constructed and maintained. Customers around the world could use their own computers to dial the bulletin board's phone number. Upon making his or her connection, a customer would be free to read any messages posted (by the TS division or other customers) on the bulletin board. The customer could also post (store) messages on the bulletin board computer for other customers or the customer support staff to read.

A PRODUCT DESIGN DECISION

Because of its extensive daily contacts with customers, Mr. Warren's division possessed a wealth of knowledge about what customers did and did not like about existing products. Using database-management techniques, his staff had developed a system for keeping track of requests for product modification (RPM). Members of either the educational or customer support division could add new RPMs to this system.

As part of its effort at providing ongoing service to its customers and being competitive in the AI software marketplace, the company was practically always involved in developing an improved, enhanced version of one or another of its products, a primary activity of the research and development division. However, the design of a new or enhanced product also involved representatives from other departments. Together, they would decide what features to include in the product design.

These design meetings would always involve a marketing manager, who wanted the design to incorporate those features that he or she deemed most important in helping sell the product. The marketing manager also had definite views on when the enhanced product would need to be available for delivery to customers, in order to meet or keep ahead of competitors. A design meeting would also typically include a production manager, who was alert to implications of a particular design for the activities of producing diskettes containing the software product, manuals documenting the product, and packaging materials to hold the diskettes and manuals.

A manager from the research and development division would also participate in design meetings. The main concern of this manager was to ensure that features included in the product design could, indeed, be implemented by R & D personnel within the time frame advocated by the marketing manager. The company's president, Christiana Whitney, was often present at meetings. She saw to it that the design would yield a product consistent with the company's overall strategic plans.

Finally, Mr. Warren was a mainstay of every design meeting. The design decision had to have his consent, because his organization would be responsible for supporting and educating customers using the resultant AI product. He was also in a position to make extremely valuable contributions to the design meeting based on his division's knowledge of customer reactions to existing products.

From their inception until a design decision was manufactured, the meetings for a given product could span several months. Disagreements about the nature or importance of proposed new features were fairly common. Ultimately, these had to be ironed out in reaching a design decision agreed to by all participants.

A BUDGET DECISION

Every November, each divisional manager submits a proposed budget to Ms. Whitney. A budget proposal shows, in detail, what expenditures the divisional manager is requesting to make during each month of the coming calendar year. This proposal includes expenses for everything from equipment and supplies to employee salaries, fringe benefits, and social security taxes. For a division that generates revenue (e.g., the TS division through its training seminars), a budget proposal also shows expected income amounts in each month.

The budgets are prepared using a spreadsheet technique of knowledge management. This technique is especially conducive to representing and easily altering budgetary relationships. For instance, it lets a manager quickly see the budgetary effect of assuming a different inflation rate or adding a new employee (e.g., effect on divisional totals for salaries, fringes, taxes, furniture, supplies, etc.). Mr. Warren's budgetary spreadsheet was prepared by combining those proposed by heads of the customer support and educational divisions with a budget for his own staff assistants.

Ms. Whitney uses the divisional budget proposals as a basis for constructing the overall corporate budget that will guide the next year's use of financial resources. Because those resources are not unlimited, she negotiates alterations in the proposals with divisional managers. These revisions can involve reducing (or increasing) the amount to be spent on some item (e.g., office furniture) or shifting expenditures to different time periods. They can cause alterations to departmental budget proposals within each division. In any event, the final budget decision for each division must be something that both its manager and Ms. Whitney feel they can live with. At a lower level, the final departmental budgets need to be agreeable to both divisional and departmental managers.

CASE STUDY QUESTIONS

1. Describe the customer support organization's environment.
2. For the news decision:

    a. What kind of multiparticipant decision maker is involved?

    b. Describe the decision context.

    c. In what ways is the decision unstructured?

    d. What managerial functions does Mr. Warren perform?

    e. Which decision strategy would you advise Mr. Warren to use, and why?

    f. Give examples of descriptive knowledge acquired and derived in manufacturing this decision.

    g. What knowledge should a DSS have in order to support Mr. Johnson's efforts? Mr. Warren's efforts?

3. For the product design decision:

    a. What kind of multiparticipant decision maker is involved?

    b. Describe the decision context.

    c. In what ways is the decision unstructured?

    d. How might the RPM system support Mr. Warren's participation in design meetings?

    e. Describe the characteristics of a DSS that would support the multiparticipant decision maker as a whole.

    f. Give an example of a team that could be a participant in this decision maker.

    g. Which decision strategy should Ms. Whitney encourage, and why?

4. For the budgeting decision:

    a. What kind of multiparticipant decision maker manufactures the overall AI Tools budget? The TS division's budget? The customer support department's budget?

    b. In what ways is a budgeting decision unstructured? In what ways is it structured?

    c. Explain the benefits of a knowledge management technique that allows rapid study of the implications of budgetary revisions.

    d. Mr. Warren's spreadsheet contains knowledge about how to calculate the TS division's total proposed expenditure in any month. What type of knowledge is this?

    e. The spreadsheet also contains an indication of how many persons will be employed in the division in each month. What kind of knowledge is this?

    f. Describe the flow of problem solving that occurs in making the overall AI Tools budget.

    g. Specify three what-if questions that Mr. Warren might need to pose to his DSS.

Part Two

FOUNDATIONS OF DECISION SUPPORT SYSTEMS

DSS pulls together three very different focusses of effort, need for knowledge and criteria for action:

"Decision" relates to the nontechnical functional and analytical aspects of DSS and to criteria for selecting applications.

"Support" focusses on implementation and understanding of the way real people operate and how to help them.

"System" directly emphasises skills of design and development and of technology.

— DR. PETER G. W. KEEN, Executive Director International Center for Information Technologies, Washington, D. C.

"Decision Support Systems: The Next Decade" *Decision Support Systems* Vol 3 (1987), no. 3; 259.

Grounded in an appreciation of decision making and knowledge, Part Two lays the foundation for understanding what decision support systems are and how they are developed. Although there is considerable diversity among specific DSSs, they also share major common features. These shared traits differentiate decision support systems from other classes of business computing systems. Individual chapters focus on the traits that DSSs can exhibit, on the architectural components that allow them to exhibit these traits, on methods used to construct decision support systems, and on software tools that DSS developers can use during construction.

Chapter 5 traces the history of DSSs, contrasting them with electronic data processing and management information systems. It summarizes technological advances that have led to the widespread use of DSSs. The chapter uses a human metaphor to outline the kinds of behaviors we might expect from DSSs. It also summarizes potential benefits and limitations of these systems.

Chapter 6 applies the human metaphor to produce a simple architecture that we can use to organize the study or design of any DSS. This generic framework identifies important components of a DSS and indicates how they are related to each other and the DSS's user. The chapter examines several special cases of the generic DSS framework. Each of these specialized frameworks emphasizes the use of a certain computer-based knowledge management technique(s).

Chapter 7 examines issues that the developer of a DSS faces. It points out the distinction between professional developers and do-it-yourself developers, each having certain advantages over the other when it comes to building a DSS. It also presents phases in the process of developing a decision support system. These may be followed in a formal, detailed fashion or they may be used as informal guides to a development approach that involves the construction of DSS prototypes.

Chapter 8 is concerned with software tools that developers can use to help implement decision support systems. We use some tools to construct or maintain one or more components of a DSS. We use others to furnish the software that actually becomes a component of the DSS. In the latter case, the tool typically embodies one or more computer-based techniques for managing knowledge. There are several distinct approaches to integrating multiple knowledge management techniques into a single DSS.

The case study for Part Two is a do-it-yourself project. It focuses on constructing a proposal for developing a particular decision support system. This DSS will differ sharply from traditional electronic data processing and management information systems. Its components will fit the generic DSS framework introduced in Chapter 6. Eventually, you will develop the proposed DSS in prototype form, most likely integrating multiple knowledge management techniques. This case gives example proposals for the kind of prototype system you might be expected to develop as a hands-on project in a DSS course.

Chapter 5

DECISION SUPPORT SYSTEM OVERVIEW

INSIGHTS

DAIRYMAN'S COOPERATIVE: A DSS FOR PRODUCTION DECISIONS

Overview

A small optimization-based decision support system was designed and implemented on a microcomputer at Dairyman's Cooperative Creamery Association. . . . Used for daily production planning and inventory forecasting, it relieves plant supervisors of . . . calculations. In addition, the system has improved interaction between all levels of management.

Daily production planning is one of the most challenging problems faced by managers in the milk processing industry. . . . Managers of milk processing plants . . . generally rely upon their past experience and intuition to make decisions about the mix of products to be produced each day. The products are all derived from raw milk, some are by-products of others, and many require the same processing equipment.

. . . MFAP was developed for planning dairy production at the Dairyman's Cooperative Creamery Association (DCCA) in Tulare, California. . . . DCCA is the largest single milk processing plant at one location in the United States. This cooperative receives about five million pounds of raw milk per day. . . . Approximately 50 products are produced at this one location.

Background

Production planning and inventory forecasting are complicated by the interrelatedness of the various milk products. For example, if raw milk is pumped to the cheese plant for processing, the plant does not just obtain cheese. In addition to cheese, there will be whey, salty whey, fines, and scrap cheese. And the interaction does not stop here since some of these products become inputs to other process "use" centers. The whey goes to the whey department where the operation produces whey concentrates at 10 percent . . . whey protein slurry, whey protein powder, whey powder, whey cream, and lactose. The whey cream is an input into the cream process department, thus affecting its production requirements and inventory levels. And the output from the cream department becomes input to the butter department, thereby affecting buttermilk quantity, which affects the evaporation department and subsequently other departments in a highly interrelated production process. . . .

Plant supervisors are responsible for allocating and estimating milk flow demand and supply. They must estimate total and available storage and equipment capacities, and anticipate personnel limitations, maintenance requirements, and customer demands, and specify quality standards. All of these factors vary each day; in fact, they may change several times on a given day, and thereby affect decisions on milk flow processing.

. . . At 4:00 A.M. each day, the following data are available for production planning:

1. Accurate estimates of milk to be received that day.
2. The exact quantity of milk to be pumped to the cheese plant.
3. Rough estimates of milk, skim milk, condensed milk, and cream to be shipped to Los Angeles.

continued

4. Accurate estimates of the quantites of cottage cheese, cream cheese, sour cream, yogurt, whipping cream, half and half, whey products, butter, and buttermilk to be produced that day.
5. Exact levels of current inventory, along with the compositional breakdown of the inventory.

This information is used for production planning and inventory forecasting for the day. . . .

Based upon the 4:00 A.M. projections, the plant supervisor makes decisions regarding production for the day. Product flow is set, equipment is allocated, personnel are assigned, transportation arrangements are made along with other decisions affecting short-term operations. . . . Rapid growth of the cooperative coupled with the complex interdependencies of the production process made production planning and scheduling increasingly difficult. . . .

System Description

. . . MFAP is an interactive and user friendly software package designed to perform daily production planning at DCCA. . . .[It] consists of two modules: (1) a preprocessor that elicits the production information and estimates available at 4:00 A.M. and uses these data to form . . . flow and capacity constraints; and (2) . . . [a] module that determines the daily production and inventory levels so as to maximize plant throughput.

The preprocessor of MFAP asks the user to respond to questions regarding what capacities will be available, current inventory levels, and supply and demand. . . . For many of the input parameters, their values rarely change from one day to the next. In such cases, the user can choose the default values of the parameters, which are the previous day's entries. Once the data have been entered, the user can review the input values and make changes as needed.

. . . The preprocessor then constructs . . . constraints. . . . These fall into the following three broad categories:

1. Product flow . . . constraints ensure that the input and output of each operation are in balance while considering the different processing speeds of each product at the required operations. . . .
2. Product conversion constraints . . . convert the input of one product into an equivalent output of a subsequent product. . . .
3. . . . Constraints ensure that the capacities of the various operations and inventory locations are not exceeded and that demand and supply restrictions are not violated. . . .

The constraints . . . can be recalled and modified. The resulting model is then solved using a primal simplex algorithm. . . . Supervisors may rerun the system several times with modified data and pose what-if questions.

A plant supervisor generally requires about 15 minues to respond to the questions presented by the preprocessor. The . . . algorithm takes another 10 minutes to provide the production plans and forecasted inventory levels for the day. This planning process that once occupied a supervisor for several hours every day now takes less than 30 minutes.

The concept underlying MFAP was developed with the cooperation of personnel at DCCA. They helped to define the specifications for such a system and

continued

provided feedback. . . . Consequently, the supervisors and managers have a strong sense of ownership.

Several plant supervisors who have been involved with production planning for more than 20 years . . . were content that the system provided structurally sound and intuitively appealing plans and forecasts and that the system would enhance plant output.

Benefits

MFAP enables the plant supervisors to make daily production plans very rapidly and to adjust these plans if unforeseen changes occur. Furthermore, the system forces the supervisors to be explicit about their objectives and to quantify and record the data . . . used in the planning process.

. . . MFAP has increased daily plant throughput by an estimated 150,000 pounds per day. . . . The estimated annual net increase in profits due to increased throughput amounts to $48,000.

. . . Monetary gains are only part of the benefits. Supervisors now have more time for communicating among themselves and with management. They are now able to pay attention to other urgent managerial and control activities. . . . Scores of related production and quality problems are being avoided.

Condensed quote from R. S. Sullivan and C. S. Secrest, "A Simple Optimization DSS for Production Planning at Dairyman's Cooperative Creamery Association," *Interfaces,* 15, no.5 (1985): 46–51.

LEARNING OBJECTIVES

In the case of the Dairyman's Cooperative, complex interdependencies of the production process were making production decisions increasingly difficult. The MFAP decision support system was devised for the purpose of capturing daily production knowledge and solving certain inventory forecasting and production planning problems. As such, MFAP is very different from conventional data processing and management information systems. It furnishes both monetary and nonmonetary benefits to production supervisors. It accepts requests both to provide knowledge and to accept knowledge. MFAP processes descriptive and procedural knowledge in its possession to arrive at requested solutions to problems. As you study this chapter, the dairy case will offer food for thought, illustrating many of the concepts introduced.

After studying this chapter, you should be able to

1. Cite the purposes for which decision support systems may exist.
2. Distinguish decision support systems from other kinds of computer-based systems, such as data processing and management information systems.
3. Describe the kinds of characteristics you would expect a DSS to exhibit.
4. Recognize the potential benefits DSSs can offer, plus limitations on DSS abilities.
5. Discuss possible behaviors that you might expect or want DSSs to exhibit.

Exercises are provided at the end of this chapter to let you apply what you have learned to an analysis of the dairy case, to review your comprehension, and to discuss various issues related to the learning objectives.

5.1 INTRODUCTION

Part One surveyed the realm of managerial work and spelled out many details of decision making and knowledge. In so doing, it staked out the boundaries and prepared the way for Part Two which lays the foundation for building an understanding of decision support systems. So far, the notion of decision support systems has been discussed only informally. Here, we define the notion in much more concrete terms, providing a firm footing for studying, developing, and using specific DSSs.

In Chapter 5, we see that, in spite of their differences in style and substance, all DSSs share similar purposes and exhibit a common set of characteristics. In Chapter 6, we see that all DSSs are designed along the lines of a single basic architecture. In Chapter 7, we examine important issues in developing DSSs. In Chapter 8, we see that this development of DSSs involves the use of various computer-based tools. Part Three surveys various knowledge-management techniques that are commonly incorporated in DSS development tools.

Unless indicated otherwise, the term *decision support system* refers to a computerized supporting participant in decision making. Recall from Figure 3.6 that a DSS may support the deciding participant either directly or indirectly through another supporting participant (e.g., a staff assistant). The team's deciding participant may be acting unilaterally or may be part of a group decision maker or organization decision maker. We focus on these kinds of decision support systems and refer to those who use them simply as *users*.

Nevertheless, much of what we learn about DSSs that support a single user is also generally valid for a DSS that supports a group as a whole, an organization as a whole, or multiple decision makers (recall Figure 3.6 (e)–(g)). However the latter kind of DSS would have some additional facilities enabling it to cope with multiple users. Specific multiparticipant features are treated in Part Five.

The present chapter is organized into four major sections. It begins with an overview that reviews the possible purposes of a DSS. The second section traces major developments in the evolution of business computing systems, from early data processing systems to the rise of management information systems to the emergence of decision support systems. Within this brief historical perspective, we identify typical traits of traditional DSSs and contrast them with traits of the earlier kinds of systems. The third section discusses potential benefits of today's DSSs and identifies their limitations. The last section looks at possibilities for tomorrow's DSSs with a special focus on the human metaphor for a DSS.

5.2 PURPOSES OF DSSs

Our overview of what a DSS is begins by asking the question, What is the purpose of a DSS? The answers to this question serve as a starting point for putting together a list of characteristics that we might expect a DSS to exhibit. Beyond these we

shall add some other traits to our list. Given that we know what a DSS's characteristics are, it becomes possible to think of a DSS in terms of its potential benefits and
to consider limits that may exist on its use. All this forms a prelude to looking at
the makeup of decision support systems in Chapter 6.

What is the purpose of a DSS? The foregoing chapters suggest several ways to
answer this questions. In very broad terms, we might say that its purpose is to
improve the decision-making ability of managers (and operating personnel) by
allowing more or better decisions within the constraints of cognitive, time, and economic limits. Its purpose is to increase a decision maker's productivity. Some
authors (e.g., Turban 1988) hold that a system that increases decision-making efficiency without increasing decision effectiveness is not a DSS. Here, we take a
broader view of DSSs. Increased effectiveness, efficiency, or both are legitimate purposes for decision support systems.

SUPPLEMENTING THE DECISION MAKER

More specifically, we can say that *the purpose of a DSS is to supplement one or more
of a decision maker's abilities*. Its intention may be to make tasks of knowledge collection easier by readily answering a user's what-is queries. (What is the present
inventory level? What is last year's sales figure?) The purpose of a DSS could be to
help a decision maker's formulation ability. It may be designed actually to formulate plans for analysis or action. A DSS's purpose could be to supplement a decision maker's ability to analyze by readily answering what-if questions. (What if the
cost of production rises by 8 percent? What would happen if a delivery is more than
2 days late?) The purpose of a DSS could be to supplement a decision maker's ability to recognize problems, be they overall decision problems or subproblems.

ALLOWING BETTER INTELLIGENCE, DESIGN, OR CHOICE

In light of Simon's characterization of decision processes, we could say that *the purpose of a DSS is to facilitate one or more of the three decision-making phases*. It might
fulfill this purpose by alerting the decision maker to a decision opportunity or supplying relevant information during the intelligence phase. A DSS could help in the
design phase by proposing alternative courses of action or analyzing the effects of
various alternatives. In the choice phase, its assistance could take the form of offering advice about what course of action to pursue or packaging the chosen alternative in a way that maximizes the likelihood of achieving expected outcomes.

FACILITATING PROBLEM SOLVING

Regarding decision making as a flow of problem-solving episodes, we could say
that *the purpose of a DSS is to help problem-solving flows go more smoothly or rapidly*. Because each problem-solving episode begins with the recognition that a problem exists, a DSS could fulfill this purpose by stimulating the user to perceive problems needing to be solved. It could go so far as to break a problem posed by the
user into subproblems, which, when solved, allow the user's problem to be solved.
Even if it doesn't offer much assistance in problem recognition, a DSS could fulfill
its purpose by actually solving problems posed by a user. Typically, the DSS reports
the solutions to the user, who then factors them into his or her efforts to solve other
problems (including the overall problem of what decision to make). The DSS may,

itself, be able to combine and synthesize the solutions of subproblems into the solution of a larger problem, which it reports to the user.

PROVIDING AID FOR NON STRUCTURED DECISIONS

Traditional definitions of decision support systems suggest that *the purpose of a DSS is to aid decision makers in addressing unstructured or semistructured decisions* (Scott Morton 1971; Keen and Scott Morton 1978; Bonczek, Holsapple, and Whinston 1981; Sprague and Carlson 1982). Although computers may also assist in the making of structured decisions, the DSS emphasis is definitely on supporting decisions that its users regard as less than fully structured. If a decision is so completely structured that no human discretion is involved, then the process for producing it could (in principle) be computerized. The resultant computer system would be called a decision-making system rather than a decision support system. But, as long as there is some lack of structure, human discretion in the recognition and/or solving of problems is important. The degree and scope of that discretion could vary from being mildly influenced by DSS activities to being a rubber stamp on decisions recommended by a DSS.

MANAGING KNOWLEDGE

One other way to assess the purpose of a DSS stems from the knowledge-management perspective. When we think of decision making as a knowledge-manufacturing process, *the purpose of a DSS is clearly one of helping the user manage knowledge.* A DSS fulfills this purpose by enhancing the user's competence in representing and processing knowledge. It supplements human knowledge-management skills with computer-based means for managing knowledge. A DSS accepts, stores, uses, derives, and presents knowledge pertinent to the decisions being made. Its capabilities are defined by the types of knowledge with which it can work, the ways in

DSS IN THE NEWS

Strategic Decision Support

. . . Consider a decision support system . . . being used primarily by the strategic planning department. Users can look at variables and at the impact these will have on the overall industry.

The biggest advantage, according to this user, is that a DSS enables people to identify the critical issues involved in a decision. The output identifies the impact that any particular variable has and that provides a way to prioritize the variables. You never know what the biggest impacts on your business are going to be, but once you begin to model it into a DSS, you can very quickly sort out which ones are significant. That is, what to look for first, where to spend your market research dollars if that's the issue, or what the biggest potential threats are likely to be.

J. Snyders, "Decision Making Made Easier," *Infosystems* 8 (1984): 54.

> ### VIEWS OF DSS PURPOSE
>
> - Increase decision maker's productivity, efficiency, effectiveness
> - Facilitate one or more of a decision maker's abilities
> - Aid one or more of the three decision-making phases.
> - Help the flow of problem-solving episodes proceed more smoothly or rapidly
> - Assist in the making of semistructured or unstructured decisions
> - Help the decision maker manage knowledge

which it can represent these various types of knowledge, and its capabilities for processing these representations.

5.3 DSSs IN A HISTORICAL PERSPECTIVE

One way to appreciate the characteristics of a DSS is to compare and contrast them with traits of two other major types of **business computing systems:** data processing systems and management information systems. Both predate the advent of computer-based decision support systems. All three share the trait of being concerned with record keeping. On the other hand, the three kinds of business computing systems differ in various ways, because each serves a different purpose in the management of an organization's knowledge resources.

DATA PROCESSING SYSTEMS

In the 1950s and 1960s, **data processing** (DP) systems dominated the field of business computing (Awad 1966; Saxon 1967; Diebold 1977; Shelly and Cashman 1980).

DSS IN THE NEWS

Variable Impacts

. . . A major tire and rubber company . . . needed to evaluate the demand of truck tires over a 10- to 15-year period. A lot of factors in the environment were changing independently of each other. The company needed a way of evaluating the impact of those variables and how that translated into either an increase or decrease in product demand. Some of the factors were the overall economy, changes in legislation that affected the size and weight of trucks and changes in productivity. . . . [This called] for a decision support system.

J. Snyders "Decision Making Made Easier," *Infosystems* 8 (1984): 54.

DATA PROCESSING EXAMPLES

Payroll   Data to be processed are gathered on weekly time sheets, showing the hours that each employee worked on each day during the week. Once this source data has been verified as being correct, a bookkeeper or data-entry clerk keys the data into the computer from the time sheets. The DPS stores that data in an organized way—grouped by department, for instance. Within each department grouping, the DPS may sort the records according to employees' identification numbers. At the direction of a system administrator in the DP department, the DPS tabulates each employee's gross pay, deductions, and net pay. The data are incorporated into an output transaction consisting of a paycheck and stub. The DPS may also produce a listing of all transactions generated or a summary report showing gross pay totals for each department.

Insurance   Insurance sales representatives submit application forms that they have filled in. A clerk enters the data from these forms into the DPS. As the data are being input, the DPS checks for accuracy. For example, the face amount of the policy is checked to ensure that it falls within an allowable range of values (say, $5,000 to $500,000). The DPS stores the entered data organized according to policy type or customer identifier. The transactions generated by the DPS are the policies it prints.

DP is sometimes referred to as **automatic data processing** (ADP) or **electronic data processing** (EDP). The main purpose of DP systems was and is to automate the handling of large numbers of transactions. For example, a bank must deal with large volumes of deposit and withdrawal transactions every day. It must properly track each transaction's effect on one or more accounts. It must maintain a history of all the transactions that have occurred in order to give a basis for auditing its operations. Other examples of heavy transaction processing include a utility company's generation of customer bills or treatment of customer payments, a government's handling of tax receipts, and a large corporation's generation of payroll checks.

The basic nature of a DP system is illustrated in Figure 5.1. At its heart lies a body of **descriptive knowledge** (i.e., data), which is a computerized **record** of what is known as a result of various **transactions** having happened. In addition, a DP system endows the computer with two major abilities related to this stored data: **record keeping** and **transaction generation.**

The first enables the computer to keep the records up to date in light of incoming transactions. It can cause the creation of new records, modification of existing records, deletion of obsolete records, or alteration of relationships among pieces of knowledge. A DP system performs these operations in response to transactions it receives from data entry clerks or various machines (e.g., a scale at a grain elevator) that monitor what is occurring in the surrounding world.

The second major ability of a DP system is concerned with the computerized production of outgoing transactions based on the stored descriptive knowledge. These transactions may be transmitted to such targets as customers, suppliers, employees, or governmental regulators. The person (or people) who administer a DP system are typically responsible for seeing that the transaction generation ability is activated at the proper times.

FIGURE 5.1   Typical Data Processing System

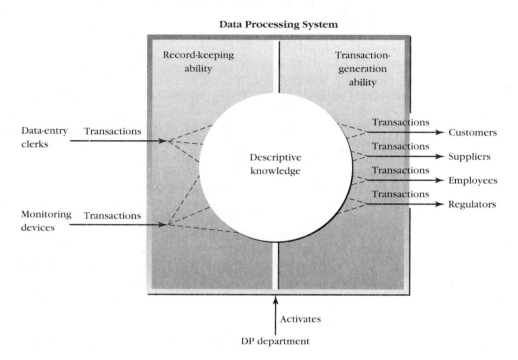

By the late 1960s, many large organizations had formed **DP departments** to create, operate, maintain, and administer DP systems to meet their own transaction processing needs. Although such systems are still very important to today's organizations, they are not of direct concern to most managers. The principal exception consists of those managers who are responsible for the performance of a DP department. As electronic data processing experience grew and computer technol-

DSS IN THE NEWS

Beyond Transactions

. . . Decision support systems . . . can be built . . . quickly. They offer a major advantage over traditional transaction processing systems . . . [A DSS developer] worked with [the] vice president of technology to quickly build a data base of all of the 200 competitive tires. . . . This includes information on construction, tread, volume and other competitive data. The decision support system allows the vice president of technology and his staff to look at competitors in ways that are not preconceived.

J. Snyders, "Decision Making Made Easier," *Infosystems* 8 (1984): 54.

ogy advanced, a different kind of business computing system began to emerge in the late 1960s and came to dominate the field well into the 1980s. These came to be known as management information systems.

MANAGEMENT INFORMATION SYSTEMS

Basic features of a **management information system** (MIS) are illustrated in Figure 5.2. Unlike a DP system, the central purpose of an MIS was and is to provide managers with periodic reports that recap certain predetermined aspects of an organization's past operations (McLeod 1986; Senn 1987; Awad 1988). Such computer-generated reports give managers at various organizational levels regular snapshots of what has been happening in the organization. Such descriptive knowledge can help them in controlling the organization's operations. For instance, an MIS might be developed to provide manufacturing managers with daily reports on parts usage and inventory levels, weekly reports on shipments received and parts ordered, a monthly report of production expenditures, and an annual report on individual workers' levels of productivity.

Record Keeping   Whereas DP is concerned with transforming transactions into records and generating transactions from records, the MIS concern with record keeping focuses on using this stored descriptive knowledge as a base for generating recurring standard reports. Of course, an MIS must have facilities for creating

FIGURE 5.2   Typical Management Information System

Management Information System

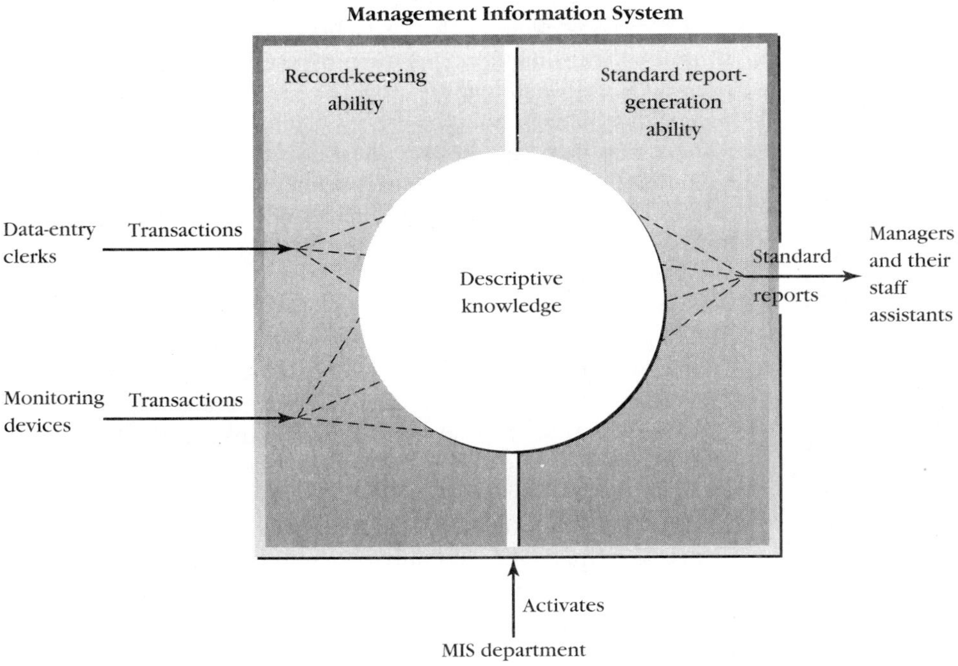

MIS EXAMPLES

Accounts Payable   An accounts payable MIS stores and processes details about money owed to vendors, suppliers, and other creditors. It maintains records of bills received from creditors, monitors due dates for making payments, and produces periodic summaries showing the amount needed to cover all bills that are due. Such a system may also automatically prepare checks and keep a record of them (thereby having a data processing function as well). Various reports produced include cash requirements reports, check registers, aged payables summaries, vendor lists, consolidated payables summary, and so forth.

Order Entry   A mail-order company accepts orders for plants and gardening supplies identified in its catalog. These orders can arrive in the mail or by telephone. The company has an MIS to help automate the handling of transactions related to customer orders. These transactions include the entry of new orders, treatment of customer inquiries, updates to customer addresses, receipt of customer payments, shipment of ordered items, and generation of mailing labels to affix to catalogs. Such transactions affect the MIS's records about customers, potential customers, orders, and inventory items listed in its catalog. Various reports produced include order-confirmation slips, daily tabulations of quantities ordered for inventory items, inventory reports showing how much of each item is on hand, sales trend reports, packing lists to guide the shipping department in filling each order, mass mailings of letters customized to each potential customer, and reports on customers whose payments are tardy.

and updating the collection of records that it keeps. As Figure 5.2 suggests, it must be able to handle transactions that affect its record-keeping chores. In the case of a manufacturing MIS, for example, there must be provisions for updating inventory records to reflect such transactions as placing orders for parts, receiving parts shipments, and using some quantity of parts in production. Thus, an MIS can be regarded as an extension of the DP idea to emphasize the generation of standard reports for managers rather than the generation of voluminous transactions for customers, suppliers, employees, or regulators.

Indeed, the notion of DP departments in many organizations has given way to what are called **MIS departments.** An MIS department typically is responsible for development, operation, and administration of both DP systems and MISs. It usually creates and operates many MISs (e.g., manufacturing MISs, a marketing MIS, a personnel MIS, a cash-management MIS) and possibly numerous DP systems. An MIS department is also responsible for coordination of all these systems, to ensure that the records kept by one are consistent with records kept by the other. (Koory and Medley 1987). In some cases, systems are devised to accomplish both DP and MIS purposes. Such a system accepts transactions, keeps records, and generates both standard reports and various transactions.

Limited Decision Support   Information contained in standard reports that an MIS furnishes to managers certainly can be factored into their decision-making activities. When this is the case, an MIS could be fairly regarded as a kind of decision support system. However, the nature of support it provides appears very limited in light of our understanding of decision making. The limits of an MIS's ability to support decision makers are due to several factors: Its reports are predefined, they tend to be issued periodically, and they are based only on descriptive knowledge.

The reports generated by an MIS are defined before the system is created by the MIS department and serve to guide the MIS department's efforts in developing the MIS. This development is typically an expensive and time-consuming affair, involving months or even years of effort by specially trained personnel. However, the situation surrounding a decision maker can be very dynamic. Except for the most structured kinds of decisions, information needs can arise unexpectedly and change more rapidly than MISs can be built or revised by the MIS department.

Even when some needed information exists in a stack of reports accumulated from an MIS, it may be buried within other information held by a report. It may be scattered across several reports. It may not be presented in a fashion that is most helpful to the decision maker. For example, it may be presented as a table of data, whereas a graph of the data would be preferable, or vice versa.

To a decision maker, the relevant information existing in MIS reports may not only be incomplete, difficult to dig out, unfocused, or difficult to grasp, it may also be in need of further processing. For instance, a series of sales reports may list daily sales levels for various products, when the decision maker actually needs a projection of future sales levels based on data in those reports. Decision making proceeds more efficiently and effectively when a decision maker can easily get complete, fully processed, focused information presented in the desired way.

The reports generated by an MIS are typically issued at periodic time intervals, such as hourly, daily, weekly, monthly, or quarterly. Set schedules of report generation are followed by the MIS personnel who operate a management information system. But decisions that are not fully structured tend to be required at irregular intervals or unanticipated times. Thus, knowledge needed for manufacturing decisions must be available on an **ad hoc,** spur-of-the-moment, basis. With an MIS, the decision maker waits until the next scheduled reports appear and wades through past reports in search of desired information. Decision making proceeds more efficiently and effectively when desired knowledge can be requested and used on an as-needed basis.

A third limit on an MIS's ability to support decisions stems from its exclusive focus on managing descriptive knowledge. The typical MIS is concerned with keeping

DSS IN THE NEWS

Demise of Hard Copy

Firestone Tire and Rubber Company . . . has done away with hard-copy summary reports because of the quick availability and ease of updating DSS reports. . . . [The] decision support system provides preformatted reports and ad hoc analysis capabilities. These let analysts look for relationships between financial and external variables, including microeconomic theories such as a total car production and gross national product.

J. Snyders, "Decision Making Made Easier," *Infosystems* 8 (1984): 54.

records that describe what has happened and later retrieving them for inclusion in reports. We have seen that several additional types of knowledge are important to a decision maker. Decision makers frequently need to manage procedural, reasoning, and other types of knowledge. But traditional MISs give little help in representing or processing such knowledge. Nor do they facilitate the integrated use of these kinds of knowledge with the more ordinary descriptive knowledge that they do help to manage. Decision making proceeds more efficiently and effectively when multiple types of knowledge can be conveniently used in tandem as the decision maker sees fit.

DECISION SUPPORT SYSTEMS

Ideally, a decision maker should have immediate, focused, clear access to whatever knowledge is needed on the spur of the moment in coping with semistructured or unstructured decisions. The pursuit of this ideal separates decision support systems from their DP and MIS ancestors. It also suggests the characteristics we might expect to observe in a DSS. These are illustrated in Figure 5.3 and can be described as follows:

1. A DSS includes a body of knowledge that describes some aspects of the decision-maker's world, that specifies how to accomplish various tasks, that indicates what conclusions are valid in various circumstances, and so forth.

FIGURE 5.3 Typical Decision Support System

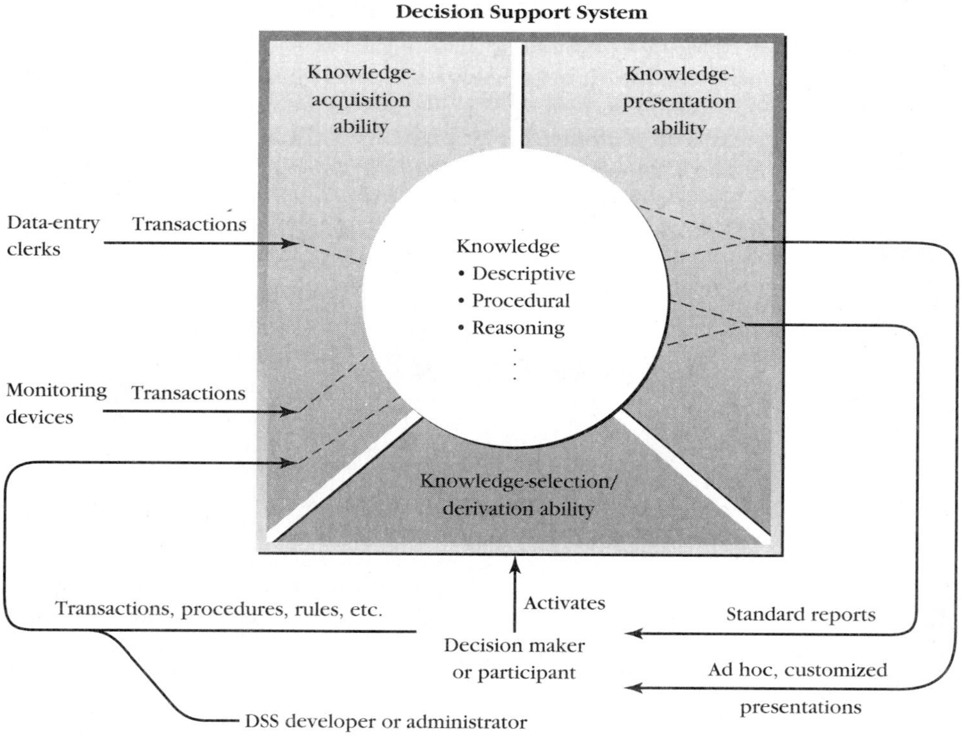

2. A DSS has an ability to acquire and maintain descriptive knowledge (i.e., record keeping) and other kinds of knowledge as well (i.e., procedure keeping, rule keeping, etc.).
3. A DSS has an ability to present knowledge on an ad hoc basis in various customized ways as well as in standard reports.
4. A DSS has an ability to select any desired subset of stored knowledge for either presentation or deriving new knowledge in the course of problem recognition and/or problem solving.
5. A DSS can interact directly with a decision maker or a participant in a decision maker in such a way that the user has a flexible choice and sequence of knowledge-management activities.

DSS EXAMPLES

Budgeting   Each department in a firm establishes an operating budget for the coming year. A budget represents a decision about how to allocate (i.e., spend, save, invest) available funds. In reaching the allocation decision, a manager has to weigh various trade-offs. For instance, to increase salaries by a certain amount, expenditures for equipment may need to be reduced. A DSS can help the manager assess the effects of making trade-offs and adjustments in the budget. For example, the DSS could be used to see what happens to the budget if a rumored increase in phone rates occurs in the middle of the year and what adjustment to other expense levels could be made to compensate for it.

Marketing   Marketing managers are responsible for making decisions that will enhance the sales of products. These decisions are concerned with such issues as product design, advertising campaigns, promotional activities, consumer education, and entry into new (e.g., foreign) markets. A marketing DSS will store and process knowledge about consumers, competitors, sales, products, ad agencies, traits of various markets, and so forth. Not only can it present selected subsets of such knowledge on an ad hoc basis, it may also offer analyses of those factors that are most important for product acceptance, forecasts of sales trends under various scenarios, solutions to the problem of how best to allocate advertising funds across different media (e.g., television, newspaper, magazine), advice about which television ad spots should be purchased, or projections of changes in competitors' shares of a market.

Investment Advice   One of the duties of a corporate treasurer is to manage the company's pool of cash. This involves making daily decisions about how to allocate available cash across an array of investment instruments ranging from money market shares and time deposits to bonds of differing yields, maturities, and quality ratings. The objective is to achieve a good return on the cash, without interfering with the firm's cash-flow needs. Such decisions can benefit from the advice of various financial specialists and experts. If the reasoning knowledge of these experts is incorporated into a DSS that also has timely knowledge about the firm's cash position, current investments, and possible investment instruments, the treasurer will be able to get investment recommendations from a computer on an ad hoc basis. In addition, the DSS may be able to explain the rationale for each piece of advice it offers. Such a DSS is an example of what is commonly called an *expert system*.

There are, of course, variations among DSSs with respect to each of these five characteristics. For instance, one DSS may possess descriptive and procedural knowledge, whereas another holds only descriptive and reasoning knowledge. Yet another DSS may store only descriptive knowledge, but a fourth DSS possesses all six types of knowledge identified in Figure 4.6. As another example, there can be wide variations in the nature of users' interactions with DSSs. One DSS may ask its user a series of questions to find out what the user wants, whereas another DS allows its user to state a command telling the DSS what is desired.

Regardless of such variations, these five characteristics combine to amplify a decision maker's knowledge-management capabilities. They can loosen cognitive, time, and economic constraints on a decision maker. They allow a computer to be responsive to the spur-of-the-moment needs that arise in the course of making semistructured or unstructured decisions. Creating such decisions usually leads a manager to request information that cannot be conveniently found in a stack of predefined reports.

The notion of decision support systems arose in the early 1970s (Scott Morton 1971; Gerrity 1971). Within a decade, each of the characteristics cited had been identified as an important DSS trait (Keen and Scott Morton 1978; Alter 1980; Bonczek, Holsapple, and Whinston 1980a, 1980b). In that period, various DSSs were proposed or implemented for specific decision-making applications such as those for corporate planning (Seaberg and Seaberg 1973), water-quality planning (Holsapple and Whinston 1976), banking (Sprague and Watson 1976), and so forth (Alter 1980). By the late 1970s new technological developments were emerging that would prove to have a tremendous impact on the DSS field. These included the microcomputer, the electronic spreadsheet, management science packages, and ad hoc query interfaces.

Microcomputers   The **microcomputer** has delivered very extensive, yet relatively inexpensive, raw computing power to the desktops and laptops of today's decision makers (Sanders 1983). This ready accessibility to computer facilities has stimulated a large increase in computer literacy beyond the doors of MIS departments. Such literacy puts decision makers in a position to develop their own DSSs, customized to their own individual needs. A typical MIS department would not have the resources to create so many individually customized DSSs in as timely a fashion.

The growth in computer literacy has allowed a MIS department's computer scientists to focus on its organization's data processing and management information systems, plus those DSSs whose development requires advanced computer expertise or involves features shared by several decision makers. In recent years, many organizations have established **information centers** where decision makers can seek advice and assistance in becoming more computer-literate and developing their own DSSs (Head 1985; Oglesby 1987).

By itself, the existence of powerful and inexpensive computer hardware was insufficient for achieving widespread DSS usage. A second key ingredient was the rise of software that could be used directly by decision makers to develop or at least operate their own DSSs, without undergoing the lengthy and extensive training required of computer professionals. As Figure 5.3 suggests, a DSS consists not only of stored knowledge, but also of software that can acquire, select/derive, and present knowledge in response to decision maker's actions.

Electronic Spreadsheets Perhaps the most significant software advance for DSSs was the invention of **electronic spreadsheet** software in the late 1970s (Lucas 1986; Parker 1991). This kind of software allows relative computer novices to build decision support systems that are very useful in supporting budgeting and other financial decisions. For instance, a DSS built with spreadsheet software could help a decision maker quickly see the effects of a 12% rise in shipping costs, a 25-unit decrease in expected sales, or a change in employee benefits. It is used to answer the many what-if questions that a decision maker considers.

Over the years, spreadsheet software has undergone a continuing evolution that has improved its knowledge-handling features and made it more convenient for managers to use. Today it is routinely used by managers and their staff assistants in support of decision-making activities. Chapter 6 considers spreadsheet-oriented DSSs, and Chapter 10 surveys the spreadsheet technique for managing knowledge.

Management Science Packages Another software advance contributing to the growth of the DSS field was the advent of **management science packages.** Management scientists invent and apply procedures for solving complex quantitative problems faced by managers. Such procedures are often called **solvers.** A management science package is software that incorporates one or more solvers. With such a package, a computer can issue a **response** to user **requests** that state problems covered by the package's solvers.

For instance, one solver might be a procedure for determining what values of some stated variables will produce an optimal result, given the existence of some

DSS IN THE NEWS

Popping Up All Over

Computers are popping up all over. From factory floor to warehouse, retail shelf to service bay, information processors are being put in the hands of new kinds of users. . . .

. . . Spurred by miniaturization and the advent of technologies that enable easier data entry and freedom of movement, computers are becoming indispensable to more and more workers outside the usual office environment.

In the Chicago futures pits, small groups of traders have just begun to use hand-held computers instead of paper to conduct their frenetic business. . . .

United Parcel Service has just finished an 18-month effort to put portable computer tablets into the hands of all its 50,000 full-time route drivers in the U.S. . . .

At Boeing Co. in Seattle, engineers are developing a set of computer-linked goggles that provide aircraft assemblers with "heads-up" displays of plans and specifications for any given part of the plane. . . .

The system is designed to give workers precise visual markers for step-by-step procedures, without requiring them to thumb through a set of blueprints or manuals.

T. Bunker, "Blue-Collar Computing Brings New Power to the Masses," *Investor's Business Daily*, 20 April 1992, p. 4.

stated constraints. A marketing manager might pose the following problem to this solver:

> Within a $50,000 advertising budget, how many magazine ads (one variable) and how many TV spots (another variable) would result in a maximal level of profits (the objective)? Each ad costs $2,000 and each spot costs $3,000. In the interest of a balanced marketing effort, there are the added constraints that no more than 70% of the budget can be used for ads and no more than 50% can be used for spots. We expect that each ad will increase sales by 5,000 units, whereas each spot will increase sales by 7,000 units. Our gross profit for each unit sold is $.75.

The solver would accept a mathematical expression of this problem and then derive the number of ads and number of spots that would maximize profits.

Query Language   A third software advance that ushered in today's decision support systems was the creation of **query languages** and the accompanying software to process requests stated in such languages (Bonczek, Holsapple, and Whinston 1981; Sprague and Carlson 1982). Three important features of such languages are that **queries**

1. Have an English-like appearance,
2. Are non procedural, and
3. Can be submitted in an ad hoc way.

The early query languages and software allowed information held in an MIS to be accessed directly by persons who were not computer scientists. Thus they formed a bridge from the MIS field into the DSS realm.

Because a query language is **English-like,** it can be learned quickly. Because the language is nonprocedural, its user does not need to give a detailed, step-by-step sequence of commands (i.e., a procedure) telling how to get at the desired information. Instead, the user issues a single command that tells what information he or she desires to see. Because such queries could be submitted in an ad hoc fashion, they began to allow MISs to be used in a much more flexible way—thereby taking a big step in the direction of decision support systems. Chapter 8 considers query languages and other kinds of DSS interface facilities.

Technologically Driven DSS Initiatives   In the 1980s, the relentless march of technological innovation presented new opportunities for realizing the five DSS characteristics, for improving on the power and flexibility of DSSs with respect to each characteristic, and for facilitating the construction of DSSs. Some of these advances were refinements or extensions to existing technology—hardware with greater storage capacity and greater speed, spreadsheet software offering greater convenience to users, more elaborate management science packages, and more versatile query languages. Other advances pioneered initiatives in the DSS field. For instance, by allowing microcomputers to communicate with each other, **local area network** technology has spurred the development of multiparticipant decision support systems, particularly DSSs for group decision makers (Gray and Nunamaker 1989). Chapter 17 examines various aspects of group decision support systems.

Artificial intelligence techniques have also emerged to guide knowledge from the ivory tower into everyday practical use. Foremost among these have been techniques for managing reasoning knowledge, which have led to a class of artificially

---

TECHNOLOGICAL ADVANCES FOR DSSs

Technological advances contributing to the spread of DSSs include

- Microcomputers,
- Electronic spreadsheets,
- Management science packages,
- Ad hoc query interfaces.

Technological advances stimulating new DSS initiatives occurred

- In computer communications such as local area networks,
- In artificial intelligence, such as practical means for building expert systems,
- In user interface construction, such as natural language, electronic forms, and direct manipulation.

---

intelligent DSSs known as **expert systems** (Bonczek, Holsapple, and Whinston 1981). An expert system draws on descriptive and reasoning knowledge to infer advice in response to a decision maker's request for a recommendation. The advice is comparable to that of a human expert; like its human counterpart, an expert system can explain its rationale to the decision maker. Part Four focuses on these artificially intelligent decision support systems.

Assorted means of interacting with computers that differ from the command orientation of query languages have also been developed. Rather than learning a query language and issuing a command phrased in terms of that language, the user simply makes requests in terms of his or her own **natural language.** Another type of interaction that became increasingly prominent in the 1980s involved filling in **electronic forms** appearing on a computer screen. This activity is analogous to making requests by filling in paper forms, except the manipulation of electronic

DSS IN THE NEWS

Redefining Corporate Computing

The days when information systems managers could dictate when and how technology evolved inside corporations are over, according to InfoWorld (June 7).

A big reason for the change is the growth in computer networks, which have given departments considerable control over their computing needs. As a result, they are demanding a greater voice in the design of information systems.

In addition, people weaned on PCs and network technologies are starting to rise to management levels. Their influence can be pegged to growing acceptance of newer network technologies.

B. Deagon, "Redefining Corporate Computing," *Investor's Business Daily,* 10 June 1993, p.4.

TYPICAL DSS CHARACTERISTICS

- Often holds other types of knowledge in addition to the descriptive variety
- Has ability to acquire and maintain each of these other types of knowledge in addition to ordinary record-keeping abilities
- Can produce ad hoc, customized presentations in addition to standard reports
- Can derive new knowledge from existing knowledge for purposes of recognizing and/or solving problems
- Can interact directly with a decision maker or decision-making participant

---

images of forms tends to be faster and more convenient than handling their paper counterparts.

Form-oriented interaction is a special case of the interaction style more broadly known as **direct manipulation.** This interaction style allows a user to make requests by directly manipulating (e.g., moving, pointing at, altering) any of a wide range of images appearing on the computer screen. These images may include such things as text, icons, drawings, and diagrams as well as electronic forms. Advances in direct manipulation technology can make DSSs more accessible and easier to use. Interfaces found in today's DSSs are considered more fully in Chapter 8.

As we approach the 21st century, the pace of the technological advances will probably not diminish. The future advances in hardware and software are likely to make further contributions to fulfilling the purposes of decision support systems and improving ways in which the five DSS characteristics are developed and delivered to users. They may even usher in new characteristics not previously recognized by DSS researchers or practitioners. In any event, the basic DSS purposes identified earlier remain the same. Moreover, the five basic DSS characteristics will not disappear, although technological advances will continue to introduce new variations for each.

EXECUTIVE INFORMATION SYSTEMS

Within the business computing field, the three most prominent and widespread kinds of systems have been those for data processing, management information, and decision support. Another related type of system is an **executive information system** (EIS). This term was coined to denote computer-based systems designed to meet the information needs of top executives such as chief executive officers, chief operating officers, and chief financial officers (Rockart 1979; Rockart and Treacy 1982; Rockart and Delong 1988). The intent of such systems is to allow top executives to get information from computers directly, without using intermediaries who interact with computers and then pass along retrieved information to the top executives. EISs can be regarded as a kind of executive support system (Kador 1989).

Like MIS, an EIS is concerned mainly with the use of descriptive knowledge. Unlike an MIS, it is intended to satisfy the ad hoc information needs of managers in response to requests they pose. Specifically, the following ten characteristics have been identified for an EIS (Turban and Schaeffer 1989):

1. Is designed to satisfy information needs of the highest executives
2. Filters, summarizes, and tracks critical information

3. Is used mainly to monitor and control an organization's activities
4. Is customized to a particular executive's approach to decision making
5. Allows information to be presented graphically in several ways
6. Is designed to present current information on a timely basis
7. Is designed to be used by persons with little computer training
8. Is tailored to conform to the organization's traits
9. Allows top-down access to information, providing summary information first and then, if desired, the more detailed information that lies behind it
10. Provides extensive information about the organization's environment.

There is nothing in these EIS characteristics that is inconsistent with the DSS characteristics noted earlier. That is, any of these ten characteristics might be observed in a particular DSS. The principal difference is that the EIS characteristics are more restrictive than those of decision support systems. Unlike the study of DSSs, a consideration of EISs is restricted to computer-based systems used by top executives, customized to an individual executive's decision-making style, needing almost no computer training, offering alternative presentation modes, concerned mainly with the management of descriptive knowledge, and emphasizing information about the organization's environment. Thus, an EIS can be fairly regarded as a special kind of DSS. Chapter 18 examines this special kind of DSS in more detail.

TASK SUPPORT SYSTEMS

Finally, we consider **task support systems** (TSS). Whereas EISs are designed to support a subset of the knowledge management needs of a certain class of decision makers (i.e., top executives), task support systems form a broader class of computer-based systems than DSSs. As Figure 5.4 indicates, the class of task support systems includes systems that support tasks of managers, operating personnel, researchers, consumers and suppliers, as well as personal tasks. Among these categories, our focus is on **management support systems** (MSSs). As we saw in Chapter 1, managers engage in a variety of activities. Each is a candidate for computer-based support.

Following Mintzberg's role-oriented view of managerial work, the class of MSSs can be divided into subclasses: informational roles being supported by the class of management information systems and, to a lesser extent, by data processing systems; decisional roles being supported by the class of DSSs; and interpersonal roles being aided by communication support systems. As Figure 5.4 suggests, data processing systems primarily support tasks of operating personnel—principally clerical kinds of tasks. Their support of managerial tasks is less direct and less pronounced. Conversely, although we consider decision support systems primarily in their support of managerial decision tasks, they can also be geared to support decisions of operating personnel (and even researchers, consumers, suppliers, etc.).

The MSS class of **communication support systems** (CSS) is extensive (Calantone, Holsapple, and Johnson 1993). Although communication support systems are not the focus of this book, various kinds of multiparticipant decision support systems can be regarded as CSSs. That is, one way of supporting a multiparticipant decision maker is to facilitate the communication among its participants. This idea is examined in Part Five.

An example of a CSS is one that allows a computer user to type in and edit messages, send the text of a message to another computer whose user will read it, see the text of a message received from another computer's user, and keep copies of

FIGURE 5.4   Some Classes of Systems in the Business Computing Field

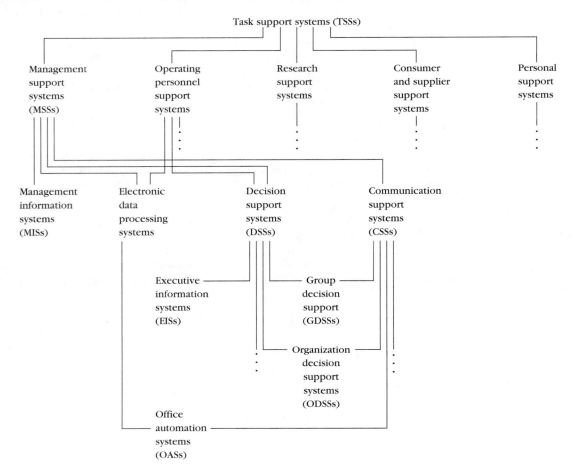

messages sent and received. These CSSs, called electronic mail systems, are common in modern offices and are a prime example of what is called office automation: automating message-passing transactions.

5.4 DSS BENEFITS AND LIMITATIONS

Computer-based systems that have the five basic DSS characteristics offer a variety of benefits. Some of these are direct and obvious. Others are somewhat indirect and more subtle. The whole issue of formally measuring the value of a particular DSS is a very complex one that is beginning to attract the attention of researchers (Keen 1981; Benbasat and Dexter 1982; Gardner 1991; Kottemann and Davis 1991; Marsden and Pingry 1993).

Here, we consider the potential benefits of DSSs in general. Some of the potential benefits cited may be achieved by one DSS and not another. A potential benefit may be only partially achieved by a particular DSS. In any event, we should be aware of the kinds of benefits that might reasonably be expected of a DSS and of limitations on the possibilities they present to us. Although DSSs can be beneficial, they are not panaceas that eliminate the need for managerial skills.

BENEFITS

The benefits of a particular DSS depend not only on the precise nature of that DSS, but also on the nature of the decision maker that uses it and on the decision context. A good fit among these three factors must exist if potential benefits of the DSS are to become practical realities. A DSS that one decision maker finds very beneficial may be of little value to another decision maker, even though both are facing similar decisions. This disparity is due to differences in the decision makers themselves.

One decision maker may be apprehensive about using a computer, whereas the other is not. One may approach the decision in a way that does not require the use of a DSS's knowledge-management capabilities. The other may take a very different approach to the decision, relying heavily on the DSS's stored knowledge and its capabilities for processing that knowledge. One decision maker may feel uncomfortable with the way in which requests are made to the DSS or the way in which its responses are presented. The other may feel entirely comfortable with the interaction style provided by the DSS. One may not have received adequate training about the uses of the DSS, whereas the other decision maker may be very experienced at using it.

Aside from such differences in decision-makers, the value of a DSS also depends on the decision type and context. In other words, a DSS that is highly beneficial to a decision maker for one decision may be of little value to the same decision maker faced with a very different decision situation. For instance, the DSS may have or be able to manufacture knowledge that is crucial for one decision-making episode but not be able to provide knowledge needed to manufacture a different decision. For one decision, a DSS may be able to respond sufficiently quickly. For another, it may be too slow. A DSS designed for use by top executives may be of little use at lower levels of management and vice versa.

Realizing that a particular DSS's benefits depend on the nature of the decision maker and the decision situation, we can nevertheless identify the potential kinds of benefits DSSs, in general, can provide. These include the following:

1. In a most fundamental sense, a DSS augments the decision maker's own innate knowledge management abilities. It effectively extends the decision maker's capacity for representing and processing knowledge in the course of manufacturing decisions.
2. A decision maker can have the DSS solve problems that the decision maker alone would not even attempt or that would consume a great deal of time due to their complexity and magnitude.
3. Even for relatively simple problems encountered in decision making, a DSS may be able to reach solutions faster and/or more reliably than the decision maker.
4. Even though a DSS may be unable to solve a problem facing the decision maker, it can be used to stimulate the decision maker's thoughts about the problem. For instance, the decision maker may use the DSS in an exploratory way to browse selectively through stored data or to analyze selectively the implications of ideas related to the problem. The decision maker may ask the DSS for advice about

dealing with the problem. Perhaps the decision maker can have the DSS solve a similar problem to trigger insights about the problem actually being faced.

5. The very activity of constructing a DSS may reveal new ways of thinking about the decision domain or even partially formalize various aspects of decision making.

6. A DSS may provide additional compelling evidence to justify a decision-maker's position, helping the decision maker secure agreement or cooperation of others. Similarly, a DSS may be used by the decision maker to check on or confirm the results of problems solved independently of the DSS.

7. Due to the enhanced productivity a DSS fosters within an organization, it may give the organization a competitive advantage over other organizations in the environment. Or, a DSS may be necessary to just stay competitive with other organizations.

Because no one DSS provides all these benefits to all decision makers in all decision situations, there are frequently many DSSs within an organization helping to manage its knowledge resources. A particular decision maker may also make use of several DSSs within a single decision-making episode or across different decision-making situations.

LIMITATIONS

Even the most carefully designed DSS has some limitations that restrict its value to decision makers. These include the following:

1. There are some innate human knowledge-management skills and talents that cannot be incorporated into today's DSSs. There are others that can be incorporated only partially into a DSS. For instance, we should not expect a DSS to exhibit such human skills as creativity, intuition, and imagination. (Penrose 1989).

2. A DSS is constrained by the knowledge it possesses. It cannot process knowledge it does not have. Its knowledge at any moment may or may not be sufficient to respond to a decision-maker's requests. Related to this point is the extent to which a DSS is able to acquire additional knowledge (i.e., learn) and the means whereby that acquisition can occur.

3. A DSS is constrained by the kinds of knowledge processing its software can perform. For instance, if a DSS does not have the ability to process reasoning knowledge, then there is little sense in storing that kind of knowledge in it. The DSS will not be able to reason in the course of producing responses to user's requests. Some DSSs are designed to process many kinds of knowledge in many ways. Others are more modest.

4. A DSS's capabilities are limited by the computer (hardware and operating system) in which it is being used. A given DSS will be more limited if it is being run on a relatively slow computer with relatively small memory capacity than if it is being used in a more powerful computer.

5. The language in which users are required to make requests limits its universe of users to those who will tolerate that mode of expression. For instance, some users prefer to make requests by responding to menus of options, whereas others prefer to state a command directly. A command-oriented DSS may be unpalatable to those who prefer menus, and vice versa. Similarly, the way in which a DSS presents responses (e.g., tabular versus graphical presentations) limits its users to those who are comfortable with perceiving that mode of pre-

sentation. Some DSSs allow multiple request languages and multiple presentation styles to relax these interaction limitations.

6. DSSs may be designed to be fairly narrow or quite specific in what they can accomplish. Thus, several such DSSs may need to be used in the course of working on problems involved in reaching a single decision. In such a case, there is the question of how to coordinate the use of multiple DSSs. For instance, the knowledge produced by one of them may need to be made available to another DSS before it can complete its processing. Thus another DSS limitation is the degree to which it can pass knowledge to and accept knowledge from other DSSs (or MISs, for that matter).

At a very fundamental level, the best DSS cannot overcome a faulty decision maker (Russo and Schoemaker 1989). It cannot force a decision maker to make requests of it, pay attention to its responses, or properly factor its responses into the decision that is made. At the opposite extreme of this DSS limitation, there is a DSS danger: the danger of over dependence on a DSS, of blindly following the DSS, or of interacting with it in an entirely mechanical and unimaginative fashion. Holding such an attitude toward a DSS relegates the user to a subservient role, whereas the proper relationship is one in which the DSS is a supporting participant in the decision making.

5.5 DSS POSSIBILITIES

Earlier in this chapter, we saw five basic characteristics that DSSs exhibit. We made the point that there are variations in the expression of each characteristic as we go from one DSS to another. For instance, every DSS has some body of knowledge about the decision-maker's world. But DSSs can differ in terms of which types of knowledge they possess. They can vary in terms of how individual pieces of knowledge are represented. Even if types and techniques are the same, two DSSs can differ in terms of what specific pieces of knowledge they hold.

In this section, we describe possible DSS variations in more detail. As prospective creators, purchasers, and users of DSSs, we need to be aware of these possibilities. Rather than just compiling and categorizing lists of possibilities that can be seen in a sampling of today's DSSs, we shall use a human metaphor to determine what possibilities could, should, and do exist for decision support systems.

Recall from Figure 3.2 that a DSS can be viewed as a supporting participant in a decision maker. Of course, humans can also serve as supporting participants. They range from staff assistants to expert consultants and can be regarded as **human decision support systems** (Huber 1980; Oberquelle, Kupka, and Maas 1983). By closely examining the activities of a human decision support system (HDSS) in relation to a decision maker, we can see possible behaviors we would like computer-based decision support systems to exhibit (Holsapple 1993).

In very broad terms, an HDSS does the following: accepts requests from a decision maker, makes responses to the decision maker, possesses knowledge, and processes knowledge. Common sense tells us that the same basic possibilities should exist for DSSs. We can take a much more detailed look at what HDSSs do and, therefore, at what DSS possibilities exist. This examination is organized according to the four basic HDSS behaviors just mentioned.

ACCEPTING DECISION MAKER'S REQUESTS

When a decision maker submits a request to an HDSS, it is a request to provide some knowledge to the decision maker, accept some knowledge from the decision maker, or both. By analogy, it seems only reasonable that a DSS should also be able to handle decision-maker requests for providing and/or accepting knowledge. Let's look first at requests to provide knowledge and then at requests to accept knowledge.

Asking for knowledge   In the course of making a decision, the decision maker identifies some problems whose solutions will be factored into the decision process. Suppose the decision maker does not have the time or ability to solve one (or more) of these problems, or the decision maker intends to personally reach a solution but wants to confirm the solution by having someone else solve it also. In such cases, the decision maker submits a request to an appropriate HDSS, asking it to provide a solution to the identified problem. This solution constitutes some knowledge desired by the decision maker. The HDSS task is then one of producing the desired knowledge, solving the identified problem, and responding to the decision maker's request. By analogy, the same should be true of a DSS.

Degrees of Procedurality   When the message to provide knowledge is sent to an HDSS, the decision maker may or may not be aware of the method that the HDSS will use to satisfy the request. At one extreme, the decision maker may be entirely unaware of what methods the HDSS will use in seeking to provide the requested knowledge. The request itself merely indicates what knowledge is desired and not how the HDSS should get it. As a middle ground, the decision maker may be aware of what methods the HDSS could use in solving the problem. In this case, the decision maker's request may directly tell the HDSS which of these methods to use in its effort to provide the requested knowledge. At the opposite extreme, the decision maker's request may include a detailed, step-by-step specification of how the HDSS is to work at providing the requested knowledge.

Thus, a decision maker's request could be **nonprocedural.** It could be **semiprocedural,** telling the HDSS which of its procedures should be exercised in providing the knowledge. Or, the request could by highly **procedural,** requiring the decision maker to communicate its own procedural knowledge to the HDSS, which then follows that procedure. Generally speaking, procedural requests are bigger and take more decision-maker effort than nonprocedural requests. They also tend to give the decision maker more flexibility and control over requesting what the HDSS will do. Conversely, semiprocedural or nonprocedural requests tend to require less decision-maker effort but also give less control over details of how the HDSS processing is accomplished. These same three approaches to making requests are also possibilities for decision makers using DSSs (Bonczek, Holsapple, and Whinston 1980a).

What the Request Seeks   When a decision maker requests knowledge from an HDSS, it may consider the request to be seeking

- The recall of some knowledge (usually descriptive) held by the HDSS;
- The derivation of some knowledge via analysis (e.g., producing expectations), via inference (e.g., producing advice), via reasoned analysis, and so forth;
- The invention of knowledge via such HDSS abilities as insight, creative synthesis, or intuition;

REQUEST TYPES

Nonprocedural Request	Semiprocedural Request	Procedural Request
Specifies what is desired, not how to produce it	Specifies which procedure to use in producing what is desired	Specifies step-by-step details of how to produce what is desired
Tends to be a short request	Tends to be a short request	Tends to be a lengthy request
Offers little control over how the request will be satisfied	Offers some control over how the request will be satisfied	Offers extensive control over how the request will be satisfied

- The collection of knowledge from sources outside the HDSS;
- Clarification, explanation, or elaboration of prior HDSS responses;
- Help in making the next request.

By analogy, DSSs should allow decision makers to have these same objectives when submitting request. However, as a practical matter, requesting a DSS consistently to invent usable knowledge is beyond the present boundary of computer technology. Requests of the other kinds can be seen in dealing with today's DSSs. We should expect to see continuing increases in the power, flexibility, and sophistication that DSSs exhibit in handling requests of each type.

Depositing Knowledge   To the preceding types of request objectives, all of which are concerned with providing knowledge to decision makers, we can add another: namely, those requests concerned with acquiring knowledge from a decision maker or other DSS users. A decision maker can request an HDSS to accept new pieces of knowledge. This knowledge furnished by a decision maker may impact later problem solving efforts of the HDSS. Similarly, an HDSS can accept new knowledge from other sources, such as newspapers, books, training seminars, conferences, and messages from others inside or outside of the organization.

By analogy, we should expect a DSS to handle requests that carry new knowledge for inclusion in its memory. These requests may come directly from the decision maker or from other persons (e.g., staff assistants, MIS department, information center) who are responsible for seeing to it that the DSS is sufficiently knowledgeable to meet the decision-maker's needs.

Interpreting Requests   Regardless of the type of request an HDSS receives, it is possible that the request may not be understood. There are two possibilities when an HDSS realizes that he or she does not understand a request. Either the HDSS makes a response seeking clarification or does not seek clarification. Following the human metaphor, it is quite possible that a DSS does not understand some request posed by a user. However, the typical DSS will not fail to seek clarification when a received request is not understood.

It is important for both HDSSs and DSSs to be able not only to interpret requests received, but also to interpret them in such a way that they accurately grasp the decision maker's intent. This brings up an obvious question. In what way does an HDSS learn to comprehend decision-maker requests? Or, is it a matter of the decision maker learning to phrase requests in a way that the HDSS can correctly interpret with minimal need for clarification? **Learning** by either an HDSS or a decision maker typically occurs through formal training (both initial and ongoing) and through experience.

By analogy, we might expect a DSS to be initially vested with knowledge necessary to comprehend decision maker's requests. We might also expect a DSS to be able to accept additional linguistic knowledge provided to it on an ongoing basis. These expectations are partially realized in some of today's DSSs, but they tend to fall far short of their HDSS counterparts. It would not be surprising if efforts by DSS developers narrowed this gap over the next decade. As this gap is narrowed, a smaller share of the learning effort will fall on the DSS user, who will need less training in phrasing requests in ways that the DSS can interpret.

In the case of learning by experience, an HDSS reviews its interpretation performance in the light of feedback from the decision maker. As a simple example, clarifications provided by a decision maker are a kind of feedback that may later help an HDSS interpret the same (or similar) kind of request without needing clarification. That is, the HDSS's linguistic knowledge is greater by virtue of having interpreted and checked the interpretation of former requests.

Metaphorically, it would be nice if a DSS could learn from its experiences. Of course this learning could involve the acquisition not only of linguistic knowledge, but of other types of knowledge as well. Computer-based decision support systems are currently far behind their human counterparts in their ability to learn from experience. The extent to which this gap is narrowed will depend on progress by researches in the fields of psychology (finding the precise mechanisms by which humans learn from experience) and artificial intelligence (finding how machines can be made to emulate intelligent human behavior).

There is one other aspect of accepting decision maker's requests that we briefly consider. A typical HDSS is able to handle syntactically different, but semantically equivalent, requests. That is, the form **(syntax)** of each differs, but the meaning **(semantics)** is identical. A decision maker can have and use several ways to say the same thing. Moreover, different decision makers may prefer to convey the same meaning via requests that have very different appearances. To handle such diversity of expression, an HDSS must have sufficient linguistic knowledge. Similarly, we might expect a DSS to accept requests that have different appearances, yet convey the same meaning. All these equivalent requests should result in the DSS solving the same problem (Holsapple et al. 1988).

MAKING RESPONSES TO DECISION MAKERS

Just as a request to an HDSS has both syntax and semantics, so does the response from an HDSS. Our metaphor suggests that the same is true of responses emanating from a DSS. Not only must a DSS determine what it means to say to a decision maker, it must also determine the way in which that response is to be presented. Will the response be presented audibly or visually? If visual, will it appear as a chart, drawing, graph, form, narrative, table of numbers, outline, or some other kind of image, perhaps as some combination of these? If the response is graphical, will it be presented as a bar, line, pie, or some other kind of graph? What colors, patterns, and labels will be used for a bar graph?

The Flexibility of Responses   Perhaps the easiest way for a DSS to cope with such presentation questions is for it to have few or no choices. A DSS may have only one prespecified way for presenting a particular piece of knowledge. For instance, it always presents forecasts as line graphs. An HDSS is typically much more flexible when it comes to making presentations, being able to give many equivalent responses that are simply different presentations of the same thing. It can package the essence of a message in various ways to suit various decision makers or support situations. This ability implies that the HDSS has considerable presentation knowledge.

Some DSSs are fairly flexible with respect to their presentation possibilities and should be even more so in the years ahead. But how can a DSS with presentation flexibility choose from among its alternatives for packaging its response to a user? Perhaps the simplest and most common approach is to require a user to specify what kind of presentation should by used. If this is not specified in the original request, then the DSS responds by seeking a **clarification.** For instance, if a decision maker requests a graph, the DSS response might be a question to clarify the kind of graph desired.

Having decision makers determine the presentation style of a response is also commonplace in the interactions that occur with HDSSs. However, in the case of human support, decision makers often leave this up to the discretion of the persons providing the support. Assuming that they do not act randomly, we must suppose that HDSSs possess some knowledge that influences the presentation styles they select for various responses. This presentation knowledge must come from somewhere. It can be changed as time goes by in order to improve HDSS responsiveness to a decision maker. Just as an HDSS can learn new linguistic knowledge, he or she can also increase presentation knowledge via training and experience. There is considerable room for improving DSS capabilities in this regard (Dos Santos and Holsapple 1989).

Types of Responses   Regardless of the presentation style used, when a human responds to a decision maker, it is to

1. Seek clarification of a request,
2. Provide knowledge to support a decision,
3. Provide clarification of a response, or
4. Seek additional knowledge.

The second of these is perhaps the most obvious kind of response that an HDSS makes. We have already touched on the importance of seeking clarification of requests that are incomplete, insufficiently detailed, or otherwise incomprehensible. The third type of response is in many ways a mirror image of the first. And the fourth forms an important basis for an HDSS's ability to actively learn, allowing for greater responsiveness in the future.

Again considering our metaphor, we might expect a DSS to be capable of all four kinds of responses. It certainly must be capable of the second. It is also likely to have at least some capacity to seek clarification of a request. However, responses of the third and fourth types tend to be less common or well developed in today's DSSs.

REQUESTS AND RESPONSES

Request	Response
Decision Maker	HDSS or DSS
• Seeks knowledge to support decision	• Seeks clarification of request
• Provides clarification of request	• Provides knowledge to support decision
• Provides knowledge (teaches)	• Provides clarification of response
• Seeks clarification of response	• Seeks knowledge (learns)

POSSESSING KNOWLEDGE

Obviously, an effective HDSS possesses knowledge. We can distinguish between the knowledge acquired by that person and his or her innate mental faculties. There is a knowledge storehouse encompassing all knowledge that has been acquired and retained. Contents of this storehouse are continually growing and changing. There is also a set of mental equipment that is able to process acquired knowledge in various ways. The extent to which a part of this mental equipment is exercised depends on such factors as personality tendencies (e.g., an analytical orientation) personal development (e.g., repeated experience in analyzing), and environing conditions (e.g., a job that requires heavy use of analytic abilities).

As mental faculty unfolds, the acquired knowledge that can be processed by that faculty is likely to increase. For instance, as one's ability to think analytically unfolds, it makes sense to have stored more descriptive and procedural knowledge for taking advantage of that ability. Or, as one's potential for making logical deductions is more fully realized, it makes sense to store more reasoning knowledge to fuel deductive efforts.

By way of our metaphor, we should expect a DSS to possess a knowledge storehouse and to have the abilities needed to process the contents of that storehouse. We should expect a DSS to be able to acquire its knowledge in much the same way that its human counterpart can. Knowledge may be acquired by direct observation, or by sensing events and objects in the surrounding world. This is not an especially common way for DSSs to acquire knowledge, even though it is common for HDSSs.

Knowledge may be acquired by instruction, or by accepting statements made by a trainer. In the DSS case, the creator of a DSS can play the trainer role by depositing the initial body of knowledge in its storehouse. As we have seen, a decision maker who uses the DSS can also be a trainer by submitting requests that cause the DSS to accept new pieces of knowledge. Knowledge may also be acquired by experience, or by self-observation and **feedback.** Although this is not yet a widespread means for knowledge acquisition among DSSs, it is likely to become more prominent as DSS technology advances.

A new piece of knowledge acquired by an HDSS may be just an additional fact for inclusion in the storehouse. On the other hand, acquisition may not be strictly additive. It could cause the alteration, adjustment, restructuring, or deletion of knowledge already possessed. The same possibilities exist when a DSS acquires knowledge. As we saw in Chapter 4, the manner in which a new piece of knowledge affects existing knowledge is governed by what we have called *assimilative knowledge*.

HDSSs can store descriptive , procedural, reasoning, linguistic, presentation, and assimilative knowledge. All these types are fair game for DSSs as well. However, typical 1990s-vintage DSSs tend to emphasize or allow the acquisition of only one or two of these types of knowledge. Most common are those that can acquire only descriptive and procedural knowledge on a continuing basis.

PROCESSING KNOWLEDGE

As mentioned before, an HDSS has an innate capacity to process the knowledge it possesses. Just as two persons' skills at processing a piece of knowledge can differ, so too can one DSS be more adept than another at processing a given piece of knowledge. Just as some HDSSs specialize in one kind of knowledge processing, many DSSs specialize in a particular kind of processing. Just as some HDSSs are talented at many kinds of knowledge processing, there are DSSs that have many processing skills.

In addition to its innate knowledge-processing (i.e., mental) abilities, an HDSS can use some pieces of acquired knowledge to help govern the processing of other pieces of knowledge. For instance, an HDSS might have acquired a procedure that it can follow in processing descriptive knowledge (e.g., procedural knowledge specifying how to compute a forecast from historical data). A similar phenomenon occurs in the knowledge processing performed by typical DSSs. They have the ability to acquire and use knowledge to guide the processing of other knowledge.

When an HDSS works at solving the problem stated in a decision maker's request for knowledge, he or she often has occasion to process different types of knowledge. An effective HDSS is able to exercise and coordinate multiple kinds of knowledge-processing abilities in a facile way during a problem-solving episode. He or she selects and sequences the use of these abilities in accordance with knowledge possessed about the use of other knowledge. Similarly, we can expect a well-versed DSS to coordinate its use of different knowledge processing abilities effectively as it solves a problem.

Knowledge processing by an HDSS or DSS is often triggered by the receipt of a clear decision-maker request. It can also be instigated by others with whom the HDSS or DSS communicates (e.g., the data-entry clerks in Figure 5.3). Finally, an HDSSs knowledge processing may be triggered by the occurrence of some event (e.g., some change in the knowledge storehouse). That is, the event is considered to be a request in the eyes of the HDSS. Similarly, event-triggered processing has been recognized as a potentially fruitful behavior for decision support systems (Holsapple 1988).

5.6 SUMMARY

Our overview of decision support systems began by noting that the purpose of a DSS could be viewed as facilitating one or more of a decision maker's abilities, aiding in one or more of the three decision-making phases, improving the flows of problem solving, assisting decision makers in dealing with unstructured and semi-structured decisions, or helping decision makers manage knowledge. We then looked at DSSs in historical perspective. We examined traits of DP and MIS fore-runners as a foundation for understanding what characteristics a DSS shares with other kinds of computer systems and what characteristics distinguish a DSS from these others. We have also traced the contributions of various technological advances to the rise of decision support systems.

Having a feel for the basic characteristics a user could expect to witness in deal-ing with a DSS, we have considered many of the possible benefits that could result from DSS usage. The extent to which these benefits are provided by a particular DSS depends not only on specific features of that DSS, but also on the natures of the decision maker and the decision situation. Even though they may offer many benefits, we have seen that DSSs are not panaceas. They do have limits of various kinds.

Finally, we turned to a consideration of possible behaviors that could be expect-ed of DSSs. To guide this exploration we adopted the metaphor of a human deci-sion support system. We identified four behavioral categories: accepting requests, making responses, possessing knowledge, and processing knowledge. For each supporting behavior of an HDSS, we identified comparable behaviors for a DSS. We commonly observe some of these in today's DSSs. Others are rarer or exist only par-tially in DSSs. Further technological advances will determine the extent to which DSSs can more fully provide the services of HDSSs.

▲ IMPORTANT TERMS

ad hoc
artificial intelligence
automatic data processing
business computing systems
clarification
communication support system
DP department
data processing
descriptive knowledge
direct manipulation
electronic data processing
electronic forms
electronic spreadsheet
English-like
executive information system
expert system
feedback
human decision support system
information center
learning
local area network
management information system

management science package
management support system
microcomputer
MIS department
natural language
nonprocedural
procedural
query
query language
record
record keeping
request
response
semantics
semiprocedural
solver
syntax
task support system
transaction generation
transactions
users

▲ APPLICATION TO THE DAIRYMAN'S COOPERATIVE CASE

1. What purpose(s) does the MFAP decision support system aim to fulfill?
2. How does MFAP differ from data processing systems? From management information systems?
3. Identify the different kinds of MFAP users and explain what each does in interacting with the system.
4. Give examples of descriptive and procedural knowledge incorporated into the DSS.
5. Give an example of ad hoc reports produced by MFAP.
6. Why has the advent of management science solvers been important for the development of MFAP?
7. Why does MFAP not qualify as an EIS?
8. Describe the main benefits of this DSS?
9. Which of the seven potential benefits accrue in the dairy case? Which of the six DSS limitations apply in this case?
10. What kinds of decision-maker requests are permitted by MFAP?
11. What kinds of responses are permitted by MFAP?

▲ REVIEW QUESTIONS

1. What decision-maker abilities could a DSS facilitate? How might it facilitate each?
2. Are there ways in which a DSS could contribute to each phase of decision making? If so, give an example of each.
3. How might a DSS assist in improving the flows of problem solving during decision making?
4. In what ways might a DSS help decision makers manage knowledge?
5. What are the important kinds of management support systems?
6. What is the main purpose of a DP system? Of an MIS? Of a DSS?
7. Are there characteristics that are shared by both DP systems and MISs? List them.
8. What characteristics differentiate an MIS from a DP system?
9. What role does a MIS department play in an organization?
10. In what respects does a DSS differ from an MIS?
11. Which traits do DSSs and MISs have in common?
12. What are the main limits on an MIS's ability to support decision makers?
13. What characteristics would you expect to observe in a DSS?
14. How did each of the following technological advances impact the rise of decision support systems?
    a. Microcomputers
    b. Electronic spreadsheets
    c. Management science packages
    d. Ad hoc query interfaces
15. Identify some important classes of task support systems.
16. How can spreadsheet software help a decision maker?
17. What does a management science package do?
18. What are the main characteristics of a query?
19. What does an expert system do?
20. In what ways do the following approaches to making requests differ from a query?

      a. Natural language statements

      b. Filling in electronic forms

      c. Direct manipulation

21. What is an executive information system?

22. Does an EIS differ from DSSs? If so, in what ways?

23. Does a DSS differ from task support systems? If so, in what ways?

24. What factors affect the benefits realized from a particular DSS?

25. How can the activity of constructing a DSS be beneficial?

26. When a DSS is unable to solve a problem facing a decision maker, can it still be beneficial? If so, how?

27. What are the major benefits that could result from using DSSs?

28. What are the major factors that can limit the value of a DSS to decision makers?

29. What does a human decision support system do?

30. When a request for knowledge is made to a DSS, what kinds of assistance might the decision maker be seeking?

31. How does a semiprocedural request differ from a procedural one? From a nonprocedural one?

32. Aside from requests that result in providing knowledge to decision makers, what other types of requests might a DSS receive?

33. When an HDSS realizes that a request is not understood, what possibilities exist?

34. How does training differ from learning by experience?

35. What is feedback?

36. How does the syntax of a request differ from the semantics of that request?

37. How can a DSS with presentation flexibility choose from among its alternatives for packaging its response to a user?

38. When an HDSS responds to a decision maker it is to satisfy one of which four objectives? Which of these four are also commonplace for DSSs?

39. What can happen when a decision maker does not understand a response?

40. In what ways can DSSs acquire knowledge?

41. How might the acquisition of a new piece of knowledge impact the body of existing knowledge?

42. How does domain knowledge differ from user knowledge?

43. What can trigger the exercise of a DSS's knowledge processing skills?

▲ DISCUSSION TOPICS

1. Discuss the importance of computer-based systems that increase decision-maker efficiency and of those that increase decision-maker effectiveness.

2. Should a computer-based system that supports the making of structured decisions be regarded as a DSS?

3. What knowledge-management activities might be most important for a DSS to handle? Comment on the feasibility of each.

4. Describe an example of a DP system.

5. Describe the behavior of an MIS with which you have had contact.

6. Is it reasonable to regard an MIS as a special kind of DSS?

7. Is it reasonable to regard a DSS as a special kind of MIS?

8. Discuss the features that make a query language more or less English-like.

9. Are there disadvantages to nonprocedural languages?

10. List the behaviors you would expect to see in an artificially intelligent computer system.

11. Identify some emerging technological advances that may affect the nature of tomorrow's DSSs.
12. Discuss the proposition that an EIS is a special kind of DSS.
13. Describe some task support systems that are not DSSs.
14. Explain the various ways in which DSSs could facilitate decision making.
15. Under what circumstances might a decision maker benefit from multiple DSSs?
16. What are the advantages and disadvantages of a DSS designed to handle a small set of tasks?
17. Discuss the dangers of overdependence on a DSS.
18. Discuss the dangers of underutilization of DSSs.
19. Debate the relative merits of procedural, semiprocedural, and nonprocedural requests.
20. When an HDSS seeks clarification of a request, what actions can he or she take? Which of these would be desirable for a DSS?
21. In what ways does an HDSS learn to comprehend decision-maker requests? Which would be desirable for a DSS?
22. Debate the relative merits of a DSS that can handle multiple syntactic variations of a request versus one that cannot.
23. Debate the relative merits of a DSS that has flexible presentation possibilities versus one that does not.
24. Discuss the distinction between acquired knowledge, derived knowledge, and innate mental faculties.
25. Invent a taxonomy that classifies various kinds of knowledge processing performed by DSSs.
26. Discuss the drawbacks of using the term *information systems* to encompass the areas of DP, MIS, and DSS.

▲ REFERENCES

Alter, S. L. 1980. *Decision support systems: Current practice and continuing challenges.* Reading, Mass.: Addison-Wesley.

Awad, E. M. 1966. *Automatic data processing: Principles and procedures.* Englewood Cliffs, N. J.: Prentice Hall.

———. 1988. *Management information systems: Concepts, structure, and applications.* Menlo Park, Calif.: Benjamin Cummings

Benbasat, I., and A. S. Dexter. 1982. Individual differences in the use of decision support aids *Journal of Accounting Research* 20, no. 1.

Bonczek, R. H., C. W. Holsapple, and A. B. Whinston. 1980a. The evolving roles of models within decision support systems. *Decision Sciences* (April).

———. 1981. *Foundations of decision support systems.* New York: Academic Press.

———. 1980b. Future directions for developing decision support systems. *Decision Sciences* (October).

Calantone, R. J., C. W. Holsapple, and L. E. Johnson. 1993. Communication and communication support: An agenda for investigation. *The Information Society* 9, no. 1.

Diebold Group, ed. 1977. *Automatic data processing handbook.* New York: McGraw-Hill.

Dos Santos, B., and C. W. Holsapple. 1989. A framework for designing adaptive DSS interfaces. *Decision Support Systems* 5, no. 1.

Gardner, C., Jr. 1991. Testing the hypotheses of a DSS framework through the integration of microeconomic theory, laboratory experiements, and the information system evaluation problem. Ph.D. diss., University of Kentucky, Lexington.

Gerrity, T. P. 1971. Design of man-machine decision systems: An application to portfolio management. *Sloan Management Review* (Winter).

Gray, P., and Nunamaker, J. F. 1989. Group decision support systems. In *Decision support systems: Putting theory into practice,* 2nd ed., edited by R. H. Sprague, Jr., and H. J. Watson, Englewood Cliffs, N. J., Prentice Hall.

Head, R. V. 1985. Information resource center: A new force in end-user computing. *Journal of Systems Management* (February).

Holsapple, C. W. 1988. Adapting demons to knowledge management environments. *Decision Support Systems* 3, no. 4.

————. 1993. A human metaphor for DSS research. *Journal of Computer Information Systems* 34, no. 2.

Holsapple, C. W., S. Park, R. Stansifer, and A. B. Whinston. 1988. Flexible user interfaces for decision support systems. *Proceedings of Hawaiian International Conference on Systems Sciences,* Kona, Hawaii, January.

Holsapple, C. W., and A. B. Whinston. 1976. A decision support system for area-wide water quality planning. *Socio-Economic Planning Sciences,* 10, no. 6.

Huber, G. 1980. Organizational science contributions to the design of decision support systems. In *Decision support systems: Issues and challenges,* edited by G. Fick and R. H. Sprague, Jr. London: Pergamon Press.

Kador, J. 1989. The paths to executive support. *Information Center* 5, no. 12.

Keen, P. G. W. 1981. Value analysis: Justifying decision support systems. *MIS Quarterly* 5, no. 1.

Keen, P. G. W., and M. S. Scott Morton. 1978. *Decision support systems: An organizational perspective.* Reading, Mass.: Addison-Wesley.

Koory, J. L., and D. B. Medley. 1987. *Management information systems: Planning and decision making.* Cincinnati, Ohio: South-Western.

Kotteman, J. E., and F. D. Davis. 1991. Decisional conflict and user acceptance of multicriteria decision-making aids. *Decision Sciences,* 22, no. 4.

Lucas, H. C., Jr. 1986. *Introduciton to computers and information systems.* New York: Macmillan.

Marsden, J. R., and D. Pingry. 1993. A theory of decision support systems design evaluation. *Decision Support Systems* 9, no. 2.

McLeod, R., Jr. 1986. *Management information systems,* 3rd ed. Chicago: SRA.

Oberquelle, H., I. Kupka, and S. Maas. 1983. A view of human-machine communication and cooperation. *International Journal of Man-Machine Studies* 19, no. 4.

Oglesby, J. N. 1987. Seven steps to a successful info center. *Datamation,* 33, no. 5.

Parker, C. S. 1991. *Microcomputers concepts and applications.* Chicago: Dryden.

Penrose, R. 1989. *The emperor's new mind,* Oxford: Oxford University Press.

Rockart, J. F. 1979. Chief executive officers define their own data needs. *Harvard Business Review* (March–April).

Rockart, J. F., and D. Delong. 1988. *Executive information systems,* Homewood, Ill.: Dow Jones–Irwin.

Rockart, J. F., and M. E. Treacy. 1982. The CEO goes on-line. *Harvard Business Review* (January–February) 1982.

Russo, J. E., and P. J. H. Schoemaker. 1989. *Decision traps.* New York: Simon and Schuster.

Sanders, D. 1983. *Computers today.* New York: McGraw-Hill.

Saxon, J. A. 1967. *Basic principles of data processing.* Englewood Cliffs, N. J.: Prentice Hall.

Scott Morton, M. S. 1971. *Management decision systems: Computer-based support for decision making.* Cambridge, Mass.: Division of Research, Harvard University.

Seaberg, R. A., and C. Seaberg. 1973. Computer based decision systems in Xerox corporate planning. *Management Science* 20, no. 4.

Senn, J. A. 1987. *Information systems in management,* 3rd ed. Belmont, Calif.: Wadsworth.

Shelly, G. B., and T. J. Cashman. 1980. *Introduction to computers and data processing.* Fullerton, Calif.: Anaheim Publishing Co.

Sprague, R. H., Jr., and E. D. Carlson. 1982. *Building effective decision support systems.* Englewood Cliffs, N. J.: Prentice-Hall.

Sprague, R. H., Jr., and H. J. Watson. 1976. A decision support system for banks. *Omega 4,* no. 6.

Sullivan, R. S., and S. C. Secrest. 1985. A simple optimization DSS for production planning at Dairyman's Cooperative Creamery Association. *Interfaces* 15, no. 5.

Turban, E. 1988. *Decision support and expert systems.* New York: Macmillan.

Turban, E., and D. M. Schaeffer. 1989. A comparison of executive information systems, DSS, and management information systems. In *Decision support systems,* 2nd ed. edited by R. Sprague, Jr., and H. Watson. Englewood Cliffs, N. J.: Prentice-Hall.

Chapter 6

DECISION SUPPORT SYSTEM ARCHITECTURE

AMERICAN AIRLINES: A DSS FOR AIRCRAFT-MAINTENANCE DECISIONS

Background

American Airlines' fleet of approximately 600 aircraft consists of 10 different fleet types including Boeing 727, 737, 747, 757, 767, and McDonnnell Douglas (MD) Super 80, DC-10, MD-11, Airbus 300, and Fokker 1000. . . . All aircraft are at various stages of existence, with each fleet having its own unique utilization and maintenance profile.

AA's Mainenance and Engineering (M&E) Long Range Planning (LRP) group develops and maintains a 5-year planning horizon schedule of base maintenance activity. . . . This 5-year plan, also known as the "dock plan," is in a state of flux as it continuously evolves due to the fleet's constantly changing size (due to retirements and new deliveries), composition (various fleet types), utilization (seasonal changes) and maintenance requirements.

American Airlines Decision Technologies (AADT) was requested . . . to formalize, automate and enhance the maintenance planning process through the development and implementation of a decision support system to aid maintenance planners in the generation of the dock plan.

System Overview

. . . [AADT] set out to design and develop a flexible, user-friendly decision support system which would allow the user to generate a maintenance plan and then perform various what-if analyses to evaluate the impact on the plan of changes in any of the key maintenance variables. The need for flexibility was of paramount importance due to the need for planners to react quickly and deftly to the rapidly changing maintenance planning environment. The system would be required to have three levels of functionality, including: 1. manage and develop maintenance planning data, 2. generate maintenance plan scenarios quickly and efficiently, and 3. generate a variety of tabular and graphical reports to describe and evaluate the maintenance plan.

. . . [A]n object-oriented, menu-driven, windows-based user interface was created to drive the system and allow for maintenance data table development. . . . Spreadsheets, with which the primary users were already intimately familiar, were used as a format for all of the tabular output reports to allow for any additional ad hoc output analyses.

DockPlan . . . includes a variety of features to enhance the dock plan development and evaluation process: [it is sufficiently] flexible to handle various problem sizes (fleet size, number of maintenance facilities and number of maintenance programs) . . . [it supports] monthly specification of daily aircraft utilization rates . . . [it] allows for new maintenance programs to be added and scheduled . . . reconfiguration, retirement and new delivery programs are considered . . . [it can adjust the] quantity of maintenance facilities available to compensate for the rise and fall of maintenance demand, and [there is] input data checking and user warnings of errors or discrepancies.

The conceptual methodology of the DockPlan system was designed to combine a planner's knowledge of and experience in overhaul scheduling with the computational power of a simple, computerized scheduling . . . algorithm. . . .

Continued

This methodology, which relies on a human's evaluative and judgmental capabilities, and a computer's number-crunching power, represents an innovative approach to the solution of complex, real-world scheduling problems complicated by a large number of dynamic, interactive variables and soft constraints.

System Usage

. . . [T]he user initially specifies the parameters of the problem (e.g., such as how many hangar spaces will be available throughout the planning horizon) and then applies the model's simple, heuristic algorithm [solver] to quickly generate a schedule. . . . The user then reviews the dock plan solution, adjusts the parameters accordingly, and re-runs the model to generate a new, and hopefully improved, solution.

The planner continues to iteratively run the model, adjusting parameters so as to "push" the schedule generation process in the right direction in order to reach an optimal or near optimal solution. . . .

. . . The user does not relinquish total control of his job funtion to the system, but is supported in his decision-making efforts by allowing the machine to handle the computational burden of generating a plan. This elevates the scheduler from the level of number-crunching "technician" to a "maintenance planner and analyst," freeing him to think about better ways to solve the problems at hand and to do exception handling, which makes better use of the human's rational capabilities.

. . . [The system] provides a vehicle for the planner to use his experience and knowledge of maintenance planning to guide the model's scheduling heuristic in the right direction toward creating an optimal dock plan. The user will be much more likely to use a system that he fits into and understands. Later, the user will also be likely to accept a more complete and total system solution, if and when one is developed. . . .

Benefits

American Airlines has derived three primary benefits from DockPlan since production usage began in October 1991: 1. planner productivity improvement, 2. maintenance cost avoidance (and reduction), and 3. revenue generation opportunity identification. These three benefits have come from a re-engineering and automation of the existing dock plan development process and an enhancement of the dock plan itself.

Automation provides dock planners the capability to generate and evaluate several sub-fleet level "what if . . . analyses" in a single day. The previous manual process required several hours, and in some cases, days, to generate and fully evaluate a single dock plan scenario.

. . . [M]aintenance planners . . . use DockPlan to significantly reduce total overhaul maintenance costs. . . . [This] equates to a potential $454 million overhaul maintenance cost avoidance over the active life of the 227 widebody aircraft in the fleet.

In a recent cost avoidance scenario, dock planners identified six months of excess 767 overhaul maintenance capacity at AA's new Alliance–Fort Worth Maintenance Base, using DockPlan's yield and resource utilization optimization

Continued

capabilities. This excess capacity was used to perform 767 airframe conversions that were previously planned to be contracted out to an outside vendor maintenance organization. Bringing this work in-house saved AA over $3 million in maintenance labor costs.

. . . Dock planners identified an opportunity to shut down a 727 overhaul line one year earlier than expected and still complete all the necessary checks, within their allowable limits, for that fleet. This equates to giving an aircraft back to the airline for an entire year which would have normally been out of service, and hence not available to generate revenue. This result will provide the airline with a considerable increase in revenue generation potential [compared to what] it would have had without DockPlan.

Condensed quotation from Douglas A. Gray, "Airworthy: Decision Support for Aircraft Overhaul Maintenance Planning," *OR/MS Today* (December 1992): 24–29.

LEARNING OBJECTIVES

The American Airlines case illustrates four important systems that make up a decision support system. There is a language system, consisting of requests a user can make. There is a presentation system, consisting of responses the DSS can make. There is a system of knowledge, consisting of representations of knowledge relevant to the maintenance decisions. At the heart of the DSS, there is a problem-processing system that accepts requests, draws on knowledge, and produces responses. Keep the American Airlines case in mind as you study this chapter.

After studying this chapter, you should be able to

1. Describe the basic architecture of a decision support system.
2. Distinguish between a system of representation and a system of processing.
3. Explain various special cases of the generic DSS framework, including
   Text-oriented DSSs,
   Database-oriented DSSs,
   Spreadsheet-oriented DSSs,
   Solver-oriented DSSs,
   Rule-oriented DSSs, and
   Compound DSSs.
4. Characterize the language system, problem-processing system, knowledge system, and presentation system of whatever DSS you happen to be developing, using, or considering.

Exercises at the end of the chapter enable you to apply what you have learned by further analysis of the case. They also include review questions and assorted topics for discussion.

6.1 INTRODUCTION

We are now in a good position to examine the architecture of decision support systems. An **architecture** is essentially a framework for organizing our thoughts and discussion about something. It identifies the major elements to be considered in developing and using something. The general architecture of houses identifies such important elements as a plumbing system, an electrical system, an air-treatment system, and a system of rooms. It also identifies relationships among these elements. Similarly, the architecture of decision support systems can be described by a generic framework that identifies essential elements of a DSS and their interrelationships. These elements are various kinds of systems that are configured in a certain way.

This chapter introduces the generic DSS framework, which views any DSS as composed of a language system, presentation system, knowledge system, and problem-processing system. By varying the makeup of these four elements, different decision support systems are produced. This generic framework will guide our exploration of DSSs in the ensuing chapters. The architecture it presents gives us the terminology for the discussion in Chapter 7 of the issues of building DSSs. It provides a uniform, organized way of looking at knowledge-management tools and techniques encountered in DSS construction and usage. These tools and techniques are considered in Chapters 8 through 11. The generic DSS framework guides our examination of artificially intelligent decision support systems in Part Four and multiparticipant DSSs in Part Five.

Here, we begin with an overview of the four generic systems that are basic elements of any DSS. Their relationships to each other and to the DSS's users are shown to be simple and straightforward. We then examine several more specialized DSS frameworks that are special cases of the **generic framework.** Each characterizes one category of DSSs, such as text-oriented DSSs, database-oriented DSSs, spreadsheet-oriented DSSs, solver-oriented DSSs, rule-oriented DSSs, and compound DSSs.

6.2 THE GENERIC FRAMEWORK FOR DSSs

A decision support system can be defined in terms of four essential aspects:

1. A language system (LS)
2. A presentation system (PS)
3. A knowledge system (KS)
4. A problem-processing system (PPS)

(Bonczek, Holsapple, and Whinston 1980, 1981a; Dos Santos and Holsapple 1989). The first three are systems of representation. A **language system** (LS) consists of all messages the DSS can accept. A **presentation system** (PS) consists of all messages the DSS can emit. A **knowledge system** (KS) consists of all knowledge the DSS has stored and retained. By themselves, these three kinds of systems can do nothing. They simply represent knowledge, either in the sense of messages that can be passed or representations that have been accumulated for possible processing.

Although they are merely systems of representation, a KS, LS, and PS are essential elements of a DSS. Each is used by the fourth element: the **problem-processing system** (PPS). This system is the active part of a DSS. A problem-processing system is the DSS's software engine. As its name suggests, a PPS is what tries to recognize and solve problems (i.e., process problems) during the making of a decision.

Figure 6.1 illustrates how the four subsystems of a DSS are related to each other and to a DSS user. The user is typically a decision maker or a participant in a decision maker. However, a DSS developer or administrator or some data-entry person or device could also be a DSS user (recall Figure 5.3). In any case, a user may make

FIGURE 6.1 Generic Framework of Decision Support Systems: Overview

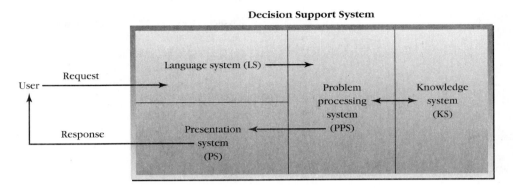

a request by selecting a desired element of the LS. As we saw in Chapter 5, it could be a request to accept knowledge, to clarify previous requests or responses, to solve some problem faced by the decision maker, and so forth. Once the PPS has been requested to process a particular LS element, it does so. This processing may very well require the PPS to draw on KS contents. The processing may also change the knowledge held in the KS. In either event, the PPS may issue a response to the user. It does so by choosing to present one of the PS elements to the user. The presentation choice is determined by the processing carried out with KS contents in response to the user's request.

In this simple architecture, we have captured the crucial and fundamental aspects common to all decision support systems. To fully appreciate the nature of any decision support system, we must know about the requests that make up its LS, the responses that make up its PS, the knowledge representations allowed or existing in its KS, and the knowledge-processing capabilities of its PPS. If we are ignorant of any of these, then we cannot claim to have a working knowledge of the DSS. Nor are we in a position to thoroughly compare and contrast the DSS with other decision support systems. Developers of DSSs are well advised to pay careful attention to all these elements when they design and build decision support systems.

APPLYING THE HDSS METAPHOR

Notice that the four DSS subsystems correspond to the four major traits we can witness in HDSSs: acceptance of requests, presentation of responses, possession of knowledge, and a capacity to process knowledge. The human metaphor can give us some insight into LS, PS, PPS, and KS details. For instance, the requests that make up a LS could be categorized as

- Those asking for the recall or derivation of knowledge (i.e., solving a problem),
- Those seeking clarification of prior responses or help in making subsequent responses, and
- Those involving the acceptance of knowledge from external sources (e.g., from the user).

Figure 6.2 shows these subsets of an LS. For a given DSS, some of these subsets may be quite small or even empty.

HISTORY OF THE GENERIC DSS FRAMEWORK

The generic framework for decision support systems began to take shape in the mid-1970s (Holsapple 1977). In this initial work, the workings of the problem processor were emphasized and encompassed such abilities as perception (including decoding of user requests and finding paths to needed knowledge in the KS), problem recognition, model formulation, and analysis. It also emphasized the integration of pieces of data and modules of procedural knowledge in a computer-based representation that the processor could access. This representation involved extensions to traditional database management notions, allowing the treatment of both descriptive and procedural knowledge.

Although the ideas of a language system and presentation system were implied in the early rendition of the framework, they did not become explicit until later (Bonczek, Holsapple, and Whinston 1980, 1981a; Holsapple 1984; Dos Santos and Holsapple 1989). The initial work on the framework recognized that a KS could hold (and a PPS could process) types of knowledge other than the descriptive and procedural varieties. Since then, the possibilities for including reasoning, linguistic, and presentation knowledge in a KS have been explored in greater depth (Bonczek, Holsapple, and Whinston 1981b; Holsapple 1983; Holsapple and Whinston 1986). The original discussion of the framework advocated incorporation of artificial intelligence mechanisms into DSSs to produce intelligent decision support systems. This idea has been further developed (Bonczek, Holsapple, and Whinston 1979, 1980, 1981a, 1981b; Holsapple and Whinston 1985, 1986). Today, it is not unusual to find such mechanisms in the PPSs and KSs of decision support systems.

Similarly, Figure 6.2 illustrates possible PS subsets suggested by the human metaphor. Again, some of these may be quite small or even empty for a particular DSS. These LS and PS categorizations are based on message semantics. Yet another way of categorizing LS requests and PS responses could be based on distinctions in the styles of messages rather than differences in their contents. These distinctions can be quite pronounced, and a particular DSS may have requests or responses in more than one stylistic category.

What does the human metaphor suggest about the details of the framework's KS? Because an HDSS can possess any of the six major types of knowledge, KS contents can be categorized as shown in Figure 6.2. For a particular DSS, one or more of these six categories may be unfilled. For example, not every DSS possesses reasoning knowledge in its KS. But, from a generic point of view, reasoning knowledge certainly is a possible part of the KS. Following the metaphor, another way of categorizing KS contents would involve the distinction between problem domain knowledge, relational knowledge of the user, and a system's self-knowledge. Because most DSSs tend to focus only on domain knowledge, we shall not pursue this alternative classification scheme here.

PROBLEM-PROCESSING ABILITIES

Observe that the KS contents identified in Figure 6.2 are entirely consistent with the conception of a DSS presented in Figure 5.3. When it comes to thinking about details of the generic framework's PPS, we can also recall what Figure 5.3 has to

FIGURE 6.2   Generic Framework of Decision Support Systems: Details

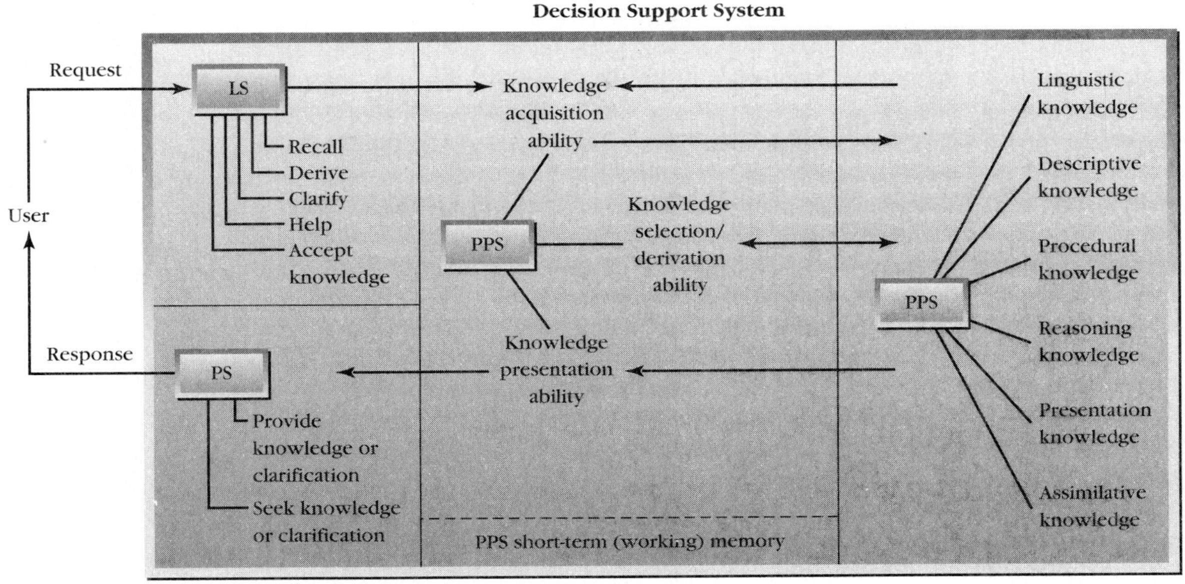

Decision Support System

say. It identifies three indispensable DSS abilities: knowledge acquisition, knowledge presentation, and knowledge selection/derivation. As Figure 6.2 indicates, these traits are shared by all problem-processing systems. Using its **knowledge-acquisition** ability, a PPS acquires knowledge about what a user wants the DSS to do or what is happening in the surrounding world. Such knowledge is carried in LS messages that serve as user requests or system observations.

As shown in Figure 6.2, the PPS may draw on KS contents when using its acquisition ability. For instance, its interpretation of a request may be based on previously acquired linguistic knowledge. Figure 6.2 also shows that the knowledge-acquisition ability can cause a change in the KS, which is influenced by existing assimilative knowledge. However, not all interpreted messages cause KS changes. An interpreted message can cause the PPS's other abilities to spring into action.

When a user's request is for the solution to some problem, the **knowledge-selection/derivation** ability comes into play. The PPS selectively recalls or derives knowledge that forms a solution. When a user's request is for clarification of a prior response or for help in stating a request, the selection/derivation ability may or may not be exercised, depending on whether it needs the KS to produce the content of its response. For instance, a user may request that a previous response consisting of a bar graph be clarified by using a line graph presentation. In such a case, a PPS may not need to repeat the selection or derivation of data on which the graphs are based. It simply retains data previously garnered for the bar graph, and its presentation ability reuses that data to respond with an equivalent line graph.

PPS USE OF SHORT-TERM, WORKING MEMORY

A PPS can have a short-term memory. Short-term memory contents are temporary compared to the KS contents. The short-term memory capacity is quite small in comparison to the KS, and it corresponds to a HDSS's span of awareness. At any moment, a person has a few things in or near the forefront of consciousness. These are pertinent to whatever mental processing is happening or has recently occurred. Typically, the contents of the focus of consciousness can change rapidly and are minuscule compared to the person's entire storehouse of knowledge. Similarly, a PPS has the capacity to keep track of a few pieces of knowledge that are of immediate or recent interest to its processing abilities. Its short-term memory may or may not hold something that also exists in the KS. It may keep a continually updated history of the past few requests and the responses to them. In brief, it contains pieces of knowledge needed during the exercise of a PPS ability.

A PPS's short-term memory can also be called its **working memory** because it aids in the current working of PPS abilities. It can be thought of as a scratch pad or a workbench of knowledge. For example, when the acquisition ability receives a LS request, the syntax of that request is held in the PPS's working memory. It may or may not be recorded in the KS. As the acquisition ability endeavors to interpret (i.e., discover the semantics of) the request, various linguistic knowledge from the KS may be brought into working memory (i.e., placed on the workbench alongside the request) for comparison and study. Ultimately, the request semantics worked out by the acquisition ability will reside in the PPS's short-term memory, where they can be detected by other PPS abilities.

By examining the interpreted request in working memory, the knowledge-selection/derivation ability determines whether selection or derivation is required. It also determines exactly what knowledge is to be selected or precisely how the derivation is to be accomplished. Any or all of the determinations may involve the bringing of other KS knowledge into working memory. The actual act of selecting or deriving knowledge also involves this short-term memory of the PPS. The semantics of the solution to a user's request will probably reside in working memory, awaiting the packaging to be performed by the **knowledge-presentation** ability. That ability may itself bring certain KS contents to the workbench as it prepares the syntax of the response.

It should be clear that the PPS concept of working memory provides a useful mechanism for allowing each PPS ability to express itself and making other PPS abilities aware of its activities. It gives the PPS abilities a workbench on which to perform their activities and a scratch pad for keeping tabs on intermediate results or temporarily needed knowledge. The KS does not become clogged, and the PPS does not have to hunt through a vast KS (i.e., knowledge warehouse) every time it needs to work on any piece of knowledge. The nature of PPS working memory causes knowledge to be dismissed from it as soon as that knowledge is no longer required for a current or expected processing activity.

DSS DIFFERENCES

Although the generic framework gives us a common base and several fundamental terms for discussing decision support systems, it also lets us distinguish among different DSSs. For instance, two DSSs could have identical knowledge and presentation systems but differ drastically in their respective language systems. Thus, the language a user learns for making requests to one DSS may well be of little use in making requests to the other DSS. The two LSs could vary in terms of the style and/or content of requests they encompass.

As another example, two DSSs could have identical PPSs and similar LSs and PSs. Even the kinds of knowledge representations permitted in their KSs could be the same. Yet, the two DSSs might exhibit very different behaviors because of the different knowledge representations actually existing in their KSs. Moreover, either could exhibit behaviors today of which it was incapable yesterday. This situation is commonly caused by alterations to its KS contents through either the acquisition or derivation of knowledge. That is, a DSS can become more knowledgeable.

Yet another common way in which DSSs differ is by having differing PPSs. Even though all PPSs possess the three basic abilities of acquisition, selection/derivation, and presentation, the exact character of each ability can differ widely from one problem-processing system to the next. For example, the selection/derivation ability of one PPS may be based on a spreadsheet technique of knowledge management, whereas that technique is entirely absent from some other PPS that emphasizes **database**- and **rule-management** techniques for handling knowledge. This implies KS differences as well. When a PPS employs a spreadsheet processing approach, the DSS's knowledge system would use a corresponding spreadsheet representation. In contrast, if a DSS's problem processor relies on database- and rule-management techniques for processing knowledge, then its KS must contain knowledge represented in terms of databases and rules. In other words, DSSs can differ with respect to the knowledge-management techniques with which their PPSs are equipped and that govern the usable representations held in their KSs.

TEAM ARCHITECTURE

Figure 6.1 showed that a DSS interacts with a user via its language and presentation systems. Certainly, there can be many differences among users, just as there are among DSSs. But what is the nature of this user? Can we characterize it in a generic way, as we have done with DSSs? To do so could give us a more complete picture of the architecture of a team decision maker. It could also portray the basic interactions that occur within a team and across its boundaries. One approach is to apply the generic DSS framework in characterizing the team member who uses a DSS (Chang, Holsapple, and Whinston 1988), as illustrated in Figure 6.3

Here, a team participant who uses a DSS is viewed as having a knowledge system holding usable representations of all knowledge the participant has either acquired or derived and then subsequently stored. The user has a problem-processing system that can employ these stored representations for purposes of problem solving (e.g., via selection or derivation), knowledge acquisition, and knowledge presentation. The user has a language system composed of all the messages that can be accepted from the DSS, from other team participants, and from sources outside the team. Conversely, the user's presentation system consists of all messages that can be sent to the DSS, other team participants, and targets outside the team.

In order for interaction (i.e., two-way communication) to be possible between a DSS and user, two conditions must be true (Dos Santos and Holsapple 1989):

1. Some elements in the user's PS must exist in the DSS's language system.
2. Some elements in the user's LS must exist in the DSS's presentation system.

When the first condition is not met, the user is unable to utter any message that the DSS is capable of processing. When the second is not met, the user is unable to process any message the DSS is capable of presenting. In either situation, there is

FIGURE 6.3   A Team Decision Maker DSS

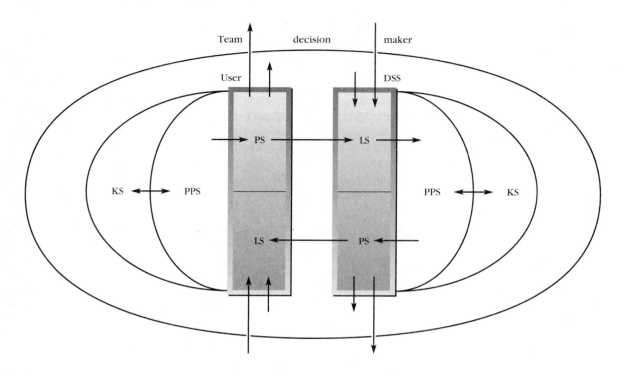

a failure to communicate. The DSS does not support the user, nor does the user really use the DSS.

At the opposite extreme, if a DSS's language system is a subset of a user's PS, then that user has fully mastered all requests that can be made of the DSS. Similarly, if a DSS's presentation system is a subset of a user's LS, then that user has fully mastered all responses that the DSS can make. Although these may be desirable conditions, they often do not exist in practice. Usually it is a matter of the user expanding his or her PS and LS to encompass increasingly larger portions of the decision support system's LS and PS, respectively. As DSS researchers make headway, we should expect to see these roles reversed. DSSs will be more adaptable, being able to expand their LSs and PSs to encompass users' PSs and LSs, respectively.

6.3 SPECIALIZED FRAMEWORKS

The different types of knowledge that might exist in a KS were illustrated in Figure 6.2. Also, PPS abilities were viewed in terms of the three basics of acquisition, selection/derivation, and presentation. Another useful way to look at KS contents and PPS abilities is in terms of the knowledge-management techniques employed by a DSS. This approach gives rise to many special cases of the generic DSS architecture. Each characterizes a certain class of decision support systems by

1. Restricting KS contents to representations allowed by a certain knowledge management-technique(s) and
2. Restricting the PPS abilities to processing allowed by the technique(s).

The result is a specialized framework with the generic traits suggested in Figure 6.1 but specializing in a particular technique or techniques for representing and processing knowledge.

For example, a special class of decision support systems uses the spreadsheet technique of knowledge management. The KS of each DSS in this class consists of descriptive and procedural knowledge represented in a *spreadsheet fashion*. The PPS of such a DSS consists of software that can accept requests for manipulating these representations, select or derive knowledge from them, and present them in a form understandable to users. In contrast, a DSS that uses a database-management technique has very different representations in its KS, and it has a PPS equipped to process them rather than spreadsheet representations. Although both spreadsheet and database DSS classes adhere to the generic framework, each can be viewed in terms of its own more specialized framework.

Several of the more common specialized frameworks are examined here: text, database, spreadsheet, solver, expert system, and compound frameworks. Many others are conceivable. Most tend to emphasize one or two knowledge-management techniques for representing KS contents and defining PPS behaviors. As we introduce these frameworks, we also present broad outlines of corresponding techniques. However, for now, we do not need to be concerned about details of the various knowledge-management techniques. Such specifics are surveyed in Part Three. Here, the focus is on how different techniques fit into the generic DSS framework to yield distinct classes of decision support systems. This gives a basis for the next chapter's discussion of alternative approaches to DSS construction.

TEXT-ORIENTED DECISION SUPPORT SYSTEMS

For centuries, decision makers have used the contents of books, periodicals, letters, and memos as textual repositories of knowledge. In the course of decision making, their contents are available as raw materials for the manufacturing process. The knowledge embodied in a piece of text might be descriptive, such as a record of the effects of similar decision alternatives chosen in the past or a description of an organization's business activities. It could be procedural knowledge, such as a passage explaining how to calculate a forecast or how to acquire some needed knowledge. The text could embody reasoning knowledge, such as rules of thumb indicating likely causes of or remedies for an unwanted situation. Whatever its type, the decision maker searches and selects pieces of text to become more knowledgeable, to verify impressions, or to stimulate ideas.

Components In the 1970s and especially in the 1980s, **text management** emerged as an important, widely used computerized means for representing and processing pieces of text. Although its main use has been for such clerical activities (preparing and editing letters, reports, and manuscripts, for instance), it can also be of value to decision makers (Keen 1987; Fedorowicz 1989). Figure 6.4 illustrates the nature of a text-oriented DSS. Its KS is made up of computer files, each of which contains a textual passage that is potentially interesting to the decision maker. We can regard these passages as electronic documents.

FIGURE 6.4   A Text-Oriented DSS

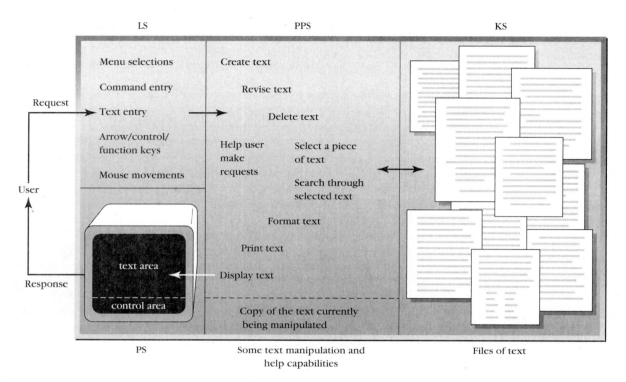

The PPS consists of software that can perform various manipulations on contents of any of the stored documents. It may also involve software that can help a user in making requests. The LS contains requests corresponding to the various allowed manipulations. It may also contain requests that let a user ask for assistance covering some aspect of the DSS. The PS consists of images of stored text that can be projected on a console screen, plus messages that can help the decision maker use the DSS. The former appears in a text area on the console screen. The latter appear in a control area that is usually at the bottom or top of the screen.

An Example   An example will help illustrate the value of text-oriented DSSs to decision makers. Imagine that you are a product manager, concerned with ensuring the success of a technically complex product. A number of the many decisions you face involve deciding about what features the product should have. Such decisions depend on many pieces of knowledge. Some tell about technical feasibility of features, whereas others indicate R&D and production costs associated with various features. You need to know about the features offered by competing products. How would potential customers assess the cost-benefit trade-offs of specific features? What legal, health, safety, and maintenance issues must you consider for each potential feature?

During the course of each week, you get an assortment of product ideas that deserve to be checked out when you get the time—if only you could remember all of them. With a text-oriented DSS, you keep electronic notes about the ideas as they arise, which consists of typing in the text that you want the PPS to create in its KS. You might put all the ideas in a single, large file of text. Or, it may be more convenient to organize them into several text files (e.g., ideas about different features are stored as text in different files).You may want to expand on an idea that has been stored in the KS. To do so, you use the LS to select the document holding that idea and to revise it. If an idea needs to be discarded, then the corresponding text is deleted instead of revised.

Suppose you want to make a decision about the inclusion or nature of some product feature. The stored text containing ideas about that feature can be selected from the KS, presented for viewing on a console screen, and perhaps printed on paper. Rather than rummaging through the selected text, you may want to restrict your attention to only those ideas concerned with the cost of the feature. Then, you use the LS to indicate that the PPS should search through the selected text for each occurrence of the "cost" keyword and display its surrounding text. The KS may hold other pieces of text entered by an assistant who has been collecting and summarizing information about features of competing products. Focused searching or browsing through such text may also support your efforts at reaching the feature decision.

Hypertext   In general, a text-oriented DSS supports a decision maker by electronically keeping track of textually represented knowledge that could have a bearing on decisions. It allows documents to be electronically created, revised, and viewed by a decision maker on an as-needed basis. The viewing can be exploratory browsing in search of stimulation or a focused search for some particular piece of knowledge needed in the manufacture of a decision. In either event, there is a problem with traditional text management: it is not convenient to trace a flow of ideas through separate pieces of text. As far as the PPS in Figure 6.4 is concerned, there is no explicit relationship or connection between the knowledge held in one text file and the knowledge in another.

This problem is remedied by a technique known as **hypertext**. With this form of text management, the KS can be pictured as shown in Figure 6.5. Each piece of text is linked to other pieces of text that are conceptually related to it. For instance, there may be a piece of text about a particular competitor. This text can be linked to pieces of text about other competitors. It can also be connected to each piece of text that discusses a feature offered by that competitor. It is probably associated with still other text summarizing current market positions of all competing products. This summary, is in turn, linked to text covering the results of market surveys, to a narrative about overall market potential, to notes containing marketing ideas, and so forth.

In addition to the PPS capabilities shown in Figure 6.4, a user could request the creation, deletion, and traversal of links. In traversing a link, the PPS shifts its focus (and the user's) from one piece of text to another. For instance, when looking at market summary text, you want more information about one of the competitors noted there. Thus, you request the PPS follow the link to that competitor's text and display it to you. In examining it, you see that it is linked to one of the features that is of special interest to you. Requesting the PPS to follow that link brings a full discussion of that feature into view. Noting that it is connected to another competitor, you move to the text for that competitor. This ad hoc traversal through associated pieces of text continues at your discretion, resembling a flow of thoughts through the many associated concepts in your own mind.

FIGURE 6.5   Knowledge System with Hypertext Framework

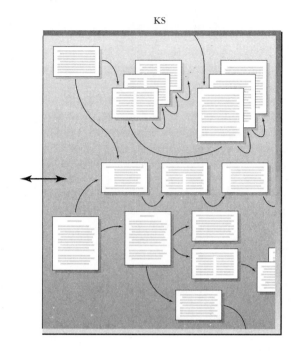

The benefit of this hypertext kind of DSS is that it supplements a decision maker's own capabilities by accurately storing and recalling large volumes of concepts and connections that he or she is not inclined personally to memorize (Minch 1989; Bieber 1992; Bieber and Kimbrough 1992). Chapter 9 gives a more detailed overview of the text-management technique (both traditional and hypertext) for knowledge representation and processing.

DATABASE-ORIENTED DECISION SUPPORT SYSTEMS

Another special case of the DSS framework consists of those systems developed with the database technique of knowledge management. Although there are several important variants of this technique, perhaps the most widely used is what is called *relational* **database management**. It is the variant we consider here. Rather than treating data as streams of text, it is organized in a highly structured, tabular fashion. The processing of these data tables is designed to take advantage of their high degree of structure. It is, therefore, more intricate than text processing.

People have used decision support systems using database management since the early years of the DSS field (e.g., Bonczek, Holsapple and Whinston 1976, 1978; Joyce and Oliver 1977; Klass 1977). Like text-oriented DSSs, these systems aid decision makers by accurately tracking and selectively recalling knowledge that satisfies a particular need or serves to stimulate ideas. However, the knowledge handled by database-oriented DSSs tends to be primarily descriptive, rigidly structured, and often extremely voluminous.

FIGURE 6.6 A Database-Oriented DSS

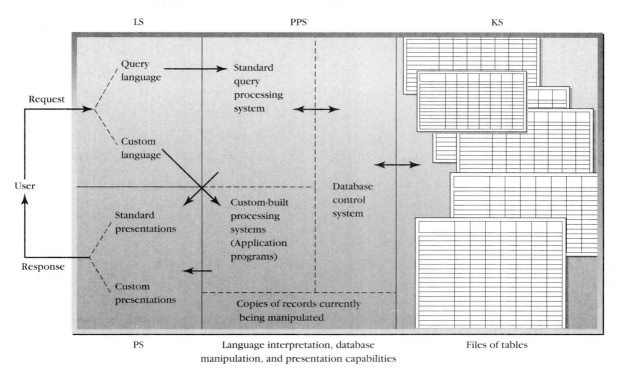

Figure 6.6 portrays the basic architecture of this kind of DSS. The computer files that make up its KS hold information about table structures (e.g., what fields are involved in what tables) plus the actual data value contents of each table. Collectively, the tables are called a database. Chapter 9 considers databases in greater depth.

The PPS has three kinds of software: a database control system, and interactive query processing system, and various custom-built processing systems. One—but not both—of the latter two could be omitted from the DSS. The **database control system** consists of capabilities for manipulating table structures and contents (e.g., defining or revising table structure, finding or updating records, creating or deleting records, and building new tables from existing ones). These capabilities are used by the query processor and **custom-built processors** in their efforts at satisfying user requests.

The **query processing system** is able to respond to certain standard types of request for data retrieval (and perhaps for help). These requests constitute a query language and make up part of the DSS's language system. Data-retrieval requests are stated in terms of the database's structure. They tell the query processor the fields and tables for which the user is interested in seeing data values. The query processor then issues an appropriate sequence of commands to the database control system, causing it to extract the desired values from the database. These values are then presented in some standard listing format for the user to view.

For a variety of reasons, users may prefer to deal with custom-built processors rather than standard query processors. They may give responses more quickly to

DATABASE TABLES

Tables are a common way of organizing data. A table has columns and rows. For instance, suppose we want to keep track of all the suppliers from whom we can order parts needed in our manufacturing operations.

The table has one column for each feature of a supplier that we want to track. Examples of such features include the supplier's name, location, sales representative, phone number, payment terms, and reliability rating. These features are often called fields.

The table has one row for every supplier of interest. Within the row is one data value for every field. Together, these data values characterize the nature of a supplier and are often called a record. Whereas fields define the structure of a table, records define its content.

Supplier Table

NAME	LOC	REP	PHONE	TERMS	RATING	] Fields
ABC Co.	NW	Linda Johnson	111-555-1111	Net 30	87	
Chances Co.	SW	Vic Raj	333-555-3333	90 SAC	58	Records
Cando, Inc.	SE	Bill Wagner	222-555-2222	COD	94	

requests a standard query processing system could not handle, presenting responses in a specially tailored fashion without requiring the user to learn the syntax of a query language or to use as many keystrokes. A custom-built processor might be built by the DSS's user but is more likely to be constructed by someone who is well versed in computer science. Such a processor is often called an *application program*, because it is a program that has been developed to meet the specific needs of a marketing, production, financial, or other application.

Embedded within a custom-built processor program is the logic to interpret some custom designed set of requests. There will be commands to the database control system, telling it what database manipulations to perform for each possible request. There will also be the logic necessary for packaging responses in a customized manner. There may even be some calculations based on values from the database. Calculation results could be included in a response.

SPREADSHEET-ORIENTED DECISION SUPPORT SYSTEMS

In the case of a text-oriented DSS, procedural knowledge can be represented in textual passages in the KS. About all the PPS can do with such a procedure is display it to the user and modify it at the user's request. It is up to the user to carry out the procedure's instructions, if desired. In the case of a database-oriented DSS, procedural knowledge cannot be easily represented in the KS. However, the application programs that form part of the PPS can contain instructions for analyzing data retrieved from the database. By carrying out these procedures the PPS can show the user new knowledge (e.g., a sales forecast) that has been derived from KS contents

THE STRUCTURED QUERY LANGUAGE

Typically, an interactive query processing system for relational databases is designed to handle ad hoc retrieval requests stated in SQL: the Structured Query Language. Using this language, we could ask for a listing of the name and terms of every supplier whose rating exceeds 80:

`SELECT NAME, TERMS FROM SUPPLIER WHERE RATING > 80`

The displayed response would be a listing similar to

Name	Terms
ABC Co.	Net 30
CANDO, Inc.	COD

Scanning this list, the user could see which suppliers with ratings over 80 offer the most favorable terms and factor that information into a decision being made.

SQL is a standard query language in the sense that all SELECT commands are basically the same regardless of the data base existing in the KS:

`SELECT field names FROM table names WHERE conditions`

The user simply fills in desired field names, table names, and conditions for the database being processed.

DATABASE APPLICATION PROGRAMS

An application program is a custom-built processing system that uses the database control system to help it satisfy a special set of user processing needs with respect to a particular database. For instance, to find out names and terms of suppliers whose reliability ratings exceed 80, we might simply type

        80

upon seeing the message "cut-off rate?" issued by the application program. The displayed responses might appear in some special format, such as

```
        Net 30              90 SAC          COD
        ABC Co. (87)        None            *CANDO, Inc. (94)
        .                                   .
        .                                   .
        .                                   .




        _____       _____         _____
Average
Rating      83                  None            96
```

*Maximum noted by an asterisk.

(e.g., records of past sales trends). But, because they are part of the PPS, a user cannot readily view, modify, or create such procedures, as can be done in the text-oriented case.

Using the spreadsheet technique of knowledge management, a DSS user not only can create, view, and modify procedural knowledge held in the KS, but also can tell the PPS to carry out the instructions they contain. This gives DSS users much more power in handling procedural knowledge than is achievable with either text management or database management. In addition, **spreadsheet management** is able to deal with descriptive knowledge. However, it is not nearly as convenient as database management in handling large volumes of descriptive knowledge, nor does it allow a user to readily represent and process data in textual passages.

Spreadsheet-oriented DSSs are in widespread use today (Cragg and King 1992a, 1992b). Figure 6.7 shows the basic architecture of DSSs that use the spreadsheet technique for managing knowledge. The knowledge system is composed of spreadsheet files, each housing a spreadsheet. Each spreadsheet is a grid of **cells**. It may be a small grid, involving only a few cells, or very large, encompassing hundreds (or perhaps thousands) of cells. Each cell has a unique name based on its location in the grid. In addition to its name, each cell can have a definition and a value.

A cell definition tells the PPS how to determine that cell's value. There are two common kinds of cell definitions:

> Constants
> Formulas

FIGURE 6.7   A Spreadsheet-Oriented DSS

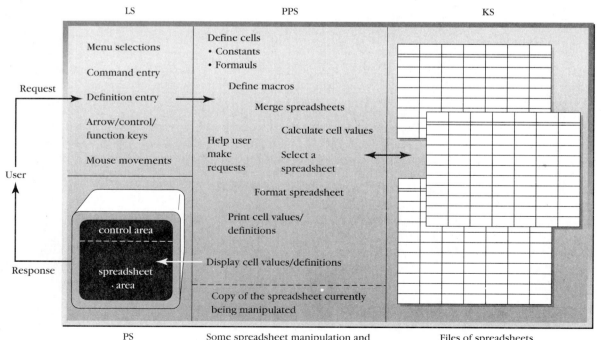

A **constant** is simply a number or a short string of text. The value of a cell defined as a constant is merely the constant itself. In contrast, a **formula** contains names of other cells, perhaps some constants, and some operators (e.g., +, *) indicating how to combine the values of named cells and constants. The result of this calculation becomes the value of the cell having a formula definition.

Taken together, the formulas of a spreadsheet constitute a chunk of procedural knowledge, containing instructions that the PPS can carry out. The results of performing this procedure are cell values of interest to the user. Spreadsheet-oriented DSSs are typically used for what-if analyses in order to see the implications of some set of assumptions embodied in the cell definitions. They support a decision maker by giving a rapid means for evaluating various alternatives.

SOME SPREADSHEET CONVENTIONS

Often, columns in a spreadsheet are designated as A, B, C, D . . . from left to right. Similarly, rows are typically designated as 1, 2, 3, 4 . . . from top to bottom. This gives a convenient way of naming cells. The cell in column A of row 1 is called A1; the cell in column B of row 1 is called B1; the cell in column B of row 2 is called B2; and so forth.

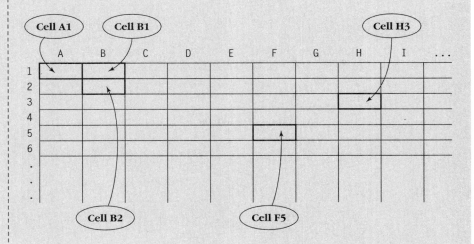

Suppose we request the PPS to make the following cell definitions in a spreadsheet:

CELL NAME	CELL DEFINITION	TYPE OF
A2	"SALES"	Constant (string)
A3	"EXPENSES"	Constant (string)
A4	"PROFIT"	Constant (string)
B1	"1992"	Constant (string)
B2	1,954,000	Constant (number)
B3	50,000 + .63*B2	Formula
B4	B2 - B3	Formula

Continued

If we request the PPS to calculate and display the cell values, we would see the following:

	A	B
1		1992
2	SALES	1,954,000
3	EXPENSES	1,731,020
4	PROFIT	222,980
.		
.		
.		

This shows what expenses and profit to expect if we assume sales of $1,954,000, fixed expenses of $500,000 and variable expenses at 63% of sales. But what if sales are only $1,700,000? To see the implications, we would change the definition of B2 to 1,700,000 and request a recalculation of the spreadsheet values, yielding

	A	B
1		1992
2	SALES	1,700,000
3	EXPENSES	1,571,000
4	PROFIT	129,000
.		
.		
.		

The profit is reduced by nearly 100,000. But what if we could reduce the variable expense rate of 0.47 by purchasing new machinery through a loan whose annual interest cost would increase the fixed portion of expenses to 650,000? To discover the answer, we would need to change the formula defining B3 (to 650,000 - 47 * B2) and request a spreadsheet calculation. In effect, each such calculation is carrying out a procedure specified by the spreadsheet's formulas and drawing on its numeric constants.

In addition to holding procedural knowledge (in the guise of formula cells) and descriptive knowledge (in the guise of numeric constant cells), a spreadsheet file can also hold some simple presentation knowledge and linguistic knowledge. When specifying a spreadsheet, a user can define some cells as string constants (e.g., "Sales") to show up as labels, titles, and explanations when the spreadsheet is displayed. This presentation knowledge makes the results of calculations easier to grasp.

Conversely, a user's task in making a request (especially to define cells) can be eased by macros. A *macro* is a name (usually short) the user can define to correspond to an entire series of keystrokes. The macro and its meaning are stored as linguistic knowledge in a spreadsheet file. For instance, the macro name D might be defined to mean the keystrokes D5*D6-D7. In subsequent requests, macro names such as D can be used instead of the lengthy series of keystrokes they represent. To interpret such a request, the PPS finds the meaning of the macro name in its KS. In effect, the LS is extended by putting linguistic knowledge into the system.

Chapter 10 considers the general elements of spreadsheet management in greater detail.

SOLVER-ORIENTED DECISION SUPPORT SYSTEMS

Another special class of decision support systems is based on the notion of solvers. A *solver* is a procedure (algorithm) consisting of instructions that a computer can carry out (execute or run) in order to solve any member of a particular class of problems. For instance, one solver might be able to solve depreciation problems. Another might be designed to solve portfolio analysis problems. Yet another might solve linear optimization problems. **Solver management** is concerned with the storage and use of a collection of solvers.

A solver-oriented DSS is frequently equipped with more than one solver, and the user's request indicates which is appropriate for the problem at hand. The collection of available solvers is often centered around some area of problems such as financial, economic, forecasting, planning, statistical, or optimization problems. Thus, one DSS might specialize in solving financial problems; another has solvers to help in various kinds of statistical analysis; and yet another might do both of these.

There are two basic approaches for incorporating solvers into a DSS: fixed and flexible. In the fixed approach, solvers are part of the PPS, which means that a solver cannot be easily added to or deleted from the DSS nor readily modified. The set of available solvers is fixed, and each solver in that set is fixed. About all a user can choose to do is execute any of the PPS solvers. This ability may be enough for many users' needs. However, other users may need to add, delete, revise and combine solvers over the lifetime of a DSS. This flexibility is achieved when solvers are treated as pieces of knowledge in the KS. With this flexible approach, the PPS is designed to manipulate (e.g., create, delete, update, combine, coordinate) solvers according to user requests.

Fixed Solvers   Let's look at the fixed approach in a bit more detail, and then we shall do the same for the flexible approach. As Figure 6.8 indicates, a fixed set of executable solvers is embedded in the PPS. In addition to these solving capabilities, such a PPS commonly has certain editing and presentation capabilities. The editing capabilities let a user make requests to store, remove, and revise specified chunks of knowledge in the KS. The presentation capabilities allow the PPS to package solver results into standard graphs, tables, or forms of various kinds. In addition, they may make use of user-specified formats that provide templates for organizing results into customized reports.

The KS for a fixed solver-oriented DSS is typically able to hold data sets. A **data set** is a parcel of descriptive knowledge that can be used by one or more solvers in the course of solving problems. It usually consists of groupings or sequences of numbers organized according to conventions required by the solvers. For example, we may have used PPS editing capabilities to create a data set composed of revenue and profit numbers for each of the past 15 years. This data set might be used by a basic statistics solver to give the average and standard deviation of revenues and profits. The same data set might be used by a forecasting solver to produce a

FIGURE 6.8   A Fixed Solver-Oriented Decision Support System

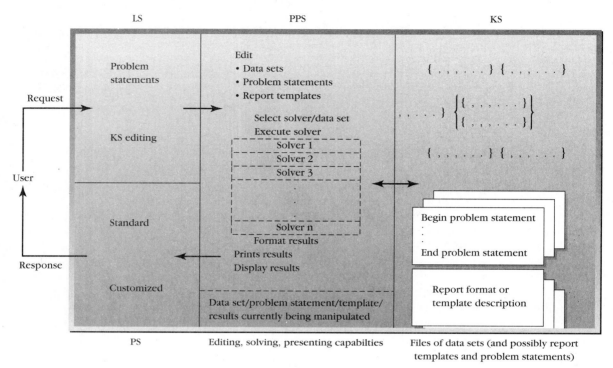

forecast of next year's profit, assuming a certain revenue level for the next year. Using a different data set, this same solver could produce a forecast of sales for an assumed level of advertising expenditures. Thus, many solvers can use a data set, and a given solver can feed on multiple data sets.

In addition to data sets, it is not uncommon for this kind of DSS to hold **problem statements** and report format descriptions in its KS. Because the problem statement requests permitted by the LS can be very lengthy, fairly complex, and used repeatedly, it may be convenient for a user to edit them (i.e., create, recall, revise them), much like pieces of text. Each problem statement will indicate the solver and mode of presentation to be used in printing or displaying the solution. The latter may designate a standard kind of presentation (e.g., a pie graph with slice percentages shown) or a customized report. The format of such a report is something the user specifies. Details of this specification can become quite lengthy and, therefore, are convenient to store as presentation knowledge in the KS.

Flexible Solvers   The flexible approach to handling solvers in a DSS also accommodates data sets and perhaps problem statements or report formats in its KS. But, as Figure 6.9 shows, the KS holds solver modules as well. A **solver module** is a piece of procedural knowledge that the PPS can execute to solve a problem. Each module requires certain data to be available for its use before its instructions can be carried out. Some of that data may already exist in KS data sets. The remaining data must either be furnished by the user (i.e., in the problem statement) or pro-

FIGURE 6.9　A Flexible Solver-Oriented Decision Support System

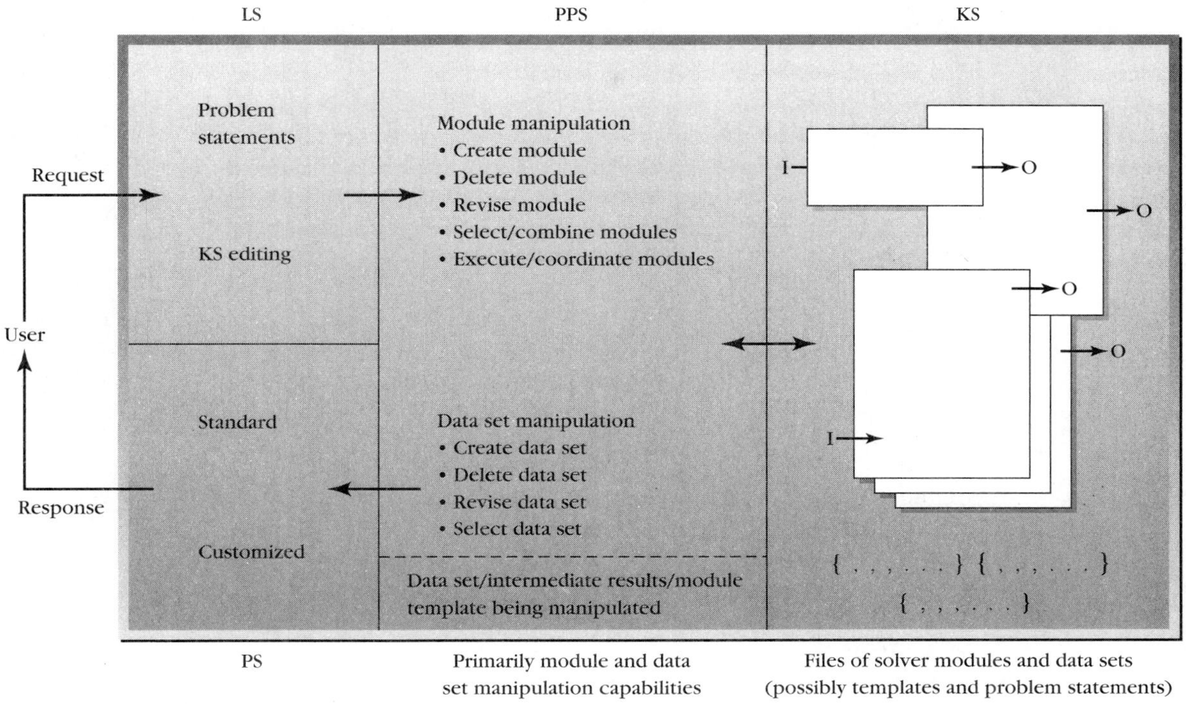

LS　　　　　　　　　　PPS　　　　　　　　　　KS

Request

User

Response

Problem
statements

KS editing

Standard

Customized

Module manipulation
• Create module
• Delete module
• Revise module
• Select/combine modules
• Execute/coordinate modules

Data set manipulation
• Create data set
• Delete data set
• Revise data set
• Select data set

Data set/intermediate results/module
template being manipulated

I → O

O

O

O

I →

$\{\,.\,,\,.\,.\,.\,\}\,\{\,.\,,\,.\,,\,.\,.\,\}$
$\{\,.\,,\,.\,.\,.\,.\,\}$

PS　　　　　Primarily module and data　　　Files of solver modules and data sets
　　　　　set manipulation capabilities　　(possibly templates and problem statements)

duced by executing other modules. In other words, a single module may not be able to solve some problems. Yet they can be solved by executing a certain sequence of modules. Results of carrying out instructions in the first module are used as data inputs in executing the second module, whose results become data for the third or subsequent module executions, and so forth, until a solution is achieved. Thus, a solver can be formed by combining and coordinating the use of available modules so that the data outputs (O) of one can be data inputs (I) to another.

As Figure 6.9 indicates, the LS contains problem statements as well as requests that let a user edit KS contents. It may also contain requests for assistance in using the system. In a problem statement, the user typically indicates which module or module sequence is to be used in addressing the problem. It may also specify some data to serve as module inputs or identify data sets as module inputs. Upon interpreting such a request, the PPS selects the appropriate module or modules from the KS. With some DSSs of this kind, the PPS is able to select modules that are implied (but not explicitly identified) in the problem statement or to combine modules into a proper sequence without being told a definite sequence in the problem statement.

By bringing a copy of a selected module into its working memory, the PPS is able to carry out the procedure of instructions its contains. The input data it needs to work on and the output data it produces are also kept in working memory while the module is being executed. After the PPS is finished executing a module, its instructions and any data not needed by the next module to be executed are eliminated from the PPS's working memory. They are replaced by a copy of the next module and data inputs it needs. The PPS may need to restructure data produced by formerly executed modules so it can be used by the module that is about to be executed. Thus, the PPS coordinates the executions of modules that combine to make up the solver for a user's problem statement.

The LS requests that a user employs to edit KS contents mirror corresponding PPS capabilities. In broad terms, they allow users to create, revise, and delete modules or data sets (and perhaps report templates or problem statements, as well). In creating a new module, for instance, a user would specify the instructions that make up this piece of procedural knowledge. Typically, this is done in much the same way that text is entered when using a text-management technique. However, the instructions are stated in a special language (e.g., programming language) that the PPS can understand and, therefore, carry out during the module execution. Creating a new module can also involve the use of PPS facilities for testing it to ensure that it produces correct results and for converting the module to an equivalent set of instructions that the PPS can process more efficiently.

As in the fixed approach, a flexible solver-oriented DSS may allow users to request a customized presentation of solver results. The desired formatting could be specified as part of the problem statement request. Alternatively, it could be stored in the KS as a template that can be revised readily and used repeatedly by simply indicating its name in problem statements.

Chapter 10 furnishes a more detailed examination of the general features of solver management.

RULE-ORIENTED DECISION SUPPORT SYSTEMS

Another special case of the generic DSS framework is based on a knowledge-management technique that involves representing and processing rules. This technique evolved within the field of artificial intelligence, giving computers the ability to manage reasoning knowledge. Remember from Chapter 4 that a piece of reasoning knowledge tells us what conclusions are valid when a certain situation exists. Rules offer a straightforward, convenient means for representing such fragments of knowledge. A rule has the basic form

If:	description of a possible situation	(premise)
Then:	indication of actions to take	(conclusion)
Because:	justification for taking those actions	(reason)

This format says that if the possible situation can be determined to exist, then the indicated actions should be carried out for the reasons given. In other words, if the premise is true, then the conclusion is valid.

As illustrated in Figure 6.10, the KS of a rule-oriented DSS holds one or more **rule sets**. Each rule set pertains to reasoning about what recommendation to give a user seeking advice on some subject. For instance, one set of rules might be concerned with producing advice about correcting a manufacturing process that is turning out defective goods. Another rule set might hold reasoning knowledge needed to produce recommendations about where to site additional retail outlets. Yet another rule set could deal with portfolio advice sought by investors. In addition to rule sets, it is common for the KS to contain descriptions of the current state of affairs (e.g., current machine settings, locations of competing outlets, an investor's

FIGURE 6.10   A Rule-Oriented Decision Support System

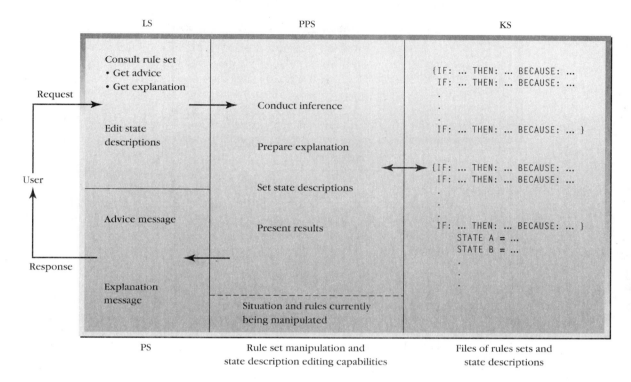

present financial situation). Such state descriptions can be thought of as values that have been assigned to variables.

Aside from requests for help and for editing state descriptions, users of a rule-oriented DSS can issue two main types of requests for decision support purposes. The LS contains requests for advice and requests for explanation. For example, in making a decision about what corrective action to take, the decision maker may request the DSS to advise him or her about the likely causes of cracks in a metal part. The decision maker may subsequently request an explanation of the rationale for that advice. Correspondingly, the PS includes messages presenting advice and explanations.

The **problem processor** for a rule-oriented DSS has capabilities for creating, revising, and deleting state descriptions. Of greater interest is the capability to do logical inference (i.e., to reason) with a set of rules to produce advice sought by a user. The problem processor examines pertinent rules in a rule set, looking for those whose premises are true for the present situation. This situation is defined by current state descriptions (e.g., machine settings) and the user's request for advice (e.g., citing the nature of the quality defect). When the PPS finds a true premise, it takes the actions specified in that rule's conclusion. This action sheds further light on the situation, which allows premises of still other rules to be established as true, causing actions in their conclusions to be taken. Reasoning continues in this way until some action is taken that yields the requested advice or the PPS gives up due

EXPERT SYSTEMS

A rule-oriented DSS is also known as an **expert system** because it emulates the nature of a human expert from whom we may seek advice in the course of making a decision (Bonczek, Holsapple, and Whinston 1980; Holsapple and Whinston 1986). An expert system is a special kind of DSS that is particularly valuable when human experts are unavailable, too expensive, or perhaps erratic. Rather than asking the human expert for a recommendation and explanation, the expert system is asked. Its rule sets are built to embody reasoning knowledge similar to what its human counterpart uses. Its inference mechanisms process those rules using basic principles of logic. Indeed, the PPS for this kind of decision support system is often called an inference engine.

An expert system is always available for consultation: 24 hours per day, 7 days per week, year-round. It does not charge high fees every time it is consulted. It is immune to "bad days," personality conflicts, political considerations, and oversights in conducting inference. To the extent that its reasoning and descriptive knowledge is not erroneous, it can be an important knowledge source for decision makers.

to insufficient knowledge in its KS. The PPS also has the ability to explain its behavior both during and after conducting the inference.

Chapter 11 gives a more detailed overview of rule management. Part Four contains extensive descriptions of the use of rule management in creating artificially intelligent decision support systems.

COMPOUND DECISION SUPPORT SYSTEMS

Each of the foregoing special cases of the generic DSS framework has tended to emphasize one knowledge-management technique, be it text, database, spreadsheet, solver, or rule management. Each supports a decision maker in ways that cannot be easily replicated by a DSS oriented toward a different technique. If a decision maker would like the kinds of support offered by multiple knowledge-management techniques, there are two basic options:

1. Use multiple DSSs, each oriented toward a particular technique.
2. Use a single DSS that encompasses multiple techniques. Some decision makers prefer the first option. Others prefer the second.

Many Assistants with One Skill Each   Recalling the HDSS metaphor advanced in Chapter 5, the first option is akin to having multiple staff assistants, each of which is well versed in a single knowledge-management technique. One is good at representing and processing text, another at handling solvers, another at managing rules, and so forth. Each has its own LS and PS, which the decision maker must learn in order to make requests and appreciate responses. When results of using one technique need to be processed via another technique, it is the decision maker's responsibility to translate responses from one DSS into requests to another DSS. For instance, a solver-oriented DSS might produce an economic forecast that a rule-oriented DSS needs to consider when reasoning about where to locate a new retail outlet.

FIGURE 6.11   A Compound Decision Support System

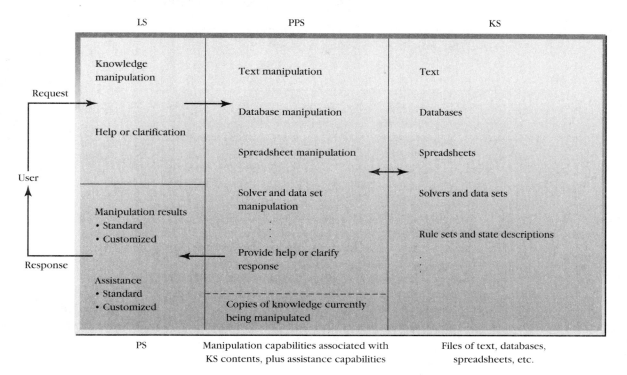

One Assistant with Many Skills   The second option is akin to having a staff assistant who is adept at multiple knowledge-management techniques. There is one LS and one PS for the decision maker to learn. Although they are probably more extensive than those of a particular single-technique DSS, they are likely less demanding than coping with the sum total of LSs and PSs for all corresponding single-technique DSSs. The effort required of a decision maker who wants to use results of one technique in the processing of another technique varies, depending on the way in which the multiple techniques have been integrated into a single compound DSS. It may range from virtually no effort to requiring that the user make requests to conduct some intermediate processing. The major integration styles found in compound DSSs are presented and discussed in Chapter 8.

Just like a single-technique DSS, a **compound DSS** is a special case of the generic framework. As Figure 6.11 shows, its PPS is equipped with the knowledge-manipulation abilities of two or more techniques. The KS holds a knowledge representation associated with each of these. Not all the techniques illustrated in Figure 6.11 need to be present. Additional techniques beyond those depicted (and discussed so far) could be included. For instance, **interface management** techniques (such as forms management, **menu management**, and graphics management) could be used to represent and process extensive linguistic and presentation knowledge. In such a case, knowledge exists in the KS that defines substantial portions of the LS and PS. The PPS is also capable of manipulating that knowledge for request interpretation and response packaging.

COMBINING DATABASE AND SOLVER TECHNIQUES

A schematic of a well-known variant of the flexible solver-oriented DSS approach (Sprague and Carlson 1982) is as follows:

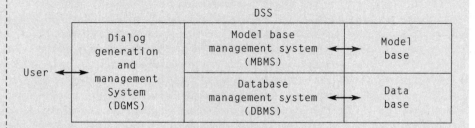

DSS

| User ⟷ | Dialog generation and management System (DGMS) | Model base management system (MBMS) ⟷ | Model base |
| | | Database management system (DBMS) ⟷ | Data base |

The KS is composed of a model base and a database. Here, **model base** is the name given to the solver modules existing in a KS. The notion of data sets in a KS is replaced by a formal database. Correspondingly, the PPS includes model base–management system software for manipulating (e.g., creating, revising, combining, or coordinating) solver modules in the model base portion of the KS. It includes database-management system software for manipulating (e.g., creating, revising, retrieving) data in the form of records held by the database portion of the KS. The dialog generation and management system is a third PPS component. It is concerned with interpreting user requests, providing help, and presenting responses to a user. Although the LS and PS elements of a DSS are not explicit in this framework, they are implicit in the notion of a dialog and have, respectively, been referred to as an action language and display language (Sprague and Carlson 1982).

The foregoing framework is often cited in DSS books and articles as "the" architecture for decision support systems (e.g., Sprague and Carlson 1982; Thierauf 1988; Turban 1988). However, it covers only a portion of the decision support possibilities permitted by the generic DSS framework. It is an important special case of the generic framework that emphasizes database and solver techniques of knowledge management. Because it combines these two techniques, it is also an example of a compound DSS.

The LS consists primarily of requests for assistance and knowledge manipulation. The former allow a user to ask for help in issuing requests or clarification of DSS responses. A knowledge-manipulation request could look very much like standard requests made to single-technique DSSs—that is, it deals with only one technique (e.g., spreadsheet) and the user is expected to understand that technique (e.g., the notion of cell definitions). Other knowledge-manipulation requests may not require such understanding and may even trigger sequences of PPS manipulations involving multiple techniques. For instance, the LS may allow a user to type

```
Show revenue projection for region = "south"
```

or to pick a comparable option from a menu. This request is not necessarily oriented toward any particular technique. The PPS interprets it as meaning that certain data need to be retrieved from a KS database, that a rule set is to be used to infer an appropriate sequence of solvers, and that those solvers are then to be executed

INTERFACE-MANAGEMENT TECHNIQUES

Interface-management techniques are the class of knowledge-management techniques concerned with representation and processing linguistic and/or presentation knowledge. By themselves, they are not an adequate basis for decision support systems. They allow requests to be interpreted and/or responses to be packaged. In the case of requests for help or clarification, some are able to match a correct response with the request. However, an interface-management technique will not carry out the added processing needed after interpretation and before packaging for other kinds of requests. For instance, it may let a user conveniently ask for a forecast and even indicate the manner in which the result is to be presented. But, by itself, the interface technique does not produce the forecast. Thus, the primary role of such knowledge-management techniques is in compound DSSs, where they can be integrated with more functional kinds of knowledge management.

Specific techniques related to interface management are described in Chapters 10 and 11. These include menu management, forms management, report management, and graphics management.

with retrieved data in order to produce the projection. The user does not need to know about database, rule set, or solver manipulations. These activities happen beneath the customized DSS surface provided by interface management facilities.

In a similar way, manipulation or assistance responses may be standardized and/or customized. Some (or all) may look much like standard responses seen from single-technique DSSs. Compound DSSs encompassing techniques for managing presentation knowledge also permit customized packaging of responses, according to presentation knowledge held in the KS. For instance, the previously requested revenue projection, along with explanatory commentary, might be presented in a multicolor form that is personalized (e.g., showing the user's name and request date) and in which the projected number blinks if it exceeds last year's revenue by more than 20%. Specifications of colors and arrangements of items in the form would exist as presentation knowledge in the KS.

MENU MANAGEMENT

Consider the incorporation of menu management into a compound DSS. The KS contains presentation knowledge about menus that can be shown to users. For each menu, this knowledge includes the identification of options existing in the menu, the positioning of those options when the menu is presented, and various cosmetics (e.g., foreground and background colors). Linguistic knowledge is also stored, indicating the interpretation to be ascribed to selecting each option. For instance, if the user's request consists of pressing the F key (i.e., choosing the Forecast option), then the stored interpretation may be to select and evaluate some spreadsheet or to execute some solver. To accompany such KS contents, the PPS would have capabilities of displaying any selected menu (in conformance with its KS characterization) and interpreting user requests with respect to that menu (by drawing on the linguistic knowledge). Chapter 10 describes menu management in greater detail.

6.4 SUMMARY

This chapter introduced the generic DSS framework. From the perspective of this framework, a decision support system can be studied in terms of four interrelated elements: a language system, a presentation system, a knowledge system, and a problem-processing system. The first three of these are systems of representation: the set of all requests a user can make, the set of all responses the DSS can present, and the knowledge representations presently stored in the DSS. The problem processor is a dynamic system that can accept any request in the LS and react with a corresponding response from the PS. The response corresponding to a request is determined by the PPS, often in light of the knowledge available to it in the KS. That is, a change in the KS could very well yield a different response for the same request. As in the case of an HDSS, some DSSs can even produce responses without having received a corresponding request. In addition to reacting to users, they take initiative in the processing of knowledge.

There are many special cases of the generic DSS framework, each characterizing a distinct class of decision support systems. Several of these more specialized frameworks have been examined here. They differ due to their emphasis on one or another popular knowledge-management technique.

Our survey of specialized frameworks serves several purposes. First, it reinforces an understanding of the generic framework by illustrating what is meant by a KS, PPS, LS, and PS. Second, it offers an overview of important kinds of DSSs. Third, the survey gives a brief introduction to various knowledge management techniques: text management, database management, spreadsheet management, solver management, and rule management. These techniques plus various techniques for managing presentation and linguistic knowledge receive additional coverage in Chapter 9. Fourth, it provides a helpful background for the next chapter's discussion of building decision support systems.

▲ IMPORTANT TERMS

architecture
cell
compound DSS
constants
custom-built processor
data set
database control system
database management
expert system
formulas
generic framework
hypertext

interface management
knowledge acquisition
knowledge presentation
knowledge selection/
    derivation
knowledge system
language system
menu management
model base
presentation system
problem-processing
    system

problem processor
problem statement
query-processing system
rule management
rule set
solver management
solver module
spreadsheet
    management
text management
working memory

▲ APPLICATION TO THE AMERICAN AIRLINES CASE

1. Sketch a diagram showing the architecture of DockPlan.
2. What conditions motivated the development of this DSS?
3. How would you characterize DockPlan's language system in terms of (a) what a user intends to accomplish with the requests and (b) the interface style used for expressing requests?
4. What was the reason for having spreadsheet presentations as part of the PS?
5. Describe the contents of DockPlan's knowledge system.
6. Is DockPlan's heuristic scheduling algorithm an example of a fixed or flexible solver approach? Why?
7. In making a language system request to run the scheduling solver, what does the user specify in the request?
8. Describe the way in which a planner uses the DSS's scheduling solver along the way toward making a decision.
9. a. Does the LS contain any requests that ask for the derivation or recall of knowledge? If so, give an example.
   b. Does the LS contain any requests that ask the system to accept new knowledge? If so, give an example.
10. Give an example of something that could be held in DockPlan's short-term, working memory.
11. Characterize the LS and PS of a DockPlan user.
12. Does DockPlan appear to be a
    a. Text-oriented DSS? Why?
    b. Database-oriented DSS? Why?
    c. Spreadsheet-oriented DSS? Why?
    d. Solver-oriented DSS? Why?
    e. Rule-oriented DSS? Why?
13. If Dock Plan can be viewed as a compound DSS, what knowledge-management techniques does it use and how is each of these used?
14. What were the main benefits that resulted from introducing this DSS into the organization?

▲ REVIEW QUESTIONS

1. What is an architecture?
2. How does a generic framework differ from specialized frameworks?
3. Why is a generic DSS framework important for the study of decision support systems?
4. Identify four essential architectural aspects of any DSS.
5. What is a language system for a DSS?
6. What is a presentation system for a DSS?
7. How does a PPS relate the other three elements of a DSS?
8. What does the human metaphor suggest about each of the following?
   a. Possible LS subsets
   b. Possible PS subsets
   c. KS contents
   d. Problem processor capabilities

9. Describe the distinction between a KS and the short-term working memory of a PPS.
10. In terms of the generic framework, how can DSSs differ?
11. Can the user of a DSS be characterized in terms of the generic framework? If so, explain.
12. What is the relationship between a specialized framework and a class of DSSs?
13. How does hypertext management differ from conventional text management?
14. In each of the following cases, what is represented in KS files?
    a. Text-oriented DSS   d. Fixed solver-oriented DSS
    b. Database-oriented DSS   e. Flexible solver-oriented DSS
    c. Spreadsheet-oriented DSS   f. Rule-oriented DSS
15. How could each of the following offer support to a decision maker?
    a. Text-oriented DSS   d. Fixed solver-oriented DSS
    b. Database-oriented DS   e. Flexible solver-oriented DSS
    c. Spreadsheet-oriented DSS   f. Rule-oriented DSS
16. How does relational database management differ from text management?
17. What kinds of software can exist in the PPS of a database-oriented DSS? What role does each play? How are they related?
18. In the spreadsheet technique of knowledge management, what is a cell? Distinguish between constants and formulas.
19. What is a macro?
20. Define a solver, data set, and solver module.
21. How does a fixed solver-oriented DSS differ from a flexible solver-oriented DSS?
22. What are a rule, a rule set, and a state description?
23. How does a rule set differ from a solver?
24. Why might an expert system be valuable to a decision maker?
25. In what ways do the PPS and KS of a compound DSS differ from those of single-technique DSSs?
26. Why are interface-management techniques, by themselves, inadequate foundations for creating DSSs?
27. How can interface-management techniques contribute to the creation of compound DSSs?

▲ DISCUSSION TOPICS

1. What features should a PPS have in order to be considered intelligent?
2. Propose a scheme for classifying LS elements based on each of the following:
    a. The style of requests
    b. The user effort in specifying requests.
3. Discuss the linkage between a DSS's language system and the linguistic knowledge held in its KS.
4. Discuss the linkage between a DSS's presentation system and the presentation knowledge held in its KS.
5. Identify two approaches to creating a DSS whose LS and PS are customized for a particular problem domain or user.
6. Explain the value of the working memory concept.
7. In what sense can a PPS be considered to be a mapping function? What is the domain? What is the range?
8. Discuss the alternatives of embedding a piece of knowledge in the PPS versus storing it in the KS.

9. What would be the traits of a PPS that are general (i.e., able to process problems in a wide range of problem domains)?

10. Describe limits on the interaction that can happen in each of the following situations:
    a. The user's PS is a superset of a DSS's LS.
    b. The user's PS is a subset of a DSS's LS.
    c. The user's LS is a subset of a DSS's PS.
    d. The user's LS is a superset of a DSS's PS.

11. Descriptive knowledge can be stored as text, in databases, or in spreadsheets. Under what circumstances would each be the most appropriate in a DSS?

12. Give a detailed enumeration of all the ways in which a decision maker might like to manipulate pieces of text.

13. What would be the benefit of being able to put names on the links among pieces of text?

14. Why might you expect a custom-built processor in a database-oriented DSS to be more efficient than a standard query processor?

15. Discuss relative advantages and disadvantages of fixed versus flexible solver-oriented DSSs.

16. What are possible benefits and drawbacks of a PPS that automatically formulates solver modules into a solver that will address a user's request for knowledge?

17. Can flexible solver-oriented DSSs provide features not available with spreadsheet-oriented DSSs? If so, what are they?

18. From the standpoint of user convenience, what properties do you think an integration approach should provide within a compound DSS?

REFERENCES

Bieber, M. 1992. Automating hypermedia for decision support. *Hypermedia* 4, no. 2.

Bieber, M., and S. Kimbrough. 1992. On generalizing the concept of hypertext. *Management Information Systems Quarterly* 16, no. 1.

Bonczek, R. H., C. W. Holsapple, and A. B. Whinston. 1976. A decision support system for area-wide water quality planning. *Socio-Economic Planning Sciences* 10, no. 6.

_____. 1978. Aiding decision makers with a generalized database management system. *Decision Sciences* (April).

_____. 1979. The integration of data base management and problem resolution. *International Journal of Information Systems* 4, no. 2.

_____. 1980. Future directions for developing decision support systems. *Decision Sciences* (October).

_____. 1981a. *Foundations of decision support systems.* New York; Academic Press.

_____. 1981b. A generalized decision support system using predicate calculus and network data base management. *Operations Research* 29, no. 2.

Chang, A., C. W. Holsapple, and A. B. Whinston. 1988. A decision support system theory. *Kentucky Initiative for Knowledge Management*, Research Paper No. 5, College of Business and Economics, University of Kentucky.

Cragg, P. B., and M. King. 1992a. A review and research agenda for spreadsheet based DSS. *International Society for Decision Support Systems Conference*, Ulm, Germany.

_____. 1992b. Spreadsheet modelling practice. *Loughborough University Management Research Series*, Paper 1992:14, Loughborough University Business School, Leicestershire, UK.

Dos Santos, B., and C. W. Holsapple. 1989. A framework for designing adaptive DSS interfaces. *Decision Support Systems* 5, no. 1.

Fedorowicz, J. 1989. Evolving technology for document-based DSS. In *Decision support systems: Putting theory into practice*, 2nd ed. edited by R. Sprague, Jr., and H. Watson. Englewood Cliffs, N. J.: Prentice Hall.

Gray, D. A. 1992. Airworthy: Decision support for aircraft overhaul maintenance planning. *OR/MS Today* (December).

Holsapple, C. W. 1977. Framework for a generalized intelligent decision support system. Ph. D. diss. Krannert Graduate School of Management, Purdue University.

_____. The knowledge system for a generalized problem processor. *Krannert Institute Paper*, no. 827, Purdue University.

_____. 1984. Synergy comes to integrated software. *Systems and Software* 3, no. 2.

Holsapple, C. W., and A. B. Whinston. 1985. Management support through artificial intelligence. *Human Systems Management* 5.

_____. 1986. *Manager's guide to expert systems.* Homewood, Ill.: Dow Jones–Irwin.

Joyce, J. D., and N. N. Oliver. 1977. Impacts of a relational information system in industrial decisions. *database* 8, no. 3.

Keen, P. G. W. 1987. Decision support systems: The next decade. *Decision Support Systems* 3, no. 3.

Klaas, R. L. 1977. A DSS for airline management. *Data Base* 8, no. 3.

Minch, R. P. 1989. Application and research areas for hypertext in decision support systems. *Journal of Management Information Systems* 6, no. 2.

Sprague, R. H., Jr., and E. D. Carlson. 1982. *Building effective decision support systems.* Englewood Cliffs, N. J.: Prentice Hall.

Thierauf, R. J. 1988. *User-oriented decision support systems.* Englewood Cliffs, N. J.: Prentice Hall.

Turban, E. 1988. *Decision support and expert systems.* New York: Macmillan.

Chapter 7

BUILDING DECISION SUPPORT SYSTEMS

INSIGHTS

CITGO: A DSS FOR SHORT-TERM PLANNING DECISIONS

Overview

Citgo Petroleum Corporation is one of the nation's largest industrial companies. . . . It is the largest independent "downstream" marketer of petroleum products. . . . Citgo is a wholly-owned subsidiary of The Southland Corporation and, as such, supplies the gasoline at most company-owned and franchised 7-Eleven convenience stores.

. . . [It is] important to maintain tight control over required working capital, as well as to incorporate its cost into all operational and strategic refining and marketing decisions. . . . This realization prompted Southland . . . to fund the development of a Supply, Distribution, and Marketing (SDM) . . . decision support system. . . . [It] provides rapid solution of large-scale problems, allowing users to respond quickly to the dynamics of a commodity market industry. . . . [It] greatly enhances user communication and understanding . . . helps top management with numerous financial short-term planning decisions and significantly enhances Citgo's ability to position itself more competitively in the marketplace.

. . . [The system] is used to help top management with their weekly decisions concerning refinery run levels, where to buy and sell products and what prices to pay or charge . . . how much product to hold in inventory at each location, how much product to ship by each mode of transportation, and how to schedule the receipt and delivery of products for exchange and purchase/sale/trade agreements with other refiners. . . . [The system is] also used by the schedulers for operational decisions. As such, the SDM system is a powerful tool to aid top management in their financial, logistical, and marketing planning.

System Development and Features

. . . [The] implementation of the SDM system posed many challenges. . . . [In developing the system] we identified four distinct users. . . . [These were] the product managers, pricing manager, the product traders, and the budget manager. Since each user is concerned with a different aspect of the operation, the input data and output reports are designed according to their styles. That is, data . . . are presented in the units and formats they normally use, such as thousands of barrels for traders, thousands of gallons for marketers, thousands of dollars for financial reports, and so forth. . . .

The product managers at Citgo are responsible for cross-functional integration and coordination with respect to the products they handle (one product manager has home heating oil and diesel fuel, and another, automotive gasolines). Product managers . . . use the . . . what-if capabilities to generate economically viable alternatives to current and forecasted operations. . . .

The pricing manager . . . uses one set of reports . . . to set ranges for terminal prices for each product. These ranges provide a management-by-exception operational mode for the regional pricing coordinators and automatically include such critical pricing variables as product cost, timing considerations, price forecasts, inventory holding costs, price-volume relationships, and so forth. In addition, the pricing manager uses the wholesale report . . . to help set prices and recommend volumes for bulk sales made to reduce excess inventories.

Continued

A third user group consists of the product traders who are responsible for product purchases and sales on the spot markets as well as trades with other refiners. Traders use the Volume Summary Report and the Infeasibility Report to determine which side of the trading board they should be on for each product. . . . They can also use the . . . what-if capabilities to determine the sensitivity of spot prices to the required purchase or sales volumes as prices fluctuate during the week.

A fourth user, the budget manager, uses the Financial Summary Report to generate various components of the monthly and quarterly budgets. . . .

The primary factor that positively influenced the success of the SDM system was the unlimited top management support received from Southland and Citgo. . . . [This] included both financial and organizational support. . . .

Benefits

The major benefit realized from the SDM Model was the reduction in Citgo's product inventory with no drop in service levels. . . .

Another direct benefit . . . was the improvement in operational decision making: improvements in coordination, pricing and purchasing decisions. . . . These improvements showed up as lower purchase prices of both spot-purchased and traded products, higher per gallon profits on terminal sales from the use of better pricing strategies, fewer distress bulk sales made from excess inventories due to better inventory control. . . . The value of these improvements in decision making and operational coordination is understandably difficult to quantify, but is estimated conservatively at . . . $2.5 million per year . . . [which] goes straight to improving Citgo's bottom line profitability.

Condensed quotation from D. Klingman, N. Phillips, D. Steiger, R. Wirth, and W. Young, "The Challenges and Success Factors in Implementing an Integrated Products Planning System for Citgo," *Interfaces* 16, no. 3, (1986): 1–16.

LEARNING OBJECTIVES

The Citgo case illustrates a decision support system built by professional developers rather than the system's ultimate users. These developers were trained in technologies and methods for building computer systems but had to acquire an understanding of the short-term planning decisions being made at Citgo as well as the needs of the four kinds of end users of the DSS. The development process extended from an initial recognition of the need for a DSS and securing top-management support to an analysis of what the four users needed, to the design of the DSS to meet those needs, to the implementation of the DSS, and to its installation and the evaluation of its benefits. To fuel your practical appreciation of ideas presented in this chapter, keep the Citgo case in mind.

After studying this chapter, you should be able to

1. Explain the relative advantages and disadvantages of do-it-yourself versus professional development.
2. Describe important steps that can occur in the process of building a decision support system.

3. Differentiate among the developmental activities of analysis, design, and implementation.
4. Discuss your role as a do-it-yourself developer.

At the end of the chapter you can apply what you have learned by doing a set of exercises pertaining to the Citgo case. Review questions and discussion topics are also provided to check on whether you have met the objectives.

7.1 INTRODUCTION

Knowing the generic DSS framework and architectural variations within that framework prepares us to study the topic of DSS development. We understand the purpose, uses, and architecture of decision support systems, but what is involved in building a DSS? Who brings a DSS into existence? What process is used to do so? How might software tools help DSS developers during the building process? This chapter helps answer such questions.

Obviously, a DSS must be built before it can be used to support decision making. We shall refer to all the activities, from the initial recognition of a need for a DSS leading up to the first use of that DSS for supporting decisions, as aspects of DSS development. The person or people who carry out the development are called DSS **developers.** Software that a developer uses in building the DSS is called a **development tool,** or tool. The quality, capacity, and capabilities of a DSS depend highly on the developer's skills, the development processes followed, and the nature of the development tool(s) used. These factors also affect the speed and cost of DSS development.

The examination of DSS development is organized into two major sections, dealing with the developer and the development process. Although they enter into our present discussion, development tools are not examined in detail until Chapter 8. Here, we shall see that developers range from professional computer scientists to do-it-yourselfers, who are often the eventual end users of the developed DSS. We shall see that there is a sequence of phases in a developmental process, including analysis, design, and implementation. We shall also see that development tools can serve as the problem-processing system (PPS) for the DSS being built.

7.2 DSS DEVELOPERS

Developers of decision support systems cover a spectrum ranging from the experienced professional developer to the novice do-it-yourself developer. A professional developer's main occupation is building decision support systems and, perhaps,

---

END-USER COMPUTING

When the ultimate user of a DSS is also the developer of that DSS, he or she is involved in doing what is often called **end-user computing** (Panko 1987).

other kinds of business computing systems as well. Such persons are usually formally trained in computer science or business computing. In contrast, a do-it-yourself developer is typically a decision maker who needs the support a DSS can provide. His or her main occupation is managerial and he or she rarely has extensive formal training in business computing systems. In this case the ultimate end user of a DSS is also the person who built it. Between the professional and do-it-yourself extremes are other developers, such as the inexperienced professional and the very experienced do-it-yourselfer. Each exhibits some characteristics of each extreme.

Both professional and do-it-yourself developers can construct successful DSSs. Both can also build failures. The degree of success of a DSS may be assessed in terms of such factors as whether it is used by the decision maker, the extent of usage, the user's impression about ease of use, the system's ability to produce correct responses, and its economic payoffs. A system that can produce correct solutions to problems is less than successful if its user regards the interface as cumbersome or awkward. Conversely, a DSS that is easy to use is of little value if the responses are incorrect or the requests involve problems that are irrelevant.

INGREDIENTS FOR SUCCESSFUL DEVELOPMENT

Regardless of whether a developer is professional or a do-it-yourselfer, key ingredients to building a successful DSS include

An appreciation of end user needs,

Selection of an appropriate development tool,

Sufficient skill in harnessing available computer technology,

Sufficient understanding of the relevant problem domain, and

Access to adequate knowledge sources.

See Figure 7.1. For some of these ingredients, the professional has an edge. For others, a do-it-yourself developer has an advantage. For instance, a professional is more likely to have superior skills when harnessing available computer technology (e.g., minimizing knowledge storage requirements) but is less likely to have superior understanding of the relevant problem domain (e.g., intricacies of economic forecasting).

Technical Skills. A professional's training in building systems delves into technical details of making computers do what is desired. These details go well beyond what is covered in this book. They give professional developers the potential to build DSSs that are more extensive, elaborate, or efficient than what the typical do-it-yourselfer could accomplish in the same time frame. However, there are many DSS opportunities that do not demand such extensiveness, elaborateness, or efficiency. These are candidates for **do-it-yourself development** and can be accomplished with the technical level offered by this book and supplemental tool-specific workbooks.

Methodological Skills In addition to technical details of how computers work and how to make them work, a professional's training involves methods governing the

FIGURE 7.1   Ingredients for Building a Successful DSS

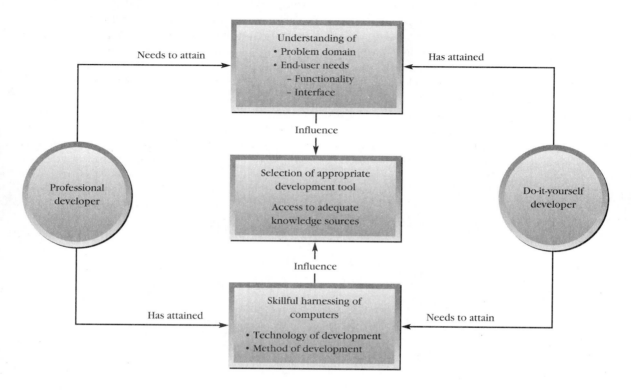

overall development process, which are variants of *systems analysis and design,* or *software engineering.* In general, systems development methods encompass analysis, design, and implementation. In the first of these phases, a developer discovers and clearly specifies what characteristics the developed system should have. The resulting specification gives guidance to and imposes restrictions on the design phase, wherein the developer formulates a detailed blueprint of what the desired system is to look like and a plan of how it is to be brought into reality. In the implementation phase, a developer's technical skills are used in making the design a reality.

Typically lacking training in development methods, do-it-yourself developers tend to approach the activity of building DSSs in a comparatively informal manner. Whereas the professional adheres to a well-defined sequence of development activities, checking off each as it is accomplished, do-it-yourself efforts have a tendency to be somewhat haphazard. Although this may not present too much difficulty for small DSS development projects, it can result in severe difficulties for ambitious DSS projects—those that are complex or broad in scope. When the discipline that guides a professional's efforts is missing, DSS development efforts are susceptible to flaws of oversight, inconsistency, and inaccuracy.

As Figure 7.1 suggests, just because a do-it-yourself developer is not a professional, there is no reason to suppose he or she cannot acquire a professional attitude toward development. Such an attitude increases the likelihood of creating successful DSSs. To help instill this attitude, the next section covers methodological aspects of harnessing computer technology. It identifies important issues and principles that deserve consideration in a DSS development process, be it conducted by a professional or do-it-yourself developer.

Satisfying the End User   As Figure 7.1 indicates, there is more to DSS development than technical and methodological skill. There must be an understanding of what the end user of the prospective DSS needs or desires. Such an understanding normally depends on familiarity with the problem domain to be addressed by the DSS. A professional developer usually needs to understand the problem domain in general and end-user needs in particular. The latter encompasses a specification of both the functionality (i.e., what problems the user wants the DSS to solve) and the interface (i.e., the language and presentation facilities the user desires for interacting with the DSS). Professional developers are wise to get end users actively involved in the analysis and design of a system. Obviously, this involvement is easily accomplished when the developer is the end user.

Selecting a Development Tool   A developer's skills and understanding combine to influence the selection of a development tool and access to knowledge sources. If a developer has the technical skill to use only one kind of tool, it is likely he or she will select that tool regardless of what is understood about end-user needs and domain traits. When a developer commands a diverse set of tools, then he or she can select the one that will best meet user needs and fit domain characteristics. For instance, a developer who is familiar only with tools that aid in spreadsheet management can reasonably choose such a tool to help build a DSS that does what-if budgeting analysis. However, these tools are far less suitable when the user needs a DSS that will recommend corrective action in a manufacturing process. For such a DSS, a tool that facilitates rule management would be a better choice (provided the developer is skilled in using it).

Knowledge Access   The developer of a DSS commonly invests the KS with some knowledge prior to its use for decision support purposes. This could include any or all of the major knowledge types (e.g., descriptive, procedural, or reasoning). The knowledge actually included in a KS depends partially on a developer's technical skills in using the selected development tool to represent knowledge accessed from various sources. For instance, a developer may have available books describing procedures for making various calculations, but if he or she does not have the technical skills needed to use selected tools to represent that knowledge, then the knowledge source is inaccessible, for all practical purposes.

The knowledge actually included in a KS also depends on a developer's mastery of the problem domain and appreciation of end-user needs. For example, a developer who does not know about the existence of a certain class of procedures for solving problems in the domain of production planning will not be able to represent them in a KS, no matter how extensive his or her technical skills may be.

HELP FOR DO-IT-YOURSELF DEVELOPERS

An important issue for the do-it-yourself developer of DSSs is getting help in a development effort. Many organizations have **information centers.** Sometimes associated with a MIS department, an information center educates end users about business computing possibilities and how to achieve them, provides continuing technical assistance to end users, and generally promotes do-it-yourself development of computing systems in the organization (Hammond 1982; Morse and Chait 1984; Head 1985; Oglesby 1987). The existence of an information center is typically a sign of an organization's strong commitment to do-it-yourself development.

An information center is usually staffed by persons well versed in computer hardware and software, the basic knowledge-management techniques (e.g., text management, database management, and rule management), an assortment of specific tools that could be used in DSS development, potential knowledge sources, and methods of system development. It is their responsibility to monitor the rapid pace of technological change and make do-it-yourself developers aware of relevant advances that could affect DSS construction and operation. This process is accomplished through seminars, newsletters, and individual consultations on an as-needed basis. For instance, suppose a prospective developer is interested in using some software tool with which he or she became familiar in college. However, upon consulting the information center about it, the developer is informed of a new tool that is similar but that has some superior features (e.g., more efficiency, less cost, greater flexibility). A developer is usually far too busy personally to track such useful technological advances.

An information center may also help developers by identifying a set of hardware or software tool candidates for a specific DSS development project, evaluating those candidates, recommending which should be used, assisting when the developer encounters problems in using chosen hardware or software tools, and perhaps even building prototypes to illustrate possible DSS features or serve as patterns that a do-it-yourselfer can emulate. Even with all this help, there are limits. Information centers normally do not build DSSs for a manager, nor do they guarantee the correctness of DSSs that are built. These jobs are the manager's responsibilities. In order to be prepared to take full advantage of help offered by an information center, do-it-yourself DSS developers should be familiar with the DSS development process. They should be conversant in basic knowledge-management techniques. They should be acquainted with one or more tools embodying at least some of these techniques.

7.3 THE DSS DEVELOPMENT PROCESS

A variety of formal approaches exist to help develop computer systems, including data-flow diagrams, hierarchical input-process-output (HIPO) forms, Warnier-Orr diagrams, structured design, and structured programming (DeMarco 1978; IBM 1974; Orr 1981; Yourdon and Constantine 1978; Jackson 1979). Such approaches are currently being used by professional developers, particularly for creating large-scale or complex computer systems. They tend to be used within the confines of the *system development life cycle* (**SDLC**). The SDLC is a formalized routine that takes considerable time, effort, and resources (Carr 1988). However, it is worthwhile when activities of the many people involved in large development projects must be coordinated (Zmud 1983).

Do-it-yourself development tends to skirt SDLC formalities and avoid the formal techniques often used within its confines. We shall do the same. However, in offering some guidelines for do-it-yourself developers, we informally consider many of the same issues that would concern a professional developer. The DSS development

SYSTEM DEVELOPMENT LIFE CYCLE

Although there are SDLC variations, a common view of the system development life cycle portrays it as a sequence of phases: problem definition, feasibility analysis, system analysis, design, programming, testing, installation, and administration. These phases, some of which may overlap in time, can be summarized as follows:

- Problem definition: A document is produced describing the nature of the organization's problem that is a candidate for being overcome by a computer system.
- Feasibility analysis: A study is performed to assess whether such a system is technically feasible (i. e., sufficient technology and skill at using it are available), economically feasible (i. e., affordable), and behaviorally feasible (i. e., likely to have positive impact on individual and organizational behaviors).
- Systems analysis: A study is performed to uncover the requirements and document enough information about the desired system and its prospective uses to allow for complete and correct design.
- Design: Based on requirements identified in the prior phase, a detailed layout of the system's parts and their interactions is created.
- Programming: The design specifications are translated into software that can drive a computer's behavior.
- Testing: The programmed software system is put through trial runs to see that it performs according to requirements.
- Installation: The tested (and corrected, if need be) system is made available to its users with any necessary training and documentation.
- Administration: Errors not detected in the testing phase are corrected, and incremental enhancements are made to system capabilities.

guidelines are organized into five topics: preliminaries, analysis, design, implementation, and operations, which are examined in sequence.

PRELIMINARIES

DSS development begins with a recognized decision support need or opportunity. Symptoms of a possible DSS need include situations where a decision maker is under stress (e.g., due to knowledge overload), overworked, (e.g., unable to make enough decisions in a normal time frame), or very expensive. A decision support system may be the solution in cases of insufficient decision maker productivity, where decisions are ineffective or decision making is inefficient.

Managers should also be alert to decision support opportunities that could give their organization a competitive advantage. A new DSS may be instrumental in implementing a competitive strategy (Holsapple and Whinston 1986). For example, an organization may initiate a new competitive strategy that provides its customers with a unique kind of service that not only retains existing customers but also lures new ones. The service might involve giving customers easy access to a DSS that can provide them with sound advice about different purchasing decisions they face.

When a manager has identified a DSS need or opportunity, he or she must also grasp the underlying causes. Suppose, for instance, that someone's decisions are ineffective. Is this because the person is not suited to the job or is it due to a lack of adequate support? In the latter case, the manager should ask further whether the support is better provided by humans, computers, or a combination of the two. This question implies an appreciation of what is possible (technically, economically, and behaviorally) with respect to DSS development and usage. For novice developers, an information center should be able to give valuable assistance in determining what is possible. As DSS development experience grows, reliance on the information center tends to diminish.

General Objectives   Within the bounds of DSS possibilities, general support objectives need to be set. The DSS can furnish the following kinds of support:

- Alert users to the need for decisions.
- Recognize problems that need to be solved.
- Solve problems recognized by itself or users.
- Facilitate or extend user ability to process (e.g., acquire, transform, explore) knowledge.
- Offer advice, expectations, evaluations, facts, analysis, and designs.
- Stimulate user perception, imagination, and creativity.
- Coordinate or facilitate interactions within multiparticipant decision makers.
- Perform some combination of the preceding.

For any designated kind of support, it should be possible to give specific examples (e.g., the DSS should be able to offer expert advice about where to set any salesperson's monthly sales quota for any product line, or the DSS should be able to show the budgetary effects of making various assumptions about sales levels and commission structures).

   The general objectives should clarify the basic types of knowledge to be managed by the DSS (e.g., descriptive, procedural). They should specify the DSS's capacity in terms of volumes of knowledge stored (e.g., historical records about dealings with 500 customers, budgetary data, and formulas for eight quarters). The capacity objectives can also be stated in terms of the prospective DSS's processing speed (e.g., able to present a response to a quota advice request in less than 2 minutes, capable of presenting budgetary effects for a new set of assumptions in less than 30 seconds).

Evaluation Standards   Coupled with setting objectives is assessing how well they are met. If an effort is going to be made to measure the DSS's success, the ground rules for doing so should be set at the outset of development and clearly related to the objectives. Because some benefits of DSSs are intangible, subjective, or difficult to quantify, the explicit setting of evaluation standards is often overlooked by do-it-yourself developers. Nevertheless, standards for gauging DSS success can be important in justifying a DSS development effort (e.g., to higher management), in learning from that effort (e.g., offering clues as to what went wrong or right), and in comparing DSS benefits to the costs incurred in developing and using it.

Development Planning   Having set the broad objectives (and perhaps evaluation standards), the developer should think out at least a rough plan of how the objectives will be met. Like any nontrivial project, a DSS development project is likely to proceed more smoothly if there is a plan to guide its activities. There are several points a do-it-yourself developer should consider including in a DSS project plan. The plan should indicate how the developer will go about securing the approval of

DSS EVALUATION

Evaluating a DSS is concerned with understanding not only what is needed or desired and what is affordable, but also with what is possible. This point is vividly made with a simple analogy from Marsden and Pingry (1986):

> Joe, a food user, is dining out. Pierre, the waiter, asks Joe what he wishes for dinner. Joe responds, "How much is a one-pound T-bone steak dinner?" "Ten dollars, gratuity included," replies Pierre. "Sounds tolerable to me," says Joe. "I'll take it medium rare." Pierre is happy for he is to receive the included gratuity. Joe too is initially happy. But his glee departs when, after dinner, he starts to the door of the restaurant and glances at a chalkboard menu he had not seen. Joe notices a special anniversary item, "FRESH ALASKA SALMON DINNER—$4.95." Joe, a true fish lover, is now saddened and decries his fate, moaning, "If only I had known. If only Pierre had aided me in searching the set of food-price pair options." Joe's satisfaction was diminished because he failed to reach the easily obtainable optimum, a failure due to a lack of search across the REVENUE (FOOD)-COST (FOOD) choice set. Further, upon arriving home, Joe is questioned by his working wife (alas, poor Joe is unemployed). "How was dinner, dear? Did you have the $4.95 salmon special?" "No, I had the $10 T-bone." "I don't understand, Joe. Salmon is your favorite food and was priced less than the T-bone you chose. I work hard all day and you throw my money out the window" "I'm sorry, dear. I thought for sure that the salmon would be much more costly than the T-bone and so I didn't even inquire about it."

higher-level management for spending time and resources on the development effort. Without at least tacit approval of superiors, the development effort will be subject to interruption or even failure. Moreover, the developer becomes vulnerable if superiors see the project as a diversion or waste of time and resources. Means for securing commitment of superiors to the development project should be part of the plan.

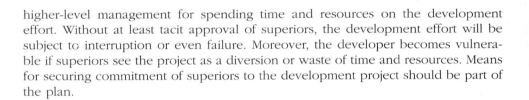

DSS IN THE NEWS

Failed Promises

Computer projects ultimately fail when senior executives frustrated by poor progress early in the projects' buildup lose their commitment and reduce funding.

Project managers also frequently fail to articulate a clear vision of what must be done for the project to work, or how it will improve business performance . . .

. . . [A] common mistake is that information technology managers shoot for perfection, wasting resources by adding equipment or personnel instead of making the system they have in place work the way it was designed to work.

B. Deagon, "Failed Promise of Automation: Why Computer Projects Often Miss Their Goal," *Investor's Business Daily* (April 21, 1992): 4.

The DSS development plan should identify the developer. If the prospective DSS will have multiple users, which users are to be involved in development and in what capacities? Some may be assigned to design the DSS, whereas others focus on implementing that design and yet another oversees the entire project. To what extent will the information center (if it is available) participate in the development effort? Even when there is only one user, the plan should indicate whether other persons will be involved in the development, not as developers but as knowledge sources for the developer (e.g., sources of expert reasoning knowledge or providers of solvers). The plan should identify all the players in a development project, indicate what their roles will be, and include some means for assuring that they will willingly participate as needed.

The DSS development plan may contain a budget showing how much can be spent on the project, where and when the expenditures can occur, and for what purposes they can be made. The plan will contain a schedule of activities that are to be carried out in the project. This helps the developer gauge the project's progress as it proceeds, giving a basis for taking corrective action if the project deviates from the schedule. The flow of scheduled activities could reasonably be organized into the phases discussed here: analysis, design, implementation, and operation.

SYSTEM ANALYSIS

The activity of **system analysis** results in a detailed statement of requirements that the prospective DSS should satisfy. These must be consistent with the broad objectives and standards set earlier but are much more specific, precise, and complete. For instance, rather than broadly indicating that the system should be able to solve what-if problems encountered in the course of deciding on budgets, system analysis results in a full list of all relevant budgetary items (e.g., sales, cost of goods sold, advertising expense), specification of their mathematical interrelationships (e.g., gross profit = sales − cost of goods sold), specific interface traits desired (e.g., menu-orientation), knowledge-management techniques to use (e.g., spreadsheet and database management), and perhaps candidate tools for implementing the DSS.

To provide details, a developer needs to study carefully the decision support situation. This effort includes study of the decision maker's tendencies and prefer-

---

DEVELOPMENT PRELIMINARIES

1. Recognizing a decision support need or opportunity
   a. Improving decision-maker productivity
   b. Pursuing a competitive strategy
2. Setting broad objectives and evaluation standards
   a. Kinds of support to be provided
   b. Capacity expectations
   c. Standards for gauging success
3. Planning for the development project
   a. Securing commitment of superiors
   b. Constructing a budget
   c. Scheduling the development activities

ROMC VIEW OF SYSTEM ANALYSIS

One way of looking at system analysis for DSSs is known as the ROMC approach (Carlson 1979; Sprague and Carlson 1982). With this approach, analysis is organized into efforts at understanding representations (R), operations (O) memory (M) aids, and control (C) mechanisms.

Representations. In terms of the generic framework, representations are elements required in the LS and PS. In identifying a DSS's representation requirements, the developer needs to characterize what representations are available for communication between the DSS and its user. Examples include graphs, charts, lists, reports, data-entry forms, menus, and text.

Operations. Operations refer to activities the DSS should be required to perform in the processing of representations. In terms of the generic framework, these include the DSS's capabilities for interpreting, producing (selection/derivation), and packaging knowledge. As such, they indicate what the PPS must be able to do relative to the DSS's knowledge system contents. Examples include operations pertaining to graphs, charts, lists, etc.

Memory Aids. These "support the use of representations and operations" (Sprague and Carlson 1982). In terms of the generic framework, such aids include KS contents operated on by the PPS (or by other KS contents) in the processing of representations. For example, a database is a memory aid that could be operated on to produce a graph. Other kinds of memory aids are PPS related, including workspaces for displaying representations and triggers to alert the user that certain operations may need to occur.

Control Mechanisms. These are mechanisms required to help the DSS user synthesize a decision-making process from the available representations, operations, and memories. In terms of the generic framework, these control mechanisms are aspects of the LS, PS, KS, and PPS that are less concerned with solving a specific problem than with facilitating use of those problem-solving capabilities. Examples include mechanisms for helping a user to make or clarify requests, to train the DSS to conform to his or her tendencies, to understand or repackage problem solutions, or to learn the system via examples.

ences, of relevant problem recognition and solving means, of knowledge relevant to the decisional activities, and of the organizational context in which the prospective system is to be used. A common way to begin this study is to examine the current approach to decision making as a basis for understanding what aspects of it will be altered or replaced by the new DSS. This examination can include observation of sample decision-making cases, interviews with the decision maker, a walkthrough of a decision episode with the decision maker, and interaction with existing decision support aids (if any). For a do-it-yourself developer, much of this study is introspective.

The detailed requirements produced by system analysis fall into three categories (Holsapple, Park, and Whinston, 1993). First, there are the **functional requirements**, which characterize the DSS's capabilities for storing, recalling, and producing knowledge (e.g., being able to store desired budgets, recall aspects of any of them, and calculate implications of changes to any). Second, there are the **interface requirements**, which characterize the DSS's knowledge-communication

FUNCTIONAL VIEW OF SYSTEM ANALYSIS

One way of beginning to think about the functional requirements for a prospective DSS is first to determine which categories of functions are needed. These broad functional categories include selection, aggregation, estimation, simulation, equalization, and optimization (Blanning 1979).

- *Selection:* finding needed knowledge within the KS as a basis for presentation to a user or for PPS derivation of new knowledge.
- *Aggregation:* derivation of summary statistics such as totals, averages, and frequency distributions.
- *Estimation:* derivations of estimates for values of parameters in a model (e. g., statistical analysis of data to estimate parameters in a probability distribution).
- *Simulation:* derivation of knowledge about expected consequences of taking an action or of changes in the organization's environment.
- *Equalization:* derivation of knowledge about what needs to occur in order for consistency conditions to be met (e. g., the solution to a set of simultaneous equations).
- *Optimization:* derivation of knowledge about what alternative maximizes (or minimizes) some overall performance measure (or cost) without violating certain constraints.

Having identified the required functional categories, a developer can undertake a more detailed analysis of needs in each.

capabilities. They indicate features of requests the DSS is required to interpret and features of responses it must be able to present. Third, there are the **coordination requirements,** which characterize the timing of events. For instance, it may be necessary for one functional event (e.g., alteration of a stored budget) always to precede some other functional event (e.g., a what-if calculation).

The functional, interface, and coordination requirements influence the choice of knowledge-management techniques to be employed in the DSS. However, the technique requirements can also be influenced by the developer's skill in using one technique versus another and by anticipated growth of the DSS (Keen 1980). A technique that is initially adequate for developing a DSS may turn out to be inadequate as the DSS encompasses greater capacity or extended capabilities. Thus, assessment of technique requirements should proceed with a growth path in mind, allowing for flexibility in future revisions to the DSS.

Having determined functional, interface, coordination, and technique requirements, the developer is in a position to identify candidate tools for DSS development. A tool (or collection of tools) is a candidate if it (or they) allows the requirements to be met. When the developer identifies multiple candidates, he or she needs to choose one. An information center may offer some advice about the choice. Generally, the developer should consider such facts as how experienced he or she is in using a candidate tool, the candidate's cost, how flexible a candidate would be in accommodating unanticipated extensions to the DSS, whether the candidate is well maintained and supported by its vendor, and how rapidly development can proceed with a candidate tool.

ANALYSIS

1. Studying the decision situations to be supported
   a. Decision-maker inclinations and tastes
   b. Relevant problem recognition and solving means
   c. Relevant knowledge used in decision making
   d. Organizational context in which the system will be used
2. Specifying detailed requirements to be met
   a. Functional requirements
   b. Interface requirements
   c. Coordination requirements
   d. Needed knowledge-management techniques
3. Identifying tool candidates

SYSTEM DESIGN

If the selection of a candidate tool or set of tools has not been finalized in the analysis phase, it needs to occur in the **system design** phase of development. If, at the onset of design, a developer knows what tool(s) will be used to implement the DSS, then the design can be created to take advantage of a selected tool's strengths and unique features, while at the same time avoiding a design that relies on the tool's weak points. Suppose, for instance, that the developer will be using a tool that makes it easy to build pop-up help windows, which can appear on the screen anytime a user is prompted to enter a request. Then screens presented to the user could be designed to have a minimal amount of explanatory text as compared to that needed when using a tool that does not offer facilities for constructing pop-up windows for help explanations.

On the other hand, selection of a tool candidate could be delayed until later in the design phase. Thus, design of a system to meet the requirements could proceed without being concerned about the tool(s) that must ultimately be selected to implement the design (Ariav and Ginzberg 1985). A possible advantage of this method is that the design does not need to be constrained by limits of a particular tool or oriented toward the features it provides. However, there is a likely disadvantage. Although the design may appear to be an excellent way to meet the analysis requirements, it may be impossible to implement easily with any of the available tool candidates. The developer must then seek new tool candidates that would make the design feasible or revamp the design to work with existing candidates.

Do-it-yourself developers should generally select a tool before getting too far into design details. We thus assume that design occurs with respect to the facilities a selected tool or tools offer. From this perspective, design is an exercise in figuring out how the system requirements can be met, given the facilities furnished by the selected tool(s). In general, many conceivable designs may satisfy system requirements. Picking a tool to use cuts down on the design choices in coming up with a blueprint of the decision support system.

Structuring the Design Effort   One way to structure the design effort is in terms of DSS architectural elements: language system (LS) design, presentation system (PS) design, knowledge system (KS) design, and problem-processing system (PPS) design. Designing the DSS's language system consists of characterizing the various requests a user will be allowed to make. These include assistance requests as well as problem-handling requests. Similarly, designing the DSS's presentation system involves characterizing the responses a user will be allowed to observe. These responses include expressions of assistance as well as presentations of problem-handling results. Taken together, the LS and PS designs tell us about the appearance of the DSS's user interface. They must, of course, be consistent with requirements specified in the analysis phase.

Designing the DSS's knowledge system begins with choosing the knowledge-representation techniques that will be adopted for those pieces of knowledge that must be stored. For each technique, the developer needs to devise a design that shows how the knowledge represented by that technique is to be organized, grouped, or structured. For instance, suppose some of the descriptive knowledge is to be represented in database tables. The developer will need to design those tables, indicating which kinds of data are to be held in each. (For example, will data about parts in inventory be held in the same table as data about suppliers of parts?) Similarly, a design is needed for spreadsheet files, rule sets, solver modules, and any other knowledge-representation technique being employed.

Designing the DSS's problem processor is a software-design task. Because the PPS is the basic dynamic component of a DSS, designing it consists of determining the flow of instructions that need to be given to the computer in order to cause it to handle LS, PS, and KS contents in accordance with the requirements identified in the analysis phase. Producing this design can be an extremely complex and time-consuming affair. Thus, PPS design by do-it-yourself developers is very uncommon and is not considered here. Fortunately, a wide variety of DSS development tools provide us with predesigned and implemented problem processors.

Effects of Tools on Design   Tools can vary widely in terms of the amount of latitude offered for each of the foregoing kinds of design. In many—if not most—cases there is no PPS design required, because the tool furnished is a ready-made problem processing system for the DSS. It is possible for a ready-made problem processor to give the developer some modest means for altering its standard default behaviors. These means consist of setting what are variously known as system parameters, environment controls, built-in variables, or switches. The settings of such switches control various aspects of PPS behavior. For instance, a developer may be given a parameter to control the screen's background color, another to control whether alphabetic case differences are ignored, and another to govern how verbose the PPS diagnostics will be.

Suppose the popular Lotus 1-2-3 spreadsheet software has been selected as a development tool. This software serves as the PPS of the DSS being built with it (recall Figure 6.7). The big advantage to a developer is that no time or effort is spent in designing and implementing a PPS. The price paid for this advantage is that the developer cannot design more problem-processing capabilities into the PPS than those already there. Thus, choosing tools with sufficient capabilities is extremely important to developers, and knowing what is sufficient depends on the analysis of system requirements.

LS and PS design are frequently minimal. For instance, there is a fixed set of requests that the 1-2-3 PPS is able to handle, regardless of whether the DSS aims to support financial, marketing, or production decisions. The developer's ability to design additional requests into the LS is limited primarily to defining synonymns for some of the requests already permitted by the tool. Similarly, there is little latitude in the kinds of presentations that the 1-2-3 PPS is able to display. For example, one of the main kinds of system responses is a visual grid of cells. A developer can design what is to appear in each cell under a given set of circumstances but cannot readily design presentations that do not conform to the standard grid view allowed by the tool.

Designing Knowledge Systems   Knowledge system design tends to be the area where there is greatest latitude and most effort. For each piece of knowledge to be represented in the KS, the developer needs to determine which technique will be used for it. For example, suppose the analysis phase identifies database, text, and spreadsheet techniques. The one assigned to represent information about a potential new product depends on the nature of that information (e. g., how structured it is, how much of it there is, how it is to be used) and on the developer's appreciation of the techniques' capabilities, strengths, and weaknesses. Often, only one technique is appropriate, but sometimes there is a good match with more than one technique. A developer is then likely to pick the one recommended by an information center, with which he or she is most familiar, or that will give the greatest flexibility for DSS evolution.

Determining the knowledge to be represented with each technique is but a first step of KS design. And, of course, this assignment is easy when only one required technique is identified in the analysis phase. The developer must next consider how a technique's representational features, as embodied in a selected tool, will be used for organizing the pieces of knowledge assigned to it. There are two important points here.

First, although all tools that offer a particular technique provide a similar functionality, there are variations. These variations can be minor, more a matter of form than substance, or they can be significant, with a tool furnishing only a limited rendition of a technique or giving useful extended features not available in most other tools offering the technique. Thus, it is worthwhile for the designer (e. g., the developer) to be aware of the particular variant of a technique embodied in the selected tool. Otherwise, the design may be infeasible or may not take full advantage of what is offered.

Second, for the variant of a technique offered by a chosen tool, there can be many possible (and even reasonable) designs for organizing knowledge. In the case of database management, a developer needs to design what is called a *database schema*. This schema is a blueprint showing categories of data to be represented in the KS's database and the relationships among those categories. In the case of solver management, a developer partitions procedural knowledge into modules and specifies a flowchart for each. The flowchart is a blueprint showing the flow of instructions for a module. In the spreadsheet case, a developer's design shows the organization of data and formulas relative to each other. For each of these cases, as well as for other techniques, the developer needs to settle on a design suitable for the knowledge processing that needs to be done. Becoming skilled at choosing designs depends on understanding a technique's knowledge-representation conventions (see Chapter 9) and practice (such as that furnished via exercises in tool-oriented supplemental workbooks that can be used with this book).

DESIGN

1. Finalize selection of tool(s) to be used.
2. LS design
   a. Assistance requests
   b. Problem-handling requests
   c. May be little design latitude, depending on tool(s)
3. PS design
   a. Assistance responses
   b. Problem-handling responses
   c. May be little design latitude, depending on tool(s)
4. PPS design
   a. Tool(s) typically furnishes ready-made PPS
   b. Little latitude without complex and time-consuming software design
5. KS design
   a. Matching and assigning pieces of knowledge to techniques
   b. For each, devising a plan for using a technique's representation conventions
      i. Be aware of variants due to tool differences.
      ii. Build design skill by learning technique possibilities and practice.
   c. Considerable design latitude

IMPLEMENTATION

Implementation is the activity of using selected tools to transform DSS designs into operational systems. For the do-it-yourself developer, this activity normally means using a development tool to create the KS on a storage medium such as a hard disc or diskette. In doing so, the developer adheres to the database design, spreadsheet design, solver design, or any other design devised in the prior development phase. If any LS or PS design occurred, then the tool's facilities are also used to store linguistic or presentation knowledge in the KS.

Typically, a tool's ready-made problem processor actually stores the knowledge in reaction to developer requests to do so. The physical details of how the problem processor accomplishes this in the computer's hardware are not especially important to us. What is important is that it is accomplished according to the developer's design and in a way that allows the PPS later to process that knowledge in response to user requests. Once the initial KS has been created, then it joins with the ready-made PPS and attendant LS and PS to constitute a DSS. One major question remains prior to putting this DSS into operation: is it the desired DSS?

Checking the DSS for Expected Behavior   The developer must examine and test the system to see whether it behaves as expected. It is quite possible that errors could have been made when creating the KS, so that its actual contents would be different from what the developer intended. To help ascertain this, the developer could request the PPS to show listings of the knowledge held in the KS. These listings could then be checked against the knowledge sources used in creating the KS. In addition, the developer could interact with the DSS as if he or she were already its user, looking for erroneous responses. These responses can be used to help pinpoint flaws in the KS contents. As implementation errors are found, the developer uses the PPS to correct KS contents and retest them.

Testing may uncover a more fundamental kind of error: a design error (e.g., omission of a needed kind of knowledge from the design). When the implementation faithfully follows a faulty design, the resultant system will probably not perform as anticipated. In such a case, the developer needs to reconsider and correct the design. KS contents are then adjusted accordingly. Depending on the nature of the design error, this adjustment may be fairly simple or it may entail reimplementing major portions of the KS. Even more fundamental and expensive to correct are analysis errors. Incorrect requirements mean reworking the design and a subsequent reimplementation effort.

In considering whether a DSS behaves as expected, we can ask the following questions:

- Are the functional requirements satisfied?
- Are the interface requirements satisfied?
- Are the coordination requirements satisfied?

As an example of the first, if functional requirements demand that the system be able to do economic order quantity (EOQ) calculations, can it? If not, was the design for an EOQ solver faulty, or was the design not properly followed during implementation of the EOQ solver module for inclusion in the KS? As an example of the second, if interface requirements demand that the EOQ result be displayed in a color-coded rectangle that also shows inputs to the solver, is it? If not, was the PS design faulty or was the corresponding presentation knowledge not correctly implemented in the KS? As an example of the third, if coordination requirements demand that a user enters a correct security code before being able to view some sensitive information, does the DSS enforce this? If not, was the PPS or KS design or implementation faulty?

Documentation   Another aspect of making a DSS operational involves the preparation of documentation telling prospective users about the system: its purposes, features, capabilities, limitations, assumption, and administration. Even though the do-it-yourself developer may have all this clearly in mind, some documentation can

---

IMPLEMENTATION

Use selected tool(s) to transform the design into an operational DSS.

1. Store knowledge into KS.
2. Test the resultant decision support system.
   a. Against functional requirements
   b. Against interface requirements
   c. Against coordination requirements
3. Make corrections, as needed.
   a. To implementation
   b. To design
   c. To requirements
4. Prepare DSS documentation.

be beneficial, particularly for a complicated DSS. There may be multiple users of the system in addition to the developer. Over time, the developer may forget about some facets of the system and be unable to remember details when needed. When the developer changes job duties, he or she may want to pass the DSS along to some other user. It is important to avoid the common problem of a do-it-yourself developer changing jobs or companies and leaving behind a crucial DSS that is not documented and thus difficult to maintain or use. Having good system documentation can help ensure smooth operation of the DSS over its lifetime.

It is a good practice for documentation to be an integral part of all preceding steps in the development process. For instance, the developer's statement of system requirements and specifications of system design form a good starting point for producing the final documentation delivered to users. They may even form the bulk of it. Indeed, as system designers, we have followed the approach of producing a system design document in the form of a user's reference manual. The system implementor then builds the actual system to match the preexisting reference manual.

PROTOTYPING: A COMMON APPROACH TO DSS DEVELOPMENT

As an alternative to the goal of an operational DSS, the analysis-design-implementation activity may have the goal of producing a **prototype** DSS (Henderson and Ingraham 1982). Rather than being intended for installation in a decision-maker team, a prototype DSS is intended to demonstrate and provoke. It can be produced much more rapidly than an operational DSS. In the analysis phase there is no effort to obtain a complete statement of requirements. Only a readily identifiable, small set of requirements (i. e., reflecting only a subset of the desired functionality) is needed. A design for these requirements is quickly created, without too much attention to details or efficiency. Implementation proceeds rapidly, without extensive testing or documentation efforts.

A prototype DSS demonstrates, on a small scale and in a partial way, what might be experienced in using the envisioned operational DSS. Such a demonstration can be helpful in several ways. First, it can aid in securing or retaining support of superiors for the development project by giving them a first-hand viewing of some of the envisioned system's support capabilities and by tangibly showing that development progress is being made. Second, if the prototype development effort is a failure (e. g., the developer is unable to implement it with a selected tool), then the plan to construct an operational DSS should be reconsidered before getting too far in the development effort. Third, when the full version of an operational DSS is unclear, a prototype DSS may provoke the user to clarify what is desired. The user can react to experience in using the prototype, indicating what features should be eliminated, changed, or added. Dealing with a "real" system in this way may clarify the requirements more rapidly than without it.

There are two kinds of prototype systems: throwaway and evolutionary (Sprague and Carlson 1982). A **throwaway prototype** is one that is discarded after the demonstration and provocation. An **evolutionary prototype** is one that is redeveloped after being demonstrated and having provoked ideas for extensions, corrections, and refinements (Keen 1980). The result is a more ambitious prototype. This iterative construction of ever-more-grand evolutionary prototypes can eventually lead to an implementation that is no longer merely a prototype but an operational DSS.

That manual is refined and extended during the implementation to reflect any deviations (e.g., the implementation may not exactly follow the original design for technical reasons or because of an oversight in the design). Any help facilities built into the DSS also contribute to its documentation.

Before declaring the DSS operational, a developer should consider documenting aspects of system not derived from analysis and design documents and not covered in the system's help facilities. These aspects include guidelines on the most efficient or effective ways to get acquainted with the system and recommended patterns of ongoing system usage. They could involve descriptions of how to administer or maintain the system (e. g., when and how KS contents are changed, who can make what changes, and what measures are to be taken to ensure the correctness of KS changes). The documentation would probably include troubleshooting advice. For instance, what is a user to do when the DSS presents a mysterious response or when the hardware suffers a power failure? Preparing documentation that addresses the foregoing kinds of issues may seem to be busy work in the short run, but it is likely to pay off handsomely in the long run.

OPERATION

The result when implementation is complete is a working, tested, corrected (if necessary), documented DSS. The system is operational and ready to be installed in the work environment. If there are users other than the developer, this installation may involve some initial hands-on training to orient them to the nature and uses of the system. Early efforts at using the DSS may well be carried out in parallel with continued use of former decision support means. This action can help ease the transition to and build user confidence in the new DSS. It also aids in an operational evaluation of the DSS, offering a benchmark against which to gauge the usefulness of the new system in actual decision-making situations.

Be it a gradual or quick process, a successful DSS will ultimately become an integral supporting participant in a team decision maker. Just as an HDSS is likely to adjust his or her knowledge to adapt to changing needs of those supported, so too is an operational DSS's knowledge system subject to change. In the course of ongoing DSS operation, a user periodically reviews its ability to offer desired support. Keep in mind the fact that a user's support desires are subject to revision, especially when confronted by unstructured decision situations (Keen 1980). When a review of the DSS indicates that its KS needs to be updated, expanded, or otherwise modified to keep pace with a user's support desires, there are two basic possibilities: incremental modification or redevelopment.

Incremental Modification   **Incremental modification** to a DSS's knowledge system is possible when needed changes can be accommodated within the already existing system design. This phenomenon is very common within the operating life of a DSS. For example, the design might specify a means for organizing profiles of stock investment candidates in terms of PE ratio, yield, relative earnings strength, relative price strength, Value Line ranking, and so forth. If, during operation, data about additional investment candidates must be stored, then this KS modification can be readily made in much the same way that initial candidates were stored during the implementation phase. Data values already stored for an investment candidate may need to be modified during operation (e.g., a company's PE ratio changes). This change is easily accomplished within the existing KS design.

Redevelopment   Although incremental modification of a DSS, in effect, gives a DSS that is more knowledgeable, that "new" DSS bears close resemblance to the original DSS from the analysis and design standpoints. Sometimes, however, the needed KS modifications are of such a nature that they cannot be accommodated within the existing design. For example, review may indicate that procedural knowledge (e. g., in the guise of spreadsheets or solvers) is desired in a KS whose design makes no allowance for such knowledge. Or, a review might indicate that entirely different kinds of data than those identified in the original development are desirable. In such cases, simple incremental modifications of the KS are not feasible. Instead, a **redevelopment** effort is in order. The developer does some more analysis to modify the original requirements and then revamps the design accordingly. Implementation proceeds based on this new design to yield the desired DSS.

Although not as frequent as incremental modification, it is not unusual for redevelopment to occur repeatedly over the life of a DSS. As a result, DSS development can be viewed as an iterative, evolutionary cycle of analysis, design, and implementation (Keen 1980; Sauter and Schofer 1988). This evolutionary development is illustrated in Figure 7.2, along with the notion of incremental modification. The dashed lines indicate the previously described possibility of implementation reverting back to design or even analysis to correct design or requirements errors uncovered during implementation.

Administration   Aside from installing the DSS into a decision-making team and reviewing it for potential improvements, operation involves some general administration. **Administration** is concerned with controlling the use of the DSS. What persons are allowed to use the DSS? When can they use it and for what purposes? How are incremental modifications controlled to ensure that the KS is maintained in a valid and consistent state? If there is a breech in this integrity of the KS, what should be done to restore it to a usable form? How can use of the DSS be effectively coordinated with the use of other DSSs?

Administration is also concerned with technology changes. For instance, if a new and improved version of a development tool used in building the system becomes available, will it work with the existing KS, should the new version be acquired, and might a redevelopment be in order to exploit new features of the revamped tool? General administration of a DSS can also involve justifying its continued operation or a redevelopment effort. As such, it entails an ongoing evaluation of the DSS's efficacy in supporting decisions (Ginzberg 1983; Blanc 1991).

OPERATION

1. Installation
2. Periodic review
   a. Incremental modifications
   b. Iterative redevelopment
3. General adminstration
   a. Controlling usage
   b. Adapting to technology changes
   c. Evaluating efficacy

FIGURE 7.2   Decision Support System Development

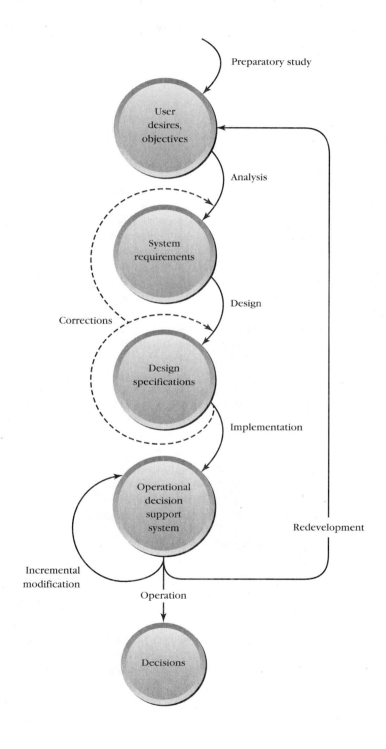

There is evidence that a person's perception of how a DSS does or could help his or her performance can be erroneous (Kottemann and Davis 1991; Kottemann, Davis, and Remus forthcoming). These studies suggest that (1) DSS evaluations should not be based entirely on users' subjective assessments, (2) independent objective valuations should be sought, and (3) ongoing training in DSS usage should incorporate means for continuing measurement of a user's effectiveness with DSS technology.

7.4 SUMMARY

This chapter has explored issues concerned with the building of decision support systems. In particular, we have looked at who builds DSSs and what steps might reasonably be taken to transform a recognized need for a DSS into an operational DSS. The spectrum of DSS developers ranges from novice do-it-yourself developers to experienced professional developers. In any case, successful DSS development depends on understanding end-user needs, familiarity with the problem domain, knowledge source access, appropriate tool selection, and skill in using computer technology. The latter two are typically strengths of a professional developer, whereas the others tend to be the strongest points of a do-it-yourself developer. The technical skills of do-it-yourself developers can be strengthened by books such as this and supplemented by technical assistance from information centers.

The process of do-it-yourself development begins with the recognition of a need or opportunity for decision support. This leads to setting broad objectives and evaluation standards for the envisioned DSS plus making a plan for the DSS development project. A typical development project includes the phases of analysis, design, and implementation. Analysis involves the production of a detailed set of requirements that the prospective DSS should meet. These include functional, interface, and coordination requirements.

The design phase is an exercise in figuring out how the system requirements can be satisfied, usually with respect to the facilities furnished by a selected development tool(s). One way to structure the design effort is in terms of DSS architectural elements: LS design, PS design, KS design, and PPS design. Often, because of the tool used, there is no PPS design needed and LS or PS design tends to be minimal. The bulk of the design effort tends to be concentrated on coming up with a blueprint for the KS.

In the implementation phase, a developer uses selected tools to transform DSS designs into an operational system. This effort usually concentrates on depositing knowledge into the KS according to the KS blueprints. Before the DSS is operational, a developer tests it to check whether it behaves as expected. If it does not, corrective action is taken. Implementation also entails documentation of the DSS to aid in smooth operation. An implemented DSS becomes operational when it is installed for use in a work environment. During the operational phase of its life, a DSS can undergo incremental modifications and redevelopment. It is also subject to general administration.

For a do-it-yourself developer, some or most parts of the development process outlined here may be carried out more or less informally. In the next chapter, we delve into the natures of development tools in more detail, classifying them by knowledge-management techniques, roles in development, interface styles, and integration traits provided.

▲ IMPORTANT TERMS

administration	incremental modification
coordination requirements	information center
developer	operation
development tool	prototype
do-it-yourself development	redevelopment
end-user computing	SDLC
evolutionary prototype	system analysis
functional requirements	system design
implementation	throwaway prototype
interface requirements	

▲ APPLICATION TO THE CITGO CASE

1. Why did Southland build the SDM decision support system?
2. Who were the prospective users of this system?
3. Why did these users not build the DSS themselves?
4. What were the general support objectives for each user?
5. What standards were used to evaluate the success of the DSS?
6. What was the primary factor affecting the success of the SDM system?
7. Why was one DSS developed to support four distinct users rather than four DSSs developed (one for each user)?
8. Outline the requirements that would have been stated during system analysis.
9. Give examples of what the design document for this DSS could have included for (a) the LS design, (b) the PS design, (c) the KS design, (d) the PPS design.
10. What kind of tool or tools would seem to be candidates for implementing the SDM system design? Why?
11. What would be furnished in the documentation delivered with the implemented system?
12. Describe the transition of the users to operational use of the DSS.
13. Give an example of how the SDM system might be incrementally modified.
14. In what part of the development effort would prototyping have been especially valuable? Why?
15. Cite the quantifiable and nonquantifiable benefits realized from the SDM decision support system.

▲ REVIEW QUESTIONS

1. In what ways do the two main classes of developers differ?
2. How can we assess the success of a DSS?
3. What advantages do professional developers have over do-it-yourself developers?
4. What are the advantages of do-it-yourself development?
5. What are three major aspects of DSS development?

6. How can an information center facilitate DSS development?
7. Why does the formal system development life cycle tend to be little used by do-it-yourself developers?
8. What preliminaries are important for DSS developers?
9. Sometimes DSS development is motivated by a sensed need and other times by recognized opportunity. Give an example of each.
10. What factors might be addressed in a DSS development plan?
11. What kinds of requirements are identified in the course of system analysis?
12. In determining the knowledge management techniques that are to be used in DSS development, what factors should be considered?
13. Why is selection of a development tool a prerequisite for completing the design and implementation phases of development?
14. How does a developer go about choosing an appropriate development tool?
15. What happens in the design phase of development?
16. What is involved in implementation?
17. Why is it beneficial to document the DSS being implemented?
18. How might periodic reviews during DSS operation be useful?
19. In what ways does incremental modification of a DSS differ from redevelopment?
20. How do evolutionary and throwaway prototypes differ?

▲ DISCUSSION TOPICS

1. Extent of usage is a factor in assessing DSS success. But is it possible for a rarely used DSS to be "more successful" than one that is routinely used? How so?
2. Under what circumstances is professional DSS development preferable to a do-it-yourself effort?
3. How would you decide whether to build a DSS yourself or have a professional developer do it?
4. Relate the symptoms of DSS need to the cognitive, economic, and temporal limits on decision makers.
5. What (if any) aspects of SDLC seem inappropriate for DSS development? How so?
6. Give a specific example of a competitive strategy. Could a DSS be helpful in implementing this strategy? How so?
7. What factors might be included in a set of standards for evaluating decision support systems?
8. What does it mean for a vendor to maintain and support a development tool?
9. Discuss the likely results if skipping the analysis phase of development.
10. Explain why LS and PS designs need to be based on functional, as well as interface, requirements.
11. Discuss what it means for a DSS to behave as expected.
12. What might be some causes of DSS inefficiency in DSS behavior?
13. Should documentation precede implementation or be developed as an afterthought?
14. If operational evaluation of a DSS indicates it is less useful than desired, what should be done?
15. Give an example of an incremental modification to linguistic knowledge in a KS. Give an example of a linguistic knowledge modification that would require redevelopment.
16. Discuss the relationship between the analysis-design-implementation cycle and prototyping.

17. Relate the ROMC approach to the human metaphor of decision support. Relate it to the generic framework of DSS.

▲ REFERENCES

Ariav, G., and M. J. Ginzberg. 1985. DSS design—A systematic view of decision support. *Communications of the ACM* 28, no. 10.

Blanc, L. A. 1991. An assessment of DSS performance. *Information and Management* 20, no. 3.

Blanning, R. W. 1979. The functions of a decision support system. *Information and Management* 2, (September).

Carlson, E. D. 1979. An approach for designing decision support systems. *Data Base* 11, (Winter).

Carr, H. H. 1988. *Managing end user computing*. Englewood Cliffs, NJ: Prentice Hall.

DeMarco, T. 1978. *Structured analysis and system specification,* New York: Yourdon Press.

Ginzberg, M. J. 1983. DSS success: Measurement and facilitation. In *Data base management: Theory and applications,* edited by C. Holsapple and A. Whinston. Dordrecht, Holland: Reidel.

Hammond, L. W. 1982. Management considerations for an information center. *IBM Systems Journal* 21, no. 2.

Head, R. V. 1985. Information resource center: A new force in end-user computing. *Journal of Systems Management* (February).

Henderson, J. C., and R. S. Ingraham. 1982. Prototyping for DSS: A critical appraisal. In *Decision support systems,* edited by M. Ginzberg et al. New York: North-Holland.

Holsapple, C. W., S. Park, and A. B. Whinston. 1993 Framework for DSS interface development. In *Recent developments in decision support systems,* edited by C. Holsapple and A. Whinston. Berlin: Springer-Verlag.

Holsapple, C. W., and A. B. Whinston. 1986. *Manager's guide to expert systems*. Homewood, Ill.: Dow Jones–Irwin.

IBM. 1974. *A design aid and documentation technique*. IBM, GC20-1851-0.

Jackson, M. A. 1979. *Principles of program design*. New York: Academic Press.

Keen, P. G. W. 1980. Adaptive design for decision support systems. *Data Base,* 12 (Fall).

Klingman, D., N. Phillips, D. Steiger, R. Wirth, and W. Young. 1986. The challenges and success factors in implementing an integrated products planning system for Citgo. *Interfaces* 16, no. 3.

Kottemann, J. E., and F. D. Davis. 1991. "Decisional conflict and user acceptance of multicriteria decision-making aids." *Decision Sciences* 22, no. 4.

Kottemann, J. E., and F. D. Davis, and W. R. Remus. n. d. Computer-assisted decision making: Performance, beliefs, and the illusion of control. *Organizational Behavior and Human Decision Processes*. Forthcoming.

Marsden, J. R., and D. E. Pingry. 1986. Generating an optimal information system: PMAX-SDLC and the redirection of MIS research (or How to help Joe eat salmon), *Journal of Management Information Systems* 3, no. 1.

Morse, J., and L. Chait. 1984. In info centers, the user always comes first, *Data Management* (February).

Oglesby, J. N. 1987. Seven steps to a successful info center, *Datamation* 33, no. 5.

Orr, K. 1981. *Structured requirements definition*. Topeka, Kan: Ken Orr and Associates.

Panko, R. R. 1987. Directions and issues in end-user computing. *INFOR* 25, no. 3.

Sauter, V. L., and J. L. Schofer. 1988. Evolutionary development of DSS, *Journal of Management Information Systems* 4, no. 4.

Sprague, R. H. Jr., and E. C. Carlson. 1982. *Building effective decision support systems*. Englewood Cliffs, NJ,: Prentice Hall.

Yourdon, E., and L. L. Constantine. 1978. *Structured design*. New York: Yourdon Press.

Zmud, R. W. 1983. *Information systems in organizations*. Glenview, Ill.: Scott Foresman.

Chapter 8

DSS DEVELOPMENT TOOLS

OLYMPICS: A DSS FOR EVENT-SCHEDULING DECISIONS

Overview

To organize the 1992 Olympic Games, the city of Barcelona needs to prepare a schedule of the games. . . . To aid the person responsible for scheduling, we developed a system that will also facilitate any rescheduling (for example, in response to weather problems).

Developing a schedule for the games is not a trivial task. . . . A huge number of schedules are possible, as more than 2,000 events have to be scheduled in a 15-day period. . . .

. . . Selecting "the best" possible schedule is not a well-defined problem at all, mainly because it is not clear what is meant by "best" in this context. The problem is one of multiple criteria; for example, a good schedule should try to ensure the maximum possible audience for each Olympic event, while avoiding inconveniences for the athletes. . . . At the same time, constraints on available equipment . . . or personnel . . . have to be met. And one would also like to avoid traffic jams caused by two or more events scheduled in facilities located near each other at approximately the same time.

. . . To help the person preparing the schedule, we built a DSS to allow him or her to develop alternative schedules and to evaluate them in the light of various criteria. We classified the criteria used and built a subsystem for each type, with the goal of evaluating proposed schedules and automatically constructing a schedule that tries to improve on a given criterion. We designed and implemented a collection of interactive algorithms [solvers] for these purposes and developed a set of graphical aids to help compare certain characteristics of a given schedule with those set at the outset as ideal.

System Development and Features

When . . . first confronted with the problem of putting together a reasonable schedule for the Olympic Games, we quickly realized that the only kind of computer-based support that would be appropriate would be a DSS. . . . We had very broad objectives for the eventual DSS:

- . . . Increase the efficiency of the process of developing the schedule for the games.
- . . . Make it possible for the person responsible for the schedule to check whether the existing hard constraints . . . were met or not by a given schedule.
- . . . Allow for the (quick) evaluation of a given schedule according to different criteria.
- . . . Compute schedules that were particularly good in some (measurable) aspects.

We started out by . . . interviewing people with experience in developing schedules for high-competition championships in different sports. . . . In the interviews with the experts we tried to obtain answers to the following questions . . .

- What is the most appropriate way to represent the structure of a given schedule? . . .
- What types of criteria are used in evaluating alternative schedules? . . .
- What computing procedures would be most appropriate? . . .

Continued

- And finally, what ways of presenting evaluation results to the user are most appropriate? . . .

At the outset, the structure of each schedule seemed to be centered around two concepts, the time slot and the Olympic activity. These concepts turned out to be insufficient. In our conversations with the experts, we discovered that they were using different kinds of groupings.

. . . One is the concept of a sport. A given sport . . . can consist of a number of *disciplines* . . . which, in turn, consists of a number of *competitions* that are to be scheduled. Going a bit further, the concept of *group* appeared. A group is just a discipline or a set of disciplines of a sport which, for schedule specification purposes, turns out to be more convenient—to the eyes of the scheduler—than a sport. . . . Experts also used the concepts of *facility* . . . and *area* (a grouping of facilities). . . . Constructing a schedule is a matter of assigning competitions in a given group to a given facility, located in a certain area, at a specific day and time. . . .

To clarify the schedule design process we made explicit distinction between a *calendar* and a *timetable*. In developing a schedule, the scheduler usually starts by putting together a calendar, assigning competitions to days, but not at first to specific time slots. Later, the timetable for each day is developed and refined. . . .

In setting up the calendar, schedulers assign competitions to days, grouping them in sets, or *events*. An event is the set of competitions that you can attend by buying a single ticket. . . . As the schedule is designed, events are also designed, by assigning competitions to them. Then events, rather than single competitions, are assigned to days.

We built the data-base structure around the concepts just introduced. . . . We implemented the data base . . . on a PC . . . to obtain maximum portability. . . . The process of defining a calendar can start once the relevant constraints have been included in the data base and all needed criteria have been defined. During this process, the user may want to introduce more constraints . . . or even to define a calendar manually—and perhaps evaluate it. The system includes these options and also permits the user to ask that a given calendar be improved by retouching it without violating any of the constraints, or that the best feasible calendar be obtained. The words *improvement* and *best* refer to a criterion that the user can specify as a weighted sum of previously defined criteria. . . .

With these objectives in mind (getting the best calendar or improving a given one), we designed a heuristic algorithm [solver]. . . . It determines a starting calendar and then tries to improve it in successive iterations. . . .

A good timetable does not require the simultaneous use of many resources, does not produce problems of traffic congestion and interference, and is well suited to the potential audience. Since timetables are developed after calendars, designing a good calendar prevents some possible problems.

. . . Criteria for evaluating timetables were related to audience issues, both the live audience and the TV audience. . . . A timetable is good to the extent that interesting things happen at the best hours. However, the same things are not equally interesting to different audiences, and the best hours are not the same

Continued

for all audiences. . . . The overall evaluation is done by weighting elementary criteria . . . with the aid of some intermediate, aggregate criteria.

. . . The system includes a greedy algorithm designed ad hoc, which . . . achieves reasonable results in helping the scheduler develop timetables with clear audience goals.

After Barcelona was selected as the site of the Games . . . members of the organizing committee tested the system (they had not participated in its design). This confirmed the usefulness of the methods, concepts, data structures, and algorithms involved. They . . . proposed no significant changes to the system but only extensions to some of the concepts employed and to the outputs generated by the system.

Condensed quotation from R. Andreu and A. Corominas, "SUCCESS92: A DSS for Scheduling the Olympic Games," *Interfaces* 19, no. 5 (1989): 1–10.

LEARNING OBJECTIVES

The Olympics case describes a DSS development process along the lines of those outlined in the prior chapter. The event-scheduling DSS is clearly different from software tools used to build it. These tools included facilities for database, solver, and graphical presentation techniques of knowledge management. The techniques needed were determined by the objectives set for the DSS. The developer selected a tool(s) that provides these techniques and built a DSS, integrating them into a single system. As you read this chapter, keep the Olympics case in mind.

After studying this chapter, you should be able to

1. Distinguish between DSSs and the tools used to build DSSs.
2. Identify important factors to consider when selecting tools for constructing a DSS.
3. Describe major interface styles that can be built into DSSs.
4. Explain the relationship between DSS development tools and knowledge-management techniques, including ways of integrating multiple techniques in the construction of a single DSS.

Exercises provided at the end of the chapter let you see how well you have met these objectives by applying your understanding to an analysis of the Olympics case, to answering review questions, and to discussing various related topics.

8.1 INTRODUCTION

In the process of DSS development, one or more tools are selected for implementing the system. In Chapter 7, we advocated a development approach in which we determine the **knowledge-management techniques** to use in a prospective DSS and then select a tool (or tools) to furnish those techniques. In practice, however, it is not uncommon for the reverse to happen: The developer selects a tool and then works within the limits of whatever technique(s) it offers.

This sequence seems to occur because a do-it-yourself developer is often familiar or comfortable with only one tool (or a very few tools). He or she is not schooled in the variety of knowledge-management techniques available, system development principles, or even the distinction between tools and techniques for managing knowledge. The all-too-frequent result is either a failed development effort or a DSS that is less effective than it otherwise could have been.

This book takes a technique-oriented view of the knowledge-management possibilities available to developers rather than a tool-oriented view. Details of a particular tool change; a tool's popularity can wax and wane; some tools fall by the wayside; new tools are introduced into the software marketplace. But, the basic techniques remain. Understanding them gives a lasting foundation for assessing the adequacy of alternative tools available when implementing specific DSSs.

It is vital to appreciate the simple relationship that exists between knowledge-management techniques and **knowledge-management tools**. A particular technique can be furnished by many different tools from various software vendors. For instance, spreadsheet management can be accomplished with Lotus 1-2-3, Microsoft Excel, and Computer Associates SuperCalc, to name a few. Detailed traits of these tools vary, but all give the ability to represent and process knowledge held in spreadsheet files.

The other side of the technique-tool relationship is that a particular tool can furnish several knowledge-management techniques to a developer. There are many examples of tools that offer one technique only (e.g., Microsoft's Word does text management). There are many that focus on one technique but offer anywhere from traces to fairly heavy doses of other techniques. For instance, the Lotus 1-2-3 tool emphasizes spreadsheet management but also gives developers a healthy graphics-management ability. Finally, there are some tools that offer multiple techniques without necessarily emphasizing any one of them. Examples include Enable, KnowledgeMan, Microsoft Works, DeskMate, LotusWorks, and PFS:First Choice (Perratore 1991).

Knowledge management cannot be exercised without corresponding tools. There are many books available that cover the detailed workings of specific tools. For instance, the *Understanding and Using* series of such books is published by West Publishing Company (e.g., Simon 1992). In this chapter, our examination of tools is more generic, looking at useful ways of classifying them. One obvious classification is based on the techniques offered in a tool. Another is based on a tool's role in DSS development. A third classification scheme distinguishes among tools in terms of the kinds of user interfaces they furnish. A fourth way to categorize tools is in terms of how they integrate multiple techniques. Appreciating these distinctions among tools leaves developers in a better position to make informed selections of development tools.

8.2 TECHNIQUE-ORIENTED TOOL CATEGORIES

A common way to classify DSS development tools is in terms of the knowledge-management techniques they offer. Thus, we can talk about spreadsheet tools, database tools, text tools, graphics tools, and so forth. If a tool provides multiple techniques, it will belong to more than one category. However, if one of the techniques is emphasized and the others are only partially offered, then the tendency is to classify it solely in the dominant technique's category. For instance, 1-2-3 is typically regarded as a spreadsheet tool, even though it has graphics capabilities.

> ### THE VALUE OF A GROWTH PATH
>
> "Today, there are many gradations of tools . . . from those suitable only for computer novices to those suitable only for computer professionals. Between the two extremes are tools that can be appropriate for both seasoned end users and for the pros. A common attitude of novice end users is to choose a tool that is just good enough for present perceived needs. It is almost inevitable that an end user's needs will grow as experience and confidence in computer usage is gained. Thus, what was once just good enough can rapidly become a dead end, forcing the end user to begin again with a more capable tool. To avoid this it is best to choose a tool that has a built-in growth path. It allows the computer novice to start out simply, to be productive quickly without having to master all aspects of the tool. It also allows the end user to incrementally progress to more advanced capabilities as the need arises" (Holsapple and Whinston 1988, 22).

If a DSS developer has determined that database, spreadsheet, and graphics techniques are to be employed, then he or she will need to select a spreadsheet tool, database tool, and graphics tool with features suitable for the implementation effort. The result may be three distinct tools, one tool that belongs to all three categories, or something between these extremes. Publications such a *PC Magazine*, *PC Week*, and *PC World* routinely print articles comparing specific features of currently available tools in one or another of the technique categories (e.g., Scoville 1991). Together with personal experience and information center advice, these resources can help in making good tool selections.

8.3 THE ROLES OF TOOLS IN DEVELOPMENT

One category of development tools consists of those that could specifically aid a developer's efforts in identifying requirements at the analysis phase or in producing design specifications. Because these tools are primarily of interest to professional developers working on large-scale DSS construction, we do not examine this category of pre-implementation tools. Instead, we focus on tools used for DSS implementation. Within the implementation tool category are intrinsic and extrinsic tools.

An **intrinsic tool** is one that serves as the problem processor of the DSS being built with it. An **extrinsic tool** is one that is used to implement the DSS but is not a part of that system's problem processor. Between these two extremes are partially intrinsic tools that furnish part of the DSS's problem processor but whose software is unable to stand on its own as a problem-processing system (PPS). Figure 8.1 summarizes these tool categories.

INTRINSIC TOOLS

An intrinsic tool is able to stand on its own as the PPS of a decision support system. As noted earlier, the 1-2-3 software is an example of such a tool (recall Figure 6.7). With an intrinsic tool, building a DSS consists of using the tool to initialize the KS contents (including possible LS or PS customization allowed by the tool). To use the

FIGURE 8.1   Categories of DSS Development Tools

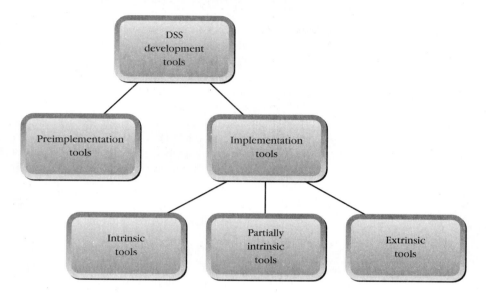

resultant DSS, a decision maker executes the intrinsic tool, using the language system (LS) it provides in order to tell what actions are to be taken with the knowledge system (KS) contents. Intrinsic tools are very popular and widely used because no effort needs to be expended in implementing the PPS software.

A partially intrinsic tool is unable to function as the entire PPS of a decision support system, yet it provides software that can function as a part of the problem processor. Some database tools fall into this category. They furnish software known as a database control system, which forms part of the PPS (recall Figure 6.6). It is up to the developer to design and implement other PPS software (e.g., a custom-built processing system) that governs the operation of the database control system. Thus, building a DSS with a partially intrinsic tool involves more than initializing the KS; it also requires development of part of the PPS. Because this task is usually challenging for do-it-yourself developers, partially intrinsic tools are used mainly by professional developers.

EXTRINSIC TOOLS

An extrinsic tool is unable to constitute any part of a PPS, yet its software can aid a developer's implementation efforts. An example of such a tool is a *compiler*, which is a piece of software that converts commands stated by a developer (in terms of a programming language) into equivalent commands that can be more readily processed by a computer. Such a tool can be used by a developer to produce parts of the decision support system's PPS (e.g., to go along with the part of a PPS provided by a partially intrinsic tool). It can also be used to produce certain KS contents (e.g., a solver). This latter use is of interest to some do-it-yourself developers.

ANOTHER VIEW OF TOOLS

There is another way of looking at development tools that has gained some prominence in the DSS literature. It involves three technology levels: specific DSS, DSS generator, and DSS tool (Sprague and Carlson 1982). We have called a *specific DSS* a DSS. A *DSS generator* is a "package of hardware/software which provides a set of capabilities to build specific DSS quickly and easily" (Sprague and Carlson 1982, 10). *DSS tools* are "hardware or software elements which facilitate the development of specific DSS or DSS Generators" (Sprague and Carlson 1982, 10–11).

The distinction between a DSS and the facilities with which it is built is an important one. The second and third levels represent an effort to suggest that DSS implementation tools differ, as indeed they do, but this dual characterization of those differences is not entirely clear. What does it mean to build a DSS quickly and easily, versus slowly and arduously? The dividing line is unclear and would seem to depend very much on the developer's traits and the nature of the DSS being built. A piece of software that qualifies as a generator for one DSS may not for another DSS (i.e., it takes longer or is more difficult). Similarly, a generator suggests that something is generated, yet very few tools exist that actually generate parts of a DSS, as opposed to aiding in their implementation. For such reasons, the DSS generator versus DSS tools classification is not

 used in this book.

8.4   INTERFACE STYLES OF TOOLS

Looking at tools in terms of the knowledge-management techniques they offer gives insight into basic functions that can be incorporated into DSSs implemented with them. Looking at tools in terms of the roles they can play during implementation gives insight into what developers will need to do in producing operational DSSs. Yet another way of looking at tools is in terms of interface styles. This view gives

A DSS DEVELOPMENT SYSTEM

Beyond the notion of using individual tools for building decision support systems is the idea of an environment for DSS construction (Ghiaseddin 1986). Called a DSS development system (DSSDS), it involves a coordinated *system* of intrinsic and extrinsic tools.

"The philosophy of the DSSDS is based on two very simple, but also very important concepts: (1) the use of highly automated tools throughout the development process and (2) the use of prefabricated pieces in the manufacturing of a whole piece whenever it is possible. The first concept increases the productivity of the developer in the same way an electric saw improves the productivity of a carpenter over a handsaw. The second concept increases the productivity of the developer analogous to the way a prefabricated wall increases the productivity of the carpenter in building a house. . . . The DSSDS environment can be thought of as a workshop with many tools and prefabricated parts that the developer can use throughout the process of building

 a new DSS or to upgrade or repair an existing DSS" (Ghiaseddin 1986, 198).

insight into how users will be allowed to interact with DSSs built via various tools. Every user does not prefer the same interface style, and user's interface style preferences can change over time. They can depend on the nature of the task a user is trying to accomplish (i.e., the substance of requests to be made or the substance of responses to be presented).

DEFINING AN INTERFACE

From a DSS perspective, an **interface** is a shorthand way of referring to the language system, the presentation system (PS), the portion of the PPS software that accepts the former and produces the latter, plus any linguistic or presentation knowledge in the KS. To a DSS user, we might say that the user interface *is* the system (Bennett 1983). It is a user's point of contact with the DSS. Ideally, the interface should be adaptable and consistent (Sanker, Ford, and Bauer 1995). Adaptability means that an interface is easy to learn (being compatible with individual users' own unique expectations and ways of doing things), allows graceful shifting from one task to the next, provides a high level of guidance and feedback based on a user's prior interactions with the system, gives each user the sense of being in control, and provides different interface styles to suit different users or the same user at different points in time. *Interface consistency* means that requests and responses should be clear and unambiguous across users, from one application to another, and over time.

Some say that a user interface is the most important aspect of a DSS (Sprague and Carlson 1982). Empirical studies have shown that the nature of its user interface can influence the impact a DSS has on decision making (Benbasat, Dexter, and Todd 1986: Dickson, DeSanctis, and McBride 1986; Sobol and Klein 1989; Webster 1990). Thus, it is vital for a developer to understand what kind of user interface a tool provides or what kind of customized user interface can be developed with the tool.

DEFINING USER FRIENDLINESS

It is often remarked that a good user interface is a **user-friendly interface** or is easy to use. But what do friendly and easy really mean? This question and its answer are often ignored, as if everyone knows and agrees about the terms' meanings. Thus, used by themselves to describe a particular user interface, the terms are

INTERFACE FLEXIBILITY

DSS development tools vary with respect to how much latitude they give for designing and implementing a DSS's interface. For an intrinsic tool, the degree of latitude available for customized interfaces depends on the nature and extent of linguistic or presentation knowledge that the tool allows to be stored in the KS. These govern how much the developer can augment the basic, ready-made LS and PS furnished by the tool. For an extrinsic tool, the degree of latitude depends on the nature and extent of facilities the tool gives a developer for producing interface portions of PPS software. For a partially intrinsic tool, interface latitude depends on what linguistic or presentation knowledge can be stored in the KS and on the latitude allowed by other tools in constructing the full PPS.

practically meaningless. However, they do begin to be sensible when we identify who the user is and in what tasks that user is engaged when interacting via the interface. As Figure 8.2 suggests, the notion of user friendliness is not only related to a specific interface, but is also user dependent and task dependent.

In the Eye of the Beholder   Like beauty, user friendliness is in the eye of the beholder (e.g., Benbasat and Dexter 1982; Dos Santos and Bariff 1988). What one person regards as an excellent interface may be seen as too primitive, inflexible, or simplistic by someone else. On the other hand, the latter's preferred interface may be viewed as overly complex, too hard to learn, or even mind-boggling by the first person. Such differences are partially due to variations in communication styles preferred by people. But they may also reflect different levels of experience in computer usage. What a novice regards as straightforward can seem too limiting to an experienced user. What an experienced user regards as straightforward can seem arduous or baffling to a novice.

Of course, a novice or occasional user may eventually become a seasoned user, meaning that he or she may outgrow what was once a satisfactory interface. Thus, it is beneficial for a tool to display interface versatility and adaptability. The first lets a user choose from among multiple interface styles to suit his or her preferences at any given time. The second lets a developer repeatedly customize a DSS's interface in response to changing user preferences. It is conceivable that a DSS could even do this adaptive customization itself based on its interactions with a user (Dos Santos and Holsapple 1989).

Task Dependency   User friendliness is also task dependent. An interface style preferred by a user for a particular problem may be seen as cumbersome when that same user faces a different kind of problem. For a certain degree of problem complexity, we would like to maximize the simplicity in stating that problem (i.e., in making a request via the interface). By simplicity, we mean conciseness (not too detailed), obviousness (unadorned, non extraneous), and consistency (familiar

FIGURE 8.2   Factors Affecting User Friendliness

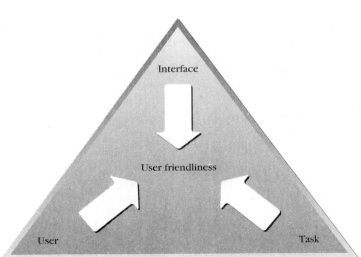

expressions). Similarly, for a certain degree of solution complexity, we would like to maximize the simplicity with which that solution is presented (i.e., simplicity of a response via the interface). In other words, the interface should provide a good fit between LS/PS and problem/solution. Because a decision maker can face a range of tasks, interface versatility and adaptability are again important.

Thus, for a given user and task, a user-friendly interface is one that minimizes user effort in expressing requests and in interpreting presented responses. What kinds of language systems do tools allow for expressing requests and what kinds of presentation systems do they allow for presenting responses? We first summarize the main LS possibilities and then the main PS possibilities. Keep in mind the fact that a particular tool may allow more than one of the LS possibilities as well as multiple PS possibilities.

LANGUAGE SYSTEM POSSIBILITIES

A common way of classifying user interfaces is based on the style of the language used for issuing requests. Prominent stylistic categories include command-oriented, natural language, menu-driven, forms-oriented, question/answer, direct manipulation, and speech-recognition interfaces (Hutchins, Hollan, and Norman 1986; Schneiderman 1987).

Command-Oriented Interface   In the command-oriented case, the LS contains statements that tell (i.e., command) the DSS what to do or how to do it. If a statement merely indicates what to do, without telling how to accomplish it, it is called a **nonprocedural** command. The LS contains a procedural command language if it takes a series of statements to tell the DSS what steps it needs to perform in order to accomplish the same task. Because less effort is needed to make a nonprocedural request than a procedural one, LSs containing nonprocedural commands tend to be more widely used. These are often called *fourth-generation languages,* in contrast to *third-generation languages*, which are procedural.

In order to use a **command-oriented interface**, a user must do some homework. He or she needs to learn what words can be used in a command and how

DSS IN THE NEWS

A Matter of Style

Graphical user interfaces are changing the way people interact with software. . . .

Windows, icons, dialogue boxes, buttons and other elements are just some of the features available to software designers building graphical applications. But graphics alone don't necessarily ensure ease of use. . . .

. . . Several training organizations have begun to offer courses to help . . . effectively implement graphical interfaces and set style guidelines. . . .

K. Doler, "Graphical Software Creates Style Questions for Corporate Programmers," *Investor's Business Daily,* 19 August 1992: 4.

REQUEST EXAMPLES

Command-Oriented Requests

Procedural commands:

```
TEMP-TABLE = PROJECT ON SUPPLIER (NAME, COST,
   LEAD-TIME)
RESULT=SELECT * FROM TEMP-TABLE WHERE PART="XJ7"
   AND COST < 7.82 AND LOCATION="MIDWEST"
LIST RESULT
```

Corresponding nonprocedural command:

```
SELECT NAME, COST, LEAD-TIME FROM SUPPLIER WHERE
PART="XJ7" AND COST < 7.82 AND LOCATION="MIDWEST"
```

Natural Language Requests

```
SHOW ME THE COST AND LEAD TIME FOR EACH MIDWEST
   SUPPLIER OF XJ7 WITH A COST BELOW 7.82
```

or

```
I WANT THE XJ7 COST AND LEAD TIME FOR ALL MIDWEST
   SUPPLIERS HAVING COSTS UNDER 7.82
```

The four sample requests shown here are equivalent, in the sense that they are asking for the same response.

they must be sequenced in the command. Simply put, the user needs to learn a language, including its vocabulary and grammar. To make this easier, the trend is toward command languages that are English-like—that is, the commands look more or less like ordinary English language statements. Nevertheless, these languages tend to be fairly rigid and restrictive about what English-like commands are acceptable to the PPS.

Natural Language Interface   A **natural language** interface also involves having the user type in nonprocedural commands. However, each request is stated in the user's own native syntax. Rather than the user learning about valid commands in the LS, the DSS tends to learn the meanings of various commands posed by the user (Holsapple and Whinston 1988). In effect, the LS grows through interaction with the user, because the PPS is able to store linguistic knowledge (such as new terms or phrases) in the KS for future use.

   With a natural language interface, a DSS tends not to be fussy about use of punctuation symbols, the sequencing of words in a command, or even misspellings of words. In addition, it is able to interpret each newly entered command in the context of preceding commands it has handled. Although some DSSs let users make natural language requests, this is not an especially common interface style. The technology underlying such interfaces has not progressed to a point where all requests users make can be interpreted or where every interpretation that is made is correct.

Menu-Driven Interface   With a menu-driven interface, a request is made by choosing one of several options presented by the PPS. Together, a collection of simultaneously displayed options constitutes a **menu**. Each option in a menu may appear on a screen as a word, phrase, number, visual button, or graphical figure (called an **icon**). Upon viewing a menu, the user will see one option highlighted by a cursor. A menu's cursor might be an arrow that points at an option, a line that underscores an option, a colored or reverse-video bar that coincides with an option (i.e., causing the option to be a different color than other options), or some other visual means of highlighting. By simply pressing arrow keys or moving a mouse device, a user brings the cursor to a desired option. Either pressing a key (e.g., the Return or Enter key) or a mouse button signals that the highlighted option is being chosen. Thus, issuing requests with this kind of interface consists of moving the cursor and signaling choices.

A typical menu is illustrated in Figure 8.3. It is composed of 11 options (Copy, database, . . . WorkSets) presented on a single line. In general a menu's options can be spread across several lines and arranged in columns. In this example, the cursor is highlighting the Copy option. Beneath the menu, a help message explaining this option appears. If the cursor were moved to another option, then a different help message concerning the newly highlighted option would automatically appear. Help messages for menu options are not found with all menu interfaces. As another variation, users are sometimes allowed to make option choices without moving a cursor. To pick the Print option, for instance, a user might merely press the P key rather than moving the cursor to that option before signaling the choice.

Sometimes a request is made not by choosing an option from a single menu but by selecting a series of options from a sequence of menus. Upon choosing an option from the first menu, a second menu is presented. Choosing an option from it may cause the presentation of a third menu of options. This sequence continues until the user has made enough choices to constitute a complete request. For instance, upon picking the Graph option in Figure 8.3, a new menu may appear with options such as Pie, Line, Area, Bar, and Scattergram. Choosing the Bar option from this second menu could yield a third menu with such options as Clustered, Stacked, and Solid to allow the user to request a graph in which bars are clustered, stacked, or three-dimensional. In summary, the LS of a DSS having a menu interface will contain a keystroke sequence (or mouse manipulations) corresponding to each request.

Forms-Oriented Interface   As with a menu-driven interface, a **forms-oriented interface** gives guidance to users. That is, a user's request is made with respect to a computer presentation. In the forms-oriented case, that presentation is an elec-

FIGURE 8.3   A Sample Menu

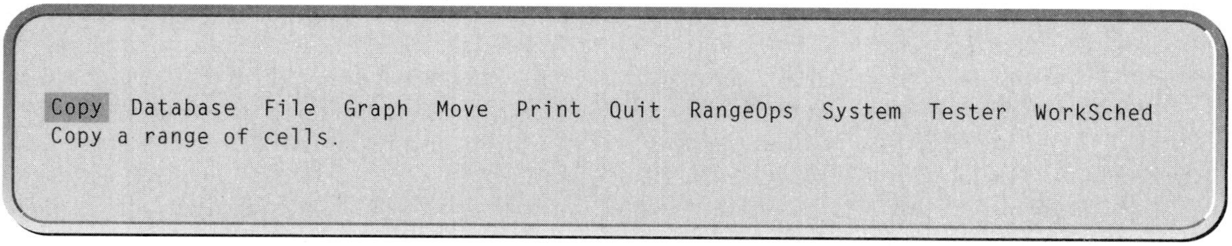

```
Copy  Database  File  Graph  Move  Print  Quit  RangeOps  System  Tester  WorkSched
Copy a range of cells.
```

tronic rendition of a common paper form. Unlike a menu, a form can contain slots that are to be filled in by the user as well as presented words, numbers, and icons. Rather than making a request by selecting from among presented options, the user fills in the blanks in the form or edits value that have been filled in previously.

Figure 8.4 shows a sample form that might be presented to a user. To request a calculation of what the new salary would be if the current monthly salary were increased by some percent, the user would type data into the Name, Monthly salary, and Increase slots. Initially, the cursor would be in the Name slot. After the user types a name and presses the Enter key, the cursor jumps to the next slot, and so forth, until all slots are filled. At any point, the cursor can be moved back to a prior slot (e.g., with arrow keys) to edit what has been filled in there. As shown in Figure 8.4, filling in the first three slots causes the requested amount to be presented in the form's New Salary slot. With a forms-oriented interface, the LS contains possible entry sequences for filling in various forms.

Question/Answer Interface   Menu-driven and forms-oriented interface styles are very common for decision support systems. Another common interface style is the **question/answer interface**. Here a user makes a request by answering a question (or series of questions) presented by the PPS. This interface is actually a very simple form, consisting of one slot to be filled in, following a slot label expressed as a question. Unlike the form case, once the user enters an answer, he or she cannot return to edit it while working on subsequent answers. That is, each answer is part of a separate, very simple form.

For instance, a user may see the question

On what drive should the results be stored?

and react by typing **B**. Then, another question is asked:

FIGURE 8.4   A Sample Form

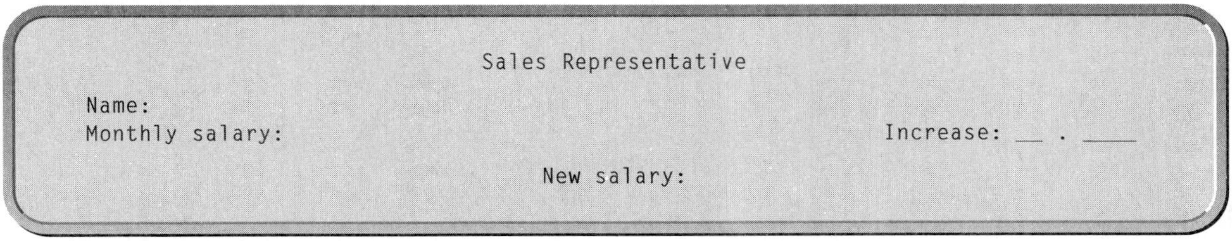

Sales Representative

Name:
Monthly salary: Increase: __ . ____

                         New salary:

a. Form before user entries

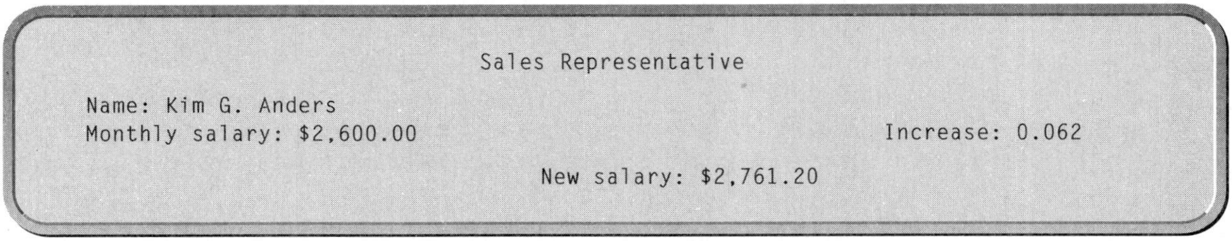

Sales Representative

Name: Kim G. Anders
Monthly salary: $2,600.00   Increase: 0.062

                         New salary: $2,761.20

b. Form after user entries and automatic calculation

```
On what drive should the results be stored: B
In which directory?
```

The user might fill in **XD**. Finally, in response to another question,

```
On what drive should the results be stored? B
In which directory? XD
In which file?
```

the user might type in **RESULT.TXT**. By answering these three questions, the user has requested the DSS to store results in a file named Result.Txt in the XD directory on drive B. In other words, the sequence B, XD, Result.Txt is one element of the LS.

Direct Manipulation and Graphical User Interfaces   Forms-oriented interfaces are a special case of **direct manipulation interfaces** (Schneiderman 1983). Generally, a direct manipulation interface lets users make requests by manipulating visual representations of familiar objects. An electronic form is a visual representation of the familiar paper form. It is manipulated by filling in (or editing) slots. A screenful of narrative text is a visual representation of the familiar printed page of text. It is manipulated by adding, deleting, moving, copying, and changing words. An electronic sketch of a machine or building is a visual representation of its physical counterpart. It can be manipulated by rotation, reorientation, scale changes, additions, deletions, and structural changes. The key idea here is that a request is made by acting on the visual representation of some object. In other words, elements in the LS are user actions for manipulating elements in the PS.

One especially prominent kind of direct manipulation interface is a **graphical user interface** (GUI). The best-known GUI is the interface provided by Microsoft's Windows operating system, although there are others. With a GUI, the software provides **graphical presentations**. Users issue requests by touching, pointing at, and clicking on displayed graphical objects (e.g., by way of manipulating a mouse). A common kind of graphical object in a GUI is an icon, which is a small picture representing some action a user could take. For instance, by pointing to and clicking on an icon consisting of a money bag with dollar signs on it, the user could request the execution of a financial application. An icon could also represent some object involved in a request. For example, a user might point to a displayed name on a file stored in the KS. Holding down the mouse button, this name could be visually dragged to an icon looking like a trash basket in order to delete the corresponding file.

With a GUI, the computer screen is organized into one or more rectangular **windows**. Each window can be regarded as giving a view into some executing application software, allowing a user to see results of its processing. Clicking on an icon that represents a window brings that window into view. Depending on the nature of the application, a window may present text, tables, graphs, diagrams, menus, forms, still pictures, motion pictures, and so forth. A window may contain other windows, or multiple windows may overlap. Because a window is often too small physically to show everything of interest, it is equipped with scrolling facilities to bring desired presentations into view. Also, window positions and sizes can be changed as desired. A window can have hot spots. When a user points to one, related information is presented (e.g., to present help text about the use of window contents).

Speech Recognition   A final interface style of making request, *speech recognition*, deserves mention, even though it is not yet available through as many tools as those noted previously (Allen 1984). A user makes a request by speaking to the system. As in the natural language case, various technological issues remain to be resolved. Nevertheless, as these are addressed, this approach to making requests may prove beneficial in at least some kinds of decision support settings (e.g., in situations of extreme crisis or demanding split-second decisions).

Having reviewed various ways of making requests, we note that it is not uncommon for a single tool to employ or make available multiple interface styles. It may allow menu and command-oriented ways of accomplishing the same decision support task. Or, it may combine menu and question/answer elements in the scope of making a single request. The important point is that, when assessing a prospective development tool, a developer should be aware of what style(s) of requests that tool will allow resultant DSSs to exhibit to their users.

PRESENTATION SYSTEM POSSIBILITIES

As we have seen, a PS consists of presentations made to assist users in making requests and those made to show users the result of some knowledge-manufacturing activity. Each of these two categories can be further subdivided.

Assistance Messages   **Assistance messages** from a DSS include responses inherent in reactive interface styles. For example, there are the questions in a question/answer interface, menu options for a menu-driven interface, labels for fill-in slots in a form-oriented interface, and displays for users to act on in a direct manipulation interface.

Assistance messages also include help information that users request and help that is automatically presented (e.g., with the menu in Figure 8.3). Diagnostics are a third kind of assistance message. These messages indicate that an error exists in

DSS IN THE NEWS

Toward More Natural Interfaces

. . . John Diebold, who has been advising corporate clients on computer automation for more than 35 years . . . is the chairman of J. D. Consulting Group Inc. . . .

One of the biggest trends, Diebold says, is that computer makers will emphasize portability and more natural ways of inputting and retrieving information.

Pen-based computers are one example. These "electronic note pads," which can read handwriting, use an electronic pen, or stylus, to input and manipulate data. . . .

Wireless communication, by satellite or radio waves, will help reduce the size of portable units to the point that only the computer screen will be visible to users, Diebold predicts.

Voice input technology will also reduce the need for keyboards in some other applications, he says. . . .

B. Deagon, "What Will Next Five Years Bring for Users of Computer-Related Technology?" *Investor's Business Daily*, (13 March 1992): 8.

the user's request or an error was encountered in the course of manufacturing knowledge. An error message can necessitate either a correction of the former request or full entry of a new request.

Result Messages   Most DSS **result messages** that show results of a knowledge-manufacturing activity tend to be textual or graphical. In **textual presentations** a basic distinction exists between free-form presentations and those that are form oriented. Some examples are shown in Figure 8.5. In the free-form case, a presentation is shown as a stream of text filling all or some portion of the video screen. This form is most appropriate when the result is a narrative passage, such as a commentary, subjective assessment, or qualitative description. It is most common when the development tool has some text-management capability.

In contrast to free-form textual messages, there are more structured textual presentations. For instance, a tool may allow results to be shown in a tabular display composed of labeled columns of words and numbers. Another common example is the presentation of results in a grid composed of cells containing words and numbers. This is typical with tools encompassing the spreadsheet technique.

Aside from tabular and grid forms, there are highly customized forms whose slots are arranged in neither tables nor grids (recall Figure 8.4 (b)) and whose slots are used to present results rather than issue requests. Tools incorporating form-management or report-generation techniques of knowledge handling allow developers to store such customized presentation knowledge in a KS.

In addition to textual messages, there are graphical presentations, as shown in Figure 8.6 on page 249. Ordinary business plots include bar charts, scattergrams, line graphs, area graphs, and pie charts. Many of these are allowed by tools having graphics-management capabilities. Less common are DSS development tools that

FIGURE 8.5   Sample Textual Presentations

```
    For each product line, a region is given an annual sales target by the KC
vice president of sales. The vice president also determines the commission rate
for each product line. In addition, each product line has a particular GMR (gross
margin rate) which indicates the percentage of its sales that constitutes the
gross profit before deducting selling expenses.
    In our region the product targets, commissions, and gross margin rates are
as follows:

        ID      Name          Target     Commission    GMR
        ---     ----------    ------     ----------    ---
        ROM     romance       235000        .024        .64
        BUS     business      175000        .022        .34
        PSY     psychology    102000        .018        .36
        REF     reference     224000        .019        .38
        PHO     photography    86000        .020        .28

The region s total target for these five products is $820,000.
```

a. Free form textual narrative

FIGURE 8.5   Sample Textual Presentations—Continued

```
Page 1

TID  FNAME   PID    Q1     Q2     Q3     Q4     QYR     S1     S2     S3     S4    SYTD MAJOR

0    Kim     ref   6040   8309   7844   9402   31595   7024   7732   8090    0    22846ture
0    Kim     bus   7320   8050   6400   8503   30275   6854   8120   6908    0    21882true
0    Kim     spo   5400   6300   7839   8390   27929   6240   5995   8032    0    20267true
1    Kris    rom   9003  10229   8340  11340   38912  10050  12453   8032    0    30535true
1    Kris    psy   8090   6209   7765   7590   29654   7540   7900   8059    0    23499true
1    Kris    bio   7400   6209   7200   8005   28895   7604   6905   8349    0    22858true
2    Kevin   pho   7400   6209   7200   8904   29794   7604   6905   8349    0    22858true
2    Kevin   sfi   9439   8378   8050   9872   35739  10390   8639   8765    0    27794true
2    Kevin   spo   6509   7734   6698   7590   28531   7773   8090   6879    0    22742true
2    Kevin   bus   3009   4321   2789   3456   13375   4321   6500   2509    0    13330false
2    Kevin   ref   3214   2345   3256   6112   14927   4322   2444   3459    0    10125false
3    Tina    psy   3214   2345   3256   6112   14927   4222   2444   3459    0    10125false
3    Tina    bus   6903   7538   8990   9311   32742   3944  10339   8004    0    24307true
3    Tina    com   5388   4399   7900   7980   25667   5944   8888   9042    0    23874true
3    Tina    rom   5000   4678   4215   3998   17889   4590   3997   5032    0    13619true
4    Toby    rom   4982   4678   8744   7432   25836   5009   3997   9037    0    18043true
4    Toby    psy   5000   4006   6007   6900   21913   2307   4839   7050    0    14496true
4    Toby    bus   4842   4006   5302   4980   19130   5003   5903   4003    0    14909true
5    Kerry   psy   4842   4006   5302   4980   19130   5003   5903   4003    0    14909true
5    Kerry   ref   6050   4985   3001   5883   19899   5590   4660   6320    0    16790true
5    Kerry   pho  10700  11009   8443   7930   38082  12222  11980   8332    0    32534true
6    Karen   bus  10700  11009   8443   7930   38082  12222  11980   8332    0    32534true
6    Karen   rom   6040   5020   5555   6666   23281   6090   5900   6904    0    18894true
6    Karen   com  12090  11069  10806   9665   43630  13121  11590  10075    0    34786true
7    Kathy   pho   8553   7543   5678   6779   28553   7884   7903   6236    0    22023true
7    Kathy   ref   4679   5568   5002   3998   19047   5032   4002   4398    0    13432true
7    kathy   sfi   4339   4229   3989   4867   17423   4360   4271   3339    0    11990true
8    Jackie  bio   4339   4229   3989   4867   17423   4360   4271   3339    0    11990true
8    Jackie  ref   5004   4678   3998   6012   19692   4996   5400   3600    0    13996true
8    Jackie  spo   5004   4468   5830   7223   22525   5345   5400   6200    0    16945true
9    Carol   rom   5004   4468   5830   7223   22525   5345   5400   6200    0    16945true
9    Carol   bus   3997   4378   4832   3901   17108   4005   4436   4998    0    13439true
9    Carol   com   6903   5882   6031   8456   27272   9488   9321   7021    0    24830true
```

b. Structured tabular display

readily allow the computerized presentation of customized drawings, sketches, and diagrams.

Another possible kind or graphical presentation involves the portrayal of pictorial images. These portrayals range from on-screen photographs to animated scenes and three-dimensional visualizations of real world objects. Although hardware requirements for the latter kinds of graphics are relatively costly, they are becoming progressively less expensive and may become ordinary parts of PSs in the not-too-distant future.

Apart from textual and graphical presentations, there is a third category of results messages: speech synthesis. Unlike the other two, it is not visual but audio. The

FIGURE 8.5   Sample Textual Presentations—Continued

```
     :A        :F        :G        :H        :I        :J        :K        :L
 1:                    Jack Vander                                                    :
 2:                         .                            Per Mile:                    :
 3:Hotel:                                                  0.22                       :
 4:Meal:                                                Mile/day:   Rate:             :
 5:                                                      110.00     0.30              :
 6:               Meal      Enter-                                                    :
 7:Name           Total     tainment   Phone    Postage   Mileage    Misc.    Totals :
 8:
 9:Kevin          284.37     71.09     155.00   118.00    580.80     80.00   1445.67:
10:Kim            273.00     68.25     155.00   118.00    562.65     83.20   1377.40:
11:Kris           284.37     71.09     155.00   118.00    580.80     76.80   1442.47:
12:Tina           307.12     76.78     155.00   118.00    617.10     89.60   1598.21:
13:Toby           293.48     73.37     155.00   118.00    595.32     64.00   1486.84:
14:Kerry          273.00     68.25     155.00   118.00    562.65     72.00   1366.20:
15:Karen          273.00     68.25     155.00   118.00    562.65     89.60   1383.80:
16:Kathy          278.69     69.67     155.00   118.00    571.72     67.20   1397.31:
17:Jackie         307.12     76.78     155.00   118.00    617.10     76.80   1585.41:
18:Carol          284.37     71.09     155.00   118.00    580.80     88.00   1453.67:
19:TOTALS:       2858.54    714.63    1550.00  1180.00   5631.60    787.20  14536.80:

\border left 1
#J3*(#J5*21  #C9*#J5*.75)
```

c. Structured grid display

FIGURE 8.6   Sample Graphical Presentations

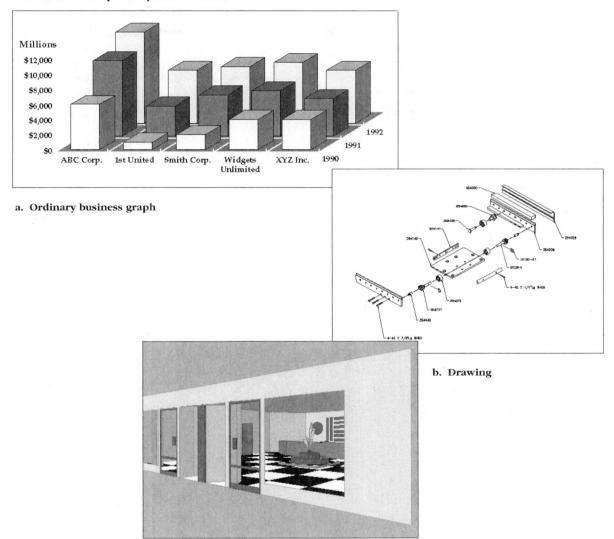

a. Ordinary business graph

b. Drawing

c. Pictoral image

DSS audibly tells a user what the results are. Of course, assistance messages could also be handled this way. Such a capability is not easily or inexpensively implemented with most DSS development tools, but with advances in technology this situation may change.

Any or all of the foregoing approaches to presenting results messages might be allowed with the chosen development tool(s), although some are more likely than others. Thus, it is possible for a DSS to employ some combination of these approaches. If a developer designs the PS before selecting a tool, then that selection can be only from among tools that allow the designed PS to be implemented. Conversely,

ARTIFICIAL REALITY

Carrying direct manipulation to an extreme is the notion of artificial reality, sometimes called virtual reality (Gupta 1992). With this as yet very expensive kind of interface, a user interacts with an artificial reality constructed by a computer. Foreshadowed by the technology of flight simulation, an artificial reality interface allows ". . . the user to inter-act with the computer in an intuitive and direct format and to increase the number of interactions per unit of time. The ultimate objective of artificial-reality research is to develop a simulated environment that seems as real as the reality it depicts. The pro-foundest strength of the interfaces, however, may lie in their ability to go beyond reality itself, by modeling in concrete form abstract entities such as mathematical equations and by enabling users to surmount problems of scale . . ." (Foley 1987, 128).

There are three main facets of an artificial reality interface: realistic visual imagery, realistic behavior of images, and interactions comparable to those with the physical world. These combine to give the user a sense of being in and acting upon an artificial-ly created reality. With present systems such as those devised by NASA, a user wears a special helmet and gloves. The helmet is equipped with viewing monitors, sensors to track head position or eye movement, and a microphone. The gloves are wired to detect finger and hand movements. The viewing monitors show graphic displays of some artificial world. To give a sense of depth, each eye is provided with a different perspective of the scene. Moving the head or eyes lets a user see a different part of the artificial world, panning the artificial vista. Images of the user's hands appear in that vista, moving and orienting themselves to reflect the actual hand and finger positioning detected by the gloves. Requests are made by pointing, gesturing, altering hand images to manipulate graphical objects, or talking into the microphone. System responses are given in terms of changes in the viewed scene (e.g., a revision to the existing scene, shift to a different vista, or movement of objects within a vista), tactile feedback via the gloves, or audio messages.

if a tool is selected before PS design, then that design must conform to what the tool allows. In any event, preferable approaches for a particular PS depend (as with the LS) on user tastes and the nature of the results that need to be packaged.

8.5 TECHNIQUE INTEGRATION IN TOOLS

Knowing about the interface styles allowed by tools gives us a way to understand the possibilities for integrating users with DSSs in decision-making teams. Another impor-tant kind of integration is concerned with the coordination of multiple knowledge-management techniques within a single DSS (Holsapple and Whinston 1984; Watabe, Holsapple, and Whinston 1991). If a development tool encompasses more than one technique, how can they be coordinated in the context of working on a single (or series of) decision problem? If multiple tools are used in the development of a DSS, how are the techniques they furnish to be coordinated when working on decision problems? Answers to these questions depend on the styles of integration offered by various development tools.

From a user's point of view, problems do not always fit neatly into traditional knowledge-management pigeonholes. For instance, a user may face a complex problem that is not strictly a spreadsheet, data-management, text-management, or rule-management issue. Rather, every one of these software approaches (and perhaps others as well) may be useful in helping a user successfully address the problem. Each technique is attuned to dealing effectively with certain aspects of a complex problem. However, no one of them is able to handle conveniently all aspects of the problem. Integrating diverse knowledge-management functionalities is an important step in the direction of supporting complex decision activities.

DSS IN THE NEWS

Virtual Reality for Decision Makers

Jeff Marshall envisions a day when securities traders will use exotic "virtual reality" computer technologies to model portfolios and execute trades with the flick of a finger or the kick of a heel.

Marshall, a senior managing director at Bear, Stearns & Co., may not have to wait long. . . .

Most people see virtual reality as little more than video arcade entertainment. . . . [R]esearchers . . . usually think of the technology in its most sophisticated form, as a computer-generated world of sights and sounds that the user enters by donning a helmet-like, stereoscopic viewer and manipulates with hand or body movements, by using "data gloves" and bodysuits covered with circuits and fiber-optic sensors.

The technology doesn't have to be so complicated, however, nor does it require exotic hardware. . . .

Some of the largest and most sophisticated financial services firms are looking at ways to use the technology. They see potent analytical tools in a technology that can provide dynamic, interactive representations of complex functions like investment portfolio modeling.

Virtual reality software can be used to provide a three-dimensional display of securities and various financial data arranged by country and industry. In some systems, an individual can use a joystick, stylus or data glove to massage the data, changing the value of one variable and prompting the program to automatically adjust the other variables to show likely results of the initial change. . . .

Researchers say imaging technologies drawn from virtual reality systems can help analysts and trainees understand complex mathematical interrelationships. An analyst can see instantly how a change in one component of a multicurrency interest rate swap—say the dollar value of yen—affects the other parts, simply by moving one part of an object depicted on a computer screen. . . .

As prices move and markets change, the symbols move around on the screen, change color and in other ways signal to the viewer the changes in their value and relationship to markets and other securities. . . .

T. Bunker, "Virtual Reality is Put to Test by Highly Demanding Securities Industry," *Investor's Business Daily*, 22 April 1993: 4.

INTERFACE OPTIONS

Language system approaches
1. Command-oriented
2. Natural language
3. Menu-driven
4. Form-oriented
5. Question/Answer
6. Direct manipulation
7. Speech recognition
8. Combinations

Presentation system approaches
1. Assistance messages
   a. Guide user's requests
   b. Help text
   c. Diagnostics
2. Results messages
   a. Textual
      i. Free-form
      ii. Form-oriented
      iii. Tabular
      iv. Grid
   b. Graphical
      i. Plots
      ii. Drawings
      iii. Images
   c. Speech synthesis
   d. Combinations

But what does *integration* really mean? In some quarters, integration is a vague notion. In others, it is nice-sounding buzzword used to characterize and market software products. Among the more serious-minded, its meaning is more definite but very often colored by familiarity with particular tools. For instance, a developer familiar only with the Lotus 1-2-3 tool is likely to have a very different idea of integration than a developer familiar only with another tool that involves a different approach to integration.

Here we focus on several distinct styles of integration. A clear grasp of these integration possibilities can be extremely helpful to DSS developers and users faced with complex problems. Researchers have devised a simple—yet powerful—framework for understanding possible types of **software integration**. It also gives a good basis for classifying, comparing, and contrasting the various software tools that are candidates for DSS development. The framework identifies five distinct types or styles of software integration. Each can be seen as a different arrangement of four elemental building blocks: program, knowledge, knowledge manipulation, and knowledge transfer.

INTEGRATING KNOWLEDGE-MANAGEMENT TECHNIQUES

1. Across tools
   a. Via knowledge format conversion utilities, export/import facilities
   b. Via a clipboard
   c. Via a common format (confederation)
2. Within a tool
   a. Via nesting of techniques
   b. Via technique synergy

In this context, a *program* is a software tool designed to manipulate knowledge in certain well-defined ways. For such manipulation to be feasible, the knowledge must be organized in computer storage in a manner required by the program. For instance, the Lotus 1-2-3 program cannot directly manipulate knowledge organized in a computer file used by Microsoft's Word program, and vice versa. *Knowledge transfer* refers to the act of copying knowledge from one repository to another, possibly reorganizing it along the way. For instance, knowledge organized in a computer file that 1-2-3 can use might be transferred to a file that Word can use.

INTEGRATION VIA KNOWLEDGE CONVERSION

Often, the knowledge that can be manipulated by one program cannot be manipulated by another, because it is not organized to be compatible with what the second program requires. Nevertheless, we may want to exercise the software capabilities of both programs in the course of working on some problem. Because these capabilities were not designed to work in tandem, they can be integrated only in an indirect way: by operating on the same knowledge. This result is possible only if a conversion facility exists that can transfer data from one kind of organization (often called a *format*) to another. This process is called **knowledge conversion**.

Converting from One Knowledge Representation to Another   Figure 8.7 summarizes this relatively weak, but common, type of integration. The indicated conversion may be accomplished by a utility that is separate from P_1 and P_2, or program P_1 may have an export facility built into it that can produce K_2 from K_1. In neither case is P_1 able to manipulate K_2. In addition, a reverse transfer may be needed, which would require another conversion utility or an export facility in P_2. Clearly, either conversion utility must comprehend the formats of both K_1 and K_2. In some cases the two formats may be so different that coming up with a meaningful conversion utility becomes exceedingly difficult or there is substantial loss of knowledge during a conversion.

Limitations   Even where a conversion is workable, this type of integration is far from ideal. It requires time and effort to carry out the knowledge transfer. The user must exit from program P_1 and invoke program P_2 before the replicated knowledge in K_2 can be manipulated. In fact, the user may need to repeat this switching process many times in the course of solving a problem. Not only is this process an

FIGURE 8.7   Integration via Knowledge Conversion

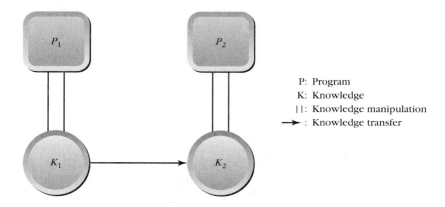

P: Program
K: Knowledge
||: Knowledge manipulation
→ : Knowledge transfer

inconvenience, having to deal with switching mechanics may disrupt the decision maker's thought process to the extent that ideas are lost. Depending on the tools used, a developer may be able to implement a part of the PPS that handles the mechanics when a user needs to switch knowledge-manipulation gears.

Because the same data exist redundantly in two places (using two different formats), maintaining consistency can become a real concern. For instance, whenever the contents of K_1 are updated, K_2 will no longer be consistent with K_1 (and vice versa) unless another conversion is performed. The cumbersome nature of this type of integration is further exacerbated as the number of programs grows. For example, when there are four formats, we need 12 conversion utilities to allow for complete knowledge transformation between any pair of formats and back again.

INTEGRATION VIA A CLIPBOARD

Another type of integration that involves switching back and forth among separate programs makes use of a common intermediate format. As Figure 8.8 shows, we transfer K_1 contents to an intermediate repository, from which they can be transferred to K_2 for later use by P_2. Each transferral involves a conversion either to or from the intermediate format, the key notion being that all knowledge transferral is mediated through this format.

A Clipboard Intermediary   The intermediate data repository is called a **clipboard** and every program designed to follow this integration style normally has two conversion facilities. One allows it to transfer (cut or copy) knowledge to the clipboard. The other allows it to transfer (paste) knowledge from the clipboard into a format that it can process. This approach to data transferral is somewhat analogous to the Federal Express system of parcel transferral, with the clipboard corresponding to Memphis.

Pros and Cons   At first glance, the clipboard approach to integration may appear more complex than the approach in Figure 8.7. But it actually has several advantages. For instance, when four formats (aside from the clipboard format) are involved, only eight conversion facilities are needed to support complete two-way knowledge transfer among four programs. Once the user transfers knowledge to the

FIGURE 8.8   Integration via a Clipboard

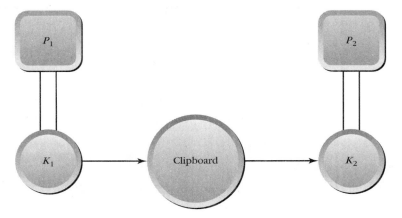

clipboard, he or she can transfer it to the formats of many other programs. The user can easily see the clipboard contents at any moment. Going a step further, the programs may even be able to manipulate directly clipboard contents, as illustrated in Figure 8.9.

Because integration via a clipboard is really a variation of the integration by conversion depicted in Figure 8.7, it shares some of the same drawbacks. To employ diverse software functionalities, the user must switch from one program to another. To achieve an integration effect, the user must explicitly engage in knowledge-transfer operations. Switching and transfer activities tend to interrupt or disrupt the flow of a problem-solving process. The practical difficulties stemming from knowledge redundancy still exist with this type of integration. For instance, the same bit of knowledge can be represented in K_1, K_2, and the clipboard. Care must be taken to maintain consistency among these multiple versions of the same knowledge as it is updated.

FIGURE 8.9   Manipulating Clipboard Contents

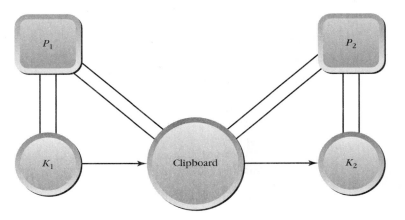

FIGURE 8.10   Integration via Common Format

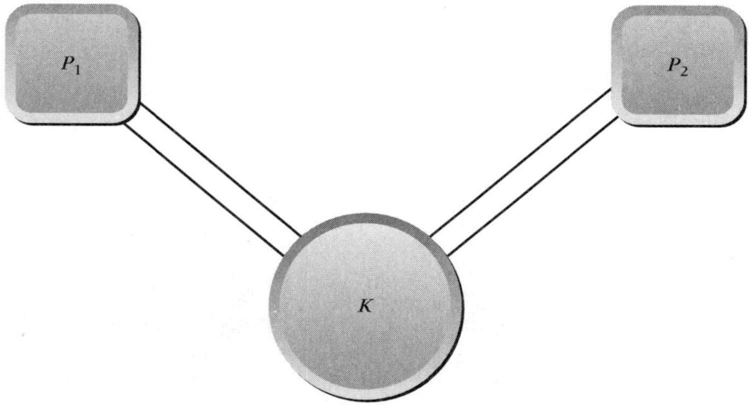

INTEGRATION VIA A COMMON FORMAT

Another strategy for integrated use of separate programs is depicted in Figure 8.10. Called the **confederation** approach to integration, it is structurally a simplification of Figure 8.9. Because there is only one format for representing knowledge, the necessity of knowledge transfer is eliminated. The idea of a clipboard is replaced by a single knowledge repository, whose format is compatible with the manipulation capabilities of multiple programs. Each tool offers a different kind of software functionality (e.g., spreadsheet, graphics). An early example of this type of integration was VisiCalc and its companion software tools, all of which were capable of manipulating the same DIF (data interchange format) file in distinctive ways.

Even though this type of integration still requires switching among programs, it does eliminate the inconvenience of knowledge transferrals. It also reduces potential consistency problems that can result from knowledge redundancy. On the other hand, the invention of a single format for knowledge representation that is universally applicable to a wide range of software functionality is difficult. As the range widens, the needed format is likely to become increasingly complicated in terms of the options it must provide. Moreover, the knowledge manipulation is likely to be less efficient than in the case of a program using a format specially designed to suit its functionality (e.g., as in Figure 8.7).

INTEGRATION VIA NESTING

Each of the preceding integration types uses knowledge to bind diverse software functionalities that are available as independent programs. In contrast to integrating multiple tools, another style of software integration incorporates functionalities of distinct knowledge management techniques into a single program. Figure 8.11 shows one way of accomplishing this, called **nested integration**. Its structure is derived from Figure 8.10 by nesting capabilities of P_2 within P_1. The result is a single program having all the P_1 functionality and serving as a host environment for P_2's functionality. The format of K is amenable to manipulation by both the P_1 and P_2 aspects of this single tool's functionality. As a variation, K may include multiple knowledge-representation formats.

FIGURE 8.11   Nested Integration

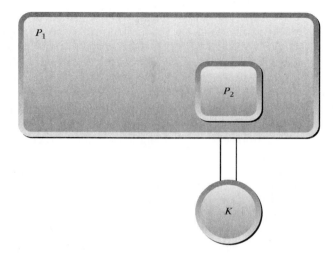

Perhaps the best-known example of the nested integration style is the Lotus 1-2-3 program, in which modest graphics functionalities are nested within an extensive spreadsheet functionality. An important advantage of this type of integration relative to those cited earlier is that there is no need to switch among programs. As with the confederation style, nested integration also eliminates the need for knowledge transfer and reduces redundancy.

On the other hand, this method of integration is not balanced. The P_1 functionality dominates the other software functionalities embedded within the tool. A user cannot readily use secondary functionality without knowing how to use the dominant functionality. In practice, the dominant functionality tends to constrain the use, capabilities, and/or capacities of secondary functionalities. In Figure 8.10, by contrast, functionalities of program P_2 can be used without even knowing about the existence of tool P_1. Its capabilities and capacities are not constrained by the independent P_1.

SYNERGISTIC INTEGRATION

An alternative strategy exists for incorporating the functionalities of multiple knowledge-management techniques into a single program. This type of integration takes a balanced view in which no functionality dominates any other. Any can be used without a knowledge of the other. For instance, graphs can be generated without knowing about or using spreadsheets. Conversely, there is no need to be familiar with graphics in order to carry out spreadsheet analyses. Thus, there is an aura of independence, even though all exist as aspects of a single program tool. However, a user is also free to exercise multiple functionalities in a single operation. For instance, a database retrieval command may also refer to spreadsheet contents and a spreadsheet-manipulation request may automatically entail some database processing.

In this approach to software integration, conventional dividing lines between knowledge-management techniques begin to disappear. For instance, where database management leaves off and spreadsheet management begins becomes somewhat unclear. Various kinds of processing that are impossible with the other types of integration suddenly become straightforward (see Holsapple and Whinston (1986, 1988) for many examples). Because the total resultant effect is more than the sum of the individual effects, this type of integration is called **synergistic integration**.

As Figure 8.12 shows, one program is able to work with knowledge in a variety of formats. This ability does not mean that the tool is merely able to import knowledge in various formats from the other programs. It can directly manipulate knowledge represented in multiple formats. Structurally, synergistic integration is the reverse of the confederation of independent (albeit compatible) programs shown in Figure 8.10. It allows the use of multiple knowledge-representation formats, each specially designed to suit a certain functionality provided by the tool P. This mitigates the convenience, efficiency, and complexity concerns noted for the confederation style.

The knowledge-manipulation facilities of P are designed such that multiple knowledge formats can be used in a single manipulation request. For instance, suppose K_1 denotes a format for representing reasoning rules and K_2 denotes a format for spreadsheet representation. Where there is synergistic integration, the program P is able to accept a request for inferring some advice from rules K_1 that make use of spreadsheet values K_2. Conversely, it can also process a request for spreadsheet evaluation if values in the spreadsheet are determined by conducting inferences with rules K_2.

Where there is synergy, no data transfer in the sense of Figures 8.7 through 8.9 is required, although it can certainly be allowed if desired. That is, P in Figure 8.12 could have the capability of converting K_1 into K_2, and vice versa. With synergistic integration, no cutting and pasting is required. There is no issue of switching among programs, because there is only one program. There is no operational imbalance in access to diverse functionalities. There are none of the inefficiencies and limitations that can result from being restricted to a single format, as in Figures 8.10 and 8.11. There may even be some program economies relative to Figures 8.7 through 8.10 by eliminating processing redundancies existing in P_1 and P_2.

FIGURE 8.12   Synergistic Integration

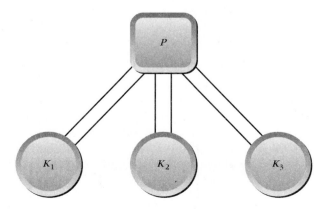

APPLYING THE INTEGRATION FRAMEWORK

Interestingly, integration framework diagrams can be used to understand integration possibilities that do not even involve software. For instance, P_1 might be interpreted as a person's problem-processing capabilities. Similarly, P_2 could be viewed as a different set of problem-processing capabilities possessed by another person. As Figure 8.7 suggests, these processing capabilities may be integrated by transferring knowledge that P_1 manipulates into a form that P_2 can manipulate. A translation (i.e., conversion) occurs during this transferral. This type of integration is roughly analogous to what happens in a meeting of the United Nations General Assembly.

In Figures 8.8 and 8.9, there is a common representation approach that every person understands in addition to his or her own native knowledge representation. Each person can manipulate a native representation and can cut and paste with respect to the "clipboard Esperanto." Figure 8.10 corresponds to an integration of human processing capabilities in which every person understands and has access to the same body of represented knowledge. A manager controls the switching among these persons with different processing specialties.

Figure 8.11 resembles the situation where one person has acquired at least some part of another person's processing capabilities and can exercise them in the context of the original, dominant capabilities. Use of the new capabilities is conditioned and colored by experience with the dominant capabilities. This is the specialist who has extended the processing specialty to encompass aspects of traditionally foreign processing methods. Figure 8.12 corresponds to the renaissance person who is more or less equally adept in a wide variety of problem-processing capabilities and conversant with many knowledge representations. Any one or more of the diverse capabilities can be exercised at will in dealing with a problem.

COMBINATIONS

To get the needed knowledge-management techniques, a developer can select and integrate multiple tools, each offering one or more of the techniques, or the developer can select a single tool in which all the needed techniques have been integrated. When integrating separate tools, some combination of integration styles may be employed. For instance, tool integration to achieve technique integration within a DSS can involve both the use of conversion utility programs and a clipboard. When a tool provides multiple techniques, some may be integrated in a nested fashion, whereas others are synergistically available. The synergy can be one-sided (e.g., a database request is able to reference spreadsheet contents, but a spreadsheet request is unable to make use of knowledge represented in a database file). Exercises in supplemental workbooks illustrate one or more of the integration styles within and across tools.

8.6 SUMMARY

Development tools are essential for building DSSs. The tools chosen for developing a particular DSS strongly influence not only the development process, but also the features that the resultant DSS can offer to a user. Available tools can be examined from several vantage points that help in understanding their influences on the process and product of DSS development. This chapter presented four of these perspectives: technique orientation, role in development, interface styles allowed, and integration approaches.

A particular tool is oriented toward one or more knowledge-management techniques. Conversely, a particular technique (in its many possible variants) is offered by more than one development tool. Thus, tools can be categorized in terms of the knowledge-management techniques they furnish. A spreadsheet tool offers some variant of the spreadsheet technique for knowledge management, a database tool provides some variant of a database technique for managing knowledge, and so on. Although many tools tend to emphasize one technique or another, vestiges of additional techniques are often apparent. Some tools furnish healthy doses of multiple techniques (such as a spreadsheet tool that is also a database tool).

A different way to classify tools is based on their roles in a development process. We can distinguish among (1) an intrinsic tool, which will serve as the PPS of the developed DSS, (2) a partially intrinsic tool, which will serve as part of the DSS's problem processor, and (3) an extrinsic tool, which does not participate in that PPS. An extrinsic tool helps the developer produce all or part of the PPS or to create some portion of the KS contents. Do-it-yourself development trends to rely primarily on intrinsic tools. Tools in the other two categories are of interest primarily to experienced or professional developers.

Development tools can be differentiated with respect to interface styles they allow to be incorporated in DSSs. A DSS's interface is defined in terms of its LS, its PS, its PPS facilities for interpreting, assisting, and packaging, and its linguistic or presentation knowledge held in the KS. With respect to the LS, an interface style refers to the means available for users to make requests. Possibilities include command-oriented, natural language, menu-driven, form-oriented, question/answer, various kinds of direct manipulation, and combination interfaces. With respect to the PS, assistance messages can follow the foregoing styles. Result messages can be classified as textual (free-form and structured) versus graphical. Developers are well advised to be familiar with all these possibilities and to be aware of which ones a tool allows.

Another important angle from which to study development tools involves the types of integration they permit within DSSs. This approach is relevant whenever multiple knowledge-management techniques are employed within the bounds of a single DSS. These techniques may be integrated within a single tool or across multiple tools. In the former case, nested and synergistic integration are distinct possibilities. In the latter case, integration can be via direct format conversion, clipboard, or confederation approaches. These five integration styles have various advantages and disadvantages relative to each other. It is not unusual for more than one of them to be employed in a single DSS. Subsequent chapters explore individual knowledge-management techniques that are subject to integration.

▲ IMPORTANT TERMS

assistance messages	command-oriented interface
clipboard	confederation

direct manipulation interface
extrinsic tool
forms-oriented interface
graphical presentations
graphical user interface
icon
interface
intrinsic tool
knowledge conversion
knowledge-management technique
knowledge-management tools
menu

natural language
natural language
nested integration
nonprocedural
question/answer interface
result messages
software integration
synergistic integration
textual presentations
user-friendly interface
window

▲ APPLICATION TO THE OLYMPICS CASE

1. Why was a DSS needed in the Olympics case?
2. From a user's point of view, what does this DSS do?
3. What were the general objectives of the DSS?
4. What knowledge-management techniques were included in the development tool(s)?
5. Describe the main concepts used to organize the DSS's database.
6. Make an educated speculation about what intrinsic (or partially intrinsic) tool may have been used in building the DSS. Explain. Do the same for an extrinsic tool.
7. Do you think a fixed or flexible solver approach was used in developing this system? Why?
8. Why was a graphical knowledge-management technique used to produce elements in the DSS's presentation system?
9. For each of the following interface styles, give an example of how such a style might have been used in the scheduling DSS:
   a. Give an example command.
   b. Give and example of a natural language request.
   c. Give an example menu.
   d. Give and example form.
   e. Give an example of a question/answer sequence.
   f. Give an example of making a request via direct manipulation.
10. Give an example of an assistance message the DSS might present. Do the same for a result message.
11. In the course of manufacturing a scheduling decision, why would it be useful to have a DSS that integrates database management and solver management? Lacking such integration, what would need to be done?
12. Suppose a tool was used that integrated database and solver management in a nested fashion. Which should be the dominant knowledge-management technique, and why? What would be the disadvantages of using such a tool?
13. If a synergistic tool were used, what could you say about the KS contents?

▲ REVIEW QUESTIONS

1. How many tools can offer a particular knowledge-management technique?
2. How many techniques can be provided by a particular tool?

3. What are the categories of implementation tools? Describe how they differ from each other.
4. Why are intrinsic tools more popular among do-it-yourself developers?
5. In terms of the generic DSS architecture, what is a DSS's user interface?
6. What major factors influence a DSS's user friendliness?
7. How does a form-oriented interface differ from a menu-oriented one?
8. What are the main approaches to presenting results of a knowledge-manufacturing activity? How do they differ?
9. What are the three basic kinds of assistance messages that can be found in a presentation system?
10. Which integration styles are concerned with integrating knowledge-management techniques that exist in separate tools?
11. Which integration styles are concerned with integrating knowledge-management techniques within the confines of a single tool?
12. Which integration styles use a single knowledge-representation format?
13. Which integration styles employ multiple knowledge-representation formats?
14. What is the role of a clipboard?
15. How do synergistic and nested integration differ from each other?
16. What are relative advantages and disadvantages of the clipboard and nested integration styles? Of the confederation and nested integration styles?
17. In what case will technique integration require the integration of independent tools?

▲ DISCUSSION TOPICS

1. What advantages might a partially intrinsic tool have over an intrinsic tool?
2. Discuss the relationship between easy-to-learn and easy-to-use systems.
3. Explain how operations activated by function keys can be thought of as forming an implicit menu.
4. Discuss advantages and disadvantages of each interface style.
5. Cite situations where each kind of result message is preferable to others.
6. Develop a general formula for the number of conversion utilities needed to permit two-way knowledge transfer among n formats in the case of integration via knowledge conversion utilities. Repeat for integration via a clipboard.
7. What are the drawbacks of knowledge redundancy? Does it have any benefits?
8. Explain why one-sided synergy is similar to nesting.
9. How does a chosen development tool influence the process of building a DSS?
10. How does a chosen development tool influence what features the resultant DSS can offer to a user?
11. Describe a decision support setting where artificial or virtual reality would be a valuable kind of user interface.

▲ REFERENCES

Allen, F. B. 1984. Cognitive factors in human interactions with computers. In *Directions for human/computer interaction*, edited by A. Barde and B. Schneiderman. Norwood, N. J.: Ablex.

Andreau, R., and A. Corominas. 1989. SUCCCES92: A DSS for scheduling the Olympic Games. *Interfaces* 19, no. 5.

Benbasat, I. and A. S. Dexter. 1982. Individual differences in the use of decision support aids. *Journal of Accounting Research* 20, no. 1.

Benbasat, I., A. S. Dexter, and P. Todd. 1986. An experimental program investigating colour-enhanced and graphical information presentation: An integration of the findings. *Communications of the ACM* 29, no. 11.

Bennett, J. L. 1983. *Building decision support systems.* Reading, Mass.: Addison-Wesley.

Dos Santos, B. L. and M. L. Bariff. 1988. A study of user interface aids for decision support systems. *Management Science* 34, no. 4.

Dos Santos, B. L., and C. W. Holsapple. 1989. A framework for designing adaptive DSS interfaces. *Decision Support Systems* 5, no. 1.

Dickson, G. W., G. DeSanctis, and D. J. McBride. 1986. Understanding the effectiveness of computer graphics for decision support: A cumulative experimental approach. *Communications of the ACM* 29, no. 1.

Foley, J. D. 1987. Interfaces for advanced computing. *Scientific American* 257, no. 4.

Ghiaseddin, N. 1986. An environment for development of decision support systems. *Decision Support Systems* 2, no. 3.

Gupta, U. G. 1992. Virtual reality: A computerized illusionary world. *Journal of Computer Information Systems* 33, no. 2.

Holsapple, C. W. and A. B. Whinston. 1984. Aspects of integrated software. *Proceedings of the National Computer Conference*, Las Vegas.

———. 1986. *Managers guide to expert systems.* Homewood, Ill.: Dow Jones–Irwin.

———. 1988. *Information jungle.* Homewood, Ill.: Dow Jones–Irwin.

Hutchins, E. L., J. D. Hollan, and D. A. Norman. 1986. Direct manipulation interfaces. In *User centered system design: New perspectives on human-computer interaction*, edited by D. Norman and S. Draper. Hillsdale, N. Y.: Lawrence Erlbaum.

Perratore, E. 1991. All together now: Integrated software under $200. *PC Magazine* 10, no. 14.

Sankar, C. S., F. N. Ford, and M. Bauer. 1995. A DSS user interface model to provide consistency and adaptability. *Decision Support Systems* 13, no. 1.

Scoville, R. 1991. Spreadsheets: Beyond number crunching. *PC World* 9, no. 9.

Schneiderman, B. 1987. *Designing the user interface: Strategies for effective human-computer interaction.* Reading, Mass.: Addison-Wesley.

———. 1983. Direct manipulation: A step beyond programming languages. *IEEE Computer* 16, no. 8.

Simon, J. C. 1992. *Understanding and using advanced Lotus 1-2-3.* St. Paul: West.

Sobol, M. G., and G. Klein. New graphics as computerized displays for human information processing. *IEEE Transactions on Systems, Man, and Cybernetics.* 19, no. 4.

Sprague, R. H., Jr., and E. C. Carlson. 1982. *Building effective decision support systems.* Englewood Cliffs, N. J.: Prentice Hall.

Watabe, K., C. W. Holsapple, and A. B. Whinston. 1991. Solving complex problems via software integration. *Journal of Computer Information Systems* 31, no. 3.

Webster, J. 1990. The relationship between playfulness of computer interactions and employee productivity. In *Desktop information technology*, edited by K. Kaiser and H. Oppelland. Amsterdam: Elsevier Science Publishers.

CASE STUDY

Using your understanding of decision support systems as a foundation, construct a proposal that characterizes the features and uses of a specific DSS for an application area in which you have direct experience or a particular interest. Your proposal should document your vision of a decision support system, which you can then develop in prototype form for demonstration to your classmates and instructor at the end of the course. As you construct the proposal, do so with the attitude that (1) the envisioned DSS can contribute to excellence within an organization in which it is installed, (2) the proposal will be submitted to managers in that organization for possible approval, and (3) if the proposed DSS development project is approved, you will be responsible for creating a prototype of the DSS to assess its feasibility, proposed features, and expected benefits.

Thus, your proposal should not merely describe what your analysis reveals that the DSS should be required to do. It should also explain how that DSS contributes to the promotion of excellence within an organization. It should convince upper management (a role played by your instructor) that the proposed DSS development project is worthy of resource commitments. It should be of a realistic magnitude—not nearly as extensive as the application cases described at the beginnings of chapters, but not entirely trivial either. The following sample proposals give a sense of what you might reasonably expect to accomplish in your own DSS development project. They are edited versions of actual project proposals submitted by students who went on successfully to develop and demonstrate the proposed DSSs. The sample proposals shown here have been selected to illustrate diverse application areas.

PROPOSAL FOR A VARIANCE ANALYSIS INVESTIGATION DSS, *BY MARY CURTIS*

ORGANIZATIONAL CONTEXT

This proposal involves an electronics company that manufactures four products that could all be classified as medium-level technology. The company is decentralized by product line and therefore uses cost control as a way to supervise the divisions. There is a high degree of command unity in the company, because each person reports to only one person, but the command chain is weak in that broad ranging and unstructured communication is encouraged. There are few layers of management—only three in the central office and three in the divisions.

The patents for all products are purchased from others, so no R&D is performed here. Company policy states that the patents can not have been used before they are bought. Therefore, all products are unique to this company, with varying degrees of competition from other similar products. Two of the current products are mature, in that the company has been making them for more than 5 years. A third product has been in production for 18 months and is "settling in." The fourth product, which was added only 3 months ago, still has a few bugs in the manufacturing process.

DECISION MAKERS

The decision makers are in middle management, at the control level. They are the highest-ranking managers in their respective divisions. The DSS will be used by four decision makers (one for each product) and may also be used by other managers for supervisory purposes or for planning.

The decision, made monthly, is semistructured because there are portions that can be programmed and other portions that require involvement of a knowledgeable decision maker. The knowledge required for the decision is strictly internal to the organization. In making the decision, a decision maker must consider some qualitative factors, such as the behavior that could result from a particular decision. The decision will affect material and human resources. The decision strategy is to optimize to the extent possible, considering that it is both semistructured and contains some qualitative factors. The phases of decision making that will be supported include both intelligence and design. The system will help gather and analyze data. It will also help solve some problems required by the decision maker. The decision spans both the financial and production functional areas.

DECISION SUPPORT PROVIDED BY THE PROPOSED SYSTEM

The decision to be supported is whether to investigate the cause of a variance when one occurs. Cost and usage of raw materials, labor hours, and overhead are budgeted for each product. When actual usage or cost exceeds these standards, variances occur. An investigation of the cause of the variance could determine if the variance is due to a factor of which management should be aware or to something that should be corrected. However, because investigations are costly, they should not be performed when the variance is minor or when the cause is cyclical and a normal occurrence for the business. The following factors should be considered in the decision:

1. Whether a variance occurred
2. Whether the variance was significant
3. The cost to investigate it
4. Other (qualitative) reasons to investigate (or not), such as the degree of need to supervise this group closely
5. Prior investigations performed for this level of variance and the cost and results of that investigation

The knowledge required during the decision making includes the following:

1. Financial data from the financial accounting system for variance calculations
2. Standard costs from the budgeting system for variance calculations
3. Prior investigation information maintained within the system, including product investigated, variance amounts, costs of investigation, and the results of investigations
4. Presentation knowledge, indicating presentation format preferences for each user.

Knowledge processing that will be required includes the following:

1. Database processing to maintain historical and current financial data for variance calculations, for historical investigation information, and also for presentation knowledge.

2. Spreadsheet processing used for handling standard costs and to make variance calculations
3. Graphical output used to contrast amounts of current variances and historical variances and also to show trends in unit costs and usages

User interfaces include these items:

1. The opening menu will allow a user to enter his or her initial request:
   a. Download financial data from a mainframe.
   b. Enter user's initials and the product in which he or she is interested.
   c. Calculate variances.
   d. Analyze the variance investigation decision.
   e. Review prior investigations.
   f. Play what-if with standard costs and variance calculation.
   g. Enter the variance decision and, if the choice is to investigate, enter the cost incurred to investigate plus the results of the investigation.
2. The analyze-variance investigation function requires the following:
   a. Calculations using two different optimization approaches.
   b. Entry of other decision factors, such as the need to supervise this production group
   c. Weighting of all factors
   d. Reporting results, including details, if requested
3. The what-if questions are as follows:
   a. Show variance calculation results in a spreadsheet format.
   b. Allow a user to change standard costs, which will not be a permanent change.
   c. Recalculate variances.
   d. Analyze a variance investigation decision for initial calculations.

DEVELOPMENT PLAN

I plan to begin developing the user interfaces immediately. I will first develop a prototype, which can then be expanded into the full system I have envisioned here. After developing the interfaces, the next step will be to build the database containing financial data and the spreadsheet, which performs the variance calculation. These will make up the bare-bones portion of the system. From there I will expand as time allows.

REQUIREMENTS FOR A QUALITY CONTROL DSS, BY DAVID COOK

ORGANIZATION CONTEXT

The proposed quality control DSS is to be used in a manufacturing environment. The DSS will aid a decision maker in making quality control decisions in a production system. Therefore, the DSS will exist in an operational control setting.

As a machine or production line produces its outputs, we must assure that those outputs are of an appropriate quality. This desire creates a need to develop a system to control quality. One of the techniques typically employed to ensure that a standard level of quality is met is statistical process control (SPC). In part, SPC involves taking samples of outputs and plotting various attributes of those outputs on control charts. A decision maker is then required to examine these control charts and determine whether the process is in or out of control. A DSS can support operating personnel in making this decision.

The organization context for the proposed DSS can be further described as mature; that is, the decision is made in the context of an established situation. A high level of knowledge about the current state of the organization typically exists and a history of previous decisions should be available. These decisions can be programmed, because there are established statistical procedures to determine whether a process is in or out of control. The DSS that is to be constructed depends upon the empowerment of employees to stop a production process if it is out of control.

DECISION MAKER

As mentioned earlier, the immediate users of the DSS are operating personnel. These are the individuals who actually operate the manufacturing process. Their need is to determine quickly and effectively whether the manufacturing process is in or out of control. It is a real possibility that without the support of a DSS, the decision maker could make poor-quality decisions. That is, the decision maker could shut down the manufacturing process when it should not be shut down; the decision maker could keep the manufacturing process running when it should actually be shut down; or the decision maker could be too slow in shutting down an out-of-control process. Other variations of poor-quality decisions are possible but are not discussed here.

The decision that is to be supported is structured. Rules exist for determining whether a process is in or out of control based on control charts. A decision is made either to shut down a manufacturing process or to allow it to continue processing each time a sample is taken from that process. The timing of decisions depends upon when the observation is made. It should also be noted that the DSS is easily adaptable to various manufacturing settings.

Although the primary (or immediate) users of the DSS are operating personnel, they are not likely to be the only consumers of the support provided by the DSS. It is possible for higher-level personnel to use the information provided by the DSS as well. For example, it is possible for the quality control manager to use the knowledge contained in the DSS's knowledge storehouse. The quality control manager may use the knowledge to examine trends in the process's output. Process engineers could use the operating personnel's corrective actions, which are stored in the DSS's knowledge storehouse, as a basis for future process improvements.

DECISION SUPPORT

The basic inputs that will be accepted into the DSS are the values of the observations taken of the manufacturing process. These are data. The other raw material necessary to make the decision is the procedural knowledge that will be programmed for inclusion in the DSS. The most basic procedural knowledge required by the DSS allows the decision maker to determine whether the process is in or out of control. For example, if there is a point outside the control limits, then it can be said that the process is out of control. Several other situations also allow the decision maker to determine that the process is out of control (e.g., trends and runs).

Each time a sample is taken, the DSS will employ its knowledge-processing capabilities to determine whether the process is in or out of control. If the DSS determines that the process is out of control, then it will inform the decision maker of its assessment of the current situation. The decision maker will then have to make the decision either to shut the process down or to allow it to continue to run.

Regardless of the decision maker's decision, the DSS will save the values of observations in each sample. Further, the DSS will store the time that each out-of-control situation takes place, the decision maker's decision, the course of action taken given that the manufacturing process was shut down, the time that the manufacturing process was allowed to resume, the amount of downtime experienced, and the decision maker's name and/or identification number.

Knowledge will be represented both numerically and via English strings. In both representation schemes, the DSS will have a limited amount of processing capability. For example, the DSS will be able to understand only such short commands as yes, no, and resume. The DSS's mathematical processing ability will also be limited to the procedures programmed into it.

In addition to the descriptive and procedural knowledge that will be managed, the DSS will also have to manage linguistic, assimilative, and presentation knowledge on a limited basis. The DSS will be allowed to assimilate only certain pieces of knowledge. Those pieces are the sample observations, the decision maker's decision, the course of action taken by the decision maker, the shut-down and resumption times of the manufacturing process, and the decision maker's identification.

The DSS's presentation will be limited so that the decision support system will have no choice with regard to the nature of the presentation of knowledge. It is anticipated at this point that the decision maker will view a computer screen that displays the control chart(s) in use. Each time a new sample is taken, the DSS will plot the result on the control chart. When a situation occurs that requires a decision, the DSS will prompt the user that a decision can be made. The decision maker then responds to the decision-making opportunity. The DSS will then ask for information from the decision maker as the decision-making episode continues.

REQUIREMENTS FOR A MUTUAL FUNDS INVESTMENT DSS, *BY MEENU SINGH*

ORGANIZATION CONTEXT

Joe is an investment counselor in a medium-sized city. In the early 1990s he experienced a large increase in inquiries about mutual funds from old as well as potential new clients who didn't know beans about these funds: How do I get started? How much do I invest? In what fund? How much risk am I taking? What is a load? What is a mutual fund? With the plummeting interest rates for traditional savings vehicles, more investors had begun to take a keen interest in mutual funds. Newspaper articles, TV business news, and heresay trumpeted benefits and successes of mutual fund investing, adding fuel to the fire of mutual funds interest.

Joe saw a golden opportunity to increase his customer base if he could offer effective and efficient mutual fund advisory services. Deciding on what advice to give a customer would be far from trivial. The number of mutual funds had grown to more than 3,800. Moreover, mutual fund investment strategies need to be tailored to individual customer situations. Could he handle this load alone? Should he look for a business partner? Always keen on obtaining a competitive advantage through increased productivity and decreased costs, Joe decided to implement a decision support system. Fortunately, he had taken a DSS course at college to help him out in this new endeavor.

DECISION MAKER

Working together, Joe and the DSS will form a team decision maker (DM) that manufactures quality decisions. It is going to be a multiparticipant DM, with Joe as the deciding participant and a computer as the supporting participant. The DSS will carry out problem-solving tasks assigned to it by Joe. There will be flows of knowledge between this team's two participants.

The kinds of decisions involved will range from structured to semistructured to unstructured. Some samples of the types of specific decisions to be made are as follows:

- How much should a customer invest in a mutual fund (MF) based on his or her income, expenses, number of dependents, etc.?
- What type of MF is appropriate for a given customer based on his or her investment objective?
- Among those specific types of funds, which one(s) should be recommended to the customer?
- If a customer wants regular income from his or her MF accounts, what kind of systematic withdrawal plan should be recommended?
- Investors often feel that the market will go down as soon as they get in. Will dollar-cost averaging or value averaging be the solution for a risk-averse investor?
- When should the customer switch to a different fund? When should he or she sell?
- How will the prime rate affect MF investments?

DECISION SUPPORT

The DSS can support the DM in various ways and at different junctures. Because knowledge is a major foundation of decision making, it is the availability of knowledge in usable forms that will dictate when and in what ways the DSS can help.

1. *Structured decisions.* All the knowledge required to make the decision is available in a form that makes it straightforward to use. The actions leading to the fully structured decision can be programmed and incorporated into the DSS. It becomes the procedural knowledge.

   For example, a program can be written to set some parameters (12-month-yield, asset size, fees, expense ratio, portfolio turnover rates, and so forth) that will whittle down the list of MFs befitting the criteria. Another example is the rate-of-return calculations.

2. *Semistructured and unstructured decisions.* Often the issues pertinent to producing a decision are not well understood. Some may be entirely unknown to the DM. The knowledge required to produce a decision is unavailable, difficult to acquire, incomplete, or in a form that cannot be readily used by the DM.

   For example, what investment amount should be recommended to a particular customer based on his or her household income, expenses, number of dependents, steadiness of income, etc.? To answer each questions, Joe has to exercise imagination and an exploratory attitude. The use of such faculties is likely to be guided by some general reasoning strategies for unstructured decisions, and these can be incorporated in the DSS.

3. *DSS architecture*

   a. *Language system.* The linguistic activities may include

- A customized main menu interface to issue requests to the DSS (also some submenus as needed);
- Customized visual forms to collect, revise customer/MF data.

For example, a form for an MF company might contain information such as total assets, current yields, turnover ratio, expense ration, and beta.

b. *Presentation System*

The messages emitted by the DSS may consist of

- Graphical presentations of some decisions;
- Textual responses;
- Displays of results via customized visual forms.

For example, a systematic withdrawal plan or dollar cost–averaging activity may be depicted with the help of a bar graph.

c. *Knowledge system.* The following types of knowledge about the DM's environment are anticipated in the knowledge system:

- Procedural knowledge
- Reasoning knowledge
- Descriptive knowledge
- Assimilative knowledge

For example, the DSS may contain assimilative knowledge about how long to retain historical data about MF companies or which MF companies should be discarded from the knowledge storehouse. Descriptive knowledge will reside in the form of MF companies' data.

The database-management techniques will be employed to accurately track and selectively recall descriptive knowledge in a relational database about MF companies that satisfy a particular need.

The spreadsheet technique may be used to manage descriptive and procedural knowledge about customers' data.

The rule-management technique will be employed to deal with two sets of rules in the KS: the first to recommend the feasible amount of investment, the second to determine the best MF category and the specific fund or funds to invest in.

REQUIREMENTS FOR A SOFTWARE MARKETING DSS, *BY SKIP BENAMATI*

INTRODUCTION

This proposal is concerned with a computer company's Kentucky trading area (KTA). It proposes to introduce a decision support system to support KTA management in managing resources. We are trying to increase revenues and profit in these areas while we continue to cut resources, especially human resources, to keep our expenses to an absolute minimum. Our main objective is profit, as we all know, and we have been given numbers to meet both for revenue and profit in the software arena. To meet these numbers with our limited marketing resources, we need to be able to make smarter decisions in the following areas: technical support training and focus, software pricing, and sales incentives.

A step was taken in this direction with a previous project that implemented the software marketing opportunity evaluation system (SMOES). Marketing representatives and systems engineers are using this expert system to assist them in choosing and prioritizing support opportunities to pursue. The proposed software marketing support system (SMSS) will build on this effort. SMSS will package SMOES with a software marketing forecasting system (SMFS) to allow decision makers to make informed decisions in the three areas just listed. A function for storing opportunities evaluated by SMOES will be added to the current system. These stored opportunities will provide the input for SMFS.

PRIMARY DECISION MAKER

The primary user of SMFS will be the manager given responsibility for software numbers. The role of this manager is to make sure that the KTA stays on a track that will allow us to reach or exceed the "software bar." To accomplish this, the abilities to track actual figures, forecast, and analyze discrepancies are essential. Typically these activities are done on a monthly basis as our month end sales totals are finalized. The kinds of questions we must consider include: Are we missing key skills that would allow us to chase other opportunities, can we offer incentives to shift some of our software marketing efforts, or can we discount some software to allow it to be more affordable to customers who are not buying because of monetary restraints. By using the information and what-if analysis that will be available in SMSS, making decisions about these questions will be easier. The software manager and SMSS will work as a team to make recommendations to the KTA management team in these areas.

SMSS OVERVIEW

SMSS will take advantage of several knowledge-management and processing techniques. SMOES already uses forms and rule management along with database management to evaluate opportunities. SMFS will add to these on-line report generations at both a summary and detail level, along with using programming and business graphics to provide information necessary to the primary decision maker.

The SMSS main menu will allow access to either SMOES or SMFS. The SMOES option will bring up the current expert system, with the added ability to store opportunities coupled with anticipated sell dates. Based on the ranking of an opportunity, it will be assigned a percentage likelihood of success. The main menu's SMFS option will bring up a forecast of planned opportunities based on time frame, revenue, and likelihood percentage. This will originally be implemented as a report, but as time allows it can be turned into a graph that portrays the information in a more meaningful format. Screen options will be given to see the detail behind the summary data from three perspectives: the forecast details by software category, the details from the software table, and the details of the stored opportunities.

An ability will be provided to do what-if analysis by changing parameters in the software, such as price, level of local expertise, and whether it is strategic or not. After making these changes, SMFS will use the SMOES rule set to reevaluate opportunities and then display the new forecast. In this way, the decision maker will be able to tinker with alternatives to find out what resource recommendations will provide the biggest payback to the KTA.

All SMSS data will be stored in relational database tables. The SMSS knowledge system will include existing SMOES data tables and two new tables. One will contain the opportunities and another will provide the numbers, which will include the yearly software quota, YTD sales, and number of the current month. The details of the opportunity table are still being determined but will include customer key, software name, likelihood of success percentage, and anticipated sale date. Existing SMOES tables for customers and software are structured as follows:

CUSTOMER

CKE	CNAME	CEXP	Revenue
AOI	Ashland Oil Inc.	HIGH	65000000
KU	Kentucky Utilities	MED	6000000
TOY	Toyota Manufacturing	MED	120000000
CSG	Cable Services Group	LOW	3000000
TJC	The Jockey Club	LOW	5000000
LEX	Lexmark	HIGH	100000000

SOFTWARE

SNAME	Cost	IMPTIM	EXPE	EMKT	EINST	ESUPP	S
Application Development	100000	6	HIGH	1	1	1	N
Case Tools	125000	2	HIGH	3	1	1	Y
Data Base Software	300000	9	HIGH	2	2	2	Y
Applications	150000	3	LOW	2	2	1	N
Office Systems	250000	3	MED	3	2	2	N
Multi Media	400000	6	HIGH	2	1	2	Y
Decision Support	150000	3	LOW	3	1	2	N
OS Performance	50000	1	LOW	1	1	1	N
Publishing	175000	2	MED	2	1	1	N
Connectivity	200000	12	MED	3	2	3	Y

DEVELOPMENT APPROACH

The approach to development will be a phased approach. The phases are as follows:

1. Create new database tables.
2. Update SMOES to allow for the storing of opportunities.
3. Create and package the forecast summary report.
4. Create and package the three detail reports.
5. Create the SMSS main menu to allow access to SMOES and SMFS.
6. Package the summary and detail reports into SMFS.
7. Add the ability to edit software parameters and rerun forecasting.
8. Alter reports where appropriate to use business graphics.

SUMMARY

The support provided by SMSS will be a further step in the right direction, given the difficult times we are facing. By adding a framework (SMSS) around SMOES and

SMFS, we are creating a base upon which we can build by plugging in additional pieces as the need arises. This truly is the basis for a KTA-wide decision support system. These are the kinds of tools that will allow us to remain competitive and continue to reach the bar in the years ahead.

PROPOSAL GUIDELINES

Ideally, you should choose an application area where you have had first-hand experience or where you have access to someone who has first-hand experience (e.g., a relative, friend, employer, or coworker). This could be experience as a decision maker, as a human decision support system, or as an observer of either of these. The main point is that prior familiarity with the chosen application area will allow you to concentrate on the intricacies of a DSS rather than identifying an application problem and learning about it from scratch. It will let you focus on how a DSS can be of value in supporting some real-world decision situation with which you are already acquainted.

Your proposal should document the results of your analysis of DSS needs and requirements in the chosen application area. As such, it should describe the organizational context in which the envisioned DSS will be used, the decision maker who will use the DSS, the nature of the decision support to be provided, and a schedule for development. The proposal's coverage of these topics can be addressed and organized in various ways. Answering the following kinds of questions can help ensure a thorough coverage.

ORGANIZATIONAL CONTEXT

1. What is the nature of the organization in which the DSS is to function?
2. What is the organization's purpose? What resources does the organization use in meeting that purpose?
3. How are the organization's managers structured?
4. Describe the main characteristics of the organization's environment.

DECISION MAKER

5. Who are the prospective users of the DSS?
6. What kind of decisions that the decision maker manufactures will be supported?
   a. What is the subject of the decision? Give examples of a couple of alternatives.
   b. Are they structured? If not, what makes them unstructured?
   c. What problems must be solved in reaching the decisions?
   d. What process or flow of steps is used in manufacturing the decisions?
   e. Describe the decision timing (e.g., hourly, daily, weekly, monthly, irregularly, once).
7. Explain how the decisions to be supported by the DSS are currently made in the organization.
8. Are there any drawbacks or limitations to the current decision approach? What are they?
9. What are the expected benefits of the envisioned DSS to the user? To the organization? To the organization's environment? Recall Section 5.4.

10. What factors (including raw materials) impact the decision making? How so?

DECISION SUPPORT REQUIREMENTS

11. What are the purposes of the proposed DSS? What is the nature of the support it is required to provide?
12. What problems will the DSS help the user solve in the course of decision making?
13. At what point(s) in a decision process will the DSS be useful?
14. Characterize the user's interaction with the DSS (e.g., LS and PS content).
15. Characterize the knowledge that is required to be managed by the DSS. What types of knowledge will be in the KS?
16. What representational techniques will be used in the KS and processed by the PPS?
17. If more than one knowledge management technique will be incorporated in the DSS, what integration approach will be used?
18. How does the proposed DSS differ from a management information system?
19. Which, if any, of the specialized frameworks described in Section 6.3 apply to the envisioned DSS?

DEVELOPMENT SCHEDULE

20. Which aspects of the proposed DSS do you plan to design and implement in your prototype?
21. Do you intend to function as a do-it-yourself developer, professional developer, or someone in between in creating the proposed DSS?
22. Describe the main activities you will perform between the time your proposal is approved and the time you will demonstrate a working prototype.
23. Prepare a schedule showing the timing of your development activities.

Part Three

KNOWLEDGE-MANAGEMENT TECHNIQUES FOR DECISION SUPPORT

Knowledge is an essential resource. Without it, a company could not operate. But knowledge in and of itself is insufficient. What good is knowledge without a mind trained to manage it? It has significance only insofar as it can be used to meet objectives, such as . . . delivering value to customers. All else being equal, an organization will be more successful if it does a good job of knowledge management. This includes the management of all types of knowledge. . . . All too often, however, knowledge management skills are taken for granted rather than being actively and explicitly cultivated.

— C. W. Holsapple and A. B. Whinston

The Information Jungle, Homewood, Ill.: Dow Jones–Irwin, 1988, p. 27.

There are numerous computer-based techniques for managing knowledge. Part Three examines more than a dozen of the most prominent and important for use in decision support systems. Each of these knowledge-management techniques is described from two angles. First, we outline the facilities a technique furnishes for representing knowledge as various kinds of objects in computer memory. Second, we consider the methods that it provides for computerized processing of those knowledge objects. The sequence in which we cover knowledge-management techniques roughly progresses from the most elementary, familiar techniques to those that are perhaps more complex or likely to be less familiar.

Implementations of each technique vary from one development tool to another. Even for a particular tool, specific features change as new and improved versions of it reach the market. Thus, we make no attempt to cover the detailed workings of an implementation of a knowledge-management technique. Instead, we focus on the core essentials of each technique. This approach provides an understanding of fundamental differences among techniques that are candidates for use in DSS development. It provides a basic grasp of the capabilities offered by each technique, thereby giving a solid foundation for learning about specific features of knowledge-management techniques embodied in various development tools.

In concert with studying Part Three, we recommend that students (or instructors) identify the techniques of greatest interest. For instance, which would be of greatest benefit in a student project that aims to build some specific DSS? The identified techniques can then be studied and used in the context of a particular tool or tools to reinforce the more general coverage offered here. The selected tool or tools can be whichever happens to be already available to students or especially appropriate to their needs. Numerous tutorial supplements (e.g., softbound use guides or exercise workbooks) are available for popular tools.

Chapter 9 begins with an examination of expression management. This is perhaps the simplest of knowledge-management techniques but one that is often integrated with other techniques in DSS development tools. The bulk of this chapter is concerned with techniques that are especially useful for representing and processing descriptive knowledge: text management, hypertext management, and database management.

Chapter 10 concentrates on knowledge-management techniques that are very suitable for the representation and processing of procedural knowledge: solver management, spreadsheet management, and program management. Closely related to these is menu management, which involves linguistic and presentation knowledge about the use of alternative procedures in a DSS.

Chapter 11 considers other techniques oriented toward managing linguistic and presentation knowledge: forms, report, and graphics management. In addition, it surveys rule management—an important technique for dealing with reasoning knowledge—and message management, which is concerned with the representation and processing of messages, regardless of the type of knowledge they carry.

The case study that concludes Part Three gives examples of DSSs that use multiple knowledge-management techniques. These illustrate the level of a DSS that you might build as a development project. Guidelines are provided for producing an interim design report for your project as well as a final project report documenting your accomplishments in a do-it-yourself case study.

Chapter 9

EXPRESSION, TEXT, HYPERTEXT, AND DATABASE MANAGEMENT

INSIGHTS

COAST GUARD: A DSS FOR PROCUREMENT DECISIONS

Overview

The Coast Guard's Office of Acquisition is interested in acquiring ships and aircraft. This costs money and must be justified with reasons. . . . Their underlying purpose for a DSS is to support the development of the best possible reasons for the best possible course of action in acquiring ships and aircraft.

. . . Acquisition recommendations are based on assumptions, some of which are solid, some of which are not . . . . [The Coast Guard was] asking for a system that could tell . . . easily and quickly the source and quality of a given assumption, as well as the assumptions underlying a given figure. . . . [They] wanted DSS support to help . . . examine the premises of arguments or the assumptions behind the reasons and reasoning presented in DSS reports.

System Features

. . . Max is a document-oriented DSS. . . . [It] provides two main classes of features: interactive (hypertext-style) documents and model management. . . . [They] support an analyst in developing a report recommending a course of action and giving the reasons for it. . . .

. . . [The] model representation and execution capabilities substantially exceed those of spreadsheet programs. . . . [It] can express essentially any information about a model or a variable for a model—for example, its source, its reliability, and its dimensional characteristics.

The . . . Max interface . . . provides the interactive documents, or hyper-text features. . . . The idea is to build reports in which items—including numbers—are linked automatically to pertinent information about them. . . .

System Usage

Max . . . has been delivered and is being used. . . . To give a sense of how Max works, we . . . discuss some of the features a user would employ . . . to work with ASSET, a model used by the Navy and the Coast Guard to estimate ship acquisition and life-cycle costs. . . .

We designed Max to support both analysts and executive browsers. Analysts execute models under various data scenarios. Information is returned in . . . reports. The analysts can then "copy and paste" from these . . . reports to create their own ad hoc final reports. The . . . reports are themselves interactive documents, dynamically generated with buttons . . . (hypertext links) automatically embedded in them. Copying and pasting preserves these links in both the original and duplicate copies. . . . Executive browsers have access to reports via generalized hypertext linking.

Imagine that an analyst wants to create a report comparing the total life-cycle costs for two different ships, a hydrofoil and a SWATH (a small waterplane area twin-hull) vessel. After starting the Max session, the analyst asks for a description of the ASSET model. To do this the analyst selects the describe command from a menu in Max's menu bar and then chooses the ASSET model as the subject of the command. The system produces a report that describes the ASSET model. The report resembles a word processing document. It contains text and mathematical formulae. Buttons . . . are highlighted in bold-face, indicating that further information is available about the objects they represent.

Next, suppose the analyst wants to execute [i.e., solve]. . . . ASSET . . . As a result, the system . . . generates . . . a report node comprising the major resulting

Continued

values. Each of these values is represented by a hypertext button and each button is generated and maintained by the . . . software.

The final report constructed for the executive browser is typically short. The analyst need do no explicit linking but may copy portions of system-produced reports into the final report, which the analyst may also edit.

Condensed quotation from S. O. Kimbrough, C. W. Pritchett, M. P. Bieber, and H. K. Bhargava, "The Coast Guard's KSS Project," *Interfaces,* 20, no. 6 (1990): 5–11, 13–15.

LEARNING OBJECTIVES

Unlike all the prior cases, the Coast Guard case involves a DSS in which hypertext knowledge management plays a central role. It is used to document models that the DSS solves, to hold the solutions, and to browse through those solutions. Hypertext, a natural extension of conventional text management, is of growing importance as a technique for handling descriptive knowledge in DSSs. Perhaps the most prominent means for representing and processing descriptive knowledge in a DSS is database management. We saw use of this technique in several of the prior cases. Here, we consider all these knowledge-management techniques after an examination of elementary expression management.

After studying this chapter, you should be able to

1. Describe the main features of each of the following knowledge-management techniques:
   - Expression management
   - Text management
   - Hypertext management
   - Database management
2. Explain the distinctions among these techniques in terms of the objects used for knowledge representation and the methods used to process those objects.
3. Assess the potential value of each technique for managing alternative types of knowledge.
4. Readily learn how to use software tools that embody these techniques as a basis for building your own DSSs.

Exercises at the end of the chapter allow you to check on your understanding of the knowledge management techniques presented here.

9.1 INTRODUCTION

Managers and other knowledge workers are today faced with masses of knowledge, some of it simple, some of it complex, and much of it interrelated. There are practical limits on the amount and variety of knowledge a mind can effectively deal with in a given period of time. However, computer systems in general, and DSSs in particular, can be a tremendous help in pushing back such limits (Keen and Wagner

> ### VALUE OF KNOWLEDGE MANAGEMENT
>
> Using computers to manage knowledge in a more efficient, effective manner is strategically very significant for both the individual and the organization. For an organization, it presents the opportunity of gaining an edge over competitors or at least keeping pace with competitors. For an individual, it can mean much the same. All else being equal, an individual with good knowledge-management skills is much more valuable to an organization than one with more limited skills.

1979). Much of the knowledge management work that is or has been done mentally or mechanically can now be accomplished electronically. As discussed in Chapter 5, automated record keeping and decision support have been major advances in this direction.

The trend toward do-it-yourself computing is continuing (McLean, Kappelman, and Thompson 1993). As explained in Chapter 7, this means that managers and other end users can increasingly handle many of their own knowledge-management needs without the intervention of computer professionals. It makes both the end

DSS IN THE NEWS

A Gold Collar

Wanted: Entry-level worker skilled in the newest word processing, spreadsheet and graphics software. Must perform work formerly done by three people.

Employees today must be better skilled than their predecessors, the American Electronics Association noted in its 1993 public policy agenda. Workers' living standards—and U.S. competitiveness—depend upon their mastering new technologies and more independent problem-solving. . . .

Developing and supporting a world-class work force is one of AEA's six major public policy priorities. . . .

Five years ago, one employee might handle word processing tasks while another handled spreadsheets.

Today, the same employee might be required to handle both functions. Employment specialists call these multitalented employees "knowledge workers" or "gold-collar" workers.

A recent Olsten study of 1,481 executives revealed that 70% had a strong need for workers with basic computing skills. The top priorities were for people with word processing, data entry and database management skills. The survey also found a strong need for computer skills at all levels of a company. . .

Computer literacy appears vital at all levels of the corporation. According to the Olsten survey, 71% of managers today are computer literate, double the level of three years ago. . . .

B. Deagon, "Computer Literacy is Necessary for Increasing Number of Employees," *Investor's Business Daily* 31 March 1993, p. 4.

users and computer professionals more productive at their respective jobs and goes a long way toward unleashing the full potential of computer technology, but there is a catch. Realizing this potential depends on a basic understanding of the computer-based knowledge-management techniques that can be employed in developing DSSs. Part Three summarizes a variety of these techniques as a foundation for building such an understanding.

The human mind has many kinds of knowledge-management abilities that can be exercised independently or together. For instance, in arriving at a decision without computer support, a knowledge worker might access descriptive knowledge from memory or from a coworker, analyze it with various mental procedures, sketch out graphs of the results, reanalyze the situation with altered assumptions, and write a report that presents a decision. That is, the decision maker is imbued with mental knowledge management techniques that can be applied to diverse problems and be used separately or together in addressing any one of those problems.

A decision maker's mental environment for managing knowledge is extended with computer-based techniques for managing knowledge. As Figure 9.1 suggests, a decision maker's mental capabilities can make use at any time of one or more computer-based techniques for knowledge management. Collectively, these techniques can be regarded as a world of hyperknowledge, supplementing and complementing

FIGURE 9.1   Supplementing Mental Knowledge-Management Capabilities with Computer-Based Capabilities

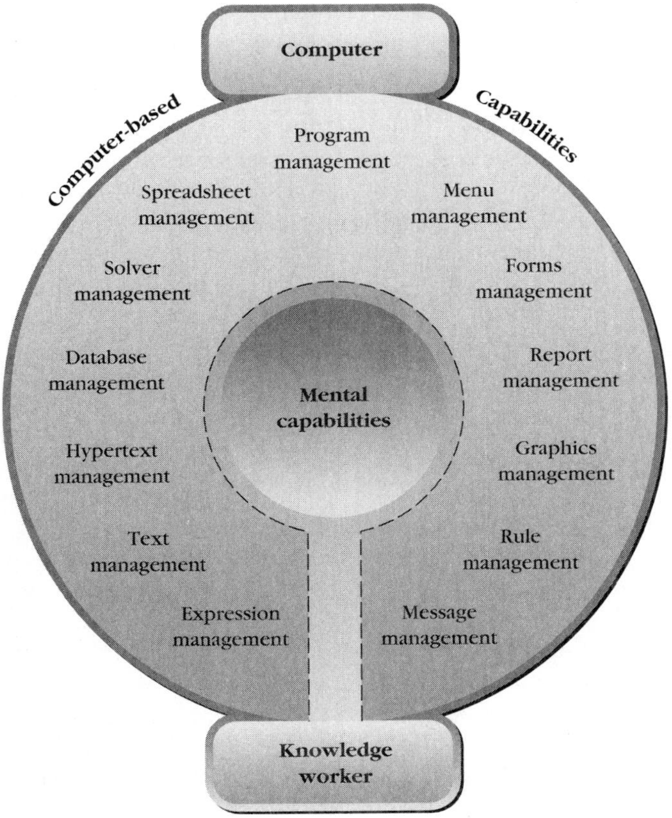

a person's innate mental capabilities (Chang, Holsapple, and Whinston 1994). The decision maker is poised at the center of this world and can use any of its capabilities at any time to supplement his or her own mental capabilities in the course of dealing with problems. From this center, the decision maker directs the computer's actions via one or more user interface mechanisms (denoted by the dashed line in Figure 9.1). As explained in Chapter 8, interface styles and the possibilities for integrating knowledge-management techniques vary considerably.

Our survey of the knowledge-management techniques shown in Figure 9.1 begins with expression management and proceeds clockwise through message management. Each technique is summarized in terms of the objects it uses for representing knowledge and the methods it provides for processing those objects. Some of the features we describe for a technique may not be available in a particular tool's implementation of that technique. Conversely, there are implementations of a technique offering features not covered in our summary of it. Our summaries focus on the common core features of each technique, leaving a consideration of variations for tool-specific books.

9.2 EXPRESSION MANAGEMENT

Expression management is concerned with (1) representing knowledge in the form of numeric, string, and logical expressions and (2) processing those representations for the ultimate purpose of evaluating them to derive new knowledge. A **numeric expression** (e.g., 12 * 2700/562) indicates how the expression manager should combine various numeric values to obtain a numeric result. A **string expression** (e.g., CITY + STATE) indicates how strings of characters should be combined to obtain a string of characters as a result. Similarly, a **logical expression** (e.g., TODAY OR TOMORROW) indicates how operands should be combined to obtain a value of true or false. In the course of making a decision, spur-of-the moment calculations such as those performed by an expression manager can be important.

Because of the universal familiarity with ordinary hand-held calculators, which are essentially rudimentary computers that do expression management, our treatment of this knowledge-management technique covers familiar ground.

REPRESENTING AND PROCESSING

A knowledge-management technique may be applicable to managing several kinds of knowledge, just as a given type of knowledge is susceptible to being handled by a mixture of one or more techniques.

Before a fragment of knowledge can be processed, it must be represented in some way. The way in which it is represented determines how it can be processed. For instance, should a sales manager represent the knowledge that Kevin is a sales representative who works in territory number 2, was hired on September 30, 1981, and has a monthly base salary of $2,500 as a sentence in a piece of text, as a record in a data base, as part of a spreadsheet, in a solver program's variables, or in some other manner? The choice depends largely on how the manager wants to process the knowledge. Just as there are many possibilities for representing a piece of descriptive knowledge, so too are there various ways for representing other types of knowledge.

Nevertheless, this coverage is important, because we use it to define some basic terms employed in describing other techniques. In fact, expression management is often integrated with other techniques. For instance, an expression-handling capability is commonly nested within tools that primarily do text, database, forms, or spreadsheet management.

We begin with an examination of objects commonly encountered in expression management. Each is concerned with a certain way for representing knowledge. We then survey basic processing methods for manipulating these objects. Each method corresponds to a type of request that can be made to the expression-management software. When that software tool serves as a problem-processing system (or part of a problem processor), these requests are in the language system, ensuing responses are in the presentation system, and objects of interest are in the knowledge system (or the problem processor's working memory) of a resultant DSS. See Figure 9.2.

OBJECTS OF INTEREST

In expression management, we want to represent knowledge in terms of such objects as variables, functions, macros, and expressions. Examples of these are given in Appendix A. Figure 9.3 illustrates components that can be involved in representing an expression, a variable, a function, and a macro. Of these, the central

FIGURE 9.2   Results of an Interactive Session Involving Variables, Expressions, and Pictures

```
_output 8*41.57 using "$ddd.dd"
$332.56
_?8*41.57 using $ddd.dd"
$332.56
_let salary=2500
_let commis=.018
_let repname="Kevin"
_let new=false
_?repname,salary,commis
Kevin    2500.00000        0.01800
_?salary+commis*10000
     2680.00000
_let salary=salary*1.1
_?salary
     2750.00000
_?salary+commis*12000>5000
FALSE
_?"Name is "+repname
Name is Kevin
_?"The salary is: ",salary using "$dddd.dd"
The salary is: $2750.00
_let pay=salary+commis*12000
_let who="Pay for "+repname+" : "
_?who,pay using "$d,ddd.dd"
Pay for Kevin: $2,966.00
```

object of interest is an expression which is either a single operand or, more interestingly, multiple operands coupled with various operators and perhaps precedence indicators. Variables and functions are important kinds of operands in expressions. Macros are objects used to save keystroke effort when interacting with expression manager software.

An **expression** tells how to calculate some desired data value. Its operands indicate what data are to be combined in producing that new data value. Its operators and precedence indicators tell how to combine them. The operands can be data values themselves (i.e., constants) or representations of data values (i.e., variables or functions).

A **variable** is merely a named storage compartment that holds a data value. Over time, a variable's value can be changed (i.e., can vary) as desired, but it must always be consistent with the variable's type (e.g., numeric, or logical). Other possible attributes of a variable include a *label* (description explaining the nature of the variable), **picture** (an indication of the format to be used in displaying its current value), and *security controls* (safeguards to govern who can access the variable's value).

A **function** is a name given to a procedure defined for calculating a desired value. A function typically has a set number of arguments, the values of which are

FIGURE 9.3   Knowledge-Representation Objects in Expression Management

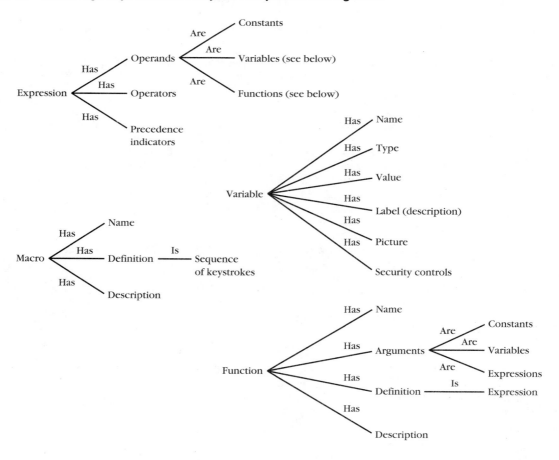

inputs to the procedure. The value that results from following the procedure becomes the value of the function. The function's definition can be a simple expression or a more complex procedure. Examples and details of functions, variables, and expressions are given in Appendix A.

A **macro** is a kind of object encountered in the implementations of many knowledge-management techniques, including expression managers. It is a name that is defined to be equivalent to a sequence of keystrokes. Whenever a macro name is entered as part of an expression, it is interpreted to be the same as having entered the corresponding keystroke sequence. Examples and details appear in Appendix A.

PROCESSING THE OBJECTS

Each kind of object just discussed is susceptible to certain kinds of processing. Each processing method corresponds to a request that can be issued to and interpreted by the expression management software. The specific syntax of these requests varies among tools that possess expression-management abilities. The extent of processing that can be requested also varies from tool to tool. Here, we make no effort to document the many variations. Rather, our approach is to identify a reasonable assortment of processing methods that could be available for each of the objects.

As shown in Table 9.1, requests can be issued to define the existence of variables, functions, and macros. Respectively, they cause space to be allocated for storing a

TABLE 9.1   Knowledge-Processing Methods in Expression Management

OBJECTS METHODS	VARIABLE	FUNCTION	MACRO	EXPRESSION
Define (Store)	For storage in KS or working memory of PPS	For storage in KS or working memory of PPS	For storage in KS or working memory of PPS	
Recall	From KS into working memory	From KS into working memory	From KS into working memory	
Show	A list of defined variables	A list of defined functions	A list of defined macros	
Specify	Variable name within an expression	Function name and names for arguments within an expression	Macro name interpretation by PPS	Expression for evaluation by PPS or in definition of function or macro
View	The name, value, type, label, picture, etc. of a specific variable	The name, definition, or description of a specific function	The name, definition, description of a specific macro	The previously specified expression
Change (edit)	The name, value, type, label, picture, etc. of a specific variable	The name, definition, or description of a specific function	The name, definition, or description of a specific macro	The previously specified expression
Delete	From KS or working memory of PPS	From KS or working memory of PPS	From KS or working memory of PPS	
Help	For assistance in understanding, defining, or using variables	For assistance in understanding, defining, or using functions	For assistance in understanding, defining, or using macros	For assistance in understanding or specifying expressions

EXPRESSION MANAGEMENT IN A NUTSHELL

Expression management is a worthwhile knowledge-management technique for inclusion in decision support systems. It involves representing knowledge in the guise of an expression and processing such knowledge to establish a value for the expression. Numeric calculations, string calculations, and logical calculations are all useful and important. Expressions can contain constants, variables, and functions plus operators to connect them. Pictures can be used to determine the appearance of calculated values when they are output. Macros facilitate a knowledge worker's flexibility in working with expressions. Using expressions for calculation recurs frequently, and development tools often integrate it with other knowledge-management techniques by nesting it within their capabilities.

variable's value, an indicated procedure associated with a function name, an indicated procedure associated with a function name, and an indicated sequence of keystrokes associated with a macro name. They also allow other attributes of these objects to be defined (e.g., labels, descriptions, pictures). Any of these three objects can also be recalled into working memory (if not already there) and then listed, viewed, changed, or deleted.

Each of the three objects can be specified within an expression. An expression can be specified for immediate problem-processing system (PPS) evaluation, with the result being displayed by the PPS. Or, it can be specified in the definition of a macro or function and thereby saved for later evaluation when that function or macro is specified in a request for expression evaluation. It is left for the reader to explore which methods are available with a specific tool and to study what the exact syntax is with that tool.

Expression-management software may respond to other kinds of requests not related to specific objects. For instance, aside from requesting help about specific objects as shown in Table 9.1, a user could request help in understanding the general nature of expression management or the specific nature of what to do in reaction to a particular error message issued by the expression manager. As noted in Appendix A, it may be possible to redefine the behavior of function keys (F1, F2, . . .). Other requests could be concerned with processing objects external to the expression-management domain. Examples include requests for executing certain operating system commands (e.g., to see a directory) or for viewing contents of disk files created and maintained by other kinds of software.

9.3 TEXT MANAGEMENT

Text management is concerned with (1) the representation of knowledge as large, free-flowing pieces of text and (2) processing those representations in various ways (Greenia 1985). Also known as *document management,* this technique has been the most widely used of all knowledge-management techniques. In their day-to-day activities, decision makers often need to prepare and use memos, letters, narrative descriptions, policy documents, directives, specifications, and notes on various topics (Fedorowicz 1989). See Appendix B for examples. These all contain knowledge, and all are susceptible to computer-based text management.

String variables are fine for storing a few strings of text, but a decision maker may need to prepare extensive notes relevant to decisions being faced. Trying to do so by assigning strings (e.g., sentences) to variables and then concatenating them in expressions would be extremely cumbersome relative to text management. Automated text management is also much faster and more convenient than conventional typing.

When composing and editing text, we work with an electronic image of the text rather than a paper version. We commit it to paper only when we are satisfied with its content. When we simply want to examine the text, it is faster to scan a single electronic image than to shuffle through several pieces of paper. Another benefit is the greater accuracy and thoroughness permitted when editing or searching through a piece of text.

It is not unusual for text-management software to include nested expression-management capabilities, giving it some capacity for carrying out simple calculations. Rudimentary spreadsheet-management capabilities are occasionally nested in text-management software (Bacon and Copeland 1991). It is also possible for implementations of the text-management technique to allow for the definition and use of macros and even the redefinition of keys. Expressions, macros, and spreadsheets are treated elsewhere in Part Three.

We begin with a simple delineation of the basic object of interest in text management: a document. See Figure 9.4. A document is characterized by the main

DSS IN THE NEWS

The Paperless Office

More than $7 billion was spent worldwide last year on products that electronically capture and digitize documents for display on computer terminals. . . .

Several image processing tools combine to make the technology work. The process usually begins with paperbound data, pictures or illustrations being electronically scanned and then digitized in computer-readable code. Images can also be directly faxed into computers, and some systems allow users to input audio and video. . . . From there, employees can retrieve and manipulate the documents on workstation terminals. . . . Users can retrieve documents in seconds instead of the several minutes or longer that it usually takes to locate paper-based data that has been filed. And the same document can be viewed by multiple people or sent electronically around the world. A third leg of image processing is a communications network to carry the data. This can range from simple computer-to-computer communication by wire on up to wireless and satellite communication. . . .

San Antonio-based United Services Automobile Association, one of the largest writers of property and casualty insurance, has linked six major regional offices through an imaging network of 1,500 terminals. Users say the system saves them a third of the time their work would take with a paper-based system. . . .

B. Deagon, "Through Image Processing, Vision of the Paperless Office is Coming Into Focus," *Investor's Business Daily* 29 June 1992, p. 3.

FIGURE 9.4   A Small Document Viewed on a Console

```
   Line:12     Col:1       a:garnote.txt   Command:
    For each product line, a region is given an annual sales target
by the KC vice president of sales. The vice president also
determines the commission rate for each product line. In
addition, each product line has a particular GMR (gross margin
rate) which indicates the percentage of its sales that constitutes
the gross profit before deducting direct selling expenses.
    In our region the product targets, commissions, and GMRs are
as follows:

        ID    Name          Target   Commission    GMR
        ---   ----------    ------   ----------    ---
        ROM   romance       235000         .024    .64
        BUS   business      173000         .022    .34
        PSY   psychology    102000         .018    .36
        REF   reference     224000         .019    .38
        PHO   photography    86000         .020    .28
```

components it can contain. We then survey basic processing methods for manipulating a document and its constituents. Each corresponds to a type of request that can be made to the text-management software—usually in the form of function keys, control keys, keystroke sequences, or mouse movements. When that software serves as a PPS (or part of a PPS), the requests are in the language system (LS), ensuing responses are in the presentation system (PS), and objects of interest are stored in knowledge system (KS) files of a resultant DSS.

DSS IN THE NEWS

No Text Processor is an Island

Suddenly, no word processor is an island. . . . Programs that once let you do little more than type and format unadorned text now serve as automated clearing-houses for spreadsheets, graphics, and databases, as well as workgroup comments and revisions . . . . All major Windows-based word processors now use OLE (Object Linking and Embedding) technology. This lets a document seamlessly incorporate "objects" created by spreadsheets, graphics packages, and sound or video recorders—even other word processors. Whereas word processors of the past often included primitive table or line-drawing functions, new versions of the same programs can use OLE to access all the functions of a full-featured spreadsheet, drawing, or graphics package.

Edward Mendelson, "Word Processors: Documents Take the Center Stage," *PC Magazine* 9 November 1993, pp. 108.

FIGURE 9.5   Knowledge-Representation Objects in Text Management

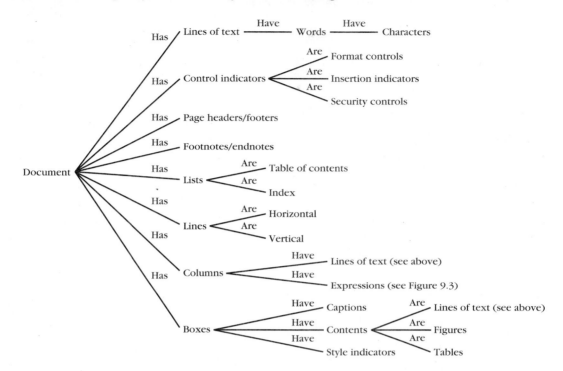

OBJECTS OF INTEREST

The central object of interest is a document. As Figure 9.5 indicates, a document can have a variety of components, ranging from ordinary lines of text to boxes holding figures or tables. Each component can itself be regarded as an object that is subject to certain kinds of processing. The textual passages contained in a document consist of lines of text. These lines may represent any of the six types of knowledge: descriptions, procedures, heuristics, and so on.

Aside from textual passages, a document may have control indicators that govern its appearance (e.g., margin width), the insertion of knowledge (e.g., text, images) from other sources, and possibly who has the ability to view or change the document. Discussion of the other objects is furnished in Appendix B. Although useful in preparing large and formal documents, they do take more time and effort to learn and use. Thus, they tend to be used less for decision support purposes than do lines of text and control indicators.

PROCESSING THE OBJECTS

Table 9.2 summarizes specific methods often encountered for processing a document, its lines of text, words in those lines, and control indicators. A document is initially specified by creating the lines of text that make up its textual passage. These may be created by simply typing words via a keyboard or by commanding the text processor to import some text from a different document into a desired position in the textual passage. Document specification can also include the activity

TABLE 9.2   Knowledge-Processing Methods in Text Management

OBJECTS METHODS	DOCUMENT	LINE OF TEXT	WORD	CONTROL INDICATORS
Specify	By creating lines of text, setting control indicators, creating headers or footers, etc.	By typing its words or importing them from another document	By typing the word	Setting format and security controls or using insertion indicators
Store	By stating the name of the KS file that will contain it	As part of the document	As part of the document	As part of the document
Show	A list of documents existing in KS			
Recall	From KS to working memory by stating name of file that contains it	As part of the document	As part of the document	As part of the document
View	By sequential scrolling, jumping to desired position, searching for a desired pattern, or printing	On a console or printed as part of a document	In current line being viewed or skipping to it as a search pattern	By examining format or security settings or insertion indicators embedded in text
Change (edit)	By editing, specifying, moving, copying, deleting lines; processing blocks; sorting entries; pattern replacement; resetting indicators; by editing, creating, deleting headers or footers, etc.	By editing, deleting, or specifying its words	By retyping, inserting, or deleting some or all of its characters by substituting a replacement pattern or thesaurus synonym for it	By altering format or security settings or insertion indicators
Check	To identify words possibly misspelled		Specific word for proper spelling	
Delete	By eliminating it from working memory and/or the KS file	By eliminating it from the document	By eliminating it from the line	By eliminating embedded indicators from document's text

of setting control indicators (e.g., to have a left margin of a desired width), creating headers and footers, specifying footnotes, endnotes, and their markers in the text, drawing lines, declaring and filling columns or boxes, and generating lists from designated words (or phrases) in the textual passage. Once a document has initially been specified, it exists in working memory, where it is subject to viewing, changing, or checking. It can also be stored in the KS for subsequent recall into working memory or eventual deletion.

Several ways of viewing a document are possible. One is to use arrow keys or a mouse to cause lines of text to scroll by in sequence on the console screen. Another is to request that lines occupying a certain position be brought into view.

LIMITS OF TEXT MANAGEMENT

Managers often need to work with pieces of text. The purpose of text-management software is to allow computers to ease tasks such as creating, storing, editing, scanning, recalling, and formatting text. Implementations of this knowledge-management technique range from rudimentary line-at-a-time editors to very extensive word processors. When text management is incorporated into a DSS, passages of text are preserved as files in the knowledge system. A user creates, edits, and scans a document by working with an electronic image of the text.

Although text management helps in storing and exploring knowledge in the guise of notes, memos, letters, and some kinds of reports, it has limitations. Suppose we want to browse through only those products whose gross margin rates exceed a certain level and whose sales target is below some specific level. We would like to do this without having to look through all the data. Text processing is little help in that regard, especially as the number of products increases. Or, suppose we try to keep track of sales representatives' performance data over the course of a year in a text file. That process involves a lot of data.

If we want to bump up everyone's third-quarter quota in a particular product line by 5.2%, how would we do it and explore its implications? Or, if we just wanted to see the first-quarter comparison of quota to sales for a particular rep on a particular product line, we would really like a more powerful processing mechanism than pattern searching through the text. Nice as text management is, there are many everyday problems of data organization and processing that it cannot handle well and some problems that it cannot handle at all.

You can request the text processor to search for and display any lines of text containing some pattern of symbols that is of interest. You can also print a document (or selected parts of it) for viewing. You can make this viewing conform to format control settings. It can include whatever is inserted in place of insertion indicators, headers and footers for pages, properly positioned footnotes and endnotes, and so forth.

In addition to viewing any of the possible contents of a document, you can request presentation of current control settings. Related to viewing is the operation of checking. Text processors equipped with spell-checkers can satisfy requests to check either the entire document or a specific word for possible misspelling.

There are numerous ways to change a document. for instance, you can issue requests to specify new lines, delete existing lines, move lines, copy lines, or edit an existing line. The latter encompasses the specification of new words, deletion of existing words, or editing an existing word. You accomplish word editing by directly retyping some of its characters, having it replaced automatically with a requested replacement pattern (e.g., requesting that Wordperfect be changed to WordPerfect throughout the document), or replacing it with a correct spelling.

It is sometimes helpful to designate some contiguous portion of text as being a block. Once you have designated it, you can process the entire block as a whole through requests to make a copy of it elsewhere in the document, to move it to another position, to delete it, to print it, to export it to another document, or to undesignate it. Other requests for changing a document include those to alter control code settings; to rotate, relocate, rescale, or use reverse video for boxes; or to specify, edit and delete headers, footers, footnotes, or endnotes.

9.4 HYPERTEXT MANAGEMENT

Although text management is good at handling individual documents, it is not well suited for rapid electronic navigation through multiple documents that have interrelated subject matter and that need to be explored in an ad hoc sequence that conforms to the decision maker's thought patterns. *Hypertext management* is more suited to such decision support needs (Minch 1989, Bieber 1990). Imagine a vice president for operations who needs to make a vehicle-procurement decision, based in part on a committee's report, consisting of a variety of documents represented and processed using text management. There are an executive summary and numerous supporting documents. Each of the supporting documents can itself have supporting documents, and so forth. Rather than a committee report consisting of documents that are handled one at a time by text-management software (see Appendix B), the report could be fashioned as a **hyperdocument.** Comprising explicitly linked individual documents, this hyperdocument is treated as a whole by the hypertext-management software.

This software handles processing requests to follow links among documents, readily navigating to and displaying any document related to the one currently being viewed (Conklin 1987). While reading the executive summary, the vice president might want to switch to the document discussing the company's projected transport needs. While reading about these projections, he or she may want to look at another document detailing the assumptions and calculations underlying the projections. Then, skipping back to the executive summary, he or she reads about one of the alternatives and determines that he or she needs to know more about it. So, he or she next views a document discussing that alternative. While doing so, the vice president makes a couple of detours to other documents examining quantitative and qualitative issues related to the analysis of that alternative. Then, it is back to the executive summary, and so forth. See Figure 9.6.

OBJECTS OF INTEREST

The major object of interest is a network of interrelated documents called a hyperdocument. As Figure 9.7 shows, a hyperdocument has individual documents, links that relate these documents into a network, and a map portraying the network's structure. Each document in a hyperdocument typically has lines of text that you can process via text-management means. Because multiple documents exist, it is convenient for each to have a unique identifying name. In some hypertext implementations, documents are called cards and are portrayed on the console as electronic images of cards (Apple 1989).

A document also contains **markers** to denote the existence of links to other documents. A marker may appear as some highlighted word or phrase (e.g., in reverse video) or as a graphical symbol called an *icon*. For instance, an executive summary document might refer to projected transport needs. If this phrase is highlighted as a marker, the VP knows that he or she could immediately follow a link to (i.e., bring into view) a related document offering more information about projected transport needs.

FIGURE 9.6   Navigating through Some of a Hyperdocument's Documents (Bieber 1992)

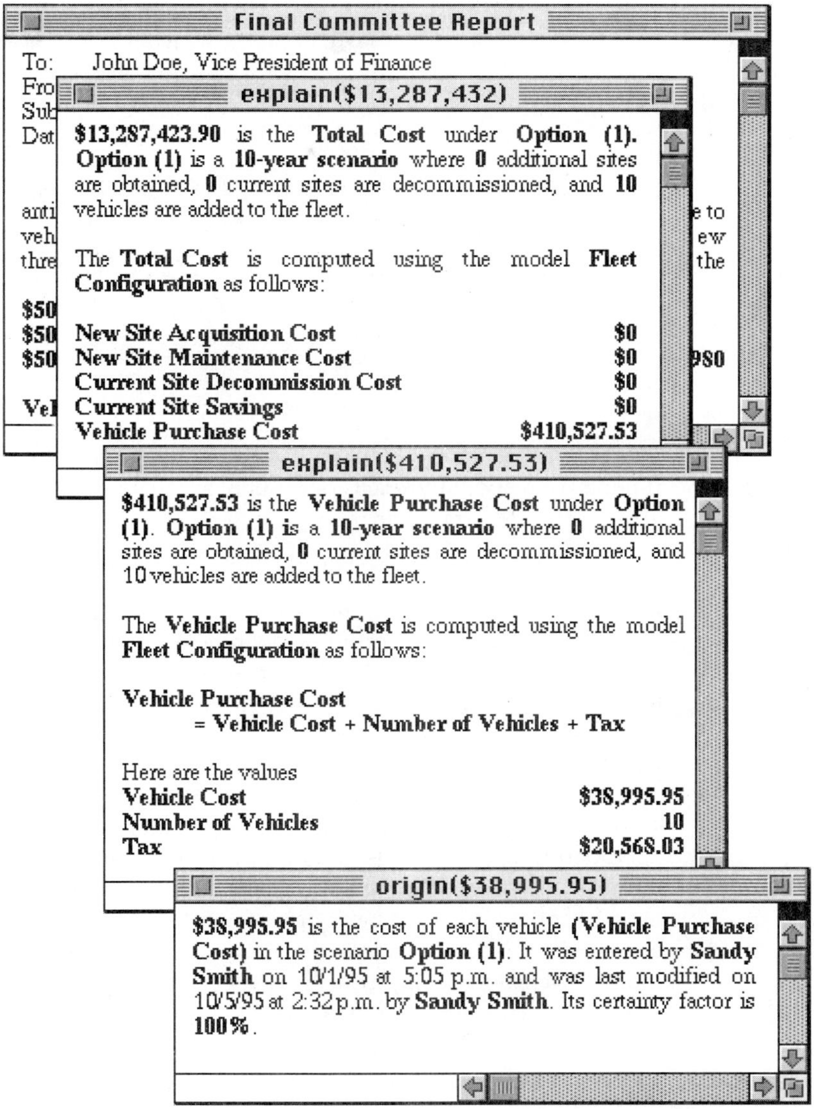

```
┌─────────────────────── Final Committee Report ───────────────────────┐
│ To:     John Doe, Vice President of Finance                          │
│ Fro┌────────────── explain($13,287,432) ──────────────┐              │
│ Sub│                                                   │              │
│ Dat│ $13,287,423.90 is the Total Cost under Option (1).│              │
│    │ Option (1) is a 10-year scenario where 0 additional sites        │
│    │ are obtained, 0 current sites are decommissioned, and 10         │
│ anti│ vehicles are added to the fleet.                 │  e to        │
│ veh │                                                   │  ew         │
│ thre│ The Total Cost is computed using the model Fleet │  the         │
│     │ Configuration as follows:                         │              │
│ $50 │                                                   │              │
│ $50 │ New Site Acquisition Cost              $0         │              │
│ $50 │ New Site Maintenance Cost              $0         │  980         │
│     │ Current Site Decommission Cost         $0         │              │
│ Vel │ Current Site Savings                   $0         │              │
│     │ Vehicle Purchase Cost          $410,527.53       │              │
│   ┌────────────── explain($410,527.53) ──────────────┐                │
│   │                                                   │                │
│   │ $410,527.53 is the Vehicle Purchase Cost under Option              │
│   │ (1). Option (1) is a 10-year scenario where 0 additional           │
│   │ sites are obtained, 0 current sites are decommissioned, and        │
│   │ 10 vehicles are added to the fleet.               │                │
│   │                                                   │                │
│   │ The Vehicle Purchase Cost is computed using the model              │
│   │ Fleet Configuration as follows:                   │                │
│   │                                                   │                │
│   │ Vehicle Purchase Cost                             │                │
│   │     = Vehicle Cost + Number of Vehicles + Tax     │                │
│   │                                                   │                │
│   │ Here are the values                               │                │
│   │ Vehicle Cost                       $38,995.95     │                │
│   │ Number of Vehicles                         10     │                │
│   │ Tax                                $20,568.03     │                │
│     ┌──────────────── origin($38,995.95) ──────────────┐              │
│     │                                                   │              │
│     │ $38,995.95 is the cost of each vehicle (Vehicle Purchase          │
│     │ Cost) in the scenario Option (1). It was entered by Sandy         │
│     │ Smith on 10/1/95 at 5:05 p.m. and was last modified on            │
│     │ 10/5/95 at 2:32 p.m. by Sandy Smith. Its certainty factor is      │
│     │ 100%.                                             │              │
│     └───────────────────────────────────────────────────┘              │
└──────────────────────────────────────────────────────────────────────┘
```

Links   A hyperdocument link electronically relates a pair of documents whose subject matter is conceptually related. A marker appearing in each of the two documents related via a link lets the user know that a link does indeed exist between them. There are two broad classes of conceptual relationships that can be handled by links: definitional and associative relationships (Bonczek, Holsapple, and Whinston 1981). The former is concerned with relating instances that define a class. For example, there is a class of procurement alternatives. Each alternative is represented by a separate document, but these documents are linked to make it easy to navigate from one to another. Collectively, all the documents defining the class of procurement alternatives are linked into what is called a *stack* (such as the stack of

FIGURE 9.7   Knowledge-Representation Objects in Hypertext Management

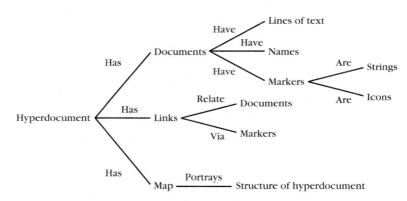

alternative documents or cards). Associative relationships, in contrast, can link documents of very different types, such as an executive summary and a document about projected transport needs.

A Map   It is common for a hyperdocument to have a **map** graphically portraying its overall structure. This graphical depiction shows nodes and arcs connecting them. The nodes correspond to documents and the arcs, to links. A map gives the user a bird's-eye view of the hyperdocument's layout and can be used to **navigate** to a desired document without having to view each of the intervening documents.

PROCESSING THE OBJECTS

Table 9.3 summarizes the basic methods commonly available for hypertext management. In effect, it adds another layer of processing possibilities to those encountered in text management. This layer is concerned mainly with establishing, navigating, and updating a network of interrelated documents. A hyperdocument is specified by means of requests to specify its documents and links between documents. Each document, in turn, is specified by typing or importing its textual passages and by designating its markers. A link is specified by matching a pair of markers, one from each document to be linked. This explicit linking helps avoid confusion in cases where a document has multiple markers and links to many other documents.

To request the storage or recall of a hyperdocument, the user must indicate the name of the KS file(s) where the hyperdocument resides. A single hyperdocument may or may not occupy multiple files, depending on its size and how the tool implements the hypertext-management technique. A user can request a listing of all hyperdocuments stored in the KS. Once one of these has been recalled, the user can see a listing of the names of its documents, along with various other attributes such as the document's size, type, date of creation, date of most recent update, and content description. The user can also see a listing of links' attributes. As another way to become familiar with a hyperdocument, a user can view a map of its structure.

For direct decision support purposes, the most important processing methods involve viewing desired portions of the hyperdocument, exploring its content for

TABLE 9.3   Knowledge-Processing Methods in Hypertext Management

OBJECTS METHODS	HYPERDOCUMENT	DOCUMENT	LINK	MAP
Specify	By specifying documents and links between documents	By typing or importing lines of text and designating markers	By relating markers in two documents	Indirectly, by specifying the hyperdocument
Store	By indicating which KS file(s) contain it	As part of the hyperdocument	As a part of hyperdocument	As part of the hyperdocument
Show	A list of all hyperdocuments existing in KS	Names (and other attributes) of all documents existing in hyperdocument	Attributes of all links existing in hyperdocument	
Recall	From KS for further processing	As part of hyperdocument	As part of hyperdocument	As part of hyperdocument
View	By giving name of desired document, searching for document with desired pattern, navigation via links through desired documents, navigation through map to desired document, printing desired portions of hyperdocument	By sequential scrolling within document, jumping to desired position in document, searching for desired pattern in document, printing document	As markers in documents	A network diagram of hyperdocument in which nodes represent documents and arcs denote links
Change	By adding, changing, or deleting its documents and/or links	By changing its contents (see Table 9.2)	By connecting different documents via markers	Indirectly, by changing the hyperdocument
Delete	By eliminating it from the KS	By eliminating it (and links involving it) from hyperdocument	By eliminating it from hyperdocument and related markers from documents	Indirectly, by eliminating the hyperdocument

needed knowledge or to stimulate insights. Typically, hypertext software allows a console screen to be partitioned into multiple viewing windows, with a different document appearing in each.

To bring a document into view in a window, a request could (1) simply call for that document by name, (2) ask that the hyperdocument be searched for the document containing some desired pattern of symbols or words, (3) navigate to it by choosing a desired marker from an already displayed document, (4) navigate through a displayed map to the node representing the desired document and then choosing to view it, or (5) print it. Within a viewing window, usual text-management methods are available to bring the desired portion of that window's current document into view.

A hyperdocument can be updated by specifying new documents, changing existing documents, or deleting documents. It can also be changed by altering the

LIMITS OF HYPERTEXT MANAGEMENT

Several limitations of the basic hypertext technique have been noted. These include no provision for automating the linking of nodes and creation of documents, possible user disorientation when exploring a complex hyperdocument, little flexibility in customizing the presentation system, and the cost of building hyperdocuments (Bieber and Kimbrough 1992). Researchers are working on overcoming such limitations, merging hypertext with nonhypertext techniques, and generalizing the basic hypertext concept to accommodate nodes that are not just documents (e.g., Bieber and Kimbrough 1992; Bieber n.d.; Chang 1988). The latter generalizations are referred to as hypermedia or hyperknowledge (Bieber 1990, 1992; Chang, Holsapple, and Whinston 1994).

links—specifying new links, changing an existing link (e.g., causing it to link a different pair of documents), or deleting links. As with other knowledge-management techniques, ancillary processing requests such as those for on-line help or file manipulation may be handled by tools implementing hypertext management.

9.5 DATABASE MANAGEMENT

In contrast to text management, database management is a highly structured approach to knowledge representation. It is a technique for record keeping frequently used in developing transaction processing and management information systems as well as DSSs (Bonczek, Holsapple, and Whinston 1984; Courtney and Paradice 1988). Generally, database management provides for the structured representation of data and the flexible processing of that data. There are several distinct approaches to database management: hierarchical, shallow network, CODASYL network, relational, associative (also called postrelational), and object oriented. They are all very similar in allowing data to be organized into records, such as sales representative records, product line records, performance records, or expense records. They differ in terms of their provisions for representing relationships among the various types of records (Holsapple 1984). Because their ways of representing data relationships can differ, the processing methods provided by these approaches can also differ.

Of these alternative approaches, relational database management has emerged as the most widely used over the past decade. It is the only database management approach considered in this book. When we henceforth refer to the database management technique, we refer only to the relational approach. Initially proposed in 1970, relational database management organizes descriptive knowledge in a tabular fashion (Codd 1970).

A **table** consists of records of a particular type. Thus, records about the various sales representatives could make up one table, records about sales performance could constitute another, and records about product lines could be the content of a third table. A collection of related tables is called a **database.** When using the relational approach, relationships among records in different tables are represented by field redundancy.

For our purposes here, database management is concerned with (1) the representation of knowledge in a database's tables and (2) the processing of these tables for the ultimate decision support aim of extracting desired data from them. See Figure 9.8. We begin with an examination of objects commonly encountered in a relational database. We then survey basic processing methods for manipulating these objects. More details and examples of database management are provided in Appendix C.

OBJECTS OF INTEREST

A knowledge system can contain one or more databases, each holding knowledge relevant to some problem domain of interest to the decision maker. As Figure 9.9 shows, each database can have a name to distinguish it from other databases. It can have one or more tables, plus a data dictionary. The **data dictionary** keeps track of what tables exist in the database (e.g., their names, structures, sizes), database usage (e.g., when a table came into existence, when it was last altered), and security authorizations (e.g., controlling who can view or update what parts of the database). With some database–management tools, tables are not partitioned into distinct databases. They all exist as one database in the KS. Also, the extent of the data dictionary facility can vary from fairly rudimentary for do-it-yourself development tools to very extensive for professional development tools.

FIGURE 9.8   SQL Database Queries—A What-If Query and a Conditional Query

```
_select name, mosal, mosal*1.06, mosal*1.07 from rep
  NAME                    MOSAL       EXPO1        EXPO2

Kevin R. Andrews          2580       2650.00      2675.00
Kim G. Anders             2600       2756.00      2782.00
Kris H. Raber             2400       2544.00      2568.00
Tina F. Lee               2800       2968.00      2996.00
Toby C. Terry             2000       2120.00      2140.00
Kerry H. Jones            2250       2385.00      2407.50
Karen V. Bruckner         2800       2968.00      2996.00
Kathy F. Smith            2100       2226.00      2247.00
Jackie V. Smith           2400       2544.00      2568.00
Carol O. Lynn             2750       2915.00      2942.50


_select fname pid q1 s1 q2 s2 from perf where s1<q1 or s2<q2
  FNAME   PID     Q1       S1       Q2        S2

Kim       bus     7320     6854     8050      8120
Kim       ref     6040     7024     8309      7732
Kim       spo     5400     6240     6300      5995
Kris      psy     8090     7540     6209      7900
Tina      bus     6903     5944     7538      10359
Tina      rom     5000     4590     4678      3997
Toby      psy     5000     2607     4006      4839
Toby      rom     4982     5009     4678      3997
Kerry     ref     6030     5590     4985      4880
```

FIGURE 9.9   Knowledge-Representation Objects in Database Management

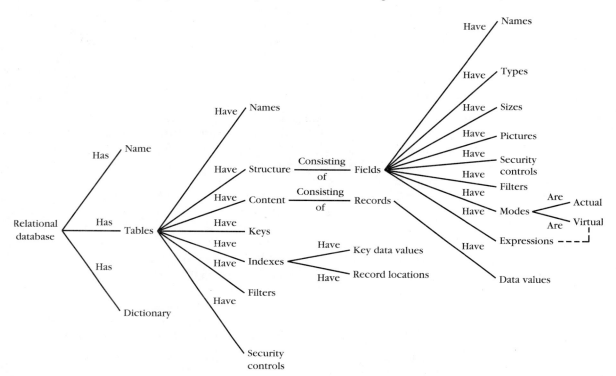

A Data Table   Each table in a database has a name to distinguish it from other tables. It has a structure consisting of fields, where each **field** identifies a category of data that can be contained in the table. A table contains records, where each **record** has one data value for each of the table's fields. A table may have a **key,** which consists of one or more fields whose value in a record uniquely distinguishes that record from all others in the table.

A table may have **filters,** each of which is an example of assimilative knowledge that prevents improper records from entering the table. For instance, we may know that the sum of values for two fields should not exceed 75% of the value for a third field in the same record. Defining such a filter for the table helps automatically safeguard the integrity of its records. A table may also have security controls to govern who can view or alter its structure or content.

RELATIONAL JARGON

In the jargon of relational database management, a table is often called a relation. A table's structure is called a relation schema. Its fields are called attributes. A table's records are called tuples.

> ### TABLE, FILE, AND DATABASE
>
> A relational database consists of all tables pertaining to a particular problem area such as sales management. A database is not a table or a file, nor is a table a file. Many different kinds of files can exist in a KS, and files holding tables are just one of the many possibilities. To qualify as a *relational* database, the relational algebra or SQL-type commands must be provided for processing tables' records.

A Data Field   Each field defined to exist in a table's structure can have a variety of attributes. It has a name that differentiates it from all other fields for the same table. It has a type, which governs what kind of data values are capable of being stored for it in the table's records. Common types are numeric, string, and logical. A very different field type allows digitized versions of audio or visual patterns to be stored for a field in each record. Retrieval of such a field value would result in the user hearing the sounds (e.g., a verbal commentary) or seeing the images (e.g., a photo, a blueprint) represented by the stored pattern.

A field's size determines how much space will be allocated to store its value in each record. Pictures, labels, and security controls for fields all serve the same purpose as they do for working variables involved in expression management. Just as filters may exist at the table level, they may also exist for individual fields. A common type of field filter consists of a range of feasible values. Attempts to give a field a value outside of the range are automatically thwarted.

Two modes of fields are possible: actual and virtual. An actual field is one whose data values in the table's records are actually stored in the database. A **virtual field** is one for which no values are actually stored and no storage space is actually allocated in the database. Yet, a user can view its value for any record, just as if it were an actual field. That value is automatically calculated whenever such viewing is requested. It is calculated by integral, nested expression-management software, which evaluates an expression defined as a part of the virtual field. This expression can include other field names as operands, using their values in a record to determine the virtual field's value in that same record.

A Key   As noted before, one or more fields may collectively be designated as a table's key. There are several uses for a key: identifying, indexing, and relating. A key value in a record helps a user to identify what the other data values in the record reference. For instance, a record may have data values for a sales target, gross margin rate, and commission rate. However, these values mean relatively little without knowing what product they describe. Thus, the record also needs the value for a product ID field (i.e., key field). The ID field tells what product is described by the other field values.

Second, a key can be used to build an index for a table. An **index** is a sorted list of the key values from the table's records, along with the corresponding locations of the records for each. By simply looking up its location in the index, the software has a fast way for accessing any record based on its key value. A third use for a table's key is to equate it with a comparable nonkey field(s) in another table in order to find records in the two tables that are related to each other. Examples of such key uses are provided in Appendix C.

PROCESSING THE OBJECTS

Here, we survey not only the most commonly encountered methods in classic relational database management but also some other methods commonly provided by database-management tools. As Table 9.4 shows, we consider methods for processing a database as a whole and for processing individual tables. Methods for table processing are divided into two classes: those that operate on a table's structure and those that operate on its content. The latter is further subdivided into those requests that process a single record at a time and those that process all or many of a table's records in a single operation. Particularly notable among the table-at-a-time methods are **relational algebra** commands, which create new tables, and **SQL** commands, which can produce listings of desired data buried in one or more tables.

A database comes into existence in a KS by giving it a name (if multiple databases are allowed) and initiating its data dictionary (if needed). We define each

TABLE 9.4   Knowledge-Processing Methods in Database Management

OBJECTS METHODS	DATABASE	TABLE STRUCTURE	TABLE CONTENTS	
			Record at a Time	**Table at a Time**
Define, Specify (create)	By indicating its name, initiating its data dictionary, and defining its tables' structures	By indicating its fields, their attributes, and the KS file(s) that will hold their contents	By assigning a value to each actual field for the record	By relational algebra or by importing records' field values from a non-database source
Use/finish	To reserve/release space in PPS working memory used in processing an indicated database	To reserve/release space in PPS working memory used in processing an indicated table		To reserve/release space in PPS working memory used in processing an indicated table
Find			A record based on its location, its key value, or its other data values	
View	List of tables in database, their fields and keys, related indexes, filters, or other aspects of data dictionary	Details of fields that make up table's structure	Data values of the most recently found record	A tabular list displaying every field's data value for every record or, via SQL, a selective listing of values for certain fields and/or records
Change (edit)	By adding, changing, or deleting tables' names, structure, content, keys, indexes, filters, security controls	By adding, changing, deleting, renaming its fields	By assigning new values for fields in the most recently found record	By reordering (e.g., sorting) records or changing data values of a field for every record meeting certain conditions
Delete	By eliminating it from the KS	By eliminating it and its contents from the database	By eliminating the most recently found record from table	By eliminating every record meeting certain conditions

RELATIONAL DATABASE DESIGN

For more than two decades computer scientists have studied the issue of what constitutes a "good" relational database design. In the course of their studies, they have invented many special notions to help in the formal design of databases. The terms to describe these include domain, candidate key, functional dependency, full functional dependence, first normal form, second normal form, third normal form, Boyce-Codd normal form, and fourth normal form (Atre 1980; Kent 1983). However, it is possible to design tables successfully for small databases without being a computer scientist. Thoughtful analysis of data-handling needs coupled with careful database design should precede the actual definition of tables and creation of records. An information center can help with this. Database design can be a much more troublesome activity than novices might expect.

table's structure by a request that characterizes the table's fields, including the attributes (e.g., name, type, size, picture, mode) of each. A table definition request may also allow an indication of the KS file(s) that will store the table's records, the table's key, its filters, and security controls. A table's index, if it exists, is either generated automatically when table contents are specified or is generated via a direct request to do so.

Once the table's structure is defined, the user can issue requests to specify its content by creating records. There are several methods for this. One involves typing in the record's data value for each actual field. A second is to devise a program that assigns a data value for each field of a record. A third involves importing the field values for multiple records from some other source (e.g., a text file). A fourth method involves the use of relational algebra commands that generate an entire new table (both contents and structure) from one or two existing tables. The most prominent of these are called PROJECT, SELECT, and JOIN. They are described in Appendix C.

The *use* method cited in Table 9.4 causes sufficient allocation of space in PPS working memory to allow a database or a table to be used in subsequent processing. When it no longer needs to be used in a session, a *finish* request is issued to release that space for other purposes. The use/finish methods are often called open/close.

For record-at-a-time processing, several methods can cause a desired record in a table to be found. We call this most recently found record the table's *current record*. For example, we could make current the record at a certain position (e.g., first, last, next, prior) or the record with a particular key value, or we could find a record whose other data values satisfy various conditions. In any event, we can then view, change, or delete the current record, as desired. It is not uncommon for a database-management tool to combine the find and view (and even change) methods for a record into a single request.

For table-at-a-time processing, one method yields an exhaustive listing of the table's records. Another, using a powerful command in the SQL, allows great selectivity as to what data are to be listed (or stored in a table, if desired). Called SELECT, this command can accomplish what could require multiple relational algebra commands. It can extract related data from multiple tables, do conditional retrieval, give

DSS IN THE NEWS

Massive Databases

. . . Database software specialist Oracle Corp. and massively parallel systems supplier nCube Corp. are the first third-party software vendor and system maker to pair up exclusively to produce massively parallel database systems for the commercial world. . . .

Oracle and nCube executives say commercial customers use massively parallel resources for two functions: decision support and transaction processing.

Decision support means the ability to track many customers' buying patterns and make more informed marketing decisions. Any PC database can track how many customers bought widgets at a hardware store. It takes an extremely powerful computer, however, to chart how different flavors of Crest toothpaste sold at Wal-Mart stores around the nation.

The more powerful the computer, the more finely these trends can be distinguished.

The same logic holds true for computers that handle transactions. Some banks are experimenting with automated teller machines that allow customers to immediately examine their last 10 checks or deposits. While the transaction is easy for the customer, it requires massive computing capability.

M. Stroud, "Massively Parallel Computer Makers Begin to Target Database Applications," *Investor's Business Daily* 23 April 1992, p. 4.

answers to what-if kinds of questions (through its integrated expression-evaluation capabilities), sort the results, and group the results—all in response to a single SELECT request issued on an ad hoc basis. Examples are provided in Appendix C. Table-at-a-time changes include a single request for record sorting or for making a uniform change for all records satisfying some condition.

There are many methods that change a database, including the methods that accomplish record-at-a-time or table-at-a-time changes to table contents. They include methods for redefining a table's structure by adding new fields, changing attributes of existing fields, or deleting fields. They also include the definition of new tables, deletion of tables, generation of new indexes, deletion of indexes, and changes to table keys, security codes, and filters.

9.6 SUMMARY

In this chapter we surveyed four knowledge-management techniques that can be usefully employed in decision support systems: expression management, text management, hypertext management, and database management. Problem processors that implement expression management are valuable for helping decision makers with ad hoc calculations that arise in the course of decision making. The main objects of interest with this technique are expressions, variables, functions, and macros.

These objects can also be manipulated within the scope of other knowledge-management techniques.

A problem processor that implements text management gives decision makers the ability to work with electronic documents. These processors are not restricted to representing any particular kind of knowledge. However, such representations are processed simply as documents, without concern for the type of knowledge held. In cases where knowledge represented in one document is logically related to that in others, a PPS that implements hypertext management is valuable. Such a PPS allows knowledge to be organized into an interconnected network of documents called a hyperdocument. The decision maker can follow markers or a map to navigate through the network to access those documents that seem relevant to the decision at hand.

Database management gives a comparatively structured way for organizing knowledge and has historically been used primarily for descriptive knowledge. When a PPS implements database management, it will contain software known as a database control system, and the KS will hold one or more databases. Using the relational approach to database management, each database is composed of one or more tables. Each table has a structure defined in terms of fields and a content organized into records. With a query facility, decision makers can extract desired data from a database on the spur of the moment.

▲ IMPORTANT TERMS

database	index	picture
data dictionary	key	record
document	logical expression	relational algebra
expression	macro	SQL
field	map	string expression
filter	marker	table
function	navigate	variable
hyperdocument	numeric expression	virtual field

▲ APPLICATION TO THE COAST GUARD CASE

1. What was the objective of building the DSS in this case?
2. What features of hypertext management made it a good choice for inclusion in the Max DSS?
3. Describe the two classes of users for which Max was designed.
4. How do the Max reports differ from conventional reports produced by an MIS?
5. Explain how the hypertext facility is used both before and after solving a model.
6. Why would it have been inappropriate for the developers to have tried to use database management for handling the knowledge they represented and processed via hypertext?
7. Why would it have been inappropriate for the DSS developers in earlier cases to have used hypertext rather than database management?

▲ REVIEW QUESTIONS

1. How can a decision maker's mental environment for managing knowledge be extended?
2. What is the relationship between a knowledge-management technique and a PPS? And a KS?
3. Define expression, variable, macro, function, and picture.
4. How can a decision maker benefit from expression management?
5. Why would someone want to use a macro? A variable? A function?
6. What happens in each case?
   a. When a function is defined
   b. When an expression is specified
   c. When a macro is viewed
   d. When a variable is deleted
7. Under what circumstances could a decision maker benefit from a DSS that employs text management?
8. What advantages does text management have over paper-based document processing?
9. How can control indicators be useful when using text management?
10. What are the main objects of interest to a decision maker using text management? What methods tend to be available for processing each?
11. Which features of text management are likely to be found in hypertext management?
12. How does hypertext management differ from ordinary text management?
13. What is a hyperdocument?
14. How does a decision maker process a hyperdocument for decision support purposes?
15. With hypertext management, what methods exist for bringing a desired document into view?
16. What is a hypertext map and how is it used?
17. What is a data dictionary and how is it used?
18. How does database management differ from text management?
19. How can database management benefit a decision maker?
20. What are a database, a table, a field, and a record?
21. How does the concept of a KS file differ from the concept of a table?
22. How does a virtual field differ from an actual field?
23. What are the advantages of a virtual field relative to an actual field, and vice versa?
24. In what way can data in two different tables be related?
25. What is a key and what are its main uses?
26. What is the result of a relational algebra command such as PROJECT or JOIN?
27. What are the advantages of using SQL queries rather than relational algebra?
28. What are filters and how are they useful for fields? For tables?

▲ DISCUSSION TOPICS

1. Characterize the mental knowledge-management techniques you use as a decision maker.
2. Explain the distinction between a variable and a macro.

3. Describe how text-management software can function as an intrinsic tool. How can it be a valuable extrinsic tool?
4. Discuss the benefits and drawbacks of making insertions into a piece of text interactively versus at print time.
5. From a decision maker's viewpoint, what are the most valuable and the least useful features of text management?
6. Give examples of descriptive, procedural, and reasoning knowledge that a decision maker might reasonably handle with text management.
7. Contrast the notions of definitional and associative relationships. Give an example of each.
8. Discuss the limitations that exist in using hyperdocuments.
9. Compare and contrast a hyperdocument with a document and with a database.
10. Discuss the similarities and differences between documents and records.
11. Describe the nature of a system that allows values of fields to be documents.
12. Describe the elements of database-management software that function as intrinsic tools and those that serve as extrinsic tools.
13. Identify the type(s) of knowledge held in a data dictionary.
14. Explain the distinction between a database's structure and its content.
15. Compare and contrast record-at-a-time versus table-at-a-time processing.
16. Although database tables are usually thought of as holding descriptive knowledge, in what sense can they also hold procedural knowledge?
17. Describe the various attributes a field could have and note the uses of each.
18. Why are *use* and *finish* methods available?
19. Describe security features for each of the knowledge-management techniques and explain why they could be important to a decision maker.

▲ REFERENCES

Apple Computer, Inc. 1989. *Hypercard user's guide.* Cupertino, Calif.: Apple.

Atre, S. 1980. *Database, structured techniques for design, performance, and management.* New York: John Wiley.

Bacon, J. P., and C. T. Copeland. 1991. *Understanding and using WordPerfect 5.1.* St. Paul: West.

Bieber, M. P. 1990. Automating hypertext for decision support. *Hypermedia and Information Reconstruction Conference,* University of Houston—Clear Lake (December).

Bieber, M. P. 1992. Automating hypermedia for decision support. *Hypermedia* 4, no. 2.

_____. n.d. On integrating hypermedia into decision support and other information systems. *Decision Support Systems,* forthcoming.

Bieber, M. P., and S. Kimbrough. 1992. On generalizing the concept of hypertext. *MIS Quarterly* 16, no. 1.

Bonczek, R. H., C. W. Holsapple, and A. B. Whinston. 1981. *Foundations of decision support systems.* New York: Academic Press.

_____. 1984. *Micro database management—Practical techniques of application development.* New York: Academic Press.

Chang, A. 1988. An environment theory of decision support. Ph.D. Diss., Purdue University.

Chang, A., C. W. Holsapple, and A. B. Whinston. 1993. Model management issues and directions. *Decision Support Systems* 9, no. 1.

_____. 1994. A hyperknowledge framework for decision support systems. *Information Processing and Management* 30, no. 4.

Codd, E. F. 1970. A relational model of data for large shared databanks. *Communications of the ACM* 13, no. 6.

Conklin, J. 1987. Hypertext: An introduction and survey. *Computer* 20, no. 9.

Courtney, J. F., and D. B. Paradice. 1988. *Database systems for management.* St. Louis: Times Mirror/Mosby.

Fedorowicz, J. 1989. Evolving technology for document-based DSS. In *Decision support systems: Putting theory into practice,* edited by R. Sprague and H. Watson. Englewood Cliffs, N.J.: Prentice Hall.

Greenia, M. W. 1985. *Professional word processing in business and legal environments,* Reston, Va.: Reston.

Holsapple, C. W. 1984. A perspective on data models. *PC Tech Journal* 2, no. 1.

Keen, P. G. W., and G. R. Wagner. 1979. DSS: An executive mind support system. *Datamation* (November).

Kent, W. 1983. A simple guide to five normal forms in relational database theory. *Communications of the ACM* 26, no. 2.

Kimbrough, S. O., C. W. Pritchett, M. P. Bieber, and H. K. Bhargava. 1990. The Coast Guard's KSS Project. *Interfaces* 20, no. 6.

McLean, E. R., L. A. Kappelman, and J. P. Thompson. 1993. Converging end-user and corporate computing. *Communications of the ACM* 36, no. 12.

Minch, R. 1989. Application and research areas for hypertext in decision support systems. *Journal of Management Information Systems* 6, no. 3.

Chapter 10

SOLVER, SPREADSHEET, PROGRAM, AND MENU MANAGEMENT

TEXACO: A DSS FOR BLENDING OPERATION DECISIONS

Overview

Gasoline blending is a critical refinery operation. In 1980, Texaco began developing an improved, optimization based, decision support system for planning and scheduling its blending operations. The system, OMEGA, is implemented on personal computers and on larger computer systems. . . .

. . . The system enables a user to retrieve a variety of data from up-to-date refinery databases and to interactively examine and modify the data after it is inserted into the OMEGA database. . . . Data include information on stock qualities and availability, as well as on blend specifications and demands. . . . The user, by selecting appropriate menu options, can construct and solve . . . an optimization problem that determines how much of each stock to allocate to each blend so that all quality specifications are met, stock availability and blend demand constraints are satisfied, and the selected objective is optimized.

OMEGA was first installed in 1983 and is now used in all seven Texaco USA refineries and in two foreign plants. . . . As OMEGA use was extended to other refineries, we encountered some resistance from users who had . . . noted differences between the blends recommended by the system and existing blending practice. Analysis showed that these differences were due to the increased accuracy of the OMEGA input data and model formulation, and to the improved robustness and accuracy of its optimizer. . . .

The economic benefits attained by using OMEGA are difficult to measure since market conditions and refinery configurations have changed since its installation. However, taking the compositions of blends used prior to OMEGA as initial values for OMEGA's optimizer, we have observed increases in gasoline profits of up to 30 percent for some batches. . . . Texaco estimates total ongoing economic gains stemming from OMEGA to be more than $30 million annually.

System Development

. . . OMEGA is . . . constantly being updated and extended. When new governmental regulations are invoked, modifications are made to OMEGA to reflect these regulations. In recent years, for example, the EPA required a lead phasedown for regular leaded gasoline. This made it necessary to modify the OMEGA model so that it would be more accurate for these lower levels of lead. The new model also reflects the fact that the laboratories are now testing the octane response of blend stocks to lead at lower levels. This phasedown also led to the use of other octane improvers, such as MMT and oxygenates, which had to be incorporated into the model.

Other business changes also led to model modifications. For instance, refinery upgrades and the refining of different crudes . . . have resulted in blend stocks with significantly different properties than those previously encountered. The quality equations in the model had to be extrapolated to predict the resulting blend qualities.

OMEGA is continually modified to reflect changes in refinery operations . . . [and] differences in refineries required changes to the system. . . . When Texaco began installing OMEGA in their foreign refineries, we had to make additional

Continued

changes to handle the different requirements for each country. . . . Furthermore, enhancements to OMEGA are constantly needed to enable it to answer the new and unanticipated what-if questions refinery engineers ask.

System Features and Usage

. . . Interactive input makes OMEGA very easy to use. . . . The user can access stock qualities, stock availabilities, blend specifications, blend requirements, starting values and limits, optimization options, automatic stock selection, automatic blend specifications selection, and several other options. . . .

Several features aid the user in performing planning functions. . . . From . . . the optimization options screen . . . the user can select one of the following objective functions: maximum profit per barrel, maximum profit, minimum octane (quality) giveaway, or a . . . combination of profit and quality giveaway. The objective function chosen depends on the problem that is being solved and the characteristics of the refinery. . . .

On a monthly basis, refineries use OMEGA to develop a gasoline blending plan for the month. The plan is generated five to 10 days before the first of the month. Planning is performed on a monthly basis because the overall refinery planning models . . . are run monthly, and because tax considerations make it desirable to minimize refinery stock inventories on the first of the month.

The refinery planning model's projected blending stock volumes are input to OMEGA. The stock qualities used in OMEGA are either the stock properties projected by the refinery-planning model or the actual average stock properties from the previous month. . . .

The blending planner typically calculates three to eight blends in a single OMEGA run. Each blend is one of the four grades of gasoline that Texaco manufactures. Often the blender will create two blends for reach grade, a blend for the fixed volume of the grade that has been committed during the planning process, called a "required" blend, and a blend for any additional amount of that grade that the refinery can make, a "holdover" blend. The blender may also create a blend for each method by which a grade of gasoline is to be transported. For example, the blender may create one unleaded regular blend for the pipeline and another for truck pickup at a terminal. . . .

The refinery planning model's blend compositions are input into OMEGA as starting values. OMEGA is then executed with a "blend-all" feature for all stocks except butane. The blend-all feature requires that all of the available stock must be blended into some blend. . . . The blend-all feature minimizes end-of-month stock inventories and prevents OMEGA from using all the high quality stocks and leaving only the low quality stocks behind.

OMEGA then creates a monthly blending plan. This blending plan displays the grade splits, that is, the proportion that each blend constitutes of the total gasoline output. This plan is reviewed to determine if it is reasonable (not all of the possible real-world constraints are part of the blending model). If not, additional constraints are placed on the blend compositions or the blend volumes, and OMEGA is rerun.

Continued

Once a reasonable blending plan has been developed, the marketing department is contacted to discuss the resulting grade splits. Marketing takes into account the current state of the gasoline market and the production by alternate refining sources and may make suggestions for modifying the grade splits. A finalized blending plan will then be developed for the month. . . .

Individual blend compositions are determined by running OMEGA with the current actual stock flow rates and stock qualities. . . . Resulting compositions are then given to the scheduler or blender. As the month progresses, these blend recipes may have to be recalculated because the availability and qualities of stock may deviate from what was expected. . . .

The scheduler determines when each of the grades will be blended. . . . If a particular stock inventory is low, the scheduler may rerun OMEGA, restricting the use of this limited stock and allowing the others to vary from the blend recipe. . . .

The scheduler gives the blender the daily blend recipe(s). The blender uses the recipe(s) to determine the flow rates for the input stocks. During blending, these rates must be adjusted to account for variations in stock properties as well as any minor inaccuracies in OMEGA's model. . . .

Benefits

. . . Installation and expanded use of OMEGA is clear evidence that OMEGA is perceived as contributing to overall profitability. . . .

More difficult to quantify are the intangible benefits . . . fewer blends fail to meet their quality specifications. OMEGA's more reliable gasoline grade split estimates provide significant aid to those developing marketing strategies and refinery production targets. . . .

Another source of intangible benefits is the use of OMEGA for what-if case studies. These studies are performed for various reasons, such as economic analysis of refinery improvement projects and analysis of how proposed governmental regulations would affect Texaco . . . some refinery and manufacturing headquarters personnel believe that these benefits are as significant as those for daily blending.

Condensed quotation from C. W. DeWitt, L. S. Lasdon, A. D. Waren, D. A. Brenner, and S. A. Melhem, "OMEGA: An Improved Gasoline Blending System for Texaco," *Interfaces,* 19, no. 1 (1989): 85–98.

LEARNING OBJECTIVES

The Texaco case describes a DSS centered around solver management as a means for handling procedural knowledge about how to solve blending problems. It uses database management for representing and processing descriptive knowledge. As we saw in the prior chapter, there are alternative techniques for coping with descriptive knowledge. As we shall see in this chapter, solver management is but one of several techniques for handling procedural knowledge, and solver management itself has major variations. Keep the Texaco case in mind as you read this chapter to refine your understanding of techniques for managing procedural knowledge.

After studying this chapter, you should be able to

1. Describe the main features of each of the following knowledge-management techniques:
Solver management
Spreadsheet management
Program management
Menu management
2. Explain the distinctions among these techniques in terms of the objects used for knowledge representation and the methods used to process those objects.
3. Assess the potential value of each technique for managing alternative types of knowledge.
4. Learn how to use software tools that embody these techniques as a basis for building your own DSSs.

Use the exercises at the end of the chapter to ensure that you have a basic understanding of the knowledge management techniques presented here.

10.1 INTRODUCTION

Continuing our survey of knowledge-management techniques for decision support, we turn to a consideration of solver management, spreadsheet management, program management, and menu management. The first three of these are related in that they are heavy-duty approaches to managing procedural knowledge—building upon and going well beyond the rudimentary capabilities of expression management. Each also has some provision for handling descriptive knowledge, albeit much more modest than what is provided by database management. Menu management gives a basis for understanding what procedure a user wants a DSS to perform at a given point in time. Like the other techniques covered in this chapter, it can involve the management of procedural knowledge. It is also not uncommon for menu management to be integrated into program management in a DSS development tool.

10.2 SOLVER MANAGEMENT

As we saw in Chapter 6, a **solver** is a chunk of procedural knowledge that can be used to derive new data—facts, estimates, projections, expectations, and solutions to problems. There are two main ways to manage solvers. One involves the incorporation of solvers into a PPS. The other allows solvers to exist as part of a KS. In the fixed-solver case, implementations of the solver-management technique are concerned primarily with characterizing the problems that are to be solved by a fixed set of predefined solvers. In the flexible-solver case, a tool that implements the solver-management technique must also be concerned with defining, viewing, changing, deleting, and integrating the solvers themselves.

Because fixed-solver management tends to take less effort, it is more widely used by do-it-yourself developers of DSSs. Fixed-solver-management software can be categorized according to the class or classes of solvers that it incorporates. These classes include statistical solvers (e.g., for regression analysis), optimization solvers (e.g., for linear programming problems), financial   solvers (e.g., for net present value or forecasting problems), and general mathematical solvers (e.g., for goal seeking or solving systems of equations). Each solver is able to solve a particular kind of problem and expects the statement of a problem to conform to a prescribed syntax. Although there is little in the way of standards for stating such problems, the **problem statements** themselves are often called models.

A **model** identifies relationships among some collection of variables and numbers (i.e., constants). As a whole, a model is a mathematical declaration that represents some situation, phenomenon, or speculation. It may relate variables and constants within a series of numeric expressions involved in equations or inequalities, within a graph of nodes and arcs (e.g., a decision tree), or via an arrangement of numbers in a data set. In effect, these are alternative ways to characterize a problem which a solver analyzes to manufacture a solution. Problems that can be analyzed by the same solver form a *model class*.

The best known DSS development tool implementing the fixed-solver-management technique is Comshare's IFPS (Gray 1983). Originally developed in the early 1970s, IFPS functions as an intrinsic tool that gives do-it-yourself developers straightforward means for specifying models and data sets. It has a large repertoire of built-in solvers that can be easily invoked for producing solutions to specified models. Originally used on mainframe computers, IFPS and a variety of other commercial tools offering fixed-solver management are now available for microcomputers (Falkner and August 1991). They have been used to solve mathematically modeled problems in such decision support applications as the following:

Asset-liability management

Bidding evaluation

Budget forecasting

Cash management

Discounted cash-flow analysis

Inventory management

Labor planning

Lease-purchase analysis

Make-buy analysis

Merger and acquisition analysis

Multiyear planning

Portfolio management

Production load management

Real estate investment

Risk assessment

Sales forecasting

Variance analysis

Flexible-solver management is concerned not only with models and related data sets but more fundamentally with the representation and processing of solver modules as well. These skills give a DSS developer the ability to build and maintain solvers that would be otherwise unavailable with fixed-solver managers, to specify **control logic** that allows solver modules to be integrated, to allow for model specifications that are otherwise unavailable, and to present solver results in ways not otherwise allowed. The price to be paid for this flexibility is the added effort of managing solvers themselves, in addition to their problem statements and data sets. See Figure 10.1

OBJECTS OF INTEREST

As Figure 10.2 suggests, models and/or solvers can be organized into what is called a **model base.** As in database management, there can be a dictionary cataloging the model base contents and keeping track of its usage (e.g., when a model or solver was last edited). Because diverse kinds of models (i.e., problem statements) exist corresponding to different types of solvers, models may be organized according to type. For instance, the way in which a linear optimization model is stated should differ from the way in which a linear regression model is characterized. Yet all linear optimization problems have certain traits in common (e.g., a linear objective function and linear constraint inequalities). So do all linear regression problems. Thus, models can be organized into classes, each of which has structurally similar problem statements.

FIGURE 10.1   Specification of a Model and Presentation of Solver Results

	1990	1991	1992	1993	1994	1995
Revenues	180000.00	225000.00	3000000.00	398437.50	498046.00	622558.59
Price	150.00	150.00	160.00	170.00	170.00	170.00
Units Sold	1200.00	1500.00	1875.00	2343.75	2929.69	3662.11
Materials per Unit	57.00	57.00	57.00	57.00	57.00	57.00
Materials	68400.00	63500.00	106875.00	133593.75	166992.19	208740.23
Labor per Unit	36.00	36.00	36.00	36.00	36.00	36.00
Labor	43200.00	54000.00	67500.00	84375.00	105468.75	131835.94
Cost of Goods Sold	111600.00	139500.00	174375.00	217968.75	272460.94	340576.17
Gross Margin	68400.00	65500.00	125625.00	180468.75	225585.94	281982.42
Utilities	4950.00	3197.50	3457.38	5730.24	6016.76	6317.59

```
Revenues = Price * Units Sold
Price = 150
Units Sold = 1000, previous * 1.15
Materials per Unit = 57
Materials = Materials per Unit * Units Sold
Case
Units Sold = 1200, Previous * 1.25
Price = 150, 150, 160, 170

What if Solution                        VIEW MODE      Model SAMPLE.MOD
What_if: Base        Set         Name      Save   Solve  Edit_case    Update
```

FIGURE 10.2   Knowledge-Representation Objects in Solver Management

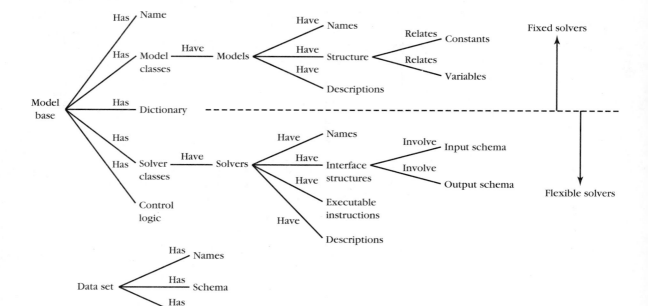

Models   A model's structure relates variables and constants to each other, which is commonly done with numeric expressions involved in equations and related numbers in a **data set.** For example, the simple model

```
COLUMNS 1-5
EXPENSES
SALES
SHARES = 1000000
NET_INC = SALES-EXPENSES
EXP_RATIO = EXPENSE/SALES
NET_INC_RATIO = NET_INC/SALES
INC_PER_SHARE = NET_INC/SHARES
```

could be related to the data set

```
EXPENSE 52, 65, 60, 75, 80
SALES 81, 86, 72, 82, 93
```

having expense and sales data for five time periods. Solving the model with this data set would derive new information about the net income, expense ratio, net income ratio, and income per share for each of the five periods. The model's equations could also be solved using other data sets, having expense and sales numbers for different companies, time periods, or scenarios.

Interestingly, we could use expression management to achieve the same results. However, it would be much more cumbersome and time consuming because it has no provision for evaluating an entire series of related expressions as a whole or for handling multiple time periods. Also, database management could be employed to achieve the same results by defining EXPENSES, SALES, and SHARES to be actual fields in a table and the other four variables to be virtual fields. The table would have five records—each with a 1000000 value for the shares field and a pair of expense and sales numbers from the data set. However, the effort involved in setting up a table for this model would probably exceed what is involved in specifying the model and data set via solver management. More generally, such a database approach is relatively limited in what it can solve.

The expressions that relate variables and constants in a model can also include functions, each of which corresponds to a solver. For instance, if fixed-solver-management software incorporates a solver that uses regression analysis to project a trend, then the following could be a model:

```
COLUMNS 1-6
SALES = 81, 86, 72, 82, 93, 95
EXPENSES = 52, 65, 60, 75, 80 TREND(SALES)
```

where the expenses number for the sixth period is determined by regression analysis on the other numbers given in the model.

Flexible Solvers   In flexible-solver management, solvers themselves will exist in a model base, where they may be organized into classes. For instance, a class of linear programming solvers could include alternative algorithms for solving linear optimization problems. Alternative solvers in a class could differ in terms of the speed, accuracy, or the extensiveness of results produced for a given problem statement. Aside from its executable instructions, which the computer follows in producing a solution, a solver will have interface structures, which are schemas that govern what it can accept as input and how its output will be arranged.

Because the input to a solver is a model characterizing some problem to be solved, a solver's input schema is concerned with detailing what conventions must be followed in stating a problem. For instance, how are multiple periods for analysis to be indicated in a model, what variable names are allowed, what symbols can be used to delimit values in a data set, and is the sequence of lines in a model important? The answers to such questions govern the appearance of model structures that can be processed by a solver. At its simplest, that structure may appear as a data set having lists of numbers to be analyzed by a solver, or it could be quite elaborate—involving many variables, operators, functions, and comments.

A solver's output schema controls the arrangement of data produced by execution of the solver instructions. The data may be for presentation to a user or for storage as a data set that is subsequently used as input to another solver module. In the latter case, it is important that the output schema of the first solver be consistent with the input schema for the second solver. At the very least, it must be possible for the output data to be readily converted to the form that is expected for input by another solver.

Recall our discussion of software integration in Chapter 8. It is just as applicable to solver integration as to the integration of knowledge-management techniques. When multiple solvers need to be treated as modules of an overall solver, there is the issue of controlling the use of those modules (e.g., the sequencing of their executions). One approach to integrating solver modules is to force the user to make requests that explicitly control their use. Alternatively, a developer may include control logic in a model base to govern integration of solver modules automatically (Bonczek, Holsapple, and Whinston 1981).

Data Sets and Templates   As Figure 10.2 indicates, a data set could contain an explicit schema to explain the layout of the numeric values it contains. This schema is an example of linguistic knowledge, enabling the interpretation of data set contents. In the foregoing example, the **schema** simply consists of the words EXPENSES and SALES, which indicate which values are to be interpreted as expense figures and which are sales data. Another object of interest is a *template,* which is a schema indicating the arrangement of a solver's results. If a solver's usual presentation is inadequate for a user's needs, he or she can develop a suitable template. Subsequently, the user can request that results be presented according to the layout detailed in that template's schema.

PROCESSING THE OBJECTS

Methods for processing a model base, model, solver, and data set are summarized in Table 10.1. In the fixed-solver case, model base definition consists primarily of specifying individual models. Model classes are predetermined to correspond to existing solver classes. Model structure is predetermined to conform to the input requirements of specific solvers. A model specification can involve the combining of previously specified models.

In the flexible-solver case, model base definition depends on solver specification. Here the options range from procuring solvers built by someone else to actually designing and implementing each solver's interface structures and executable instructions. Specification of data sets and templates is straightforward and must conform to what is allowed by the solvers in the model base or PPS.

DSS IN THE NEWS

Number Crunching

The emergence of desktop computers has had immense effects on statistical analysis. Not only has access to these tools increased dramatically, but the automated collection of data by computers and their connection to other computers by communications networks has profoundly altered how we collect data and perform analysis. Whereas classical data analysis generally emphasized small data sets, nowadays data sets may be huge. Commercial operations in transportation, telecommunications, marketing and retail may generate tens of thousands of observations to draw upon. With personal computers, analysis can proceed interactively, perhaps beginning with graphical summaries of the data and continuing with more than one numerical approach to gain a deeper understanding of what the data may reveal.

James J. Swain, "Crunching Numbers," *OR/MS Today,* October 1994, p. 48.

TABLE 10.1   Knowledge-Processing Methods in Solver Management

OBJECT METHOD	MODEL BASE	MODEL	SOLVER	DATA SET
Define, specify (create)	By indicating its name, initiating its model dictionary, defining its model classes and/or solver classes, and specifying its control logic.	By indicating its name, specifying its description, or defining its structure in terms of temporal or equational relationships among variables and constants.	By indicating its name, specifying its description, defining its interface structures in terms of schemas, or providing executable instructions	By indicating its name and specifying its data values organized via some schema
Use/finish	To reserve/release space in PPS working memory used in processing an indicated model base	To reserve/release space in PPS working memory used in processing an indicated model.	To reserve/release space in PPS working memory used in processing an indicated solver	To reserve/release space in PPS working memory used in processing an indicated data set
Execute			Solver with an indicated model and/or data set	
View	List of models, solvers, and/or data sets in model base; control logic; aspects of model dictionary	Its structure relating variables and constants (e.g., in expressions) or model description	Its interface structures, instructions, description, or results of solver execution	Its data contents
Change (edit)	By adding, changing, or deleting models, solvers, control logic	By changing its structure or description	By changing its interface structures, instructions, or description	Its data contents
Delete	By eliminating it from KS	By eliminating it from model base	By eliminating it from model base	By eliminating it from KS

Using and finishing refer to processing any of the objects held in the KS. They cause the object to be accessed for use from KS files and stored in KS files for later use, respectively. The execute method applies only to solvers. A request to execute a solver, be it fixed or flexible, causes the solver's instructions to be performed for a particular model and/or data set, thereby producing the solution to a problem and presenting it as a response. Any of the objects held in the KS are subject to viewing, change, and deletion.

10.3   SPREADSHEET MANAGEMENT

Aside from text management, spreadsheet management is probably the most widely used technique for do-it-yourself computing. This is due in large measure to the convenience with which spreadsheets can handle such ubiquitous tasks as budgeting and managing cash flow (Glau 1987). They can also be helpful for activities such as project planning and scheduling, network analysis forecasting, decision tree analysis, and even optimization (Carroll 1986). Today's widespread use of spread-

MODEL MANAGEMENT

Solver management is concerned not only with the management of solvers, but also with managing the statements of problems they can solve and managing data involved in those problem statements. Various authors sometimes refer to solvers as models, to problem statements as models (as we have done here), or to data sets as models (Chang, Holsapple, and Whinston 1993). As a result, the term model management is often applied to any or all of these topics. For clarity, we have adopted only one meaning of the word *model* in our characterization of the solver management technique.

There is a significant and growing area of research commonly known as *model management* bridging the fields of DSS and management science. Solver-management techniques have their roots in that research area and are likely to evolve as progress is made in it. Among the many important issues investigated by model management researchers are these.

1. A means for adapting database–management ideas to the management of solvers, their problem statements, and data inputs (Bonczek, Holsapple, and Whinston 1978, 1983; Stohr and Tanniru 1980; Blanning 1983, 1987b; Dolk 1986; Lenard 1986; Ramirez, Ching, and St. Louis 1993).

2. A means of specifying problem statements for solvers (Bonczek, Holsapple, and Whinston 1981; Geoffrion 1987, 1989a; Ma, Murphy, and Stohr 1989; Jones 1990, 1991; Bhargava and Kimbrough 1993; Chari and Krishnan 1993; Courtney and Paradice 1993; Hong, Mannino, and Greenberg 1993; Lee 1993).

3. Approaches to integrating problem statements into larger models (Bonczek, Holsapple and Whinston 1978; Geoffrion 1989b; Krishnan 1990; Dolk and Kotteman 1993; Jones 1993).

4. Facilities for supporting the developers of solvers and their problem statements (Ghiaseddin 1986; Eck, Philippakis, and Ramirez 1990; Dhar and Jarke 1993; Bhargava and Krishnan 1993).

5. Facilities for helping users understand solver results (Greenberg 1983, 1987; King 1986).

6. Use of artificial intelligence mechanisms for handling control logic or automated learning (Bonczek, Holsapple, and Whinston 1981; Dutta and Basu 1984; Blanning 1984, 1987a; Fedorowicz and Williams 1986; Binbiasioglu and Jarke 1986; Shaw, Tu and De 1988; Jarke and Radermacher 1988; Liang 1993).

sheets owes much to the popularity of two spreadsheet implementations called VisiCalc and 1-2-3.

VisiCalc was the first significant software for spreadsheet management and in many respects defined the basic traits of this knowledge-management technique (Allen 1984). It appeared on the scene in the late 1970s at about the same time as the first usable microcomputers. In fact, VisiCalc made a major contribution to the usability of these machines by beginning to make their latent power accessible to large numbers of people who were not computer scientists and programmers. At the time VisiCalc appeared, no appreciable microcomputer software for text management or database management existed. Decision support was previously confined to the mainframe-computer domain.

In the early 1980s a new class of faster and higher-capacity microcomputers became available. New spreadsheet software geared to take advantage of these more potent machines were developed. Among these, one of the earliest was 1-2-3 (Cain 1984). Introduced by Lotus Development Corporation in 1983, this second-generation spreadsheet package is today one of the most widely used and recognized.

Spreadsheet management lets us represent procedural and descriptive knowledge in a grid of cells called a **spreadsheet,** or worksheet. Each **cell** can have a definition and a value. A **cell definition** is an expression that specifies what is to be calculated when that cell is encountered in the course of evaluating the spreadsheet. Collectively, all the cell definitions for a spreadsheet are sometimes called a *spreadsheet template.*

Spreadsheet evaluation consists of processing cell definitions, step by step, to determine values for the cells. **Cell values** can be seen through a viewing window on the spreadsheet screen. By altering cell definitions and recomputing the spreadsheet, the effects of different assumptions can be readily seen on the screen. This kind of what-if investigation lies at the heart of spreadsheet processing and makes spreadsheet analysis valuable in supporting decision-making activities.

OBJECTS OF INTEREST

A knowledge system can hold one or more spreadsheets. Each is typically stored in its own disk file. Every spreadsheet has the same gridlike structure and can be thought of as a matrix of cells. When presented on a console (e.g., Figure 10.3), a

FIGURE 10.3   Viewing the Cell Values in a Spreadsheet

```
      :A      ·     :B         :C        :D        :E        :F        :G          :H
  1:                     MONTHLY EXPENSE ALLOCATION                   Jack Vander         :
  2:                                                                                      :
  3:Hotel:        39.10                                                                   :
  4:Meal:         22.75                                                                   :
  5:                                                                                      :
  6:              Monthly              Hotel               Meal      Enter-               :
  7:Name          Salary     Nights    Total     Meals     Total     tainment    Phone:
  8:                                                                             155.00:
  9:Kevin         2500.00    4.00      156.40    12.50     284.37    71.09       155.00:
 10:Kim           2600.00    3.00      117.30    12.00     273.00    68.25       155.00:
 11:Kris          2400.00    4.00      156.40    12.50     284.37    71.09       155.00:
 12:Tina          2800.00    6.00      234.60    13.50     307.12    76.78       155.00:
 13:Toby          2000.00    4.80      187.68    12.90     293.48    73.37       155.00:
 14:Kerry         2250.00    3.00      117.30    12.00     273.00    68.25       155.00:
 15:Karen         2800.00    3.00      117.30    12.00     273.00    68.25       155.00:
 16:Kathy         2100.00    3.50      136.85    12.25     278.69    69.67       155.00:
 17:Jackie        2400.00    6.00      234.60    13.50     307.12    76.78       155.00:
 18:Carol         2750.00    4.00      156.40    12.50     284.37    71.09       155.00:
 19: TOTALS:      24600.00   41.30     1614.83   125.65    2858.54   714.63      1550.00:
```

spreadsheet appears to comprise rows and columns. At the left edge of the screen there are row numbers. Across the top, each column is usually designated by a letter. The screen serves as a viewing window for looking into a spreadsheet. Because of the physical limitations of a screen, all the rows and columns in a spreadsheet may not be visible at the same time.

As Figure 10.4 suggests, the most important thing to understand about spreadsheet structure is the notion of a cell. A cell is the place where a row intersects a column, and its position in the grid determines its name. For instance, the place where column A and row 1 intersect is called cell A1, the place where column B and row 5 intersect is called cell B5, and so forth.

The two most common kinds of definitions allowed by spreadsheet-management software are constants and expressions whose values can be calculated. When the definition of a cell is a constant (e.g., a number or string of text), that cell's value is simply that constant. When a cell definition is an expression involving operators, cells as operands, and perhaps functions, then that cell's value is determined by calculating the expression's value in the course of spreadsheet evaluation.

In essence, a spreadsheet gives us a convenient way to organize interrelated expression-management activities into a structure of rows and columns that we can process as a whole rather than in the piecemeal one-at-a-time fashion allowed by simple expression managers. Viewed in another way, a spreadsheet is a matrix of variables. Those cells having constants as definitions are much like the variables we encountered in expression management. Those with more elaborate expressions as definitions can be thought of as virtual variables (akin to virtual fields), whose values are calculated as needed by evaluating their definitions.

If a cell is given a picture, that picture will control the appearance of the cell's value whenever it is presented on the screen or printed. Some spreadsheet man-

FIGURE 10.4   Knowledge-Representation Objects in Spreadsheet Management

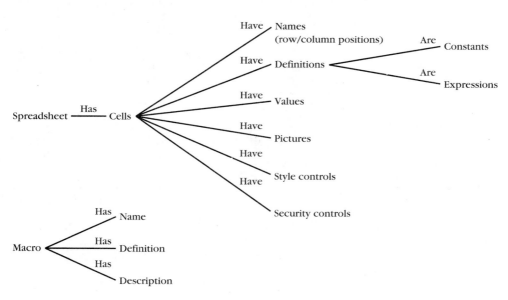

agers allow a cell's presentation on the screen to be stylized. For instance, the manager allows a cell to be given a red background, black foreground, and high-intensity mode in order to highlight it relative to other cells. Some spreadsheet managers also allow a cell to have security controls that govern who can view or change its definition. Finally, it is common for spreadsheet management software to allow macros as another object of interest. A macro name may be defined to represent a few keystrokes or an entire procedure. The macro name may then be referenced interactively or in a cell definition.

PROCESSING THE OBJECTS

Once a spreadsheet is specified to exist, by indicating how many rows and columns it has, any of its cells can be specified. As Table 10.2 shows, this processing method lets us give a definition to a selected cell. Indicating its picture, style, and security codes may involve separate requests. We can specify cell definitions one at a time by moving a cursor to the cell of interest and then typing in a constant or an expression involving other cells (whose values are to be used in calculating this cell's value). Alternatively, we can specify definitions for a block of cells en mass. For instance, we can import data values already existing elsewhere (in the KS or in a file outside of it) to become the constant definitions for a cell block. Or, we can make requests to copy or move definitions already existing in a spreadsheet to be definitions of some other cells. If the copied or moved definitions are not constants, the software may automatically adjust their references to cells to reflect the new positions in the spreadsheet.

When finished using a spreadsheet, we can issue a request indicating that the current rendition of the spreadsheet is to be stored on a disk file in the KS. This releases the PPS working memory that had been consumed by its cells. Later, when we again want to process that spreadsheet, we issue a request identifying the file of the spreadsheet we now want to use. The program allocates working memory space accordingly to allow the PPS to work with its cells.

TABLE 10.2 Knowledge-Processing Methods in Spreadsheet Management

OBJECT METHOD	SPREADSHEET	CELL
Specify	By indicating the number of rows and columns to allocate space for	By indicating its definition, picture, style, and security controls
Use/finish	To reserve/release space in PPS working memory for holding cell specifications while the spreadhseet is being processed	
Evaluate	All cell definitions to calculate current values for all cells	As part of spreadsheet evaluation
View	Values of desired blocks of cells on the screen or on a printout	A cell's definition, picture, style, security controls
Change	By specifying/changing/deleting cell characteristics or by copying or moving cell characteristics	By changing its definition, picture, style, or security controls
Delete	By eliminating it from the KS	

Spreadsheet-management software always provides a method for evaluating a spreadsheet's cells by calculating each cell's value based on its definition. Evaluation methods can vary in terms of the pattern and timing of cell evaluations. For instance, the pattern might be to evaluate cells row by row from the top to the bottom of the spreadsheet or column by column from left to right. The pattern may be based on the dependencies among cell definitions. For example, cell B12 must be evaluated before all cells whose definitions include B12. At one extreme, the timing of spreadsheet evaluation is completely at the user's discretion, a request for evaluation being issued whenever desired. At the opposite extreme, evaluation is automatic—being performed by the spreadsheet manager each time the definition of a cell is changed.

Typically, the most recently calculated values for cells are displayed for viewing on the console screen. However, because a spreadsheet can have too many cells to be seen simultaneously, methods exist for bringing other cells into sight through the console screen's viewing window, breaking the screen into multiple viewing windows (each looking into a different part of the spreadsheet) and freezing the display of certain rows and columns in a window while scrolling other rows and columns into and out of view. There are methods for producing printouts of a spreadsheet's cell values or of its cell definitions.

Changing a spreadsheet involves requests for specifying previously undefined cells, changing characteristics of already defined cells, or deleting characteristics of

SPREADSHEET MANAGEMENT

The technique of spreadsheet management gives a relatively simple way of representing procedural knowledge and relatively small amounts of descriptive knowledge. Each cell definition functions as a step in the overall spreadsheet procedure. Each of these steps involves the evaluation of an expression and assigning the result to a variable that is traditionally called a cell. In the case of a constant definition, the evaluation is trivial and amounts to the storage of a piece of descriptive knowledge. The act of spreadsheet evaluation is one of performing the steps in a spreadsheet's procedure. When a user changes a cell definition for what-if purposes, a step in the procedure has been altered. This new procedure may yield results very similar to or quire different from those of the original spreadsheet procedure.

Software that implements spreadsheet management commonly has a nested graphics capability with features along the lines of those described in the discussion of graphics management in Chapter 12. These implementations also furnish commands that allow a block of cells to be treated as a small table of data—with each row in the block corresponding to a data record. Thus, it is sometimes claimed that such spreadsheet tools have a database management capability nested within them. Although the commands involved in this can be useful (e.g., sorting cell rows within a cell block), the net effect falls far short of the functionality and capacity afforded by true database-management techniques summarized in the prior chapter.

In handling macros, it is common for spreadsheet management software to allow a macro to be defined in terms of branching or looping commands that are commonly available in ordinary programming languages. Defining a cell in terms of such a macro effectively nests the programming technique of knowledge management within the spreadsheet technique in a DSS development tool.

previously specified cells. These requests can work on individual cells or entire blocks of cells (as in copying or moving definitions). There are also requests for changing the appearance of a spreadsheet through a viewing window, such as suppressing the display of row numbers and column letters, making columns wider or narrower, and designating different foreground and background colors. Of course, the most important change for what-if analysis is to change the definition of one or more cells. The impacts of such what-if changes can then be examined when the spreadsheet is evaluated.

10.4 PROGRAM MANAGEMENT

Spreadsheets are handy for presenting the results of a series of steps in a special matrix form. They are very workable when procedural knowledge can be naturally organized into a sequence of assignment statements, each assigning a value to a cell by evaluating the cell's definition. There is added flexibility when cell definitions can include commands embedded in macros. Valuable as they are, however, spreadsheets are no panacea when it comes to representing and processing procedural knowledge.

For some procedures, the mode of presentation embodied in a spreadsheet screen is inappropriate. It may be that we do not need a presentation of values as a procedure's steps are followed. Some procedures may be highly interactive. In such a procedure there can be many steps that involve getting inputs from the user, interspersed with other steps that do calculations, data management, graphics, and so forth. Customized user interfaces may be desired for this interaction. With ordinary spreadsheets, the following of a procedure is not at all interactive. Once the computation begins, it proceeds without user interaction until the last cell definition has been processed.

Aside from presentation limitations, the restriction of conventional spreadsheets to a sequence of calculations makes them inappropriate for many procedures. A more flexible way of representing procedural knowledge would be quite beneficial. The ability to embed **commands** in cell definitions is a dramatic step toward increased flexibility, but there is an alternative way to represent procedural knowledge. It offers the same degree of flexibility and is much more convenient for specifying many kinds of procedures.

Instead of embedding commands in a spreadsheet, we simply type them into a file much like ordinary text. We type the first command as the first line of text, the next command as the second line, and so forth. It is usually permissible for a large command to extend across multiple lines. Each command represents a step in a procedure. As a whole, the command file represents a procedure. A request to perform such a procedure causes each of its commands to be executed in sequence.

Because the procedure's commands are stored like text in a file, all the usual text-management facilities are available for reviewing, inserting, and deleting individual commands as needed. This feature makes it possible to see the entire flow of commands in a glance, rather than looking at cell definitions one at a time on a spreadsheet's message line. A procedure represented and processed in the foregoing manner is commonly called a **program** (Figure 10.5). The activity of specifying the commands that make up a program is commonly called programming (Higgins 1979; Jackson 1979). Program management involves (1) representing procedural

FIGURE 10.5   A Simple Program

```
   Line:35      Col:1      a:scalc.ipf
   15    ! The program will allow repeated calculations with SCALC as long
   16    ! as the variable MORE has "y" as its value. While MORE has this
   17    ! value, the calculation process will iterate.
   18       more="y"
   19       while more in ["y","Y"] do
   20
   21       ! Find out what rep the user wants and then obtain that record
   22         input who using "%8r" \
   23          with "For which rep do you want to make a salary calculation?"
   24         obtain from rep where fname=who
   25         if #found then perform "a:repfound"
   26               else output trim(who), "is not a valid rep name"
   27                    output "Enter one of the following names:"
   28                    select fname using "%35 %8r" from rep
   29                    #found=false !SELECT finds records, but not WHO
   30                    while not #found do
   31                       input who using "%8r" with "Enter desired name:"
   32                       obtain from rep where fname=who
   33                    endwhile
   34                    perform "a:repfound"
   35         endif
   36         input more using "a" with "Do you want more calculations?(y/n) "
   37         if more in ["Y","y"] then clear; endif
   38       endwhile
```

knowledge in command files (i.e., programs), and (2) the processing of those programs.

OBJECTS OF INTEREST

A knowledge system can contain many programs.. Each is typically held in its own file. Each program is specified in terms of some language consisting of commands that can be executed by the computer. Some of the most widely used languages include BASIC, COBOL, C, Pascal, and FORTRAN (Bohl 1984; Kazmier and Philippakis 1991; Purdum 1985; Kiebwitz 1978; Schriber 1969). In addition, a variety of popular software tools have their own built-in programming languages. For instance, although the dBASE tool is widely regarded as a database manager, it also can execute files holding commands specified in the dBASE programming language (Ross 1990).

Although each programming language has its own unique commands and syntax, they all tend to share common traits. As Figure 10.6 shows, a program can contain not only commands, but also declarations and comments. A **declaration** is a statement that declares the existence of some object that the program will use. For instance, it may declare that a particular working variable or array will be used by the program's commands, thereby causing space to be allocated for it in working memory. Other common declarations include those that detail the structure of a data file or the definition of a macro that the program will use. **Comments** can be interspersed among commands or declarations in a program. They serve to docu-

DSS IN THE NEWS

Most Widely Used Programming Language

Cobol, which stands for common business-oriented language, is the most widely used computer programming language in the world. It's the primary or secondary software used on 83% of mainframes made by International Business Machines Corp.

B. Degan, "CEO Briefing on Information Technology," *Investor's Business Daily,* 10 December 1992, p. 4.

ment what the program is intended to do and are ignored by the computer when the program's commands are executed.

For do-it-yourself developers of DSSs, program commands can be considered to fall into four main categories: assignment commands, input/output (I/O) commands, control commands, and utility commands. When executed, an **assignment command** causes a variable to take on a value that is determined by evaluating an expression specified in that command. **I/O commands** fall into two categories: those that allow a program to interact with its user and those that allow it to retrieve and store data in disk files. An input command results in a new value (from the user or a file) for an indicated variable. An output command results in the value of a variable or expression being displayed to a user or stored in a file.

Control commands determine the number of times and order in which other commands are executed. Without control commands, the contents of a command file are executed one time in sequence. Common control commands include IF, TEST, WHILE, and PERFORM. The IF command executes one series of commands if a specified condition is satisfied and a different series if it is not. The TEST command gives a way of controlling which one (or more) of many command series will be executed, depending on the value of some variable or expression specified in the command. The WHILE command lets a series of commands be executed repeatedly while a specified condition is satisfied. As soon as it is not satisfied, execution proceeds to other commands. The PERFORM command givers a program a means for executing other programs as if their commands were actually included there. Further discussion of these commands is provided in Appendix D.

FIGURE 10.6   Knowledge-Representation Objects in Program Management

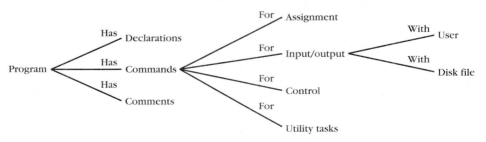

Finally, various utility commands can appear in a program. These help make the activity of programming more convenient or the execution of a program more efficient. For instance, utility commands may be available for indicating what disk drive is to be assumed when none is specified, for releasing the memory allocated to variables that are no longer needed, or for saving and restoring screen images.

PROCESSING THE OBJECTS

There are five major methods for processing programs. First, we can specify a program. As previously noted, we typically accomplish this in the same way as we specify a document in text management, except that each line specified in a program must conform to the conventions of the programming language being used. Second, we can change the lines in a program in the same way we can change lines in a document. Changes may be for the purpose of expanding the program to accomplish new tasks or with the intent of correcting errors (i.e., "bugs") in the program.

Third, many implementations of program management let us request help in debugging a program. Once a program is initially specified, we should always test it thoroughly to be sure that it behaves in the way we expect (Cougar 1979). If it does not, then there is a bug in it. The activity of finding the error and fixing it is

DSS IN THE NEWS

The World of Multimedia

Multimedia is a growing technology area with as many definitions as potential applications.

. . . The term multimedia software basically refers to advanced programs that use a mixture of elements—text, graphics, sound, video and animation—to convey information.

The idea behind multimedia is to build software that communicates in a more human and more interesting way than just displaying text for a user to read.

But making applications easier to use isn't easy for software developers. In fact, dealing with multiple inputs like sound and video dramatically complicates the development process.

Fortunately, the process can be streamlined with some of the new programming tools . . . that provide an object-based visual programming environment. This approach allows users to avoid writing code in a traditional computer language and instead develop programs by linking predefined, reusable objects that describe program features. . . .

. . . In the future, . . . real estate agents could use a multimedia computer listing of properties to pull up all the data on a house along with a video of the property, audio narrative and perhaps even a schematic showing the lot size and easements. . . .

K. Doler, "New Software Development Tools Help Move Users into World of Multimedia," *Investor's Business Daily* 21 May 1992, p. 3.

THREE CLASSES OF PROGRAMS

There are three basic classes of programs: host software, application software, and tools. Just as hardware is an environment in which software is used, host software, such as an operating system, serves as an environment within which the other two types of programs can be executed. Host software is created by computer professionals.

As its name implies, an application program is designed to handle a particular application, such as the support of gasoline-blending decisions. The program is devised by a do-it-yourself developer and kept in a KS, as are application programs. They embody knowledge that applies to a particular user or problem area. Examples include programs that govern a DSS's interactions with a user or database and programs that are solvers of problems peculiar to a user's decision support needs.

In contrast to application programs, widely used tools are not application specific. They are programmed by computer professionals. As we have seen, a tool is an implementation of one or more knowledge-representation and processing techniques. For instance, a tool that embodies a spreadsheet approach to managing knowledge awaits to be applied to supporting budgeting, scheduling, or other specific kinds of decisions.

called **debugging.** One approach to debugging a program is to mentally step through its commands, thinking out the effect of each step. It can sometimes be helpful to put extra commands in the program to output the effects of individual commands, allowing us to focus in on where things begin to go astray. The most common kinds of bugs are due to improper command syntax, omitted commands, and illogical sequencing of commands. Program-management software can help in detecting such bugs by automatically tracing the effects of commands on variables and by analyzing the syntax and logic of a program's commands.

Fourth, many program managers let us (or require us to) request that a program be compiled before it can be executed. This kind of processing is accomplished with an extrinsic tool called a **compiler.** It results in a new, but equivalent, version

DSS IN THE NEWS

Objects of Attention

. . . [The] potential payoff from object technology stems from binding programming and data . . . [A]n object called "customer X" would include not only all data about the customer but also some computer code [i.e., methods] for communicating with other objects. . . . [This lets it] respond when an object called "marketing survey," asks for data on customers. . . . [T]hese objects can also work across networks. . . . A searcher object, asked to find the gross national product of Peru, would relentlessly scour the network until it came to an object that "knew" the answer. The same technique might make it easy for a chief executive to glean important facts about a client or competitor. . . .

F. Guterl, "Software: Object Programming," *Business Week*, Special 1994 Bonus Issue, p. 64.

of the program. The instructions in the compiled program can be directly executed by the host computer. Program managers that do not compile programs provide an intrinsic software tool called an **interpreter,** which carries out a program's instructions.

Fifth, a request can be issued to execute a program. A user or another program (via a PERFORM command) can invoke such a request directly. In either case, it causes the program's instructions to be carried out by the host computer.

10.5 MENU MANAGEMENT

A program involving ordinary input and output commands can be used to provide customized question/answer interfaces for a DSS. As we saw in Chapter 8, customized menu interfaces are another common way for accepting user requests. However, they are not so easily constructed with traditional programming languages. The menu-management technique greatly facilitates the creation and operation of menu interfaces. Menu management is concerned with (1) the representation of presentation, linguistic, and perhaps procedural knowledge as menus and (2) means for processing those menus.

Menu-management software is often used in conjunction with a programming language. Rather than using an input command to get data from a user, the software presents a **menu** of data options, and the user picks one option. In either case, the entered data or the selected option becomes the value of a variable that is subsequently used in the program execution.

A menu manager can be treated as a prefabricated procedure that can be executed via a PERFORM command within any program. For example, the command

PERFORM MENU USING REP, CHOICE

causes the menu manager (i.e., a program called MENU) to present a menu previously defined and stored with the name REP, allow a user to pick one of the presented **menu options,** and assign a value to the CHOICE variable reflecting the selected option.

Alternatively, a menu manager can be integrated into program-management software (i.e., into a compiler or interpreter) so that menu presentation and input can be invoked as a function in the programming language. For instance, a program might have the assignment command

CHOICE = MENU (REP)

to have the REP menu presented to a user, allow the user to pick an option, and then assign a value to CHOICE reflecting the selected option.

A third alternative for integrating menu management and program management allows programs to be associated with options when a menu is defined. That is, each option in a menu can be defined to have a set of instructions that tells the menu manager what to do if that option happens to be chosen by a user. As a variation, no programs are associated with a menu's options. Instead, a submenu is associated with each option. In this case, selection of an option causes the menu manager to present the associated submenu (Figure 10.7). Only those menus not having associated submenus would have associated programs.

FIGURE 10.7   A Menu and the Submenu for One of Its Options

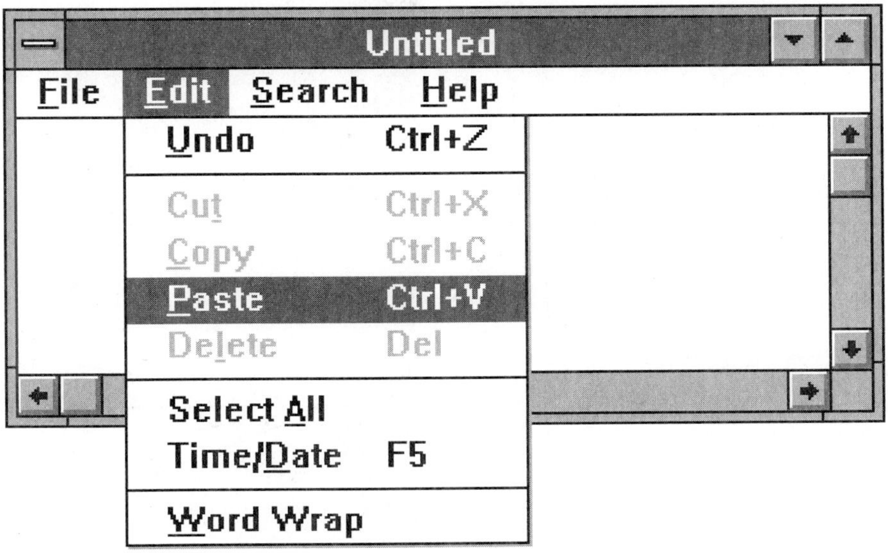

OBJECTS OF INTEREST

The central object of interest in menu management is a menu. As Figure 10.8 indicates, a menu can have a name, position for display on the screen, a set of options, an explanation, and a specified style. Each option is usually a word, number, phrase, or icon that will appear on the screen as a candidate for user selection. Each option can have some help text describing what will happen if this option is selected. When a user highlights an option, the menu manager will display its help text. As noted previously, with some menu managers an option may also be defined to have either a sequence of commands that are executed when the option is chosen or a submenu that is presented when the option is chosen.

If a menu has an explanation, it will be displayed along with the options. An explanation tells the user what the menu is about and how to use it. There are numerous possibilities for a menu's style, including its type, layout, border characteristics, color combinations, and processing conventions. The menu type can range from fixed, which means the menu remains displayed even after an option is selected, to pop-up, which means the menu pops up on the screen only until an option is selected and then vanishes.

Menu layout is concerned with how the options are displayed relative to each other. Possibilities range from a horizontal bar or row of options to a vertical list of options to multirow, multicolumn arrangements. Border characteristics are concerned with how a menu is visually separated from other screen contents (e.g., thick versus thin lines or double versus single lines). Foreground and background color combinations can exist for a menu as a whole, its options, its explanation, or help text. Processing conventions include indications of how an option should be highlighted (e.g., reverse video, high intensity) and what option should be the default (i.e., the initially highlighted option).

FIGURE 10.8   Knowledge-Representation Objects in Menu Management

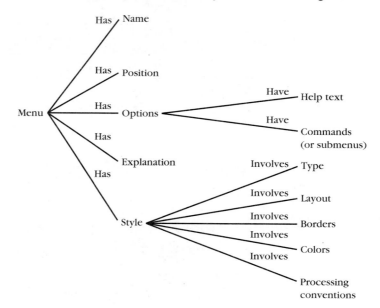

PROCESSING THE OBJECTS

There are six basic methods for processing a menu. We can define it, use/finish it, view its characteristics, change them, delete the menu, or activate it. A menu is defined by specifying its name, position, options, explanation, and style. Some menu-management implementations may not handle all these characteristics. Implementations also vary in terms of how the definition is made. For some, the act of defining a menu is itself menu-driven, with the resultant menu being stored in a KS file. For others, menus may be defined in a special language using text management or specified in the arguments of a function for menu processing.

Once a menu is defined, we may store it in the KS when we are finished using it. Later we can recall it for use, as needed. Once a menu is in use (i.e., in the PPS working memory), the DSS developer can view, change, or delete it or activate it. This method causes the menu manager to present the menu to a user, highlight any option the user desires, display help text for whatever options the user highlights, accept the option selected by the user, and carry out any commands or submenu processing that may have been defined for the selected option.

A menu manager can be designed to combine the definition and activation methods into a single request. That is, a menu is defined as it is activated, without storing it for subsequent use. This "on-the-fly" menu management does not make use of use/finish, view, change, or delete requests.

10.6 SUMMARY

In this chapter we have surveyed four techniques particularly concerned with the management of procedural knowledge: solver, spreadsheet, program, and menu management. The first three of these also have some capabilities for handling descriptive knowledge. The fourth is oriented toward managing linguistic and presentation knowledge. Additional techniques that focus on representing and processing these two knowledge types are surveyed in the next chapter. Important classes of objects covered in this chapter include solvers, models, data sets, spreadsheets, programs, and menus. Each of these is a candidate for inclusion in a decision support system's KS.

A solver is an executable algorithm that can solve any problem belonging to a certain class of problems. In a fixed-solver DSS, solvers are part of the PPS software. In flexible-solver DSSs, they are held in KS files and are subject to creation, revision, and deletion. The statement of a specific problem that we want a solver to solve is often called a model. Sometimes models explicitly include data. Alternatively, a model may refer to data sets containing data that helps characterize the problem. A software tool that implements solver management gives the ability to create, combine, revise, and delete both models and data sets in a DSS's knowledge system as well as to execute a solver to get the solution of a problem.

A spreadsheet is a gridlike arrangement of expressions into cells. A cell's expression effectively defines how the value of that cell is to be calculated. This calculation is trivial for cells that are defined in terms of constant expressions. However, a cell's definition can involve operators, functions, and operands (i.e., references to other cells). Spreadsheets can be specified, modified, and deleted in a DSS's knowledge system. Most important, a spreadsheet can be evaluated to study the collective implications of assumptions captured in its cells' definitions. Exploring implications is a common activity within decision making.

A program existing in a KS is a sequence of commands that instruct a computer what to do in support of a decision maker. These commands may evaluate expressions, assigning the results to variables rather than cells. The commands may be to interact with a user or with other KS contents or to control the use of other commands in the program by way of conditional branching or iteration. Program management is a versatile, flexible means for managing procedural knowledge. However, it generally requires more skill and training than is needed to use solver- or spreadsheet-management implementations effectively.

A menu is an object for presenting a set of options to a user, capturing a user's selection, and either reporting that selection to a program or initiating further processing based on that selection. This further processing could be either the presentation of an appropriate submenu (for further processing itself) or the execution of a procedure defined for the selected option when the menu was initially created.

▲ IMPORTANT TERMS

assignment commands	interpreter
cell	I/O commands
cell definition	menu
cell value	menu options
commands	model
comments	model base
compiler	problem statement
control commands	program
control logic	schemas
data set	solver
debug	spreadsheet
declarations	

▲ APPLICATION TO THE TEXACO CASE

1. How is the OMEGA decision support system used before the start of each month?
2. How is OMEGA used as a month progresses?
3. What kind of input does the OMEGA solver need?
4. What kind of output does the OMEGA solver produce?
5. This case refers to a model. What is the nature of this model?
6. Does this DSS appear to use a fixed or flexible approach to solver management?
7. Aside from solver management, what other knowledge-management technique is used?
8. What kinds of factors cause OMEGA models to change?
9. Do you think OMEGA could have been developed more easily, using a spreadsheet rather than solver management? Why or why not?
10. In what way do you suspect the OMEGA developers used programming?
11. Explain the connection between OMEGA's optimization options screen and menu management.
12. If OMEGA is able to produce a truly optimal blending plan, why is a human participant needed in the decision making? That is, why is OMEGA a decision support system rather than a decision-making system?
13. Describe the benefits that Texaco realized from the DSS.

▲ REVIEW QUESTIONS

1. In what way is procedural knowledge represented and processed by each of the following?
   a. Solver management
   b. Spreadsheet management
   c. Program management
   d. Menu management
2. Contrast the treatment of solvers in fixed-solver versus flexible-solver management.
3. What are the relative benefits and drawbacks of each approach to solver management?
4. How does a solver differ from a model?
5. What is the relationship between a model and a data set?
6. How can a DSS that incorporates solver management assist a decision maker?
7. What is a model base? A model?
8. Why are input schemas and output schemas for a solver important?
9. How can the use of multiple solvers be coordinated when they are all needed to solve a given problem?
10. How does processing differ in the fixed- versus flexible-solver cases?
11. How can a DSS that incorporates spreadsheet management benefit a decision maker?
12. What is a spreadsheet? A cell?
13. How does a cell definition differ from a cell value?
14. In what way do macros extend conventional spreadsheet capabilities?
15. What capabilities are offered by program management that are not readily available with spreadsheet management?

16. What are the main types of commands commonly found in a program?
17. How do commands, comments, and declarations differ?
18. What are the two categories of I/O commands?
19. In what way does conditional branching differ from conditional iteration?
20. How can a DSS that incorporates program management benefit a decision maker?
21. How do compilers and interpreters of programs differ?
22. What methods are generally available for processing programs?
23. What is a menu?
24. What are the major ways of relating menu management to program management?
25. What are the major attributes of menus?
26. How do fixed menus differ from pop-up menus?
27. Why is menu management relevant to DSS development and usage?

▲ DISCUSSION TOPICS

1. Contrast the efficacy of solver management with that of database management for handling (a) procedural knowledge and (b) descriptive knowledge.
2. Are tools that implement (a) solver management, (b) spreadsheet management, (c) program management, and (d) menu management intrinsic, partially intrinsic, or extrinsic?
3. What does spreadsheet management have in common with solver management? With program management?
4. How does spreadsheet management differ from solver management? From program management?
5. Discuss the relationship between expression management and spreadsheet management.
6. Explain why spreadsheet management falls far short of database management as a means for representing and processing descriptive knowledge.
7. Compare and contrast solver management and program management.
8. Discuss the implications of compiled versus interpretive program management for DSS developers and DSS users.
9. What kinds of debugging methods would be helpful for a program manager to provide?
10. Describe the different uses of the term *model* in the DSS field.
11. Tools that implement spreadsheet or database management are often called *applications* by vendors. Critique this nomenclature.
12. Solver-management techniques have their roots in an area of research known as model management. Describe the major research initiatives in this area of research.

▲ REFERENCES

Allen, B. R. 1984. *VisiCalc—IBM PC: An executive's guide*. Reston, Va.: Reston.

Bhargava, H. K., and S. O. Kimbrough. 1993. Model management: An embedded languages approach. *Decision Support Systems* 10, no. 3.

Bhargava, H. K., and R. Krishnan. 1993. Computer-aided model construction. *Decision Support Systems* 9, no. 1.

Binbiasioglu, M., and M. Jarke. 1986. Domain specific DSS tools for knowledge-based model building. *Decision Support Systems* 2, no. 3.

Blanning, R. W. 1983. Issues in the design of relational model management systems. *Proceedings of the National Computer Conference* (June).

———. 1984. A PROLOG-based framework for model management. *Proceedings of the First International Workshop on Expert Database Systems* (October),

———. 1987a. A framework for expert modelbase systems. *Proceedings of the National Computer Conference* (June).

———. 1987b. A relational theory of model management. In *Decision support systems: Theory and applications,* edited by C. Holsapple and A. Whinston. Berlin: Springer-Verlag.

Bohl, M. 1984. *Information processing with BASIC.* Chicago: SRA.

Bonczek, R. H., C. W. Holsapple, and A. B. Whinston. 1978. Mathematical programming within the context of a generalized database planning system. *Recherche Operationnelle* 12, no. 2.

———. 1981. *Foundations of decision support systems.* New York: Academic Press.

———. 1983. Specifications of modeling knowledge in decision support systems. In *Processes and tools for decision support,* edited by H. G. Sol. Amsterdam: North-Holland.

Cain, N. W. 1984. *1-2-3 at work.* Reston, Va.: Reston.

Carroll, T. O. 1986. *Decision power with supersheets.* Homewood, Ill.: Dow Jones–Irwin.

Chang A., C. W. Holsapple, and A. B. Whinston. 1993. Model management issues and directions. *Decision Support Systems* 9, no. 1.

Chari, S., and R. Krishnan. 1993. Toward a logical reconstruction of structured modeling. *Decision Support Systems* 10, no. 3.

Cougar, J. D. 1979. *The art of software testing.* New York: John Wiley.

Courtney, J. F., and D. B. Paradice. 1993. Studies in managerial problem formulation systems. *Decision Support Systems* 9, no. 4.

DeWitt, C. W., L. S. Lasdon, A. D. Waren, D. A. Brenner, and S. A. Melhem. 1989. OMEGA: An improved gasoline blending system for Texaco. *Interfaces* 19, no. 1.

Dhar, V., and M. Jarke. 1993. On modelling processes. *Decision Support Systems* 9, no. 1.

Dolk, D. R. 1986. Data as models: an approach to implementing model management. *Decision Support Systems* 2, no. 1.

———. 1988. Model management and structured modeling: The role of an information resource dictionary system. *Communications of the ACM* 31, no. 6,

Dolk, D. R., and J. E. Kottemann. 1993. Model integration and a theory of models. *Decision Support Systems* 9, no. 1,

Dutta, A., and A. Basu. 1984. An artificial intelligence approach to model management in decision support systems. *IEEE Computer* 17, no. 9.

Eck, R., A. Philippakis, and R. Ramirez. 1990. Solver representation in model management systems. *Proceedings of Hawaiian International Conference on System Sciences* (January).

Falkner, M., and R. A. August. 1991. The Price Waterhouse report: Financial modeling software. *PC Magazine* 10, no. 4.

Fedorowicz, J., and G. D. Williams. 1986. Representing modeling knowledge in intelligent decision support systems. *Decision Support Systems* 2, no. 1.

Geoffrin, A. M. 1987. An introduction to structured modeling. *Management Science* 33, no. 5.

———. 1989a. The formal aspects of structured modeling. *Operations Research* 37, no. 1.

———. 1989b. Integrated modeling systems. *Computer Science in Economics and Management* 2, no. 1.

Ghiaseddin, N. 1986. An environment for the development of decision support systems. *Decision Support Systems* 2, no. 3.

Glau, G. R. 1987. *Controlling your cash flow with 1-2-3 or Symphony.* Homewood, Ill.: Dow Jones–Irwin.

Gray, P. 1983. *Student guide to IFPS.* New York: McGraw-Hill.

Greenberg, H. J. 1983. A functional description of ANALYZE: A computer assisted analysis system for linear programming models. *ACM Transactions on Mathematical Software* 9, no. 1.

_____. 1987. A natural language discourse model to explain linear programming models and solutions. *Decision Support Systems* 3, no. 4.

Higgins, D. A. 1979. *Program design and construction.* Englewood Cliffs, N.J.: Prentice Hall.

Hong, S. N., M. V. Mannino, and B. Greenberg. 1993. Measurement theoretic representation of large, diverse model bases. *Decision Support Systems* 10, no. 3.

Jackson, M. A. 1979. *Principles of program design.* New York: Academic Press.

Jarke, M., and F. J. Radermacher. 1988. The AI potential of model management and its central role in decision support. *Decision Support Systems* 4, no. 4.

Jones, C. V. 1990. An introduction to graph-based modeling systems, Part I: Overview. *ORSA Journal on Computing* 2, no. 2.

_____. 1991. An introduction to graph-based modeling systems, Part II: Graph-grammars and their implementation. *ORSA Journal on Computing* 3, no. 3.

_____. 1993. An integrated modeling environment based on attributed graphs and graph-grammars. *Decision Support Systems* 10, no. 3.

Kazmier, L. J., and A. S. Philippakis. 1991. *Comprehensive COBOL.* New York: McGraw-Hill.

Kiebwitz, R. B. 1978. *Structured programming and problem-solving with Pascal.* Englewood Cliffs, N.J.: Prentice Hall.

King, D. 1986. The ERGO project: A natural language query facility for explaining financial results. *DSS-86 Transactions* (April).

Krishnan, R. 1990. A logic modeling language for automatic model construction. *Decision Support Systems* 6, no. 2.

Lee, R. 1993. Direct manipulation of graph-based decision models. *Decision Support Systems* 9, no. 4.

Lenard, M. 1986. Representing models as data. *Journal of Management Information Systems* 2, no. 4.

Liang, T. 1993. Analogical reasoning and case-based learning in model management systems. *Decision Support Systems* 10, no. 2.

Ma, P. C., F. H. Murphy, and E. A. Stohr. 1989. Graphics interface for linear programming. *Communications of the ACM* 32, no. 8.

Purdum, J. 1985. *C programming guide.* Indianapolis, Ind.: Que.

Ramierez, R. G., C. Ching, and R. D. St. Louis. 1993. Independence and mappings in model-based decision support systems. *Decision Support Systems* 10, no. 3.

Ross, S. C. 1990. *Understanding and using dBASE IV.* St. Paul: West.

Schriber, T. J. 1969. *FORTRAN case studies for business applications.* New York: John Wiley.

Shaw, M. J., P. L. Tu, and P. De. 1988. Applying machine learning to model management in decision support. *Decision Support Systems* 4, no. 3.

Stohr, E. A., and M. R. Tanniru. 1980. A database for operations research models. *International Journal of Policy Analysis and Information Systems* 4, no. 2.

Chapter 11

FORMS, REPORT, GRAPHICS, RULE, AND MESSAGE MANAGEMENT

SOUTHLAND: A DSS FOR ROUTING DECISIONS

Overview

A geographic-based decision support system has been developed to help Southland Corporation traffic managers choose routes for trucks that deliver to convenience stores. The system, implemented on a microcomputer, presents information on routes and accounts, uses flexible computer graphics and interactive text screens to help a traffic manager analyze routes, and produces maps for drivers and reports for management.

The Southland Corporation is the . . . world's largest operator and franchisor of convenience stores . . . known throughout the world as "7-11 stores." . . . To keep over 7,000 stores well-stocked, frequent delivery of small quantities of goods (usually in less than case lots) is required. . . .

Several approaches exist for formulating and evaluating a set of routes for a fleet of vehicles. The principle optimization methods proposed for assigning delivery points to routes are dynamic programming . . . and integer programming. . . . Although these methods produce optimal solutions, they are often unable to solve reasonable-sized problems efficiently. For this reason heuristic approaches to the routing problem have been developed. . . . They are computationally feasible, and they have produced near optimal solutions for a number of actual delivery problems.

A semiautomated system based on computer graphics provides an alternate way to perform the routing and scheduling function. . . . Computer graphics present large amounts of data in an efficient and effective way that is easily understood by decision makers, who can then quickly and easily identify trends in performance and initiate corrective action in a timely fashion.

System Features

. . . The system . . . developed for the Southland Corporation's Orlando, Florida, distribution center . . . is a geographic-based decision support system and report generator. . . . Various graphics features are provided which enable the user to build or view a route on a map, zoom in on a specific area of a map, locate accounts, extract information on the account from the database, and determine the exact distance in miles from any account or landmark to a distribution center. The data for map displays are divided into two categories. The fixed geographic data—roads, coastlines, and water—are stored as line segments to be plotted whenever a map is requested. Whenever needed, stores and connecting routes are plotted from the store data file which includes location coordinates.

The system can best be explained by describing its four major components, the main menu:

1. INPUT DELIVERY REQUIREMENTS AND ROUTES,
2. BUILD ROUTES,
3. MAINTAIN STORE FILE, AND
4. SORT ON SELECTED FIELDS.

These components are separate activities required for routing and reporting.

. . . INPUT DELIVERY REQUIREMENTS AND ROUTES allows the user to originate, add to, and modify a set of routes. Through this option, the traffic manager

Continued

supplies information unique to each route, such as route number, total weight and volume, and vehicle type and capacity. The BUILD ROUTES option graphically displays routes on maps and displays charts on a text screen which show each stop on a route. The traffic manager can shuffle deliveries among routes, add, eliminate, or consolidate routes through an interactive process. The option MAINTAIN STORE FILE allows relatively permanent information about stores, such as location and acceptable delivery times, to be easily modified. . . . SORT ON SELECTED FIELDS enables the user to search the store file on seven fields and print out reports that include store specific data such as addresses, feasible delivery times and days, and specific delivery instructions.

The system is extremely flexible. . . . Menu and submenu options offer the traffic manager a number of ways to use the system. Because modular design methodology has been used to develop the system, it can be enhanced easily and used in other settings.

Benefits

. . . Feedback indicates that the system is a success. Traffic managers have fully accepted the system and are using it to perform a number of activities that improve the quality of the daily dispatch, such as consolidating routes, detecting overlaps, and modifying delivery sequences. Southland management has reported that use of the system has reduced the number of routes scheduled daily. On the average, the system has reduced the number of routes by one, resulting in a net savings of a thousand dollars per day.

Recently, the graphics features discussed here have been employed to develop a system for crisis management. The flexible graphics and interactive database capabilities have been used to simulate emergency evacuation scenarios. . . . This system enables the users to plot a route and implement changes in variables as conditions warrant. For example, the user may change the capacity of a route to reflect changes in weather conditions, or changes in conditions that initially precipitated the evacuation decision.

Condensed quotation from S. Belardo, P. Duchessi, and J. P. Seagle, "Microcomputer Graphics in Support of Vehicle Fleet Routing," *Interfaces* 15, no. 6 (1985): 84–91.

LEARNING OBJECTIVES

In the Southland case, graphics management is crucial to the success of the DSS. As discussed in this chapter, there are other forms of graphs that can be very helpful to decision makers (e.g., bar graphs or scattergrams). As with graphics management, forms management and report management are concerned with the representation and processing of presentation knowledge, and the latter plays a part in Southland's DSS. The case alludes to heuristics, which may be characterized as rules along the lines described in this chapter. Although not mentioned in the case, it may well be that some form of message management would be helpful (e.g., in informing others about route decisions made). As you read this chapter, keep the Southland case in mind.

After studying this chapter, you should be able to

1. Describe the main features of each of the following knowledge-management techniques:
   - Forms management
   - Report management
   - Graphics management
   - Rule management
   - Message management
2. Explain the distinctions among these techniques in terms of the objects used for knowledge representation and the methods used to process those objects.
3. Assess the potential value of each technique for managing alternative types of knowledge.
4. Learn how to use software tools that embody these techniques as a basis for building your own DSSs.
5. Recognize and assess the integration of multiple techniques in DSS development tools.

Exercises at the chapter's end will help you see how well you have met these objectives.

11.1 INTRODUCTION

Concluding our survey of knowledge-management techniques for decision support, we examine means for managing forms, reports, graphics, rules, and messages. Relative to menus, forms provide a more open-ended way for users to interact with a DSS. Rather than controlling DSS behavior by selecting one of several prespecified options, a user can make requests by filling in blank slots in a form. Forms can also be used by a DSS strictly for presentation purposes. Report management gives a DSS even more elaborate presentation capabilities than forms management. Graphics management gives a way for treating the values held in some data source as presentation knowledge, using them to control the appearance of graphs produced by a DSS.

Rule management is an important technique for representing and processing reasoning knowledge. It gives a basis for building artificially intelligent decision support systems. Part Four provides a more detailed examination of the value, development, and operation of such DSSs. Finally, we consider message management. A message can embody any of the six knowledge types. As with text management, however, messages are processed without regard to which types of knowledge they represent. This processing allows messages to be created, stored, modified, sent, and received by a DSS.

Having surveyed 13 knowledge-management techniques, each of which can be implemented in DSS development tools, we conclude with a discussion of the growing trend toward integration of multiple techniques in individual decision support systems. Synergistic integration of conventional techniques effectively yields a new knowledge-management technique whose processing capabilities are greater than the simple sum of conventional capabilities. In considering a particular tool as a candidate for DSS development, it is important to appreciate which techniques are provided by that tool, the degree to which each is provided, and the nature of technique integration. These factors strongly influence what kinds of DSSs can be built with the tool and what kinds of decision support are possible by using the tool.

11.2 FORMS MANAGEMENT

Forms management deals with the representation of presentation knowledge as a form and with the processing of such forms (Kaiser 1968; Myers 1976; Tsichritzis 1982; Betts 1991). Virtually every day, decision makers process various forms. They look at forms that others have filled in, such as product progress forms and monthly expense account forms. They also fill in forms and send them to others, such as the form used when reviewing an employee's performance.

A **form** is a way of presenting data. It imposes a certain visual organization on some data values with the intent of making it easy to convey or grasp the story that those values have to tell. Of course, the same collection of data could be presented through alternative forms that visually arrange the same values in different ways to suit different purposes or tastes. But most forms have certain basic traits in common.

A form normally has some preprinted strings of text arranged on the page. There is usually a title, perhaps some instructions to the person filling out or reading the form, and then some description that accompanies each place where data are to be filled in. Thus, there are two kinds of elements in a form. The literal, or preprinted slots, are constant and unchanging. They are literally always presented, no matter whether anything has been filled in or not. There are also the nonliteral slots in a form, where various things can be filled in as needed, as in a tax form.

Depending on the purpose of a form, the two kinds of **form slots** can be laid out in various ways. That is, any element—be it literal text or a nonliteral slot—has a certain physical location in the form. Many times elements might be grouped into a box or color block because they are related in some way.

All the traits we have identified for paper forms are also traits of electronic forms that can be presented on a console screen. See Figure 11.1. In addition, data can be entered into the nonliteral slots for electronic storage (e.g., as variable values or field values in a database record). Moreover, forms-management software can use the nonliteral slots to display values of variables or results of expression evaluation. As in the case of menu management, it is not unusual for a forms manager to be integrated with a programming facility for use in place of ordinary line-at-a-time input and output.

OBJECTS OF INTEREST

The main objects of interest in forms management are forms (also called electronic forms or e-forms). In addition, there are variables (or fields), whose values are entered through a form's slots, and expressions, whose values are presented in a form's slots. As Figure 11.2 shows, a form can have a name that distinguishes it from other forms that are stored in the KS or are simultaneously in use in working memory. Visually, a form can also have elements, boxes, and color blocks. These fit within the rectangular boundary of a form. That rectangular area may be smaller than, the same size as, or larger than the console screen.

Form Elements   Each element has a designated location in a form. **Literal elements** can be textual or graphical icons displayed at designated locations.

FIGURE 11.1   A Blank Form Ready for a User to Insert Sales Representative Data

```
                        Sales Representative


  Name:                    Spouse:_____   Phone: (___) ___-____
  Address:


        Major products are __:__:__

                                          Monthly salary
                                             $__,_____.__

                                          Monthly expense (budgeted)
                                             $__,_____.__



  Territory:
```

Nonliteral elements are of two basic kinds. A nonliteral element can be defined for getting a value entered by a user at a designated location in the form and assigning it to a specified variable, or it can be defined by specifying an expression whose value will be calculated and presented at the element's designated location. If this expression is simply a variable, then the nonliteral element could be used as a slot to both get a value from a user and to put the variable's value on the screen for a user to see.

FIGURE 11.2   Knowledge-Representation Objects in Forms Management

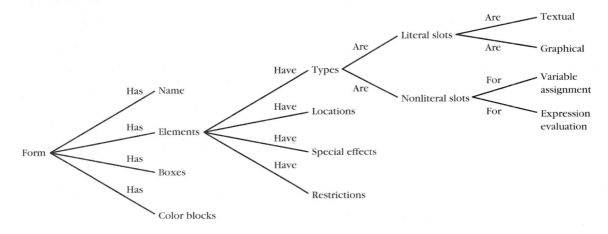

An element can be specified to have various special visual effects. For instance, it may have a picture to govern its appearance (and restrict the values that can be typed into it by a user). It can be specified as having a reverse video display, as blinking, as being low intensity, or as having sound effects (e.g., a beep whenever the user enters a value for it). A nonliteral element, in which a user can enter a value, may also be specified to have certain restrictions for that value. The forms manager uses those restrictions as assimilative knowledge to prevent an improper value from being assigned to the element's variable.

Boxes and Color Blocks   The boxes specified in a form are rectangles encompassing certain areas. Each can be specified to have stylistic traits (e.g., single line versus double line, thick line versus thin line, line intensity, line colors). Similarly, a color block is a rectangular area having a specified background color and foreground color. All elements in a box take on those colors.

DSS IN THE NEWS

E-Forms Perform

Many vendors are still peddling virtual paper products, but a few are adding smarts to their e-forms products, essentially turning them into low-end workflow tools. The ground is still shifting, however, and some of the things you should consider—and that the market is still sorting out—are workflow capabilities, integration with e-mail, cross-platform support, database integration, and the package's scripting language.

The original lure to using e-forms was to avoid paying for all those paper forms. But the real payoff can come from transforming the process and thus lowering the cost of processing the form. That's not small change. Paul Clandillon, IBM's brand manager for forms products, says that, for every dollar American businesses spend on printed forms, they spend $14 processing them.

Take an e-forms pilot project under way at KFC headquarters in Louisville, Ky. According to Lori King, a senior programmer/analyst at KFC, the pilot project observes: "benefits stuff; payroll stuff. Letting facilities know who this person is, where they're going to sit, what equipment they need to have and have access to, and what areas they'll have access to. IT needs to know to get them a PC and what kind, as well as adding their name and privileges to the card key access system and getting them a card. They'll also need appropriate access to the LAN, the mainframe, and the e-mail system."

In most companies, the new hire has to fill in one form or another, often with much the same information. And other people have to process, approve, track, and store all the forms. So King says, "Why don't we combine those processes into one PC-based employee profile application? Then the employee name and demographic information would be populated automatically on the appropriate forms sent to each department. All the pieces can be tied together in a systematic way, eliminating redundant data entry. And with all those little pieces, something always gets left out, like ordering the nameplate."

L. The, "E-Forms Get Smarter," *Datamation* 1 December 1994, pp. 67–68.

PROCESSING THE OBJECTS

Typical methods available for form processing fall into three main classes: those concerned with specifying the customized nature of a form, those that allow forms to be transferred between disk files and working memory, and those that control interaction with a form on the console screen.

Defining a Form   The first of these classes involves requests for defining the nature of a form, changing its characteristics, showing those characteristics, and deleting it from the KS. There are two general approaches to defining a form. One is to specify its elements, boxes, and color blocks by making statements in a special form declaration language that the forms-management software can interpret. The second is to interactively "paint" the form's elements, boxes, and color blocks on the screen. This allows the software to give immediate visual feedback about the appearance of a form as it is being invented. Once a form is defined, either its declaration or its appearance on the screen can be viewed or changed. Changing a form's characteristics (e.g., moving an element, adding a box, enlarging a color block) can be accomplished by altering the form's declaration or through the form manager's extrinsic painting facility.

Saving and Loading Forms   The second class of methods allows the specification of a form's characteristics to be saved in a KS file, once the form is initially defined or the definition is changed. It allows for requests to load a form from the KS into working memory prior to changing its characteristics or using it for interaction with a user. It allows requests to show the names of forms currently in use. The working memory that a form occupies can later be released when interaction with the form is finished.

DSS IN THE NEWS

Reforming the Way Things Are Done

. . . Time can be saved and calculation errors minimized by creating and filling out expense forms, review forms, purchase orders and the like on personal computers. . . .

. . . Many corporations have built their own custom forms-processing applications using database software and programming languages. . . .

The Edison Electric Institute, a Washington-based trade association serving investor-owned electric utilities, recently completed a forms automation project that allows travel expense forms to be filled out and filed electronically. Institute officials say automation has cut the time required to reimburse employees for expenses to one day from three weeks and has increased the accuracy of the data submitted. . . .

K. Doler, "How to Speed Forms Processing, Cut Down Errors with PC Software," *Investor's Business Daily* 2 March 1993, p. 4.

FORMS MANAGEMENT IN RELATION TO PROGRAMS AND SPREADSHEETS

Used within a program, forms management offers several advantages to customary line-oriented, question-answer interaction with a user. It gives a relatively convenient way to let users interact through electronic replicas of familiar paper forms. It affords greater flexibility and ease of interface construction, especially for producing fancy, eye-catching presentations. It reduces programming effort, permitting an entire series of input/output commands to be replaced with a couple of commands that process a form as a whole.

Forms management can also be seen as an alternative to spreadsheet management, and vice versa. A spreadsheet can be regarded as a form whose elements are organized into a grid. Each spreadsheet cell corresponds to a form element. Cells with constant definitions are akin to literal elements. Those with formula expressions as definitions are similar to nonliteral cells. Spreadsheet evaluation is comparable to form evaluation. However, spreadsheet processing does not have a direct counterpart to the form-processing method of accepting data values typed into slots. Although a spreadsheet can be regarded as a special kind of form, a form can be regarded as a generalization of the spreadsheet idea, in which there is a free-form layout of cells (i.e., form elements) that can be used for direct entry of data values as well as display of results from expression evaluation.

Controlling Interaction via Forms   The third class of forms-management methods involves a set of requests that can be invoked for any form currently in use. Ordinarily, a series of such requests is embedded within a program (in place of conventional input/output commands) or a macro. Available requests in this class include those that (1) cause a form's literal elements, boxes, and color blocks to be presented on the screen, leaving blank slots for nonliterals, (2) accept user-typed data values in each of the nonliteral slots for assignment to variables, (3) evaluate all expressions for nonliteral slots and display the results in those slots, (4) clear the form from the screen, and (5) print the form's current image.

11.3   REPORT MANAGEMENT

Report management involves (1) representing presentation knowledge in terms of templates and (2) processing those templates to produce customized reports. Each **report template** consists of one or more forms that control a report's appearance. The report's content is commonly extracted from a database, but it could come from other sources such as working variables or spreadsheet cells. Because templates are comprised of forms (recall Figure 11.2), our treatment of report management is relatively brief. Moreover, this knowledge-management technique is not especially likely to be employed for coping with ad hoc decision support needs. Its primary decision support value is in presenting information in a customized way when (1) there is time to prepare the necessary template and (2) customized presentation is helpful in gaining acceptance for a particular alternative.

Recall that results of an ad hoc SQL SELECT command can be thought of as a tabular report consisting of lines of data. Some degree of control over the presentation of these lines may be furnished (e.g., pictures, column headings, intercolumn spacing). Nevertheless, this capability falls far short of the free-form layouts provided by forms and necessary for elaborate reports. Report management is a technique that gives extensive control over the presentation of report contents.

OBJECTS OF INTEREST

Like ad hoc inquiry processing, report-management software can present results on a line-by-line basis. Each such line is called a **report detail.** However, unlike query results, a report detail can be spread over several lines if desired. The arrangement of data values of each report detail is determined by a form. This detail form has nonliteral elements where the data values are to appear and can also have literal elements. Figure 11.3 shows a report consisting of ten details, each occupying two lines. Notice that each detail has the same pattern of literal and nonliteral elements. Only the values of nonliterals differ from one detail to the next.

In addition, report-management software allows a report to have **header** and **footer** forms. A header form appears before report details, whereas a footer appears after report details. Three kinds of headers and footers are commonly supported. First, there is a report header and footer pair that encases all details in the report. For instance, a report header might consist of a title, date, and underlined column headings. A report footer might consist of a line after all the details, identifying the person who requested the report.

Second, there can be a pager header and footer pair that surrounds all details on each page of a report. For instance, page headers might consist of page numbers and the report title. Third, a group header and footer pair can denote the beginning and end of each group of report details, where the group is defined according to some **control break** criterion. In Figure 11.4, territory ID is the control break

FIGURE 11.3   Report with Two-Line Report Details

```
Name: Kevin R. Andrews        Addr: 25 Stratton Ave. Bloomington IL 54321
    (123) 456-1111 Sal: $2,500  Exp: $1.025.68    sfi"pho:spo 08/30/1981   Kris
Name: Kim G. Anders           Addr: 8242 Wabash, Chicago IL 68909
    (312) 553-6754 Sal: $2,600  Exp: $896.74      ref:bus:spo 04/06/1979
Name: Kris H. Raber           Addr: 314 Miami, Dayton OH 46783
    (513) 333-9989 Sal: $2,400  Exp: $1.132.61    fom:psy:bio 04/08/1982   Kevin
Name: Tina F. Lee             Addr: 7892 Meridian, Indianapolis IN 46662
    (317) 299-8393 Sal: $2,800  Exp: $988.20      bus:com:rom 12/13/1981   Ben
Name: Toby C. Terry           Addr: 2028 Prescott, Fort Wayne IN 45567
    (345) 123-4567 Sal: $2,000  Exp: $1,080.53    rom:psy:bus 02/25/1985
Name: Kerry H. Jones          Addr: 128 Spiceland, Grand Rapids MI 35988
    (632) 098-7654 Sal: $2,250  Exp: $1.229.64    pho:ref:psy 06/10/1983   Kendra
Name: Karen V. Bruckner       Addr: 44 Tan Ave., Madison WI 66667
    (433) 442-8201 Sal: $2,800  Exp: $1.335.00    com:bus:rom 05/14/1982
Name: Kathy F. Smith          Addr: 85 Griese Ln. Milwaukee WI 65543
    (415) 567-8901 Sal: $2,100  Exp: $882.74      pho:ref:sfi 07/03/1984   Tom
Name: Jackie V. Smith         Addr: 32 New Jersey, Columbus OH 33464
    (322) 861-6543 Sal: $2,400  Exp: $1.006.45    spo:ref:bio 04/12/1980   David
Name: Carol O. Lynn           Addr: 58 Cater Dr., Midland MI 40098
    (412) 832-5643 Sal: $2,750  Exp: $1.229.73    com:rom:bus 11/01/1979
```

FIGURE 11.4   Report with Group Headers and Footers

```
Territory 0          Name: Kim B. Anders

    Product            Sales              Quota          Sales - Quota
    -------            -----              -----          -------------

      bus            $21,882            $30,273              $-8,391
      ref            $22,846            $31,595              $-8,749
      spo            $20,267            $27,929              $-7,662
                                                           $-24,802

    Totals:          $64,995            $89,797


Territory 1          Name: Kris H. Raber

    Product            Sales              Quota          Sales - Quota
    -------            -----              -----          -------------

      bio            $22,858            $28,895              $-6,037
      psy            $23,499            $29,654              $-6,155
      rom            $30,535            $38,912              $-8,377
                                                           $-20,569

    Totals:          $76,892            $97,461


Territory 2          Name: Kevin R. Andrews

    Product            Sales              Quota          Sales - Quota
    -------            -----              -----          -------------

      bus            $13,330            $13,575                $-245
      pho            $22,858            $29,794              $-6,936
      ref            $10,125            $14,927              $-4,802
      sfi            $27,794            $35,739              $-7,945
      spo            $22,742            $28,531              $-5,789

    Totals:          $96,849           $122,566             $-25,717


Territory 3          Name: Tina F. Lee

    Product            Sales              Quota          Sales - Quota
    -------            -----              -----          -------------

      bus            $24,307            $32,742              $-8,435
      com            $23,874            $25,667              $-1,793
      psy            $10,125            $14,927              $-4,802
      rom            $13,619            $17,889              $-4,270

    Totals:          $71,925            $91,225             $-19,300
```

criterion. The group of details for each territory has a header showing the territory ID, representative name, and underlined column headings. Each group footer consists of column totals for the group's details. Thus, the template used in producing this report consisted of three simple forms: one for each group header, one for each report detail, and one for each group footer.

> ## CONTROLLING REPORT STRUCTURE AND CONTENT
>
> A template gives a way of representing presentation knowledge. When a command is executed to generate a report with a template, the template's patterns control both the structure and content of the report. The report's content is also restricted and ordered by including a condition and ordering clause in the request. As with ad hoc queries, report generation can involve the simultaneous retrieval of related data from multiple tables.
>
> Customized reports can assume several distinct styles, depending on the nature of headers and footers. If no header or footer pattern is designed in a template, a report will consist only of details in which each conforms to the same pattern. A report header and footer pair embraces all report details. A page header and footer pair appears on each page of a report and embraces only those details that are on a page. A group header and footer pair embraces each group of details, where the desired grouping criterion is specified in the report-generation request, just as it can be specified in a SELECT command. Typically, a group footer shows some statistics or calculations pertaining to its group.

PROCESSING THE OBJECTS

The template used for generating the report in Figure 11.4 may have been defined via either a declarative or painting approach. Suppose this template's nonliteral slots are specified to correspond to fields in the PERF and REP tables of Appendix C. Assume the template is given the name TERREP and stored in a KS file. Then the report in Figure 11.4 results from a request such as

```
REPORT TERREP FROM PERF, REP WHERE PERF.PID=REP.PID AND TID
<"4" GROUP BY TID ORDER BY TID, PID
```

Notice that this request is practically identical to a SELECT request. The main difference is that rather than a list of fields following the word SELECT, the name of a template follows the word REPORT.

As with a SELECT command, when data are extracted from two tables, both are specified and the condition contains a term equating their matching fields. Observe that the report is ordered by territory ID and, within each TID group, by product ID. Each group header has related data values drawn from two different tables. Each detail in a group contains a calculated value. Each group footer has the appropriate sums of data values from the group's details. This same template can be used in generating many different reports, involving different territories or various subsets of the products. But each report has the same structural appearance.

11.4 GRAPHICS MANAGEMENT

Several kinds of graphics management exist. One lets us treat the computer like an electronic Etch-a-Sketch machine, allowing us to draw diagrams on the console screen by rolling a mouse around on the desktop (Greitzer 1986). Going beyond line drawings, we could sketch out scenes and color in various parts of the landscape.

Some development tools even permit an animation effect on the console screen, involving the rapid-fire or slow-motion display of a sequence of scenes.

Another kind of graphics management is used by engineers in the course of designing and manufacturing products. For instance, a graphical image of a car's design may be shown on a console screen, where it can be rotated, magnified, and modified. Such software is known as CAD or CAM: computer-assisted design or computer-assisted manufacturing (Medland 1993).

Here, however, we focus on bread-and-butter business graphics: pie charts, bar graphs, line plots, scattergrams, and so on (Cooper 1984). We have seen that data can be presented via customized forms, via reports, and via ad hoc queries. Data can be presented by incorporating it into a piece of text or displaying it in a spreadsheet grid. In each of these presentation approaches, the data values are presented as numbers or strings. It can often be useful to see those values presented graphically (Cleveland and McGill 1984).

Plotting graphs can help a decision maker quickly spot patterns, trends, and proportions that exist in a collection of data values. See Figure 11.5. Graphics management, then, is concerned with (1) the representation of data sources for producing graphs and the representations of graphs and (2) the processing of graphical data sources and graphs themselves.

FIGURE 11.5 Two Vertical Bar Graphs Showing Sales Quotas of Three Product Lines for Each of Two Sales Representatives

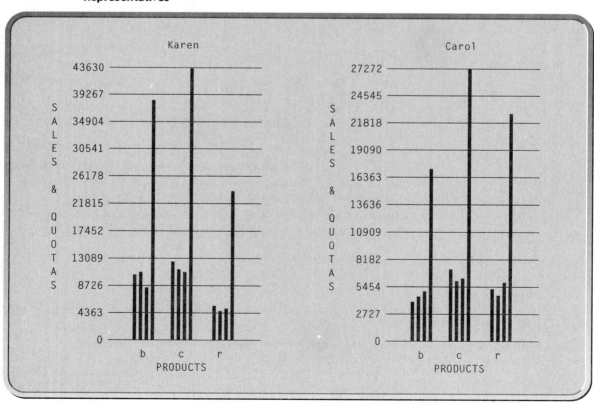

OBJECTS OF INTEREST

A **graph** is generated from a **data source** that serves as a kind of presentation knowledge. This presentation knowledge controls the sizes, heights, and locations of a graph's contents. When generating a bar chart, the data source controls how many bars will be in the chart, how they will be clustered in the graph, and how high the individual bars will be. When generating a pie graph, the data source determines the relative sizes of slices in the pie and the labeling of those slices. In general, it may be possible to plot different kinds of graphs from a single data source or the same kind of graph using different portions of that data source.

Data Sources   An **array** structure is typically used as a data source. Values of the array's elements provide the data for generating graphs. As Figure 11.6 shows, the data values that make up a graphical data source could have various origins. These include the user (1) directly assigning a data value to each array element, (2) using the values of some designated block of spreadsheet cells, (3) letting the tabular result of a database query serve as an array, (4) using array structures permitted by programming languages, or (5) using solver results. All but the first of these imply an integration of graphics management with another knowledge-management technique. Depending on the type of integration (recall Chapter 8), data values are either imported or converted into a data source array or the object holding the data values (e.g., a spreadsheet block) is treated as being a graphical data source array. In the former case, each data source can have a name to distinguish it from other arrays held in the KS or working memory.

FIGURE 11.6   Knowledge-Representation Objects in Graphics Management

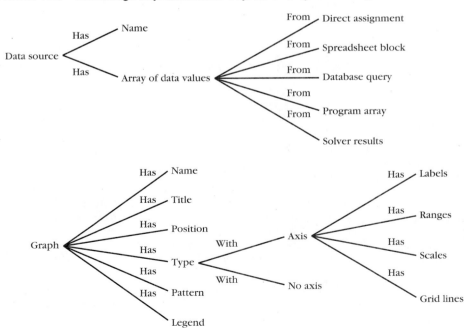

For purposes of our description here, we shall simply regard a data source as being an array. A two-dimensional array is made up of multiple columns as well as multiple rows of elements. For instance, an array called DS (i.e., data source) might be dimensioned to have 4 rows and 3 columns. It would thus be capable of holding 12 values in its elements. Suppose these values are

4	2800	4000
5	2950	3014
6	2500	2820
7	3005	2400

Each element is referenced by indicating its row and column. For instance, DS(2,3) has the value 3014.

An array is just a grid of storage compartments or elements. We can put any value we want in any compartment, and we can tell the graphics management software to plot a graph based on whatever values happen to be there. We can plot many kinds of graphs from a single data source: pies, lines, bars, areas, and more.

Graphs   Once we have generated a graph from a data source, it can be regarded as an object that is itself subject to various kinds of processing. As Figure 11.6 shows, a graph may be given a name to distinguish it from other graphs. Often, a graph will have a title describing the subject matter with which it is concerned. A graph can have a position on the screen, which can range from the entire screen to some portion of it (e.g., the lower-right screen quadrant). Each graph is of a certain type: It either has axes (e.g., a bar graph) or it does not (e.g., a pie graph). In the former case, the graph may also have a label, range of values, scaling factor, and grid lines for each axis.

Every graph has certain patterns for features such as colors (e.g., pie slices alternating between red and green), lines (e.g., solid versus dashed lines), areas (e.g.,

DSS IN THE NEWS

Snazzy Graphics

Computers have made snazzy graphics a standard feature of reports and meetings everywhere. But old-fashioned tables full of numbers often may work better.

So says Iris Vessey, an associate professor of information systems at Pennsylvania State University. In a recent study, she found that graphs allow people to grasp trends among numbers more quickly, but less accurately, than when they spend a few more seconds with tables. Many study participants, when given a choice, felt more comfortable turning to rows of numbers on a table than comparing lines on a graph.

"We tend to just give decision makers more options to choose from" in presenting information, she says. "But there's a lot of evidence that they don't always choose the best way.". . .

G. Fuchsberg, "Tabling the Move to Computer Graphics," *Wall Street Journal* 30 January 1991, p. 131.

crosshatched versus solid bars), and markers (e.g., circles versus squares to plot points). A graph may also have a legend showing the meaning of each kind of color, line, area, or mark. For instance, a legend may indicate that white bars denote sales quotas and blue bars represent sales achieved.

PROCESSING THE OBJECTS

Graphics-management software implements methods for processing data sources, generating graphs from data sources, and manipulating generated graphs. With respect to the first of these, there are methods for defining the existence of a data source (e.g., allocating space to hold values of array elements), specifying or changing values in a data source (e.g., assigning a value to an array element), storing or recalling a data source, viewing the values in a data source, and deleting or releasing a data source from the KS or working memory.

Graph Generation   Graph-generation methods allow a user to request that a certain kind of graph be generated from an indicated data source, subset of a data source, or multiple data sources. For instance, a request such as

PLOT BAR FROM DS

yields a bar graph having four clusters of two bars each. The four numbers in the array's first column will appear along the x-axis. For each, there will be two bars whose heights are governed by the two data values remaining in its row of the array. Thus, above 6 on the x-axis, there will be one bar that corresponds to 2500 on the y-axis and another higher bar at the 2820 level.

Before making a request for a specific kind of graph, it is important to know what conventions the graphics-management software uses for transforming a data source into such a graph. In the foregoing example, the convention is that the first column furnishes x-axis values, the second column furnishes the y-axis height of the first bar in each cluster, and each succeeding column furnishes the y-axis heights of succeeding bars in each cluster. Such conventions for other kinds of graphs are similarly straightforward.

Common kinds of business graphs that can be generated by graphics management software include

- Bar graphs
- Area graphs
- Line graphs
- Point graphs (i.e., scattergrams)
- High-low-close graphs
- Pie charts

Variants of these graphs exist. For example, some software allows the use of horizontal rather than vertical bars or lets bars be stacked on top of each other within a cluster as an alternative to placing them side by side. It may also allow the generation of three-dimensional versions of graphs in addition to ordinary flat graphic presentations.

Viewing Controls   Recalling the features of a graph identified in Figure 11.6, a data source by itself may not be sufficient for producing the final graph to be viewed. An ordinary data source does not indicate what title a graph should have, where it

> ### ORDINARY BUSINESS GRAPHICS
>
> Business graphics is important in managing presentation knowledge. Implementations of this technique provide facilities for constructing data sources, generating graphs, and processing those graphs. These facilities add a valuable dimension for supporting decision-making activities.
>
> Once the elements of a data source array have been filled in, any block of these values can be graphed at some position on the screen. There are several basic kinds of graphs that can be generated from a data source, including bar charts, area graphs, pies, line graphs, high-low-close plots, and scattergrams. In addition, there are implementations of graphics management that can produce less well known kinds of graphs (e.g., Stoll 1986).
>
> The order and selection of patterns for filling areas, drawing lines, making marks, and using colors in a graph can be controlled. Where applicable, x- and y-axis ranges are determined automatically from the data source. Numeric ranges can also be directly specified and scaled.
>
> An existing graph is subject to various kinds of processing. It can be kept in main memory for later viewing, printed, redisplayed, stored in a KS disk file, brought into main memory for processing, enhanced (e.g., to include a legend), and modified (e.g., by superimposing text or additional graphs on it).

should be positioned on the screen, what patterns to use, what descriptions should appear in a legend, what labels to use along axes, and so forth. Depending on the graphics manager implementation, the user may specify such features at the time of graph generation or after the initial graph is generated. As an example, a graphics-generation request such as

    PLOT BAR FROM DS AT BOTTOM RIGHT

causes the bar graph to be positioned in the lower-right quadrant of the screen.

On the other hand, suppose we have just generated a graph, named it G1, and now want to give it a legend. Then a request such as

    PLOT BAR LEGEND ON G1 USING "SALES" , "QUOTA"

processes the existing graph, modifying it to contain a legend in which the pattern for the first bar in each cluster is denoted as SALES and the second, as QUOTA. In general, the methods available for processing an existing graph include naming it, storing it in the KS, recalling it from the KS, viewing it (via the console screen or printer), and changing it. Requests to change a graph include the specification or modification of its title, axis labels, position, axis ranges, axis scales (e.g., powers of 10 or logarithmic), display of horizontal or vertical grid lies, various patterns, and its legend.

11.5 RULE MANAGEMENT

Rule management emerged from the field of artificial intelligence as an important technique for representing and processing reasoning knowledge. It has been implemented in a variety of commercially available tools and plays an important role in the construction of expert systems. Because we focus on rule management in the examination of artificially intelligent DSSs in Part Four, our treatment here is fairly brief, touching only on some of its highlights.

The main purpose of an expert system is to serve as the computerized counterpart to a human expert. When a decision maker needs some expert advice about a problem, a human expert may not be available. Instead of waiting to consult a human expert, the person could immediately consult an expert system to get comparable advice. The value of expert systems in providing decision support has long been recognized (Bonczek, Holsapple, and Whinston 1980) and is widely accepted today (Olson and Courtney 1992; Turban 1993).

An expert system can be consulted in much the same spirit as advice is sought from a human expert. A user poses a specific problem to the expert system. Like its human counterpart, it will probably ask the user for further information to help clarify or more fully describe the exact nature of the problem. Like a human expert, its objective is to offer some advice, recommendation, or solution to the user. To meet this objective, the software portion of an expert system draws on reasoning expertise. Thus, an expert system must somehow capture a human expert's reasoning knowledge. Otherwise, the computer could not possibly emulate the human.

As a result of training and experience, a human expert acquires the reasoning knowledge that allows him or her to function as an expert in a particular problem domain. When a specific problem is posed, the expert draws on relevant fragments of that stored reasoning knowledge as needed in the course of deriving some advice. Similarly, in the case of an expert system, reasoning knowledge for a particular problem domain must be acquired and stored in the computer. Furthermore, there must be software that is able actively to process that knowledge to derive advice.

Rule management is a valuable technique for representing and processing reasoning knowledge. Reasoning knowledge can be represented as rules that tell what conclusions can be drawn under various circumstances. See Figure 11.7 for an example of a rule specification. We can request the rule-management software to process a set of rules. The processing result could be some advice or an explanation of the rationale behind that advice. The software that does this processing is commonly called an **inference engine.**

OBJECTS OF INTEREST

A **rule** is a fragment of reasoning knowledge that tells an inference engine what to do if a certain situation exists. Each rule has a name, **premise, conclusion,** and reason. If it can be established that the premise is true, then the rule's conclusion can be regarded as valid. A premise is simply a logical expression, and a conclusion consists of one or more actions. If a rule is used to draw an inference, then its reason serves as part of the explanation offered to a user.

A rule's premise can be a single condition or a compound logical expression formed from multiple conditions. It can involve constants, functions, and working variables. A rule's conclusion typically involves a command for assigning a value to a variable, perhaps involving a calculation. Consider the following example:

```
RULE: R1
   IF:   SALES > 1.5 * QUOTA
   THEN: BASE = QUOTA + (SALES - 1.15 * QUOTA)
```

FIGURE 11.7   Specifying a Rule

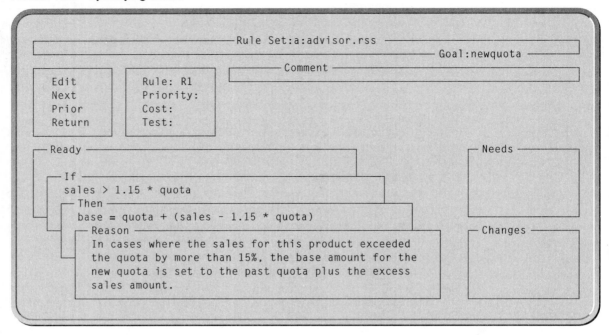

Here the rule is named R1. Its premise is a single condition involving the variables SALES and QUOTA. When the inference engine determines that this premise is true, then it will take the single action specified in R1's conclusion, thereby establishing a new value for the BASE variable.

As Figure 11.8 suggests, rules representing expertise about some problem domain are specified to form a **rule set.** This rule set is consulted by the inference engine when a user wants advice about some problem in that domain. A rule set can contain more than just rules. It may have an initialization sequence, which is a series of commands that the inference engine will execute before actually beginning to reason with the rules. For instance, it may have commands that establish initial values for some variables referenced in the rules. Similarly, a rule set may have a completion sequence, which is a series of commands that tell the inference engine what to do when the reasoning with rules has been completed. These are typically commands for presenting or storing the generated advice. Another part of a rule set involves variable descriptions, which characterize the variables referenced in the rules. For instance, a variable description might tell the inference engine how to find the value of a variable when there are no rules that can determine its value.

PROCESSING THE OBJECTS

The major methods that rule-management software provides for processing rule sets include means for (1) specifying and modifying a rule set as a KS file, (2) analyzing or testing the soundness of its reasoning knowledge, (3) compiling it into a representation that can be rapidly processed by an inference engine, (4) conducting inferences with the rule set to derive advice about a stated problem, and

FIGURE 11.8   Knowledge-Representation Objects in Rule Management

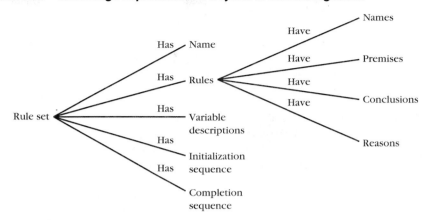

(5) explaining the rationale underlying the advice that is derived. Here, we focus on the fourth of these, because inference lies at the heart of rule management.

Inference   When someone invokes an inference engine to request some advice, it is a sign that something is unknown. For instance, we might ask for quota advice because we do not know what the new quota should be. Because an inference engine does not already know what new quota value to recommend, it will try to reason out a solution using a rule set that embodies expertise about quota setting.

Thus, when we invoke an inference engine with a particular rule set, normally one or more of the variables referenced in the rules have no known values. For instance, NEWQUOTA might be the name of a variable having no initial value when the rule set is consulted. If the inference engine succeeds in deriving a value for it by processing the rules, then that value becomes the advice.

The inference engine will first execute any commands that exist in the rule set's initialization sequence. There are probably commands to input a sales representative name, product name, quarter, and past performance data. Thus, the values of some variables, such as SALES and QUOTA (referred to in Rule R1), become known. Then, rules are processed in an attempt to establish values for remaining unknown variables—NEWQUOTA, in particular. There are two basic strategies inference engines follow when reasoning with rules: forward chaining and backward chaining. Some inference engines are capable of only one of these two approaches to reasoning. Others can do either kind of reasoning and even hybrid types of reasoning that mix the two basic approaches.

Forward Reasoning   **Forward reasoning,** or chaining, is based on the idea of examining each rule in a forward direction, looking first at its premise. The inference engine ignores a rule's conclusion until it can determine that the premise is satisfied. When that happens, the rule is fired. Firing a rule means that the inference engine takes whatever actions are specified in the rule's conclusion. If a rule's premise is not satisfied—the logical expression's value is either false or unknown—then the rule is not fired. The inference engine goes on to consider another rule.

Forward reasoning continues in this way until either a value has been established for a specified unknown variable such as NEWQUOTA or all the rule set's rules have been considered. In the latter case, the inference engine makes a second pass through the rule set, reconsidering the unfired rules. As a result of firing some rules in the first pass, some previously unknown variables may have known values and some previously known variables may have different known values. So, rules that previously had a false or unknown premise could have a true premise on the second pass. The inference engine then fires them and continues making passes.

The inference engine continues reasoning and drawing conclusions in this way until either some user-specified variable attains a known value or no further rules can be fired. In either event, any variables whose values changed or became known during the reasoning process can have their values presented as advice to the user. Commands in the rule set's completion sequence can control the inference engine's presentation of these values.

Reverse Reasoning   **Reverse reasoning** is based on the idea of considering rules in a reverse direction. The inference engine looks first at a rule's conclusion rather than its premise. It looks to see whether the conclusion contains an action that could change a certain unknown variable by giving that variable a value. At any

DSS IN THE NEWS

The Expert Sniffer

An expert system gathers up the knowledge of experts on a given topic and loads that knowledge into a computer. Users can draw on that information to make decisions and identify problems by entering queries into the system. . . .

The Expert Sniffer is designed around an expert system that recognizes patterns in cryptic network protocols and then provides English-language diagnoses, such as "slow file server" or "duplicate network addresses. . . ."

Expert Sniffer also will map out the network structure on a computer screen, identifying servers, routers and other devices. Specific problem areas can be diagrammed or highlighted. . . .

. . . Ed Goddin . . . with Home Insurance, a casualty insurance company, tested Expert Sniffer on a problem encountered earlier at the company's Dallas office.

The problem, which rendered the office's network almost unusable, had stumped local network administrators. Goddin was forced to fly out and spend a couple of days investigating the problem before tracking it down to a faulty wire.

When Goddin first received Expert Sniffer, he entered the symptoms of the Dallas problem into it, and it correctly identified the problem in a matter of minutes.

Another early user, Ron Tipton, a network manager at the University of Tennessee, says Expert Sniffer has allowed him to identify network problems and potential snafus before users start to complain.

"I use it proactively, rather than reactively," he said.

In one instance, Tipton said he was able to identify a server that had slowed down because it was being overloaded before users began to call. He then reallocated some of that server's functions to other machines.

K. Doler, "Pinpointing Network Problems is Becoming Easier with New Software Products," *Investor's Business Daily* 5 May 1992, p. 4.

> ## THE RISE OF RULES
>
> Rule management is likely to be an increasingly important knowledge-management technique. It is particularly valuable as a means for representing and processing reasoning knowledge. Such knowledge is the cornerstone of artificially intelligent decision support systems. These DSSs may take the form of stand-alone expert systems or may be full-scale, integrated environments (recall Figure 9.1), in which rule management is but one contributor to decision support activities (Holsapple and Whinston 1987). The use of rule management to realize such possibilities is more fully explored in Part Four.

moment during the reverse-reasoning process, the inference engine is focusing its efforts on trying to establish a value for a particular unknown variable. This value is called the *current goal variable*. For instance, when the overall goal of a consultation is to generate a new quota, NEWQUOTA is the current goal variable at the outset of inference engine processing.

The inference engine detects which of the rule set's rules could possibly establish a value for the current goal variable. These are treated as candidate rules for the current goal. The inference engine selects one of these rules and examines its premise. If its premise is true, the rule is fired to establish a value for the current goal. If the premise is false, then the rule is not fired, and another of the candidate rules for the current goal is selected for consideration.

If the premise is unknown, then each unknown variable can, in turn, become the current goal and be subjected to the same reverse-reasoning process. Reverse reasoning works by using rules to break the overall problem into subproblems. Each unknown variable in the premise of a candidate rule becomes a subproblem. Each subproblem may itself be broken into its own subproblems, and so on. By establishing values for the subproblems identified in a premise, the inference engine can determine whether the premise is satisfied. If it is, then the rule can be fired to establish variable values according to the conclusion's actions.

During the course of reasoning, an inference engine may ask the user to provide the value for a variable. The user may want to know why such a request is being made. On demand, the inference engine can explain why. Once a solution is reported, the user may want to know what line of reasoning was constructed in the course of the inference. An inference engine is able to explain itself, stating why the inferred recommendation is justified in light of the specified problem and available expertise for reasoning about that problem.

11.6 MESSAGE MANAGEMENT

Decision makers routinely send and receive **messages** for purposes of knowledge acquisition and to stimulate or enable knowledge derivation. For instance, a regional manager's decision may depend on information existing at corporate headquarters, advice from an expert at a consulting firm, data collected by sales representatives in the region, and interaction with a supervisor. To alert others about his or her knowledge needs, the manager creates and sends messages. Their responses are messages that the manager receives and perhaps stores for later reference. This message passing depends on the existence of **communication networks,** which can link people in the same building or scattered throughout the world. The telephone system is perhaps the best-known example of a communication network.

A decision maker's message-handling activities are not restricted to telephone conversations. They can involve other kinds of communication networks and can be facilitated via computer-based message management. This knowledge-management technique is concerned with (1) the representation of knowledge as messages that a computer can send and receive and (2) the computer-based processing of those messages until they have been sent and upon receiving them. Message-management software helps a user create, send, receive, and use messages that traverse a communication network to and from specific locations. At each of these locations is a computer equipped to engage in message-management activities.

There are many technical details involved in fully understanding telecommunications networks. For instance, there are coding and digitizing considerations, various transmission mechanisms, alternative topologies (e.g., star versus ring versus bus), and geographic classifications (e.g., local area networks versus wide area networks) (Rose 1991). These are beyond the scope of our brief survey. Familiarity with them is not essential for using message-management software.

VARIATIONS

If a computer on the network has a user, then message-management activities at that location probably involve message receiving, construction, and sending. A widely used example of such message management is **electronic mail,** or E-mail. E-mail software lets a user prepare and send memos and letters through a network. The contents of a file (e.g., from a database or a spreadsheet) can also serve as an E-mail message. Each message can be sent to certain designated locations. The electronic mail software keeps track of everything that is sent. It alerts a user that mes-

DSS IN THE NEWS

Beyond a Quiet Dinner for Two

"Personal" communication is the latest buzzword among consumer electronics and computer companies—and they don't mean a quiet dinner for two.

This more businesslike tête-á-tête involves using a "personal digital assistant" or "personal communicator" that will let you fax, phone, transmit data and keep electronic notebooks and diaries in your own handwriting, all on a compact and mobile hand-held device. . . .

PDAs will cost less than personal computers, which will help them exploit sales channels that most computer manufacturers only recently entered. The absence of uniform standards for digital communications poses challenges for offering the more advanced PDA functions worldwide.

Reuters, " 'Personal' Communication Era Nears, but Market Remains Ill-Defined," *Investor's Business Daily* 21 April 1993, p.4.

sages have been received for his or her viewing. Replies, in the guise of amendments to a received memo or as new memos, can be routed to the senders.

It is possible that a computer in the network does not have a user who directly participates in message management. In this case, its message-management activities commonly involve construction or modification of files based on messages received or the transfer of file contents as a message across the network to the location that requested it. Examples of this kind of message-management occur with electronic bulletin boards, information- or news-retrieval services, file-transfer facilities, cooperative authoring systems, and group decision support systems.

Bulletin Boards An **electronic bulletin board** is a computer that collects messages sent to it by users of other computers connected to it. It also allows any of these users to view the messages that exist in its files. Decision makers can use such a facility to gather information, stimulate ideas, or solicit assistance.

Retrieval Services A **retrieval service,** such as the Dow Jones Information Services, allows a subscriber to link his or her computer into a network to retrieve knowledge held in a remote computer's files. For instance, upon connecting to a remote Dow Jones computer, a user can retrieve excerpts of the *Wall Street Journal*

DSS IN THE NEWS

Knowledge Exchange without Thumbtacks

. . . A rising number of corporations have installed their own bulletin board systems to exchange messages and data among employees and customers at various locations. . . .

Personal computer users simply dial a telephone number to connect to a computer that acts as the bulletin board's server. . . . They can access various types of information on the bulletin board and communicate with other bulletin board users.

. . . Bulletin boards provide messaging services. . . .

. . . There are currently 60,000 bulletin boards in the country, a number that has doubled in the past 18 months. More than 12 million Americans call into a public or private bulletin board system every day.

. . . Companies want to set up bulletin boards . . . to provide an electronic means of exchanging information with customers . . . to streamline customer service and support. . . .

Bulletin boards are an inexpensive means of exchanging data within corporations. . . . Citibank . . . runs a bulletin board that's used by about 650 people in the bank's corporate audit and financial control divisions.

. . . Divisions around the world send in data to the bulletin board each month to be consolidated into reports. . . . Information also is disseminated to all the sites using the system.

K. Doler, "Bulletin Board Systems: A Inexpensive Data Communications Option," *Investor's Business Daily* 17 February 1994, p. 4.

to view business, economic, and financial data or to see general news of the day as messages on his or her computer's console screen (Woodwell 1986).

File Transfer   A **file-transfer** is one that allows two computers to be connected such that one is a receiver and the other is a sender. The receiver computer is attached to a communication channel (e.g., to a phone line via a *modem*) and waits to be called by the sender computer. Also attached to the communication channel, the sender initiates contact (e.g., by calling the phone number of the receiver computer). When this connection is established, the sender transmits a message naming certain files existing in the receiver computer. The receiver computer responds by transferring copies of the indicated files as messages to the sender computer, whose user can then process their contents as desired.

Cooperative Authoring   In a **cooperative authoring** system, several people use their computers to create a document residing in a file(s) on another computer in the network. Each author can construct and send messages that alter the document. The computer's message-management software controls who can make what changes and when by accepting only certain kinds of messages from a given author at a given time. For instance, one author may be allowed to send messages at any time to view the whole document but be allowed to change only its introduction and conclusion—and only when another author is not in the process of changing them.

Electronic Brainstorming   A group decision support system typically implements message management to facilitate brainstorming among group participants. Each has a computer with which to issue messages that offer ideas and opinions about some topic of interest to the decision being made. The ideas in these messages are accumulated and organized into files by message-management software on another computer. This computer, in turn, can send messages consisting of comments

DSS IN THE NEWS

Wireless Messaging

Wireless messaging is well on its way to becoming the lifeblood for workers who need up-to-the-minute information. . . .

One billion people could be using wireless modems for mobile communications by the year 2000, a figure that approaches the size of the TV market, projects American Telephone & Telegraph Co.

Only a few years ago, the cost of sending or receiving a wireless electronic-mail message was about $1 for the equivalent of 500 letters or digits. The cost since has dropped to about 13 cents.

An editorial in *Network Computing* magazine (April) said wireless E-mail could be the single most important technology this decade for the mobile professional.

B. Deagon, "Electronic Mail Advantage," *Investor's Business Daily* 22 April 1993, p. 4.

accumulated from participants to any individual participant's computer. There, all the contributed comments can be viewed to stimulate further comments from that participant. These additional comments take the form of further messages sent to the accumulating computer for storage and subsequent routing to other participants.

OBJECTS OF INTEREST

In spite of its many variations, message management does involve a common object of interest: a message. Messages differ in terms of type and content. Two fundamental types of messages are those that are requests for another computer to do something and those that are responses from another computer. The content of a message often contains text, akin to a simple document in text management. A message may also consist of a user's entries into a form, a file existing in a computer, or even **multimedia** presentations involving graphical, video, or audio elements. Although the bulk of messages are typically representations of descriptive or procedural knowledge, each of the six types of knowledge can be represented in a message to be transferred.

PROCESSING THE OBJECTS

Major message-processing methods fall into four main classes: methods for message preparation, network access, message transferral, and message use. For message preparation, message-management software often furnishes what amounts to a simple text-management capability—allowing users to prepare messages in much the same way as specifying and editing documents. In response to a message-preparation request, some message managers present a user with a form with slots to enter such items as the message's destination, its purpose, its date of preparation, and its text. These entries constitute the message to be sent. Message preparation can also occur external to message-management software. In this case, a file that will serve as the message is prepared via text-management, database–management, solver-management, spreadsheet-management, or other software.

Network access methods are concerned with connecting a computer to the other computer(s) with which it needs to communicate. In some cases (e.g., for a typical GDSS), no explicit connection requests are needed, because the computers are already connected in a network. In other cases, the computer's message-management software carries out explicit requests to connect with or disconnect from another computer. For example, before messages can be exchanged with an electronic bulletin board or information-retrieval service, the user issues a request to have the message-management software establish a connection with the remote computer. Once that connection is made, message transferral can occur. Similarly, when the exchange of messages ends, a request is issued to disconnect from the remote computer.

Message-transferral methods are concerned with sending and receiving messages among computers connected in a network. As with network access methods, there may or may not be specific requests required for sending messages. For instance, the act of preparing a message (e.g., typing a comment in a GDSS or an announcement for a bulletin board) can automatically cause it to be sent to another computer. On the other hand, preparing a memo or file to be sent via E-mail is a separate operation from requesting that it be sent. A request to send a message needs to indicate the desired destination(s). It may also indicate whether the receiving

> ### COMMUNICATION SUPPORT SYSTEMS
>
> The technique of message management, in its many variations, is not only important for the development of decision support systems, but it is also fundamental to the creation of communication support systems. As a field of research and study, the field of computer-based communication support systems is not nearly as well developed as the DSS field (Calantone, Holsapple, and Johnson 1991; Holsapple, Johnson, and Waldron 1996). However, as it matures it is likely to have useful implications for decision support systems. Although communication does not always occur to support decision making, such support can be one important purpose of communicating. Systems that facilitate communication therefore have a potential for supporting decision making as well.

computer should acknowledge receipt of the message, the message's priority, and the speed with which it should be delivered (e.g., regular, express, or immediate).

Message-management software that receives a message either takes immediate action in response to the message content or stores it in a manner that allows it to be used subsequently. As an example of the former, a message asking to examine the material posted on a bulletin board results in a return message displaying bulletin board contents. As an example of the latter, an E-mail message is stored in a *mailbox* file. Over time, many messages can accumulate in this mailbox.

A message that has been prepared or received can be used in various ways, provided it has been retained. In the case of E-mail, for instance, the message-management software will notify a user of messages in the mailbox, allow the user to view any of these messages (on the screen or printed), store messages in a KS for later use, forward a message to another destination, type in a response to the message, and delete it from the mailbox.

11.7 INTEGRATING TOWARD A GENERAL PROBLEM PROCESSOR

There is a trend toward the integrated use of multiple knowledge-management techniques in a single DSS. Aside from the assortment and extensiveness of techniques being integrated, the style with which they are integrated is significant. As we saw in Chapter 8, basic styles of software integration include nesting, confederation, and synergy. The nested style yields a single software tool that treats one knowledge-management technique as dominant and the others as secondary. The secondary techniques can be exercised within the confines of the dominant technique but cannot be used independently. The confederation style involves multiple compatible software tools, normally one for each knowledge-management technique. These are "integrated" by data import and export or by cut-and-paste operations. By switching back and forth among the separate programs, knowledge-management techniques can be exercised independently, but they cannot be used together in a single operation.

Like the nested style, synergy integrates multiple techniques into a single software tool. However, all are on an equal footing without any dominant component. Like a confederation, any technique can be exercised independently of the others. However, techniques can also be used together without switching among programs, importing and exporting, or cutting and pasting. As a result, the total effect that can be achieved is much greater than the sum of the individual techniques' effects, and no technique interferes with the capacity or capability of another technique. The techniques are blended and fused into a unified whole such that there are no barriers separating them and each is an equal to the other.

A SUPER KNOWLEDGE-MANAGEMENT TECHNIQUE

In a sense, synergistic integration gives us new knowledge-management techniques that are hybrid fusions of the techniques being integrated (Holsapple 1984; Holsapple and Whinston 1984, 1988). For example, consider the synergistic integration of all knowledge-management techniques surveyed so far in Chapters 9–11. The result can be regarded as a super, or universal, knowledge-management technique. Its objects of interest include all those of the more traditional individual techniques discussed so far plus hybrid objects. For instance, a spreadsheet cell could be defined in terms of a program and a program could be specified in terms of cells. The super technique's processing methods consist not only of those for the individual techniques, but also those methods capable of processing the hybrid objects or multiple objects in a single operation. For instance, a SQL request could have a condition involving spreadsheet cells, or text-management requests could include SQL retrieval for depositing database values in documents.

Table 11.1 provides some examples of the new knowledge-management abilities that can result from synergistic integration of conventional techniques. Such capabilities do not exist within an individual conventional technique.

New versions of tools that emphasize the implementation of knowledge-management techniques are increasingly tending toward the incorporation of additional techniques in either a nested or synergistic way. Full-scale commercial implementations of tools that synergistically integrate most of the techniques surveyed in Part Three first began to appear in the mid-1980s (Holsapple and Whinston 1988). A variety of tools adopting assorted approaches to integrating selected knowledge-management techniques are commercially available today (Perratore 1991).

TOWARD A GENERALIZED PROBLEM PROCESSOR

The principle of synergy in software integration is a crucial step in the direction of a **generalized problem processor.** A generalized problem-processing system (GPPS) is an intrinsic DSS development tool that can function as the PPS for diverse decision support systems, without regard to the knowledge representation and processing requirements for any one of them (Bonczek, Holsapple, and Whinston 1980).

If the problem processor of a DSS is general, then it stores all application-specific knowledge in the knowledge system. We can transform a DSS based on a generalized problem processor into a DSS for some other decision support application by exchanging one knowledge system for another. We can extend such a DSS simply by modifying its knowledge system contents. The advantages that a GPPS offers for rapid, inexpensive development and maintenance of decision support systems are obvious.

We have seen that a particular type of knowledge is susceptible to being represented in various ways. For instance, descriptive knowledge might be represented in text files, a database, a spreadsheet, and so on. Clearly, no single representation method is superior to all others in all situations. Thus, a GPPS must be able to

TABLE 11.1   Examples of Pairwise Synergy among Knowledge-Management Techniques

USING IN	TEXT MANAGEMENT	DATABASE MANAGEMENT	FORMS MANAGEMENT	GRAPHICS MANAGEMENT
Text Management		Field values consisting of text	Form elements that are textual	Graphics screen with textual display
Database Management	Direct incorporation of field values or query results in text (immediate or delayed)		Specifying fields for nonliteral form elements	Generating graphs using fields' values or as data source
Forms Management	Direct incorporation of forms in text (immediate or delayed)	Create, modify, or view data via forms		Graphics screen with form display
Graphics Management	Direct incorporation of graphs into text (immediate or delayed)	Field values consisting of graphs	Form elements that are graphs	
Solver Management	Direct incorporation of solver results in text (immediate or delayed)	Virtual fields defined in terms of solver results	Solver results specified as nonliteral form elements	Graph generated using solver results as data source
Spreadsheet Management	Direct incorporation of cell values in text (immediate or delayed)	Cell references embedded in database operations and virtual field definitions	Cells specified for nonliteral form elements	Graph generated using cells as data source
Program Management	Direct incorporation of program results in text (immediate or delayed)	Virtual field defined in terms of a program	Program variables specified for nonliteral form elements	Graph generated using program variables as data source
Rule Management	Direct incorporation of inference results in text (immediate or delayed)	Inferred variable embedded in database operations	Inferred variables specified for nonliteral form elements	Graph generated using inferred variables as data source

accommodate knowledge systems that utilize all these various representation methods. For each knowledge-representation method that can be used in a knowledge system, a GPPS must possess a corresponding knowledge-processing ability.

The Key to Generality   The key to problem processor generality is the ability to handle many different knowledge-representation methods. The knowledge system of one DSS may involve knowledge represented in text files, spreadsheets, and relational data tables. The knowledge representation of another DSS's knowledge system might include structured programs, spreadsheets, and rule sets. If these two decision support systems are to have the same problem processor, that problem processor must be able to work with all the various representation methods that can be employed across the universe of knowledge systems.

The major hurdle that we had to overcome before the idea of a GPPS could become a reality was how to combine effectively the processing methods of so

SOLVER MANAGEMENT	SPREADSHEET MANAGEMENT	PROGRAM MANAGEMENT	RULE MANAGEMENT
Solver results with textual display	Cells defined in terms of text contents	Enabling program to manipulate text as variables	Enabling rules to manipulate text as variables
Database values or query results used in place of data sets	Cells defined in terms of field or database operations	Fields used as program variables; database operations embedded in program	Rules reference fields; database operations embedded in rule conclusions
Model specification or solver result via form	Cells defined in terms of form manipulations	Forms management operations embedded in program	Forms management operations embedded in rule conclusions
Graphics operations embedded in solver	Cell defined as graphics generation request	Graphics operations embedded in program	Graphics operations specified in rule conclusions
	Cell defined as the invocation of a solver	Solver processing requests embedded in program	Solver processing requests embedded in rule conclusions
Cell values used in place of data sets		Cells used as program variables; spreadsheet operations embedded in program	Rules referencing cells; spreadsheet operations embedded in rule conclusions
Model defined in terms of program	Cell defined as the execution of a program		Rules referencing program variables; program executions embedded in rule conclusions
Model defined in terms of consultation results	Cell defined as the consultation of a rule set	Consultation requests embedded in program	

many knowledge-management techniques into a single invariant program. The knowledge-processing abilities had to be combined in such a way that each individual ability could be used without the others. For instance, a DSS developer creating a knowledge system should not be forced to represent knowledge in a spreadsheet in order to make use of nonspreadsheet-processing abilities. The developer should be able to use a database method of representing knowledge without being required to use a spreadsheet method, and vice versa.

Although this independence of knowledge-processing abilities is essential, it does not imply that a GPPS is merely a hodgepodge of separate components. Such segregation would not permit multiple abilities to work together simultaneously. It would require switching back and forth among various components. Instead, the component abilities of a GPPS have to be combined in such a way that several of them can be exercised in a single operation. The traditional barriers that separated various knowledge-representation and -processing methods had to be removed for a GPPS to become a reality (Holsapple and Whinston 1983).

Implications of Generality   This conception of a GPPS presents a host of challenging questions to the business computing community. Why should there be any rigid separation between spreadsheets and databases? Shouldn't a spreadsheet cell be able to access data held in a database? Shouldn't an SQL query be able simultaneously to access knowledge held in a spreadsheet and a database? Shouldn't the values of database fields be able to be dynamically determined by a spreadsheet computation? Why should knowledge represented in a textual fashion be separate? In the midst of editing some text, shouldn't a user be allowed to make database and spreadsheet references to incorporate knowledge from these sources into the text—either immediately or on a dynamic basis as the text is printed? Why should a programming language be separate? Shouldn't spreadsheet cells and database fields be available as variables in the procedural knowledge captured by a program? Shouldn't it be possible to define a spreadsheet cell in terms of an entire program?

These questions illustrate a small sampling of the possibilities available with a GPPS. A full exploration of such possibilities could easily fill an entire book (Holsapple and Whinston 1988). The main points to keep in mind here are these:

1. A GPPS must have a broad range of knowledge-processing capabilities for working with a broad range of knowledge-representation methods.
2. The knowledge-processing abilities or components of a GPPS must be able to operate independently of each other.
3. The components must be blended together into a single program (i.e., PPS software) in such a way that there are no barriers among them and so their abilities can be used together in a single operation.

The Human Metaphor   Interestingly, this blending resembles what goes on within human consciousness. A bit of introspection makes it clear that our own minds have

---

MULTIMEDIA

Multimedia technology is emerging as a potentially valuable aid for decision makers. This technology is concerned with integrating distinct modes of presentation (Hofstetter 1994). It includes, but goes beyond, combining presentations from conventional knowledge-management techniques such as graphs, forms, documents, and tabular listings. It also allows visual presentation on the same screen of photographs, films, maps, drawings, and so forth. It allows audio presentation of recordings. The knowledge underlying such presentations tends to be stored on high-capacity peripheral media such as CD-ROMs (which could be regarded as a KS extension).

When used on a DSS, multimedia presentations enrich the PS, with the potential for facilitating a decision maker's capacity to grasp what the DSS has to convey. Beyond allowing the retrieval of prerecorded visual and audio material, multimedia technology may allow audio/visual presentation of events that are simultaneously occurring elsewhere. That is, conventional message management can be supplemented by seeing and/or hearing the sender and/or recipient of the message.

multiple kinds of knowledge-processing abilities that can be exercised independently or together. For instance, in arriving at a decision without computer support, the human decision maker might access descriptive knowledge from memory or from a coworker, analyze it with various mental models, sketch out graphs of the results, consult an expert for advice, reanalyze the situation with altered assumptions, and write a report that shows the decision.

Clearly, a decision process can involve a broad range of knowledge-processing activities manipulating diverse knowledge-representation objects. This same mental processing tool can be applied to diverse decision problems, and its component capabilities can work separately or together. The goal of a GPPS is to supplement the innate human tool with an analogous computer-based tool. In so doing, we get a super knowledge-management technique that involves much more than the mere sum of conventional individual techniques for knowledge management.

11.8 SUMMARY

In this chapter we surveyed five more knowledge-management techniques: forms, report, graphics, rule, and message management. The first is oriented toward treating linguistic and presentation knowledge. The next two are primarily means for dealing with presentation knowledge. Rule management is intended principally for coping with reasoning knowledge. Message management is not particularly focused on treating one or another knowledge type.

The main knowledge-representation objects relevant to the five surveyed techniques are forms, templates, data sources, graphic images, rule sets, rules, and messages. Each can be stored in the KS of a decision support system. Methods for

DSS IN THE NEWS

In the Right Place at the Right Time

Operations planning, scheduling and control (OPSC) problems arise in all sorts of industries, including transportation. These problems are typically centered around the deployment of scarce resources (planes, trains, trucks, and machines) among competing activities (flights, routes, and products) in such a way that some objective (revenue or profit maximization, cost minimization, or customer service) is optimized while adhering to operational constraints (regulatory authority-imposed rules, weather patterns, and equipment limitations).

Planning assesses demand vis-a-vis resource availability, usually in strategic, aggregate, and general terms. . . . What-if scenario analysis, sometimes spreadsheet-based, has put a new spin on the concepts of sensitivity analysis in order to provide management planners with the capability to quickly assess the impact of changing parameters. . . .

The problem of controlling an airline's flight operations is inherently reactive by nature. Murphy's Law rules: What can go wrong, will go wrong. Count on it!

Continued

The approach taken in dealing with this situation is, "What's done is done. Now what are we going to do about it to minimize further down-line disruptions, such as flight delays, cancellations, and passenger replacement?" . . . Besides access to and display of information, what types of decision support tools are most useful to flight operations controllers? Four levels of decision support are typically applied in this arena: information processing, operations monitoring and alerting, what-if scenario analysis, and flight re-scheduling and resource reassignment decision support models.

. . . Filtered information displays that allow controllers to quickly assess flight activities at a given airport are invaluable. Such displays provide rapid response to commands like, "List all of the flights arriving at DFW between 0800 and 1000, which are wide-body aircraft, with less than 50 passengers." Using these flexible displays, which are based on multiple key searches and sorts, controllers can selectively filter data to support ad hoc analysis and real-time decision-making.

Monitoring and alerting functions allow controllers to use the computer to track flight operations conditions and notify them about situations which are out of kilter. Computers are good at processing large amounts of information quickly, whereas humans are best at exception handling. Rather than having flight operations staff continuously sifting through large amounts of incoming data to identify the few situations needing attention, the computer does the sifting and flags exceptional conditions to the controller's attention.

Using multi-color graphical Gantt-chart displays, alert conditions are coded according to problem severity, e.g., all flights which are 30 minutes late are highlighted in yellow, whereas flights more than 30 minutes late are highlighted in red. Controllers can even change the tolerance on disruption notification, since direness of the situation is relative. . . . Alerts are also used to flag other noteworthy conditions, such as insufficient ground time for baggage and crew connections and violation of airport closure or curfew requirements.

Using a computer model-based representation of the flight schedule network, what-if scenario analysis is employed to simulate flight operations in an attempt to determine the down-line impacts of pending flight decisions. Controllers can specify a set of conditions such as flight delays, cancellations or aircraft reassignments to identify and rectify potential conflicts. Smart simulations supported by databases provide a mechanism to assess the feasibility of flight operations and answer questions such as, "Can this aircraft be assigned to this flight routing which goes over water?" or "Is this aircraft's noise profile suitable to the noise abatement and curfew profiles at the destination airport?"

Experimentation with more sophisticated . . . systems that support flight re-scheduling and aircraft re-assignment decision-making has begun to bear fruit. In a recent paper in *Transportation Science,* Jarrah et al. reported on development and implementation of a minimum-cost network flow model framework for supporting flight cancellation and delay decision-making at United Airlines. . . . The model generated effective, implementable solutions in reasonable time, which were in many cases superior to solutions generated by experienced flight controllers in terms of the number and magnitude of flight delays and cancellations required.

Douglas Gray and Nader Kabbani, "Right Tool, Place, Time," *OR/MS Today* (April 1994): 35–36, 40–41.

processing each are candidates for inclusion in a problem-processing system. Such processing methods can be valuable contributions to the capabilities of decision support systems.

Hybrid knowledge-management techniques result from the integration of two or more conventional techniques. A universal, or super, technique comprises a synergistic integration of all of the conventional techniques. Objects of interest for it include all those objects identified in Chapters 9–11 plus their hybrids. Its processing methods include all those noted in Chapters 9–11 plus those able to process conventionally unrelated objects in a single operation. Implementations of this universal knowledge-management technique can function as generalized problem-processing systems.

▲ IMPORTANT TERMS

array	graph
communication network	header
conclusion	inference engine
control break	literal element
cooperative authoring	nonliteral element
data source	message
electronic bulletin board	multimedia
electronic mail	premise
file transfer	report detail
footer	report template
form	retrieval service
form slot	reverse reasoning
forward reasoning	rule
generalized problem processor	rule set

▲ APPLICATION TO THE SOUTHLAND CASE

1. What decisions are being supported?
2. Why were graphics so important for this DSS?
3. What kinds of graphics did the user see?
4. What other knowledge-management techniques appear to have been employed in developing this DSS?
5. If message management were integrated into Southland's DSS, whom might it help and in what ways?
6. What were the main benefits of graphical presentations?
7. What served as the data source for graph generation?
8. Explain how the system can be adapted to use for a different application.
9. What advantages did Southland's DSS provide to its user?
10. Explain each of the main menu's four primary options.

▲ REVIEW QUESTIONS

1. What is a form and what objects can be defined to exist within it?

2. Give an example of each of the following types of knowledge being represented in a form.
   a. Presentation knowledge
   b. Procedural knowledge
   c. Linguistic knowledge
   d. Assimilative knowledge
3. How is the concept of a form related to that of a report template?
4. In what ways do nonliteral elements differ from a form's literal elements? What features do these two kinds of slots have in common?
5. What are the two main uses of nonliteral slots?
6. During interaction with a user, what major form-processing methods can be used?
7. How does forms management assist a decision maker when it is incorporated into a decision support system?
8. What is a report detail?
9. How do the various kinds of header-footer pairs in a report template differ from each other?
10. Under what circumstances is report management likely to have its greatest decision support value?
11. If a report is being generated from a database, explain how the request for the report differs from a SQL request. How does it resemble a SQL request?
12. What role does a data source play in graphics management?
13. How do the processing methods available for operating on a data source differ from those that can process graphs generated from that source?
14. What knowledge-management techniques can yield arraylike structures of data values amenable to graph generation?
15. How can many graphs of the same type be generated from the same data source?
16. For axis-type graphs, what graphical characteristics cannot be determined from a data source? In terms of processing methods, how might these be requested?
17. Why is it beneficial to be able to preserve a graphical image in memory, even though it is not currently being viewed?
18. What is an expert system?
19. Which rule-management software is extrinsic and which is intrinsic?
20. What does an inference engine do?
21. How do forward reasoning and reverse reasoning differ?
22. In a rule, what is a premise? A conclusion? A reason?
23. From a decision support point of view, what is the value of a message-management capability?
24. What are the main traits of each of the following approaches to message management? How can each be beneficial to a decision maker?
   a. E-mail
   b. Electronic bulletin board
   c. Retrieval service
   d. File transfer
   e. Coauthoring
   f. Electronic brainstorming in a GDSS
25. What are the main classes of message-processing methods?
26. When two knowledge-management techniques are integrated into a single tool, what considerations are important for a DSS developer who might use that tool?

27. What is a hybrid knowledge-management technique? A universal knowledge-management technique?

▲ DISCUSSION TOPICS

1. Explain how a spreadsheet can be regarded as a special kind of form.
2. Give an example of a form that is not a spreadsheet.
3. Why are color blocks and boxes useful in forms?
4. Discuss the relative merits and drawbacks of declaring a form versus painting it.
5. Explain how forms management differs from the use of I/O commands in program management.
6. Explain why forms management is not just a special case of report management in which a template consists of a single form.
7. Can CAD/CAM software form the PPS of a decision support system?
8. For each of the main types of graphs, indicate the nature of its data source and a decision-making situation where it would be preferred to other graph types.
9. What are the relative advantages and disadvantages of storing a graphical image in the KS versus regenerating it on an as-needed basis?
10. From what sources do rules come?
11. As a decision maker, when do you tend to use forward reasoning and under what situations do you prefer reverse reasoning?
12. How does a rule differ from an IF-THEN command in program management with respect to (a) the possible values for a premise and (b) the way it is processed?
13. Discuss the similarities and differences between message management and text management.
14. Describe the nature of a GPSS. What are its benefits to a DSS developer? What are its disadvantages relative to more specialized PPSs?
15. When database management is synergistically integrated with spreadsheet management, what useful processing capabilities could result that are not possible with the individual techniques?
16. Discuss the relevance of software integration to the creation of GPSSs.
17. Discuss the relative advantages and disadvantages of graphs compared to tabular presentations.

▲ REFERENCES

Belardo, S., P. Duchessi, and J. P. Seagle. 1985. Microcomputer graphics in support of vehicle fleet routing. *Interfaces* 15, no. 6.

Betts, K. 1991. Form and content: Five electronic forms packages. *PC Magazine* 10, no. 19.

Bonczek, R. H., C. W. Holsapple, and A. B. Whinston. 1980. Future directions for developing decision support systems. *Decision Sciences* (October).

Calantone, R. J., C. W. Holsapple, and L. E. Johnson. 1991. Communication and communication support: An agenda for investigation. *Information Society* 9, no. 1.

Cleveland, W. S., and R. McGill. 1984. Graphical perception: Theory, experimentation, and application to the development of graphical methods. *Journal of the American Statistical Association* 79, no. 387.

Cooper, M. S. 1984. Micro-based business graphics. *Datamation* 30, no. 6.

Greitzer, J. 1986. Freehand-graphics. *PC Week* 3, no. 33.

Hofstetter, F. T. 1994. *Multimedia presentation technology*. Belmont, Calif.: Wadsworth.

Holsapple, C. W. 1984. Synergy comes to integrated software. *Systems and Software* 3, no. 2.

Holsapple, C. W., and M. D. Gagle. 1987. Expert system development tools. *Hardcopy* 7, no. 2

Holsapple, C. W., L. E. Johnson, and V. Waldron. 1996. A formal model for the study of communication support systems. *Human Communication Research* 22.

Holsapple, C. W., and A. B. Whinston. 1983. Software tools for knowledge fusion. *Computerworld* 17, no. 15.

————. 1984. "Integrated DSS Development Tools for Micro Computers," *Data Pro Research Reports,* MC51-050, December, 1984.

————. 1987. *Business expert systems.* Homewood, Ill.: Irwin.

————. 1988. *The information jungle.* Homewood, Ill.: Dow Jones–Irwin.

Kaiser, J. B. 1968. *Forms design and control.* New York: American Management Association.

Medland, A. J. 1993. *CAD./CAM in practice: A manager's guide to understanding and using.* New York: John Wiley.

Myers, G. 1976. Forms management. *Journal of Systems Management* (October).

Olson, D. L., and J. F. Courtney. 1992. *Decision support models and expert systems.* New York: Macmillian.

Perratore, E. 1991. All together now: Integrated software under $200. *PC Magazine* 10, no. 14.

Rowe, S. H., II. 1991. *Business telecommunications.* New York: Macmillian.

Stoll, M. 1986. Charts other than pie are appealing to the eye. *PC Week* 3, no. 12.

Tsichritzis, D. 1982. Form management. *Communications of ACM* 25, no. 7.

Turban, E. 1993. *Decision support and expert systems,* 3rd ed. New York: Macmillian.

Woodwell, D. R. 1986. *Using and applying the Dow Jones information services.* Homewood, Ill.: Dow Jones–Irwin.

CASE STUDY

This case study is a continuation of the do-it-yourself case begun in Part Two. Upon receiving approval for your proposal, you can begin the schedule of development activities that it contains. Although this may involve some additional analysis to address any concerns raised in the proposal review process (e.g., by your instructor), what remains is largely a design and implementation effort involving one or more of the knowledge-management techniques described in Part Three. At the end of this effort, you should demonstrate your DSS and submit the following items for evaluation:

- Any amendments or alterations to the proposal involving the project's scope, aims, or methods
- An explanation of what you accomplished, including listings of knowledge system contents you created (e.g., database table structures, records in database tables, definitions in spreadsheets, textual passages, program listings, form declarations, rule set specifications, and so forth)
- Knowledge system files and a user's manual, explaining how to use the system and including characterizations of the LS and PS, instructions on how to invoke the system, a sample session(s) showing interactions with the system, and guidelines indicating what system features to use for what purposes
- An explanation of how you tested the system, plus any ancillary files used in that testing
- A discussion of possible future extensions (or revisions) to the system
- A retrospective description of insights you gained by undertaking the project

The next two sections contain abbreviated examples of materials submitted after implementing DSSs proposed at the end of Part Two. Detailed examples of the knowledge system contents for these two cases appear in Appendix G. Following these descriptions of implementations, we suggest how you may want to document your own DSS design activity as an interim project report.

A VARIANCE ANALYSIS INVESTIGATION DSS, *BY MARY CURTIS*

OVERVIEW

This system was designed to help factory managers analyze their product variances and determine if those variances are significant enough to investigate. There is a trade-off in the investigation, because the investigation of a potential problem can be expensive. Additionally, it is possible that a variance can occur when there is no real problem, merely a seasonal fluctuation or self-correcting deviation in the production process. Therefore, the cost of investigation must be weighed against the risks: not investigating when there is a problem and investigating when no real problem exists.

The variances computed include

Labor efficiency variance: Using too many labor hours for a product

Labor cost variance: Using labor that is too expensive for a production process or product

Materials quantity variance: Using too much raw material for a product

Material price variance: Paying too much for raw materials or parts

Overhead efficiency variance: Applying too much overhead to the product

Overhead spending variance: Incurring too much overhead for the plant

The use of the system follows this basic process:

1. Compute the amounts of variances and, for preliminary evaluation, compare to companywide exception parameters.
2. Compute a variance measure that is a factor of
   a. The product's risk of being out of control;
   b. The manager's need to supervise this particular product;
   c. The magnitude of the variance.
   These three factors are weighted and an overall measure is calculated for each type of variance.
3. Review prior investigations for a type of variance to give the manager an idea of what has happened in past investigations. This can be shown by descending cost or descending variance measures.
4. Allow complete discretion to play what-if with the spreadsheet without permanently changing the contents or format.
5. Enter the results of an investigation into the history file for future reference in step 3.

The system is tailored to each manager. Each manager and the products he or she manages are stored in the VARUSER database. Also in this database is the presentation format preference of that manager. This format can be changed at any time while using the investigation routine (step 2). When the manager changes his or her preference, that change is permanently reflected in the VARUSER database.

SYSTEM DEVELOPMENT

I developed the system in phases. First, the variance spreadsheet was built to allow managers to get comfortable with its appearance and to decide what further evaluations they would like. Then, the what-if portion was built to allow them to see the impact of alternative standards and performance. Next, the variance measure calculation was designed with the input of all managers. (See the user documentation for more detailed discussion of this calculation.) Next, the history database was set up to keep a record of investigations and their results and the reporting capabilities for this database were written. Also, at this time the internal controls that had been previously designed were implemented to prevent unauthorized access to or use of the system.

Appendix G shows the structure of relevant tables, declarations of forms, and programs coded to govern the flow interactions.

USER GUIDE

Place the accompanying floppy in the A drive. To start the system, enter PERFORM "A:VARMAIN". The first screen to come up is the user logo screen. The user is prompted for his or her initials and the product he or she wishes to analyze at this

Main Menu

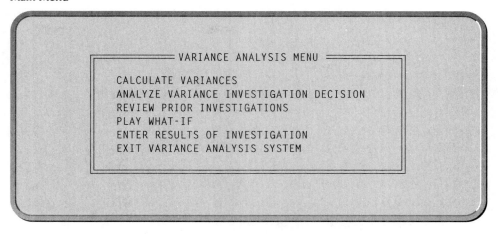

```
                    ═══ VARIANCE ANALYSIS MENU ═══

         CALCULATE VARIANCES
         ANALYZE VARIANCE INVESTIGATION DECISION
         REVIEW PRIOR INVESTIGATIONS
         PLAY WHAT-IF
         ENTER RESULTS OF INVESTIGATION
         EXIT VARIANCE ANALYSIS SYSTEM
```

time. The user must be preauthorized to use the system on each product. The two users who are authorized at this time include

Initials	Product
MBC	01
MBC	02
CWH	02
CWH	04

The main menu will then appear as shown above.

Calculate Variances Option   This option allows you to enter the standard costs and actual costs for

Labor per-hour rate and the number of hours used
Materials per-unit cost and the number of units used
Variable overhead per-unit rate and the number of units used

The system will enter spreadsheet mode. A sample is illustrated on page 376.

1. Enter the amounts discussed into the green areas.
2. The software automatically calculates the variances for each and compares them to an "exception rate" for each type of variance. (These rates are below the screen in row 24.) The measure compared to the rate is the absolute value of variance/standard rate.
3. If the variance exceeds the exception rate, asterisks appear below the variance cell, indicating that the variance is considered unacceptable by management's pre-established standards.
4. When you are finished, type \BYE to exit this phase.

Analyze Variance Investigation Decision   This phase of the system performs more detailed analysis on the variances to help you decide if any of them should be investigated. It is broken into three steps:

Spreadhseet Mode

```
enter rates into green areas                                    type BYE to exit
                                                       *** indicates significance
                               LABOR VARIANCES
        EFFICIENCY VARIANCE                           RATE VARIANCE
    STANDARD  ACTUAL  VARIANCE              STANDARD  ACTUAL  VARIANCE
      3.00     3.20    -0.20                  25.00    23.00     2.00
                                                               ***


                             MATERIALS VARIANCES
        QUANTITY VARIANCE                            PRICE VARIANCE
    STANDARD  ACTUAL  VARIANCE              STANDARD  ACTUAL  VARIANCE
     19.00    15.00     4.00                  65.00    70.00    -5.00
                        ***


                         VARIABLE OVERHEAD VARIANCES
        EFFICIENCY VARIANCE                          SPENDING VARIANCE
    STANDARD  ACTUAL  VARIANCE              STANDARD  ACTUAL  VARIANCE
    200.00   245.00   -45.00                 197.00   150.00    47.00
```

1. Change the exception rates in the spreadsheet, if desired. This screen is labeled CHANGE VARIANCE INVESTIGATION PARAMETERS. These rates are not only changed in the spreadsheet, but are also used in a later calculation. An example of the screen is shown below.

Change Variance Investigation Parameters Screen

```
    CHANGE VARIANCE INVESTIGATION PARAMETERS


    Change Variance Investigation Cutoff For Each Type of Variance

              LABOR EFFICIENCY:          0.10

              LABOR RATE:                0.05

              MATERIALS QUANTITY:        0.03

              MATERIALS PRICE:           0.10

              OVERHEAD EFFICIENCY:       0.25

              OVERHEAD RATE:             0.20
```

Variance Decision Screen

```
                         VARIANCE DECISION SCREEN

                  Enter on a scale of 1=low     10=high

                        What is the degree of:


    RISK OF PRODUCT                NEED TO SUPERVISE

         2                               4




               What is the Relative Importance of:

    RISK OF PRODUCT           NEED TO SUPERVISE          EXTREMITY OF VARIANCE

         4                          _5                           3
```

2. The next screen, labeled VARIANCE DECISION SCREEN, prompts for two sets of variables. A sample appears above.
   a. First, you are prompted for measures for two factors, other than the variances, that may indicate the need to investigate a production function. These include the risk of poor performance you perceive the product to have at this time and the extent to which you feel that this product should be closely supervised by management investigations. Note that the scale is 1 for low and 10 for high.
   b. Next, you are asked to identify the relative weight that the three factors (risk, need to supervise, and variance) should carry in the overall determination to investigate. Again, note that the scale is 1 for relatively little weight and 10 for the most weight. For example, your ratio could be 2 to 5 to 8 if you felt that variance was the most important. Alternatively, if you felt each was relatively equal and not very great, you might use the 2 to 2 to 2. Press Enter when you have finished reading this screen and are ready to continue.
3. Finally, the system will show the results of the variance investigation calculation for each type of variance. An example is shown on page 378.
   a. The formula is

   ```
   If the absolute value of variance/standard rate is
   greater than the exception rate discussed before,
   then the investigation measure is
        (relative weight given for risk * risk factor)
   plus (relative weight given for supervision *
        supervision factor)
   plus (relative weight given for variance * absolute
        value of variance/standard rate).
   ```

Variance Investigation Calculation Screen

```
        RESULTS OF VARIANCE INVESTIGATION CALCULATION

           LABOR EFFICIENCY:          11.0

           LABOR RATE:                 8.2

           MATERIALS QUANTITY:         0.6

           MATERIALS PRICE:           11.0

           OVERHEAD EFFICIENCY:       11.0

           OVERHEAD RATE:              0.7
```

b. The software presents these results in one of two ways, depending on how you viewed the results the last time you analyzed this product. Users who prefer a graphical format are shown a graphical format, and those preferring tabular format are shown a tabular format. A tabular example is shown here.
c. After you have finished viewing, press Enter. You will be given the opportunity to view the results in an alternative mode. Respond Y or N to the question that follows.

Review Prior Investigations   This screen allows you to review the history database to see how prior investigations have fared. You can view the history for any of the six kinds of variances.
1. Select one of the types of variances. The labor efficiency variance contains the most history at this time.
2. Indicate what sort order you would like: Calculate variance measure (M) or cost (C). Either is listed in descending order.

Play What-If   This screen puts you into the spreadsheet mode. You may change anything you wish in this screen. Your changes will not be saved. Enter \BYE when you have completed the what-if analysis.

Enter Results of Investigation   This option gives an input screen used to report the results of investigations. Your data are entered into the variance history database (VARHIST) for future reference via the "Review Prior Investigations" option. An example of the input screen appears on page 379.

Variance Investigation Results Record Screen

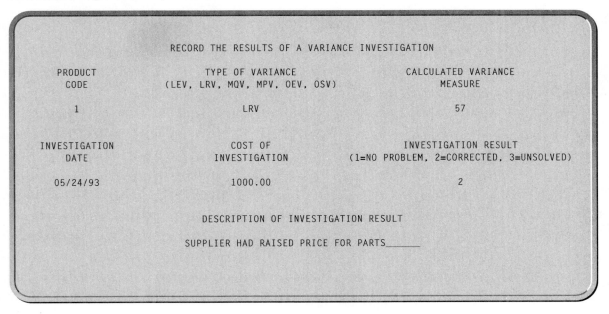

```
          RECORD THE RESULTS OF A VARIANCE INVESTIGATION

  PRODUCT              TYPE OF VARIANCE                CALCULATED VARIANCE
   CODE           (LEV, LRV, MQV, MPV, OEV, OSV)            MEASURE

     1                      LRV                              57


INVESTIGATION             COST OF                    INVESTIGATION RESULT
    DATE               INVESTIGATION          (1=NO PROBLEM, 2=CORRECTED, 3=UNSOLVED)

  05/24/93               1000.00                            2


              DESCRIPTION OF INVESTIGATION RESULT

          SUPPLIER HAD RAISED PRICE FOR PARTS_____
```

You are prompted for the following
a. Product code: Enter a number 1 through 4.
b. Type of variance: Enter the type of variance investigation you are reporting.

LEV	Labor efficiency variance
LRV	Labor rate variance
MQV	Material quantity variance
MPV	Material price variance
OEV	Overhead efficiency variance
OSV	Overhead spending variance

c. Calculated variance measure: Enter the measure that prompted you to make this investigation.
d. Investigation date: Give the date of the investigation you are reporting.
e. Cost of investigation: Enter the overall cost of the investigation you are reporting.
f. Investigation result: Enter
   (1) No problem found—no need to have investigated
   (2) Problem corrected—successful investigation
   (3) Problem unresolved—further investigation needed
g. Description of investigation result: Use the 40 characters to make (limited) notes regarding the investigation for future reference.

Press Escape when you have no more investigations to report. Select Exit on the main menu when you have finished using the system

A SOFTWARE MARKETING DSS, *BY SKIP BENAMATI*

INTRODUCTION

Welcome to SMSS. The purpose of this system is to support the software marketing efforts of the Kentucky Trading Area, KTA, by providing decision-making support at multiple levels. Using this system should allow field personnel to make appropriate decisions about software opportunities to pursue and at the same time allow management to analyze current forecasting information to make decisions that could alter the course of the KTA software-marketing effort.

Presented here is a prototype of a proposed solution. The important thing to evaluate is the types of functions and data-analysis techniques provided. The packaging and alternative ways of "cutting" the information in the system can be altered with relative ease to meet the preferences of the primary decision maker at the management level.

APPROACH

SMSS provides a software platform to which marketing support applications can be added. The current SMSS prototype includes two such applications: Software Marketing Opportunity Evaluation System (SMOES) and the Software Marketing Forecasting System (SMFS).

SMOES is an expert system that provides decision support to systems engineers and marketing representatives in evaluating software-marketing opportunities. SMFS is a management tool that forecasts and analyzes information about marketing opportunities. It shows overall forecast information and then allows decision makers to look deeper into the information behind the numbers. This process provides support for making changes in our software-marketing strategy as we drive to meet our annual numbers.

A wide variety of knowledge-management techniques are employed in SMSS, including forms management, database management, business graphics, on-line reporting, rule management, flexible solver management, and programming. All are synergistically integrated in the development tool. These, combined with a menu-driven user interface, make the applications easy to learn and use.

Invoking SMSS brings up a main menu that provides access to either of the two applications. As more applications become available to the KTA, they can be added to SMSS as other support options. A user invokes SMSS by typing PERFORM "A:SMSSMN" and then selecting either application option or the exit option from the menu presented.

When an opportunity is ranked during SMOES usage, it is also assigned a percentage likelihood of success based on its position in the customer and software tables (recall the description of these in the Part Two Case Study): the better the opportunity, the higher the likelihood of success. The SMOES action menu has an option that will allow for the storing of the opportunity in the OPPORTUNITY database table. The user is prompted for the anticipated sale date in MM-YY format for the opportunity. This information provides the basis for SMFS forecasting.

By selecting the SMFS option from the SMSS main menu, a user sees a bar graph of the forecast for the remaining portion of the current fiscal year. The system is set up to handle any fiscal year-end through the YRENDMNT attribute of the QUOTA table. Also from this table comes the number of months recorded via the MNTH-SRCR attribute, the annual quota, and year-to-date sales. The graph is created using this information and any recorded opportunities that are past the last recorded month.

The number of bars will vary, depending on where in the fiscal year the records are. The quota bar on the first set of bars is adjusted to reflect the quota for the remaining months in that quarter only. Opportunity dollars are forecast by multiplying the software cost by the percentage of likelihood of success. In this way, although not all software will hit, the high-percentage opportunities will make up for the low-percentage ones that probably won't hit. Any low-percentage hits will do wonders for the numbers.

Pressing any key will clear the graph and present the SMFS main menu. This menu consists of five options.

1. Review forecast: This option reviews the remaining year's forecast graph as described before and returns control to the main menu.
2. Review opportunity details: This option presents details about opportunities in the form of two percentage bar charts. The first is the percentage of total opportunities for a given software group, and the second is the percentage of forecasted dollars for a given software group. Before presenting the graphs, the user will be given a choice of analyzing any one of the remaining quarters.
3. Review forecast details: This option allows for the analysis of opportunities in tabular format by either the customer or the software group. The user selects one of these from a menu. The choice among particular or all remaining quarters is presented as in Option 2. Then, based on the selection of software group or customer, a user is given the option of viewing opportunities for any particular or all software groups or customers. If all is selected, those with opportunities are displayed one at a time. Each screen can be cleared by pressing any key. If a software group or customer is chosen that has no opportunities for the time period selected, a message is presented and another selection must be made.
4. Alter software details: This option is not currently available but follows naturally from the existing effort. It is envisioned as a way to provide a decision maker with what-if analysis capabilities. Analysis will be done by changing software parameters such as price, level of expertise, and whether it is strategic or not. All can affect the ranking of opportunities. Each opportunity affected will then be reranked and temporarily stored, and a new forecast will be produced. When finished, the software will offer the ability to save the changes permanently or to reset the software and opportunities to their base. This piece of the application, although originally in the scope of the current effort, should still be considered as a valuable future add-on.
5. Exit to SMSS: This option returns the user to the SMSS main menu.

As a prototype, there is some editing that is not done for SMSS. For instance, opportunities can be stored that have anticipated sale dates in the past. However, the forecasting system ignores all opportunities that have anticipated sale dates less than or equal to the last month recorded from the QUOTA table.

There is no real data entry in SMFS. All user interaction is through menu selection. In this way, it is fairly failure resistant.

TECHNICAL REFERENCE

The knowledge system includes four database tables, 11 pieces of procedural code, and the SMOES rule set. The four table structures, sample records, and the 11 programs are listed in Appendix G. A brief description of each procedure follows.

SMSSMN.IPF	The SMSS control program; initializes the environment and presents the SMSS menu.
DTCHOICE.IPF	Presents a menu to allow for the selection of the type of detail desired, customer or software group.
FORECAST.IPF	Prepares and presents the forecast bar graph for the remaining quarters of the fiscal year. Also presents year-to-date numbers.
FOREDET.IPF	Used to create the forecast detail report by software group. Creates the report based on the quarter or all quarters and a software group or all groups, depending on menu selections.
FOREDET2.IPF	Used to create the forecast detail report by customer. Creates the report based on the quarter or all quarters and a customer or all customers, depending on menu selections.
GETQTR.IPF	Performs the calculation to determine the remaining quarters in the fiscal year and presents a menu for selecting from a list of quarters or all remaining.
OPPDET.IPF	Plots the percentage of dollars forecast and the percentage of the total opportunity count by software group in percentage pie chart format.
SMFSMN.IPF	Presents the SMFS main menu and guides the user through the use of SMFS.
SMOESBIB.IPF	SMOES solver that calculates the benefit to the company.
SMOESGGL.IPF	SMOES solver that calculates the overall goal and the percent likelihood of success for an opportunity.
SMOESMN.IPF	SMOES main procedure.

EXPERIENCE NOTES

The development of SMSS was indeed a learning experience. First, I approached decision making in a very different manner. Thanks to the readings and lectures from the course, I was much more in tune with what was happening as opposed to the act of doing it. This helped me in designing the application, because I was able to put a decision maker's hat on and think about the processes that our management goes through in first forecasting our numbers and then making sure we are on track to get there.

I considered myself a do-it-yourself developer while doing this application. I can see why a design and scope are necessary prior to starting development. I could have gotten off onto many tangents as a do-it-yourselfer in the course of development. It was actually fun exploring some of these, but I knew what I needed going in and tried to stick to it as much as I could. The possibilities are endless, though, because the type of decisions can vary widely. A system with plenty of flexibility in the types of analysis and data that can be used is paramount.

Because of this need, I am not sure that all of the flexibility in the SDLC is always good for do-it-yourselfers. I can see certain individuals never finishing anything, because there are always other avenues to explore.

AN INTERIM REPORT

Based on your analysis of the appearance and behavior that are required for your envisioned DSS, it is probably worthwhile to spend some time producing a design that will guide your implementation efforts. You may be tempted to proceed immediately from requirements to implementation, doing ad hoc design concurrently with implementation and making things up as you go along. As a discipline to help control such an urge, consider preparing an interim project report that spells out a design to guide the implementation. This interim report should clearly answer such questions as the following:

1. What tool(s) will be used for development?
2. Which knowledge-management technique(s) furnished by the tool(s) will be used to satisfy which system requirements?
3. For each technique used, what objects are to be implemented? For example, in the case of database management, what tables will be defined and what are examples of records for each? In the case of forms management, what forms will be declared and what form elements will each contain? In the case of hypertext management, what types of documents will there be and what interrelationships will exist among them? In the case of spreadsheet management, what spreadsheets will be defined and what will be the arrangement of cell definitions for each? In the case of flexible solver management, what modules will make up solver libraries and in what ways can the modules be combined to synthesize solvers? In the fixed-solver case, what data sets will be implemented and what problem statements (i.e., models) will be stored? For program management, what programs are needed, what is the logical structure of each, and what are their inputs and outputs?
4. Where will the implementor get the knowledge that is stored according to the designs?
5. If the developer is not using an intrinsic tool, what PPS design will guide the problem processor implementation?
6. How should the implementor test for the correctness of DSS behavior?
7. How should the implementor test for ease of use in DSS interactions?
8. What provisions exist for design revision during implementation?
9. What system documentation will be implemented for users?
10. Beyond the design implemented in the prototype, what further design effort will be required for implementing subsequent versions of the DSS?

Part Four

ARTIFICIALLY INTELLIGENT DECISION SUPPORT SYSTEMS

. . . As a consequence of continuing progress in such domains as artificial intelligence . . . new tools have been emerging—not to replace the time-tried ones, but to supplement them. . . . [T]he major force that has been driving this gradual enlargement of aids to decision making is the nature of the decision-making task itself. Many important decisions (some would say "most") have important qualitative components that do not lend themselves easily to the calculus of real numbers. . . . [M]uch decision making leads to complexities beyond the reach of optimizing techniques, requiring approaches that are more heuristic than algorithmic. A major testing ground for new ideas about computer-aided and automated decision making has been the discipline of artificial intelligence. . . . The AI path has been characterized by attention to goal-seeking systems . . . to systems that draw on large knowledge bases. . . . The number of real-world applications of AI systems is now growing rapidly.

—DR. HERBERT SIMON, Nobel Laureate, Carnegie-Mellon University

Forward to R. Bonczek, C. Holsapple, and A. Whinston, *Foundations of Decision Support Systems.* New York: Academic Press, 1981, pp. xi–xii

The rule-management technique surveyed in Chapter 11 emerged within the field of artificial intelligence (AI). By incorporating this or other AI techniques in a decision support system, we make that DSS artificially intelligent—capable of displaying behavior that would be regarded as intelligent if observed in humans. Artificially intelligent DSSs are becoming increasingly common. Perhaps the most prominent of these are expert systems, which support decision making by giving advice comparable to what human experts would provide. Such systems are the focal point of Part Four.

Chapter 12 provides an overview of artificially intelligent decision support systems. It examines major branches of study in the AI field and how each may contribute to injecting artificially intelligent behavior into DSSs. It traces the history of technological advances leading to a class of artificially intelligent DSSs known as expert systems. It also examines the potential benefits of these systems to individuals and organizations.

Chapter 13 concentrates on how to represent reasoning knowledge as rules and how to process those representations. Two of the most prominent processing methods are forward chaining and backward chaining. These are alternative approaches for using a set of rules to draw inferences about the values of variables. Chapter 13 considers both of these inference methods in detail.

Chapter 14 is concerned with developing rule-based decision support systems. Some important aspects of this expert system development differ from conventional DSS development. One of these involves the acquisition of reasoning knowledge for incorporation into a knowledge system. This chapter considers both the context and process of knowledge acquisition. Both fit within a seven-step development cycle for building expert systems.

Chapter 15 presents a variety of advanced topics related to reasoning with rules: how rigorous the inference will be, in what order rules will be selected for processing, what strategy will guide the evaluation of a rule's premise, and the timing of when inference will happen. It also examines the incorporation of uncertainty into reasoning and the treatment of fuzzy (multivalued) variables.

The case study that concludes Part Four offers guidelines for the development of an artificially intelligent DSS. It provides examples of three expert systems conceived and built by students in the course of a semester. They are symptomatic of what you should be able to develop in a hands-on project of your own.

Chapter 12

OVERVIEW OF ARTIFICIALLY INTELLIGENT DECISION SUPPORT

INSIGHTS

CADILA LABS: AN ARTIFICIALLY INTELLIGENT DSS FOR DRUG PREFORMULATION DECISIONS

Overview

The chief executive of Cadila Laboratories, a major pharmaceutical company . . . thought the firm would achieve a distinct competitive advantage over other pharmaceutical companies in India by having . . . an expert system . . . on drug preformulation.

Preformulation consists of investigating a drug's physical, chemical, and biological properties alone and in combination with other chemicals (called excipients) used to develop a stable dosage form. A preformulation study identifies compatible, potentially useful pharmaceutical excipients and determines their relative proportions in the final formulation. A computer-based expert system for preformulating drugs would reduce total costs by reducing R and D time and identifying good stocking policies for excipients.

The biggest . . . challenge . . . was getting the experts to articulate their R and D analysis for preformulations. . . . The main task of acquiring knowledge from experts and representing it in a structured form . . . lasted for six or seven months. . . . [It was] a learning process for the experts as well as for the expert system.

System Development

Developing an expert system for drug preformulation includes various stages: acquiring knowledge about the main drug, excipients, and their interactions; organizing the knowledge; and designing the inference engine.

The information about the main drug to be included consists of its physical, chemical, and biological properties. . . .

Excipients are included for their therapeutic and production-process properties. For example, disintegrants, such as cornstarch, ensure that the tablet crumbles after it is swallowed. Binders and adhesives, such as gelatin, are used to bind the powder particles together to form a tablet. Lubricants . . . reduce friction as tablets and capsules are compressed. . . . Diluents . . . are added to increase the tablet's bulk to make it a practical size for compression.

Most of the rules in our expert system concern the interaction between a main drug and its excipients. We give a few ES rules below:

- If the functional group of the main drug is "highly acidic," then it needs a "moderate" binder and adhesive, a "moderate" disintegrant, and starch is to be avoided.
- If the solubility of the main drug is "soluble," then it needs a "weak" binder and adhesive, and a "weak" disintegrant.
- If the melting point of the main drug is "low," then it needs a diluent.
- If the density of the main drug is "high," then it needs a "weak" binder and adhesive, and a "weak" disintegrant.
- If the rate of dissolution of the main drug is "fast," then it needs a "weak" disintegrant.
- If the rate of absorption of the main drug is "fast," then it needs a diluent.

Continued

. . . Our expert system for preformulation contains the knowledge the preformulator requires to select compatible excipients for a given main drug . . . .

System Usage

. . . In our expert system, the user first inputs the properties of the main drug. The expert system then draws inferences in two steps. . . . First it infers the desirable properties of the excipients for compatibility with the main drug. . . . Then the expert system selects the appropriate excipients and their recommended proportions in the drug. . . . Usually several alternate preformulations are generated one after another. If requested, the expert system also provides an explanation for selecting a particular preformulation.

The expert system . . . is interactive and is driven by various menus. The New Drug menu prompts the user to input the properties of a new drug by providing a list of the main drug properties. . . . Using the Edit Drug menu, the user can edit information on the properties of any main drug entered earlier.

. . . [T]he Consult menu lets the software consult the knowledge . . . on the interaction between the main drug and excipients. . . . The software then consults the knowledge . . . on excipients . . . and identifies compatible excipients from the list of excipients possessing the required characteristics. The system then suggests a preformulation consistent with the knowledge already built in. If this preformulation is not acceptable, it will provide alternate preformulations.

The user can obtain the reasons for selecting the preferred preformulation through the Explain menu and can then judge whether it is acceptable or based on incorrect or insufficient information. . . .

Benefits

Cadila Laboratories has reported a number of benefits: The expert system greatly aids R and D experts in identifying compatible excipients. It has reduced the number of trials needed to determine the exact proportion of the excipients in the final formulation. The expert system identifies "almost compatible" excipients and determines their proportions quite satisfactorily. . . . In its present form, the expert system has led to a savings of about 35 percent of the total R and D time needed for preformulations.

Condensed quotation from K. V. Ramani, M. R. Patel, and S. K. Patel, "An Expert System for Drug Preformulation in a Pharmaceutical Company," *Interfaces* 22, No. 2 (1992); 101–108.

LEARNING OBJECTIVES

The Cadila Labs case gives an indication of what is involved in the development and use of a particular kind of artificially intelligent DSS called an expert system. The system was devised to give Cadila a competitive advantage. A major benefit realized from the system was the 35% reduction in time required to make preformulation decisions. This chapter explores the many potential benefits of expert systems and suggests ways in which they can be helpful in implementing competitive strategies. It also furnishes an overview of other artificial intelligence features that could be incorporated into a DSS aside from an expert reasoning capability. Keep the Cadila Labs case in mind as you study the reasons for artificially intelligent DSSs.

After studying this chapter, you should be able to:

1. Trace the technological advances in AI that contributed to today's artificially intelligent DSSs known as expert systems.
2. Characterize major branches of study in the AI field that have a potential for contributing to the realization of artificially intelligent DSSs.
3. Recognize the potential benefits expert systems offer for decision makers, experts, and organizations.
4. Explain ways in which expert systems can be instrumental in implementing competitive strategies.

Exercises at the end of the chapter reinforce and check the mastery of these objectives.

12. 1 INTRODUCTION

Artificially intelligent decision support systems are DSSs that make use of computer-based mechanisms from the field of **artificial intelligence** (AI). Researchers in the AI field endeavor to make machines such as computers capable of displaying intelligent behavior, or behavior that would reasonably be regarded as intelligent if it were observed in humans. A cornerstone of intelligence is the ability to reason. This ability, in turn, represents a principal area of research in the AI field, concerned with the discovery of practical mechanisms that enable computers to solve problems by reasoning. Although these mechanisms may not be identical to those a human uses in reasoning, they do produce results that are more or less comparable to what would be expected of a human.

AI PAYOFFS

The application of artificial intelligence techniques will play an increasing role in reshaping traditional notions of what organizations are, how they are managed, and how decisions are made. All of this presents a major challenge and an important opportunity to today's managers and organizations. Although the transition will not be without growing pains, it will likely lead to increases in the productivity of managers and organizations. Those organizations in the forefront of applying AI methods to aid decision making will have distinct competitive advantages over those that lag.

Perhaps the largest AI payoff will come in the realm of expert systems. These artificially intelligent DSSs employ AI reasoning techniques in order to offer expert advice about problems posed by decision makers. An expert system makes use of expertise that has been gathered (e. g., from a human expert) about reasoning used to solve a specific type of problem or class of related problems. The potential benefits of such systems range from the distribution and omnipresence of expertise to the formalization and preservation of an organization's reasoning knowledge.

Perhaps the most important AI mechanism to date has been the inference engine. As discussed in Chapter 11, it lies at the core of the rule-management technique—having the ability to make inferences from reasoning knowledge represented in rule sets. Just as a human decision support system can make inferences to derive knowledge in support of decision making, so too can a DSS whose problem processor is or includes an inference engine. Although our main focus in Part Four is on this kind of artificially intelligent DSS, we must point out that other AI mechanisms have been devised that are capable of incorporation into a DSS to make it artificially intelligent.

In this chapter we examine the reasons artificially intelligent DSSs are important. Such systems can be and are built because of (1) technological advances in the AI field that make them feasible and (2) their potential benefits to decision makers and organizations. We begin by tracing the evolution of reasoning systems within the AI field, culminating in the appearance of practical expert systems and powerful tools for creating them. By way of contrast, we then briefly consider other technological advances in AI, including natural language processing, knowledge representation, and machine learning. Each could be used to make DSSs more artificially intelligent. The remainder of this chapter focuses on the value of expert systems as DSSs, including an examination of their potential benefits to users, experts, and organizations. Having established an understanding of the reasons for which expert systems exist, we are then prepared for Chapter 13's detailed examination of how automated inference with a set of rules works.

12. 2 THE EVOLUTION OF REASONING SYSTEMS

The quest for computer systems that can reason about facts and assertions in order to solve problems lies at the heart of the AI field. In general, **reasoning systems** can be regarded as fitting the same generic architecture as DSSs. Typically, a reasoning system will have

- A knowledge system that holds facts and assertions about some problem area,
- A language system for stating specific problems to be solved,
- A problem-processing system that draws on the content of the knowledge system in order to infer solutions to problems stated with the language system, and
- A presentation system for conveying inferred solutions.

Research into the nature of reasoning systems has been concerned primarily with developing increasingly powerful and flexible approaches to representing KS contents and making inferences from them.

KNOWLEDGE BASE

In the jargon of the AI field, a reasoning system's KS is often called a *knowledge base*. For consistency and clarity, we shall avoid this term and continue to use the more general notion of a knowledge system in our examination of artificially intelligent DSSs.

Suppose that a reasoning system is built to solve the problem of how much an individual should invest in growth stocks. Its knowledge system would contain various facts about the present status of the stock market and assertions about how an individual should invest under a variety of circumstances. The user of this system would state a specific problem by typing in answers to a predetermined series of questions regarding the nature of the individual (e. g., assets, income level, age, and dependents). These answers characterize a particular individual and therefore constitute a particular problem statement. Some reasoning systems would incorporate this knowledge provided by a user into the KS. Others would not consider the problem statement to be part of the KS. In either case, the problem-processing system would reason with the KS contents in order to solve the investment problem of a particular individual.

INFERENCE

AI research into reasoning systems has concentrated on the inference mechanism to be used in a PPS, because that is what actually does the reasoning about facts and assertions held in a knowledge system. For a specific problem, the objective is to examine the *relevant* facts and assertions in a *sequence* that results in deriving or discovering a solution to the problem. At various steps in a reasoning process, the problem processor may need to ask the user for further information or clarification of problems being considered.

Just as in human reasoning, it is important for the problem processor to be able to differentiate between knowledge that is relevant and knowledge that is irrelevant to the specific problem at hand. It is also important to consider the relevant knowledge in a logical sequence, rather than with random browsing or jumping to conclusions. Otherwise, the problem "solution" may be unsound or may take a relatively long time to derive. AI researchers and logicians have devised many strategies for deciding what knowledge to examine next at each step in a reasoning process.

In general, the reasoning strategies fall into two broad categories: forward reasoning and reverse reasoning. **Forward reasoning** begins with the basic knowledge about the problem area. This knowledge is examined in a particular sequence, with the problem processor keeping track of the implications of examined fragments of knowledge each step of the way. This examination proceeds until the implications are discovered that provide a solution to the specific problem being processed.

Reverse reasoning, on the other hand, begins with the original problem statement. This problem is decomposed into subproblems, which are, in turn, broken into further subproblems, and so forth. The idea is that a small subproblem will be easier to solve than a large problem. That is, the DSS may solve the problem by simply looking up a relevant fact or assertion in the knowledge system. By solving all (or even some) of a problem's subproblems, the DSS can then easily solve the problem itself.

EARLY REASONING SYSTEMS

One of the earliest centers for research into reasoning systems in the mid-1950s was a management school: the Graduate School of Industrial Administration at the Carnegie Institute of Technology (now, Carnegie-Mellon University). Although artificial intelligence is often regarded as a field within the area of computer science, not a single computer science department existed in any university at the time that Carnegie's Herbert Simon and Allen Newell began their investigations into the nature of reasoning systems.

Together with J. C. Shaw of the RAND Corporation, Simon and Newell developed the Logic Theorist in 1956 (Newell, Shaw, and Simon 1963). This system used reverse reasoning to solve problems (i. e., prove theorems) in propositional calculus, with a small set of axioms as its initial knowledge system. In 1957 they began a much more ambitious project that was to extend over the next decade. This was the landmark General Problem Solver (GPS) (Newell and Simon 1963; Ernst and Newell 1969). Unlike the Logic Theorist, GPS was not specifically targeted toward solving propositional calculus problems—or problems in any other specific area. Instead, it endeavored to embody general reasoning methods that were applicable to a wide range of problem areas. In other words, it attempted to specify a general approach to problem solving.

DSS IN THE NEWS

Tackling Tough Retail Problems

For some Disney Store managers, finals week can be a real headache. . . .

. . . Because retailers employ many college students and other part-timers, scheduling can eat up hours of a manager's time. . . .

Disney management wants to give that time back to store managers by giving them a personal computer program that automatically draws up schedules for them.

Disney's system is just one example of how retailers are applying computers that can reason and use rules or case histories to draw inferences from data.

Some, like Circuit City Stores Inc., use such systems to help customers resolve problems. Others, like The Limited Inc. and Kmart Corp., use these artificial intelligence systems to tackle their toughest problems—like inventory management and forecasting sales of promotional items. . . .

Dale D. Achabal, director of the Retail Management Institution at Santa Clara University, says one company he knows of figures artificial intelligence can save $20 million a year by cutting its usual number of overstocked items by 10%.

Retailers working with researchers at Santa Clara University have built three artificial intelligence systems to forecast promotional, markdown and overall sales. Each system tries to identify causal relationships—say, a certain discount will boost sales by a specific amount. . . .

Rule-based reasoning, a key type of artificial intelligence system, requires software developers to devise and computer users to follow complex sets of very specific rules that guide the computer's judgments.

Also, a company must first locate the expertise to be captured and utilized by the system. . . . Typically, the expertise needed resides in some expert's head. . . .

. . . Rule-based reasoning systems can be useful for such highly complex tasks as managing inventory and forecasting markdown sales. . . . Coopers & Lybrand built one for TJ Maxx, the off-price clothing chain. . . .

T. Bunker, "How Artificial Intelligence Can Solve Real Problems in Retail Business," *Investor's Business Daily* 3 February 1993, p. 4.

The intent of GPS was to furnish a problem-processing system whose software never had to change, regardless of the problem area being addressed. GPS accomplished this result by storing all problem-specific knowledge, including reasoning knowledge peculiar to a problem area, in the knowledge system rather than weaving it into the problem processor software. Thus, by changing the content of its knowledge system, GPS was capable of solving problems in diverse areas, including propositional calculus, symbolic integration, resolution theorem proving, and various reasoning puzzles.

A specific problem was described to GPS in terms of an existing initial situation and a desired goal situation. The knowledge system contained operators (reasoning knowledge), each allowing the problem processor to determine that one situation can be reached from another given situation. To solve a problem, the problem-processing system searched through the operators to discover a sequence of operators—a flow of logic—that led from the initial situation through various intermediate situations to the goal. By establishing this flow of reasoning, the problem was solved. Such searches are governed by heuristics—problem-solving processes that are generally effective, yet do not completely ensure that an optimal solution will be found.

Although GPS itself turned out to have limited generality in terms of the breadth and depth of problems it actually solved, the principles it embodied were significant (Newell and Simon 1972). Reasoning systems research is greatly indebted to the trailblazing work of Simon and Newell for insights into the nature of reasoning and for the guiding spirit it provided to other researchers during the formative years of the field.

THE RISE OF EXPERT SYSTEMS

By the early 1970s a major new thrust was underway. This development involved the creation of reasoning systems that concentrated on solving difficult problems in very narrow problem areas. Real-life problems such as diagnosing diseases, assessing the chemical structures of unknown molecules, and applied mathematical analysis were emphasized. Because these systems are able to solve problems that would otherwise require the services of experts in their respective problem areas, they have come to be known as **expert systems**. Work on the earliest of these, DENDRAL, began in the mid-1960s (Lindsay et al. 1980). By the late 1970s a flurry of expert systems had burst upon the scene.

Table 12.1 shows a representative sampling of these pioneering expert systems. The most important thing to note about these expert systems is that *they work,* which is indisputable. They solved practical problems that would otherwise have required the services of human experts. Unlike the General Problem Solver, the problem processors of these expert systems were not designed to be general. They were custom built for very specific problem areas.

Reasoning methods peculiar to a specific problem area were incorporated into an expert system's problem-processing software. Thus the problem-processing system of DENDRAL is not suited for diagnosing bacterial blood infections. Conversely, the MYCIN problem processor is not sufficiently general to undertake molecular analysis. The implementers of expert systems each built their own problem-processing software from scratch, usually using special programming languages such as LISP. The time required to implement each of these expert systems normally

TABLE 12.1   Representative Pioneering Expert Systems

EXPERT SYSTEM	PROBLEM AREA
CASNET (Weiss, Kulikowski, and and Safir 1978)	Diagnoses glaucoma and recommends therapies
CRYSALIS (Englemore and Terry 1979)	Determines the protein structures of unidentified molecules from electron density maps
DENDRAL (Lindsay et al. 1980)	Determines the chemical structures of unidentified molecules
INTERNIST, CADUCEUS (Pople, Myers, and Miller 1975)	Diagnoses internal medical ailments
MACSYMA (Martin and Fateman 1971)	Solves differential and integral calculus problems in applied mathematics
MYCIN (Shortliffe 1976)	Diagnoses and prescribes treatments for bacterial blood infections
PROSPECTOR (Duda, Gaschnig, and Hart 1979)	Determines the major types of ore deposits present in a geological site
PUFF (Kunz et al. 1978)	Diagnoses lung dysfunctions
R1, XCON (McDermott 1981)	Determines an appropriate computer system configuration for a customer's needs
SACON (Bennett and Englemore 1979)	Advises how to analyze mechanical structures

amounted to many worker-years of effort. Implementation was expensive and required AI specialists rather than mainstream professional developers.

TOOLS FOR BUILDING EXPERT SYSTEMS

The effectiveness of expert systems having been proven, attention began to turn toward the invention of general-purpose tools for building expert systems more quickly and inexpensively. This was perhaps the central AI challenge as the 1980s began—a challenge that had to be met before expert systems could come into widespread use. Through their experiences in implementing expert systems, AI researchers noted certain commonalities across problem areas and began to design problem processors whose reasoning mechanisms were independent of the problem areas being addressed and in which all problem-specific reasoning knowledge could be held in the knowledge system.

One of the earliest such tools was EMYCIN—a somewhat general problem processor patterned after MYCIN's problem-processing system (Van Melle 1979). As such, it is oriented toward certain kinds of diagnosis problems, and it is restricted to operating on MYCIN-style knowledge systems. There are many real-world problem areas whose reasoning knowledge is not amenable to being represented in this kind of knowledge system. Nevertheless, for someone faced with the task of developing an expert system whose problem area closely resembles that of MYCIN, EMYCIN would be a useful tool. Because it provided a ready-made problem processor for reverse reasoning, there was no need to program a new problem processor for the expert system. The developer could concentrate on filling the knowledge system with problem-specific reasoning knowledge. Tools such as EMYCIN are often called *expert system shells*.

Considerably more general tools for developing expert systems are the OPS5 (McDermott 1981) and ROSIE (Fain et al. 1981) interpreters. These tools are problem processors that use forward reasoning to solve problems. To build an expert system with such tools, the developer creates a program consisting of statements describing a flow of reasoning to be followed when solving a problem. Although this involves considerably less effort than programming an expert system from scratch in the LISP language, it does not offer many of the built-in conveniences available with tools such as EMYCIN. On the other hand, tools such as OPS5 have been helpful in developing expert systems that do not naturally fit into the confines of more specialized tools like EMYCIN.

Expert System Shells   Since the mid-1980s, many tools for building expert systems have become available commercially. Although there are interesting differences among them, as a group they have tended to follow the EMYCIN rather than OPS5 philosophy. The appearance of these **shells** represented an important step beyond commercial LISP and PROLOG interpreters. Each shell is an implementation of the rule-management technique summarized in Chapter 11. An expert system shell typically consists of two main modules: a rule set builder and an inference engine. The rule set builder is software for creating, maintaining, and compiling rule sets pertaining to various problem areas. Creating a rule set consists of specifying its rules, characterizing the variable to be used by them, and indicating the usage of those rules. Rule set maintenance involves changing this specification to correct errors discovered during testing and to incorporate new reasoning expertise as it becomes known. The software for creation and maintenance may be menu-guided or may involve a text-oriented specification.

After a rule set is created or changed, the developer uses the rule set builder to compile it. The compilation activity checks the validity of the rule set and reports any errors to the developer. If the rule set specification is valid, then the software generates a new version of the rule set. This compiled version of the rule set is what the inference engine actually draws on during a reasoning process. It consumes less computer memory than the original source version and it also allows the inference engine to solve problems much more rapidly than would be possible if only a

---

FITTING THE DSS MOLD

When consulting an expert system, a user states a problem and then interacts with the system via its user interface. This interaction can occur both during the reasoning process and after the reasoning is concluded. An expert system's inference engine is the problem processor software that actually carries out the reasoning needed to solve a problem. In so doing, it draws on the stored reasoning expertise about the problem area. In addition, it may interact with the user to find out further details about the nature of the problem being solved. When the problem is solved, the inference engine reports the solution to the user and is able to explain its line of reasoning in reaching that solution.

The stored expertise about a problem area can be represented as a rule set. A rule set contains a collection of rules, each of which captures some piece of knowledge about how to reason in the specific problem area addressed by the expert system.

source version of the rule set were available for processing. Some shells do not support the compilation feature. Their inference engines can only interpret source versions of the rule sets.

The second major software module of an expert system shell consists of an inference engine that can reason with any rule set that has been created and compiled via the rule set builder software. Such an inference engine is therefore general with respect to the rule sets that can be specified with its rule set manager. This reduces the activity of creating an expert system to that of creating, revising, and compiling its rule set.

Some inference engines work with a single, rigid user interface. With the exception of furnishing content for prompts presented to a user, these inference engines give the developer little control over the nature of user interfaces. Regardless of the problem area addressed by an expert system, its user interface is essentially the same as those of all other expert systems that use the inference engine. The developer is left without such niceties as control over prompt positionings, use of form-oriented interaction, color and intensity selection, customized menus for user input, and so on.

Integrated Environments   Advancing beyond the idea of a shell was another kind of commercial tool specifically geared toward building artificially intelligent decision support systems that were not simply expert systems. Called an **integrated environment**, this kind of tool synergistically integrates rule management with other knowledge-management capabilities discussed in Chapters 9–11 (Holsapple and Whinston 1986). Using just its rule-management capabilities, we can build ordinary expert systems like those constructed with shells. However, if we use its other knowledge-management capabilities as well, we produce DSSs whose support features can go beyond the bounds offered by traditional expert systems. In the spirit of GPS, an integrated environment functions as a generalized problem processor for DSS construction (Bonczek, Holsapple, and Whinston 1981), whereas a shell, database manager, or other technique-specific software is more specialized.

GENERIC EXPERT SYSTEMS

Overview
- Computer-based system able to emulate reasoning behavior of a human expert
- Consulted by users seeking advice
- Traditional applications in medical and scientific areas

Traits
- Accepts requests for advice in some problem domain
- Interacts with user to clarify the nature of the problem
- Can explain why a particular interaction is needed
- Draws on stored reasoning expertise to infer a solution
- Presents the solution to the user
- Can explain the line of reasoning that led to the solution

BUSINESS EXPERT SYSTEMS

Overview
- Applies expert system technology to managerial problems
- Employs more than just reasoning knowledge
- Also uses conventional knowledge management techniques when working on a problem

Traits
To truly emulate business expert, a business expert system should

- Possess generic expert system traits
- Possess other knowledge-management capabilities
- Be able to exercise all in a coordinated, integrated fashion

12. 3 OTHER BRANCHES OF AI

Artificially intelligent DSSs can also result from the use of AI mechanisms coming from other branches of the AI field. These include natural language processing, knowledge representation, machine learning, automatic programming, and pattern recognition (Barr and Feigenbaum 1982). Here, we briefly survey each branch and point out what it can contribute to the construction of artificially intelligent decision support systems.

NATURAL LANGUAGE PROCESSING

The central AI objective of **natural language processing** is to allow humans to interact with computers in their own natural language rather than a computer language (Horwitt 1984). As noted in Chapter 8, the user of a natural language processor does not need to learn or remember any special language before asking for desired information. Talking to the computer is just about like talking to a human assistant. The only difference is that requests are typed out on a keyboard rather than spoken—and even this difference may disappear as advances in voice-recognition technology occur.

When conversing with a natural language system, a decision maker does not need to be concerned about adhering to a rigid computer language syntax. He or she can use everyday words, sentences, and even sentence fragments. Just as in a human conversation, a decision maker may make a request that is not fully understood. It might contain a new word whose meaning is unknown, a word that is known to have multiple meanings, a word that has been inadvertently misused, and so forth. Just as in a human conversation, the natural language system will interact with a user to clarify the request. It is able to learn the meanings of new terms as they are introduced into the conversation. It then understands all future references to those terms. This is a handy way for customizing the system's vocabulary to include a decision maker's favorite terms, jargon, and abbreviations.

Some natural language processors are able to detect typing or spelling errors in a request and automatically correct them. For instance, if we inadvertently type lsit rather than list, the processor would surmise that we really meant to enter list. As a courtesy, it would ask whether this interpretation is correct. Alternatively, we may define lsit to be a new term in the system's vocabulary.

Just as in a human conversation, a natural language system is able to understand a request in the context of the requests that preceded it. For instance, we might ask,

Who is in New York?

The system might respond by asking whether we mean the state or the city. After we indicate that we are referring to the city, the system will respond with a listing of employees based in New York City. Next, we might ask,

What are their salaries?

The system will respond with a two-column report showing names of New York City employees in one column and their respective salaries in the second column. If we then decide to see this information shown as a pie graph, our next request might be,

Plot them in a pie.

The result would be a pie graph showing the relative salary percentages for New York City employees. If we next wanted to see the same information portrayed as a bar graph, we might say,

Graph it as bars.

The information that was formerly shown as a pie chart would then be shown in a bar graph.

The most widespread use of natural language processing is for retrieving information from data files or databases (Rauzino 1983; Eptein 1985; Allen 1987). In the course of understanding a request, the natural language system builds a comparable retrieval command in the language that can be processed by a particular file or database–management system (e. g., in SQL). The file or database–management software then executes the resultant command in order actually to retrieve the desired information and present it to the user. In this way, the user is insulated from any need to know about how the file or database is organized. Some of the more advanced natural language processors do computations, statistical analyses, graphics generation, solver execution, and even expert system consultation.

When a natural language processor is part of a DSS's PPS, the vocabulary that it feeds on and expands is stored in the KS. Giving a DSS this kind of interpretation ability can increase the productivity of decision makers. It allows those who are only occasional or casual computer users to get answers directly to ad hoc information needs. Without such a system, the decision maker must either go to the information center for help or learn how to use the database–management system's query language or menu interface (if it exists). Neither is a particularly satisfying strategy: The first ends up overloading the information center, which is expensive and time consuming, whereas the second forces the manager to learn a new language and use it enough so that it does not have to be relearned from time to time. The natural language solution frees the user to concentrate on decision making rather than computerese.

KNOWLEDGE REPRESENTATION

The effective management of knowledge is an essential ingredient of intelligent behavior. Thus, the exploration of methods for **knowledge representation** is an important AI research topic. As might be expected, there is no single knowledge-representation method that is best for all types of knowledge or for all problem areas. The prevalent method for representing reasoning knowledge in an expert system is to use *productions.* Newell and Simon introduced this approach in the models of human thinking that they developed (Newell and Simon 1972). A production is simply a rule. It says that if a particular situation exists, then a particular conclusion can be drawn; or if certain conditions are satisfied, then a certain action can be produced.

Many other mechanisms for knowledge representation have been devised by AI researchers (Winston 1984; Ringland and Duce 1988; Bench-Capon 1990). Two of the most prominent of these are semantic nets and frames, each of which is oriented mainly toward handling descriptive knowledge.

Semantic Networks   A **semantic network** consists of nodes and arcs (Quillian 1968). Each node represents a concept, which could be some concrete entity (e. g., "IBM") or a more abstract notion (e. g., "corporation"). Each arc represents a relationship between the two nodes it connects. The arc's label (e. g., "is-a") denotes the nature of that relationship (e. g., "IBM is-a corporation"). Formal languages for specifying the structure of semantic nets have been devised (Raphael 1968), but no standards for semantic net representation and processing have emerged. Further discussion and examples of semantic nets are provided in Appendix E.

Frames   A **frame** consists of slots, each of which is somewhat similar to the idea of a field in database management. Collectively, a frame's slots are used to describe the nature of some object of interest (Minsky 1975). For instance, a corporation frame might have such slots as corporation name, ticker symbol, current share price, 52-week high, 52-week low, and yield. Like a field, each of these slots can have a value, an expression for computing a value, a filter, and so forth. In addition, procedures can be attached to slots. For instance, the current share price slot could have a procedure attached to it that would be activated whenever the price value increased. If the new value were to exceed the value of the 52-week high slot, then the procedure would update the latter to reflect the new 52-week high. Such a procedure is an example of what is called a **demon**—an object that watches for some event to happen and then takes some specified actions in response. Demon management has been recognized as a potentially valuable technique for decision support (Holsapple 1987). Slots can also involve such representations as semantic nets and rules (Fikes and Kehler 1985; Thuraisingham 1989).

Frames can be related to each other. For instance, we could have many instances of the corporation frame (i. e., one for IBM, one for GE, etc). These are related in that they all have the same kinds of slots. They are instances of the more general concept of a corporation, and each inherits all the traits defined for a corporation. At an intermediate level, there could be additional frames corresponding to various classes of corporations. Each of these would inherit all the corporation slots but could have additional slots peculiar to a class of corporations. For instance, a frame for the class of retail corporations might have one or more slots for same-store sales comparisons, whereas a frame for semiconductor manufacturers could have a slot for the book-to-bill ratio. A Walmart frame would have data for retail corporation slots, including same-store sales. A semiconductor manufacturing frame, such as one for Intel, would have book-to-bill data. Further discussion and examples of frames are provided in Appendix E.

MACHINE LEARNING

Incorporating the ability to learn into a software system is another subject of AI investigation. A good natural language system is able to interact with its user to

DSS IN THE NEWS

Learning from Experience

. . . Computers and software that do indeed learn from experience are finding their way into a broad range of software and hardware products used in everything from financial services to handwriting recognition.

. . . The market for neural net products . . . will mushroom from this year's projected $236 million to more than $2.2 billion by 1998.

. . . Neural net products use rudimentary artificial intelligence technology.

. . . Creating such devices is easier said than done.

. . . The problem is that "nobody knows how to write down a step-by-step procedure for remembering," noted Stewart Personick, a manager at the Morristown, N. J., information networking research laboratory of Bellcore. . . .

. . . Like the brain, a neural network consists of "neurons" that are linked together through communication conduits called synapses.

Depending on how these neurons are stimulated, the system can be imprinted with the "memory" of an experience. You can either simulate such neuron-synapse connections in a software program that runs on an ordinary computer or etch them on a silicon chip.

Classically, computers depend on one large "brain" processor called the central processing unit. These units are perfectly adapted for applications that require organizational abilities, such as listing every name that begins with the letter "S" in a telephone book.

But they tend to fall apart when they must choose between variables. Ask a traditional computer to figure out, on the basis of experience, what factors are important in stock investing, and you're out of luck.

Neural networks, however, can be trained to do just that. The key is to train computers to recognize patterns or trends. . . .

. . . Nikko Securities Co. has already developed a neural net system that can develop stock purchase criteria. . . .

. . . Security Pacific Corp. and Chase Manhattan Corp. reportedly used neural networks to help determine which loans would go bad. . . .

. . . An Eastman Kodak Co. chemical plant in Texas has developed a neural net software model to simulate the plant's performance. . . .

M. Stroud, "Are Neural Networks About to Come Into Their Own?," *Investor's Business Daily* 2 June 1992, p. 4.

learn the meaning of an unfamiliar term, adding it to the vocabulary so it will be understood in future conversation. Tools for developing expert systems normally allow incremental additions and changes to the reasoning knowledge stored in a knowledge system, letting an expert system developer "teach" the system over time. Of course, there is much more to learning than the accumulation of facts.

Machine learning involves devising mechanisms that allow computers to learn from experience, learn by examples, and learn by analogy. Some of these mechanisms modify the basic behavior (i. e., the program) that acts on stored knowledge. Others yield behavioral changes based on modifications to the stored knowledge. Machine learning mechanisms form the basis for adaptive decision support systems (Holsapple, Park, and Whinston 1993). Two of the most prominent approaches to machine learning are neural networks and genetic algorithms.

Neural Networks   A **neural network** is a system of independent processing elements, often called *neurons,* that aims to solve classification problems (Feldman et al. 1988; Wasserman 1989). For instance, it might determine that shares of a particular company's stock can be expected to underperform the market while classifying some other company in the outperform category. As it is trained, a neural network is given more and more problems and receives feedback on its success in correctly classifying each. Its learning mechanism adjusts the network's behavior in an effort to improve its classification capabilities. Because solutions to classification problems can be useful ingredients in decision making, a neural network can be

DSS IN THE NEWS

Emergency!

A computer network diagnosed heart attacks in emergency room patients more accurately than physicians, but researchers said the system should be used as an aid rather than a replacement.

The computer network could tell with 97 percent accuracy that a patient was having a heart attack and could specify or better analyze the probable cause 96 percent of the time, said a study in Sunday's Annals of Internal Medicine.

Emergency room doctors could detect heart attacks 78 percent of the time and specify the cause 85 percent [of the time]. . . .

The computer program, called an artificial neural network, tries to mimic the way a physician diagnoses a patient using observation and intuition.

Both the neural network and the physicians used the same information to make their diagnoses. . . .

The neural network's ability to "boost" a physician's accuracy by at least 10 percent could potentially save $280 million a year in preventing unnecessary hospitalization and malpractice suits. . . .

Associated Press, "Computers Beat Doctors at Diagnosing Heart Attacks," *Lexington Herald-Leader* 1 December 1991, p. A22.

DSS IN THE NEWS

Computer Genes

Researchers in the field of artificial life . . . are creating artificial organisms from the primordial soup of digital bits that pulse through silicon chips.

. . . [They] unleash "genetic algorithms," strings of computer code that automatically generate new code. . . . At the Tokyo Institute of Technology, researchers are building genetic algorithms that may learn to schedule hundreds of processes in a factory. . . . Thinking Machines Corp. is testing a genetic algorithm program called Star-Gene to sift thousands of pieces of data on millions of credit-card users to predict how the cards will be used. Several researchers are nurturing A-life programs to predict swings in the stock market.

R. Brandt, "Software: Agents & Artificial Life," *Business Week,* Special 1994 Bonus Issue, pp. 64–68.

viewed as a type of decision support system (Schocken and Ariav 1994). Further details on neural networks are provided in Appendix F.

Genetic Algorithms   Within a given application domain, a **genetic algorithm** aims to improve on a population of candidate solutions to domain problems (Davis 1989; Goldberg 1989). The improvement occurs across time periods of dealing with the same problem. Each time period is called a *generation*. A genetic algorithm evaluates the solution effectiveness of the population during a generation as a basis for producing a new population of candidate solutions. The new population is produced by means of reproduction, crossover, and mutation operators. A description of these operators and other genetic algorithm highlights appears in Appendix F. Genetic algorithms have been advocated as a means for imbuing some DSSs with an unsupervised learning capability (Pakath 1993).

AUTOMATIC PROGRAMMING

Automatic programming involves mechanisms for automatically generating a program that will carry out some prescribed task (Bierman 1976). Thus, a person who is not a programmer can describe the nature of a desired task. This description specifies the characteristics and behavior that the program should exhibit but does not need to specify how to actually build the program. The description is input to automatic programming software, which actually builds a program that can accomplish the described task.

An example of an automatic program generator used in managerial settings is software that generates programs capable of producing varied reports for decision makers. A generated program contains all input and output logic necessary for interacting with the user, all computational logic for needed calculations, all access logic for retrieving desired data from a database, and all formatting logic for controlling the layout of reports produced. Thus, the automatic program generator is able to create programs comparable to those of a human programmer.

From a DSS developer's point of view, an automatic program generator would be a valuable extrinsic tool for creating programs that are to be installed in a KS (e. g., Holsapple, Park, and Whinston 1992, 1993). It also has potential as an intrinsic tool, incorporated into a PPS. In this capacity, its function would be to formulate solvers (e. g., from KS modules) that need to be executed in the course of providing responses to user requests.

PATTERN RECOGNITION

Another topic of AI investigations is concerned with **pattern recognition,** including both visual and audio patterns. The ability to exhibit intelligent behavior in relation on one's surroundings depends in part on the ability to perceive those surroundings. To the extent that a computer system's perception is limited to sensing keystrokes or mouse movements, the end user is somewhat burdened relative to normal interhuman communication. Pattern recognition research aims to ease this burden (Fu and Whinston 1977). As progress is made, we move closer to systems (expert systems, for instance) that will be driven by spoken words and visual images. In addition, progress in pattern recognition has had and will continue to have an important impact in the entire field of robotics.

12. 4 POTENTIAL BENEFITS OF EXPERT SYSTEMS

Managerial applications of expert systems are virtually endless (Eom, Lee, and Ayaz 1993; Wong and Monaco 1995). They include both small and large expert systems to give advice to decision makers in such areas as the following:

- Establishing sales quotas
- Recommending acquisition strategies
- Generating project proposals
- Planning advertising spot layouts
- Scheduling job shops
- Maintaining facilities
- Selecting forecasting models
- Determining credit limits
- Selecting transport routes
- Providing investment counseling
- Analyzing market timing situations
- Offering job-costing advice
- Assessing job qualifications
- Evaluating performance
- Planning requirements
- Applying discounting policies
- Responding to customer inquiries
- Conducting trainee orientations

In short, any repository of problem-solving expertise that a decision maker needs to consult is a candidate for expert system development. Consider the example of setting sales quotas.

AN APPLICATION SCENARIO

The company of interest here is KC, Inc., a book publisher. KC has a national sales staff that covers 12 geographic regions. In each region there is a sales manager, who is responsible for the sales representatives working within that region. Each sales representative services a prescribed territory within the region. This service includes visiting each retail bookstore in the region on a regular basis to promote existing books, introduce new books, take orders, and inquire about bookstore needs that KC may be able to fulfill. A sales representative is also able to solicit and take book orders via the telephone. In addition to a base salary, each sales representative receives a commission for all books sold to retail bookstores within his or her territory. The company establishes different commission rates for different product lines.

There are currently 14 product lines. One product line consists of general reference books. Another comprises romance novels. Other lines include science fiction, psychology, photography, and computer books. Toward the end of each year, each regional manager is responsible for deciding on quarterly sales quotas for each of the sales representatives in the region. Each sales representative is assigned a quota for each product line for each quarter of the upcoming year. A sales manager therefore needs to decide on 56 quotas for each sales representative. Because a region may have 7 to 12 sales representatives, a sales manager must set from 400 to 700 quotas at the end of each year.

KC's vice president of sales realizes that establishing quotas is not only a big task, but a complicated one as well. Each quota could possibly be influenced by a wide variety of factors, including product line characteristics, seasonal trends, territory demographics, past performance of the salesperson, sales training programs, the expected number of new titles in a product line, expenditures for local and national advertising, and general economic conditions (e. g., unemployment and growth expectations) in the territory. The vice president is concerned about the consistency and fairness of quotas assigned to sales representatives both within a region and across regions. These ideas are important, because various bonuses are paid to sales representatives who exceed their quotas. Also, the three sales representatives who exceed their total quotas by the greatest amounts receive expense-paid vacations to overseas resort areas.

To help sales managers quickly establish reasonable and fair quotas, the vice president has budgeted funds for developing a computer-based system that can support decisions about quotas. This program is actually part of a larger project that will supply each sales manager with a microcomputer to be used for a variety of purposes beyond supporting quota decisions. It will also be used throughout the year to track and analyze the performance of sales representatives, for preparing reports and letters, for exchanging messages with the computers at KC's corporate headquarters, and for various budgeting activities.

The problem of setting quotas requires considerable expertise. Some sales managers seem to have a knack for it, whereas for others it is a struggle. The vice president has, over the years, been especially impressed with the quota decisions made by a sales manager named Jack Vander and plans to capture Jack's expertise in an expert system that is able to recommend quota levels. The resultant expert system will then be made available to all sales managers for use in their microcomputers. It will be able to offer advice about each quota decision faced by each manager.

The company and its employees described here are hypothetical. Although KC is unrelated to any actual company, it is typical. We shall refer to this application scenario often in the remainder of Part Four. It is used to illustrate many of the important points about expert systems as they are introduced. The principles and techniques reinforced via KC examples can, of course, be applied broadly to build and use artificially intelligent DSSs for a wide range of decision support applications.

OPERATIONAL BENEFITS

To the extent that expert systems can be built successfully for such applications, they offer many benefits. These potential benefits make the study of expert systems interesting and worthwhile. An overview of the benefits is presented here; keep them in mind while reading the chapters that follow. These chapters will help develop a fuller appreciation of how the benefits can be achieved.

Timeliness   An expert system is able to provide timely advice when a human expert is unavailable. Unlike its human counterpart, an expert system can operate around the clock, seven days per week, every day of the year. An expert system does not get sick, take holidays, go on vacations, or resign. An expert system is not tied up in meetings, away on business, or otherwise incommunicado. In the case of KC, Jack Vander is simply unavailable as a consultant for other sales managers to contact for help in setting their quotas: Jack has his own sales representatives to manage.

Replication   Unlike the human experts that it emulates, an expert system can easily be replicated. The same expert system can be used simultaneously in many sites across the country or around the world. Once an expert system has been constructed, it is relatively inexpensive to distribute. A good expert system functions as a clone of the human expert. Each of the KC sales managers will, in effect, have Jack at his or her side to provide advice if and when it is desired. Notice that this does not threaten to put either Jack or the other sales managers out of work. The expert system is not a substitution for Jack. Instead, it provides an expert advisory service not previously available, with the intention of improving KC's overall sales effort. The impact on Jack is likely to be a bonus, raise, or promotion in recognition of his contribution. Nor is the expert system a substitute for the other sales managers. It simply offers quota advice to them as an aid to managerial effectiveness.

Increased Expert Productivity   In some cases, a human expert may already be in place to provide advice. The introduction of an expert system that can offer comparable advice should have a very positive impact on the human expert. It can reduce the demands on that human expert's time by insulating him or her from many kinds of consultation requests. This allows the human expert to focus on the most challenging problems and to concentrate on new creative activities. Human experts are normally a scarce resource for an organization. To the extent that their productivity can be increased by off-loading consultation activity to expert systems, the organization's human resources can be more effectively utilized. The human expert does not have to spend as much time directly providing advice and those seeking advice do not encounter the usual bottleneck of competing for the human expert's attention.

Consistency   Another benefit of an expert system is that it provides consistent, uniform advice. It is thorough and methodical. Unlike the human expert, an expert system does not have lapses that cause it to overlook important factors, skip steps, or forget. It is not politically motivated, temperamental, or biased (unless the developer designs it to be so). An expert system functions as a standardized problem solver that can be a substitute, supplement, or verifier for a human expert. Once Jack has built the expert system for providing quota advice, he will probably consult it himself when he sets quotas for his sales representatives. Not only might it suggest quotas faster than Jack could himself, it will do so in an entirely consistent and error-free manner.

Explanations   Like a human expert, an expert system is able to explain the line of reasoning it uses for each problem it solves. The flow of reasoning used for one problem may be quite different than that used for a different problem. This explanation ability enables the expert's advice to be critiqued. A user can study the rationale on which the advice is based and is free to accept it or reject it. A sales manager may want to see why a particular quota level is being recommended as a basis for assessing whether to accept the advice, modify it in light of additional factors, or entirely reject it. The built-in explanation ability sets expert systems quite apart from traditional application systems for record-keeping and decision support. Because those traditional systems were unable to reason, there was never an issue of explaining their lines of reasoning.

Uncertainties   Human experts are able to reason with uncertainties. These uncertainties are reflected in the advice given. Although all expert systems do not have a comparable capacity, many do. For instance, Jack may want his expert system to take uncertainties about possible states of the local economy into account when it reasons about quotas. As a result, the expert system might indicate that it is 80% confident that $20,000 is a proper quota and 60% confident that $18,500 is a reasonable quota. This built-in ability to reason about uncertainties and alternative (fuzzy) values is yet another potential benefit that differentiates expert systems from traditional applications systems (see Chapter 15).

Evolution   Expert systems are able to evolve in a straightforward manner. Because the reasoning knowledge is represented as rules in a rule set, new expertise can be added by simply adding new rules or modifying existing rules. This modularity of rules means that there is no issue of programming or reprogramming. The developer of an expert system need not be a programmer, provided the development tool is a shell or integrated environment. Jack Vander is certainly not a programmer. As examples in the following chapters illustrate, Jack can start out with a simple rule set that is initially useful, yet easily capable of many kinds of elaboration. Over time, the reasoning knowledge embodied in the rule set can be tailored, revised, and expanded, allowing the expert system's expertise to evolve gradually, just as human expertise evolves.

Formalization of Knowledge   A somewhat subtle, yet quite significant, benefit of expert systems is their effect of formalizing an organization's reasoning knowledge. Converting an expert's reasoning knowledge into explicit rules can lead to a better understanding of the nature of an application problem area as well as clearer insight into how the application's problems are solved. This introspection may well result in better decision making. At the very least, an expert system's formalization of reasoning knowledge provides a way of preserving that knowledge long after its human progenitor has left the scene. It can also provide a valuable basis for training new human experts.

In addition to the foregoing operational benefits of business expert systems, there is also an important strategic role that such systems can play in contributing to an organization's competitive position (Holsapple and Whinston 1987). The remainder of this chapter is concerned with the strategic benefits and opportunities that business expert systems can offer. Top-level management should be aware of (or be made aware of) the far-reaching implications that business expert systems have for an organization's competitive strategy or outright survival. In what ways can business expert systems give an organization an edge over its competitors? What impacts can business expert systems have on a competitive environment and on the implementation of a competitive strategy?

COMPETITIVE STRATEGY[1]

A company's long-term viability depends on its ability to maintain an effective **competitive strategy**. Business researchers have pointed out that management information systems can be used to achieve competitive advantages (McFarlan 1984; Cash and Konsynski 1985). For instance, a large airline carrier's reservation system is used not only to book its own flights but also those of its competitors. As a result, the large airline has access to reservation levels of all flights offered by those competitors. This information, which is not fully available to its competitors, enables the large airline to identify competing flights that are performing well and install aggressive competitive countermeasures for those routes. Other examples include interorganizational information systems for order entry and purchasing. These systems provide electronic pathways between companies, pathways that not only can yield competitive advantages but can also shift the balance of power between buyers and suppliers.

These systems are concerned with the storage, maintenance, retrieval, and transmission of information. As discussed in Chapter 4, what we normally think of as information or data is but one kind or knowledge: descriptive knowledge about an organization's state and environment. Of course, reasoning knowledge is also important to an organization. Just as the computerization of descriptive knowledge in the guise of management information systems can lead to a competitive edge, so too can the computerization of reasoning knowledge in the guise of artificially intelligent DSSs. Although expert DSSs do not have the same long history as management information systems, it is not premature to consider their strategic implications for an organization's competitive stance.

Traditionally, the expertise embodied in an organization's employees has provided an important basis for achieving, improving, and maintaining its competitive position. All else being equal, organizations without comparable expertise are at a disadvantage. With expert decision support systems, there is an opportunity to amplify the competitive advantage derived from superior expertise. To the extent that the expertise captured in an expert system is unique or not widely known, a sustained advantage results. Unlike management information systems, interesting

---

1. *Source:* The part of section 12.4 titled "Competitive Strategy" is adapted by permission of the IEEE from Clyde W. Holsapple and Andrew B. Whinston, "Business Expert Systems—Gaining a Competitive Edge," *Proceedings of Hawaiian International Conference on Systems Sciences,* Kona, Hawaii, January 1990. © 1990 IEEE.

expert systems cannot be readily reproduced without access to the details of their stored expertise. Such an expert system can be used openly, but as long as it has sufficient security provisions to protect the details of its reasoning knowledge from disclosure, the competitive advantage it furnishes endures. In a sense, it is an intellectual property right, similar to a patent without a predetermined expiration date.

Like management information systems, expert systems can be used to implement a competitive strategy (Holsapple and Whinston 1987; Sviokla 1989, 1990). Competitive strategies fall into three categories (Porter 1979). One strategy is based on the idea of producing goods or services at a lower cost than competitors. Another strategy is based on brand differentiation, which involves offering a unique and attractive mix of product features. A third basic strategy is to concentrate in a special market niche with a product that has little direct competition because of its remarkable features or cost advantages. These basic strategies suggest three ways in which artificially intelligent DSSs can contribute to an organization's competitiveness:

- Enhance internal productivity.
- Provide enhanced services.
- Provide new services.

On a larger scale, an organization could even look to expert systems as part of a strategy aimed at spawning a completely new industry.

Enhancing Internal Productivity   The purpose of the expert system for setting sales quotas is to enhance sales manager productivity. It does so in two ways. First, it can increase efficiency by reducing the time and effort that a sales manager expends on this activity. The gain can be applied to other activities (e.g., representative training) that have a positive impact on sales within the region. As a result, the company is more competitive, because its sales managers have an efficiency advantage over their counterparts in competing companies.

Second, the expert system can increase effectiveness by utilizing expertise that is otherwise unavailable to many sales managers. The best that the company can

DSS IN THE NEWS

Doing More With Less

GTE Corp.'s operations in Florida's Tampa-Sarasota region is more the rule than the exception. Over the past five years, the area's population and telephone system have grown by about 7% annually, yet GTE still employs the same number of service people, about 250. Laptops let repair crews plan their daily schedules efficiently and allow customers to get a more accurate time of arrival from repair folks. The staff backing up these technicians has dropped from 45 to 11 as software-driven "expert" systems take customer requests and arrange them in the most efficient order.

C. Farrell, M. Mandel, and J. Weber, "Riding High," *Business Week*. 9 October, 1995, p. 142.

offer in this area is replicated in a consistent fashion throughout the organization. A competitor may have employees whose expertise rivals Jack's; however, as long as that expertise is not distributed within the competing organization, it operates at a disadvantage relative to KC. It does not maximize the productivity of its sales managers. All else being equal, KC has a competitive advantage due to a more cost-effective use of its sales management resources.

The sales quota case is just one example of how an organization can use expert system technology to implement a competitive strategy that aims at enhanced internal productivity. It can be applied at all levels of organizational decision making. Anthony (1965) has identified three levels in the continuum of decision processes: strategic planning, management control, and operational control. At one end of the decision-making spectrum, strategic planning is concerned with decisions about objectives and policies. Management control is concerned with managing resources to meet objectives and conform to policies. At the other end of the spectrum, operational control involves the exercise of precisely specified decision rules to decide what actions to undertake. At one extreme, operational control problems tend to be routine and highly structured. At the other extreme, strategic planning problems tend to be less routine and less structured (Simon 1960).

In the case of KC, setting sales quotas is an example of a management control problem. An expert system that offers sales quota advice can assist in the effective utilization of a sales manger's resources. A different kind of problem that confronts KC from time to time is whether to take on a new product line or eliminate an existing product line. These are examples of strategic planning problems. They require considerable expertise to solve and could also benefit from expert systems. Many of KC's operational control problems are also appropriate for expert systems. For instance, the shipping department has a few simple rules that clerks use to determine how regular shipments are to be sent. But rush orders are not unusual, and they require much greater expertise to handle effectively. The carrier selected for such a shipment depends on factors such as the time of day, day of the week, holiday proximity, destination, and shipment size. An expert system that can offer customized shipping advice for the exceptional cases enhances the productivity of the clerks and their supervisor alike.

At each level of decision making, there are problems amenable to expert system assistance. All these problems should be considered as opportunities for implementing a competitive strategy based on the notion of enhancing internal productivity. Some of these productivity increases may lead to cost advantages, as suggested by Porter. But lower cost is not the only possible manifestation of enhanced productivity. As in the case of the quota expert system, there may also be more effective and efficient decision making. Although this expert system will not significantly impact the cost or price of books, it can still lead to a competitive advantage. It can yield increased sales or market share through the more responsive and motivated sales force that results from fair and consistent quotas, as well as through the removal of a burden to the sales managers.

Providing Enhanced Services   An important part of a large chemical company involves the marketing of numerous chemicals to industrial customers. Many of the chemicals have multiple uses; there may be several chemicals that could, alternatively or in tandem, meet a particular customer need. Sometimes a customer already knows what chemicals it wants and the needed amount of each. However, in many cases a customer does not know what amounts of what chemicals will satisfy its needs. Management decides to implement a competitive strategy that aims to enhance the service provided to customers. Instead of merely selling chemicals, the company will provide solutions. The company will help a customer to clarify the problem faced, offer expert advice about a purchase decision for solving that problem, and justify the advice that is offered.

Sufficient in-house expertise exists for handling the diverse technical problems that customers face. But the catch to implementing the full-solution strategy lies in the delivery of this expertise. Training technical sales representatives to communicate the traits and uses of the company's products effectively is already a costly, lengthy, and ongoing endeavor. Even with extensive training, sales representatives often find it difficult to match a customer's perceived needs (typically described in very technical terms) with product offerings.

Further training that enables a representative to help in clarifying a customer's actual problem, to offer expert advice about solutions, and to justify that advice convincingly may have some value. However, such training cannot be expected to result in a satisfactory implementation of the competitive strategy. There is the prospect that highly trained representatives can be lured away by competitors, so that the company serves as a training ground for its competitors. Furthermore, there are limits to what a sales representative can absorb while still actively making sales calls. Even the problem-solving ability of an in-house expert has limits. Individuals who are experts about everything are rare indeed. However, the collective know-how of these experts is formidable.

A possible alternative to implementing the full-solution strategy would be to make the in-house experts directly accessible to customers. Together they would form a technical sales support staff. When a representative encountered a problem that he or she could not handle, it would be referred to an appropriate expert in the support staff. This expert would then help define and solve the problem and explain the solution. There are several difficulties with this implementation approach. The experts typically are not especially skilled in sales techniques. Their expertise is important for postsale customer support and for the research and development of new products. The experts are neither numerous nor inexpensive. As a result, customer referrals would need to be queued. Responses might not be timely, and unhealthy contention for expert support might arise among the sales representatives.

If it were not for the scarcity and cost of experts, the ideal implementation strategy would be for each sales representative to have an agreeable technical support staff at his or her side as sales calls are made. The representative would be in control of the sales call as it unfolded and would be able to draw directly on the staff's expertise if and when it was needed for clarifying customer problems, offering recommendations, and justifying advice that is given. The company's top management has opted for this approach to implement its competitive strategy, but with one exception. Rather than the impracticality of a technical support team physically accompanying each sales representative, the team's expertise is captured in one or more expert systems. With a portable microcomputer, each sales representative will be accompanied by an appreciable portion of the support team's expertise. Rather than attempting to train representatives to an expert level, the in-house experts train expert systems. The company therefore has a controllable asset that cannot be lured away by the competition.

The competitive advantage that results from enhanced service may or may not be reproducible. To the extent that a competitor has equivalent (or superior) in-house expertise and can harness it in a comparable way, the initial competitive edge may not be fully sustainable. Nevertheless, the first entrant into the marketplace with this enhanced service may have created some entry barriers for competitors that consider following its lead. For instance, it may establish itself in customers' eyes as the leader in providing this service. This positive image can be difficult to overcome. As customers become accustomed to the leader's expert systems, they may find it inconvenient or uninteresting to bother with others. Furthermore, the leader has a learning curve edge in applying the technology to achieve a competitive advantage. Followers are likely to be a step behind as the expert systems supporting purchase decisions continue to evolve.

Providing New Services   Related to the idea of enhanced services is the notion of new services. As in the case of the chemical company, an enhanced service is concerned with improved features, greater timeliness, greater thoroughness, and so on. A competitive strategy could also be aimed at furnishing a new service that draws customers to a company. For instance, top management personnel of a retail bank have decided to introduce a new service that has not been offered by other banks of its type and size. In considering consumer loans, these banks presently use rigid scoring protocols that lead to either the acceptance or rejection of a loan request. This retail bank intends to increase its customer base by offering an investment banker's services to its customers.

In traditional investment banking, an expert works out a customized financing arrangement suitable to a client company's needs. Thus, the retail bank's competitive strategy is based on providing a new service in which loan instruments are tailored to individual consumer situations. In considering how to implement this strat-

---

POTENTIAL BENEFITS OF EXPERT SYSTEMS

Automated Consultation
- Provides easy distribution of expertise
- Available when human experts are scarce, overburdened, expensive, and unavailable when needed
- Benefits both the expert and those seeking advice

Formalization
- Provides a discipline for formalizing an organization's expertise
- Serves as a basis for generating new experts
- Presents a way to preserve valuable reasoning expertise

Strategic Potential
- Is a basis for achieving competitive advantage (or remaining competitive)
- Improves internal productivity
    Quota advice
    Shipping advice
- Provides enhanced services
    Chemical sales support
- Offers new services
    Retail banks and customized financing

egy, substantial expertise would clearly be required to handle effectively the creation of customized consumer loans. However, the bank would not be financially justified in hiring sufficient investment bankers to handle the relatively large number of relatively small (dollar-wise) applicants. But an expert system that embodies the sophisticated reasoning behavior that an investment banker would display for consumers could be financially attractive, especially if it were shared by a consortium of banks. Loan officers could base their decisions about what financing to offer on advice from such an expert system. As in the case of enhanced services, reproducibility and entry barriers are important issues when considering new services implemented via expert systems.

12. 5 SUMMARY

Artificially intelligent decision support systems exist for two main reasons. First, advances in AI technology have made it practical to build systems whose behaviors resemble some aspects of human intelligence. We can expect such advances to continue, leading to new dimensions for DSSs. Second, decision makers can benefit from DSSs that exhibit more, rather than less, intelligence. Such systems become closer approximations to HDSSs than they would in the absence of AI technology.

As does human intelligence, artificial intelligence has many aspects. One of the most significant is the ability to reason. The AI quest for reasoning systems has matured to the point where computers are able to display expert behavior. To assist in the construction of these expert systems, numerous software tools are now commercially available. These include both shells and integrated environments.

Although expert systems are the most prominent kind of artificially intelligent DSSs and form our focus here, there are other branches of AI that can contribute to the realization of artificially intelligent decision support systems. These include natural language processing, which effectively allows a DSS user to specify the LS, knowledge representation, which offers alternative kinds of KS contents, machine learning, which provides mechanisms that could be incorporated in a PPS to allow a DSS to learn, automatic programming, which has potential to aid in the construction of DSS solvers and user interfaces, and pattern recognition, which could yield DSSs with nontraditional modes of interaction.

The potential benefits of expert systems are numerous, ranging from operational to strategic. They give decision makers uninterrupted access to consistent advice. They relieve experts from having to give that advice. They allow an organization to formalize and retain some of the expertise that exists within it. The strategic implications of expert systems for business present a challenge and opportunity for top-level management. Management that pays attention to these implications and is alert to the possibilities can find itself with a competitive edge, rather than being out on a competitive ledge. The remaining chapters in Part Four are concerned with fostering a sufficient technical understanding to turn the potential benefits of expert systems into realities.

▲ IMPORTANT TERMS

artificial intelligence	competitive strategy
automatic programming	demon

expert system
forward reasoning
frame
genetic algorithms
integrated environment
natural language processing

neural networks
pattern recognition
reasoning system
reverse reasoning
semantic network
shell

▲ APPLICATION TO THE CADILA LABS CASE

1. What decisions were supported by Cadila's expert system?
2. What was the nature of the support provided?
3. In what way did the artificially intelligent DSS contribute to Cadila's competitiveness?
4. In what sense was development of the expert system a learning experience for (a) the expert system and (b) the experts?
5. What kind of development tool was used in building this expert system?
6. What application-specific knowledge exists in the knowledge system?
7. What is the nature of the advice offered by the expert system?
8. Aside from advice, what other kind of decision supporting response can the system make to a user's request?
9. What primary benefit(s) did R and D users of the system realize?
10. What benefit(s) not noted in the case may also have accrued to Cadila Labs by having developed and used the expert system?

▲ REVIEW QUESTIONS

1. What kinds of factors should be considered when assessing the capabilities of a natural language?
2. What are some potential drawbacks of a natural language interface?
3. What are the main subsystems of a reasoning system? How do they differ from those of a DSS?
4. What are the advantages of keeping all application-specific reasoning knowledge seperate from the software that uses that knowledge?
5. What is the difference between an expert system shell and an expert system?
6. What are the main classes of tools available for developing expert systems?
7. How does a shell differ from an integrated environment?
8. In what sense can natural language processing be considered to be a type of automatic programming?
9. How does an expert system differ from a conventional decision support system?
10. What are two software components of an expert system development tool? What role does each play in the development process?
11. What are the major operational benefits of expert decision support systems?
12. Why should a business expert system not be regarded as a threat to the human expert who furnishes its rules?
13. Why should a business expert system not be regarded as a threat to non-experts?
14. What properties must a system have in order to qualify as an expert system?
15. What are three classic types of competitive strategy, and what is their relevance to artificially intelligent DSSs?

16. In what ways can expert system technology be instrumental in implementing a competitive strategy?

▲ DISCUSSION TOPICS

1. Give three examples of rules that might govern human reasoning in the course of solving a business problem.
2. Discuss the relevance of each AI branch for building artificially intelligent DSSs.
3. Describe the notion of a general problem solver.
4. List some of the different kinds of knowledge-processing abilities that a GPPS could possess.
5. Explain the kinds of processing that are available when there is a synergistic integration of spreadsheet and rule-management capabilities.
6. Describe how expert system capabilities can be incorporated into a decision support system.
7. Contrast inference with machine learning mechanisms.
8. Using the HDSS metaphor, how does a human consultant to a decision maker behave, and which of these behaviors should an artificially intelligent DSS exhibit?
9. Identify three kinds of problem areas where expert systems could help a salesperson.
10. Give an example of a business problem that is not particularly well suited to expert system development.
11. How do business expert systems differ from conventional expert systems?
12. What are some of the important ways in which inference engines can differ from one another?
13. Discuss the importance of inexpensive expert systems to small businesses and Third World countries.
14. Discuss the difference between using an expert system in strategic planning and using an expert system in the implementation of a strategic plan.
15. Give examples of how expert systems can be applied at each level of decision making.
16. Explain how a competitive strategy implemented with expert systems can lead to a sustainable competitive advantage.

▲ REFERENCES

Allen, J. 1987. *Natural language understanding*. Menlo Park, Calif.: Benjamin Cummings.

Anthony, R. N. 1965. *Planning and control systems*. Boston: Harvard Business School. 1965.

Barr, A., and E. A. Feigenbaum, eds. *The handbook of artificial intelligence*. Vols. 1–3. Los Altos, Calif.: William Kaufmann.

Bench-Capon, T. 1990. *Knowledge representation*. New York: Academic Press.

Bennett, J. S., and R. S. Englemore. 1979. SACON: A knowledge-based consultant for structural analysis. *International Joint Conferences on Artificial Intelligence 6*.

Bierman, A. W. 1976. Approaches to automatic programming. *Advances in computers. Vol. 15*. Edited by M. Rubinoff and M. C. Yovits. New York: Academic Press.

Bonczek, R. H., C. W. Holsapple, and A. B. Whinston. 1981. *Foundations of decision support systems*. New York: Academic Press.

Cash, J. I., Jr., and B. R. Konsynski. 1985. IS redraws competitive boundaries. *Harvard Business Review* (March-April).

Davis, L. 1989. *Handbook of genetic algorithms*. New York: Van Nostrand Reinhold.

Duda, R. O., J. G. Gaschnig, and P. E. Hart. 1979. Model design in the PROSPECTOR consultant system for mineral exploration. In *Expert systems in the micro-electronic age,* edited by D. Michie. Edinburgh: Edinburgh University Press. 1979.

Engelmore, R. E., and A. Terry. 1979. Structure and function of the CRYSALIS system. *International Joint Conference on Artificial Intelligence 6.*

Eom, H. B., S. M. Lee, and A. Ayaz. 1993. Expert systems application development research in business: A selected bibliography (1975–1989). *European Journal of Operational Research* 68, no. 2.

Epstein, J. A. 1985. Natural phenomenon. *Digital Review* 1, no. 3.

Ernst, G. W., and A. Newell. 1969. *GPS: A case study in generality and problem solving.* New York: Academic Press.

Fain, J., D. Gorlin, F. Hayes-Roth, S. J. Rosenschein, H. Sowizral, and D. Waterman. 1981. *The ROSIE language reference manual.* Santa Monica, Calif.: Rand Corporation.

Feldman, J. A., M. A. Fanty, N. H. Goddard, and K. J. Lynne. 1988. Computing with structured connectionist networks. *Communications of the ACM* 31, no. 2.

Fikes, R., and T. Kehler. 1985. The role of frame-based representation in reasoning, *Communications of the ACM* 28, no. 9.

Fu, K. S., and A. B. Whinston, eds. 1977. *Pattern recognition: theory and applications.* Layden, The Netherlands: Noordhoff International Publishing Co.

Goldberg, D. E. 1989. *Genetic Algorithms in Search, Optimization and Machine Learning.* Reading, Mass. Addison-Wesley.

Holsapple, C. W. 1987. Adapting demons to knowledge management environments. *Decision Support Systems* 3, no. 4.

Holsapple, C. W., V. S. Jacob, R. Pakath, J. S. Zaveri. 1993. Learning by problem processors: Adaptive decision support systems. *Decision Support Systems* 10, no. 2.

Holsapple, C. W., S. Park, and A. B. Whinston. 1992. Generating structure editor interfaces for OR procedures. *Zeitschrift fur operations research* 36, no. 3.

———. 1993. A framework for DSS interface development. In *Recent developments in decision support systems,* edited by C. Holsapple and A. Whinston. Berlin: Springer-Verlag.

Holsapple, C. W., and A. B. Whinston. 1986. *Manager's guide to expert systems using GURU,* Homewood, Ill.: Dow Jones-Irwin. 1987.

———. 1987. *Business expert systems.* Homewood, Ill.: Dow Jones–Irwin.

Horwitt, E. 1984. Natural languages improve the user-computer dialogue. *Business Computer Systems* 3, no. 11.

Kunz, J. C., R. J. Fallat, D. H. McClung, J. J. Osborne, R. A. Votteri, H. P. Nii, J. S. Aikens, L. M. Fagen, and E. A. Feigenbaum. 1978. A physiological rule-based system for interpreting pulmonary function test results. HPP-78-19, Computer Science Department, Stanford University.

Lindsay, R. K., B. G. Buchanan, E. A. Feigenbaum, and J. Lederberg. 1980. *Applications of artificial intelligence for chemical inference: The DENDRAL project.* New York: McGraw-Hill.

Martin W. A., and R. J. Fateman. 1971. The MACSYMA system. *Proceedings of the Second Symposium on Symbolic and Algebraic Manipulation,* Los Angeles.

McDermott, J. 1981. R1: The formative years. *AI Magazine,* 2.

McFarlan, E. W. 1984. Information technology changes the way you compete. *Harvard Business Review* (May–June).

Minsky, M. 1975. A framework for representing knowledge. In *The psychology of computer vision,* edited by P. Winston. New York: McGraw-Hill.

Newell, A., J. C. Shaw, and H. A. Simon. 1963. Empirical explorations with the logic theory machine: A case history in heuristics. In *Computers and thought,* edited by E. A. Feigenbaum and J. A. Feldman. New York: McGraw-Hill.

Newell, A., and H. A. Simon. 1963. GPS: A program that simulates human thought. In *Computers and thought,* edited by E. A. Feigenbaum and J. A. Feldman New York: McGraw-Hill.

_____. 1972. *Human Problem Solving*. Englewood Cliffs, N. J.: Prentice-Hall.

Pakath, R. 1993. Genetics-based machine learning: A promising tool for developing business computing systems? *Journal of Computer Information Systems* 33, no. 4.

Pople, H. E., Jr., R. D. Myers, and R. A. Miller. 1975. DIALOG: A model of diagnostic logic for internal medicine. *International Joint Conferences on Artificial Intelligence 4*.

Porter, M. E. 1979. How competitive forces shape strategy. *Harvard Business Review* (March-April).

Quillian, M. R. 1968. Semantic memory. In *Semantic information processing,* edited by M. Minsky. Cambridge, Mass.: MIT Press.

Ramani, K. V., M. R. Patel, and S. K. Patel. 1992. An expert system for drug preformulation in a pharmaceutical company. *Interfaces* 22, no. 2.

Raphael, B. 1968. SIR: A computer program for semantic information retrieval. 1968. In *Semantic information processing,* edited by M. Minsky. Cambridge, Mass.: MIT Press.

Rauzino, V. C. 1983. Natural language processors. *Computerworld* (September 5).

Ringland, G. A., and D. A., Duce. 1988. *Approaches to knowledge representation: An introduction*. New York: John Wiley.

Schocken, S., and G. Ariav. 1994. Neural networks for decision support: Problems and opportunities. *Decision Support System* 11, no. 5.

Shortliffe, E. H. 1976. *Computer-based medical consultation: MYCIN*. New York: Elsevier.

Simon, H. A. 1960. *The new science of management decision*. New York: Harper & Row.

Sviokla, J. J. 1989. Expert systems and their impact in the firm. *Journal of Management Information Systems* 6, no. 3.

_____. 1990. An examination of the impact of expert systems on the firm. *MIS Quarterly* 14, no. 2.

Thuraisingham, B. 1989. Rules to frames and frames to rules. *AI Expert* (October).

Van Melle, W. 1979. A domain-independent production rule system for consultation programs. *International Joint Conferences on Artificial Intelligence 6*.

Wasserman, P. D. 1989. *Neural computing: Theory and practice*. New York: Van Nostrand Reinhold.

Weiss, S. M., C. A. Kulikowski, and A. Safir. 1978. A model-based consultation system for the long-term management of glaucoma. *International Joint Conferences on Artificial Intelligence 5*.

Winston, P. H. 1984. *Artificial intelligence,* 2nd ed. Reading Mass.: Addison-Wesley.

Wong, B. K., and J. A. Monaco. 1995. Expert system applications in business: A review and analysis of the literature (1977–1993). *Information and Management* 29, no. 3.

Chapter 13

RULE MANAGEMENT

AUSTRALIA: AN ARTIFICIALLY INTELLIGENT DSS FOR CROP DECISIONS

Background

Lucerne or alfalfa . . . is the major perennial forage legume grown in Australia. It is grown for both grazing and hay production. . . .

. . . There are thirty-one lucerne varieties available for sowing by farmers in New South Wales. These varieties vary markedly in their dormancy (growth habit) and their levels of susceptibility or resistance to a number of major insect pests and disease, which may severely affect their performance and production characteristics. There are four distinct dormancy categories, two major insects and five diseases to which varieties have varying levels of resistance.

With such a widespread distribution and a large number of varieties to choose from, and because of its agricultural importance, farmers are continually asking extension agronomists which recommended lucerne variety should be grown for satisfactory long-term production. The answer to this apparently simple question involves the consideration of a number of important, complex and interacting factors. For example, irrigated heavy textured soils or poorly drained soils prone to waterlogging would require varieties with higher levels of resistance to debilitating disease . . . than those required for lighter textured, well-drained soils. Similarly, if the crop is to be sown in an area where either bacterial wilt or stem nematodes are known to occur, then only varieties with high levels of resistance should be recommended.

. . . Before making a recommendation an extension expert would need to know information on factors such as: the proposed stand use and management practices; the previous cropping history . . . the type of dormancy . . . required by the farmer; the expected stand life; the stand situation, and the soil type. The extension expert would then use this information supplied by the farmer, together with required experience and district knowledge . . . to make an appropriate recommendation.

Expert systems are a major developing area for both agricultural research and application. Many problems encountered by extension specialists are unstructured and so do not lend themselves to mathematical optimization. In these difficult decision-making areas rule based . . . expert systems . . . offer a means of assembling and interrogating knowledge about a particular subject. . . . Use of a computerized expert consultation system has several advantages over conventional advisory methods. Firstly and most importantly it provides farmers with a rapid, concise answer based on the most up-to-date information, enabling informed management decisions to be made. For the experienced advisor it reduces traveling time to conduct field inspections, allowing their expertise to be more widely applied; for newly appointed staff it provides a knowledgeable source of advice which they can also use as a learning tool.

Consultation sessions can also be logged and stored . . . [A]dvice can be output directly in letter format. . . . [E]xpert systems provide a mechanism for documenting the private knowledge of experienced personnel. . . . They provide an interactive means of transferring technology. . . .

Continued

System Overview

To assist extension agronomists to make the correct decision when recommending lucerne varieties to farmers we have constructed an expert consultation system, LUCVAR. It is designed to be used by agricultural advisors when being consulted by farmers and to operate on either a desk-top microcomputer or a portable lap-top. . . .

Lucvar contains 268 parameters. . . . Parameters may be:

1. facts which have true, false or unknown values
2. numbers which may be expressed as integers, decimal or scientific notation or may take the value of a numeric expression
3. categories which have defined options, or phrases of text.

The value of each parameter can in turn be conditional on other parameters being true or false. Lucvar also contains 142 individual pieces of advice in text form. The display of this advice is also generally conditioned by the truth value or numeric expressions being evaluated, ensuring that irrelevant advice is not given. . . .

Lucvar was developed using . . . a . . . shell designed for the construction and consultation of expert systems of an advice-giving nature. . . .

. . . A Lucvar consultation takes the form of an interactive dialogue. . . . Questions are asked of the user who supplies yes/no answers, chooses an option from a menu screen, or enters a numerical value or a text phrase. . . . The consultation shell never asks a question unless it needs to evaluate the answer and it never asks a question to which it already knows the answer. . . .

. . . Lucvar knowledge . . . was gathered from a number of published . . . as well as undocumented "private" sources. . . . Knowledge acquisition and knowledge engineering was not a difficult process. . . . [The system was] developed by people with a knowledge of the domain. . . . [Thus,] problems that may occur in expert system construction as a result of conflict between computer scientists, experts and project administrators were overcome.

. . . The system contains 560 rules and has undergone extensive preliminary testing prior to its final release. Care has been taken to provide a system that is easy to use. . . .

Condensed quotation from G. M. Lodge and T. C. Frecker, "LUCVAR: A Computer-Based Consultation System for Selecting Lucerne (Alfalfa) Varieties," *Expert Systems* 6, no. 3 (1989): 166–176.

LEARNING OBJECTIVES

From the Australia case, we can see that deciding what variety of alfalfa to plant is far from trivial. Farmers often seek the advice of agricultural extension experts in the course of making this kind of decision. Their expertise has been captured in a set of 560 rules involving 268 variables (parameters). In this chapter, we look at just how such rules can be expressed. We also consider, in detail, how a set of rules can be processed to establish values for variables that were initially unknown, thereby inferring some advice about the specific situation faced by the expert system's users. Keep the Australia case in mind as you cultivate an understanding of rule management in the expert system field.

After studying this chapter you should be able to

1. Express reasoning knowledge as rules and interpret the reasoning knowledge represented in rules.
2. Explain the role of unknown variables in a reasoning process.
3. Give detailed descriptions of how forward and reverse reasoning work.
4. Apply either forward or reverse reasoning to a set of rules to infer advice for a stated problem.
5. Describe the main ways in which a user can interact with an inference engine.

Check your achievement of these objectives by answering questions about the Australia case, by responding to the review questions, and by considering the discussion topics found at the end of the chapter.

13.1 INTRODUCTION

Basic features of rule management were outlined in Chapter 11. Here, we revisit this knowledge-management technique—taking a much more detailed look at the representation and processing of rules. This level of understanding not only takes the mystery out of expert systems, it is also an important prelude to developing these artificially intelligent DSSs (as described in Chapter 14) and turning their potential benefits into realities.

The KC application scenario is used to illustrate our consideration of rules for reasoning and our examination of reasoning with rules. The formal language used in examples throughout this chapter is typical of what would be used with commercial shells or integrated environments. Because there is no standard language for expressing rules, a given shell's language for specifying rule set contents will likely differ somewhat in style and capability from what is illustrated in our examples. Nevertheless, enough similarity exists among such languages that an understanding of examples presented here will enable rapid gains in proficiency with a specific shell's language.

We begin with a description of how the developer of an artificially intelligent DSS can express reasoning knowledge in the form of rules. This description leads to a set of 18 rules for the KC application. Using these rules, we examine the inference mechanisms of forward and reverse reasoning. In so doing, we introduce the notion of unknown variables and identify parts of a rule set other than its rules. We also discuss possibilities that result from using an integrated environment as the development tool. After establishing an appreciation of how inference engines work on a rule set, we conclude the chapter by looking at the various ways in which users can interact with an inference engine: directly or indirectly and during or after a consultation.

13.2 RULES FOR REASONING

Recall that a **rule** tells an **inference engine** what to do if a specified situation exists. A rule therefore has a **premise** and a **conclusion.** If the inference engine can determine that the rule's premise is true, then the rule's conclusion is known to be valid. A premise consists of one or more conditions. A conclusion consists of one or more actions. If the inference engine discovers that a rule's conditions are satisfied, then the engine will carry out whatever actions are contained in the rule's conclusion.

EXPRESSING RULES

When Jack Vander (recall Chapter 12) thinks about setting a new quarterly quota for a product, his overall strategy is to come up with some reasonable base amount and adjust that amount based on a variety of factors. He likes to set the base to reflect the sales representative's past performance. If the sales representative's sales exceeded his or her quota by more than 15%, then the excess is combined with that quota to determine the base amount. This idea is easily expressed in a rule set.

```
RULE: R1
    IF: SALES > 1.15*QUOTA
    THEN: BASE = QUOTA + (SALES - 1.15*QUOTA)
```

In this way, Jack has formally expressed a fragment of the reasoning knowledge he uses in setting quotas. Another similar piece of knowledge is that he uses the present quota as the base amount if the sales did not exceed the quota by at least 15%.

```
RULE: R2
    IF: SALES <= 1.15*QUOTA
    THEN: BASE = QUOTA
```

Each rule has a single condition for its premise and a single action in its conclusion.

Multiple Conditions　　One of the factors Jack uses to adjust a base amount is related to local advertising expenditures for a product line. He believes that if the local economy is good and the advertising expenditure exceeds $2,000, then the local advertising factor should be 1% for every $1,000 spent. The rule incorporating this knowledge into the rule set is

```
RULE: R10
    IF: ECONOMY = "good" and LOCALADS > 2000
    THEN: LAFACTOR = LOCALADS/100000
```

Notice that this premise has two conditions that must be met before the conclusion is valid.

NAMING FLEXIBILITY

The developer of a rule set has discretion over the names of variables specified in rules as well as the names of the rules themselves. For conciseness, most example rules in this chapter are designated by the names R1, R2, ... In practice a developer may want to use a rule name that somehow reflects the nature of the rule. For instance, we could refer to R1 and R2 as HIGH_SALES and REGULAR_SALES, respectively.

Multiple Actions   Similarly, it is permissible to have a rule with multiple actions in its conclusion. For example, Jack expects that if the economy is fair, then the local advertising factor should be 1% for every $1,200 spent, and the economic factor should be one-third of the anticipated economic growth rate. He realizes that values must be known for both the LOCALADS and GROWTH variables before LAFACTOR and EFACTOR can be calculated. These ideas are concisely expressed as follows:

```
RULE: R4
     IF: ECONOMY="fair" AND KNOWN("LOCALADS") AND KNOWN "GROWTH")
     THEN: EFACTOR = GROWTH/3
           LAFACTOR = LOCALADS/120000
```

Rule R4 has three conditions in its premise and two actions in its conclusion.

Notice that the KNOWN functions were not used in the premises of rules R1, R2, and R10 because each of those premises already contained references to all the variables needed in order to carry out their respective actions. Therefore, it is guaranteed that values of these variables will be known before the rules' actions are taken. In the case of R4, the KNOWN functions ensure that values are known for LOCALADS and GROWTH before the actions in R4's conclusion are taken. In general, our examples will use the KNOWN function as needed to ensure that a variable on the right side of an assignment statement in a rule action appears in the rule's premise. With some tools this action may not need to be explicit (i.e., the inference engine could assume that such functions were meant to be included in the premise).

Disjunctions and Negation   Disjunctions may be allowed in a premise. For instance, Jack needs to represent the fact that he considers the economic outlook to be poor if growth projections fall below 2% or it appears that the unemployment rate will exceed 8.2%:

```
RULE: R9
     IF: GROWTH < .02 OR UNEMPLOYMENT >= .082
     THEN: ECONOMY = "poor"
```

This rule's premise is an example of a disjunction. It says that if either condition is satisfied, then the conclusion is valid.

Negation can be an important ingredient of problem-solving rules. For instance, Jack decides that once a base and factors for the economy, product, and local advertising are known, then they can be combined in a certain way to determine the new quota for the product. However, he believes that this formula is valid only if the product is neither a strong nor weak product. Thus, his rule might be stated:

```
RULE: R17
     IF: NOT(WEAK OR STRONG) AND KNOWN("BASE") AND
         KNOWN("EFACTOR") AND KNOWN("PFACTOR") AND
         KNOWN("LAFACTOR")
     THEN: NEWQUOTA + BASE*(1+EFACTOR+LAFACTOR+PFACTOR)
```

Here again the KNOWN function is used to ensure that the values of certain variables are known before an attempt is made to use them in a calculation.

Integrating Expression Management   Notice that some of Jack's rules involve numeric calculations. In some cases the rule may need these calculations in its premise (e.g., rules R1 and R2). In other cases, the rule may need them in its conclusion (e.g., rules R1 and R17). Because such calculations are commonplace in reasoning, it is very beneficial for a development tool to integrate expression management with its rule-management capabilities. This practice allows rules to involve all the common numeric operations of addition, subtraction, multiplication, division, and exponentiation. It also provides the person developing rule sets with built-in math functions for automatically calculating square roots, logarithms, and so forth.

Beyond Assignment Actions   All the foregoing rules have had conclusions consisting of one or more assignment actions. An assignment action merely indicates what value to assign to a variable. For instance, in rule R2 the value of QUOTA is assigned to the BASE variable if the premise is true. Another kind of action that could appear in a rule's conclusion is an *input statement,* which will prompt the user to type in the value for a variable.

For instance, if there is strong interest in a particular product, the base amount is known, and various adjusting factors are known, then Jack wants to prompt the expert system's user for a subjective estimate of the percentage of sales increase due to rising interest in the product line. This percentage is then used in determining the new quota for the product. The corresponding rule is

```
RULE: R15
   IF: STRONG AND KNOWN("BASE") AND KNOWN("EFACTOR")
       AND KNOWN("PFACTOR") AND KNOWN("LFACTOR")
 THEN: INPUT RISE NUM WITH\
       "Enter percent increase due to rising interest in "+PROD
       NEWQUOTA=BASE*(1+EFACTOR+LAFACTOR+PFACTOR+RISE/100)
```

If the premise is true, the conclusion's first action is to input the desired percentage into the RISE variable. The NUM in this INPUT command guarantees that the user's entry will be numeric. The prompt that the user will see consists of the quoted message with the product of interest concatenated to it. If the product line happens to be computers, then the user sees the prompt:

Enter percent increase due to rising interest in computers _____

The user's response becomes the value of RISE, which is used in the conclusion's second action for determining the new quota.

The backslash at the end of the conclusion's first line is used to indicate that the command is continued on the next line. In order to fit within the margins of this book, commands shown in subsequent examples are sometimes broken into multiple lines, indicated with backslashes.

The foregoing examples illustrate basic features of rules. More advanced kinds of rules are possible, having more elaborate actions or allowing varying degrees of uncertainty to be expressed. We present examples of these rules later in this chapter and in Chapter 15. We shall also see that there can be more to a rule than just its premise and conclusion. Furthermore, a **rule set** can contain much more than just rules.

SOFTWARE FOR BUILDING RULE SETS

An expert system development tool must provide some way of creating, revising, and deleting a rule set's rules. We call software for accomplishing this a **rule set builder.** Various kinds of rule set builders are possible. At one extreme, a text manager can serve as a rule set builder. At the other extreme is software that allows rules to be created and revised by responses to menu options. Yet another possibility is software that itself invents rules without having a developer specify them. This process involves a kind of machine learning known as rule induction.

Text-Oriented Rule Building Jack could use a text manager to build and maintain a rule set's rules in a text file. Each rule would be added, revised, deleted, or viewed just like any other textual representation of knowledge. When Jack has finished entering the rule set's rules, he can save them as a file in the KS. Suppose this disk file is called ADVISOR.RSS, where the RSS file extension indicates that this file contains the source version of a rule set. Jack is free to use the text manager later to make changes to the rules held in a rule set's source file. A sample of text entry for rules is shown in Figure 13.1.

When Jack is satisfied with a rule set, he then compiles it in order to generate a version of the rule set that can be efficiently processed by the inference engine. This compilation is accomplished by rule builder software that is able to interpret the language employed in specifying rules and restate them in a form that can be directly processed by the tool's inference engine. Compilation results in a new KS file. We call Jack's new file ADVISOR.RSC, where the RSC file extension indicates that it contains the compiled version of the ADVISOR rule set.

During this compilation process, the rule builder software analyzes the rules that Jack has constructed. The compilation analysis looks for possible oversights, inconsistencies, syntactic mistakes, and logical errors in the rule set. If the rule builder detects any potential problems, it issues pertinent warning messages to Jack. If

FIGURE 13.1   Entering Rules via a Text-Oriented Rule Set Builder

```
Line:13        Col:53      a:advisor.ras

rule: r1

     if: sales > 1.15 * quota
     then: base = quota + (sales - 1.15 * quota)
     reason: In cases where the sales for this product exceeded
             the quota by more than 15%, the base amount for the
             new quota is set to the past quota plus the excess
             sales amount.

rule: r2

     if: sales <= 1.15 * quota
     then: base = quota
     reason: The base amount for the new quota is the same as the
             past quota because this product's sales did not
             exceed the past quota by more than 15%.
```

warning messages do appear, Jack can immediately use the text manager to correct the source version of the rule set. It is then recompiled.

Menu-Oriented Rule Building   A different approach to rule set building presents the developer with a menu interface, which provides an alternative way for creating and revising the source version of a rule set. In order to work on rules for the ADVISOR rule set, Jack would select a Rules option for a main menu. This selection typically causes a submenu to appear, whose options allow Jack to work on the rules in various ways, including browsing through selected rules and possibly editing them as the browsing proceeds, looking up a specific rule, creating a new rule, renaming a rule, and deleting a rule.

For instance, to create a new rule Jack would be prompted to enter the new rule's name. Once the name has been provided, he could type in the rule's premise and conclusion. A sample screen for creating rule R1 is shown in Figure 13.2. Notice that other optional characteristics of a rule could also be entered. We ignore them for the present. These advanced options are discussed later. The remaining ADVISOR rules are created in the same way.

Having prepared the set of rules, Jack selects a menu option to save the source version of the rule set. He could also choose a menu option to compile the rule set. He can modify the source rule set file later, as needed. Menu-oriented rule set building is probably more appropriate for beginning and infrequent rule set developers than is text-oriented rule set building. Experienced rule set developers are likely to prefer a text-oriented rule set builder.

Induction-Oriented Rule Building   For some applications, rule **induction** may be a workable alternative to specifying and modifying rules directly with a rule set builder. Rule induction is based on the idea of translating specific examples into

FIGURE 13.2   Entering a Rule via a Menu-Oriented Rule Set Builder

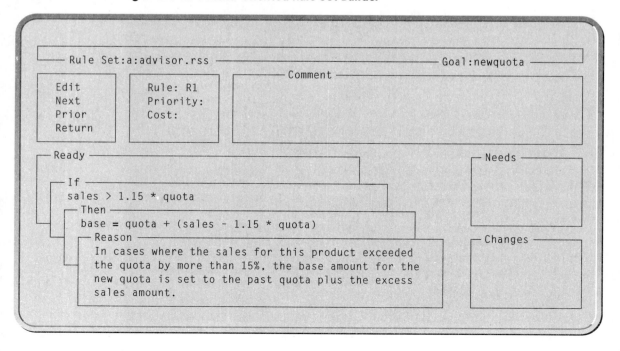

one or more general rules. For example, if Jack used a rule set builder that performed induction, he would specify a collection of examples rather than directly stating the desired rules. In each example, Jack would need to supply a value for every variable that could influence the new quota. He would also need to specify what new quota should correspond to those values. For instance, Jack would need to indicate that for SALES of $8,729, QUOTA of $9,205, GROWTH of 0.024, UNEMPLOYMENT of 0.055, LOCALADS of $875, and so on, the NEWQUOTA should be $9,472. It would be up to Jack to invent and type in enough of these examples to allow the rule induction software to produce the necessary rules for solving quota problems. Even for the modest quota application, this would be quite a challenge.

Contriving and entering enough examples to cover clearly all possibilities for a particular problem area can become extremely cumbersome for nontrivial problems. How can the developer be sure all possibilities are covered and that the induction software will produce the desired rules? This uncertainty is especially problematic when the advice to be given by an expert system is not categorical.

For instance, suppose we want an expert system that gives advice about creditworthiness of loan applicants. The advice will fall into two categories: worthy or unworthy. Plenty of case histories are available as examples to feed into a rule induction mechanism. On the other hand, quota advice does not fall into some small number of categories. It involves calculations that can generate values along a continuum. Attempting to give sufficient examples to allow inductive identification of the underlying calculations in rules would probably be futile. In contrast, the direct specification of rules immediately captures a pattern of reasoning without the need to make up sufficient examples to convey the same knowledge to an induction mechanism.

Although useful in some categorical situations, the limited applicability of rule induction leads us to dismiss it from further consideration here. We assume a more general text- or menu-oriented rule set builder is being employed for expert system construction. Of course, using such a tool requires that the developer somehow come into possession of the reasoning expertise to be directly represented in rules. If the developer is also the expert, then he or she has the needed information. Otherwise, the developer will need to acquire the knowledge (e.g., from a human expert) before directly representing it. Expert system development issues are explored further in Chapter 14.

13.3 REASONING WITH RULES

Once a rule set has been built, the reasoning knowledge it contains can be used by an inference engine. Remember that each rule is a module of knowledge that tells

IMPORTANCE OF TOOL FACILITIES

The facilities that a tool provides for rule set management are important for developer productivity. They should, of course, be carefully considered when selecting an expert system development tool. Extensive guidelines for tool selection have been assembled (Holsapple and Whinston 1987). These are summarized in the next chapter's consideration of expert system development.

the inference engine what actions to take, provided the conditions stated in its premise are satisfied. When confronted with a problem, the inference engine reasons with the rules in an effort to derive a solution to the problem. This reasoning involves the ability to select those rules that are pertinent to the specific problem, determine whether a rule's premise is satisfied, carry out the actions specified in a rule's conclusion, and acquire additional knowledge (e.g., from the user) if an impasse is reached. Each of these abilities is explored in the discussion that follows.

DSS IN THE NEWS

A Knowledge Highway

Buried in trillions of bits of data in an American Express Co. complex in Phoenix lie the answers to literally millions of questions.

It would take a small army of analysts to dig out the answers to the 60 million credit authorization inquiries received by the company each year. Instead of hiring an army, Amex gave the computers that held the data the tools to do much of the work.

By applying rules and conditions to each inquiry, Amex's "authorizer assistant" computers respond to more than 30 million of the credit inquiries each year. The five-year-old system does the work of at least 500 analysts.

Now Amex is rolling out two similar systems, one to help Amex employees sort through new account applications and another to help keep track of millions of card-holder credit histories. All three employ software that gives the computers the rules and conditions needed to complete the task at hand, such as determining if a purchase should be approved or credit should be extended.

Once linked together and able to share information, the three systems will form what Amex has dubbed its Knowledge Highway. . . .

Many banks, securities firms and financial markets are trying to implement similar systems to do things like monitor regulatory compliance, detect fraud and spot money-laundering operations.

Computers that can analyze data could help improve the quality of decision making and lead to fewer losses from mistakes. . . . Systems like those in Amex's Knowledge Highway are known as "inference engines" to dig into huge piles of data and come up with high-quality answers, fast . . . .

Much of the Knowledge Highway's design derives from what Amex learned in setting up and using its authorizer assistant.

In use since 1987, the authorizer assistant presorts inquiries, categorizing them as routine or requiring examination by an analyst. It spots and flags unusual buying patterns that could be fraud.

This improves the quality of the information once an authorization request is passed to an analyst for action . . . .

. . . Reduced costs and improved decision making have translated into a return of at least $10 for each $1 invested by the company . . . .

T. Bunker, "American Express to Shift Much Processing to 'Knowledge Highway'," *Investor's Business Daily* 24 August 1992, p. 3.

THE ADVISOR RULE SET

Suppose that Jack Vander has developed the ADVISOR rule set having the 18 rules shown in Figure 13.3. Notice that in addition to its premise and conclusion, each of

FIGURE 13.3   Sample Rules in the ADVISOR Rule Set

```
RULE: R1
    IF: SALES > 1.15 * QUOTA
    THEN: BASE = QUOTA + (SALES - 1.15 * QUOTA)
    REASON: In cases where the sales for this product exceeded the quota by more than 15%, the
            base amount for the new quota is set to the past quota plus the excess sales amount.

RULE: R2
    IF: SALES <= 1.15 * QUOTA
    THEN: BASE = QUOTA
    REASON: The base amount for the new quota is the same as the past quota, because this product's
            sales did not exceed the past quota by more than 15%.

RULE: R3
    IF: ECONOMY = "good" AND KNOWN ("GROWTH")
    THEN: EFACTOR = GROWTH
    REASON: When the local economic outlook is good, the economic factor is equal to the economy's
            anticipated growth rate.

RULE: R4
    IF: ECONOMY = "fair" AND KNOWN ("LOCALADS") AND KNOWN ("GROWTH")
    THEN: EFACTOR = GROWTH/3: LAFACTOR = LOCALADS/120000
    REASON: When the local economic outlook is fair, the economic factor is one third of the growth
            rate and the local advertising factor is 1/120,000 of the amount budgeted for local
            advertising.

RULE: R5
    IF: ECONOMY = "poor" AND KNOWN ("GROWTH") AND KNOWN ("UNEMPLOYMENT")
    THEN: EFACTOR = MIN (GROWTH, .085 - UNEMPLOYMENT)
    REASON: If the local economic outlook is poor, then the economic factor should be the lesser
            of the growth rate and the result of subtracting the unemployment rate from 8.5%.

RULE: R6
    IF: GROWTH >= .04 AND UNEMPLOYMENT < .076
    THEN: ECONOMY = "good"
    REASON: The economic outlook is good, because the projected unemployment is below 7.6% and
            the anticipated growth rate is at least 4%.

RULE: R7
    IF: GROWTH >= .02 AND GROWTH < .04 AND UNEMPLOYMENT < .055
    THEN: ECONOMY = "good"
    REASON: The economic outlook is good, because projected unemployment is less than 5.5% and
            the anticipated growth rate is between 2% and 4%.

RULE: R8
    IF: GROWTH >= .02 AND GROWTH < .04 AND UNEMPLOYMENT >= .055 AND UNEMPLOYMENT < .082
    THEN: ECONOMY = "fair"
    REASON: The economic outlook is fair because of moderate growth and unemployment expectations.

RULE: R9
    IF: GROWTH < .02 OR UNEMPLOYMENT >= .082
    THEN: ECONOMY = "poor"
    REASON: The economy outlook is poor, because either the anticipated growth rate is very low or
            projected unemployment is high or both.

RULE: R10
    IF: ECONOMY = "good" AND LOCALADS > 2000
    THEN: LAFACTOR = LOCALADS/100000
    REASON: When the economy is good and local advertising exceeds $2,000, the local advertising
            factor is 1% for every $1,000 expenditure.
```

FIGURE 13.3   Sample Rules in the ADVISOR Rule Set—Continued

```
RULE: R11
    IF: ECONOMY = "poor" AND LOCALADS < 1500
    THEN: LAFACTOR = -.015
    REASON: When the economic outlook is poor and local advertising expenditures for the product
            are modest, then the local advertising factor is negative.

RULE: R12
    IF: (ECONOMY = "poor" AND LOCALADS >= 1500) OR (ECONOMY = "good" AND LOCALADS <= 2000)
    THEN: LAFACTOR = 0
    REASON: The local advertising factor is negligible because of low advertising in a good economy
            or a poor economy coupled with substantial local advertising for the product line.

RULE: R13
    IF: PROD IN ["computer", "romance", "scifi"]
    THEN: PFACTOR = (NEWTITLES + OLDTITLES)/OLDTITLES - 1
          STRONG = TRUE
          WEAK = FALSE
    REASON: This is a strong product line. The product factor is based on the growth in the
            number of titles in this line.

RULE: R14
    IF: PROD IN ["reference", "biography", "psychology", "sports"]
    THEN: PFACTOR = .75 * ((NEWTITLES + OLDTITLES)/OLDTITLES - 1)
          STRONG = FALSE
          WEAK = FALSE
    REASON: This is neither a strong nor weak product line. The product factor is proportional
            to three-fourths of the growth in the number of titles in this line.

RULE: R15
    IF: STRONG AND KNOWN ("BASE") AND KNOWN ("EFACTOR") AND KNOWN ("PFACTOR") AND KNOWN ("LAFACTOR")
    THEN: INPUT RISE NUM\
          WITH "Enter estimate of percentage sales increase " + "due to rising interest in" + PROD
          NEWQUOTA = BASE * (1 + EFACTOR + LAFACTOR + PFACTOR + RISE/100)
    REASON: This is a strong product line. The base amount, economic factor, product factor, and
            local advertising factor for calculating the new quota are all known. A subjective
            assessment of the expected sales increase due to general rising interest in the
            product is requested. The new quota is then calculated.

RULE: R16
    IF: WEAK AND KNOWN ("BASE") AND KNOWN ("EFACTOR") AND KNOWN ("PFACTOR") AND KNOWN ("LAFACTOR")
    THEN: INPUT FALL NUM\
          WITH "Enter estimate of percentage sales decrease " + "due to falling interest in" + PROD
          NEWQUOTA = BASE * (1 + EFACTOR + LAFACTOR + PFACTOR - FALL/100)
    REASON: This is a weak product line. A subjective assessment of the expected sales decrease due to
            general declining interest in this product line is requested. The new quota can then be
            calculated.

RULE: R17
    IF: NOT (WEAK OR STRONG) AND KNOWN ("BASE")
        AND KNOWN ("EFACTOR") AND KNOWN ("PFACTOR") AND KNOWN("LAFACTOR")
    THEN: NEWQUOTA = BASE * (1 + EFACTOR + LAFACTOR + PFACTOR)
    REASON: This is neither an especially strong nor weak product line. Its new quota is calculated from
            the base amount and factors for the economy, local advertising, and product line expansion.

RULE: R18
    IF: NOT (PROD IN ["computer", "romance", "scifi", "reference", "biography", "psychology", "sports"])
    THEN: WEAK = TRUE; STRONG = FALSE
          PFACTOR = .45 * ((NEWTITLES + OLDTITLES)/OLDTITLES - 1)
    REASON: This is a weak product line. The product factor is proportional to less than
            half of its growth in titles.
```

the rules has a reason. This **reason** is simply an English description of the rule. If a rule is involved in solving a problem, then its reason can be displayed to the user when the inference engine is asked to explain the line of reasoning used to reach a solution. The developer of a rule set is free to make a rule's reason as specific (e.g., rule R1) or general (e.g., rule R8) as warranted by the application. It may be desirable to avoid overly specific reasons, especially if the rule is too technical or complex for a user to understand in detail or if the rule's reasoning knowledge cannot be disclosed to users for security reasons. A rule's reason can be omitted from the rule set if desired.

A sales manager may now want to consult the ADVISOR rule set to get advice about what quarterly quota to set for a particular sales representative on a particular product line. Imagine for a moment that you are the inference engine. You have access to all 18 rules. How will you reason with these rules in order to derive the desired quota advice? How will you select which rule to consider next as your reasoning proceeds? How will you carry out the actions in its conclusion if the premise is satisfied? These are the issues confronting the inference engine each time a consultation is requested.

CHALLENGE OF THE UNKNOWN VARIABLES

It is clear that the user wants you (the inference engine) to reason with the expertise embodied in the ADVISOR rule set in order to determine a value for the NEWQUOTA variable. If you pause to examine the rules in Figure 13.3, you will notice that the variables in the rules are **unknown variables.** In rule R1 for instance, you do not presently know the value of SALES or the value of QUOTA. Therefore, you have no way of determining whether the premise of R1 is true or false. Because the premise is unknown, you do not know whether it is permissible to **fire** the rule (i.e., to take the action specified in its conclusion).

Look at rule R16. Even if you knew the value of WEAK (true or false), the rule could not be fired, because the base amount and various factors indicated in the premise are unknown. The KNOWN function has an unknown value if the indicated variable's value is unknown but could perhaps become known in the reasoning process. If the inference engine has discovered that the variable's value cannot become known during the reasoning process, then the KNOWN function has a false value. Initially, the KNOWN functions in R16 are unknown (not false), because their variable's values could possibly become known during the reasoning process. As a result, R16 cannot presently be fired. In fact, you are currently unable to fire any rule in the ADVISOR rule set because the premise of each rule is presently unknown.

Approaches to Knowing   The conventional way for an inference engine to overcome this apparent impasse is to ask the user to supply the values of unknown variables. Of course, the inference engine needs to know precisely what question to ask for each variable that could be unknown. This presentation knowledge can be incorporated into the rule set in any of several ways: as a rule's conclusion, as a variable description, or in an inference initialization sequence.

Rule Conclusion   In looking at R13, for instance, Jack notices that a value must be established for PROD before the premise can be determined to be either true or false. Because none of the other rules has a conclusion that could change the value of PROD, Jack decides that the user of the ADVISOR system should be prompted to indicate which product is of interest for a particular consultation. This can be accomplished by adding the following rule to the ADVISOR rule set:

```
RULE: VARPROD
    IF: NOT KNOWN("PROD")
    THEN: INPUT PROD STR WITH "Enter product line:"
    REASON: You must tell me what the product line is
            before I can determine what its new quota
            should be.
```

The inference engine now has a way of getting a string value for PROD when the product line is not known during a consultation. Jack could devise similar rules for acquiring values of other variables that could be unknown during a consultation.

Variable Description   A drawback of inventing rules such as VARPROD is that many of them may be necessary in a rule set that has many variables. In general, increasing the number of rules in a rule set slows the expert system's response time. All else being equal, an inference engine can normally reason with a small number of rules faster than it can reason with a significantly larger number of rules. A more important drawback for advanced expert system developers is that a rule such as VARPROD gives no way of characterizing the nature of the variable itself. Such characterizations are of no concern for the moment but will be examined later.

Rather than the VARPROD rule, Jack could incorporate the following **variable description** into the ADVISOR rule set:

```
VARIABLE: PROD
    FIND: INPUT PROD STR WITH "Enter product line:"
```

This approach yields the same prompting effect as the VARPROD rule but without the cost of processing a rule. The FIND portion of a variable description simply tells the inference engine how to find a value for the variable when the value is needed but unknown during a reasoning process. Thus, in addition to rules, a rule set can contain descriptions of variables used in those rules.

Inference Initialization   Some development tools allow a rule set to contain an inference **initialization sequence** in addition to rules and variable descriptions. An initialization sequence is simply a series of actions that the inference engine will automatically carry out as soon as a user consults the rule set. These actions are taken before the inference engine even begins to consider how the rules will be used in reasoning about the specific problem that has been posed. The initialization sequence is an ideal spot to include a sequence of input actions for the following:

1. All the rule set variables that are needed for every consultation, regardless of the specific problem posed by the user
2. All the rule set variables whose values are known to the user at the start of every consultation

For instance, Jack might build the following initialization sequence into the ADVISOR rule set.

```
INITIAL:
    INPUT REP STR WITH "What is the sales rep's name?"
    INPUT PROD STR WITH "Enter product line:"
    INPUT SALES NUM WITH "How much " +\
```

```
        TRIM(PROD) + " did " + TRIM (REP) + " sell?"
INPUT QUOTA NUM WITH "What was the " + TRIM(PROD)\
        + " quota for " + TRIM(REP) + "?"
```

Whenever the ADVISOR rule set is consulted, the inference engine carries out the four INPUT actions before considering any of the rule set's rules. It first asks the user which sales representative is of interest and then asks which product line is of interest. The user's responses become the new values of the REP and PROD variables, respectively. Furthermore, these responses automatically become part of the subsequent sales and quota questions. TRIM is an example of a built-in function. It automatically trims off any blanks from the end of a string variable's value.

A sample of the user interaction for this initialization sequence is shown in Figure 13.4. Notice that an initialization sequence allows Jack easily to control the order in which questions are posed to the expert system user. Of course, many more INPUT actions could have been included in the initialization sequence (e.g., for GROWTH and UNEMPLOYMENT).

Automatic Prompting   In lieu of any other way to establish a variable's value, an inference engine may directly prompt the user. This automatic prompting consists of displaying the variable's name and waiting for a user to type in a value for it. To make use of this approach, a user must know what is referred to by the variable name. For instance, a user must know that PROD refers to the product line of interest.

Customizing the User Interface   The foregoing approaches made use of one or more INPUT commands. A development tool may allow alternatives to such commands, giving more flexibility in customizing the expert system's user interface. Such tools have been commercially available for many years (Holsapple and Whinston 1986). For example, if there is an integral menu-management capability, a developer could opt to use it in place of an INPUT command. A good candidate for this is the PROD variable, which has a limited number of legitimate values. The variable description for PROD could consist of a command that displays those values in a menu and assigns the user's selection as the variable's value, reducing user effort and the chance of input errors.

A tool may incorporate an integral forms-management capability. This integration would allow a developer to build a collection of forms that the inference engine can use for interacting with a user. The developer could design or modify each form by painting its layout, colors, contents, and special effects directly on the console screen (recall Chapter 11). These forms would be stored in the KS along

FIGURE 13.4   A Sample of Inference Initialization

```
What is the sales rep's name? Toby
Enter product line: romance
How much romance did Toby sell? 13750
What was the romance quota for Toby? 12560
```

with rule sets. Commands available for processing an entire form at a time could be built into a rule set in place of INPUT commands. These commands include displaying a form to the user at a desired screen location, assigning values that the user types into the form to proper variables, resetting the form's contents, and clearing a form from the screen. For instance, the entire series of INPUT commands could be replaced by a couple of simple form commands.

Although the user interface examples shown in this chapter deal primarily with the line-oriented INPUT and OUTPUT commands, expert system developers should remember that more sophisticated alternatives are available.

BEYOND USER INTERACTION

The rules of an interesting rule set will inevitably refer to some variables whose values are unknown at the outset of a consultation. In order to grasp fully the nature of a problem posed by an end user, the inference engine needs to somehow establish the values for at least some of these unknown variables. A human expert can draw on expertise about a problem area in order to know what questions to ask of a client and when to ask them. Similarly, an expert system's inference engine is able to draw on a rule set to determine what questions to ask of a user and when to ask them. As briefly described before, the interface styles (line-oriented, menu-oriented, forms-oriented) for getting values from the user can also be designed into a rule set.

If an expert system is to be truly able to emulate the human expert, it must not be limited merely to asking the user for a variable's value whenever there is insufficient knowledge to continue reasoning about a problem. A tool that imposes this restriction on developers leads to expert system behavior that could well be regarded as mentally handicapped if it were observed in a human. Resultant expert systems may not resemble outstanding human experts as closely as we might like. Expert system development tools have made a start at addressing this restriction.

Tools commonly support **hooks** to outside data files or programs. A hook allows a rule set to access data in files that have been produced as a result of executing external programs or to request the execution of an external program. The exact details of these hooks vary widely from one tool to another, but all fall far

---

ALTERNATIVE KNOWLEDGE SOURCES

A human expert is not limited to asking the client questions whenever the reasoning process pauses because of insufficient knowledge. The client may not know all the answers anyway. Thus, instead of always asking the client, the expert gets the knowledge needed to continue the reasoning process from other sources. This could involve reading a textual passage, making a calculation, conducting an analysis with some solver (e.g., regression analysis), looking up values that exist in a database, telephoning an external source to ask for needed knowledge, consulting other experts, and so forth. Any or all of these could happen as the expert ponders a particular problem. Because there are no barriers in the human mind, these kinds of activities can be blended together as desired in the course of reasoning about a problem. This synergy is an important factor in effective human problem solving. It can be just as important for problem solving by an artificially intelligent DSS.

short of the effects that can be achieved with synergistic integration. Hooks, therefore, receive little consideration here. However, we do examine some possibilities that result from integrating conventional knowledge-management techniques into expert system development tools.

Recall that there are three distinct approaches to incorporating desired prompting behavior into a rule set: as the conclusion of a rule, in the find action of a variable description, or in the rule set's initialization sequence. In each case, it is possible to replace or supplement INPUT commands with other kinds of commands not involving user interaction. This feature is valuable when the developer believes that it makes more sense to acquire an unknown variable's value without asking the user. In other situations, the developer may want the inference engine to do some preliminary work and present the results (e.g., a graph or report) to the user before asking for user input. Consider the following possibilities, all of which can be achieved with a commercially available tool.

Database Management within a Rule Set   Suppose the technique of relational database management is synergistically integrated into an expert system development tool. KC's vice president of sales has decided that each sales manager will use this database–management facility to track quarterly sales and quotas of all their sales representatives for each product. KC's MIS department has designed the data table structure shown in Figure 13.5 for this purpose. The table's name is THISYR, and it identifies five categories of data that are of interest: sales representative name, product line name, quarter number, quota, and sales. Each category is called a *field* and has its own unique name (REPNAME, PRODNAME, QTRNAME, QUOTA, SALES).

Figure 13.6 shows some actual data content of this table for one of the sales managers. Each row in the table depicts a record. It records the quota and sales of a particular product in a particular quarter by a particular sales representative. For instance, in this year's second quarter, Toby's romance sales were $13,750, against a quota of $12,560. Each sales manager maintains his or her own representatives' data in a THISYR table. The manager can use ad hoc query capabilities to monitor and evaluate sales representatives performance during the course of the present year.

Jack realizes that a sales manager's THISYR table contains data that are pertinent to the expert system he is developing. For instance, why should his expert system force a user to look up and then type in sales and quota figures when they are already available in the THISYR table? Not only does this activity take more time and place a burden on the user, it also increases the chance of errors due to unde-

FIGURE 13.5   Structure of the THISYR Table

THISYR

REPNAME	PRODNAME	QTRNUM	QUOTA	SALES

FIGURE 13.6   Sample Records in the THISYR Table

THISYR

REPNAME	PRODNAME	QTRNUM	QUOTA	SALES
Toby	computer	1	14051	11010
Toby	romance	1	16820	17520
Toby	computer	2	18000	16958
Toby	romance	2	12560	13750
Kim	scifi	1	6750	7120
Kim	computer	1	14444	12982
Kim	romance	1	12820	12147
Toby	scifi	1	7980	8796
Kim	computer	2	15582	16125
⋮	⋮	⋮	⋮	⋮

tected typing mistakes. As a convenience to the user, Jack might build the following initialization sequence into the ADVISOR rule set:

```
INITIAL:
    INPUT REP STR WITH "What is the sales rep's name?"
    INPUT PROD STR WITH "Enter product line:"
    INPUT QTR STR USING "n" WITH "Enter quarter:"
    IF NOT INUSE("THISYR") THEN USE THISYR; ENDIF
    OBTAIN RECORD FROM THISYR FOR\
        REPNAME=REP & PRODNAME=PROD & QTRNUM=QTR
```

This initialization sequence begins in much the same way as the one presented earlier. Here, the user is prompted for the quarter number in addition to the representative's name and product line. The "n" picture means that only a single numeric character will be accepted in response to the "Enter quarter:" prompt. If the THISYR table is not already in use, then the USE command tells the inference engine the THISYR is going to be used (the database could consist of many tables, not all of which need to be used by the expert system). The OBTAIN command obtains the THISYR record whose representative's name, product, and quarter match those specified by the user.

After the inference engine carries out this initialization sequence, both the SALES and QUOTA variables will have the correct values. The inference engine simply obtains them from the table, rather than forcing a user to look them up and enter them in response to prompts. It is now in a position to evaluate the premises of rules R1 and R2 of the ADVISOR rule set.

Spreadsheet Management within a Rule Set   Just as it is commonplace to have data values stored in a database, a spreadsheet often contains values that could be pertinent to expert system processing. If spreadsheet management is an integral capability of an expert system development tool, the inference engine always has immediate access to the value of any cell of the spreadsheet presently in use. The spreadsheet need not be showing on the screen in order to access its contents. Thus, there is no need to prompt a user to reenter any value that already exists in a spreadsheet.

KC's sales managers use the integrated tool's spreadsheet capabilities for preparing advertising budgets. Each quarter, the manager receives a discretionary amount to spend on local advertising. Sales managers use their own formulas for allocating advertising funds to product lines and sales representatives. In general, a sales manager's spreadsheet will contain many local advertising amounts, but only one is pertinent to a particular consultation. Jack wants the inference engine to look up the proper value for a consultation's LOCALADS variable in the sales manager's spreadsheet. He has reached an agreement with the sales managers that certain rows of their spreadsheets will always contain budgeted advertising amounts by product line and that a particular cell block will show which column of advertising amounts belongs to which sales representative.

To let the inference engine know how to find a value for the LOCALADS variable, Jack could build a variable description into the ADVISOR rule set that indicates where to find the budgeted amount for any designated sales representative and product line and then assigns that value to LOCALADS. Thus, when the inference engine needs to find a value for LOCALADS during a consultation, it simply looks up the proper value in the sales manager's own advertising spreadsheet. A manager can use the DSS to work on an advertising budget and then immediately consult the ADVISOR rule set. As soon as the consultation is completed, the manager may decide to adjust some of the spreadsheet assumptions and then immediately reconsult ADVISOR to see the effect on the recommended new quota amount.

Solver Management within a Rule Set　　In order to carry out its reasoning about quotas, the inference engine will need to know about the growth and unemployment outlooks for the local economy. The sales managers themselves are unable to make such projections. In the past, Jack has relied on KC's economic forecasting staff for producing reliable growth and unemployment estimates for the various territories in his own region. In building the ADVISOR expert system, he would like the inference engine to rely similarly on the economic forecasting staff. These economists have invented an economic model for making growth and unemployment projections.

If the expert system development tool incorporates solver management, it is straightforward to represent the model (and perhaps even its solver) in the KS. As a result, the inference engine can itself invoke a solver in the course of a consultation to perform an economic analysis with the model, thereby determining the growth and unemployment rates. Suppose the model is named ECON. Jack adds the following action to ADVISOR's initialization sequence:

    SOLVE ECON

This command performs the desired economic analysis, producing values of the GROWTH and UNEMPLOYMENT variables based on solving the model.

Program Management within a Rule Set　　Alternatively, the KC economic forecasting staff may have implemented a program called ECON that, when executed, sets values for the GROWTH and UNEMPLOYMENT variables. Assuming that program management is synergistically integrated, the initialization sequence would contain a command to execute ECON. The ECON program may draw on KC databases and spreadsheets, prompt the user for various inputs, make use of values of any variables that have been previously set by the inference engine, get needed input messages from the mainframe computer at KC's headquarters, and so forth. A program can itself use all knowledge that is available to the inference engine and can derive new knowledge that is directly available to the inference engine as soon as the program's execution terminates.

Rule Management within a Rule Set   Suppose that KC's economists had implemented their forecasting knowledge as an expert system rather than a model or program. Then the SOLVE command shown above would be replaced by one such as

```
CONSULT ECON
```

This command allows the ADVISOR expert system to consult an ECON expert system. The ECON rule set would contain the expertise needed to establish values for the GROWTH and UNEMPLOYMENT variables. As soon as the inference engine finishes consulting ECON, it continues the ADVISOR consultation, with all the ECON results available to it.

Graphics within a Rule Set   In reviewing the ADVISOR rules, Jack decides that rule R2 should give the user some discretion in determining the base amount for the new quota. So he uses the rule set builder to alter R2:

```
RULE: R2
     IF: SALES <= 1.15 * QUOTA AND KNOWN("SUBJ")
     THEN: BASE = QUOTA * (1 + SUBJ/100)
     REASON: If the sales-to-quota ratio is not exceptional,
             then the base amount will be based on your
             subjective assessment of how reasonable last
             year's quota was. The subjective assessment
             indicates the percentage by which the base
             should differ from last year's quota.
```

Here, Jack has introduced a new variable, SUBJ. He wants the inference engine to ask the manager for the value of SUBJ in the event that R2 is considered during a consultation. But he wants the inference engine to put the past sales and quota levels in perspective before prompting the user.

Specifically, Jack wants the inference engine to produce a bar graph comparing the representative's quotas to sales for the product line over the last four quarters. He also wants the inference engine to generate a pie graph portraying the relative percentage breakdown of quota amounts by quarter. For convenient viewing, both graphs should appear on the console screen at the same time. When the manager has finished viewing the graphs, the inference engine should prompt for a subjective opinion based on the graphical content.

If graphs management is a part of an integrated environment for building expert systems, these results can be accomplished via database-retrieval and graphics-generation commands in a variable description for SUBJ instead of simply having the inference engine use a solitary INPUT command to get a value for SUBJ. These results would help the user make a reasonable response to the INPUT prompt. If the inference engine needs to find a value for SUBJ during a consultation, it will carry out the actions in this variable description.

REASONING FLOWS

With this background, it is time to take a look at how an inference engine actually reasons with the rules in a rule set as it attempts to solve a problem. The following

BENEFITS OF INTEGRATION

There is no need for a modern expert system blindly to prompt the user every time it has insufficient knowledge to continue its reasoning about a problem. When an inference engine is effectively integrated with conventional knowledge-management capabilities, it can use any of them to acquire the knowledge needed to continue its reasoning. This results in expert systems that much more closely resemble human experts' problem-solving abilities.

Sometimes it is best to prompt a user for the value of an unknown variable. Other times it places an unnecessary burden on the user, decreasing the efficiency of both the user and the inference engine. It increases the likelihood of erroneous consultation responses due to undetected mistakes in user responses. In yet other cases, the user may not possess a meaningful answer. These issues are resolved by an integrated environment that encompasses the knowledge-management facilities that are so well known in the business-computing world (Holsapple, Tam, and Whinston 1987).

discussion assumes that Jack has augmented the ADVISOR rules shown in Figure 13.3 with the initialization sequence appearing in Figure 13.7 and a variable description to look up the proper LOCALADS value in a spreadsheet.

Notice that the initialization sequence explicitly gives an unknown value to variables whose values are not set by the preceding actions in the sequence. This initialization is important when an inference engine remembers the values of variables

FIGURE 13.7   Initialization Sequence for the ADVISOR Rule Set

```
INITIAL:
    INPUT REP STR WITH "What is the sales rep's name?"
    INPUT PROD STR WITH "Enter product line:"
    INPUT QTR STR USING "n" WITH "Enter quarter:"
    INPUT OLDTITLE NUM WITH "How many oldtitles for " + \
        TRIM(PROD) + "?"
    INPUT NEW TITLE NUM WITH "How many new titles?"
    IF NOT INUSE ("THISYR") THEN USE THISYR; ENDIF
    OBTAIN RECORD FROM THISYR FOR REPNAME = REP & \
        PRODNAME = PROD & QTRNUM = QTR
    SOLVE ECON
    ECONOMY = UNKNOWN; EFACTOR = UNKNOWN
    LOCALADS = UNKNOWN; LAFACTOR = UNKNOWN
    PFACTOR = UNKNOWN; BASE = UNKNOWN
    STRONG = UNKNOWN; WEAK = UNKNOWN
    NEWQUOTA = UNKNOWN
GOAL:
    NEWQUOTA
```

even after a consultation terminates. If a user requests two consecutive consultations, the second should not normally begin with variable values determined by the first consultation. The values should be reinitialized. Figure 13.7 also shows that the default goal of the rule set is NEWQUOTA. If a consultation request does not explicitly identify a goal for the consultation, the rule set's default goal is assumed.

When a user makes a consultation request, the inference engine first carries out all actions specified in the rule set's initialization sequence. What happens next depends on the kind of reasoning that has been requested. As explained in Chapters 11 and 12, there are two basic kinds of reasoning: forward and reverse. Variations of these two are possible (see Chapter 15), but the focus here is first on basic forward reasoning and then on basic reverse reasoning. In both explanations, it is instructive to imagine that you are the inference engine. You have carried out the initialization actions and are now ready to begin reasoning with the ADVISOR rules in Figure 13.3.

Forward Reasoning   **Forward reasoning,** sometimes called **forward chaining** or *data-driven reasoning,* is based on the idea of examining each rule in a forward direction, looking first at its premise. The conclusion is ignored until the premise is determined to be true. When a rule's premise is found to be true, the rule is fired (i.e., the actions in its conclusion are taken). If the rule's premise is false, then the rule is not fired and another rule is considered. A rule whose premise is currently false may be reconsidered later. The firing of other rules may change variables in such a way that its premise could become true.

There is one other possibility when considering a rule during forward reasoning. Its premise may be neither true nor false—it may be unknown. This situation occurs if one or more of the variables referenced in the premise are still unknown. The values of these variables were not established either during the initialization sequence or as a result of firing previously considered rules. If the rule set contains variable descriptions for these unknown variables, then the inference engine can find values for them by carrying out the prescribed actions in these variable descriptions. However, if there are some unknown variables that do not have variable descriptions and for which a user cannot provide values in response to automatic prompts (if any), the premise is still unknown. In such a case, the rule is not fired, and another rule is considered. A rule whose premise is currently unknown may be reconsidered later. The firing of other rules may establish values for the unknown variables, so that the premise can later be evaluated as either true or false.

After the inference engine has made a pass through all the rules and at least one has been fired, another pass is made to examine the remaining unfired rules. Reasoning stops when either a pass is made without firing a rule or a value has been established for the goal variable.

An Example of Forward Reasoning   To see how forward reasoning works in practice, think of yourself as the inference engine. A user has just asked you for a consultation to test the effects of applying the ADVISOR expertise. You conduct the initialization actions of Figure 13.7 to establish initial values for the rule set's variables. Suppose that the following variable values result from the prompts, database retrieval, and model solution:

```
REP:   "Toby"          SALES:  24000
PROD:  "romance"       QUOTA:  20000
QTR:   "3"             GROWTH: .03
```

```
OLDTITLES: 100      UNEMPLOYMENT: .06
NEWTITLES: 10
```

As Figure 13.7 shows, you do not know values of other variables at the present time. Now, you turn your attention to forward reasoning with the ADVISOR rules.

The first issue that arises is the order in which rules should be selected for consideration. Should you consider the rules in the order in which they appear in the rule set (see Figure 13.3) or should you select them in some other order? An alternative selection order might be to consider the rules with the fewest number of unknown variables in their premises before considering those with more unknowns. Here, we consider the rules based on their rule set order. This kind of sequencing is typical of inference engines that do forward reasoning.

From Figure 13.3 you can see that rule R1 is first in the rule set, so you consider it before any other rule. When you evaluate the R1 premise, you discover that it is true. Sales of 24,000 do indeed exceed the quota of 20,000 by more than 15%. You therefore fire the rule by taking the action specified in R1's conclusion. As a result, the BASE variable is no longer unknown but now has a value of 20,000 + 24,000 − 23,000 = 21,000. You proceed to the next rule, R2. When you evaluate its premise, you see that it is false and thus go on to consider rule R3. Because the ECONOMY variable is presently unknown and has no variable description in the rule set, you cannot determine whether R3's premise is true or false. Hence, you continue to R4. Its premise is similarly unknown, as is the premise of R5.

When you consider the first condition in the premise of R6, you see that it is false (the growth of 0.03 is not at the 0.04 level). Thus, you know that the overall premise will also be false, regardless of the unemployment rate. You can immediately discard R6 and go on to rule R7. Here you find that the first two conditions in the premise are satisfied. However, the third is not, because the unemployment rate of 0.06 is not less than 0.055. As a result, the R7 premise is false and you move on to consider rule R8. All four conditions in the premise of this rule are true, so the overall premise is true. You fire rule R8 to give ECONOMY a "fair" value. When you evaluate the next rule's premise, the first condition is false, but you cannot stop there. Because the OR (rather than AND) operator appears, you must try the second condition also. In this case, it too is false. Thus R9's premise is false and you consider the next rule.

The premises of R10, R11, and R12 are successively discovered to be false. When you reach R13, you find that its premise is true. You therefore fire this rule to take the three actions specified in its conclusion. First, you calculate PFACTOR to be (10 + 100)/100 − 1 = 0.10; then you let the STRONG and WEAK variables have values of TRUE and FALSE, respectively. The premises of each of the remaining rules (R14–R18) are either unknown or false. At this point you have considered all 18 rules and you have fired 3 of them: R1, R8, and R13. By taking the actions indicated by these rules, you realize that some previously unknown or false premises may now be true. Therefore, you make another pass through the rule set to consider the unfired rules.

R1 was already fired. The premises of R2 and R3 are false. When you then consider the R4 premise, you see that the first condition is true. However, the second condition is unknown because the LOCALADS variable value is still unknown, although it could possibly become known. You (the inference engine) notice that there is a variable description for LOCALADS, so you can find a value for LOCALADS by taking the spreadsheet lookup actions specified there. Suppose that this results in a value of 1200. This makes the second condition true, because a value is now known for LOCALADS. The third condition is true, so the premise of R4 is true. When you fire this rule, 0.01 is assigned to both EFACTOR and LAFACTOR. You proceed to R5. Its premise is false, as are the premises of R6 and R7.

Rule R8 has already been fired. The premises of rules R9 through R12 are false. Rule R13 has already been fired, and rule R14's premise is false. Because STRONG is true and all the indicated variables are known, the premise of rule R15 is true. You can now fire that rule. In so doing, you first ask the user to enter a subjective assessment of the percentage increase in romance books due to the general rise of public interest in this kind of book. Suppose the user responds to the input prompt by entering 5. You then take the action of calculating the new quota:

```
NEWQUOTA = BASE*(1+EFACTOR+LAFACTOR+PFACTOR+RISE/100)
         =21000*(1+.01+.01+.10+5/100)
         =21000*(1.17)=24750
```

The premise for each of the remaining three rules is false. On this second pass through the ADVISOR rules, you fired R4 and R15.

If you were to make one more pass through the unfired ADVISOR rules, you would see that none of them can be fired. By firing R4 and R15, you have done nothing to change the falseness of the other rules' premises. You have reached a point where you can reason no further. You have fully tested the effects of applying the ADVISOR expertise to a particular sales representative for a particular product line in a particular quarter. One effect is that you can now offer advice about what the new quota should be. You also now know what the economic prognosis is, what the base amount is, and what the various adjusting factors are. The consultation is almost done. You still need to do something with the results of your reasoning.

Presenting Results of a Consultation   An expert system will report the value of the rule set's goal variable to the user. Expert system development tools vary in terms of how much control they give developers over the appearance of this report. A human expert, of course, has broad flexibility when it comes to presenting advice. It is important to present advice in a manner that is conducive to user understanding. Furthermore, the human expert is not limited just to presenting the reasoning results; he or she can immediately process this newly derived knowledge in various ways. It can be stored away (i.e., remembered or recorded) for later reference, used as input to solver analysis of some model, used as a basis for graphics generation, incorporated into a textual description, communicated to people at distant sites, used as a basis for data recall, incorporated into a spreadsheet, and so forth.

There are tools that tend to resemble real human experts by supporting all these capabilities after reasoning has concluded but before a consultation terminates. This effect is accomplished by building a **completion sequence** into a rule set. Like an initialization sequence, this sequence is simply a series of one or more commands that can be processed by the PPS. However, the PPS executes these commands after reasoning with the rules has concluded rather than before it begins. A very simple completion sequence for the ADVISOR rule set is shown in Figure 13.8. It begins with the CLEAR command, which simply clears the screen. The OUTPUT commands allow Jack to control the console screen position where each output is to appear. The last two actions are examples of how Jack can have the PPS carry out desired actions if specified conditions are met.

FIGURE 13.8   A Completion Sequence for the ADVISOR Rule Set

```
DO:
   CLEAR
   AT 5,1 OUTPUT "Sales Rep:", REP
   AT 6,1 OUTPUT "Product Line:", PROD
   AT 5,20 OUTPUT "Quarter:", QTR
   AT 8,1 OUTPUT "The recommended new quota is:", NEWQUOTA
   AT 12,20 OUTPUT "Basis for the recommendation."
   AT 14,20 OUTPUT "Base Amount:", BASE
   AT 14,40 OUTPUT "Economic Factor:", EFACTOR
   AT 15,40 OUTPUT "Product Factor:", PFACTOR
   AT 16,40 OUTPUT "Local Ads Factor:", LAFACTOR
   IF STRONG THEN AT 17,40 OUTPUT "Rise Factor:", RISE/100; ENDIF
   IF WEAK THEN AT 17,40 OUTPUT "Fall Factor:", FALL/100; ENDIF
```

Figure 13.9 shows results of the completion sequence. For a fancier presentation, Jack could replace the nine OUTPUT commands of Figure 13.8 with a couple of form-management commands. In addition to presenting consultation results, Jack may want the inference engine to preserve the results as a record in a table. He accomplishes this result by assigning variable values to the fields of a new record in that table. In general, any of the knowledge-management techniques covered in Part Three can be employed in a completion sequence provided they have been integrated into the development tool.

FIGURE 13.9   Presentation of Results by the Completion Sequence

```
Sales Rep:Toby        Quarter:3
Product Line:romance

The recommended new quota is:24750

                    Basis for the recommendation.

                    Base Amount:21000    Economic Factor:.01
                                         Product Factor:.1
                                         Local Ads Factor:.01
                                         Rise Factor:.05
```

Reverse Reasoning   **Reverse reasoning** is sometimes called **backward chaining** or *goal-directed reasoning*. It is based on the idea of considering rules in a reverse direction—looking first at a rule's conclusion, rather than its premise. At any moment during the reasoning process, the inference engine is focusing its efforts on trying to establish the value of a particular unknown variable, called the **current goal** variable. At the outset of a consultation, the user can specify the goal to be sought by the inference engine if it is not the **default goal** named in the rule set. As an alternative to NEWQUOTA, for instance, any unknown variable in the ADVISOR rule set could be specified as the overall goal of the consultation.

Reverse reasoning is a much more intricate process than forward reasoning. Forward reasoning is a relatively "blind," or brute-force, method for using rules to discover the value of an initially unknown variable. It therefore involves a comparatively brief explanation. Reverse reasoning is a much more sophisticated method of reasoning and requires a more lengthy explanation.

As reverse reasoning begins, the inference engine focuses on the consultation's overall **goal variable** (e.g., V1 in Figure 13.10). For the moment this is the current goal, and its value is unknown. By looking at the conclusions of rules in the rule set, the inference engine can detect which of these rules could possibly establish a value for the goal variable. These rules are candidates for further consideration. The inference engine selects one of these **candidate rules** (e.g., RA in Figure 13.10) and examines its premise.

If the premise is true, then the rule is fired to establish a value of the goal variable. Because remaining candidate rules may also affect the value of the goal variable, they too may then be considered in the same way. If the premise is false, then the rule is not fired, and another of the candidate rules is selected for consideration. The other possibility is that a candidate rule's premise is unknown. When this situation occurs, the inference engine attempts to make the premise known by trying to determine values for the unknown variables in the premise.

There are two ways for the inference engine to make an unknown variable known during reverse reasoning. As with forward reasoning, the inference engine can carry out the actions specified in a variable description. If there is no variable description for an unknown variable, then that variable temporarily becomes the current goal (e.g., V2 in Figure 13.10). The inference engine works on this goal in exactly the same way as the consultation's overall goal. It detects which of the rule set's rules could possibly establish a value for this current goal variable. These rules are treated as candidate rules for the new current goal (e.g., RB and RC in Figure 13.10). The inference engine selects one of these rules and examines its premise (e.g., RB in Figure 13.10).

If its premise is true, the rule is fired to establish a value for the current goal. If the premise is false, then the rule is not fired and another of the candidate rules for the current goal is selected for consideration. If the premise is unknown, then its unknown variables (e.g., V3 and V4 in Figure 13.10) can, in turn, be subjected to the same reverse-reasoning process. If an unknown variable does not have a variable description showing how to find its value, then that variable temporarily becomes the new current goal.

Thus, reverse reasoning works by using rules to break the overall problem into subproblems. Each of these may itself be broken into its own subproblem. In other words, it meets the current goal (e.g., V4) by giving a value to the unknown variable that is of immediate interest (e.g., by firing RE). If there are any candidate rules for that goal that have not yet been considered, then they too may be processed in

FIGURE 13.10 Using Rules to Break Goals into Subgoals

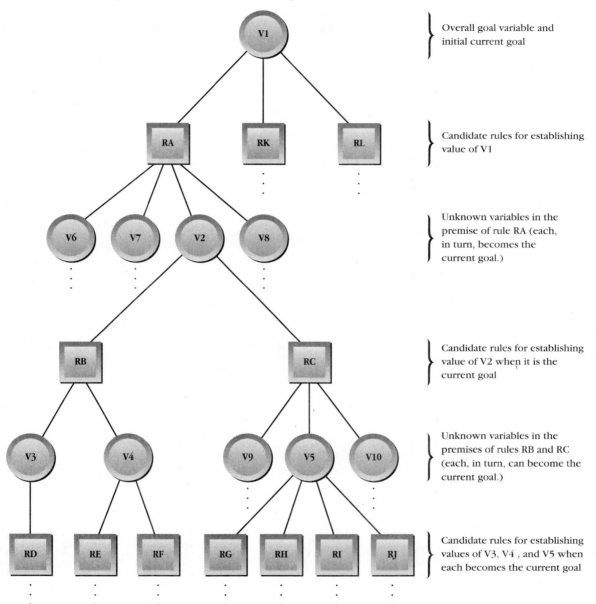

Overall goal variable and
initial current goal

Candidate rules for establishing
value of V1

Unknown variables in the
premise of rule RA (each,
in turn, becomes the
current goal.)

Candidate rules for establishing
value of V2 when it is the
current goal

Unknown variables in the
premises of rules RB and RC
(each, in turn, can become the
current goal.)

Candidate rules for establishing
values of V3, V4 , and V5 when
each becomes the current goal

the same manner (e.g., RF for the goal V4). At this point, the inference engine focuses on a different goal (i.e., problem, unknown variable). There are two possibilities for the variable that is now focused on as the current goal. If solving the former goal (e.g., V4) does not allow the premise (e.g., of RB) that contains it to be evaluated as being either true or false, then another unknown variable (e.g., V3) in that premise becomes the new current goal. The inference engine uses reverse reasoning to try to solve the problem posed by this goal.

The second possibility is that the just-solved goal (V4) allows the premise (of RB) containing it to be evaluated as either true or false. The last unsolved goal (V2) to have previously been the current goal (before it was broken into subproblems of V3 and V4) again becomes the current goal. If the premise (of RB) is true, the rule is fired and this goal variable's value can therefore change. If the premise is false, the rule is not fired, and the goal variable's value remains unchanged. In either case, another candidate rule (RC) for that goal variable (V2) is selected for consideration. If there are no further candidate rules for the current goal, then no further reasoning is possible for that variable. If this variable (e.g., V2) is the goal of some subproblem, the inference engine focuses on another subproblem (e.g., V8) that has yet to be solved.

Eventually—when all its pertinent subproblems have been processed (e.g., V6, V7, V2, and V8 via RA, as well as those found via RK and RL)—the overall goal will again become the current goal. Depending on which of its candidate rules have been fired, this variable (e.g., V1) now has a value that has been determined by rea-

VARIATIONS IN REASONING

Aside from the basic flow of reverse reasoning, there are a number of more subtle issues involved. First is the issue of the selection order that will be used for considering candidate rules that have been identified for a goal.

Second is the issue of when the inference engine should use a variable description to establish a value for an unknown variable. Should this happen before (i.e., instead of) having the inference engine try reverse reasoning to determine a value for the variable? Or, should it happen only as a last resort—in cases where reverse reasoning is unable to determine a value? Depending on the nature of the application, one of these alternatives may be preferable to another.

Third is the issue of how rigorous the inference engine should be. Although it is highly rigorous to consider exhaustively all candidate rules for a variable, this may be excessive for some rule sets. For instance, a rule set may have been built in such a way that no more than one candidate rule's premise will ever be true for a given problem. In such a situation, it is probably a waste of time for the inference engine to consider the remaining candidate rules once one candidate rule has been fired. On the other hand, a rule set may be built so that the premises of multiple candidate rules could be true for a given problem. In such situations it may be important for all candidate rules to be considered.

Fourth is the issue of how an inference engine should go about trying to evaluate the premise of a rule. In what sequence should its unknown variables be considered? Should the inference engine try to evaluate the premise only after all of its unknown variables become known? Or, should the inference engine try to evaluate the premise as each of its unknown variables becomes known? Should a rule be fired as soon as its premise is determined to be true, regardless of whether all of its unknown variables have been processed?

Fifth is the issue of how many times a rule can be fired. Is the firing cap 1, or should an inference engine be permitted to reconsider already-fired rules—firing them again if they still have true premises?

Variants of inference engine behavior with respect to the forgoing issues as well as the treatment of uncertainty are examined in Chapter 15.

soning with the expertise embodied in the rule set. If the overall goal variable ends up with an unknown value, then the rule set has insufficient expertise to solve the user's problem. Once reverse reasoning terminates, the inference engine performs the rule set's completion sequence.

An Example of Reverse Reasoning   To see how reverse reasoning works in practice, once again imagine that you are the inference engine. The user has asked you to seek the value of the NEWQUOTA variable. You first carry out the commands in ADVISOR's initialization sequence. Suppose that this yields the same variable values that were used in the forward-reasoning example.

```
REP: "Toby"            SALES: 24000
PROD: "romance"        QUOTA: 20000
QTR: "3"               GROWTH: .03
OLDTITLES: 100         UNEMPLOYMENT: .06
NEWTITLES: 10
```

As Figure 13.7 shows, other variables are presently unknown. Now you turn your attention to reverse reasoning with the ADVISOR rules depicted in Figure 13.3. Remember that you will be examining a rule's conclusion before you look at its premise.

You know that NEWQUOTA is the overall goal variable, and at this moment it is also your current goal. Its value is presently unknown. You need to identify those rules whose actions could possibly change the value of NEWQUOTA. These rules will be the candidate rules for NEWQUOTA. By looking at the conclusions of the ADVISOR rules, you can easily pick out those that have a potential for affecting the value of NEWQUOTA. When you look at the conclusion of rule R1, you see that even if R1 is fired, it could not alter the present value of NEWQUOTA. It can affect only the BASE variable. Similarly, R2 does not qualify as a candidate rule for NEWQUOTA. As you scan the 18 rule conclusions, you can see that there are only 3 rules that have a chance of giving a value to NEWQUOTA. These NEWQUOTA candidate rules are R15, R16, and R17.

Suppose you select R15 to consider first. When you look at its premise, you see that it is unknown. In fact, you will need to know the values of five presently unknown variables and STRONG will have to be true before you can fire this rule and produce a value for NEWQUOTA. Finding out the value of STRONG becomes a new subproblem, and the STRONG variable becomes your current goal. There is no variable description that gives you actions to take for finding a STRONG value. Therefore, you identify the candidate rules for STRONG, which are rules R13, R14, and R18.

You consider R13 first. When you examine its premise, you can evaluate it immediately. Because the premise is true, you fire rule R13 (see point 1 in Figure 13.11). Not only does this result in a value of TRUE for STRONG, but two other actions are also taken. The WEAK variable becomes FALSE, and a value of 0.10 is calculated for PFACTOR. Rule R14 is another candidate rule for STRONG. Because its premise is false, you proceed to the last STRONG candidate rule. The premise of this rule (R18) is also false, so you are done processing the STRONG variable. Because the value you have inferred for STRONG does not make the premise of R15 false, you proceed to another subproblem for that rule. In particular, you need to establish a value for the BASE variable before R15 can be fired. Thus, BASE is now your current goal.

FIGURE 13.11 A Reverse-Reasoning Example

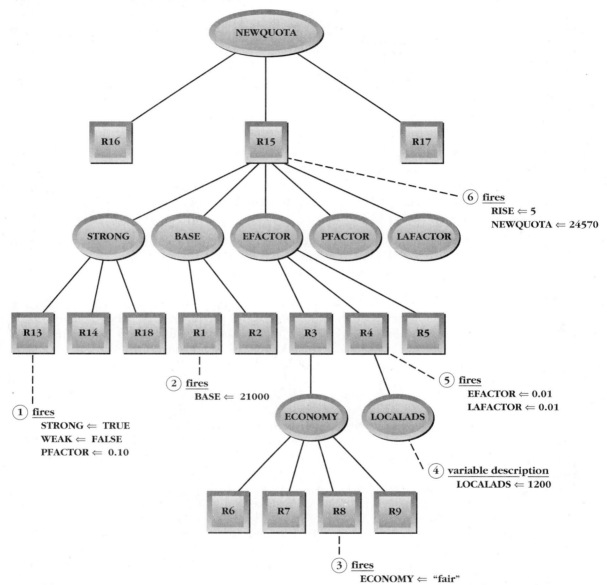

There is no variable description for BASE, so you use reverse reasoning in an effort to establish its value. You see that there are two rules that could possibly change the value of BASE from its present unknown status. These candidate rules are R1 and R2. You consider R1 first. When you evaluate its premise, you discover that the premise is true. You therefore fire R1, which calculates a value of 2100 for BASE. (See point 2 in Figure 13.11.) Considering the other candidate rule for BASE, you discover that its premise is false. Thus, you are finished processing BASE. Because BASE now has a known value, you continue working with rule R15 by focusing on the next subproblem: establishing a value for EFACTOR.

With EFACTOR as your current goal, you identify its candidate rules, R3, R4, and R5. Because there is no variable description for EFACTOR, you immediately consider R3. When you try to evaluate its premise, you discover that you cannot, because ECONOMY is unknown. Thus, you now have a subproblem for EFACTOR that involves establishing a value for the ECONOMY variable. ECONOMY temporarily becomes your current goal. It has no variable description that tells how to find its value, so you identify ECONOMY candidate rules, R6, R7, R8, and R9. When you examine the premise of R6, you see that it is false. Similarly, the premise of R7 is false. However, when you evaluate the premise of R8, you discover that it is true. Thus you fire R8 and a value of "fair" is assigned to ECONOMY. (See point 3 in Figure 13.11.) Because the premise of R9 is false, you are finished processing the ECONOMY variable, and EFACTOR is once again your current goal.

You can now evaluate the premise of EFACTOR's first candidate rule (R3), and you discover that it is false. Proceeding to R4, you see that LOCALADS needs to become known before this rule can be fired. Using the actions specified in the LOCALADS variable description, you find its value by looking it up in a spreadsheet. (See point 4 in Figure 13.11.) The resultant value for LOCALADS is 1200. The premise of R4 is now true, so you fire it. This establishes a value of 0.01 for both EFACTOR and LAFACTOR. (See point 5 in Figure 13.11.) The last candidate rule for EFACTOR is R5. Because its premise is false, you are now done processing the EFACTOR variable and continue working with rule R15. All variables in R15's premise are now known, and you discover that the premise is true when you evaluate it. You now fire R15. Assuming that the user responds with 5 to the RISE prompt, a value of 24,570 is calculated for the NEWQUOTA goal. (See point 6 in Figure 13.11.)

You consider the other two candidate rules for NEWQUOTA (R16 and R17) but quickly see that each has a false premise. As a result, your reasoning for this consultation is finished, and you complete the consultation by taking the actions specified in the ADVISOR's completion sequence. In the course of your reverse reasoning, you fired five rules in the order R13, R1, R8, R4, R15. Notice that these are the same five rules that were fired in the forward-reasoning example, though the firing order differs (R1, R8, R13, R4, R15 in the forward case).

13.4 INTERACTING WITH INFERENCE ENGINES

Once a rule set exists, a user should be able to ask the inference engine to consult that rule set. There are several important aspects related to this activity of invoking an inference engine. First is the issue of **consultation environment.** Is it rudimentary, allowing the user to do nothing more than make requests of the inference engine? Or is it a rich environment, allowing a user to intermix such requests with data-management, spreadsheet, graphics, and other common decision support requests?

Second is the issue of how a consultation request is actually made. Is it made via a natural language conversation, by selecting desired options presented in menus, by a simple consultation command, or through some special user interface that has been custom-built by the expert system developer?

Third, what kinds of requests can be made of the inference engine? Beyond the choice of what type of reasoning (forward, reverse, etc.) is to be employed, there are requests that ask the inference engine to explain itself. For instance, when a consultation ends, how can a user ask the inference engine to explain its line of reasoning? How elaborate can the inference engine's responses be?

THE CONSULTATION ENVIRONMENT

In a human decision-making process, the mind provides an environment for exercising various knowledge-processing activities (recall Figure 9.1). One such activity is the consultation of experts, which is by no means the only kind of knowledge-processing activity that is possible. And when consultation occurs, it normally happens within the context of other kinds of knowledge processing. Certain activities may stimulate the need for a consultation, and the consultation results may make still other activities possible. For instance, as a result of exploring some descriptive knowledge, a person may discover that advice is needed about some particular problem. Once the advice is received, it may be incorporated into various calculations, used for selective examination of further descriptive knowledge, used as a stimulant for seeking additional expert recommendations, treated as an input for analytical modeling, presented in various guises to other persons, and so forth.

The important point is that human consultation needs arise and are fulfilled within a rich environment that supports many other varieties of knowledge processing. All these kinds of knowledge processing (including the capacity to consult experts) are available for use at any time and in any sequence, giving a person great discretion about how to employ them with respect to any particular decision situation. It is possible to provide expert system users with a similar environment, where the user is free to request a consultation whenever he or she deems it appropriate. Such requests can be freely intermixed with requests for any of the other kinds of knowledge processing. The possibilities arising from this flexibility are virtually unlimited.

For example, a KC sales manager might begin an interactive session by working on a spreadsheet for the local advertising budget. While working on the local advertising budget, the sales manager wants to selectively retrieve a list of all sales representatives whose sales in the fourth quarter for romance books exceeded $8,000. So, she simply types the appropriate SQL query. The manager may then decide to use the rule set that Jack built to get advice about a new quota for one of the listed sales representatives.

When the calculation is completed and the manager sees the advice offered, she can follow up with any of many possible actions. Suppose the inference engine prompted for a value for the RISE variable. The manager may want to rerun the consultation but give a different response to the prompt this time to observe the impact on the recommended new quota. The manager may also want to study the effect of changing some aspect of the advertising budget. As soon as the consultation ends, the manager brings the spreadsheet into view. The desired change is made to the spreadsheet, and its cell values are recomputed. ADVISOR is again consulted immediately to see the impact of the budget change.

The foregoing examples suggest the versatility that a decision maker might expect from the environment within which an inference engine is invoked. It should be possible to intermix consultation requests with requests for other useful kinds of knowledge processing surveyed in Part Three. Ideally, the decision maker should be able to intermix these requests on a spur-of-the-moment basis. The creative flow that can so often happen in a decision process should not be interrupted or destroyed by such crude requirements as having to switch among separate programs, produce intermediate files of data, cut and paste data values, and so on. As far as possible, an artificially intelligent DSS should stimulate and enhance (i.e., truly support) the flow of a decision process rather than impede it.

METHODS FOR REQUESTING A CONSULTATION

Regardless of the environment richness within which consultation is requested, there are several alternative means for invoking an inference engine. These means include commands or menu responses that the inference engine has been designed to recognize. The possibility of a customized LS that depends on the developer incorporating linguistic knowledge into the KS also exists. All may be present in a single decision support system, enabling it to be conveniently accessed by many different kinds of users, from computer novices to professional systems developers.

Ready-Made Methods   A command to consult the ADVISOR rule set might be as simple as:

```
CONSULT ADVISOR
```

Using the same tool to build other rule sets would allow them to be consulted with the same command, except that ADVISOR would be replaced by the name of the desired rule set. Such a CONSULT command could be directly used at any time in an interactive session. It might also be used in various indirect ways, depending on the type and extent of integration provided by the tool.

For instance, a CONSULT command might serve as the definition of a spreadsheet cell. Whenever a user requests a spreadsheet recomputation, the PPS would carry out the desired consultation within the midst of the recomputation. A CONSULT command could be embedded by a developer in the logic of a program. For example, an ECON program may itself consult an expert system to get advice that helps establish the growth and unemployment projections. This invocation of the inference engine would take place during the execution of ECON, so that the user of ECON may even be unaware that ECON is consulting a rule set.

Another indirect usage of the CONSULT command happens when it is embedded within a rule set. It may appear in the initialization sequence, in a rule's conclusion, in a variable description's find actions, or in the completion sequence. When a user consults an expert system, that expert system can itself consult other expert systems in order to produce the advice that will be reported to the user. The user may be unaware of these additional consultations going on behind the scenes. All these consultations are processed by the same inference engine.

As an alternative to invoking the inference engine with a CONSULT command, the user may have a menu-guided interface provided by an inference engine. This type of interface allows a user to request a consultation by choosing a consult option. The resulting submenu might consist of an option for each rule set name. Upon choosing one of these, the user might indicate the kind of reasoning desired (forward or reverse) by selecting an option from yet another submenu.

Customized Methods   Some tools allow the entire appearance of interactions with an expert system to be custom built by the developer. An integral programming language is one such means for building a customized interface. The developer devises a program that embodies linguistic and presentation knowledge, storing it in the

KS. By executing this program, the flow of a user's interaction with the expert system is governed by logic built into the program. What the user sees on the console screen is controlled by this interface program. It also determines what user requests are legitimate and how they are interpreted.

An interface program may interact via line-oriented input and output, forms management, graphics generation, menu management, or some combination of these. At the developer's discretion, an interface program may accept user input via keystrokes, mouse manipulation, function keys, or some combination of these. Depending on what request a user enters, the program initiates appropriate actions (i.e., interprets the request).

Notice that all these are the same interface facilities that can be embedded in a rule set for governing the user interface during consultation. Here, the focus is on using them to govern the user interface before (and after) a consultation. The user never sees the actual CONSULT commands for invoking the inference engine, because they are embedded in the interface program. By executing this program, the user will be presented with a customized interface for repeatedly invoking the inference engine and perhaps accomplishing other decision support tasks as well. Such interface programs are distributed as KS components to all of an expert system's users. When a user wants to consult the expert system, he or she executes the interface program.

EXPLANATION ABILITIES

When a person consults a human expert, the resultant advice is, of course, important. It may also be puzzling, surprising, or somewhat less than obvious. In such situations, the expert may be asked to explain the line of reasoning. Explanations may even be desired when the advice is not surprising. There are many reasons for asking the expert for an **explanation.** For example, an explanation can help the person to assess how reasonable the advice is or to understand more clearly the rationale for the advice. Like human experts, an expert system should be able to explain itself. There are basically two times when an expert system's inference engine is able to explain itself: during a consultation and after a consultation.

Explanations during a Consultation During a consultation, an inference engine may ask the user for an input of some kind. Before answering, the user may want to know why the question is being asked. The developer of the rule set may have anticipated some such situations by preceding commands that ask for input with output commands that explain why the ensuing input is being requested. As a result, the inference engine automatically causes the explanation (of why an input is being requested) to be presented to the user before the question is asked. Such an explanation can be as detailed and parameterized as the developer wants it to be. Instead of or in addition to this detailed explanation approach, an inference engine may also be able to offer explanations on a more ad hoc basis.

For example, if a user is being prompted because a particular rule is being considered, that rule's reason may help to explain why the user is being prompted. Suppose the inference engine is in the process of firing rule R15. The user sees the input prompt and wonders why the expert system is asking for this input. If the user presses a designated key at this point, the console screen displays the reason for rule R15 (and perhaps other information about the current status of the consultation). To avoid interfering with other screen contents, the explanation may appear in a pop-up window that vanishes when the user indicates he or she is finished with viewing it.

Explanations after a Consultation An inference engine must also be able to explain itself after a consultation terminates. How did it reach the advice that it reported? Why did it fire the rules that it fired? It is typical that an inference engine answers these questions in response to HOW and WHY types of commands (or menu options). As with the CONSULT command, an end user can directly request these commands or embed them at desired points in a customized interface program.

Suppose a sales manager invokes the inference engine to have it use reverse reasoning in deriving new quota advice. Assume that the user's responses were the same as they were for the reverse reasoning example summarized in Figure 13.11. By the end of the consultation, the inference engine has fired rules R13, R1, R8, R4, and R15 and has calculated a value of 24,750 for NEWQUOTA. Figure 13.12 shows an exploration of the line of reasoning following an actual consultation of the ADVISOR rule set.

The user types in the HOW command to see how the new quota was determined. The inference engine replies that it was determined by firing rule R15, yielding a new quota of 24,750. Notice that a descriptive label of "Recommended new quota" appears alongside the variable name. This effect is achieved by incorporating

```
VARIABLE:NEWQUOTA
     LABEL:Recommended new quota
```

as a variable description in the ADVISOR rule set. For the discussion that follows, assume that the following variable descriptions have also been included in the ADVISOR rule set.

```
VARIABLE STRONG
     LABEL:Product is strong
VARIABLE:BASE
     LABEL:Base amount
VARIABLE:EFACTOR
     LABEL:Economic factor
VARIABLE:PFACTOR
     LABEL:Product factor
VARIABLE:LAFACTOR
     LABEL:Local advertising factor
VARIABLE:LOCALADS
     LABEL:Local advertising amount
VARIABLE:GROWTH
     LABEL:Anticipated growth rate
```

After seeing that the inference engine fired R15 to achieve a quota recommendation, the user may want to see why R15 was fired. As shown in Figure 13.12, a WHY command accomplishes this result. The WHY command causes the inference engine to report whether an indicated rule (R15, in this case) has been fired. The screen then displays the rule's reason, followed by a portrayal of variables pertinent to the firing of that rule. Notice that variables are mentioned in terms of their descriptive labels rather than their actual names. The value for each variable is displayed.

FIGURE 13.12   Exploring the Line of Reasoning

```
> HOW
NEWQUOTA — Recommended new quota
Rule    Value
------------
R15     24570
> WHY R15
Rule R15 fired because:
This is a strong product line. The base amount, economic factor,
product factor and local advertising factor for calculating the
new quota are all known. A subjective assessement of the
expected sales increase due to general rising interest in the
product is requested. The new quota is then calculated.

        (2) Product is strong              true
        (3) Base amount                    2100
        (4) Economic factor                0.01
        (5) Product factor                 0.10
        (6) Local advertising factor       0.01

> HOW 4
EFACTOR — Economic factor
Rule    Value
------------
R4      0.01
> WHY R4
Rule R4 fired because:
When the local economic outlook is fair, the economic factor
is one third of the growth rate and the local advertising factor
is 1/120000th of the amount budgeted for local advertising.

        (7) Local advertising amount       1200
        (8) Economic outlook               fair
        (9) Anticipated growth rate        0.03
```

The parenthesized number preceding each variable label makes subsequent "how" questions very convenient. Suppose that in examining why R15 was fired, the user decides that it would be useful to know how the economic factor was determined (as a basis for firing R15). The user accomplishes this result by specifying the corresponding number (4, in this case) when again executing the HOW command. The inference engine responds by explaining that rule R4 was fired in order to produce the economic factor of 0.01. The final WHY command in Figure 13.12 asks the inference engine why rule R4 was fired. These how and why questions can proceed for as long as the user desires.

Because a rule set's developer has control over the contents of each rule's reason and each variable's label, the explanations that the inference engine can produce can be customized to suit the nature of the application. A development tool may permit reasons and labels to be more than literal text, allowing the use of parameters as well. This lets the explanation be customized to include current values of variables. In some cases, a developer may want rule reasons to be detailed, explicit restatements of the rules' premises and actions. In other cases, it may be undesirable for a rule's reason to be too explicit. Compare, for instance, the reasons of rules R7 and R8 in Figure 13.3. The former is fairly specific, whereas the latter is not. In general, reasons and labels should be constructed so that they are meaningful to potential users of the expert system, without unnecessarily disclosing reasoning knowledge that should remain hidden (e.g., for security purposes).

13.5 SUMMARY

As the rule examples in this chapter suggest, rules provide a modular way of representing reasoning knowledge. This concept is different than that of trying to use a programming language to embed such knowledge in a program. Instead of sequencing program statements within traditional control structures, we assemble a modular collection of fragments of reasoning knowledge. This result is accomplished with a development tool's rule building software, which may be a text-oriented or menu-driven facility. The inference engine determines how to make use of these pieces of reasoning knowledge in response to a particular problem posed by a user.

We have taken an inside look at how an inference engine works during a consultation. We explored the mechanics of both forward and reverse reasoning. With forward reasoning, an inference engine takes the attitude of carrying out every action that is logically valid. The user can then study the results. Reverse reasoning is much more focused. The inference engine limits itself to taking only those actions that might help to meet some specified goal. Due to its focused approach, reverse reasoning is often preferable because it may be able to determine a variable's value much more rapidly than forward reasoning. Forward reasoning is of special interest in situations where we do not have a specific goal, where we know that most rules are to be considered, or where there are relatively few rules in a rule set.

We have also seen various ways that an inference engine can acquire knowledge needed in its reasoning process: from the user (or other external sources) or from its own integral knowledge system, which holds databases, spreadsheets, solvers, other rule sets, and so forth.

The environment available for invoking an inference engine is important to both developers and users of expert systems. A consultation environment may range from rudimentary and rigid to powerful and flexible. We have highlighted some of the most important factors to examine when evaluating a consultation environment and have examined alternatives that could be available within a consultation environment for invoking an inference engine. No matter what interface methods are supported, an expert system's inference engine must be capable of explaining its behavior to a user. Ideally the expert system developer should easily be able to customize these explanations.

▲ IMPORTANT TERMS

backward chaining	completion sequence
candidate rules	conclusion

consultation environment   inference engine
current goal   initialization sequence
default goal   premise
explanation   reason
fire   reverse reasoning
forward chaining   ruler
forward reasoning   rule setu
goal variable   ule set builder
hooks   nknown variable
induction   variable description

▲ APPLICATION TO THE AUSTRALIA CASE

1. Why was Lucvar developed? What kind of decision does it support?
2. Give an example of a numeric variable used in Lucvar's rule set. Give an example of a string variable. Give an example of a logical variable.
3. Using the syntax shown in this chapter, state a rule that concludes something about the level of resistance.
4. Describe the rule set's overall goal variable in terms of the values it could have.
5. Might rule induction have been helpful in specifying the rule set? Explain.
6. What type of tool was used to develop Lucvar?
7. How does Lucvar's inference engine establish values for unknown variables?
8. If Lucvar uses forward reasoning, what is the minimum number of rules for which an attempt must be made to do premise evaluation? Is this more, less, or the same as the number of premises that would be evaluated via reverse reasoning?
9. What expert source(s) did the developers use to acquire the reasoning knowledge represented in the rule set?
10. What benefit(s) did the expert system provide to extension agronomists? To farmers?

▲ REVIEW QUESTIONS

1. What is the relationship between conditions and a rule's premise?
2. Give an example of a condition involving a relational operator.
3. Give an example of a condition involving no relational operators.
4. What possible values can the condition SALES <= 1.15*QUOTA have? Describe situations that lead to these values.
5. What is the relationship between actions and a rule's conclusion?
6. What kinds of actions are useful in the conclusions of rules existing in an expert system?
7. Why are the two KNOWN conditions necessary for rule R4?
8. Why is a KNOWN condition unnecessary in rule R10?
9. What is the relationship between a rule's premise and conclusion?
10. What is the purpose of rule-builder software?
11. Contrast the text-oriented and menu-oriented approaches to rule set building.
12. What are some of the advantages of rule set compilation?
13. How is rule set building with induction limited relative to direct specification of rules?

14. Beyond its premise and conclusion, what else might be involved in a rule specification?
15. Beyond its rules, what else might a rule set contain?
16. What are three ways of incorporating prompts for further information into a rule set?
17. What is the role of a rule set's initialization sequence?
18. Beyond line-oriented input and output, what other kinds of interface facilities could be of value to a developer?
19. During a consultation, the inference engine may encounter many unknown variables whose values may need to become known if a solution is to be derived. Suppose the user does not know the value for such a variable. How can the inference engine establish a value for it?
20. Why are hooks to external software valuable? What are their limitations relative to synergistic integration?
21. Step through the inference engine's reasoning with the ADVISOR rule set where the initial variable values are as follows:

```
REP: "Kevin"        SALES: 10000
PROD: "scifi"       QUOTA: 9000
QTR: "3"            GROWTH: .04
OLDTITLES: 50       UNEMPLOYMENT: .06
NEWTITLES: 10
```

Assume that the spreadsheet contains a value of 200 for Kevin's local advertising budget for the science fiction product line. Use reverse reasoning first; then solve the same problem with forward reasoning.

22. Repeat Question 21 using the following different initial values:

    a. **SALES: 8000; PROD: "sports"**
    b. **SALES: 9000; GROWTH: .01; NEWTITLES: 40**
    c. **GROWTH: .03; PROD: "reference"**

23. What methods may be available to a user for requesting a consultation?

▲ DISCUSSION TOPICS

1. What are the advantages of having extensive freedom and flexibility in the specification of a rule?
2. Suppose your inference engine permits only one action per conclusion. How would you capture the reasoning knowledge represented in rule R4?
3. Suppose your inference engine is unable to comprehend the OR operator. If you need a premise of GROWTH<.02 OR UNEMPLOYMENT>=.082, what would you do?
4. Instead of determining the BASE with respect to a fixed 15% criterion, Jack wants the percentage to be the ratio of the square root of twice the quota relative to half the quota. Assume that the inference engine is able to recognize and process a square root function named SQRT. Restate rules R1 and R2 accordingly.
5. How would the prior situation be handled if the inference engine were unable to compute square roots with a built-in function?
6. Explain the difference between inference performed by an expert system and rule induction performed by a rule set builder.

7. Why is it valuable to have a variety of ways available for customizing an expert system's user interface?

8. Compare the conditional clauses allowed in SQL inquiries with the premises allowed in rules.

9. Describe several alternative strategies that you would like an inference engine to support for the selection order used when considering a group of candidate rules.

10. What is meant by inference engine rigor?

11. What kinds of capabilities would you expect to find in an AI environment for business computing? Why?

12. Identify various places in a joint human-computer decision-making process where the ability to consult an expert system could be valuable.

13. What is knowledge security and why is it important?

14. Explain how the ability to specify a reason for each rule is useful from a security standpoint.

▲ REFERENCES

Holsapple, C. W., K. Tam, and A. B. Whinston. 1987. Expert system integration. In *Expert Systems for Business,* edited by B. Silverman. Reading, Mass.: Addison-Wesley.

Holsapple, C. W., and A. B. Whinston. 1986. *Manager's guide to expert systems using GURU.* Homewood, Ill.: Dow Jones–Irwin.

————. 1987. Artificially intelligent decision support systems—Criteria for tool selection. In *Decision support systems: Theory and applications,* edited by C. Holsapple and A. Whinston. Berlin: Springer-Verlag.

Lodge, G. M., and T. C. Frecker. 1989. LUCVAR: A computer-based consultation system for selecting lucerne (alfalfa) varieties. *Expert Systems,* 6, no. 3.

Chapter 14

DEVELOPING AN ARTIFICIALLY INTELLIGENT DSS

INSIGHTS

BANKING: AN ARTIFICIALLY INTELLIGENT DSS FOR COMMERCIAL LOAN DECISIONS

Overview

. . . [The] Commercial Loan Analysis Support System (CLASS) . . . uses rules . . . obtained from a commercial lending expert to analyze the first four Cs of lending (credit, collateral, capital, and capacity). The system is intended for commercial loans to medium and large sized companies.

Commercial loan officers examine numerous financial factors to uncover a company's financial weaknesses. Their evaluation begins with a general analysis involving an examination of key financial trends and factors. When one of those factors does not meet the industry norm, commercial loan officers must perform a more detailed analysis to uncover the causes.

The general analyses consist of general trend analysis, and separate analyses of credit, collateral, capital, and capacity. General trend analysis provides loan officers with a quick indication of a company's performance in several key areas: sales, operating income, net income, selling/administrative expenses, working capital, and cash flow. Five year trends of these data permit loan officers to determine quickly whether a company's performance has improved, declined, or remained stable. Credit, capital, and capacity analyses involve a comparison of a company's financial ratios against industry standards.

A detailed analysis is performed whenever a general analysis indicates a weakness. For example, if inventory turnover is below the industry average, commercial loan officers examine additional factors such as source prices and gross margin. Moreover, for any measure that is below the industry norm, loan officers examine its historical trend to determine if the condition is temporary or chronic.

As problem areas are identified and examined, the loan officers accumulate loan covenants, or restrictions, which become part of the final loan agreement. For example, if long-term debt to total assets is above the industry average, a loan officer may recommend reducing long-term debt. A covenant may also be written prohibiting additional long-term borrowing. . . .

To thoroughly evaluate a company, a loan officer must know which financial factors require consideration and their interrelationships, how to interpret and integrate the results of multiple analyses, and when to proceed with additional analyses. The voluminous data and complexity of the problem make the loan decision difficult for even the most seasoned loan officers. . . .

System Features and Development

CLASS is an expert system designed to evaluate a company's financial posture, recommend commercial loan decisions and pertinent covenants, and document the loan analysis. CLASS's interface provides substantial opportunity for human interaction. Commercial loan officers can easily enter and view financial data, choose execution options through menus, respond to queries, and obtain reports.

The knowledge engineering team that built CLASS consisted of one expert . . . [a] consultant with over ten years of hands-on experience in commercial lending, and two knowledge engineers . . . [who] employed a method similar to protocol

Continued

analysis. They asked the expert to solve many small, difficult problems that require interpretation of the results of several financial analyses. The knowledge engineers recorded the expert's logic and behavior, and analyzed the subsequent protocols to develop procedures, rules, and loan covenants. . . .

. . . The knowledge engineering team used several commercial loan cases for validation purposes. For each case, the expert's opinions were compared to the system's results. The system was modified until the results reflected the expert's judgements. . . . The expert also evaluated the interface and improvements were made accordingly. The system was continually revised until the expert was satisfied with its performance and interface.

System Usage

. . . Financial facts about the borrower are recorded by using standard spreadsheet software. The logical capabilities of the spreadsheet are then used to convert the numerical data into symbolic evaluations. For example, the numerical result that return on assets exceeds the industry standard is converted into a symbolic fact by marking the fact called "ROA ok" as true. Then spreadsheet software is used to write the symbolic information to a file which is read by the expert system.

CLASS is designed to utilize up to five years of financial data. . . . Rows in the spreadsheet represent ratios, percentages, and financial statement line items (sales, selling and administrative expenses, inventory). Columns typically represent years. The knowledge engineering team chose this representation because commercial loan officers are familiar with spreadsheets and regularly use them for loan analysis. The logic for converting the numerical data into symbolic facts for the expert system . . . has been developed as a spreadsheet template into which the financial data are inserted.

The first analysis that CLASS performs is general trend analysis. CLASS superimposes each major financial trend of the firm on the corresponding industry trend, and asks the user to evaluate the trend as improving, stable, or deteriorating . . . CLASS relies on the expertise of the user, assisted by the graphics capabilities of the computer. . . . Based upon the user's response for each kind of trend, CLASS uses a simple averaging and rounding heuristic to decide whether the trends are collectively improving, stable, or deteriorating.

CLASS then moves on to evaluate credit by examining the three primary components of credit: efficiency, profitability, and liquidity. Each category is evaluated as strong, normal, weak, or poor. Based upon the separate evaluations, CLASS concludes that overall credit is strong, normal, weak, or poor. Similar procedures are used to analyze collateral, capital, and capacity. . . . Finally, CLASS makes a final recommendation about the loan by combining general trend analysis with category-specific evaluations. When it identifies weaknesses, CLASS examines additional measures, displays trends, and recommends loan covenants. CLASS continuously spawns detailed analyses until it uncovers all weaknesses and isolates the causes of those weaknesses. Thus, CLASS reasons about loans in the same way as the expert.

Continued

   . . . Like a loan officer, CLASS consistently synthesizes a large number of detailed facts into a loan recommendation. CLASS has been designed to seek out any potential weakness in the prospective borrower and conduct an extensive detailed analysis of each weakness. Weaknesses may be over-analyzed, but none will be overlooked. This approach is consistent with the general notion in commercial lending that one is primarily concerned with weaknesses instead of strong points, which are taken for granted.

Condensed quotation from Peter Duchessi, Hany Shawky, and John P. Seagle, "A Knowledge-Engineered System for Commercial Loan Decisions," in *Financial Management* (Autumn 1988).

LEARNING OBJECTIVES

As the banking case indicates, developers of expert systems are commonly called knowledge engineers. In this case, two of them act as agents in the transformation of a human expert's knowledge into a computerized representation of it (i.e., into a rule set). Often referred to as a knowledge-acquisition process, this particular transformation used a method called protocol analysis, in which the knowledge engineers observed the expert's responses to a variety of credit-application problems representative of those that might be posed to the expert system. This chapter provides a broader and more detailed view of the task of developing expert systems. As you read the chapter, consider how the additional development issues it presents would have been handled by the banking case's expert system developers.

   After studying this chapter you should be able to

1. Describe the activities involved in developing a rule-based decision support system.
2. Explain how development of an artificially intelligent DSS differs from conventional DSS development.
3. Discuss the major factors that furnish a context for knowledge acquisition and the important factors to consider within a knowledge-acquisition process.
4. Construct and interpret dependency diagrams.
5. Describe approaches to testing the correctness of reasoning knowledge represented in a rule set.

   The chapter ends with exercises you can use to ensure that you have met these objectives.

14.1 INTRODUCTION

Being acquainted with the basic structure, characteristics, and operation of rule-based DSSs, we are ready to take a look at how they are built. In particular, we are interested in how the expertise in the mind of an expert (or perhaps held in another source) is transformed into a set of rules that a particular inference engine can process to yield correct advice. Determining this information involves special considerations beyond the approaches to conventional DSS development outlined in Chapter 7.

The activity of rule set development is perhaps more an art than a science—for the present at least. Practice may well be the best teacher. Nevertheless, there are a number of considerations that, if you keep them in mind, can greatly facilitate the development of expert systems for decision support. These considerations are explored in this chapter.

First, there is the issue of how to identify an expert system opportunity. Once you identify such an opportunity, you should clearly state the proposed expert system's objectives and establish a plan for meeting those objectives. Then the actual development of an expert system's rule set can begin. This activity is generally called **knowledge acquisition** and is widely regarded as a bottleneck in the activity of **rule set specification.** We examine both the context and process of knowledge acquisition. The evolutionary and iterative nature of expert system development can be viewed as forming a development spiral. Each cycle in this spiral consists of seven stages. As we explore these stages, we introduce several aspects of the rule-management technique not presented in earlier chapters.

14.2 EXPERT SYSTEM OPPORTUNITIES

Rule set development begins only after an expert system opportunity has been identified. Such opportunities are abundant in most organizations, but managers must develop the ability to see them. Nearly every person in an organization is (or should be) an expert at playing some role that is important to the organization's viability. In some cases, an expert system could help the human expert in carrying out particular activities demanded by a role, freeing the person to concentrate on other aspects of that role. This allows the productivity of both the expert and the expert system's users to increase. To help recognize such situations, it is useful to recall the discussion in Chapter 12 of potential benefits offered by expert systems.

The manager should look for problem-solving activities where human experts are in short supply, overburdened, unavailable when needed, or very expensive. An expert system opportunity may well exist if such an activity involves reasoning for the purpose of

- Diagnosing the cause of a situation (e.g., auditing, troubleshooting, debugging),
- Prescribing a course of action (e.g., planning, designing, repairing),
- Predicting what will happen (e.g., forecasting, speculating),
- Understanding what is happening (e.g., interpreting, teaching, monitoring),
- Governing what is happening (e.g., implementing, controlling, managing),
- Evaluating a happening (e.g., judging results, assessing impacts).

Expert system opportunities exist not only where human experts need relief or need to be replicated, they also exist where human experts have not yet ventured. For instance, an expert stock trader may be limited to following a small number of stocks because of the large amount of time required in making daily or hourly trading decisions about each one of them. If an expert system were developed, the trader's expertise could be applied to a larger number of stocks than the trader could possibly handle personally. The expert system would simply make the same trading recommendations that the trader would make, given enough time to do so. In this way, the trader's expertise is highly leveraged. Thus, managers should be alert for expert system opportunities even where a single human expert has been unsuccessful (e.g., to trade effectively 50 stocks rather than 5).

PROGRAMS VERSUS RULE SETS

Sometimes persons who have experience in writing programs will ask, "Why not develop a program instead of developing a rule set?" This is a reasonable question. A program could be written in COBOL or C that has roughly (or even exactly) the same effect as any expert system. Are there, then, really any expert system opportunities as opposed to programming opportunities? This is a commonly asked question, but it confuses the ends (expert systems) with the possible means (program development versus rule set development). Such confusion should be avoided when looking for expert system opportunities.

Just because you can solve a problem with a program does not mean that it is not an expert system opportunity. Nor does it mean that you should solve the problem with a program. Recall from the knowledge-management discussion in Part Three that there may be many ways to represent and process a particular kind of knowledge. You can represent the reasoning knowledge that is essential for an expert system in a rule set and process it by an inference engine. Alternatively, you can represent and process the same reasoning knowledge within a program.

Trying to create an expert system by writing a program rather than developing a rule set has many drawbacks. First, and most importantly, the developer must be a programmer, devising and debugging what amounts to an inference engine. In contrast, rule set developers need not be programmers, because a rule set is basically nonprocedural rather than algorithmic. The developer simply states reasoning facts and leaves to the inference engine the activity of processing them in a correct sequence.

Unlike a developer using rule management, the programmer must build a reasoning explanation mechanism into the program. If reasoning with uncertainty is needed, a programmer must program all the necessary certainty calculations. The program must be devised to allow a user to optionally get explanations for any input prompts. All this amounts to reinventing the inference engine "wheel" that is already available to a rule set developer.

The relationship of an expert system development tool to programming is somewhat similar to the relationship of a spreadsheet package to programming. A programmer can certainly write programs to solve the same problems that are handled by a spreadsheet, but why bother? Moreover, persons who are not programmers are able to meet many of their own knowledge-management needs with a spreadsheet package, because it provides a convenient way for viewing, maintaining, and thinking about certain kinds of procedural modeling problems. Similarly, a tool for developing rule sets provides a convenient way for viewing, maintaining, and thinking about reasoning knowledge. On the other hand, neither a spreadsheet package nor an expert system development tool supplants a programming language. Neither would be appropriate for implementing a large-scale optimization algorithm, for example. They simply make it easier to accomplish certain kinds of knowledge-management tasks, compared to what would be required with a programming language.

Of course, reasoning expertise about the problem area must exist or be capable of being acquired. Otherwise, an expert system's rule set cannot be developed. Furthermore, it must be possible to represent the reasoning knowledge formally (e.g., as rules). KC's expert system for quota advice was built to handle a situation where sufficient expertise (i.e., Jack's) was not available for all managers at the same time (i.e., year's end). The problem area involved prescribing a course of action (i.e., setting quotas). The desired reasoning expertise for this problem area existed (i.e., Jack's) and could be represented as rules (e.g., Figure 13.3). As a result, each sales manager can exploit Jack's expertise while leaving Jack free to pursue his role within the organization.

Expert system opportunities exist for both small and large problems. A small problem is one that requires only modest effort on the part of a human expert. It typically involves a fairly small number of variables and takes the expert anywhere from a few minutes to an hour to solve. Large problems are those that might require hours, days, or even weeks for an expert to solve. These problems usually involve many variables. Because rule set development for large problems requires greater development time and expense, an expert system for a small problem will typically have a more immediate impact and payback. Its benefits will be visible more quickly.

Expert systems are not panaceas. On the other hand, their possibilities should not be underestimated. When looking for expert system opportunities, it is important to keep an open mind. Candidate problem areas range from large to small. Some may have a very narrow focus, whereas others involve a broad class of problems. They invariably involve reasoning and may involve reasoning about uncertain situations. The problems to be solved may be wholly or partially numeric in nature. They may need to be solved frequently or rarely, regularly or sporadically, in bunches or in isolation. The reasoning knowledge applied to the problem area may be stable or it may be undergoing continuing change.

Expert systems are particularly appropriate where those who ask for advice also want to explore the line of reasoning that has led to a recommendation. Perhaps the best way to begin looking for expert system opportunities is to identify those areas in an organization where human experts are pressured, overloaded, not always available when needed, unable to take the time to enlarge their expertise, and so on. Also be on the lookout for situations where consultation services are not presently available but could be valuable.

14.3 SEIZING AN EXPERT SYSTEM OPPORTUNITY

Once an expert system opportunity has been identified, there are a few preliminaries to undertake before actual development of the rule set begins (Holsapple and Whinston 1986). For the most part, these involve the normal managerial actions that precede most projects: specifying objectives and planning how to meet them. For small problems, the manager may do all this rather quickly and even informally. For a major development effort, greater detail and formality in accordance with the organization's customary project management methods are usually advisable.

OBJECTIVES

From the outset it is a good idea to be clear about what the proposed expert system will and will not do. One way to begin is by characterizing the organizational setting within which the expert system will be used. The developer should give a clear statement of the expert system's purpose within that setting. What kind of problem will it solve (e.g., sales representative names)? How fast must a typical consultation be if it is to be of value to a user? What style of user interface is appropriate? How "good" must the expert system's advice be? Why is the expert system being constructed (e.g., for better, more timely, or less expensive decision support)? What is its expected benefit? In view of these benefits, how much is it reasonable to spend for the expert system's construction and ongoing operation? When must it be ready for operation? Will it be an ad hoc or institutional system? The developer should include answers to these kinds of questions in a statement of objectives. They will form a basis for planning and later evaluation.

PLANNING

Planning identifies resources that will be needed to construct the desired expert system. It prescribes a flow of actions that will use those resources to meet the objectives. It establishes a budget for the construction project. For small problems, you can produce the development plan quickly. Larger problems typically require greater planning effort.

Resources that are essential for expert system construction include an expert, a developer, a development tool, and a host computer. You should select each in light of overall objectives, and together they should be compatible with each other. You should probably select the specific resources in the given order—the expert first, the developer next, the tool, and, finally, the host computer.

Choosing an Expert   The chosen expert must be both able and willing to participate in the development process on a continuing basis. Choosing an expert who is uninterested in or feels threatened by the proposed expert system will inevitably result in the failure of the entire project. You must make it clear to the expert that the proposed expert system will contribute to the productivity of coworkers. It may be regarded as an extension of the expert, leveraging his or her expertise and increasing personal productivity. You may need to offer additional incentives to ensure expert cooperation. For some projects, a group of experts might be necessary. You might use a book or document as the source of expertise about a problem area.

Choosing a Developer   Ideally, the developer should already have some familiarity with the expert system's problem area. The developer and the expert may very well be the same person. At any rate, they should be capable of maintaining a good working rapport with each other. For large problems, a team of developers may be

---

ESSENTIAL RESOURCES FOR EXPERT SYSTEM DEVELOPMENT

- Expert
- Developer (knowledge engineer)
- Development tool
- Host computer

warranted, allowing parallel development of various aspects of a rule set. Different developers might work on various rule sets that are consulted by a primary rule set. Some developers may work exclusively on the user interface cosmetics, on procedural models used by the rule set, and so forth. Those who are involved with acquiring reasoning knowledge from experts are often called **knowledge engineers.**

All else being equal, an experienced developer is preferable to an inexperienced one, but the developer may or may not have formal training as a knowledge engineer. An appreciation of conventional knowledge-management techniques is also very helpful for building artificially intelligent DSSs. These techniques are just as concerned as AI techniques with the engineering of knowledge.

Regardless of the extent of training and experience, there are several basic traits that good rule set developers have. They are talented designers and investigators. They pay attention to details. They are skilled at self-expression, interpersonal relationships, and interviewing techniques. Above all, a good developer has a positive attitude toward learning, with both a willingness and ability to be an inquisitive, fast-learning student or apprentice of the expert.

Choosing a Development Tool Selecting a development tool for the proposed expert system is also an important decision. The tool should fit the developer and the problem area. In practice, it is a good idea to select a development tool that can be used repeatedly for building a variety of expert systems. Purchasing and learning five different tools for five different expert systems is a more expensive and time-consuming proposition than using the same tool for building all five systems. This situation, of course, implies that the tool should be flexible and versatile. It may well have many features that are not pertinent to a particular expert system development effort, but these features may be essential for later development efforts and enhancements.

TOOL SELECTION

Criteria for tool selection fall into several major categories:

1. *Rule set characteristics:* How much flexibility and power does a tool provide for representing reasoning knowledge?
2. *Rule set building:* What facilities does the tool provide for constructing, testing, and revising a rule set?
3. *Consultation traits:* To what extent can an inference engine's consultation behavior be controlled or adjusted, and what is the nature of the environment within which it can be invoked?
4. *Integration:* What additional knowledge-management techniques are integrated into the tool, and what is the nature of that integration?
5. *Vendor support:* What is the history of the tool's vendor, and what services does it provide to the tool's adopters?
6. *Performance:* Will the tool perform satisfactorily (e.g., in terms of inference speed) for the intended applications?
7. *Pricing:* What is the cost of purchasing the tool and of using it on a continuing basis?

Researchers have published detailed guidelines to consider when selecting a development tool for expert decision support systems (Holsapple and Whinston 1987). Perhaps the most important factor to keep in mind is that the tool should enhance a developer's productivity by providing natural ways of representing knowledge. Regardless of what a developer wants to represent, the ideal tool allows the representation to be accomplished in a direct, straightforward manner. It should not be an obstacle course that tests the developer's ingenuity at overcoming its limitations. It might help to consider whether the tool would be able conveniently to handle the relatively modest quota advisory expert system presented in Chapter 13. This example is quite typical of what we should expect to encounter in developing a business expert system.

Choosing the Computer   Finally, you need to select a computer for development needs, including both the hardware and operating system. Obviously, the chosen computer must be one that accommodates the selected development tool. To the extent that it supports other software, it may have additional value beyond the scope of expert system development. Remember that you will need to install additional units of the development machine (or one that is compatible with it) at every site where the expert system will eventually be used. If a tool works with a variety of machines, then the resultant expert system could be used on different computers at different sites.

Planning the Use of Resources   Having identified the resources that will be used for expert system construction, a plan for using them can begin to take shape. Planning involves establishing milestones for the development project and setting target times for reaching each of them. The time to develop a rule set depends very much on the nature, size, and scope of the problem area. It also depends heavily on the resources that have been selected. All else being equal, faster development times should result from a powerful and flexible development tool, an actively cooperative expert, a seasoned developer, and so on. The plan of action should be accompanied by a budget for expenditures on resources during the life of the development project. Both the timing and budget for the project should satisfy the objectives specified earlier.

A plan may involve several phases. At the end of each phase, you should evaluate the progress in meeting the objectives. If the development during a phase is satisfactory, the work proceeds to the next phase. You may adjust or flesh out the plan for the next phase in more detail before work actually begins. If you do not complete a phase in a satisfactory manner, you may need to revise substantially the plans for subsequent phases or even terminate the entire project.

Prototyping   The initial phase of a plan, especially for a large or expensive project, is usually a **feasibility study.** The intent is to gain some relatively quick confirmation that the selected resources will work for constructing an expert system for the target problem area. The centerpiece of this study is a working **prototype,** which is a bare-bones expert system, having a subset of the capabilities envisioned for the full-fledged expert system. In the case of Jack's expert system, a prototype might have been developed first that gave quota recommendations based only on the base amount and product factors. Or the rules shown in Figure 13.3 might be considered as the prototype for a more refined ADVISOR rule set involving still other factors that Jack considers pertinent to giving quota advice.

In any event, the prototype concentrates on some subset of the project's objectives. If this subset cannot be developed in fairly short order, the reason will usually become obvious during the prototyping experience. One or more of the resources will be inadequate for developing the desired expert system, or there will be some mismatch or incompatibility among the selected resources. In such a situation, you should reconsider the selected resources and make necessary changes. If it is not feasible to make the needed changes, then you might abandon the project or revise its objectives to conform with available resources.

Not only is prototype development an inexpensive trial run for highlighting glitches (if any) in the plan, it is an important part of selling the overall development plan to management (Drenth and Morris 1992). Solid managerial backing of the project is essential for eventual success of an expert system. Rapid development of a prototype that addresses some interesting subset of the problem area can give fairly compelling evidence that shows support for the project is warranted. Demonstrations of prototypes should convey a sense of what expert systems are, highlight their potential benefits, and instill confidence in their practicality.

Through its suggestion of technical feasibility, a prototype can help gain project approval, but this by itself is not sufficient. In addition, the project objectives must be clearly presented. The remaining phase(s) of the plan must be well conceived vis-à-vis the objectives. Economic feasibility needs to be shown by detailing why and how the benefits that would result from meeting the objectives justify the costs identified in the plan's budget.

14.4 THE DEVELOPMENT PROCESS

Once a plan has been accepted, actual development can begin. A typical cycle of activities recurs repeatedly during the development of a rule set (Holsapple and Whinston 1986). As shown in Figure 14.1, this cycle consists of several stages: study, problem definition, rule set specification, expert testing, interface construction, user testing, and installation. These stages are the major considerations facing a rule set developer, but they are not engraved in stone. Novice developers may want to follow them fairly closely, whereas experienced developers can adapt them to suit their own needs and tastes.

FIGURE 14.1   Stages in a Development Cycle

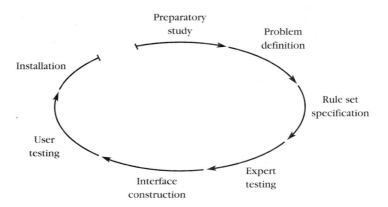

Each iteration through the **development cycle** results in a more complete realization of the expert system than the former iteration. You may think of each iteration as corresponding to a phase in the project's overall plan. Even the construction of a prototype normally consists of an iteration through the development cycle. Thus the development of a rule set tends to be incremental and evolutionary in nature. Put together, repeated iterations through the development cycle form the development spiral shown in Figure 14.2. Each iteration builds and expands on the result of the prior iteration, broadening the rule set's scope and more nearly approaching the overall project objectives. As the spiral grows, these objectives may themselves grow (or change), based on what is gleaned from the development experience. Due to the dynamic nature of certain problem areas, a final expert system may never be reached. Objectives can be open-ended, allowing the expert system to grow perpetually.

Rule set development is a learning process for the developer and should be approached with an experimental, investigating spirit. The developer is out to explore the mind of the expert, to discover what the expert knows, and to understand the expert's reasoning behavior. Typically, the expert's reasoning knowledge has not previously been formalized. It exists informally and may never have been systematically scrutinized before—not even by the expert. Therefore, rule set development is a process of formalizing the informal, of making the implicit explicit. A developer, then, is a student, a transformer, a designer, and an organizer. He or she grasps the heretofore unseen and gives it a form that is understandable to an inference engine. In developing a rule set, the developer documents expertise. This rule set document is then used by an inference engine in solving problems.

14.5 STUDY AND PROBLEM DEFINITION

A developer begins by doing his or her homework. Before interrogating the expert, the developer should get acquainted with the problem area and its terminology. First-hand familiarity with prospective users should also be acquired, as well as an appreciation of the circumstances in which the expert system will be consulted. Finally, the developer should have an understanding of the knowledge-representation methods supported by the chosen tool.

After this preparatory study, the next stage in a development cycle is to meet with the expert for the purpose of jointly defining the problem domain that will be addressed. This **problem definition** must, of course, be consistent with the project's objectives and plan. It should also be quite detailed. It identifies the variable (or variables) that will serve as the expert system's goal. The problem definition provides a very specific characterization of those problems that the expert system should be able to solve. One way to create this characterization is to come up with a representative series of sample consultation problems. These problems may be actual consultation problems that the expert has previously handled or hypothetical problems that the expert considers to be typical or those encountered in the problem domain. For the ADVISOR rule set, this process could involve a sampling of specified quota-setting problems from various regions using different sales representatives and product lines.

FIGURE 14.2 The Development Spiral

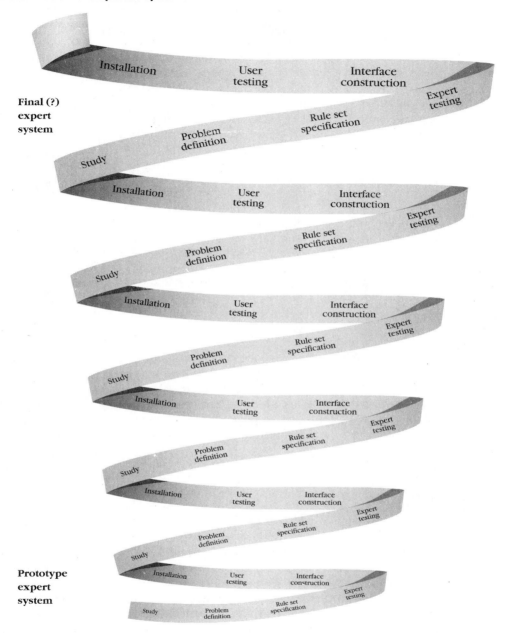

14.6 RULE SET SPECIFICATION

The problem definition stage begins to give the developer an appreciation of the kinds of inputs that the expert system will need for reasoning as well as the kinds of output that should result from the reasoning. The third stage of a development cycle involves the actual specification of rules that can transform inputs into desired outputs. Because the rule set–specification stage involves acquiring reasoning knowledge from an expert and representing it in a computer-usable way, it is the heart of *knowledge acquisition*. The preparatory phases of study and problem definition, plus the follow-up phase of expert testing, may also be regarded as being parts of knowledge acquisition.

The phenomenon of knowledge acquisition always occurs in a particular context and involves a particular process (Holsapple, Raj, and Wagner 1993). The context and process can vary widely from one expert system development effort to another. However, certain context and process factors are always present in knowledge acquisition—regardless of their variations. Following an overview of knowledge acquisition, including its general context and process factors, we offer a few practical guidelines to govern rule set specification.

KNOWLEDGE ACQUISITION

The **knowledge-acquisition** (KA) **process** involves the elicitation, analysis, and interpretation of knowledge used by a human expert in solving a particular problem, plus the subsequent transformation of that knowledge into a computer-usable representation (Kidd 1987). It involves obtaining, structuring, and formalizing the knowledge of experts (Breuker and Wielinga 1987). Knowledge acquisition is a complex phenomenon having many diverse facets.

Various frameworks have been advanced to assist in organizing and structuring an understanding of KA. Some are concerned with prescribing a sequence of steps that rule set development should follow when performing knowledge acquisition. Others prescribe the type of KA approach to select in varying situations. Here, we briefly consider examples of both development-oriented and selection-oriented frameworks (Holsapple and Wagner 1993) as a prelude to examining the more general framework of KA context and process factors.

Steps in Knowledge Acquisition   One kind of development-oriented KA framework takes a systems analysis perspective. For example, Figure 14.3 shows one process (Tuthill 1990). Observe that this process is iterative. Its first two steps, plus steps 7 and 8, are very broad descriptions of what happens during the rule set–specification stage in the development cycle of Figure 14.1. Steps 3–6 broadly describe what happens during the **expert testing** stage. Most interesting, perhaps, is the loop that indicates an iteration between the rule set specification and expert testing until the rule set is deemed to be satisfactory.

Some development-oriented frameworks organize steps into phases (e.g., McGraw and Harbison-Briggs 1989; Liou 1990). For example, KA has been characterized in terms of four phases called planning, extraction, analysis, and verification (Liou 1990). The steps in these phases are as follows:

Planning
1. Understand the problem domain.
2. Identify domain expert(s) and user(s).
3. Define the problem scope.
4. Identify the type of application.
5. Develop process models.
6. Plan KA sessions.

FIGURE 14.3   A Systems Analysis Framework for Knowledge Acquisition

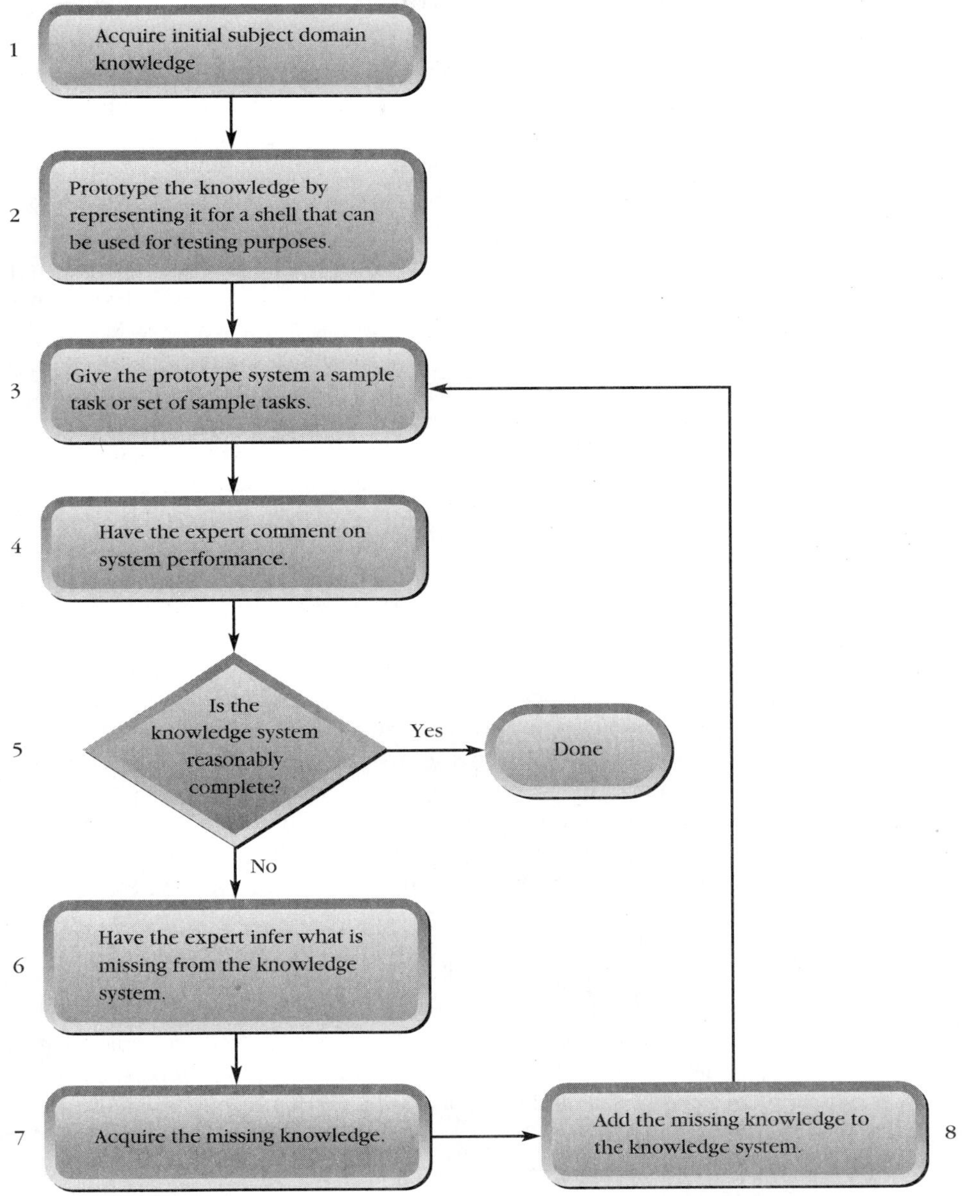

Extraction
  7. Explain the KA approach to the expert(s).
  8. Conduct KA sessions following the approach.
  9. Debrief experts on their views of the sessions.

Analysis
  10. Analyze KA session outputs.
  11. Represent acquired knowledge.

Verification
12. Develop test scenarios.
13. Verify knowledge with experts.

Unlike the framework in Figure 14.3, this one views KA as encompassing the study (step 1) and problem definition (steps 3 and 12) stages of the development cycles in Figure 14.1. These steps are mixed with initial planning activities (e.g., steps 2 and 4–6) that precede the development cycles in Figure 14.1. This framework breaks the rule set–specification stage into two phases: extraction and analysis. It also encompasses the expert testing stage via step 13.

Selection of Knowledge-Acquisition Methods   Selection-oriented frameworks are very different in that they identify a set of **knowledge-acquisition methods** and then indicate which should be used for various KA situations. A knowledge-acquisition method is simply a means of directing an expert's attempts at divulging reasoning knowledge. Two of the most prominent KA methods are known as **interviewing** and **protocol analysis** (Hayes-Roth, Waterman, and Lenat 1983; Hart 1986; Tuthill 1990). Although there are others, we focus on these two.

With the interviewing method, a knowledge engineer plays the role of an interviewer. Iteration with an expert amounts to an interview in which the knowledge engineer attempts to learn an expert's reasoning knowledge by asking relevant questions and recording the expert's answers. Interviews can be highly structured, involving a predefined series of questions. Or, they can be more open-ended, allowing the knowledge engineer to pursue unanticipated lines of questioning stimulated by an expert's responses. Within the scope of KA for developing an expert system, many interviews can occur. As development proceeds, interviews may tend to become more structured and focused (McGraw and Harbison-Briggs 1989).

An alternative KA method is protocol analysis (Ericsson and Simon 1984). In this approach, a knowledge engineer observes as the expert solves problems like those that the intended expert system should solve. The knowledge engineer prods the expert to think aloud and to explicitly describe his or her reasoning throughout the problem-solving exercise. The knowledge engineer records the expert's protocols (i.e., behaviors) and subsequently analyzes them in the course of transforming them into rules that an inference engine can process.

A knowledge-acquisition process can include mixed usage of interviewing and protocol analysis. Whatever the mix, the knowledge engineer typically analyzes and structures knowledge gleaned as a means of discovering gaps or inconsistencies in what has been learned. Such shortfalls are then remedied by further targeted use of KA methods, until the knowledge engineer has learned enough about the expert's reasoning to specify a set of rules. In the process shown in Figure 14.3, KA methods are employed in steps 2 and 7. They are employed in step 8 of the 13-step process.

Regardless of whether a knowledge engineer adheres to the steps in Figure 14.3, the 13 steps, or another sequence of KA steps, there is the issue of what KA method(s) to employ when interacting with an expert. Selection-oriented frameworks attempt to answer that question. For example, one such framework distinguishes among KA applications in terms of such characteristics as problem size and complexity (Kim and Courtney 1988). It then prescribes which KA method should be used for small, large, complex, or simple reasoning problems. Researchers have only just begun to study such prescriptions under controlled experimental conditions (Burton et al. 1987; Holsapple and Raj 1994). Although early results from these studies indicate differing levels of effectiveness or efficiency for distinct KA methods, under varying circumstances, such as simple versus complex problem domains, they do not yet allow us to make conclusive prescriptions.

Although development-oriented and selection-oriented frameworks of knowledge acquisition touch on some KA aspects and possibilities, they do not give us a full overview of knowledge acquisition. There is a phenomenon-oriented framework that endeavors to identify the key considerations influencing the conduct and outcome of knowledge acquisition (Holsapple and Wagner 1995a, 1995b). According to this framework, an understanding of knowledge acquisition depends on understanding both the KA context and the KA process. Here, we briefly review highlights of these two major aspects of knowledge acquisition.

Knowledge-Acquisition Context   **Knowledge-acquisition context** refers to the environment within which knowledge acquisition occurs. As such, it facilitates, conditions, and constrains KA processes. Knowledge acquisition can be understood in terms of the organization context, immediate context, and project context (Holsapple and Wagner 1995a).

The organizational context can be understood in terms of managerial support, prior experience, organization design, and technological culture (Dhaliwal and Benbasat 1990). Management support refers to the extent of commitment and organizational resources furnished by the organization for a particular expert system project, including material, financial, human, and knowledge resources. Prior experience refers to an organization's past efforts at knowledge acquisition. It is characterized in terms of the number of expert systems developed, the type of each (e.g., predictive versus diagnostic, simple versus complex), the RA methods used, and the outcomes for each of these methods. With respect to organization design, the structure and size of an organization can affect the nature of knowledge sources available and the ways in which a knowledge engineer can interact with them. Technological culture refers to the degree to which new technology is readily learned and incorporated into the operations and planning of an organization. All foregoing organizational context factors can influence what happens in the conduct of knowledge acquisition.

The immediate context of KA is concerned with characteristics of the physical environs within which knowledge acquisition happens. For instance, if an expert perceives the KA surroundings to be sterile, cramped, or uncomfortable, then the quality of knowledge acquired may suffer. In some cases, such as when protocol analysis is used, a knowledge engineer may need to reproduce the problem-solving environment so that it "feels right" to an expert.

Project context is somewhat of a middle ground between the organizational context and the immediate context of knowledge acquisition. A project involves the plan, resources, and activities devoted to developing a particular expert system. Knowledge acquisition is influenced by the project within which it occurs. One way to think about this influence is in terms of project objectives and project constraints (Holsapple and Wagner 1995a). As we have seen, some project objectives are concerned with the technical performance of a system (e.g., system response-time objectives), whereas others are task performance objectives (e.g., making recommendations of a certain quality). Both can influence the way in which a knowledge engineer conducts knowledge-acquisition activities.

Project constraints are concerned with the financial, temporal, and participant resources available. Because some KA approaches may be more costly or time consuming than others, a project's budget and schedule are important contextual influences on knowledge acquisition. A project also defines who will participate in a KA process and what roles each will play. The capabilities and interactions of these persons go a long way toward shaping the outcome of knowledge acquisition and should be taken into account when selecting KA methods or structuring KA processes.

Knowledge-Acquisition Process   A **knowledge-acquisition process** links together elements existing in the available KA context. It consists of a sequence— or perhaps even a parallel pattern—of episodes governed by a set of process regulations (Holsapple and Wagner 1995b). In the simplest case, an entire KA process may be regarded as a KA episode. Or, it could be viewed as a sequence of three episodes, such as knowledge elicitation, structuring, and representation. From another perspective, each application of a KA method can be regarded as an episode. For example, initial KA episodes may be unstructured interviews, followed by episodes using structured interviews or protocol analysis. Even certain activities within the use of a KA method could be regarded as an episode.

Whatever episode perspective is adopted, it is important for a knowledge engineer to be clear about the kinds of episodes that will occur in an unfolding KA process. In addition, the knowledge engineer needs to be clear about the process regulations that govern the execution of KA episodes within a KA process. These regulations include initiation conditions, termination conditions, and activity regulations. Initiation conditions specify what circumstances must exist before an initial episode in a KA process can commence. It may be the arrival of an appointed time, the availability of certain resources, or a collection of more specific conditions related to a prospective KA method. Similarly, termination conditions determine when the KA process ends. A developer must be aware of both the initiation and termination conditions for the specific KA process in which he or she will engage.

An awareness about activity regulations that determine how the KA episodes can unfold must also exist. They may require that structured interview episodes precede protocol analysis episodes, that certain episodes proceed in parallel, or simply that episodes unfold at the discretion of the knowledge engineer. The guidelines that we now offer for rule set specification are activity regulations that prescribe the following: Episodes for identifying variables and their interdependencies must occur before episodes for determining rules, which must precede episodes for specifying initialization and completion sequences.

GUIDELINES FOR RULE SET SPECIFICATION

We conclude our consideration of knowledge acquisition with a few guidelines for specifying a rule set. First, two basic strategies for guiding a knowledge-acquisition process are discussed. These strategies are examples of activity regulations. Second, we propose a sequence of activities to follow in the specification of a rule set. Each activity is discussed in detail. It suggests that variables be identified first, that their interdependencies then be recognized, that these interdependencies be used to structure the discovery of rules, and that specification of initialization and completion sequences then take place.

One strategy for knowledge elicitation is to concentrate on one sample problem at a time. This strategy is inherent in protocol analysis. If it is used for the interview KA method, the developer's style and line of questioning should encourage the expert to explain in detail how and why the solution is derived for that problem—in a spirit similar to an expert system user invoking HOW and WHY commands (Chapter 13) to examine the line of reasoning employed during a consultation. In either case, the developer then translates the expert's explanations into specifications of the reasoning knowledge (i.e., rules) needed to solve the sample problem. Next, the developer and expert focus on another sample problem, enlarging and generalizing the existing rule set to handle this new case as well. This incremental approach continues until the rule set handles all problems defined in the previous stage of the development cycle.

Another strategy is to specify directly needed reasoning knowledge without considering the samples one after another. Instead, the developer's line of questioning in an interview might try to elicit general reasoning principles or patterns from the expert. This reasoning knowledge is general in the sense that it is applicable to the problem domain as a whole. The sample problems drawn from that domain can be used in the developer-expert interchanges to illustrate the general rules that are being explained and specified. This process continues until the developer and expert agree that sufficient rules have been specified to handle the defined problem domain.

Regardless of whether a developer is working on discerning rules for a specific sample problem or for the problem domain as a whole, he or she is confronted with the issue of sequencing the knowledge-acquisition activities. For instance, if conducting interviews, what should the developer ask about first? One interrogation strategy might be described as random—posing whatever questions happen to come to mind in the course of discussions with the expert. Such wandering may be fine for getting acquainted with the expert but is ill advised once serious rule specification work has begun. It is likely to result in gaps and to require frequently recovering the same ground. A more structured approach could conceivably begin in various places. Its first questions might be directed toward acquiring an under-

KNOWLEDGE ACQUISITION AND LEARNING

Interestingly, the incremental and direct strategies for guiding a knowledge-acquisition process mirror two popular approaches to learning within management schools: the case study method and the systemic method. In the former, learning is accomplished by working through specific cases that have been chosen to be representative of common situations. Generalizations to other situations may be made based on what is gleaned from specific cases. In the latter approach to learning, the student works at understanding a system of ideas (e.g., a theory) or techniques (e.g., mathematical modeling) that are generally applicable to numerous situations. For illustration and reinforcement, the relatively abstract system may be examined in the contexts of specific situations. Just as both learning methods can be applied in the same curriculum, a mix of the two specification strategies could be used by the developer. The approach taken depends on the knowledge-acquisition context (e.g., nature of the problem domain and the inclinations of the developer and expert).

standing sufficient for specifying the rule set's initialization sequence, or it might begin by asking questions that allow the rules to be specified before the initialization or completion sequences.

Discovering the Variables   Of the several possibilities, we here explore an approach that begins with rule set variables. The developer pursues a sequence of episodes aimed at discovering the variables that will ultimately be referenced by the rules, initialization sequence, and completion sequence. These variables include goal variables, input variables, and intermediate variables. From the preparatory study and problem-definition stages, the developer already has an inkling of the kinds of variables that will be needed. Rather than directly asking the expert to name all variables, the developer asks the expert questions such as: what kinds of things do you like to know about when you begin to ponder a problem? What facts or hypotheses do you try to establish when thinking about a problem? What are the factors that influence how you reason about a problem? Does this factor depend on other factors? If so, which ones?

Each factor that an expert identifies is recorded, because it will probably become a variable referenced in the rule set. For instance, when developing the ADVISOR rule set, Jack may have asked himself what factors he considers when setting a quota. He would have answered with questions such as, Who is the sales representative? What is the product line? How well did the representative perform last year for this product line? Is the product line strong or weak? How much local advertising is there? What is the economic outlook? Each of these factors led to at least one corresponding variable in the ADVISOR rule set: REP; PROD; QUOTA and SALES; STRING, WEAK, PFACTOR; LOCALADS; and ECONOMY. Notice that sales representative performance led to the QUOTA and SALES variables, which together characterize performance. Alternatively, a PERFORMANCE variable could have been designated. When Jack then asked himself on what an assessment of performance depends, he would have thought of the two additional factors of quota and sales levels.

It may turn out that not all variables identified in this way are used in the eventual rule set. Conversely, some additional variables may need to be specified later if the expert has overlooked some factors. In any event, the initial identification of pertinent variables is a good basis for later talking about and specifying rules. Variables furnish the basic raw materials for actually specifying each rule.

As an expert identifies each factor, the developer invents a corresponding variable name, which should be reasonably descriptive of the factor described by the expert. No two variables should be given the same name. Before proceeding to the next factor, it is worthwhile to quiz the expert about the nature of the variable. What type of values can it have? What range of values is permissible? From what source(s) could the variable's value be acquired—a rule or rules, a database, a solver, a spreadsheet, the user, a remote computer system, a computation, or a consultation? That is, where would the expert turn to get its value during a consultation?

When is the variable's value established, before a consultation begins, during the initialization, in the course of reasoning, or after the reasoning? Is the variable's value usually known to the expert before any reasoning actually happens, or might it be unknown? Is the factor (i.e., variable) needed for solving all (or nearly all) problems within the defined problem domain, or is it needed only for some problems but not for others? For practical purposes, does the expert assume that a value for this variable is known with certainty, or does the expert sometimes ascribe some degree of uncertainty to a value? Does the variable always have only one value at a time, or does the expert sometimes conceive of it as having several possible values at the same time? The latter two possibilities are described in Chapter 15.

Variable specification forms similar to those shown in Figures 14.4 and 14.5 are useful in keeping track of the expert's characterization of each variable. They also serve as handy reminders of the kinds of questions a developer should ask the expert for each variable that is invented.

As a further design aid, **dependency diagrams** such as the one shown in Figure 14.6 can be helpful in visualizing relationships among variables. For instance, this dependency diagram shows that ECONOMY can depend on GROWTH and UNEMPLOYMENT. In turn, ECONOMY can lead to values for EFACTOR and LAFACTOR. To construct a dependency diagram, a left-to-right approach is recommended. First, we write a variable for a goal factor (e.g., NEWQUOTA) and then decide on what factors this goal might depend. The answer allows us to write variables for additional factors (e.g., BASE, EFACTOR, etc.), each pointing to the goal. The process is then repeated for each of the newly specified variables, and so on. In the resulting diagram, each variable that depends on other variables necessitates one or more rules for establishing its value.

Discovering the Rules   Having reached an understanding of the variables that will be referenced in a rule set, the developer's KA episodes can turn to the rules. The variable specification forms give good clues about what questions should be asked. In Figure 14.5, for instance, notice that the BASE variable's value is set (by a computation) during the reasoning portion of a consultation. In other words, one or more rules need to be specified to indicate the reasoning an expert uses to establish a value for the BASE variable. From Figure 14.5, the developer should expect the expert's explanation to be contingent on sales and quota levels. The developer transforms the expert's conversational explanations into rules R1 and R2:

FIGURE 14.4   Variable Specification Form for a Single Variable

Variable name: SALES
Description: The amount of a product line actually sold by a rep in particular quarter.
Type of values? ____✓____ Numeric _____ String _____ Logical
Size of values: _____
Range of values: __0–100,000__
Value can be uncertain? ____✓____ No _____Yes
Maximum values at a time: 1
Source of values?   _____ User   _____ Statistical analysis
                             ____✓____ Database   _____ Computational expression
                             _____ Spreadsheet   _____ Assignment
                             _____ Model   _____ Remote communication
                             _____ Consultation   _____ External file/external program
Status when reasoning begins: _____ Unknown ____✓____ Known
Value established?   ____✓____ Before consultation begins
                             _____ During consultation's initialization sequence
                             _____ During consultation's reasoning with rules
                             _____ During consultation's completion sequence
Depends on other variables? none

FIGURE 14.5   Variable Specification Form for Multiple Variables

Variable Name	Type Num	Type Str	Type Log	Size	Range	CF N	CF Y	Values (max)	Source User	Source SpSh	Source DB	Source Model	Source Comp	Source Assn	Source Comm	Source Ext	Init U	Init K	Value Set Pre	Value Set Int	Value Set RComp	Depends on
BASE	✓				0 to 2,000,000	✓		1					✓				✓				✓	SALES QUOTA
SALES	✓				0 to 200,000	✓		1			✓							✓		✓		
QUOTA	✓				0 to 200,000	✓		1			✓							✓		✓		
PFACTOR	✓				-0.5 to 0.5	✓		1					✓					✓		✓		PROD OLDTITLES NEWTITLES
LOCALADS	✓				0 to 5,000	✓		1		✓							✓				✓	
PROD		✓		12	Products	✓		1	✓									✓		✓		
REP		✓		10	Valid reps	✓		1	✓									✓		✓		
NEWQUOTA	✓				0 to 250,000	✓		1				✓					✓				✓	BASE EFACTOR LFACTOR WEAK STRONG RISE FALL
ECONOMY		✓		4	good, fair, poor	✓		1						✓			✓					GROWTH UNEMPLOY-MENT
GROWTH	✓				-0.5 to 0.5	✓		1						✓				✓		✓		
STRONG			✓			✓		1					✓				✓				✓	PROD

FIGURE 14.6   A Dependency Diagram for ADVISOR

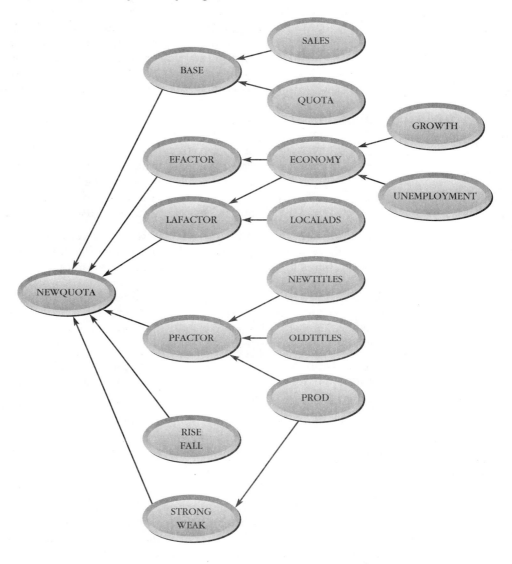

EXPLOITING INTEGRATION

As an interesting exercise, a development tool's forms management and database-management facilities could be used to keep track of variables during the development process. Rather than filling in a paper form, the developer would fill in a comparable electronic form on the console screen—with the information being automatically stored in a database. Alternatively, a tool's facilities for incorporating variable descriptions within a rule set (e.g., within a menu-oriented rule set builder) give a somewhat similar effect.

```
RULE: R1
      IF: SALES > 1.15 * QUOTA
      THEN: BASE = QUOTA + (SALES - 1.15 * QUOTA)
      REASON:  In cases where the sales for this product
               exceeded the quota by more than 15%, the
               base amount for the new quota is set to the
               past quota plus the excess sales amount.

RULE: R2
      IF: SALES <= 1.15 * QUOTA
      THEN: BASE = QUOTA
      REASON:  The base amount for the new quota is the
               same as the past quota because this
               product's sales did not exceed that past
               quota by more than 15%.
```

The reason specified with each rule may well be a verbatim or paraphrased rendition of the expert's explanation. This process can be repeated for each variable whose value is to be set during the reasoning portion of a consultation.

In looking at the Reas (reasoning) column under the heading Value Set in Figure 14.5, the developer might next ask how the expert reasons about the product factor (PFACTOR). As each rule is specified, the developer should ask the expert whether there are other conclusions implied by the rule's premise. For instance, when the rule

```
IF: PROD IN ["computer","romance","scifi"]
THEN: PFACTOR = (NEWTITLES + OLDTITLES)/OLDTITLES - 1
```

is first specified, the developer might ask if there are any other conclusions that can be drawn about the computer, romance, and science fiction product lines. The expert would reply that these are strong, not weak, product lines. The developer would then specify two additional actions in the rule's conclusion, yielding Rule R13:

```
RULE: R13
      COMMENT:  The premise of this rule will need to be
                changed when additional product lines
                become strong or when the product lines
                shown are no longer strong.
      IF: PROD IN ["computer", "romance", "scifi"]
      THEN: PFACTOR = {NEWTITLES + OLDTITLES)/OLDTITLES - 1
            STRONG = TRUE
            WEAK = FALSE
```

Notice that in addition to its premise and conclusion, this rendition of rule R13 also contains a **rule comment.** A tool may allow the developer to optionally specify a comment for any rule in the rule set. Rule comments are ignored by the inference engine and are never seen by end users. A comment is visible when working on the rule with a rule set builder. It is used to document the rule in some way, such as providing an explanation of why the rule is specified the way it is or a reminder of what things to consider if the rule needs to be modified.

When extra actions are put into a conclusion, the developer should recheck the premise with the expert to be sure that its truth is sufficient to imply that all of the conclusion's actions be taken. This is clearly the case for R13, but think about how rule R4 might have come into being. Suppose that when the expert explains how the local advertising factor is determined, the rule

```
IF: ECONOMY = "fair" AND KNOWN("LOCALADS")
THEN: LAFACTOR = LOCALADS/120000
```

is specified by the developer. As a follow-up question, the developer asks whether there are any other implications of a fair economy. The expert replies that the economic factor should be set at one third of the growth rate in such a situation. The developer expands the conclusion to be

```
THEN: EFACTOR = GROWTH/3;LAFACTOR = LOCALADS/120000
```

However, this conclusion is incorrect unless the premise is also expanded to indicate that the GROWTH variable must be known before the conclusion's actions could be taken. The correct specification is

```
RULE: R4
      IF: ECONOMY = "fair" AND KNOWN("LOCALADS") AND
          KNOWN("GROWTH)
      THEN: FACTOR = GROWTH/3;LAFACTOR = LOCALADS/120000
```

By the time the expert has explained the reasoning for each variable whose value can be set after initialization and prior to completion, the developer will have specified the rule set's rules (and variable descriptions, if any). Some developers may want to elicit the rules in a *top-down* fashion, beginning first with rules that affect the goal variable (e.g., NEWQUOTA), proceeding to rules that affect variables in the premises of rules for the goal, and so forth. Other developers may prefer to discover rules in a *bottom-up* fashion, beginning with rules for variables (e.g., BASE) that depend on other variables whose values are known when reasoning begins, proceeding to rules for variables that depend on other variables for which rules have just been specified, and so forth.

Initialization and Completion Sequences   After the variable descriptions and rules have been specified, the developer constructs the rule set's initialization sequence.

GUIDELINES FOR RULE SET SPECIFICATION

1. First, clarify the factors involved in reasoning. These become variables in the rule set. Specify a variable description for each and specify the rule set's default goal.
2. Identify dependencies that exist among the factors. These can be illustrated in a dependency diagram.
3. Use the dependency diagram to guide systematically the elicitation of rules, where each rule explicitly captures certain dependencies that exist among variables.
4. Construct the initialization and completion sequences to be consistent with the variable descriptions and rules.

Here, all variables that should be unknown before the reasoning begins are explicitly assigned the UNKNOWN value. Furthermore, appropriate commands are included for all variables whose values are to be set in the initialization sequence (see the Init (initialization) column under the Value Set heading in Figure 14.5). For variables involving input from a user, elaborate prompting and screen cosmetics are unnecessary at this stage of the development cycle. Similarly, when the completion sequence is specified, an elaborate presentation of results is not yet needed. The completion actions are the final aspect of rule set specification.

The rule set can be compiled when the initialization and completion sequences have been specified. Any errors detected by the rule set builder's compiler should be corrected. Any warning messages about possible errors or inconsistencies should also be heeded. Once the rule set is successfully compiled, the expert system will be ready for expert testing.

14.7 EXPERT TESTING

In this stage of the development cycle, an expert tests the expertise that has been captured in a rule set. The developer normally sits with the expert during this testing stage. Together they consult the expert system, with the expert critiquing the system's reasoning behavior, advice, and explanations. They are on the lookout for indications that the rule set may be inaccurate, incomplete, or inconsistent. The sample problems produced in the cycle's problem definition stage should offer a good set of consultation **test cases.** If the expert agrees that the expert system offers sufficiently good and timely advice with respect to project objectives, then the developer goes on to the next stage. Otherwise, the rule set needs to be modified.

Suppose the expert believes that the expert system's advice is invalid for some consultations. Who is right, the expert or the expert system? What is the cause of this apparent discrepancy between the expert system's advice and the advice that the expert would have given? How can the developer determine where the inference engine began to go off track? Once the answers to these questions are known, the developer can make corrections to the rule set and again work through test cases with the expert. There are at least three methods that could be used to answer such questions: a query to the inference engine for an explanation, automatic tracing of the reasoning process, and customized tracing.

HOW AND WHY REVIEW

The first method makes use of the HOW and WHY types of commands introduced in Chapter 13 (recall Figure 13.11). By using these commands, the developer and expert can examine the line of reasoning that was used for the sample problem. The expert can either agree or disagree with how a particular variable's value was determined or why a particular rule was fired. If there is disagreement, then one or more of the rules may need to be altered. The HOW and WHY commands help identify sources of disagreement and targets for alteration.

Using a HOW command, the expert may see that a rule was fired that should not have been fired. The expert and developer should examine this rule's premise for errors and oversights. The premise may need to be adjusted by changing its existing conditions or incorporating new conditions into it. For instance, if Jack had forgotten to include the GROWTH>=.04 condition in R6's premise, rule R6 would sometimes fire when it really should not. By seeing that R6 fired when it should not have, Jack is alerted to the fact that its premise is incomplete. The rule set manager is then used to add the omitted condition, yielding the R6 rule shown in Figure 13.3.

If the expert believes that the premise is correct, then at least one of the variables in the premise must have received an unexpected value; otherwise, the rule would not have been fired. A WHY command lets the developer and expert see what values of the premise's variables allowed the rule to be fired. To see how a variable with an unexpected value received that value, a HOW command is used for that variable. It shows the rule or rules that led to the unexpected value. One or more of these rules should not have fired, some additional rule affecting the variable should have fired, or a fired rule's conclusion may have been erroneous or incomplete. The rules should be revised accordingly.

If HOW and WHY review of a consultation detects that the premises of all fired rules are correct, then rule conclusions may be the source of the expert's disagreement. For example, if the conclusion of R16 incorrectly multiplies EFACTOR with LAFACTOR (instead of adding them), then the resultant NEWQUOTA value will not agree with the expert's advice. Here again, the developer uses HOW and WHY to discover which variable's value does not conform to the expert's expectations. He or she also examines the fired rules' actions that affect that variable for correctness. There may be an inaccurate calculation, erroneous database–retrieval request, improper solver invocation, and so on. If the developer finds such an error, he or she can make the needed corrections with the rule set builder (e.g., changing an erroneous * to a +, yielding the correct R16).

It is possible that a HOW and WHY review will show that all premises and conclusions are correct, even though the expert disagrees with the advice generated for a test case. This outcome is probably due to a failure to recognize some important factor (i.e., variable) that influences the expert's reasoning. For instance, if Jack had forgotten about the UNEMPLOYMENT variable, then unexpected quota advice could have resulted. ECONOMY would have been based only on GROWTH. The developer needs to prompt the expert to identify such an oversight. When the developer recognizes the new variable, it is incorporated into existing rules or new rules. If he or she originally overlooked UNEMPLOYMENT then it would not appear in rules R5 through R9. Once the oversight is recognized, the developer incorporates it into those rules, as shown in Figure 13.3.

It may be that no additional variables are identified. In such a situation, the developer should prompt the expert for additional fragments of reasoning knowledge (i.e., rules) that may have been overlooked. For example, if the developer had inadvertently omitted rule R2 from the ADVISOR rule set, then the inference engine would have given an "unknown" recommendation for NEWQUOTA whenever sales did not exceed the quota by more than 15%. The expert would, of course, disagree with this advice. In examining the rule set, he or she would see that all rules are correct and all important variables have been used in the rules. He or she would also see that NEWQUOTA is given an unknown value because BASE has an unknown value. This should suggest to the developer that an additional rule is needed for assigning known values to BASE. In examining the incomplete rule set, the developer can see that BASE is set only for one possible relationship between sales and quota. By conferring with the expert, the developer would be able to add R2 to the rule set to cover the other possibility.

TRACING

The HOW and WHY review examines what the inference engine has done. A second method for diagnosing problems in a rule set allows the expert and developer to examine what the inference engine is doing. In other words, the inference engine gives an automatic step-by-step account of its activities while the reasoning is taking place.

The **tracing** of reasoning behavior appears on the console screen or can be routed to a printer. It portrays the detailed dynamics of reasoning by showing such activities as the selection of a rule for consideration, encounters with unknown variables, and the firing of rules. As a result, the developer and expert can study a record of all steps taken by an inference engine to see where the reasoning is going astray.

Automatic tracing is of primary interest during the testing of a rule set's expertise. In fact if that expertise needs to be hidden from view, then it is important to have a way of disabling the tracing capability after testing is completed. Otherwise, important knowledge about the internal functions of the reasoning process will be readily available to any user of the expert system as well as any competitor who gains access to it.

There may be certain aspects of reasoning with a particular rule set that are not covered by the built-in automatic tracing mechanism. For instance, more elaborate reporting of rule firing may be desired. This customized tracing is handled very easily if the inference engine can execute an OUTPUT type of command. Suppose that a developer wants the inference engine to display the values of BASE, QUOTA, and SALES as soon as rule R1 fires to see if they are as expected. This is accomplished by inserting an OUTPUT command into R1's conclusion:

```
RULE:  R1
       IF: SALES > 1.15 * QUOTA
       THEN: BASE = QUOTA + SALES - 1.15 * QUOTA
             OUTPUT "Sales:",SALES,"Quota:",QUOTA, "Base:", BASE
```

The OUTPUT command can be used in a similar way to produce customized tracing messages during the execution of an initialization or completion sequence, of any rule conclusion's actions, or of any variable description's actions for finding that variable's value.

There is yet another place to use OUTPUT commands for tracing. We have seen that each rule can be declared to have a premise, a conclusion, and a reason. An inference engine may also allow any rule to be given a sequence of preactions. **Rule preactions** are simply a sequence of one or more commands (e.g., OUTPUT) that the inference engine will automatically execute as soon as the rule is selected for consideration. Because a rule's preactions are carried out before an attempt is made to evaluate the premise, using OUTPUT there gives a way to generate customized messages showing the state of variables before any premise evaluation attempt is made.

As an example, the word READY (as in "ready, aim, fire") might denote the beginning of a preaction sequence. If so, rule R3 might be expanded to be

```
RULE:  R3
  READY:  OUTPUT "Now about to consider R3."
          OUTPUT "Will attempt to set EFACTOR."
          OUTPUT "ECONOMY must be good to fire. ECONOMY:", ECONOMY
```

```
OUTPUT "GROWTH must be known to fire. GROWTH:", GROWTH
IF: ECONOMY = "good" AND KNOWN("GROWTH")
THEN: EFACTOR = GROWTH
REASON: When the local economic outlook is good, the
        economic factor is equal to the economy's
        anticipated growth rate.
```

In addition to their use in tracing the flow of reasoning, preactions can also be a valuable aspect of the reasoning itself (Holsapple, Tam, and Whinston 1985). They give the developer a convenient way to be sure that certain actions are always taken before a given rule's premise is evaluated.

SAVING AND USING STORED TEST CASES

When testing the correctness of an expert system's reasoning behavior HOW/WHY review, automatic tracing, and customized tracing are all helpful. Any or all of them can be employed for each test case that is examined. In situations where there are many test cases or when the testing of each sample problem requires a considerable amount of user input, it is worthwhile to be able to save the input values of each case. You should save these values in such a way that the input does not have to be reentered directly to the inference engine each time a case is tested. You should also be able to pick any one of these stored cases for individual testing or to iterate through the entire series of sample problems. In other words, it is important that you can conveniently manage the test cases.

SPEEDING UP THE CONSULTATIONS

When rule set testing has progressed to the point where the expert agrees that it provides sufficiently good advice, the developer should examine the expert system from a performance viewpoint. Does testing show that the expert system meets the project's processing speed objectives? Have both forward and reverse reasoning speeds been tested, with the fastest one being compared to the objectives? A developer can try to speed up consultations in any of three ways: changing the inference engine behavior, modifying the rule set, and converting to a different computer or inference engine.

Reasoning Controls   The first way may be the least expensive, because it often does not require even a recompilation of the rule set. However, it depends on the existence of built-in means for controlling the inference engine's behavior. Several kinds of reasoning controls were discussed briefly in Chapter 13, and they are dealt with in more detail in Chapter 15. Because they affect the inference engine's reasoning behavior, they can affect consultation speeds. For example, a developer can test the effects of different rule-selection orders on sample problems, noting which selection order for competing candidate rules yields the fastest consultation. A major benefit of such reasoning controls is that they can be used to tune the inference engine's performance for a particular rule set.

Reducing the Number of Rules   Just as reasoning controls can influence expert system performance, the rule set contents can also affect consultation speed. In general, a small number of rules will yield faster reasoning than a large number of rules.

A tool that provides a rich assortment of knowledge-representation methods permits more concise, parsimonious rule sets than less sophisticated tools; but regardless of what tool is being used, the developer should consider whether there is a way to reduce the number of rules in a rule set. For instance, if two rules have the same premise, then the developer may collapse them into a single rule having that premise together with a conclusion formed from the conclusions of the two original rules. The developer can also collapse rules if the premise of one is a special case of or is subordinate to the premise of the other.

There is yet another general approach to reducing the number of rules. Consider the rules R1 and R2:

```
RULE:  R1
       IF: SALES > 1.15*QUOTA
       THEN: BASE = QUOTA + SALES - 1.15 * QUOTA
       REASON: In the cases where the sales for this
               product exceeded the quota by more than 15%
               the base amount for the new quota is set to
               the past quota plus the excess sales amount.

RULE:  R2
       IF: SALES <= 1.15 * QUOTA
       THEN: BASE = QUOTA
       REASON: The base amount for new quota is the same
               as the past quota because this product's
               sales did not exceed that past quota by
               more than 15%.
```

Notice that together they cover all possible relationships between sales and a quota. There is an easy way to combine them into a single rule that is equivalent from a reasoning viewpoint. The new rule is

```
RULE:  RSQ
       IF: KNOWN("SALES") AND KNOWN("QUOTA")
       THEN: IF SALES <= 1.15 * QUOTA THEN BASE = QUOTA
               ELSE BASE = QUOTA + SALES - 1.15 * QUOTA
             ENDIF
       REASON: If sales do not exceed the quota by more
               than 15%, then the base amount is the same
               as the past quota; otherwise the base
               amount is set to the past quota plus the
               excess sales amount.
```

Replacing rules R1 and R2 with RSQ would result in the same advice, while giving the inference engine one less rule to consider.

Initialization Actions   In addition to rule reduction, a developer should consider the actions appearing in the initialization sequence. Generally, actions that establish values of variables that are not frequently needed in consultations should be removed from the initialization sequence. Instead, they should appear in a variable description (or rule conclusion). If the initialization sequence executes a solver (e.g., the ECON solver in ADVISOR), it may be prudent to remove that action from the initialization sequence. The alternative is to preexecute the solver and have it store its results where they are accessible to the inference engine (e.g., in a data table or spreadsheet). Preexecution can lead to faster consultations if the solver is large and the same solver results are used repeatedly by many consultations. On the other hand, it yields slower overall processing if different results are needed from an interactive solver by different consultations.

Other Measures   When performance gains through reasoning controls and rule set alterations are insufficient to meet project objectives, the developer should reevaluate and possibly revise performance objectives. If actual performance still falls short, the developer may need to take more drastic measures to enhance the expert system's performance. One possibility is to acquire a new, faster computer that still supports the development tool (and, therefore, its rule set). Another possibility is to acquire a different development tool and restate the rule set in a form that can be processed by its inference engine. However, on the same computer, there is no prior guarantee this new rendition of the expert system will be faster than the earlier one.

There is one final point to keep in mind when changes are made for the purpose of speeding up consultation performance. The changes must be made in a way that does not alter consultation results produced by the original rule set. To this end, the new expert system should again be tested for correctness after efficiency adjustments have been made and before proceeding to the stage of interface construction.

14.8   INTERFACE CONSTRUCTION

At this point in a development cycle, the necessary reasoning knowledge has been correctly captured in a rule set. However, little attention has been paid to the ergonomics of the expert system's user interface. While concentrating on getting the rules right, a developer normally does not want to bother with constructing an elaborate user interface at the same time. For this reason, the initial user interface built into a rule set typically consists of line-oriented INPUT and OUTPUT statements. The prompts and messages generated by these commands may be cursory or skeletal in nature—sufficient for interaction during expert testing but not appropriate for end users of the expert system. At the very least, these will need to be made palatable for end users.

What is an appropriate user interface? The answer to this question depends on both user tastes and the facilities provided by the development tool for **interface construction.** Facilities a tool might provide for customized user interfaces include line-oriented input/output, forms management, menu processing, function key definition, graphics management, and combinations of these.

The project objectives may be detailed enough to prescribe the exact nature of the desired interface. If they are not, the expert may be able to provide further guidance based on prior interaction with prospective users. But the best source for details (e.g., wording, colors, screen layout) about a suitable interface is the expert system's ultimate user(s). As a useful starting point, the developer can pose alternate interface styles to the user for reactions and suggestions.

In addition to the aspect of the user interface built into the rule set, there is also the interface used for invoking the inference engine. The developer might simply allow the user to request a consultation with the native command language or menus provided for inference engine invocation. As explained in Chapter 13, another option is to construct a customized interface for making consultation requests. Here again, it is worthwhile to have the user actively involved in deciding the characteristics of this custom interface.

Another part of the user interface that a developer may wish to customize is the operation of the postconsultation explanation ability. Although an inference engine has built-in HOW and WHY capabilities that allow users to explore the line of reasoning employed in a consultation, this may not suit the tastes of some users. A developer can customize these standard explanation abilities to some extent by controlling the textual description that makes up each rule's reason in the rule set. With some tools, a developer can construct more specialized explanation abilities to accompany or replace standard HOW and WHY facilities (Holsapple and Whinston 1986).

A remaining activity in constructing a user interface consists of devising documentation for the user. This documentation should, of course, provide a clear explanation of the expert system's purpose, scope, and operation. Practice consultation sessions should be included to give the user a first-hand feel for the expert system's capabilities. The documentation can be in the form of manuals and/or on-line descriptions if the latter are permitted by the development tool.

14.9 USER TESTING AND INSTALLATION

Once the user interface has been constructed, the expert system is ready for **user testing.** The same series of sample problems that were used in expert testing may also be used here. The purpose of this testing is to check not the advice that is given, but rather the way in which it is requested, presented, and explained. The documentation is also being tested in these final trial runs of the expert system. The developer (and expert, if possible) should closely monitor user reactions to the expert system to ascertain what aspects of the user interface need adjustment. If the user was involved in the prior interface construction phase, these adjustments should normally be relatively minor.

DSS IN THE NEWS

Frequent updating is needed by some expert systems, users find. Digital Equipment developed one of the world's largest expert systems to figure out what combinations of computers, disk drives, terminals and communications cables a customer needs. Some 30 people work full time to change the expert as Digital introduces products and new communications standards emerge.

Du Pont had to add rules to a system used to diagnose problems at a chemical plant. The system didn't spot a clogged valve caused when a bird fell in a tank's open hatch and drowned.

W. M. Bulkeley, "Expert Systems are Entering into Mainstream of Computers," *Wall Street Journal* 5 December 1986, p. 29.

After any needed adjustments are made in the user-testing stage, the developer is ready for the final stage of a development cycle: installation. Installation involves the introduction of the expert system into the workplace, where it is consulted as desired by end users. During the installation stage, these users are instructed about how to invoke the inference engine, what kinds of inputs they may need to provide, and how to correctly interpret or apply consultation results. All the conventional wisdom about successfully introducing technological change into an organization is valid when installing an expert system (Lucas 1976).

Installation can be followed by another cycle that is one turn higher on the development spiral. For a developer, this means that the learning process continues. Taking the existing expert system as the starting point, the developer studies the problem area in greater depth or breadth, defines an expanded set of problems that the new expert system will address, specifies and tests its rule set, constructs and tests its interface, installs it, and proceeds to the next cycle in the development spiral.

14.10 SUMMARY

Opportunities for building business expert systems abound for both small and large problems. In each case, the expert system is built by developing its rule set. The planning that precedes rule set development is much like the planning that would precede any project of comparable magnitude within the organization. The development process itself follows an evolutionary spiral composed of development cycles.

Each cycle picks up where the last ended, building on the prior rule set. For a developer, the spiral represents a continuing education process in which more and more of an expert's reasoning knowledge is discovered and formalized in the rule set. Here, each development cycle was presented in terms of seven consecutive stages. Other characterizations of a development cycle (involving different stages or sequences) may be equally valuable. Many aspects of traditional systems analysis and project management can be applied to the development of expert systems.

Rule set development is a process of discovery and documentation. Research continues in search of ways of automating various aspects of the process (Boose 1989). It would not be surprising eventually to see expert systems that can assist in this process—that is, an expert system that "picks the mind" of a human expert in order to build new expert systems. Until that time comes, the topics discussed in this chapter should serve as reminders to developers of expert decision support systems about issues to consider during the development process.

▲ IMPORTANT TERMS

dependency diagram	knowledge acquisition
development cycle	knowledge-acquisition context
expert testing	knowledge-acquisition methods
feasibility study	knowledge-acquisition process
interface construction	knowledge engineer
interviewing	problem definition

protocol analysis   tracing
prototype   test cases
rule comment   user testing
rule preaction   variable specification form
rule set specification

▲ APPLICATION TO THE BANKING CASE

1. Who is the user of CLASS? What decision does CLASS support?
2. What are the three main functions of CLASS?
3. Describe the knowledge source for CLASS.
4. Describe the agent (knowledge engineer).
5. What knowledge-acquisition method was used in developing CLASS?
6. Beyond knowledge acquisition, what else was involved in the development of this expert system?
7. How was the expert testing performed?
8. In what way is CLASS integrated with spreadsheet software?
9. Does the case imply that forward or reverse reasoning is used? Explain.
10. Whom did this expert system benefit and how?

▲ REVIEW QUESTIONS

1. What must be true in order for expert system opportunities to exist for small problems?
2. What factors influence the success of an expert system development process?
3. Once an expert system opportunity has been identified and before a plan for its development is devised, what crucial managerial action must take place?
4. What are the main resources required for developing an expert system? In what order should they be selected and why?
5. What kinds of personality traits will a good rule set developer have?
6. What is one sequence of activities that constitute a development cycle?
7. What is the advantage of discovering a rule set's variables prior to discovering its rules?
8. How do the KA methods of interviewing and protocol analysis differ?
9. To understand the phenomenon of knowledge acquisition, what factors do we need to study?
10. What is a dependency diagram?
11. How can a dependency diagram benefit a developer?
12. What is the purpose of a rule's comment?
13. What is a rule preaction and how might it be usefully applied?
14. How can a developer check out an expert systems' reasoning behavior?
15. What is the advantage of avoiding an unnecessarily large number of rules in a rule set?

▲ DISCUSSION TOPICS

1. What is the single most important factor influencing the expert system–development process?
2. Contrast programming with rule management.
3. Contrast conditional branching in a program with a rule in a rule set.

4. Discuss the value of a prototype.
5. Discuss the relationship between knowledge acquisition and rule set specification.
6. Give examples of ways in which contextual factors can influence a KA process.
7. In some quarters there is a tendency to judge the magnitude of an expert system in terms of how many rules it has. Explain the flaw in this viewpoint.
8. What are the drawbacks of collapsing too many rules into a single rule?
9. Explain how to construct an initialization or completion sequence in such a way that its behavior can be easily altered without changing the rule set and requiring recompilation.
10. How can a developer specify a rule's conclusion in such a way that the effect of firing that rule can be altered from one consultation to the next without requiring a recompilation of the rule set?

▲ REFERENCES

Boose, J. 1989. A survey of knowledge acquisition techniques and tools. *Knowledge Acquisition* 1, no. 1.

Breuker, J., and B. Wielinga. 1987. Use of models in the interpretation of verbal data. In *Knowledge elicitation for expert systems: A practical handbook,* edited by A. Kidd. New York: Plenum Press.

Burton, A. M., N. R. Shadbolt, A. P. Hedgecock, and G. Rugg. 1987. A formal evaluation of knowledge elicitation techniques for expert systems: Domain 1. In *Proceedings of the First European Workshop on Knowledge Acquisition for Knowledge-Based Systems,* Reading University (September).

Dhaliwal, J. S., and I. Benbasat. 1990. A framework for the comparative evaluation of knowledge acquisition tools and techniques. *Knowledge Acquisition,* 2, no. 2.

Drenth, H., and A. Morris. 1992. Prototyping expert solutions. *Expert Systems* 9, no. 1.

Duchessi, P., H. Shawky, and J. P. Seagle. 1988. A knowledge-engineered system for commercial loan decisions. *Financial Management,* (Autumn).

Ericsson, K. A., and H. A. Simon. 1984. *Protocol analysis, verbal reports and data.* Cambridge, Mass.: MIT Press.

Hart, A. 1986. *Knowledge acquisition for expert systems.* New York: McGraw-Hill.

Hayes-Roth, F., D. Waterman, and D. Lenat. 1983. *Building expert systems.* Reading, Mass.: Addison-Wesley.

Holsapple, C. W., and V. Raj. 1994. An exploratory study of the two KA methods. *Expert Systems* 11, no. 2.

Holsapple, C. W., V. Raj, and W. Wagner. 1993. Knowledge acquisition: Recent theoretic and empirical developments, In *Recent Developments in Decision Support Systems,* edited by C. Holsapple and A. Whinston, Berlin: Springer-Verlag.

Holsapple, C. W., K. Tam, and A. B. Whinston. 1985. The synergistic integration of expert system technology with conventional knowledge management facilities. In *Symposium on the Impact of Microcomputers on Operations Research,* Denver (March).

Holsapple, C. W., and W. P. Wagner. 1993. Knowledge acquisition frameworks: A survey, assessment, and implications. *Kentucky Initiative for Knowledge Management,* Research Paper No. 48, College of Business and Economics, University of Kentucky.

———. 1995a. Contextual factors in knowledge acquisition. *International Journal of Expert Systems: Research and Applications,* forthcoming.

———. 1995b. Process factors in knowledge acquisition. *Expert Systems,* forthcoming.

Holsapple, C. W., and A. B. Whinston. 1986. *Manager's guide to expert systems using Guru.* Homewood, Ill.: Dow Jones–Irwin.

———. 1987. Artificially intelligent decision support systems—Criteria for tool selection. In

Decision support systems: Theory and application. edited by C. Holsapple and A. Whinston. Berlin: Springer-Verlag.

Kidd, A. 1987. Foreword. In *Knowledge elicitation for expert systems: A practical handbook,* edited by A. Kidd. New York: Plenum Press.

Kim, J., and J. Courtney. 1988. A survey of knowledge acquisition techniques and their relevance to managerial problem domains. *Decision Support Systems* 4, no. 3.

Liou, Y. 1990. Knowledge acquisition: Issues, techniques, and methodology. In *Proceedings of the 1990 ACM SIGBDP Conference on Trends and Directions in Expert Systems,* Orlando, Fla.

Lucas, H. 1976. *The analysis, design, and implementation of information systems.* New York: McGraw-Hill.

McGraw, K. L., and K. Harbison-Briggs. 1989. *Knowledge acquisition: Principles and guidelines.* Englewood Cliffs, N.J.: Prentice Hall.

Tuthill, G. S. 1990. *Knowledge engineering: Concepts and practices for knowledge-based systems.* Blue Ridge, Penn.: TAB Books.

Chapter 15

ADVANCED REASONING TOPICS

DSS INSIGHTS

ONTARIO: AN ARTIFICIALLY INTELLIGENT DSS FOR TILLAGE DECISIONS

Overview

Intensive Row-Crop production of corn . . . and soybeans . . . is reducing the productivity of prime agricultural land and contributing to the contamination of surface and groundwater. . . . Alternative tillage practices for crop production are available that significantly reduce the impact of corn and soybean production on the environment. However, farm producers are reluctant to adopt these alternative practices because there is a lack of readily available expertise regarding the selection and implementation of the practices.

In agriculture, problems are often characterized by uncertain, imprecise, or unknown information and problem-solving knowledge. Although experts cannot always state with 100% confidence that a particular fact, conclusion, or piece of knowledge is true or false, they can still make useful and meaningful recommendations based on uncertain and imprecise information.

A system that models the inexact reasoning process of an expert will consist of many . . . rules and must be able to propagate uncertainties through the inference . . . as various rules fire. . . .

System Description

Intensive production of corn and soybeans with conventional tillage practices in southwestern Ontario has resulted in serious soil degradation . . . reducing the productivity of the land and contributing to the contamination of surface and ground water. . . . In Ontario, several factors make conservation tillage . . . difficult to implement. . . . To successfully adopt a conservation practice, a farm manager needs expert advice on (1) the selection of an appropriate practice and (2) the implementation of the selected practice.

A rule-based expert system was developed to select tillage alternatives for corn and soybean production in Ontario. Various pieces of evidence . . . are used to reach a recommendation. Each piece of evidence either increases or decreases the expert's belief that a tillage practice is appropriate. The various pieces of evidence are used to select between the following tillage alternatives: NO-TILL, MODIFIED-NO-TILL, RIDGE-TILL, DISK, CHISEL-PLOW, MODIFIED-PLOW, SPRING-PLOW, and FALL-PLOW. The tillage alternatives are ranked according to the expert's belief in the success of the alternative under a specific set of farm constraints.

The expert system was validated by comparing the output from the system to the expert's recommendation. . . . The expert agreed with 86% of the recommendations given by the expert system. . . .

During a consultation, the user is prompted for values . . . [of] parameters. . . . Based on the parameter values, rules are fired that conclude the tillage alternatives with various degrees of certainty . . . At the end of the consultation, the preferred alternatives are ranked and presented to the user. . . .

Condensed quotation from N. D. Clarke, M. D. McLeish, T. J. Vyn, and J. A. Stone, "Using Certainty Factors and Possibility Theory Methods in a Tillage Selection Expert System," *Expert Systems With Applications* 4, no. 1, (1991), 53–54.

LEARNING OBJECTIVES

The Ontario case describes an expert system that reasons with uncertainties and presents multiple pieces of advice, each with varying degrees of certainty. In this chapter, we consider how inference engines can accomplish such feats by using certainty factors. We also cover the related subject of processing fuzzy variables. Another advanced topic that we examine is concerned with reasoning controls and variations. This topic is analogous to the "manual transmission" of an inference engine, whereas what we have looked at so far is an "automatic transmission" that gives developers little choice in how the engine will work at reasoning.

After studying this chapter, you should be able to

1. Describe major variations in inference engine behaviors and determine how to choose among them.
2. Explain major alternatives for reasoning rigor, rule-selection order, premise evaluation, and inference timing.
3. Understand how an inference engine can use certainty factors to incorporate expressions of uncertainty into advice that is derived.
4. Discuss the role of fuzzy variables in automated reasoning.
5. Make use (as needed) of reasoning controls, certainty factors, or fuzzy variables in the development and operation of expert systems.

Exercises at the end of the chapter are provided to help reinforce and check on what you have learned.

15.1 INTRODUCTION

This chapter presents some of the more advanced aspects of automated reasoning. They are concerned with variations in the details of forward and reverse reasoning, plus mechanisms for handling uncertainty within inference processes. To the extent that a developer has control over exactly what variations and mechanisms will be used for a particular expert system, there is a greater possibility of adjusting the inference engine to emulate more closely the expert's recommendations and/or to perform inferences more quickly.

People reason differently with the knowledge available to them. Some are more rigorous than others in using all available knowledge. The order in which people examine reasoning knowledge can vary. Human experts can use different strategies in their attempts to establish that some situation exists (i.e., that some premise is true). Variation exists in the timing of when to use inference versus other possible means (e.g., database retrieval) to find a value for something that had been unknown. Any or all of these variations can exist for inference engines. The first major section of this chapter examines them.

People are not always certain about all the knowledge they use. Human experts are able to work with various uncertainties when they reason about problems. There may be uncertainty about the precise nature of a problem, about the factors involved in reasoning about that problem, or about some of the reasoning knowledge itself. Nevertheless, all these factors are somehow taken into account in arriving at some advice for the problem. Any or all of these issues can confront inference engines that cope with uncertainty. The second major section of this chapter examines the certainty factor approach to dealing with uncertainty during inference engine processing. It also includes an introduction to the use of fuzzy variables for treating uncertainty during inference. All examples in this chapter are based on the ADVISOR rule set introduced in Chapter 13.

15.2 REASONING VARIATIONS

The development cycle presented in Chapter 14 concentrates on the construction of a rule set. Although the advice generated by an expert system depends heavily on the rule set that has been built, it also depends on the way in which the inference engine reasons with that rule set. Two different inference engines, both performing forward (or reverse) reasoning for the same problem and using the same rule set, could carry out different lines of reasoning and/or produce different advice. The line of reasoning pursued by one may yield a faster consultation than the other. These differences exist when the two inference engines use distinct variations of forward (or reverse) reasoning.

Here, we discuss several variations that govern the exact nature of an inference engine's reasoning behavior. One controls how rigorous the inference engine will be as it considers rules. Another variation concerns the order in which an inference engine selects rules for consideration. There is also the issue of the strategy an inference engine employs when trying to evaluate a premise. Yet another reasoning variation deals with when (if at all) the inference engine executes any find actions defined for an unknown variable. Still another concerns how many times a given rule can be fired within a single consultation.

Some inference engines are implemented in a way that lets a developer control which of the reasoning variations are to be used. With this built-in variability, the developer sets a few of the engine's **reasoning controls** as a way of adjusting its reasoning behavior in order to see which behavior gives advice closest to that of the human expert. All reasoning variations discussed in this chapter have been implemented in commercial development tools (Holsapple and Whinston 1986). However, not all tools provide all of these variations.

To select a particular reasoning variation other than the built-in default behavior, the developer issues a command to the inference engine indicating which variation is desired. For instance, an inference engine's default behavior might be to use absolute rigor by considering all the reasoning knowledge in a rule set. If we do not think the inference engine needs to be so thorough for a particular consultation, then we would issue a command to change the setting of the engine's rigor control.

REASONING RIGOR

A human expert may reason about a problem in a very meticulous and exhaustive way, rigorously using all reasoning knowledge at his or her disposal in arriving at a recommendation. On other occasions that same expert may put less effort into solving a problem, halting as soon as some advice can be offered. Thus, the expert expends minimal effort and does not rigorously apply all available reasoning knowledge. The person requesting advice may not have the time to wait for fully rigorous reasoning, may not have the money to pay for it, or may need only rough advice. The degree of reasoning **rigor** that is needed, desired, or permitted depends on the situation surrounding a consultation session. Both the advice that is offered and the speed with which it is produced depend, in turn, on the degree of rigor.

It is not unreasonable to expect an expert system to be capable of emulating the human capacity for reasoning with varying degrees of rigor. Thus, there should be some way of controlling how rigorous an inference engine is during a consultation. During one consultation it may exhaustively use all pertinent rules in arriving at a recommendation. In the very next consultation with the same rule set, the inference engine could stop as soon as the goal variable has a known value—even though further reasoning might produce a different value for that variable. Absolute rigor may not be needed or desired in all situations.

Forward-Reasoning Rigor   When forward reasoning is requested, the current setting of the rigor control determines when the inference engine will stop considering further rules. Remember that forward reasoning begins by checking the first rule's premise. If it is true, the engine fires the rule. If the premise is either false or unknown, the inference engine does not fire the rule and then checks the next rule's premise. The inference engine considers rules one after another in this manner, possibly iterating through the rule set's rules many times, until it has been rigorous enough in its efforts to establish a value for the goal variable. The meaning of *rigorous enough* is governed by the rigor-control setting. When the reasoning stops, the rule set's completion sequence is executed.

If the rigor-control switch is set to be absolute when the reasoning begins, then the inference engine repeatedly iterates through the rule set's rules. In each iteration it checks the premises of rules that have not yet fired. Thus, in the second and subsequent iterations, it considers every rule whose premise was formerly found to be false or unknown. If any of these now has a true premise, then the engine fires it. These iterations through the rule set continue until an iteration occurs in which no rule is fired. At that point, the inference engine has done all that it can possibly do. It has gleaned all that it can about the effects of the presented problem. It can now report these effects to the user. The inference engine has been absolutely rigorous in its forward reasoning.

At the opposite extreme is minimal rigor. When the rigor-control switch is set to be minimal, the inference engine stops considering rules as soon as the goal variable has a known value. It may stop before there has been even one full iteration through the rule set, or it may carry out multiple iterations. At any rate, this setting nearly always results in fewer rule considerations and faster reasoning than the setting for absolute rigor. It may or may not produce the same value for the goal variable and other variables reported via the rule set's completion sequence.

In the case of the ADVISOR rules of Chapter 13, minimal rigor will always yield the same value as absolute rigor for the NEWQUOTA goal, because the rules for establishing a NEWQUOTA value happen to be mutually exclusive. If one of them fires, then it is assured that none of the others will fire. On the other hand, if a rule set contains multiple rules that could possibly fire for determining a value for the same variable, then absolute rigor and minimal rigor can give different values to the variable. This variation occurs because absolute rigor will consider all the rules and fire all that are appropriate, whereas minimal rigor may consider and fire only one of them.

Between the two extremes is a compromise rigor. With this control setting, the inference engine goes beyond minimal rigor but stops short of absolute rigor. It is like minimal rigor, except the inference engine continues to consider every remaining unfired rule that could affect the goal variable if it were fired. If such a rule's premise is true, then the engine fires the rule. If the premise is false or unknown, then the inference engine does not consider this rule again in the current consultation. Typically, this compromise approach to reasoning rigor will cause the inference engine to consider more rules (i.e., take more time) than with minimal rigor but fewer rules (i.e., less time) than with absolute rigor. If rules are not mutually exclusive, the compromise could yield different variable values than either minimal or absolute reasoning.

To observe the processing differences between the rigor-control settings, a developer can pick a sample problem and use the automatic tracing mechanism to see how far the inference engine goes for each. No matter what degree of rigor is chosen, the usual HOW and WHY review will indicate the line of reasoning employed.

Reverse-Reasoning Rigor   When reverse reasoning is requested, the rigor-control setting determines how exhaustive the inference engine will be in considering the candidate rules for determining the value of an unknown variable. Remember that at various times during reverse reasoning, the inference engine will identify candidate rules for establishing the value of an unknown variable. A candidate rule is one whose action could possibly change the variable's value if it were fired. Therefore, the rigor setting controls how much effort the inference engine expends in attempting to establish an unknown variable's value. The same degree of rigor is applied to each unknown variable encountered during reverse reasoning.

If the rigor is set to absolute when reverse reasoning begins, the inference engine will consider all candidate rules identified for an unknown variable. A candidate rule is considered by checking its premise. If the premise is true, the engine fires the rule and considers the next candidate rule. If it is false, the engine does not fire the rule but instead considers the next candidate rule. If the premise is unknown, further reverse reasoning occurs in order to determine whether the premise is true or false, with the engine then firing or not firing the rule accordingly. This continues until it has considered all candidate rules for an unknown variable. Thus, the inference engine has been absolutely rigorous in its reverse reasoning.

At the opposite extreme, a minimal rigor setting means the inference engine will stop considering the variable's candidate rules as soon as the unknown variable is given a known value. In other words, as soon as the inference engine fires a candidate rule to establish a known value for the variable, it declares a cease fire for that variable and goes on to another unknown variable (if any). Because it never considers more rules than absolute rigor, reasoning with minimal rigor will always be at least as fast as the more exhaustive approach. Minimal rigor may or may not produce the same value as absolute rigor for an unknown variable.

In the case of the ADVISOR rules of Chapter 13, as with forward reasoning, both approaches always yield the same values for unknown variables, because the candidate rules for establishing any unknown variable's value happen to be mutually exclusive. If one of the candidate rules fires, none of the others can. However, if a rule set contains multiple rules whose actions could change a variable's value and whose premises could all be true, then absolute rigor and minimal rigor can yield different values for the variable, because absolute rigor will consider all candidate rules and fire those whose premises can be determined to be true, whereas minimal rigor may consider and fire only one of them.

As with forward reasoning, there is a compromise between the two extremes in reverse reasoning rigor. In this case, the inference engine goes beyond minimal rigor for an unknown variable but stops short of absolute rigor. This setting is like minimal rigor, except the inference engine continues to examine each remaining candidate rule. If the premise is true, the engine fires the rule. If the premise is false or unknown, the inference engine proceeds to the next candidate rule, and so forth, until it examines all candidate rules. This procedure differs from absolute rigor in that no reverse reasoning will occur in an attempt to ascertain values of unknown variables in premises of residual candidate rules. Typically, the compromise approach causes an inference engine to consider more rules (i.e., take more time) than with minimal rigor but fewer rules (i.e., less time) than with absolute rigor. If candidate rules are not mutually exclusive, the compromise could yield a different value for the unknown variable than either minimal or absolute reasoning rigor.

To observe the processing differences between various degrees of rigor, a developer can pick a sample problem and use the automatic tracing mechanism to compare how far the inference engine goes when working on unknown variables. Regardless of the rigor setting, a HOW and WHY review will show the extent of the reasoning employed. Suppose a user consults the ADVISOR rule set using reverse reasoning. NEWQUOTA will be one of the unknown variables encountered by the inference engine. It is clear that the inference engine will identify three candidate rules (R15, R16, and R17) for NEWQUOTA. In the case of absolute rigor, the inference engine will consider each one, complete with reverse reasoning for all unknowns in the premise of each. On the other hand, suppose minimal rigor is used. If reverse reasoning determines that the premise of R15 is true, then the engine fires R15 and ignores the remaining two candidate rules. If it cannot fire R15, then it considers R16 and fires it if reverse reasoning finds that its premise is true. It ignores Rule R17 unless R16 did not fire, in which case it considers R17 as a way for establishing a NEWQUOTA value. As with forward reasoning, minimal rigor is the most efficient choice when using reverse reasoning with the ADVISOR rule set.

RULE-SELECTION ORDER

As an inference engine reasons about a particular problem, it must select and process the rules in some order. The order in which it examines rules can affect both the speed with which advice is generated and the actual nature of the advice. At any moment during the reasoning, one or more rules compete for the inference engine's attention. All prior discussion of reasoning processes has assumed that the competing rules are considered according to their relative positions in the rule set. However, other selection orders are also possible.

In the case of forward reasoning, the group of competing rules consists of all unfired rules that have not yet been considered in the present iteration. When the first iteration begins, all rules are competing for consideration. Which one should be considered first, which one second, and so forth? As each subsequent iteration begins, the number of competing rules diminishes, because some rules have been fired in the prior iteration. Regardless of which iteration it is in and which degree of rigor is being used, an inference engine examines competing rules according to a specific **selection order.**

In the case of reverse reasoning, the currently competing rules are all the unconsidered rules that are candidates for establishing an unknown variable's value. When the inference engine begins working on an unknown variable, all that variable's candidate rules are competing for consideration. Regardless of which unknown variable is being worked on and which degree of rigor is being used, an inference engine examines the competing candidate rules according to a specific selection order.

During the expert-testing stage of a development cycle, a developer is free to experiment with the different selection strategies offered by an inference engine. The developer simply changes the setting of the reasoning control for selection order. If the rule set does not contain multiple rules that can all fire in a consultation and can all change the value of the same variable, then the chosen selection strategy will not affect the consultation results or efficiency—provided absolute rigor is used. If the reasoning is less rigorous, different selection orders can yield different reasoning speeds. If a rule set contains multiple rules whose conclusions could change the same variable and whose premises are not mutually exclusive, then the value of that variable is sensitive to the selection order.

The main point is that some inference engines permit a developer to use a selection order mechanism to adjust the reasoning behavior for a particular problem or rule set. The adjustment may be for the purpose of more nearly replicating the advice a human expert would give or for the purpose of optimizing reasoning speeds. Many selection strategies are conceivable. Here, we focus on four basic selection criteria:

1. *First criterion:* Select the competing rule closest to the first rule in the rule set, then the next-closest competing rule, and so on.
2. *Priority criterion:* Select the competing rule with the highest priority, then the one with the next-highest priority, and so on.
3. *Cost criterion:* Select the competing rule with the cheapest action, then the one with the next cheapest action, and so on.
4. *Unknown criterion:* Select the competing rule with the fewest unknown variables in its premise, then the one with the next-fewest unknowns, and so on.

The First Criterion   With the first criterion setting for selection order, competing rules will be selected according to their relative order in the rule set. For instance, suppose rule R2 has been listed prior to rule R1 in the ADVISOR rule set. When these two rules are competing, the inference engine will select R2 for consideration before R1. Such a rearrangement would be preferable if Jack happens to know that for most consultations the sales will not exceed the quota by more than 15%. With minimal reasoning rigor, this means that most reverse reasoning consultations will be faster, because they do not need to consider rule R1, whose premise will be more often false than true.

This same technique of rule arrangement can be usefully applied throughout a rule set. As rules for determining a variable's value are elicited from an expert, the developer can ask which are most and least likely to be needed. The rules are then arranged accordingly—most likely to least likely. Even if the selection order is not set to the first criterion, such an arrangement can still be worthwhile, because the relative order of rules in a rule set is typically the tiebreaker: whenever the specified selection strategy results in a tie between two competing rules, the rule that appears closest to the start of the rule sets is selected.

The Priority Criterion   Using the priority criterion, the selection order among competing rules is determined by rule priorities. When a rule is being specified, the developer can give it a priority. As an example, rule R1 might be specified as

```
RULE: R1
  PRIORITY: 70
  IF: SALES > 1.15*QUOTA
  THEN: BASE = QUOTA + SALES - 1.15 * QUOTA
  REASON: In cases where the sales for this product
          exceeded the quota by more than 15%, the base
          amount for the new quota is set to the past
          quota plus the excess sales amount.
```

If the priority selection criterion is in force and R1 is a candidate rule, then R1 will be selected before other candidate rules having lower priorities and after those with higher priorities. If some other rule also has a priority of 70, then the priority tie is broken by selecting the one that appears nearest the start of the rule set.

You can give any rule any priority in some range (e.g., from 0 through 100). If you have not explicitly specified a priority for a rule, then the inference engine assumes it has a default priority (e.g., 50). Generally, a rule's priority is easier to change than the rule's relative position in a rule set. Some inference engines even allow rule priorities to change in the midst of a consultation (e.g., based on what has occurred so far).

Rule prioritization gives a handy way of forcing one competing rule to be considered before another. Sometimes an expert will describe two rules, both of which can affect the same variable, and make the additional comment that one must be considered before the other. This is easily accomplished by giving that rule a higher priority than the other rule and designating that a prioritized selection order should be used.

The Cost Criterion   In reasoning about a problem, it is not unusual for a human expert to postpone expensive actions as long as possible. It may turn out that a solution can be reached before a costly action has to be taken, resulting in savings of time and effort. The same effect can be achieved in inference engine reasoning by letting the selection order be cost-based. This causes the least costly competing rule to be selected first, then the second cheapest competing rule, and so on. When less than absolute rigor is employed, this selection order can affect the inference engine's reasoning speed and advice—just as it does for the human expert.

A rule set developer has full discretion over specifying the relative costs of rules. A rule's cost reflects the developer's assessment of how expensive it would be to take the rule's preactions, test its premise, and/or carry out its conclusion if the premise happens to be true. Suppose rules R1 and R2 are revised to have both priorities and costs.

```
RULE: R1
  PRIORITY: 70
  COST: 15
  IF: SALES > 1.15 * QUOTA
  THEN: BASE = QUOTA + SALES - 1.15 * QUOTA

RULE: R2
  PRIORITY: 60
  COST: 10
  IF: SALES <= 1.15 * QUOTA
  THEN: BASE = QUOTA
```

Jack has given rule R1 a somewhat higher cost than R2, because its conclusion involves greater computational effort. If rule selection is priority based, rule R1 will be selected before R2 when the two rules compete. However, if it is cost based, rule R2 is selected before R1 because of its lower cost.

The Unknown Criterion   When confronted with several competing rules, a plausible strategy is to select the one with the fewest unknown variables in its premise. If one of the rules has no unknown variables in its premise, the truth or falseness can be determined very rapidly. It will take longer to make this determination for a rule with one unknown variable in its premise. For ten unknown variables, it is likely that even more time and effort are required. By focusing first on rules about which the least is unknown, an inference engine may be able to achieve a faster reasoning speed—provided the degree of rigor is less than absolute.

Combining Selection Criteria   Selection criteria can be combined in various ways to yield additional selection orders. Basically, these give alternatives to using the

---

SELECTION ORDER CONTROL FOR INDIVIDUAL VARIABLES

In the case of reverse reasoning, there may be a need to use different selection orders for different sets of candidate rules. For instance, the variable description for NEWQUOTA might look something like

```
VARIABLE: NEWQUOTA
  RIGOR: A
  ORDER: UC
```

to cause the processing of its candidate rules to be based primarily on the unknown (U) criterion and secondarily on the cost (C) criterion (regardless of what the overall selection order setting happens to be).

rule set order to break ties. For instance, we might designate that selection order is to be based on both priority and cost, with priority being given precedence.

PREMISE-EVALUATION STRATEGY

Think of yourself as an inference engine engaged in reverse reasoning. You have just selected some rule for consideration. Having carried out its preactions (if any), you are now ready to check its premise. You notice that the premise cannot be immediately evaluated as either true or false, because it has several unknown variables. You realize that a value needs to be determined for at least one (and perhaps all) of these unknown variables before you can evaluate the premise as being either true or false. You will use reverse reasoning to establish values for one or more of the unknown variables.

But which unknown variable will you work on first, second, and so on? Will your work on getting values for all the unknowns or only some of them? When will you actually test the premise to try to see whether it is true or false? These are some of the issues facing an inference engine as it endeavors to evaluate the selected rule's premise. Reasoning controls can help a developer adjust the **premise-testing strategy** an inference engine uses to address these issues—in the interest of faster reasoning or closer approximation of experts.

Sequence of Unknowns   A straightforward way to process unknowns in a premise is from left to right. However, a developer may desire some other sequence. One way to instruct the inference engine to use a certain sequence is to extend the rule's definition with another clause. For instance, rule R16 could be defined as

```
RULE: R16
   NEEDS: BASE,PFACTOR,EFACTOR,LAFACTOR,WEAK
  IF: WEAK AND KNOWN("BASE") AND KNOWN("EFACTOR")
      AND KNOWN("PFACTOR") AND KNOWN("LAFACTOR")
  THEN: INPUT FALL NUM WITH\
       "Enter percent sales decrease due to falling interest in "\
          + PROD
      NEWQUOTA=BASE*(1+EFACTOR+LAFACTOR+PFACTOR-FALL/100)
```

Here, the NEEDS clause will cause the inference engine to work on BASE first, then PFACTOR, and so on. In general, such a clause lets a developer easily control the order in which unknown variables are subjected to reverse reasoning.

Think about a premise comprising multiple conditions connected by the AND operator. For such a premise, the developer might position the conditions that are least likely to be true at the beginning of the premise. In other words, if one of the conditions in this premise turns out to be false, we would like the inference engine to discover that fact as soon as possible. Once the inference engine finds a condition to be false, it knows that the entire premise must be false. Values will not need to be found for any unknown variables that remain in the premise's other conditions. This yields faster processing than a situation where all the premise's unknown variables are worked on before the very last condition in the premise is discovered to be false.

A reverse strategy for sequencing conditions (and therefore variables) in a premise should be used when they are connected by the OR operator. As soon as any condition is found to be true, the overall premise is known to be true, regardless of whether the remaining conditions are true, false, or unknown. This suggests that the developer should sequence OR conditions from the one that is most likely to be true to the one that is least likely to be true.

Evaluation Time   Aside from the sequence of variable examinations, there can be variations in the timing of premise evaluation attempts. Three possible settings for this reasoning control include the eager, patient, and strict approaches. An *eager setting* causes the inference engine to evaluate the premise's conditions each time one of its unknown variables becomes known via reverse reasoning. If this evaluation of conditions provides sufficient evidence to make the premise either true or false, testing of the premise halts and the rule is fired or not fired accordingly.

The *patient setting* involves a more prolonged strategy in which the inference engine does not try to evaluate the premise until it has made an attempt to establish a value for each of the premise's unknown variables. For a *strict setting,* the inference engine works on each unknown variable until it either cannot establish a value for one of them or has established values for all of them. In the former case, the premise remains unknown, so the rule does not fire. In the latter case, the premise is then evaluated and the rule is fired if it is true. In either case, processing proceeds to the next candidate rule.

Which of these settings should be chosen for consulting a particular rule set? The answer depends on what kinds of premises need to be tested. It is fair to say that no one strategy for testing premises is "best" for all kinds of premises. Suppose, for instance, that variables in the conjunctive (i.e., ANDed) premises of ADVISOR rules have been arranged so that the variables most likely to be unknown appear to the left of their respective premises. A good choice would then be the strict strategy. However, this is not such a good strategy for rules R9 and R12, whose premises contain OR operators. If their conditions are organized from most to least likely to be true, then the eager strategy would be preferable to the strict one.

WORKING ON AN UNKNOWN VARIABLE

Once again, think of yourself as an inference engine engaged in reverse reasoning. In the course of evaluating the premise of some selected rule, you encounter an unknown variable. You know that there may be two approaches to establishing its

---

PREMISE-TESTING CONTROL FOR INDIVIDUAL RULES

To make exceptions to the overall premise-testing strategy, a developer may be able to specify the testing strategy that should be used for individual rules. For instance rule R9 might be specified in the rule set as

```
RULE: R9
   TEST: E
   IF: GROWTH < .02 OR UNEMPLOYED >= .082
   THEN: ECONOMY = "poor"
```

As a result, the inference engine will ignore the overall premise-testing setting whenever rule R9's premise is being checked. For R9, it will use the eager (E) premise-testing strategy. This same testing strategy could be specified for R12 in a similar fashion.

value. You could use reverse reasoning, which begins by identifying candidate rules for the unknown variable and endeavors to fire at least one of them. Or, if the rule set contains a variable description for the unknown variable, you could carry out the actions specified in that description. Which approach should you take?

Suppose an inference engine's default behavior is to attempt first to establish the variable's value by reverse reasoning. If it is successful, processing for the premise proceeds. However, if reverse reasoning is unable to infer a value, the inference engine executes the variable's find actions (if any exist) before proceeding. This strategy could be reversed by changing the setting of the reasoning control that governs when find actions are used. Rather than executing find actions as a last resort, the developer may decide that the inference engine should execute an unknown variable's find actions first. Only if they do not make the variable known will the inference engine attempt reverse reasoning for that unknown variable.

Because the execution of find actions is typically less time consuming than reverse reasoning, the setting that uses find actions as a first resort may result in faster reasoning. On the other hand, it may give a different consultation result than the last-resort strategy when both the find actions and reverse reasoning could potentially establish values for the variable. With some inference engines, the developer is free to choose either approach for a particular consultation or a particular variable, depending on the desired effect.

FIRING CAPS

So far we have always assumed that once an inference engine fires a rule, that rule is ignored for the rest of the consultation. This behavior is typical for inference engines. However, for some applications it may be desirable for a rule to be eligible for multiple firings within a single consultation. As an example, a rule's action may involve a conditional (e.g., IF . . . THEN . . . ELSE . . .) command. On the first firing of this rule, some actions in this command may not be taken. It may be desirable to consider the rule again in the consultation, with the possibility of taking those actions during a second firing.

Some inference engines give developers a reasoning control whose setting determines the maximum number of times a rule can be fired in a single consulta-

---

TIMING CONTROL FOR INDIVIDUAL VARIABLES

It is common for the developer to want some variables to be handled in one way (e.g., find actions as a first resort), whereas others are to be handled in a different way (e.g., find actions as a last resort). In such a situation, each variable description can contain an indication of when its find actions are to be executed. For example, the variable description

```
VARIABLE: LOCALADS
   WHEN: F
   FIND: REPCOL=LOOKUP(REP,#Y2,#Y13,#Z2)
         LOCALADS=LOOKUP(PROD,#A18,#A31,#(18,REPCOL))
```

could force the inference engine to always execute the find actions as a first (F) resort when working on LOCALADS.

SUMMARY OF REASONING VARIATIONS

Reasoning Aspect	Variations
Rigor in attempting to determine an unknown variable's value	Absolute, minimal, compromise
Rule-selection order used in attempting to determine an unknown variable's value	First, priority, cost, unknown
Premise evaluation strategy:	
Sequence in which values for unknown variables are sought	Left-to-right, specified order
Timing of premise evaluation attempts	Eager, patient, strict
Seeking a value for an unknown variable	Consider find actions first, attempt backward chaining first
Cap on the number of times a rule can fire	One, specified number

tion. The default setting for this **firing cap** is typically 1. The inference engine may override the firing cap setting for an individual rule by using a clause for that purpose in the initial specification of that rule.

15.3 DEALING WITH UNCERTAINTY

Human experts sometimes need to reason about uncertain situations. The person asking for advice may not be completely sure about all the inputs he or she provides to the expert during a consultation. The expert might not have complete confidence in all the knowledge acquired from external sources during a consultation. Even if the expert is completely certain about all aspects of the problem being faced, he or she could have some uncertainty about the validity or applicability of some of the expertise that will be used in reasoning about the problem. All these uncertainties are factored into the human reasoning process. As a result, the advice that the expert gives may be qualified by some degree of certainty. Jack might say, "I'm 80% certain that this is a fair quota."

Similarly, techniques exist for factoring varying levels of certainty into the reasoning performed by an expert system. These include Bayesian statistics (Spiegelhalter 1986, Lindley 1987), belief functions (Shafer 1987) belief networks (Pearl 1988), fuzzy logic (Zadeh 1983), and certainty factor approaches (Shortliffe and Buchanan 1975; Shortliffe 1976; Holsapple and Whinston 1986; Wise and Henrion 1986). Representative viewpoints about such alternatives for treating uncertainty can be found in Kanal and Lemmer (1986). Relative to other alternatives, certainty factors have been widely adopted for dealing with uncertainty in expert systems (Heckerman and Shortliffe 1992) and are the most commonly available means offered by expert system development tools (Kopcso, Pipino, and Rybolt 1988; Tonn and Goeltz 1990). Thus, our coverage of uncertainty in expert systems focuses on certainty factors.

Some expert system development tools do not have built-in mechanisms for dealing with uncertainty. Others are able to deal with certainty factors. The method that one tool uses for handling certainty factors may be different than the method used by another tool. Ideally, a tool should take its cue from human experts who are able to deal with uncertainties in different ways, depending on the nature of the problem.

CERTAINTY FACTORS

A **certainty factor** is a number that can be assigned to the value of a variable. It is a measure of how certain or confident the inference engine is about the value for the variable. For our discussion here, certainty factors are in the range 0 through 100, although some tools use ranges such as 0 through 10 or -1 through 1. A certainty factor of 0 is the lowest possible certainty. In the ADVISOR rule set, no certainty factors are explicitly assigned to any of the variable's values. When no certainty factor is mentioned for a variable's value, a certainty factor of 100 is assumed.

EMPIRICAL STUDIES ON THE VALUE OF CERTAINTY FACTORS

There have been repeated studies showing that human judgment about uncertainty often deviates from the prescriptions of probability theory (Kahneman, Slovic, and Tversky 1979; Tversky and Kahneman 1983; Favere and O'Leary 1991). In a similar vein, there have been a few studies to see whether experts tend to combine certainties in ways that match the certainty-combining mechanisms commonly implemented in inference engines. Perhaps the earliest of these found that the MYCIN expert system yielded results comparable to or better than a panel of independent experts (Yu et al. 1979).

More recently, researchers have conducted studies independent of any particular expert system (Tonn and Goeltz 1990; Holsapple and Wu 1993, 1994; Holsapple, Rayens, and Wu 1993, 1994). The findings generally reveal that anywhere from 25% to 90% of subjects combine certainties in ways consistent with conventional certainty factor methods. In other words, anywhere from 10% to 75% of human behaviors are inconsistent with these behaviors. Thus, depending on the expert being modeled, conventional certainty factor methods may or may not be a good fit. If not, a developer may choose to use some way for treating uncertainty that does not rely on certainty factors or to use some unconventional certainty factor methods (Calantone, Holsapple, and Wu 1990).

Aside from empirical evidence about the applicability of certainty factor methods, they have been challenged on analytical grounds. For instance, an analysis of the specific use of certainty factor methods in the MYCIN expert system reveals some theoretical shortcomings that appear to limit its applicability [Heckerman and Shortliffe 1992]. These shortcomings are concerned with (1) combining certainties across rules and (2) conceptual difficulties that arise if a probabilistic interpretation of certainty factors is adopted. Such concerns may also be relevant for non-MYCIN certainty factor approaches described in this chapter. However, in trying analytically to assess diverse ways of handling uncertainty in expert systems it is worth noting that they tend to make different or even unstated assumptions about the very nature of uncertainty (Magill and Leech 1991).

CONTROL OVER CERTAINTY FACTOR ALGEBRAS

The method an inference engine uses to derive a new certainty factor from existing certainty factors is called a **certainty factor algebra.** This algebra is merely a mathematical convention that determines how the new certainty factor is computed. Some inference engines do not allow a choice among different certainty factor algebras. They are akin to a human expert that is able to think in only one way, regardless of the problem being faced. Nevertheless, it is still worthwhile for a developer to understand the single algebra that is employed.

Many human experts tend to be more adaptable. Their methods of dealing with uncertainty differ, depending on the situation. In one situation, an expert may be daring about the way in which uncertainties are combined. For another problem, the expert may be risk averse. In yet another context, the expert's handling of uncertainty may fall between these extremes. In order to approximate this adaptability, an inference engine needs to have reasoning controls whose settings control what certainty factor algebras are to be used.

If a rule set does not involve any explicit certainty factors (i.e., everything has a certainty of 100), then the settings of certainty controls are of no interest. Inexperienced rule set developers will probably be unconcerned about alternative settings and just stay with the standard default values for the certainty controls. However, as a developer becomes more experienced, he or she may fruitfully explore alternative settings during the expert-testing stage of a development cycle. The developer accomplishes this exploration by simply trying different algebras in successive consultations with a sample problem. He or she can examine the settings from the standpoint of which one causes the inference engine to generate advice that most closely replicates the expert's advice.

Jack realizes that the growth and unemployment projections made by the ECON solver are not guaranteed to be completely accurate. In conferring with the economics staff, he finds that they can revise the ECON solver slightly so that it will set two additional variables: CGROW and CUNEMP. The values of these variables will indicate the solver's level of confidence in the GROWTH and UNEMPLOYMENT values that it produces. Jack decides to incorporate the uncertainty about growth and unemployment into the rule set. He accomplishes this result by including two additional commands following SOLVE ECON in ADVISOR's initialization sequence:

```
SOLVE ECON
LET GROWTH = GROWTH CF CGROW
LET UNEMPLOYMENT = UNEMPLOYMENT CF CUNEMP
```

When the initialization sequence is carried out at the start of a consultation, the CGROW and CUNEMP confidence levels calculated by ECON become the certainty factors for GROWTH and UNEMPLOYMENT. This is accomplished by the CF clause in each assignment statement. But, how do we now assess the certainty of an expression involving these two variables (or any other variables)?

THE CERTAINTY OF AN EXPRESSION

An inference engine is apt to encounter many expressions during a consultation. Some of these expressions are likely to be numeric, such as 1.15*QUOTA. Others will most certainly be simple logical expressions, such as GROWTH >= .04 or SALES > 1.15*QUOTA. Such conditions can themselves contain numeric expressions and can be connected by Boolean operators (e.g., AND, OR) to form compound logical expressions such as GROWTH >= .04 AND UNEMPLOYMENT < .076. The premise of every rule is a logical expression.

Whenever it encounters an expression, an inference engine will try to evaluate it using the values of the variables involved. If it can evaluate a numeric expression, then the value is a number. Similarly, a logical expression is either TRUE or FALSE. In situations where the engine cannot successfully evaluate an expression, its value is said to be unknown.

If the inference engine's evaluation is successful, then the expression's value is known with a specific degree of certainty. This certainty depends on three things. First, there are the certainty factors of the variables' values that were used in evaluating the expression. Second, there are the kinds of operations (e.g., +, *, >, =, AND, OR) specified in the expression. Third, there is the algebraic method used in combining certainty factors.

Certainty-combining methods available in commercial inference engines fall into two classes: joint methods and confirmative methods. Some of these engines give developers a choice of which joint method is to be used in calculating an expression's certainty. Similarly, they provide a reasoning control for setting the confirmative method to be used.

Bear in mind that an expression's value is always computed according to the operators and is unaffected by individual certainties of variables in the expression. Those certainties are combined to yield a certainty factor for the expression's value. A joint certainty-combining method is used for numeric expressions, conditions, and logical expressions involving AND. For a logical expression of the form

```
condition-1 OR condition-2
```

the certainties of condition-1 and condition-2 are combined in a confirmative fashion. We now look at details of using joint and confirmative methods for calculating expression certainties.

Joint Certainty   Table 15.1 shows examples of the kinds of expressions whose certainties are calculated in a joint fashion. Here, we step through a couple of examples in detail: first, a premise comprising a compound logical expression and then a simple numeric expression. We focus on two of the most widely encountered joint certainty-combining methods: the minimum method and the product method.

Suppose ECON projects a growth rate of 0.05 with 80% confidence and an unemployment rate of 0.075 with 90% confidence. After the initialization, GROWTH has a value of 0.05 with a certainty factor of 80; the UNEMPLOYMENT variable has a value of 0.075 with a certainty factor of 90. When the inference engine evaluates the premise of R6, it discovers that the premise is true. (See Chapter 13 for rule R6 and other rules mentioned in this chapter.) But how true is it? The 0.05 value of GROWTH exceeds 0.04 in the first condition, so that condition is true with a certainty of 80. Similarly, the second condition is true with a certainty of 90. The question then becomes how the inference engine should combine these two certainty factors to determine an overall certainty factor for the premise.

Keeping in mind that both conditions must be true in order for the premise to be true, it is reasonable that the overall certainty of the premise should not exceed that of the least certain condition. If you are only 80% sure about the growth rate, then your **joint certainty** about both unemployment and growth cannot reasonably

TABLE 15.1   Examples of Expressions Having Joint Certainties

TYPES OF EXPRESSION	EXAMPLES
Numeric	`LOCALADS/1000`
	`MIN(GROWTH,.085-UNEMPLOYMENT)`
	`I + J + 2`
	`(28 + X)**3`
	`SQRT((QOH - 50)/5)`
	`REVENUE - EXPENSE`
String	`TRIM(FNAME)+" "+LNAME`
	`TRIM(STREET)+" "+TRIM(CITY)+" "+STATE+" "+ZIP`
	`"This is the report for "+ REP`
Condition	`GROWTH>=.02`
	`PROD IN ["computer","romance","scifi"]`
	`EOQ < SQRT((QOH - 50)/5)`
	`ECONOMY = "good"`
Logical (compound)	`ECONOMY="good" AND KNOWN("GROWTH")`
	`GROWTH >= .04 AND UNEMPLOYMENT < .076`
	`GROWTH >= .02 AND GROWTH < .04`
	`            AND UNEMPLOYMENT >= .055`

exceed 80. This method is called the *minimum method*. Intuitively, it is equivalent to the old argument that a chain is no stronger than its weakest link.

Others might reasonably push this argument further, claiming that the joint certainty should actually be calculated by taking the product of the two individual certainties. If one of the certainty factors is 100, then this yields the same result as the approach of taking the minimum certainty factor. However, if both are less than completely certain, then the *product method* yields a lower certainty than the minimum method. In this case, a joint certainty of 72 would result from the product method (90 · 80/100), versus a joint certainty of 80 for the minimum method (minimum of 80 and 90).

As a second example consider the expression

REVENUE-EXPENSE

and assume REVENUE's value has a certainty factor of 50, whereas the EXPENSE value has a certainty factor of 70. Using the minimum method, the joint certainty that should be attributed to the difference between revenues and expenses is MIN (50, 70) = 50. If we're 50% sure about revenues and 70% sure about expenses, the minimum method says that we should not be more than 50% sure about the difference between them. If the certainty factor of 70 is replaced by 60, the result is the same: MIN(50,60) = 50.

The product method is more conservative than the minimum method. The product will always be less than or equal to the minimum. In thinking about the minimum method, we cannot deny that a chain is no stronger than its weakest link. The product method says it is not even as strong as its weakest link. It says that both uncertainties should be reflected in the joint certainty. Thus, assuming certainty factors of 50 and 70, respectively, for REVENUE and EXPENSE, the joint certainty computed for the difference is (50 · 70)/100 = 35. Both certainty factors contribute to a joint certainty that is less than either of them. Reducing the 70 certainty factor to 60 yields an even lower certainty of (50 · 60)/100 = 30 for the expression.

Regardless of the calculation method, the important point is that all joint certainty factors are automatically calculated by the inference engine during a consultation. However, a joint certainty–calculation method that is well suited for one application may be poorly suited for some other application area. Commercial inference engines that support several built-in methods for calculating joint certainty factors date back to the mid-1980s (Holsapple and Whinston 1986). These methods include both the minimum and product methods, which are graphically contrasted in Figure 15.1. Each graph shows how the joint certainty (vertical axis) is affected as one certainty factor varies from 0 to 100 while the other is fixed at 45.

A developer may be able to designate which of the joint certainty factor methods will be used by the inference engine in a particular consultation. This result is accomplished by setting a joint reasoning control to indicate the desired method. Because it is concerned with determining joint certainties for expressions, we refer to this control as the JCFE switch.

Confirmative Certainty   Suppose that SOLVE ECON yields a growth rate of 0.01 with a confidence of 70 and an unemployment rate of 0.085 with a confidence of 50. When the inference engine evaluates the premise of rule R9, the first condition is true (0.01 < 0.02) with a certainty factor of 70. The second condition is true (0.085 ≥ 0.082) with a certainty factor of 50. The major difference between this rule and R6 is that the two conditions are connected by the OR rather than AND operator.

Keeping in mind that only one condition needs to be true in order for this premise to be true, it is reasonable that the overall certainty of the premise should be at least as large as the most certain of the two true conditions. Intuitively, the rationale is that when two "chains" are offered, the strongest will be chosen. Others might reasonably push this argument further, claiming that both can be chosen, with one reinforcing the other. In any event, one certainty factor acts to confirm the other.

One approach to calculating the **confirmative certainty** is to take the maximum of the two certainty factors. Another approach, which yields a higher confirmative certainty, is called the *probability sum*. It causes the product of the two certainty factors to be subtracted from their sum. In the preceding example, a

FIGURE 15.1 Comparing Results of Joint Methods (with One Contributing Certainty Fixed at 45)

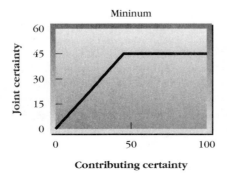

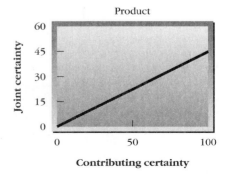

A COMPROMISE JOINT ALGEBRA

In thinking about which joint certainty algebra to adopt for a particular problem area, a developer may find it useful to ask the expert about which of the available methods matches his or her own way of jointly combining uncertainties (Holsapple, Rayens, and Wu 1993), which can be done by using a few examples drawn from expressions specified in the rule set. For each, the developer can ask whether the expert deems a minimum or product more reasonable, or the developer could ask what joint certainty the expert would invent and then check to see whether it is closer to the minimum, the product, or some other joint certainty method. If neither the minimum nor product methods seems to fit the expert or problem area, then the joint average method offers a compromise between the two (Holsapple and Whinston 1986; Holsapple and Wu 1994). For the growth and unemployment example, it yields a joint certainty of $(MIN(90, 80) + (90 \cdot 80)/100) / 2 = (80 + 72) / 2 = 76$.

confirmative certainty of 70 would result from the maximum method (maximum of 70 and 50) versus a confirmative certainty of 85 for the probability sum method ($70 + 50 - 70 \cdot 50/100$). Figure 15.2 contrasts results of the two confirmative methods. Each graph shows how the confirmative certainty (vertical axis) is affected as one certainty factor varies from 0 to 100 while the other is fixed at 85.

Suppose that the certainty factor of 50 is replaced by 10. The probability sum philosophy says we should be less certain than with 50; the confirmative certainty would be $(70 + 10) - (70 \cdot 10/100) = 73$, which is less than 85. In contrast, the maximum method would still give a confirmative certainty of MAX (70, 10) = 70, even though there is now less certainty about one of the pieces of evidence. In fact, the second condition's certainty factor could fluctuate from 0 to 70 without affecting the maximum method's joint certainty.

As in the case of joint certainty factors, all confirmative certainty factors are automatically calculated by the inference engine during a consultation. Here, too, inference engines may support several built-in methods for determining confirmative certainty factors. These methods include the maximum and probability sum methods. A developer is able to designate which of the confirmative certainty factor methods will be used by the inference engine in a particular consultation by setting

FIGURE 15.2 Comparing Results of Confirmative Methods (with One Contributing Certainty Fixed at 85)

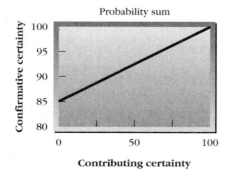

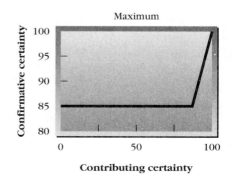

A COMPROMISE CONFIRMATIVE ALGEBRA

In thinking about which confirmative certainty algebra to adopt for a particular problem area, the developer may want to quiz the expert in a similar way to the approach used when deciding on a JCFE setting. The only difference is that the example expressions involve conditions connected by the OR operator. There are other confirmative certainty methods to accommodate experts whose reasoning falls between the maximum and probability sum extremes (Holsapple and Whinston 1986; Holsapple and Wu 1994). One of these is the average method, which offers a compromise between the conservative maximum method and the venturesome probability sum method. For the growth and unemployment example, it yields a confirmative certainty of

$$(MAX(70, 50) + ((70 + 50) - 70 \cdot 50/100))/2$$
$$= 70 + 120 - 35$$
$$= 77.5$$

▲ which is halfway between the maximum of 70 and the probability sum of 85.

a confirmative reasoning control to indicate the desired method. We refer to this control as the CCFE (confirmative certainty for expression) switch.

THE CERTAINTY OF A VARIABLE'S VALUE

You now see how an inference engine can reason with uncertainty when evaluating expressions. But in order to deal with uncertainty, an inference engine must be able to do more than compute certainties for expressions appearing in premises and actions. It must also be able to compute certainty factors for variables' values. Suppose the inference engine has established that the R6 premise is true with a certainty of 72. This certainty is very simply reflected for the ECONOMY variable's value of *good* when the rule is fired: if the inference engine is 72% certain that the premise is true, then it is also 72% sure that the ECONOMY value of good is correct. This is carried even further when rule R3 is later considered, but the reasoning is a bit more involved for this rule.

As in the case of R6, the R3 premise is true with a certainty of 72. But unlike R6, the R3 action does not consist of assigning a constant to a variable. Instead, it assigns the GROWTH variable's value to EFACTOR. Thus, there are two sources of uncertainty that jointly contribute to the certainty factor that will result for EFACTOR: the certainty factor of the premise (72) and the certainty factor of GROWTH (80). A joint method is appropriate for combining these values to arrive at a certainty factor for the EFACTOR variable.

Some inference engines let a developer designate which of the joint certainty methods should be employed for computing a variable's certainty. The developer sets a reasoning control that we call the JCFV (joint certainty for variable) switch. As with JCFE, the minimum, product, and perhaps other joint methods are possible settings. Do not confuse the JCFE switch with the JCFV switch. The former controls joint certainty computations for expressions such as the premise of a rule and arithmetic formulas in a rule's conclusion. The latter controls the joint certainty computation for a variable. The flexibility that results from differentiating between these two distinct uses of joint certainty computation is important for expert system developers.

Suppose that JCFV is set to have the inference engine use the minimum method for computing a variable's certainty factor when a rule fires. This setting results in a certainty factor of 72 (the minimum of 72 and 80) for EFACTOR's value when rule R3 is fired. The product method would yield a certainty factor of 58 ($72 \cdot 80/100$, rounded). In either case, a value of 0.05 is assigned to EFACTOR. If the inference engine later fires rule R15, then the EFACTOR value of 0.05 is used in computing the NEWQUOTA value. The certainty factor of this NEWQUOTA value is influenced by the certainty factor that exists for EFACTOR. Suppose this certainty factor is 72. Assuming that BASE, STRONG, LAFACTOR, PFACTOR, and RISE all have certainties of 100, the certainty factor for NEWQUOTA is then 72.

Capturing a User's Uncertainty   The certainty factors for GROWTH and UNEMPLOYMENT were acquired from the execution of a solver. Alternatively, certainty factors may be taken from other integral sources—a spreadsheet, a data table, statistical calculations, and so forth. An inference engine can also acquire the certainty factor for a variable's value from the expert system's user. For example, when rule R15 is fired, the inference engine asks the user to provide a value for the RISE variable. It would not be unusual for a user to feel somewhat uncertain about his or her response. Jack can easily have the inference engine capture this uncertainty by inserting the actions

```
INPUT CRISE USING "nnn" WITH\
"On a scale of 0 to 100, how sure are you?"
LET RISE = RISE CF CRISE
```

immediately after the input action that already exists in rule R15. When the inference engine fires this revised R15, the engine prompts the user for a rise response. It then prompts the user to indicate how sure he or she is about this response. This degree of certainty becomes the value of the CRISE variable, which is then used to set the certainty factor for the RISE variable.

Suppose the user is 75% sure about the rise response. The user inputs 75, and this becomes the certainty factor for the RISE value. The inference engine calculates a new quota according to the formula in R15. The inference engine also determines a certainty for this NEWQUOTA value, based on the certainty factors of all variables involved in the formula. If the minimum method has been selected for JCFV and the product method has been chosen for JCFE, then EFACTOR has a certainty factor of 72, as described earlier. Assume that, with the exception of RISE and EFACTOR, the other variables in the NEWQUOTA formula have certainty factors of 100. Thus, the inference engine needs to compute the joint certainty of 100, 72, 100, 100, and 75.

Computation Method   The computation method for joint certainties in an expression is controlled by the JCFE setting. No matter what this setting is, the three certainty factors of 100 do not affect the result. Because the product method has been designated for JCFE, the joint certainty is $72 \cdot 75/100 = 54$. The inference engine would report a certainty of 54 out of 100 for its new quota recommendation. If the minimum method had been selected for both JCFE and JCFV, then EFACTOR would have had an 80 certainty factor and the resultant certainty factor for NEWQUOTA would have been 75 (the minimum of 80 and 75).

Remember that the availability of JCFE, CCFE, and JCFV controls allows the expert system developer (or user) to choose the method that has the most intuitive appeal for a particular application. Selecting the product approach for reasoning about joint certainties is relatively conservative. For some applications it may result in an understatement of joint certainty levels. On the other hand, the minimum approach is relatively venturesome and may result in an overstatement of joint certainties for some applications. The important point is that a tool should allow a choice between these (and perhaps other) methods, rather than forcing the inference engine always to employ the same method. This choice lets expert systems be more easily tailored to the needs of their respective application areas. It also permits the impacts of different certainty methods on the same rule set to be observed and contrasted by simply changing control switch settings.

THE CERTAINTY OF A RULE ACTION

The foregoing discussion described how an inference engine can acquire the certainty factor for a variable's value from various integral sources (e.g., via solver execution) and from external sources (e.g., from the expert system's user). It also described (1) how the certainties of a premise can be combined (via JCFE and CCFE settings) in either a joint or confirmative fashion to yield an overall certainty for the premise, (2) how the certainty of a premise affects (via the JCFV setting) the certainty factors of variables changed by the conclusion when a rule is fired, and (3) how the certainties of variables in a numeric expression jointly contribute (via the JCFE setting) to the certainty of that expression's value. However, these topics do not involve any uncertainties about the rules themselves. They all assume that Jack is completely certain about the reasoning expertise embodied in every rule.

What happens if Jack is not fully certain about the goodness or validity of some rule? Perhaps a rule is usually applicable but may not be good in some unspecified circumstances. Think about rule R6 for example:

```
RULE: R6
  IF: GROWTH >= .04 AND UNEMPLOYMENT <.076
  THEN: ECONOMY = "good"
```

This rule says Jack is certain that if growth and unemployment are at specified levels, then the economy should be regarded as good. The validity of this rule itself is absolute. As long as the premise is true, the conclusion is completely valid. However, suppose the premise is true with 72% certainty. When the engine fires the rule, this same certainty is passed along to the conclusion, where it is factored into the certainty of the variable that is changed there. As result, ECONOMY will have a value of good with a certainty factor of 72.

Passing an Action's Certainty Along to a Variable   Now let's say Jack has some second thoughts about the validity of rule R6. He still feels 90% comfortable with it, but he realizes that it may not be valid all the time. To incorporate this uncertainty into the rule set, he revises rule R6, using CF as an abbreviation for certainty factor:

```
RULE: R6
  IF: GROWTH >= .04 AND UNEMPLOYMENT < .076
  THEN: ECONOMY = "good" CF 90
```

This revised R6 indicates that Jack is only 90% certain about giving ECONOMY a good value when the premise is true. Whenever the engine fires the revised R6, the 90% certainty about the rule's action is factored into the certainty that results for ECONOMY's value of good.

Suppose, for example, the inference engine has determined that the premise is true with a certainty of 100. When the revised R6 is fired, the certainty of a good economy will then be 90. If there had been no CF 90 for the action ECONOMY = good, then the certainty of a good economy would have been 100. During a different consultation, suppose the inference engine has determined that the premise is true with a certainty of 70. When the revised R6 is fired, the inference engine will base the certainty of a good economy on both 70 (because of uncertainty about the premise) and 90 (because of uncertainty about the action). The inference engine will compute a joint certainty from 70 and 90, using the method indicated by the JCFV setting. This value becomes the certainty factor for ECONOMY's value. For the minimum method, the joint certainty determined from the premise and action for this variable would be 70. The greater uncertainty about the premise overshadows the mild uncertainty about taking the action. For the product method, the joint certainty would be 63 (70 · 90/100). The uncertainty about the premise is multiplied by the uncertainty about taking the action, resulting in an even lower joint certainty for the variable.

Different Certainties for Different Actions in a Conclusion   An inference engine may allow Jack to specify a different certainty for each action in a rule's conclusion. For instance, the conclusion of rule R4 might be altered as follows:

```
THEN: EFACTOR = GROWTH/3 CF 95
      LAFACTOR = LOCALADS/120000 CF 88
```

This conclusion tells the inference engine that Jack is 95% sure about the validity of taking the first action and 88% sure about the second. When the rule is fired, the certainty of EFACTOR is jointly based on the certainty factor of GROWTH, the certainty of the premise, and 95. The certainty factor of LAFACTOR is jointly based on the certainty factor of LOCALADS, the certainty of the premise, and 88.

Variable Degrees of Certainty   All these examples of specifying a certainty for taking the action of a rule have explicitly stated the certainty. Such certainties can also be indicated implicitly with a variable rather than an integer constant. For example, rule R6 might be stated as

```
RULE: R6
IF: GROWTH >= .04 AND UNEMPLOYMENT < .076 AND KNOWN ("CR6")
THEN: ECONOMY = "good" CF CR6
```

where CR6 is a variable whose value can be established in any of a wide variety of ways. It might be set in the initialization sequence or based on the region of the country, some user input, or the results of performing the ECON solver. Or, there may be some new rules added to ADVISOR that determine how certain the inference engine should be about taking the R6 action when its premise is true. This ability to treat certainty factors as variables gives the rule set developer added flexibility.

FIRING MULTIPLE RULES FOR THE SAME VARIABLE VALUE

The ADVISOR rule set contains two rules that can give a value of good to the ECONOMY variable: R6 and R7. However, the premises of these two rules are specified in such a way that it would be impossible for both of them to be true within a consultation. But consider what can happen if the second condition in R7's premise is eliminated:

```
RULE: R7
   IF: GROWTH >= .02 AND UNEMPLOYMENT < .055
   THEN: ECONOMY   = "good" CF 80
```

This revised version of R7 also indicates that Jack is 80% sure about the validity of the rule's action when the rule is fired. Along with the previously revised R6,

```
RULE: R6
   IF: GROWTH >= .04 AND UNEMPLOYMENT < .076
   THEN: ECONOMY = "good" CF 90
```

it is now possible for the inference engine to fire both R6 and R7 during a consultation. In such a case, the value of ECONOMY is good, but what is its certainty factor?

Suppose that the initialization sequence for a consultation has given GROWTH a value of 0.045 with a certainty factor of 85 and UNEMPLOYMENT a value of 0.05 with a certainty factor of 70. Assume that the minimum method is being used to determine the joint certainty of conjunctions in a premise (i.e., based on the JCFE setting). When the inference engine evaluates the premise of R7, it discovers that the premise is true with a certainty of 70. Similarly, it discovers that the premise of R6 is true with a certainty factor of 63. When R6 is fired, the value of ECONOMY becomes good with a certainty factor of 63. This example assumes that JCFV is set to use the product method for computing a variable's joint certainty from a rule's premise and action certainties (70 · 90/100). When R7 is fired, the value of ECONOMY now becomes good with a certainty of 56 (70 · 80/100). Thus, the certainty for a good economy depends on which rule fired last (as determined by the settings of rigor and selection order controls).

Replacement versus Additive Assignments   Because the actions of rules R6 and R7 involve commonplace assignment statements, the result of the most recently executed statement replaces the prior value and certainty for ECONOMY. Although this replacement behavior may be desired for some variables in some expert system applications, a different kind of behavior is probably warranted for the ECONOMY variable. That is, if two rules suggesting a good economy have fired, then the two certainties resulting for ECONOMY should be combined in a confirmative fashion. The resultant certainty factor should be at least as great as the largest of these two. To cause the inference engine to process the ECONOMY variable in this way, Jack would revise the conclusions of R6 and R7 by inserting a + symbol ahead of the = symbol:

```
RULE: R6
   IF: GROWTH .= .04 AND UNEMPLOYMENT < .076
   THEN: ECONOMY += "good" CF 90

RULE: R7
   IF: GROWTH >= .02 AND UNEMPLOYMENT < .055
   THEN: ECONOMY += "good" CF 80
```

The += indicates that the action is an additive assignment. Rather than replacing the former evidence about a variable's value and certainty, the action provides additional evidence about the variable.

Confirming a Variable's Value The CCFV (confirmative certainty for variable) setting controls how this additional evidence about a variable is combined with existing evidence in a confirmative fashion. The most conservative method is to use the maximum of the existing certainty factor and the just-computed certainty factor. The most venturesome method is to use the probability sum of these two certainty factors, subtracting their product from their sum. Thus, we have two controls for governing methods used in calculating the certainty of a variable's value. Joint certainty for a variable involves the combination within a rule (intrarule) based on the premise and action certainties. Confirmative certainty for a variable is concerned with combining joint certainties across multiple rules (interrule).

Assume that we have set the controls to the product method of computing joint certainties for variables (JCFV) and the probability sum method of computing confirmative certainties for variables (CVFV). Suppose you (i.e., the inference engine) have established that the premise of R6 is true with a certainty of 70 and then you fire R6. This gives ECONOMY a value of good with a certainty of 63 ($70 \cdot 90/100$). Suppose you later discover that the premise of R7 is true with a certainty of 70 and then you fire R7. In isolation, this rule would tell you to let ECONOMY's value be good with a certainty of 56 ($70 \cdot 80/100$). However, because the action involves an additive assignment, you check to see whether ECONOMY already has a value of good. It does. Therefore, you use the probability sum method to combine the existing certainty factor of 63 with the new certainty of 56:

$$63 + 56 - (63 \cdot 56/100) = 119 - 35.28 = 83.72$$

As a result of firing these two rules, you are now 84% sure that the economy is good. This is a greater certainty than either rule can give individually. The rules tend to confirm each other, which is reflected in the variable's certainty factor.

CONTROL OF CERTAINTY ALGEBRA USAGE FOR INDIVIDUAL VARIABLES

The JCFV and CCFV settings indicate which certainty algebras the inference engine will use for each variable that is processed during a consultation. Suppose the expert tends to be cautious (e.g., product and maximum) about designating the certainty for one variable, venturesome (e.g., minimum and probability sums) for another variable, and in between these extremes for a third variable. Can these different attitudes all coexist within a single consultation? Inference engines exist that allow reasoning about uncertainty to be fine-tuned on a variable-by-variable basis (Holsapple and Whinston 1986). For example, a variable description such as

```
VARIABLE: ECONOMY
   LABEL: Economic Outlook
   JOINT: A
   CONFIRM: P
```

could cause an inference engine always to use the joint average (A) and the probability (P) sum algebras when computing the intrarule and interrule certainties for values of the ECONOMY variable—regardless of the current JCFV and CCFV settings. Such flexibility adds another dimension to the developer's world of controlling how an inference engine reasons about uncertainties.

If you had fired R7 before R6, you would produce exactly the same result. If the values of GROWTH and UNEMPLOYMENT had allowed you to fire only one of these rules, then there would have been no confirmative boost in certainty about a good economy. After you fire R6 and R7, there are no further ADVISOR rules that could affect the ECONOMY variable. However, imagine that ADVISOR were expanded to include other rules that could indicate a good economy within the rule being fired. If this certainty is low, then the new evidence for a good economy is weak, and 84 increases very little. If the certainty is high, then the new evidence is strong, and the certainty factor rapidly approaches 100.

THRESHOLD OF THE UNKNOWN

When a human expert reasons about a problem, the degree of certainty about something may be so low that it is regarded as being unknown. But, what does "low" mean? Where is the dividing line between the known and the unknown? Depending on the nature of an application area, we could draw this line in different places. For one application, a certainty of 70 might be too low to allow a value to be regarded as being sufficiently known. That is, it should be excluded from the reasoning efforts. For another application, a certainty of 25 might be high enough for a value to be regarded as being known.

In a similar way, an inference engine that processes certainty factors will typically have a threshold of the unknown. If the certainty of a value falls below this threshold, then the value is considered to be unknown. A typical default **unknown threshold** is 20, which means that a variable is considered to be unknown if none of its values has a certainty factor in excess of 20. Some inference engines allow a developer to control the level of the uncertainty threshold by setting a reasoning control to the desired level. There are even those that allow this to be overriden on an individual variable basis by specifying a threshold in its variable description.

15.4 FUZZY VARIABLES

Often a human expert is confronted with the task of making some sense out of a fuzzy situation (Zadeh 1965; Kosko 1993). One or more of the factors involved in the reasoning process is unclear or out of focus, in the sense that it has simultaneously several plausible appearances. The economic outlook may appear to be both good and fair at the same time—each with a certain degree of plausibility. Some inference engines can track and propagate a variable's multiple values (and their respective certainties) during the reasoning process. This manipulation of fuzzy variables can be considered to be an implementation of some aspects of fuzzy set theory (Zadeh 1983).

In all the examples shown to this point, no variable had more than one value at a time. For instance, the ECONOMY variable could either be unknown or have a value of poor, fair, or good at any given point in a consultation. However, it could not be both fair and good at the same time during a consultation with the ADVISOR rule set shown in Chapter 13. In contrast, a human expert who reasons about the economic outlook might be unclear about what that outlook is. The outlook might be fuzzy. At a given moment, the expert might simultaneously think that the outlook is good or fair, each with some degree of certainty. The expert may be equally certain about both values or be more sure about one than the other. The expert uses both economic outlooks in subsequent reasoning, yielding two possibilities for the economic factor that will be used to produce new quota advice. Each possible economic factor has its own certainties. Similarly, two possibilities result for the local advertising factor, each with a particular degree of certainty. Ultimately, the expert arrives at two new quota recommendations—each with some appropriate degree of certainty.

In order for an inference engine to emulate the human's ability to reason about fuzzy situations, it must have the capacity to simultaneously keep track of different values for the same variable. It must be able to deal with differing degrees of uncertainty about each of those values. It must be able to incorporate the multiple values and their respective certainty factors into subsequent reasoning activity. Some expert system development tools do not have built-in mechanisms for supporting reasoning abut fuzzy situations. Others provide this support.

REASONING WITH FUZZY VARIABLES

A **fuzzy variable** is simply a variable that has more than one value at a time. Each value of a fuzzy variable has its own certainty factor. If a variable has one value, then it becomes fuzzy by assigning an additional value to the variable. This is easily accomplished by using an additive assignment ($+=$) action rather than the traditional assignment ($=$) action.

DSS IN THE NEWS

Fuzzy Logic in the Workplace

Picture a factory that can automatically switch from manufacturing one product to another. Or a computerized secretary that can take dictation. Or, for that matter, a vacuum cleaner that automatically adjusts suction as the amount of dirt to pick up changes.

These are some of the innovations that could attend the increasing acceptance of fuzzy logic. . . .

Once considered an obtuse mathematical theorem, fuzzy logic is finding practical applications in an array of computers and appliances. Fuzzy logic gives the machines the ability to choose among several "decisions" just as human beings do. . . .

The concept behind fuzzy logic is simple. Computers are digital, meaning they translate all data into 1s and 0s, "ons" and "offs." The problem is that most physical phenomena tend to be complicated. Expressing them digitally can be extraordinarily difficult.

. . . A traditional computer might be able to call a six-foot man tall and a five-foot man short, if those parameters were specifically programmed in. It would fall apart if it were asked to judge whether a five-foot, 11-inch man was tall or short. Fuzzy logic devices are designed to deal with such gradations. . . .

M. Stroud, "Companies Finding Practical Applications for Fuzzy Logic in Products, Factories," *Investor's Business Daily* 29 May 1992, p. 3.

Recall that R6 and R7 were revised to use additive assignment actions. Because both actions resulted in the same value (good) for ECONOMY, this variable had only one value during a consultation. Now suppose Jack revises R8 by eliminating its second condition and using an additive assignment in its action:

```
RULE: R8
  IF: GROWTH >= .02 AND UNEMPLOYMENT >= .055
      AND UNEMPLOYMENT < .082
    THEN: ECONOMY += "fair" CF 80
```

If this rule is fired, then ECONOMY will have a value of fair in addition to whatever other known value it may already have. The certainty factor for ECONOMY's value of fair is automatically computed in the usual way.

Suppose that a particular consultation's initialization sequence has given GROWTH a value of 0.04 with a certainty factor of 60 and UNEMPLOYMENT a value of 0.06 with a certainty factor of 75. Assume that JCFE is set to use the minimum method for calculating the joint certainty of a conjunctive premise. Assume that JCFV and CCFV are set to use the product (within a rule) and probability sum (across rules) methods for combining certainties when determining the certainty factor of a variable's value. Imagine that you are the inference engine.

When you consider the revised R6, you discover that its premise is true with a certainty of 60 (minimum of 60 and 75). You fire R6 to give ECONOMY a value of good with a certainty of 54 (60 · 90/100). When you consider the revised R7, you see that its premise is false because the unemployment rate exceeds 5.5%. When you consider the revised R8, you discover that all three conditions in the premise are satisfied. The certainty of this premise being true is 60 (minimum of 60, 75, and 75). When you fire R8, you give ECONOMY a value of fair in addition to the value of good that it already has. The certainty factor for this value of fair is 48 (60 · 80/100). Thus, the ECONOMY variable now has two values, and you are slightly more certain about the value of good than about the value of fair.

As the reasoning proceeds, both values of ECONOMY are available for use. For instance, if you now consider rule R3 you will discover that its premise is true with a certainty of 54. When you fire this rule you establish a value for EFACTOR. If you next consider R4, you see that its first condition is true with a certainty of 48. You use the LOCALADS variable description to look up a value for local advertising. As a result, you now know LOCALADS. GROWTH already has a value. Therefore, the premise of R4 is now true with a certainty of 48 (minimum of 48, 100, and 100). If you now fire R4, the value of EFACTOR that resulted from R3 is replaced by the value of GROWTH/3. Replacement is undesirable here because Jack really wants you to explore the implications of both economic outlooks. In other words, EFACTOR should be a fuzzy variable, capable of having multiple values simultaneously.

To achieve the desired reasoning behavior, Jack revises the R3 and R4 actions by inserting the + symbol ahead of the = symbol. As a result, you (the inference engine) know that Jack desires an additive assignment for EFACTOR rather than a traditional replacement action. Thus, firing R3 and R4 results in two values for EFACTOR—each with its own certainty. This fact illustrates a simple, but important, point for rule set developers. A developer should identify which of a rule set's variables should be capable of being fuzzy during a consultation. Wherever a value is assigned to such a variable in rule actions, an additive, (+=) assignment should be specified.

In view of the revised R6, R7, and R8 ADVISOR rules, the potential fuzziness of ECONOMY implies that the following variables could also potentially be fuzzy: EFACTOR, LAFACTOR, and NEWQUOTA. Thus, the actions of rules R3, R4, R10, R12, R15, R16, and R17 that result in values for these variables should be additive assignments. For instance, the revised rule R4 is

```
RULE: R4
   IF: ECONOMY = "fair" AND KNOWN ("LOCALADS") AND KNOWN ("GROWTH")
 THEN: EFACTOR += GROWTH/3; LAFACTOR += LOCALADS/120000
```

Notice that it would do no harm to employ additive assignments in the actions of rules R9, R5, and R11. However, it is unnecessary for this rule set, because the conditions that lead to a poor economy preclude the possibility of simultaneously having any value other than poor for ECONOMY.

REPORTING VALUES AND CERTAINTIES OF A FUZZY VARIABLE

Suppose you continue the inference started here until you have established two values for the NEWQUOTA variable, each with a particular degree of certainty. You are now ready to take the actions specified in the completion sequence. However, completion sequences in Chapter 13 were not designed to handle the output of multiple values for a fuzzy variable. The completion sequence shown in Figure 15.3 can be used instead. Its commands make use of three functions for processing individual values of a fuzzy variable: VALN, CFN, and NUMVAL.

The VALN function provides the nth value of a specified variable, where the order of values is from the one with the highest certainty to the one with the lowest certainty. Similarly, CFN provides the certainty factor of the nth value. The NUMVAL function is used to find out the number of values a specified variable has. Thus, at coordinates 9, 5 on the console screen, the inference engine outputs the value of NEWQUOTA having the highest certainty factor. That certainty factor is output on the same line by the CFN function. If NEWQUOTA was assigned more than one value in this consultation, then the second value and its certainty factor are output on line 10 (and so forth until all are displayed).

FIGURE 15.3 A Completion Sequence Using Iteration

```
DO:
    CLEAR
    AT 5,1 OUTPUT "Sales Rep:", REP
    AT 6,1 OUTPUT "Product Line:", PROD
    AT 5,20 OUTPUT "Quarter:", QTR
    AT 8,1 OUTPUT "The recommended quota is:"
    LET I = 1
    WHILE I <= NUMVAL(NEWQUOTA) DO
        AT 8 + I,5 OUTPUT VALN(NEWQUOTA,I) USING "nnnnn",\
                "with certainty of", CFN(NEWQUOTA,I) USING "nnn"
    ENDWHILE
```

Fuzzy variable values and certainties can be displayed in other ways than those shown here (e.g., via forms or graphs). As described earlier, they can also be available for use in nonoutput actions, such as spreadsheet processing, procedural modeling, database-management operations, and so on (Holsapple and Whinston 1986).

MULTIVALUE ASSIGNMENT WITHIN A RULE'S CONCLUSION

We have seen that an inference engine can assign multiple values to a single variable as the result of firing multiple rules that lead to different conclusions about that variable. This result is accomplished by specifying an additive (+=) assignment in each rule's action. As shown next, there is a more direct way to give a variable multiple values.

During the expert-testing stage of a development cycle, Jack reconsiders rule R6. This rule was originally stated as

```
RULE: R6
    IF: GROWTH >= .04 AND UNEMPLOYMENT < .076
    THEN: ECONOMY = "good"
```

But Jack now wants to refine this piece of reasoning knowledge. Although it is usually the case that the economy is good for the indicated growth and unemployment levels, Jack realizes that the economy will sometimes be only fair for those levels and occasionally will even be poor.

To capture this realization in the rule set, he alters R6 to make ECONOMY into a fuzzy variable.

```
RULE: R6
 IF: GROWTH >= .04 AND UNEMPLOYMENT < .076
 THEN: ECONOMY += {"good" CF 95, "fair" CF 30, "poor" CF 10}
```

If R6 fires, then ECONOMY will have all three values. The certainty for each value is computed just like the certainty of a single-valued variable, based on its intrarule certainty and its interrule certainty (if any). As usual, the computation method is controlled by the JCFV and CCFV settings.

The Processing Flow   Now think of yourself as the inference engine, considering whether to fire rule R6. Suppose that the ECON program yielded values of 0.04, 0.05, and 0.03 for the GROWTH variable, with respective certainty factors of 80, 70, and 50. Suppose it also produces a value of 0.07 for UNEMPLOYMENT with a certainty factor of 90. Should you fire R6? If so, what would be the intrarule certainties for each of ECONOMY's three values? To answer this question, you must first determine whether the premise of R6 is true. If it is true, you will need to combine your certainty about the premise's truth with the certainty of each value assigned to ECONOMY. You will then have the three intrarule certainties for the three values of ECONOMY.

Looking at the first condition in R6's premise, is it true that GROWTH is at least 0.04? Because GROWTH is fuzzy, the condition that contains it is a fuzzy expression. In general, if an expression contains one or more fuzzy variables, then the expression itself is probably fuzzy. When you evaluate a fuzzy expression, you will probably end up with more than one value, each with its own certainty factor. In the case of

```
GROWTH >= .04
```

you will end up with two values for the expression —namely, TRUE and FALSE— because two of GROWTH's values (0.04 and 0.05) make the expression true, whereas the other GROWTH value (0.03) makes it false.

How certain are you that the condition is true and how certain are you that it is false? Think about the FALSE value first. There is only one GROWTH value (0.03) that results in a FALSE value for the expression. Because 0.03 has a certainty factor of 50 and no other uncertainty is involved in the expression, you are 50% sure that the condition is false. The certainties (80 and 70) for the other GROWTH values need to be combined to find out how sure you are that the condition is true. Clearly, these should be combined in a confirmative fashion. Because both 0.04 and 0.05 yield a TRUE value, the certainty factor for TRUE should be at least as large as the largest of the certainties for the two GROWTH values. As usual, the CCFE setting controls how the confirmative certainty will be computed. Suppose it is set to the probability method sum. You then compute that the certainty for the condition's TRUE value is $80 + 70 - 80 \cdot 70/100 = 94$.

The second condition in the premise is evaluated in the usual way, resulting in a TRUE value with a certainty of 90. Because both conditions are true, the premise as a whole is true. Your certainty about the truth of the premise is computed from the certainties (94 and 90) about the truth of its two conditions. If JCFE is set to the minimum method, this yields a certainty factor of 90 for the truth of the premise. Assuming the unknown threshold is set below 90, you fire rule R6.

Firing rule R6 results in three values for the ECONOMY variable: good, fair, and poor. The intrarule certainty that you attribute to each value is computed from the premise's certainty and the certainty factor specified for that value in the rule's conclusion. Supposing JCFV is set to the minimum method, the intrarule certainty for good is MIN (90, 95) = 90, for fair is MIN (90, 30) = 30, and for poor is MIN (90, 10) = 10. Thus, you have evaluated a premise containing a fuzzy variable, fired the rule, and computed the certainty factor for each value of the conclusion's fuzzy variable. Fuzzy variables are handled in this same manner throughout an inference engine's reasoning activities.

Accounting for Falseness   If desired, the developer might construct R6 in such a way that the certainty of falseness for the premise influences the intrarule certainties for ECONOMY's values when the rule is fired. For instance, Jack might restate R6 as

```
RULE: R6
  READY: LET ENOUGHGROWTH = GROWTH>=.04
  IF: ENOUGHGROWTH AND UNEMPLOYMENT < .076
  THEN: IF MORETRUE(ENOUGHGROWTH) THEN D = 0
        ELSE D = CFV(ENOUGHGROWTH, FALSE) * .1
        ENDIF
        ECONOMY += {"good" CF 95-D, "fair" CF 30-D, "poor" CF 10-D}
```

The preaction results in a fuzzy logical variable called ENOUGHGROWTH. It is given a value of TRUE with certainty 94 and a value of FALSE with a certainty of 50. The premise is still discovered to be true with a certainty of 90.

In the rule's actions, the MORETRUE and CFV functions appear. The first of these tests the certainties of ENOUGHGROWTH's TRUE and FALSE values to see whether

SUBTRACTIVE ASSIGNMENT

As Jack ponders rule R6, he recognizes that there is a growth rate beyond which he is sure that the economy cannot be poor. If this is 0.05, then he no longer wants poor to be a value of ECONOMY. This might be achieved by altering R6 as follows:

```
RULE: R6
  IF: GROWTH >= .04 AND UNEMPLOYMENT < .076
  THEN: ECONOMY += {"good" CF 95, "fair" CF 30,\
        "poor" CF 10}
        IF GROWTH >= .05 THEN ECONOMY -= "poor"; ENDIF
```

Now as Jack continues to ponder rule R6, he decides that if the growth is high, then the certainty about a fair economy also should be reduced. Furthermore, he reasons that the certainty of ECONOMY's value of good should be increased in such a situation. To accomplish this, he revises R6:

```
RULE: R6
  IF: GROWTH >= .04 AND UNEMPLOYMENT < .076
  THEN: ECONOMY += {"good" CF 95, "fair" CF 30, \
        "poor" CF 10}
        IF GROWTH >= .05 THEN
            ECONOMY -= "poor"
            ECONOMY -= "fair" CF 80
            ECONOMY += "good" CF 20
        ENDIF
```

The second subtractive assignment command within the conclusion's IF statement indicates that Jack is 80% sure about getting rid of ECONOMY's "fair" value when growth is high. When the inference engine fires R6, it checks to see whether the growth is at least 5%. Because GROWTH is a fuzzy variable (values of 0.04, 0.05, and 0.03, with certainties of 80, 70, and 50), the expression

```
GROWTH >= .05
```

will have both a FALSE value and a TRUE value. One GROWTH value (0.05) makes the expression TRUE with a certainty of 70. Thus, poor is eliminated from ECONOMY's values and the certainty of the value of fair needs to be diminished.

To reduce a value's certainty during a subtractive assignment, the inference engine takes the complement of the certainty factor that is specified in the assignment. The complement is then combined in a joint fashion with the value's existing certainty. In this example, the complement is 100 − 80 = 20. If JCFV is set to the minimum method, combining 20 and 30 yields a new certainty of 20 for ECONOMY's value of fair.

the certainty of truth exceeds the certainty of falseness. If it does, then no deduction will be made (D = 0) when the certainties of ECONOMY's values are computed. However, if ENOUGHGROWTH is not more true than false, a deduction is calculated (with the CFV function) that is equal to one tenth of the certainty factor for ENOUGHGROWTH's FALSE value. This deduction is used to adjust each of the three certainties for ECONOMY prior to the intrarule certainty computations by subtracting it from 95, 30, and 10.

The important point of this example is not the formula used to compute D nor the manner in which D is used to adjust some certainties. These methods could be varied in a multitude of ways. The important point is that a developer is able to construct rules that treat individual certainties of a fuzzy variable's values in specially customized ways. This result is made possible by built-in functions such as MORETRUE and CFV, which allow a rule to reference individual fuzzy variables and their certainties.

15.5 SUMMARY

Forward and reverse reasoning are two fundamentally different approaches to reasoning. Within each approach, many variations are possible. There are many kinds of reverse reasoning and many kinds of forward reasoning. Because no single kind of reasoning is best in all situations, skilled developers find it valuable to have mechanisms for easily adjusting an inference engine's exact reasoning behavior so it can differ from one consultation to another and from one rule set to another. Such adjustments can help the developer build an expert system whose advice more closely resembles that of the human expert. They can also allow the developer to tune the inference engine in the interest of maximizing consultation speeds.

Aspects of reasoning that can be adjusted include the degree of reasoning rigor, the selection order for considering competing rules, the testing strategy employed for premise evaluation, and the timing of reverse reasoning for unknown variables. The controls are also meaningful on a rule-by-rule and variable-by-variable basis. It is possible to set the reasoning controls prior to a consultation or have them set by the inference engine whenever it executes the rule set's initialization sequence. There can be additional reasoning controls that pertain specifically to reasoning with uncertainty and with fuzzy variables.

The topics of certainty factors and fuzzy variables are extensive. Only a brief overview of some of the basics has been presented here. Certainty factors are numbers that reflect the degree of certainty about a variable's value, an expression's value, or the appropriateness of a rule's action. In the course of reasoning, certainties need to be combined to derive other certainties. We have distinguished between two major certainty-combining situations: (1) combining certainties about the components of an expression to get a certainty factor for the expression's value, and (2) combining certainties involved in the firing of a rule to get a certainty factor for the value assigned to a variable in the rule's action.

Multiple methods exist for combining certainty factors. The traditional methods fall into two categories: joint (e.g., minimum and product methods) and confirmative (e.g., maximum and probability sum methods). Both categories come into play for each of the certainty-combining situations. Some inference engines give developers reasoning controls to govern which joint and confirmative certainty-combining methods are to be used in the situation of evaluating an expression (JCFE, CCFE) and in the situation of assigning a variable's value (JCFV, CCFV). The settings for such controls are chosen to yield certainties that most nearly approximate those of the expert being modeled.

Fuzzy variables are variables that have multiple values. Each value of a fuzzy variable has a certainty factor. In the course of inference, the multiple values of fuzzy variables (and their certainties) are propagated via additive assignments in fired rules. The result is typically multiple values for the consultation's goal variable, each with some reported degree of certainty. More-detailed explorations of these topics appear in Holsapple and Whinston (1986).

It should be kept in mind that an understanding of certainty factors and fuzzy variables is not necessary in order to use an expert system. Furthermore, interesting expert systems can be developed without using such features. However, there are many applications where uncertainty arises. It is therefore valuable for an expert system development tool to support the kinds of built-in certainty factor and fuzzy variable capabilities described here. They may not be required for some applications, yet they are always available when needed. Obviously, the degrees of flexibility, power, and convenience that a tool provides for reasoning with uncertainty are also very significant.

▲ IMPORTANT TERMS

certainty algebra	premise-testing strategy
certainty factor	reasoning controls
confirmative certainty	rigor
firing cap	selection order
fuzzy variable	unknown threshold
joint certainty	

▲ APPLICATION TO THE ONTARIO CASE

1. What decision does this expert system support?
2. Why did the developer of the system need to deal with certainties in this application?
3. Identify the sources of uncertainty for this application.
4. What kinds of parameter (i.e., variable) values is a user prompted to provide?
5. Describe the nature of the system's response to a user upon completion of a consultation.
6. What were results of the expert testing for this system?
7. What inference controls could have conceivably been used to enhance the expert testing results?
8. Suppose an overall fuzzy goal variable of tillage alternative was designed into the system. What is the maximum number of values this variable could have during a consultation?

▲ REVIEW QUESTIONS

1. What is a reasoning control?
2. Why is it beneficial for an inference engine to provide an assortment of reasoning controls?
3. What kinds of reasoning controls might an inference engine reasonably be expected to support?
4. What role does a rule's NEEDS clause play?
5. Describe three distinct strategies for trying to evaluate a premise that contains unknown variables.

6. What is a certainty factor?
7. In addition to values of variables, what else can have a certainty factor?
8. What are some possible sources of certainty factors?
9. The two conditions in a conjunctive premise are true with certainties of 60 and 80, respectively. What is the joint certainty for this premise using (a) the product method and (b) the minimum method?
10. The two conditions in a disjunctive premise are true with certainties of 60 and 80, respectively. What is the confirmative certainty for this premise using (a) the maximum method and (b) the probability sum method?
11. If X={2 CF 20, 1 CF 60} and Y={3 CF 70, 6 CF 80}, what are the values of the fuzzy expression X*Y? What are the certainties of those values (a) if the minimum and maximum methods are used, and (b) if the product and probability sum methods are used?
12. For what kinds of expressions is a joint certainty computation appropriate?
13. For what kinds of expressions is a confirmative certainty computation appropriate?
14. Suppose we are 70% certain that X has a value of 12 and 80% sure that Y has a value of 100. What is the value of the expression X+Y, and how sure are we about this value for each of the joint certainty algebra methods?
15. Suppose the inference engine has determined that A>B with a certainty of 30 and that B=C with a certainty of 60. What is the value of the premise A>B OR B=C, and how sure is the inference engine about this value for each of the confirmative certainty algebra methods?
16. What is the most conservative approach to determining a variable's certainty?
17. What is the least conservative approach to determining a variable's certainty?
18. Rule XA has the action

    `X+=200  CF  70`

    in its conclusion. Rule XB has the action

    `X+=200  CF  50`

    in its conclusion. Suppose XA is fired with a premise certainty of 90 and then XB is fired with a premise certainty of 80. How certain are we that X has a value of 200 if (a) the minimum and maximum methods are used? (b) The product and maximum methods are used? (c) The most venturesome methods are used? (d) The most conservative methods are used and XB's action is X=200 CF 50?
19. How does a fuzzy variable differ from a traditional variable?
20. Explain what an uncertainty threshold is.
21. How does conventional assignment (i.e., replacement) differ from additive assignment when multiple rules are fired to yield the same value for a variable?

▲ DISCUSSION TOPICS

1. Why might the rigor setting affect the solution derived by the inference engine?
2. Describe a situation where priorities are a worthwhile selection criterion.
3. What premise-testing strategy should usually be avoided for a disjunctive premise involving certainty factors below 100? Why?
4. Someone claims that the availability of many reasoning controls makes the development process more difficult and complex than it would otherwise be. Explain why the exact opposite can be true.

5. Explain why certainty factors should not be referred to as probabilities.
6. Under what two circumstances will the product and minimum methods yield the same joint certainty?
7. Suggest an alternative method for determining joint certainties that is always more venturesome than the product method and always more conservative than the minimum method.
8. Someone suggests that an alternative method for computing a joint certainty factor would be to take the average of the two contributing certainty factors. Discuss this suggestion.
9. Under what two circumstances will the probability sum and maximum methods yield the same confirmative certainty?
10. Suggest an alternative method for determining confirmative certainties that is always more venturesome than the maximum method and always more conservative than the probability sum method.
11. Someone suggests that an alternative method for computing a confirmative certainty would be to take the average of the two contributing certainty factors. Discuss this suggestion.
12. What is a certainty algebra?
13. What is the human analog for an inference engine that does not support multiple certainty algebras?
14. Under what circumstances is the average method appropriate for joint certainty computation?
15. Explain why the confirmative average method can be regarded as a compromise between the maximum and probability sum methods.
16. Regardless of the algebra being used, what are the two basic aspects of computing a variable's certainty factor?
17. How is it possible to allow different certainty factor algebras to be used for different variables within a single consultation? What is the value of such a capability?
18. Why is it important for an inference engine to be able to use different certainty factor algebras?
19. Describe a situation where it is valuable to use a fuzzy variable whose values all have a certainty of 100.
20. Why is it important to have functions for working on individual values of a fuzzy variable?

▲ REFERENCES

Calatone, R. J., C. W. Holsapple, and J. Wu. 1990. Certainty factor algebras. *Kentucky Initiative for Knowledge Management,* Research Paper No. 26, College of Business and Economics, University of Kentucky.

Clarke, N. D., M. D. McLeish, T. J. Vyn, and J. A. Stone. 1991. Using certainty factors and possibility theory methods in a tillage selection expert system. *Expert Systems With Applications* 4, no. 1.

Favere, M., and D. E. O'Leary. 1991. Conditional, conjunction and disjunction fallacies in probability judgements. *Carnegie Conference on Decision Making, Cognitive Science, and Accounting,* Pittsburgh (June).

Heckerman, D., and E. Shortliffe. 1992. From certainty factors to belief networks. *Artificial Intelligence in Medicine* 4.

Holsapple, C. W., W. S. Rayens, and J. Wu. 1993. Operator effects in the choice of certainty factor algebras: An experimental study. *Knowledge Acquisition* 5, no. 4.

————. 1994. An experimental study of magnitude effects in the choice of certainty factor algebras. *International Journal of Expert Systems: Research and Applications* 7, no. 3.

Holsapple, C. W., and A. B. Whinston. 1986. *Manager's guide to expert systems.* Homewood, Ill.,: Dow Jones–Irwin.

Holsapple, C. W., and J. Wu. 1993. Psychological validity of certainty factor algebras: An empirical study. *Expert Systems* 10, no. 2.

————. 1994. Certainty factor algebras: Comparing conventional mappings and experimental results. *Intelligent Systems in Accounting, Finance, and Management* 3, no. 1.

Kahneman, D., P. Slovic, and A. Tversky. 1979. *Judgement under uncertainty: Heuristics and biases.* Cambridge: Cambridge University Press.

Kanal, L. N., and J. F. Lemmer, eds. 1966. *Uncertainty in artificial intelligence.* New York: North-Holland.

Kopcso, D., L. Pipino, and W. Rybolt. 1988. A comparison of the manipulations of certainty factors by individuals and expert system shells. *Journal of Management Information Systems* 5.

Kosko, B. 1993. *Fuzzy thinking: The new science of fuzzy logic.* New York: Hyperion.

Lindley, D. V. 1987. A statistical view of uncertainty in expert systems. In *Artificial intelligence and statistics,* edited by W. Gale. Reading, Mass.: Addison-Wesley.

Magill, W., and S. Leech. 1991. Uncertainty techniques in expert system software. *Decision Support Systems* 7.

Pearl, J. 1988. *Probabilistic reasoning in intelligent systems.* San Mateo, Calif.: Morgan Kaufman.

Shafer, G. 1987. Probability judgement in artificial intelligence and expert systems. *Statistical Science* 2.

Shortliffe, E. H. 1976. *Computer-based medical consultations: MYCIN.* New York: American Elsevier.

Shortliffe, E. H., and B. G. Buchanan. 1975. A model of inexact reasoning in medicine. *Mathematical Biosciences* 23.

Spiegelhalter, D. J. 1986. A statistical view of uncertainty in expert systems. In *Artificial intelligence and statistics,* edited by W. Gale. Reading, Mass.: Addison-Wesley.

Tonn, B. E., and R. T. Goeltz. 1990. Psychological validity of uncertainty combining rules in expert systems. *Expert Systems,* 7.

Tversky, A., and D. Kahneman. 1973. Availability: A heuristic for judging frequency and probability. *Cognitive Psychology* 5.

Tversky, A., and D. Kahneman. 1983. Exceptional versus intuitive reasoning: The conjunction fallacy in probability judgement. *Psychological Review* 90.

Wise, B. P., and M. Henrion. 1986. A framework for comparing uncertain inference systems to probability. In *Uncertainty in artificial intelligence,* edited by L. Kanal and J. Lemmer. New York: North-Holland.

Yu, V. L., L. M. Fagan, S. M. Wraith, W. J. Clancy, A. C. Scott, J. F. Hannigan, R. L. Blum, B. G. Buchanan, and S. N. Cohen. 1979. Antimicrobial selection by a computer: A blinded evaluation by infectious disease experts. *Journal of the American Medical Association* 242.

Zadeh, L. A. 1965. Fuzzy Sets. *Information and Control* 8.

————. 1983. The role of fuzzy logic in the management of uncertainty in expert systems. *Fuzzy Sets and Systems* 11.

CASE STUDY

A good way to build your conceptual understanding of artificially intelligent DSSs into a practical understanding is to develop your own expert system. Here, we present samples of student work along those lines involving three very different application areas. You are encouraged to identify an application area of interest to you and for which you have access to reasoning expertise. This may be your own expertise, that of an expert or experts to whom you have access, or perhaps expertise embodied in books. In any event, your project should revolve around the formal representation of that reasoning knowledge in the KS of an artificially intelligent DSS. Guidelines for this do-it-yourself case study are presented following the three sample projects.

AN ARTIFICIALLY INTELLIGENT SYSTEM TO SUPPORT SITE-SELECTION DECISIONS, BY DAN JACOVITCH AND DOUG MAXWELL

IMPORTANCE OF SITE SELECTION

No decision is more important to Pump-n-Save than selecting the location for our gasoline/convenience stores. Even ample financial resources and above-average managerial skills cannot offset the handicap of a poor location. Moving is costly. Legal complications of a lease can be difficult to untangle—not to mention other location-related problems that could arise. Clearly, careful examination of alternative sites is a worthwhile endeavor. By studying the relevant reports from the Bureau of the Census, we can develop valuable insights about the characteristics of prospective customers and gain knowledge about the economic strengths and weaknesses of specific trading areas.

When a large corporation such as ours is faced with selecting sites for gasoline/convenience stores, it must first select the areas in which to conduct detailed reviews (i.e., involving traffic counts, property surveys, etc.). The costs involved with these detailed surveys preclude their use over widespread areas. As such, our marketing and development departments need to focus their efforts on areas of potential success.

CURRENT APPROACH TO SITE SELECTION

Presently, Pump-n-Save uses the expertise of the manager of development in limiting the areas for review. A county is divided into tracts by the Bureau of the Census, where an average tract has about 4,000 to 5,000 residents. Before conducting detailed reviews within a given county of interest, the manager considers two primary pieces of tract-level information: consumption profiles of the population and the number of competitors' locations.

The consumption profiles are purchased and are available in printed and electronic format. The competitor locations are organized by census tract and are maintained by the marketing department; these are filed by county. When development is expected in a new county, one of the first steps performed by marketing is to create a competitor location file for that county. This information on the competitor location is used in different ways, depending on the level of aggression aimed for in this site. If the site is highly aggressive, it will be located in competitive areas; if it is not aggressive, the areas selected for development will not contain as many competitors.

The manager of development combines the demographic and consumer behavior knowledge with the competitive positioning knowledge to determine the areas that call for detailed surveys. This initial screening is critical in keeping development costs to a minimum while ensuring that successful units meet competitive positioning objectives.

SHORTCOMINGS OF THE CURRENT APPROACH

The critical initial screening process is performed by one person. This process requires a heavy use of judgment, and the logic involved is not documented. If we want to maintain consistent development criteria over time, it would be in our best interest to formalize the process. If we lost the expertise of the manager of development, the person taking on his responsibilities would apply his or her own experience and judgment; these would probably be inconsistent with the present unformalized criteria.

Other concerns relate to human limitation factors. When the manager of development is working on a county with many tracts, it is very likely that they will not all be reviewed in a consistent manner due to the sheer volume. Also, the degree to which the competitive positioning objectives are taken into consideration is not clear.

ADVANTAGES OF A BUSINESS EXPERT SYSTEM

A business expert system (BES) will, most importantly, provide a formal reasoning process that consistently screens tracts based on desired objectives. It will also provide documentation of this process. Although the expert does not presently spend a great deal of time on this process, he will be confident that his ideas for tract review have been consistently applied. He will also have the ability to alter the nature of competitive aggression and quickly see the results of this what-if analysis. Forced selection of aggression ensures that aggression will be considered in all decisions.

SPECIFIC FEATURES OF THE BES

The initial screen will allow the user to select the county to be considered in the study. This selection forces the system to look at the tracts that correspond to the selected county. Because the expert needs to consider the competitive nature of the area when determining appropriate site locations, the system should also have this ability. Therefore, the system will next ask the user to select whether they are aggressive or nonaggressive or if aggression should be ignored. This aggression selection will be compared to the number of competitors in the tracts to determine if the level of competition matches the desired level of aggression.

At this point, the system will prompt the user as to whether the system should list only tracts that are deemed by the system to be desirable. The system will then provide a list of the appropriate tracts from which the user can choose. After a tract selection, the system has all the user-supplied information that it needs to analyze and provide advice and attributes about this tract.

The system will use the Census Bureau reports (CACI), which index consumer consumption on a tract level. Instead of receiving the reports on hard copy, they are on computer disks. The system also will use the company's information on competitor locations that has been supplied by the marketing department and updated by the user.

LIMITATIONS AND FUTURE POSSIBILITIES

In its initial planned form, the system will not look at trends in CACI data (e.g., multiple-year comparisons). This feature can be incorporated into the logic at a later date.

Presently, site development is conducted one county at a time. The planned system is designed to continue this tradition. In the future, the system could be modified to review groups of counties or even entire states.

The design of the system relies heavily on analysis of the composition of small areas. As such, it will not detect the obvious sites for gas stations that exist along large flows of traffic from one area to another. These sites are more apparent and can be selected from maps and air surveillance.

The system is also not sensitive to the nature of bordering tracts. It is possible that many competitors may be on the border of a tract and yet not be considered during the screening process. This system is designed as an initial screening tool; as such, as long as these limitations are known, they can be accounted for during the detailed review.

It is important to reiterate that this system is not meant to select an actual site. It is meant as an initial screening device to direct a decision maker's efforts to a limited number of tracts and therefore minimize detailed site-survey costs.

MAINTENANCE REQUIREMENTS OF THE BES

The system will require that CACI information continue to be purchased annually in electronic format. The CACI tables will have to be converted to a format with which the system can work. Marketing will have to continue updating their competitor location files and make those available to the development area.

DEVELOPMENT

The goal of the system is to minimize the expense of locating decisions and maximize the quality and consistency of those decisions. The factors that will aid in this goal are the CACI data and the competitor location information.

Of particular interest in the CACI data are the following: population by age, income, gasoline consumption, automobile supply purchases, VCR ownership, and grocery items. The CACI values are in the form of indexes, with 100 being the national average.

To perform its analysis, the system evaluates the nature of the market, the degree to which competitive units match the level of aggression desired, and the prospects of the tract based on the market and the level of gas consumption. The market is qualified as GOOD, FAIR, or POOR (with varying levels of certainty) based on income and demographics. The prospect and degree of match determine whether further analysis should be conducted on this tract (e.g., traffic counts, property surveys).

While the system is processing the tract, it also considers additional indexes to determine levels of grocery, video, and automotive product consumption. This consumption knowledge is calculated and output on all processed tracts to provide additional insight to the user. If friendly units are found to exist in the tract being processed, the system informs the user.

The rule set is formulated with the aid of the manager of development. His apparent success indicates that he has a good sense of judgement regarding where to conduct detailed surveys.

ACTION PLAN

Convert CACI format to BES tables.

Generate competitor/friendly unit location fields.

Formulate the MARKET portion of the rule set.

Test the MARKET rule set module.

Develop the entire rule set.

Test the entire rule set.

Incorporate certainty factors.

Test the rule set (Compare with the expert's results).

Design initial user interface menus and prompts.

Design user interface outputs.

Test the workability of the interface and output.

Demonstrate the BES to the class.

Turn in the disk, proposal, documentation, variable list, and dependency diagram.

DEVELOPMENT DISCUSSION

We found that creating the dependency diagram was the most important step performed in early and middle development. Without it, we would have had difficulty determining relationships among variables. We did not, however, treat the diagram as being a final document. It was revised repeatedly during development. The result is shown in the following figure.

For debugging, we used automatic tracing to determine what rules were not firing and thus causing a variable to remain unknown. We encountered problems with rule set variables that had the same name as table fields. We cured this by placing a T in front of the table field names and assigning their values to variables in the rule set's initialization sequence.

For testing the system, we used a looping program and placed print lines in the rule set's completion sequence. These printed key values and showed all fuzzy values with their certainties. Each iteration of the loop used a consultation to process information for a different record in the CACI90 table. After printing 30 or more values, we examined the output to see if it made sense. If it didn't make sense, we rethought the logic, made changes where appropriate, and then ran the looping program again.

Dependency Diagram

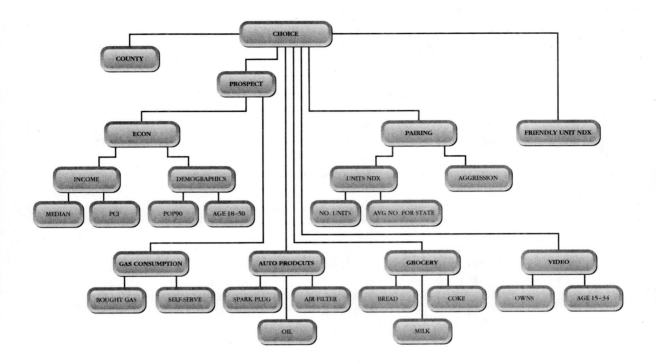

We opted for a menu-driven system that would provide as much flexibility as possible. Initially, each menu screen creation was placed in its own KS file. This practice helped in terms of clarity, but we found that during a particular series of menu steps, the problem processor would respond with "unable to open caci-cho.rsc." We felt that this problem occurred because too many KS files were being opened as we stepped through the menu. To correct the problem, we moved the menus into one file called "KYGAS." This change to one file also made the system faster.

Another problem related to speed is one that addresses the size of the CACI90 table (more than 840 records). By creating a relational table that just had county IDs and names, we made things somewhat faster. However, the one big time-saver of table indexing has not yet been incorporated. This modification is easily done, but we have not yet made it. Our goal was to get a fairly flexible menu-driven system that gave good advice about whether particular tracts are attractive enough to warrant further research.

Appendix H shows a listing of the main program (KYGAS) controlling the user interface, a summary of variables used by the inference engine, and a listing of the rule set itself.

USER GUIDE

This expert system is executed by typing PERFORM KYGAS and pressing Enter. The following menu is then presented. Menu 1 lists Kentucky's counties. You should arrow to the county of interest and press Enter. (You can also press the first letter of the county desired to move the highlight bar to counties that start with that letter.)

MENU 1
WHICH COUNTY ARE YOU INTERESTED IN? (USE CURSOR KEYS TO SELECT)

ADAIR	EDMONSON	KNOX	NICHOLAS
ALLEN	ELLIOTT	LARUE	OHIO
ANDERSON	ESTILL	LAUREL	OLDHAM
BALLARD	FAYETTE	LAWRENCE	OWEN
BARREN	FLEMING	LEE	OWSLEY
BATH	FLOYD	LESLIE	PERRY
BELL	FRANKLIN	LETCHER	PIKE
BOONE	FULTON	LEWIS	POWELL
BOURBON	GALLATIN	LINCOLN	PULASKI
BOYD	GARRARD	LIVINGSTON	ROBERTSON
BOYLE	GRANT	LOGAN	ROCKCASTLE
BRACKEN	GRAVES	MADISON	ROWAN
BREATHITT	GRAYSON	MAGOFFIN	RUSSELL
BRECKINRIDGE	GREEN	MARION	SCOTT
BULLITT	GREENUP	MARSHALL	SHELBY
BUTLER	HANCOCK	MARTIN	SIMPSON
CALDWELL	HARDIN	MASON	SPENCER
CALLOWAY	HARRISON	MCCRACKEN	TAYLOR
CAMPBELL	HART	MCCREARY	TODD
CARLISLE	HENDERSON	MCCLEAN	TRIGG
CARROLL	HENRY	MEADE	TRIMBLE
CARTER	HICKMAN	MENIFEE	UNION
CASEY	HOPKINS	MERCER	WARREN
CLARK	JACKSON	METCALFE	WASHINGTON
CLAY	JEFFERSON	MONROE	WAYNE
CLINTON	JESSAMINE	MONTGOMERY	WEBSTER
CRITTENDEN	JOHNSON	MORGAN	WHITLEY
CUMBERLAND	KENTON	MUHLENBERG	WOLFE
DAVIESS	KNOTT	NELSON	

After the user selects a county of interest, the system prompts the user for the level of AGGRESSION desired. The level of aggression chosen will be used by the system to screen out tracts that do not satisfy the level of aggression desired. The user can also select a different county by returning to the county listing menu.

Hint: Select DO NOT CARE the first time through to see output based only on demographics and consumption levels.

MENU 2
SELECT THE LEVEL OF ABGRESSION DESIRED.
DO NOT CARE   - competitors are of no importance
AGGRESSIVE   - favor tracts with higher level of
                       competition
NONAGGRESSIVE   - favor tracts with lower level of
                       competition
SELECT A DIFFERENT COUNTY

After the user selects the level of aggression, the system asks the user whether it should list all tracts in the selected county or show only the tracts that should or should not be considered based on the tract prospect and level of aggression desired. The user can also return to the AGGRESSION menu.

Hint: If there are many tracts in the county selected, you should allow for an adequate amount of time (about 10–15 seconds per tract). The first time through you should select NO on this menu. If you select YES, the system will tell you which tract it is currently processing and the total number of tracts that will be processed.

MENU 3
WHICH TRACT IN THIS COUNTY WOULD YOU LIKE THE EXPERT
SYSTEM TO SCREEN?

0001.00.000	0018.00.000	0033.00.000
0002.00.000	0019.00.000	0034.01.000
0003.00.000	0020.00.000	0034.02.000
0004.00.000	0021.00.000	0034.03.000
0005.00.000	0022.00.000	0035.01.000
0006.00.000	0023.01.000	0035.02.000
0007.00.000	0023.02.000	0036.00.000
0008.00.000	0024.00.000	0037.00.000
0009.00.000	0025.00.000	0038.01.000
0010.00.000	0026.00.000	0038.02.000
0011.00.000	0027.00.000	0039.01.000
0012.00.000	0028.00.000	0039.02.000
0013.00.000	0029.00.000	0040.01.000
0014.00.000	0030.00.000	0040.02.000
0015.00.000	0031.01.000	0041.01.000
0016.00.000	0031.02.000	0041.02.000
0017.00.000	0032.00.000	0042.01.000

After the expert system processes the tract information, it outputs the nature of the MARKET, GAS consumption, the PROSPECT value and certainty, whether the tract matches the level of AGGRESSION desired, and if the company SHOULD or SHOULD NOT conduct further analysis on this tract. Additional information includes: automotive product, grocery, and video consumption and whether the company currently has a friendly unit in this tract.

OUTPUT FORM
    COUNTY: FAYETTE
    TRACT MCD: 0018.00.000
    The MARKET (based on income and demographics) in
    this tract is FAIR. Given this market condition and
    the LOW level of gas consumption in this tract, the
    Expert System is 66% sure the PROSPECT is FAIR.

    **AGGRESSION information will be displayed here **
    Given the above, further analysis of this tract
    SHOULD NOT be performed.

    The following levels of consumption were found:
                        GROCERY VIDEO GAS
                          LOW   LOW   LOW

When the user is finished viewing the output, the system displays a final menu that asks WHAT NOW? One of two menus will show up: If the user selected from a screened listing of the tracts, the menu will look like the following:

```
LAST MENU
WHAT NOW?
      PROCESS A DIFFERENT TRACT FROM SCREENED LISTING
      SELECT A DIFFERENT COUNTY
      ESCAPE TO PPS PROMPT (for how/why explanations)
      QUIT TO DOS PROMPT
```

otherwise, it will look like this:

```
WHAT NOW?
      SELECT A DIFFERENT TRACT IN CURRENT COUNTY (list all
      tracts)
      SELECT A DIFFERENT COUNTY
      ESCAPE TO PPS PROMPT (for how/why explanations)
      QUIT TO DOS PROMPT
```

AN ARTIFICIALLY INTELLIGENT SYSTEM TO SUPPORT RESOURCE-ALLOCATION DECISIONS, *BY LINDA JOHNSON*

RUOLF CORPORATION

Ruolf Corporation, an international engineering, construction, maintenance, and related services firm, reported over $6 billion in revenue last year. Ruolf's primary strategic business unit has five primary sectors: industrial, process, power, hydrocarbon, and government. Five business-unit vice presidents report to the president of the industrial sector, Frank Stein. These vice presidents oversee the pulp and paper; metals; food, beverage, and consumer products; commercial; and automotive and electronics units.

Last year, the industrial sector obtained $2.4 billion in revenues. The primary responsibility for each vice president is to obtain construction projects for their business unit that meet the strategic goals of the industrial sector. Joan Hatcher, vice president of metals, is particularly adept at accomplishing this goal. In fact, in 1989 for every dollar she spent on project proposals, her business unit received ten contract dollars. Several vice presidents insist that their efforts to obtain projects are compromised by lack of resources to prepare project proposals.

President Stein believes that although he has provided the vice presidents with adequate budgets, they have allocated funds to projects unwisely—that is, vice presidents spend too much on projects that are of relatively small strategic importance to the company, while not spending enough to maintain relationships with valued customers. In fact, a very important Fortune 500 client almost awarded its plant-expansion project in Kentucky to a competitor because Ruolf's vice president of commercial was overly confident that the client would once again sign with his unit. Had it not been for Stein's last-minute intervention, a valuable client who has provided the company with billions of dollars in revenues over the years could have been lost.

Each vice president is responsible for overseeing approximately 50 project proposals per year. It is impossible for Frank Stein to be involved in each proposal to assure that the firm's strategic mission is being fulfilled. While Stein was wondering what could be done to improve this situation, Joan Hatcher appeared in his office for a meeting. Before Joan even had a chance to speak, Frank asked, "How do you determine the allocation of resources from your budget to project proposals?" Joan replied, "Frankly, I haven't thought about it. But, I suppose I take three main factors into consideration: the strategic importance of obtaining the project, the available resources at my disposal, and the estimated project proposal resource requirements." Frank then asked Joan if she could prepare a report containing the details of how she arrives at resource allocation for project proposals. The next section is an overview of that report.

PROJECT PROPOSAL RESOURCE-ALLOCATION SYSTEM

After considerable thought, Joan was able to diagram what she felt were the most important factors that she took into consideration when deciding on the allocation of resources to obtain a project. The dependency diagram below illustrates the knowledge that Joan has available during her decision-making process.

Dependency Diagram

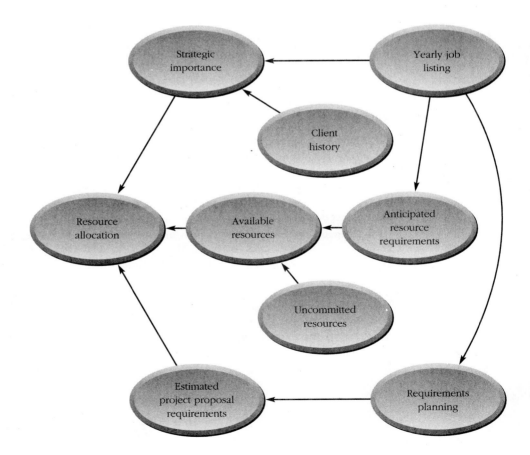

She determines the strategic importance of the project by considering the value of the client to Ruolf and the monetary value of the project itself. A factor that affects her decision of client value is whether the project is for an existing client or a new client. In the case of existing clients, Joan considers historical records to determine the client's contribution to profit and the quality of past working relationships. This information is currently contained in a database table. In considering potentially new clients, Joan assesses the volume of construction business let by the client on a yearly basis, and she subjectively assesses the strategic importance of this client to Ruolf. These data are obtained from a national job listing and downloaded to a database table to permit ad hoc inquiry.

To determine available resources, Joan must consider already encumbered resources as well as anticipated resource requirements for upcoming projects. At the beginning of the fiscal year, Joan commits 1/2% of the total projected revenue from a project to the preparation of the project proposal. This amount is then adjusted either up or down as needed. Joan maintains these data in a spreadsheet.

Among the most important factors considered in determining the budget per project is the estimated project proposal requirement. Not only is this value important in determining the overall goal, but it also plays a part in framing the proposal and determining specific resources necessary to obtain a project. The necessary requirements to prepare a proposal can exceed the amount that a unit is willing to spend to obtain the project. This fact can result in the abandonment of a proposal process altogether. A chart of accounts listing pertinent categories of costing for each project proposal is given below.

Not only does this categorization provide Joan with a way to determine the cost of seeking a project, but it also allows her to determine whether particular departments are overburdened with proposal responsibilities and allows her to shift resources to cover peak loads.

SYSTEM DEVELOPMENT

After Joan explained the way in which she achieved resource allocation, Stein requested that the in-house expert system developer look over the documentation and consult with Hatcher to determine if a system could be developed to advise the vice presidents of the other operating divisions. Although the expert system devel-

Chart of Accounts

```
               CHART OF ACCOUNTS

        001    Engineering resources

        002    Personnel resources

        003    Accounting resources

        004    Services resources

        005    Construction resources
```

oper noted that the system would certainly need to be augmented by the knowledge of the other vice presidents in their particular area of construction expertise, Stein, Hatcher, and the expert system developer were optimistic that a system could be developed that could assist the other vice presidents in systematically determining resource allocation. In addition, it would allow Stein to understand more accurately special resource requirements not allowed for in the budget.

THE DEVELOPER'S PLAN OF ACTION

After consulting with both Frank Stein and Joan Hatcher, the expert system developer was able to outline a schedule of activities that would culminate in the development of an expert system to support the project proposal resource allocation process. The schedule is shown here.

Development Schedule

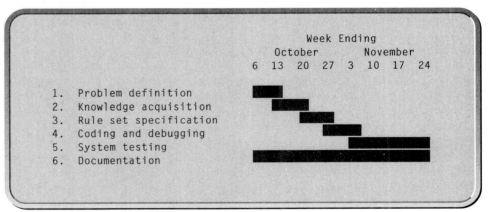

The expert system developer plans to use an integrated environment as the development tool. A menu-driven interface will be created for this expert system, because the vice presidents are currently unfamiliar with many capabilities provided by the environment. The vice presidents will specify the project names for which resource allocation figures are requested. In addition, the vice presidents might be required to supplement the knowledge contained in the knowledge system by answering appropriate questions, particularly questions regarding the certainty of obtaining a project. The vice presidents will also be able to seek a recommendation for the allocation of a particular project's budget into cost account categories. These figures will be shown graphically as well as in tabular form.

After reviewing the plans outlined by the expert system developer, Stein granted permission to the expert system developer to proceed with prototype development. Some of the resultant KS contents are shown in Appendix H.

USER GUIDE

The Project Proposal Resource Allocation System (PPRAS) is provided to all vice presidents of the industrial division. It is an expert system designed to assist vice presidents in determining resource-allocation requirements for upcoming projects to be bid on by their divisions.

The PPRAS can be run entirely from one diskette provided to each user. It is recommended that each user make a backup copy of this diskette. To begin a decision support system session, the user issues a DOS command to begin execution of the integrated environment as the PPRAS problem processor. A consultation session begins by entering the command

```
consult "a:resource" to test
```

where resource.rsc is the name of a KS file containing the rule set.

The first screen the user will see provides an overview of PPRAS. The user should note that most of the screens during the consultation session are similar. This similarity provides continuity of a frame of reference. The lines at the bottom of the screen (generally lines 18 to 24) instruct the user what keys to press to continue the consultation process.

First Screen

```
       PROJECT PROPOSAL RESOURCE ALLOCATION SYSTEM


        This system has been designed to assist
        you in determining resource allocation
        requirements for upcoming project
        proposals. You are required to know the
        name of the project for which assistance
        is needed.
```

The second screen provides the user with a choice of proceeding with the consultation process or exiting the system. The user selects the PROCEED option by pressing the Enter key.

Second Screen

```
        PROJECT PROPOSAL RESOURCE ALLOCATION SYSTEM


        At this point you may exit the system by
        positioning the highlight bar on EXIT and
        pressing ENTER or proceed with the
        consultation by pressing the ENTER key.


                        Proceed
                        Exit
```

The third screen allows the user to decide whether to consult the system for a recommendation regarding a project for a new client or an existing client.

Third Screen

```
        PROJECT PROPOSAL RESOURCE ALLOCATION SYSTEM


            Project for a New Client
            Project for an Existing Client



            Select one of the items above by
            positioning the highlight bar on
            your choice and pressing enter.
```

Regardless of which option the user enters on the third screen, a list of clients will appear on the fourth screen. As indicated by the box at the bottom of the screen, the user can select a client by positioning the cursor (highlight bar) on the choice and pressing Enter.

Fourth Screen

```
            PROJECT PROPOSAL RESOURCE ALLOCATION SYSTEM

        Atlantic Richfield              Kimberly Clark
        ALCOA                           Western Steel
        Reynolds Metals                 CWP Transportation
        U.S. Steel                      Illinois Copper
        Canadian Metals                 Glasgow Zinc
        Butler Copper                   Birmingham Aluminum

        Select one ot the items above by positioning the
        highlight bar on your choice and pressing enter.
```

Once a client (either new or existing) has been selected, the fifth screen lists the projects being let for bids by the client selected *with one exception*. Existing clients found in the OLDCLI.ITB database table may not have any projects to let for the current year. If this is the case, a message will be displayed to the user indicating the client selected has no new projects. If the user receives this message, he or she should press the space bar. PPRAS will then provide the user with the option of exiting the system or consulting the system again.

Fifth Screen

```
        PROJECT PROPOSAL RESOURCE ALLOCATION SYSTEM



    CWP Transportation does not have any new projects this year.




                Press Space Bar to Continue
```

It is possible that the PPRAS will not be able to assign the project's strategic importance to the firm. Although the system generally assigns a project either a PRIMARY, SECONDARY, or TERTIARY rating, in borderline cases the system relies on the user to determine the project's strategic importance to Roulf and the industrial division. In such a case, a sixth screen will appear that requires the user to select the strategic importance of the project. This selection ultimately factors into the calculation of resource requirements.

Sixth Screen

```
        PROJECT PROPOSAL RESOURCE ALLOCATION SYSTEM


                        PRIMARY
                        SECONDARY
                        TERTIARY


            Select one of the items above by
            positioning the highlight bar on
            your choice and pressing enter.
```

Prior to asking the user to input engineering and construction expenses, the seventh screen will display for the user the name of the client, the name of the project, the dollar value (in millions of dollars) of the project, and the client's rating. This information might be useful to the user in determining the engineering and construction expenses.

Seventh Screen

```
              PROJECT PROPOSAL RESOURCE ALLOCATION SYSTEM


     We are currently considering the Jackson Warehouse project.
     This project is for Anaconda.
     The project is valued at 100 million.
     The client's rating is assessed to be 6.




                      Press Space Bar to Continue
```

Because engineering and construction expenses are values that rely heavily on the expertise of the vice president or his or her staff assistants, it is necessary for the user to enter a number between 0 and 99, which represents the percent of total resource requirements that would be necessary to obtain the project. This is accomplished by inputting the values into the blanks provided in the eighth screen.

Eighth Screen

```
             PROJECT PROPOSAL RESOURCE ALLOCATION SYSTEM

     ┌─────────────────────────────────────────────────────┐
     │    Input a number between 0 and 99 to               │
     │    indicate the percentage of resources             │
     │    to be spent on each item.                        │
     └─────────────────────────────────────────────────────┘


     Percent of Engineering Expenses? 23
     Percent of Construction Expenses? 14
```

Given the percentages assessed by the user in screen 8, PPRAS will then conduct inference with a rule set to provide a recommendation of the required resources necessary to obtain the project. In addition to providing a total resource allocation recommendation, a list is displayed of the chart of accounts for the five primary resources with recommended allocations for each account. The ninth screen displays two other important pieces of information. The anticipated resource requirements are displayed, along with the difference between anticipated and estimated resources.

Ninth Screen

```
               PROJECT PROPOSAL RESOURCE ALLOCATION SYSTEM

                                                    Estimated

          Engineering expenses                    $ 22,869
          Personnel expenses                      $ 14,914
          Accounting expenses                     $  7,954
          Services expenses                       $  4,971
          Construction expenses                   $ 13,920
          Total resource requirement is           $ 64,628

          This differs from anticipated by        $ 34,800

          You will now see two graphs of these expenses
          Press the SPACE BAR after viewing each graph


                    Press Space Bar to Contine
```

Anticipated resource requirements are determined annually by the board of directors, which mandates a fixed percentage of total construction dollars available on the market. *Estimated resource requirements* are determined by reasoning with knowledge contained in PPRAS and user input.

The total estimated resource requirements are then graphed using a pie chart, which slices the total estimated resource requirements into chart of account categories with associated percentages. The total estimated resource requirements are next graphed as a bar chart showing side-by-side the *anticipated* and *estimated* resource requirements by chart of account.

Under certain circumstances, PPRAS may deem it necessary to ask the user if certain values should be revised. If so, screens already explained in this documentation will appear, and questions should be answered in the manner described.

AN ARTIFICIALLY INTELLIGENT SYSTEM TO SUPPORT ROBOT GRIPPER DECISIONS, BY BOPANA GANAPATHY

The gripper (or end-effector) is the device attached to the end of a robot arm. Specifically, its purpose is to grasp objects during a manipulation task. Typically, a robot arm is designed to interface with different types of grippers. This feature provides robots the flexibility to be used in a variety of applications, especially in flexible manufacturing environments. Clearly, selecting the correct gripper for an application is essential to the success of the task to be performed.

In a manufacturing firm, a robot-applications engineer matches grippers to tasks. In a highly flexible manufacturing environment, these decisions have to be made several times a day for each robot. Gripper selection is a nontrivial task and depends on several factors. In arriving at his or her decision, the robot-applications engineer considers the following criteria:

1. Characteristics of the component to be handled
   a. Geometry
   b. Weight
   c. Material
   d. Surface quality
   e. Temperature
2. Task specification
   a. Type of task (pick-and-place, machining process, or assembly)
   b. Number of different components in a cycle
   c. Position accuracy
   d. Cycle time
3. Environmental conditions
   a. Presence of contaminants
   b. Available work envelope (collision avoidance)
4. Capability of robot
   a. Repeatability
   b. Accuracy
   c. Speed
   d. Acceleration
   e. Payload capacity
   f. Type of actuation

The goal is to determine the gripper characteristics (and hence a gripper) that best meets the requirements for a particular application:

5. Gripper characteristics
   a. Grasping action (mechanical, vacuum, or magnetic)
   b. Grasping type (internal or external contact with component)
   c. Inherent weight
   d. Gripping force
   e. Type of actuation (electrical, pneumatic, or hydraulic)
   f. Operating temperature
   g. Maximum and minimum size component that can be handled (range of jaw opening)
   h. Area of contact with component
   i. Compatibility with robot to be used

At the outset, the robot-applications engineer has some (but not all) of the information needed to arrive at a decision. As an example, the weight of the component [COMPWT] (characteristic 1(b)) is known. In addition, it is known that contaminants [CONTAM] (characteristic 3(b)) are present. The coefficient of friction [FRICT] needed to estimate the gripping force [GFORCE] (characteristic 5(d)) depends on the type of contaminant present, as in:

```
IF: CONTAM = "OIL"
THEN: FRICT = 0.9
```

The following is a sample rule that may be used to estimate the gripping force:

```
IF: KNOWN ("FRICT") AND KNOWN ("COMPWT") AND KNOWN
    ("SAFEFAC")
THEN: GFORCE = FRCIT*COMPWT*SAFEFAC
```

where SAFEFAC is a factor of safety and can vary from one application to another.

The estimated GFORCE is then calculated with respect to other criteria such as component geometry (characteristic 1(a)) and component material (characteristic 1(c)) to determine the grasping action (characteristic 5(a)) and grasping type (characteristic 5(b)). The preceding analysis serves only to illustrate a part of the reasoning process and is by no means complete. During this process, the robot-applications engineer may use knowledge from a variety of sources: his or her own experience and training, handbooks and other technical literature, gripper manufacturer catalogs (either in printed form or in a computer database) or even consultations with other robot-applications engineers.

Considering the complexity of the task involved, the firm could be severely handicapped if the robot-applications engineer were to be unavailable for some reason. Most firms cope with such exigencies by using the services of other manufacturing engineers within the firm. However, these engineers typically have little training and experience in robot applications. As a result, they require more time to select a gripper for an application. Moreover, this process can be laborious, because they try to compensate for their lack of experience by referring extensively to technical literature and other sources of knowledge. Finally, they are usually unable to provide a convincing justification for a particular selection.

An expert system (ES) that emulates the robot-applications engineer could help remedy this problem. The purpose of the ES is to provide advice on robot gripper selection, both to determine the desired characteristics and to explain why the characteristics are appropriate for the application under consideration. The user of the ES should be a technically literate person (ideally, a manufacturing engineer). However, the user is not required to possess any specific training and/or experience in robot applications.

The ES will be useful as long as the user is familiar with and capable of understanding technical terminology. If this basic requirement is not met, there can be no meaningful interaction between the user and the ES. Assuming that the user meets the minimal technical competency requirements, at the end of a consultation, the ES will recommend gripper characteristics suitable for a particular application. If requested, it will provide explanations as to why these characteristics are appropriate.

In a typical flexible manufacturing environment, the user may consult the ES several times a day. The response time of the ES is expected to be 3 to 5 minutes per consultation. It is anticipated that the user will interact with the ES via a customized user interface, consisting of a collection of forms. The interface program will accept user input via keystrokes.

At the start of a consultation, the user will have to specify descriptive knowledge (problem definition) for a particular application. This knowledge includes data on characteristics such as component specification, task specification, environmental conditions, and the capability of the robot. The descriptive knowledge pertaining to these criteria is assumed to be known with certainty and is represented by single-valued variables. Therefore, certainty factors and fuzzy variables are not considered relevant in this application. Once the known variables are initialized, the expert system may obtain additional data from several other sources (e.g., a database containing information from a gripper manufacturer's catalog). Thus, it is expected that the knowledge system will consist of variables, rule sets, databases, procedures, and text. The problem-processing system abilities will include database management, forms management, text processing, procedure execution, inference engine reasoning, and report generation. The ES will thus be implemented using an integrated environment as the development tool.

Once a prototype of the ES has been built, its behavior will be tested by using a number of test cases. Here, a distinction must be made between software testing and expert testing. Software testing involves testing the validity of the code, whereas expert testing involves testing the expert system's reasoning behavior. A number of test cases will be constructed to reflect typical robot gripper-selection problems. The general techniques of software testing may be employed to generate a coverage matrix of suitable test cases.

If the robot-applications engineer believes that the advice offered by the ES is invalid for some test cases, the rule set will need to be modified. Here, one or more of the following three techniques may be used to detect and isolate the inaccuracies, incompleteness, or inconsistencies in the rule set: asking the inference engine for an explanation (HOW and WHY), automatic tracing of the reasoning process, and customized tracing.

If the robot-applications engineer agrees that the ES offers good advice on a timely basis for all test cases, he or she will further develop the prototype system. This process will involve interface construction and user testing before installation. During user testing, the user will employ the same test cases from expert testing. Here the purpose of testing is to check the manner in which advice is requested, presented, and explained. At this stage, adjustments will be made to the user interface, if needed.

Once the ES is installed, it is expected to provide the following benefits:

1. The user will have ready access to expert advice that will help him or her better perform the task of robot gripper selection. The user will be able to complete the task not only in less time, but also by expending less effort. Thus, the user will have more time available to perform other tasks. Also, repeated interaction with the ES will help improve the user's skills for gripper-selection tasks.
2. At the firm level, a reduction in time required to make a gripper selection implies that job completion times are reduced, offering increased flexibility in job scheduling. Ultimately, this translates into improved operational efficiency. In terms of traditional competitive strategies, the firm improves productivity and becomes a low-cost competitor. Also, because the ES is designed for use in a flexible manufacturing environment, it helps reinforce the strategic implications of flexible manufacturing. Thus, in terms of traditional competitive strategies, the firm can better achieve its product differentiation goals.

AMENDMENTS TO THE PROPOSAL

With the exception of the following, the implemented prototype possesses all of the features and meets all of the objectives specified in the foregoing project proposal. In the prototype, the knowledge system does not contain a database. During the project proposal stage, it appeared that a database would be necessary. However, as the development cycle progressed, this need became less obvious. Also, numeric calculations were implemented in the rule conclusions themselves rather than as separate programmed solvers. Finally, the prototype does not currently possess any report-generation capabilities. KS files for the prototype implementation appear in Appendix H.

USING THE EXPERT SYSTEM

Upon entering the integrated environment, issue the command

```
perform "a:session"
```

to bring up the main menu. Much of the remaining interaction between the user and the expert system is aided by on-line documentation. It is suggested that first-time users review the "About gripper-section" option from the main menu before attempting a consultation.

During a consultation, six forms (labeled FORM 1 through FORM 6) are presented onscreen. You are required to input, via keystrokes, values for several parameters on each form. The forms are self-explanatory and, where appropriate, provide guidelines on the choice of appropriate input values. After a consultation, the results are displayed onscreen. You may view the line of reasoning and/or the results as many times as you wish. If you indicate that you *do not* wish to view the line of reasoning and/or the results the system returns to the main menu.

A FEW THOUGHTS ON THE EXPERT SYSTEM DEVELOPMENT PROCESS

For the most part, I followed the seven-stage development procedure. Although I am not sure whether a different and better method exists, from my own experience I found the prescribed method to be very useful. Further, if I had to undertake a similar project again, I am not sure that I have any reason to consider using any other method. In short, my experiences with both the development methodology and the development tool have been very positive.

YOUR OWN PROJECT

In order to concentrate on the use of technology to develop an expert system, you should choose an application with which you already have some familiarity. Construct a proposal for your project, describing the application area and outlining the envisioned system's features. Take the attitude that the green light for proceeding with development of your expert system will depend on the proposal's ability to convince your supervisor (e.g., instructor) that your project is feasible and beneficial. Your proposal should explain the organizational context for the envisioned system, describe the system from a prospective user's perspective, characterize the proposed system from a developer's viewpoint, and present a schedule of development activities.

In explaining what you intend to accomplish, organize your proposal's content in the clearest presentation possible for securing project approval and support. Minimally, your proposal should answer the following questions:

1. In what organizational setting will the expert system be used and for what purpose?
2. How often will it be used and with what response requirements?
3. Who is the anticipated user, and what user traits will influence the design and use of the system?
4. What benefits is your expert system expected to provide for its user? The expert? The organization?

5. In the current absence of the expert system, how (if at all) is expert reasoning incorporated into the decision process?
6. Does the proposed expert system have any strategic implications for the organization?
7. From the intended user's viewpoint, what will the expert system do? How will it be used in the course of decision making?
8. From the user's perspective, what will this artificially intelligent system not do?
9. What is the nature of the interface a user will experience when interacting with the system?
10. In this project, who (or what) is the expert being emulated? As the developer, what tool(s) will you use?
11. What goal(s) will the expert system address?
12. What factors contribute to achieving the goal? Can you sketch at least a rough, tentative dependency diagram?
13. What knowledge-management techniques will be employed? How will integration (e.g., of database management) with the inference engine be accomplished?
14. Are certainty factors and/or fuzzy variables relevant to the application? Give an example.
15. How will expert testing be accomplished? User testing?
16. What aspects of the expert system described in your proposal will be incorporated into your first pass through the development cycle (i.e., into your prototype)?
17. What is your schedule of activities for developing the expert system once the proposal is approved?

Upon completion of a pass through the development cycle, you should be able to demonstrate your expert system and submit the following materials for evaluation:

- Any amendments or alterations to the proposal involving the project's scope, aims, or methods.
- An explanation of what you accomplished, including listings of knowledge system contents you created (e.g., database table structures, records in database tables, definitions in spreadsheets, textural passages, program listings, form declarations, rule set specifications, and so forth).
- Knowledge system files and a user's manual explaining how to use the system and including characterizations of the LS and PS instructions on how to invoke the system, a sample session or sessions showing interactions with the system, and guidelines indicating what system features to use for what purposes.
- An explanation of how you tested the system, plus any ancillary files used in that testing.
- A discussion of possible future extensions (or revisions) to the system.
- A retrospective description of insights you gained by undertaking the project.

Part Five

MULTIPARTICIPANT AND EXECUTIVE DECISION SUPPORT SYSTEMS

. . . A so-called knowledgeable person usually has solid knowledge only within some special area, representing a tiny fraction of the whole spectrum of human concerns. Humorist Will Rogers said, "everyone is ignorant, only on different subjects."

How does an ignorant world perform intricate functions requiring enormous knowledge? These intricate functions include not only such scientific feats as air travel and space exploration, but also the complex economic processes which bring a slice of bread and a piece of butter to your plate at breakfast. Anyone who has studied the actual process by which everyday food items are planned, produced, and distributed knows that the complexity staggers the mind. Many highly intelligent and highly trained people spend a lifetime studying it, and learning more all the time. Among those who speculate financially in such commodities, economic disaster is commonplace, even after they have spent years studying the market. In short, individually we know so pathetically little, and yet socially we use a range and complexity of knowledge. . . . The question is not only how given institutions . . . . manage to do this, but how various institutions . . . differ in the manner and effectiveness with which they do it"

— DR. THOMAS SOWELL, Senior Research Fellow, Hoover Institute

Knowledge and Decisions (New York: Basic Books, 1980), p. 3

A decision support system can support a decision maker by recalling or deriving knowledge in order to find or solve problems affecting the decision at hand. A decision support system can also be instrumental in the sharing of knowledge among decision-making participants, perhaps even stimulating them jointly to create new knowledge that would not otherwise exist. It is this support of multiparticipant decision making that we explore in Part Five. We also examine the special nature of decision support systems for top-level executives and close with some exploratory ideas about the nature of tomorrow's knowledge-based organizations.

Chapter 16 lays a foundation for understanding multiparticipant decision support systems (MDSSs). It shows that these systems are part of the field known as organizational computing. As such, MDSSs are closely related to such organizational computing topics as groupware, computer-mediated communication, computer support cooperative work, and coordination technology. Chapter 16 reviews each topic as a background for appreciating the next chapter's coverage of MDSSs.

Chapter 17 introduces a generic framework for MDSSs that is an extension of the generic DSS framework introduction in Part Two. Three important kinds of systems adhering to this MDSS framework are group decision support systems, organizational decision support systems, and negotiation support systems. The natures and uses of each of those types of MDSSs are examined as the chapter unfolds.

Chapter 18 is devoted to executive information systems. It begins by considering the information needs of top executives and how such needs differ from those of other decision makers. This examination leads to a consideration of the nature of executive information systems. We also look at how such systems are developed, what their limitations are, and what conditions lead to their development and adoption.

Chapter 19 looks into the future, signs of which can already be seen in the present. This future is populated with knowledge-based organizations and knowledge workers. We describe the broad outlines of these knowledge-based organizations. We indicate the challenges and opportunities that await these knowledge workers. The intent is to provide a useful mindset for understanding the organizational and global context in which tomorrow's DSSs will be used and for appreciating the needs of the knowledge workers who will use those DSSs.

Chapter 16

ORGANIZATIONAL COMPUTING FOR DECISION SUPPORT

MCI: A GROUPWARE SYSTEM TO SUPPORT RESEARCH REQUEST PROCESSING

Overview

MCI Communications . . . strives to disseminate information to its employees through the most technologically-advanced means available. As such, MCI supports three information resource centers. . . . This article describes Lotus Notes applications developed in the Corporate Information Resources Center (CIRC) in Washington.

All three information resource centers (IRCs) are accessible to MCI's 35,000 employees via telephone, electronic mail or personal visit; however, the focus of each IRC varies. The CIRC . . . primarily handles strategic planning, sales and marketing questions. . . .

Prior to the implementation of Notes, all reference queries were tracked manually. Requests come into the CIRC primarily by MCI Mail and the telephone. These requests were scribbled onto green sheets of paper . . . and completed by the librarian who took the request. When a library user inquired about the status of a research request, we were powerless to help unless we had taken the request personally. This situation occurred frequently, frustrating both CIRC staff and users. . . . [In response,] we developed . . . the Green Sheets Application. . . .

System Features

. . . Using a look-up function, we can type in the first letter of a patron's name to see if the CIRC has done work for that patron in the past. If so, Notes fills in the patron's name, department/location code, telephone and fax numbers, and mailing address. If not, information can be entered by the new user that will be retrieved the next time she calls in. Next, there is a free-text field for describing the work to be done, and check-off boxes to indicate the type of project and resources used. The date the request was received and the name of the person keying in the request is filled in automatically—the request can be "assigned" to any CIRC staff member. . . .

When the research work is completed, the librarian who worked on the request fills in the date completed, checks off how the information was sent (helpful for tracing mis-directed packages), and how long the project took. The librarian can include notes on the project, such as online search strategies, sources consulted, or whether any information was found. . . .

The Green Sheets Application on Notes lets us monitor workload, reassign work as necessary, check on the status of a request, compile statistics on CIRC reference work, and search for prior projects similar to a new request. ("Didn't we find information last month on the number of airline passengers to and from South America? Where did we find the numbers?") . . . The Green Sheets Application has greatly enhanced our ability to manage the primary work of the CIRC.

Organizational Memory

. . . Next . . . we developed . . . the CIRC Memory, our institutional memory of the CIRC department. . . . We use this . . . as a "brain dump," a place to

Continued

put information that staff members have learned that the rest of the staff should know. Examples of CIRC Memory records include:

. . . • a downloaded sample search session to retrieve the Dow Jones Industrial Average for 1988
   • a procedures manual detailing how to respond to typical CIRC reference requests
   • pointers to Internet resources on the telecommunications industry. . .
   • a reminder that statistics on the number of rotary telephones in the U.S. are kept in a particular vertical file.

Each record is full-text searchable, so staff members can type in a keyword or combine keywords and a subject category, for example, to retrieve the information needed. . . . [This is] popular with the CIRC staff members as a way to share their knowledge. . . . [It] allows the newer librarians to tap into the experiences of the more-seasoned librarians. . . .

Collaborative Authoring

One of the most basic functions of Notes is . . . an electronic bulletin board. One user can post a message and others can post responses to that message. . . . We post questions on policy, the status of ongoing projects, [etc. The bulletin board is] . . . also used . . . to write graduate school recommendations jointly for two of our student clerks. We posted the graduate school questionnaire . . . restricted access to the posting to CIRC librarians only, then had each librarian post her comments and feedback into the questionnaire.

This article was jointly written. . . . One of the convenient features of Notes is the ability to change the color of the text as well as fonts. When either of the authors wanted to include notes to the other (e.g., "think this makes sense?" "Do you have a good example of this?"), we could put the note in red so the other person would notice the annotation immediately.

Condensed quotation from M. E. Bates and K. Allen "Lotus Notes in Action: Meeting Corporate Information Needs" *Database* 17, no. 4 (1994); 27–33.

LEARNING OBJECTIVES

The MCI case illustrates how groupware can be used in an organization to track and facilitate information flows. Groupware, such as Lotus Notes, forms a part of the large and growing field of organizational computing. This field is concerned with the features, development, operation, and management of computing systems that aim to promote organizational (in contrast to individual) productivity. As such, it overlaps with the DSS field, which is concerned with promoting decision-making productivity. The intersection of the two fields is an area called multiparticipant decision support systems. It is concerned with how decision makers, who are organized in varying ways, can be supported by computing systems. Here, we begin to address this topic by examining groupware and other areas of the organizational computing field from the perspective of how they can contribute to support of multiparticipant decision makers. As a prelude, we begin with an organizational perspective relating the kinds of DSSs found in organizations.

After studying this chapter, you should be able to

1. Offer an organizational perspective that identifies and relates multiple kinds of decision support systems found in an organization.
2. Outline the organizational computing field and discuss its relevance to the decision support system field.
3. Identify the categories of multiparticipant decision support systems.
4. Describe the nature of groupware, computer-mediated communication, computer-supported cooperative work, and coordination technology.

Exercises at the end of the chapter enable you to check that you have met these objectives.

16.1 INTRODUCTION

The reason that organizations exist is because an organization allows participants to accomplish collectively more than they could individually. As we saw in Chapter 3, organizations range from hierarchic teams to unstructured groups to a wide variety of hybrid organizations that incorporate aspects of both. In each case, an organization's knowledge resources are distributed among participants. The sum total of this knowledge, plus the potential for distributed pieces of knowledge to act on each other and produce new knowledge, yields a range and complexity of organization knowledge that goes far beyond that of any single participant (Ching, Holsapple, and Whinston 1991). For an organization's work to be accomplished, this distributed knowledge must be properly processed. How it is processed depends heavily on the organizational infrastructure and its supporting technological infrastructure.

DSS IN THE NEWS

Wanted: New Approaches and Experience

Speedy delivery and analysis of knowledge requires mastery of many new tools and techniques, say experienced chief information officers. Among those tools and techniques are Notes or other groupware, rapid and joint application development, object-oriented programming, "scrubber" software to improve data quality, middleware for accessing legacy databases, search engines, data warehousing and enterprise reference systems.

Moreover, heavy communications and infrastructure experience is needed to support complex knowledge delivery systems that increasingly include images, video and voice. Leadership and decision-making skills also are key.

J. Maglitta "Smarten up!" *Computerworld* 5 June 1995, p. 86.

ORGANIZATIONAL INFRASTRUCTURE AND TECHNOLOGICAL INFRASTRUCTURE

Organizational infrastructure refers to the roles that have been defined for participants to fill, the relationships among those roles, and regulations that govern the use of roles and relationships (Holsapple and Luo 1995). In a simple group, for

---

REENGINEERING

According to proponents of reengineering, it "is time to stop paving the cow paths. Instead of embedding outdated processes in silicon and software, we should . . . 'reengineer' our businesses: use the power of modern information technology to radically redesign business processes in order to achieve dramatic improvements in their performance . . . use information technology not to automate an existing process but to enable a new one." (Hammer 1990).

Critics of reengineering point to failed efforts. Three-fourths of all reengineering projects are failures, according to an article in *Computerworld*. (3 October, 1994) This perception should not lead us to ignore the many successes. The fault is not necessarily with the principle of reengineering but may well lie in a flawed implementation of it.

Guidelines that have been advanced to help a reengineering effort include

1. Design each individual's work to focus on achieving a certain outcome, rather than carrying out a single task;
2. Let individuals who need the results of a process perform the process themselves;
3. Let the individuals who produce information process it as well;
4. Use technology to treat distributed resources (e.g., human or knowledge) as if they were centralized;
5. Link and coordinate parallel activities as they proceed, rather than waiting to integrate their results upon completion;
6. Let the one who does the work make decisions about that work (subject to regulations); and
7. Capture and enter information only once and do so as it is generated.

As an example, consider Ford's handling of accounts payable (Hammer 1990). A copy of each purchase order written by the purchasing department was sent to the accounts payable department. When the goods were later received by receiving clerks, accounts payable was sent a copy of the receiving documents. At the same time, the vendor supplying the goods sent an invoice. The accounts payable department in North America consisted of more than 500 people, who would match 14 items between a purchase order, the receiving document, and the invoice. Payment was issued when a match was found. By comparison, Mazda's accounts payable group employed 5 people.

Ford reengineered, resulting in an organization that eliminated the need for invoices and purchase order copies, paid vendors upon receipt of goods, yielded greater financial accuracy, and reduced accounts payable workforce requirements by 75%. Now, upon initiating an order, the purchasing department enters it directly into a database. When goods arrive, a clerk at the receiving dock uses the database to confirm that they match an outstanding order. If they do, the clerk accepts them and logs the receipt in the computer system. The system generates the check that accounts payable sends to the vendor.

instance, there are several similar roles—each being defined as a representative (e.g., of some viewpoint or special interest). Relationships among roles permit a participant filling one role to communicate those filling any other roles in the group infrastructure. Regulations might require that at most one participant can send a message at a time and that any group decision be determined by majority rule.

Technological infrastructure refers to computer-based means for designing, enabling, monitoring, evaluating, enforcing, and modifying organizational infrastructure (Holsapple and Luo 1995). In the group, for instance, technology may allow relationships among roles that are otherwise impractical due to time and space differences among participants. Or, technology may permit regulations that allow several participants to send messages simultaneously, to communicate anonymously, or to reach a group decision via electronically enforced market-oriented rules.

In the interest of strong organizational performance, a good fit should exist between technological infrastructure and organizational infrastructure. There are two basic approaches to achieving a good fit. For an existing organizational infrastructure, we can seek the technology that best enhances performance (e.g., for a specific group infrastructure, what technology is well suited to helping the group accomplish its task?). A very different approach, called *business process reengineering,* is concerned with redefining an organization's infrastructure to fit or take advantage of currently available technologies (Hammer 1990). That is, advances in technology can make previously infeasible organizational infrastructures possible and even preferable.

ORGANIZATIONAL COMPUTING

Research in the field known as **organizational computing** is concerned with creating new kinds of technological infrastructure for organizations and with studying the fit between technology and organizational infrastructure. The part of this field that is of particular interest here involves decision support systems for supporting multiple persons jointly involved in making a decision, as opposed to DSSs for an individual making a decision. These **multiparticipant DSSs** are subject to all the generic features of decision support systems described in prior chapters. However, they have added features, making them suitable for supporting multiple participants organized according to some structure of interrelated roles and operating according to some set of regulations.

The multiparticipant features of such DSSs come from various sources, including groupware technology, computer-supported cooperative work technology, and computer-mediated communication technology. These technologies are still evolving and unfolding. Consequently, the features of multiparticipant DSSs continue to grow in an ongoing effort to form improved fits with various kinds of organization infrastructure.

In this chapter, we begin with an organizational perspective of DSSs. It identifies the kinds of DSSs found in organizations for both individual and multiparticipant support. This perspective relates the various kinds of DSSs in a unified view of decision support efforts within an organization. We then examine the organizational computing field in more depth, noting that it overlaps with the DSS field and encompasses several subject areas. We examine four of these areas that are especially relevant to the support of multiparticipant decision makers: groupware tech-

DSS IN THE NEWS

The Center of the Company

[T]he current corporate interest [in knowledge management] is no passing fad, says Harvard Business School professor Christopher A. Bartlett. . . . "Knowledge is now the center of the company. It is needed to free the creativity and initiative of frontline managers . . .," Bartlett says.

Why now? Companies have fewer people, more technology and more information . . . Rapid growth of groupware and networks are big factors. So is widespread business process reengineering.

J. Maglitta "Smarten up!" *Computerworld* 5 June 1995, p. 85.

nology, computer-mediated communication, computer-supported cooperative work, and coordination technology.

Building on this background, Chapter 17 considers the different kinds of multi-participant DSSs that have been proposed or developed, emphasizing the distinction between DSSs that support groups and those that support other types of organizational infrastructure. Chapter 18 covers systems that support decision making at the highest organizational levels: executive information systems. In Chapter 19, we conclude by examining knowledge-based organizations that are increasingly being enabled by technological advances. In such organizations, knowledge is regarded as the preeminent resource. The organization infrastructure and technological infrastructure are highly integrated for purposes of knowledge management and multi-participant decision making.

16.2 ORGANIZATIONWIDE DECISION SUPPORT SYSTEMS

So far in this book, the emphasis has been on understanding what a DSS is, what its potential benefits are, and how it can be developed. It is now time to step back and take a look at the bigger picture of multiple DSSs existing simultaneously within an organization. Such a picture has been provided by Philippakis and Green (1988) in the form of a framework that encompasses the various DSS practices that can be found in an organization. The discussion here is based on their framework and analysis. The picture it provides is a valuable foundation for thinking about, planning, and managing an organization's DSSs.

TYPES OF DSSs IN THE ORGANIZATIONAL CONTEXT

From an organizationwide perspective, four types of DSSs can be identified (Philippakis and Green 1988). We shall refer to these as corporate planning systems, functional decision support systems, executive information systems, and local decision support systems. Although all have the common traits of a DSS, each has distinctive traits that set it apart from the others.

MULTIPLE DSS PROJECTS IN AN ORGANIZATION

Philippakis and Green (1988) report on a meeting with executives from government and industry who wanted to benefit from sharing views about the issues of developing, managing, and controlling the diverse DSS projects evolving in their respective organizations. As the meeting progressed, it became apparent that there were different views on means for supporting DSS development and considerable variations in DSS applications. For instance, four of the executives offered the following contrasting views on how DSSs were regarded in their respective organizations:

1. A DSS consisted of a centralized model-based corporate planning system that was in the process of being made available for distributed access by multiple managers.
2. DSSs were targeted at supporting specific functions of financial management and customer analysis.
3. DSSs were developed on personal computers throughout the organization with assistance from an information center.
4. A DSS was concerned with tapping into a corporate database to provide responses to top executives' ad hoc data analysis requests.

Even though such diverse DSS applications and orientations were discussed, the meeting's participants concluded that they were not mutually exclusive. They could coexist within an organization. However, they also concluded that a comprehensive perspective encompassing the diverse views would be beneficial in understanding and managing the diversity of DSS-related activities that were occurring in organizations. Philippakis and Green conducted a more extensive and detailed field study of DSS practices in organizations. Their findings and insights led to an organizationwide DSS perspective that includes the identification of four basic DSS types and the integration of those types into a framework encompassing all organizational DSS practices.

Corporate Planning Systems   A **corporate planning system** (CPS) is a DSS that holds and derives knowledge relevant to the overall planning decisions of an organization's top-level managers. These decisions cut across departments and divisions. They involve and affect all the organization's functions—its operations, marketing, personnel, and financing activities. A CPS's knowledge includes extensive data pertaining to the corporation itself (e.g., internal cost information) and to its environment (e.g., national economic statistics). Also included are solvers that mathematically model the organization's processes (Naylor and Mansfield 1977).

Often called *corporate planning models,* these solvers are programs designed to respond to what-if requests of a corporate planning executive. The corporate planner states a set of assumptions characterizing some prospective plan or situation in the environment. Based on these, one or more CPS solvers draw on pertinent stored data to derive the outcomes that should be anticipated if the assumptions come to pass. It determines the corporatewide implications of scenarios posed by the planner—the impacts of a particular plan or situation on operations, marketing, personnel, finance, and the corporate environment.

Corporate planning systems predate the appearance of the term decision support system in the early 1970s (Scott Morton 1977). For instance, Boulden and Buffa (1970) describe an elaborate CPS used at Potlatch Forests, Inc. More generally,

Gershefski (1970) discusses the CPS state of the art that evolved during the 1960s. Nevertheless, CPSs have long been recognized as an important kind of DSS (Bonczek, Holsapple, and Whinston 1980; Scott Morton 1982). A study in the mid-1980s found that half of the reported DSS applications were for corporate planning and forecasting (Hogue and Watson 1985).

Today, nearly all large organizations use CPSs to support their long-range planning decisions. These systems tend to be created and maintained by professional developers who are assigned to formal corporate planning departments rather than MIS departments. They are large-scale DSSs, requiring considerable resources to develop and keep up to date.

Functional Decision Support Systems   A **functional decision support system** (FDSS) is one that holds and derives knowledge relevant to decisions about some function an organization performs. This function could be a marketing function, production function, financial function, etc. Examples of FDSSs include those that support decisions about budgeting an advertising campaign across alternative media, about scheduling the production of back-ordered products, or about deploying cash on hand among alternative short-term investment vehicles. Decision support systems having a functional orientation are commonplace (Alter 1980; Keen and Scott Morton 1978).

Functional DSSs differ from corporate planning systems in several ways. Although a CPS supports decisions affecting multiple organizational functions, an FDSS supports decision making about problems within a single function. A CPS supports decisions that tend to take a relatively long time to make and have long-term implications, but an FDSS supports decisions with shorter time horizons. A CPS is used by corporate planners and other high level executives, whereas an FDSS is used mainly by lower-level decision makers. Compared to a CPS, the typical FDSS does not require as much commitment of time and effort to create and maintain. It tends to be developed by computing professionals and/or fairly experienced end users.

Executive Information Systems   An **executive information system** (EIS) is a DSS that holds knowledge relevant to the wide-ranging decisions made by a high-level executive. These decisions are not restricted to planning or any particular organizational function. Although a CPS supports an executive's long-range planning decisions, it offers little help for the diverse mix of more immediate, short-term decisions that an executive must make. This gap is filled by an EIS (Rockart and Treacy 1982).

Also called an executive support system, this kind of DSS is designed to satisfy a top executive's ad hoc needs for information about the organization's current performance and for forecasts about anticipated activities over the short run. Compared to a CPS, its modeling capabilities are not nearly as complex, elaborate, or extensive. Compared to an FDSS, its capabilities are not so narrowly oriented. Although end users may participate in the development of an EIS, this effort is generally spearheaded by a professional developer (e.g., a member of the executive's staff). Several studies have documented the widespread use and perceived benefits of EISs in large organizations (Rockart and Treacy 1982; Friend 1988; Rockart and De Long 1988).

Local Decision Support Systems   According to Philippakis and Green (1988), the fourth major type of DSS is a **local decision support system** (LDSS). This kind of DSS supports decision makers below the top executive level. Rather than cutting across functional lines like a CPS and EIS, a LDSS tends to be localized within some function. It tends to be more specialized in scope than an FDSS, intended to handle the ad hoc information needs related to some limited aspect of a function such as marketing, finance, or production. A local decision support system is usually conceived, developed, and maintained by its end user (and perhaps his or her support staff). It is under that end user's control. The rise of computer literacy coupled with the appearance of convenient, powerful, inexpensive development tools has led to today's extensive use of LDSSs in both large and small organizations.

AN ORGANIZATIONAL FRAMEWORK FOR DECISION SUPPORT SYSTEMS

All four types of DSSs can exist in a single organization. How should an organization's DSSs be managed, coordinated, and evaluated? The organizational activity of managing DSSs has received little attention among DSS researchers, and that attention has focused mainly on the management of individual DSSs (Hogue and Watson 1983; Ariav and Ginzberg 1985). Young (1984) recognized the value of a corporate strategy for DSS deployment and administration. However, researchers have yet to advance such a strategy that accounts for the four main types of DSSs.

Should an organization's LDSSs be actively managed to avoid duplicated effort or ensure the consistency of their KSs and their responses to requests? Can or should LDSSs draw on the knowledge system contents of FDSSs, or vice versa? Similarly, should CPS creation and maintenance be coordinated with development of FDSSs and EISs? Specifically, what FDSSs should be developed in an organization, and is there any need or value to linking their development or operation? At what point can multiple LDSSs in a functional area be integrated to form (or be superseded by) an FDSS? How such questions are addressed in an organization may depend on the organizational infrastructure and can strongly influence the value that an organization realizes from the potential of DSS technology.

Three Dimensions   As a foundation for studying these organizational issues of DSS management, Philippakis and Green (1988) introduced a framework that shows relationships among the four DSS types. Illustrated in Figure 16.1, this framework relates the four DSS types in terms of three dimensions: organizational level and scope, degree of system formality, and user class. The first of these distinguishes between DSSs used at the operational level and focused on relatively narrow decision domains (i.e., FDSSs and LDSSs) versus DSSs used at a higher strategic level and supporting decisions that involve multiple functions (i.e., CPSs and EISs). The formality dimension distinguishes between DSSs that tend to be relatively formal in their design and documentation because they support recurring types of decisions (i.e., CPSs and FDSSs) versus DSSs that are less formal due to their support of more unanticipated or one-shot types of decisions (i.e., LDSSs and EISs). The user class dimension acknowledges that some DSSs are intended to support individual decision makers, whereas others support multiparticipant decision makers. In principle, any of the four DSS types could be designed for either user class.

DSS Planning   Planning is an important and well-studied part of administering an organization's management information systems (Lederer and Sethi 1991a, 1991b, 1992; Lederer and Gardiner 1992a, 1992b). There is a need for organizations to devote similar attention to decision support systems (Henderson, Rockart, and Sifonis 1987). The foregoing framework suggests that administrators involved in DSS

FIGURE 16.1 An Organizational Framework for Decision Support Systems Adapted from Philippakis and Green (1988)

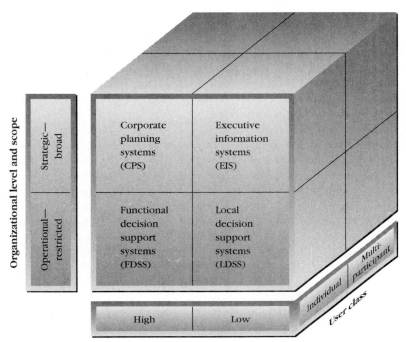

planning need to recognize that different kinds of users are served by DSSs and that each DSS type will require different resources. The user differences imply that there will be variations in how DSSs are evaluated and controlled, depending on their planned uses and the productivity gains planned for their users. The resource differences include variations in hardware, development tools, knowledge to be stored (e.g., what data or solvers are needed), user interfaces, and developer skills.

Creating an organization plan for decision support involves recognizing and grappling with these variations. It also involves recognizing commonalities in resource needs. For instance, there can be both advantages and drawbacks to a plan that standardizes on a particular tool (or tool set) for developing all LDSSs—and perhaps even using the same tool for all FDSS development as well. In general, the plan should

1. Assign responsibility for development, maintenance, control, and evaluation of each DSS type;
2. Specify whether the specific types of DSSs are to be developed in some sequence or developed in parallel;
3. Indicate how, if at all, the various DSSs or DSS types are to be linked;
4. Identify development resources (i.e., tools, personnel, finances, and knowledge) and methods to be used for each DSS type;
5. Clarify the relationships that the developers and users of each DSS type can have with other computer-related elements in the organization (e.g., the information center, the MIS department, developers and users of other DSS types); and

6. Establish oversight authority and regulations to ensure consistency across DSS knowledge systems.

The organization must develop such a plan either to fit, support, and enhance the organization's existing infrastructure or as part of a broader plan that revamps the organization's infrastructure to take advantage of the various types of DSS technology.

16.3 ORGANIZATIONAL COMPUTING

Understanding the types of DSSs available for enhancing organizational productivity, organizationwide planning for their deployment and coordination, and evaluation of their collective economic impacts on an organization are all aspects of a field of study called *organizational computing*. This field is also concerned with exploring similar issues for computing systems other than DSSs. Organizational computing (OC) studies ways in which computing technologies can promote improved performance and competitiveness of organizations, as distinct from improved individual performance (Applegate et al. 1991). Although the latter can contribute to the former, it is not the focus of OC study.

A major area of overlap between the OC field and the DSS field is shown in Figure 16.2: multiparticipant decision support systems. As indicated by the user class dimension in the framework of Figure 16.1, each of the four major DSS types (CPS, EIS, FDSS, LDSS) could be intended for supporting an individual decision maker or a multiparticipant decision maker. Those that support multiparticipant decision makers are of particular interest in the OC field. Not only are multiparticipant DSSs an important subject within the OC field, they are related to other major OC subjects. As indicated by the double arrows in Figure 16.2, these subjects include groupware, computer-mediated communication, computer-supported cooperative work, and coordination technology, which are themselves interrelated.

Figure 16.2 indicates that multiparticipant DSSs fall into two major categories, **group decision support systems** and **organizational decision support systems.** As their names imply, they differ in terms of the kind of multiparticipant decision maker they are intended to support. A group decision support system (GDSS) is devised to support a group decision maker. Recall from Chapter 3 that a group is a flat organization, one whose infrastructure is very simple—involving little in the way of role specialization, communication restrictions, or formal authority differences.

An organizational decision support system (ODSS) is intended to support a decision maker with more elaborate organizational infrastructure—involving specialized roles, restricted communications patterns, or important differences in authority over the decision. Recall from Chapter 3 that a hierarchic team is a common example of such a decision maker.

Cutting across the GDSS and ODSS categories is another class of systems known as negotiation support systems. A negotiation is an activity in which participants representing distinct (often conflicting) interests or viewpoints attempt to reach an agreement about some controversial issue. A **negotiation support system** (NSS) is intended to help the participants achieve an agreement. In so doing, it supports the participants' efforts at reaching a joint decision about how to resolve a controversial issue. Thus, an NSS is a kind of multiparticipant DSS. If the negotiating par-

FIGURE 16.2   Relating the Fields of Decision Support Systems and Organizational Computing

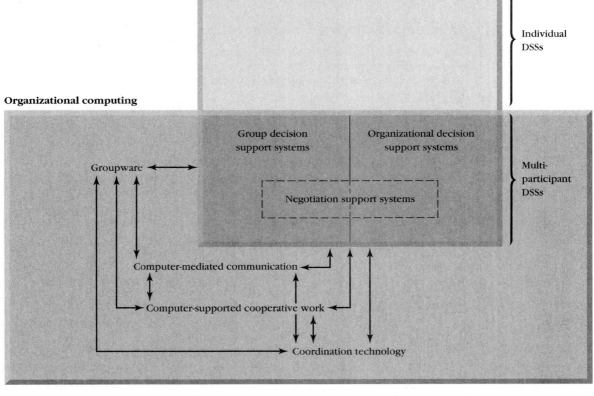

ticipants are structured as a group, then the NSS is a special kind of GDSS. If they have a more elaborate infrastructure, then the NSS is a special kind of ODSS.

Before exploring multiparticipant DSSs in more detail in Chapter 17, we briefly examine the other four OC subjects identified in Figure 16.2: groupware, computer-mediated communication, computer-supported cooperative work, and coordination technology. This study furnishes a useful background for appreciating multiparticipant DSSs. Developments in these OC areas have had and will continue to have considerable influence in the multiparticipant DSS realm.

GROUPWARE

Groupware refers to various kinds of computer-based systems, each of which satisfies the following two conditions:

1. It provides an interface to an environment shared by a group of persons.
2. It supports that group in carrying out a common task or meeting a common goal (Ellis, Gibbs, and Rein 1991).

DSS IN THE NEWS

Companies Employing Groupware

Organizing and coordinating a group project is always a tedious, time-consuming job—something many managers would love to hand off to someone else.

Fortunately, personal computers are now being enlisted to deal with this thankless task. . . .

When used in a local area network, or LAN, Notes enables PC users to gather, share, catalog and sort important business information on projects, as well as electronic mail about those projects. . . .

Notes falls into a category of software loosely called "groupware," programs that enable several users to work together across a network.

"Groupware is an easy bucket to toss in any application that's beyond personal productivity, but in fact there are many different kinds of groupware applications, some focused on communications and some focused on authoring and other tasks," explained Ann Palermo, director of office systems at market researcher International DataCorp. . . .

International Data estimates that 900,000 groupware user licenses were sold in 1990 and that by 1995 yearly worldwide sales will reach 3.2 million. . . .

. . . At PeopleSoft, Inc., . . . customer-service representatives use Notes to track and store customer-service reports, but its ability to sort different views or slices of stored data has been particularly helpful. . . .

. . . PeopleSoft is planning to expand its use of Notes by building a customer-service application and communications system for its clients. . . . PeopleSoft will give its customers the Notes software as part of its customer-support contract.

"We looked at other options . . . bulletin board software and electronic mail, but with those applications you can't structure the data and capture it in forms and fields," said Bergquist. . . .

. . . Metropolitan Life Insurance Co. is evaluating a Notes application for tracking, storing and sharing the status reports generated during the evaluation and closing of private placements.

This project, if approved, would involve multiple offices communicating about potential investment deals across a network. . . .

K. Doler, "Firms are Employing 'Groupware' to Manage Projects," *Investor's Business Daily* 21 November 1991, p. 10.

Because systems can provide shared environments and support common tasks to varying degrees, a spectrum of groupware exists, rather than a clear dividing line between groupware and systems that are not groupware. One way to get a sense of systems on the groupware spectrum is to consider a classification of groupware provided by Ellis, Gibbs, and Rein (1991). Each class of groupware is oriented toward offering a distinct kind of support.

Message Systems   A **message system** is a kind of groupware that allows persons to pass messages among themselves. Such systems make use of some form of the message-management technique discussed in Chapter 11. Common examples of

SIX CLASSES OF GROUPWARE

- Message systems
- Conferencing systems
- Collaborative authoring systems
- Group decision support systems
- Coordination systems
- Intelligent agent systems

message-management systems are **electronic mail** and electronic bulletin board systems. In the former case, the groupware lets a user specify a textual message, routes that message to the computer having the electronic address specified by the user, and serves as a "mailbox" for receiving messages sent by other users of the electronic mail system. In the case of a bulletin board system, messages are not sent directly to other users' computers but to a computer that serves as a message repository. Users can then use their own computers to browse through the messages posted on the bulletin board computer and post messages of their own if desired.

The communication that occurs with these kinds of message systems is called **asynchronous,** which means that the sending of a message does not have to be synchronized with the viewing of that message. A message is sent with no requirement that the receiver has to view it at a certain time. Message systems can furnish a limited decision support capability in the sense of helping a decision maker acquire knowledge needed for producing a decision. The acquired knowledge could stimulate the recognition of a decision problem or be instrumental in solving that problem.

Impacts of message systems on both individuals and organizations have been studied. For instance, studies of managers using electronic mail found that their satisfaction with this kind of groupware stemmed mainly from time savings (Panko and Panko 1980; Foster and Flynn 1984; Long 1987). The asynchronous communication was found to reduce both telephone tag and telephone interruptions. Electronic mail systems were also found to (1) make it easier to broadcast a message to multiple receivers and (2) result in messages containing more information than would have been received without the use of this groupware technology. To combat problems of information overload (Hiltz and Turoff 1985) and junk mail

FIRST- AND SECOND-LEVEL EFFECTS OF MESSAGING SYSTEMS

Researchers have observed that messaging systems have two levels of effects (Sproull and Kiesler 1991). First, there are productivity gains from reducing the cost of work—reducing telephone delays and hard copy. For instance, Manufacturer's Hanover Trust realized a saving of 36 minutes per employee per day through use of electronic mail, for an annual opportunity savings of $7 million. Similarly, Digital Equipment Corporation estimated a $28 million annual marginal cost saving due to its managers' use of electronic mail. Second-level effects are perhaps more important. They are the result of connecting people with new people and new knowledge. For instance, interpersonal relationships tend to be more open, meaning increased self-disclosure and candidness.

DSS IN THE NEWS

Countrywide Funding Corp., the nation's largest mortgage lender, provides a good example of how Lotus Development Corp.'s Notes software can creep slowly into an organization and win it over completely in time. . . .

Bartlett wanted to automate the tedious process of filling out and routing forms for loans that required exceptions to the company's lending guidelines. The exception approval process used to take weeks and require the physical routing of a multipart form among several company divisions.

Now Notes' electronic mail handles it all.

Using Notes, loan officers requesting exceptions fill out a form, then press a button and mail it off to a group that researches exceptions.

The assigned researcher adds his or her comments to the exception record. When finished, the request is sent by E-mail to the secondary marketing group, which must approve exceptions. A lending expert in the group adds his or her comments, and if the expert approves of the loan, the loan officer is immediately notified by electronic mail.

Since information on the whole process is stored electronically, . . . [decision makers] can use Notes to learn important facts about lending trends—for example, on which branches are requesting the most exceptions and what the most common requests are. . . .

Countrywide now has "hundreds of applications on Notes."

K. Doler, "How Notes is Put to Use at Countrywide," *Investor's Business Daily* 29 December 1993, p. 4.

(Denning 1982), filtering mechanisms have been added to electronic mail systems (Malone et al. 1987; Mackey 1988). These filters let a user store rules that the system will use automatically to discard, file, or reroute each incoming message based on its content.

Conferencing Systems   Persons with common interests or working on common or similar tasks often travel to a common site where they interact face-to-face, exchanging and developing knowledge. What happens when people who need to hold such a conference are unable to convene due to travel that is too time consuming and expensive or scheduling conflicts that do not permit all to be in the same place at the same time? A kind of groupware known as a **conferencing system** provides one answer to this question. With such a system, each participant is able to interact via his or her own computer with the other participants in a computer conference. Ellis, Gibbs, and Rein (1991) have identified three approaches to groupware conferencing which they call real-time computer conferencing, computer teleconferencing, and desktop conferencing.

A **real-time computer conferencing** system allows participants to interact with each other at the same time through their respective computers (Sarin and Greif 1985). The system can be supplemented by a simultaneous audio linkage among the participants (e.g., via a telephone conference call).

Computer teleconferencing refers to telecommunication support of simultaneous interactions among participants by such means as conference calls or video conferencing (Johansen 1984). A common video conferencing setup involves a small number of active participants located in a specially equipped room and an audience composed of a larger number of participants at other sites. The room has a video camera that zooms in on the active participant who is speaking and voice-activated microphones to pick up the audio. Resultant audio-visual signals are broadcast to the audience participants, who may contact the panel of active participants to pose questions, make requests, and provide feedback.

Real-time computer conferencing lacks the video capabilities of teleconferencing. On the other hand, teleconferencing systems lack the ability to share text and graphic images, which are exchanged via real-time computer conferencing. The third groupware approach to conferencing systems incorporates the strengths of the other two approaches while avoiding their shortcomings. Called **desktop conferencing,** this approach allows participants to interact through their desktop computers. Each participant's display screen is partitioned into multiple windows. Some are for textual and graphical interaction, whereas others are for video images of participants (Watabe et al. 1990). The computers are also equipped for audio interaction of participants. To the extent that a conference aims to support a decision being made by participants, conferencing system groupware functions in a decision support capacity.

DSS IN THE NEWS

Coming of Age

Dorothy Mulligan is deep in a discussion about computer repair.

To make a point, the coordinator for academic computing and educational technology at Jersey City State College in New Jersey pulls out a computer board. She points to one tiny numbered chip. "That could be the part that has the problem," she observed.

What makes this scene unusual is that Mulligan is actually thousands of miles away from her audience. Her demonstration is being transmitted to Los Angeles through a videoconferencing device.

Videoconferencing has finally come of age. For as little as $30 an hour, you too can connect branch offices and headquarters, teachers and students, manufacturers and subcontractors. . . .

Today's prices are possible because of dropping costs for digital transmission, advances in computer technology and the ability to compress data. . . .

. . . Its main advantage is eliminating the time and expense of travel. . . .

. . . The systems provide flexibility that a telephone just can't match. You can catch the subtle facial cues with body language lost in ordinary telephonic communication. With overhead projector attachments, you can transmit images of everything from photographs to electronic parts. A computer optical disk system can even allow you to transmit moving images. . . .

M. Stroud, "With New Prices and Technology, Videoconferencing Units May Merit a Look," *Investor's Business Daily* 2 April 1992, p. 4.

Collaborative Authoring Systems   A **collaborative authoring system** is groupware that lets a group of people collaborate in the creation and revision of a document. Generally, the document's text is divided into sections. At any moment, the groupware allows any participant to view any segment. Only one participant at a time is allowed to modify a segment. However, while viewing a segment participants may be able to comment about it (e.g., expressing agreement or objections or suggesting revisions). These comments are recorded by the system as separate text for consideration by the segment's author and other reviewers (Leland, Fish, and Kraut 1988). If the collaborating authors are working on crafting a document that describes their collective decision about some issue, then this type of groupware is being used as a kind of multiparticipant DSS.

Collaborative authoring systems can function in either an asynchronous or real-time mode. In the asynchronous case, participants work on the same document at the same time. Collaborative authoring systems can track participant activity and provide notification of approaching deadlines. Some have the ability to explicitly notify participants of each others' actions. For instance, the groupware could inform one participating author that he or she will need to consider making changes to a document segment because of alterations another participant has made to a different segment (Kaiser, Kaplan, and Micallef 1987).

Group Decision Support Systems   Unlike the other kinds of groupware, which may be used for decision support but which were not created with a decision support focus, group decision support systems are designed specifically to assist a

DSS IN THE NEWS

Beyond Talking Heads

Forget ho hum travel cost savings, there's much more to videoconferencing. Turns out, it can help companies make money, too. Costs have dropped, and by using the technology in exciting new ways, some smart companies are making networked video a strategic part of their business. . . .

Adding videoconferencing to its plastics blow-molding machines gives Wheaton Industries in Millville, N.J., two advantages. It helps the company meet the strategic objectives of its own plastic bottle-making operations by making the machines easier to service. And, Wheaton's General Machinery Co. unit plans to sell the video-capable machines against the machines of other makers that haven't yet awakened to the advantages of video.

Most banks have TV cameras at their automated teller machines, but that's for security. Turn that camera into a two-way videoconferencing application, and you can staff bank branches remotely, letting bankers sell investments day and night. Huntington Bancshares of Columbus, Ohio is doing just that. . . .

Using videoconferencing as a business tool has endless possibilities that we are only just beginning to see.

P. A. Strauss, "Beyond Talking Heads: Videoconferencing Makes Money," *Datamation* 1 October 1994, pp. 38, 41.

group of persons meeting to reach a decision. This assistance includes the removal of communication barriers among participants and provision of facilities for structuring the flow of deliberations (DeSanctis and Gallupe 1985). A group decision support system (GDSS) can help participants generate ideas, organize comments on topics related to the decision, analyze issues, rank alternatives, and so forth.

With a typical GDSS implementation, participants meet in a room equipped with a network of computers and large computer-controlled public display screens. This arrangement is often called an *electronic meeting room,* and the GDSS groupware is called an **electronic meeting system** (Stefik et al. 1987; Dennis et al. 1988). Each participant's computer has a private viewing space that displays his or her own contributions to the electronic meeting (e.g., text of ideas the participant enters during a group brainstorming session). Each computer also provides a public viewing space for examining collective results of the group work (e.g., text of ideas offered by all participants during brainstorming). All participants can also see the large public display screen, which can display collective results, individual screens, or various other textural or graphical images relevant to the meeting.

DSS IN THE NEWS

Electronic Travel

Will technology kill off the business trip?

The Geneva-based International Air Transport Association reported in its annual Corporate Air Travel Survey last month that half of those questioned on the issue felt telecommunications developments will permit them to cut back on travel. . . .

The economic weakness and the 1990–91 Persian Gulf crisis together marked a turning point in many companies' decisions to seek alternatives to travel, analysts say. . . .

The market for large, studio-based systems has become saturated, analysts say. The next step is desktop units and then personal computer-based video systems, both of which offer greater flexibility.

PC-based systems display the video image in one corner of the screen while showing other software in separate "windows." When a video phone call is in progress, data from spreadsheets or work processing programs can be displayed for all parties to view. . . .

Desktop and PC systems require new digital network technologies such as ISDN, short for integrated services digital network. . . . ISDN can carry images such as moving pictures as well as computer data and voice signals. . . .

. . . One recent example is Olivetti SpA and British Telecom's new multimedia Personal Computer Communication system. . . . It combines a personal computer, video camera and an ISDN network telephone to offer an integrated system capable of organizing audio, video and data. . . .

Reuters, "Videoconferencing Appears to Gain as Alternative to Business Travel," *Investor's Business Daily,* 4 May 1993, p. 4.

Some GDSSs are designed to be used by participants who are physically separated (Bui and Dolk 1986; Jacob and Pirkul 1992). Even though the meeting participants do not all meet in the same room, they do meet at the same time, and their group decision is supported by the GDSS groupware. Today, GDSSs are the most studied and used kind of multiparticipant decision support system. As such, Chapter 17 is devoted to a more detailed examination of GDSS development, features, and usage.

Coordination Systems   Where multiple participants are involved, coordination of their individual activities to achieve a larger goal is important. That larger goal may be to reach a decision or to accomplish something else, such as ensuring that a customer's order is processed, that a student's application for admission is fully considered, or that there is compliance with some set of governmental regulations. **Coordination systems** can help in the integration and harmonizing of participant activities in various ways. These groupware systems can show each participant the status of his or her own actions as well as what others have done in working toward the overall goal. A coordination system may issue an alert to a participant when others have completed enough of their activities to allow him or her to proceed. As a deadline approaches, it may issue a reminder to a participant that work needs to be completed.

DSS IN THE NEWS

Noteworthy Collaboration

. . . Lotus Notes, introduced in 1989, allows computer users to access, track, organize and collaborate together on documents residing on a shared database. Besides supporting traditional desktop computer applications like word processing and spreadsheets, the Notes program also can manage electronic mail, video and audio communication. . . .

Notes is used principally to organize the work of a group of people cooperating together on projects involving activities like customer service, account management and product development.

Such work is often referred to as electronic collaboration. . . . [The] global market for products and services related to electronic collaboration is estimated by industry analysts at $3 billion a year and is expected to grow as much as 30% annually.

. . . AT&T Network Notes will allow users to collaborate on the preparation of documents that include text, image and video. A sales representative making a presentation to a customer could make information . . . products or services available from a Notes computer server electronically and instantly.

Medical specialists across the U.S. could use the network to videoconference and collaborate on the best way to treat a patient. They could view the patient's latest test results simultaneously while their comments are stored in a central database. . . .

B. Deagon, "AT&T, Lotus Seek to Simplify Network Chores While Extending Reach," *Investor's Business Daily* 18 March 1994, p. 4.

One class of coordination systems has a form orientation. Such systems route electronic forms to appropriate participants at appropriate times in accordance with well-defined organizational procedures. When a participant receives a form, he or she may fill in blank portions of it or review its contents. When the participant finishes with the form, he or she notifies the coordination system, and it passes the original form, the modified form, or other kinds of forms to other participants. In effect, the coordination system shepherds the flow of work among participants according to a fixed process (Lochovsky et al. 1988).

Another class of coordination system has a conversational orientation. Such systems recognize a set of speech acts (e.g. the act of making a request or a commitment) and require participants to engage in such acts in valid ways (Flores et al. 1988). For instance, such a system might consider making a commitment to be an invalid act if not preceded by a request. Hence, it would not allow such a sequence to occur. In general, all coordination systems employ coordination technology of one kind or another. Such technology and the theory that underlies it are examined in more detail later in this chapter.

Intelligent Agent Systems   The emergent study of intelligent agents is highly multidisciplinary and has progressed to a point where the technology is beginning to be offered commercially (Riecken 1994). Generally, an **intelligent agent** is software (and accompanying hardware) that employs some artificial intelligence mechanisms to carry out a certain set of tasks. We can think of expert systems as intelligent agents. The filters used with messaging systems are intelligent agents. An important class of intelligent agents involves those that behave like personal assistants collaborating

DSS IN THE NEWS

Delivering Intellectual Global Assets

Like many of its Big Six consulting and accounting firm brethren, KPMG Peat Marwick is rolling out a corporatewide groupware system meant to help its professionals more efficiently share their expertise. . . . Dubbed Knowledge Manager . . . this . . . system allows KPMG personnel . . . to click on icons and access remote databases that contain, for instance, examples of successful proposals for floor space utilization. . . . A pilot version of Knowledge Manager helped KPMG win a bid at a Northeast insurance concern. At 3 P.M. on a Friday in August, the insurer asked KPMG for a proposal for a major technology overhaul.

Four partners working in different cities collaborated over the weekend using Knowledge Manager to gather background information, access graphics libraries and communicate. By noon Monday, they delivered a thick proposal to the insurer, complete with graphics and diagrams. . . .

"We want to deliver to every individual in the firm the combined intellectual global assets of the firm," said Allan Frank, managing partner at the enabling technologies division.

L. Radosevich, "KPMG Turns to FirstClass Groupware," *Computerworld* 21 November 1994, p. 58.

with users in various work environments (Maes 1994). Such an agent assists a user by concealing the complexity of tasks, performing tasks on behalf of the user, monitoring events for the user, notifying the user about situations of interest as they arise, and so forth.

One branch of intelligent agent study extends into the groupware area. It is concerned with intelligent agent systems that function as participants in group work, help participants involved in group work to collaborate, or assist participants in using other groupware. In the first of these cases, the agent's actions resemble those of human participants. It may be devised to represent a particular point of view that contrasts with those of other participants or to perform a certain task that other participants might overlook. For instance, an agent may monitor group activity and then offer suggestions to other participants (Gibbs 1989). A branch of artificial intelligence called *distributed artificial intelligence* is concerned with the study of groups of autonomous intelligent agents (Bond and Gasser 1988).

Second, intelligent agents can help participants coordinate their efforts. They can, for example, aid participants by scheduling meetings, administering meetings, or managing conference activities such as dismissal and introduction of participants (Maes 1994; Edmonds et al. 1994). Third, intelligent agents can facilitate the use of other groupware. For instance, agents for electronic mail can prioritize, forward,

DSS IN THE NEWS

Handheld Decision Support

[As an example of a new generation of] Personal digital assistants (PDAs) . . . Sony Electronics Inc. this week released its first PDA, . . . five-inch by seven-inch, battery-powered device as thick as a paperback book. . . .

The Magic Cap software used to operate Sony's new PDA works by touch-screen menus, using icons to represent commands. Magic Cap has absolutely no handwriting recognition, so there's no fussing with a technology not yet ready for use.

Using the Magic Cap as a simple interface, roving executives with Magic Link can send and receive electronic mail, make hotel and airline reservations, keep an appointment book and check stock quotes.

Most of those capabilities owe to AT&T's PersonaLink network. PersonaLink uses telephone lines to enable executives to easily send and receive electronic mail and faxes—and check stocks.

In a big step forward, PersonaLink also has "intelligent agent" software that could put a lot of the "personal" in personal digital assistant.

Personal agents can be programmed to make intelligent decisions for the PDA user. Based on instructions such as "Page me if I receive e-mail from so-and-so" or "Page me if ABC Co. stock falls below $30," personal link alerts its owner to important events.

PersonaLink also helps PDA users solve a conundrum in the age of ever-expanding E-mail use: the agent enables a message to find the recipient—even if the sender has no address.

S. Higgins, "New Generation of Handheld Data Assistants Come Closer to Ideal," *Investor's Business Daily* 30 September 1994, p. A4.

BUILDING GROUPWARE SYSTEMS

Building groupware systems involve all the challenges of developing systems for individuals, plus additional challenges stemming from the social dynamics of group processes. Grudin (1994) has identified eight of these additional challenges to the development and installation of groupware:

1. Groupware systems often require additional work from users who may not see direct, personal benefits from using the groupware.
2. A groupware system may not attract a sufficient number of users to be beneficial.
3. Groupware may be resisted when it requires users to break out of ingrained ways of doing things.
4. Groupware systems may not be sufficiently flexible to accommodate improvisation and exception handling that often occurs in group processes.
5. Groupware needs to be integrated with systems that users need for supporting their own individual activities.
6. Difficulty in evaluating a groupware system's impacts both within and across specific settings makes it difficult to use experience in learning how to build better groupware systems.
7. Using intuition to design groupware systems is less valuable than using it in building single-user systems, owing to the relative novelty and added complexity of groupware.
8. Introducing groupware into the workplace needs to be carefully planned, orchestrated, and considered from the outset of system development.

 Despite these challenges, there is evidence of progress in the groupware realm.

DSS IN THE NEWS

Collaborative Organizations

Groupware . . . potential is unleashed only if an organization is structured to take advantage of group work . . . If groupware is inserted into a flat, horizontal organization, it can boost productivity sharply. To make this new technology work, organization and culture are as important as PCs and software. . . . Preaching collaboration is not enough. It is as important . . . to create incentives for people to share as it is . . . to buy the latest groupware. . . . [G]roupware is a technology for managing relationships, not just information. Companies must design collaborative organizations for the tools of collaboration. Once they do, the power of groupware manifests itself.

Editorial, "Groupware Requires a Group Effort," *Business Week*, 26 June 1995, p. 154.

discard, sort, and archive a participant's incoming messages. Such an agent can learn to do so by monitoring how the participant handles messages and then behaving in the same way for future messages (Lashkari, Metral, and Maes 1994). Although research into intelligent agent groupware is at a fairly early stage, it promises to increase productivity of multiparticipant decision making.

COMPUTER-MEDIATED COMMUNICATION

The subject area of **computer-mediated communication** (CMC) is concerned with systems that use computers to create, store, deliver, and process communications (Kerr and Hiltz 1982). As such, it overlaps with the groupware subject area. The focus in both message systems and conferencing systems (real-time and desktop) is on computer-based means for handling communications. Although other kinds of groupware depend on computer-mediated communications, it is not the sole focus. Communication is crucial for a decision maker's ability to acquire knowledge. As earlier chapters showed, acquiring and deriving knowledge are cornerstones of decision making. It follows that computer-mediated communication can be an important form of decision support.

Here, we look at traits that CMC systems tend to have in common and at what researchers have discovered about the impacts of CMC systems. Rapaport (1991) discusses the history of CMC as an area of study and provides a survey of CMC uses and applications.

CMC System Traits   With CMC systems, communication occurs by typing and reading. The communication may be real-time or asynchronous in nature. A CMC system itself usually includes some or all of the following five elements (Kerr and Hiltz 1982):

1. A text-management tool for creating and modifying messages
2. A notebook for each participant, which is storage space for keeping notes, drafts of messages, documents of personal interest, and so forth
3. Messages, each of which is sent to one or more participants, is either identified with its sender or anonymous, is held at the receiving computer until discarded by the receiver, and may trigger an automatic confirmation (showing the date and time of receipt) for the sender
4. Journals, which are shared storage spaces for posting and viewing messages (from short items to long documents)
5. Conferences, each of which is a storage space common to a set of participants determined by an organizer or moderator, in which each participant can add comments or view comments (to keep up to date on the proceedings) and which may remain open for hours, weeks, or even years

More elaborate CMC systems may have additional elements for activities such as maintaining calendars, data storage and retrieval, merging text, issuing reminders, or participant voting. Turoff and Hiltz (1982) discuss desirable options for designing CMC systems and strategies for implementing such systems. Rapaport (1991) lists and discusses more than 50 features that would ideally be designed into CMC implementations.

CMC System Impacts   Researchers have been studying the impacts of CMC systems for at least two decades, including their impacts on society (Hiltz and Turoff 1978;

COMMUNICATION SUPPORT SYSTEMS

Progress in CMC research has led to several useful technologies. However, after almost two decades of empirical research exploring impacts of communication technology, there is little in the way of theoretical frameworks for integrating these findings and guiding the development of computer-based systems to support communications (Steinfield and Fulk 1990). Indeed, the underlying study of organizational communication itself lacks theoretical frameworks for integrating its researchers' results (Krone, Jablin, and Putnam 1987). Recently, steps to remedy this situation have begun to emerge. Authors have advanced a research agenda spanning the boundaries of organizations, communications, and computers (Calantone, Holsapple, and Johnson 1993). From that starting point, others have devised a framework formally characterizing the nature of communication support systems (Holsapple, Johnson, and Waldron 1996). This framework—involving such concepts as communicate-abilities and knowledge-management episodes—is developed within the same knowledge-management perspective used for understanding decision support systems. Thus, we eventually may closely link the study of communication support systems with the study of DSSs.

O'Hara-Devereaux and Johansen 1994), on jobs and job performance (Hiltz 1982; Zuboff 1982), on the organizations in which they are used, and on relationships among participants. We briefly summarize findings for the latter two topics. Users of CMC systems have reported that communications increase once a CMC system is installed (Hiltz 1984). In a successful CMC installation at Hewlett-Packard, the company found that a high activity level by a conference's organizer resulted in greater use of the system by participants and in the most successful conferences (Fanning and Raphael 1986).

Some of the studies have examined CMC impacts on a group decision maker. Comparing decision making by a CMC-supported group versus face-to-face, non-computer-supported communication, studies found that supported groups were less likely to reach a total consensus, less likely to have a dominant participant, more prone to request and furnish opinions, inclined to use many fewer words in producing a decision, and likely to have higher-quality decisions (Turoff and Hiltz 1982) A separate study with a different CMC system again found that groups using CMC systems made fewer remarks, had less consensus, and had less tendency for dominant participants to emerge (Siegel et. al. 1986). There was also a greater tendency for supported participants to use strong expressions in interacting and to reach a decision farther away from their individual preferences. Other studies have indicated that CMC systems promote consensus among decision-making participants (Applegate and Hertenstein 1988).

COMPUTER-SUPPORTED COOPERATIVE WORK

Varying views exist about what is included in the subject area of **computer-supported cooperative work** (Greif 1988; Bannon and Schmidt 1991). To some it is just another term for groupware—concerned with the development and installation of computer systems that support group work. However, not all cooperative work is done by groups. As we saw in Chapter 3, there are other kinds of multiparticipant ensembles. This fact is recognized by most groupware advocates (Schmidt and Bannon 1992). Computer-supported cooperative work (CSCW) has a more comprehensive scope than the groupware area (Greenberg 1991). Because communication is a key ingredient in cooperative work, the CMC area can also be seen as fitting within the CSCW realm.

As an area of study, CSCW is concerned with attempts to understand the nature and characteristics of cooperative work as a basis for designing supportive computer-based systems (Schmidt and Bannon 1992). This interdependence leads to various secondary (i.e., coordination) activities that are distinct from the work to be accomplished. These activities include securing commitments by participants to accomplish specific tasks in certain time frames, with particular quality levels, and in return for specified compensation. Such coordination activities impose overhead costs on cooperative work. Designers of CSCW systems aim to reduce the overhead coordination costs of cooperative work and/or improve the outcome of that cooperative work.

Thus, CSCW is not defined by a set of computer-based technologies such as electronic mail, computer conferencing, intelligent agents, and the like. Instead, it attempts to produce systems for a particular category of human work—cooperative work—using whatever existing or future technology is helpful. Some existing technology that handles the processing of requests by multiple users is definitely not helpful, actually preventing cooperative work (Applegate et al. 1991; Rodden, Mariani, and Blair 1992). An example is multiuser database technology, which has been used to build many applications that give users simultaneous access to large shared databases while allowing each user to work without concern about the actions of other users. Each user is unaware of the data storage and retrieval activities of the others, behaving as if he or she is the only user of the system. Rather than promoting the illusion of isolation, a CSCW system makes participants aware of each other's actions, helps propagate results of those actions to others, facilitates

DSS IN THE NEWS

Keeping Up with Ideas and Events

. . . Andersen Consulting. . . . built a system . . . called Knowledge Exchange [to support] 20,000 consultants around the world. . . . [It] consists of over 2,000 databases that consultants can tap into. Each specialized group has a database on the system and a "page" summarizing its contents and any relevant news. As employees add to their database, they build a library to store the group's collective experience and knowledge. So when a question relating to a project arises, consultants can check the . . . database to find an answer quickly. . . . [The system lets employees conduct] electronic consultations with each other. The result: Problems that once took two weeks and thousands of dollars to figure out are solved overnight. . . .

J. W. Verity, "Cyber-Networks Need a Lot of Spackle," *Business Week,* 25 June 1995, pp. 93–94.

participant interactions, and explicitly deals with participant interdependencies in the interest of maximizing cooperative work.

Although people are still researching what is needed for computer-supported cooperative work, it appears that we can distinguish support provided by CSCW systems from other computing applications in three ways (Rodden, Mariani, and Blair 1992). First, a CSCW system is likely to be distributed across multiple computers in such a way that they can function together to support the participants' cooperative work. We have made considerable progress in distributed computing technology over the past two decades, but CSCW needs are likely to make demands for further advances. Second, a CSCW system will probably establish, maintain, and process a representation of the cooperative work context. Such a representation includes knowledge about the participants being supported, their interdependencies, and the transactions they generate. Third, a CSCW system will probably try actively to support the cooperation taking place as well as keeping a record of it. This suggests the system may have abilities to monitor, alert, coordinate, advise, and perhaps even learn from experience.

CSCW is a large area within the organizational computing field, an area in which there are many unanswered questions beyond the scope of groupware and computer-mediated communication. As researchers discover more about computer-supported cooperative work, our ability to build and successfully use multiparticipant decision support systems will also grow, because multiparticipant decision making is frequently a cooperative work effort. Indeed, decision making can be seen as a major application area for researching and developing CSCW systems that will also be either group or organizational decision support systems.

COORDINATION TECHNOLOGY

Coordination technology refers to the use of technology to help people in activities that may be cooperative, competitive, or involve conflicts of interest (Malone 1988). It is rooted in coordination theory, which refers to theories about managing dependencies among activities (Malone and Crowston 1994). These theories come from and are influenced by various disciplines, such as organization science, computer science, management science, economics, law, social psychology, and linguistics. From the definition it is clear that coordination technology and CSCW are related. In the context of cooperative work, technological support of coordination can be useful. However, coordination (and technology to support it) is also important in accomplishing work that is not cooperative. For instance, in the case of competitive bidding, participants are at odds with each other. Yet, dependencies among them in the bidding process need to be managed (i.e., coordinated) and can be computer supported (Malone 1987; Ching, Holsapple, and Whinston 1993).

Thus, coordination technology overlaps with CSCW. But it also includes support of noncooperative work. Because communication is an important aspect of coordination, the CMC subject area is related to coordination technology. But coordination technology is much broader, including support of tasks other than communication. Coordination technology is also related to groupware, which includes the category of coordination systems. But coordination technology (like CSCW) is not restricted to the support of groups. Indeed, its greatest potential benefit may well be for other organizational forms, where the activities and interdependencies being managed are more numerous, intricate, and complex (Watabe, Holsapple, and Whinston 1992; Ching, Holsapple, and Whinston 1993).

Regardless of whether a multiparticipant decision maker is a group or a more complex organization (such as a hierarchic team) and regardless of whether the participants are cooperative or in conflict, there are dependencies among participants' activities. When computer-based technology is used to help manage these dependencies, it is called coordination technology. It is also called a decision support system: a GDSS, ODSS, or NSS, depending on the nature of the multiparticipant decision maker being supported. Some of the relationships among OC subject areas are shown in Figure 16.3.

Coordination technology forms a very large subject area, encompassing much of the other OC areas we have described—and more. We do not attempt to survey it fully here. Instead, we provide a flavor of the area's scope and diversity as a basis for appreciating its connections to the study of decision support systems. Our examination is guided by a framework that identifies common types of dependencies that need to be managed (Malone and Crowston 1994). These dependencies are shown in Table 16.1, along with examples of approaches to managing each dependency. When these coordination approaches (and others that have yet to be invented) are supported or performed by computer-based systems, the result is coordination technology.

At a very broad level, there is a need for coordination among all of an organization's activities within the constraints imposed by its environment (e.g., legal constraints, market constraints). That is, the dependencies among operations, finance, marketing, research and development, personnel, computing, and other functional activities need to be recognized and managed. The field of strategic management is largely concerned with this high-level coordination. The corporate planning systems noted in Figure 16.1 model dependencies across different functional activities and are examples of coordination technology. Coordination also happens within an organizational function. In many organizations, for instance, the operations function

FIGURE 16.3   Directions and Connections in the OC Field

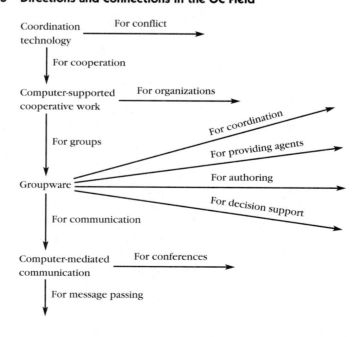

TABLE 16.1   A Framework for Studying Coordination

TYPE OF DEPENDENCY	COORDINATION EFFORT	EXAMPLES OF COORDINATION METHODS FOR MANAGING DEPENDENCY
The same resource is needed in multiple activities.	Managing the allocation of resources	First come, first served Based on priorities of activities Determined by managerial decision Based on budget or plan for resource utilization Competitive bidding for the resource
The result of one activity is needed by another activity: sequencing, transfer, and usability.	Managing supplier-consumer relationships	Supplier notifying consumer of status Project-management techniques (scheduling, PERT, CPM) Inventory-management techniques (just-in-time, economic order quantity) Product design techniques (standardization, participatory design)
Multiple activities must occur simultaneously.	Managing simultaneity constraints	Scheduling techniques
One activity involves multiple subactivities.	Managing task-subtask relationships	Organization design Management by objectives
Multiple activities jointly need to produce a single decision.	Managing multiparticipant decision making	Nominal group technique Delphi method Nemawashi-based process Arbitration procedures Structured argumentation

involves the manufacture of goods. Computer-integrated manufacturing (CIM), which refers to the integration of all manufacturing activities through computer-based systems, plays a key role in coordinating manufacturing activities (Gurbaxani and Shi 1992). Thus, such systems form another class of coordination technology. At a more elemental level, there are coordination efforts such as the five identified in Table 16.1. We now elaborate on each.

Managing the Allocation of Resources   **Resource allocation** occurs when multiple activities need some limited resource. The resource could be material, human, monetary, or knowledge (recall Chapter 1). For instance, multiple jobs may need the same machine, multiple tasks may need the same worker, multiple projects vie for a limited pool of funds, multiple products may require the same kind of parts, or multiple decisions may need the same expert's advice or the same DSS. Dependencies among the activities arise due to their shared need for the limited resource. Managing such dependencies is a kind of coordination that has been extensively studied in economics, organization science, management science, and computer science.

Economists recognize markets as coordination mechanisms for the allocation of resources (Simon 1981). Organization science studies hierarchical coordination mechanisms whereby managers at different organizational levels control the usage of certain resources (e.g., workers) and determine how they are to be allocated to various activities. Management science studies how resource-allocation problems can be mathematically modeled and solved, in quest of good or optimal coordination. Computer scientists are concerned with devising algorithms for effectively coordinating the use of limited computing resources (i.e., processors, memory, and I/O devices).

These fields contribute various coordination methods, including those examples identified in Table 16.1, that have potential for inspiring coordination technology. For instance, computer-based systems that permit widely scattered participants to bid for securities are already a reality in the financial world. These electronic markets are an example of coordination technology. Similarly, Smith and Davis (1991) have formalized the notion of competitive bidding schemes for computer networks and Ching, Holsapple, and Whinston (1992, 1993) have done so for interorganizational coordination. Because the ultimate result of using electronic markets is a decision about resource allocation, the coordination technology can be regarded as a kind of multiparticipant DSS.

Managing Supplier-Consumer Relationships   Both within and across organizations, **supplier-consumer relationships** are very common. The supplier activity yields some material product or knowledge that the consuming activity seeks. In such a relationship, there are three major types of dependency to be managed: sequencing, transfer, and usability dependencies (Malone and Crowston 1994). Coordination methods for each of these can spawn corresponding coordination technologies.

A sequencing dependency refers to the fact that a supplier must be ready to supply and the consumer must be ready to receive before the transaction can occur. Managing this aspect of a supplier-consumer relationship may simply involve monitoring the supplier activity and notifying the consumer of the current status. However, the supplier activity may be very complex (e.g., the manufacture of a machine). In such a case, coordination demands careful sequencing and tracking of processes and events in the supplier activity. Project-management techniques function as coordination methods. These include the use of PERT (project evaluation and review technique), CPM (critical path method), and other scheduling techniques. Computer implementations of these methods have been available for many years, serving as a kind of coordination technology to help decision makers' scheduling efforts.

Transfer dependency refers to coordinating the transfer of material goods or knowledge from a supplier activity to a consumer activity. This process includes the management of inventory as a buffer between the two activities. Examples of coordination methods used for this dependency include just-in-time planning (to reduce the need for inventory) and various inventory-management practices. Usability dependency is concerned with ensuring that what the supplier transfers to the consumer is usable. Relevant coordination methods include such product-design techniques as establishing product standards or participatory design in which a customer actively participates in product design. The latter may well benefit from groupware of the collaborative authoring variety.

Managing Simultaneity Constraints   Coordination is needed when multiple activities must occur simultaneously. Simultaneity constraints occur when two or more activities must occur in parallel. A common example is a meeting, in which several people's activities intersect at the same time and in the same place. Related coordination technology includes meeting-scheduling software and groupware conferencing systems in that they relax physical constraints that would otherwise make a meeting difficult or impossible to coordinate.

Managing Task-Subtask Relationships   If an activity is thought of as a task, then many other activities (i.e., subactivities) can be initiated by decomposing the task into subtasks. Each task can be accomplished by accomplishing its subtasks. Each subtask can be decomposed into a lower level of subtasks, and so forth. Some or all subtasks may be performed by computers. Coordination in this case is concerned with recognizing alternative **task decompositions,** choosing an appropriate decomposition from among them, and ensuring timely subtask completions (Mintzberg 1979; Bonczek, Holsapple, and Whinston 1979). To the extent that a decomposed task is to make a decision (as in the case of a hierarchic team) or to solve a problem as part of a decision process, any assisting coordination technologies can be regarded as providing decision support.

The recognition and selection of decomposition alternatives may be managed through the design of an organization. That is, coordination is built into the design, and the act of designing is an exercise in coordination. A pioneering coordination technology along these lines is a system that all organization participants can use to collectively redesign their organization on a continuing basis (Rein, Holsapple, and Whinston 1993). Related to organization design is another coordination approach called *management by objectives* (Odiorne 1965). It consists of a manager designing explicit objectives for each subordinate manager. Managers carry out tasks accordingly and are evaluated on the extent to which they met their objectives. Related coordination technology would include expert systems for setting objectives and monitoring systems for tracking progress in meeting objectives.

Managing Multiparticipant Decision Making   When multiple activities jointly need to produce a single decision, those activities are typically coordinated. That is, the multiple participants' activities are usually not intertwined in an entirely random manner. How their dependencies are or can be managed is strongly influenced by the organization of a decision maker. If the participants are organized as a group, then Robert's rules of order may serve as the coordination method. On the other hand, this coordination method is not applicable if the organization is a hierarchic team. In that case, the coordination method would probably involve task decomposition, where the task being decomposed is the making of a decision. Applicable coordination methods also depend on whether the participants are related in a cooperative or conflicting manner. Here, we consider coordination methods shown in Table 16.1.

Nominal Group Technique   The **nominal group technique** is a coordination method primarily applicable to a group engaged in cooperative decision making. It imposes the following steps on participants' activities (Van de Ven and Delebecq 1971):

1. Each participant individually writes down his or her ideas about what the decision should be.
2. In a round-robin fashion, each participant presents one of his or her ideas. It is listed in summary form on a wall chart or white board for all to see, with no discussion about its desirability.
3. After all ideas are presented and listed, the participants clarify and evaluate the alternative ideas.
4. Each participant individually votes on each idea by rating it on some scale or giving a rank ordering of the ideas. These votes are then pooled to determine the group's preferred alternative (i.e., its decision).

All these steps are candidates for computerization. Participants type in their ideas on their own computers. These computers are networked so the accumulated ideas can be presented to each participant. The discussion can occur electronically, with each participant typing in comments about the various ideas. Each participant votes by rating or ranking ideas displayed on his or her computer. Such coordination technology is commonplace in today's group decision support systems.

Delphi Technique The **Delphi technique** is also a coordination method geared mainly toward groups of participants who are cooperating. It resembles the nominal group technique in some respects, but the decision-making participants do not actually convene in a meeting. This coordination method imposes the following structure on participants' activities (Lindstone and Turoff 1975):

1. Identify a group of persons who have expertise in the decision area.
2. Send a questionnaire to all participants to survey their views about the decision problem.
3. Organize and analyze the participants' responses.
4. Send a summary of the survey results to each participant. Send another questionnaire to be filled out after they consider the results. When a participant's view is very different from those of the others, he or she can be requested to explain, with that rationale being forwarded to other participants.
5. Steps 2–4 are repeated until a consensus emerges about what the decision should be. If none emerges within some time limit, questionnaire responses are pooled, and the most preferred alternative becomes the decision.

Coordination technology supporting the Delphi technique can form the backbone of group decision support systems.

Nemawashi A coordination method widely used in Japanese organizations is the **nemawashi-based process.** It is a process that is not applicable to groups, because it involves restricted communication patterns among participants who play diverse roles and are situated at all levels of authority. Nor is it especially applicable to hierarchic teams, because it involves reaching a decision consensus among all who participate. Nemawashi-based coordination imposes the following structure on participants' activities (Watabe, Holsapple, and Whinston 1992):

1. When a major decision about some project is required, one participant (or a group of participants) is designated to be the coordinator. The coordinator identifies other important persons involved in the project to serve as participants in making the decision and solicits their views about the decision to be made. They can range from a few persons to many dozens of participants.
2. From their views, the coordinator produces a set of decision alternatives (i.e., project plans). Experts on various aspects of the project are asked to specify criteria for evaluating each of the alternatives and then to rate each alternative with respect to each of their specified criteria.
3. Based on results from Steps 1 and 2, the coordinator selects a candidate alternative.
4. The coordinator constructs an informal document for this alternative and shows it to other participants. Through negotiation and persuasion, the coordinator seeks a consensus. This process can require revisions to the document or a return to the prior step to choose a different candidate alternative.
5. The coordinator prepares a formal document detailing the candidate alternative. This document is circulated among participants, beginning with those at the low-

est organizational level and proceeding toward the top. Each participant affixes a personal seal to the document to indicate that it has been examined and is supported. If the alternative, as formally documented, elicits strong objection, the participant's seal is affixed upside down. The alternative is considered to be formally approved as the decision if it garners sufficient properly oriented seals (sufficiency differs from one organization or project to another).

This coordination method has been mathematically formalized as a basis for designing coordination technology that can provide organizational (as distinct from group) decision support (Watabe, Holsapple, and Whinston 1992).

Arbitration   **Arbitration procedures** are coordination methods that can apply when there is decision making under conflict. That is, participants in decision making are in conflict with each other about what alternative is preferable, but they still need to agree on some alternative as the decision. The participants engage in bargaining interactions in search of a mutually acceptable alternative. In the background, there is the promise that an arbitration procedure will be triggered if an agreement is not reached (e.g., by a certain time). This procedure could be conventional arbitration in which an outside party (the arbitrator) considers the participants' conflicting arguments and then selects an alternative that he or she regards as most appropriate. That alternative becomes the participants' decision. A different arbitration procedure, called final-offer arbitration, requires each participant to submit a final offer, from which the arbitrator must choose one (Stevens 1966; Farber 1980). This process greatly limits the alternatives compared to conventional arbitration. As a basis for coordination technology, arbitration procedures have been little studied.

Structured Argumentation   **Structured argumentation** is a coordination method that channels the interactions that can occur among participants by requiring them explicitly to represent and adhere to a pattern of arguments and counterarguments about decision alternatives. Perhaps the best known method of this kind is IBIS (issue-based information system), which is intended to bring structure to the consideration of unstructured problems (Kunz and Rittel 1970). An IBIS argumentation process is represented by a graph of nodes and links. The basic types of IBIS nodes include issue, position, and argument nodes. An issue node represents a problem posed in the form of a question. (For instance, What overseas market, if any, should our firm attempt to enter?) A position node corresponds to an alternative solution for the problem. An argument node involves one or more statements that either support or object to a suggested solution. Creation of an **issue net** begins with the specification of a root issue node. Then, various position nodes can be linked to it. Positions are evaluated by posting the pros and cons of each position in the form of argument nodes linked to it. Depending on the validity and strength of these arguments, a position is selected to resolve the issue.

A hypertext implementation of IBIS, offering a graphical interface, is available; it allows multiple participants to contribute to the construction of an issue net and monitor progress in that construction in an asynchronous manner (Conklin and Begeman 1988). An extension to IBIS replaces the idea of argument nodes with structured dialogue sequences to impose greater organization on the discourse among participants (Hamalainen et al. 1992). Such coordination technology is relevant not just to multiparticipant decision support, but also to other kinds of computer-supported cooperative work such as collaboration among persons tackling a research or design issue.

SEVEN CLASSES OF COORDINATION METHODS

Coordination is an important issue for both the management of an organization's many DSSs and for implementing multiparticipant DSSs. Many coordination methods have been developed and continue to be invented. In some situations multiple coordination methods may be beneficial. Shaw and Fox (1993) identify seven classes of coordination methods relevant to multiparticipant decision support systems.

1. *Coordination by revising actions:* Plan to avoid conflicts among participants by helping each to adjust its activity. For instance, frequent passing of information among participants in air-traffic control allows each to adjust the guidance of an aircraft to avoid conflicts (Cammarata, McArthur, and Steeb 1983).

2. *Coordination by synchronization:* Promote regular interactions among participants by controlling the timing and sequencing of those interactions.

3. *Coordination by structured techniques:* Follow a defined series of steps that systematically guides participants toward a decision (e.g., nominal group technique, Delphi method).

4. *Coordination by negotiation:* Use bargaining among participants to achieve a mutually acceptable decision. For instance, the negotiation process may be one of participants bidding for the opportunity to perform tasks (Smith 1980; Ching, Holsapple, and Whinston 1992).

5. *Coordination by opportunities:* Each participant has the opportunity to contribute to decision making by posting ideas and requests that all others can see (perhaps in reaction to ideas posted by others). In effect, the "board" for posting ideas and requests serves as a coordination mechanism that can be distributed or support concurrent problem solving (Shaw and Whinston 1989; Nii, Aiello, and Rice 1989).

6. *Coordination by game theory:* Game theory examines means to enable self-interested participants achieve globally satisfactory solutions. This process can involve the use of payoff matrices (showing expected payoffs to participants from alternatives) and participant's utility functions (Genersereth and Rosenschein 1985; Genersereth, Ginsberg, and Rosenschein 1986).

7. *Coordination by constraint reasoning:* Find a common set of solutions by analyzing differing constraints attributed to each participant. For instance, constraint reasoning can direct multiple participants' problem-solving processes (Fox et al. 1992).

16.4 SUMMARY

The study of organizational computing is a vast endeavor, beyond the scope of a single chapter or perhaps even a single book. The organizational computing field is also rapidly growing and changing, with new concepts and technologies appearing every year. Of particular interest here are those parts of the OC field related to decision support systems. They form an important basis for achieving an organizationwide perspective on DSSs and for beginning to appreciate multiparticipant DSS possibilities.

In connection with the first of these, four types of DSSs were identified, characterized, compared, and contrasted: corporate planning systems, functional decision support systems, executive information systems, and local decision support systems. These DSSs were integrated into a framework that relates them along three dimensions: organizational level or scope, degree of system formality, and user class (individual versus multiparticipant). The organizationwide view provided by this framework is a good starting point for beginning to think about planning for and managing an organization's DSSs.

In connection with the second point, not only does the OC field overlap with the DSS field, it encompasses several subject areas that have strong relationships with multiparticipant decision support. The OC-DSS overlap consists of multiparticipant DSSs, which can be classified into those that support group decision makers (GDSSs) versus those that support more complex kinds of organizational decision makers (ODSSs). Cutting across these two classes is a type of multiparticipant DSS called a negotiation support system (NSS).

Four OC subject areas that contribute to the study of multiparticipant DSSs are groupware, computer-mediated communication, computer-supported cooperative work, and coordination technology. A survey of each of these areas indicates that they are related to each other and they offer technologies that can be adapted for decision support purposes. Continuing advances of researchers in these four areas are likely to help shape the multiparticipant DSS landscape for years to come. In Chapter 17, we look at GDSSs, ODSSs, and NSSs in greater detail.

▲ IMPORTANT TERMS

arbitration procedures
asynchronous
collaborative authoring system
computer-mediated communication
computer-supported cooperative work
computer teleconferencing
conferencing system
coordination system
coordination technology
corporate planning system
Delphi technique
desktop conferencing
electronic mail
electronic meeting system
executive information system
functional decision support system
group decision support system
groupware

intelligent agent
issue net
local decision support system
message system
multiparticipant decision support system
negotiation support system
nemawashi-based process
nominal group technique
organizational infrastructure
organizational computing
organizational decision support system
real-time computer conferencing
reengineering
resource allocation
structured argumentation
supplier-consumer relationship
task decomposition
technological infrastructure

▲ APPLICATION TO THE MCI CASE

1. Give an example of organizational infrastructure at MCI.
2. Give an example of supporting technological infrastructure at MCI.
3. What does an information resource center at MCI do?
4. In what way does CIRC support decision makers?
5. Why was the Green Sheets Application developed?

6. How does the Green Sheets Application improve productivity of the CIRC organization?
7. Explain how the organizational memory can serve a decision support role.
8. How does the organizational memory improve the productivity of the CIRC organization?
9. Explain how the electronic bulletin board was used for collaborative authoring.
10. In what way is collaborative authoring a group decision effort?
11. What was the advantage of using the electronic bulletin board for collaborative authoring rather than having a meeting for that purpose?
12. What Green Sheets Application features could be accomplished via desktop conferencing? What additional features could be provided?
13. How might intelligent agents enhance the Green Sheets Application? The organizational memory? The collaborative authoring?
14. Which of the five CMC elements does the Green Sheets Application appear to possess?
15. Why does the Green Sheets Application not qualify as a CSCW system?
16. If coordination technology were to be used for the Green Sheets Application, which of the five coordination efforts from Table 16.1 would come into play? Briefly explain.

▲ REVIEW QUESTIONS

1. What are the three main components of organizational infrastructure?
2. How are organizational infrastructure and technological infrastructure related?
3. What are two basic approaches to achieving a good fit between technological and organizational infrastructure?
4. In what way is each of the following OC subject areas relevant to the study of multiparticipant DSSs?
   a. Groupware
   b. Computer-mediated communication
   c. Computer supported cooperative work
   d. Coordination technology
5. Taking an organizationwide perspective, what are four major types of DSSs found in organizations today?
6. How do the following differ in terms of what they do, who develops them, who uses them, and what resources they require?
   a. Corporate planning systems
   b. Functional DSSs
   c. Executive information systems
   d. Local DSSs
7. What should an organization's plan for decision support include?
8. What is organizational computing?
9. Why is the study of organizational computing important for understanding the DSS field?
10. In what way does the OC field overlap with the DSS field?
11. What is a multiparticipant DSS?
12. How do GDSSs differ from ODSSs?
13. What is the relationship of negotiation support systems to multiparticipant DSSs?

14. Identify four OC subject areas that are related to the study of multiparticipant decision support systems.
15. What is groupware? Identify major classes of groupware.
16. How might each class of groupware be used for decision support purposes?
17. What is asynchronous communication? Give an example.
18. In connection with electronic mail, what does a filtering system do?
19. What are advantages and disadvantages of messaging systems relative to face-to-face or telephonic means of passing messages?
20. What are advantages and disadvantages of real-time computer conferencing relative to (a) video conferencing, (b) desktop conferencing, and (c) face-to-face conferences?
21. What is the typical layout of an electronic meeting room in which a GDSS is used?
22. What are some of the basic elements that are found in CMC systems?
23. How are CSCW systems distinguishable from other computing applications?
24. Why are systems built with multiuser database technology not examples of CSCW systems?
25. What is coordination?
26. According to coordination theory, what kinds of dependencies need to be managed?
27. What is the purpose of task decomposition?
28. In coordinating a supplier-consumer relationship, what kinds of dependencies need to be considered?
29. What are four coordination methods for managing dependencies among activities in a multiparticipant decision maker?
30. How does each of the following work?
    a. Nominal group technique
    b. Delphi method
    c. Nemawashi-based process
31. Why are different coordination methods of interest in managing dependencies involved in multiparticipant decision making?

▲ DISCUSSION TOPICS

1. Discuss what features a multiparticipant DSS might usefully possess beyond the features of a DSS for an individual decision maker.
2. Why is it important to have an organizationwide perspective of decision support systems?
3. What issues should planners and managers consider with respect to the various kinds of DSSs that can exist in an organization?
4. Position the four types of DSSs in an integrated framework.
5. Can you think of another useful dimension to extend the framework shown in Figure 16.1?
6. Can you devise an alternative classification of DSSs from an organizationwide perspective? What are its advantages and disadvantages relative to the classification presented in this chapter?
7. Why is it useful to distinguish between GDSS and ODSS? What are other ways to classify multiparticipant DSSs?
8. Discuss how a NSS for a group might differ from a NSS for an organization.

9. Describe the connection between groupware and computer-mediated communication.

10. Speculate on useful benefits from integrating intelligent agents with each of the other kinds of groupware.

11. What might be advantages and disadvantages of using a GDSS in an electronic meeting room versus having a face-to-face meeting?

12. What useful role might an intelligent agent play as a participant in a multiparticipant decision maker?

13. Describe the relationship between groupware and coordination technology.

14. How does the development of a groupware system differ from developing a system for an individual user?

15. Discuss the effects that CMC systems have been found to have on organizations and offer a rationale for those effects.

16. Distinguish between cooperative work and noncooperative work. Give examples.

17. Distinguish between cooperative decision making and noncooperative decision making. Give examples.

18. Can you enlarge Table 16.1 with other kinds of dependencies?

19. Why is coordination important to a group decision maker? To a team decision maker? To more complex organizational decision makers?

20. For each of the five coordination methods that Table 16.1 identifies as means for managing multiparticipant decision making, describe how it might serve as the basis for building coordination technology for incorporation in multiparticipant DSSs.

▲ REFERENCES

Alter, S. 1980. *Decision support systems: Current practice and continuing challenges.* Reading, Mass.: Addison-Wesley.

Applegate, L., C. Ellis, C. W. Holsapple, F. J. Rademacher, and A. B. Whinston. 1991. Organizational computing: Definitions and issues. *Journal of Organizational Computing* 1, no. 1.

Applegate, L. M., and J. J. Hertenstein. 1988. *Westinghouse electric corporation: Automating the capital budgeting process.* Boston: Harvard Business School Case Services.

Ariav, G., and M. J. Ginzberg. 1985. DSS design: A systemic view of decision support. *Communications of the ACM* 28, no. 10.

Bannon, L., and K. Schmidt. 1991. CSCW: Four characters in search of a context. In *Studies in computer supported cooperative work, theory, practice and design,* edited by J. Bowers and S. Benfor. Amsterdam: North-Holland.

Bates, M. E., and K. Allen. 1994. Lotus notes in action: Meeting corporate information needs. *Database* 17, no. 4.

Bonczek, R. H., C. W. Holsapple, and A. B. Whinston. 1979. Computer-based support of organizational decision making. *Decision Sciences* (April).

————. 1980. The evolving roles of models within decision support systems. *Decision Sciences* (April).

Bond, A. H., and L. Gasser. 1988. An analysis of problems and research in DAI. In *Readings in artificial intelligence,* edited by A. Bond and L. Gasser, San Mateo, Calif.: Morgan Kaufmann Publishers.

Boulden, J. B., and E. S. Buffa. 1970. Corporate models: On-line, realtime systems. *Harvard Business Review* 48, no. 4.

Bui, T., and D. Dolk. 1986. Communications design for co-op: A group decision support system. *ACM Transactions on Office Information Systems* 4, no. 2.

Calantone, R. J., C. W. Holsapple, and L. E. Johnson. 1993. Communication and communication support: An agenda for investigation. *The Information Society* 9, no. 1.

Cammarata, S., D. McArthur, and R. Steeb. 1983. Strategies of cooperation in distributed problem solving. *Proceedings of the Eighth International Joint Conference on Artificial Intelligence.*

Ching, C., C. W. Holsapple, and A. B. Whinston. 1991. Computer support in distributed decision environments. In *Environments for Supporting Decision Processes,* edited by H. Sol and J. Vecsenyi, Amsterdam: North-Holland.

_____. 1992. Reputation, learning, and organizational coordination. *Organization Science* 3, no. 2.

_____. 1993. Modeling network organizations: A basis for exploring computer supported coordination possibilities. *Journal of Organizational Computing* 3, no. 3.

Conklin, J., and M. Begeman. 1988. gIBIS: A hypertext tool for exploratory policy discussion. In *Proceedings of CSCW '88 Conference on Computer Supported Cooperative Work.* New York: ACM Press.

Denning, P. J. 1982. Electronic junk. *Communications of the ACM* 26, no. 3.

Dennis, A. R., J. F. George, L. Jessup, J. F. Nunamaker, and D. R. Vogel. 1988. Information technology to support electronic meetings. *MIS Quarterly* 12, no. 4.

DeSanctis, G., and B. Gallupe. 1985. Group decision support systems: A new frontier. *Data Base* 16, no. 4.

Edmonds, E. A., L. Candy, R. Jones, and B. Soufi. 1994. Support for collaborative design: Agents and emergence. *Communications of the ACM* 37, no. 9.

Ellis, C. A., S. J. Gibbs, and G. L. Rein. 1991. Groupware: Some issues and experiences. *Communications of the ACM* 34, no. 1.

Fanning, T., and B. Raphael. 1986. Computer teleconferencing: Experience of Hewlett-Packard. *CSCW '86 Proceedings,* Austin, Texas (December).

Farber, H. S. 1980. An analysis of final offer arbitration. *Journal of Conflict Resolution* 24.

Flores, F., M. Graves, B. Hartfield, and T. Winograd. 1988. Computer systems and the design of organizational interaction. *ACM Transactions on Office Information Systems* 6, no. 2.

Foster, L. W., and D. M. Flynn. 1984. Management information technology: Its effects on organizational form and function. *MIS Quarterly* 8, no. 4.

Fox, M., E. Gardner, S. Safier, and M. J. Shaw. 1992. The role of architecture in computer-assisted design systems. In *Knowledge-aided design,* edited by M. Green. New York: Academic Press.

Friend, D. 1988. EIS: Straight to the point. *Information Strategy: The Executive's Journal* 4, no. 4.

Generesereth, M. R., M. L. Ginsberg, and J. S. Rosenschein. 1986. Cooperation without communication, *Proceedings of the Fifth National Conference on Artificial Intelligence.* Philadelphia.

Generesereth, M. R. and J. S. Rosenschein. 1985. Deals among rational agents. *Proceedings of the Ninth International Joint Conference on Artificial Intelligence.*

Gershefski, G. W. 1970. Corporate models—The state of the art. *Management Science* 16, no. 6.

Gibbs, S. J. 1989. LIZA: An extensible groupware toolkit. *Proceedings of the ACM SIGCHI Conference on Human Factors in Computing Systems,* Austin, Texas (May).

Greenberg, S. 1991. Computer-supported cooperative work and groupware. In *Computer-supported cooperative work and groupware,* edited by S. Greenberg.) London: Academic Press.

Greif, I., ed. 1988. *Computer-supported cooperative work: A book of readings.* San Mateo, Calif.: Morgan Kaufmann Publishers.

Grudin, J. 1994. Groupware and social dynamics: Eight challenges for developers. *Communications of the ACM* 37, no. 1.

Gurbaxani, V., and E. Shi. 1992. Computers and coordination in manufacturing. *Journal of Organizational Computing* 2, no. 1.

Hamalainen, M., S. Hashim, C. W. Holsapple, Y. Suh, and A. B. Whinston. 1992. Structured discourse for scientific collaboration: A framework for scientific collaboration based on structured discourse analysis. *Journal of Organizational Computing* 2, no. 1.

Hammer, M. 1990. Reengineering work: Don't automate, obliterate. *Harvard Business Review* (July–August).

Henderson, J. C., J. F. Rockart, and J. G. Sifonis. 1987. Integrating management support systems into strategic information systems planning. *Journal of Management Information Systems* 4, no. 1.

Hiltz, S. R. 1982. *Online scientific communities: A case study of the office of the future.* Norwood, N.J.: Ablex.

———. 1984. *Online communications: A case study of the office of the future.* Norwood, N.J.: Ablex.

Hiltz, S. R., and M. Turoff. 1978. *The network nation: Human communication via computer.* Reading, Mass.: Addison-Wesley.

———. 1985. Structuring computer-mediated communication systems to avoid information overload. *Communications of the ACM* 29, no. 7.

Hogue, J. T., and H. J. Watson. 1983. Management's role in the approval and administration of decision support systems. *MIS Quarterly* 7, no. 2.

———. 1985. An examination of decision-maker's utilization of decision support system output. *Information and Management* 8, no. 4.

Holsapple, C. W., L. E. Johnson, and V. Waldron. 1996. A formal model for the study of communicaiton support systems. *Human Communicaiton Research* 22.

Holsapple, C. W., and W. Luo. 1995. A framework for studying computer support of organization infrastructure. *Information and Management,* forthcoming.

Jacob, V. S., and H. Pirkul. 1992. A framework for supporting distributed group decison making. *Decision Support Systems* 8, no. 1.

Johansen, R. 1984. *Teleconferencing and beyond: Communications in the office of the future.* New York: McGraw-Hill.

Kaiser, G. E., S. M. Kaplan, and J. Micallef. 1987. Multiuser, distributed langauge-based environments. *IEEE Software* 4, no. 6.

Keen, P. G. W., and M. S. Scott Morton. 1978. *Decision support systems: An organizational perspective.* Reading, Mass.: Addison-Wesley.

Kerr, E. B., and S. R. Hiltz. 1982. *Computer-mediated communication systems.* New York: Academic Press.

Krone, K. J., F. M. Jablin, and L. L. Putnam. 1987. Communication theory and organizational communication: Multiple perspectives. In *Handbook of Organizational Communication,* edited by F. M. Jablin, et al. Newbury Park, Calif.: Sage Publications.

Kunz, W., and H. Rittel. 1970. Issues as elements of information systems. Working Paper No. 131, *Center for Planning and Development Research,* University of California, Berkeley.

Lashkari, Y., M. Metral, and P. Maes. 1994. Collaborative interface elements. In *Proceedings of the National Conference on Artificial Intelligence.* Cambridge, Mass.: MIT Press.

Lederer, A. L., and V. Gardiner. 1992a. The process of strategic planning. *Journal of Strategic Information Systems,* 1, no. 2.

———. 1992b. Meeting tomorrow's business demands through strategic information systems planning. *Information Strategy: The Executive's Journal* 8, no. 4.

Lederer, A. L., and V. Sethi. 1991a. Guidelines for strategic information planning. *Journal of Business Strategy* 12, no. 6.

———. 1991b. Critical dimensions of strategic information systems planning. *Decision Sciences* 22, no. 1.

———. 1992. Meeting the challenges of information systems planning. *Long Range Planning* 25, no. 2.

Leland, M. D., R. S. Fish, and R. E. Kraut. 1988. Collaborative document production using quilt. *CSCW '88 Proceedings,* Portland, Ore. (September).

Lindstone, H., and M. Turoff. 1975. *The Delphi Method: Technology and applications.* Reading, Mass.: Addison-Wesley.

Lochovsky, F. H., J. S. Hogg, S. P. Weiser, A. O. Mendelzon. 1988. OTM: Specifying office tasks. *Proceedings of the Conference on Office Information Systems,* Palo Alto, Calif.

Long, R. J. 1987. *New office information technology: Human and managerial implications.* New York: Croom-Helm.

Mackey. W. 1988. Diversity in the use of electronic mail: A preliminary inquiry. *ACM Transactions on Office Information Systems* 6, no. 4.

Maes, P. 1994. Agents that reduce work and information overload. *Communications of the ACM* 37, no.7.

Malone, T. W. 1987. Modeling coordination in organizations and markets. *Management Science* 33.

Malone, T. W. 1988. What is coordination theory? *National Science Foundation Coordination Theory Workshop,* Massachusetts Institute of Technology, Cambridge, Mass. (February).

Malone, T. W., and K. Crowston. 1994. The interdisciplinary study of coordination. *ACM Computing Surveys* 26, no. 1.

Malone, T. W., K. R. Grant, F. A. Turbak, S. A. Brobst, and M. D. Cohen. 1987. Intelligent information sharing systems. *Communications of the ACM* 31, no. 5.

Mintzberg, H. 1979. *The structuring of organizations.* Englewood Cliffs, N.J.: Prentice Hall.

Naylor, T. H. and M. J. Mansfield. 1977. The design of computer based planning and modeling systems. *Long Range Planning* 10.

Nii, H. P., N. Aiello, and J. Rice. 1989. Experiments on cage and poligon: Measuring performance of parallel blackboard systems. In *Distributed artificial intelligence,* vol. II, edited by L. Gasser and M. Huhns. London: Pitman.

Odiorne, G. S. 1965. *Management by objectives.* New York: Pitman.

O'Hare-Devereaux, M., and R. Johansen. 1994. *Globalwork: Bridging distance, culture, and time.* San Francisco: Jossey-Bass Publishers.

Opper, S. 1988. A groupware toolbox. *Byte* (December).

Panko, R. R., and R. U. Panko. 1980. A survey of EMS users at DARCOM. *Computer Networks* 5, no. 1.

Philippakis, A. S., and G. I. Green. 1988. An architecture for organization-wide decision support systems. *Proceedings of the Ninth International Conference on Information Systems,* Minneapolis (December).

Rapaport, M. 1991. *Computer-mediated communications.* New York: John Wiley.

Rein, G. L., C. W. Holsapple, and A. B. Whinston. 1993. Computer support of organization design and learning. *Journal of Organizational Computing* 3, no. 1.

Riecken, D. 1994. Intelligent agents. *Communications of the ACM* 37, no. 7.

Rockart, J. F., and D. W. DeLong. 1988. *Executive support systems, the emergence of top management computer use.* Homewood, Ill.: Dow Jones–Irwin.

Rockart, J. F., and M. E. Treacy. 1982. The CEO goes on-line. *Harvard Business Review* 60, no. 1.

Rodden, T., J. A. Mariani, and G. Blair. 1992. Supporting cooperative actions. *Computer Supported Cooperative Work* 1, no. 1.

Sarin, S., and I. Greif. 1985. Computer-based real-time conferencing systems. *IEEE Computer* 18, no. 10.

Schmidt, K., and L. Bannon. 1992. Taking CSCW seriously: Supporting articulation work. *Computer Supported Cooperative Work* 1, no. 1.

Scott Morton, M. S. 1971. *Management decision systems: Computer-based support for decision making.* Division of Research, Harvard University, Cambridge, Mass.

––––––. 1982. The role of decision support systems in corporate strategy. In *Corporate strategy,* edited by T. Naylor. New York: North-Holland.

Shaw, M. J., and A. B. Whinston. 1989. Learning and adaptation in distributed artificial intelligence systems. In *Distributed Artificial Intelligence,* vol. II, edited by L. Gasser and M. Huhns. London: Pitman.

Shaw, M. J., and M. S. Fox. 1993. Distributed artificial intelligence for group decision support: Integraton of problem solving, coordination, and learning. *Decision Support Systems* 9, no. 4.

Siegel, J., V. Dubrovsky, S. Kiesler, and T. W. McGuire. 1986. Group processes in computer-mediated communication. *Organizational Behavor and Human Decision Processes* 37, no. 2.

Simon, H. A. 1981. *Sciences of the artificial,* 2nd ed., MIT Cambridge, Mass: MIT Press.

Smith, R. G. 1980. The contract net protocol: High level communication and control in a distributed problem solver. *IEEE Transactions on Computers* 29.

Smith, R. G., and R. Davis. 1981. Frameworks for cooperation in distributed problem solving. *IEEE Transactions on Systems, Man, and Cybernetics* 11, no. 1.

Sproull, L., and S. Kiesler. 1991. Two-level perspective on electronic mail in organizations. *Journal of Organizational Computing* 2, no. 1.

Stefik, M., G. Foster, D. G. Bobrow, E. Kahn, S. Lanning, and L. Suchman. 1987. Beyond the chalkboard: Computer support for collaboration and problem solving in meetings. *Communications of the ACM* 31, no. 1.

Steinfield, C. W. and J. Fulk. 1990. The theory imperative. In *Organizations and Communication Technology,* edited by J. Fulk and C. Steinfield. Newbury Park, Calif.: Sage Publications.

Stevens, C. M. 1966. Is compulsory arbitration compatible with bargaining? *Industrial Relations* 5.

Turoff, M., and S. R. Hiltz. 1982. Computer support for group versus individual decisions. *IEEE Transactions on Communications* 30, no. 1.

Van de Ven, A. H., and A. L. Delebecq. 1971. Nominal versus interacting group processes for committee decision making. *Academy of Management Journal* 14.

Watabe, K., C. W. Holsapple, and A. B. Whinston. 1992. Coordinator support in a nemawashi decision process. *Decision Support Systems* 8, no. 2..

Watabe, K., S. Sakata, K. Maeno, H. Fukuoka, and T. Ohmori. 1990. Distributed multiparty desktop conferencing system: MERMAID. *CSCW '90 Proceedings,* Los Angeles.

Young, L. F. 1984. A corporate strategy for decision support systems. *Journal of Information Systems Management* 1, no. 1.

Zuboff, S. 1982. New worlds of computer-mediated work. *Harvard Business Review* 60, no. 2.

Chapter 17

MULTIPARTICIPANT DECISION SUPPORT SYSTEMS

BURR-BROWN: COMPUTER-BASED SUPPORT OF A GROUP'S ANNUAL STRATEGIC PLANNING DECISIONS

The Decision Room

The . . . facility . . . consists of the main meeting room, a control room and a small conference room. . . . The main room has two rows of . . . computers, arranged in concentric arcs on tiered flooring to provide excellent sight lines for each participant. . . . The facilitator's station at the front of the room has two computers of its own and the ability to control all the technology in the room. . . . The atmosphere of the room is comfortable and professional. . . .

Supporting Software

The system uses . . . an integrated set of tools . . . each . . . designed to work as a part of a unified system: receiving inputs from other tools, providing outputs to other tools, or both. . . .

Electronic Brainstorming (EBS) allows participants to share comments anonymously on a specific question. Each participant works simultaneously, sharing information on the same question, but without interacting directly. The ideas generated with this tool become the input to the Issue Analyzer (IA). This facilitates the analysis and organization of the ideas generated. The VOTE module allows a variety of voting options; it is often used in conjunction with IA to aid the participants in developing a rank ordering of key issues. Discussion of topics is facilitated through the use of the Topic Commenter (TC) tool. This allows interactive simultaneous input by all participants on the issues raised. . . .

Using the System

Because the tools are flexible in their application and because they can be strung together in a variety of ways, the system has the ability to meet the needs of many different groups. The procedures, which are tailored to each group's needs in a pre-planning session, map the intended process to the use of computer tools. . . .

. . . Facilitation provided . . . helped the participants to use the various hardware and software features of the room. . . . The facilitator's role is that of implementing the plan for the sessions, keeping the participants on track, assessing the need for modifications to the plan . . . [This] provides a focal person who is responsible for the implementation of the plan for the session. . . . [Use of the facilitator] provides a relatively neutral leader for the meeting—one whose role was that of monitoring the process, rather than pressing for a particular goal. . . .

The Burr-Brown Application

Burr-Brown . . . is a publicly held corporation which manufactures and sells parts to other electronics manufacturers. It has approximately 1500 employees and $150 million in annual sales. . . .

. . . [It was] decided to use the system for Burr-Brown's annual strategic planning meeting. This meeting is a regular part of their organizational

Continued

process. In past years, it had been carried out at off-site locations using manual methods. . . .

The participants were all senior managers at the division manager level and above. Thirty-one members of the organization participated over a three day period. . . .

Three pre-planning meetings were held with representatives of the company. Through these, company goals for the sessions were defined. . . . Prior to the planning meeting, each division prepared brief one-year and five-year proposed plans. These provided general and specific divisional objectives supported by projected budgets. They were distributed to participants in advance. . . .

. . . Three days were divided between long term strategic planning (day one), short range action planning (day two) and a wrap-up of the two processes (day three). The planning needs of each of the organization's eleven divisions were addressed in these areas. Both automated and face to face discussions were used to maximize the effectiveness of the process. . . .

On the first morning, Electronic Brainstorming (EBS) was used to generate ideas about expected corporate performance in the coming years. The comments from this session were then organized and sorted using Issue Analyzer (IA). This information formed the basis from which each of the divisional plans was to be considered. Through the rest of day one, each of the divisional 5-year plans was examined using the Topic Commenter (TC) tool.

Day two was used to consider each of the divisions again—this time in light of a one-year action plan. TC was again used for this task. Late in the afternoon, EBS and IA were used to generate and organize ideas on how to accomplish the next year's overall corporate objectives.

Day three began with a continuation of the process of identifying ways to accomplish the next year's goals. The VOTE module was used to rank order the generated ideas three times—first by overall benefit to the firm, second by time (short-term versus long-term) and third, feasibility. The top five issues from the benefit ranking were then entered into TC for further group discussion. After lunch on the third day, the participants were divided by the CEO into four work groups, with each examining the developed issues from one of the following considerations: gross margin improvement, spending control and overall perspective.

At the end of this process, each work group presented its findings to the entire group. Finally, an overview of what had been accomplished was presented by the CEO.

Results

. . . At the conclusion of the process, 22 of the 26 participants responding to a post-session questionnaire indicated that they believed that the automated process was better than a manual one. The other four expressed no preference. . . .

Continued

The following testimonial was obtained from a Group Vice-President . . . "The process allowed us to do in three days what would have taken months to do. In addition, if we had done it manually, we could not have brought more than 9 or 10 people into the process . . . and there would have been less interaction."

An additional comment from the CEO . . . [stated that it] " . . . lets so many participate. The comments were much more open than we could get with a manual session. If that had been a manual process, only two or three out of the group would have spoken up. . . . The primary difference is that with the manual system used in the past, only 8–10 people could participate."

. . . "The anonymity allowed people to ask questions that would not have been asked if names were tagged to the questions," and the comments and suggestions generated by these questions are now being applied. . . .

"A lot more people are on board with an understanding of what went on. Thus, there is a stronger sense of understanding and agreement among the employees. A lot of education happened that previously hasn't happened during one of these things. . . . People walked in with narrow perceptions of the company and walked out with a CEO's perception. This is the view that is sought in strategic planning, but is usually not achieved."

Condensed quotation from A. Dennis, D. Vogel, J. Nunamker, Jr., and A. Heminger, "Bringing Automated Support to Large Groups: The Burr-Brown Experience," *Information & Management* 18, no. 3 (1990); 113–117.

LEARNING OBJECTIVES

The Burr-Brown case gives a good sense of typical features offered by a group decision support system. It also gives a feel for what happens during the use of a GDSS. This chapter examines group decision support systems in more detail, including what researchers have discovered about their benefits and limitations. It also examines two other kinds of multiparticipant DSSs: organizational decision support systems and negotiation support systems. We begin with a discussion of distinctions and commonalities among the three types of multiparticipant decision support systems, including the introduction of a unifying generic framework for them.

After studying this chapter, you should be able to

1. Distinguish between group decision support systems and organizational decision support systems.
2. Describe a generic architecture for multiparticipant decision support systems.
3. Discuss what has been discovered about the benefits and limitations of group decision support systems.
4. Identify important issues in the design and usage of organizational decision support systems.
5. Explain various ways in which negotiation support systems can help in the resolution of conflicts among a decision maker's participants.

By successfully doing the exercises provided at the end of this chapter, you can verify that these objectives have been met.

17.1 INTRODUCTION

In this chapter, we take a closer look at the intersection of the organizational computing and decision support system fields portrayed in Figure 16.2. This intersection is the area of multiparticipant decision support systems. When a computer-based system supports the decision-making efforts of a decision maker composed of multiple participants, then it is a **multiparticipant decision support system** (MDSS). In the simplest case the decision maker is working on single decisions, but more complex possibilities can occur. For instance, a decision maker may be working on a series or orchestrated collection of minor decisions that lead to a major decision, or the decision maker may be engaged in making multiple concurrent decisions that can affect each other or in their totality significantly affect organizational performance without being tied to an overall grand decision (recall Chapter 2).

As we saw in Chapter 3, there are different kinds of multiparticipant decision makers. These include groups, hierarchic teams, and other types of organizations. An MDSS that supports a group decision maker is called a **group decision support system.** An MDSS that supports other kinds of multiparticipant decision makers, such as hierarchic teams or nemawashi project organizations, is called an **organizational decision support system** (ODSS). It is possible that an MDSS supports negotiations among participants to resolve points of contention. If so, it is called a **negotiation support system** (NSS) in addition to being either a GDSS or ODSS.

In the next section, we more fully develop distinctions among the types of MDSSs. We also highlight commonalities, including a generic MDSS architecture based on the DSS framework introduced in Chapter 6. The three sections that follow examine GDSSs, ODSSs, and NSSs in turn. The emphasis is on GDSSs because, to date, they have been the most intensively studied of the three. Each of the three is still evolving through active investigation by researchers. The treatment here provides a platform for appreciating the results of those research efforts as they unfold.

17.2 MDSSs: DISTINCTIONS AND COMMONALITIES

FITS WITH ORGANIZATION INFRASTRUCTURE

An organization's infrastructure has three major aspects: the **roles** that can be played by organization participants, the **relationships** among those roles, and the **regulations** that govern role and relationship creation, modification, and usage (Holsapple and Luo 1995a). **Technological infrastructure** exists for the purpose of improving the performance that an organization's participants can achieve through the roles, relationships, and regulations. As Figure 17.1 suggests, there can be good or poor fit between technological infrastructure and the particular **organization infrastructure** being applied to some task (e.g., a decision-making task). We can assess the impact of a particular technological infrastructure on the performance that can be realized with a particular organization infrastructure in terms of the efficiency with which a task is accomplished, the quality of the task's result, participant satisfaction, participant motivation, and innovations that result (Holsapple and Luo 1995b). In Figure 17.1 for instance, using X will yield better performance than Y on one or more of these performance measures.

A multiparticipant DSS's technological infrastructure is intended to improve an organization's performance in decision-making tasks. The three Rs of organization

FIGURE 17.1   Technological Infrastructure Impacts Organization Performance

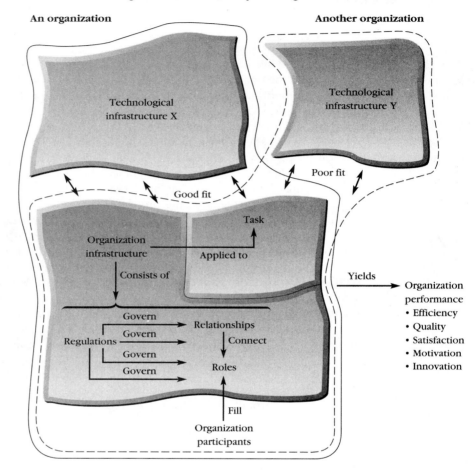

infrastructure (roles, relationships, regulations) help distinguish among the types of MDSSs by allowing us to classify these systems in terms of how they fit with organization infrastructure. We first consider how technology fits with roles, then with relationships, and finally with regulations.

Role Fits   Roles may reflect very little functional differentiation. In other words, a particular role is replicated throughout an organization, and all participants fill that same kind of role. For instance, every participant in a committee fills a role of committee member; every participant in a jury fills a juror role. Diverging from such a pure case, a more complex organizational infrastructure involves two distinct kinds of roles. For example, the committee could have a chairperson role in addition to its member roles; the jury could have a foreman role in addition to its ordinary juror roles. At the opposite extreme from little differentiation among roles, we have organizations in which participants play numerous highly differentiated roles as they jointly work on completing a decision-making task. Hierarchic teams are good examples of this, where the roles reflect an extensive division of labor into diverse specialties.

Roles that an organization's participants can fill may reflect very little differentiation in authority over the decision task. On a jury, for instance, each juror has an equal vote in determining the outcome. Committees also tend to give equal weight to the votes of its members. This is certainly the case when they are regulated by the nominal group technique. At the other extreme, there are extensive differences in the authority of different roles over a decision task. In a strictly hierarchical team, one role is vested with all authority, the other roles having none. Participants in a nemawashi process all have some authority by virtue of their roles, but the degree of authority differs. An upside-down seal affixed by a lower-level role carries less weight than one from a high-level role.

Uniting the functional and authority dimensions gives the axes shown in Figure 17.2. The GDSS and ODSS placements indicate where the best fits are likely to occur. Group decision support systems tend to fit well with decision makers having relatively little in the way of functional or authority differences among roles played by participants. In contrast, ODSSs are generally intended for decision makers encompassing a more complex assortment of roles. The dividing line between GDSSs and ODSSs in Figure 17.2 should be regarded as an approximation that is not entirely rigid or clear-cut. It simply shows where ODSSs and GDSSs are likely to form the best fits.

Looking at roles from another perspective gives a way to identify good fits between negotiation support systems and organization infrastructure. Roles involved in a multiparticipant decision maker can be designed to foster cooperation and avoid severe conflict. This situation is typical in a hierarchic team and in many groups as well. Conversely, roles may be designed in such a way that major conflict is permissible or inevitable. The only sense in which they cooperate is that they all aim to reach a binding decision. As an example, consider the negotiator roles involved in trying to decide about the content of a labor contract.

As shown in Figure 17.3, this spectrum of role designs from cooperative to conflicting gives a way to describe NSS fits with organization infrastructure. Observe that even where there is a cooperative role design, an NSS could be beneficial. For

FIGURE 17.2   MDSS Fits Based on Role Differences

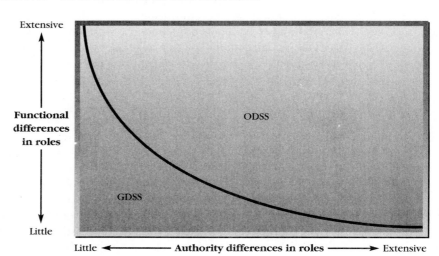

FIGURE 17.3   NSS Fits Based on Role Differences

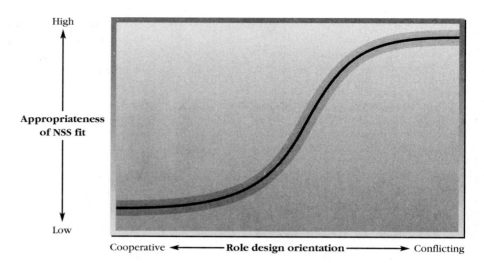

instance, participants assigned to such roles may harbor conflicting views that are not entirely held in check by a cooperative role design. Indeed, it can be very difficult to design and enforce a total absence of conflict without hampering organizational performance (e.g., reducing quality, motivation, or innovation). The line in Figure 17.3 should be interpreted as being more or less the center of a swath that indicates some variation in appropriateness due to factors other than the orientation of role design.

Relationship Fits   Roles are linked by lines of communication (Boulding 1956). Many patterns of communication channels are possible for a given set of roles. As one extreme is the pattern in which every role is linked to every other role, either directly (as with electronic mail) or indirectly (via an electronic bulletin board). In contrast, communication channels can be restricted. The participant filling one role may not need to communicate with all participants filling other roles. Communication channels are sometimes restricted to avoid chances of information overload or distraction. The nemawashi coordinator may never converse with the top-level participants. The lowest-level participants do not have channels to the top. Even if a channel is electronic, there is still a cost associated with it. Thus, if it is not necessary, certain roles in an infrastructure can remain disconnected. This is usually the case with hierarchic teams, with channels being used only between one level of roles and the next.

Figure 17.4 shows the appropriateness of MDSS fits across the spectrum of communication channel variations, from unrestricted to very restricted channel patterns. GDSSs, as they have evolved over the years, tend to exhibit open communication patterns. This result is reasonable when we consider that a free exchange and airing of ideas to and by group members is typically an objective—as in the nominal group technique. On the other hand, ODSSs tend to be designed to account for restrictions in communication channels that exist in comparatively complex organizations. NSSs can fall anywhere in either the GDSS or ODSS swath.

FIGURE 17.4 MDSS Fits Based on Role Relationship Differences

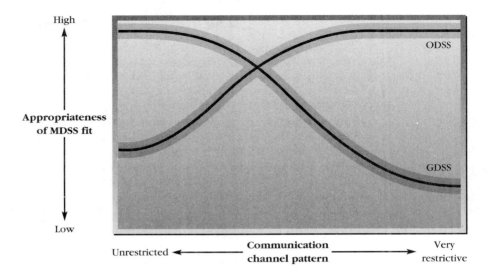

Regulation Fits   As Figure 17.1 suggests, regulations govern the design and use of roles and relationships, plus the assignment of participants to roles. Coordination methods are ways of regulating organization infrastructure. Regulations range from being few and simple to numerous and complex. This variation gives yet another way to characterize MDSS fits with organization infrastructure.

Figure 17.5 indicates that GDSSs are not particularly well suited to offering technological support in situations of complex regulations. For instance, regulations imposed by the nominal group technique are relatively simple compared to those of a nemawashi process. Present-day GDSSs would be of limited value as technological infrastructure for the latter. Although developers of ODSSs may build systems to fit with comparatively simple regulations, the focus in ODSS research and

FIGURE 17.5 MDSS Fits Based on Regulation Differences

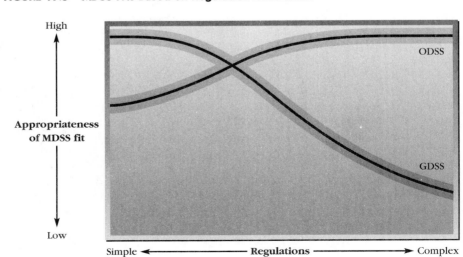

development is on fitting with more complex regulations. NSSs can fall anywhere on either the GDSS or ODSS swath.

MDSS COMMONALITIES

Having seen how ODSSs and GDSSs tend to differ in terms of organizational traits with which they fit, it is useful to consider what they have in common. First, we look at possible arrangements of participants in time and space, finding that the same possibilities exist for all types of multiparticipant decision support systems. Second, we introduce a generic architecture for designing and studying all types of MDSSs.

Participant Arrangements   Any MDSS will fall into one (or more) of the four categories shown in Figure 17.6 regardless of whether it is a GDSS, ODSS, or NSS. Interestingly, we can associate some kinds of groupware with particular categories (Johansen 1988). For instance, conferencing systems link participants who are in different places at the same time. Messaging systems and collaborative authoring systems are oriented toward connecting participants in different places who read and send messages at different times. In the same place–different time category is what has been called shift work groupware (Johansen 1991). It supports situations where subgroups of a group work in shifts, needing access to a group memory, to keep track of group progress, and to coordinate with other subgroups' activities. Although GDSSs can fit any category, most implementations of this groupware have been designed to support participants meeting at the same time in the same place.

Perhaps the most distinctive feature of a same time–same place MDSS is that it functions on a networked system of computers residing in a high-tech decision room. All participants gather in that room at the same time to work toward a decision. Each participant typically sits at one of the computers, using it to offer his or her input to the decision process as well as to monitor what has happened so far. Participants often use large public viewing screens for monitoring purposes also.

FIGURE 17.6   Possible Participant Arrangements for MDSSs

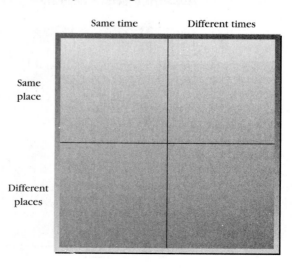

Verbal interaction may or may not be approved at various points in the decision process. The MDSS and/or a facilitator coordinates the participants' activities on the path toward a decision. A facilitator usually is not a decision-making participant but rather is an intervenor who instructs the participants about MDSS usage, ensures the technical MDSS operation goes smoothly, or otherwise facilitates the participants' work with the MDSS.

A different time–same place MDSS also functions in a high-tech decision room. However, not all participants simultaneously work on reaching a decision. Some are there at one time and others are there at a different time—yet all are participating in making a single decision or set of related decisions. Laboratory experiments have shown there can be significant advantages of partitioning a group into subgroups that work at different times rather than having all participants work simultaneously (Holsapple and Luo 1994). It was found that if a group's experienced members worked on a decision problem separately from those with less experience, then the decision quality was significantly better, although decision-making efficiency was better when all worked at the same time. This result occurred regardless of whether the experienced subgroup met first and passed its findings on to the relatively inexperienced subgroup, or vice versa.

A same time–different place MDSS does not depend on a single decision room. Participants convene in time but not in space. Laboratory experiments indicate that, in the case of supporting a group decision, a same time–different place system tends to increase the shifts that individual participants make between their original positions and the ultimate group decision (Gallupe and McKeen 1990). Compared to the same time–same place decision support, the efficiency was not as high. However, support of remote meetings did produce decision quality comparable to those in the same time–same place case.

A different time–different place MDSS needs neither a decision room nor simultaneous work by the participants. Messaging systems can be regarded as MDSSs in this category to the extent that the messages being passed are important for the participants' decision making. However, without added capabilities beyond simple communication support, they must be regarded as relatively primitive MDSSs. An example of a more extensive MDSS in this category is a system to support coordination

---

ANYTIME-ANYPLACE

Although there is much research to be done before the full potential of any time-any place MDSSs will be realized in practice, Johansen (1991, 225) points out that ". . . Doug Englebart, one of the early groupware pioneers, had a system in the late 1960s (NLS) that had capabilities touching on all four time/place cells. . . . For same time/same place Englebart had a. . . . room where the moderator had a full workstation and each of the participants had a mouse and screen. For different times/different places, there were shared journals and group writing capabilities. For same time/different places, there was screen sharing and remote multimedia (including audio and full-motion video). Finally, same place/different time capabilities were in place in Englebart's Augmentation Research Center. . . . Members could use the center anytime of the day or night—even if other . . . members were not present simultaneously. Englebart's broad vision is now becoming practical."

of decision making in a nemawashi process (Watabe, Holsapple, and Whinston 1992). It would, for instance, include means for automatically routing both informal and formal documents to the appropriate participants at appropriate times, plus capturing, organizing, and analyzing their feedbacks for the coordinator.

As MDSS research continues, more will become known about each of the four categories for GDSSs, ODSSs, and NSSs. New technological means for support will be devised and tools for building MDSSs will increasingly provide an integrated set of these technologies. Any time–any place MDSSs are emerging (Johansen 1991). This kind of MDSS—whether it supports groups, more complex organizations, or both—is able to function in any of the four cells of Figure 17.6. Depending on the decision support needs, it could operate in two or more of the categories simultaneously or in a desired sequence.

A COMMON ARCHITECTURE

One thing all MDSSs have in common is that they fit into the time-place categories of Figure 17.6. Another commonality is that all MDSSs adhere to the generic DSS framework introduced in Chapter 6. However, we can elaborate on that framework to get a more detailed picture of the architecture of a multiparticipant DSS, as distinct from a DSS for an individual. As with the time-place classification, this characterization of MDSS commonalities also becomes a basis for appreciating how one MDSS can differ from another.

A multiparticipant DSS has a language system (LS), problem-processing system (PPS), knowledge system (KS), and presentation system (PS). The language system is composed of all requests users can make of the MDSS. The knowledge system consists of all stored knowledge: descriptive, procedural, reasoning, linguistic, presentation, and assimilative. The presentation system comprises all responses that can be issued to users. The problem-processing system is the software that interprets requests, takes appropriate actions (perhaps using the KS to do so), and issues responses. But, as Figure 17.7 indicates, quite a bit more can be said about these four elements of an MDSS.

First, note that four kinds of users can interact with an MDSS: participants in the decision maker being supported, a **facilitator,** who helps the participants make use of the MDSS, external knowledge sources that the MDSS monitors or interrogates in search of additional knowledge, and an administrator, who is responsible for assuring that the system is properly developed and maintained. Not all MDSSs need or make use of a facilitator. Also, some MDSSs are not designed to interact with external knowledge sources—be they computerized (e.g., Dow Jones News Retrieval Services) or human.

The MDSS itself is generally distributed across multiple computers linked into a network. That is, the PPS consists of software on multiple computers. That distributed PPS software works together in supporting the multiparticipant decision maker. The associated KS consists of a centralized knowledge storehouse accessed through one of the linked computers (called a server) by the other computers (called clients) and/or decentralized KS components affiliated with many or all of the computers and accessories across the network.

Language System   The language system consists of two kinds of messages: public and private. Public LS messages are the kind that any user is able to submit as a request to the MDSS. A private LS message is one that only a single, specific user

FIGURE 17.7   A Generic MDSS Architecture

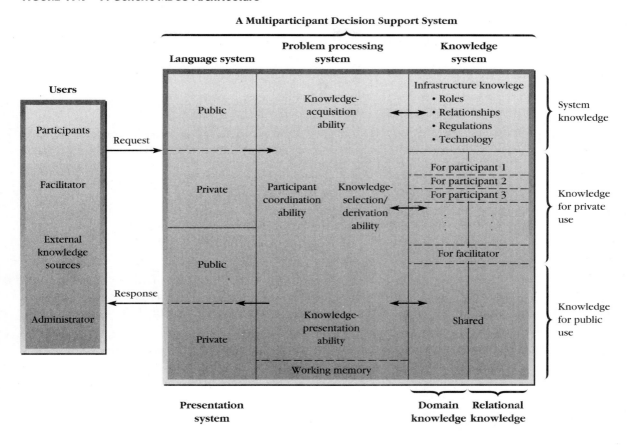

knows how to submit to the MDSS. Semiprivate LS messages are those that can be submitted by more than one—but not all—users. Some MDSSs employ a strictly public LS; every user is able to (indeed, required to) issue requests with exactly the same language. When an MDSS allows private or semiprivate messages in its LS, at least some users are either (1) allowed to issue requests that are off limits to others or (2) able to make requests in ways unknown to others. For instance, a facilitator may make requests that are unavailable to participants, and vice versa, or an MDSS may permit each participant to use an individually customized language reflecting his or her own preferred way of interacting.

Regardless of whether they are public or private, the basic kinds of requests that can be made of a MDSS are to

1. Recall some knowledge from the KS,
2. Acquire some new knowledge (e.g., from an external source),
3. Derive some new knowledge,
4. Clarify (i.e., provide additional knowledge about) a response,
5. Accept some new knowledge into the KS,
6. Route a message (i.e., some knowledge), or
7. Provide help in (i.e., knowledge about) using the system.

Messages to accomplish such activities exist in the LS. The first two kinds of requests are likely to be made by participants, a facilitator, and an administrator. Derivation requests are made primarily by participants or a facilitator. The remaining four kinds of requests can be made by any of the users identified in Figure 17.7.

Presentation System   The presentation system consists of two kinds of messages: public and private. Public PS messages are those that do or can serve as responses to any user. A private PS message is a response that can go to only a single, specific user. A semiprivate PS message is a response available to some—but not all—users. An MDSS that has only a public PS presents the same kind of appearances to all users. When private or semiprivate messages are permitted in a PS, some users are either (1) allowed to see information that is off limits to others or (2) able to see information presented in a way unavailable to others. For instance, some participants attempting to reach a negotiated decision may be blocked from viewing knowledge available to others, or the MDSS may customize presentations for each participant to reflect his or her own preferred way of viewing.

Regardless of whether they are public or private, responses made by an MDSS are to

1. Provide knowledge that has been selected or derived from the KS, sent as a message by a user, or embedded within the PPS (e.g., for clarification or help), or
2. Seek knowledge to be stored in the KS, sent as a message to a user, or used by the PPS to clarify a request.

Messages that accomplish these activities exist in the PS. Subject to the MDSS's security controls and the regulating PPS coordination ability, any of the four types of users can receive such responses.

A response can be triggered by a request from the user receiving the response or by a request from a different user. A response may not be directly triggered by any particular request. It could be the PPS's response to recognizing that some situation exists (e.g., in the KS, in the working memory, or in the environment). For instance, the passage of a certain amount of time or the appearance of certain knowledge in the KS could be events that trigger the PPS to issue notifications to participants that they should proceed to a vote. A knowledge-management technique for implementing this event-triggered processing is called *demon management* (Holsapple 1987).

Knowledge System   As noted before, each of the six knowledge types is a candidate for inclusion in the knowledge system of a MDSS (recall Figure 6.2). However, rather than depicting these in the KS of Figure 17.7, we use a threefold classification of knowledge: knowledge about the system itself, knowledge about those with whom the system is related, and knowledge about the decision domain (Dos Santos and Holsapple 1989; Holsapple, Johnson, and Waldron 1996).

MDSSs can be implemented such that some (or even a large portion) of this knowledge is embedded in the PPS software rather than the KS. To the extent it is programmed into the PPS, the MDSS becomes relatively inflexible and expensive to alter. To the extent it is in the KS, the MDSS is easier to alter—involving a revision to KS contents rather than reprogramming.

System knowledge includes knowledge about the particular infrastructure of which the MDSS is the technological part. This includes knowledge about the roles and relationships with which the MDSS must be concerned, plus knowledge of the

INTERFACE DESIGN ISSUES

Together, the LS and PS are what users know of an MDSS's user interface. As we have seen earlier, the composition of the LS and PS are very much tied to aspects of the PPS and KS as well. To the extent that a PPS gives the developer of an MDSS latitude in designing its LS and PS (i.e., by allowing the developer to specify linguistic and presentation knowledge in the KS), there are a variety of interface design issues to consider. Gray et al. (1993) point out that

1. From the standpoint of what users see, there are such issues as the design of public screens, interactions between public and private screens, and the design of private screens.
2. From the standpoint of what users must know about what they see, there are such design issues as accounting for cultural and individual differences among participants.
3. From the standpoint of what users do by working with what they see, there are design issues such as permissible interaction patterns among participants and accounting for the possible existence of a facilitator.

They go on to offer a variety of guidelines for addressing these design issues in the case of the same time–same place GDSSs.

regulations that it must follow, facilitate, or enforce (Ching, Holsapple, and Whinston 1993). This knowledge of regulations is the key for coordinating the activities of the decision-making participants (and other users too). System knowledge also includes knowledge about technical specifics of the computers involved and their network linkages.

Domain knowledge pertains to the subject matter about which decisions are to be made. It can involve any mix of the six knowledge types (descriptive, procedural, reasoning, and so forth). Some of this is public—available to be shared by all interested users. Other domain knowledge is private, being accessible only to a particular individual user. In Figure 17.7, this knowledge is designated by identifying a private knowledge store in the KS for each decision-making participant and the facilitator. **Relational knowledge** can also be public or private and can involve a mix of the six types. It is concerned with characterizing the users of the MDSS, as distinct from roles they fill. For instance, in the case of a negotiated decision, participants may benefit from profiles of those with whom they deliberate.

Problem-Processing System   Observe that the problem-processing abilities identified in Figure 17.7 include all those shown in Figure 6.2: knowledge acquisition, knowledge selection or derivation, and knowledge presentation. Depending on the MDSS implementation, each of these abilities can be exercised by a user doing some individual work and/or by all participants doing some collective work. As an example of the former, a participant may work to produce a forecast as the basis for an idea to be shared with other participants. As an example of the latter, participants may jointly request the MDSS to analyze an alternative with a solver or provide some expert advice. As we saw in Chapter 6, any or all of these can draw on KS contents.

In addition to the three familiar abilities, the problem processor for an MDSS has some kind of participant-coordination ability. This coordination ability embodies the technological support for an organizational infrastructure's regulations. It helps regulate the filling of roles, behaviors of roles, and relationships between roles. It draws heavily on the KS's system knowledge; if there is no or little knowledge, the coordination behaviors are programmed directly into the PPS. In the latter case, the PPS rigidly supports only one approach to coordination. In the former case, it begins to approach the ideal of a generalized problem processor—serving as a general-purpose tool for building a wide variety of MDSSs involving diverse coordination mechanisms. With such a tool, development of each MDSS is accomplished by specifying the coordination mechanism (along with other knowledge) in the KS.

Examples of participant coordination abilities that a PPS could exhibit are as follows (Ching, Holsapple, and Whinston 1992; Turoff et al. 1993; Hoffer and Valacich 1993):

1. *Channel control:* The PPS controls what communication channels are open for use at any given time during the decision making.
2. *Decision-process guidance:* The PPS guides the deliberations in such ways as (a) giving special support to a facilitator (e.g., for monitoring and adjusting for the current state of participants' work; (b) requiring input from all participants or permitting that input to be anonymous); (c) enforcing a particular coordination method (e.g., the nominal group technique or Delphi method); (d) handling participant voting (e.g., rating or rank ordering of alternatives).
3. *Information distribution:* The PPS continually gathers, organizes, filters, and formats public materials generated by participants during the decision-making process, electronically distributing them to participants periodically or on demand; it permits users to transfer knowledge readily from private to public portions of the KS (and vice versa) and perhaps even from one private store to another.
4. *Communication synchronizing:* The PPS continually tracks the status of deliberations as a basis for giving cues to participants (e.g., who has viewed or considered what, where are the greatest disagreements, where is other clarification or analysis needed, when is there a new alternative to be considered, and who has or has not voted).
5. *Role assignment:* The PPS regulates the assignment of participants to roles (e.g., furnishing an electronic market in which they bid for the opportunity to fill roles).
6. *Incentive management:* The PPS implements an incentive scheme designed to motivate and properly reward participants for their contributions to decisions.
7. *Learning:* By tracking what occurred in prior decision-making sessions, along with recording feedback on the results of those sessions (e.g., decision quality, process innovation), a PPS enables the MDSS to learn how to coordinate better or to avoid coordination pitfalls in the future.

For each of these coordination abilities, a PPS may range from offering relatively primitive to relatively sophisticated features. As the MDSS field continues to develop, we expect to see a trend toward more sophisticated coordination features (i.e., toward more ODSS implementations) and toward GPPSs as powerful, flexible tools for developing multiparticipant decision support systems. For the remainder of the chapter we summarize highlights of what is known about GDSSs, ODSSs, and NSSs.

17.3 GROUP DECISION SUPPORT SYSTEMS

Group decision support systems have been the most extensively studied type of MDSS, although the current understanding of GDSSs has by no means reached a point where it could be called mature. Here, we trace major developments in the evolution of knowledge about GDSSs, furnishing a foundation for using current GDSS technology and appreciating future GDSS developments as they unfold in the years ahead.

BACKGROUND

The appearance of group decision support systems predates the GDSS term. For instance, in 1971 a system called EMISARI was implemented at the U.S. Office of Emergency Preparedness to support the decision making of 100 to 200 people scattered around the country during declared national emergencies. For more than a decade it was used to help participants monitor, interpret, and organize information relevant to group decision making in quickly changing, unpredictable situations (Turoff 1991).

In the late 1970s, a **decision room** called the Planning Laboratory was implemented, serving as an inspiration for much of the same time–same place GDSS software developed since that time (Gibson 1991; Wagner, Wynne, and Mennecke 1993). It consisted of computer terminals recessed into a conference table, a public display screen, and software. One of the elements of this software, Mindsight, supported the generation of ideas by participants stationed at the terminals. An important lesson of the Planning Lab experience was that psychological aspects of GDSS were just as challenging as technological aspects.

Definitions The GDSS term began to appear prominently in the early to mid-1980s (Huber 1982; Kull 1982; Lewis 1982). Yet, it has seldom been defined explicitly by those who use it, and there are somewhat differing views on what it includes (Kraemer and King 1988). For our purposes here, the following two definitions cover the main points of a GDSS:

> A set of software, hardware, language components, and procedures that support a group of people engaged in a decision-related meeting (Huber 1984);

> An interactive, computer-based system that facilitates solution of unstructured problems by a set of decision makers working together as a group (DeSanctis and Gallupe 1985).

Both definitions are consistent with the way we have previously characterized GDSSs in this book.

The study of GDSSs is a natural outcropping from the DSS field's early emphasis on DSSs for individuals. It is also a response to the perceived need for developing better ways to aid the group decision processes that are so commonplace today (Kraemer and King 1988). On the one hand, managers are faced with more and longer meetings to cope with knowledge-intensive issues. On the other hand, participating in such meetings takes time away from other important matters, thus increasing resistance to participation (Huber 1984). One possible solution to this dilemma is to reduce the time and effort required of participants without reducing (and perhaps even enhancing) decision quality. In a broad sense, this is the goal of GDSSs.

Objectives   With a GDSS we seek to reduce the losses that can result from working as a group, while keeping (or enhancing) the gains that group work can yield. Drawing on the large body of social science research into group work, Nunamaker et al. (1993) enumerate major sources of potential gains and losses from group work as opposed to individual work. These are summarized in Tables 17.1 and 17.2.

Nunamaker et al. (1993) identify four approaches whereby a GDSS can influence the balance of these gains and losses. First, a GDSS could provide process support, which means that it serves as a computer-mediated communication system for allowing the group's process of participant interaction to occur. Second, a GDSS could provide process structure. Process structure refers to regulations that govern the pattern, timing, and contents of communications among participants. Third, a GDSS could provide task support, which means that it can select and/or derive

DSS IN THE NEWS

We've Got to Start Meeting Like This

If computers can speed data and word processing, how about meetings?

A growing number of companies are adopting computer-aided meetings, and reporting that the systems cut costs and boost a session's productivity. . . .

The idea is that, at key points during a discussion, participants in a meeting use personal computers to vote on key decisions or type in anonymous messages. The vote tallies or individuals' comments appear on a projection screen. . . .

. . . Users claim this is a quick, painless way of winnowing down ideas to those deemed of greatest value. The anonymous comments and votes may be ego-bruising to an idea's creator, but they're impersonal and quick because the system avoids up-and-back arguments and keeps participants focused on the meeting's purpose.

The benefits of using computers during meetings also include increased participation by the people attending them and enhanced communication because of the removal of inhibitions to speaking. The system also generates greater agreement on decisions because everyone participates.

BellSouth uses the system in brainstorming sessions. Meeting participants contribute ideas that are written on a flip chart. When the brainstorming ends, the list of 20 or more ideas is entered into the computer and everyone is asked to pick the five most important ones by voting with his keypad. The ideas receiving the most votes then get further consideration.

"With limited time and resources, we have to narrow the viable options," said Joseph Gier, staff manager . . . at BellSouth. "It used to take forever to arrive at a consensus. But with the meeting software, we can do it quickly. . . ."

And computer-aided meetings' anonymity reportedly promotes candor.

"We find it especially useful when discussing key priority or sensitive issues such as work force diversity," said Cathy Johnson, manager of company planning with Motorola. . . . "The keyboards allow for anonymous voting, but the major issues are unearthed so they can be discussed openly". . . .

R. J. Maturi, "Computers Can Improve the Efficiency of Meetings," *Investor's Business Daily,* 2, November 1990, p. 6.

TABLE 17.1   Major Sources of Gains from Group Work

TYPE OF GAIN	SOURCE OF THE GAIN
Greater knowledge	A group has greater knowledge than any individual participant.
Synergy	Participants' differing knowledge and processing skills allow results that could not be achieved individually.
Stimulation	As part of a group, a participant can be stimulated to acquire or derive knowledge that would otherwise be unavailable.
Learning	Participants can improve their own performance by learning from the behaviors of others in the group.
Better evaluation	A group is better than an individual participant at detecting flaws in proposed ideas.

knowledge relevant to decision tasks faced by the group. Fourth, a GDSS could provide task structure. Task structure refers to techniques that help the group to better appreciate and analyze task knowledge by filtering it, organizing it, combining it, and controlling the timing of its generation.

A particular GDSS takes one or more of these four approaches to dealing with the gains and losses that would otherwise occur in group decision making. Of course, there can be many variations on each approach. For instance, process support can vary in terms of the group memory features a GDSS provides, the extent

TABLE 17.2   Major Sources of Losses from Group Work

TYPE OF LOSS	SOURCE OF LOSS
Air time	Available speaking time must be allocated among participants.
Production blocking	Because only one person can express ideas at a time, fewer ideas are produced and expressed.
Information overload	Information is presented faster than it can be absorbed.
Forgetting	Participants can fail to remember contributions of others.
Pressure to conform	Out of fear or politeness, participants can be hesitant about disagreeing with the positions or ideas of others.
Evaluation apprehension	Participants can be reluctant to share their ideas for fear of getting a negative evaluation of their contribution.
Free riding	Some participants can rely on the others to accomplish the group work due to a disinterest in competing for air time, a perception that their inputs would not be useful, or laziness.
Cognitive inertia	Group work proceeds in a narrowly focused direction, because participants are reluctant to offer comments that do not seem to be directly related to the focus.
Socializing	The group work loses focus and accomplishes less due to excessive socializing about matters unrelated to the work.
Domination	Dominating personalities or positions of some participants give them greater influence or allow them to unproductively monopolize group time.
Coordination problems	Without appropriate coordination to integrate participants' contributions, discussion cycling, incomplete discussion, and premature decisions can result.
Partial use of knowledge	Incomplete access to knowledge can hamper successful completion of the group work.
Partial task analysis	Incomplete appreciation of the group work to be done can result in superficial or irrelevant discussions.

to which a GDSS enables participants to contribute anonymously, the extent to which it permits participants to communicate in parallel, and the particular electronic media effects a GDSS provides. Table 17.3 shows potential impacts of each of the four approaches on the various types of gains and losses (Nunamaker et al. 1993). An up-arrow indicates that the approach increases the corresponding gain or loss. Down-arrows denote decreases in the gain or loss.

For instance, parallel communication allowed by a GDSS permits an increase in group knowledge gains by allowing multiple participants to express themselves simultaneously. On the other hand, media effects from a GDSS can lead to a decrease in the knowledge gained by group work (e.g., typing comments is slower than speaking and does not have the information richness of a face-to-face conversation). We do not discuss all the entries in Table 17.3. Instead, they are meant to convey an impression of the many issues involved in developing, using, and evaluating various GDSSs—as well as the many reasons why GDSSs can be beneficial. Later, we summarize what researchers have discovered about GDSS benefits. First, however, we take a look at ways of classifying GDSSs, tools for developing GDSSs, and the operation of GDSSs.

TABLE 17.3   Potential Effects of GDSS Approaches

| | GDSS APPROACHES TO INFLUENCING GROUP WORK | | | | | | |
| | PROCESS SUPPORT | | | | | | |
Effects on Group Work	**Group Memory**	**Anonymity**	**Parallel Communication**	**Media Effects**	**PROCESS STRUCTURE**	**TASK SUPPORT**	**TASK STRUCTURE**
Type of Gain							
Greater knowledge	↑		↑	↓		↑	↑
Synergy	↑		↑			↑	
Stimulation			↑				
Learning		↑	↑				
Better evaluation		↑		↑			↑
Type of Loss							
Air time			↓				
Production blocking	↓		↓				
Information overload	↓		↑	↓			
Forgetting	↓						
Pressure to conform		↓					
Evaluation apprehension		↓					
Free riding		↑	↓				
Cognitive inertia							
Socializing			↓				
Domination			↓				
Coordination problems					↓		
Partial use of knowledge	↓			↑		↓	
Partial task analysis						↓	↓

GDSS TYPES

By identifying different types of GDSSs, classification schemes can help both developers and prospective installers of GDSS technology. In developing a GDSS, we need to know what type of GDSS is intended. We then design it to have the features of that GDSS type, rather than features of another type. If we consider installing a GDSS, we need to be clear about our options. Which of the available GDSS types would be best for us to install in the particular decision making circumstances that we face? Knowing about alternative GDSS types can help in answering this question.

Although all GDSSs conform to the architecture given in Figure 17.7, they also differ in varying ways. Looking at that architecture, we can see many ways to classify GDSSs:

1. A GDSS requiring a facilitator versus a GDSS that operates with no facilitator;
2. A GDSS with a public interface (LS, PS) only versus a GDSS having both private and public inferences;
3. A GDSS that lets participants have their own private knowledge stores versus a GDSS in which all domain and relational knowledge is public;
4. A GDSS with infrastructure knowledge held in its KS versus a GDSS in which such knowledge is not allowed (i.e., it is embedded in the PPS).

GDSSs can also be classified in terms of the exact natures of each of the four PPS abilities illustrated in Figure 17.7. For example, some GDSSs are capable of coordinating participants via a nominal group technique, whereas others are not.

Aside from classifying GDSSs based on architectural features, we could categorize them based on the time-place categories shown in Figure 17.6. That is, some GDSSs are designed to support a same time–same place arrangement of participants. In contrast, another type of GDSS might be designed for different times–different place arrangements. Two other GDSS classification schemes are described here. One is based on the level of support provided to the group. The other is based on the technology used for group decision support.

Three GDSS Levels   DeSanctis and Gallupe (1987) identify three levels of GDSSs. These differ in terms of features they offer for supporting a group decision maker. The features of a Level 1 GDSS reduce or remove communication barriers that would otherwise occur among participants in a group decision maker. The idea is to stimulate and hasten the exchange of messages. Table 17.4 summarizes what a group needs in order to overcome communication barriers. It shows corresponding GDSS features intended to meet those needs. A Level 1 GDSS is designed to have such features.

The features of a Level 2 GDSS reduce uncertainty and "noise" that can occur in a group's decision process. This is accomplished by the participants' use of systematic methods in the decision process. Table 17.4 summarizes what a group needs in order to overcome process difficulties. It shows corresponding GDSS features intended to meet those needs. A Level 2 GDSS is designed to have such features.

The features of a Level 3 GDSS allow it to control the timing, content, or pattern of messages exchanged by participants—that is, the GDSS actively drives or regulates a group's decision process. In the Level 1 and Level 2 cases, GDSSs are more reactive or subservient than active. Table 17.4 indicates the kinds of group needs

TABLE 17.4   Examples of Group Needs and Corresponding GDSS Features

GDSS LEVEL		GROUP NEEDS TO BE ADDRESSED	CORRESPONDING GDSS FEATURE
1	a.	Efficient message passing among participants	Uses electronic messaging
	b.	Access to personal or corporate data files during meeting	Links computer for each participant to computers holding data
	c.	Simultaneous display of ideas, data, graphs, votes, etc., to all participants	Has large shared viewing screen; public window display on each participant's computer
	d.	Relaxing inhibitions of some participants about contributing	Allows anonymous contributions
	e.	Avoiding free riders or disinterested participants	Actively solicits contributions from each participant
	f.	Efficiently organizing and analyzing ideas and votes	Summarizes/displays ideas; tabulates/displays votes
	g.	Quantification of preferences	Furnishes rating scales or ranking schemas
	h.	Planning a meeting agenda	Provides agenda templates to be selected or filled in
	i.	Staying on schedule according to planned agenda	Provides continuous display of agenda and clock
2	j.	Structuring and scheduling problem solving	Uses automated planning methods (e.g., PERT)
	k.	Analysis of uncertainties	Provides solvers for probability problems (e.g., decision tree analysis)
	l.	Decision analysis for resource-allocation problems	Provides solvers for allocation (e.g., optimizers)
	m.	Data analysis	Provides solvers for data analysis (e.g., statistics)
	n.	Analysis of preferences	Provides solvers for preference analysis problems
	o.	Use of a structured method for guiding the deliberations, but lack of know-how or time to do so	Has automated idea generation/compilation technique (e.g., nominal group); provides on-line help about various methods
3	p.	Enforcement of formal decision procedure	Automates the procedure (e.g., parliamentary procedure)
	q.	Greater clarity about options for decision procedure	Has automated advisor giving recommendations on available approaches
	r.	Structuring and filtering messages to adhere to rules	Provides filtering/structuring of intelligent agents
	s.	Developing rules to govern the deliberations	Provide rule set construction/inference facilities

that a Level 3 GDSS could address. For each, it shows corresponding features to design into this type of GDSS.

Six GDSS Technologies   Kraemer and King (1988) derived a GDSS classification scheme from available technologies that can be applied when groups need to make decisions They identify the six kinds of GDSSs shown in Table 17.5: electronic boardrooms, teleconference rooms, group networks, information centers, collaboration laboratories, and decision rooms.

The most primitive of these GDSSs uses electronic boardroom technology. It involves equipping an ordinary conference room with a computer that can control audiovisual projections of maps, drawings, blueprints, photos, charts, diagrams, etc., onto a large screen for easy shared viewing by the participants. Teleconference rooms involve videoconferencing facilities that support idea exchanges among

TABLE 17.5   GDSS Classification Based on Technology

GDSS TYPE	FACILITY/HARDWARE USED	SOFTWARE USED	OTHER CONSIDERATIONS
Electronic boardroom	Conference room; computer-controlled audiovisual projections on a screen	For storage and retrieval of previously prepared presentations	Same time–same place; audiovisual technician present
Teleconference rooms	Conference rooms; computer-controlled audiovisual transmissions between rooms	For handling digital transmission of audio, video, and data	Same time–different place; teleconference facilitator present
Group network	Separate offices; computer network	For real-time or asynchronous desktop conferencing; for real-time meeting scheduling	Same (or different) time–different place; one participant serves as conference chair
Information center	Conference room; video projector for large screen; computer(s) with display terminals	For database management, statistical analysis, graphics, and text processing	Same time–same place; modeling and software specialists present
Collaboration laboratory	Conference room; electronic chalkboard computer workstations	Software for collaborative writing or outlining and perhaps structured argumentation	Same (or different) time–same place
Decision room	Conference room, video projector for large screen; networked computers	For brainstorming, topic commenting, voting, modeling, decision analysis	Same (or different) time–same place; group process facilitator present

decision-making participants located in two or more specially equipped rooms (recall the groupware discussion in Chapter 16). Similarly, a group network GDSS employs either real-time or desktop conferencing technology (recall the groupware discussion in Chapter 16).

Chapter 8 introduced the notion of an information center, which is equipped with technology and personnel to aid end-user computing efforts. An information center can focus on aiding the participants in a specific decision-making group (e.g., a marketing group). The group's use of computer technology in the course of their deliberations is supported by the center's software and modeling specialists. Such an information center functions as a joint computer-human GDSS. A collaboration laboratory GDSS uses collaborative authoring groupware and perhaps some coordination technology (e.g., based on structured argumentation) to help participants organize outlines of ideas, prepare associated text detailing ideas, and evaluate proposals.

A GDSS in the decision room class operates on a network of computers, including one linked to a large-screen projection device. A sample decision room layout is shown in Figure 17.8. The software and perhaps a facilitator coordinate the work that is done by the participants. The software permits parallel communication and

FIGURE 17.8   Decision Room Layout at University of Kentucky

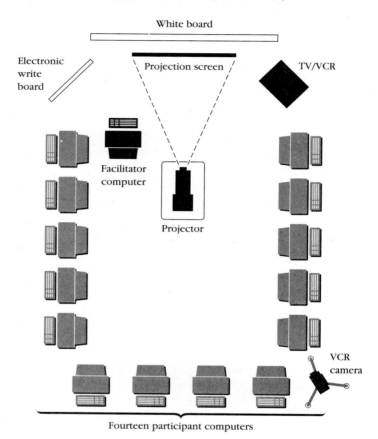

Fourteen participant computers

anonymous contributions to the deliberations. It can encompass a variety of tools for supporting such activities as brainstorming, issue analysis, topic commenting, and voting. We take a more extensive look at such tools in the next section.

GDSS DEVELOPMENT AND USAGE

All the aspects of DSS development discussed in Chapter 8 apply to GDSSs as well. That discussion is not repeated here. But we do consider a few additional topics especially relevant to GDSS development. A first step in GDSS development is to identify a group or groups that are candidates for decision support. Then, the developer needs to determine what type of GDSS is needed. Should it be a Level 1, 2, or 3 GDSS? Should it be group network type of GDSS, a decision room DSS, etc.? Having settled on the GDSS type, a developer needs to specify precisely what features are desired. This specification is made in consultation with both the prospective users of the GDSS (participants, facilitator, administrators) and the upper-level management committed to introducing the GDSS. The activity of feature identification may reveal that the type of GDSS needed is different from what was initially identified.

The type of GDSS desired, along with a detailed list of desired features, narrows the consideration of what tools are to be used for development. To date, there is no tool that provides a generalized problem-processing system (GPSS) for GDSSs. That is, no tool furnishes a single PPS that may be used for GDSSs of all three levels and all six technologies. Following from the original idea of a GPPS in the 1970s, researchers have advocated the creation of GPPSs for group decision support systems (DeSanctis and Gallupe 1987). These GPPSs would give researchers a single software environment for more readily assessing the comparative effectiveness of alternative GDSS designs and features. This environment would give developers a single tool with which to build many types of GDSSs, by creating different knowledge systems to go along with the prefabricated GPPS.

GDSS Development Tools   The tool chosen for building a particular GDSS normally provides a ready-made PPS, LS, and PS. Some may allow for customization of the LS and PS by storing linguistic and presentation knowledge in the KS. A developer will, at the minimum, need to load some system knowledge into the KS (e.g., identifying users, computers, and linkages). For some GDSSs, little or no domain and relational knowledge is specified by the developer. The users are given a mostly "blank slate," which they fill in as the decision process unfolds. For other GDSSs, the developer needs to design the structure of domain and relational knowledge that can be held in the KS (e.g., design the structure of data tables). The developer may preload some knowledge into those KS structures. In the course of decision making, users also furnish knowledge for the PPS to store in the KS.

The KS contents are sometimes referred to as the **group memory.** It includes knowledge that is deposited by the developer and, over time, by the GDSS administrator. It includes knowledge of what has transpired as the participants interact about the decision. The group memory supports an ongoing group process within a session, and perhaps even across sessions, in several ways (Hoffer and Valacich 1993). First, it can provide participants with a common perspective of objectives and regulations. Second, it can provide uniform, consistent knowledge acquired from external sources and from its records of prior similar sessions. Third, it gives a way to bring new participants up to speed by browsing through knowledge about the current session and former sessions. Fourth, it forms the basis for coordinating participant activities and regulating the group's process. Fifth, it becomes a foundation for learning about effectiveness of group decision making.

The PPS provided by a development tool may actually be organized as a collection of distinct processors, each with its own LS and PS but sharing the same knowledge system. Vendors often refer to each of these processors as being a *tool,* because it can be used separately from any of the PPS's other processors. Frequently, the group will use one processor, then another, yet another, and so forth, in the course of decision making. The sequence for using these processors is typically planned in advance of the deliberations, and a facilitator is often responsible for switching from one to the next.

For example, decision support processors that can make up the PPS for a decision room kind of GDSS may include the following (Vogel et al. 1989):

1. *Electronic brainstorming:* This processor allows participants simultaneously and anonymously to type in their own ideas about a specific question. These textual passages are stored in the KS along with the text of questions relevant to the decision making. They are circulated among participants for viewing and

comment. An individual participant's screen shows the question of interest, ideas that participants have so far entered about addressing the question, and any comments participants may have entered concerning those ideas. The screen also has an area for the participant to type in new ideas or comments as they come to mind. The purpose is to exchange ideas rapidly in the interest of critiquing them and to stimulate further ideas that participants would likely not have come up with if working individually. At the end of a brainstorming session, this processor can produce a report showing all generated ideas and related comments.

2. *Topic commenting:* With this processor, one or more topic descriptions are stored in the KS. Each of these can be broken into subtopics, which are also stored in the KS. In an electronic meeting, a participant can choose any topic or subtopic. He or she can then enter comments about the topic (for storage in the KS) and also view comments that others have made on that topic. Participants enter their comments in parallel and can do so anonymously. Each participant has the freedom to switch from working on one topic to another whenever he or she desires. The purpose is to solicit participant ideas about a set of topics related to the decision, collectively reaching a more detailed understanding of those topics through the entry, exchange, and review of comments.

3. *Issue analysis:* This processor helps participants organize results of idea generation to identify those items of greatest importance. It also allows information from external sources to be merged into the issue analysis to further elaborate on the focus items. Thus, it reorganizes and enlarges KS contents.

4. *Voting:* This processor allows each participant to indicate his or her preferences anonymously. For instance, it may present each participant with a set of options in a multiple-choice manner, allowing each user to pick one. It could also have each participant rank-order the alternatives. As another possibility, each participant can rate each alternative (e.g., agree versus disagree or on a numeric scale to show degrees of agreement). The voting processor records all participants' votes, tabulates them, and displays results for all to see. The results either become the decision or form a basis for further deliberation.

5. *Policy formulation:* Participants use this processor to jointly create a document that states a policy or mission. A facilitator enters an initial rough draft of the policy for circulation to all participants. Each then proposes changes by editing the draft. Group discussion of these leads to a second draft. The group iterates through drafts in this way until a consensus is achieved.

6. *Stakeholder analysis:* This processor helps participants in systematically evaluating the implications of a prospective plan or policy. As stakeholders in the policy are identified, they are recorded in the KS, along with descriptions of their assumptions and expectations. For instance, the proposed policy might involve raising the minimum grade-point average for business students at a state-assisted university. Stakeholders would include students, faculty, potential employers, and taxpayers. Participants in deciding whether to enact the policy would identify the assumptions or positions of these various interested parties (e.g., a high-quality program is preferable to a large one, or all citizens in the state should be served). Using the stakeholder analysis processor, they would also rate the importance of these assumptions to the stakeholders and to enactment of the policy. The ratings are automatically tabulated and graphically displayed to the group for discussion and analysis.

7. *Idea organizer:* The processor administers the nominal group technique. Participants individually develop lists of alternatives or issues. These issues are then shared in a round-robin fashion, discussed, and prioritized.

8. *Alternative evaluator:* With this processor, participants evaluate alternatives with respect to multiple criteria, taking into account their differing views on the differing importance of criteria as well as the differing degrees to which each alternative meets each criterion. Results are presented in various graphical and tabular ways. The purpose is to identify the "best" alternative.

9. *Questionnaire:* This processor lets a facilitator create an electronic questionnaire for participants to answer. It summarizes their answers for storage and shared viewing. The questionnaire can have conditional parts, which a user will see only if prior questions were answered in a specified way.

10. *File reader:* This processor lets any participant immediately view the contents of files previously stored in the KS. For instance, while engaged in topic commenting, a participant may want to refer to contents of some file that is relevant to the topic. The file reader processor permits this, allowing the participant to browse through the file's contents and then return to topic commenting when desired.

11. *Group dictionary:* This processor allows a group to define terms formally as part of a KS dictionary. Creating a definition is an interactive, iterative activity for the participants, continuing until a consensus definition is achieved. Not only does this provide reference points for future group work, it can help focus participants' attention.

12. *Enterprise analysis:* This processor is used to create a KS representation of an organizational enterprise in terms of its structure, processes, and relationships among processes. It is intended to give participants a foundation for assessing potential impacts a decision could have on the represented organization.

13. *Session manager:* This processor is used before a GDSS session involving all participants begins. With it, a facilitator and others produce a session plan indicating what processors will be used and when. It can be used during the session to keep activities on track. It can also facilitate the linkage of one session to another by enabling information sharing sessions.

GDSS Success Factors   Based on GDSS experiences at IBM, researchers have identified a number of factors as contributing to implementation success (Grohowski et

---

GROUP SUPPORT SYSTEMS

Some authors, researchers, and vendors use the term group support system (GSS) instead of GDSS. They regard a GDSS as a special kind of GSS intended to support group decision-making tasks. Other GSSs are oriented strictly toward other kinds of group tasks such as communicating or creating (without the ultimate purpose of deciding).

Tools for building GDSSs can also be used for developing other kinds of GSSs. For instance, a topic commenter could be used for a GSS intended to gather comments about certain issues in a structured way. The collected comments may be intended to stimulate someone's creativity, and providers of these comments are not participants in a group decision.

Because of this book's focus on decision support systems, we use GDSS instead of the broader GSS term.

al. 1990). Not only should GDSS developers be aware of such factors, they are also of interest to prospective GDSS users and to those who sponsor the introduction of a GDSS into an organization. Success factors include the following:

1. *Organizational commitment:* It is important that the organization in which the GDSS is to be installed is committed to making use of it. This commitment is fostered by giving potential users practical demonstrations and experience in using a sample GDSS prior to installation. It also depends on ensuring the GDSS is being developed to meet real needs and objectives of the organization (e.g., more effective group meetings).

2. *Executive sponsor:* It is vital that there be one or more executives who stay informed about and committed to the GDSS development and usage. The executives make the request for GDSS development, allocate resources to it, monitor the development project, give high-level feedback to the developer, and promote the system's usage among group decision makers.

3. *Operating sponsor:* Development and operation of the GDSS need to be managed (e.g., by an administrator in charge of decision room facilities). This kind of sponsor gives quick feedback and assistance during development.

4. *Dedicated facilities:* In cases where special rooms are used, care should be given to ensuring user comfort and freedom from distraction. The facilities should appear to have been designed with the central intention being an environment to support group decision making rather than being treated as an afterthought.

5. *Site visits:* In the case where special rooms are used, being able to visit other sites where GDSSs are operating can be beneficial to sponsors (to see what is possible), to developers (to see how others develop GDSSs and what features they have), and to users (to see how other groups benefit from GDSSs).

6. *Liaisons:* Beyond site visits, ongoing liaisons among developers, users, and tool vendors are beneficial. Users can inform developers of the improvements they would like to see in a GDSS. Developers can inform vendors of the added tool capabilities that would be useful.

7. *Responsiveness:* The relative novelty of emerging GDSS technology in organizations implies that developers employ prototyping, be capable of making an ongoing series of changes, and adopt an evolutionary view of GDSS development.

8. *Training:* Training programs need to be created for all users of the GDSS being developed. Participants, facilitators, and system administrators all need to know about certain aspects of the system. Having them engaged in the GDSS development process can be beneficial.

9. *Cost-benefit analysis:* Beyond initial trial use of a GDSS prototype, expanded use of a more complete system should be subjected to a cost-benefit evaluation. This assists in either securing ongoing commitment or recognizing that further evolutionary development would not be fruitful.

10. *Software flexibility.* It is important to select (or build) a PPS that is flexible in the sense of allowing a GDSS to evolve over time, to be used eventually in ways not envisioned, and to be used in changing situations.

11. *Managing expectations:* Developers (and sponsors) must strike a realistic balance between offering a GDSS as the solution to all group decision-making difficulties and the position of detractors who see it as a costly or fanciful technology with little payoff. As described a bit later, researchers have demonstrated that GDSSs can indeed improve the decision-making performance of groups.

GDSS PREPLANNING

The development effort for some GDSSs is fairly minimal, aside from providing system knowledge (e.g., about the networked computers to be used). For instance, in the following scenario it consisted of preplanning the use of processors ("tools") available in the PPS and loading a question for brainstorming into the KS. The resultant GDSS was intended to support the decision about a plan of action. The scenario is a condensed quote from a description of GDSS experiences at IBM (Nunamaker et al. 1989, 186–187):

> A manager responsible for improving shop floor control was having difficulties identifying problem areas that were hindering the process. Those persons knowledgeable about each of the subfunctions seemed unable to isolate primary causes and identify potential solutions that could result in improved productivity. In fact, a two hour meeting of half a dozen of the key participants had resulted in a number of arguments and no solutions.
>
> The manager elected to try the Group Support System in an attempt to resolve issues and develop a plan of action including information system requirements to improve the shop floor control process. The manager met with the facilitator to express the objective she sought and to understand how the Group Support System might be used. It was mutually decided to use the Electronic Brainstorming tool with the question "What are the key issues in improving shop floor control?" followed by Issue Analysis and Voting. A session agenda and time was established for 10 of the key participants including the manager.
>
> The Brainstorming session lasted for 35 minutes during which time the participants generated 645 lines of comments. Comments included issues, ideas, and clarifications as group members shared information. At the end of the brainstorming session, the manager reflected that for the first time she was able to get meaningful answers to questions associated with shop floor control issues.
>
> A 30 minute period of focus item identification followed by 45 minutes of issue consolidation and face-to-face discussion resulted in a generalized list of requirements for effective shop floor control improvement. Each group member prioritized the list in terms of importance to improved shop floor control and cast a private ballot using the Voting tool. The accumulated results were displayed to the group. After 10 minutes of discussion, the session was concluded with comments from the manager thanking the participants and directing the analysts to proceed towards the development of information systems support for the shop floor control process.
>
> It was found that such GDSS usage at IBM resulted in greater efficiency, effectiveness, and satisfaction than was achieved without automated support.

GDSS Facilitation   The facilitator is a key user whose activities can strongly influence group performance when using a GDSS (Bostrom, Anson, and Clawson 1993). A facilitator serves one or more of four main functions (Nunamaker et al. 1993). First, a facilitator helps the participants in technical aspects of using the GDSS—starting and stopping various PPS processors, assisting participants in interacting with their computers, and so forth. Second, a facilitator helps in planning the agenda of a particular session.

Third, a facilitator guides the session. He or she ensures that the agenda of the meeting plan is followed, monitors group progress to assess whether agenda changes may be needed, encourages constructive behavior by the participants, and deals with disruptive influences. Fourth, a facilitator can provide continuity across sessions that use the GDSS, setting standards for how it is used.

A facilitator affects group decision making in two main ways: effects related to the task domain and effects of a relational nature (Bostrom, Anson, and Clawson 1993). That is, a facilitator's intervention can promote better group decisions in a particular decision domain and can foster positive relationships (e.g., cohesiveness, rapport, commitment) among group participants. Of course, the quality of relationships among participants can influence the decision process and its results.

There are three kinds of facilitators: internal, external, and automated (Bostrom, Anson, and Clawson 1993). Any or all may be present for a GDSS session. An internal facilitator is also a decision-making participant. In addition to participating in domain-specific discussions related to the decision-making task, this individual must also be concerned with guiding the group's use of the GDSS and fostering positive group relationships. These multiple responsibilities, coupled with a lack of facilitation skill or training, are a main reason why meetings using this kind of facilitator often end up being ineffective (Mosvick and Nelson 1987).

An external facilitator tends to be trained or experienced in designing and conducting GDSS-based meetings. He or she has no interest in what decision is ultimately made but focuses instead on accomplishing the decision task and on cultivating participant relationships. This kind of facilitator may be composed of two persons. One is a technical facilitator who operates the GDSS technology. The other is a process facilitator who interacts directly with participants. An automated facilitator is a Level 3 GDSS. Both external and automated facilitators are neutral, focusing on facilitation rather than deciding.

GDSS RESEARCH FINDINGS

There is a growing body of empirical research that has examined the effects of GDSS use on group performance. This research includes both laboratory experiments in controlled settings and field studies of GDSS usage in actual work environments. Based on an extensive review of this research, Dennis and Gallupe (1993) have summarized what is known about GDSS effects. In broad terms, GDSS effects appear to depend both on situational factors and specific aspects of the technology itself.

Three prominent situational factors are group size, task complexity, and task type. Research results consistently show that a GDSS increases group performance (versus not using a GDSS) more for larger groups than for smaller ones. Satisfaction of participants also tends to be greater as group size increases. There is evidence suggesting that GDSSs may be more appropriate for relatively complex decision tasks. For decision-related tasks of generating ideas, knowledge, alternatives, and so on, GDSSs have been found to increase greatly performance and satisfaction. They also appear to be somewhat beneficial for choice tasks, but the evidence is not as strong.

Researchers have also studied factors related to GDSS technology itself: anonymity, parallelism, structuring, and facilitation. The evidence is split on whether participant anonymity yields better performance than lack of anonymity. It appears that the value of anonymity depends on the task being done and on the specific participants involved. Research has shown that enabling participants to work in parallel is a major benefit of GDSS technology. Investigation of structuring has found that group performance generally increases when a GDSS structures participant interactions. However, the specific structuring used must fit the situation; otherwise performance is impaired. Studies of using a facilitator versus not using one with a GDSS indicate that outcomes are better with a facilitator. Researchers have also found that repeated participant experiences with a GDSS tend to yield increased group performance.

Summing up why GDSSs may benefit group decision makers, Nunamaker et al. (1993) draw the following conclusions from their observations of GDSSs in the lab and the field:

- Parallel communication encourages greater participation and reduces the likelihood of a few participants dominating the proceedings.
- Anonymity reduces apprehensions about participating and lessens the pressure to conform, allowing for more candid interactions.
- Existence of a group memory makes it easier for participants to pause and ponder the contributions of others during the session, as well as preserving a permanent record of what has occurred.
- Process structuring helps keep the participants focused on making the decision, reducing tendencies toward disgression and unproductive behaviors.
- Task support and structuring give participants the ability to select and derive needed knowledge.

Although the study of GDSSs is at an early stage, there is already sufficient evidence to indicate that this technology is altering the conduct of group decision making.

17.4 ORGANIZATIONAL DECISION SUPPORT SYSTEMS

To date, organizational decision support systems have not received nearly as much attention as group decision support systems. However, research and development in this part of the DSS field is likely to grow dramatically over the next decade. For this reason, we sketch out the broad outlines of this kind of multiparticipant decision support system. We look at various conceptions of what an organizational decision support system (ODSS) is, at suggested architectures to guide the development of ODSSs, and at the array of technologies that could be useful in that development.

The notion of an ODSS has been recognized for a long time in the DSS field. One early framework viewed an organizational decision maker as a knowledge processor having multiple human and multiple computer components, organized according to roles and relationships that divided their individual labors in alternative ways in the interest of solving a decision problem facing the organization (Bonczek, Holsapple, and Whinston 1979). Each component (human or machine) is an intelligent processor capable of solving some class of problems either on its own or by coordinating the efforts of other components—passing messages to them and receiving messages from them. The key ideas in this early framework for ODSS are the notions of distributed problem solving by human and machine knowledge processors, communication among these problem solvers, and coordination of interrelated problem-solving efforts in the interest of solving an overall decision problem.

Also noting that ODSSs are vehicles for problem solving, communication, and coordination, Hackathorn and Keen (1981) maintain that organization support concentrates on facilitating an organization task involving multiple participants engaged in a sequence of operations. They also contend that an ODSS is distinct from a GDSS. As we saw earlier in this chapter. ODSSs tend to be better fits for organizational infrastructure where there are considerable differences in functionality and authority among roles (Figure 17.2), considerable restrictions in communication channels (Figure 17.4), and relatively complex regulations (Figure 17.5). In contrast, GDSSs are designed to suit multiparticipant decision makers with little role differentiation, few communication channel restrictions, and comparatively simple regulations: flat organizations. Recall that either kind of MDSS fits into one or more of the time-place categories shown in Figure 17.6.

ODSS DEFINITIONS

To get a further sense of what an ODSS is (or could be), it is useful to review several definitions that have been advanced:

1. The organization's DSS resources (software, hardware, knowledge, people) that are shared by its corporate planning systems, executive information systems, functional DSSs, and local DSSs in order to function in a coordinated way (Philippakis and Green 1988).
2. Collection of software, hardware, procedures, and personnel that "keeps the organization alive" (Bots and Sol 1988).
3. Computer and communication technology that coordinates and distributes decision making across an organization's hierarchical levels and functional areas so that decisions are consistent with the organization's competitive environment (Watson 1989).
4. A distributed system that supports the division of labor involved in an organization's decision making (Swanson 1989).
5. Computer and communication technology that enhances an organization's decision-making processes, leaping beyond GDSS notions in much the same way that they go beyond DSSs that support individual users (King and Star 1989).
6. Technological infrastructure that provides an environment that enhances, facilitates, or enables organizational and individual decision making (Fedorowicz and Konsynski 1992).
7. A common set of tools (e.g., solvers) used by multiple participants from more than one organizational unit who make interrelated, but autonomous, decisions (Carter et al. 1992).

In an effort to distill the essence from definitions of ODSS, George (1991) identifies three main themes that they tend to have in common. First, an ODSS involves computer-based technologies and may involve communication technology as well. Second, an ODSS accommodates users who perform different organizational functions and who occupy different positions in the organization's hierarchic levels. Third, an ODSS is primarily concerned with decisions that cut across organizational units or impact corporate issues. Although this third theme may be suggested in several definitions, it should not be regarded as a necessary condition for all ODSSs. For instance, ODSSs that support hierarchic teams (as discussed in Chapter 3) do not necessarily need to address corporatewide issues or multiunit decisions. This observation suggests that different types of ODSSs are possible (e.g., those concerned with corporatewide, multiunit decisions versus those that support decisions making of a single organizational unit within a corporation).

Another way of classifying ODSSs is based on emerging organizational trends of downsizing, self-managing teams, and outsourcing (George, Nunamaker, and Valacich 1992). That is, such trends are either permitted or made possible by different types of ODSSs. Downsizing refers to a reduction in the number of employees and the number of hierarchic levels. ODSSs in this situation act as knowledge filters and amplifiers, handle the additional communications resulting from increased spans of control, and help integrate results of employee's varied knowledge work. These are all functions traditionally performed by middle managers.

A self-managing team is responsible for the complete effort involved in producing some good or service. It forms (and reforms) its own organizational infrastructure in order to meet this responsibility. The ODSS features to facilitate decision making in this kind of situation have been little studied but would seem to include a high degree of flexibility to match (e.g., coordinate) whatever the current infrastructure happens to be (Busch et al. 1991). *Outsourcing* refers to purchasing a service from another organization rather than performing it in-house. Although outsourcing allows an organization to focus on what it does best, it requires greater coordination among organizations. ODSSs to facilitate decision making in such circumstances have recently begun to be studied, with features related to coordination among networks of organizations appearing to be very prominent (Ching, Holsapple, and Whinston 1993, 1995).

One other classification approach recognizes four ODSS types, which differ in terms of how they relate to organizational infrastructure: structure enforcing, structure preserving, structure independent, and structure transforming (Fedorowicz and Konsynski 1992). A structure-enforcing ODSS is one that reinforces conventional processes in an organization, perhaps even embedding traditional processes and policy in the system's PPS and KS. A structure-preserving ODSS does not directly affect an organization's business processes, even though it yields changes in the way decisions are made. Structure-independent ODSSs are those that do not depend on a particular kind of infrastructure or deviate from conventional organizational processes. A structure-transforming ODSS is one that enables nontraditional organizational infrastructures.

Classification schemes such as these add depth to ODSS definitions by indicating alternative ODSS objectives. In addition, they are starting points for thinking about designing and implementing specific organizational decision support systems. Prospective ODSS developers also need to have an architectural framework of ODSS components in mind as a basis for development, plus an appreciation of relevant technologies that can be brought to bear in an ODSS implementation.

ODSS ARCHITECTURES

The MDSS architecture presented in Figure 17.7 can be readily applied to ODSSs, because they are particular kinds of MDSSs. In using this architecture you must remember that the PPS and KS can be distributed across a network of numerous computers at numerous sites and the participants communicate across the network. Also note that this architecture gives the ODSS developer and the creator of ODSS development tools considerable flexibility in determining particular features to be included. More specific perspectives on ODSS architecture have been advanced. They amount to special cases of the architecture shown in Figure 17.7. Here, we look at two.

Swanson and Zmud (1989) propose an architecture that sees an ODSS as providing distributed support for multiple concurrent decision-making situations by way of two sets of components: general and situation-specific. As illustrated in Figure 17.9, the general components consist of facilities for communication (e.g., messaging systems), process governance (e.g., coordination systems), data handling (e.g., text-management and database-management systems), and public data management for creating and maintaining public data. The situation-specific components consist of representations of the contexts in which decision processes occur (giving participants a shared frame of reference), local or private databases for each participant's individual work, and representations of participants and tasks (allowing them to be monitored across various decision situations). The general components are processors that are candidates for inclusion in an ODSS's problem processing system. The situation-specific components are candidates for inclusion in an ODSS's knowledge system.

The second architecture we consider is even more specialized, being the design for a particular ODSS that has been implemented. Figure 17.10 illustrates the architecture for an ODSS called the Enlisted Force Management System (EFMS) (Carter et al. 1992). The EFMS problem-processing system is not depicted, but it clearly has database- and solver-management capabilities. The KS consists primarily of an

FIGURE 17.9   An Alternative View of ODSS Architecture

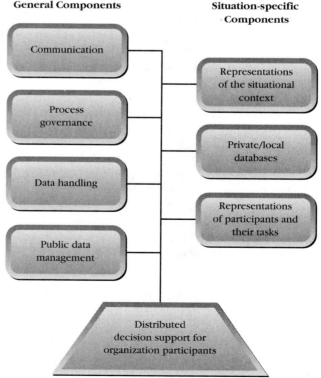

FIGURE 17.10   Architecture of the Enlisted Force Management System

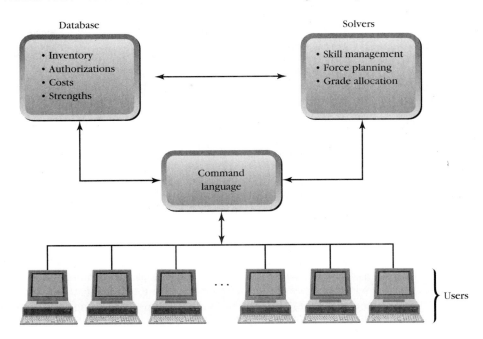

application-specific database and solver modules. The users consist of various organizational units in the U.S. Air Force spread over three locations. They use EFMS to make decisions about their hundreds of thousands of enlisted personnel. This ODSS required more than 125 person-years to develop during a 9-year period.

ODSS DEVELOPMENT

Developing an ODSS such as EFMS is a much larger undertaking than constructing more traditional kinds of DSSs. It is not amenable to end-user development. It requires a more formal approach, such as the system-development life cycle discussed in Chapter 8 (Carter et al. 1992). Today there are few tools that can serve as ready-made problem processors for ODSS development. Rather, there are a variety of technologies from which the developer can select and then integrate into a problem-processing system for the ODSS. According to Fedorowicz and Konsynski (1992), the available and useful technologies for ODSSs cover the entire gamut of computer-based technology available for business computing systems—from the knowledge-management techniques covered in Part Three to the artificial intelligence technologies outlined in Chapter 12 to the organizational computing technologies summarized in Chapter 16.

George (1991) organizes candidate technologies to be considered for use in ODSS development into several categories:

- *Communication technologies* to facilitate communication within the organization and across the organization's boundaries;
- *Coordination technologies* to coordinate the use of resources involved in decision making;

- *Filtering technologies* to filter and summarize knowledge (e.g., intelligent agents);
- *Monitoring technologies* to track the status of the organization and its environment;
- *Knowledge-management technologies* to represent and process diverse kinds of knowledge needed in decision making; and
- *Decision support technologies* to help the organization and its participants make decisions.

As ODSS development tools with ready-made PPSs begin to appear, we should expect to find all or some of these technologies integrated within them. Integration approaches can range from the confederation to the nested to the synergistic styles.

17.5 NEGOTIATION SUPPORT SYSTEMS

An organization—be it a group or something more complex—can be viewed as a network of agreements among its participants and with outside parties in its environment (Lax and Sebenius 1986). Inside an organization, an entity may reach agreements with subordinates about task assignments and performance evaluation; with peers about cooperative efforts, mutual obligations, and resolution of conflicts; and with superiors about compensation plans, budget allocations, new projects, and so forth. Across organizational boundaries, the agreements can take the form of contracts or may be more informal understandings that regulate relationships between organizations. All agreements are multiparticipant decisions. All are candidates for negotiations and perhaps for computer-based negotiation support.

A negotiation involves two or more participants who represent either themselves or others. Negotiation can result from conflict and competition, or it could be undertaken to realize some potential gain expected to result from cooperation among participants. The negotiations may be acrimonious, contentious, or harmonious. They may or may not be face-to-face. They may or may not involve explicit offers or counteroffers (Bazerman 1986). Agreements resulting from negotiation are joint decisions that guide and shape the behavior of organizations (Lax and Sebenius 1986).

Although some GDSSs and ODSSs have features that can benefit negotiators, these features have not been the central motive or interest of such systems. There is a growing interest in computer-based systems designed specifically for supporting negotiation activities. We refer to these as *negotiation support systems*. If an NSS

NEGOTIATION

Negotiation is a widespread, multifaceted, complex phenomenon. We can view it as both an art and a science. Researchers in a variety of disciplines, including economics, political science, industrial relations, social psychology, and applied mathematics, have studied it. Social scientists have explored negotiation in terms of broad practical maxims and game theorists have considered it in terms of mathematical abstractions. These studies form the roots for appreciating NSS possibilities (Holsapple, Lai, and Whinston 1991).

is supporting negotiation within a group, then it is a special kind of GDSS. If it is supporting negotiation within an organization, then it is a special kind of ODSS.

Among the earliest NSS examples was the Conflict Analysis Program, developed to provide support for an arbitrator during prenegotiation strategy formulation (Fraser and Hipel 1981). It was designed to help arbitrators eliminate infeasible agreements, order feasible ones according to participants' preferences, and assess the stability of agreements. Pioneering tools for NSS development included NEGO, DECISION CONFERENCING, NEGOPLAN, and MEDIATOR. Each provided a PPS that could work with the KS constructed by the NSS developer and/or the negotiation's participants.

The NEGO problem processor was designed to help negotiators change their strategies, form coalitions, and evaluate compromises (Kersten, 1985). DECISION CONFERENCING was designed to help participants decompose complex issues into simpler ones, create new alternatives, anticipate others' positions, and facilitate communication among negotiators (Quinn, Rohrbaugh, and McGrath 1985). NEGO-PLAN is an expert system shell for negotiation support (Matwin et al. 1989). It uses a rule-based system in representing negotiation issues and decomposing negotiation goals to help a participant examine consequences of different negotiation scenarios. MEDIATOR was designed to support a human mediator in a negotiation activity by integrating participant views to build a joint problem representation (Jarke, Jelassi, and Shakun 1987). The system also provided access to data and solvers and furnished structured communication facilities for both participants and the mediator.

More extensive surveys of NSS software have been prepared (Jelassi and Foroughi 1989; Anson and Jelassi 1990). However, they are beyond the scope of this book. Here, we present a framework identifying the major ingredients of a negotiation. Based on this framework, we identify functions that could be useful to have in an NSS. Our consideration of negotiation support systems concludes with a consideration of alternative types of NSSs.

INGREDIENTS OF NEGOTIATION

A negotiation activity can be characterized in terms of eight major elements: the issue to be negotiated, the set of participants involved, the participant's acceptance regions, their locations, their strategies, their movements, rules of negotiation, and assistance from an intervenor (Lai 1989; Holsapple, Lai, and Whinston 1995c). To understand negotiations in general or in particular cases, it is important to understand these eight elements. Each is described briefly and informally in the discussion that follows.

An *issue* is the matter of contention that is the focus of a negotiation. The issue can have several aspects or dimensions. For instance, the issue may be the launch of a new product with such dimensions as its timing, product features, and pricing. The set of all possible positions that could be taken concerning the issue can be thought of as an **issue space.**

A *participant* in a negotiation is one whose agreement must be attained in order for a solution to exist. A participant could be a person, several people (e.g., a group), a computer, or a human-machine combination. Participants negotiating about the product launch issue might include representatives of marketing, research and development, finance, manufacturing, and customer service. Each participant has an **acceptance region** within the issue space. It is composed of positions that would be acceptable to that participant. The intersection of all participants' acceptance regions forms an **agreement region,** which is a basis for the decision reached by the negotiating participants.

A *location* is a particular position in an issue space. At any moment, each participant will prefer a location that is within its acceptance region and will occupy it. Each participant has the freedom to move to a different location. At any moment, the set of all participants' locations defines the current state of a negotiation process. The goal of a negotiation activity is to reach a state in which all participants are at the same location in the agreement region.

Each participant has a strategy for negotiating. **Coalition** formation can be an important aspect of participants' strategies when more than two participants exist. Once participants form a coalition, they are at the same location and move together as long as they stay in that coalition. However, participants may occupy the same location coincidentally rather than intentionally. In order to distinguish this latter circumstance from a coalition, it is called a *rendezvous.* Some coalitions may not be allowed due to restrictions in the rules of negotiation.

Rules of negotiation define what interactions are allowed among participants, what movements are permissible within an issue space, and when and how a negotiation ends. They therefore play an extremely important role in a negotiation process. Five major categories of rules are those involving time constraints, regulation of coalition formation, governance of communications patterns, conflict-resolution policies, and intervention by outside agents.

An **intervenor** is an active agent with a purpose of directly or indirectly helping the participants reach an agreement. An intervenor can play such roles as mediator, arbitrator, rule manipulator, or facilitator (social or technical). Not every negotiation will have or even allow an intervenor. However, once an intervenor is drawn into a negotiation activity, it plays an extremely.important role. Like a participant, each intervenor could be a person, multiple persons acting as a whole, a computer system, or a human-machine combination. Because negotiation is a kind of multiparticipant decision-making process, an intervenor actually functions as a decision support system for the set of entities (or perhaps some subset of them).

NSS FUNCTIONS

The eight negotiation elements just identified suggest possible kinds of support that an NSS might provide (Holsapple, Lai, and Whinston 1994). Some of these have already been implemented in specific NSSs or investigated in NSS research. Others have not. Support possibilities for each element are summarized in Table 17.6. The support possibilities identified here are not necessarily exhaustive, but they are representative of features for developers to consider and researchers to study. Which of these are incorporated into a specific NSS is the choice of its developer.

Issues Because the notion of an issue is at the very root of negotiation activity, an NSS is likely to have some means for representing the issue space. For this reason, the developer of an NSS should ask, What is the issue space? How might it be represented? Could a general tool be devised to represent and manipulate issue spaces in much the same way as a database-management tool can represent and manipulate databases? An issue space representation should help NSS users achieve and maintain a complete and correct understanding of the characteristics of an issue space. It also forms a basis for the NSS performing various analyses.

TABLE 17.6 Some NSS Support Possibilities

PARAMETERS	SUPPORT POSSIBILITIES
Issues	To determine the dimensions of a negotiation issue
	To determine the value of each dimension to each participant
	To formally represent the issue space
	To identify the feasible portion of an issue space
	To process the representation of an issue space
	To update and keep track of changes in an issue space
Participants	To accommodate knowledge about participants
	To update knowledge about participants
Acceptance Region	To identify the acceptance region of one or more participants
	To change a participant's own acceptance region.
	To monitor and catalogue all participants' acceptance regions
	To compute the agreement region
Locations	To represent a location within the issue space
	To portray all possible locations within an acceptance region or agreement region
	To evaluate the relative values of all locations within the acceptance region of a participant
	To detect whether a location is within the acceptance region
	To keep track of all participants' locations and analyze the changes
	To measure the dispersion of current or potential locations
	To detect the trend of dispersion among locations at each state of a negotiation process
Strategies	To track participants' previous strategies and analyze their changes
	To forecast participants' strategies
	To design, select, and review strategies
	To analyze likely effects of possible coalition formations
Movements	To derive all candidate locations for moving based on a selected strategy
	To select or recommend a new location from candidate locations
	To keep track of all entities' historical movements and analyze their changes
	To forecast other participants' movements
Rules of Negotiation	To collect and maintain knowledge about rules of negotiation
	To prevent participant behavior that would violate the rules
	To detect whether prospective behavior would violate the rules
	To recognize the existence of impasses, adjournment, or breakdown situations
	To recognize whether a termination rule is satisfied
Intervenor	To keep participants informed about intervenor actions, and vice versa
	To recognize the time and situation in which an intervenor is likely to act
	To accommodate knowledge characterizing the nature of a particular intervenor

SOURCE: Holsapple, Lai, and Whinston (1995b)

Researchers have begun to explore such NSS abilities (Kersten, et al. 1988; Matwin et al. 1989; Koperczak, Kersten, and Szpakowicz 1990; Kersten and Mallory 1990; Kilgour, Fang, and Hipel 1990; Bui 1992; Bui and Strand 1993). If an NSS represents an issue space within its KS, then its PPS must be able to process the representation in some way. For instance, an issue or a dimension could be added. A minimal processing capability would be able to retrieve an issue space for presentation purposes.

One benefit of an NSS's ability to manage issue space representations is the foundation it provides for a participant's negotiation efforts. Without a clear appreciation of the issue space, a participant's efforts at devising strategies and selecting movements are hampered. Another benefit may come from the NSS functioning as a reminder or monitor of issue space boundaries. For multiple users, there is the benefit of participants being able to obtain a consistent specification of the issue space. Indeed, some NSS research has studied how a negotiation issue can be restructured during a negotiation process (Shakun 1990, 1991; Kersten et al. 1990; Sycara 1991; Matwin, Szapiro, and Haigh 1991).

Participants   Like issues, participants have a large influence on a negotiation. They are prime movers in the dynamic interactions that make up negotiation activity. Because the outcome of a negotiation depends on these interactions, a participant must not only know itself, it must also be informed about other participants. The more it knows about other participants, the better it understands a negotiation situation. By accommodating knowledge about participants within its KS, a negotiation support system can foster such understanding. Conceivably, an NSS should have the ability to acquire, use, and present knowledge about participants' acceptance regions, locations, strategies, movements, value systems, objectives, social roles, and so forth.

In this direction, some NSS researchers have studied cognitive difficulties, thought, emotion, preference, and confidence of participants (Faure, Dong, and Shakun 1990; Lim and Benbasat 1993; Bui 1994). Some research has examined how an NSS can forecast an opponent's behavior or represent the nature of an opponent (Kersten et al. 1991). Bui (1992) has proposed an individual DSS that offers its user analytical and strategic insights about other participants in a negotiation. Because some knowledge about a participant is likely to change rapidly, it is important for an NSS to have a capability for making timely updates to such knowledge. Retentive update can be important, allowing an NSS to keep and use knowledge about participants' past behaviors (e.g., case-based reasoning that draws on past experiences has been used in NSS research [Sycara 1990b; Bui 1992]). How training and/or preparation of a participant affects its performance has also been explored (Gauvin, Lilien, and Chatterjee 1990; Eliashberg et al. 1992).

Acceptance Regions   How participants' acceptance regions intersect forms a basis for reaching an agreement (i.e., a decision). Andriole (1993) pointed out that to "identify the range of acceptable negotiation outcomes" is one of main tasks in defining a problem or opportunity. Under pressure and facing a complicated negotiation issue, a participant can get lost and even attempt to move to a location that is not in its acceptance region. Therefore, we might expect an NSS to be able to help participants correctly identify their own acceptance regions as well as those of other participants. For instance, Matwin, Szapiro, and Haigh (1991) discuss how the aspiration levels of each entity form an *aspiration grid*. An aspiration grid is a way of defining an entity's acceptance region.

By tracking participants' acceptance regions, an NSS provides a foundation for forecasting their behaviors, such as selected strategies and movements. Certainly, this forecasting also depends on knowledge of the issue space and the involved participants. If an NSS is able to keep track of all participants' acceptance regions, it should also be able to compute the agreement region at any moment. A user of this NSS can understand the situation more clearly and completely as a basis for contemplating an appropriate strategy. In all, little NSS research has explicitly explored acceptance region topics (Holsapple, Lai, and Whinston 1995a).

Locations   Even when a participant can identify its acceptance region, it may not be easy to recognize and evaluate all locations that exist in the region (especially when the number of issue dimensions is large). An NSS may be able to help. For instance, it may graphically portray all possible locations that exist within an acceptance region and ensure that a prospective new location is within the acceptance region. A prerequisite for such abilities is that an NSS can represent a location (Hipel, Fang, and Kilgour 1990; Kersten et al. 1990). Considerable research has concentrated on the search for optimal or final locations (Kersten and Mallory 1990; Sycara 1990a; Matwin, Szapiro, and Haigh 1991; Bui 1992; Quaddus 1993; Iz 1994; Zigurs et al. 1994). The methods applied in this work include multiple-criteria decision methods, simulation, economic models, rule-based formalisms, neural network mechanisms, case-based reasoning, machine learning, graph model analysis, and fuzzy logic.

The location of a participant directly influences a negotiation process and result. A participant can benefit from keeping track of other participants' locations and recognizing how they change over time. Therefore, an NSS might be expected to take care of location tracking and analysis. For instance, researchers have attempted to maintain logs to keep records of collaborators' interactions (Carmel, Herniter, and Nunamaker 1993). Conceivably, an NSS may have a mechanism to measure the distance between a participant's current location and each candidate location and to evaluate the relative values among these locations. It may also have the ability to measure the dispersion of locations in each state of the negotiation process. An NSS may provide a mechanism to detect whether the dispersion of locations at each state of a negotiation process is decreasing.

Strategies   Because of the uncertain and dynamic nature of some negotiations, a participant may desire to review, create, and choose varying strategies over time. These alternative strategies can be numerous and complex. One potential function of an NSS is to keep track of all of a participants' previous strategies as a basis for review. From the review, a participant may decide to keep the same strategy, shift to another strategy selected from recorded strategies, or devise a new strategy. To aid in such deliberations, an NSS could have some procedural and reasoning knowledge, allowing it to recommend or derive candidate strategies. Strategy selection could be aided by NSS-generated comparisons of strategies with respect to a participant's value system and objectives. Some reported NSSs (e.g., DECISION CONFERENCING) provide strategy-planning abilities (Jelassi and Foroughi 1989).

The ability to help a participant correctly discern strategies of others is another potential NSS function. This ability depends on knowledge about other participants' previous strategies and may take into account probabilities of the possible strategies. Thus, it can be beneficial for an NSS to keep track of other participants' strategies as well as those of its user. For example, Negotiation Edge has been developed to help a negotiator identify strategies derived from self-assessment of its own personal negotiation style as well as from assessments of other participants' negotiation styles (Jelassi and Foroughi 1989).

Coalition formation can be an important part of a participant's strategy in negotiations having more than two participants (Shakun 1990, 1991). Conceivably, developers could implement an NSS to recognize coalition states, track their shifts over time, support participants' decisions about whether to ally themselves with other entities, and offer advice about the activity of forming and maintaining a coalition (Holsapple, Lai, and Whinston 1995b). For example, an NSS might help a participant recognize feasible coalitions and then evaluate and compare benefits it would enjoy by participating in them. Once a participant makes a decision to attempt to form a particular coalition, the NSS may assist its efforts at persuading target participants to agree on the coalition formation. Among developed NSSs, NEGO is one that allows negotiators to change their strategies and to form coalitions (Kersten 1985).

Movements   For a particular strategy, there can be multiple candidate locations to which a participant could move. An NSS could offer support by deriving all such candidate locations, ensuring all candidate locations are within an acceptance region, and helping a participant evaluate the candidate locations. Selection of a particular location may depend on other participants' movements. An NSS that provides forecasting mechanisms, allowing a participant to analyze other participants' movements, could be beneficial. Tracking all participants' movements and analyzing their changes could be prerequisites for applying such a forecasting mechanism. For example, NEGO simulates movements based on anticipated behaviors of both parties (Kersten 1985). NEGOPLAN allows a participant to investigate the consequences of its own location and the anticipated location of the other side (Koperczak, Kersten, and Szpakowicz 1990).

Rules of Negotiation   All aspects of a negotiation are constrained by the rules of negotiation. Anson and Jelassi (1990) contend that such rules should be established at the start of a negotiation. A possible NSS function is to help participants keep the rules of negotiation in mind and ensure that their actions do not violate those rules. We could extend this concept to an NSS that monitors other participants' behaviors with respect to the rules. For example, an NSS may remind a participant about approaching time expirations, check to see if a desired coalition formation violates regulations on coalition formation, aid in recognizing the existence of negotiation impasses, detect when a termination rule is satisfied, or aid in recognizing situations where an intervenor might or should come into the negotiation (Holsapple, Lai, and Whinston 1995b).

Intervenor   Upon being drawn into a negotiation, an intervenor can play an extremely important role. It can influence the negotiation process or its outcome. If a participant can stay informed about the intervenor as well as the other participants, it will have a better appreciation of the negotiation situation. Thus, it can be desirable for an NSS to provide knowledge about the intervenor as well as about participants. This knowledge should include information about when the intervenor might or should be involved, what kind of role the involved intervenor will play, the constitution of the involved intervenor, and the influence wielded by the intervenor (Valley, White, and Iacohucci 1992).

Desired NSS abilities can also be considered from an intervenor's viewpoint, providing an intervenor with full knowledge about the state of a negotiation. The more complete this knowledge is, the better is an intervenor's ability to assist participants in reaching an agreement. If an NSS serves as an intervenor, it is essential for that NSS to be able to communicate with every entity. In addition, we might want the ability to give suggestions, execute termination rules, or provide decision techniques or final arbitration (Holsapple, Lai, and Whinston 1995b).

TYPES OF NSSs

It is important for both NSS users and developers to appreciate the types of negotiation support systems that are possible. This lets them settle on the type of NSS most suitable for the negotiation situation at hand. One way to classify negotiation support systems is based on the extent by which each NSS possesses functions such as those noted in Table 17.6. Similarly, we could classify NSS development tools in terms of which of these functions their PPSs perform.

Here, we look at a simpler way of classifying NSSs into distinct types. It is based on the kind of participants who are negotiating (i.e., a group versus a more complex organization) and the nature of an NSS's role in the negotiation (Holsapple, Lai, and Whinston 1995b). As Figure 17.11 shows, an NSS can support negotiation within a group of participants or an organization of participants. It can support a negotiation by either assisting participants or serving as a participant. In the former case, it can assist an individual participant, a subset of the whole set of participants (which may or may not form a coalition), the entire set of participants, or an intervenor. In the latter case, an NSS serves either as an entity or an intervenor. Figure

FIGURE 17.11   A Framework for Classifying NSSs

Name of NSS's role / Name of participants	Participant	Subset of whole participant set — Coalition — Individually	Subset of whole participant set — Coalition — Whole	Subset of whole participant set — Noncoalition — Individually	Subset of whole participant set — Noncoalition — Whole	Whole participant set — Individually	Whole participant set — Whole	Whole participant set — Intervenor	Serves as — Participant	Serves as — Intervenor
Group										
Organization										

SOURCE: Adapted from Holsapple, Lai, and Whinston (1995b).

17.12 shows the types of NSSs graphically. Each part of Figure 17.12 corresponds to a column in Figure 17.11.

Compared to NSSs that support organization negotiation, NSSs supporting a group negotiation could presumably be simpler and more uniform. In the organization case, an NSS's KS may need to hold knowledge about the organization's structure (i.e., its authority, communication, and role structures). Negotiating participants are likely to have different levels of access to a shared organizational NSS, reflecting different authorities, communication restrictions, and roles. NSS support of a coalition may be worthwhile only when the coalition is strong in terms of its stability. More generally, participation in an NSS-aided subset is based on the cost of NSS usage.

FIGURE 17.12 Types of Negotiation Support Systems

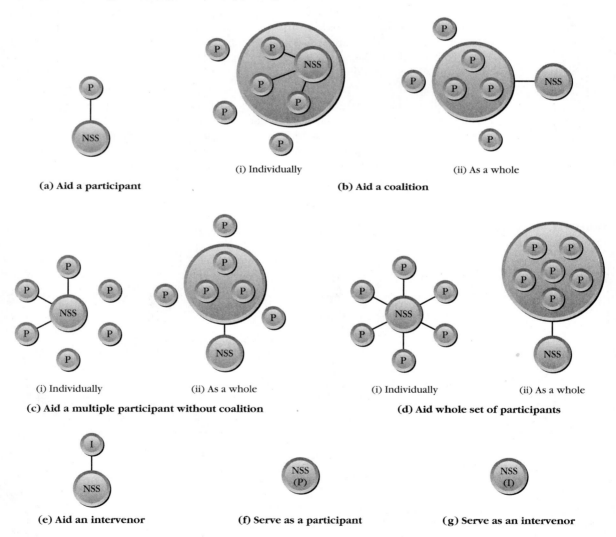

(i) Individually

(a) Aid a participant

(b) Aid a coalition (ii) As a whole

(i) Individually (ii) As a whole

(c) Aid a multiple participant without coalition

(i) Individually (ii) As a whole

(d) Aid whole set of participants

(e) Aid an intervenor (f) Serve as a participant (g) Serve as an intervenor

SOURCE: Adapted from Holsapple, Lai, and Whinston (1995b).

When an NSS supports multiple participants, it may provide support for each individually or for all as a whole. If an NSS supports participants individually, then it may provide customized support for each. Differences among participants are a major focus of an intervenor's effort. We may devise an intervenor's NSS for tracking and analyzing such differences. We may also design it to support participants in some respects.

The classification suggests that an NSS can serve as a substitute for a human entity. For instance, it may serve as an entity to help prevent an overly risky or overly cautious solution. Research has indicated that risky shift and cautious shift can arise in group behavior. When an NSS serves as an intervenor, it may implement various techniques for consensus seeking. Developing NSSs that serve as participants or intervenors will depend heavily on research advances concerned with intelligent agents.

To date, negotiation support systems have been discussed, designed, or developed to assist an individual participant (Matwin, Szapiro, and Haigh 1991; Bui 1992) or intervenor (Anson and Jelassi 1990; Lim and Benbasat 1991; Shakun 1991; Carmel, Herniter, and Nunamaker 1993; Quaddus 1993), to support an entire set of participants (Lim and Benbasat 1991; Carmel, Herniter, and Nunamaker 1993; Iz 1994) or a coalition, and even to serve as an intervenor (Jones and Jelassi 1990; Sycara 1991). Some types of NSSs have received little attention so far.

We should expect further advances in all NSS categories. Especially important is the creation of general-purpose tools for NSS construction. Such a tool would consist of a PPS geared toward one (or more) of the 20 categories identified in Figure 17.11. Its processing capabilities would include applicable functions such as those identified in Table 17.6. Its LS, PS, and KS representation structures would be consistent with these PPS abilities. The KS contents (including linguistic and presentation knowledge that help define a LS and PS) would be what distinguishes one NSS built with this tool from others built with the same tool, including knowledge about which of the potential PPS behaviors is to be in force for a particular negotiation support application.

17.6 SUMMARY

This chapter has examined computer-based systems that support the decision-making efforts of decision makers comprising multiple participants. These multiparticipant decision support systems (MDSSs) can be categorized into those that support groups (GDSSs) and those that support more complex organizations of decision-making participants (ODSSs). Cutting across these two categories are MDSSs specifically oriented toward supporting negotiated decisions (NSSs). Depending on the organizational infrastructure of a decision maker, one or another of these MDSS types will be most appropriate. We can gauge the appropriateness of an MDSS's fit with a particular decision maker in terms of the natures of the roles, relationships, and regulations that make up its infrastructure.

MDSSs do have various traits in common. All fit into one or more of the time-place categories. That is, every MDSS is oriented toward some arrangement of decision-maker participants in time and space. All MDSSs adhere to the generic DSS architecture introduced in Chapter 6. However, we can elaborate on that framework to get a more detailed architecture that is common to MDSSs. With this architecture, four potential kinds of users are identified. The PPS and/or KS can be distributed across several linked computers. The LS and PS can have public and private messages. The KS can hold system knowledge, domain knowledge, and relational knowledge. The KS can hold public and private knowledge. The PPS has a participant-coordination ability in addition to knowledge-acquisition, selection or derivation, and presentation abilities. Some PPS abilities may be exercised by individuals doing individual work, whereas others involve joint work.

Group decision support systems have been the most extensively studied and widely implemented type of MDSS. Relative to individual work, group work has the potential for certain gains and losses. GDSSs are intended to help the potential gains from group work to become actual gains, while helping prevent potential losses due to group work. GDSSs can be classified into various types based on their architectural features, the time-place categories into which they fit, levels of support they offer to a decision maker, or available technologies that can be applied.

Tools for building GDSSs encompass a considerable variety of processors that are ready-made for inclusion in a PPS. Choosing appropriate tools is one of a variety of factors that have been found to be important for GDSS success. Unlike DSSs for individuals, usage of a GDSS often involves a facilitator, who can strongly influence group performance with the GDSS. Researchers have discovered that effects of GDSS usage depend on situational factors as well as the technology itself.

Organizational decision support systems are for multiparticipant decision makers that are more complex than groups. ODSS research and practice are not as well developed as in the case of GDSSs. Yet, researchers have identified different types of ODSSs, advanced specialized ODSS architectures, recommended development guidelines, and identified candidate technologies for use in ODSS development. In the case of negotiation support systems, researchers have recognized a wide range of support possibilities and implemented and studied a number of them in NSSs. Also, they have advanced a way for categorizing NSSs. Exploration of the diverse kinds of ODSSs and NSSs that are possible is still in an early stage, but it is likely to mature rapidly in the years ahead.

▲ IMPORTANT TERMS

acceptance region

agreement region

coalition

decision room

domain knowledge

facilitator

group decision support system

group memory

intervenor

issue space

multiparticipant decision support system

negotiation support system

organization infrastructure

regulations

relational knowledge

relationships

roles

system knowledge

technological infrastructure

▲ APPLICATION TO THE BURR-BROWN CASE

1. What is a decision room?
2. What decisions was the GDSS intended to support?
3. Characterize the group decision maker.
4. Explain how each of the following was used: (a) electronic brainstorming, (b) issue analyzer, and (c) topic commenter.

5. Why were preplanning meetings held, and what was their outcome?
6. What role did the facilitator play?
7. Why was the GDSS-supported approach more effective than the manual approach?
8. Why would ODSSs and NSSs have been inappropriate for this application?
9. This GDSS fits into which of the categories in Figure 17.6?
10. Describe the contents of this GDSS's knowledge system.
11. Is this a Level 1, 2, or 3 GDSS? Explain.
12. Which of the six technologies identified in Table 17.5 was used for the GDSS?
13. Identify four kinds of decision support processors included in the problem-processing system of Burr-Brown's DSS.
14. Which of the three kinds of facilitators was used?

▲ REVIEW QUESTIONS

1. What are the three major aspects of organizational infrastructure?
2. Why is an appreciation of organizational infrastructure important for the study of MDSSs?
3. How do GDSSs and ODSSs differ in terms of role characteristics for which they are most appropriate?
4. How do GDSSs and ODSSs differ in terms of relationship characteristics for which they are most appropriate?
5. How do GDSSs and ODSSs differ in terms of regulation characteristics for which they are not appropriate?
6. What do MDSSs have in common?
7. How do the four main categories of participant arrangements differ from each other?
8. What are four classes of users who could interact with an MDSS?
9. What aspects of an MDSS tend to be distributed across multiple computers?
10. How do public and private messages in an MDSS's language system differ?
11. What basic kinds of requests can be made to an MDSS?
12. How do public and private messages in an MDSS's presentation system differ?
13. What basic kinds of responses can be made by an MDSS?
14. How do system knowledge, domain knowledge, and relational knowledge differ? How can each be beneficial for inclusion in the knowledge system of an MDSS?
15. What problem processing abilities can be found in MDSSs?
16. What participant coordination abilities might a PPS be expected to exhibit?
17. What is a group decision support system?
18. In contrast to individual work, what are four potential gains from group work? What are four potential losses? What GDSS features could prevent these losses?
19. How can each of the following GDSS features benefit a group?
    a. Group memory
    b. Parallel communication
    c. Anonymous interaction
20. How do Level 1, 2, and 3 GDSSs differ?
21. For each of the following, what are the features provided and how do they support a group decision maker?
    a. Electronic boardroom
    b. Teleconferencing rooms
    c. Group networks
    d. Information centers

e. Collaboration laboratories

f. Decision rooms

22. How is a GDSS of the decision room variety developed? Who provides the KS contents?

23. What are four distinct kinds of decision support processors that may be found in the PPS of a GDSS? How does each benefit a group decision maker?

24. What are six factors that have been found to be important for successful development and installation of a GDSS?

25. What do GDSS facilitators do?

26. How do internal, external, and automated facilitation differ?

27. What has GDSS research found about the effects of each of the following on GDSS usage and performance?

a. Group size

b. Task complexity

c. Anonymity

d. Parallelism

e. Structuring

f. Facilitation

28. What is an ODSS?

29. How do structure enforcing ODSSs differ from those that are structure transforming?

30. What are the main technologies relevant to ODSS development?

31. What is an NSS?

32. What are the main elements of negotiation activity? For each, give an example of a related NSS feature.

33. How are acceptance regions related to an issue space and to an agreement region?

34. What is a coalition and how does it differ from a rendezvous?

35. What does a negotiation intervenor do?

36. In terms of the nature of an NSS's role in negotiation, what are the main types of negotiation support systems that can exist?

▲ DISCUSSION TOPICS

1. Discuss the relationships among organizational infrastructure, technological infrastructure (e.g., MDSSs), task, and organization performance.

2. In what ways can we assess the impact of a particular MDSS on the performance that can be achieved with a particular organizational infrastructure?

3. Give examples of both groups and more complex organizations in which you have participated. How could each have benefitted from an MDSS?

4. Describe the features of an anytime-anyplace MDSS.

5. Why might different time–same place decision making have some advanges over same time–same place decision making?

6. Discuss the relative advantages and disadvantages of LSs that furnish private-only, public-only, or public-private messages.

7. Discuss the relative advantages and disadvantages of PSs that furnish private-only, public-only, or public-private messages.

8. Discuss the relative advantages and disadvantages of KSs that handle private-only, public-only, or public-private knowledge.

9. Which PPS coordination abilities are especially useful for GDSSs? For ODSSs? For NSSs?
10. What features of group behavior suggest that computerized support of group decision making could be beneficial?
11. Under what circumstances is the anonymous interaction permitted by a GDSS a negative influence on group behavior? Explain.
12. Are there any disadvantages to the parallel communication permitted by a GDSS? If so, what are they?
13. Describe situations where each of the following would benefit group decision makers.
    a. Electronic brainstorming
    b. Topic commenting
    c. Issue analysis
    d. Voting
14. What difficulties can arise when a facilitator is also a participant in the decision making?
15. Relate ODSSs to the notions of outsourcing and downsizing.
16. Explain how the ODSSs in Figures 17.9 and 17.10 are special cases of the MDSS architecture shown in Figure 17.7.
17. Why is ODSS development likely to require more effort than development of GDSSs?
18. What are the main differences between NSSs for groups and NSSs for other kinds of organizations?
19. Discuss the distinctions among mediators, arbitrators, and facilitators as types of negotiation intervenors.
20. Explain how rules of negotiation are related to organizational infrastructure.

▲ REFERENCES

Andriole, S. J. 1993. Information management support for international negotiation. *Theory and Decision* 34.

Anson, R. C., and M. T. Jelassi. 1990. A developmental framework for computer-supported conflict resolution. *European Journal of Operational Research* 46.

Bazerman, M. 1986. *Managerial decision making.* New York; John Wiley.

Bonczek, R. H., C. W. Holsapple, and A. B. Whinston. 1979. Computer based support of organizational decision making. *Decision Sciences* (April).

Bostrom, R. P., R. Anson, and V. K. Clawson. 1993. Group facilitation and group support systems. 1993. In *Group support systems: New perspectives,* edited by L. Jessup and J. Valacich. New York: Macmillan. York, 1993.

Bots, P. W. G., and H. G. Sol. 1988. Shaping organizational information systems through co-ordination support. In *Organizational Decision Support Systems,* edited by R. Lee, A. McCosh, and P. Migliarese. New York: North-Holland.

Boulding, K. E. 1956. *The image.* Ann Arbor, Mich.: University of Michigan Press.

Bui, T. 1992. Building DSS for negotiators: A three-step design process. *Proceedings of Hawaiian International Conference on System Sciences,* Hawaii (January).

———. 1994. Evaluating negotiation support systems: A conceptualization. *Proceedings of Hawaiian International Conference on System Sciences,* Hawaii (January).

Bui, T., and M. Jarke. 1986. Communications design for co-op: A group decision support system. *ACM Transactions on Office Information Systems* 4, no. 2.

Bui, T., and N. Strand. 1993. A neural net model to represent negotiators' heuristics. *Proceedings of the Hawaiian International Conference on System Sciences,* Hawaii (January).

Busch, E., M. Hamalainen, C. W. Holsapple, Y. Suh, and A. B. Whinston. 1991. Issues and obstacles in the development of team support systems. *Journal of Organizational Computing* 1, no. 2.

Carmel, E., B. C. Herniter, and J. F. Nunamaker, Jr. 1993. Labor-management contract negotiations in an electronic meeting room: A case study, *Group Decision and Negotiation* 2, no. 1.

Carter, G. M., M. P. Murray, R. G. Walker, and W. E. Walker. 1992. *Building organizational decision support systems*. San Diego: Academic Press.

Ching, C., C. W. Holsapple, and A. B. Whinston. 1992. Reputation, learning, and organizational coordination. *Organization Science* 3, no. 2.

_____. 1993. Modeling network organizations: A basis for exploring computer supported coordination possibilities, *Journal of Organizational Computing* 3, no. 3.

_____. 1995. IT support for coordination in network organizations. *Information and Management*, forthcoming.

Dennis, A. R., and R. B. Gallupe. 1993. A history of group support systems empirical research: Lessons learned and future directions. In *Group Support Systems: New Perspectives*, edited by L. Jessup and J. Valacich. New York: Macmillan.

Dennis, A., D. Vogel, J. Nunamaker, Jr., and A. Heminger. 1990. Bringing automated support to large groups: The Burr-Brown experience. *Information and Management* 18, no. 3.

DeSanctis, G., and R. B. Gallupe. 1985. Group decision support systems: A new frontier. *Data Base* (Winter).

_____. 1987. A foundation for the study of group decision support systems. *Management Science* 33, no. 5.

Dos Santos, B., and C. W. Holsapple. 1989. A framework for designing adaptive DSS interfaces. *Decision Support Systems* 5, no. 1.

Eliashberg, J., S. Gauvin, G. L. Lilien, and A. Rangaswamy. 1992. An experimental study of alternative preparation aids for international negotiations. *Group Decision and Negotiation* 1, no. 3.

Fang, L., K. W. Hipel, and D. M. Kilgour. 1989. Conflict models in graph form: Solution concepts and their interrelationships. *European Journal of Operational Research* 41.

Faure, G. O., V. L. Dong, and M. F. Shakun. 1990. Social-emotional aspects of negotiation. *European Journal of Operational Research* 46.

Fedorowicz, J., and B. Konsynski. 1992. Organization support systems: Bridging business and decision processes. *Journal of Management Information Systems* 8, no. 4.

Fraser, N., and K. Hipel. 1981. Computer assistance in labor-management negotiation. *Interfaces* 11, no. 1.

Gallupe, R. B., and J. D. McKeen. 1990. Enhancing computer mediated communication: An experimental investigation into the use of a group decision support system for face-to-face versus remote meetings. *Information and Management* 18, no. 1.

Gauvin, S., G. L. Lilien, and K. Chatterjee. 1990. The impact of information and computer based training on negotiators' performance. *Theory and Decision* 28.

George, J. F. 1991. The conceptualization and development of organizational decision support systems. *Journal of Management Information Systems* 8, no. 3.

George, J. F., J. F. Nunamaker, Jr., and J. S. Valacich. 1992. ODSS: Information technology for organizational change. *Decision Support Systems* 8, no. 4.

Gibson, D. V. 1991. Executive GDSS: Behavioral considerations at individual, organizational, and environmental levels of analysis. *Journal of Organizational Computing* 1, no. 3.

Gray, P., M. Mandviwalla, L. Olfman, and J. Satzinger. 1993. The user interface in group support systems. In *Group support systems: New perspectives,* edited by L. Jessup and J. Valacich. New York: Macmillan.

Grohowski, R., C. McGoff, D. Vogel, B. Martz, and J. Nunamaker. 1990. Implementing electronic meeting systems at IBM: Lessons learned and success factors. *MIS Quarterly* 14, no. 4.

Hackathorn, R. D., and P. G. W. Keen. 1981. Organizational strategies for personal computing in decision support systems. *MIS Quarterly* 5, no. 3.

Hipel, K. W., L. Fang, and D. M. Kilgour. 1990. A formal analysis of the Canada–U.S. softwood lumber dispute. *European Journal of Operational Research* 46.

Hoffer, J. A., and J. S. Valacich. 1993. Group memory in group support systems: A foundation for design. In *Group support systems: New perspectives,* edited by L. Jessup and J. Valacich. New York: Macmillan.

Holsapple, C. W. 1987. Adapting demons to knowledge management environments. *Decision Support Systems* 3, no. 4.

Holsapple, C. W., L. E. Johnson, and V. Waldron. 1996. A formal model for the study of communication support systems. *Human Communication Research* 22.

Holsapple, C. W., H. Lai, and A. B. Whinston. 1991. Negotiation support systems: Roots, progress, and needs. *Journal of Information Systems* 1, no. 4.

———. 1995a. Analysis of negotiation support system research. *Journal of Computer Information Systems.* 35, no. 3.

———. 1995b. Implications of negotiation theory for research and development of negotiation support systems. *Group Decision and Negotiation,* forthcoming.

———. 1995c. A formal basis for negotiation support system research. *Group Decision and Negotiation,* forthcoming.

Holsapple, C. W., and W. Luo. 1994. Using a GDSS: Effects of experience patterns on decision efficiency, quality, and participant satisfaction. Research Paper No. 79, *Kentucky Initiative for Knowledge Management,* College of Business and Economics, University of Kentucky.

———. 1995a. A framework for studying computer support of organization infrastructure. *Information and Management,* forthcoming.

———. 1995b. Dependent variables for organizational computing research: An empirical study. *Journal of Organizational Computing* 5, no. 1.

Holsapple, C. W., and A. B. Whinston. 1988. Distributed decision making: A research agenda. *ACM SIGOIS Bulletin* 9, no. 1.

Huber, G. P. 1982. Group decision support systems as aids in the use of structured group management techniques. *Proceedings of Second International Conference on Decision Support Systems,* San Francisco (June).

———. 1984. Issues in the design of group decision support systems. *MIS Quarterly* 8, no. 3.

Iz, P. H. 1994. Application of fuzzy arithmetic in group decision and negotiations involving multicriteria and conflicting priorities. *Proceedings of Hawaiian International Conference on System Sciences,* Hawaii (January).

Jarke, M. 1986. Knowledge sharing and negotiation support in multiperson decision support systems. *Decision Support Systems* 2, no. 1.

Jarke, M., M. Jelassi, and M. Shakun. 1987. MEDIATOR: Towards a negotiation support system. *European Journal of Operational Research* 31.

Jelassi, M., and A. Foroughi. 1989. Negotiation support systems: An overview of design issues and existing software. *Decision Support Systems* 5, no. 2.

Johansen, R. 1988. *Groupware: Computer support for business teams.* New York: The Free Press.

———. 1991. Groupware: Future directions and wild cards. *Journal of Organizational Computing* 2, no. 1.

Jones, B. H., and M. T. Jelassi. 1990. The effect of computer intervention and task structure on bargaining outcome. *Theory and Decision,* no. 28.

Kersten, G. 1985. NEGO—Group decision support system. *Information and Management* 8.

Kersten, G. E., L. Badcock, M. Iglewski, and G. R. Mallory. 1990. Structuring and simulating negotiation: An approach and an example. *Theory and Decision* 28.

Kersten, G. E., and G. R. Mallory. 1990. Supporting problem representations in decisions with strategic interactions. *European Journal of Operational Research,* no. 46.

Kersten, G. E., W. Michalowki, S. Matwin, and S. Szpakowicz. 1988. Representing the negotiating process with a rule-based formalism. *Theory and Decision* 25.

Kilgour, D. M., L. Fang, and K. W. Hipel. 1990. A decision support system for the graph model of conflicts. *Theory and Decision* 28.

King, J. L., and S. L. Star. 1989. Conceptual foundations for the development of organizational decision support systems. *Proceedings of the Hawaiian International Conference on System Sciences,* Kona, Hawaii (January).

Koperczak, Z., G. Kersten, and S. Szpakowicz. 1990. The negotiation metaphor and decision support for financial modelling. *Hawaiian International Conference on System Sciences,* Hawaii (January).

Kraemer, K. L., and J. L. King. 1988. Computer-based systems for cooperative work and group decision making. *ACM Computing Surveys* 20, no. 2.

Kull, D. 1982. Group decisions: Can a computer help. *Computer Decisions* 14, no. 5.

Lai, H. 1989. *A theoretical basis for negotiation support systems,* Ph.D. diss., Purdue University.

Lax, D., and J. Sebenius. 1986. *The manager as negotiator: Bargaining for cooperation and competitive gain.* New York: The Free Press.

Lewis, L. F. 1982. *Facilitator: A microcomputer decision support system for small groups,* Ph.D. diss., University of Louisville.

Lim, F. J. and I. Benbasat. 1991. A communication-based framework for group interfaces in computer-supported collaboration. *Proceedings of Hawaiian International Conference on System Sciences,* Hawaii (January).

————. 1993. A theoretical perspective of negotiation support systems. *Journal of Management Information Systems* 9, no. 3.

Matwin, S., T. Szapiro, and K. Haigh. 1991. Genetic algorithms approach to a negotiation support system. *IEEE Transactions on Systems, Man, and Cybernetics* 21, no. 1.

Matwin, S., S. Szpakowicz, E. Koperczak, G. Kersten, and W. Michalowski. 1989. Negoplan: An expert system shell for negotiation support. *IEEE Expert* 4, no. 1.

Mosvick, R., and R. Nelson. 1987. *We've got to start meeting like this! A guide to successful business meeting management.* Glenview, Ill.: Scott Foresman.

Nunamaker, J. F., Jr., A. R. Dennis, J. S. Valachich, D. R. Vogel, and J. F. George. 1993. Group support systems research: Experience from the lab and field. In *Group support systems: New perspectives,* edited by L. Jessup and J. Valachich. New York: Macmillan.

Nunamaker, J., Jr., D. Vogel, A. Heminger, B. Martz, R. Grohowski, and C. McGoff. 1989. Experiences at IBM with group support systems: A field study. *Decision Support Systems* 5, no. 2.

Philippakis, A. S., and G. I. Green. 1988. An architecture for organization-wide decision support systems. *Proceedings of the Ninth International Conference on Information Systems,* Minneapolis (December).

Quaddus, M. A. 1993. Group decision and negotiation support in multiple criteria decision making: An interactive approach. *Proceedings of Hawaiian International Conference on System Sciences,* Hawaii (January).

Quinn, R., J. Rohrbaugh, and M. McGrath. 1985. Automated decision conferencing: How it works. *Personnel* 62, no. 1.

Shakun, M. F. 1990. Group decision and negotiation support in evolving, nonshared information contexts. *Theory and Decision* 28.

————. 1991. Airline buyout: Evolutionary systems design and problem restructuring in group decision and negotiation. *Management Science* 37, no. 10.

Swanson, E. B. 1989. Distributed decision support systems: A perspective. *Proceedings of the Hawaiian International Conference on System Sciences,* Kona, Hawaii (January).

Swanson, E. B., and R. W. Zmud. 1989. Organizational decision support systems: Conceptual notions and architectural guidelines. Information Systems and Decision Processes Workshop, Tucson, Ariz. (October).

Sycara, K. P. 1990a. Negotiation planning: An AI approach. *European Journal of Operational Research* 46.

————. 1990b. Persuasive argumentation in negotiation. *Theory and Decision* 28.

————. 1991. Problem restructuring in negotiation. *Management Science* 37, no. 10.

Turoff, M. 1991. Computer-mediated communication requirements for group support. *Journal of Organizational Computing* 1, no. 2.

Turoff, M., S. R. Hiltz, A. N. F. Bahgat, and A. R. Rana. 1993. Distributed group support systems. *MIS Quarterly* 17, no. 4.

Valley, K. L., S. B. White, and D. Iacobucci. 1992. The process of assisted negotiations: A network analysis. *Group Decision and Negotiation* 1, no. 2.

Vogel, D. R., J. F. Nunamaker Jr., W. B. Martz, Jr., R. Grohowski, and C. McGoff. 1989. Electronic meeting system experience at IBM. *Journal of Management Information Systems* 6, no. 3.

Wagner, G. R., B. E. Wynne, and B. E. Mennecke. 1993. Group support systems facilities and software. In *Group Support Systems* edited by L. Jessup and J. Valacich. New York: Macmillan.

Watabe, K., C. W. Holsapple, and A. B. Whinston. 1992. Coordinator support in a nemawashi decision process. *Decision Support Systems,* 8, no. 2.

Watson, R. T. 1989. A design for an infrastructure to support organizational decision-making. *Proceedings of the Hawaiian International Conference on System Sciences,* Kona, Hawaii (January).

Zigurs, I., E. V. Wilson, A. M. Sloane, R. F. Reitsma, and C. Lewis. 1994. Simulation models and group negotiation: Problems of task understanding and computer support. *Proceedings of Hawaiian International Conference on System Sciences,* Hawaii (January).

Chapter 18

EXECUTIVE INFORMATION SYSTEMS

PRATT & WHITNEY: AN EXECUTIVE INFORMATION SYSTEM

Overview

Pratt & Whitney . . . is a multi-billion dollar operating unit of United Technologies Corporation. Executives at Pratt & Whitney's Commercial Engine Business (CEB) developed a strategic plan to increase market share through focused improvements in its products and customer service. In response to increasing competitive pressures, management wanted to set and monitor new corporate Critical Success Factors. This would help keep them focused on the "heart of the business"—the quality of its customer services and the performance of its products. A key area for this quality-based focus was the company's commercial jet engine business.

. . . Management wanted . . . a consistent "theme" throughout their marketing plans—all areas of the company needed to understand and support the same goals if they were to become more competitive. . . . Berson, President of CEB, wanted to automate the coordination of those marketing plans across the company's business units.

System Development and Features

. . . Study found that executives need timely access to strategic information to improve Pratt & Whitney's competitive posture in the commercial jet engine marketplace. They knew that it would require more than standard application software to get this access, so they looked for an interactive system with hands-on tools for investigating performance and tracking issues.

. . . Search led them to Comshare's Commander EIS, which is strong in colorful presentations, and features a pictorial menu that can be learned intuitively and rapidly. It has a cooperative processing approach, using the PC and the host, according to which machine can best accomplish a particular task. . . .

They began implementation of their EIS system by building a prototype application of a Fleet Management System for Berson. The system drew data from three existing production systems. It tracked key quality and reliability measures of each Pratt & Whitney jet engine model by customer. Details included the reliability of jet engines in operation, spare engine availability, spare parts delivery and work stoppages. . . .

The application gave Berson details on each engine model's numbers and reasons for shop visits, shutdowns, and flight delays and cancellations. Berson could track this information by individual customer to see where quality improvements were needed and where products and performances had changed over time. This, in turn, helped Berson and other executives to make changes in plans and procedures to address the specific needs of each customer.

Since development of that initial prototype, the system has been expanded to include details of multiple products across various classes and levels. It now tracks three categories of information: key initiatives (quality indicators), competitive support (marketing information), and customer-specific information, such as critical issues for each customer, parts availability by product, and so forth.

Results

Currently, Berson and 25 senior executives in various areas of the organization use the system, including executives in the Human Resources and Finance areas. . . . That number could expand to more than 200 users. . . . All functions

Continued

contribute to the bottom line, and an EIS can help them make that contribution by giving them greater insight into why things work the way they do, and how some of their business processes need to change to better serve their customers.

. . . An EIS highlights what is important. It creates an organizational focus and an alignment within the company so that managers and executives are working towards common goals. An EIS encourages management to ask questions, such as "What's working? What isn't? How can we improve our processes to make things work better?" . . . It is impossible to cost-justify that kind of benefit, but it is clearly what makes an EIS the valuable tool that it is.

Condensed quotation from W. C. Burkan, "The New Role for 'Executive' Information Systems," *I/S Analyzer* 30, no. 1 (1992): 4–5.

LEARNING OBJECTIVES

The Pratt & Whitney case illustrates the need for an executive information system (EIS), a prototyping approach to its development, and common kinds of EIS features. Such systems are designed for the most expedient conveyance of focused information to the executives who need it. In this chapter, we examine the information needs of top executives and the nature of EISs that can be built to meet those needs. EIS development issues are discussed, as are limitations on EIS usage.

After studying this chapter, you should be able to

1. Describe what executive information systems are.
2. Explain how and why executive information systems are developed.
3. Identify factors that should be considered when development of an executive information system is proposed.
4. Comment on how to avoid EIS failures.

Exercises at the end of this chapter test the extent to which you have met these objectives.

EXECUTIVE SUPPORT SYSTEMS

The terms executive information system and executive support system are sometimes used interchangeably. However, many people use the latter to refer to a system with broader capabilities than an EIS (Rockart and De Long 1988). Whereas an EIS focuses on providing information to executives, an executive support system (ESS) can have additional support capabilities. For instance, an ESS might include some electronic communication or data analysis facilities (Watson, Rainer, and Koh 1991). Thus, an ESS has a superset of EIS capabilities. Because the distinction between EISs and ESSs is not crucial for our purposes here, we do not belabor it. We simply use the EIS term, with the understanding that what is said also applies to ESSs.

18.1 INTRODUCTION

As we saw in Chapter 16, an **executive information system** (EIS) is a distinct type of decision support system. Its basic architecture is like that of other DSSs, but it differs from them by occupying a particular niche in an organization's structure—that of meeting the ad hoc decision analysis needs of top executives in large organizations (Philippakis and Green 1988). The use and benefits of EISs in large organizations has been well documented (Rockart and Treacy 1982; Rockart and DeLong 1988; Burkan 1991; Watson, Rainer, and Koh 1991). In this chapter, we take a more detailed look at EISs. We see why and how they are developed. We also consider what factors to keep in mind when contemplating the development of an EIS.

18.2 THE INFORMATION NEEDS OF TOP EXECUTIVES

The information needed by a top executive for decision making tends to be much broader and more diverse than that required by functional managers (e. g., a production manager) or front-line supervisors. The local DSSs and functional DSSs that work for managers beneath the top level do not individually provide what is needed by a top executive. Although these DSSs may collectively be able to produce much of the information required by a top executive, they are generally not geared toward doing so. Much of what they produce is not relevant to a top executive's decision making. The top executive cannot be expected to deal with a dozen different DSSs in trying to discover the pieces of information that are critical for his or her decision making.

A study by McLeod and Jones (1986) found that executives use most information in handling disturbances (i.e., exceptions) and in entrepreneurial efforts. Exactly what information does a top executive need? We must have an answer to this question before developing an EIS.

FIVE APPROACHES TO EXECUTIVE INFORMATION NEEDS

Rockart (1979) has identified five approaches to determining and satisfying executive information needs: the by-product, null, key indicator, total study, and critical success factor methods. We consider each of these in turn. Any of the last three could be a basis for developing an executive information system.

By-Product Method   With the *by-product method,* little effort is spent in trying to determine what information is needed by top executives. Electronic data processing systems and management information systems are built to handle transactions, maintain current and historical records, and provide predefined reports mainly to lower-level managers. Results from some of these reports are passed on to top executives in aggregate form or to highlight some exceptional situation. Thus, the information received by top executives is contained in a collection of reports that are by-products of the organization's ongoing operations.

Null Method   With the *null approach,* no formal or systematic effort (e. g., preparation of reports) is made to supply top executives with needed information. Their needs are viewed as being so dynamic and unpredictable that computer systems producing predefined reports are not helpful. Instead, they informally collect information, much of it subjective, from trusted sources by word of mouth. Although the null approach recognizes the importance of informal, subjective acquisition of information, it also ignores the value of supplementing such information with computer-based systems.

Key Indicator Method   The **key indicator** method for furnishing executive information is based on three ideas. First is the idea that the health of a business can be gauged in terms of a set of key financial indicators. Once these are identified, information about each is gathered in a continuing basis. The second idea is exception reporting, where the executive is made aware only of those indicators for which performance is off target. Executives can then examine further information about these exceptions as a basis for deciding about corrective action. The third idea involves using flexible visual display technology, ranging from computer-generated graphics to wall-size visual displays such as those in electronic boardrooms. Thus, key indicator information is made available to executives in full, by exception, and graphically.

Total Study Method   The *total study approach* consists of asking a sample of executives about their total information needs. Developers then compare the results of the study with what existing computer-based systems produce. Where gaps exists, developers design new subsystems to provide the missing information. This tends to be an expensive approach—one where it is difficult to design subsystems that serve any single executive well.

Critical Success Factor Method   The *critical success factor approach* endeavors to overcome shortcomings in each of the other approaches. For any organization, **critical success factors** are certain areas of activity in which satisfactory results will

---

EXAMPLES OF CRITICAL SUCCESS FACTORS

The top executive of a major division in a decentralized electronics company has return-on-investment as the chief goal, with the following critical success factors (Rockart 1979):

1. Strengthening customer relations
2. Supporting the sales force in the field
3. Improving productivity
4. Securing R&D support from the government
5. Developing new products
6. Acquiring new technological capabilities
7. Improving production facilities

The first two indicate the executive's desire to put greater emphasis on marketing in this engineering-oriented company. The third, sixth, and seventh factors are related to achieving more cost-effective facilities for production. The other two are concerned with keeping pace in a rapidly changing market. Quantitative indexes were developed to measure progress in some of these areas. For other factors, subjective judgment proved most effective.

ensure that the organization's performance is competitive. Things must go right in this handful of areas if the organization is to survive or be successful. Thus, critical success factors demand careful and continuing attention from executives. They must continually receive information about the current level of performance in each of the critical areas as a basis for decision making. An analyst identifies critical success factors through a formal process of interviewing executives. The interviews first uncover executive's goals, then the critical success factors that underlie them, and, finally, an agreement in how to measure and report progress in the factors and goals. The focus of this approach is on individual executives and the current objective and subjective information needs of each.

KINDS OF INFORMATION NEEDED

Based on experiences in applying the critical success factor approach, Rockart (1979) makes the following observations about the kinds of information top executives need:

1. Traditional financial accounting systems do not furnish the kinds of information needed for tracking critical success factors. However, cost accounting information is often useful in monitoring these factors.
2. Information from sources external to the organization is often important to critical success factors (e. g., information about markets, customers, competitors).
3. Many critical success factors require the coordination of information that is spread across computers and throughout the organization.
4. Objective measures are likely to be capable of being developed for many critical success factors. Yet, a small (but substantial) portion of information about the status of critical success factors involves gathering subjective assessments of others in the organization.
5. There are two categories of critical success factors. One type involves monitoring current results and is prevalent in situations where the executive feels competitive pressure for achieving certain short-run performance levels. The other type is oriented toward building for the future by reshaping the organization to survive in an anticipated new environment.
6. A considerable portion of the information about critical success factors is short term and volatile.

The foregoing characteristics of information needed by top executives have definite implications for the nature and development of executive information systems.

18.3 THE NATURE OF EXECUTIVE INFORMATION SYSTEMS

The notion of an executive information system as a distinct type of DSS was introduced in the early 1980s (Rockart and Treacy 1982). Some representative EIS definitions are as follows:

- A decision support system that assists top executives in conducting ad hoc analysis of current performance and projected operations (Philippakis and Green 1988)
- A computerized system that gives executives easy access to internal and external information relevant to their critical success factors (Watson, Rainer, and Koh 1991)
- A system that helps executives request and monitor key information from both

internal and external sources via customized presentations (Millet and Mawhinney 1992).

Beyond such definitions, it is useful to consider specific characteristics of executive information systems. Generally speaking, an EIS tends to have the following traits (Zmud 1986; Watson, Rainer, and Koh 1991; Watson et al. 1995). It is

1. Used directly by top-level executives,
2. Designed to require little or no user training,
3. Designed to be "easy" to operate, often being customized to the needs of an individual executive user,
4. Able to present information in textual, tabular, and/or graphical ways (see Figure 18.1),
5. Able to access and combine information from a broad range of sources both within and outside of the organization,
6. Able to select, filter, compress, and track critical success factor or key indicator information, and
7. Able to do status reporting, exception reporting, trend analysis, and drill-down investigation.

Drill-down investigation refers to the ability to look at more detailed information that underlies the data being displayed. Some EISs may have messaging capabilities and personal organizers (e.g., electronic calendars, reminder files). Equipping an EIS with sophisticated data analysis capabilities (e. g., involving various solvers) yields a more extensive kind of executive support system. However,

FIGURE 18.1   EIS with a Graphical User Interface

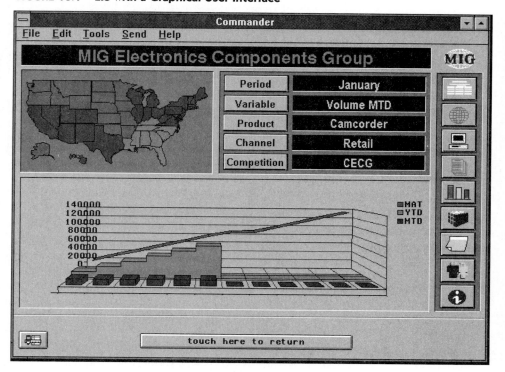

> ### DRILL DOWN
>
> "Duracell CEO C. Robert Kidder manipulated a mouse attached to his workstation to search for data comparing the performance of the Duracell hourly and salaried work forces in the U. S. and overseas. Within seconds the computer produced a crisp, clear table in colors showing that the U. S. salaried staff produced more sales per employee. He asked the computer to drill down for more data, looking for reasons for the difference. By the time he finished browsing, he had determined that Duracell had too many salespeople in Germany wasting time calling on small stores" (Main 1989, 77).

studies of top executives have found that they use computers primarily for selecting, summarizing, and presenting stored information rather than for automated analysis (Rockart and De Long 1988; Millet and Mawhinney 1992; Rainer and Watson 1995).

HOW AN EIS FITS IN AN ORGANIZATION

The typical EIS is mainly a monitoring device that supports executive decision making by providing information about certain factors or indicators of particular interest. Its customized, focused presentations of information aim to stimulate insights by helping an executive rapidly grasp the organization's current situation. The insights could take the form of recognizing problems or identifying opportunities. Figure 18.2 illustrates how a typical EIS fits into an organization.

The internal sources on which an EIS draws are usually the databases of an organization's management information systems (which may, in turn, draw on records from EDP systems). The external information sources include commercial data banks, such as those offered by market research companies, and commercial information services such as the Dow Jones News Retrieval Service. The EIS integrates information from such sources, focusing only on what interests the executive, and packages it in customized presentations that can be readily interpreted as a basis for decision making.

An executive can also obtain information from sources other than an EIS. Some of these may be computer-based, such as a corporate planning system (recall Chapter 16). Others are not computerized. Examples from within an organization include trusted advisors and staff. Some of their information may well come from local decision support systems and functional decision support systems. Other noncomputerized information sources exist in the organization's environment.

EVOLUTION OF EISs

The nature of executive information systems has been evolving from early systems with narrow capabilities used only by the very top-level executives to EISs with wider capabilities used by more levels of management (Burkan 1992). The first generation of EISs consisted mainly of electronic **briefing books** targeted at a small number of executives. They took data from a company's MISs, organized it into visual tables and graphs, and presented it directly to these executives. The information included mainly accounting and operational data. Users could drill down to

FIGURE 18.2   The Role of an EIS in Supporting Executive Decision Making

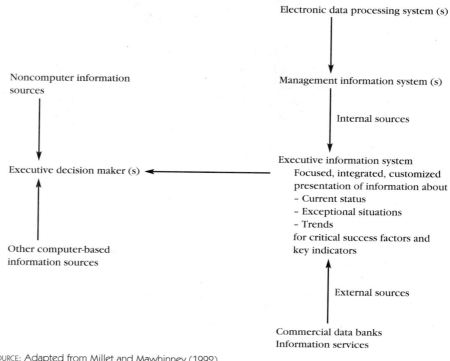

SOURCE: Adapted from Millet and Mawhinney (1992).

get greater detail in areas of particular interest. However, they could request little in the way of additional analyses. Although such EISs have been beneficial, many failures of this briefing book kind of EIS have also been reported (Burkan 1992). The main reasons seem to be that top executives are not computer-oriented, only a modest amount of really useful information was provided by early systems, and senior management lacked interest in EISs.

Trends   Three trends have changed (and are still changing) the nature of executive information systems to go beyond being electronic briefing books for the highest echelon of executives (Burkan 1992). The first trend is the recognition that top executives and lower levels of managers should get information that is consistent in form and content. Lacking this consistency, a top executive would ask questions of lower-level managers, to which they could not readily respond. The executive's questions would stem from using an EIS, but the managers would have no direct knowledge of the EIS-provided information on which the questions were based, hampering their ability to respond. Thus, there is a trend toward giving other managers access to the EIS that top executives use—allowing everyone to be on the same footing when questions are raised and problems are addressed.

Second, the trend toward networked desktop computers provides a technological mechanism for accurate sharing of information resulting from computerized analysis, as well as sharing of stored information. These analyses may be performed by solvers (e.g., statistical procedures) or take the form of expert system recommendations. This makes the traditional briefing book type of EIS much more dynamic and flexible by allowing needed information to be generated on the fly in response to current executive needs.

Third, there is the trend toward achieving competitive advantage by making information directly available to executives in related organizations (e.g., customer, supplier, and distributor organizations)—that is, the scope of an EIS is expanding to include not only internal executives, but external executives as well. A large volume of information is made accessible to customers, suppliers, and others to rummage through, manipulate, and drill into using their own selected presentation modes. This service can help secure valuable ties to those other organizations.

The result of these trends is a second generation of executive information systems. These EISs extend beyond the highest executives to additional managers. The information they furnish is under someone's control to ensure consistency. They provide greater flexibility to users in making requests and viewing responses. This greater functionality and ease of use is delivered via desktop computers networked to each other and larger computers. In effect, an EIS manages an up-to-date representation of an organization and its environment. That representation can be accessed by all affected managers to get information of critical interest (Volonino, Watson, and Robinson 1995). EISs increasingly provide analytical capabilities that can be exercised to give added value to stored information by helping to detect why things are the way they are, how they could be otherwise, and what they should be.

Perhaps the most important emerging EIS features are greater abilities to perform analyses (functioning as executive support systems), to do multimedia presentations, to communicate with other executives, and to incorporate artificial intelligence (e.g., functioning as software agents; see Figure 18.3 [Chi and Turban 1995]).

FIGURE 18.3 Personalized News Alert Compiled from External Sources by a Software Agent

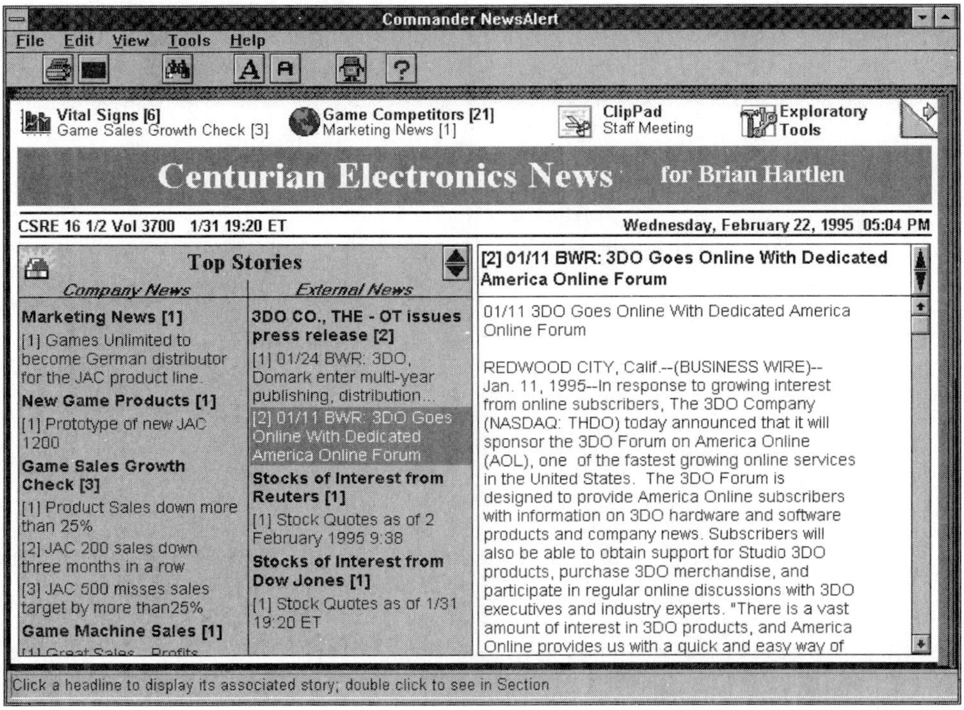

It is these features that most strongly differentiate EISs from executive's briefing books. Technologies influencing the nature of emerging EISs include client-server architectures, open architectures, information customization, and audio input/output (Burkan 1992). Each is summarized here.

Technologies   Early EISs were implemented on organizations' mainframe computers, with responses being presented to executives on terminal screens. Others transferred data from mainframes to executives' desktop computers, where it could be interrogated. As EIS usage has grown to encompass more levels of executives, EIS information has come to be stored as a set of precompiled reports on the file server

DSS IN THE NEWS

Surviving the Margin Squeeze

. . . Hertz Corp. . . . has built an agent application that helps managers make car-rental pricing decisions.

The rent-a-car business is characterized by intense price competition. . . . Industry margins have been squeezed as carmakers boosted fleet prices.

As a result, rental car companies are constantly evaluating prices to remain competitive and profitable.

Hertz installed Comshare's executive information system a couple of years ago to compile pricing information.

. . . Pricing agents had to sift through reams of data to spot trends and analyze pricing changes. In fact, Hertz' pricing database—including competitive pricing information gleaned from travel agent databases—amounts to 28,000 spreadsheets with 250,000 daily price quotes.

. . . [They] had to evaluate literally millions of price changes in the market . . . [and] needed a way to cut through that data to execute price changes in the right priority, in the right markets, quickly with a few people. . . .

With the Exception Monitor (agent application), rate data is retrieved daily and sifted according to pre-set parameters. It then delivers highlighted reports to pricing managers on significant changes made by competitors in their geographic regions.

. . . Hertz was able to get the first application up and running in about 90 days. The company continues to enhance it with new features.

Because . . . [it] enables Hertz to comb through large volumes of pricing data efficiently . . . pricing managers are able to look at more markets more often.

. . . [Managers] can also look at more types of cars. . . . When the data was overwhelming . . . managers just concentrated on looking at a few cars.

Also because pricing is reviewed regionally, nationwide price changes by competitors weren't immediately apparent. Now, Exception Monitor can find those types of changes as well. And the alert system can be set up to automatically notify upper managers when a competitor makes a dramatic pricing change.

Kathleen Doler, "Corporate, Government Users Call Exception Monitor a Useful Tool," *Investor's Business Daily,* 31 August 1994, p. A3.

of a local area network. When a user requests one of these reports, a particular presentation format (e.g., tabular or graphical) can be requested for it.

A newer approach makes use of client-server architectures, dividing the production of reports into two parts. Each client is an executive's desktop workstation,

DSS IN THE NEWS

Exceptional Help

Wouldn't it be nice if you could hire a personal assistant to act as a researcher and comb through corporate data searching for trends and useful bits of information?

. . . Software makers are now letting corporate computer users create . . . software agents . . . [that] can filter through databases or other electronic data sources and glean important, relevant information for computer users. . . . Analysts describe these agents as a form of "business intelligence". . . .

. . . What makes agent technology so important in general is there's just too . . . much information. And, with the promise of the information highway, it's just going to get worse. . . . Agents are going to be absolutely essential for us to survive through this information age that's evolving.

Software that can apply filters or exception rules to data has been around for a long time. But what's different about agent technology is it seeks out exceptions and then applies rules to those exceptions.

The first of the EIS software makers to employ agent technology is Comshare Inc. . . . [which] released its Exception Monitor, an agent-technology addition to its Commander executive information system. . . .

The Exception Monitor has three components: the monitor builder, the exception engine and desktop alerting. . . . Monitor builder . . . enables users to create exception detection rules. The exception engine is what enables the software to scan through tables of data looking for the trend the user has specified. . . . Desktop alerting routes, formats and prioritizes the communication of exception records created by the exception engine. It then delivers alerts to users according to each user's requirements and priorities.

For instance, the system could be set up to deliver a once-a-month alert for every department that is more than 5% over budget and has a monthly budget of greater than $500,000.

. . . The alert could be sent to a varied list of executives depending on which department was over budget. An exception definition can include computations and comparisons involving dozens of different pieces of information.

Initially, the Exception Monitor can only access data in Comshare's EIS software. However, the company plans to open the program up enabling it to access other data sources including a variety of database programs and text information sources such as Dow Jones and Reuters. . . .

Also, the Exception Monitor is designed to not only identify exceptions, but it also tells you exactly where the exception took place and has a tool that lets you go find it. . . .

K. Doler, "New Software Helps Decision Makers Sift Through Reams of Data," *Investor's Business Daily* 30 August 1994, p. A4.

which gathers information needed for a requested report from one or more servers. It then presents the collected information in a manner conducive to the executive's needs. Each server is typically a more powerful computer that does information storage and retrieval while enforcing security restrictions on what data can be accessed by a user.

An open architecture is one in which EIS software on client machines is designed to be compatible with diverse software (e.g., various database management systems) on servers, as well as other software on the client itself. This enables the EIS to "plug in" to huge data stores and to analytical software for modeling, forecasting, statistical analysis, and other kinds of problem solving. As the move toward more open architectures for EISs increases, it is likely that results will include much larger volumes of accessible information, easier development, faster processing, and more up-to-date information.

Information customization refers to the ability to customize an EIS for each executive user. This customization can involve information content and presentation. Content customization involves focusing and filtering, enabling an executive to see only what he or she regards as essential. For security reasons, customizing information content is especially important where an EIS serves executives in other organizations, because information that should not go beyond organizational boundaries is filtered out. Intelligent agents and expert systems have a potentially large role to play in content customization. Eventually, we can expect an executive's EIS to be on the lookout for—as well as actively search for—any information of interest to that executive, customizing it and delivering in the executive's electronic mailbox.

Direct manipulation and multimedia EIS interfaces will increasingly become the norm. An example of the latter involves audio EIS input and output. As an alternative to reading text on a computer screen, the executive will listen to it. Audio explanations and commentary will also accompany what is seen on the screen—commenting on graphs, diagrams, and video clips. As an alternative to typing, the executive will simply verbalize requests for data exploration and messages for transmission.

MOST COMMON EIS CAPABILITIES

In a study of 50 firms using executive information system, Watson, Rainer, and Koh (1991) found that the following were the most frequent EIS capabilities:

- Providing access to the current status (88%)
- Electronic mail (65%)
- Access to external databases (57%)
- Access to external news services (56%)
- Spreadsheet management (34%)
- Text management (34%)

The percentages indicate what proportion of firms use EISs having the indicated capabilities (e.g., 65% use EISs with electronic mail capabilities).

18.4 DEVELOPING AN EXECUTIVE INFORMATION SYSTEM

Executive information systems are usually built by professional developers (Watson et al. 1995). Few top executives have the time or training for successful do-it-yourself development. However, executives do initiate EIS development in the majority of cases (Watson, Rainer, and Koh 1991). In some cases EIS development is initiated by an organization's MIS department. But even then, there is usually a top executive (e.g., CEO, president, or vice president) who sponsors the EIS development effort. This **executive sponsor** oversees the development project, offers developers guidance and feedback about what the EIS should do, and conveys a strong commitment for the EIS to those affected by it (e.g., staff or managers who furnish data for it) (Rockart and De Long 1988).

SPONSORS AND DEVELOPERS

An executive sponsor's motivation for developing an EIS can be the result of pressures from both inside and outside the organization (Houdeshel and Watson 1987; Rockart and De Long 1988). The most critical internal pressure is the need for timely information, with needs for better communication, access to operational data, and rapid status updates also being important (Watson, Rainer, and Koh 1991). An increasingly competitive environment is the most critical external pressure, with other major influences being rapid change in the environment, a need to be more proactive in dealing with the environment, and increasing government regulation (Watson, Rainer, and Koh 1991). Because of difficulties in quantifying an EIS's benefits before it is developed, EIS development projects are rarely subjected to or justified by cost-benefit analysis. Instead, a sponsor's intuition about EIS impacts on decision making is usually the prime justification for beginning EIS development (Watson, Rainer, and Koh 1991).

HOW TO DISCOVER WHAT INFORMATION EXECUTIVES NEEDS

Turban (1993) offers the following guidelines for discovering what information executives need:

1. Use the critical success factor approach.
2. Quiz executives about what questions they would ask upon returning from a vacation.
3. Quiz executives about what information they would least like their competitors to obtain.
4. Conduct interviews with executives to find what information they regard as most important.
5. Identify the information requirements for the organization's short-term and long-run objectives.
6. Determine what information executives actually use from the reports they currently receive.
7. Furnish on-line access to current reports and ask how the resultant system can be customized to better meet their needs.
8. Build prototype EISs through the use of show-criticize-improve iterations.

An executive sponsor normally assigns someone to serve as an EIS's **operating sponsor.** This person manages the day-to-day activities involved in the EIS development project. In doing so, he or she interacts with executives, their staffs, professional developers from the MIS department, hardware and software vendors, and those who will be providing information to the EIS. The operating sponsor will probably be a senior executive (Rockart and De Long 1988) or manager of the MIS department (Watson, Rainer, and Koh 1991).

The EIS developer typically comprises a few people, including systems analysts, programmers, executives' staff members, and information center personnel. Collectively, it is important that the developer has both technical skills and a thorough knowledge of the organization's business. The former come from MIS department personnel. The latter comes mainly from executive staff. In addition, good interpersonal skills and an ability to work well with executives are essential in an EIS developer (Armstrong 1990). A developer's first task is to clarify the executive sponsor's motivation for wanting an EIS. Once there is an understanding of what capabilities the EIS needs to have, the developer can begin to think about what tool(s) should be selected to create the desired EIS.

DEVELOPMENT TOOLS AND METHODS

As part of tool selection, the developer determines what criteria will be used to evaluate the software alternatives. These criteria are tied to the capabilities desired by the sponsor. Tool vendors are contacted, and their offerings are evaluated. At the same time, prototype development can begin to (1) explore the accuracy and availability of data from internal and external sources, (2) give the executive sponsor some rapid feedback and a rough sense of what the envisioned EIS might be like, and (3) get a better appreciation of what tool features would be especially beneficial. The tool used in EIS prototype development may or may not be the one that is ultimately selected for building the actual EIS. In any event, it should be sufficiently flexible to readily accommodate expansion and modification of EIS outputs.

There are several commercially available software products specifically intended for EIS development. In general, they facilitate the creation of easy-to-use EIS interfaces, diverse screen designs, access to needed data, and integration with other software (e.g., a spreadsheet-management tool). As an alternative to purchasing an EIS development tool from a vendor, a developer may choose to custom-build an EIS's problem-processing system in-house (Paller and Laska 1990; Rainer, Snyder, and Watson 1992). Many organizations use a combination of in-house and vendor-supplied software in EIS development.

The development of an executive information system tends to be an ongoing, evolutionary activity (Houdeshel and Watson 1987; Rockart and De Long 1988; Burkan 1992; Watson et al. 1995). The personnel involved in developing an EIS do not simply disband once executives begin using the EIS. Instead, they continue to enhance the EIS, giving it new information-reporting and analyzing capabilities. This process includes adding new screens for users to see, deleting outdated presentations, adapting screen content and format to meet changing executive information needs, and tapping new data sources. In a study of actual EISs, the average number of information-providing screens was initially 55 (Watson, Rainer, and Koh 1991). One year after initial introduction, researchers found EISs to have more than 300 screens on average. At 3 years, researchers found the average to be nearly 500.

As executives become more familiar with an EIS, they tend to want more and more information from it.

As a successful EIS evolves, the numbers of users also tends to grow. This growth is often referred to as increasing the EIS's **spread** (Rockart and De Long 1988). When a manager becomes aware that peers or superiors are using an EIS, he or she may be more inclined to use it as well (e.g., to see what information the boss is using). In a study of organizations using EISs, the average initial spread for an EIS was found to be almost 8 users (Watson, Rainer, and Koh 1991). On average, 3 months after installation the spread nearly doubled. At the 1-year point, the average spread had increased to more than 40 users. At 2 years, the average was 70—with a steady increase beyond that point to more than 100 users.

Overall, EIS development can follow the traditional system analysis and design life cycle described in Chapter 8. However, it tends to move through the steps more rapidly and with prototyping iterations. Continuing **evolutionary development** tends to occur after the initial EIS has been installed for usage (Watson et al. 1995). Having established what EIS capabilities and features are wanted, the developer selects a development tool, while keeping in mind the fact that the EIS will need to expand and evolve over time. The tool should ideally allow fast modifications and extensions to the EIS. The development effort must, of course, have the cooperation of those in charge of data sources on which the EIS will draw.

It is important to get EISs to executives as soon as possible. A survey of EIS projects indicates that the average time required to deliver a working EIS to executives' desktops is about 5 months (Watson, Rainer, and Koh 1991). It is imperative that this first delivery works and provides useful information. After initial installation, developers can polish and further develop the EIS on a continuing basis.

18.5 LIMITATIONS ON EXECUTIVE INFORMATION SYSTEMS

Executive information systems are expensive to develop and operate. A survey of organizations using EISs indicate an average development cost of $365,000 (Watson, Rainer, and Koh 1991). This cost includes $128,000 for software, $129,000 for hardware, $90,000 for personnel, and $18,000 for training. The same survey found that annual operating costs (including ongoing development) averaged over $200,000. These costs include $46,000 for software, $29,000 for hardware, $117,000 for personnel, and $16,000 for training. However, there are large variations in EIS software prices, hardware needs, and operating costs (e. g., depending on the system size and complexity). Beyond the economic considerations, there are also technical and organizational limitations on EIS development and usage (Millet and Mawhinney 1992). Here, we summarize some of the main issues related to each.

TECHNICAL ISSUES

EIS developers face a variety of technical issues that limit what they can accomplish. The many sources of data for an EIS can reside in a wide variety of media and can be represented according to diverse formats. Ultimately, developers have to transfer each to the EIS. To accomplish the format conversions, developers may need to learn new languages and seek the assistance of data providers, data keepers, and other MIS department personnel (Armstrong 1990). **Data providers** control where the information transferred to an EIS comes from, what level of detail is eligible for transferral, and how often updates to the EIS can occur. **Data keepers** are those who create and maintain the data sources on which an EIS draws. Data providers and keepers exist for both internal and external data sources.

EIS developers must determine whether an executive request will be satisfied by drawing on contents of the EIS's own knowledge system versus drawing directly from one or more data sources maintained separately from the EIS. In the former case, the KS is refreshed from time to time, making it consistent with the data sources. This approach generally yields faster responses to executive requests but may give responses that are not as up-to-date as the data sources. The **refresh rate** may range from every time there is an executive access to some periodic cycle. The latter approach of drawing directly from data sources in responding to a query gives the most up-to-date information. However, the data sources are not generally organized in a way that permits efficient EIS retrieval, possibly resulting in an EIS that seems relatively cumbersome and slow.

In the case where the KS is loaded from data sources as a basis for responding to executive requests, there is the question of how data providers can manipulate the data before they are loaded (Armstrong 1990). Permitting such manipulation gives data providers a chance to reduce data errors, saving executives from mistakes and confusion. It also lets data providers feel less exposed to executives seeing every detail of their operations. They maintain control over the information they provide. The limitation of such manipulation is that it takes time, making the EIS knowledge system less up-to-date.

An EIS is no better than the information it delivers. It is, therefore, limited by the quality of data held in available data sources. *Quality* refers to the correctness, completeness, and currency of data. Data providers are accountable for the quality of data they make available to an EIS. One way to ensure this is to identify data providers on the screens executives see. If an executive has a question about something he or she sees on a screen, the name and phone number of the provider appear there for easy contact.

EIS limitations resulting from technical issues will be relaxed as EIS development tools become more flexible and powerful. In addition, increased availability of relevant data via commercial external data sources can help. Technical issues are also addressed by executives becoming more technically and analytically skilled. This will result, in part, from formal training of those who step into executive roles. Repeated usage of EISs is also beneficial. Studies of executives using EISs found that as the frequency and duration of EIS use increases, there are also increases in the speed of problem identification, the speed of decision making, and the extent of analysis in decision making (Leidner and Elam 1993; Elam and Leidner 1995).

ORGANIZATIONAL ISSUES

EIS limitations stemming from organizational issues can be more difficult to surmount than those from technical constraints. Three potential adverse impacts of EISs on organizations are biased agendas and time orientations, loss of managerial synchronization, and organizational distablization (Millet and Mawhinney 1992). We briefly consider each of these in turn.

It is possible that an EIS could bias an executive's agenda and/or time horizon. Information that an EIS can provide is usually only a part of the whole body of information that an executive should ideally consider (recall Figure 18.1). It accounts for only part of what an executive's full agenda should be. It tends to emphasize measurable aspects of an organization's activity. Information about less quantifiable aspects typically comes from other sources. Overreliance on an EIS can result in an executive paying too much attention to what is measurable—to whatever slice of relevant information happens to be presented by the EIS. Such channeling of attention can bias an executive's agenda, causing it to omit or gloss over important areas.

Because of the greater frequency and depth of information an EIS can supply, there may be a tendency for an executive to concentrate more on short-run, lower-level decisions, loosening or losing a grasp on the long-range, big picture. Excessive micromanagement can also disrupt the activities of lower-level managers. When they know that an executive can drill down to monitor particular aspects of their activity, they may shift their own agendas and shorten their time horizons to focus on improving the closely monitored aspects of work in favor of others or of long-term performance.

One way of synchronizing management processes is through periodic reporting. The periodic shared review of all key indicators across managerial levels lets sensing, deciding, and acting be orchestrated in phases. Although many EISs are still heavily oriented toward periodic reporting, their ability to produce ad hoc reports is very valuable for executives. However, reliance on ad hoc EIS reports has a potential for disrupting reporting cycles and the managerial activities that they synchronize. In making ad hoc requests, an executive must remember not to overlook information that is always included in predefined reports and should attempt to avoid reacting to isolated ad hoc information in a shortsighted way.

When large organizations are forced to react too quickly to internal or external circumstances, they can become destablized. By providing fast responses for spur-of-the-moment requests, an EIS gives executives information needed to react more rapidly. Without an EIS, the information is received later and reaction time is lengthened. Frequent feedback and up-to-date information are actually a major benefit. However, if an executive overreacts to EIS-supplied information by making organizational adjustments that are too frequent or too strong, damaging destabilization can result.

EIS FAILURES

Aside from the technical and organizational limits on EIS usability, there is the possibility that a particular EIS will be an outright failure. An EIS failure occurs when development fails to result in the installation of the system or in the use of an installed system to full advantage (Barrow 1990). Many of the factors that can contribute to EIS failure are outlined in Table 18.1 (Curtis 1994). By being aware of EIS limitations and the potential for EIS failure, the sponsors and developers of these systems are in a better position to fend off difficulties.

An EIS development effort that fails to satisfy users can be a setback for an organization and the individuals involved (Curtis 1994). The organization can lose a competitive edge or opportunity. It will likely be reluctant to engage into other EIS development efforts. Executives who were expecting the system to meet some of their needs may not only be disappointed, but may have no other viable alternatives for improving their decision making. Of course, the careers of development personnel may also be adversely affected by EIS failure.

Preventing an EIS failure involves many factors. Beyond an executive sponsor, it helps to have a broad base of executive support for the project. This can be

TABLE 18.1   Causes for EIS Failure

1. Management failures and/or political problems
   a. Lack of sponsorship
   b. Perception of the system as unimportant
   c. Lack of commitment by management
   d. Resistance by middle management
   e. Misrepresentation of true potential
   f. Unknown objectives or inability to define information requirements
   g. Requirement for cost-justification of the EIS
   h. Insufficient information system department resources
   i. Loss of interest by executives
   j. Unwillingness to train
2. Developer failures
   a. Failure of the system to meet objectives
      (i)   Inadequate consideration of the reasons for developing an EIS
      (ii) Inadequate analysis of needs
      (iii) Poor development-tool selection
   b. Doubtful data integrity
   c. Insufficient depth of information
   d. Slow application development
3. Technology failures
   a. Hardware
      (i)   Problems accessing data
      (ii) Inability to support required functions including simultaneous processing
      (iii) Inadequate capacity and speed, resulting in poor response time
   b. Software
      (i)   Problems accessing data
      (ii) Insufficient functions
      (iii) Lack of user-friendliness
      (iv) Inability to integrate software packages
   c. Users
      (i)   Inability to maintain databases
      (ii) Inability to learn to use the system
      (iii) Resistance to the system or its use
4. Cost
   a. In dollars, to develop
   b. In users' time, to analyze and train
   c. In political terms
5. Time
   a. Too much time to develop
   b. Too much time to train
   c. Too much time to maintain

SOURCE: Curtis (1994)

fostered through training seminars to remove executive apprehension of computer usage (Karten 1989). It is especially useful if the training includes demonstrations of sample EIS capabilities. To maintain broad-based support, the potential users should be involved in discussions about the system's intended features, capabilities, and uses. Rapid **prototyping** to give a quick, firsthand impression of the EIS's value and potential is also important for maintaining support (Armstrong 1990; Barrow 1990).

An enthusiastic operating sponsor and competent development personnel are vital for preventing EIS failure. In addition to technical and managerial participation in the developer, some advocate accountants for the design and review of internal controls to safeguard sensitive data used by an EIS (Curtis 1994). Where a thorough analysis of system requirements is lacking, the chance of EIS failure is higher (Wetherbe 1991). Prototyping can help uncover previously overlooked requirements. To meet user requirements, the EIS developer must select appropriate tools.

Appropriate data sources must also be identified. When an organization's management information systems are not extensive, then internal data sources can be inadequate for successful EIS development. Thus, both initial and ongoing cooperation of data providers and data keepers must be secured (Armstrong 1990). If the EIS cannot acquire needed data on a timely, reliable, accurate basis, what it reports to executives will be of little value. This situation should not be taken for granted, because it can be a notable source of organizational resistance to an EIS. In order for an EIS to be a continuing success, ongoing developmental support is required (Watson 1990). This support staff may well contain personnel from the initial developer.

18.6 CONDITIONS LEADING TO EXECUTIVE INFORMATION SYSTEMS

Even though there are some obstacles in the path of creating a successful executive information system, they can be circumvented and overcome. Many successful EIS implementations have been documented (Rockart and De Long 1988; Watson, Rainer, and Koh 1991; Rainer, Snyder, and Watson 1992). Investments in EISs are significantly motivated by executives' needs for improved ways of getting at and viewing information—by their needs for integrated, combined, unified information in presentation formats tailored to their individual tastes (Millet and Mawhinney

---

IMPORTANT FACTORS FOR SUCCESSFUL EIS DEVELOPMENT

EIS researchers have identified eight factors that are important for successful development of executive information systems (Rockart and De Long 1988):

1. An executive sponsor who is informed and committed
2. An operating sponsor
3. Appropriate EIS development personnel
4. Appropriate EIS development tools
5. Effective data management
6. Clear linkage of EIS to the organization's objectives
7. Management of organizational resistance
8. Management of EIS evolution and spread

1992). EISs can be the technical solution to integrating data from diverse internal and external sources, providing a unified reporting system that disguises the fact of multiple underlying data sources.

Rather than being pulled by executive needs, the impetus for developing an EIS can be a push from the technology side. That is, the MIS department, the vendor of an EIS tool, or a consulting firm can be the original advocate of an EIS development project (Watson, Rainer, and Koh 1991; Millet and Mawhinney 1992; Watson et al 1995). For instance, the MIS department may see an EIS project as a way to help coordinate its MISs, as a way to learn and experiment with new technology, or as a means for gaining greater access to top executives, or as a way to expand or retain its current budget level. The vendor of an EIS development tool may offer special introductory pricing. A consultant may develop an EIS at little or no charge as a way to gain entry into an organization, increasing its prospects for subsequent contracted work.

As an organization becomes larger and its environment becomes more fast-paced and complicated, the pressure for an EIS becomes greater. In such a setting, it can help meet the executive need for frequent monitoring of operations and details to shore up the problem solving that goes into decision making. An EIS can be used to help implement a competitive strategy, project an organizational image of being technologically up-to-date, solidify ties with top executives in consumer and supplier organizations, or justify and sell executive decisions. It may give an organization an edge in attracting and retaining executives. As the number and sophistication of EIS users grow, so does the benefit that EISs can provide to an organization. Finally, a successful EIS fosters the development of extensions to that EIS or of new EISs within an organization.

18.7 SUMMARY

Executive information systems are increasingly important means for supporting the decision making of top executives. An EIS allows an executive to request information directly that portrays trends, highlights exceptions, and stimulates insights as a basis for high-level decision making. The EIS responses are presented in ways attuned to an executive's individual needs and tastes. Because it is designed specifically to support executives, an EIS permits executives to review information needed for decision making in a faster and more focused way than pouring through conventional reports provided by management information systems.

As a basis for building an EIS, various approaches can be used to discern the information a top executive needs. These approaches include the by-product, null, total study, key indicator, and critical success factor methods. Critical success factors are those areas of activity where satisfactory results will ensure that organizationai performance is competitive. To support decision making, executives continually need to receive information about the current status of performance in these areas. Generally, this involves information from both internal and external sources, held in multiple MISs and on multiple computers, much of which is short-term and subject to rapid change, oriented toward monitoring current performance and/or building for the future.

In being created to meet such information needs, today's EISs tend to have several common traits, including sufficient ease of use to be employed directly by top executives; also, it can draw on a wide variety of data sources; can deal with critical success factor information; can present information in ways customized to executive desires; can perform reporting of status, trends, and exceptions; and allows drill-down investigation. Emerging trends in EIS characteristics include broadening accessibility to managers below the top executive level, increasing abilities for electronic communication and automated analysis of information, and provision of EIS access for executives in certain external organizations (e.g., customers or suppliers).

Executive information systems are usually built by professional developers, with general oversight by an executive sponsor. The development task can be greatly facilitated by various commercial software offerings specifically designed to function as EIS development tools. Rapid EIS prototyping, quickly traversing a life cycle of system analysis and design, and evolutionary improvement are advocated in the development of EISs. Evolutionary EIS development requires the ongoing availability of development personnel to implement EIS extensions.

There are various technical limitations on what an EIS can do. There are potential organizational liabilities that can limit the value of an EIS. There is also the possibility of outright EIS failure. Preventing such failure depends on a variety of factors, including enthusiastic sponsorship, cultivation of executive users' interest, a skilled developer, appropriate development tool(s), accessible data sources, and ongoing development support. Successful EIS development efforts pay close attention to such factors. As an organization and its environment become increasingly complex and dynamic, the pressure for successful implementation of this kind of decision support system grows.

▲ IMPORTANT TERMS

briefing book	executive sponsor
critical success factor	key indicator
data keeper	operating sponsor
data provider	prototyping
drill-down investigation	refresh rate
evolutionary development	spread
executive information system	

▲ APPLICATION TO THE PRATT & WHITNEY CASE

1. What decision did the Fleet Management System support?
2. What information did the Fleet Management System provide to its users?
3. Why was the EIS needed to provide information to users given that it already existed in three production systems?
4. What interface features were especially important for this EIS?
5. Identify some of the critical success factors tracked by this EIS.
6. What information might the user see during drill-down investigation of a particular jet engine model?
7. What additional useful features could be incorporated into the Fleet Management System through the use of intelligent software agents?
8. Who was the executive sponsor for this EIS?
9. What development tool was used?

10. Why was a prototype, evolutionary approach to development used?
11. What appears to be happening to the EIS's spread at Pratt & Whitney?
12. Describe the main benefits that resulted from installing this EIS.

▲ REVIEW QUESTIONS

1. How do information needs of top executives differ from those of other managers?
2. What approaches can be used to determine and satisfy executive information needs?
3. What is the key indicator approach to furnishing executive information?
4. What are critical success factors and how are they relevant to EISs?
5. How do the two categories of critical success factors differ?
6. What is an executive information system?
7. What are the common capabilities that an EIS has?
8. How is drill-down investigation beneficial to an executive?
9. What are the internal and external sources of information for an EIS?
10. What is an electronic briefing book?
11. What three trends are changing the nature of EISs?
12. In what ways have EISs gone beyond electronic briefing books?
13. How is client-server architecture being used in EISs?
14. What are the advantages of an EIS with an open architecture?
15. What are the advantages of an EIS that does extensive information customization?
16. Who typically builds an EIS?
17. What kinds of sponsors can be involved in an EIS development project, what does each do, and why is each important?
18. What motives can underlie the launching of an EIS development project?
19. What skills should an EIS developer have?
20. In what ways is prototype EIS development useful?
21. How does the spread for a successful EIS tend to change?
22. What does an EIS developer do after the initial installation of the system?
23. How do data providers and data keepers differ?
24. What technical issues limit EIS development?
25. What is meant by the refresh rate for an EIS? What happens if it is too slow or too fast?
26. What are potential liabilities to an organization from using an EIS?
27. What are common causes of EIS failure?
28. For what kinds of organizations are EISs potentially most valuable?

▲ DISCUSSION TOPICS

1. How does an EIS differ from other kinds of DSSs?
2. Why is an EIS preferable to MISs as a source of information for top executives?
3. What are relative advantages and disadvantages of each of the following methods: by-product, null, key indicator, total study, and critical success factor?
4. In the absence of an EIS, how does an executive get the information he or she needs?
5. Discuss potential advantages and drawbacks of including an extensive assortment of solvers in an EIS.

6. Give an example of a situation where it could be desirable to provide an EIS to executives in a different company.
7. What would be the main features of an EIS intended to support (a) a group of executives working on a common decision, (b) an organization of executives working on the same or interrelated decisions, and (c) multiple executives negotiating among themselves about some issue of shared interest?
8. Discuss the interplay between identifying a developer, identifying a development tool, and creating a prototype.
9. Sometimes prototyping is regarded as very different than traditional systems analysis and design. Discuss the compatibilities that can exist for these two views of development.
10. What features should an EIS development tool have?
11. Why is cost-benefit analysis often difficult for EISs?
12. What roles might accountants play in EIS development?
13. Discuss security issues related to building and using an EIS.
14. Discuss the relative advantages and disadvantages of an EIS that provides information from its own KS versus one that dynamically collects it from data sources on an as-needed basis.
15. As the developer of an EIS, what steps would you take to ensure that the project does not result in failure?
16. Does it make a difference whether the impetus for EIS development is executive pull or technological push? Explain.

▲ REFERENCES

Armstrong, D. 1990. The people factor is EIS success. *Datamation*. (April 1).

Barrow, C. 1990. Implementing an executive information system: Seven steps for success. *Journal of Information Systems Management*. (Spring).

Burkan, W. C. 1991. *Executive information systems*. New York: Van Norstrand Reinhold.

————. 1992. The new role for "executive" information systems. *I/S Analyzer,* 30, no. 1.

Chi, R. T. and E. Turban. 1995. Distributed intelligent executive information systems *Decision Support Systems*. 14, no. 2.

Curtis, M. B. 1994. The accountant's contribution to executive information systems. *Journal of End User Computing* 6, no. 3.

Elam, J. J. and D. G. Leidner. 1995. EIS adoption, use, and impact: the executive perspective. *Decision Support Systems* 14, no. 2.

Houdeshel, G., and H. J. Watson. 1987. The management information and decision support (MIDS) system at Lockheed-Georgia. *MIS Quarterly* 11, no. 1.

Karten, N. 1989. Why executives don't compute. *Information Strategy: The Executive's Journal* (Fall).

Leidner, D. G, and J. J. Elam. 1993. Executive information systems: Their impact on executive decision making. *Journal of Management Information Systems* 10, no. 3.

Main, J. 1989. At last, software CEOs can use. *Fortune* (March 13).

McLeod, R., Jr., and J. W. Jones. 1986. Making executive information systems more effective. *Business Horizons* (September).

Millet, I., and C. H. Mawhinney. 1992. Executive information systems—A critical perspective. *Information and Management* 23, no. 1.

Paller, A., and R. Laska. 1990. *The EIS book*. Homewood, Ill.: Dow Jones–Irwin.

Philippakis, A. S., and G. I. Green. 1988. An architecture for organization-wide decision support systems. *Proceedings of the Ninth International Conference on Information systems*. Minneapolis, Minn. (November).

Rainer, R. K., Jr., C. A. Snyder, and H. J. Watson. 1992. The evolution of executive information system software. *Decision Support Systems* 8, no. 4.

Rainer, R. K., Jr., and H. J. Watson. 1995. What does it take for successful executive information systems? *Decision Support Systems* 14, no. 2.

Rockart, J. F. 1979. Chief executives define their own data needs. *Harvard Business Review* (March).

Rockart, J. F., and D. W. De Long. 1988. *Executive support systems, the emergence of top management computer use.* Homewood, Ill.: Dow Jones–Irwin.

Rockart, J. F., and M. E. Treacy. 1982. The CEO goes on-line. *Harvard Business Review* (January).

Turban, E. 1993. *Decision support and expert systems: Management support systems,* 3rd ed. New York: MacMillan.

Volonino, L., H. J. Watson, and S. Robinson. 1995. Using EIS to respond to dynamic business conditions. *Decision Support Systems* 14, no. 2.

Watson, H. 1990. Avoiding hidden EIS pitfalls. *Computerworld* (December 4).

Watson, H. J., R. K. Ranier, Jr., and C. E. Koh. 1991. Executive information systems: A framework for development and a survey of current practices. *MIS Quarterly* (March).

Watson, H. J., R. T. Watson, S. Singh, and D. Holmes. 1995. Development practices for executive information systems: findings of a field study. *Decision Support Systems* 14, no. 2.

Wetherbe, C. J. 1991. Executive information requirements: Getting it right. *MIS Quarterly* (March).

Zmud, R. W. 1986. Supporting senior executives through decision support technologies: A review and directions for future research. In *Decision Support Systems: A Decade in Perspective,* edited by E. McLean and H. Sol. Amsterdam: Elsevier.

Chapter 19

KNOWLEDGE-BASED ORGANIZATIONS

INSIGHTS

BOEING: SYSTEMS TO LINK AND COORDINATE KNOWLEDGE WORKERS

Overview

Boeing Co. officials didn't need the 50th anniversary of the end of World War II to remind them of the old days of airplane production. A walk around Boeing's shop floor is a nostalgia trip in itself, as the company's approach to building aircraft hasn't changed much since the mid-1940s.

"What we've had up to now is a process designed for a time when we had one customer, the federal government, and we were building B-29s that had almost no variables," explained Douglas Frederick, an information systems support manager at Boeing.

About 16 months ago, Boeing's commercial airplane group in Renton, Wash., launched a radical three-year redesign of the "configuration" process, or the way it produces aircraft tailored to its customers' needs. The process starts with the initial customer contact and continues through after-sale support.

The redesign effort is employing a variety of software technologies to break down the barriers between functional departments and eliminate bottlenecks that lengthen the production cycle and add unnecessary costs.

Less than halfway into the multimillion-dollar project, it is too early to quantify benefits, Frederick says. He adds, however, that Boeing ultimately expects to reduce its time-to-market by 50% and its production costs by 25%.

The reengineered process recognizes that Boeing's business is characterized by multiple customers, thousands of product features and options such as the number of aircraft seats, galleys, engines and lavatories, and countless on-the-fly engineering changes.

Ron Woodard, the commercial airplane group's president, has said that overhauling the configuration process offers "the single biggest opportunity to get quality up and cost and cycle down."

Current Approach

The current process begins when the customer decides on the configuration of its new airplane and signs a contract, according to Frederick, one of the project directors. At that time, a customer identification number is assigned to the engineering drawings.

Each functional group—such as engineering, manufacturing and shipping—has its own bill of materials, or list of parts required for that job.

Every time a drawing or related document passes between these groups, the different bills of materials have to be reconciled. Each department has its own computers and business systems, some of them decades old.

When the original engineering bill of materials goes to production, for example, it has to be broken down line by line, converted into the codes and formats used with that department's systems and manually reentered to create a new bill of materials.

Boeing officials say a typical customer order might create up to 13 renditions of the original parts list and pass through dozens of different computer systems, making the process or reconciling lists extremely costly and time-consuming.

Another problem involves the customer ID number. If parts are changed for any customer's plans or an airplane's position on the production line is changed, the drawings must be "retabbed" with a modified customer ID.

Continued

New Approach

The new process does away with the system of reconciling different parts lists and carrying customer IDs on drawings.

It makes "product data manager" software the single source of all product information, which is made available to engineering, manufacturing, tooling, planning and other divisions on an as-needed basis. With everyone using a single database, changes need only be noted once, saving considerable time and expense.

"The PDM will keep track of every part and every design change," said Frederick. "It replaces all the old bills of materials and keeps track of the customer ID numbers."

Another enabling type of software, an "enterprise resource planner," will manage the entire work flow, automatically routing documents as needed from parts ordering, to purchasing, planning and scheduling. . . .

Two other types of software also play key roles in Boeing's new configuration system. A "process planner" is used by manufacturing engineers to create a computerized instruction guide for building every plane. The how-to plan covers every part number, every individual assembly task and the order of those tasks. . . . A "linkage shop view" system allows users in any department to pull information from the product data manager, computer-aided design system or any other Boeing database and view all that data on a single computer screen. . . . [These] two software products were supplied by Cimlinc Inc. of Itasca, Ill., under a $6.8 million contract.

"Typically, building a plane involves integrating information from multiple places," noted Richard Hahn, a Cimlinc vice president. "Our software creates the links between the application and the database."

"Before, it might take two or three days for someone to get an engineering drawing, and very often, nobody bothered to document (where all the drawings were and who had made changes in them). . . . Now, everyone gets immediate access to the information they need in a format they can use."

The overall computing environment for Boeing's new business process is a distributed "client-server" model in which applications are split between specialized network servers and desktop personal computers. Nearly all the computers run the Unix operating system.

Condensed quotation from M. Mehler, "Boeing Leaves Past Behind With Production Redesign," *Investor's Business Daily* 23 May 1995, p. A8.

LEARNING OBJECTIVES

The Boeing case outlines systems of the kind that will be of increasing importance in the transition to knowledge-based organizations. These are organizations where the flows of knowledge among participants are regarded as the foundation for organizational productivity and success. Participants in such organizations are first and foremost regarded as knowledge workers, regardless of whether they are top executives or operating personnel and regardless of their functional areas of activity (e.g., engineering, manufacturing, or planning). These knowledge workers need to be linked, supported, and coordinated so that their highly interrelated decisions (and other knowledge-processing activities) fit well together, avoiding ineffi-ciencies, inconsistencies, and chaos. Computer-based technology has a major role to play in the support of knowledge workers.

The systems being developed by Boeing illustrate ways in which computers can support knowledge workers through desktop computers that are connected to large knowledge storehouses. This effectively links knowledge workers by joint partic-ipation in creating and using the flow of knowledge that accompanies customized aircraft production. The computer support even goes so far as to coordinate the entire stream of interrelated decision making by the knowledge workers involved in the complex task of producing an airplane. Keep the Boeing case in mind as you read this chapter's view of knowledge-based organizations.

After studying this chapter you should be able to

1. Describe the broad outlines of emerging knowledge-based organizations.
2. Discuss the challenges and opportunities that will face knowledge workers in the years ahead.
3. Understand the broad outlines of the emerging global knowledge society.

Exercises at the end of the chapter will help you reinforce and check on the meeting of these objectives.

19.1 INTRODUCTION

Over the past 40 years, advances in computer-based technology have had an impor-tant impact on the way in which organizations operate. Over the next few decades, such advances will revolutionize the way in which we think about organizations. The very nature of organizations is changing from an emphasis on working with materials to an emphasis on working with knowledge (Holsapple and Whinston 1987; Drucker 1988). We will eventually come to view work with material goods as a secondary or almost incidental aspect of an organization's mission. It will be lit-tle more than an automatic consequence of knowledge processing. Furthermore, managing an organization's human and financial resources will also become exer-cises in knowledge management.

The knowledge-based perspective of decision making and decision support, as laid out in prior chapters, is symptomatic of a major shift in the way in which orga-nizations are viewed. This shift is still in a relatively early stage, but it will strongly

---

KNOWLEDGE-BASED ORGANIZATIONS

In predicting the coming of a new kind of organization, management scholar and social philosopher Peter Drucker (1988, 45, 50) states that ". . . the typical business will be knowledge based, an organization composed largely of specialists who direct and dis-cipline their own performance through organized feedback from colleagues, cus-tomers, and headquarters. . . . The center of gravity in employment is moving fast from manual and clerical workers to knowledge workers. . . . To remain competitive—maybe even to survive—businesses will have to convert themselves into organizations of knowledgeable specialists."

A PERVASIVE PERSPECTIVE

". . . [The] context [for exploring knowledge management] is extremely extensive; it encompasses every function from research to service, including marketing as well as engineering, and design as well as manufacturing . . . [M]anagers involved in *any* aspect of product or process development [can and need] to view every day's activities from the perspective of knowledge management and growth. Products are physical manifestations of knowledge, and their worth largely, if not entirely, depends on the value of the knowledge they embody. The management of knowledge, therefore, is a skill, like financial acumen, and managers who understand and develop it will dominate competitively . . . [F]lows of appropriate knowledge into and within companies enable them to develop competitively advantageous capabilities." — **Dorothy Leonard-Barton** in *Wellsprings of Knowledge*, p. xiii.

affect the management of organizations, decision manufacturing processes, decision support needs, and even the fabric of society. In a most fundamental sense, organizations will increasingly be regarded as joint human-computer knowledge-processing systems. Human participants in these systems, from the most highly skilled to the least-skilled positions, can be regarded as **knowledge workers** (Holsapple and Whinston 1987; Drucker 1988, 1994). Collectively, they will work with many types of knowledge in a variety of ways and with various objectives.

The knowledge-management efforts of these knowledge workers will be aided and supported by computers in ways we have seen in earlier chapters as well as in ways just beginning to be apparent. Computer coworkers will not only relieve us of the menial, routine, and repetitive. They will not only be reactive, responding to users' explicit requests. They will also actively recognize needs, meet some of those

DSS IN THE NEWS

Developing Knowledge Management Expertise

. . . McKinsey & Co., Anderson Consulting, Price Waterhouse, Gemini Consulting and other big consultancies are developing knowledge management expertise internally and with clients.

Ernst & Young recently started a Knowledge Management Practice and opened a Center for Business Knowledge in Cleveland last year. Two dozen major U.S. corporations have joined its new research consortium on the topic.

Moreover, some 200 top executives jammed a Planning Forum/Ernst & Young conference in Boston last fall. Another is set for November.

Interest is worldwide: Kao, the Japanese soap and detergent giant, is a pioneer manager of knowledge. "The Japanese Procter and Gamble" is noted for savvy use of expert systems and open decision-making.

J. Maglitta, "Smarten up!" *Computerworld*, 5 June 1995, p. 85.

needs on their own, stimulate insights, offer advice, and facilitate knowledge flows. They will highly leverage an organization's uniquely human skills, such as intuition, creative imagination, value judgment, and the cultivation of effective interpersonal relationships.

The potential of such **knowledge-based organizations** for increased human productivity will be realized to the extent that these organizations are successfully inaugurated and managed. This prospect impacts each of the traditional functional areas of management (e.g., marketing or operations management) in two significant ways. First, it presents an opportunity to enhance the performance of practitioners in each functional area. Second, it presents challenges to investigators in each functional area, because they are now confronted with a new kind of organization. This chapter provides a characterization of knowledge-based organizations that can serve as a foundation for understanding these opportunities and chal-

ORGANIZATIONS OF THE FUTURE

In predicting the nature of business organizations for the 21st century, Applegate, Cash, and Miles (1988) indicate that emerging technologies will expand the options managers have for structuring and operating their businesses. New organizational structures will become possible. New management processes will arise. New strategies for human resource management will develop. Their predictions are consistent with the idea of knowledge-based organizations sketched here. Specifically, they predict that emerging technologies will permit the following.

Organizational Structure
- Large organizations will have benefits previously enjoyed by small ones and small organizations will realize benefits previously in the domain of larger ones.
- Organizations (even large ones) will be able to operate with more flexible, dynamic structures.
- Distinctions between decentralized and centralized control in organizations will become fuzzy.
- The focus of work will be on task forces dealing with projects.

Management Processes
- Decision processes will become more explicit and well defined.
- Formal control systems will not need to be embedded in an organization's communication relationships.
- More creative thinking will be enabled throughout an organization.
- An organization's history, experience, and expertise will be retained despite turnover in personnel.

Human Resources
- Workers will be better trained in knowledge management, more autonomous, and more mobile.
- The work environment will be intellectually engaging.
- Job descriptions involving narrow task definitions will decline.
- Compensation will more closely reflect contributions.

Such changes will make the business world a very different place than it is today.

lenges. It also gives a basis for speculating on the nature of tomorrow's decision support systems—particularly for multiple participants and top executives.

19.2 KNOWLEDGE WORKERS

Knowledge workers are concerned with procuring, storing, organizing, maintaining, creating, analyzing, presenting, distributing, and applying knowledge in order to meet an organization's goals. Some knowledge workers may be involved with all these aspects of knowledge management, whereas others specialize in one or a few of these activities. There are also various types of knowledge to be managed: descriptive, procedural, reasoning, linguistic, presentation, and assimilative knowledge. Here, too, knowledge workers may specialize.

Figure 19.1 portrays the activities of a knowledge worker with respect to various types of knowledge. Each type of knowledge is susceptible to each of the knowledge-management activities. At the same time, one or more of the various types of knowledge are typically used in carrying out a particular activity. For instance, procedural knowledge is the basis for analysis; when descriptive knowledge is the subject of analysis, facts or expectations about the organization and its environment may be derived. The maximization of knowledge worker productivity is a paramount issue whose resolution lies in technological advances, appropriate training, and an administrative atmosphere that fosters cooperation among knowledge workers.

TECHNOLOGICAL ADVANCES

On the technology front, several crucial footholds have already been established beyond the apparently never-ceasing per-dollar improvements in hardware speeds and storage capacities. One of these is the technology for intercomputer communications, including local area networks, mainframe-micro linkages, and global networks. Continued development of this technology is a key for promoting knowl-

FIGURE 19.1 Activities of a Knowledge Worker

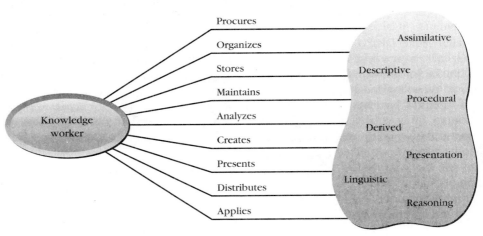

Types of knowledge

edge sharing, cooperative (and consistent) problem solving among knowledge workers, distributed knowledge processing, and coordinated decision making.

Another crucial technological element for the realization of knowledge-based organizations is the existence of software tools designed specifically for use by knowledge workers. Each tool brings with it an environment for working with (i.e., managing) knowledge of various kinds. Knowledge workers do not have the technical skills of computer professionals, yet they need tools to support their knowledge-management activities. By allowing knowledge workers to handle directly many of their own needs, such tools can enable an organization's computer professionals to concentrate on the most technically demanding tasks, such as developing extensive customized software systems. Although the whole area of generic software tools for knowledge workers is still at an early state, the direction of its evolution should be clear in light of the preceding chapters.

Knowledge-management software tools can be examined from several interrelated perspectives, including capacities, capabilities, and convenience. This software will increasingly be designed so that it is the hardware rather than the software that imposes practical capacity limits. To the extent that the software does impose limits, those limits will tend to be so high that they do not interfere with needs of the most demanding knowledge workers. That is, they will not inhibit the convenient exercise of software capabilities.

The capabilities of a knowledge-management tool should be assessed in terms of their *breadth* and *depth*. Breadth refers to how many classes of diverse knowledge-management tasks the software can peform and/or support: storing procedural knowledge, analyzing descriptive knowledge, and so forth. Depth refers to the extent of the capabiltiies within each class, ranging from superficial to comprehensive. The knowledge-management techniques presented in Part Three provide a background for gauging both the depth and breadth of a tool's capabilities.

We should expect the capabilities of knowledge-management tools to continue to increase in both breadth and depth; that is, they will become increasingly flexible. It is likely that tools will increasingly integrate many traditionally separate functionalities in a synergistic way, so that the total effect is much more than the sum of the individual effects and the existence of one functionality in no way constrains the exercise of other functionalities. The result will be a generation of knowledge-management tools that enable knowledge workers to work with a single tool for solving a wide variety of computer-based knowledge-management activities.

Such a tool sacrifices nothing relative to the depth of traditional stand-alone software and actually gains through the synergy of its breadth. It effectively avoids the inconvenience of switching among multiple tools in order to accomplish a task. It furnishes a uniform user interface regardless of the activity being exercised. Perhaps most important is the growth path it offers to knowledge workers. Starting out with the simple aspects of one functionality, workers can grow into its deeper capabilities as needed. The growth path can also progress horizontally into other functionalities supported by the tool. Knowledge workers will be free from dead-end tools and tool fragmentation.

Although knowledge-management software will enable knowledge workers to solve many of their own needs, it will not be a substitute for the professional application systems developer. Professional developers will support knowledge workers by providing them with customized application systems for record-keeping and decision support. These are systems whose scale, complexity, performance, integrity, or security characteristics would not allow them to be constructed by end users in a timely, cost-effective manner.

TRAINING

Rudimentary computer literacy is, of course, a necessary foundation for knowledge worker training. It is rapidly becoming just as much a basic skill as reading, writing, and mathematics. But basic computer literacy by itself is insufficient preparation for knowledge workers.

If truly knowledge-based organizations are to be realized, people must have a keen appreciation of the very nature of knowledge, including a taxonomy of knowledge types, a repertoire of knowledge-representation techniques, a familiarity with knowledge-processing methods, and an understanding of knowledge utilization in solving problems in the traditional functional areas of management. This formal study of the fundamentals of knowledge is concerned more with practicalities than abstract issues.

The cube in Figure 19.2 suggests possibilities that can confront knowledge workers as they attempt to solve a problem. Workers must select and utilize some combination of one or more cells. As the practicalities of knowledge are more fully comprehended, they will become an essential aspect of knowledge worker training. They will also stimulate the appearance of new kinds of facilities in knowledge-management software tools. Knowledge worker training must obviously encompass the subject of advanced knowledge-management software tools. This subject includes not only tool characteristics, but also tool selection and effective tool application within each of the functional areas of management. Finally, we note that training for each knowledge worker will be a continuing effort that will itself be aided by technological advances (Drucker 1994; Whinston 1994).

FIGURE 19.2   Knowledge-Management Possibilities

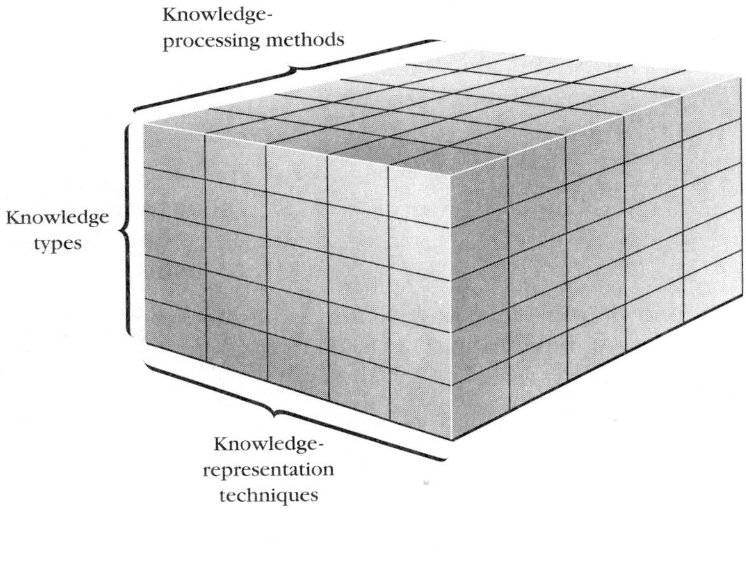

DSS IN THE NEWS

A Tangled Unusable Thicket

Anyone with Notes experience knows that even a single discussion database can quickly become a tangled unusable thicket. "Be prepared to invest a lot of energy on the quality of information," Goldman [CIO of The Chase Manhattan Bank NA] warns.

To cope, Anderson Consulting, Buckman Laboratories and others have created positions for "knowledge managers" responsible for knowledge base quality and content.

J. Maglitta, "Smarten up!" *Computerworld*, 5 June 1995, p. 86.

COOPERATION

In addition to technological advances and proper training, cooperation among knowledge workers will be essential to collective knowledge worker effectiveness and productivity with respect to overall organizational goals. This cooperation must be manifest in the sharing of knowledge, in a coordinated reasonable division of labor among the knowledge workers, and in the coordinated timing of knowledge-processing tasks.

The sharing of an organization's knowledge resources among knowledge workers is essential from two standpoints. First, it avoids duplication of effort in knowl-

CONTINUOUS RENEWAL

". . . [There are] a few characteristics that, repeated throughout the organization and embedded in the actions of its managers, create an atmosphere for continuous renewal.

The first characteristic is an *enthusiasm for knowledge*—that is, for the knowledge content of every activity. The managers respect and encourage the accumulation of knowledge as a legitimate undertaking and one for which they are responsible . . .

The second characteristic . . . is a *drive to stay ahead in knowledge,* to surf the waves of technological innovation . . . This drive to access the latest and best knowledge, wherever it originates, keeps people *listening*—another absolutely critical skill. . . .

A third characteristic is the *tight coupling among complementary skills*. . . . The nature of the knowledge reservoirs to be linked will undoubtedly change in the future. . . . However, we will still need specialists and groups . . . who concentrate on developing particular knowledge bases. . . . [O]rganizations will continue to need tight coordination among self-reliant, knowledge-rich groups and individuals . . .

The fourth characteristic is an appreciation for the *iterative, return-loop nature of all activities*. . . . [M]anagers . . . know that they can never walk away from that activity with the assumption that it is now perfected. . . . Closely related to this acknowledgement. . . . is that the emphasis on *higher-order learning*. . . . For every activity the manager asks, What is the potential knowledge-building import of this action?"

—**Dorothy Leonard-Barton** in *Wellsprings of Knowledge*, pp. 261–265.

edge collection and maintenance. Second, it promotes consistent decision making, because all knowledge workers have access to the same body of knowledge (or subsets thereof). The shared knowledge may be centralized and/or distributed. In any case, knowledge-management software must be capable of ensuring the integrity of shared knowledge, enforcing security restrictions that apply to various classes of knowledge workers, and supporting reasonable access speeds. Furthermore, the knowledge workers must be motivated to exercise these software capabilities conscientiously.

The division of labor among knowledge workers has significant implications for the total productivity of the workers. A division along traditional functional lines will probably continue to be prominent. However, interdisciplinary knowledge workers will become increasingly apparent in knowledge-based organizations. These people are functional generalists rather than functional specialists. Division of labor will also come to be viewed from the complementary, yet very different, perspective suggested by Figure 19.2. Knowledge workers will specialize in handling certain types of knowledge, in utilizing certain knowledge-representation techniques, and in exercising particular knowledge-processing methods. That is, different classes of knowledge workers will be experts in working with a certain cell or group of cells in the knowledge cube represented in Figure 19.2.

The streamlined coordination of knowledge-processing tasks is of obvious importance. This coordination must be based on a valid (and perhaps dynamically changing) prioritization of problems. The assignment of tasks to workers must, of course, match task requirements with knowledge workers' skills. The scheduling or timing of knowledge-processing tasks for solving these problems should be designed to avoid knowledge worker contention for the same resource and to promote parallel knowledge worker activity in the solving of each high-priority problem. Automatic triggering mechanisms will exist to notify each knowledge worker involved in solving a problem when progress has reached the point where that worker can begin to take action.

According to Drucker (1988), knowledge workers will tend to operate more in **task forces** than conventional departments. A task force will involve specialists from various functions (e.g., research, manufacturing, marketing, or personnel) who work together to accomplish some task (e.g., taking a product from the idea stage to the market stage). Each participant in the task force brings special knowledge and knowledge-handling skills to the combined effort. When a task force of knowledge workers needs to be formed is an open question. The structure of a task force (e.g., group versus more complex organization), the assignment of specific knowledge workers to it, and its regulations (e.g., incentive and compensation schemes, evaluation mechanisms, leadership controls) are also open issues—perhaps needing to be addressed on a case-by-case basis. In any event, knowledge workers will be expected to exhibit greater self-discipline and assume greater responsibility for relationships and communications than is currently the case in a typical organization (Drucker 1988).

19.3 KNOWLEDGE-BASED ORGANIZATIONS

Having focused on the characteristics of the knowledge workers who will populate tomorrow's knowledge-based organizations, we can now step back to view the overall landscape of such an organization. The dominant technological features of

KNOWLEDGE MANAGEMENT IN THE WORKPLACE

"What does an organization managed by and for the growth of knowledge look like? How do managers think and behave in a learning organization? What activities create the knowledge assets? There are probably no perfect examples. In fact, many institutions have knowledge management and learning capabilities. However, to penetrate the mist . . . that enshrouds the term *knowledge management,* let us place a real organization under the microscope. Chaparral Steel, a minimill that is the tenth largest U.S. steel producer, offers an interesting example of a company focused on knowledge management. . . . The steel production process is a weird combination of impressive brute physical force and highly skilled finesse. How can one apply a fragile, academic sounding term . . . to a production facility where raw physical power so predominates and where productivity is such a major concern that every second counts? Do these people really think about "knowledge management"? They do, from CEO down to the line operator who is standing, stopwatch in palm, persistently trying to better the speed of the rolling mills—just because he thinks it is possible. . . .

Knowledge management demands the ability to move knowledge in all directions—up, down, across. At Chaparral, knowledge flows readily . . . because considerable effort has been made to minimize both vertical and horizontal barriers. . . . Chaparral competes through constantly improving production processes. . . . Decisions about production methodologies are pushed down to the lowest possible supervisory level, "where the knowledge is." . . . Lead operators are selected for their knowledge transmitting as well as knowledge creating skills. . . . Work is structured with the objective of disseminating knowledge. . . . Creating knowledge requires constant pushing beyond the familiar, and Chaparral employees are skilled experimenters. . . . An important source of knowledge is found in other organizations. Chaparral employees constantly benchmark and scan the world for technical expertise.

. . . Chaparral Steel . . . claims as a core capability its ability to transform technology rapidly into product . . . [This involves] competencies in the form of: (1) people's *skills* and (2) the knowledge embedded in *physical systems.* In addition to these important knowledge repositories, capabilities have two other highly interdependent dimensions that channel and control knowledge: (3) *managerial systems* that support and reinforce the growth of knowledge through carefully designed education and incentives and (4) *values* that serve to screen and encourage or discourage the accumulation of different kinds of knowledge." —**Dorothy Leonard-Barton** in *Wellsprings of Knowledge,* pp. 5, 7, 10–12, 27.

this landscape are local workstations, support centers, communications paths, and distributed knowledge storehouses (Holsapple and Whinston 1987). These technological components, coupled with organizational infrastructure, will greatly influence what knowledge workers can accomplish.

MAIN COMPONENTS IN THE TECHNOLOGICAL INFRASTRUCTURE

A local **workstation** is the immediate computer-based extension to a knowledge worker's own innate knowledge-management capabilities. The type of knowledge-management software that resides at a particular workstation depends on the nature of the knowledge worker. It may be a customized application built with some knowledge-management tool or it may be a tool itself. In any case, the workstation software will increasingly be based on technical advances in decision support systems, software integration, artificial intelligence, and organizational computing.

Communication paths enable workstations—and hence knowledge workers— to interact with each other. They also allow a workstation to request and receive knowledge-management assistance from other workstations or from various support centers. Thus, a communications capability is a crucial aspect of the workstation software.

A **support center** is a computer that can provide services to one or more workstations. These centers are typically equipped to carry out processing that would be inefficient or infeasible for a particular workstation or some group of workstations. A local workstation's use of a support center (or communications with other workstations, for that matter) may be entirely invisible to the knowledge worker who operates that workstation.

A support center may also serve as a mechanism for coordinating the activities of multiple workstations. For instance, in the course of solving a decision problem, a knowledge worker may identify various subproblems whose solutions require the expertise of other knowledge workers or of expert systems. Requests to solve these subproblems are initiated (either explicitly or implicitly) at the local workstation and routed along communications paths to other workstations where the subproblems are to be resolved. A support center can serve as a clearinghouse for such communications, coordinating the assignments, timings, and responses of requested knowledge-processing tasks in accordance with the organizations's priorities and objectives. In addition to its service work, a support center may carry out certain kinds of processing that are so highly structured and predictable that no knowledge worker discretion or interaction is needed.

The storehouses of knowledge available to knowledge workers may be distributed throughout an organization (Radding 1995). Potentially large volumes of knowledge could be stored at each individual workstation. Knowledge can also be stored at support centers. Wherever it is, knowledge can be shared by all knowledge workers having security clearance to use it. Its location is generally influenced by its magnitude, its combined storage access cost, who its primary users are, and who is responsible for creating and maintaining it. A **knowledge storehouse** may even exist outside of the organization proper.

Together, the four components—local workstations, support centers, communications paths, and knowledge storehouses—provide a basis for studying and designing the technological infrastructure of knowledge-based organizations. Clearly, there are many possible ways to configure these components. Figure 19.3 suggests some of the possibilities. The formal study of knowledge-based organizations that emerges over the next few years will be concerned with classification and evaluation of various archetypal infrastructures for uniting an organization's knowledge workers.

Beyond structural variations, there will also be alternatives for the constitution of each **knowledge-management infrastructure** component. Some local workstations may be mere terminals connected to a support center. Others will be microcomputers with their own indigenous processors and large local storage capacities. In addition to common present-day input approaches, knowledge workers will have workstations capable of accepting instructions vocally and optically. Multimedia workstation responses will also complement the more traditional presentation methods.

FIGURE 19.3   Sample Infrastructure for a Knowledge-Based Organization

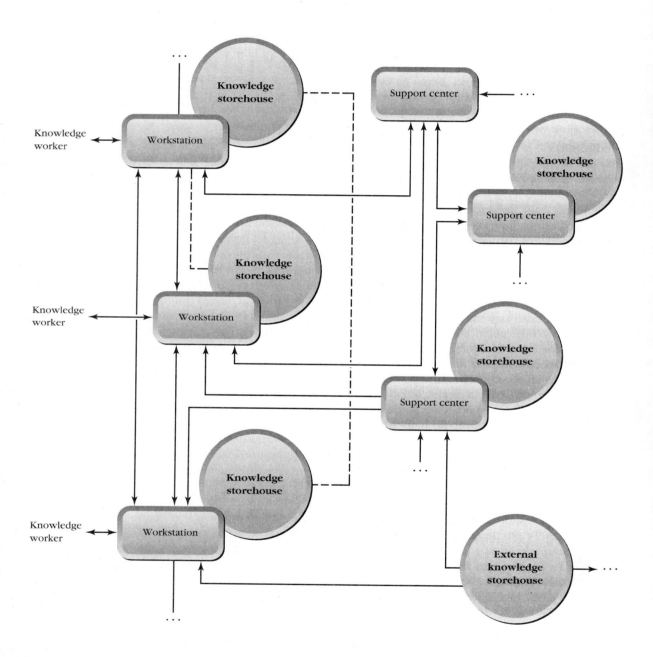

Some workstations will have a broad knowledge-management orientation. Others will have a deep orientation, specializing in a particular kind of knowledge processing. In both cases, decision support system techniques such as those described in this book will have major impacts on the knowledge-management software's facilities.

DSS IN THE NEWS

Another Revolution is Brewing

"Jim, what if the clients have questions about our proposal while you're in Hawaii?" The image of Jim's perennially nervous New York partner flits on to Jim's three-foot color video-phone.

Jim sighs, "Relax. I've already sent full-motion explanation videos to 50 computer mailboxes," he says soothingly, gazing out the window at the rolling New Mexico hills. "Besides, my palmtop's wireless fax and phone will be switched on the whole vacation. If you want me, you can reach me."

This scenario is imaginary today. But it may not be by the end of the decade.

Just over a decade after the personal computer grabbed the American public's imagination, another revolution is brewing. Futurists call it the personal communication revolution, or the age of electronic assistants.

The personal computer made a lot of people a lot more efficient. It rarely changed how or where they lived. . . .

By the end of the decade, thousands of Americans could use videophones to telecommute like the fictitious worker Jim. School children could do their homework on interactive television. Shut-ins could communicate with other people over vast networks. Newspaper readers could receive customized papers reflecting their interests. . . .

If all this sounds utopian, consider that only a tiny minority of American businesses used PCs and fax machines in 1980. Today, it's tough to imagine running a business without them.

M. Stroud, "The Next Computer Revolution: The Individual, Not Business, May Benefit Most," *Investor's Business Daily* 6 May 1992, p. 1.

Support centers will range from microcomputers to mainframe computers, the choice being made among technically adequate alternatives on economic grounds. Microcomputers will make up a significant proportion of support centers. The choice of communications technology will be very much influenced by desired coordination regulations and by the nature of what is being communicated.

PLUGGING INTO EXTERNAL TECHNOLOGICAL STRUCTURES

Beyond any organization's infrastructure, there are larger-scale technological structures. The communication paths, support centers, and knowledge storehouses of which they are composed can be valuable supplements to an organization's infrastructure. These external technological structures are truly massive and are growing daily, adding a global dimension to what exists within a knowledge-based organization. By plugging into such structures, an organization's infrastructure is virtually extended to encompass far more knowledge than would be possible to maintain internally.

Some of these external structures are commercial information service ventures. Examples include those of America Online, Compuserve, and Prodigy. Plugging into them is a matter of paying a subscription fee that is far less than the cost of maintaining the information internally. These information service ventures can also serve as conduits into noncommercial networks of knowledge, although they are not necessary to get to those networks.

The best-known external structure into which links can be readily made by an organization (or individual) is the **Internet.** The Internet is a set of more than 40,000 interconnected computer networks sprawled across more than 75 countries, with an estimated user base in excess of 20 million (Widdifield and Grover 1995). It is noncommercial in the sense that it is not controlled by any single company. To use the Internet, a knowledge worker's desktop computer can be equipped with programs that permit the exchange of electronic mail messages, the running of computers at other sites, tapping into remote databases, brainstorming via electronic bulletin boards, and so on.

Two recent developments have greatly enhanced the value of the Internet as a technological structure of support centers, knowledge storehouses, and communication paths: the World Wide Web and Web browsers. The **World Wide Web** is the Internet's collection of thousands of hyperlinked sites, each of which has a storehouse of knowledge that can be presented in graphical, multimedia fashion on desktop computers that access the Web. Each site has a computer, called a *Web server,* that manages a knowledge storehouse at the site and handles the dispatch of its contents across the Internet. Currently, the number of Web servers is more than doubling every year.

DSS IN THE NEWS

Electronic Eyes on the World

A marketing manager for an up-and-coming Silicon Valley computer company starts his day by reading intelligence on what the competition has been up to over the last 24 hours.

The information doesn't come from corporate spies—rather, the marketing man (who prefers to remain anonymous) is a subscriber to the Genie information service. He has instructed Genie's mainframe computer to comb news wires for stories of particular interest to him.

He also can use a variety of financial analysis features on the service to obtain everything from a credit rating on a potential customer to the latest research reports written by Wall Street analysts. . . .

Welcome to the leading edge of the information services revolution. Researchers believe about one million people use "dial-up" services for on-line shopping, banking, game playing or just plain chatting electronically. . . .

. . . There are hundreds of special-interest services like NewsNet, which provides on-line coverage of industry newsletters and wire services.

. . . Most of the large information providers offer a wealth of business news, financial analysis, stock trading and electronic mail. . . .

All it takes to connect to these services is a computer and a modem. . . . Users are given a password and a local telephone number for logging onto the systems, thereby escaping expensive long-distance charges. . . .

S. Silverthorne, "Computer Systems Become Eyes on Financial World," *Investor's Business Daily* 6 July 1990, p. 6.

EVOLUTION OF THE INTERNET

In the late 1960s the U.S. Department of Defense asked computer scientists to design a way for an unlimited number of computers to communicate in such a way that the destruction of any one (or more) of them would not prohibit the communications of those that remained. The scientists responded with a communication technology called packet switching, which originated at the National Physical Laboratories in the United Kingdom. This led to the implementation of a system that allowed transmissions among four main computers over nuclear-safe lines. Sponsored by the Advanced Research Projects Agency of the Department of Defense, this implementation came to be known as ARPANET. The ARPANET quickly expanded to include computers at dozens of universities and corporations, with many improvements and refinements being made along the way.

A major innovation in the early 1970s was the advent of ARPANET protocols known as Transmission Control Protocol/Internet Protocol (TCP/IP). These protocols are sets of codes that are to be sent or received in a prescribed sequence to ensure that desired computers are linked and can engage in intelligible message passing. One of the most important aspects of TCP/IP is that it is not restricted to any particular type of computer or communications technology. ARPANET, combined with other networks, became the Internet in the early 1980s. TCP/IP is still the protocol used on the Internet today.

The Internet's World Wide Web was launched in 1989. It was conceived by the European Laboratory for Particle Physics as an easy way to route graphical documents around the world. Publishing within the Web is straightforward using commands of its relatively simple hypertext markup language. This ease of publishing has led to the daily appearance of hundreds of new home pages on a wide variety of topics.

Interest in the Web exploded after the introduction of Mosaic. Released in 1993 by the National Center for Supercomputing Applications at the University of Illinois, Mosaic was the first easy-to-use graphical software for browsing the World Wide Web. Currently, Netscape's Navigator is the best known commercially available Web browser.

DSS IN THE NEWS

Planet Internet

. . . [T]hanks to . . . the World Wide Web, the Internet is beginning to eclipse—more accurately, to subsume—the PC. . . . [It] will soon be so ubiquitous, or "transparent," as experts say, that we'll take it for granted, as we do the phone system today. . . . All major software . . . will be "aware" of the Net and depend on it for a continuous stream of new data and updated functions. [You will no longer] . . . have to make a conscious decision to "get on the Internet". . . . Whenever it needs to, your PC will reach into the Web. . . . The boundary between your computer's contents and the rest of cyberspace will be almost imperceptible. . . .

J. Verity and R. Hof, "Planet Internet," *Business Week.* 3 April 1995, pp. 118–121.

A **Web browser** is software that allows the Web to be explored from a desktop computer, effortlessly jumping from one Web server to another—giving the illusion of dealing with a single large computer. Browsers, such as Mosaic or Netscape's Navigator, present accessed knowledge on the desktop in multimedia fashion, including text, colorful photos, graphics, and video. Web-browsing programs let users click with a mouse on displayed graphical buttons to browse though multimedia documents stored at Web sites around the world. Because these documents are linked in hypertext fashion, a user can click on a marker in one document to bring up a related document from the same or an entirely separate Web site.

To plug into the external technological structure provided by the World Wide Web, a knowledge worker's workstation needs to be equipped with a Web browser and an Internet connection. The search for knowledge on the Web typically begins by specifying the address of a **home page.** A home page is associated with a particular site and is a starting point for hypertext exploration of documents pertaining to a certain topic at the home page's site or at other sites.

Table 19.1 shows information about a few home pages for various sites, along with the addresses that can be used to access them. The first three are essentially directories that have long lists of links to other sites organized into useful categories. Web-browsing software usually includes a hot-list feature that allows any page of interest to be added to a personal directory. Later, you can reaccess the page with a mouse click rather than again typing in its address. The next three entries in Table 19.1 are for companies and the last three are concerned with business uses of the Internet. Figure 19.4 shows a page from IBM's web site.

The immense and growing body of knowledge that exists in the World Wide Web can support a knowledge worker's decision making in various ways. The general browsing activity can be undertaken to stimulate ideas in the course of deci-

TABLE 19.1   A Few Sites of Interest on the World Wide Web

SITE	ADDRESS	TOPIC
WebCrawler	http://webcrawler.com	Hundreds of thousands of Web documents indexed for searches on keywords
WWW Virtual Library	http://www.w3.org/hypertext/DataSources/bySubject/Overview.html	Topical and graphic indexes to Web pages for those who have a topic in mind
Yahoo	http://www.yahoo.com	Huge index of web pages organized into categories
IBM	http://www.ibm.com	IBM products and services
Microsoft	http://www.microsoft.com	Microsoft and its products
Novell	http://www.novell.com	Novell products and services
CommerceNet	http://www.commerce.net	How to use the Internet for business; links to business-related sites
FinanceNet Electronic Commerce	http://www.financenet.gov/ec.htm	Small-business Internet uses
Internet Business Center	http://www.tig.com/IBC/	Doing business on the Internet

FIGURE 19.4   A Page from IBM's Web Site

sion making or even to help recognize the need for a decision. Highly selective browsing may be used to satisfy the need for some specific piece of knowledge required in decision making. Of course, the ultimate value of the Web's knowledge for a particular decision maker depends on exactly what knowledge happens to exist there and on how easy it is to access.

Managing an organization's use of the Internet is not without its challenges. For instance, the organization has no control over what is published in the World Wide Web. What a knowledge worker accesses may be outdated, inconsistent with knowledge held in the organization, or just plain incorrect. How is a knowledge worker to be aware of such situations, and what can management do to lessen the likelihood of resultant injury to the organization? Although there may be a temptation to tightly control and monitor knowledge workers' Internet communications, a better answer appears to lie in focusing on training these workers to be alert to and effectively respond to inappropriate (and even dangerous) communication behavior (Cash 1995).

As technical and managerial obstacles are overcome, the full potential of the Internet will become clearer. Presently, its maximum potential is unknown. But what we can say with certainty is that knowledge-based organizations will increasingly plug into external technological structures to draw on knowledge resources that they themselves are unable or unwilling to manage internally.

This trend is part of a larger one toward virtual corporations (Byrne, Brandt, and Port 1993). Also called modular corporations (Tully 1993) or network organizations (Snow, Miles, and Coleman 1992), they consist of separate firms that function as

DSS IN THE NEWS

Let Your Agents Do The Navigating

The good news is that news filtering software is getting better. These programs choose important articles from the thousands that gauge readers' interests better and track more publications than before. They're also cheaper. "Publishers are recognizing the incredible opportunity to publish electronically," said Richard Vancil, vice president of marketing for Burlington, Mass.-based Individual Inc. . .

. . . Individual and two other software companies in nearby Cambridge, Mass., have new products that advance the field of news filters. All use software agents, programs that use artificial intelligence to carry out complex tasks that require judgments.

On Monday, Individual formally launched NewsPage, an information service on the Internet's World Wide Web. NewsPage draws on more than 500 news service, papers, trade magazines, industry newsletters, and government sources. From these, it compiles more than 25,000 pages of information each day. The articles are organized under 1,000 topics. Customer "user profiles" can slim down the content sent to each user. If a user sought news from three magazines on the finances of Internet service companies, the software could hunt it down for the user. Individual's NewsPage service can be reached at http://www.newspage.com.

OneSource Information Services Inc. launched a filtering service of its own last month. The service is called Company Watch. It gives daily news and database updates for a customer-picked watch list of up to 100 companies. Company Watch uses Individual's NewsPage—and other sources like news services publications, SEC documents, and analyst reports. It pulls all relevant information together in a single Notes database. The database is built from scratch each day and E-mailed to customers.

A third new entry is Bolt Beranek & Newman Inc.'s Personal Internet Newspaper, or PIN. PIN searches the Internet and other services for articles, with software agents that make use of user-defined profiles. PIN offers three agents, also called "bots." Web Bot scans the World Wide Web, News Bot scans Usenet discussion groups on the Internet, and Mail Bot scans users' Internet E-mail. Pricing hasn't been set.

S. Higgins, "How New Software Can Select the On-Line News You Need," *Investor's Business Daily,* 20 July 1995.

DSS IN THE NEWS

Navigating through a Labyrinth of Knowledge

Every day, 75,000 new documents appear on interconnected networks known as the Internet.

No source of information has ever been as comprehensive and or up-to-date as the Internet. But even for the most proficient users, much of the network's valuable information is inaccessible.

Information stored on thousands of Internet databases remains unused because users don't know how to get it. . . .

While taking full advantage of the Internet still requires technical proficiency, the level of proficiency required is decreasing. Software companies are offering new programs designed to help computer users more easily find their way around the Internet's vast pools of data.

. . . Other programs under development will let companies put their own databases on the Internet—with new security designed to keep that data secure from unauthorized users.

. . . The programs that point users toward important data and those that let corporations "post" their own databases on the Internet can potentially reduce the cost of business research and communications. . . .

S. Higgins, "New Tools Emerge for Navigating Internet's Labyrinth of Databases," *Investor's Business Daily* 6 May 1994, p. A3

integral parts of a greater organization, with each retaining authority in its own major budgeting and pricing matters. In the case of the Internet, firms that provide Web servers, home pages, and related electronic documents are separate entities, but they function as integral hyperlinked participants in a greater virtual knowledge-based organization.

19.4 MANAGEMENT OF A KNOWLEDGE-BASED ORGANIZATION

Various organizations have begun to create the position of **chief knowledge officer** (CKO) to manage the capture, distribution, and productive use of knowledge (Davenport 1994). Chief knowledge officers will play key roles in the transformation to knowledge-based organizations. Potential aspects of the CKO job include the following (Davenport 1994):

1. Being an advocate for knowledge and learning, changing organization culture and individual behavior to focus on the importance of knowledge management.
2. Designing, implementing, and overseeing an organization's computer-based knowledge-management facilities, human knowledge-management resources,

ORGANIZATIONAL LEARNING

". . . [K]nowledge reservoirs in organizations are not static pools but wellsprings, constantly replenished with streams of new ideas and constituting an ever-flowing source of corporate renewal . . . inextricably linked to learning; knowledge is both raw material and finished goods in today's corporations." —**Dorothy Leonard-Barton** in *Wellsprings of Knowledge*, p. 3.

research units, libraries, and conduits to external knowledge sources—all of which contribute to an organization's knowledge management infrastructure.
3. Serving as the main liaison with external knowledge providers.
4. Instigating, fostering, and shaping the internal creation of knowledge.

Qualifications for a CKO include deep experience in the creation, dissemination, and application of knowledge, familiarity with knowledge-management technologies and companies, familiarity with development of human resources (e.g., training, cultivating creativity and effective human relations), and the ability to set a good example as a knowledge worker.

In light of his or her duties, a CKO's job must be coordinated with executives in charge of the organization's human relation and information technology functions. It could possibly be merged into one of these functions. However, both human relation executives and chief information officers already have their hands full. Thus, the best position for a CKO in an organization chart could well be a senior independent role that fosters productive knowledge management throughout an organization, coupled with ongoing organizational learning (Davenport 1994).

In organizations without a CKO, there is no single person or unit responsible for these interrelated activities. This responsibility may be shared by all participants as part of the organizational culture. In any event, an organization's knowledge resources need to be consciously and carefully managed. Otherwise, the notion of a knowledge-based organization will likely remain just a concept rather than a reality. As Figure 19.5 indicates, a CKO integrates and melds technological and organization infrastructure into a unified knowledge-management infrastructure. The CKO harnesses both technology and human resources to create and administer a human-computer infrastructure specifically geared toward maximizing knowledge utilization in the interest of fulfilling an organization's purpose. Figure 19.3 illustrates an example of such an infrastructure. Here, we consider how a CKO might view the creation and administration of a knowledge-based organization.

CREATION

The management of a knowledge-based organization begins with careful planning of its design and construction (Holsapple and Whinston 1987). Where such a plan is absent, the result will probably be a haphazard organization emerging out of a series of uncoordinated and ad hoc responses to short-term knowledge-processing needs. This haphazardness is characterized by redundant effort, inconsistency, inefficiency, and managerial control difficulties. All these traits tend to place an organization at a serious disadvantage relative to its well-planned competitors.

A plan for increasing, using, and preserving an organization's knowledge resources should have long-term, strategic aspects that provide a framework for

FIGURE 19.5 Conventional versus Knowledge-Based Organization

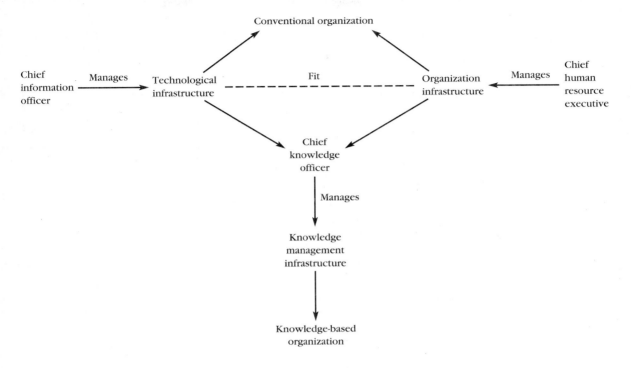

DSS IN THE NEWS

Knowledge Work to Be Done

Business leaders recognize the power of managing organizational knowledge, but doing it effectively remains an enigma for many, according to the initial findings from a benchmarking study conducted by Arthur Andersen. Among other results the study found:

- A solid majority (79%) of the executive respondents said it's important for knowledge management to be central to an organization's business strategy. Yet 59% said they're doing a poor job of implementing an effective strategy.
- Ninety-one percent said their companies have not yet linked knowledge management to financial results.
- Forty-seven percent encourage and facilitate a knowledge sharing culture.

CEO Briefing, "Knowledge Management Is Coming of Age," *Investors Business Daily,* 16 November 1995, p. A4.

developing operational plans. The prospects of ongoing technological advances, increasing knowledge worker expertise, and new environmental challenges suggest that planned flexibility will be very important. This flexibility can take many forms, such as selecting workstation software that supports growth in knowledge worker expertise, choosing workstation and support center hardware standards that are extensible, adopting communication path technology that maximizes communications options, and selecting software that can effectively handle both large and complex knowledge storehouses.

Companies and in-house CKO units specializing in the customized design and building of technological and organization infrastructures for knowledge-based organizations will become increasingly prominent. These organizations will be very much analogous to the traditional architectural and construction industries that create and remodel manufacturing, warehouse, and transportation facilities. However, they will be concerned with the creation and remodeling of knowledge processing,

DSS IN THE NEWS

Surrendering the Mainframes

Some U.S. steel companies are surrendering their mainframe computers to outside information specialists to boost manufacturing efficiency and customer service.

Instead of spending millions of dollars to manage and run routine data processing functions like payroll and human resources with an army of information systems troops, steel companies are deploying an elite core of technology experts.

"Many manufacturers have spent so much time developing and maintaining their in-house computer systems that they haven't been able to focus on the competitive advantage that technology offers, like serving customers more efficiently," said Ted Rybeck, research director with Advanced Manufacturing Research Inc. . . .

Bethlehem Steel Corp. typifies the trend . . . [and] signed a 10-year outsourcing deal with . . . Electronic Data Systems Corp. that was estimated to be worth $500 million. With EDS managing many of its computer services, Bethlehem has cut its information workers to less than 30. Most of the remaining 400 computer specialists who were on its staff now work for EDS. . . .

At about the same time . . . Armco Steel Co. signed a similar 10-year outsourcing contract with Integrated Systems Solutions Corp. . . . Armco has reduced its information systems staff down to a small core from 200 workers. . . .

By passing much of their computer work to systems integrators, both companies hope to free up scarce capital needed to upgrade their manufacturing systems infrastructure. . . .

Big U.S. steelmakers need to find ways to compete with smaller, more nimble minimills that use technology to help lower inventory costs and improve manufacturing efficiency. Outsourcing can help by freeing companies from getting bogged down in traditional computer services, allowing them to focus on manufacturing. . . .

While outsourcing isn't new, the number of large, long-term contracts—ranging from $50 million to $500 million—has exploded over the past few years. . . .

B. Deagon, "Big Steel Hopes it Will Pay to Outsource Some Computer Operations," *Investor's Business Daily* 6 May 1993, p. 4.

knowledge storage, and communication facilities. They will also be concerned with the design of knowledge worker roles, relationships, and regulations. Just as their traditional counterparts do, these new-age architects and builders will employ a variety of tools, techniques, prefabricated components, and subcontracted work efforts in devising the blueprints and building the customized infrastructure for a knowledge-based organization. All this effort occurs within the scope of an organization's strategic plan for knowledge management.

Although entirely prefabricated technological infrastructures may be installed in some cases, customized infrastructures will be very prominent. Their typically higher initial cost can be more than offset by the ongoing productivity advantages they can offer. A customized infrastructure is specially tailored to fit the organization's idiosyncracies and to conform ergonomically to knowledge worker needs. Clearly, the creators of an organization's knowledge-management infrastructure must be highly skilled in technical, organizational, economic, and ergonomic considerations.

Technically, they must have expertise at least comparable to today's computer professionals. Using ergonomic principles, they design and build customized software for knowledge workers to use via local workstations. This customized software handles knowledge-processing activities that are beyond the ability of individual knowledge workers to accomplish directly with available knowledge-management tools. Creators of the infrastructure will also specify the structural, security, and integrity characteristics of knowledge storehouses and may even be responsible for furnishing the initial contents (e.g., data, solvers, rule sets, forms) of these repositories.

Comprehension of an organization's existing or planned control structure must be coupled with an appreciation of economical technical options to arrive at a workable configuration of workstations, support centers, knowledge storehouses, and communications paths. The configuration must not only be technically workable, it must also be organizationally workable from such standpoints as knowledge worker coordination, consistency with knowledge worker incentives, consistency with organizational priorities, and maximizing collective productivity. Increasingly, the creation or modification of a knowledge-management infrastructure will be considered to be inseparable from the creation or modification of an organization. The two issues are so inextricably interrelated that they will come to be regarded as practically identical for future knowledge-based organizations.

ONGOING OPERATION

Once in place, the knowledge-management infrastructure must be effectively managed. Via each of its workstations, this infrastructure is an extension of or enhancement to a knowledge worker's own innate knowledge-processing abilities. Managing the infrastructure and managing those who use its knowledge resources are inseparable issues for purposes of effective organizational functioning. Coordination and control are the keynotes of this managerial effort, whose goal is to maximize the decision-making effectiveness of the organization subject to constraints imposed by its human, material, capital, and knowledge resources.

Administration and maintenance of the infrastructure and the knowledge it holds will draw heavily on the technical expertise of computer professionals. Local management of the knowledge resources will be carried out by knowledge workers using the software available via their workstations. Knowledge-processing activities will be managed by the combined actions of knowledge workers and software. In the course of arriving at a problems' solution, a knowledge worker may request the assistance of other knowledge workers and/or various expert systems.

Knowledge-Processing Requests   Specialized knowledge-processing requests may be explicitly stated by the knowledge worker through the local workstation. Alternatively, a request may be generated by the workstation itself (or one of its support centers) as it endeavors to carry out some knowledge-processing task instigated by the knowledge worker (Holsapple and Whinston 1987; Tesler 1995). In the latter case, the knowledge worker may even be unaware that the workstation is consulting other human knowledge workers or artificially intelligent systems as it performs its task.

Thus, a knowledge worker will be capable not only of explicitly or implicitly issuing requests, but also of receiving requests for assistance. As far as possible, workstation and support center software should manage these requests in a manner consistent with the organization's goals and priorities. That is, knowledge workers should be relieved from the burden of managing requests. When a request is made that is not directed at a specific knowledge worker, the software should route the request to one of the knowledge workers (human or artificially intelligent) capable of responding to that request.

The selection of target processors for undirected tasks will be determined on the basis of relative load factors, relative costs, and response-time objectives. This selection process presupposes that the software is capable of understanding the nature of each request in order to identify the set of targets that are feasible in terms of their capacity to respond to the request. Of course, this understanding might be accomplished by an expert system.

Knowledge Preprocessing   The requests for assistance that are pending or in process at a given workstation will be managed by software. This action includes both the automatic scheduling of request processing and the preprocessing of requests as they arrive. Before a knowledge worker begins to process a request, the software will preprocess in a variety of ways. It will automatically check the appropriateness of the request for this knowledge worker. It will examine the request to detect any ambiguities, inconsistencies, or incompleteness that may exist in it. These

DSS IN THE NEWS

Too Complex

British Telecom is preparing to launch software agents using artificial intelligence to help manage its networks, which are becoming . . . [too] complex to be managed by people alone. *New Scientist* reports in its July 30 issue that these agents would "negotiate with each other on behalf of their respective owners—the caller and telecom companies—to find the optimum mix of bandwidth, price and time for making a call." The work of the agents will be invisible to the caller, with the exception of being asked about a desire for "a low-quality . . . cheap connection or a more expensive, high-bandwidth link."

"AI-Based Agents to Trade on Nets," *Datamation* (September 15, 1994): 95.

problems are automatically clarified by conversing with the workstation (or perhaps knowledge worker) that initiated the request, resulting in a new statement of the problem to be processed.

The workstation **preprocessor** then undertakes a preliminary analysis of the problem posed by the request to determine whether the workstation itself can generate a solution without knowledge worker effort. If knowledge worker effort is required, then the preprocessing software automatically does as much as it can to lay the groundwork for the actual processing to be carried out by the knowledge worker. This action could include a broad range of activities, such as gathering needed knowledge from various storehouses, conducting basic analyses whose

DSS IN THE NEWS

Knowbots

With thousands of readily accessible computer databases on line around the world, finding specific bits of information takes more work than ever.

Though still rudimentary, some new tools can help those who want to dip into these pools of electronic information and get out with minimal fuss and expense.

Several of these are loosely based on an idea kicked around for years by computer scientists: to get computer programs to do basic research legwork, like finding data about a specific topic in any of a hundred databases, with little involvement on the part of the person seeking the information.

Developers call these software tools by a variety of names, including wide-area information servers, information agents and Knowbots, short for knowledge robots. . . .

Sandpoint Corp. . . . markets a product called Hoover. . . . Hoover works in conjunction with wide-area networks. . . .

Hoover can be set up to automatically update a file it has created—say, a client profile for a banker. It can update the file with items such as the client's current stock price, product changes and personnel moves, drawing on any of the databases connected to its network.

A Hoover user need not know where requested information can be found. . . . The user simply makes the request. Hoover figures out where the information resides, links to that database and retrieves the data. . . .

. . . Hoover is set up to allow customers to limit the cost and extent of searches, including automatic updates. . . .

. . . In theory, a user would teach a Knowbot his or her interests and then release it to cruise any and all accessible data sources. The user ideally would not have to lift a finger to direct the Knowbot's inquiries. The program would seek information on its own, returning from its network cruises only when it ferreted out something of interest to its master. . . .

. . . Development of Knowbots has been driven by explosive growth of Internet, the global collection of thousands of smaller computer networks that grew out of a U.S. government effort to facilitate military research two decades ago. . . .

T. Bunker, "With Knowbots, Users Need Not Know Complexities of Database Hunts," *Investor's Business Daily* 10 February 1993, p. 4.

DSS IN THE NEWS

My Agent Will Handle It

. . . Professional athletes, movie stars, . . . and television anchors all have agents. Why not you?

. . . New software will be used by electronic shoppers to create and dispatch so-called software agents, which will travel over phone lines to almost any computer database and carry out tasks on the user's behalf. . . .

M. Mehler, "CEO Briefing on Information Technology," *Investor's Business Daily* 13 January 1994, p. 4.

results will be needed by the knowledge worker, reducing the problem into sub-problems and initiating assistance requests for each, and so forth.

To summarize, a workstation's preprocessor organizes, schedules, and lays the foundation for a knowledge worker's problem-solving sessions. It is essentially a decision support system or part of a multiparticipant DSS. It is very likely artificially intelligent. In the course of a problem-solving session, the knowledge worker employs knowledge-management tools and/or customized knowledge-management software to solve the problem(s) inherent in a request that has been received. The emphasis is on enhancing knowledge worker productivity by eliminating the routine and repetitive, providing greater processing speed and accuracy, stimulating insights, furnishing advice, and fostering a synergy based on communication with other knowledge workers. In these ways, a workstation and the infrastructure that it opens into constitute a significant extension to an individual's knowledge-management capabilities.

DSS IN THE NEWS

Softbots

. . . Research also promises advanced software "agents," handy little programs that someday will sit in your computer and assist with tasks such as scheduling meetings or screening e-mail . . . [The] agents [are] called "softbots" or "nobots." An e-mail soft-bot might spot patterns in the way you screen your e-mail and encode the routine in software, say putting memos from the boss on top.

R. Brandt, "Software: Agents & Artificial Life, *Business Week* (Special 1994 Bonus Issue): 68.

19.5 REALIZATION OF KNOWLEDGE-BASED ORGANIZATIONS

Clearly, software based on continuing developments in the interrelated fields of artificial intelligence, decision support systems, and organizational computing will play a crucial role in the design, construction, and ongoing management of knowledge-based organizations (Applegate, Cash, and Mills 1988). Traditional functional areas of management will also make important contributions to the realization of effective knowledge-based organizations (Holsapple and Whinston 1987).

ECONOMIC ISSUES

At a fundamental economic level, practical ways of measuring knowledge and assessing the value of knowledge are needed. These methods will stem from an understanding of knowledge types and representation techniques. Knowledge measurement and valuation can provide an objective basis for tracking knowledge worker productivity, evaluating alternative knowledge-processing methods and infrastructure designs, deciding whether to make or buy some piece of knowledge, pricing (internal and/or external) for knowledge that is to be distributed, studying economies of scale, the general accounting of knowledge assets, and so on.

REQUIREMENTS AND PROBLEMS IN REALIZING KNOWLEDGE-BASED ORGANIZATIONS

Drucker (1988) has outlined requirements for achieving knowledge-based organizations and has identified some of the likely management problems in doing so.

Requirements

- Common objectives that are simple, clear, and translate into specific actions.
- Organizational concentration on a small number of objectives.
- A realization that most knowledge workers are specialists who cannot be told how to play their roles but rather need to be focused on jointly achieving something.
- A clear statement of management's performance expectations for the organization, task forces, and individuals.
- Organized feedback for comparing results with performance expectations—as a basis for evaluation, learning, and knowledge worker self-control.
- An organizational culture in which all participants practice knowledge responsibility, with each constantly thinking through what knowledge he or she needs to make a contribution and what knowledge is possessed that could benefit others in performing their duties.

Problems

- Developing incentives, compensation and recognition schemes, and career opportunities for knowledge worker specialists.
- Designing the management structure for an organization of task forces.
- Creating and instilling a unified vision across the organization's specialized knowledge workers.
- Ensuring that top executive knowledge workers are in ample supply, are well prepared, and adequately tested.

Classical economics can contribute to the development of incentive allocation schemes for ensuring that both technology and human expertise are harnessed to meet the organization's objectives. Such schemes are of obvious importance for promoting knowledge worker cooperation and effective utilization of technological infrastructure (Ching, Holsapple, and Whinston 1992). Thus, when a knowledge worker receives a request, there must be some incentive for acting on that request in accordance with the request's priority. Furthermore, the fact that the action has taken place must be tracked. Conversely, when a request is issued, the cost of fulfilling that request should be apparent to discourage injudicious use of scarce knowledge-processing resources. There must be economic incentives to prevent a knowledge worker from passing along all work to other knowledge workers without having added any value.

Understanding the pertinence of economies of scale for knowledge management is another important issue. Compared to a small organization, a large-scale organization may be able to spread the cost of manufacturing a particular parcel of knowledge across many more decision makers that will use it. Because of its larger internal market, the large organization may be able to exploit the knowledge in many more ways, giving the large organization a competitive advantage over smaller organizations. However, this also suggests interesting opportunities for knowledge-service organizations that specialize in the generation and external marketing of knowledge (e.g., rule sets, solvers, solver results) to relatively small organizations. Such a service organization together with its clients may collectively achieve economies of scale that rival (or perhaps surpass) those of a large organization.

FINANCE AND ACCOUNTING ISSUES

The issue of budgets for knowledge processing deserves investigation from such standpoints as appropriate aggregation, automated tracking, variance-approval mechanisms, and knowledge worker evaluation. Knowledge-based organizations will routinely choose among alternative investments aimed at augmenting their

DSS IN THE NEWS

Every Executive: A Chief Knowledge Officer

Within the next 20 years, you'll see over half of the information technology assets moving into the hands of commercially run service utilities. "Outsourcing" is just a name that masks a profound change in the way technology may support the majority of customers in the future. What you see is the end of the craft guild mode and the beginning of the industrialization of information processing. Corporations will be able to take their IT budget out of overhead and make it a variable cost, just as labor and materials are now a cost of production. For that they will not need a CIO, but a chief technical officer that will assure enterprise-wide systems integration, because every executive will be a chief information officer.

P. A. Strassmann, "CIOs Should Get Back to Basics," *Datamation* (September 15, 1994): 72.

knowledge assets. This choice will involve financial analysis that can determine present values for various bodies of knowledge. Prospective mergers will be formally examined in terms of knowledge resources and the potential for exploiting complementary infrastructures and knowledge.

It will be vital for a knowledge-based organization to maintain an account of the present state of its knowledge resources as a basis for control and analysis. Balance sheets specifically citing knowledge assets will permit an analysis of trends in knowledge formation and provide a basis for understanding how well the organization is poised to cope with anticipated growth and needs. Some kinds of knowledge are consumed in the production of new knowledge and have no independent existence after being used in a particular knowledge-processing task. More durable kinds of knowledge can be used repeatedly in a variety of processing tasks. However, a specific parcel of durable knowledge typically becomes less useful or obsolete over some period of time. Thus, issues related to knowledge aging, depreciation, and replacement must be addressed. Yet another important aspect of knowledge accounting is the auditing of knowledge assets and inventories.

MARKETING ISSUES

To the extent that an organization markets the knowledge it creates, there must be a means for fairly capturing the costs of producing that knowledge. This process provides a basis for knowledge pricing. Although the sale of knowledge will involve new media and techniques for knowledge delivery, it will have many similarities to today's publishing industry. However, the emphasis will increasingly be on the sale of knowledge (be it descriptive, procedural, reasoning, etc.) rather than the sale of an object that conveys that knowledge. It is important that the knowledge be immediately processible in a variety of ways via the purchaser's workstation and/or support centers. For instance, the knowledge (e.g., rule sets) may be packaged in such a way that it can be immediately deposited in a workstation's knowledge storehouse, where it is directly susceptible to processing with a standard tool.

OPERATIONS ISSUES

As suggested in the prior section, operations management of a knowledge-based organization is not at all trivial. Experts in this area will be heavily involved in the design of infrastructure. They will be responsible for devising regulations for software that coordinates knowledge worker activities. These activities may very well take place in the context of a nonstop organization that provides very flexible conditions (times, locations) for knowledge workers. Critical path project-management techniques may be employed for complex problems that involve the participation of many knowledge workers.

Scheduling an organization's knowledge-processing activities may come to be viewed from a job shop perspective, in which each job is a problem whose completion (i.e., solution) is accomplished through the coordinated actions of multiple specialized knowledge workers. We should expect to see certain material requirements planning principles and quality control techniques adapted to the manufacture of knowledge and decisions (i.e., problem solutions). Operations research models based on simulation or optimization have the potential for extensive application in these various aspects of managing a knowledge-based organization.

Mechanisms for guaranteeing the security of knowledge are vital from the accounting, operations, and legal standpoints. Knowledge workers must be auto-

DSS IN THE NEWS

Taking Care of Business

Congratulations. You and the rest of the business process reengineering team have finally completed your company's first major project. . . . New systems and a stream-lined process are in place, and results are close to targets.

Now what?

That's the question companies are asking themselves today. . . . For an increasing number, the answer is integrated process management. Companies like Pacific Bell, Xerox, and $2.1 billion automobile fleet management firm PHH are creating high-level process management functions that, in many cases, are closely allied with central IS organizations. IS is being called on to support process management by, among other things, evaluating and recommending—or even developing—a new class of process-modeling and simulation tools.

"I do see the practice of process management emerging right now," says Thomas H. Davenport, director of the information systems management program at the University of Texas. . . . "The problem is it's not as sexy as pure BPR where you say, 'Let's throw away everything we have and start over.' But process management is more realistic."

Process management essentially surrounds classic BPR with consistent practices, methodologies, and procedures that, one hopes, will make BPR more effective.

J. Moad, "After Reengineering: Taking Care of Business," *Datamation* (October 15, 1994): 40.

---

matically prohibited from making unauthorized alterations to knowledge. Also, the infrastructure must be able to prohibit the disclosure of various subsets of its global knowledge resources to knowledge workers who do not have the authority to view it. The security mechanisms built into the infrastructure should support situations where a knowledge worker needs to use some parcel of knowledge without being able either to view it or to alter it.

KNOWLEDGE MANAGEMENT

We envision the emergence of a new functional area of management: knowledge management (KM). It will have close interdisciplinary links with the traditional areas, along the lines just described. It will subsume and reorient such areas as management information systems and decision support systems. KM will be concerned with the study of infrastructures for knowledge-based organizations. It will take advantage of past work on such topics as database management, artificial intelligence, generalized problem processors, and linguistic analysis. It will devise a taxonomy of knowledge and create new approaches to knowledge representation and processing. The KM field will both stimulate and assimilate technological advances in software and hardware.

The foregoing considerations are important for the realization of viable knowledge-based organizations. They are, of course, suggestive rather than exhaustive. As such, they are indicative of research directions for the functional areas of management. In some cases, this research will involve the adaptation or extension of exist-

THE CHALLENGE OF THE FUTURE

Drucker (1988, 53) nicely sums up the current state: "Now we are entering a . . . shift from the command-and-control organization, the organization of departments and divisions, to . . . the organization of knowledge specialists. We can perceive, though perhaps only dimly, what this organization will look like. We can identify some of its main characteristics and requirements. We can point to central problems of values, structure, and behavior. But the job of actually building . . . is still ahead of us—it is the managerial challenge of the future."

ing concepts and methods to the new organizational context. In other cases, it will lead to the development of fundamentally new concepts and methods. Results of these research efforts, coupled with continuing technological advances, will define the possible constitutions for future knowledge-based organizations and will significantly impact the future curriculum of management schools.

19.6 THE EMERGING KNOWLEDGE SOCIETY

We close with a brief sketch of Drucker's vision of the emerging **knowledge society** (Drucker 1994). This society is the environment in which knowledge-based organizations and individual knowledge workers will operate. By the turn of the century, he projects that knowledge workers will make up at least a third of the United States' workforce. By comparison, manufacturing workers have never made up a larger percentage than this (except in wartime). Regardless of the actual timing of this projection, the trend is clear.

Most knowledge workers will receive compensation at least as great as manufacturing workers have ever achieved. There will be many new job opportunities for knowledge workers at the same time that the proportion of manufacturing positions continues to shrink. These opportunities will require considerable formal education, a capacity to acquire and apply both conceptual and concrete knowledge, and an attitude that pursues continuous learning.

In many developed countries, knowledge workers will form the largest single segment of the workforce. They will give the emergent knowledge society its leadership, character, and social profile. Education, which involves acquiring and distributing formal knowledge, will form the knowledge society's core. Increasingly, knowledge will be acquired beyond the traditional means of formal schooling and will involve new learning technologies (Whinston 1994).

The idea that an educated person is someone who has acquired a basic stock of knowledge will be superseded by the notion of someone who has learned how to learn and who continues to do so throughout a career. In the knowledge society, a key competitive factor for knowledge workers and organizations (and even countries) will be the proficiency in acquiring and using knowledge.

Highly specialized people will make up the knowledge society's central workforce. Generalist knowledge workers will be those who are able to acquire knowledge rapidly in new specialty areas, thereby having greater job mobility. The high degree of specialization has two major implications: Much knowledge work will be multiparticipant, and a knowledge worker will need to be affiliated with at least one organization. The first implication stems from the difficulty of an individual having sufficient knowledge (i.e., spanning specialties). Much more needs to be understood about the many possible multiparticipant configurations: groups, teams, task forces, and other organizational types. The second implication stems from the inability of specialized knowledge to itself yield performance. In the knowledge society, it is not the individual knowledge worker who performs, but rather the organization that performs by converting specialized knowledge of knowledge workers into performance.

DSS IN THE NEWS

Now You Know

If Peter Drucker is right, and knowledge is "the only meaningful economic resource," many firms—especially western ones—may be in deep trouble. According to a new study by Ikujiro Nonaka and Hirotaka Takeuchi of Hitotsubashi University, it is the ability to create new knowledge, rather than manufacturing prowess, that puts firms ahead. And many western managers are not much good at it.

At first sight, this seems a bit unfair. Mr. Drucker, the dean of American management gurus, has been banging on about "knowledge workers" for decades. It is not unusual nowadays to run into managers at conferences whose name-tags proclaim them "Vice-President, Knowledge." The problem, according to the two Japanese academics, is that the name-tag-wearers are thinking of the wrong sort of knowledge. For most western companies "knowledge" means hard data, numbers, and words—or "explicit" knowledge. Japanese firms, by contrast, are more concerned with "tacit" knowledge—the sort of know-how embodied in employees' hunches, ideals, and skills.

Tacit knowledge is often deeply ingrained and hard to share. But, once converted into explicit knowledge, it can be a key part of innovation. When members of Honda's design team decided to build a radical new car for the 1980s, they at first framed their ideas using concepts such as "automobile evolution," "short and tall," and "man-maximum, machine-minimum." Woolly though such phrases sound, they helped create the innovative little Honda City car. Nissan designed its Infinity luxury cars from a similar start.

Many small firms have passed on tacit knowledge through apprenticeship systems for generations. It is harder to do this in big companies—and to do it instantaneously. The Japanese academics think three things can help. First, ensure that employees share as many of each other's experiences as possible. That means creating lots of shifting, flexible teams. Second—and unfashionably—make use of middle managers. Lots of tacit knowledge is created on the factory floor, whereas vision tends to be the province of the boardroom. Middle managers can tie the two together.

Lastly, reckon Messrs. Nonaka and Takeuchi, a company must shape itself into a "hypertext" organization, comprising three separate structures. One is a traditional hierarchy: this is both a good way to run the day-to-day business of a company and to spread explicit knowledge throughout the firm. For the creative side of the business, however, another structure should take the form of teams that form and re-form to generate new ideas. Underpinning all this is the third structure—a "knowledge base" where tacit and explicit knowledge come together and are readily accessible. This could include anything from computer databases to corporate culture and the collected wisdoms of all a firm's older citizens.

"Now You Know," *The Economist*, 27 May 1995, p. 58.

The essential purpose of management in the knowledge society will be to make knowledge productive. In Chapter 1, we identified knowledge as one of four key organizational resources—one that has often been largely overlooked. Drucker sees knowledge as *the* key resource in the emerging knowledge society. Every organization and every country will have to consider carefully the competitiveness of its knowledge competencies in a world economy whose key resource is knowledge. The same may be said for every knowledge worker in the global knowledge society.

19.7 SUMMARY

We are rapidly entering an era that will be dominated by knowledge-based organizations. Each such organization will be populated by a community of knowledge workers who are interconnected by a computer-based infrastructure. Each knowledge worker will be an expert in carrying out certain kinds of knowledge-management activities. The worker's knowledge-processing efforts will be supported by a workstation equipped with an artificially intelligent environment for business computing, customized knowledge-processing software, and perhaps some problem-preprocessing rule sets. The workstation will also serve as the knowledge worker's entry point into the infrastructure's knowledge storehouses, support center capabilities, and other workstations. The infrastructure will be virtually extended by plugging into external technological structures such as the Internet.

The design, construction, and ongoing management of an effective infrastructure presents challenges to each of the traditional functional areas of management. Each area can make important contributions to the realization of viable knowledge-based organizations. The focal point for study and research into such organizations will be a new field, referred to as knowledge management, which transcends the more narrow interests of fields such as MIS and DSS. Its mission involves the identification and creation of concepts, methods, and tools for maximizing the global productivity of knowledge workers in an organization.

▲ IMPORTANT TERMS

chief knowledge officer	knowledge-based organization
home page	preprocessor
Internet	support center
knowledge-management infrastructure	task force
knowledge society	web browser
knowledge storehouse	workstation
knowledge worker	World Wide Web

▲ APPLICATION TO THE BOEING CASE

1. Describe the four systems involved in the redesign of production at Boeing.
2. For each system, explain how it could support decision making.
3. Who are the knowledge workers in this case?
4. How do the new systems help improve decision making in the organization?

5. Explain the nature of each of the following in the case of Boeing's new systems:
   a. Local workstations
   b. Support centers
   c. Communication paths
   d. Knowledge storehouses
6. Propose a feature or system not described in the case that would further enhance knowledge workers' decision making performance.
7. What tangible benefits does Boeing's management expect to realize from its new knowledge-based approach to production?
8. How is the Boeing case related to the concept of reengineering?
9. What type of knowledge is a decision made with the aid of the *process planner* system?
10. How does the *enterprise resource planner* system help coordinate decisions by diverse knowledge workers? How does the *product data manager* system do the same?

▲ REVIEW QUESTIONS

1. How do knowledge-based organizations differ from more traditional organizations?
2. What does a knowledge worker do?
3. Software tools for knowledge management can be examined from what perspectives?
4. What is the distinction between the breadth and depth of a knowledge management tool's capabilities?
5. What are the main components of a knowledge-based organization's infrastructure and how are they interrelated?
6. What is the Internet? The World Wide Web? Web-browsing software?
7. What must be in place on a workstation in order to make use of the Internet?
8. What is a Web server? A home page?
9. How does plugging into an external technological structure benefit a knowledge worker?
10. How does a workstation's preprocessor help a knowledge worker?
11. How does an organization of task forces differ from one with traditional departments?
12. What is the function of a support center?
13. What does a chief knowledge officer do?
14. What qualifications should a CKO have?
15. How can research advances in various functional areas of management contribute to the realization of knowledge-based organizations? Give an example.
16. What are the main features of the emerging knowledge society?

▲ DISCUSSION TOPICS

1. Give several examples of knowledge workers.
2. Differentiate between knowledge workers who are specialists and those who are generalists.
3. Beyond basic computer literacy, what should knowledge workers appreciate in order to be effective?

4. What roles can expert systems play in the realization of knowledge-based organizations?
5. Discuss the relevance of ODSSs to a knowledge-based organization.
6. Should the CKO role be separate from the chief information officer?
7. Debate the advantages and disadvantages of infrastructure development by a CKO's unit versus a company that specializes in such work.
8. What needs to be done to make a knowledge-based organization a reality?
9. What limitations or pitfalls exist for knowledge workers who browse the World Wide Web?
10. If you were to design a course concerned with knowledge management, what would the course outline look like?
11. Discuss the impact that the emerging knowledge society might have on (a) knowledge workers, (b) organizations, (c) countries, (d) you, and (e) educational institutions.
12. Explain how a workstation can be regarded as a knowledge worker.
13. Discuss the relationship between reengineering and knowledge-based organizations.

▲ REFERENCES

Applegate, L. M., J. I. Cash, Jr., and D. Q. Miles. 1988. Information technology and tomorrow's manager. *Harvard Business Review* (November).

Byrne, J. A., R. Brandt, and O. Port. 1993. The virtual corporation. *Business Week* (February 8).

Cash, J. I., Jr. 1995. Protecting your Net assets. *Information Week* (May 22).

Ching, C., C. W. Holsapple, and A. B. Whinston. 1992. Reputation, learning, and organizational coordination. *Organization Science* 3, no. 2.

Davenport, T. 1994. Coming soon: The CKO. *Information Week* (September 5).

Drucker, P. F. 1988. The coming of the new organization. *Harvard Business Review* (January).

———. 1994. The age of social transformation. *Atlantic Monthly* 274, no. 5.

Holsapple, C. W., and A. B. Whinston. 1987. Knowledge-based organizations. *The Information Society* 5, no. 2.

Leonard-Barton, D. 1995. *Wellsprings of knowledge*. Boston: Harvard Business School Press.

Radding, A. 1995. Support decision makers with a data warehouse. *Datamation* 41, no. 5.

Snow, C. C., R. E. Miles, and H. J. Coleman. 1992. Managing 21st century network organizations. *Organizational Dynamics* 20, no. 3.

Tesler, L. G. 1995. Networked computing in the 1990s. *Scientific American*. Special issue: The Computer in the 21st Century.

Tully, S. 1993. Modular corporation. *Fortune* (February 8).

Whinston, A. B. 1994. Reengineering education. *Journal of Information Systems Education* 6, no. 3.

Widdifield, R., and V. Grover. 1995. Internet & the implications of the information superhighway for business. *Journal of Systems Management* (May).

EXPRESSION MANAGEMENT

Suppose you manage eight sales representatives. What would be the added monthly cost of giving each a $41.57 increase in the entertainment allowance? Using expression management, we might type the request

`OUTPUT 8*41.57`

The expression manager evaluates the arithmetic expression (8*41.57) and outputs the result of 332.56.

Suppose you want to save this result to use in later calculations. You might type the request

`M = 332.56`

Later, this value of the variable M could be used to calculate and view the annual increase by typing

`OUTPUT M*12`

or, perhaps,

`OUTPUT M*12 USING "$d,ddd.dd", "annual increase for $41.57"`

In the former case the output is 3990.72, whereas in the latter case there is a more elaborate presentation:

`$3,990.72 annual increase for $41.57`

which might be printed for later reference or circulation. The USING clause tells the software what conventions to use when portraying a value on the screen. The series of characters enclosed in quotes is often called a *picture*. This picture of $d,ddd.dd says that the result should be displayed with a dollar sign in front, followed by one digit (d stands for digit), a comma, three digits, a decimal point, and—finally—two more digits.

If you want to use this picture frequently, you might give the expression manager the command

`MACRO PIC USING "$d,ddd.dd"`

to define a new term (i.e., PIC) that will thereafter be interpreted as meaning the same thing as an entire series of keystrokes (i.e., using "$d,ddd.dd"). Such user-defined terms are commonly called *macros* and are often used to save keystroking effort (e.g., allowing a user to simply type the 3 characters of PIC instead of the 17 keystrokes involved in USING "$d,ddd.dd").

Suppose you frequently need to convert monthly figures to daily rates. This conversion can be facilitated by defining a function to do the necessary calculations, no matter what the monthly figure happens to be. For instance, typing something like

FUNCTION MTOD (@1,@2) (@1*12)/(366-@2)

could create a function named MTOD (i.e., Month-TO-Day), having two arguments that are used in calculating a value according to the specified expression. The first argument, @1, is the monthly value to be converted. The second argument, @2, should have a value of 0 for a leap year and 1 otherwise. Applying the MTOD function to the variable M for the year 1995, you would type

OUTPUT MTOD (M,1)

to display the result calculated from (332.56*12)/(366–1). The MTOD function is a very simple example of a flexible solver. Expression-management software typically furnishes a set of built-in, predefined functions for very common calculations (e.g., a square root calculation). They are examples of fixed solvers.

From the foregoing example, it is clear that an expression is a representation of simple procedural knowledge. It uses operators to indicate the step(s) that should be taken to calculate a desired value. Each variable an expression manager keeps track of represents a fragment of descriptive knowledge. A picture is a simple example of presentation knowledge, governing the packaging of a response. Conversely, a macro definition is a common example of linguistic knowledge, being needed for the interpretation of certain requests. Part Three surveys other techniques for managing descriptive, procedural, presentation, and linguistic knowledge. They are better able to cope with more complex and larger volumes of knowledge than expression management.

OBJECTS OF INTEREST

Of the objects shown in Figure 9–2, our focus here is primarily on expressions. Because variables and functions are important kinds of operands in expressions, this examination of them is embedded within the larger discussion of expressions. Following that discussion, we briefly consider macros and two special classes of built-in variables that serve as control switches and sensors.

Expressions   Expressions can contain three basic kinds of operands: constants, variables, and functions. A *constant* is simply an unchanging, literal value (and thus is sometimes called a literal). A numeric constant is simply a number. It may be an integer or a decimal number. A *string constant* consists of a string of text involving any characters that have corresponding keys on the keyboard. All the characters that make up a string are interpreted as a whole, literally and verbatim. We enclose each string constant in quotes to differentiate it from individual words used in commands. A logical constant consists of either the word TRUE or the word FALSE (or perhaps the letters *T* and *F*). Whereas a constant value is fixed, the value of a *variable* can vary. Minimally, a variable has a name, a type (e.g., numeric, string, logical), and a value. Its value is always consistent with its type. For instance, a numeric variable always has a numeric value. A variable may have other traits, such as a picture, an explanatory label, and security codes, to control who has access to its value. Each variable can be thought of as being a storage compartment where we can place a value for later use. Whenever we want to use a variable's value, we simply type its name.

In addition to constants and variables as operands, an expression can contain *functions*. A function carries out a specific kind of procedure to produce a value. The procedure may be one that is not easily or concisely expressed in terms of operators such as +, −, **, /, or *. However, it can be easily expressed by referring to the function by name. Each function typically has a name that is suggestive of the kind of operation it carries out. For instance, SQRT might be the name of a built-in function that calculates square roots. The value produced by a function may depend on arguments specified with the function. Arguments are traditionally enclosed in a matching pair of parentheses following the function's name. For instance,

```
SQRT(25)
```

has one argument (25) and yields a result of 5.

A function can appear anywhere that a constant or variable could be used in an expression that is being evaluated. A function's arguments do not have to be constants, as in the example just shown. Arguments can be variables or expressions involving operators and even other functions. Functions are traditionally classified according to the kinds of values they can produce. Thus, SQRT is an example of a numeric function, because it always produces a numeric result. Similarly, string functions produce strings of text as values. Logical functions are those that yield either TRUE or FALSE as a value.

If expression-management software gives us the ability to define our own functions (such as the previous MTOD example), then we can store the procedures embodied in these definitions in a KS, where the PPS can access them as needed in manufacturing responses for requests. For each, we may also be able to store a description that explains the nature of the function and its arguments. The PPS then uses such descriptions in responding to assistance requests. Similarly, if a variable has a label stored along with its value in the KS, then the PPS could use it to offer explanatory help in response to a request for assistance concerning the nature of that variable. We can combine variables and constants of the same type into an expression by means of operators, which indicate how the expression is to be evaluated. An expression's type is determined by the result of this evaluation.

A *numeric expression* consists of one or more numeric constants, numeric variables, and/or numeric functions connected by numeric operators, such as +, -, /, *, and ** (exponentiation). Examples of numeric expressions are

```
SALARY
2800
SALARY+COMMIS*10000
2800+.018*10000
(2800+.018)*10000
```

The first two have no operators, because they each involve only one term. The third is an expression involving two variables, a constant, and two operators. The last two expressions are similar except for the parentheses which are precedence indicators. When calculated, their values will be different.

Terms inside parentheses are always evaluated first. The exponentiation operator (if present) gets the next-highest precedence, followed by division and multiplication and, finally, addition and subtraction. Thus, the expression

2800+.018*10000 represents a procedure that causes 0.018 to be multiplied by 10,000 before adding 2,800 to the result. In contrast, the expression (2800+.018)*10000 represents a procedure that causes 2,800 and 0.018 (within parentheses) to be added together before multiplying the result by 10,000.

A *string expression* comprises one or more string constants, string variables, or string functions. These are connected by a string operator such as + (concatenation). Examples of string expressions include

```
"2820 Elm Street"
TRIM(STREET)+", "+CITY
"The rep's name is "+REPNAME
```

The first is just a single string constant and involves no operator. The second concatenates the values of the three strings. The first is the value of a string function, TRIM, which trims any trailing blanks off of the value of its argument (i.e., the STREET variable in this case). The second is the string constant composed of a comma followed by a space. The third is the value of the CITY variable. The third example concatenates the value of REPNAME to the end of a four-word string constant.

Just as numeric expressions have numeric values and string expressions have string values, a *logical expression* always has a logical value. When calculated, its value will be either TRUE or FALSE. The simplest kind of logical expression is a single logical constant or variable. More interesting logical expressions involve comparisons of the "is this greater than that" variety. A comparison, formally called a *relational expression,* is concerned with the relationship between two things of like type. Common relational operators include

```
GT   GE   LT   LE   EQ   NE
```

or, equivalently,

```
>   >=   <   <=   =   <>
```

Examples of relational expressions include

```
SALARY GE 2000
COMMIS*10000<185.2
"Kris" GT "Kevin"
STATE IN ["Indiana", "Kentucky", "Illinois", "Ohio"]
```

The first expression compares the value of the SALARY variable to the numeric constant 2000. When this expression's value is calculated, the result will be TRUE if the present value of SALARY is greater than or equal to 2,000; otherwise it will be FALSE. Similarly, the second expression evaluates to TRUE if 10,000 times the COMMIS value is less than 185.2; otherwise it is FALSE.

The third expression shows that we can compare strings as well as numbers. Its value is TRUE because Kr is greater than Ke in alphabetic sequence. The fourth example, involving the relational IN operator, is TRUE only if the STATE variable's value matches one of the four bracketed string constants.

Aside from relational expressions, another common type of logical expression is a compound logical expression involving the AND or OR operators. For example,

```
REPNAME GE "Kevin" AND SALARY<=2900
```

will evaluate to TRUE if and only if both of the comparisons are TRUE. In general, multiple relational expressions can be connected as a single compound logical expression by logical operators such as AND and OR. If OR had been used in this example, the evaluation would yield TRUE if either or both of the comparisons were TRUE.

Why should we care about calculating strings and things? Isn't numeric calculation enough? String and logical calculations are important. In fact, they are so pervasive in our own mental endeavors that we tend to take them for granted. Think about how many times a day you put together strings of text and store away or present the result. Think about how often you compare one thing to another, where the result of the comparison (either TRUE or FALSE) influences what you will do next or what conclusion you will draw about some situation.

Macros   A macro is nothing more than a name that we give to an entire series of keystrokes, so that when we need to enter those keystrokes we can merely enter the macro name instead of all the keystrokes it represents. When we invent a new macro, we should choose a name that does not conflict with words already in the language system (e.g., SQRT, OUTPUT, EQ). We identify some keystroke sequence that we expect to type over and over again in various requests. For instance, suppose we want to use SALARY+COMMIS in several calculations. We might define a macro called SC by typing

    MACRO SC SALARY+COMMIS

Now, instead of typing out SALARY+COMMIS every time we need it, we simply type SC.

It is important to understand the difference between a macro and a variable. Whenever we want, we can invent a new variable or new macro. Either can be held in a problem-processing system's short-term working memory or stored in a knowledge system for later use. A variable is a storage compartment that holds a value, allowing us to get at that value again by mentioning the variable's name. On the other hand, a macro is a user-defined term that is essentially a synonym for some series of keystrokes. In effect, this feature allows us to add new words to a command language. Whenever we use one of these words, the expression manager will know what we mean.

Because a variable can have a value, we can classify variables according to the types of values they have: numeric, string, or logical variables. In contrast, macros do not have values; therefore, there is no notion of different types of macros. In knowledge-management terms, a variable is concerned with descriptive knowledge, whereas a macro is concerned with linguistic knowledge.

Function keys (labeled F1, F2, ... on a keyboard) can be used to achieve results similar to macros. Instead of defining a new term and its associated keystroke sequence, we can define a keystroke sequence for an existing function key. Whenever we later press that key, its entire sequence of associated keystrokes automatically appears on the screen, beginning at the present cursor position. It is just as if we actually typed them all, except we merely pushed a single key.

Built-in Variables   So far, we have considered variables that are invented by users of an expression manager to meet their needs for storing data values. Because these are the variables with which we usually work, they are often called *working variables*. Aside from working variables, expression-management software may recognize a number of built-in variables. The values of these predefined variables can be viewed and changed like those of working variables. However, built-in variables can never be eliminated, and their values have a special significance related to governing and monitoring the processing performed by the expression management software. Here, we look at how built-in variables can serve as control switches and sensors that facilitate interaction with an expression manager.

A control switch gives a user a way of controlling some aspect of the software's behavior, thereby shaping the environment within which processing occurs. Some pieces of software have no control switches. Others have many switches, allowing users to tailor the software behavior to suit their respective tastes and needs. Control switches can take various forms. One of the most common of these involves built-in variables that we refer to as *environment variables*.

For the most part, the settings of environment variables are a way of representing certain linguistic and presentation knowledge. The PPS software uses this knowledge in understanding user requests and in presenting responses to the user. For example, an expression manager might maintain an environment variable that lets a user control the number of decimal digits displayed for numerical results when a picture is not specified. Suppose this built-in variable is named E.DECI. Then, if we generally want three digits displayed to the right of a decimal point in numerical results, we would set the E.DECI variable to have a value of 3. As other examples, there may be environment variables whose values control the foreground and background colors of console displays, whether output is to be routed to a printer or disk file, and how verbose error messages should be. Aside from environmental variables, there is another class of built-in variables that may be available, when managing expressions. We shall call these *utility variables*. Unlike other kinds of variables, the values of utility variables can be automatically changed by the software itself to reflect some happening. In effect, they are sensors that allow a user to examine the present state of affairs while interacting with the software. For instance, such variables might give the most recent error or the present date. At any time, a user can look at the value of a corresponding utility variable to get a current reading. The reading seen may well be different from the reading that is seen later for the same sensor.

PROCESSING THE OBJECTS

Variables   Defining the existence of a variable involves a request that indicates the variable's name and perhaps its type, picture, label, security controls, and initial value. The result is that space is allocated to hold a value for the variable either temporarily in the short-term, working memory of the PPS or more permanently on a disk file in the KS. In the former case, the variable will cease to exist when interaction with the PPS is terminated. In the latter case, the variable (including its most recent value) will be available to be recalled into working memory for use in subsequent sessions of interaction with the PPS. The KS disk file in which it is stored likely contains other variables and perhaps functions and macros as well.

Predefined variables, of course, cannot be defined. Nevertheless, their values can be preserved in a KS disk file if desired and later recalled, making it easy to pick up a later processing session with the same control settings in force as when the prior session ended.

Once variables exist or have been recalled, it is possible to request that a listing of their names (and labels, if any) be shown. More specifically, a request can be made to view a particular variable's value or all that variable's attributes. In the former case, the value that is output will be presented according to the variable's picture, if any. However, if the request to view the value contains a picture, that picture will override any pictures specified when the variable was defined. A request to view all of a variable's attributes will show its name, current value, type, and any other traits optionally allowed by the expression manager (e.g., picture or label).

Analogous to viewing requests are requests to change a specific variable's value or some of that variable's other attributes (e.g., its name, picture, or label). In the case of built-in variables, however, such attributes cannot be changed. Another method for processing a working variable is to delete it either from the KS or from working memory by releasing the storage space it occupied.

Functions If an expression manager allows functions to be defined, such definitions could be for short-run use, only within the current processing session, or they could be stored in a KS disk file, available for recall whenever needed. It is possible to request that a listing of a function's names (and descriptions) be shown in order to see those currently available for use or available for recall. More specifically, you may issue a request to view a particular function's definition or that function's value for a specified argument(s) value. Another kind of processing involves changing a function's attributes by editing its definition, description, or name. Finally, a function can be deleted from either working memory or the KS.

Macros Like variables and functions, macros can be defined to exist in working memory for short-run use by the PPS and/or preserved in the KS for longer-term survival. Once in the KS, a macro definition can be recalled for use in the current processing session. You can request a list of all macro names that can be interpreted. You can also view and edit the definition of a specific macro, if desired. Macros can be deleted from working memory and/or a KS disk file.

Expressions The most common processing for an expression is to specify it in a request that asks the PPS to compute a value for it. This specification may be for the purpose of displaying the expression's value or for assigning that value to a variable. In the former case, the request may include a picture to enhance the output. In the later case, the variable's prior value is changed to be the same as the expression's value. Expressions can also be specified as part of the activity of defining a function or macro instead of for immediate evaluation. Another method of expression processing is to request that the previously specified expression be displayed for view and possible editing if desired. You can then evaluate the edited expression specification to see the effect of the change.

TEXT MANAGEMENT

Suppose the vice president (VP) for operations needs to make a decision about procuring vehicles for her company. The decision will be based in part on the recommendation of a procurement committee assigned to study and analyze alternative vehicle fleet configurations. The committee's report to the VP consists of a collection of documents: a one-page executive summary showing the cost of each alternative and the final recommendation, a background account of the company's projected transport needs, a description of each of the alternatives to be considered, a document showing detailed financial and other data used as a basis for analysis, a statement of the procedures for and results of quantitative analysis for each alternative, a discussion of qualitative issues relevant to each alternative, and so forth.

In the course of its development, this report underwent many extensions, refinements, and other modifications. Text-management software was used to create initial versions of the report's text, with distinct documents being stored on separate disk files. In some cases, an expression manager integrated into the software may have been used to calculate some numbers appearing in the documents. The same text manager was used by committee members in revising contents of the documents to reflect new data as they were gathered, improved analytic procedures as they were devised, and current reasoning about each alternative based on quantitative and qualitative analyses. Ultimately the final modifications to the report were made in order to present the knowledge it contained in as clear a manner as possible for the VP's consumption.

The resultant electronic report became part of the KS in the DSS used by the VP. With the text-management software in this DSS's problem processing system, the VP could not only read the report's documents in a linear fashion, but could have a lengthy document quickly scanned to see only those portions containing a particular phrase of interest. For instance, on the spur of the moment, the VP may want to see all passages referring to a particular vehicle vendor or a particular procurement alternative. Aside from both structured and unstructured explorations of the text, the VP could enter additional text into the KS. For example, she may want to make notes electronically in the margins of existing text to keep track of ideas and questions stimulated by her explorations.

From the foregoing example, it is clear that a textual passage can be a representation of descriptive knowledge (e.g., a description of an alternative, a column of financial data), procedural knowledge (e.g., steps to follow in analyzing an alternative), or even reasoning knowledge (e.g., specification of heuristics used to derive a recommendation). However, conventional text management is unable to distinguish among types of knowledge represented textually. A piece of text is a piece of text and is processed as such. Text processing allows creation, modification, viewing, and deletion of text. It does not automatically carry out the steps in procedures that happen to be represented textually or carry out inferences on reasoning knowledge that is represented as text.

OBJECTS OF INTEREST

A document's lines of text are made up of strings of words (with punctuation marks). Words include not only terms that could be found in a dictionary, but also abbreviations, special names, numbers, mathematical formulas, and so forth. From a text-processing perspective, a word is some string of contiguous symbols delineated by other symbols, such as spaces or punctuation marks.

Although a document may have control indicators, they are not part of textual passages per se. Instead, they govern the appearance and use of the document. Among the various kinds of control indicators are those that control the format of a textual passage, those that indicate what is to be inserted at designated places in a document, and those that govern security of the document's contents.

Format controls are essentially a kind of presentation knowledge used to determine various aspects of a document's appearance, such as margins, spacings, alignments, and page numbers. An insertion indicator is embedded in a document as a placeholder, indicating what should be put in that place when the document is presented (e.g, printed). Insertion possibilities include some text from another document (e.g., a name and address), the result of evaluating an expression, or a graphical image. Some security controls are a kind of assimilative knowledge, restricting what can be entered into a document by preventing unauthorized persons from making alterations. There may also be security controls that restrict the presentation of the document—or parts of it—to certain persons.

A page header is a chunk of text that will appear at the top of some or every page when the document is presented. Similarly, a footer appears at the bottom of pages. Footnotes and endnotes are chunks of text related to marked positions in the main textual passages of a document. A document can have lists, each of which consists of words or phrases coupled with the corresponding page numbers indicating where they can be found in the document. Two common kinds of lists are a table of contents and an index. Lists, footnotes, endnotes, and even insertion indicators are relatively primitive forerunners of the hypertext concept. As discussed in Chapter 9, this concept involves electronically linking logically related pieces of text so that a user can quickly follow a link from the currently viewed text to bring some other relevant piece of text into view.

For highlighting purposes, it is common to allow the incorporation of horizontal and vertical lines into documents. A document (or portions of it) may be structured into columns. These may be textual columns, with lines of text snaking from one column to the next (as in a newspaper) or with textual passages developed separately in each column (as in a two-column listing of products and their sales levels). Alternatively, columns may have numeric expressions. For instance, the first column might contain employee salaries (numeric constants), the second might have their fringe-benefit values (numeric constants), and the third could be defined as an expression consisting of sums of the first two columns to show each employee's total compensation.

Within a document, boxes may be sprinkled throughout the main textual passage. Each box could have a caption, some style indicators, and contents. A caption is a string of symbols identifying the box (e.g., by numbering it) and characterizing its contents. Style indicator settings control such presentation aspects as the shading of box contents and the type of box border (e.g., its thickness). Box contents may simply be lines of text. More elaborate contents include figures and tables, such as those in this book.

PROCESSING THE OBJECTS

In addition to the processing methods summarized in Table 9.2, there are processing methods for other textual objects. Headers, footers, footnotes, and endnotes are typically specified by typing their contents. In the cases of the latter two, a marker (e.g., number) relating it to some point in the text must also be specified. Each of these objects is stored or recalled as part of the document. Each can be edited, deleted, and viewed on the console or positioned in the printed document.

A text manager can be requested to generate a list (e.g., index or table of contents) and position it at a desired place in the document. However, before this can be done, the user must view the text and flag every item (e.g., word or phrase) that is to be included in the list. When the list-generation request is subsequently issued, the text manager assembles the flagged items into a list with corresponding page numbers for each item.

Line processing in text involves requests for specifying a line (indicating its position, orientation, length, thickness, shading, etc.), changing some aspects of it or deleting it. Lines are stored, recalled, and viewed as part of the document. Columns are specified by indicating their type (e.g., snaking versus parallel) and typing text lines or expressions into them. Their contents can be changed or deleted. They can be stored, recalled, or viewed as part of a document.

When a box is specified it is given a caption, its style indicators are set (to determine the border style and box shading), its contents are created or inserted (from a separate file), and its position in the document is specified. Boxes are stored, recalled, and viewed as part of a document. Aside from changing its contents and style, there may be methods for rotating, shrinking, or enlarging the box as a whole. Finally, a box can be deleted from a document.

Implementations of the text-management technique typically permit on-line help to be requested for each object and its methods, plus requests not tied to any particular object. The latter include requests to change environment variable settings such as the console foreground and background colors, the identifier for the kind of printer that will be used, and the number of text display windows to allow on the screen at any one time. They also include basic file-manipulation requests, such as those to see a directory, rename a file, or copy a file.

DATA MANAGEMENT

Data management in its various guises is an extremely valuable way of structuring and processing descriptive knowledge. Broadly speaking, there are two main branches in the data-management field. One is data file management, which often allows data to be structured in a more or less tabular fashion but which does not support either of the standard relational command languages.

The other branch is database management. Here there are classic, well-defined approaches (called data models) for representing and processing a database. These include the relational data model (which is our focus here), with its two standard languages. One of these languages involves commands (e.g., PROJECT and JOIN) that operate on existing tables to produce new tables. The other is a higher-level language that can avoid the production of intermediate tables in achieving a desired processing result.

A database is not a file; instead it is a collection of interrelated records of many different kinds (e.g., performance, sales representative, product, and expense records). These records and their relationships are represented according to the structuring conventions of a data model and processed with the data model's commands. Together, a data model's structuring conventions and processing language form a database-management technique.

The relational database-management technique organizes a database's records into tables. Relationships between tables' records are established by repeating one table's data in another table, as described here.

OBJECT OF INTEREST

Tables   A table's structure is defined in terms of the columns or categories of data that can exist in the table. Traditionally, a table's data categories are called *fields*. Each field is given a name that indicates the kind of data it holds. For instance, we might define a table named PROD to hold records about the various product lines. This table's structure might involve fields named PID (product ID), PNAME (product name), TARGET (product's sales target), GMR (product's gross margin rate), and CRATE (commission rate for a product). This structure will allow each product record we create in the table to have five data values: an ID, name, target, gross margin rate, and commission rate.

Figure C.1 shows two conventional and equivalent ways of diagramming the PROD table's structure. Sketching diagrams of this kind can be a useful shorthand way of conveying table structures for purposes of discussion. In each case, a rectangle encloses the table's field names, and the rectangle is labeled with the name of the table. As the number of fields per table becomes larger, the top style of diagram becomes increasingly unwieldy relative to the second kind of diagram.

FIGURE C.1   Alternative Diagrams of the PROD Table's Structure

```
PROD
┌───────┬───────┬────────┬───────┬───────┐
│ PID   │ PNAME │ TARGET │ GMR   │ CRATE │
└───────┴───────┴────────┴───────┴───────┘
PROD
┌────────┐
│ PID    │
│ PNAME  │
│ TARGET │
│ GMR    │
│ CRATE  │
└────────┘
```

A table can contain records. Each record conforms to the table's structure by having one value for each field. A table's records are stored in a disk file.

Physically, the content of a table file is arranged very differently than the content of a text file. A table file's content may be encrypted, which means that if we were to try to view it like a piece of text, it would appear to be gibberish. This is a security feature that helps prevent unauthorized persons from seeing a table's content.

Fields   A field has other characteristics aside from its name. Whenever we invent a field, we need to indicate what its type is. A field's stated type controls what kind of data values are permissible for it. As with a variable in expression management, a field can be either string, numeric, or logical in type. Once a type has been stated, all values of that field throughout the table must adhere to that type. For example, the GMR field would be declared to be numeric, which means the database-management software will permit only numeric values to be stored for the GMR field.

Field size indicates the maximum number of characters allowed for any value of the field. For example, PID would be designated as a string field of size 3 if a product ID never exceeds three characters. If we use a picture in our specification of a field, that picture will control the appearance of any of that field's values when it is presented on the screen or printer. The picture also determines what values are valid for the field on a character-by-character basis. For example, if the third placeholder in a field's picture is *d,* then the database manager will prohibit a nondigit from appearing in that position for any of the field's values. Filters give another way of helping to ensure the validity of a field's data values. For example, we may restrict values of CRATE to the range 0.01 to 0.20.

When declaring a field, we can give it a label if we like. A label is just a description of the meaning of a field. For instance, a label of "gross margin rate" might be given to the GMR field. Labels are most useful when we give a field a short name whose meaning is not immediately obvious.

Most fields tend to be actual. That is, their values are actually stored in a table. However, some fields may be virtual. Their values are never stored and do not actually exist anywhere until the very moment we want to look at one of them. At that moment, the value materializes. Their values take up no storage space but yet are always present when we need to see them. Moreover, there is never any need for changing the values for this kind of field.

A virtual field is defined just like an actual field, with one exception. It includes an expression that tells the database manager how to calculate the field's values whenever a value is needed. All five fields discussed for the PROD table are actual fields. We might include a sixth field in the table called CTARG, whose value in a particular record would be the product line's commission target. If this were an actual field, we would need to type in the product of a record's CRATE and TARGET values as being the actual CTARG value when creating each record. In addition, whenever a CRATE or TARGET value changes, we would have to make a corresponding change to the actual CTARG value. But, if we let CTARG be a virtual field, we just define its values as always being equal to CRATE*TARGET. Then we never actually have to enter or change a value for the CTARG field.

PROCESSING THE OBJECTS

Once a table's structure has been envisioned (e.g., via a diagram), it needs to be defined. For example, the PROD table structure of Figure C.1 must be defined before records can be created in it. The definition of a table includes such items as the table name, the name of a disk file that will hold the table, and declarations of the table's fields, along with their respective characteristics.

Figure C.2 shows diagrams for the REP and PERF table structures. In addition to the table and field names, these diagrams show descriptive labels for each. Virtual fields are indented. Along with PROD, these tables will be used in the discussion that follows. An example of a command to define the PERF table is given in Figure C.3. User entries are lowercase and the database manager prompts (i.e., FILE? and FIELD?) are uppercase.

Notice that the PERF table definition has two numeric virtual fields: QYR and SYTD. The value of QYR for any record is always guaranteed to be the sum of the present Q1, Q2, Q3, and Q4 values for that record. Similarly, a record's SYTD value is always calculated to be the sum of whatever its S1 through S4 values happen to be at the moment that the SYTD value is accessed.

In this table there is a label for almost every field. The table definition also has an example of a logical field. Because each PERF record will pertain to a particular representative's performance figures for a particular product line, that record either will or will not involve one of the representative's major product lines. Thus, we have

FIGURE C.2   Diagrams of REP and PERF Table Structures

REP	Representative		PERF	Performance
FNAME	First name		TID	Territory ID
MIDI	Middle initial		FNAME	First name
LNAME	Last name		PID	Product ID
NAME	Full name		Q1	Quota for quarter 1
SPOUSE	Spouse name		Q2	Quota for quarter 2
HDATE	Hire date		Q3	Quota for quarter 3
PHONE	Phone number		Q4	Quota for quarter 4
TID	Territory ID		QYR	Quota for the year
STREET	Street		S1	Sales for quarter 1
CITY	City		S2	Sales for quarter 2
STATE	State		S3	Sales for quarter 3
ZIP	Zip		S4	Sales for quarter 4
ADDR	Full Address		SYTD	Sales year to date
MOSAL	Monthly salary		MAJOR	Major product
MOEXP	Monthly budgeted expense			
MAJORP	Major products			

FIGURE C.3   Defining the PERF Table

```
define perf
FILE? "a:perf.itb"
FIELD? tid str 3 using "n  " labeled "Territory ID"
FIELD? fname str 8 using "uaaaaaaa" labeled "First name of rep"
FIELD? pid str 3 using "aaa" labeled "Product ID"
FIELD? q1 num using "ffffff" labeled "Quota: quarter 1"
FIELD? q2 num using "ffffff" labeled "Quota: quarter 2"
FILED? q3 num using "ffffff" labeled "Quota: quarter 3"
FILED? q4 num using "ffffff" labeled "Quota: quarter 4"
FIELD? qyr num =q1+q2+q3+q4 using "nnnnnn"
FIELD? s1 num using "ffffff" labeled "Sales: quarter 1"
FIELD? s2 num using "ffffff" labeled "Sales: quarter 2"
FIELD? s3 num using "ffffff" labeled "Sales: quarter 3"
FIELD? s4 num using "ffffff" labeled "Sales: quarter 4"
FIELD? sytd num =s1+s2+s3+s4 using "nnnnnn" labeled "Sales year to date"
FIELD? major logic using "lllll" labeled "Major prod for rep"
FIELD?
```

included the MAJOR field, whose value will be TRUE for major performance records and FALSE for records that do not deal with a representative's major products.

As soon as we define a table, it is in use. That simply means we are free to process it. If a table is not in use, we cannot process it. At any moment, we can request a list of what tables happen to be in use. For any of these, we can request that its structure be shown. Or, we may be interested in the characteristics of only one particular field. Then, we can ask to be shown that field's traits without having to step through all the other fields. Processing requests for showing tables and their structures can be quite handy if at some moment we happen to forget which tables are in use, what their fields are, or the characteristics of some field.

Many tables can be in use simultaneously. This fact is extremely important, because we often want to work on several tables in a single operation. Just as there is a processing method to put a table in use, there is also one to indicate when we are finished using it. Finishing a table frees up some of the PPS's working memory for other purposes.

Whenever a table is put in use, a portion of the work area is allocated for managing the transfer of records between disk and main memory, where they can actually be acted on by the database-management software. This portion of main memory is often called a *buffer*. It contains images of those records that are susceptible to immediate processing.

If a record whose image is not in the buffer is needed, the database manager takes care of bringing it into the buffer, where it can be processed. At the same time, it also takes care of sending images that were in the buffer back out to the disk file. Whenever something comes into the buffer, something that was already there has to go out to make room for the new images.

We do not have to worry about explicitly telling the software to bring individual records into the work area from disk or to save individual records from the work area to disk. All that is handled automatically for us beneath the surface—as long as the table is in use. When we finish a table, the images in its buffer are flushed out to disk, and we cannot process it further until it is again put in use.

Among the tables in use at any given time, we may designate one as the default table. Many database-management commands normally require us to specify the table to which we are referring. However, if we do not specify a table in the command, the database manager assumes that we want it to process the default table. For example, if instead of typing FINISH REP, we just type FINISH, the default table will be finished instead of REP. When the concept of a default table is supported, there will be a command that can be used to make a different table the current default.

Creating Records   Once we have defined a table, we can create records in it either immediately or at some later date. The only requirement is that the table must be in use. Generally speaking, there are two basic approaches to record creation: interactive and batch. Interactive creation means that a user types in a record's data values as the record is being created. Although it is not part of the standard relational data-management languages, some software packages facilitate the interactive creation activity by prompting the user with field names. The user can then type the record's data values in alongside their corresponding field names. Batch creation means that a batch of records is created by taking data from some nontable source and attaching it to the table. The nontable source might be a text file or file produced by some other external software.

Accessing an Individual Record   Here, we look at two of the simplest viewing methods, which we will call *obtain* and *browse*. An obtain request obtains a specific record from a table and displays its field values (if desired). A browse request lets us browse through a table's records in either a forward or reverse direction, viewing one at a time. It also gives the chance to edit the values of records as we browse.

To obtain the first record from the PROD table, we might type

OBTAIN FIRST RECORD FROM PROD

The software's response would be a display of all the field values for that record. To obtain the next record in the PROD table, we type

OBTAIN NEXT FROM PROD

and the values of its fields come into view. Similarly, we could obtain last and prior records for viewing.

We can also obtain records conditionally by incorporating logical expressions into requests. For instance, to obtain the next record whose TARGET value exceeds 221,000, for example, the request is

OBTAIN NEXT FROM PROD WHERE TARGET>221000

or, to obtain the record having information about romance books, the request is

OBTAIN RECORD FROM PROD WHERE PID="ROM"

Notice that the logical expression in the second example involved a string field and a string constant, whereas the prior example's logical expression involved a numeric field and a numeric constant. As we saw with expression management, a logical expression can itself have numeric calculations on either side of a relational operation. For instance, the request

OBTAIN FIRST RECORD FROM PROD WHERE TARGET*CRATE>5640

obtains the first PROD record whose total targeted commission exceeds 5640. We can also use compound logical expressions as conditions.

Although obtain requests are worthwhile for getting at a particular record, we might want to view all the REP records that have a monthly salary in excess of $2,400, for instance. Rather than repeatedly executing obtain requests, we could issue a single browsing request to rummage about in the table. It lets us browse in either direction through all the records that satisfy whatever condition we are interested in without having to issue more than one command.

Entering a command such as

BROWSE REP FOR MOSAL>2400

causes the screen to clear momentarily before the first REP record with a MOSAL in excess of 2,400 appears. In addition to viewing the record's values, we can edit them as desired by simply moving the cursor to a value and retyping it. Pressing a key (e.g., Page Down) would bring into view the next representative having a monthly salary greater than $2,400.

Any kind of condition that can be specified for an obtain request can also be specified for a browse request. The browsing behavior with the ability to edit values is the same, regardless of what condition is stated. The condition just restricts which of a table's records will be accessible during browsing. For instance, a request such as

BROWSE REP FOR LNAME="Smith"

browses through only those REP records with a last name of Smith,

BROWSE PERF FOR QYR*.75<SYTD

browses through the performance records for which year-to-date sales have not yet surpassed three-fourths of the annual quota, and

BROWSE PERF FOR QYR*.75<SYTD AND MAJOR

does the same as the previous command but with the further restriction that only those records with MAJOR values equal to TRUE are browsed. The command

BROWSE REP FOR TID IN ["3","9","2"]

browses through REP records whose territory ID is 3 or 9 or 2.

It may be possible to focus on certain fields while browsing. For instance, we might want to focus on third-quarter performance while browsing through performance records without visually wading through all the data. Suppose we would like to see the representative's name, the product ID, the third-quarter sales figure, and the third-quarter quota. We want to see only that information for each record while browsing. This result is accomplished with the request

BROWSE PERF WITH FNAME,PID,S3,Q3

While browsing through successive PERF records, their values for these four fields are the only ones displayed. Notice that the fields are requested in a different order than the order in which they have been defined for the table.

Relational Algebra Relational algebra commands make new tables from existing tables. The new table may contain a subset of the data in an existing table. The subset may be formed by pulling out only those records that satisfy some condition, by pulling out the data values for selected fields, or both. Alternatively, a new table contains data from two existing tables. Unlike obtain and browse methods, an algebraic command processes an entire table at a time.

Basic relational algebra commands include PROJECT, SELECT, JOIN, and UNION. There are others, but these are the main ones. PROJECT produces a new table by extracting a copy of certain columns (i.e., field values) from an existing table. The algebraic SELECT produces a new table by extracting a copy of certain rows (i.e., records) from a single existing table. Unlike these two commands, the JOIN command produces a new table from two existing tables. The new table's fields are the same as those defined for the two existing tables. The new table's records are formed by joining together matching rows from the two existing tables. Two rows match if they have the same value for some designated pair of fields, where one field is from one table and the other field is from the other table. The UNION command produces a new table by attaching the records of one existing table to those in another table. The two tables must be structurally the same.

Suppose we want to make a new table consisting of the third-quarter data from the PERF table. Let's call it PERF3. It would have the same number of records as PERF, but each PERF3 record would have data only for the PID, FNAME, TID, Q3, and S3 fields. We can do all this with a single PROJECT request:

```
PROJECT PID,FNAME,TID,Q3,S3 FROM PERF TO PERF3
```

The contents of the PERF table are unaffected. PERF3 is now available for use.

We could now make a new table from PERF3 itself, consisting of only those records for which sales are at least as great as the quota. Call it TOPPERF3. The SELECT command is

```
SELECT FROM PERF3 FOR Q3 GE S3 TO TOPPERF3
```

and it results in the new table of top performances in the third quarter.

Suppose we had made a new table called MIDPERF3, having the same fields as TOPPERF3. This new table might have performance records that are not at the top level but have sales within, say 10% of their quotas. We could add the MIDPERF3 records into the TOPPERF3 table of records with a single UNION command:

```
UNION FROM MIDPERF3 TOPPERF3
```

Imagine that we have made a table called BRIEFREP whose records contain the TID, MOSAL, and MOEXP field values from REP. We would like to produce a new, enlarged version of the PERF3 table. Each record of this new table should have the monthly salary and monthly budgeted expenses for the representative whose performance has been recorded there. Our request will need to identify two source tables, and we will have to indicate what basis to use for determining which record in BRIEFREP is related to which record in PERF3.

The following JOIN command accomplishes this:

```
JOIN FROM PERF3, BRIEFREP FOR PERF3.TID=BRIEFREP.TID to MIX3
```

The condition gives the software a basis for relating each PERF3 record to a corresponding BRIEFREP record. As each PERF3 record is considered, its TID value is noted. The software identifies the BRIEFREP record whose own TID value matches that of the PERF3 record. Together the data values of these two records form a new record in the MIX3 table whose structure involves all fields from both tables. This process is repeated for every PERF3 record until each has been examined and mated with its matching BRIEFREP record.

Table Modification   There are two distinct kinds of modifications that can be made to a table: those that modify its structure and those that modify its content. The create and browse methods modify a table's content, but in no way do they affect its structure. There are other methods for modifying table content, such as change and sort requests. Also, a redefine method modifies a table's structure. Before making significant modifications to a table, it may be prudent to make a backup copy. In the event that a problem arises during or because of the modification, we can restart the modification with the backup copy of the table.

If we want to make the same kind of change to many values of a field, we can use the change method. It is also a good way to make a change to a single field value based on some calculation. Suppose we need to reduce all sales targets by 45%. We can accomplish this result by the request

    CHANGE TARGET IN PROD TO TARGET—.45*TARGET

To increase each TARGET value by its corresponding commission rate, but only for those product lines having a gross margin rate of at least 60%, the corresponding command is

    CHANGE TARGET IN PROD TO TARGET*(1+CRATE) WHERE GMR>=.6

where each new TARGET value is calculated from the record's existing TARGET and CRATE values. The command's condition ensures that such a change is made only to those PROD records for which the GMR value is greater than or equal to the 0.6 level.

Relational database-management theory is very clear on the topic of ordering a table's records. No particular order is to be assumed, and the standard relational processing commands make no provision for reordering the sequence of records in a table. Nonetheless, having a table's records sorted in a particular order can be quite useful during browsing and for examining a listing. Thus, it is not unusual for a sort method to be available.

We may like to browse through PROD records alphabetically based on their respective IDs. If they are not already in that sequence, we can sort the product records based on the PID field:

    SORT PROD BY PID

Unless otherwise indicated in the SORT command, the sorting occurs in an ascending sequence. The records can be sorrted from highest to lowest sales targets:

    SORT PROD BY DESCENDING TARGET

Complex expressions involving multiple fields can be used as sort criteria. As an example, the command

    SORT PERF BY DESCENDING TID,ASCENDING(QYR—SYTD)/Q4

would sort the PERF records first by descending territory IDs. Among records with the same TID value, there is a secondary sorting. It is based on how close, in percentage terms, the representative is to achieving the fourth-quarter quota.

A redefine type of request lets us rename, delete, or alter the characteristics of existing fields. Because structural modification can be a fairly drastic action, potentially affecting every record as well as the structure, it may be advisable to make a backup copy of a table before modifying its structure. This advice is particularly pertinent for large tables with many thousands, or even hundreds, of records.

Figure C.4 gives an example of a redefine request. The first entry adds a new integer field named OLDTITLE to the table's structure. It could be used to keep track of the number of titles in a product line that were carryovers from prior years. The next entry adds another field to PROD's structure. This NEWTITLE field could be used to hold a count of new titles introduced into a product line in the current year. Then, an entry adds a virtual field whose value would be the commission target. The next entry changes the GMR field name to GMRATE. The final entry defines new characteristics for the existing TARGET field.

As the number of records in a table increases, we would naturally expect a database manager to take longer to access a particular record based on some condition. On the average, there are more records to look through in order to find the one we want. Access to individual records in a table can be speeded up by making and using an index. Just as we use an index to locate quickly some desired topic in an encyclopedia, a database manager uses an index to locate quickly some desired record in a table. All we have to do is request that an index be made and then have the software use the index when we desire.

Figure C.5 illustrates the connection between an index and a table. It shows a subset of the PERF records. Imagine that the PERF table contains only these 14 records. We know that each record can be uniquely identified by its territory ID and product ID. But neither a TID value nor a PID value by itself is sufficient to identify an individual PERF record. Many records can have the same TID value and many records can have the same PID value, but no more than one PERF record has a particular pair of TID and PID values.

Because the joint value of these two fields uniquely identifies each record in the table, we might want to base an index on them. For each possible value pair, the index will contain location information that tells the database manager where the corresponding PERF record is located. We traditionally call the fields on which an index is based the *key*. We call the location information that accompanies each index key value in the index a *pointer*. It commonly consists of the physical address of the corresponding record in the disk file holding the table. Rather than write out physical disk addresses in this diagram, we use arrows to show where the pointers lead.

Suppose we want to access the com record for territory 6. We would issue a command indicating an index key value of 6 and com. Once the database manager knows the index key value in which we are interested, it looks up that value in the

FIGURE C.4   Adding, Renaming, and Altering Fields

```
_redefine prod
FILE?
FIELD? +oldtitle int using "nnnn"
FIELD? +newtitle int using "nnnn"
FIELD? +ctarget num =crate*target using "fffff"
FIELD? *gmrate,gmr
FIELD? target num using. "$f,fff,fff"
FIELD?
```

FIGURE C.5   Visualization of an Index for the PERF Table

TID	FNAME	PID	Q1	...	MAJOR
1	Kris	bio	7400	...	true
8	Jackie	bio	4339	...	true
6	Karen	bus	10700	...	true
3	Tina	bus	6903	...	true
0	Kim	bus	7320	...	true
4	Toby	bus	4842	...	true
9	Carol	bus	3947	...	true
2	Kevin	bus	3009	...	false
6	Karen	com	12090	...	true
9	Carol	com	6903	...	true
3	Tina	com	5388	...	true
2	Kevin	spo	6509	...	true
0	Kim	spo	5400	...	true
8	Jackie	spo	5004	...	true

Index column:
```
0  bus
0  spo
1  bio
2  bus
2  spo
3  bus
3  com
4  bus
6  bus
6  com
8  bio
8  spo
9  bus
9  com
```

index to see where the corresponding record is located. Knowing that location, it can then directly access the record without having to rummage through any other PERF records in search of the one with a TID of 6 and a PID of com.

In actual practice, a database manager may employ *B-tree indexing*. B-tree and its several variants, involve a particular way of organizing and processing the entries in a multilevel index. It is quite different than a linear sequencing of entries in sorted order based on their key values. However, it is not necessary to know details about the insides of indexes in order to make good use of them.

Query Processing (Relational Calculus)   All kinds of facts are buried in a table like PERF. Beyond the raw numbers there is much more. There's the fact that Kim's second-quarter quota for reference books is higher than her first-quarter reference quota but less than her fourth-quarter reference quota. There is the fact that she will need fourth-quarter reference sales of at least 8,749 to meet her annual quota. There are the facts that reference performance data exist for five of the representatives, one of these has a lower annual quota than the others, and some are above the annual average quota.

It would be beneficial to have software discern such facts quickly. The decision maker would like a way to automate the focusing, combining, calculating, grouping, and ordering of data. As we work on making a decision, we reach a point where we need to find out something from a database of tables before moving ahead. We would like to make a spur-of-the-moment, ad hoc inquiry that would show us no more and no less than what it is we are trying to discover. This could well be a once in a lifetime query, something we have never thought of exploring before and may never need to examine again.

In any event, upon seeing the query result, the decision process can continue. Of course, the result will probably influence the direction of thinking and may well stimulate another ad hoc inquiry, and so on, until the process gathers sufficient knowledge along the way to make a decision.

Carrying this idea one step further, our inquiry may involve more than what is visible in the table. In supporting a decision process, we may want to make hypothetical queries. This process is often referred to as what-if analysis. For instance, what if all romance quotas were suddenly increased by 8%. Who would now have romance shortfalls and how large would they be?

An entire wish list for what-is and what-if explorations is satisfied with a single standard command called SELECT. Each SELECT command is an ad hoc query that can draw on data held in one or more tables to satisfy spur-of-the-moment information needs. The result of a SELECT command is a tabular display of desired data (which can be stored in a new table, if desired).

The SELECT command forms the core of SQL, an English-like rendition of the relational calculus access language. In its most basic form, the SELECT command lets us identify for which of a table's fields we are interested in seeing values. We merely list the desired fields' names following the word SELECT, and they become column headings for the command's result. We can pick any subset of the fields we want and they can be in any order. Figure C.6 shows an example of the command and its result.

A very handy feature of queries is that they are not limited just to fields. Expressions can be requested along with the fields. Suppose we want to examine the representatives' weekly salaries. The numbers we desire are not explicitly stored in the REP table, but there are sufficient data there to determine what the weekly salary rates are. We can let SELECT dig it out for us by including an appropriate numeric expression:

SELECT TID NAME MOSAL*12/52 FROM REP

The proper calculation is performed for each row of the query result. As another example, the query

SELECT NAME MAJORP MOSAL*MOEXP (MOEXP+MOSAL)*12 FROM REP

lets us view the monthly and annual sums of budgeted expenditures for each of the sales representatives. The final two columns contain data derived from the table's contents.

FIGURE C.6 Designating Query Fields

```
_select tid,city,name,phone,mosal from rep
TID   CITY            NAME              PHONE            MOSAL

 2   Bloomington     Kevin R. Andrews  (123) 456-1111   2500
 0   Chicago         Kim G. Anders     (312) 553-6754   2600
 1   Dayton          Kris H. Raber     (513) 333-9989   2400
 3   Indianapolis    Tina F. Lee       (317) 299-8393   2800
 4   Fort Wayne      Toby C. Terry     (345) 123-4567   2000
 5   Grand Rapids    Kerry H. Jones    (632) 098-7654   2250
 6   Madison         Karen V. Bruckner (433) 442-8201   2800
 7   Milwaukee       Kathy F. Smith    (415) 567-8901   2100
 8   Columbus        Jackie V. Smith   (322) 861-6543   2400
 9   Midland         Carol O. Lynn     (415) 832-5643   2750
```

Expressions in queries can be very useful for what-if analysis, in addition to what is analysis. For instance, what if all salaries were increased by 6% or 7%? We could compare the effects of such increases against the current monthly salaries with a single query, without affecting the table's data in any way whatsoever. The query

```
SELECT NAME, MOSAL, MOSAL*1.06, MOSAL*1.07 FROM REP
```

results in columns comparing the three salary options for each representative, giving a feel for the effects of making salary adjustments.

Unconditional queries are those whose results contain one line for each record existing in a table. In contrast, a conditional query usually will result in fewer lines than there are records in the table, because it has a condition that excludes undesired records from being processed. When we pose a conditional query for some table, a line will be displayed for each record whose field values make that condition TRUE.

Suppose we want to identify quickly all performance records that were below quota in both of the first two quarters in order to take corrective action. The query

```
SELECT FNAME PID Q1 S1 Q2 S2 FROM PERF WHERE S1<Q1 & S2<Q2
```

has a compound condition composed of the conjunction of two relational expressions. The six selected field values will be displayed for each of the records satisfying the condition.

Another query, intending to discover those performance records for which the improvement in second-quarter sales over first-quarter sales exceeded the improvement expected with respect to quotas, is as follows:

```
SELECT FNAME,PID,Q1,S1,Q1,S2,Q22 Q1,S22 S1 FROM PERF\
WHERE S22 S1>Q22 Q1 & Q2>Q1
```

The second part of the condition ensures that only those records for which there is an expected improvement will be considered. The backslash indicates that the command is continued on the next line.

Relational calculus, of which SQL is an embodiment, allows data to be garnered from two or more tables in a single operation. It obviates the need to put together a proper procedure of PROJECT, JOIN, and algebraic SELECT commands in order to produce a table with the desired data. A SELECT query is a realization of the non-procedural relational calculus approach to retrieval. One query can display results, where each line is based on related data from multiple tables.

Suppose we need to examine the performance data for products having a commission rate of at least 2.4% and included there we want to see the year-to-date commissions paid for each. Of course, this request involves related records stored in the PERF and PROD tables. Neither table by itself would have enough data to address our needs. The appropriate query is as follows:

```
SELECT TID, PID, PNAME, SYTD*CRATE FROM PERF, PROD\
WHERE PERF.PID=PROD.PID & CRATE GE .024
```

Unlike the earlier queries, we indicate two tables from which the data are to be retrieved and include a record-matching criterion in the query's condition. This criterion says that a PERF record is to be considered as being related to a PROD record if their PID values are equal.

We can request sorting as part of an ad hoc query. This sorting will not affect the order of records in the table or tables being queried. It affects only the ordering of lines in the query's result. It is, therefore, referred to as *dynamic sorting*. The command

SELECT TID NAME SPOUSE ADDR FROM REP ORDER BY ASCENDING LNAME FNAME

causes query results to be sorted first on the basis of LNAME values and secondarily on the basis of FNAME values. Notice that it is permissible to order the query results based on fields that are not included in those results.

In general, we can dynamically sort on as many fields as we like, and any can be prefaced by ASCENDING or DESCENDING. The ORDER BY fields can actually come from different tables. Suppose we need to see the first-quarter quotas for the representatives for whom the commission rates are greater than 2.2%. We might want the results ordered by product ID and, within each product ID, the lines ordered by descending quota. The command

```
SELECT PID, NAME, Q1, FNAME FROM PERF, PROD WHERE CRATE\
GT .022 & PERF.PID=PROD.PID ORDER BY ASCENDING PID,\
DESCENDING Q1
```

makes it very easy to see quickly the progression from highest to lowest quota for each of the high-commission product lines. If the query results were not ordered, such patterns would not be as obvious.

In addition to the foregoing basics of the SQL SELECT command, there are some additional features involving control breaks, statistics calculations, and query nesting. In some implementations of SQL, the focus is on its query ability as embodied in the SELECT command. In other implementations, additional SQL commands that really have nothing to do with queries are provided. They are often intended for use by programmers, and they fall into two categories: DDL (Data Description Language) and DML (Data Manipulation Language). The SQL DDL includes data-management commands that a programmer would use to define, delete, and structurally alter tables. It also allows *views* to be defined, where a view can be thought of as a virtual table whose "content" is defined in terms of a query. The SQL DML includes commands for manipulating (i.e., creating, modifying, deleting, or listing) records in a table. It also includes a "cursor" mechanism that has nothing to do with the usual notion of a cursor on a console screen. In SQL terminology, a cursor is an ordered collection of records in a table or view. It gives a limited way of accessing records on a one-at-a-time basis (à la the NEXT variation of the OBTAIN command).

The capacity to receive quick answers to ad hoc queries is extremely important to effective decision making. Thus, a versatile ad hoc query capability is crucial in supporting the exploratory aspects of a decision process. These explorations may aid in picking out relevant facts from large volumes of data. Alternatively, they may also involve what-if analyses. The SQL SELECT command is an extremely potent and flexible realization of the ad hoc inquiry aspect of database management.

PROGRAM MANAGEMENT

Programming is the most versatile and general-purpose technique for managing procedural knowledge. It is employed in specifying solvers for inclusion in a KS and in defining the more elaborate kinds of macros used in spreadsheet cell definitions. It is very useful in customizing the appearance and flow of a user's interactions with a DSS. In such a capacity, it embodies not only procedural knowledge, but linguistic, presentation, and assimilative knowledge as well.

CONTROL LOGIC

In simplest terms, a program is a sequence of commands existing in a disk file. When a program is performed (i.e., executed), the commands are executed in sequence. There are certain commands that can divert the flow of command execution in various ways via conditional branching (IF, TEST), conditional iteration (WHILE), and nested program execution (PERFORM).

Although the syntax and names of these commands vary from one programming language to another, the basic logic and structure of each is as follows. An IF command has the form

```
IF conditions
   THEN commands
   ELSE other commands
ENDIF
```

Collectively, the conditions constitute a logical expression such as those described for expression management. If values of this expression's variables make the expression true, then the first series of commands is executed. Otherwise, the other series of commands is executed. That is, the flow of the program branches in one of two ways, depending on whether the conditions are true or false. After the branching occurs, the next command in the program (following the end of the IF command) is processed.

The TEST command is a more general form of conditional branching, allowing the program to branch in more than two ways. It has the basic form

```
TEST expression
   CASE expression: commands
   CASE expression: commands
```

•
•
•

```
    OTHERWISE: commands
ENDTEST
```

Here, the TEST expression is evaluated. Its value is compared to those of the CASE expressions. If a match is found, that case's commands are executed. If no match is found, the OTHERWISE commands are executed. After the branching occurs, the next command in the program (following the end of the TEST command) is processed.

The WHILE command is an instruction that causes the repeated execution of series of commands embedded within it. It has the basic form

```
WHILE conditions
    DO commands
ENDWHILE
```

The conditions constitute a logical expression. While its value is true, the indicated commands are performed. Those commands can change values of variables involved in the conditions. If these changes make the expression false, then control passes to the next command following the end of the WHILE. The commands included within WHILE could also include an instruction to jump immediately to the command following the end of the WHILE command.

The PERFORM command causes a specified program in a separate command file to be executed. This is valuable when there is some sequence of steps that needs to be used repeatedly within one or more programs. Rather than repeat the full sequence of steps every place it is needed, those steps become a separate program in their own right. They are represented and maintained in their own command files. Wherever another program needs to use these steps, it simply has a PERFORM command that will cause them to be performed. Mechanisms are available to pass data values to the program being performed and to pass results of its execution back to the original program for further processing.

When a tool integrates a programming language with other techniques of knowledge management, then requests for carrying out their processing methods can be placed between or within the commands that control the program's flow of execution. Thus, a program can do calculations, initiate text management, carry out database management, execute SQL queries, process model bases, create or alter spreadsheet templates, carry out operations on cells or the spreadsheet as a whole, and so forth.

PROGRAM DEVELOPMENT

Programming gives both do-it-yourself computer users and professional application developers a valuable way of automating procedural knowledge. A program can be stored in a DSS's knowledge system along with other kinds of knowledge. Once it is there, the DSS will perform it instead of the user having to enter and carry out the steps one by one. Our treatment of programming in Chapter 10 was far from exhaustive. The remainder of this appendix gives a few additional observations about program development.

It is a good idea to document the steps in a program with plenty of comments. Even though the purpose of all steps may seem clear as we are developing a program, when we take a look at it a month or year later, it may not be as clear if we do not use any comments. Yet we may want to expand it at that time to make it more powerful or flexible. Without comments, we might need to expend a good deal of effort to become sufficiently reacquainted with a program to be able to make such changes correctly. Putting in a little more effort up front is worth it in the long run.

Good documentation in a program is essential to maintaining that program over time. Not only that, documenting things as we go along can help avoid oversights in devising program logic. Ideally, a professional programmer documents a program before actually typing in its commands.

Programmers often use—or are advised to use—modular, or structured, programming, in which procedural knowledge is structured into separate program modules. Each module is designed to represent a unit of procedural knowledge that may need to be performed many times. A module at a lower level in the flow of execution is often referred to as a subprogram, or subroutine, with respect to the higher-level module.

When it is possible to identify a chunk of procedural knowledge that may need to be used in several places within the flow of higher-level procedures, we should develop it as a distinct program module. This action greatly facilitates the use and maintenance of that procedural knowledge. Modular programming can also be helpful even when a chunk of procedural knowledge is needed in only one place in only one larger procedure. It can help structure the program-design process and break a large programming problem into smaller, more easily managed modules. The approach of first developing the top-level module and then developing lower-level modules is often referred to as top-down design and is commonly employed by professional programmers.

With a basic knowledge of programming, do-it-yourself developers can begin to appreciate what professional application developers do in constructing complex or large-scale DSSs. Some of these developers are systems analysts who determine or discover the requirements of how prospective application software should behave. Because this is normally accomplished by understanding the needs and problems of potential users of the software, effective interpersonal skills and a good background in the functional areas of management are important for successful systems analysis.

Other developers are systems designers who take specifications of what an application system is required to do and create plans of how those requirements can be met. Still other developers are the programmers who actually implement full-scale application systems by writing programs corresponding to the designs. The resultant application software (i.e., programs) gives its users customized interfaces for dealing with various record-keeping and decision support activities. Once a user executes such a program (e.g., via an operating system command), the interaction begins and follows the flow dictated by the program's commands.

Unlike professional application software developers, do-it-yourself developers are managers who use what they themselves develop. Each manager who writes a program also does preliminary analysis and design for that program. Wearing an analyst hat, the manager thinks out what it is that he or she needs the program to do. Wearing a designer hat, the manager then plans a flow of steps that will meet the analyzed needs. Wearing a programmer hat, the manager formally specifies and tests the commands corresponding to the plan. Then, the manager actually uses the developed program via its custom-built user interface.

As explained in Chapter 7, the activities of analysis and design are not peculiar to using the programming technique of knowledge management. Effective use of any knowledge-management technique depends on analyzing what the needs are (i.e., understanding what problem is being faced) and designing a plan for meeting those needs (e.g., selecting suitable knowledge management capabilities).

Programs written in C, Pascal, or COBOL languages must be compiled before they can be executed. The programmer typically uses text-management software to prepare a file containing commands allowed by the programming language. This file is called the source program and it is saved in a disk file. The source program is then processed by a special program called a compiler. For instance, COBOL programs are processed by a COBOL compiler, programs written in the FORTRAN language are processed by a FORTRAN compiler, and so forth. A compiler examines the source program for syntactic errors. If any are detected, they are reported to the programmer, who then debugs the program and again tries to process it with the compiler.

When the compiler detects no errors in a source program, it generates a new version of the program in a different language, whose commands can be more directly and rapidly executed by the computer hardware. This new version of the

FIGURE D.1   Program Creation with a Compiled Language

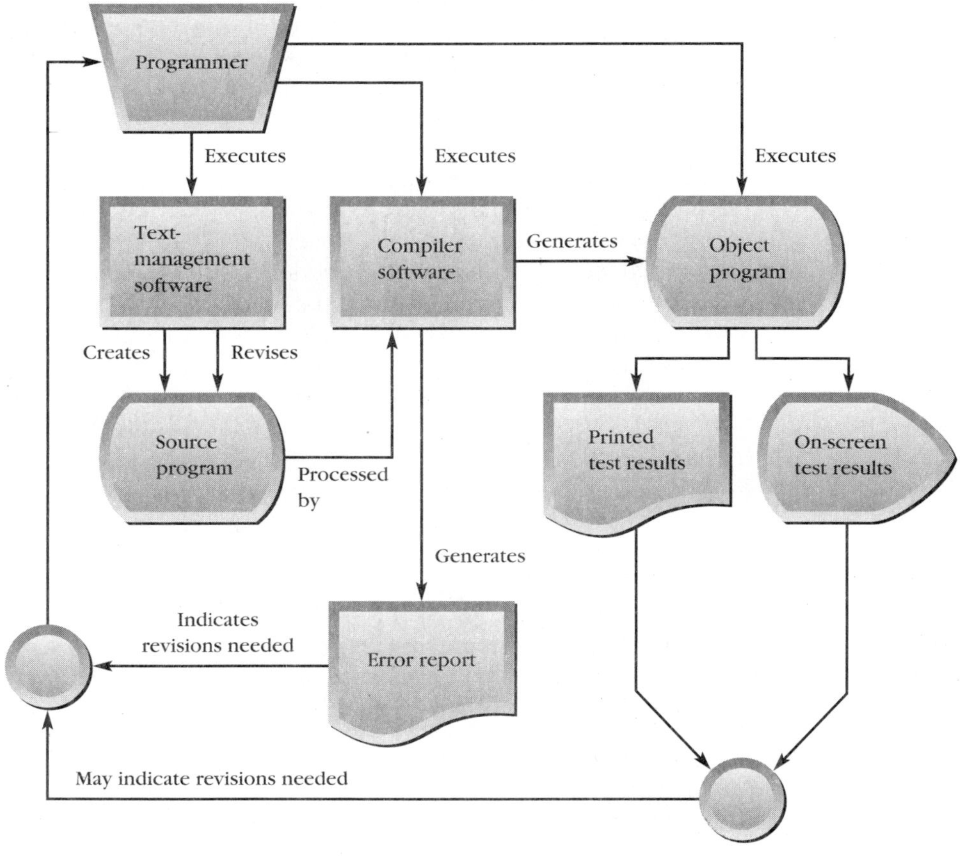

program is saved on a file and is called the object program, or executable program. Once an object program is acquired from the compiler, a programmer can execute it to begin testing its behavior and logic. If bugs are found, the source program is edited and again submitted to the compiler for generating a new object program. The new object program is then tested. As Figure D.1 suggests, the debugging process of editing the source program, compiling, and testing the object program continues until the programmer is satisfied with the program's behavior.

Programming languages that do not require the use of a compiler (e.g., BASIC) are called interpretive languages. Generally, the execution speed of a program written with a compiled language is faster than a comparable program written with an interpretive language, because much of the work of translating a programmer's commands into commands that the hardware can process is done prior to execution rather than during the execution of the program. For large, extensive, or complex programs, the difference in execution times can be significant. For most do-it-yourself programming efforts, the difference will not be significant. The added convenience of avoiding the compilation step and having a wealth of commands that normally do not exist in compiled languages is the positive trade-off that results from an interpretive language.

For large programming projects, it is important first to understand the potential users' requirements. This job belongs to the systems analyst. Second, it is important to think out the flow of a program's logic in advance of actually creating the program. Professional systems designers do this preliminary design work by sketching diagrams called flowcharts. A flowchart shows the procedural flow of steps that should be followed when a program executes. It provides a highly visual guideline for the programmer who specifies and tests a program's commands.

Figure D.2 shows a flowchart that a designer might have designed prior to creating a program. By convention, the various geometric shapes in the diagram represent different kinds of steps in a procedure. The meaning of some commonly used flowcharting shapes are explained in Figure D.3. Although do-it-yourself developers often do not design explicit flowcharts for small programs, flowcharts become increasingly beneficial as the size of a programming task grows. Even for a small program, a flowchart can be beneficial. For instance, it is immediately obvious in Figure D.2 that there is a duplicate series of steps. Seeing this, a developer might want to revamp the program design to eliminate the duplication and produce a more efficient program.

FIGURE D.2 **Sample Flowchart for Calculating Information about a Sales Representative Based on Database Contents**

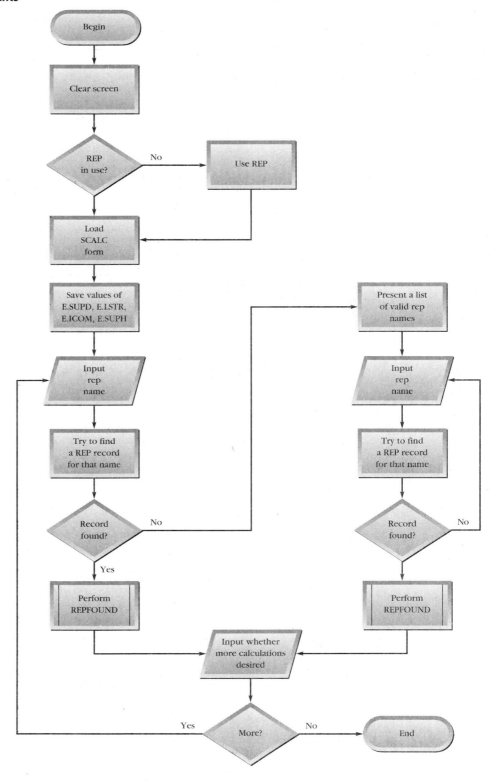

FIGURE D.3   Some Common Flowcharting Conventions

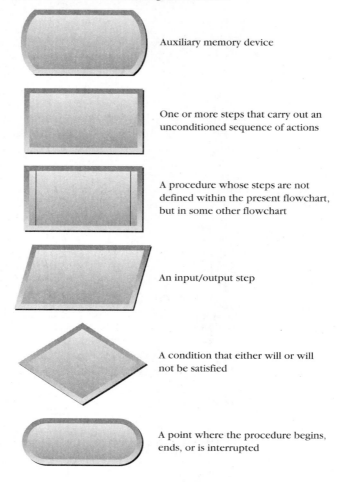

Auxiliary memory device

One or more steps that carry out an unconditioned sequence of actions

A procedure whose steps are not defined within the present flowchart, but in some other flowchart

An input/output step

A condition that either will or will not be satisfied

A point where the procedure begins, ends, or is interrupted

AI KNOWLEDGE REPRESENTATION

Rules provide a very natural, convenient, nonprocedural way of representing reasoning knowledge. This is knowledge for reasoning about the use of other knowledge: procedural, presentational, assimilative, linguistic, reasoning, and so on. Of these, the ability to reference descriptive knowledge in a rule is essential. Tools for developing reasoning systems must have facilities for managing descriptions of the current state of the world about which reasoning is to occur.

As we saw in Part Three, a development tool may furnish numerous methods for representing descriptive knowledge, including databases, spreadsheets, text, arrays, and variables. All these methods are familiar to the business computing community, and their popularity is a testimony to their value. Clearly, these techniques are valuable to any tool concerned with the construction of expert systems for diverse business applications. However, a development tool could support other approaches to representing descriptive knowledge: approaches that arose in the AI field.

Here, we focus on two of these approaches for handling descriptive knowledge: semantic nets and frames. Many of the aspects of these approaches are actually quite similar to aspects of familiar business computing approaches to knowledge representation. Several of these correspondences are noted in the description that follows.

REPRESENTING THE STATE OF THE WORLD

As it reasons about a problem, an inference engine must be able to track the state of the world. We can view any application world in terms of various concepts and their interrelationships. In the sales quota world, for example, there are concepts such as product name, quarter number, representative name, this year's sales, this year's quota, local advertising amount, and so forth. At a more concrete level there are concepts such as romance, 2, Toby, 13,750, 12,560, and 2,820. As introduced in the hypertext discussion in Chapter 9, there are two kinds of relationships that can exist among concepts: definitional and associative.

One concept can define or more closely specify the meaning of another. For instance, product name and romance have a definitional relationship, in which the latter is one way of defining the former. In a definitional relationship, one concept is an instance, an occurrence, or a value of a more abstract concept. Toby is an instance of a sales representative name, 13,750 is an occurrence of this year's sales, and 2 is one of the possible values of quarter number. Conversely, concepts that are legitimate definitions, instances, or values of the product-name concept include romance, scifi, and computer, but not Toby or 13,750.

Product name and this year's sales are two concepts that are related, but the relationship is not definitional. Neither is an instance of the other. Nevertheless, they are associated with each other in the sense that any instance of this year's sales (e.g., 13,750) has been produced for a particular product (e.g., romance). The concept of this year's sales is similarly associated with the quarter number and sales representative name concepts. A sales amount is made by a specific representative in a specified quarter.

Consider the concepts of product name, product ID, and commission rate (for a product). These three concepts are associated with each other in the sense that they are all attributes of a broader concept, namely, the concept of a product; that is, the concept of a product is an aggregate of three other concepts. Similarly, an instance of the product concept is an aggregate of three values (e.g., romance, ROM, and 0.03), one for each of the three associated concepts that make up the notion of a product.

A concept that is an aggregate of other concepts is sometimes called an *entity,* or an object. The concepts of which it is composed are sometimes called *attributes.* Thus, we can say that a product is a type of object or entity whose attributes are its name, ID, and commission rate. There may be many instances of this object, each comprising three values (one value for each of the three attributes). Interestingly, this object-attribute-value notion is one AI way of representing descriptive knowledge.

SEMANTIC NETS

Semantic net representation is rooted in AI researchers' efforts at modeling memory. Although there is no operational standard for semantic net specification and usage, basic notions that are generally shared by implementations of this technique are examined here. A semantic net is composed of nodes that represent concepts, be they objects or attributes, concrete instances or abstractions. The relationships between concepts are represented by named arcs between the nodes. An arc's name indicates the meaning (i.e., semantics) of the relationship it represents. Definitional relationships are commonly called *is-a* relationships. Associative relationships between an attribute and its object are commonly called *has-a* relationships. Other associative relationships are typically given names that reflect their respective meanings.

Specification   Figure E.1 shows typical pictorial portrayals of semantic net relationships. A formal language can be used to actually specify a semantic net for computer storage. Such languages can vary widely from one implementation to another. As an example, the knowledge in Figure E.1(a) might be formally specified as

    ISA(Toby,rep name)

to indicate that Toby is a representative's name. We call this kind of formalization a *predicate*. Similarly, the arcs in Figure E.1(b) and (c) could also be formally stated as predicates:

    HASA(product,product name)
    HASA(product,product ID)

FIGURE E.1   **Semantic Net Representations**

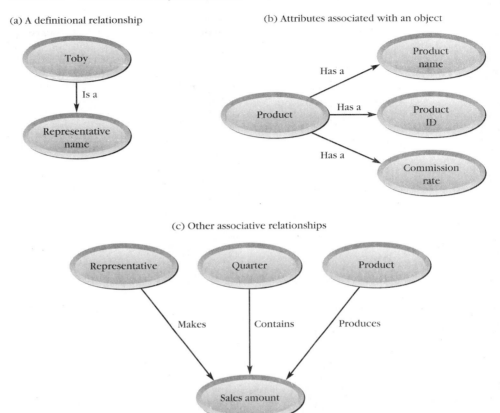

(a) A definitional relationship

(b) Attributes associated with an object

(c) Other associative relationships

```
HASA(product,commission rate)
MAKES(rep,sales amount)
CONTAINS(quarter,sales amount)
PRODUCES(product,sales amount)
```

Thus, a semantic net can be specified in terms of a series of predicate statements.

Processing   The ways in which semantic net representations are processed vary from one implementation to another. However, the available processing generally allows the net to be created, modified, and traversed. Traversal refers to the ability to move along the net's arcs to find related concepts. For example, in Figure E.2, we can begin with Toby and traverse the net to discover that Toby is the name of a sales representative whose phone is 317-925-8068, who has made a performance of the sales amount 13,750 versus the quota amount 12,560 in the quarter whose number is 2 for the year 1985, and who has produced this performance for the product whose name is romance. Traversal can normally begin with any node and proceed along arcs in any direction.

Figure E.3 shows another semantic net with the same basic structure. The only difference is that the instances of three attributes (quarter number, sales amount, and quota amount) are not the same as in the semantic net of Figure E.2. Thus, this

FIGURE E.2   Toby's Romance Performance in Quarter 2

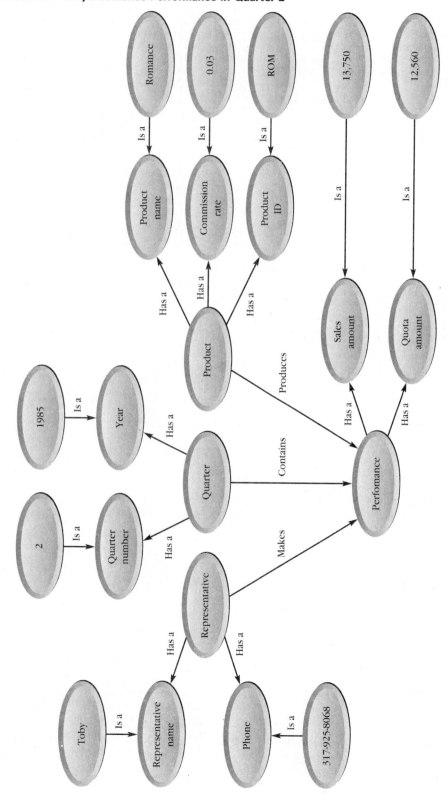

FIGURE E.3   Toby's Romance Performance in Quarter 1

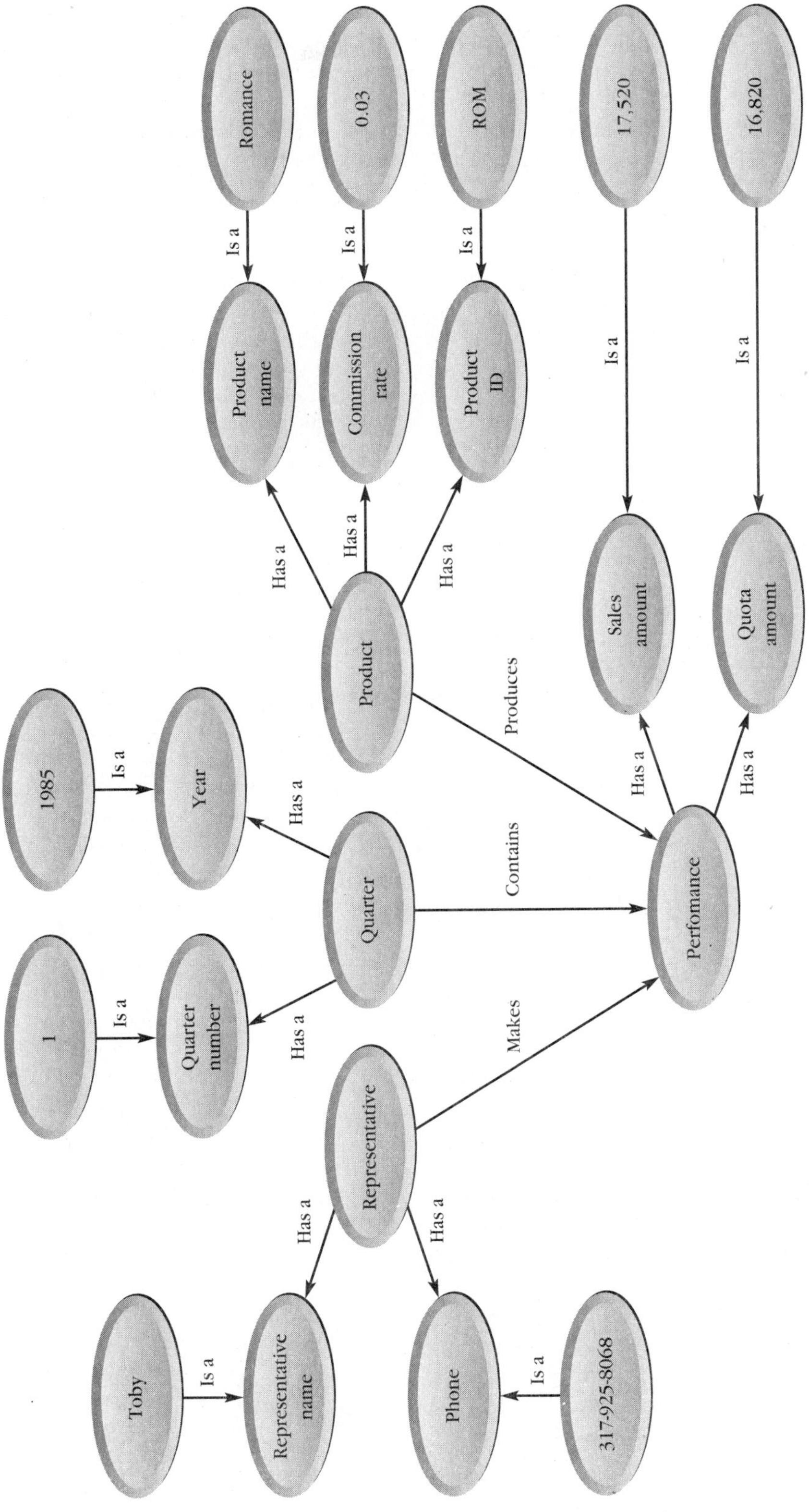

net describes Toby's performance for romance in the first, rather than second, quarter. Notice that a large portion of the net will not change regardless of which representative, quarter, or product is involved. Only those nodes at the heads of is-a arcs vary from one net to another. The other nodes and arcs are structurally static.

Retrieval versus Inference   Sometimes the activity of traversing a semantic net to retrieve related data values is called *inference*. Consider the rule

```
IF:REPNAME="Toby" & QTRNUM="2" & PRODID="ROM"
THEN:SALES=13750 ;QUOTA=12560
```

It could be argued that this captures some of the same knowledge represented in Figure E.2. Thus, traversal to retrieve related values from a net would be replaced by customary inference. In this sense, traversal of a semantic net—or retrieval from a data table, for that matter—can be regarded as a sort of pseudoinference. Although it is conceptually equivalent to inference, it is quite different operationally. Retrieval of desired sales and quota amounts will be significantly faster than inference based on rules such as the one shown here. It also takes less effort by the rule set developer and allows the descriptive knowledge to be used easily for other purposes beyond the scope of reasoning about new quotas.

In general, it is a poor practice to try to represent descriptive knowledge (e.g., about a representative's performance) as if it were reasoning knowledge. A human expert would not reason that if the sales representative's name is Toby, the quarter is 2, and the product ID is ROM, then the sales must be 13,750 against a quota of 12,560. The human expert would simply look up (i.e., retrieve) the pertinent sales and quota amounts in a filing folder, a report, and computerized database, or some other source.

Conversely, it would be a poor practice to try to represent a reasoning knowledge as if it were descriptive knowledge. This would involve an enumeration of all possible new quota problems and their solutions. Each enumerated case would be stored as descriptive knowledge in a table or a semantic net. A quota advice problem would then be solved not by actual inference, but by finding the matching case and retrieving its new quota value. For nontrivial problems, enumeration and retrieval are impractical. Think about what it would entail as an alternative to inference with the ADVISOR rule set in Part Four. The process of representing and processing reasoning knowledge as rules is far more efficient and effective than trying to generate and use all possible pieces of advice that would result from those rules.

FRAMES

Frame representation of knowledge originated with Minsky's pattern recognition and analysis research in the 1970s. Since then, various frame formalisms have been proposed. Although there is no universally adopted standard for frame specification and processing, we shall examine here some of the more interesting aspects that might be encountered in a frame representation supported by an expert system development tool. It should be noted that variations exist not only in features and usage, but also in the terminology used to discuss frames. For instance, frames themselves are sometimes called *units, concepts,* or *flavors*.

Slots   A frame is used to represent a type of object, entity, or class. The frame's name is indicative of the object being represented. A frame is composed of *slots*.

Each slot corresponds to an attribute that is possessed by the type of object that a frame represents. A slot's name is normally descriptive of the attribute that it represents. Consider the PROD table in Figure C.1. That table's structure could be represented as a frame named PROD and having five slots named PID, PNAME, TARGET, GMR, and CRATE. In this example, the PROD frame represents a type of abstract entity or object, namely, the notion of a product. An instance of a frame consists of specific data values for the frame's slots. Thus, a record in the PROD table corresponds to an instance of the PROD frame.

Just as a table field has various characteristics, so does a frame slot. Slot characteristics are often called *facets*. A slot typically has a type (e.g., string, numeric, logical) that specifies what kind of data values it can have, a size indicating how large its values can be, and a label commenting on the nature of the slot. Slots with pictures or security access codes are less common.

We can specify virtual fields, as well as elements in forms and report templates, in terms of expressions, allowing us to compute their values dynamically on a when-needed basis. Similarly, frame implementations may allow instructions to be attached to a slot. The PROD frame could have a slot named COMTARG with an attached procedure (e.g., written in LISP) that calculates the product's commission target. When we need the value of COMTARG for frame instantiation, we calculate it by executing the procedure.

Procedural Attachment   Allowing a slot value to be specified in terms of a procedure (or even a rule set consultation) goes a step beyond the usual notion of a virtual field, form element, or template element whose value is specified in terms of an expression. Interestingly, a slot is, in this sense, equivalent to the notion of a cell whose definition is a procedure involving any of the customary control structures, such as those for conditional iteration, case processing, and conditional branching. A collection of related cells in a spreadsheet is thus comparable to slots of a frame.

Various frame implementations support differing approaches to procedural attachment. For instance, a procedure may be attached to a frame (rather than a slot) and stored as the value of a special type of slot. A procedure stored in this way can be invoked by a command designating the slot that holds it, plus any arguments needed by the procedure. In frame parlance, such a procedure is sometimes called a *method*, or *operator*, and using a command to cause its execution is thought of as *sending a message* to the frame. Because a frame represents an object, frames are usually regarded as an object-oriented approach to knowledge representation and processing.

Another variation of procedural attachment that may be found in a frame implementation is the attachment of a procedure to a slot with the stipulation that it should behave as a demon. Computer scientists have long used the term demon to refer to processing that is automatically activated when a certain event takes place. A slot's demon procedure might be executed whenever the slot's value is viewed or altered. The procedure could serve any of a variety of purposes, such as logging the activity for a slot's value, checking on the validity of the value, updating another slot that might serve to hold a measure of certainty about the present slot, or changing other slot values to be consistent with the present slot's new value.

Inheritance   Frame implementations typically provide a way for representing definitional relationships between objects (i.e., frames). These are the is-a relationships

PREDEFINED OBJECT CLASSES

As noted in Part Three, many other depictions of objects are possible: tables, records, spreadsheets, forms, graphs, and so forth. In implementations of conventional knowledge-management techniques, these are predefined classes of objects, and there are many built-in methods attached to each kind of object. These built-in methods constitute a large portion of a tool's software. They are indigenous, object code procedures that do not need to be programmed by a developer. Nor do they need to be explicitly attached to objects. Attachment is automatic. Some methods may be attached to (i.e., meaningful for) diverse types of objects, whereas other methods are pertinent to only a specific kind of object.

For example, the OBTAIN method always exists for each tabular object (i.e., for each table). Invoking OBTAIN for a particular table is in essence sending a message to that table indicating that a particular procedure is to be executed. In the case of sending such a message to the PROD table, the argument needed by the OBTAIN method might be the condition specified in the message:

```
OBTAIN RECORD FROM PROD FOR PID="scifi"
```

One object can send a message to another object. The message indicates which of the recipient's methods should be used. For instance, the preceding message to obtain a record may have been sent by a rule set (another kind of object), which in turn has received a message to carry out its CONSULT method from another object, such as a cell, piece of text, or procedural model.

As shown in Part Three, there is no need to have slots in each object for holding all the possible methods that could be requested for that object. A developer does not need to devise procedures for carrying out commonplace operations for an object. On the other hand, if specialized processing is needed for an object, the developer can specify procedures with a tool's integral programming language (if one exists). These problems need not be explicitly bound to particular types of objects. Notice that procedures themselves can be treated as objects and that PERFORM is a built-in method that is applicable to all custom-built procedures.

discussed earlier with respect to semantic nets. Direct representation of associative relationships such as MAKES, CONTAINS, and PRODUCES in Figure E.2 are generally not supported. The result is a hierarchy of frames that represents a taxonomy, or classification scheme.

For instance, the general class of employees could be thought of as comprising three subclasses: hourly employees, salaried employees, and commissioned employees. There is an is-a relationship between employees and each of its subclasses (e.g., salaried employee is-a employee). Each subclass is itself defined in terms of individual employees. Toby is a commissioned employee, which is an employee. All attributes existing for the general class of employees should pertain to all commissioned employees, and all attributes existing for commissioned employees pertain to Toby. Thus, Toby inherits the properties of the employee concept.

Clearly, this taxonomic inheritance can be depicted in a semantic net. It can also be represented by means of links between frames. When the EMPLOYEE frame is defined, it could be specified as being linked to the SAL, HRLY, and COMM frames. When the COMM frame is defined, it could be specified as being linked to frames for each of the commissioned employees. Such links might be visualized as shown in Figure E.4. Some frame systems make a distinction between two kinds of is-a links. There are those that connect a subclass (e.g., COMM) to a broader class (e.g., EMPLOYEE) and those that connect a frame that is not a class (e.g., TOBY) to one that does represent a class (e.g., COMM). The former could be termed *subclass links,* whereas the latter could be called *terminal links.*

Each frame in Figure E.3 will have slots. As shown there, the slots of a frame in an is-a hierarchy fall into two categories: those that are inherited by the frame's subclass or terminal frames and those that are not. The former are sometimes called *member slots,* and the latter called *own slots.* The EMPLOYEE frame has two member slots (NAME and ADDR) that will serve as attributes for each of its subclass frames. The SAL frame has a slot named HIGH, which is its own attribute, indicating the highest salary for the class of salaried employees. This frame also has three member slots that are attributes for each of its members. Two of these (NAME and ADDR) are inherited from the EMPLOYEE frame. The three member slots of SAL are inherited as own slots by each of the terminal frames linked to SAL. Similar member slots are specified for COMM, except the monthly salary attribute is replaced by the commission base attribute. Hourly employees have slots for hourly and overtime rates.

A frame implementation typically provides processing commands for adding slot values to a frame hierarchy and for retrieving those values by navigating through the links. As in the case of semantic net processing, we might regard retrieval through a frame structure as a kind of pseudoinference. For instance, we can use the links to discover that Jack is salaried and that salaried persons are employees. Therefore, we know that Jack is an employee.

FIGURE E.4   Representing a Taxonomy

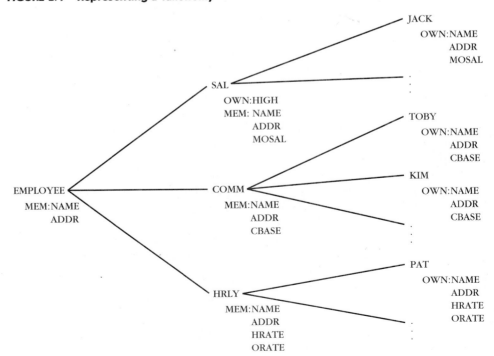

Frames to Organize Rules   When an expert system development tool supports a frame approach to representing descriptive knowledge, the rules that are specified can typically draw on data values held in slots. Such a tool may also allow (or in some cases require) that each rule be stored in a frame. A rule set, then, would correspond to a frame representing a class (e.g., the class of quota ADVISOR rules). Each terminal frame linked to this class would have slots holding a particular rule (e.g., rule R1 is-a ADVISOR rule). A slot would need to be defined for each of the various attributes a rule can have, such as its name, premise, conclusion, priority, cost, preaction sequence, comment, reason, and so forth.

Benefits   Proponents of development tools that support frames correctly point out that rules provide a very convenient way for representing reasoning knowledge but are not good at representing structured descriptive knowledge. They correctly argue that frames provide more versatility than the shells that go no further than the simple idea of representing descriptive knowledge in the guise of variables (often called *attributes*) and their values. They try to address the knowledge representation and processing deficiencies of such shells by using frames in addition to rules. This is similar in spirit to the motivation behind synergistically integrating rule management with conventional knowledge-management techniques. The principal difference is that the latter has opted for commonplace business-computing methods of knowledge management rather than the explicit use of less familiar frames (or semantic nets, for that matter).

Tools that combine frames and rules provide three benefits. First, frames furnish a structural language for describing the objects and attributes referred to in rules. Spreadsheets, databases, forms, text, and all the rest do the same, while providing greater specialization to the kinds of objects commonly used in business problem solving. Second, frames are said to support a layer of *generic deductive* capability about those objects that need not be represented explicitly as rules (i.e., pseudoinference via retrieval). In problem areas requiring extensive categorization, this result is beneficial. However, many business problems (e.g., setting sales quotas) do not tend to be heavily involved with taxonomy issues. They often involve a much richer array of associative interrelationships among masses of data values that can be handled quite nicely with appropriate database-management techniques. Third, frames can be used as an aid to organizing and managing rules. As described in Part Four, this result can be accomplished without the developer even being conscious of the notion of a frame.

SUMMARY

Attempts to augment conventional rule specification with frame or semantic net mechanisms are symptomatic of the need for rich knowledge-management capabilities when it comes to developing expert systems. Other mechanisms, such as predicate calculus or scripts, are also candidates. For the developers of business applications, none of these is an adequate substitute for a healthy assortment of conventional business computing techniques for knowledge management. Nevertheless, frames and semantic net mechanisms may increasingly become available as additional facilities in the repertoire of DSS development tools.

Appendix F

MACHINE LEARNING

by Ram Pakath

GENETIC ALGORITHMS

A genetic algorithm (GA) is one that seeks to improve upon the quality of a problem solution through a process that mimics that of natural selection and adaptation of species in nature. The method begins with a set of initial solutions (called an initial population) to a complex problem. It then crosses and mutates selected solutions from this initial set to develop a new set of solutions. The procedure is repeated to create successive generations of solutions until a predefined stopping criterion is met. This criterion may be based on a threshold value for effort expended, solution quality, or a combination.

The philosophy behind the method is that if we conduct a search for a better answer simultaneously from multiple locations within a complex space of solutions, we stand a better chance of locating the globally optimal solution. Consequently, the GA approach has generally been advocated for complex, multimodal solution spaces where there is high likelihood of a search strategy being trapped at a local optima. The probability of entrapment is generally higher for methods that localize their search efforts to a specific region of the solution space.

The initial set of solutions is either entirely randomly chosen or determined through a deliberate strategy that involves both deterministic and random choice. The former approach is used when the decision maker has no particular reason for wanting to choose a starting set otherwise and is generally how a GA operates. In certain instances, however, it is worthwhile to seed the starting solution set with some carefully chosen set of initial solutions along with some randomly generated solutions, usually because the population of solutions is of fixed, limited size.

It is likely that a random starting solution set may, coincidentally, be not representative of the entire space when the space is very large in relation to population size. The method prefers that the set be as diversified as possible to enable it to search for improved solutions from multiple, well-dispersed points in the space. A second reason is that the random starting population may be made up entirely of very poor quality solutions. This situation increases the likelihood of being trapped at a local optima. Also, while it may at times be possible to wade through such solutions and ultimately locate the globally best answer, the effort required may be highly prohibitive. Deliberately seeding the starting population with some high-quality solutions may help accelerate the move toward the desired solution.

Given a starting population, a GA would start its processing by selecting a set of members from this set to populate a gene pool. New solutions are generated using members picked randomly from the gene pool. The general strategy is to associate selection probabilities with individual members of the current population that reflect the standing or strength (called the fitness) of each member in relation to other members in the set. Usually, we convert the quality measure of each solution in the population into a selection probability measure for that member by converting the fitnesses to relative fitnesses. Solutions of higher quality (i.e., highly fit solutions) have higher likelihood of being selected to participate in the gene pool.

It is possible that the gene pool could contain multiple copies of the same population member because of its relatively high selection probability. On the other hand, even the worst current solution has some nonzero probability of being selected for participation in the pool. Note that it is also likely that highly fit members could dominate the gene pool and, hence, heavily influence subsequent generations of solutions to the problem. If this happens, then population diversity is reduced in later generations, increasing the likelihood of premature convergence to some suboptimal solution. The likelihood of this occurring is lessened by using a procedure called *fitness scaling*.

A popular fitness scaling approach is *linear scaling*. The general idea behind linear scaling is to ensure that the actual fitnesses of the most highly fit current population members are scaled down to a predetermined multiple of the average population fitness. Thus, the *scaling parameter* (i.e., multiplier) in effect determines the expected number of copies of the most highly fit member in the gene pool. Further, linear scaling also ensures that the average population fitnesses before and after scaling are the same. Thus, we may expect to have one copy of each member of average fitness in the current population in the gene pool. With linear scaling, however, it is also possible for very poor quality solutions to be scaled to zero fitness and thus be disallowed from participation in the pool.

Once the gene pool is determined, a GA begins the next phase of its operations by using members of the gene pool for procreation. That is, members from the pool are randomly selected to act as parents. Parents are either mutated or crossed with one another to generate new solutions. These new solutions replace existing solutions in the population. The general procedure is as follows. Associated with any GA is a set of genetic operators called mutation, crossover, and reproduction. Each of these has a predetermined probability of application. The GA selects two members at random from the gene pool.

Based on the crossover probability, it is first determined whether the two parents must be crossed. If the answer is yes, they are crossed with one another, yielding either one or two offspring solutions, depending on the type of crossover being applied. At this stage one is left with either the original parents (if the decision was not to cross them) or the offspring generated via crossover. A determination is then made on whether each of the currently available solutions ought to be mutated, based on the mutation probability. Each available solution is either mutated or left untouched. Thus, at this stage we are left with a set of one or two offspring, each of which may be either an original parent (if the decision was neither to cross nor mutate), generated solely through crossover of the original parents (if the decision was to cross but not mutate), generated solely through mutation of an original parent (if the decision was to mutate but not cross), or generated through crossover of the original parents followed by mutation of a resultant offspring (if the decision was to cross and mutate). The first of these possible cases where the resultant offspring is actually a copy of an original parent is tantamount to reproduction of the parent.

We have outlined the general procedure. Some applications decide on mutating before deciding on crossover. Further, a number of mutation and crossover operators have been identified in the literature. Several of these are known to perform well in specialized problem circumstances. Some of these are intended for general use. Usually a GA is equipped with one type each of the crossover and mutation operators. Some studies involve the use of multiple operators of each kind, with different operators being utilized at various stages of the solution process. One recent study examines the viability of letting the algorithm pick the best mutation and/or crossover operators given past experience with various types of operators of each kind. Likewise, although the traditional approach requires that the mutation and crossover probabilities be predefined, some recent research attempts to alter these probabilities dynamically at run time such that the current probability levels reflect the past success rate at using each operator for the problem under consideration. A third strategy that has also been recently explored is to allocate different crossover and mutation probability levels to different members of the population and to alter these at run time based on performance.

The three classes of operators play distinct roles. Reproduction seeks to preserve what is good in the current generation in subsequent generations. Crossover seeks to mingle the attributes of two solutions to create a new solution that could possess the more desirable traits of each parent. Mutation seeks to inject some novelty into the population by attempting to generate offspring quite unlike any in existence. Its role is rejuvenation. Mutation is especially useful in jolting the process out of entrapment at a local optima. The usage rate of each operator depends on the statically or dynamically assigned probabilities. Generally, the probabilities are such that crossover is heavily used, with mutation being resorted to only when crossover fails to bring about any improvement. Too high a mutation probability would reduce the process to a random walk.

Having generated offspring, a GA may use one of two strategies in deciding how to create a new population. One strategy, called *generational replacement,* is to eliminate the entire current population and replace it with newly generated offspring. A potential weakness of this approach is that it is possible that the current population of solutions would be replaced by a poorer one.

A second strategy is called *steady-state replacement.* With this approach, as and when an offspring is generated it is used to replace the worst member of the current population. The same approach is used even when two offspring are generated in one procreational effort. The two offspring replace the worst two members of the current population. A variation on this idea is temporarily to append the offspring to the current population, reassess the relative fitnesses or relative scaled fitnesses of the entire population, and then decide which member(s) ought to be discarded. The motivation here is that any generated offspring must compete with existing population members for a place in the population (which is of finite size).

A third strategy is called *elitism.* With elitism, the current best (i.e., most highly fit) population member is reproduced in the new population. Elitism is usually pursued with generational replacement. All these approaches seek to enhance the likelihood of subsequent generations of solutions improving upon prior solutions, with mutation and fitness scaling reducing the likelihood of premature convergence.

Once a new population is generated, the three-step process of gene-pool selection, offspring creation, and new population generation is reiterated until the predefined stopping rule is satisfied. Note that the manner in which we encode solutions should permit the performance of mutation and crossover. The most widely used encoding method is to represent population members as binary strings. Generally, population strings are of fixed size. In some numerical optimization contexts, populations are encoded as strings of integers of arbitrary size.

Any GA requires a number of parameters to be specified. At the very minimum, these include the population size, the population encoding scheme and string length, the types of genetic operators, the operator probabilities, and the stopping rule. Beyond this, particular implementations require the specification of a number of other parameters based on the level of sophistication involved.

Given the random (or mixed random and deterministic) starting population of a GA, it is imprudent to rely upon the answer provided by one GA run of a certain number of generations. Usually, the findings from several independent runs are pooled in determining the solution to a problem. We conclude by noting that GA-based systems are reasoning systems that employ a technique of reasoning called *unsupervised inductive learning.* Traditionally, GA-based systems have been designed as application-specific systems in the sense that a system is designed for a specific application, and the benefits that accrue through learning are applied only to that application.

There has been some research on generating GA-based systems with the ability to generalize learned knowledge (i.e., fruitfully apply knowledge learned in one application to another). An example of such generalization is the use of character-istics of some or all of the members of the final generation in one application in creating the initial population of another similar (though not identical) problem instance. Such efforts, however, have been sporadic and scattered.

Good overviews on GAs may be found in Goldberg (1989), Forrest (1993a), and Pakath (1994a). Articles focusing on specific issues of theoretical and/or practical interest are found in Belew and Booker (1991), Forrest (1993b), Grefenstette (1985, 1987), Schaffer (1989), and in several well-known, refereed journals, including the relatively more recent *Evolutionary Computation* (published by the MIT Press). Other sources of information on GAs include an international conference held bien-nially since 1985, as well as an electronic Genetic Algorithm Digest to which one can subscribe (send a subscription request to GA-list-request@aic.nrl.navy.mil), which is in volume 8 at the time of this writing.

NEURAL NETWORKS

A neural network (NN) is a model of reasoning based on the human brain. The human brain is made up of a densely interconnected set of simple processing units called *neurons.* The brain employs multiple neurons simultaneously in carrying out its functions. Although each neuron by itself is a relatively weak entity, an army of such entities constitutes a formidable processing force. The interconnections between neurons are called *synapses.* Neurons coordinate their processing efforts by means of chemical signals exchanged through synapses. An NN applies this approach to problem solving (on a much smaller scale) to solving complex prob-lems. In NN parlance, neurons are called units and synapses are called connections, or links. Given some input stimuli or signals, an NN is designed to provide the desired output signals. In an optimization context, for instance, given a set of input parameter values, an NN should deliver the optimal solution to a problem.

The basic elements of an NN are its units, its topology, and the learning algo-rithm it employs. The topology refers to the layout of the units and their connec-tions. Any NN is made up of a heirarchy of layers. The units in the network are arranged along these layers. The topmost layer is referred to as the *output layer,* and the bottommost is called the *input layer.* All other, intermediate layers are referred to as the *hidden output layers,* or simply hidden layers. In traditional NNs, each unit in one layer is connected to all units in the next-higher layer via direct connections between units in the two layers. Such NNs are called *output-feed forward* networks. The outputs of each unit flow in one direction only, which is toward the output layer. Special structures allow outputs to feed backward or sideways as well.

The function of the units in the input layer is to provide the input stimuli (i.e., signals) applied to the NN. These stimuli cause the units in the output layer of the NN to generate output signals. The hidden and output layers of an NN facilitate the transformation of the input to the output. When referring to a NN by the number of layers it contains, it is customary to ignore the input layer and merely state the number of output layers it contains, because the input layer does no real processing apart from supplying the inputs to the rest of the network. Thus a one-layer net actually contains two layers—the input layer and one output layer (i.e., it has no hidden layers). It has been established that for all practical purposes we do not need anything more than a three-layer net.

Neural nets also differ in the makeup of their neurons, or units. Each unit has a state, or activity level, associated with it. This state is determined by the input stimuli that the unit receives. These stimuli are an aggregation of the activity levels of all units in the layer below. Each connection from a unit in the layer below to the unit in question has a weight or strength value associated with it. Generally (i.e., in nonadaptive NNs), these weights are allowed to adapt only during the training phase of an NN and remain constant during actual use. The activity level of each lower-layer unit is multiplied by the weight of the link connecting it to the unit whose activity level is being determined. All such weighted inputs to the unit in question are summed. A quantity called the threshold level, or bias, for the unit under consideration is subtracted from the weighted sum to yield the actual total input to the unit. Thus, the total input to the unit may be positive, negative, or zero, depending on the relative sizes of the sum of weighted inputs and its bias. A unit's threshold is also a quantity that is dynamically determined and is not predefined.

Once the total input to a unit is determined, we need another mechanism to convert it to an activity level for the unit. This conversion is usually achieved using a special function called a sigmoid nonlinearity, which converts the total input value into a quantity between 0 and 1, with the output being 0.5 when the total input is zero. In some instances functions other than the sigmoid nonlinearity are used.

The third element in an NN is some mechanism for adjusting its weights and biases. As mentioned, this adjustment usually occurs during a phase called the training phase of an NN, when the net is a nonadaptive net. The relatively more recent adaptive NN also allows adaptation to occur during actual use. Regardless, all such adaptation is done using some algorithm. The most popular of the many available strategies is the back propagation algorithm. The back propagation algorithm is one that propagates some measure of the error in a network's output back through the various layers of the network in the direction of the input layer. This activity implies that the output generated by each unit in the output layer (which actually is the activity level for that unit) is compared with a desired output value for the unit to determine some measure of error. The method uses an error function based on the sum of squared errors to generate an aggregate measure of error. The algorithm focuses on progressively adjusting the weights and biases of a network using the aggregate error measure along with a quantity called the learning rate of the network, which is specified by the trainer.

In operationalizing this strategy for training a net, the trainer begins with a set of training problem cases. Usually, the training process itself is supervised, with the trainer offering the net the correct answer to each training case. Thus, the net does not have the responsibility of inferring the correct responses, as in the case with unsupervised training. Training begins with initial, trainer-specified choices for critical parameters in the network, such as its learning rate, weights, and biases. A typical choice for the learning rate is between 0 and 1, with 0.5 being tried first. The appropriate learning rate choice for the net under consideration (and for the type of problem to which the net is being applied) can be determined only through a process of manual trial and error.

The weights and biases are quantities that the net learns during the training process. However, starting values must be specified by the trainer. Usually, these are randomly chosen between −0.5 and 0.5. For each member of the training suite, a forward pass is conducted, and the errors are propagated back once. The procedure is repeated over and over again, where all members in the suite are applied to the net successively in each pass. The training terminates when all the weights and biases stabilize. At this point, the net has learned all that it can from the example instances. Its knowledge is embodied in the adapted weight and bias values. The net is now ready for use in actual applications from the domain under consideration.

Given this understanding of the basic components of an NN, a critical concern in practice is the topology of the net itself. Typically, a net would contain one input unit for each member of an input vector of signals. The act of generating an output signal may be viewed as assigning the input as belonging to a certain class. Thus, typically, we would have one output unit for each possible class. The number of hidden units may be one or two, as already mentioned, with no more than two such layers required under any circumstance.

Unfortunately, for the type of nonlinearity commonly used in practice (namely, sigmoids), no insights are presently available on the number of hidden units required in the hidden layer(s). Thus, the number of hidden units must be chosen through trial and error. Researchers have shown that too many hidden units negatively impact network performance. Further, there is research evidence showing that when two networks perform identically during training, it is more likely that the one with fewer hidden units will do better in actual application than the one with more such units. This observation also apparently holds good even if the net with fewer hidden units performs somewhat worse than the other during training.

Just as with GAs, NNs are sensitive to starting conditions, including the sequencing of training instances. Usually, several independent replications of the training process described are conducted, with the weights and biases picked to have the smallest minimum error value for the actual application. As with GA-based systems, NNs are also reasoning systems that learn through induction, with the process usually being supervised induction. Unlike GA-based systems however, NNs generally are intended as generalizable systems, with the system being applied to a variety of actual problem instances from the training domain.

Good overview articles on NNs are Lippmann (1987), Waite and Hardenbergh (1989), and Weiss and Kulikowski (1991). Rummelhart, Hinton, and Williams (1986) describe in detail the back propagation algorithm . Various learning procedures for NNs are discussed in Ackley, Hinton, and Sejnowski (1985), Lippman (1987), Hinton (1989), and Pakath (1994b). Current sources of information include well-known refereed journals such as *Neural Networks* (published by the International Neural Network Society) and the IEEE Transactions. Other information sources include the numerous annual conferences, some held by the INNS in isolation and others in conjunction with societies such as the Institute of Electrical and Electronics Engineers (IEEE), and their proceedings.

REFERENCES

Ackley, D. H., G. E. Hinton, and T. J. Sejnowski. 1985. A learning algorithm for Boltzmann machines. *Cognitive Science, 9.*

Belew, R. K., and L. B. Booker, eds. 1991. *Proceedings of the Fourth International Conference on Genetic Algorithms,* San Mateo, Calif.: Morgan Kaufmann.

Forrest, S. 1993a. Genetic algorithms: Principles of natural selection applied to computation. *Science* (August 13).

———. ed. 1993b. *Proceedings of the Fifth International Conference on Genetic Algorithms.* San Mateo, Calif.: Morgan Kaufmann.

Goldberg, D. E. 1989. *Genetic algorithms in search, optimization and machine learning.* Reading, Mass.: Addison Wesley.

Grefenstette, J. J., ed. 1985. *Proceedings of an International Conference on Genetic Algorithms and Their Applications.* Hillsdale, N.J.: Lawrence Erlbaum Associates.

———. 1987. *Genetic algorithms and their applications: Proceedings of the Second International Conference on Genetic Algorithms.* Hillsdale, N.J.: Lawrence Erlbaum Associates.

Hinton, G. E. 1989. Connectionist learning procedures. *Artificial Intelligence, 40.*

Lippmann, R. 1987. An introduction to computing with neural nets. *IEEE Acoustics, Speech, and Signal Processing Magazine* (April).

Pakath, R. 1994a. Machine learning and the genetic algorithm strategy. In *Operations research and artificial intelligence,* edited by C. W. Holsapple, V. S. Jacob, A. B. Whinston. Norwood, N.J.: Ablex.

———. 1994b. Neural networks: Concepts, learning, and applications. In *Operations research and artificial intelligence.* edited by C. W. Holsapple, V. S. Jacob, and A. B. Whinston. Norwood, N.J.: Ablex.

Rumelhart, D., G. E. Hinton, and R. Williams. 1986. Learning internal representations by back-propagating errors. *Nature, 323.*

Schaffer, J. D. ed. 1989. *Proceedings of the Third International Conference on Genetic Algorithms.* San Mateo, Calif.: Morgan Kaufmann.

Waite, T., and H. Hardenbergh. 1989. Neural nets. *Programmers Journal 7.*

Weiss, S. M., and C. A. Kulikowski. 1991. *Computer systems that learn: Classification and prediction methods from statistics, neural nets, machine learning and expert systems.* San Mateo, Calif.: Morgan Kaufmann.

Appendix G

SAMPLE KNOWLEDGE SYSTEM CONTENTS

VARIANCE ANALYSIS INVESTIGATION DATA TABLES: STRUCTURES AND SAMPLE CONTENTS

```
Table: VARUSER          Created:    04/18/93     Read Access: A........
Header Size: 295        Modified:   04/24/93     Write Access: A.......
Access Mode: Local      Record Size:  9          Number of Records:   4
File: B:\VARUSER.ITB
```

Field	Type	Size	Picture	
#MARK	LOGIC	1	(default)	
DNAME	STR	3	%3a	
DPROD	INT	2	(default)	
DVAROUT	INT	2	n	"VARIANCE OUTPUT FORMAT"

VARUSER TABLE CONTENTS

DNAME	DPROD	DVAROUT
MBC	1.00	1
CWH	2.00	1
MBC	2.00	1
CWH	4.00	2

```
Table: VARPROD          Created: 04/23/93        Read Access: A.........
Header Size: 1147       Modified: 04/23/93       Write Access: A........
Access Mode: Local      Record Size: 39          Number of Records: 5
File: B:\VARPROD.ITB
```

Field	Type	Size	Picture	
#MARK	LOGIC	1	(default)	
PPROD	INT	2	nn	
PLES	INT	2	%4n.nn	"LABOR USAGE STANDARD"
PLEA	INT	2	%4n.nn	"LABOR USAGE ACTUAL"
PLRS	INT	2	%4n.nn	"LABOR RATE STANDARD"
PLRA	INT	2	%4n.nn	"LABOR RATE ACTUAL"
PMQS	INT	2	%4n.nn	"MATERIAL QUANTITY STANDARD"
PMQA	INT	2	%4n.nn	"MATERIAL QUANTITY ACTUAL"
PMPS	INT	2	%4n.nn	"MATERIAL PRICE STANDARD"
PMPA	INT	2	%4n.nn	"MATERIAL PRICE ACTUAL"
POES	INT	2	%4n.nn	"OVERHEAD USAGE STANDARD"
POEA	INT	2	%4n.nn	"OVERHEAD USAGE ACTUAL"
POSS	INT	2	%4n.nn	"OVERHEAD RATE STANDARD"
POSA	INT	2	%4n.nn	"OVERHEAD RATE ACTUAL"
PLEV	INT	2	n.nn	
PLRV	INT	2	n.nn	"LABOR RATE MAX"
PMQV	INT	2	n.nn	"MATERIAL QUANTITY MAX"
PMPV	INT	2	n.nn	"MATERIAL PRICE MAX"
POEV	INT	2	n.nn	"OVERHEAD USAGE MAX"
POSV	INT	2	n.nn	"OVERHEAD RATE MAX"

```
Table: VARHIST               Created: 04/24/93        Read Access: A........
Header Size: 497             Modified: 04/25/93       Write Access: A........
Access Mode: Local          Record Size: 63          Number of Records: 8
File: B:\VARHIST.ITB
```

Field	Type	Size	Picture	
#MARK	LOGIC	1	(default)	
VPROD	INT	2	nn	"PRODUCT CODE"
VVAR	STR	3	%3a	"TYPE OF VARIANCE"
VCALC	INT	2	%5n	
VDATE	STR	8	nn/nn/nn	"INVESTIGATION DATE"
VCOST	INT	2	%6n.nn	"COST OF INVESTIGATION"
VRESULT	INT	2	n	"RESULT OF INVESTIGATION"
VDESC	STR	40	%40a	

VARHIST TABLE CONTENTS

VPROD	VVAR	VCALC	VDATE	VCOST	VRESULT	VDESC
1	LEV	37	11/11/55	0.00	1	FOUND NO PROBLEMS
1	LEV	123	12/19/90	100.00	2	MINOR DISAGREEMENT RESOLVED
1	LRV	24	11/11/92	250.00	2	OVERPAYMENT OF OVERTIME WAS CORRECTED
1	LEV	37	05/06/92	1000.00	3	A MACHINE IS REQUIRING MORE

3	MQV	12	04/10/93	1000.00	3	TIME THAN BEFORE
						UNUSUAL AMOUNT OF MATERIAL
						USED UNKNOWN
1	LRV	125	05/04/93	100.00	1	FOUND ONLY SEASONAL VARIANCE
1	LRV	57	05/24/93	1000.00	2	SUPPLIER HAD RAISED PRICE
						FOR PARTS
2	LEV	255	04/31/93	2556.00	3	SEE FILE LEVAAA

VARIANCE ANALYSIS PROGRAM LISTINGS AND FORM DECLARATIONS

```
!! THIS IS THE MAIN PROGRAM OF THE VARIANCE INVESTIGATION SYSTEM

!! STORE ORIGINAL VALUES OF ENVIRONMENT VARIABLES
MSUPD = E.SUPD
MSTAT = E.STAT
MPAUS = E.PAUS
MLSTR = E.LSTR
MBACG = E.BACG
MFORG = E.FORG
MICAS = E.ICAS
MICOM = E.ICOM


!! SUPPRESS SHOWING LOCATED TABLE RECORD
E.SUPD = TRUE


!! SUPPRESS CALCULATING AND SHOWING STATISTICS ON OBTAIN
E.STAT = FALSE
!! PAUSE AFTER A FULL PAGE IS DISPLAYED
E.PAUS = TRUE
!! STRING LENGTH IS 80 CHARACTERS
E.LSTR = 80
!! BACKGROUND COLOR IS BLUE
E.BACG = "B"
E.FORG = "C"
!! ignore upper/lower case differences !
E.ICAS = TRUE
!! turn on recompute for spreadsheet !
E.ICOM = TRUE
!! initialize variance decision variables !
DP = 0
DS = 0
DV = 0
RP = 0
RS = 0
RV = 0


LOAD "b:VAR.ICF"
USE "b:VARUSER"
USE "b:VARPROD"
```

```
USE "b:VARHIST"
PERFORM "b:VARFORMS"
NAME = " "
!! TURN OFF BORDERS ON SPREADSHEET
CALC BORDER

CLEAR

PERFORM "b:VARINTRO"

MCONTINUE = 1
WHILE MCONTINUE = 1 DO

CLEAR

DIM opt (6)
        opt(1) = "CALCULATE VARIANCES               "
        opt(2) = "ANALYZE VARIANCE INVESTIGATION DECISION"
        opt(3) = "REVIEW PRIOR INVESTIGATIONS       "
        opt(4) = "PLAY WHAT-IF                     "
        opt(5) = "ENTER RESULTS OF INVESTIGATION      "
        opt(6) = "EXIT VARIANCE ANALYSIS SYSTEM      "
choice   =    MENU(opt,1,6,7,12,0,41,1,10,-1,1,"WMMGWWMG","FDCP",\
"VARIANCE ANALYSIS MENU",)

IF CHOICE = 1
        CALC
        SAVE TO "b:VAR.ICF"
ENDIF
IF CHOICE = 2
        PERFORM "b:VARINVEST"
        SAVE TO "b:VAR.ICF"
ENDIF
IF CHOICE = 3
        PERFORM "b:VARVIEW"
ENDIF
IF CHOICE = 4
        CALC
        LOAD FROM "b:VAR.ICF"
ENDIF
IF CHOICE = 5
        PERFORM "b:VARRPTIN"
ENDIF
IF CHOICE = 6
        MCONTINUE = 0
ENDIF

ENDWHILE

E.SUPD = MSUPD
```

```
E.STAT = MSTAT
E.PAUS = MPAUS
E.LSTR = MLSTR
E.BACG = MBACG
E.FORG = MFORG
E.ICAS = MICAS
E.ICOM = MICOM
```

```
VARFORMS.IPF

!! DECLARATIONS OF FORMS GENERATED VIA INTERATIVE PAINTING
FORM VARINTRO
      AT 2, 6 TO 10, 66 PUT BORDER "FCBA"
      AT 3, 21 PUT "   VARIANCE ANALYSIS SYSTEM   " WITH "R"
      AT 6, 21 PUT "ENTER YOUR 3 INITIALS:"
      AT 6, 45 GET NAME USING "aaa" WITH "R"
      AT 8, 21 PUT "ENTER YOUR PRODUCT NUMBER:"
      AT 8, 48 GET MPROD NUM USING "nn" WITH "R"
ENDFORM

FORM VARMAX
      AT 4, 16 PUT "CHANGE VARIANCE INVESTIGATION PARAMETERS"
      AT 8, 10 PUT "Change Variance Investigation Cutoff For Each Type "+\
"of Variance"
      AT 11, 20 PUT "LABOR EFFICIENCY:"
      AT 11, 48 PUT #A25 USING "n.nn"
      AT 11, 48 GET #A24 NUM USING "n.nn"
      AT 11, 48 PUT #A24 USING "n.nn"
      AT 13, 20 PUT "LABOR RATE:"
      AT 13, 48 GET #B24 NUM USING "n.nn"
      AT 13, 48 PUT #B24 USING "n.nn"
      AT 15, 20 PUT "MATERIALS QUANTITY:"
      AT 15, 48 GET #C24 NUM USING "n.nn"
      AT 15, 48 PUT #C24 USING "n.nn"
      AT 17, 20 PUT "MATERIALS PRICE:"
      AT 17, 48 GET #D24 NUM USING "n.nn"
      AT 17, 48 PUT #D24 USING "n.nn"
      AT 19, 20 PUT "OVERHEAD EFFICIENCY:"
      AT 19, 48 GET #E24 NUM USING "n.nn"
      AT 19, 48 PUT #E24 USING "n.nn"
      AT 21, 20 PUT "OVERHEAD RATE:"
      AT 21, 48 GET #F24 NUM USING "n.nn"
      AT 21, 48 PUT #F24 USING "n.nn"
ENDFORM

FORM VARIMPORT
      AT 2, 26 PUT "VARIANCE DECISION SCREEN"
      AT 4, 18 PUT "Enter on a scale of 1=low   10=high"
      AT 6, 24 PUT "What is the degree of:"
```

```
        AT  8,  1 PUT "RISK OF PRODUCT"
        AT  8, 29 PUT "NEED TO SUPERVISE"
        AT 10,  6 GET DP NUM USING "nn"
        AT 10,  6 PUT DP USING "nn"
        AT 10, 36 GET DS NUM USING "nn"
        AT 10, 36 PUT DS USING "nn"
        AT 16, 21 PUT "What is the Relative Importance of:"
        AT 18,  1 PUT "RISK OF PRODUCT"
        AT 18, 29 PUT "NEED TO SUPERVISE"
        AT 18, 58 PUT "EXTREMITY OF VARIANCE"
        AT 20,  6 GET RP NUM USING "nn"
        AT 20,  6 PUT RP USING "nn"
        AT 20, 36 GET RS NUM USING "nn"
        AT 20, 36 PUT RS USING "nn"
        AT 20, 68 GET RV NUM USING "nn"
        AT 20, 68 PUT RV USING "nn"
ENDFORM


FORM VARCALC
        AT  5, 16 PUT "RESULTS OF VARIANCE INVESTIGATION CALCULATION"
        AT  3,  5 TO 21, 69 PUT BORDER "FGBC"
        AT  9, 20 PUT "LABOR EFFICIENCY:"
        AT  9, 50 PUT INVLE USING "nnnnn.n"
        AT 11, 20 PUT "LABOR RATE:"
        AT 11, 50 PUT INVLR USING "nnnnn.n"
        AT 13, 20 PUT "MATERIALS QUANTITY:"
        AT 13, 50 PUT INVMQ USING "nnnnn.n"
        AT 15, 20 PUT "MATERIALS PRICE:"
        AT 15, 50 PUT INVMP USING "nnnnn.n"
        AT 17, 20 PUT "OVERHEAD EFFICIENCY:"
        AT 17, 50 PUT INVEO USING "nnnnn.n"
        AT 19, 20 PUT "OVERHEAD RATE:"
        AT 19, 50 PUT INVOS USING "nnnnn.n"
ENDFORM
```

```
VARINTRO.IPF


!! THIS PROGRAM GETS THE USER'S INITIALS AND THE PRODUCT THEY WORK WITH
E.SUPD = TRUE

CLEAR
PUTFORM VARINTRO
GETFORM VARINTRO
CLEAR

!! load this user's database info and save to context file !
OBTAIN RECORD FROM VARUSER FOR DNAME = NAME AND DPROD = MPROD
IF #FOUND = FALSE THEN
```

```
        AT 18, 30 OUTPUT "INVALID USER-ID / PRODUCT COMBINATION"
        AT 20, 34 OUTPUT "ACCESS DENIED     HIT ENTER TO CONTINUE"
        WAIT
        STOP
ENDIF

-------------------------------------------------------------------------------

VARINVES.IPF

!! CALCULATE VARIANCE INVESTIGATION MEASURES AND DISPLAY IN APPROPRIATE FORM

CLEAR
! get cut-off percentages for variances
PUTFORM VARMAX
GETFORM VARMAX
CLEAR


! get relative importance of investigation factors
PUTFORM VARIMPORT
GETFORM VARIMPORT

ADDIT = (DP * RP) + (DS * RS)
IF ABS(#C7/#A7)>#A24 THEN INVLE = ADDIT + (ABS(#C7/#A7)) * RV;
        ELSE INVLE = ADDIT + (RV);
 ENDIF;


IF ABS(#G7/#E7)>#B24 THEN INVLR = ADDIT + (ABS(#G7/#E7)) * RV;
        ELSE INVLR = ADDIT + RV;
 ENDIF;


IF ABS(#C13/#A13)>#C24 THEN INVMQ = (ABS(#C13/#A13)) * RV;
        ELSE INVMQ = ADDIT + RV;
 ENDIF;


IF ABS(#G13/#E13)>#D24 THEN INVMP = (ABS(#G13/#E13)) * RV;
        ELSE INVMP = ADDIT + RV;
 ENDIF;


IF ABS(#C19/#A19)>#E24 THEN INVOE = (ABS(#C19/#G19)) * RV;
        ELSE INVOS = ADDIT + RV
 ENDIF;
WAIT

MMORE = "Y"
WHILE MMORE = "Y" DO


! output the results of the calculation !
IF VARUSER.DVAROUT = 1 THEN
```

```
        CLEAR
        PUTFORM VARCALC
        AT   9, 50 OUTPUT INVLE USING "nnnnn.n"
        AT  11, 50 OUTPUT INVLR USING "nnnnn.n"
        AT  13, 50 OUTPUT INVMQ USING "nnnnn.n"
        AT  15, 50 OUTPUT INVMP USING "nnnnn.n"
        AT  17, 50 OUTPUT INVOE USING "nnnnn.n"
        AT  19, 50 OUTPUT INVOS USING "nnnnn.n"
        WAIT
ELSE
        DIM DS(6,2)
        DS(1,1) = "LE"
        DS(2,1) = "LR"
        DS(3,1) = "MQ"
        DS(4,1) = "MP"
        DS(5,1) = "OE"
        DS(6,1) = "OS"
        DS(1,2) = INVLE
        DS(2,2) = INVLR
        DS(3,2) = INVMQ
        DS(4,2) = INVMP
        DS(5,2) = INVOE
        DS(6,2) = INVOS
        #TITLE = "RESULTS OF VARIANCE MEASURES CALCULATION"
        #XLABEL = "TYPE OF VARIANCE"
        #YLABEL = "VARIANCE MEASURE"

        PLOT BAR FROM DS(1,1) TO DS(6,2)
ENDIF

CLEAR
AT 5,10 INPUT MANS WITH \
   "CHANGE THE PRESENTATION MODE AND REDISPLAY? (Y/N)"
IF MANS = "N" THEN
   MMORE = "N"
ENDIF

IF MANS = "Y"
        IF VARUSER.DVAROUT = 1 THEN
           VARUSER.DVAROUT = 2
        ELSE
           VARUSER.DVAROUT = 1
        ENDIF
ENDIF

ENDWHILE
RETURN
```

VARVIEW.IPF

```
! THIS PROGRAM LETS USER REVIEW PRIOR INVESTIGATION DECISIONS !
E.STAT = FALSE
MVIEW = 1

WHILE MVIEW = 1 DO

CLEAR
DIM MTYPE(7)
MTYPE(1) = "   LABOR EFFICIENCY VARIANCE    "
MTYPE(2) = "   LABOR RATE VARIANCE    "
MTYPE(3) = "   MATERIALS QUANTITY VARIANCE    "
MTYPE(4) = "   MATERIALS PRICE VARIANCE    "
MTYPE(5) = "   OVERHEAD EFFICIENCY VARIANCE    "
MTYPE(6) = "   OVERHEAD RATE VARIANCE    "
MTYPE(7) = "   EXIT MENU             "
MSELECT = MENU(MTYPE,1,7,08,20,0,38,1,11,-1,1,"WUUWWRUW","FDC",\
"REVIEW PRIOR INVESTIGATIONS RESULTS")
IF MSELECT = 7 THEN
     MVIEW = 0
     RETURN
ENDIF

DIM MCODE(6)
MCODE(1) = "LEV"
MCODE(2) = "LRV"
MCODE(3) = "MQV"
MCODE(4) = "MPV"
MCODE(5) = "OEV"
MCODE(6) = "OSV"

MVAR = MCODE(MSELECT)

AT 18, 15 INPUT MANS WITH \
"DO YOU WANT TO SORT BY CALC MEASURE(M) OR BY COST(C)?"

LET #TITLE = "   REVIEW OF PREVIOUS INVESTIGATIONS RESULTS"

IF MANS = "C" THEN
SELECT * FROM VARHIST WHERE VPROD = MPROD AND VVAR = MVAR ORDER\
BY ZA VCOST
ELSE
SELECT * FROM varhist WHERE VPROD = MPROD AND VVAR = MVAR ORDER BY\
ZA VCALC
ENDIF

WAIT

ENDWHILE
```

```
VARRPTIN.IPF


! THIS PROGRAM ADDS RECORDS TO VARIANCE HISTORY FILE FROM RESULTS
! OF INVESTIGATIONS
CREATE RECORD FOR VARHIST WITH VARADDHS
```

SMSS DATA TABLES: STRUCTURES AND SAMPLE CONTENTS

```
Table: CUSTOMER           Created:  04/25/93      Read Access:  A.........
Header Size: 321          Modified: 04/25/93      Write Access: A.........
Access Mode: Local        Record Size: 39         Number of Records: 6
File: a:customer.itb


Field       Type      Size      Picture
-----       ----      ----      -------
#MARK       LOGIC     1         (default)
CKEY        STR       3         %3r
CNAME       STR       20        %20r
CEXPER      STR       4         %4r
REVENUE NUM 8         $%3f,%3f,%3f,%3f




Page    1 of                        CUSTOMER Table Contents


CKEY            CNAME             CEXPER       REVENUE


AOI     Ashland Oil Inc.          High         $65,000,000
KU      Kentucky Utilities        MED           $6,000,000
TOY     Toyota Manufacturing      MED         $120,000,000
CSG     Cable Services Group      LOW           $3,000,000
TJC     The Jockey Club           LOW           $5,000,000
LEX     Lexmark                   HIGH        $100,000,000
```

```
Table: OPPORTTY           Created:  04/25/93      Read Access:  A.........
Header Size: 466          Modified: 04/25/93      Write Access: A.........
Access Mode: Local        Record Size: 81         Number of Records: 13
File:  a:opportty.itb


Field       Type      Size      Picture
-----       ----      ----      -------
#MARK       LOGIC     1         (default)
OPCKEY      STR       3         %3r
OPSNAME     STR       25        %25r
OPPCT       NUM       8         d.dd
SALEMNTH    NUM       8         dd
SALEYR      NUM       8         dd
```

```
OPTYPE      STR     1       %1r
SCOST       NUM     8       $%3f,%3f
QTR         NUM     8       d
MNTHINYR    NUM     8       ff
```

Page   1 of   OPPORTTY Table Contents

OPCKEY	OPSNAME	OPPCT	SALEMNTH	SALEYR	SCOST	QTR	MNTHINYR
KU	OS PERFORMANCE	0.90	2	93	$50,000	1	2
TOY	DATA BASE SOFTWARE	0.80	3	93	$300,000	1	3
CSG	CASE TOOLS	0.80	6	93	$125,000	2	6
LEX	OS PERFORMANCE	0.65	6	93	$50,000	2	6
KU	MULTI MEDIA	0.80	5	93	$400,000	2	5
TJC	APPLICATION DEVELOPMENT	0.55	8	93	$100,000	3	8
TJC	CASE TOOLS	0.55	9	93	$125,000	3	9
LEX	APPLICATIONS	0.15	9	93	$150,000	3	9
TJC	OS PERFORMANCE	0.65	9	93	$50,000	3	9
TOY	PUBLISHING	0.80	7	93	$175,000	3	7
LEX	APPLICATION DEVELOPMENT	0.80	10	93	$100,000	4	10
TJC	PUBLISHING	0.15	12	93	$175,000	4	12
KU	PUBLISHING	0.50	10	93	$175,000	4	10

```
Table: SOFTWARE          Created:  04/25/93      Read Access:  A..............
Header Size: 423         Modified: 04/25/93      Write Access: A..............
Access Mode: Local       Record Size: 74         Number of Records: 10
File: a:software.itb
```

Field	Type	Size	Picture
-----	----	----	-------
#MARK	LOGIC	1	(default)
SNAME	STR	25	%25r
COST	NUM	8	$%3f,%3f
IMPTIME	NUM	8	(default)
EXPER	STR	4	%4r
EMKT	NUM	8	(default)
EINST	NUM	8	(default)
ESUPP	NUM	8	(default)
STRAT	STR	1	%1r

Page   1 of   SOFTWARE Table Contents

SNAME	COST	IMPTIME	EXPER	EMKT	EINST	ESUPP	STRAT
APPLICATION DEVELOPMENT	$100,000	6	HIGH	1	1	1	N
CASE TOOLS	$125,000	2	HIGH	3	1	1	Y

DATA BASE SOFTWARE	$300,000	9	HIGH	2	2	2	Y
APPLICATIONS	$150,000	3	LOW	2	2	1	N
OFFICE SYSTEMS	$250,000	3	MED	3	2	2	N
MULTI MEDIA	$400,000	6	HIGH	2	1	2	Y
DECISION SUPPORT	$150,000	3	LOW	3	1	2	N
OS PERFORMANCE	$50,000	1	LOW	1	1	1	N
PUBLISHING	$175,000	2	MED	2	1	1	N
CONNECTIVITY	$200,000	12	MED	3	2	3	Y

```
Table: QUOTA            Created:  04/18/93    Read Access:  A............
Header Size: 315        Modified: 04/18/93    Write Access: A............
Access Mode: Local      Record Size: 33       Number of Records: 1
File: a:quota.itb


Field      Type      Size      Picture
-----      ----      ----      -------
#MARK      LOGIC     1         (default)
QUOTA      NUM       8         $%3f,%3f,%3f
YTDSALES   NUM       8         $%3f,%3f,%3f
YRENDMNT   NUM       8         (default)
MNTHSRCR   NUM       8         (default)
```

```
Page    1 of                        QUOTA Table Contents

    QUOTA          YTDSALES       YRENDMNT     MNTHSRCR

  $3,000,000      $800,000       12           4
```

SMSS PROCEDURAL CODE

```
!SMSSMN
!This is the main driver app for the SMSS system. It will guide the user
!into SMOES or SMFS and any other apps that are added in the future.
!

IF NOT INUSE ("CUSTOMER") THEN USE "A:CUSTOMER.ITB";ENDIF
IF NOT INUSE ("SOFTWARE") THEN USE "A:SOFTWARE.ITB";ENDIF
IF NOT INUSE ("OPPORTTY") THEN USE "A:OPPORTTY.ITB";ENDIF
IF NOT INUSE ("QUOTA") THEN USE "A:QUOTA.ITB";ENDIF
LOAD "A:SMSSFRM.FRM"

CLEAR
CONT=TRUE
!Loop until Exit is pressed
```

```
WHILE CONT DO
    PUTFORM SMSSMAIN
    DIM SMSSCH(3)
    SMSSCH(1) = "SMOES - Software Marketing Opportunity Evaluation System"
    SMSSCH(2) = "SMFS - Software Marketing Forecasting System"
    SMSSCH(3) = "Exit SMSS"
    SMSSCTL = MENU(SMSSCH,1,3,13,15,1,58,1)
    IF (SMSSCTL=1) THEN PERFORM "A:SMOESMN.IPF";ENDIF
    IF (SMSSCTL=2) THEN PERFORM "A:SMFSMN.IPF";ENDIF
    IF (SMSSCTL=3) THEN
        CLEAR
        CONT=FALSE
    ENDIF
ENDWHILE
```

```
!DTCHOICE
```

```
!Allows for the selection of the type of detail to examine.
!Customer and Software group details are available. Once a selection is
!made, control is passed to the appropriate program.
```

```
PUTFORM SMFSFORM
PUTFORM DTCHOICE
DIM CH(3)
CH(1)="Software Details"
CH(2)="Customer Details"
CH(3)="Return to Main"
CHCTL=MENU(CH,1,3,10,30,1,18,1)
IF (CHCTL=1) THEN PERFORM "A:FOREDET.IPF";ENDIF
IF (CHCTL=2) THEN PERFORM "A:FOREDET2.IPF";ENDIF
IF (CHCTL=3) THEN CLEAR;ENDIF
```

```
!FORECAST
```

```
!This is the module that presents the forecast for the remaining quarters
!in the fiscal year. YTD numbers are also presented.
```

```
#TITLE=" "
E.WFU=FALSE
E.DECI=0
E.DSUM=FALSE
!E.SERR=TRUE
E.STAT=FALSE
RQUOTA=QUOTA.QUOTA/4
```

```
!Calculate the factor to use for determining YTD numbers
YTDQUOTA=(QUOTA.QUOTA/12)*QUOTA.MNTHSRCR
```

```
IF (QUOTA.MNTHSRCR > 1) THEN
    TMPMNTH=QUOTA.MNTHSRCR - 1
ENDIF
FSTQTR=TRUNC(TMPMNTH/3)
QFACTOR=3 - (QUOTA.MNTHSRCR-(3*FSTQTR))

!Prepare and present the graph

DCTR=1
DIM SLSQTA(4,3)
DCTR=1
IDX=0

!Fill the array containing the information for the remaining quarters

WHILE (DCTR < 5) DO
        STAT OPPORTTY.SCOST*OPPORTTY.OPPCT USING "$fff,fff,fff" \
                FROM OPPORTTY for OPPORTTY.QTR=DCTR AND \
                OPPORTTY.MNTHINYR > QUOTA.MNTHSRCR;
        IF #FOUND THEN
            IDX=IDX+1
            SLSQTA (IDX,1) = OPPORTTY.QTR
            IF (IDX=1) THEN
                SLSQTA (IDX,2)=(RQUOTA*QFACTOR)/3
            ELSE
                SLSQTA (IDX,2) = RQUOTA
            ENDIF
            SLSQTA (IDX,3) = #SUM(1)
        ENDIF
        DCTR = DCTR + 1
ENDWHILE

!Plot the graph

#TITLE="KTA Software Forecast"
#XLABEL="Quarter"
#YLABEL="Dollars"
DIM #LEGEND (2)
#LEGEND(1)="Quota"
#LEGEND(2)="Actual/Forecast"
E.PAUS=FALSE
PLOT BAR FROM SLSQTA(1,1) TO SLSQTA(IDX,3) AT BOTTOM;
PLOT LEGEND FOR BAR AT 11,22
PLOT ONTOP TEXT "KTA YTD Numbers and Software Forecast" at 1,2
SYTDS=TOSTR(QUOTA.YTDSALES,10,0)
PLOT ONTOP TEXT SYTDS AT 7,13
PLOT ONTOP TEXT "QUOTA" AT 8,5
SQTA=TOSTR (YTDQUOTA,10,0)
E.WFU=TRUE
PLOT ONTOP TEXT SQTA AT 8,13
```

```
CLEAR

----------------------------------------------------------------------

!FOREDET

!This module is used to create the forecast detail report by software
!group. It can also be done for all groups.

E.SUPH=FALSE
E.PAUSE=TRUE
E.LEGH=TRUE

!Set up headings for the reports

DIM #LEGEND(6)
#LEGEND(1)="Software Group"
#LEGEND(2)="CKey"
#LEGEND(6)="Qtr."
#LEGEND(4)="Software Cost"
#LEGEND(5)="% Frcst"
#LEGEND(6)="$$$$ Frcst"

!Get the Desired Quarter

PERFORM "A:GETQTR.IPF"

!Get the software for analysis

SWFOUND=FALSE
PUTFORM SMFSFORM
PUTFORM GETSFW

!Loop until a software group with opportunities stored is selected

WHILE NOT SWFOUND DO
    OPTIONS = LASTREC(SOFTWARE)
    DIM SW(OPTIONS+1)
    CONVERT TRIM(SNAME) FROM SOFTWARE TO ARRAY SW(2) ORDER BY SNAME
    SW(1) = "ALL"
    CHOICE = MENU(SW,OPT,OPTIONS+1,7,25,0,30,1)
    CLEAR

!Create report for a single software group

    IF (CHOICE > 1) THEN
        OBTAIN RECORD FROM SOFTWARE FOR SNAME=SW(CHOICE)
        #TITLE="                    Software Detail Report for "+SOFTWARE.SNAME
        IF (REQQTR=5) THEN
            SELECT UNIQUE OPSNAME, OPCKEY USING "aaaa", \
```

```
              QTR USING "fff", SCOST USING "$ff,fff,fff,fff", \
              OPPCT*100 USING "ffffffff", \
              SCOST*OPPCT USING "$fff,fff,fff" FROM OPPORTTY \
              FOR OPSNAME=SOFTWARE.SNAME \
              GROUP BY OPSNAME, ORDER BY OPSNAME
          ELSE
            SELECT UNIQUE OPSNAME, OPCKEY USING "aaaa", \
                QTR USING "fff", SCOST USING "$ff,fff,fff,fff", \
                OPPCT*100 USING "ffffffff", \
                SCOST*OPPCT USING "$fff,fff,fff" FROM OPPORTTY \
                FOR OPSNAME=SOFTWARE.SNAME AND OPPORTTY.QTR=REQQTR \
                GROUP BY OPSNAME, ORDER BY OPSNAME
          ENDIF
          ELSE
              #TITLE="                            Software Detail Report for All Groups"
          IF  (REQQTR=5) THEN
              SELECT UNIQUE OPSNAME, OPCKEY USING "aaaa", \
                  QTR USING "fff", SCOST USING "$ff,fff,fff,fff", \
                  OPPCT*100 USING "ffffffff", \
                  SCOST*OPPCT USING "$fff,fff,fff" FROM OPPORTTY \
                  GROUP BY OPSNAME, ORDER BY OPSNAME
          ELSE
            SELECT UNIQUE OPSNAME, OPCKEY USING "aaaa", \
                  QTR USING "fff", SCOST USING "$ff,fff,fff,fff", \
                  OPPCT*100 USING "ffffffff", \
                  SCOST*OPPCT USING "$fff,fff,fff" FROM OPPORTTY \
                  FOR OPPORTTY.QTR=REQQTR GROUP BY OPSNAME, ORDER BY OPSNAME
          ENDIF
      ENDIF


!Was data found??

    IF #FOUND THEN
        SWFOUND=TRUE
        WAIT
        CLEAR
    ELSE
        PUTFORM SMFSFORM
        PUTFORM GETSFW
        PUTFORM NORECS
    ENDIF
ENDWHILE

-------------------------------------------------------------------------------

!FOREDET2

!This routine creates the forecast detail report for a given customer.

E.SUPH=FALSE
```

```
    E.PAUSE=TRUE
    E.LEGH=TRUE


    !Prepare the column headings for the report

    DIM #LEGEND(6)
    #LEGEND(1)="CKey"
    #LEGEND(2)="Software Name"
    #LEGEND(6)="Qtr."
    #LEGEND(4)="Software Cost"
    #LEGEND(5)="% Frcst"
    #LEGEND(6)="$$$$ Frcst"


    !Get the Desired Quarter

    PERFORM "A:GETQTR.IPF"


    !Get the Customer for analysis

    SWFOUND=FALSE
    PUTFORM SMFSFORM
    PUTFORM GETCUST


    !Loop until a customer with opportunities is found

    WHILE NOT SWFOUND DO
        OPTIONS = LASTREC(CUSTOMER)
        DIM CS(OPTIONS+1)
        CONVERT TRIM(CNAME) FROM CUSTOMER TO ARRAY CS(2) ORDER BY CNAME
        CS(1) = "ALL"
        CHOICE = MENU(CS,OPT,OPTIONS+1,7,25,0,30,1)
        CLEAR
        IF (CHOICE > 1) THEN
            OBTAIN RECORD FROM CUSTOMER FOR CNAME=CS(CHOICE)
            #TITLE="                 Customer Detail Report for "+CUSTOMER.CNAME
            IF (REQQTR=5) THEN
                SELECT UNIQUE OPCKEY USING "aaaa", OPSNAME, \
                    QTR USING "fff", SCOST USING "$ff,fff,fff,fff", \
                    OPPCT*100 USING "ffffffff", \
                    SCOST*OPPCT USING "$fff,fff,fff" FROM OPPORTTY \
                    FOR OPCKEY=CUSTOMER.CKEY \
                    GROUP BY OPCKEY, ORDER BY OPCKEY
            ELSE
                SELECT UNIQUE OPCKEY USING "aaaa", OPSNAME, \
                    QTR USING "fff", SCOST USING "$ff,fff,fff,fff", \
                    OPPCT*100 USING "ffffffff", \
                    SCOST*OPPCT USING "$fff,fff,fff" FROM OPPORTTY \
                    FOR OPCKEY=CUSTOMER.CKEY AND OPPORTTY.QTR=REQQTR \
                    GROUP BY OPCKEY, ORDER BY OPCKEY
            ENDIF
```

```
        ELSE
            #TITLE="                            Customer Detail Report for All Customers"
            IF (REQQTR=5) THEN
                SELECT UNIQUE OPCKEY USING "aaaa", OPSNAME, \
                    QTR USING "fff", SCOST USING "$ff,fff,fff,fff", \
                    GROUP BY OPCKEY, ORDER BY OPCKEY
            ELSE
                SELECT UNIQUE OPCKEY USING "aaaa", OPSNAME, \
                    QTR USING "fff", SCOST USING "$ff,fff,fff,fff", \
                    OPPCT*100 USING "ffffffff", \
                    SCOST*OPPCT USING "$fff,fff,fff" FROM OPPORTTY \
                    FOR OPPORTTY.QTR=REQQTR \
                    GROUP BY OPCKEY, ORDER BY OPCKEY
            ENDIF
        ENDIF
        IF #FOUND THEN
            SWFOUND=TRUE
            WAIT
            CLEAR
        ELSE
            PUTFORM SMFSFORM
            PUTFORM GETCUST
            PUTFORM NORECS
        ENDIF
ENDWHILE


-------------------------------------------------------------------------------


!GETQTR

! This routine allows users to pick the quarter to work with for viewing
! detail information

CLEAR
PUTFORM SMFSFORM
PUTFORM GETQTR
GQQTR=FSTQTR+1
CNTR = (4-GQQTR)+2
DIM GQCTL (CNTR)
GQINX=1
WHILE (GQQTR < 5) DO
    GQCTL(GQINX) = TOSTR(GQQTR,1,0)
    GQINX = GQINX + 1
    GQQTR = GQQTR + 1
ENDWHILE
ALLR = "All Remaining"
GQCTL (GQINX) = ALLR
CTLVAR= MENU(GQCTL,1,CNTR,10,30,1,15,1)
IF (GQCTL(CTLVAR) = ALLR) THEN
        REQQTR=5
```

```
ELSE
            REQQTR=TONUM(GQCTL(CTLVAR))
ENDIF
CLEAR

--------------------------------------------------------------------------------

!OPPDET


! This routine will plot in pie format, the percentage of dollars forecast,
! and the percentage of the total opportunity count of software group.
! This can be done for any quarter remaining or the remainder of the year.

#TITLE=" "
E.DCNT=TRUE

!Get the quarter that is desired

PERFORM "A:GETQTR.IPF"

!Set up control variables and array and loop selecting the numbers for
!each software group and storing them in the array and legend for using
!to create the pie charts.

IDX=0
DIM #LEGEND (20)
DIM OPPDT (20,3)
OPPDT(1,1) = "DDD"
OBTAIN FIRST FROM SOFTWARE
MORESFW=TRUE
CNTTOT=0
WHILE MORESFW DO
        IF (REQQTR=5) THEN
            STAT OPPORTTY.SCOST*OPPORTTY.OPPCT USING "fff,fff,fff" \
                FROM OPPORTTY FOR OPPORTTY.OPSNAME=SOFTWARE.SNAME
        ELSE
            STAT OPPORTTY.SCOST*OPPORTTY.OPPCT USING "fff,fff,fff" \
                FROM OPPORTTY FOR OPPORTTY.OPSNAME=SOFTWARE.SNAME \
                AND OPPORTTY.QTR = REQQTR
        ENDIF
        IF #FOUND THEN
            CNTTOT=CNTTOT + #CNT
            IDX = IDX + 1
            OPPDT (IDX,1) = "   "
            OPPDT (IDX,2) = #CNT
            OPPDT (IDX,3) = #SUM(1)
            #LEGEND(IDX) = SOFTWARE.SNAME
        ENDIF
        OBTAIN NEXT FROM SOFTWARE
        IF NOT #FOUND THEN MORESFW=FALSE; ENDIF
```

```
ENDWHILE

!Plot both pie charts and the legend

E.WFU=FALSE
IF REQQTR=5 THEN TQTR="All"
ELSE TQTR=TOSTR(REQQTR,1,0);ENDIF
#TITLE="Dollars Pct."
PLOT LABELED % PIE FROM OPPDT(1,1) TO OPPDT (IDX,3) USING 1,3 AT TOP RIGHT
#TITLE="Opp Count Pct."
PLOT ONTOP LABELED % PIE FROM OPPDT(1,1) TO OPPDT (IDX,3) \
    USING 1,2 AT TOP LEFT
PLOT ONTOP TEXT "QUARTER "+TQTR AT 25,17
PLOT ONTOP TEXT "# Opps. "+TOSTR(CNTTOT,2,0) AT 25,2
E.WFU=TRUE
PLOT LEGEND FOR PIE AT 14,9
CLEAR
```

```
!SMFSMN

!Main module for the Software Marketing Forecasting System. Guides the
!user through the various options of the application.

E.LSTR=50
PERFORM "A:FORECAST.IPF"
SMFSCTLV=0
PUTFORM SMFSFORM

!Loop until exit.

WHILE (SMFSCTLV<5) DO
        AT 7,15 OUTPUT "Select the Option Desired and Press Enter"
        DIM SMFSCTL (5)
        SMFSCTL(1) = "Review Forecast"
        SMFSCTL(2) = "Review Opportunity Details"
        SMFSCTL(3) = "Review Forecast Details"
        SMFSCTL(4) = "Review/Alter Software Details"
        SMFSCTL(5) = "Exit SMFS"
        SMFSCTLV = MENU(SMFSCTL,1,5,10,20,1,30,1)

!Execute the forecast graph.

        IF (SMFSCTLV=1) THEN
                CLEAR
                PERFORM "A:FORECAST.IPF"
                PUTFORM SMFSFORM
        ENDIF
```

```
!Execute the Opportunity pie graphs

        IF (SMFSCTLV=2) THEN
                CLEAR
                PERFORM "A:OPPDET.IPF"
                PUTFORM SMFSFORM
        ENDIF

!Execute the Detail reports

        IF (SMFSCTLV=3) THEN
                CLEAR
                PERFORM "A:DTCHOICE.IPF"
                PUTFORM SMFSFORM
        ENDIF

!Option Not available

        IF (SMFSCTLV=4) THEN
                PUTFORM NOTYET
        ENDIF
ENDWHILE
CLEAR
```

```
!SMOESBIB

! This program is used to calculate the overall Benefit of using the BCOMP
! (Benefit to Company), BREP (Benefit to Rep), and RISK variables. It is
! invoked by the BENIBM ruleset once these three variables have values.

IF BREP = "YES" THEN \
        IF (RISK = "MED" & BCOMP="HIGH") OR \
           (RISK = "LOW" & (BCOMP= "HIGH" or BCOMP = "MED")) \
                THEN BIBM = "HIGH"
        ENDIF

        IF RISK = BCOMP THEN BIBM = "MED"
        ENDIF

        IF (RISK = "HIGH" & BCOMP = "MED") OR \
           (RISK = "MED" & BCOMP = "LOW") \
                THEN BIBM = "LOW"
        ENDIF

        IF RISK = "HIGH" & BCOMP = "LOW" THEN BIBM = "NONE"
        ENDIF
ELSE
```

```
    IF BREP = "NO" THEN \
        IF (RISK = "MED" & BCOMP="LOW") OR \
            (RISK = "HIGH" & (BCOMP = "LOW" OR BCOMP = "MED")) \
                THEN BIBM = "NONE"
        ENDIF

        IF RISK = BCOMP THEN BIBM = "LOW"
        ENDIF

        IF (RISK = "MED" & BCOMP = "HIGH") OR \
            (RISK = "LOW" & BCOMP = "MED") \
                THEN BIBM = "MED"
        ENDIF

        IF RISK = "LOW" & BCOMP = "HIGH" THEN BIBM = "HIGH"
        ENDIF
    ENDIF
ENDIF
```

```
!SMOESGGL

! This program is used to calculate the overall goal of the consultation
! Using the BCUST, Benefit to customer, the BIBM, and the
! FUNDS, Funds available Variables. It also assigns a percentage
! likelihood of success to the cpportunity.

IF FUNDS = "YES" THEN \
        IF (BCUST="HIGH" AND BIBMG <> "NONE") OR \
            (BCUST="MED" AND (BIBMG="HIGH" OR BIBMG="MED")) \
                THEN OPPORT = "Premier"
        ENDIF

        IF (BCUST="HIGH" AND BIBMG="NONE") OR \
                (BCUST="MED" AND BIBMG="LOW") OR \
                (BCUST="LOW" AND BIBMG="HIGH") \
                THEN OPPORT = "Pursue"
        ENDIF

        IF (BCUST="MED" AND BIBMG="NONE") OR \
                (BCUST="LOW" AND BIBMG="MED") OR \
                (BCUST="NONE" AND BIBMG="HIGH") \
                THEN OPPORT = "OK"
        ENDIF

        IF (BCUST="NONE" AND BIBMG <> "HIGH") OR \
            (BCUST="LOW" AND (BIBMG="LOW" OR BIBMG="NONE")) \
                THEN OPPORT = "Bad"
        ENDIF
```

```
            IF (OPPORT="Premier" AND BCUST="HIGH") \
                    THEN PCT = 90
            ENDIF
            IF (OPPORT="Premier" AND BCUST="MED") \
                    THEN PCT = 80
            ENDIF
            IF (OPPORT="Pursue" \
                    THEN PCT = 65
            ENDIF
            IF OPPORT="OK" \
                    THEN PCT = 50
            ENDIF
            IF (OPPORT="Bad" AND ((BCUST="MED" AND BIBMG="LOW") OR \
                (BCUST="NONE" AND BIBMG="MED"))) \
                    THEN PCT = 15
            ELSE
                    IF OPPORT="Bad" \
                                THEN PCT = 0
                    ENDIF
            ENDIF
ELSE
    IF FUNDS = "NO" THEN \
        IF (BCUST="HIGH" & BIBMG="HIGH") \
                THEN OPPORT = "Premier"
        ENDIF

        IF (BCUST="HIGH" & (BIBMG="MED" OR BIBMG="LOW")) OR \
                (BCUST="MED" AND BIBMG="HIGH") \
                THEN OPPORT = "Pursue"
        ENDIF
        IF (BCUST="HIGH" AND BIBMG="NONE") OR \
                (BCUST="LOW" AND BIBMG="HIGH") \
                THEN OPPORT = "OK"
        ENDIF

        IF (BCUST="LOW" AND BIBMG <> "HIGH" OR \
                BCUST="NONE" OR (BCUST="MED" AND BIBMG="NONE") \
                THEN OPPORT = "Bad"
        ENDIF

        IF OPPORT="Premier" \
                THEN PCT = 75
        ENDIF
        IF OPPORT="Pursue" \
                THEN PCT = 55
        ENDIF
        IF OPPORT="OK" \
                THEN PCT = 35
        ENDIF
        IF OPPORT="Bad" AND (BIBMG="HIGH" OR BCUST="MED") \
```

```
                    THEN PCT = 10
        ELSE

                    IF OPPORT="Bad" AND BIBMG="MED" AND BCUST="LOW" \
                            THEN PCT = 5
                    ELSE

                            IF OPPORT="Bad" \
                                    THEN PCT = 0
                            ENDIF
                    ENDIF
        ENDIF
    ENDIF
ENDIF
```

```
!SMOESMN
```

! This program invokes and controls the SMOES system. It uses the
! CUSTOMER and SOFTWARE tables as well as user input to evaluate
! the rank of a given software opportunity. The user is given the
! option of continuing with different input for the same customer,
! changing customers, viewing consultation details or exiting.

```
CTLVAR=2
```

! The main control loop until exit

```
WHILE (CTLVAR=2) DO
    CUSTKEY=UNKNOWN
    CMNTHSAV=0
    CSTRAT="N"
    SCRFUNDS="Y"
    OPT=1
    PUTFORM CUSTFORM
    PUTFORM GETCKEY
    TALLY GETCKEY
    GETFORM GETCKEY
    E.STAT=FALSE
    E.SUPD=TRUE
    E.SUPH=TRUE
    E.DECI=1
    OBTAIN RECORD FROM CUSTOMER FOR CKEY=CUSTKEY
```

! The control loop until the customer changes

```
    CTLVAR = 1
    WHILE (CTLVAR = 1) DO
        CLEAR
        PUTFORM CUSTFORM
        PUTFORM CUSTDATA
```

```
              TALLY CUSTDATA
              GETFORM CUSTDATA
              PNEED=UNKNOWN


! Build the Software Menu Category and get the Software Record

              PUTFORM MENUFORM
              OPTIONS = LASTREC(SOFTWARE)
              DIM SW(OPTIONS)
              CONVERT TRIM(SNAME) FROM SOFTWARE TO ARRAY SW(1) ORDER BY \
                    SNAME
              CHOICE = MENU(SW,OPT,OPTIONS,17,14,0,30,2)
              OPT=CHOICE
              OBTAIN RECORD FROM SOFTWARE FOR SNAME=SW(CHOICE)


! Calculate Customer % Annual Savings and Payback Period

              IF SCRFUNDS = "Y" THEN FUNDS = "YES" ELSE FUNDS = "NO"; ENDIF
              PBPERIOD = SOFTWARE.IMPTIME + (SOFTWARE.COST/CMNTHSAV)
              ANNSAV=CMNTHSAV*12
              IF CSTRAT="Y" OR ANNSAV > 300000 THEN PNEED=3; ENDIF
              PCTANNSV = (ANNSAV/CUSTOMER.REVENUE) * 100


! INVOKE THE INFERENCE ENGINE TO FIND OPPORTUNITY RATING

              CLEAR


! Display the Results

              PUTFORM CUSTFORM
              PUTFORM RESULTS
              TALLY RESULTS
              IF OPPORTG="Premier" \
                        THEN PUTFORM PREMIER; ENDIF
              IF OPPORTG="Pursue" \
                        THEN PUTFORM PURSUE; ENDIF
              IF OPPORTG="OK" \
                        THEN PUTFORM OK; ENDIF
              IF OPPORTG="Bad" \
                        THEN PUTFORM BAD; ENDIF
              CTLVAR=3


! Control loop with menu to allow user to view details before continuing

              WHILE (CTLVAR=3 OR CTLVAR=4) DO
                  PUTFORM CONTROL
                  DIM CTL(5)
                  CTL(1) = "Cont. With "+TRIM(CUSTOMER.CKEY)
                  CTL(2) = "Cont./New Cust."
                  CTL(3) = "Details?? "
```

```
              CTL(4) = "Save Opportunity."
              CTL(5) = "Exit SMOES"
              CTLVAR = MENU(CTL,1,5,20,7,1,20,3)
              IF CTLVAR=3 THEN PUTFORM DETAILS
                               TALLY DETAILS
              ENDIF
              IF CTLVAR=4 THEN OPCKEY=CUSTOMER.CKEY
                   ATTACH 1 TO OPPORTTY
                   OBTAIN FIRST FROM QUOTA
                   OPSNAME=SOFTWARE.SNAME
                   PUTFORM SAVEOPP2
                   TALLY SAVEOPP2
                   GETFORM SAVEOPP2
                   IF OPPORTTY.SALEMNTH <= QUOTA.YRENDMNT THEN \
                            FSMNTH=(12-QUOTA.YRENDMNT) + OPPORTTY.SALEMNTH
                            ENDIF
                   IF OPPORTTY.SALEMNTH > QUOTA.YRENDMNT THEN \
                            FSMNTH=OPPORTTY.SALEMNTH - QUOTA.YRENDMNT; ENDIF
                   OPPORTTY.MNTHINYR=FSMNTH
                   IF FSMNTH > 1 THEN FSMNTH=FSMTH-1; ENDIF
                   TQTR=TRUNC(FSMNTH/3) + 1
                   OPPORTTY.OPCKEY=CUSTOMER.CKEY
                   OPPORTTY.SCOST=SOFTWARE.COST
                   OPPORTTY.OPPCT = PCT/100
                   OPPORTTY.QTR = TQTR
                   OPPORTTY.OPSNAME = SW(CHOICE)
                   PUTFORM OPPSAVED
              ENDIF
         ENDWHILE
    ENDWHILE
ENDWHILE
MARK RECORDS IN OPPORTTY FOR OPPCT=0
COMPRESS OPPORTTY
SORT OPPORTTY BY QTR
CLEAR
```

SAMPLE KNOWLEDGE SYSTEM CONTENTS FOR ARTIFICIALLY INTELLIGENT DECISION SUPPORT SYSTEMS

INTERFACE PROGRAM FOR THE SITE-SELECTION DSS

```
LET e.lstr=80;LET e.supd=true;LET e.pdep=60; E.BACG="UUUUA"; E.FORG="WWWWC"
MENU1="YES";MENU2="NO";MENU3="NO";MENU4="NO"
MENU4A="NO";MENUL="NO";MENULS="NO"
CLEAR
WHILE MENU1="YES" OR MENU2="YES" OR MENU3="YES" OR MENU4="YES" OR \
MENU4A="YES" OR MENUL="YES" OR MENULS="YES" DO
! MENU1 (COUNTY LISTING)

IF MENU1="YES" THEN CLEAR
        LOAD SUMM1
        IF NOT INUSE("CACI90") THEN USE CACI90;ENDIF
        IF NOT INUSE("COUNTY") THEN USE COUNTY;ENDIF
        OPTIONS=LASTREC(COUNTY)
        DIM WHATCNTY(OPTIONS)
        CONVERT CNYTST FROM COUNTY TO ARRAY WHATCNTY(1) ORDER BY CNTYST
        output "WHICH COUNTY ARE YOU INTERESTED IN? (use cursor keys to select)"
        CHOICE1=MENU(WHATCNTY,1,OPTIONS,2,2,0,15,5)
        OBTAIN RECORD FROM COUNTY WHERE COUNTY.CNTYST=WHATCNTY(CHOICE1)
MENU1="NO"
MENU2="YES"
ENDIF
```

```
!MENU2 (AGGRESSION)
IF MENU2="YES" THEN CLEAR
        AT 2,2 OUTPUT "SELECT THE LEVEL OF AGGRESSION DESIRED."
        DIM SCRN2(4)
        LET SCRN2(1) = "DO NOT CARE  - competitors are of no importance"
        LET SCRN2(2) = "AGRESSIVE   - favor tracts with higher level of competition "
        LET SCRN2(3) = "NONAGGRESSIVE - favor tracts with lower level of competition "
        LET SCRN2(4) = "SELECT A DIFFERENT COUNTY"
                LET CHOICE2=MENU(SCRN2,1,4,5,3,0,80,1)
                TEST CHOICE2
                CASE 1: aggress = "null"
                        MENU3="YES"
                        BREAK
                CASE 2: aggress = "yes"
                        MENU3="YES"
                        BREAK
                CASE 3: aggress = "no"
                        MENU3="YES"
                        BREAK
                CASE 4: clear
                        output "WHICH COUNTY ARE YOU INTERESTED IN? (use "+\
                        "cursor keys to select)."
                        choice1 = menu(whatcnty,1,120,2,2,0,15,5)
                        obtain record from caci90 where cntyst=whatcnty (choice1)
                        MENU2="YES"
                        BREAK
                OTHERWISE: OUTPUT "DO YOU KNOW WHAT YOU ARE DOING?"
        ENDTEST
MENU2="NO"
ENDIF


!MENU3 (SCREENED)

IF MENU3="YES" THEN CLEAR
        AT 2,2 OUTPUT "WOULD YOU LIKE THE EXPERT SYSTEM TO SCREEN THE "+\
        "TRACTS IN THIS COUNTY?"
        DIM SCRN3(4)
        LET SCRN3(1) = "NO  - DO NOT SCREEN THEM (list all tracts)       "
        LET SCRN3(2) = "YES - screen them and list DESIRABLE tracts      "
        LET SCRN3(3) = "YES - screen them and list UNDESIRABLE tracts    "
        LET SCRN3(4) = "CHANGE AGGRESSION DESIRED                        "
                LET CHOICE3 = MENU(SCRN3,1,4,5,3,0,50,1)
        TEST CHOICE3
        CASE 1: AT 10,2 OUTPUT "The system is processing your request."
                SCREENED="NO"
                DIM WHATRACT(120)
                CONVERT TTRACTMC FROM CACI90 FOR TSTCNTY=COUNTY.STCNTY \
                        TO ARRAY WHATRACT(1)
                menu3="no";MENU4="YES"
```

```
            BREAK
  CASE 2: AT 10,2 OUTPUT "The system is processing your request."
            SCREENED="YES"
            #found=true
            DIM WHATRACT(120)
            CONVERT TTRACTMC FROM CACI90 FOR TSTCNTY=COUNTY.STCNTY \
            TO ARRAY WHATRACT(1)
            AT 10,2 OUTPUT WHATCNTY(CHOICE1) USING "uuuuuuuuuuu",\
            "county has ",#row using "nnn"," tracts."
            at 12,2 input yn str using "u" with\
            "Do you want to continue? (N/Y)"
  if yn ne "y" then menu3="yes"
  else      at 10,2 output "  "

            DIM ATRACTS(120)
            X=0;J=0
            WHILE #FOUND DO
                    SUP="TRUE"
                    X=X+1;J=J+1
                    OBTAIN RECORD FROM CACI90 WHERE CACI90.TSTCNTY\
                    =COUNTY.STCNTY AND CACI90.TTRACTMC=WHATRACT(X)
                    if #found then at 12,2 output "Processing tract#"\
                    X using "nn"," out of a total of ",#row using "nnn","."
                    CONSULT CACICHOI TO TEST
                    endif
                    IF CHOICE="YES" THEN ATRACTS(J)=WHATRACT(X)
                    ELSE J=J-1
                    ENDIF
            ENDWHILE
            IF J=0 THEN CLEAR;AT 2,2 OUTPUT "NO DESIRABLE TRACTS WERE FOUND."
            WAIT;MENU3="YES"
            ELSE menu3="no";MENU4A="YES"
            ENDIF
  endif
            BREAK


  CASE 3: AT 10,2 OUTPUT "The system is processing your request."
            SCREENED="YES"
            #found=true
            DIM WHATRACT(120)
            CONVERT TTRACTMC FROM CACI90 FOR TSTCNTY=COUNTY.STCNTY \
            TO ARRAY WHATRACT(1)
            AT 10,2 OUTPUT WHATCNTY(CHOICE1) USING "uuuuuuuuuuu",\
            "county has ",#row using "nnn"," tracts."
            at 12,2 input yn str using "u" with\
            "Do you want to continue? (N/Y)"
  if yn ne "y" then menu3="yes"
  else      at 10,2 output "  "
            DIM ATRACTS(120)
```

```
                X=0;J=0
                WHILE #FOUND DO
                        SUP="TRUE"
                        X=X+1;J=J+1
                          OBTAIN RECORD FROM CACI90 WHERE CACI90.TSTCNTY=\
                          COUNTY.STCNTY AND CACI90.TTRACTMC=WHATRACT(X)
                          if #found then at 12,2 output "Processing "+\
                          "tract#" X using "nn"," out of a total of ",#row using "nnn","."
                          CONSULT CACICHOI TO TEST
                          endif
                        IF CHOICE="no" THEN ATRACTS(J)=WHATRACT(X)
                          ELSE J=J-1
                        ENDIF
                ENDWHILE
                IF J=0 THEN CLEAR;AT 2,2 OUTPUT "NO UNDESIRABLE TRACTS WERE FOUND."
                at 4,2 output "(press enter to continue)"
                WAIT;MENU3="yes"
                ELSE menu3="no";MENU4A="YES"
                ENDIF
        endif
                BREAK
        CASE 4: menu3="no";MENU2="YES"
                BREAK
        OTHERWISE: OUTPUT "DO YOU KNOW WHAT YOU ARE DOING?"
        ENDTEST
ENDIF
!MENU4 (LIST ALL TRACTS)
IF MENU4="YES" THEN CLEAR; SUP="FALSE"
                CHOICE3A=#ROW
                IF CHOICE3A/24 <=1 THEN CHOICE3B=1
                ELSE IF CHOICE3A/24 <=2 THEN CHOICE3B=2
                ELSE IF CHOICE3A/24 <=3 THEN CHOICE3B=3
                ELSE IF CHOICE3A/24 <=4 THEN CHOICE3B=4
                ELSE IF CHOICE3A/24 <=5 THEN CHOICE3B=5
                ELSE IF CHOICE3B=6
                ENDIF;ENDIF;ENDIF;ENDIF;ENDIF
                AT 2,2 OUTPUT "WHICH TRACT MCD ARE YOU INTERESTED IN?"
                LET CHOICE4 = MENU(WHATRACT,1,CHOICE3A,3,2,0,13,CHOICE3B)
                OBTAIN RECORD FROM CACI90 WHERE CACI90.TSTCNTY=\
                COUNTY.STCNTY AND CACI90.TTRACTMC=WHATRACT(CHOICE4)
                CONSULT CACICHOI TO TEST
MENU4="NO"
ENDIF


!MENU4A (LIST OF SCREENED TRACTS)
IF MENU4A="YES" THEN CLEAR;SUP="FALSE"
                IF J/24 <=1 THEN CHOICE4A=1
                ELSE IF J/24 <=2 THEN CHOICE4A=2
                ELSE IF J/24 <=3 THEN CHOICE4A=3
```

```
                ELSE IF J/24 <=4 THEN CHOICE4A=4
                ELSE IF J/24 <=5 THEN CHOICE4A=5
                ELSE CHOICE4A=6
                ENDIF;ENDIF;ENDIF;ENDIF;ENDIF
                AT 2,2 OUTPUT "WHICH TRACT MCD ARE YOU INTERESTED IN?"
                LET CHOICE4 = MENU(ATRACTS,1,J,3,2,0,13,CHOICE4A)
                OBTAIN RECORD FROM CACI90 WHERE CACI90.TSTCNTY= \
                COUNTY.STCNTY AND CACI90.TTRACTNC=ATRACTS(choice4)
                CONSULT CACICHOI TO TEST
MENU4A="NO"
ENDIF


!MENUL (LOOP TO UNSCREENED ONES)
IF MENUL="YES" THEN
        e.bacg="UUUUA";E.FORG="WWWWC";AT 18,2 OUTPUT "WHAT NOW?"
        DIM SCRNL(4)
        LET SCRNL(1) = "SELECT A DIFFERENT TRACT IN CURRENT COUNTY       "
        LET SCRNL(2) = "SELECT A DIFFERENT COUNTY                        "
        LET SCRNL(3) = "ESCAPE TO PROMPT (for how/why explanations)"
        LET SCRNL(4) = "QUIT TO DOS PROMPT                               "
                LET CHOICEL = MENU(SCRNL,1,4,20,3,0,50,1)
                TEST CHOICEL
        CASE 1: CLEAR
                AT 2,2 OUTPUT "WHICH TRACT MCD ARE YOU INTERESTED IN?"
                LET CHOICE4 = MENU(WHATRACT,1,CHOICE3A,3,2,0,13,CHOICE3B)
                OBTAIN RECORD FROM CACI90 WHERE TSTCNTY=STCNTY AND\
                TTRACTMC=WHAT RACT(CHOICE4)
                CONSULT CACICHOI TO TEST
                BREAK
        CASE 2: CLEAR
                OUTPUT "WHICH COUNTY ARE YOU INTERESTED IN?"+\
                "(use cursor keys to select)."
                LET CHOICE1 = MENU(WHATCNTY,1,120,2,2,0,15,5)
                OBTAIN RECORD FROM COUNTY WHERE CNTYST=WHATCNTY(CHOICE1)
                MENU2="YES"
                BREAK
        CASE 3: CLEAR
                at 2,2 output "COUNTY     TRACT          MARKET PROSPECT CHOICE"
                at 3,2 output whatcnty(choice1) using "%10r",tractmed using "%11u"," ",\
                market using "uuuu","   ",prospect using "uuuu","     "\
                choice using "uuu"
                AT 5,2 OUTPUT "You can now HOW & WHY to understand the values"
                AT 6,2 OUTPUT "obtained for this tract"
                AT 7,2 OUTPUT " "
                wait
                BREAK
        CASE 4: AT 25,2 OUTPUT "HAVE A NICE DAY!"
                BYE
                BREAK
```

```
        OTHERWISE: OUTPUT "DO YOU KNOW WHAT YOU ARE DOING?"
        ENDTEST
MENUL="NO"
ENDIF


!MENULS (LOOP TO SCREEN OTHERS)
IF MENULS="YES" THEN
        e.bacg="UUUUA";e.forg="WWWWC";AT 18,2 OUTPUT "WHAT NOW?"
        DIM SCRNL(4)
        LET SCRNL(1) = "SELECT A DIFFERENT TRACT FORM SCREENED LISTING"
        LET SCRNL(2) = "SELECT A DIFFERENT COUNTY"
        LET SCRNL(3) = "HOW/WHY EXPLANATIONS"
        LET SCRNL(4) = "EXIT TO DOS"
                LET CHOICEL = MENU(SCRNL,1,4,30,3,0,50,1)
                TEST CHOICEL
        CASE 1: CLEAR
                AT 2,2 OUTPUT "WHICH TRACT MCD ARE YOU INTERESTED IN?"
                LET CHOICE4s = MENU(ATRACTS,1,J,3,2,0,13,CHOICE4a)
                OBTAIN RECORD FROM CACI90 WHERE TSTCNTY=STCNTY AND\
                TTRACTMC=ATRACTS(CHOICE4)
                CONSULT CACICHOI TO TEST
                BREAK
        CASE 2: CLEAR
                OUTPUT "WHICH COUNTY ARE YOU INTERESTED IN?"
                LET CHOICE1 = MENU(WHATCNTY,1,120,2,2,0,15,5)
                OBTAIN RECORD FROM COUNTY WHERE CNTYST=WHATCNTY(CHOICE1)
                MENU2="YES"
                BREAK
        CASE 3: CLEAR
                at 2,2 output "COUNTY     TRACT          MARKET PROSPECT CHOICE"
                at 3,2 output whatcnty(choice1) using\
                "rrrrrrrrrr",tractmcd using "uuuuuuuuuuu"," ",\
                market using "uuuu","   ",prospect using "uuuu","   ", choice using "uuu"
                AT 5,2 OUTPUT "You can now HOW & WHY to understand the values"
                AT 6,2 OUTPUT "obtained for this tract"
                AT 7,2 OUTPUT " "
                wait
                BREAK
        CASE 4: AT 25,2 OUTPUT "HAVE A NICE DAY!"
                BYE
                BREAK
        OTHERWISE: at 25,2 OUTPUT "DO YOU KNOW WHAT YOU ARE DOING?"
        ENDTEST
MENULS="NO"
ENDIF
ENDWHILE
RETURN
```

SUMMARY OF VARIABLES USED IN SITE-SELECTION INFERENCE

VARIABLE LISTING

	DESCR	TYPE	VALUES	MAX # OF VALS	CF	DEPENDS ON
TABLE FIELDS						
=============						
TABLE: CACI90						
=============						
1 TSTCNTY	STATE COUNTY ID	STR	'21001' – '21239'	1		USER
2 TRACTMC	TRACT MCD ID	STR	(EG. '0703.02.000')	1		USER
3 TPOP90	POPULATION 1990	NUM		1		1,2
4 TAGE1534	POP AGES 15-34	NUM		1		1,2
5 TAGE1864	POP AGES 18-64	NUM		1		1,2
6 TGAS	GAS PURCHASES	NUM NDX	100 = AVG	1		1,2
7 TSELFSRV	SELF SERVE PURCH	NUM NDX	100 = AVG	1		1,2
8 TOIL	OIL PURCHASES	NUM NDX	100 = AVG	1		1,2
9 TPLUGS	SPARK PLUG PURCH	NUM NDX	100 = AVG	1		1,2
10 TFILTER	AIR FILTER PURCH	NUM NDX	100 = AVG	1		1,2
11 TSODA	SODA PURCHASES	NUM NDX	100 = AVG	1		1,2
12 TVCROWN	VCR OWNERSHIP	NUM NDX	100 = AVG	1		1,2
13 TBREAD	BREAD PURCHASES	NUM NDX	100 = AVG	1		1,2
14 TMILK	MILK PURCHASES	NUM NDX	100 = AVG	1		1,2
15 TMEDHHI	MEDIAN HSHLD INCOME	NUM		1		1,2
16 TPCPI	PER CAPITA PERS INC	NUM		1		1,2
17 TCOMPETE	# OF COMPET. UNITS	NUM		1		1,2
18 TFRIEND	FRIENDLY UNITS 1 = YES	NUM	0 OR 1	1		1,2
19 TMEDAGEP	MEDIUM AGE PCNT	NUM VIRTUAL	TAGE1864/TPOP90	1		5,3
20 TYOUTHP	YOUTH AGE PCNT	NUM VIRTUAL	TAGE1534/TPOP90	1		4,3
21 TGROCNDX	GROCERY INDEX	NUM VIRTUAL	F(TBREAD,TMILK,TSODA)	1		13,14,11
22 TGASNDX	GAS INDEX	NUM VIRTUAL	F(TGAS,TSELFSRV)	1		6,7
23 TAUTONDX	AUTO INDEX	NUM VIRTUAL	F(TOIL,TPLUGS,TFILTER)	1		8,9,10
24 TUNITNDX	COMPETITION INDEX	NUM VIRTUAL	(TCOMPETE/14)*100	1		17
TABLE: COUNTY						
-------------						
25 STCNTY	STATE COUNTY ID	STR	'21001' – '21239'	1		1
26 CNTYST	COUNTY NAME	STR	(EG. 'ADAIR')	1		26
USER SUPPLIED						
=============						
27 AGGRESS	AGGRESSION	STR	YES,NULL,NO	1		USER
RULE CREATED						
=============						
28 CHOICE (GOAL)	SHOULD THE TRACT BE EXAMINED?	STR	YES,NO	1		29,33
29 PROSPECT	LIKELIHOOD OF SUCCESS	STR	GOOD,FAIR, POOR	1	Y	30.34
30 MARKET	MARKET CONDITIONS	STR	GOOD,FAIR, POOR	1	Y	31.32
31 INCOME	INCOME	STR	HIGH,MEDIUM,LOW	1		15.16
32 DEMO	DEMOGRAPHICS	STR	LARGE HIGH,LARGE LOW MEDIUM HIGH,MEDIUM LOW SMALL HIGH, SMALL LOW	1		3,19
33 PAIRING	COMPETITION MATCH W/AGGRESSION	STR	GOOD,FAIR,POOR	1		24,27
34 GAS	OVERALL GAS PURCHASES	STR	HIGH,MEDIUM,LOW	1		22
35 AUTO	AUTO PARTS PURCHASES	STR	HI,MED,LOW	1		23
36 GROCERY	GROCERY PURCHASES	STR	HI,MED,LOW	1		21
37 VIDEO	VIDEO POTENTIAL	STR	HI,MED,LOW	1		12,20

RULE SET FOR THE SITE SELECTION DSS (RULE SET FILE NAME: CACICHOI.RSC)

```
INITIAL:

        let e.cfva="pp";e.cfjo="p";e.cfco="p"
        LET E.whn="F";LET E.RIGR="M"
        LET E.TRYP="P";let e.sord="p"
        STCNTY=CACI90.TSTCNTY;TRACTMCD=CACI90.TTRACTMC
        POP90=CACI90.TPOP90;PCPI=CACI90.TPCPI
        MEDHHI=CACI90.TMEDHHI;MEDAGEP=CACI90.TMEDAGEP
        COMPETE=CACI90.TCOMPETE;FRIEND=CACI90.TFRIEND
        YOUTHP=CACI90.TYOUTHP;GROCNDX=CACI90.TGROCNDX
        GASNDX=CACI90.TGASNDX;AUTONDX=CACI90.TAUTONDX
        VCROWN=CACI90.TVCROWN;UNITSNDX=CACI90.TUNITNDX
        income=unknown;demo=unknown;market=unknown
        GROCERY=UNKNOWN;VIDEO=UNKNOWN;GAS=UNKNOWN;AUTO=UNKNOWN
        PROSPECT=UNKNOWN;WORDS=" ";CHOICE=UNKNOWN;
        PAIRING=UNKNOWN;KCHOICE="NO";WORDS2=" "


GOAL:   CHOICE


RULE:   GROC
        PRIORITY: 60
        IF:     KNOWN("GROCNDX")
        THEN:   IF GROCNDX <= 105 THEN GROCERY = "LOW"
                ELSE IF GROCNDX >= 120 THEN GROCERY = "HI"
                ELSE GROCERY = "MED"
                ENDIF
                ENDIF
        REASON: IF MILK, BREAD, AND SODA CONSUMPTION IS BELOW
                THE NATIONAL AVERAGE IN THIS TRACT, GROCERY
                CONSUMPTION IS CONSIDERED "LOW" AND IT IS
                CONSIDERED "HIGH" WHEN THESE LEVELS ARE WELL
                ABOVE THIS AVERAGE.


RULE:   VIDEO1
        PRIORITY: 60
        IF:     VCROWN >= 100 AND KNOWN("YOUTHP")
        THEN:   IF YOUTHP >= .3 THEN VIDEO = "HI"
                ELSE VIDEO = "MED"
                ENDIF
        REASON: VIDEO PROSPECTS ARE BASED ON VCR OWNERSHIP
                AND INDIVIDUALS BETWEEN THE AGES OF 15 & 34.
                HIGH VCR OWNERSHIP AND A LARGE CONSUMER BASE
                YIELD A "HIGH" VALUE FOR VIDEO.


RULE:   VIDEO2
        PRIORITY: 60
        IF:     VCROWN < 100
        THEN:   VIDEO = "LOW"
```

```
        REASON:  IF VCR OWNERSHIP IS BELOW THE NATIONAL AVERAGE,
                 VIDEO PROSPECT IS SET TO "LOW".

RULE:   FRIEND
        PRIORITY: 60
        IF:      FRIEND >= 1
        THEN:    WORDS2="THIS TRACT CONTAINS AT LEAST ONE COMPANY UNIT"
        REASON:  IF A FRIENDLY UNIT IS FOUND IN THIS TRACT, THE
                 SYSTEM PROMPTS THE USER OF THIS OCCURRENCE.

RULE:   AUTO
        PRIORITY: 60
        IF:      KNOWN("AUTONDX")
        THEN:    IF AUTONDX < 100 THEN AUTO = "LOW"
                 ELSE IF AUTONDX >= 115 THEN AUTO = "HI"
                 ELSE AUTO = "MED"
                 ENDIF
                 ENDIF
        REASON:  IF AUTOMOTIVE PRODUCT CONSUMPTION IN THIS TRACT
                 IS LESS THAN THE NATIONAL AVERAGE, THEN AUTO
                 PROD IS SET TO "LOW". MUCH GREATER THAN THIS
                 AVERAGE WILL SET IT TOO "HIGH".

RULE:   GAS
        PRIORITY: 60
        IF:      KNOWN("GASNDX")
        THEN:    IF GASNDX < 100 THEN GAS = "LOW"
                 ELSE IF GASNDX >= 108 THEN GAS = "HIGH"
                 ELSE GAS = "MEDIUM"
                 ENDIF
                 ENDIF
        REASON:  IF GAS CONSUMPTION IN THIS TRACT IS LESS THAN
                 THE NATIONAL AVERAGE, GAS IS DEEMED TO BE "LOW".
                 MUCH GREATER THAN THIS AVERAGE WILL SET IT "HIGH".

RULE:   INC1
        IF:      MEDHHI > 23000
        THEN:    INCOME = "HIGH"
        REASON:  MEDIAN HOUSEHOLD INCOME IS GREATER THAN 23000
                 THEREFORE, THIS TRACT IS CONSIDERED
                 TO HAVE HIGH INCOME.

RULE:   INC2
        IF:      MEDHHI > 13000 AND MEDHHI <= 23000 and known ("pcpi")
        THEN:    IF PCPI > 14000 THEN INCOME = "HIGH"
                       ELSE IF PCPI > 10000 THEN INCOME = "MEDIUM"
                           ELSE INCOME = "LOW"
                           ENDIF
                 ENDIF
        REASON:  THE MEDIAN HOUSEHOLD INCOME IS MORE THAN 13000 BUT
```

LESS THAN OR EQUAL TO 23000. THIS TRACT IS CONSIDERED
TO BE HIGH INCOME IF THE PER CAPITA INCOME (PCI) IS
GREATER THAN 13000, MEDIUM INCOME IF PCI IS BETWEEN
10000 AND 13000, AND LOW INCOME IF PCI IS LESS THAN
10000.

RULE: INC3
    IF: MEDHHI < 13000
    THEN: INCOME = "LOW"
    REASON: THE MEDIAN HOUSEHOLD INCOME FOR THIS TRACT IS LESS
              THAN 13000; THERFORE, THIS TRACT IS LOW INCOME.

RULE: DEMO1
    IF: POP90 >= 3500 and known("medagep")

    THEN: IF MEDAGEP > .60 THEN DEMO = "LARGE HIGH"
                        ELSE DEMO = "LARGE LOW"
              ENDIF
    REASON: THIS TRACT HAS A LARGE POPULATION. IF THE PERCENT OF
              PEOPLE IN THE MEDIUM AGE BRACKET IS GREATER THAN 60,
              THIS TRACT HAS A LARGE HIGH DEMOGRAPHIC, OTHERWISE IT
              IS LARGE LOW.

RULE: DEMO2
    IF: POP90 >= 2000 AND POP90 < 3500 and known("medagep")
    THEN: IF MEDAGEP > .60 THEN DEMO = "MEDIUM HIGH"
                    ELSE DEMO = "MEDIUM LOW"
              ENDIF
    REASON: THIS TRACT IS A MEDIUM POPULATION SIZE. IF THE PERCENT
              OF MEDIUM AGE PEOPLE IS GREATER THAN 60, THIS TRACT HAS
              MEDIUM HIGH DEMOGRAPHICS; OTHERWISE, IT IS MEDIUM LOW.

RULE: DEMO3
    IF: POP90 < 2000 and known("medagep")
    THEN: IF MEDAGEP > .60 THEN DEMO = "SMALL HIGH"
                    ELSE DEMO = "SMALL LOW"
              ENDIF
    REASON: THIS TRACT HAS A SMALL POPULATION. IF THE PERCENT OF
              MEDIUM AGE POPULATION IS GREATER THAN 60, THE TRACT HAS
              SMALL HIGH DEMOGRAPHICS; OTHERWISE, IT IS SMALL LOW.

RULE: MRK1
    IF: DEMO = "LARGE HIGH" and known("income")
    THEN: MARKET += {"GOOD" CF 100,"FAIR" CF 60,"POOR" CF 20}
              IF INCOME = "MEDIUM" THEN MARKET -= "GOOD" CF 10
                        MARKET += {"FAIR" CF 10,"POOR" CF 10}
              ELSE IF INCOME = "LOW" THEN MARKET -= "GOOD" CF 25
                        MARKET += {"FAIR" CF 25,"POOR" CF 25}
                  ENDIF
              ENDIF

REASON: THE DEMOGRAPHICS FOR THIS TRACT ARE THE BEST POSSIBLE.
         THIS INDICATES A GOOD MARKET; HOWEVER, THE SURENESS OF
         THE QUALITY OF THIS MARKET IS TEMPERED BY THE LEVEL OF
         INCOME (E.G. IF INCOME IS LOW, WE CAN ONLY BE 75 PERCENT
         SURE THAT THIS IS A GOOD MARKET).

RULE: MRK2
    IF: DEMO = "LARGE LOW" and known("income")
    THEN: MARKET += {"GOOD" CF 90,"FAIR" CF 70,"POOR" CF 30}
            IF INCOME = "MEDIUM" THEN MARKET -= "GOOD" CF 10
                        MARKET += {"FAIR" CF 10,"POOR" CF 10}
            ELSE IF INCOME = "LOW" THEN MARKET -= "GOOD" CF 25
                        MARKET += {"FAIR" CF 25,"POOR" CF 25}
                ENDIF
            ENDIF
    REASON: THIS TRACT HAS A LARGE POPULATION, BUT THE PERCENT OF
             MEDIUM AGE POPULATION IS NOT HIGH. WE CANNOT BE
             ENTIRELY SURE THAT IT IS A GOOD MARKET, AND IF INCOME
             IS LOW, THE MARKET IS CLASSIFIED AS FAIR.

RULE: MRK3
    IF: DEMO = "MEDIUM HIGH" and known("income")
    THEN: MARKET += {"GOOD" CF 70,"FAIR" CF 80,"POOR" CF 50}
            IF INCOME = "MEDIUM" THEN MARKET += "FAIR" CF 10
                        MARKET -= {"GOOD" CF 10,"POOR" CF 10}
            ELSE IF INCOME = "LOW" THEN MARKET += "FAIR" CF 25
                        MARKET -= {"GOOD" CF 25,"POOR" CF 25}
                ENDIF
            ENDIF
    REASON: THIS TRACT HAS A MEDIUM POPULATION WITH A HIGH
             PERCENT OF MEDIUM AGE. IF INCOME IS HIGH, THEN
             THE MARKET IS CONSIDERED TO BE GOOD. HOWEVER,
             IF INCOME IS MEDIUM OR LOW, THE MARKET IS CONSIDERED
             FAIR WITH DECREASING CERTAINTY.

RULE: MRK4
    IF: DEMO = "MEDIUM LOW" and known("income")
    THEN: MARKET += {"GOOD" CF 50,"FAIR" CF 90,"POOR" CF 70}
            IF INCOME = "MEDIUM" THEN MARKET += "POOR" CF 10
                        MARKET -= {"GOOD" CF 10,"FAIR" CF 10}
            ELSE IF INCOME = "LOW" THEN MARKET += "POOR" CF 25
                        MARKET -= {"GOOD" CF 25,"FAIR" CF 25}
                ENDIF
            ENDIF
    REASON: THIS TRACT HAS A MEDIUM POPULATION WITHOUT A
             HIGH PERCENT OF PEOPLE IN THE MEDIUM AGE GROUP. IT
             IS CLASSIFIED AS A FAIR MARKET UNLESS THE INCOME IS
             LOW, IN WHICH CASE IT IS CLASSIFIED AS POOR -- POOR
             MARKETS ARE NOT CONSIDERED FURTHER.

```
RULE:    MRK5
    IF:     DEMO = "SMALL HIGH" and known("income")
    THEN:   MARKET += {"GOOD" CF 30,"FAIR" CF 80,"POOR" CF 90}
            IF INCOME = "MEDIUM" THEN MARKET += "POOR" CF 10
                    MARKET -= {"GOOD" CF 10,"FAIR" CF 10}
            ELSE IF INCOME = "LOW" THEN MARKET += "POOR" CF 25
                    MARKET -= {"GOOD" CF 25,"FAIR" CF 25}
                ENDIF
            ENDIF
    REASON: THIS TRACT HAS A SMALL POPULATION, A FAIRLY LARGE
            PORTION OF WHICH IS OF MEDIUM AGE. AS SUCH, ITS MARKET
            IS CLASSIFIED AS FAIR WITH A CERTAINTY THAT DECREASES
            WITH INCOME, IF THE INCOME IS LOW, THE MARKET IS
            CLASSIFIED AS POOR -- POOR MARKETS ARE NOT CONSIDERED
            FURTHER.


RULE:    MRK6
    IF:     DEMO = "SMALL LOW"
    THEN:   MARKET += {"POOR" CF 100,"GOOD" CF 20,"FAIR" CF 60}
    REASON: THIS TRACT IS SMALL IN POPULATION AND DOES NOT HAVE A
            HIGH PORTION OF PEOPLE IN THE MEDIUM AGE BRACKET; AS
            SUCH, ITS MARKET IS CLASSIFIED AS POOR -- POOR MARKETS
            ARE NOT CONSIDERED FURTHER.


RULE:    PROSP1
    IF:     KNOWN("MARKET")
    THEN:   PROSPECT = MARKET
    REASON: ASSIGN THE FUZZY VARIABLE MARKET TO PROSPECT. THIS ALLOWS
            THE SYSTEM TO MODIFY PROSPECT BASED ON THE GAS CONSUMPTION.
    COMMENT:THIS IS DONE TO KEEP THE NATURE OF MARKET CLEAR.


RULE:    PROSP2
    IF:     KNOWN("GAS") AND KNOWN("PROSPECT")
    THEN:   IF GAS = "HIGH" THEN PROSPECT += {"GOOD" CF 40,"FAIR" CF 10}
            ELSE IF GAS = "LOW" THEN PROSPECT -= {"GOOD" CF 40,"FAIR" CF 20}
                ENDIF
            ENDIF
    REASON: IF GAS CONSUMPTION IS HIGH OR LOW, INCREASE OR DECREASE THE
            CERTAINTY OF PROSPECT, RESPECTIVELY.


RULE:    PAIRING1
    IF:     AGGRESS = "NO" AND KNOWN("UNITSNDX") AND KNOWN("PROSPECT")
    THEN:   IF UNITSNDX >= 130 THEN pairing = "POOR"
            CHOICE = "NO" ;KCHOICE="YES"
            ELSE IF UNITSNDX >=80 THEN pairing = "FAIR"
                ELSE pairing = "GOOD"
                ENDIF
            ENDIF
    REASON: IF LOW AGGRESSION IS DESIRED AND THE NUMBER OF COMPETITORS
            IS HIGH, THE PAIRING IS "POOR." IF THE NUMBER OF COMPETITORS
```

                     IS LOW, THEN ITS PAIRING IS "GOOD."

RULE: PAIRING2
         IF: AGGRESS = "NULL" AND KNOWN("PROSPECT")
         THEN: pairing = "NULL"
         REASON: IF AGGRESSION IS OF NO INTEREST TO THE USER, SET THE
                  PAIRING TO NULL ALSO.

RULE: PAIRING3
         IF: AGGRESS = "YES" AND KNOWN("UNITSNDX") AND KNOWN("PROSPECT")
         THEN: IF UNITSNDX >= 140 THEN pairing = "GOOD"
                  ELSE IF UNITSNDX >=80 THEN pairing = "FAIR"
                       ELSE pairing = "POOR"
                       ENDIF
                  ENDIF
         REASON: IF HIGH AGGRESSION IS DESIRED AND THE NUMBER OF COMPETITORS
                  IS HIGH, THE PAIRING IS "GOOD." IF THE NUMBER OF COMPETITORS
                  IS LOW, THEN SET ITS PAIRING TO "POOR."

RULE: CHOICE1
         IF: HIVAL(PROSPECT) = "GOOD" AND KNOWN("pairing") and KCHOICE <> "YES"
         THEN: CHOICE = "YES"
         REASON: A GOOD PROSPECT VALUE SHOULD BE FURTHER ANALYZED.

RULE: CHOICE2
         IF: HIVAL(PROSPECT) = "FAIR" AND KNOWN("pairing") AND KCHOICE <> "YES"
         THEN: IF pairing = "GOOD" OR pairing = "FAIR" THEN CHOICE = "YES"
                  ELSE CHOICE = "NO"
                  ENDIF
         REASON: IF THE PROSPECT IS "FAIR" AND THE AGGRESSION MATCHED WITH
                  THE NUMBER OF COMPETITORS IS FAIR OR GOOD, THE TRACT SHOULD
                  HAVE FURTHER ANALYSIS CONDUCTED ON IT, ELSE IT SHOULD NOT.

RULE: CHOICE3
         IF: HIVAL(PROSPECT) = "POOR" AND KNOWN("pairing") AND KCHOICE <> "YES"
         THEN: IF CFV(PROSPECT,"POOR") < 65 AND pairing = "GOOD" THEN CHOICE = "YES"
                  ELSE CHOICE = "NO"
                  ENDIF
         REASON: IF PROSPECT HAS A VALUE OF POOR WITH CERTAINTY LESS THAN 65%
                  AND THE PAIRING IS GOOD BASED ON AGGRESSION, THE TRACT SHOULD
                  HAVE FURTHER ANALYSIS CONDUCTED ON IT.

RULE: CHOICE4
         IF: PAIRING ="NULL"
         THEN: IF HIVAL(PROSPECT)="GOOD" OR HIVAL(PROSPECT)="FAIR" THEN CHOICE= "YES"
                  ELSE CHOICE="NO"
                  ENDIF
         REASON: IF THE USER DOES NOT CARE ABOUT COMPETITOR LOCATIONS, THEN
                  LET THE PROSPECT VALUE DETERMINE IF DETAILED ANALYSIS SHOULD
                  BE CONDUCTED.

```
DO:

IF SUP="FALSE" THEN CLEAR
      e.bacg="uuuuu";E.FORG="WWWWW"
      IF choice="yes" then txt=" SHOULD "; ELSE TXT="SHOULD NOT";ENDIF
      PUTFORM SUMM1;TALLY SUMM1
      AT 6,66 OUTPUT MARKET USING "uuuu"
      AT 8,36 output cfn(prospect,1) using "nnn"
      AT 8,62 output prospect using "uuuu"
      if aggress<>"null" and pairing<>"fair" THEN
            if pairing="poor" then txt1="DOES NOT";else if pairing="good" then \
            txt1="DOES";endif
            if aggress="yes" then agg="HIGH";else agg="LOW";endif
            at 10,3 output "This tract ",txt1 using "uuuuuuuu"," satisfy the criteria"
      endif
            at 16,2 output "(press enter to continue)"
            at 14,53 output grocery using "uuu","   ",video using "uuu"
      WAIT
      IF SCREENED="YES" THEN MENULS="yes"
      ELSE MENUL="yes"
      ENDIF
ENDIF
!      THIS IS FOR TESTING PURPOSES ONLY
!LET I=1
!WHILE I <= 3 DO
!IF I=1 THEN
!OUTPUT STCNTY, " ",tractmcd," ",INCOME USING "uuuuuu"," ",demo using "%llu"
!ELSE OUTPUT "                                        ",VALN(MARKET,I),"CF"
!ENDIF
!I=I+1

!ENDWHILE
END:
```

KNOWLEDGE SYSTEM FILES FOR THE PROPOSAL RESOURCE-ALLOCATION DSS

Program Files	Report Files
SCREEN.IPF	NEWONE.TPL
SCREEN2.IPF	OLDONE.TPL
SCREEN3.IPF	PLIST.TPL
SCREENE.IPF	
NEW.IPF	Rule Set File
EXIST.IPF	
NEWPROJ.IPF	RESOURCE.RSC
PROJECT.IPF	
UINPUT.IPF	
RESREQ.IPF	

```
RESBAR.IPF
CHANGE.IPF
FINAL.IPF
STRATEGY.IPF
RESOURCE.IPF
```

Form Files

```
MAINFORM.ICF
SCN1FORM.ICF
WAITFORM.ICF
SCN2FORM.ICF
LINEFORM.ICF
UFORM.ICF
EXITFORM.ICF
```

Database Files

```
OLDCLI.ITB
NEWCLI.ITB
PROJECT.ITB
```

Spreadsheet File

```
ROA.ICF
```

PROGRAM LISTINGS FOR THE PROPOSAL RESOURCE-ALLOCATION DSS

```
!                              SCREEN.IPF
! First screen user sees which loads initial forms for
! explanation purposes.




e.lstr=50
e.supd=true
e.serr=true
!e.echo=true  used for testing purposes
!e.trac="v" used for testing purposes
!e.odsk=true used for testing purposes
!e.secb=true using for testing purposes

release all
load "A:"roa.icf" with "c"
load "A:mainform"
load "A:scn1form"
```

```
load "A:waitform"
load "A:scn2form"

putform scn1form
putform mainform
putform waitform

wait
perform "a:screen2.ipf"
```

                                     SCREEN2


```
! This screen provides the user with a choice of continuing
! or exiting the program.


clear
putform scn1form
putform scn2form

dim FOPTS(2)
FOPTS(1) = "Proceed "
FOPTS(2) = "Exit    "

let choice = MENU(FOPTS,1,2,15,35,0,12,1)

        TEST CHOICE
                CASE 1:  EXIT=FALSE
                         A=10
                         perform "a:screen3.ipf"
                         break
                CASE 2:  EXIT=TRUE
                         A=100
                         CLEAR
                         break
                OTHERWISE:
                         AT 20,20 OUTPUT "Your request is invalid"; CLEAR
        ENDTEST
```

                                     SCREEN3
```
! This screen provides the user with the option of an
! existing client or a new client.


clear
putform scn1form
```

```
load "a:lineform"
putform lineform


dim NEWOLD(2)


NEWOLD(1) = "Project for a New Client        "
NEWOLD(2) = "Project for an Existing Client "


let newmtwo = MENU(NEWOLD,1,2,10,25,0,35,1)


        TEST NEWMTWO
                CASE 1:   perform "a:new.ipf"
                          Break
                CASE 2:   perform "a:exist.ipf"
                          Break
                OTHERWISE:
                          AT 17,20 OUTPUT "Your request is invalid"; CLEAR
        ENDTEST
```

```
                        SCREENE
! This program loads EXITFORM and exists the user.



clear

load "a:exitform"
putform scn1form
putform exitform
release all
finish all

wait
clear
```

```
!                           NEW
! This program allows the user to select a new client from
! the NEWCLI database to be used to match it with a project
! that the new client may have available for bid this year.
! This database is maintained by the VP's staff assistants.

clear
putform scn1form
putform lineform

test not inuse("newcli")
   case true: use "A:newcli.itb"
endtest
```

```
opts=lastrec(newcli)
dim WHO(opts)
convert trim(cname) from newcli to array WHO(1)

        NEW = MENU(WHO,1,opts,8,20,0,30,2)
        OBTAIN from newcli where cname=who(NEW)
        y=crating
        perform "a:newproj.ipf"
```

```
!                       EXIST
! This program allows the user to select an existing client
! from the OLDCLI database. This is subsequently matched with
! a project that the client may have available this year.


clear
putform scn1form
putform lineform

test not inuse("oldcli")
    case true: use "A:oldcli.itb"
endtest

options = lastrec(oldcli)
dim WHO(options)
convert trim(cname) from oldcli to array WHO(1)

        OLD = MENU(WHO,1,options,8,20,0,30,2)
        OBTAIN from oldcli for cname=who(old)
        x=cname
        y=ocrating
        perform "a:project.ipf"
```

```
!                       NEWPROJ
! This program retrieves the project for the new client from
! PROJECT, assigns variable values for rule set consultation,
! and then performs uinput to ascertain additional variable
! values.


putform scn1form
putform lineform

test not inuse("project")
    case true: use "A:project.itb"
endtest
```

```
opt4=lastrec(project)
dim PROJECT(opt4)

convert trim (pname) from project for project.clname=newcli.cname \
to array PROJECT(1)

        PROJ = MENU(PROJECT,1,opt4,10,30,0,30,2)
        OBTAIN from project where pname=PROJECT(proj)
        ncrating=y
        OCRATING=-1
        PROJRANK=PRANK
        PVALUE=SIZE
        CALC COMPUTE
```

```
!                       PROJECT
! This program retrieves the project for the old client from
! Project, assigns variable values for rule set consultation,
! and then performs input to ascertain additional variables'
! values.

putform scn1form
putform lineform

test not inuse("project")
    case true use "A:project.itb"
endtest

opt = lastrec(project)
dim PROJECT(opt)

obtain from project where clname=who(old)

if #found then
convert trim(pname) from project for project.clname=oldcli.cname to array PROJECT(1)

        PROJ = MENU(PROJECT,1,opt,10,30,0,30,2)
        OBTAIN from project where pname=PROJECT(proj)
        cname=x
        ocrating=y
        NCRATING=-1
        PROJRANK=PRANK
        PVALUE=SIZE

else clear
    putform scn1form
    at 12,15 output trim(who(old))," does not have any new projects this year."
    putform waitform
    EXIT=TRUE
```

```
      A=100
      wait

endif

-------------------------------------------------------------------------------------

!                              UINPUT
! This program allows the user to provide percentage estimates
! of engineering and construction expenses.

e.lstr=50
c=""

clear
!load "a:scn1form"
putform scn1form

at 10,15 output "We are currently considering the ",trim(pname), " project"

at 11,15 output "This project is for ", trim(clname), "."
at 12,15 output "The project is valued at " ,pvalue using "ddd", " million

at 13,15 output "The client's rating is assessed to be ", y using "dd", "."

perform waitform
wait
CALC COMPUTE

clear
load "A:uform"
putform scn1form
putform uform

eng=100
const=100

at 16,20 input eng using "dd" with "Percent of Engineering Expenses?"
at 17,20 input const using "dd" with "Percent of Construction Expenses?"

CALC COMPUTE

clear
putform scn1form
putform waitform

RES=#(15,4)
at 7,15    OUTPUT "                               Estimated"
at 8,15    OUTPUT ""
```

```
at 9,15     OUTPUT "Engineering expenses                   ",#(10,4)
at 10,15    OUTPUT "Personnel expenses                     ",#(11,4)
at 11,15    OUTPUT "Accounting expenses                    ",#(12,4)
at 12,15    OUTPUT "Services expenses                      ",#(13,4)
at 13,15    OUTPUT "Construction expenses                  ",#(14,4)
at 14,15    OUTPUT "Estimated requirements are              " RES using "$ddd,ddd"
at 15,15    OUTPUT "Anticipated requirements were           ",#(17,1)
at 16,15    OUTPUT "This differs from anticipated by ", #(13,1)
at 18,15    OUTPUT "You will now see two graphs of these expenses"
at 19,15    OUTPUT "Press the SPACE BAR after viewing each graph"
wait
perform "a:resreq.ipf"
```

```
--------------------------------------------------------------------------------
```

```
!                        RESREQ
! This program will display the results to the user
! using a pie graph.

#TITLE = "PERCENTAGE OF RESOURCES TO ACCOUNTS"

plot labeled percent pie from #a10 to #d14 using 2,4

perform "a:resbar.ipf"
```

```
--------------------------------------------------------------------------------
```

```
!                        RESBAR
! This program will show the results to the user using
! a bar graph.

e.deci=0

#TITLE = "RESOURCES BY ACCOUNTS"
#XLABEL = "Account Name"
#YLABEL = "Dollar Amount"

plot bar from #a10 to #d14 using 2, 4
```

```
--------------------------------------------------------------------------------
```

```
!                        CHANGE
! Allows user to change engineering and construction estimates.

Clear

putform scn1form
putform lineform
```

```
dim NEWCHO(2)
NEWCHO(1) = " Revise Estimate "
NEWCHO(2) = " Exit the System "

let chose = menu(NEWCHO,1,2,10,30,0,20,1)

        test chose
                case 1:  perform "a:uinput.ipf"; EXIT=FALSE
                         break
                case 2:  EXIT=true
                         break
                otherwise:
                at 20, 20 output "Your request is invalid"; CLEAR
        ENDTEST
```

```
!                         FINAL
! This program allows the user to exit or consult the
! rule set again.

CLEAR
putform SCN1FORM
load "a:lineform"
putform lineform
e.lstr=50

dim FINAL(2)
FINAL(1) = "Exit"
FINAL(2) = "Consult System Again"

let AGAIN = MENU(FINAL,1,2,11,30,0,30,1)

        TEST AGAIN
                CASE 1:  EXIT=TRUE
                         break
                CASE 2:  EXIT=FALSE
                         break
                OTHERWISE:
                         at 20,20 output "Your request is invalid"; CLEAR
        ENDTEST
```

```
!                         STRATEGY
! This program allows the user to alter the strategy.
!

CLEAR
PUTFORM scn1form
```

```
PUTFORM lineform
DIM STRAT(3)
STRAT(1)="PRIMARY          "
STRAT(2)="SECONDARY        "
STRAT(3)="TERTIARY         "


let NEWSTRA = MENU(STRAT,1,3,10,30,0,15,1)


        test NEWSTRA
                CASE 1:  PRIMARY=TRUE
                        BREAK
                CASE 2:  SECONDARY=TRUE
                        BREAK
                CASE 3:  TERTIARY=TRUE
                        BREAK
        OTHERWISE:
                AT 20,20 OUTPUT "Your request is invalid"; clear
        ENDTEST
```

FORM DECLARATIONS FOR THE PROPOSAL RESOURCE-ALLOCATION DSS

```
FORM MAINFORM
        AT 7, 15 TO 18, 64 PUT BORDER "FGBR"
        AT 10, 21 PUT "Thank you for considering the use of the "
        AT 11, 21 PUT "project proposal resource allocation       "
        AT 12, 21 PUT "system.                                    "
        AT 13, 21 PUT "                                           "
        AT 14, 21 PUT "      Press Any Key to Return to the       "
        AT 15, 21 PUT "                  Command Line    "
        AT 6, 7 TO 20, 73 PUT "FWBU"
        AT 8, 16 TO 17, 63 PUT "FUBW"
ENDFORM
```

```
FORM SCN1FORM
        AT 5, 16 PUT " PROJECT PROPOSAL RESOURCE ALLOCATION SYSTEM " WITH "R"
        AT 3, 6 TO 21, 75 PUT BORDER "FCBA" WITH "D"
        AT 1, 1 TO 24, 80 PUT "FWBU"
ENDFORM
```

```
FORM WAITFORM
        AT 23, 24 PUT " Press Space Bar to Continue " WITH "R"
ENDFORM
```

```
FORM SCN2FORM
        AT 7, 15 TO 12, 65 PUT "FUBW"
        AT 8, 16 PUT "       At this point you may exit the system by     " WITH "R"
        AT 9, 16 PUT "       positioning the highlight bar on EXIT or      " WITH "R"
        AT 9, 21 PUT "positioning the highlight bar on EXIT and" WITH "R"
        AT 10, 16 PUT "     you may proceed with consultation by          " WITH "R"
        AT 10, 21 PUT "pressing ENTER or proceed with the " WITH "R"
        AT 11, 16 PUT "     pressing the ENTER key.                       " WITH "R"
        AT 11, 21 PUT "consultation by pressing the ENTER key. " WITH "R"
ENDFORM
```

```
FORM LINEFORM
        AT 17, 23 PUT "Select one of the items above by"
        AT 18, 23 PUT "positioning the highlight bar on "
        AT 19, 23 PUT "your choice and pressing enter."
        AT 17, 20 TO 19, 60 PUT "FUBW"
ENDFORM
```

```
FORM UFORM
        AT 7, 15 TO 14, 64 PUT BORDER "FGBR"
        AT 10, 21 PUT "Input a number between 0 and 100 to       "
        AT 11, 21 PUT "indicate the percentage of resources    "
        AT 12, 21 PUT "to be spent on each item.      "
        AT 13, 21 PUT "                                    "
        AT 6, 7 TO 16, 73 PUT "FWBU"
        AT 8, 16 TO 13, 63 PUT "FUBW"
ENDFORM
```

```
FORM EXITFORM
        AT 7, 15 TO 18, 64 PUT BORDER "FGBR"
        AT 10, 21 PUT "Thank you for considering the use of the "
        AT 11, 21 PUT "project proposal resource allocation    "
        AT 12, 21 PUT "system.                         "
        AT 13, 21 PUT "                                   "
        AT 14, 21 PUT " Press Any Key to Return to the         "
        AT 15, 21 PUT " Command Line              "
        AT 6, 7 TO 20, 73 PUT "FWBU"
        AT 8, 16 TO 17, 63 PUT "FUBW"
ENDFORM
```

LISTINGS OF SAMPLE CONTENTS IN DATABASE TABLES FOR THE PROPOSAL RESOURCE-ALLOCATION DSS

EXISTING CLIENT LISTING

Client Name	Client Rating
Atlantic Richfield	3
ALCOA	1
Reynolds Metals	7
U.S. Steel	5
Canadian Metals	10
Butler Copper	6
Kimberly Clark	11
Western Steel	8
CWP Transportation	2
Illinois Copper	9
Glasgow Zinc	12
Birmingham Aluminum	4

POTENTIAL NEW CLIENTS

Client Name	Client Rating
Anaconda	6
Richmond Steel	2
Minnesota Mining and Minerals	3
Medusa Aggregrates	5
Newport Mining	4
Echlin Engines	1

MOODY'S PROJECT LISTING

Client Name/ Project Name	Project Size (in millions)	Bid Date	Project Rating
Atlantic Richfield Logan Aluminum	400	02/15/	10
Anaconda Jackson Warehouse	100	02/21/	12
Richmond Steel Eastern Mill	159	03/01/	5
Reynolds Metals Fulton	250	03/15/	18
Minnesota Mining and Minerals Brainerd	85	03/25/	7
Reynolds Metals Cairo	550	03/30/	1

U.S. Steel Cleveland	300	04/01/	17
Medusa Aggregrates Central City	105	05/15/	19
ALCOA Pittsburgh	350	05/31/	4
Canadian Metals Ontario	175	06/01/	3
ALCOA NYC	95	06/15/	8
Newport Mining Grand Junction	65	07/13/	13
Atlantic Richfield Warren Copper	150	07/30/	11
Reynolds Metals McCracken Recycling	89	08/15/	14
Echlin Engines Nashville DC	70	09/16/	2
ALCOA Atlanta	245	09/25/	15
Kimberly Clark Grenada	300	10/15/	9
Medusa Aggregrates Madisonville	65	10/31/	9
Richmond Steel Western Mill	220	11/10/	16
Minnesota Mining and Minerals MSP	450	12/10/	6

LISTING OF SPREADSHEET CELL VALUES AND DEFINITIONS FOR THE PROPOSAL RESOURCE-ALLOCATION DSS

Definitions are denoted by "Expr" (they are expressions to be evaluated).

#A1
```
    Value    :  21
    Expr.    :  ENG
    Picture  :  "ff"
```

#B1
```
    Value    :              CHART OF ACCOUNTS
    Expr.    :  "          CHART OF ACCOUNTS"
```

#A2
```
    Value    :  32
    Expr.    :  CONST
    Picture  :  "ff"
```

#A3
```
    Value    :  100
```

```
     Expr.    :  pvalue
     Picture  :  "fff"


#A4
     Value    :  2
     Expr.    :  #a3/4023*100


#A6
     Value    :  ACCOUNT
     Expr.    :  "ACCOUNT"


#B6
     Value    :  ACCOUNT
     Expr.    :  "ACCOUNT"


#C6
     Value    :  PERCENT
     Expr.    :  "PERCENT"


#D6
     Value    :  DOLLAR
     Expr.    :  "DOLLAR"


#A7
     Value    :  NUMBER
     Expr.    :  "NUMBER"


#B7
     Value    :  NAME
     Expr.    :  "NAME"


#C7
     Value    :  ALLOCATED
     Expr.    :  "ALLOCATED"


#D7
     Value    :  AMOUNT
     Expr.    :  "AMOUNT"


#A10
     Value    :  001
     Expr.    :  "001"


#B10
     Value    :  ENG
     Expr.    :  "ENG"


#C10
     Value    :  0.21
     Expr.    :  #a1/100
```

```
   Picture :  "d.dd"


#D10
   Value   :  $ 20,880
   Expr.   :  #a17*#c10
   Picture :  "$ddd,ddd"


#A11
   Value   :  002
   Expr.   :  "002"


#B11
   Value   :  PERSON
   Expr.   :  "PERSON"


#C11
   Value   :  0.15
   Expr.   :  if crank = "Top" OR PRIMARY then p=.20; else p=.15; endif; p
   Picture :  "d.dd"


#D11
   Value   :  $ 14,914
   Expr.   :  #a17*#c11
   Picture :  "$ddd,ddd"


#A12
   Value   :  003
   Expr.   :  "003"


#B12
   Value   :  ACCOUNT
   Expr.   :  "ACCOUNT"


#C12
   Value   :  0.08
   Expr.   :  .08
   Picture :  "d.dd"


#D12
   Value   :  $  7,954
   Expr.   :  #a17*#c12
   Picture :  "$ddd,ddd"
#A13
   Value   :  004
   Expr.   :  "004"


#B13
   Value   :  SER
   Expr.   :  "SER"
```

#C13
    Value   : 0.05
    Expr.   : If TERTIARY then .05; else .10; endif
    Picture : "d.dd"

#D13
    Value   : $ 4,971
    Expr.   : #A17*#c13
    Picture : "$ddd,ddd"

#A14
    Value   : 005
    Expr.   : "005"

#B14
    Value   : CONST
    Expr.   : "CONST"

#C14
    Value   : 0.32
    Expr.   : #a2/100
    Picture : "d.dd"

RULE SET FOR THE PROPOSAL RESOURCE-ALLOCATION DSS

```
1       INITIAL:
2
3               OCRATING = UNKNOWN; NCRATING = UNKNOWN
4               CRANK = UNKNOWN; PVALUE = UNKNOWN
5               PRIMARY = UNKNOWN; SECONDARY = UNKNOWN
6               TERTIARY = UNKNOWN
7               E.RIGR="C"
8               Perform "a:screen.ipf"
9
10      GOAL:   RESOURCE
11
12      Rule: EXIT
13
14              IF:     EXIT and A>99
15              THEN:   RESOURCE = 0
16              REASON: The user chose to exit the system or the existing
17                      client had no projects for the upcoming year.
18
19      Rule: R2
20              IF:     (OCRATING > 0 AND OCRATING <= 3) OR
21                      (NCRATING > 0 AND NCRATING <= 3)
22              THEN:   CRANK = "Top"
23              REASON: When the client's rating is in the top three the
```

```
24                          client is assessed to have a top ranking.
25
26      Rule: R3
27              IF:     NCRATING > 3 OR (OCRATING > 3 AND OCRATING <= 8)
28              THEN:   CRANK = "Moderate"
29              REASON: When a new client's rating is greater than three or
30                      an existing client's rating is between four and eight
31                      the client's rank is assessed to be moderate.
32
33      Rule: R4
34              IF:     OCRATING > 8
35              THEN:   CRANK = "Low"
36                      TERTIARY = TRUE CF 90
37              REASON: When an existing client's rating is greater than eight,
38                      the client's rank is assessed to be low and priority of
39                      the project is tertiary.
40
41      Rule: R5
42              IF:     PROJRANK < 5 OR CRANK = "Top"
43              THEN:   PRIMARY = TRUE CF 95
44              REASON: When the project is priority ranking is greater than five
45                      and the client ranking is assessed to be top, then project
46                      is of primary strategic importance.
47
48      Rule: R6
49              IF:     CRANK <> "Top" and PROJRANK > 5 AND PVALUE >= 250
50              THEN:   SECONDARY = TRUE CF 92
51              REASON: A project is assigned as being of secondary strategic
52                      importance when the client's rating is not top, the
53                      project's ranking is greater than five and the project's
54                      value is greater than or equal to 250 million.
55
56      Rule: R7
57              IF:     CRANK = "Moderate"
58              THEN:   PERFORM "a:strategy.ipf"
59                      CALC COMPUTE
60              CHANGES:PRIMARY, SECONDARY, TERTIARY
61              REASON: When a client's ranking is moderate, then the user
62                      must determine the strategic importance of the project.
63
64      Rule: R8
65              TEST:   E
66              IF:     PRIMARY OR SECONDARY OR TERTIARY
67              THEN:   PERFORM "A:UINPUT.IPF"
68                      RESOURCE = RES
69              REASON: Once the strategic importance of the project is determined
70                      the user must determine the percentage of resources to be
71                      allocated to engineering and construction expenses.
72
73      Rule: R9
```

```
74              IF:     KNOWN("RESOURCE") AND PRIMARY
75              THEN:   PERFORM "A:CHANGE.IPF"
76              CHANGES:RESOURCE
77              REASON: If the project is of primary strategic importance, the user
78                      is given the opportunity to revise engineering and
                        construction projections and review again.
79
80
81      Rule: R10
82              IF:     KNOWN("RESOURCE") AND CRANK="Moderate" AND EXIT=FALSE
83              THEN:   PERFORM "A:STRATEGY.IPF"
84                      CALC COMPUTE
85                      PERFORM "A:CHANGE.IPF"
86              CHANGES:RESOURCE
87              REASON: The user has an opportunity to change the strategic
                        importance of a project when the client ranking is moderate.
88
89
90
91
92
93      DO:     PERFORM "A:FINAL"
94              If EXIT then perform "a:screene"; endif
95              If EXIT=FALSE then release consult ALL
96              RELEASE ALL
97              consult "a:RESOURCE" to test
98              endif
99
100
```

KNOWLEDGE SYSTEM FILES AND VARIABLES FOR THE ROBOT GRIPPER-SELECTION DSS

File Description

(1) .IPF files

indata.ipf: used to obtain valid input from user via forms
initial.ipf: used to set environment variables and initialize unknown variables in rule set
outdata.ipf: used to present results of consultation
reasons.ipf: used to present customized line of reasoning after a consultation
review.ipf: used to present user with option of repeatedly viewing both the results of a
   consultation and the line of reasoning after a consultation
session.ipf: used to present the MAIN MENU from which the user can
   consult the expert system

(2) .RSS files

gripper.rss: contains the rules that represent the reasoning knowledge for the application

(3) .ICF files

acomform.icf: represents the form labeled FORM 4

applform.icf: represents the form labeled FORM 1

bcomform.icf: represents the form labeled FORM 5

ccomform.icf: represents the form labeled FORM 6

envrform.icf: represents the form labeled FORM 2

grpaform.icf, grpbform.icf: used to present results of consultation

instform.icf: used to present user with instructions, prior to the start of a consultation

intrform.icf: used to present user with an introduction to the expert system

resaform.icf, resbform.icf, rescform.icf: used to present user with the option of viewing
   line of reasoning and reviewing results of a consultation

robtform.icf: represents the form labeled FORM 3

sesaform.icf, sesbform.icf: used in conjunction with "session.ipf" to present MAIN MENU

valdform.icf: used to present user with error message for invalid input(s)

waitform.icf: used to present user with wait message during a consultation

Rule Set Variables

(1) Known variables

COMPGEOM: identifies type of component geometry (cylindrical, spherical, arbitrary, flat)

COMPLNTH: identifies largest dimension (length) on component (in m.)

COMPMAT: identifies type of component material (ferrous, nonferrous)

COMPNAT: identifies nature of component (robust, fragile)

COMPSURF: identifies type of component surface (porous, nonporous)

COMPTEMP: identifies degree of component temperature (low, high)

COMPWT: identifies weight of component (in Kgs.)

CONTAMIN: identifies degree of contamination in work environment (low, medium, high)

CYCLTIME: identifies degree of cycle time required (low, high)

DIFFPRES: identifies maximum differential pressure between component
   surface and gripper (in Pascal)

MAGCONST: identifies magnetic constant of component material (in Tesla)

POSITACC: identifies degree of positional accuracy required (low, high)

PRESSURE: identifies compressive strength of component material (in Pascal)

RBTACT: identifies type of actuation for robot used (electrical, pneumatic, hydraulic)

RBTPLOAD: identifies pay load capacity of robot used (in Kgs.)

TASKTYPE: identifies type of task (assembly, machining, pickplace)

(2) Unknown variables

FRICTION: intermediate variable, value depends on CONTAMIN and is used to
   calculate GRIPFORC

GRIPACT: returns type of actuation for gripper (possible values:
   electrical, hydraulic, pneumatic)

GRIPAREA: returns value of minimum contact area on gripper

GRIPCHAR: goal variable, returns TRUE if gripper characteristics
   (GRIPTYPE, GRIPWT, GRIPFORC, GRIPAREA, JAWSIZE, GRIPACT) are all known

GRIPFORC: returns value of minimum gripping force to be generated

GRIPTYPE: returns type of gripper selected (possible values: jaw, magnetic, vacuum)

GRIPWT: returns value of maximum allowable weight for gripper

GTYPE1, GTYPE2, GTYPE3, GTYPE4, GTYPE5: intermediate variables, used in
   determining GRIPTYPE (possible values: all, magvac)

JAWDIM: returns value of minimum jaw opening for jaw type grippers

JAWSIZE: returns TRUE if jaw dimension is to be calculated

SAFEFAC: intermediate variable, value depends on CONTAMIN and is used to calculate GRIPFORC

PROGRAMS FOR THE ROBOT GRIPPER-SELECTION DSS

SESSION.IPF

_____

```
!This program generates the main menu from which the user can
!choose to learn more about gripper selection, proceed with a
!consultation, or quit to the operating system.
!
LET E.LSTR=50
WANTMORE=TRUE
DIM VAROPT(3)
LET VAROPT(1)="About robot_gripper selection"
LET VAROPT(2)="A consultation"
LET VAROPT(3)="Exit and return to DOS"
WHILE WANTMORE DO
  RELEASE VARIABLE; WANTMORE=TRUE
  LOAD "a:sesaform"; CLEAR; PUTFORM SESAFORM
  LET CHOICE=MENU(VAROPT,1,3,5,6,1,50,1)
  TEST CHOICE
    CASE 1: CLEAR
        LOAD "a:intrform"; PUTFORM INTRFORM; GETFORM INTRFORM
        IF INTR="Y" THEN
          LOAD "a:applform"; LOAD "a:envrform"
          LOAD "a:robtform"; LOAD "a:acomform"
          LOAD "a:bcomform"; LOAD "a:ccomform"
          CLEAR; PUTFORM APPLFORM; WAIT
          CLEAR; PUTFORM ENVRFORM; WAIT
          CLEAR; PUTFORM ROBTFORM; WAIT
          CLEAR; PUTFORM ACOMFORM; WAIT
          CLEAR; PUTFORM BCOMFORM; WAIT
          CLEAR; PUTFORM CCOMFORM; WAIT
        ENDIF
        BREAK
    CASE 2: CLEAR
        CONSULT "a:gripper" to seek GRIPCHAR
        BREAK
    CASE 3: RELEASE ALL
        BYE
  ENDTEST
  CLEAR
  LOAD "a:sesbform"; PUTFORM SESBFORM; GETFORM SESBFORM; CLEAR
  IF YN NE "Y" THEN
    WANTMORE=FALSE
  ENDIF
```

```
ENDWHILE
RELEASE VARIABLE
```

```
INTIAL.IPF
_____


!This program sets the environment variables and initializes
!the unknown variables for the rule set <gripper.rss>.
!
LET E.LSTR=50; LET E.SUPD=TRUE
LET E.RIGR="A"; LET E.SORD="R"
LET E.TRYP="S"; LET E.WHN="N"
GRIPTYPE=UNKNOWN; GTYPE1=UNKNOWN
GTYPE2=UNKNOWN; GTYPE3=UNKNOWN
GTYPE4=UNKNOWN; GTYPE5=UNKNOWN
FRICTION=UNKNOWN; JAWDIM=UNKNOWN
JAWSIZE=UNKNOWN; GRIPACT=UNKNOWN
SAFEFAC=UNKNOWN; GRIPFORC=UNKNOWN
GRIPAREA=UNKNOWN; GRIPWT=UNKNOWN
GRIPCHAR=UNKNOWN
RETURN
```

```
INDATA.IPF
_____


!This program presents the user with a set of forms, accepts user
!input for various parameters via the forms and verifies the input
!values.
!
LET E.LSTR=50
LOAD "a:applform"; LOAD "a:envrform"
LOAD "a:robtform"; LOAD "a:acomform"
LOAD "a:bcomform"; LOAD "a:ccomform"
LOAD "a:valdform"; LOAD "a:instform"
PUTFORM INSTFORM; GETFORM INSTFORM; CLEAR
!
! Obtain and validate variable values in form <applform>
!
LET APPL=FALSE
PUTFORM APPLFORM; GETFORM APPLFORM; CLEAR
IF TASKTYPE IN ["assembly", "machining", "pickplace"]
  IF POSITACC IN ["low", "high"]
    IF CYCLTIME IN ["low", "high"] THEN
      APPL=TRUE
    ENDIF
  ENDIF
```

```
  ENDIF
WHILE APPL=FALSE DO
 PUTFORM VALDFORM; GETFORM VALDFORM; CLEAR
 PUTFORM APPLFORM; GETFORM APPLFORM; CLEAR
 IF TASKTYPE IN ["assembly", "machining", "pickplace"]
  IF POSITACC IN ["low", "high"]
   IF CYCLTIME IN ["low", "high"] THEN
    APPL=TRUE
   ENDIF
  ENDIF
 ENDIF
ENDWHILE
!
! Obtain and validate variable values in form <envrform>
!
LET ENVR=FALSE
PUTFORM ENVRFORM; GETFORM ENVRFORM; CLEAR
IF COMPTEMP IN ["low", "high"]
 IF CONTAMIN IN ["low", "medium", "high"] THEN
  ENVR=TRUE
 ENDIF
ENDIF
WHILE ENVR=FALSE DO
 PUTFORM VALDFORM; GETFORM VALDFORM; CLEAR
 PUTFORM ENVRFORM; GETFORM ENVRFORM; CLEAR
 IF COMPTEMP IN ["low", "high"]
  IF CONTAMIN IN ["low", "medium", "high"] THEN
    ENVR=TRUE
  ENDIF
 ENDIF
ENDWHILE
!
! Obtain and validate variable values in form <robtform>
!
LET ROBT=FALSE
PUTFORM ROBTFORM; GETFORM ROBTFORM; CLEAR
IF RBTPLOAD>0
 IF RBTPLOAD<10000
  IF RBTACT IN ["electrical", "pneumatic", "hydraulic"] THEN
    ROBT=TRUE
  ENDIF
 ENDIF
ENDIF
WHILE ROBT=FALSE DO
 PUTFORM VALDFORM; GETFORM VALDFORM; CLEAR
 PUTFORM ROBTFORM; GETFORM ROBTFORM; CLEAR
 IF RBTPLOAD>0
  IF RBTPLOAD<10000
   IF RBTACT IN ["electrical", "pneumatic", "hydraulic"] THEN
```

```
      ROBT=TRUE
     ENDIF
   ENDIF
 ENDIF
ENDWHILE
!
! Obtain and validate variable values in form <acomform>
!
LET ACOM=FALSE
PUTFORM ACOMFORM; GETFORM ACOMFORM; CLEAR
IF COMPGEOM IN ["cylindrical", "spherical", "arbitrary", "flat"]
 IF COMPLNTH>0
  IF COMPLNTH<10000
    IF COMPWT>0
     IF COMPWT<10000 THEN
       ACOM=TRUE
      ENDIF
     ENDIF
    ENDIF
  ENDIF
ENDIF
WHILE ACOM=FALSE DO
 PUTFORM VALDFORM; GETFORM VALDFORM; CLEAR
 PUTFORM ACOMFORM; GETFORM ACOMFORM; CLEAR
  IF COMPGEOM IN ["cylindrical", "spherical", "arbitrary", "flat"]
   IF COMPLNTH>0
    IF COMPLNTH<10000
     IF COMPWT>0
      IF COMPWT<10000 THEN
        ACOM=TRUE
       ENDIF
      ENDIF
     ENDIF
    ENDIF
  ENDIF
ENDWHILE
!
! Obtain and validate variable values in form <bcomform>
!
LET BCOM=FALSE
PUTFORM BCOMFORM; GETFORM BCOMFORM; CLEAR
IF COMPNAT IN ["robust", "fragile"]
 IF COMPMAT IN ["ferrous", "nonferrous"]
  IF COMPSURF IN ["porous", "nonporous"] THEN
    BCOM=TRUE
   ENDIF
  ENDIF
ENDIF
WHILE BCOM=FALSE DO
```

```
  PUTFORM VALDFORM; GETFORM VALDFORM; CLEAR
  PUTFORM BCOMFORM; GETFORM BCOMFORM; CLEAR
  IF COMPNAT IN ["robust", "fragile"]
   IF COMPMAT IN ["ferrous", "nonferrous"]
    IF COMPSURF IN ["porous", "nonporous"] THEN
     BCOM=TRUE
    ENDIF
   ENDIF
  ENDIF
ENDWHILE
!
! Obtain and validate variable values in form <ccomform>
!
LET CCOM=FALSE
PUTFORM CCOMFORM; GETFORM CCOMFORM; CLEAR
IF MAGCONST>0
  IF MAGCONST<1000000000
   IF PRESSURE>0
    IF PRESSURE<1000000000
     IF DIFFPRES>0
      IF DIFFPRES<1000000000 THEN
       CCOM=TRUE
      ENDIF
     ENDIF
    ENDIF
   ENDIF
  ENDIF
ENDIF
WHILE CCOM=FALSE DO
  PUTFORM VALDFORM; GETFORM VALDFORM; CLEAR
  PUTFORM CCOMFORM; GETFORM CCOMFORM; CLEAR
  IF MAGCONST>0
   IF MAGCONST<1000000000
    IF PRESSURE>0
     IF PRESSURE<1000000000
      IF DIFFPRES>0
       IF DIFFPRES<1000000000 THEN
        CCOM=TRUE
       ENDIF
      ENDIF
     ENDIF
    ENDIF
   ENDIF
  ENDIF
ENDWHILE
!
! Display wait message
!
LOAD "a:waitform"; PUTFORM WAITFORM
```

```
RETURN
```

```
OUTDATA.IPF
```

_____

```
! This program writes the results of a consultation to a form.
!
LET E.LSTR=50
LOAD "a:grpbform"; LOAD "a:grpaform"; CLEAR
IF JAWSIZE=TRUE THEN
  PUTFORM GRPBFORM; TALLY GRPBFORM
ENDIF
IF JAWSIZE=FALSE THEN
  PUTFORM GRPAFORM; TALLY GRPAFORM
ENDIF
PERFORM "a:reasons.ipf"
PERFORM "a:review.ipf"
RETURN
```

```
REASONS.IPF
```

_____

```
! This program explains the line of reasoning after a consultation by
! making use of utility variables
!
LET E.LSTR=79
NEEDMORE=TRUE
WHILE NEEDMORE DO
  LOAD "a:resaform"; PUTFORM RESAFORM; GETFORM RESAFORM
  IF RESA="Y" THEN
    CLEAR
    LOAD "a:resbform"; PUTFORM RESBFORM
    AT 5,1 ? "The goal variable was determined from the following rule(s):"
    AT 7,1 HOW
    WAIT
    CLEAR
    PUTFORM RESBFORM
    AT 5,1 ? "The following rules were considered because ..."
    AT 7,1 WHY
    WAIT
    I=1
    WHILE I<=#HCNT DO
      R=#HOW(I)
      CLEAR
      PUTFORM RESBFORM
      AT 5,1 ? "The following rules were considered because ..."
      AT 7,1 WHY R
      WAIT
```

```
    I=I+1
  ENDWHILE
 ENDIF
 IF RESA NE "Y" THEN
   NEEDMORE=FALSE
 ENDIF
  CLEAR
 RELEASE RESA
ENDWHILE
CLEAR
RETURN
```

REVIEW.IPF

_____

```
! This program allows the user to review both the results of a
! consultation and the line of reasoning before returning to the
! main menu.
!
LET E.LSTR=50
ONCEMORE=TRUE
WHILE ONCEMORE DO
  RELEASE RESC
  LOAD "a:rescform"; PUTFORM RESCFORM; GETFORM RESCFORM
  IF RESC="Y" THEN
    PERFORM "a:outdata.ipf"
  ENDIF
  IF RESC NE "Y" THEN
    ONCEMORE=FALSE
  ENDIF
  CLEAR
ENDWHILE
CLEAR
RETURN
```

RULE SET FOR THE ROBOT GRIPPER-SELECTION DSS

GRIPPER.RSS

_____

```
INITIAL:
  PERFORM "a:intial.ipf"
  PERFORM "a:indata.ipf"
GOAL: GRIPCHAR

RULE: R1
```

PRIORITY: 90
IF: TASKTYPE IN ["assembly", "machining"]
THEN: GRIPTYPE="jaw"
REASON:
Only jaw-type grippers provide the high degree of dexterity required in assembly and machining operations.

RULE: R2
PRIORITY: 50
IF: TASKTYPE="pickplace" AND POSITACC="low"
THEN: GTYPE1="all"
REASON:
Pick-and-place operations require a low degree of dexterity. Further, because the specified operation requires only a low degree of positional accuracy, all gripper types are feasible and other discriminatory criteria must be applied.

RULE: R3
PRIORITY: 90
IF: POSITACC="high"
THEN: GRIPTYPE="jaw"
REASON:
Because the specified operation requires a high degree of positional accuracy, only jaw-type grippers are appropriate.

RULE: R4
PRIORITY: 90
IF: COMPGEOM IN ["cylindrical", "spherical", "arbitrary"]
THEN: GRIPTYPE="jaw"
REASON:
Because the component geometry is cylindrical, spherical or arbitrary, only jaw-type grippers are appropriate.

RULE: R5
PRIORITY: 55
IF: GTYPE1="all" AND COMPGEOM="flat"
THEN: GTYPE2="all"
REASON:
Because this is a pick-and-place operation requiring low positional accuracy and the component geometry is flat (i.e., planar), all gripper types are feasible, and other discriminatory criteria must be applied.

RULE: R6
PRIORITY: 85
IF: COMPTEMP="high" OR CONTAMIN IN ["medium", "high"]
THEN: GRIPTYPE="jaw"
REASON:
Because the specified operation involves a component with high temperature (greater than 200°C) or the operating environment is contaminated with grease, oil, or other lubricants; water or other coolants; or particulate matter such as swarf from machining; only jaw-type grippers are appropriate.

```
RULE: R7
  PRIORITY: 60
  IF: GTYPE2="all" AND COMPTEMP="low" AND CONTAMIN="low"
  THEN: GTYPE3="all"
  REASON:
  This is a pick-and-place operation requiring low positional accuracy for component with
  flat geometry and low temperature (less than 200°C). Further, the operating environment
  is relatively clean. Hence, all gripper types are feasible, and other discriminatory
  criteria must be applied.


RULE: R8
  PRIORITY: 85
  IF: CYCLTIME="low"
  THEN: GRIPTYPE="jaw"
  REASON:
  Because the specified application is a high-speed operation—that is, the time interval
  between a gripper deactivation and the next activation is small (less than 5 seconds)—only
  jaw-type grippers are appropriate.


RULE: R9
  PRIORITY: 65
  IF: GTYPE3="all" AND CYCLTIME="high"
  THEN: GTYPE4="all"
  REASON:
  This is a pick-and-place operation requiring low positional accuracy for a component with
  flat geometry and low temperature in a relatively clean operating environment. Further,
  the specified application is a low-speed operation; that is, the time interval between a
  gripper deactivation and the next activation is greater than 5 seconds. Hence, all gripper
  types are feasible, and other discriminatory criteria must be applied.


RULE: R10
  PRIORITY: 70
  IF: GTYPE4="all" AND COMPNAT="fragile"
  THEN: GTYPE5="magvac"
  REASON:
  This is a pick-and-place operation requiring low positional accuracy for a component with
  flat geometry and low temperature in a relatively clean operating environment. Further,
  the specified application is a low-speed operation. Hence, all gripper types are feasible,
  and other discriminatory criteria must be applied. Because the component is fragile, only
  magnetic or vacuum type grippers are recommended. Additional criteria must be used to
  discriminate between magnetic and vacuum-type grippers. Jaw-type grippers are not
  preferred, because the grasping action may damage or destroy fragile components.


RULE: R11
  PRIORITY: 75
  IF: GTYPE4="all" AND COMPNAT="robust"
  THEN: GRIPTYPE="jaw"
  REASON:
```

This is a pick-and-place operation requiring low positional accuracy for component with flat geometry and low temperature in a relatively clean operating environment. Further, the specified application is a low-speed operation and component is robust. Hence, all gripper types are feasible for this application. With all other factors equal, jaw-type grippers are preferred because they are more reliable.

RULE: R12

    PRIORITY: 80

    IF: GTYPE5="magvac" AND COMPMAT="ferrous" AND

    COMPSURF="porous"

    THEN: GRIPTYPE="magnetic"

    REASON:

This is a pick-and-place operation requiring low positional accuracy for component with flat geometry and low temperature in a relatively clean operating environment. Further, the specified application is a low-speed operation. Hence, all gripper types are feasible, and other discriminatory criteria must be applied. Because the component is fragile, only magnetic or vacuum type grippers are recommended. When the component material has magnetic properties (ferrous) and the component surface is porous (or is granular and has air pockets), then magnetic grippers are appropriate.

RULE: R13

    PRIORITY: 80

    IF: GTYPE5="magvac" AND COMPSURF="nonporous"

    THEN: GRIPTYPE="vacuum"

    REASON:

This is a pick-and-place operation requiring low positional accuracy for component with flat geometry and low temperature in a relatively clean operating environment. Further, the specified application is a low-speed operation. Hence, all gripper types are feasible and other discriminatory criteria must be applied. Because the component is fragile, only magnetic or vacuum type grippers are recommended. When the component surface is non-porous, then vacuum grippers are preferred to magnetic grippers, because they are more reliable in operation.

RULE: R14

    PRIORITY: 80

    IF: GTYPE5="magvac" AND COMPMAT="nonferrous" AND COMPSURF="porous"

    THEN: GRIPTYPE="jaw"

    REASON:

This is a pick-and-place operation requiring low positional accuracy for component with flat geometry and low temperature in a relatively clean operating environment. Further, the specified application is a low-speed operation. Hence, all gripper types are feasible and other discriminatory criteria must be applied. Because the component is fragile, only magnetic or vacuum type grippers are recommended. When the component material is non-ferrous and the component surface is porous, neither magnetic nor vacuum type grippers can be used. In this case, the jaw type gripper is the only available option.

RULE: R15

    PRIORITY: 50

    IF: GRIPTYPE IN ["vacuum", "magnetic"]

    THEN: JAWSIZE=FALSE

    REASON:

Because a vacuum or magnetic-type gripper is chosen, the jaw-size criterion (recommended size of jaw opening) is not applicable. This criterion is applicable only for jaw-type grippers.

RULE: R16

  PRIORITY: 50

  IF: GRIPTYPE="jaw" AND KNOWN ("COMPLNTH") AND KNOWN ("FRICTION")

  THEN: JAWSIZE=TRUE; JAWDIM=COMPLNTH/FRICTION

  REASON:

Because a jaw-type gripper is chosen, the jaw-size criterion (recommended size of jaw opening) is applicable and is calculated based on the component's largest dimension and the coefficient of friction at gripper-component interface.

RULE: R17

  PRIORITY: 50

  IF: KNOWN ("COMPWT") AND KNOWN ("RBTPLOAD")

  THEN: GRIPWT=RBTPLOAD-COMPWT

  REASON:

The maximum inherent weight of the gripper depends on the payload capacity of the robot being used and the component being manipulated.

RULE: R18

  PRIORITY: 50

  IF: GRIPTYPE="jaw" AND KNOWN ("SAFEFAC") AND KNOWN ("COMPWT")

     AND KNOWN ("FRICTION") AND KNOWN ("PRESSURE")

  THEN: GRIPFORC=SAFEFAC*COMPWT/(2*FRICTION)

     GRIPAREA=GRIPFORC/PRESSURE

  REASON:

The gripping force to be generated by the gripper depends on the weight of the component, the coefficient of friction at the gripper-component interface, and a factor of safety that depends on the level of environmental contamination. The desired area of the gripping surface depends on the gripping force to be generated and allowable compressive strength of the component material.

RULE: R19

  PRIORITY: 50

  IF: GRIPTYPE="magnetic" AND KNOWN ("SAFEFAC") AND KNOWN ("COMPWT")

     AND KNOWN ("FRICTION") AND KNOWN ("MAGCONST")

  THEN: GRIPFORC=SAFEFAC*COMPWT/FRICTION

     GRIPAREA=GRIPFORC/MAGCONST

  REASON:

The gripping force to be generated by the gripper depends on the weight of the component, the coefficient of friction at the gripper-component interface, and a factor of safety that depends on the level of environmental contamination. In this case, only one surface is used to grip the component. The desired area of the gripping surface depends on the gripping force to be generated and magnetic constant for the component material.

RULE: R20

  PRIORITY: 50

```
IF: GRIPTYPE="vacuum" AND KNOWN ("SAFEFAC") AND KNOWN ("COMPWT")
       AND KNOWN ("FRICTION") AND KNOWN ("DIFFPRES")
THEN: GRIPFORC=SAFEFAC*COMPWT/FRICTION
         GRIPAREA=GRIPFORC/DIFFPRES
REASON:
```

The gripping force to be generated by the gripper depends on the weight of component, the coefficient of friction at the gripper-component interface, and a factor of safety that depends on the level of environmental contamination. In this case, ony one surface is used to grip component. The desired area of the gripping surface depends on the gripping force to be generated and differential pressure that exists at the component-gripper interface.

```
RULE: R21
  PRIORITY: 50
  IF: GRIPTYPE="magnetic"
  THEN: GRIPACT="electrical"
  REASON:
```

For a magnetic gripper, activation is achieved electrically by energizing an electro-magnet and is independent of method of robot activation.

```
RULE: R22
  PRIORITY: 50
  IF: GRIPTYPE="vacuum"
  THEN: GRIPACT="pneumatic"
  REASON:
```

For a vacuum gripper, activation is achieved pneumatically and is independent of method of robot activation.

```
RULE: R23
  PRIORITY: 50
  IF: GRIPTYPE="jaw" AND KNOWN ("RBTACT")
  THEN: GRIPACT=RBTACT
  REASON:
```

For a jaw-type gripper, the form of activation depends on the method of robot activation used. Hence, if a robot is activated electrically, the gripper is activated electrically; if a robot is activated hydraulically, the gripper is activated hydraulically and if the robot is activated pneumatically, the gripper is activated pneumatically.

```
RULE: R24
  PRIORITY: 95
  IF: CONTAMIN="high"
  THEN: FRICTION=0.2
        SAFEFAC=4.0
  REASON:
```

Environmental contamination is considered to be high if oil, grease, or other lubricants are present. Other substances such as water and particulate matter may or may not be present. Under such conditions, the coefficient of friction is low and affects the grasping ability of the gripper. Hence, a high factor of safety is employed.

```
RULE: R25
```

```
PRIORITY: 95
IF CONTAMIN="medium"
THEN: FRICTION=0.6
      SAFEFAC=2.0
REASON:
```
Environmental contamination is considered to be medium if water or other coolants are present and particulate matter may or may not be present. Under such conditions, friction coefficient is moderately high, with a moderate negative effect on the grasping ability of the gripper. Hence, a factor of safety is employed and has a value that reflects the intermediate state between the two possible extremes of high and low environmental contamination.

```
RULE: R26
  PRIORITY: 95
  IF: CONTAMIN="low"
  THEN: FRICTION=0.95
        SAFEFAC=1.2
  REASON:
```
Environmental contamination is considered to be low when no contaminant is present. Under such conditions, the friction coefficient is high and any adverse effects on the grasping ability of the gripper are minimal. Although a factor of safety is not strictly required, a small value is employed in keeping with generally accepted engineering practice.

```
RULE: R27
  PRIORITY: 100
  IF: KNOWN ("GRIPTYPE") AND KNOWN ("GRIPWT") AND KNOWN ("GRIPFORC")
  AND KNOWN ("GRIPAREA") AND KNOWN ("JAWSIZE") AND KNOWN ("GRIPACT")
  THEN: GRIPCHAR=TRUE
  REASON:
```
The following factors define desired gripper characteristics for an application-type gripper, maximum inherent weight of gripper, minimum grasping force to be generated, minimum area of grasping surface, desired opening of jaw (if a jaw-type gripper is selected) and method of gripper activation. When all these factors are assigned values, then the gripper characteristics are known.

```
DO:
  PERFORM "a:outdata.ipf"
```

Glossary

Access code   A security mechanism that controls the users that have access to specified knowledge.

Acceptance region   The positions in an issue space that are acceptable solutions to a negotiator.

Active cell   The cell highlighted by the cell cursor.

Ad hoc   Unplanned; spur of the moment.

Administration   The act of managing or supervising the use of resources.

Agreement region   The intersection of negotiators' acceptance regions during a negotiation.

AI   See *artificial intelligence*.

AI environment   A piece of software that integrates traditional (e.g., business) computing capabilities with AI technology such as natural language processing and inference. Within this environment, natural language conservation can be used to exercise many of the traditional capabilities (e.g., business graphics, statistics generation), expert systems that employ those capabilities (e.g., spreadsheet analysis, database management) can be built, and the traditional capabilities (e.g., procedural models, spreadsheets) can themselves carry out expert system consultations. Thus, in a single piece of software, the capabilities of an inference engine, rule set manager, and natural language processor are blended with traditional capabilities.

Alternative   One of the possible decisions that a decision maker can choose.

Analysis   The activity of subjecting data to a procedure, thereby producing some beliefs, expectations, or solutions for some problem; the part of system development concerned with identifying what the system is required to do.

Analytical hierarchy process   An approach to decision making that involves structuring multiple criteria for deciding into a hierarchy, assessing the relative importance of these criteria, comparing alternatives for each criterion, and determining an overall ranking of the alternatives.

Announcing   Conveying the result of a decision-making process.

Application developer   Someone who develops (e.g., conceives, designs, implements, tests, delivers) application software.

Application software   Program that manages knowledge pertaining to a specific application area (e.g., payroll, order entry, market analysis).

Application system   The combination of application software, the knowledge managed by that software, and the interface that allows a user to interact with the software.

Arbitration   Coordination methods that can apply when there is conflict among the multiple participants engaged in decision making.

Architecture   A design that can be used to guide the implementation of a system or a framework that can be used to guide the study of a subject.

Argument   An input to a function.

Array   A named collection of elements arranged into columns and rows, where each element behaves and can be processed as a variable.

Artificial intelligence (AI)   A field of study and application concerned with identifying and using tools and techniques that allow machines to exhibit behavior that would be considered intelligent if it were observed in humans.

ASCII   American Standard Code for Information Interchange; commonly used for representing textual characters.

Assignment   The act of assigning a new value to a variable.

Assignment command   A command to assign a value to a variable.

Assimilative knowledge   Knowledge that controls what knowledge is acceptable for assimilation into a knowledge system.

Assistance messages   Messages issued by a DSS to assist the user in using the system (e.g., help messages).

Asynchronous communication   Communication in which the message passing is not synchronized. Participants send messages to each other at different times that suit their own individual needs.

Asynchronous transmission   A method of transmission in which the sending and receiving machines are synchronized by signals indicating the start and end of each transmitted character.

Authority   The power possessed by a participant in an organization to make decisions on behalf of the organization regarding the structuring of its resources and the cultivation of relationships to its environment.

Authority level   The relative extent of a decision maker's authority, ranging from the power to make day-to-day operating decisions for some small slice of organizational activity to the power to make strategic decisions with a pervasive impact on organizational activities.

Automatic data processing   A type of business computing that is primarily concerned with systems that handle the processing of data that describe transactions and with updating records based on transactions data.

Automatic programming   The generation of a desired program by another program that accepts a description of the generated program's desired traits.

Auxiliary memory   Memory used for temporary, intermediate, or long-term storage of knowledge, usually in the form of various kinds of files held in secondary storage media (e.g., a diskette or computer tape).

Backup   Additional copy of some knowledge that can be used in the event of the loss of or damage to the original.

Backward chaining   An approach to rule-based reasoning in which the inference engine endeavors to find a value for an overall goal by recursively finding values for subgoals. At any point in the recursion, the effort of finding a value for the immediate goal involves examining rule conclusions to identify those rules that could possibly establish a value for that goal. An unknown variable in the premise of one of these candidate rules becomes a new subgoal for recursion purposes.

BASIC   Beginner's All-purpose Symbolic Instruction Code. A programming language commonly used on microcomputers.

Baud rate   Communications transmission speed.

Bit   A binary digit (i.e., either a 0 or 1) used to represent "on" or "off" states in a computer or on auxiliary memory media.

Block   A contiguous series of characters or lines in a piece of text; an adjacent group of array elements; a rectangle of spreadsheet cells; a rectangle of color in a form or template.

Booting   The activity of initiating the execution of a computer's operating system.

B-tree   A multilevel approach to implementing indexes for rapid direct access to individual records in a file.

Buffer   Portion of a work area that serves as a loading and unloading zone during the transferral of

knowledge to and from a CPU.

Bug   An error in a program that causes undesirable results when the program is executed.

Bus   A connection allowing transmissions between computer components.

Business computing systems   Computer-based systems used for business purposes. These include automatic data processing systems, management information systems, and decision support systems.

By-products   Knowledge produced in the manufacture of a decision (e.g., solutions to intermediate problems) in addition to the decision itself.

Byte   A contiguous series of bits (e.g., often eight) representing a single character or digits in a number.

C   A programming language used by professional programmers to develop efficient host, tool, and application system software.

Candidate rules   A group of rules that the inference engine has determined to be of immediate relevance at the present juncture in a reasoning process. These rules will be considered according to a particular selection order and subject to a prescribed degree of rigor.

Cell   The smallest constituent of a spreadsheet. Visually, a spreadsheet's cells are arranged into rows and columns. Each cell is referenced by the row and column in which it exists. A cell can have a definition that indicates how to compute the value of that cell. Advanced spreadsheets allow cells to be defined in terms of commands in addition to traditional expressions.

Cell definition   An indication of what actions the spreadsheet software should take when processing the cell (e.g., an expression that the software evaluates, with the result being displayed to a user).

Cell value   The value (if any) most recently calculated for a cell.

Central memory   See *main memory.*

Central processing unit   A computer's electronic circuitry that carries out software instructions. Main memory is often considered to be a part of the central processing unit.

Centralization   An organization design in which authority is concentrated in a relatively few power centers.

Certainty algebra   The mathematical conventions that are used to combine two or more certainty factors to yield a single certainty factor.

Certainty factor   A numeric measure of the degree of certainty about the *goodness, correctness, likelihood,* etc., of a variable value, an expression value (e.g., a premise), or an assignment action.

Chief information officer   A high-level executive in charge of managing an organization's information who participates with other executives in strategic decision making.

Chief knowledge officer   A high-level executive who

manages the capture, production, and productive use of knowledge in an organization, championing a knowledge-based culture in the organization and contributing a knowledge-based perspective to strategic decision making.

Choice The phase of decision making concerned with choosing one of the alternatives identified via the prior phases of intelligence and design.

Clarification message A message to or from a DSS that requests or provides clarification of some prior message.

Client/server architecture A distributed computing system in which multiple personal computers called clients share the memory and processing capabilities of another (typically larger) computer called a server.

Clipboard A place where data cut or copied from one program's work area may be deposited for subsequent pasting into another program's work area.

Coalition A collection of two or more participants in a negotiation who have agreed to take the same position on issues as the negotiation unfolds.

COBOL Common Business-Oriented Language; a widely used programming language designed for developing business application software.

Codasyl-network Conference on Data Systems Languages; the leading example of the network data model.

Cognitive limit A limit on the human mind's ability to represent or process knowledge.

Cognitive style An individual's approach to acquiring, organizing, discarding, and using knowledge (e.g., during decision making). For instance, the approach may emphasize qualitative knowledge versus quantitative knowledge.

Collaborative authoring system A system that allows multiple authors to collaborate in the production of a document (e.g., a document needed during the process of manufacturing a decision or needed to announce a decision).

Command An imperative statement telling a computer to carry out some task.

Command chain A linkage of decision makers across differing authority levels in an organization.

Command interface A user interface in which a user communicates via a command language.

Command language A language consisting of all commands that a piece of software can understand.

Command unity A situation in which a decision maker is the direct subordinate of no more than one other person in the organization.

Commanding A managerial function concerned with issuing specific instructions to cause things to happen.

Comment A portion of a program (or rule) consisting of internal documentation about the program (or rule).

Communication The exchange of messages resulting in the transferral or creation of knowledge.

Communication network Computer and communication technology that links multiple participants in a joint activity that can range from simply passing messages to group decision making to project management.

Communication support system A computer-based system that enhances its user's ability to communicate.

Communications paths The interconnection of two (or more) devices that allows the transmission of knowledge and requests between them.

Competing rules Those candidate rules that have yet to be considered.

Competitive strategy An organization's plan for staying competitive or achieving a competitive advantage relative to other organizations in its environment.

Compile The act of producing an object program (or rule set) from a source language version of the program (or rule set). The object program can be executed by a computer, whereas the source version cannot.

Compiler Software that carries out the compilation of a set of valid statements in some designated (i.e., source) language.

Completion sequence A portion of a rule set composed of actions that the inference engine will carry out after all reasoning with the rule set's rules has been completed.

Compound DSS A decision support system that incorporates two or more knowledge-management techniques.

Computer-mediated communication The use of computers to create, store, deliver, and process communications.

Computer-supported cooperative work The use of computers to support cooperative work among multiple participants (e.g., collaborative authoring), as distinct from work that may not be cooperative.

Computer teleconferencing Audio-video telecommunication support of simultaneous interactions among participants (e.g., involving conference calls or videoconferencing).

Conclusion A portion of a rule composed of series of one or more actions that the inference engine can legitimately carry out if a rule's premise can be established to be true.

Concepts Pieces of knowledge (ranging from abstract to concrete, from qualitative to quantitative) that can be represented and processed.

Concurrency The situation that exists when a decision maker is working on multiple decision problems simultaneously.

Condition A logical expression composed of a logical variable, of a logical function, or of two expressions connected by a relational operator such as >, =, <=, IN, and so on. The two participating expressions must be of the same type (e.g., both numeric). In the case of the IN operator, the second expression is typically a collection of expressions.

Conditional branching   A programming method that causes the flow of command execution to branch in a certain direction, depending on whether a specified condition is satisfied.

Conditional iteration   A programming method that causes the flow of command execution to iterate through a sequence of commands for as long as a specified condition is satisfied.

Console screen   A device that allows a computer user to view requests he or she makes of the computer and the computer's responses to those requests.

Confederation   An approach to software integration that involves multiple functionally distinct pieces of software, each of which can access the same knowledge representation.

Conferencing   The use of computer and communication technology to conduct a conference without requiring participants to convene in the same place at the same time.

Confirmative certainty   The certainty factor that results from combining two or more certainty factors in such a way that they confirm each other. The resultant confirmative certainty factor is at least as large as the largest contributing certainty factor.

Constant   A known value that never changes.

Consultation   The activity of acquiring or producing expert advice or solutions to a problem.

Consultation environment   The knowledge-processing environment within which expert system consultation occurs.

Control break   A means for separating presented knowledge into groups, where each member of a group has some value in common.

Control commands   Commands in a programming language that are used to control the flow of program execution (e.g., conditional branching commands).

Controlling   A managerial function concerned with ensuring that plans are carried out properly.

Control logic   The logic embedded in a procedure to govern what will happen when and under what circumstances.

Coordinating   A managerial function concerned with harmonizing activities in an organization; ensuring that proper resources are brought into play at appropriate times and that they adequately relate to each other during the course of some activity (e.g., decision making).

Coordination requirements   The requirements for relating a prospective system's interface behavior and its functional behavior.

Coordination system   A system that helps integrate and harmonize the activities of individuals working toward the achievement of some shared goal.

Coordination technology   A field of study concerned with the uses of technology in coordinating the efforts of multiple participants in cooperative, competitive, or conflicting situations.

Corporate planning system   A decision support system that holds and derives knowledge relevant to planning decisions that cut across organizational units and involve all of an organization's functions (i.e., its operations, finance, marketing, personnel, etc.).

Criteria   Standards by which alternatives are judged.

Critical success factors   The factors that have been identified as most important to the success of an organization.

Current state   The present configuration of an organization's resources.

Data processing   See *automatic data processing.*

Data set   A collection of data organized into the format required for input to a particular program (e.g., for numeric analysis by a solver).

Data source   A data set, database, file, or other repository of data that can be used for processing (e.g., for graph generation).

Data warehousing   A strategy of extracting data from large databases (and other sources) for storage in smaller databases, giving managers the ability more easily to explore and analyze data as a basis for faster and improved decisions.

Database control system   Software that accomplishes creation, modification, and retrieval of data for a database in response to a user's data manipulation requests.

Debugging   The activity of identifying and eliminating bugs from a program.

Decentralization   An organization design in which authority is distributed among a relatively large number of participants.

Decisional role   One of the three major types of roles a manager plays, the others being informational and interpersonal.

Decision   The choice of one from among a number of alternatives; a piece of knowledge indicating a commitment to some course of action.

Decision context   The situation within which a decision is made.

Decision maker   An individual, group, team, or other type of organization having the authority to make a decision about what to do.

Decision making   The activity that culminates in the choice of an alternative; the activity of using knowledge as raw materials in the manufacture of knowledge about what to do.

Decision-making phase   One of the three (possibly overlapping) phases in a decision-making process: intelligence, design, and choice.

Decision-making strategy An approach to guiding a decision-making process (e.g., satisficing, optimizing).

Decision room A specially equipped room in which participants in group decision making use computers to mediate and facilitate their interactions in the course of reaching a decision.

Decision support system A computer-based system composed of a language system, presentation system, knowledge system, and problem-processing system whose collective purpose is the support of decision-making activities.

Decision type A particular kind of decision. There are multiple ways to classify decision types (e.g., structured versus unstructured, unilateral versus negotiated).

Declarations Nonexecutable statements that establish a context for actions that will be taken (e.g., the declaration of variable names, types, or sizes in a program).

Default goal The goal that an inference engine pursues if none is specified by the user at the outset of a consultation.

Default table Table that is used in database-management processing if no other table is explicitly specified.

Default value A value that exists unless explicitly changed by a user or program.

Delphi technique A formal approach to collecting views from several people about some topic (e.g., a forecast, a decision problem). The approach is iterative, involving each participant independently providing views in writing to a leader, who provides feedback for the next round in an attempt to foster convergence of views with each successive round.

Demon Procedural knowledge that is automatically executed when certain prespecified events occur.

Dependency diagram A diagram containing nodes for the variables (i.e., factors) that are pertinent to a problem area. The nodes are connected by arrows that portray the dependencies that exist among the variables.

Descriptive knowledge Knowledge about past, present, and hypothetical states of an organization and its environment.

Design A phase of decision making that involves the identification of alternatives, analysis of the likely outcomes of each, and evaluation of those outcomes with respect to the organization's purpose; a part of system development concerned with creating a blueprint to guide the implementation of the system.

Desktop conferencing Allows participants in a joint activity to interact simultaneously through their desktop computers, whose display screens are partitioned into multiple windows for textual, graphical, and video interaction. The computers are also equipped for audio interaction.

Desktop publishing The use of desktop computers for producing high-quality page layouts.

Developer The person(s) involved in specifying system requirements (interface, functional, coordination), designing the system to meet the requirements, and implementing the system according to the designed blueprint.

Development cycle A sequence of steps undertaken in the development of a system, following the identification of a need for the system and proceeding through the installation of the system for operational use. The latter can trigger the former, leading to another cycle of development.

Development tool Software that a developer uses to facilitate the analysis, design, or implementation of a system.

Dictionary Linguistic knowledge consisting of a vocabulary of words available for natural language interaction.

Direct manipulation interface A type of interface in which a user makes requests by manipulating items displayed on a console screen. The displayed items are visual replicas or indicators of nonelectronic counterparts.

Disk A common auxiliary memory medium that stores data magnetically.

Disk drive A common auxiliary memory device that is able directly to store and retrieve knowledge on a disk.

Diskette A floppy (i.e., flexible) disk.

Document An object in which knowledge is represented as pages in a book (e.g., as text, perhaps with pictures and tables). These may be organized sequentially or linked to each other in hypertext fashion.

Do-it-yourself computing The use of software tools by people who are not computer professionals.

Do-it-yourself development Development of a system by the system's intended user (who is typically not a computer professional).

Domain knowledge Knowledge about a particular application area or problem domain.

DP department An organizational unit that builds, manages, and operates data processing systems.

Drill down The ability to see increasingly detailed information about some topic of interest.

DSS See *decision support system*.

Economic limit A limit on knowledge processing or decision making that is due to funding constraints.

Electronic bulletin board A repository of messages that have been sent to it, any of which can be viewed by the bulletin board's users.

Electronic data processing See *automatic data processing*.

Electronic forms An electronic version of traditional paper forms that can be filled in and read, but with calculations being done automatically. Also see *form*.

Electronic mail A communication service that allows

messages to be sent electronically by one person to other specifically designated persons, where they are stored until read.

Electronic meeting system   A computer-based system that facilitates a meeting. When the purpose of the meeting is to make a decision, the system is a DSS (e.g., for a group decision maker).

Electronic spreadsheet   An electronic version of traditional paper grid-like worksheets allowing rapid calculations and what-if analysis.

Elimination-by-aspects   A decision-making strategy that eliminates all alternatives not passing the most important decision criterion (i.e., aspect), then eliminates all that do not pass for the second aspect, and so forth.

Emergent situation   A decision-making context that involves some facets not previously experienced by the decision maker.

Emulation   An activity in which one entity (e.g., a computer) offers the same observable behavior as another (e.g., a human or a computer).

End user   The user of application software; one who is not a computer professional, yet directly uses software tools to meet some of his or her own knowledge-management needs.

End-user computing   See *do-it-yourself computing*.

Environment   An organization's surroundings.

Environment knowledge   See *descriptive knowledge*.

Environment variable   A variable whose value controls the behavior of some aspect of a system.

Established situation   A decision-making context that the decision maker has repeatedly experienced in the past.

Evaluation   The activity of assessing the quality (i.e., validity and/or utility) of a system or the knowledge it contains.

Evolutionary prototype   A partial or simplified version of a system that is developed in a relatively short time with the intent of getting feedback about it as a basis for seeing how to improve it in an iterative way.

Execution   The activity of performing a program's commands.

Executive information system   A decision support system customized to satisfying wide-ranging needs of top executives in selectively filtering, extracting, compressing, and viewing information about the organization and its environment.

Executive support system   A decision support system having features of an executive information system and other capabilities, such as the execution of solvers or the provision of communication support.

Expert system   A computer-based system composed of a user interface, an inference engine, and stored expertise (i.e., a rule set or an entire knowledge sys-

tem). Its purpose is to offer advice or solutions for problems in a particular problem area, thereby functioning as an artificially intelligent DSS. The advice is comparable to that which would be offered by a human expert in that problem area.

Expert system development tool   Software used to facilitate the development of expert systems. The three types of tools are programming languages (and their respective interpreter or compiler software), shells, and AI environments.

Expert system environment   A knowledge-management environment supporting the technique of rule management.

Expert system shell   See *shell*.

Expert testing   The stage of an expert system development cycle in which the advice offered by the system is tested (e.g., by the expert) for correctness.

Explanation   The response that an expert system gives when asked to justify why it gave the advice it did for a particular consultation.

Export   The act of outputting some knowledge system contents into a file whose format is acceptable to another program.

Expression   A constant, variable, or function or a series of constants, variables, and/or functions connected by meaningful operators.

Expression management   A knowledge-management technique in which expressions serve as the representation method and evaluation serves as the processing method.

Extrinsic tool   A development tool that does not become part of the system being developed.

Facilitator   A person or persons who manage the use of a group decision support system from initial planning through actual operation.

Feasibility study   A study of the technical and economic prospects for developing a system prior to actually committing resources to developing it.

Feedback   Knowledge about the behavior of a system or its outcomes that is fed back into the system (e.g., as a basis for system changes that will affect its future behavior and outcomes).

Field   A named category of data. Fields are used in defining the structure of a database.

File   A collection of knowledge that is treated as a whole by the operating system; a collection of data records of some type that can be processed by file management (as opposed to database management) operations.

File-management system   A type of data management that organizes data into files without adhering to any of the major data models.

File transfer   A kind of remote communications in which files are sent and received by connected computers.

Filter A mechanism that excludes unwanted knowledge (e.g., from being assimilated into a knowledge system or from being displayed to a user).

Find actions Those actions stated in a variable description that an inference engine can use (e.g., as an alternative to backward chaining) to find the value of that variable when it is unknown.

Fire See *firing a rule*.

Firing a rule The activity of carrying out the actions in a rule's conclusion once it has been established that the rule's premise is true.

Flowchart A diagram showing the flow of steps for accomplishing some procedure.

Footer A portion of a customized report that appears at the end of the report, at the end of a page, or at the end of each group of report details.

Form A piece of presentation knowledge that indicates the visual layout to display slots, the source of the value that can appear in each slot, and special attributes for the slot (e.g., reverse video, blinking).

Format Same as *picture;* the way in which a file's contents are arranged; the layout of a form, template, or menu.

Format code A code embedded in a piece of text to control some aspect of the way the text will be formatted as it is printed.

Form management The ability to define forms and to subsequently process an entire form at a time with any one of several commands.

Form slot An element of a form through which information can be displayed to and/or collected from a user.

Forms-oriented interface An interface style in which a user interacts by filling in and viewing electronic forms.

FORTRAN FORmula TRANslator; a programming language oriented toward mathematical calculations.

Forward chaining An approach to rule-based reasoning in which the inference engine determines the effect of currently known variable values on unknown variables by firing all rules whose premises can be established as being true.

Forward reasoning See *forward chaining*.

Frame A representation of an object in terms of slots, where there is one slot for each of the object's characteristics. A particular instance of an object consists of a value for each of the frame's slots. The value may be assigned or determined by a procedure attached to the slot. Frames can be related to each other via inheritance slots.

Function A named object whose value is determined by performing a particular kind of operation. The function name (e.g., SQRT) indicates the nature of the operation (e.g., finding a square root). A function typ-

ically has one or more arguments, whose values are operated on in order to determine the function's value. Each argument is an expression.

Functional DSS A decision support system that holds and derives knowledge relevant for decisions about some function an organization performs (e.g., a marketing function, a production function).

Functional requirements A specification of what problem-solving activities a system needs to perform.

Function keys Special keys (labeled F1, F2, etc.) that, when pressed, cause the executing software to take prescribed actions.

Fuzzy set A generalization of the traditional mathematical notion of a set that permits partial membership in a set.

Fuzzy variable A variable that simultaneously has two or more values. The certainty factor of one value may differ from that of another value.

GDSS See *group DSS*.

Generalized problem solver A system developed by Newell and Simon that had the ability to solve a variety of problems that could be expressed in terms of finding a path connecting an initial state and a goal state, involving the discovery of a proper sequence of operators, each of which transforms one state into another.

Genetic algorithm A kind of artificial intelligence procedure that uses biological principles (e.g., reproduction, crossover, mutation) to improve a system's performance based on its problem solving experiences.

Global A variable, form, macro, etc., that continues to exist outside the scope of a single program's execution.

Goal variable A variable whose value an inference engine attempts to determine in the course of a consultation.

Graphical data source Data values that can be used to generate a graphical presentation.

Graphics A knowledge-management technique concerned with the generation and manipulation of figures, plots, and geometric shapes.

Group A simple kind of organization characterized by participants having comparable authority about the group's task (e.g., decision making), little in the way of formal divisions of labor, and few restrictions on who can communicate with whom.

Group DSS A decision support system designed to support a decision or decisions made by a group.

Group memory A facility for recording what a group has discovered and accomplished.

Groupware Computer/communication technology used to facilitate the work of a group (e.g., a GDSS).

Hard copy A copy of computer output, usually on paper.

Hardware   Physical devices that employ electrical, magnetic, and mechanical technology.

Header   A portion of a customized report that appears at the start of the report, at the start of a page, or at the start of a group of report details.

Help text   A textual description that appears on the console screen to help a computer's user.

Heuristic   A rule of thumb. The rules in a rule set may be thought of as being heuristics.

Hierarchical   An early type of data model that allows limited (i.e., treelike) direct representation and processing of one-to-many relationships.

Home page   A World Wide Web site's starting point for hypertext exploration of documents about a particular topic.

Host   A type of software in which other software executes (e.g., operating system, windowing shell).

Human decision support system   A person whose function in an organization is to carry out various knowledge-management tasks for the purpose of supporting the deliberations of a decision maker.

Hyperdocument   A document composed of pages that are linked to represent relationships among them. A user can access pages related to a topic of interest by following a path of links.

Hypertext   A knowledge-management technique in which knowledge is represented in linked documents and processed in a way that allows a user to select a highlighted marker on the currently viewed page to access a linked page about a topic indicated by the marker.

Implementation   A stage of system development in which a system design is transformed into an actual system that operates according to that design.

Import   The act of assimilating the output of another program into the knowledge system being used by the present software.

Incrementalism   The decision strategy of muddling through by picking an alternative that is expected to produce an improvement over the current situation.

Incremental modification   Modification of a system by making refinements, extensions, and corrections to it rather than redeveloping it from scratch in order to meet user needs.

Index   A file that contains index key values and indications of where to find the records having those values, as a basis for fast record access.

Index key   A collection of one or more fields whose collective value for some record serves as a basis for quickly accessing that record.

Induction   A process that attempts to derive general rules (or to build a decision tree) based on example problems and their solutions.

Inference engine   A piece of software that is able to

accept a problem statement from the user, use reasoning knowledge about the problem area in attempting to derive a solution, gather needed problem-specific information (e.g., from the user) in the course of reasoning, explain why it needs this added information, present the solution to the user, and explain the line of reasoning used in reaching the solution.

Information   Descriptive knowledge (characterizing the state of some past, present, future, or hypothetical solution).

Informational role   One of the three major types of roles a manager can play; it is concerned with acquiring, maintaining, and distributing information (and other types of knowledge).

Information center   A component of an organization that helps facilitate do-it-yourself computing.

Information system   See *application system*.

Infrastructure knowledge   Knowledge about an organization's roles, their relationship, and regulations on activities of those who fill the roles.

Initialization sequence   A portion of a rule set composed of actions that the inference engine will carry out before considering the rule set's rules.

Input device   Hardware that allows a user to make requests of or enter knowledge into a computer.

Integrated environment   A tool for building expert systems that integrates the capabilities of a shell with other knowledge-management techniques such as database management, spreadsheet management, and programming.

Integrated software   Software that allows multiple knowledge-management techniques to be coordinated in some way (i.e., confederation, nesting, or synergy).

Intelligence   The first of Simon's three phases of decision making, concerned with recognizing the need for a decision and acquiring knowledge about the decision situation.

Intelligent agent   A computerized mechanism (usually employing artificial intelligence techniques) that carries out certain specialized tasks.

Interactive computing   A mode of computer usage permitting frequent interchanges between a user and the computer in the course of program execution.

Interface   See *user interface*.

Interface requirements   A specification of the style and appearance that a system's user interface needs to possess.

Internet   A global set of interconnected computer networks that gives a knowledge worker access to vast stores of knowledge.

Interpersonal role   One of the three major types of roles a manager can play; concerned with establishing, cultivating, and fulfilling relationships with others.

Interpreter   Software that carries out commands that

have not been previously compiled. These commands may be submitted interactively or in a batch (i.e., as a program).

Interpreting A problem processor's activity of translating a language system request into some action that it can perform.

Interpretive software A program that processes user requests one at a time, immediately processing each.

Intervenor A person, persons, or computer that helps participants in a negotiation reach an agreement.

Interviewing A common approach to knowledge acquisition in which a system developer (e.g., knowledge engineer) interviews a knowledge source (e.g., an expert) in an effort to understand what should go into a knowledge system.

Intrinsic tool A development tool that becomes part of the system being developed.

Invoking Requesting the execution of a particular piece of software.

I/O commands Commands that request some input be accepted or some output be presented.

Issue space All possible positions that can be taken in a negotiation about some matter of contention.

Iteration The repeated execution of a series of commands.

Joint certainty The certainty factor that results from combining two or more certainty factors in such a way that they detract from each other. The resultant joint certainty factor is no larger than the smallest of the contributing certainty factors.

Knowledge An organizational resource consisting of the sum of what is known.

Knowledge acquisition The part of expert system development concerned with eliciting, structuring, and representing an expert's reasoning knowledge.

Knowledge acquisition context The setting within which knowledge acquisition occurs, characterized by the organization, project, and immediate surroundings that influence the outcome of a knowledge acquisition's process.

Knowledge acquisition methods Methods used by knowledge engineers to acquire knowledge from experts (e.g., interviewing, protocol analysis).

Knowledge acquisition process The flow of activities undertaken in the course of knowledge acquisition within some context, involving one or more episodes, one or more participants, and regulations governing the episodes and participants.

Knowledge base That part of an expert system containing application-specific reasoning knowledge that the inference engine uses in the course of reasoning about a problem. In expert systems whose reasoning knowledge is represented as rules, the knowledge base is a rule set or rule base. In some expert systems,

a knowledge base can also contain initial values for variables. The traditional AI notion of "knowledge base" is a small, yet interesting and important, aspect of the much more all-encompassing DSS notion of a knowledge system.

Knowledge-based organization An organization in which the primary, driving activity is the management of knowledge.

Knowledge-based system An AI term that is typically taken to be synonymous with the notion of an expert system. Of course, management information systems and conventional decision support systems are also knowledge-based (i.e., concerned with the representation and processing of knowledge).

Knowledge conversion The conversion of one representation of knowledge (used by a particular program) into another representation of the same knowledge (that can be used by a different program).

Knowledge engineer A person (or group) that acquires reasoning knowledge from a human expert in the course of building an expert system. From the broader DSS viewpoint, anyone who is concerned with building any kind of knowledge into a knowledge system can be considered to be a knowledge engineer.

Knowledge management The activity of representing and processing knowledge.

Knowledge-management environment A type of software tool in which multiple knowledge-management techniques are blended together in a balanced way for use by end users and application software developers.

Knowledge-management technique A technique for representing knowledge in terms of certain kinds of objects and for processing those objects in various ways.

Knowledge-management tool Software that furnishes a developer with one or more knowledge-management techniques.

Knowledge preprocessing The ability of a knowledge worker's workstation to work on responding to requests posed to the knowledge worker before the knowledge worker devotes attention to them.

Knowledge presentation The activity of presenting knowledge in one of many possible modes.

Knowledge processing Actions that are taken to manipulate knowledge representations (e.g., adding, modifying, deleting, and using them).

Knowledge representation The way in which knowledge is symbolized and structured (e.g., in computer memory).

Knowledge selection/derivation The way in which a decision support system's problem processor attempts to satisfy a user's request: by selecting knowledge or by deriving it.

Knowledge system That subsystem of a decision support system in which all application-specific knowledge is represented for use by the problem-processing system. This includes knowledge of any or all types (e.g., descriptive, procedural, reasoning) represented in a variety of ways (e.g., as databases, spreadsheets, procedural solvers, rule sets, text, graphs, forms, templates).

Knowledge type A category or class of knowledge (e.g., descriptive knowledge, procedural knowledge).

Knowledge worker A person who manages various kinds of knowledge in the course of filling some role in an organization.

LAN See *local area network*.

Language system The subsystem of a decision support system that consists of (or characterizes the class of) all acceptable problem statements.

Learning The activity of altering a knowledge system.

Legend An explanatory guide for output such as a graph or a query's result.

Linguistic knowledge Knowledge about languages used for communication purposes.

LISP A programming language that has been used for more than a quarter of a century by computer scientists who work in the AI field. It is oriented toward the processing of symbolic data represented as linked list structures (i.e., LISt Processing). A list structure is processed with various functions such as CAR (returns the first element of a list), CDR (returns all but the first element of a list), and CONS (prefixes one list to another).

Literal element A constant in a form or template.

Local A variable, form, macro, etc., whose existence is local to the program in which it is declared.

Local area network A communications system designed to allow transmissions among two or more devices (e.g., computers) within a small geographic area.

Local DSS A decision support system designed to support ad hoc needs pertaining to some limited aspect of a main organizational function. LDSSs are often developed by their users.

Logical constant A constant that is true or false.

Logical data structuring The knowledge representation (as opposed to processing) aspect of a data model.

Logical expression An expression whose value (if it is known) is either true or false.

Logical function A function whose value is true or false.

Logical variable A variable whose value is at present either true or false.

Loop A series of commands that can be executed repeatedly during the execution of a program; usually the commands involved in conditional iteration.

Machine learning The ability of a computer system to alter its behavior through either supervised or unsupervised learning.

Macro A name that is given to a sequence of keystrokes such that the name can be used instead of the keystroke sequence when interacting with computer software.

Mail merge The merging of different data values into repeated copies of the same basic text in order to produce customized versions of the text.

Mainframe A large-scale computer, generally having greater capacity and processing power than a microcomputer.

Main memory The portion of a CPU whose contents (i.e., data, programs, rules, forms, graphs, etc.) can be immediately processed by the CPU's arithmetic, logic, and control circuitry.

Management control A decision-making context in which decisions are concerned with ensuring that resources are acquired, utilized, and released to meet organizational objectives.

Management information system An application system for keeping current records about some aspect of an organization or its environment.

Management science The formal (e.g., mathematical) study of methods for solving managerial problems, from the operational to strategic level and including all functional areas of management.

Management science package Software that implements one or more solvers devised by management scientists and requiring a particular data set format.

Management support system A computer-based system that facilitates a manager's tasks (e.g., knowledge-management, communication, decision-making tasks).

Manager One who uses available resources to achieve some objective; a decision maker.

Managerial functions The functions that a manager performs (e.g., planning, organizing, commanding, coordinating, controlling).

Managerial roles The roles that a manager plays (e.g., interpersonal, informational, decisional).

Many-to-many relationship A relationship in which each instance of either object can be related to many instances of the other object.

Many-to-one relationship A relationship in which many instances of one object are related to at most one instance of another object.

Map An overview of the documents linked in a hypertext knowledge-management system.

Marker A highlighted indicator in a hypertext document indicating a link to another document whose content is related to the passage containing the marker.

Menu A collection of options available for user selection.

Menu management A knowledge-management technique concerned with the storage and processing of knowledge about menus.

Menu options The items in a presented menu that

are available for a system's user to select.

Message   A particular knowledge representation assembled by a sender for transmission to a receiver(s).

Message system   Computer/communication technology that accomplishes message passing among senders and receivers (e.g., electronic bulletin board, electronic mail).

Meta-knowledge   Knowledge about knowledge.

Microcomputer   A small (desktop or laptop) computer consisting of a system unit, keyboard, auxiliary memory devices, console screen, and perhaps a speaker and printer.

Minicomputer   A medium-sized computer whose capacity, processing power, and cost generally fall between those of microcomputers and mainframes.

MIS   See *management information system.*

MIS department   An organizational unit responsible for building, maintaining, operating, and managing management information systems (and perhaps other kinds of business computing systems as well).

Model   A solver; a problem statement for a solver; data input to a solver.

Model base   A computerized collection of knowledge about models.

Modem   MOdulator-DEModulator; a device that connects a computer to a communications line, handling the conversion between digital and analog signals.

Module   A program that can be performed by other programs.

Mosaic   Software for multimedia browsing on the World Wide Web.

Multiparticipant DSS   A decision support system that supports multiple participants engaged in a decision-making task (or functions as one of the participants).

Multiparticipant task   A task that involves multiple participants, each of which could be an individual, a computer, or some unit composed of persons and/or computers.

Natural language   A kind of user interface that allows the user to carry on a conversation with a computer-based system in much the same way as he or she would converse with another human. The system is able to learn new terms, understand new requests in the context of prior requests, overlook grammatical errors, and carry out actions implied by the conversation.

Navigation   The activity of following markers to find desired knowledge in a hypertext system.

Negotiation   A give-and-take interchange among multiple participants that proceeds until all agree on a particular alternative (or a breakdown occurs to terminate the negotiation).

Negotiation support system   A system that helps those involved in a negotiation to reach an agreement.

Nemawashi-based process   A decision-making process involving a coordinator's efforts to achieve a consensus of participants across multiple levels of authority in an organization.

Nested integration   The approach to software integration in which all secondary components are constrained to being used within the confines of a single dominant component.

Network   A collection of devices connected in such a way that they can communicate with each other via transmission of requests and/or knowledge; a type of data model that is less restrictive than the hierarchical in allowing direct representation and processing of one-to-many relationships.

Network organization   See *virtual corporation.*

Neural network   An approach to machine learning (inspired by biological studies of the brain and nervous system) in which simple processors are organized into layers. Collectively, they "learn" from experience by a process of adjusting weights that determine the activation levels of individual processors (i.e., neurons).

Nominal group technique   A series of activities intended to aid group decision making; individuals write down their own ideas, the ideas are shared in a round-robin fashion, they are discussed in sequence, alternatives are individually listed and ranked, and the votes are pooled to determine the group's decision.

Nonliteral element   A position in a form where a value of a nonconstant expression can be presented or where a value can be accepted for assignment to a variable (e.g., working variable, field, cell).

Nonprocedural   Indicates that a procedure (i.e., a definite *sequence* of steps) is not specified. That is, there is no programming. Reasoning knowledge captured in the guise of a rule set's rules is nonprocedural. Queries are nonprocedural.

Numeric constant   A number composed of digits, an optional decimal point, and optional sign.

Numeric expression   An expression whose value (if it is known) is a number. The expression can involve numeric constants, numeric operators such as +, -, *, /, **, and MOD (modulus).

Numeric function   A function that yields a numeric value with respect to its argument(s).

Numeric variable   A variable whose value is presently a number. An integer variable is a special case of a numeric variable in that its value is an integer.

Object-oriented language   A language for representing objects and processing those representations with various methods. The methods available for processing an object (e.g., a spreadsheet cell, a database record, a graph, a form, a variable, etc.) depend on the nature of that object.

Object program   A program whose commands are in a language that can be immediately understood (i.e., carried out) by a particular computer.

Off-line   Situation in which a device is not actively connected to, under the direct control of, or in direct communication with a computer's CPU.

Off-the-shelf software   Generic software designed for a class of users rather than for the customized needs of a specific user.

One-to-many relationship   A relationship in which each instance of one object can be related to many instances of a second object, but no occurrence of the second object is related to more than one occurrence of the first object (i.e., a reverse way of viewing a many-to-one relationship).

One-to-one relationship   A relationship in which each instance of either object is related to no more than one instance of the other object.

On-line   Situation in which a device is actively connected to, under the direct control of, or in direct communication with a computer's CPU.

Open architecture   An approach to software design in which the software can make use of the output from other software (imports), furnish inputs that can be used by other software (exports), run other software (as a host), and/or communicate with other computers.

Operating system   A common type of host software that controls the operation of a computer in such a way that other programs can be executed.

Operation   The portion of a system life cycle involving the use of an implemented system, including an evaluation of its practical capabilities.

Operational control   A decision-making context in which decisions are concerned with ensuring that specific tasks are performed efficiently and effectively by operating personnel.

Option   One of the user-selectable processing alternatives presented in a menu.

Optimize   The decision strategy of choosing the alternative that gives the best overall value.

Organization   A system of resources structured by power centers according to some purpose within the context of some environment.

Organizational DSS   A multiparticipant DSS designed to support a decision maker having a more elaborate infrastructure than a group (i.e., involving specialized roles, restricted communication patterns, differing authority levels).

Organization design   The particular relationships that exist among an organization's managers (e.g., authority relationships, communication relationships).

Organization infrastructure   An organization's roles, the relationships among them, and regulations governing the filling of roles and utilization of relationships.

Organization resources   The money, material, people, and knowledge that belong to an organization.

Organizing   A managerial function concerned with selecting, training, assigning, and evaluating workers.

Output device   Hardware that displays a computer's requests or knowledge to a user.

Package   A program, usually with accompanying documentation, written by a software vendor and typically offered for sale.

Packaging   The part of a decision-manufacturing process concerned with determining appropriate presentations for responses.

Parameter   A term whose value influences the behavior of a program when the program is executed.

Parity bits   Extra bits that accompany bytes for the purpose of checking the validity of the byte during communications or transfer from auxiliary memory to main memory.

Pascal   A programming language popular among computer scientists.

Password   A sequence of characters that must be entered in order to gain access to the processing capabilities of a program or to some stored knowledge resource.

Pattern recognition   A branch of artificial intelligence concerned with recognizing the meaning of a visual or audio pattern.

Peripheral device   A device (e.g., printer, auxiliary memory) that complements a computer's CPU.

Personal computer   See *microcomputer.*

Picture   A sequence of placeholders and possibly some literal symbols that control the appearance of a value as it is being displayed.

Planning   A managerial function concerned with making forecasts, formulating outlines of things to do, and identifying methods to accomplish them.

Pointer   An internal indicator telling where a record is located within a table or on disk.

Postrelational database   A database whose records are not restricted to tabular, hierarchical, or network organization and processing. All types of real-world relationships (e.g., one-to-one, one-to-many, recursive, forked) can be directly represented in a semantically lucid manner and can be processed with various postrelational access languages. This kind of database is sometimes called a multiarchical, associative, or extended-network database.

Power centers   Those within an organization who direct the structuring of its resources.

Preactions   A portion of a rule consisting of actions that the inference engine will carry out before examining the rule's premise.

Premise   A portion of a rule composed of one or more conditions connected by Boolean operators such as AND, OR, XOR (exclusive OR), and NOT. If a rule's premise can be established as being true, then the rule's conclusion is valid. A premise is an example of a logical expression.

Premise-testing strategy The strategy that an inference engine uses when trying to establish the truth of a rule's premise.

Presentation knowledge Knowledge that control's the way in which presentations are made.

Presentation system The component of a DSS that consists of all responses a problem processor can make.

Primary memory See *main memory*.

Problem definition An early part of system development involving a specification of what problems the system will address.

Problem-processing system That subsystem of a decision support system that accepts problems stated in terms of the language system and draws on the knowledge system in an effort to produce solutions.

Problem processor See *problem-processing system*.

Problem recognition The activity of detecting that a problem exists that needs to be solved (e.g., in the course of decision making).

Problem solving The activity of manipulating knowledge to arrive at a solution for a stated problem.

Problem statement A user's request that characterizes the nature of a problem that a system is to solve.

Procedural Indicates that a procedure (i.e., an explicit *sequence* of steps) has been specified. A program has been devised stating, in detail, how to accomplish a task.

Procedural knowledge Knowledge about how to produce a desired result by carrying out a prescribed series of processing steps.

Procedural model A program that represents a piece of procedural knowledge about how to analyze some set of input data. When a procedural model (e.g., for regression analysis) is executed, it carries out a prescribed algorithm and reports the results. See *solver*.

Procedure The step-by-step specification of how to accomplish some task. Also see *program*.

Program A sequence of commands that a computer can execute.

Programmer One who captures procedural knowledge as a program.

Programming language A formal language for representing procedural knowledge as a program.

PROLOG A programming language that has been used for more than a decade by computer scientists who work in the AI field. It is oriented toward processing Horn clause axioms (a particular kind of axiom allowed in first-order predicate calculus). These axioms are processed by a resolution theorem prover using the principle of unification.

Prompt A program's way of alerting the user that it is awaiting either a request or some additional knowledge before continuing its processing activities.

Protocol analysis An approach to knowledge acquisition in which an expert "thinks aloud" for a knowledge engineer during the process of reasoning about particular problems.

Prototype A sketchy, tentative, incomplete version of an envisioned system. It can be developed relatively quickly to get feedback about its features and feasibility.

Purpose The specific reason for which an organization exists.

Query A nonprocedural request (e.g., for some database manipulation to be performed).

Query language A nonprocedural language for exploring, and analyzing (e.g., what-if processing) descriptive knowledge.

Query processing system Software that transforms requests stated in a query language into data-manipulation commands that a database control system can execute.

Question/answer interface An interface style in which the system poses questions to a user who must answer each question before processing proceeds.

RAM Random Access Memory; a kind of main memory whose contents can be altered by the CPU.

Raw materials Knowledge used in the making of decisions.

Real-time computer conferencing system A system that allows participants in a joint activity to interact with each other at the same time through their respective computers using text and graphical images.

Reason The part of a rule that explains its rationale.

Reasoning knowledge Knowledge about what circumstances allow particular conclusions to be considered to be valid.

Reasoning system A system that employs reasoning knowledge in the course of solving problems.

Record A group of data values consisting of one value for each of a prescribed set of relational fields; an occurrence of a record type.

Record-keeping The activity of keeping records about some subject matter as a basis for subsequent retrieval and calculation.

Record type An aggregate of conceptually related fields that represents the attributes of some real-world object (concept or entity).

Redevelopment The development of a new system to replace an existing one (in contrast to making incremental modifications to the existing system).

Redundancy The repetition of the same field in multiple record types (e.g., as the means for representing relationships in a relational data base); the repetition of the same data value in multiple records.

Regulations Constraints governing the assignment of participants to roles and the interactions that can occur among them.

Relation   See *table*.

Relational algebra   The low-level access language whose commands produce new intermediate tables by operating on one or two existing tables.

Relational calculus   The high-level access language whose commands operate on multiple tables simultaneously without requiring any intermediate tables.

Relational database   A database whose records are organized into tables that can be processed by either the relational algebra or relational calculus. Relationships between tables are represented by field redundancy.

Relational knowledge   Knowledge about those with whom interactions can occur (e.g., a DSS's knowledge about idiosyncrasies of its users).

Relational operator   The operator in a condition that relates one expression to another (e.g., >, <, =).

Remote communications   The transmission of requests and knowledge between two computers that may be far apart geographically.

Report details   The primary contents of a customized report in which each report detail adheres to the same form.

Report generation   A technique of presenting descriptive and calculated (i.e., derived) knowledge in a customized manner without needing to write a program.

Report template   A characterization of the layout and content of a type of report.

Request   An element of a DSS's language system.

Resource structuring   A manager's effort at arranging an organization's resources in order to accomplish its purpose with a high degree of productivity (i.e., with little waste of resources).

Response   An element of a DSS's presentation system.

Retrieval service   A service that lets a subscriber link his or her computer to a network to allow retrieval of knowledge held in a remote computer's files.

Reverse reasoning   See *backward chaining*.

Rigor   An indication of how exhaustive an inference engine is in considering candidate rules. Will all rules be considered (full rigor), or is it possible for some competing rules to be disregarded?

Role   A prescribed set of activities and duties to be performed within an organization.

Rule   A named fragment of reasoning knowledge consisting of a premise and a conclusion. In addition, a rule may have other attributes, such as a textual description and an internal comment.

Rule base   The collection of all rule sets available to an inference engine.

Rule comment   A developer's documentation on the nature of a rule.

Rule management   A technique of knowledge management concerned with rule representation and processing.

Rule set   A named collection of rules that represent reasoning knowledge about some problem area. A rule set is used by an inference engine to solve specific problems in that area. In addition to rules, a rule set may also contain an initialization sequence, a completion sequence, and variable descriptions.

Rule set developer   A person who uses a rule set development tool to capture an expert's reasoning knowledge in the guise of a rule set (see *knowledge engineer*).

Rule set manager   Software that is used to formally specify, modify, analyze, and compile a rule set.

Rule set specification   The formal representation of an expert's reasoning knowledge about some problem domain.

Run   The activity of executing a program.

Satisficing   A decision-making strategy of selecting the first alternative discovered that happens to be good enough with respect to some minimal criteria.

Schema   The logical data structure designed for a particular application, representing all types of relevant objects (in terms of record types) and their interrelationships.

SDLC   See *system development life cycle*.

Secondary memory   See *auxiliary memory*.

Secondary storage   See *auxiliary memory*.

Security   Deals with the protection of knowledge from unauthorized disclosure, modification, and usage.

Selection order   The order in which the competing rules remaining for a group of candidate rules are to be considered (e.g., based on relative rule priorities, costs, positions, numbers of unknown variables in premises, etc.).

Semantic net   A graphical representation of binary relationships between objects. Each node in the net represents an object. Two nodes are related by an arrow that points from one to the other. The arrow is labeled to indicate the semantics of the relationship. The postrelational data model's logical structuring facilities have a great deal in common with semantic nets.

Semantics   The meaning of a symbol, expression, or relationship; the meaning of a representation.

Semiprocedural   Requests that are neither procedural nor nonprocedural.

Sensor   Hardware or software that records the occurrence of some event.

Shell   A kind of expert system development tool consisting of two stand-alone pieces of software: a rule set manager and an inference engine capable of reasoning with rule sets built with the rule set manager; a kind of host software for executing other software.

Software   See *program*.

Software integration   Designing a problem processor to allow the use of multiple knowledge-management techniques via a single decision support system.

Solver A program that solves problems of a particular type in response to corresponding problem statements.

Solver management A knowledge-management technique concerned with representing and processing solver modules.

Solver module A solver that may be used with other solver modules to form a larger solver.

Sort key One or more fields whose values in records are used as a basis for sorting those records.

Source program A program written in a language that a computer's hardware cannot directly execute. The source program is either compiled into an object program whose commands the machine can understand or its commands are interpreted one at a time by another piece of software.

Spreadsheet A collection of cells whose values can be displayed on the console screen. By changing cell definitions and having all cell values reevaluated, a user can readily observe the effects of those changes.

Spreadsheet management A knowledge-management technique concerned with representing knowledge in terms of spreadsheets and processing those representations.

SQL See *structured query language.*

Staff assistant An individual who assists a manager (e.g., as a human decision support system).

Stand-alone tool A software tool that supports one knowledge-management technique in isolation from other techniques.

State The structure and content of an organization's monetary, human, material, and knowledge resources.

Strategic planning A decision-making context in which decisions are concerned with establishing organizational purposes, determining objectives, and setting policies on the handling of resources.

String constant A string of text composed of alphabetic characters, digits, punctuation, and/or other recognizable symbols.

String expression An expression whose value (if it is known) is a string of text. The expression can involve string constants, string variables, and/or string functions connected by the string concatenation (+) operator.

String function A function that yields a text string value with respect to its arguments.

String variable A variable whose value is presently a string of text composed of alphabetic characters, digits, punctuation, and/or other recognizable symbols.

Structured argumentation A coordination method that channels interactions that can occur among participants by requiring them to represent explicitly and adhere to a pattern of arguments and counterarguments about decision alternatives.

Structured decision The result of a routine or repetitive decision-making process.

Structured query language A query language designed for processing descriptive knowledge represented as relational data tables; a collection of commands that, in addition to the query capability, gives application developers data-management capabilities for creating and manipulating tables of data.

Subprogram See *module.*

Substitution indicator An indicator that, when prefacing a variable, causes the value of the variable to be substituted for the variable in a command.

Switch See *environment variable.*

Symbol An arrangement (e.g., visual, electronic) that represents some elemental piece of knowledge.

Synergistic integration The approach to software integration in which each component can be used independently or multiple components can be used in tandem to produce an overall effect that is greater than the sum of the individual component effects. There are no clear dividing lines between component capabilities, and no component limits the use of any other.

Syntax The way in which symbols are (or can be) arranged to represent relationships among pieces of knowledge; the form of a representation.

System An organized collection of components, designed and coordinated for the purpose of filling some defined role.

System analysis The activity of studying a phenomenon or a need in order to more fully understand it and to determine ways to improve or address it.

System design The activity of formulating a plan to guide the implementation of a system that will meet the requirements identified by a systems analyst.

System development life cycle A systematic approach to developing computing systems, especially large-scale systems built by professional developers.

System knowledge A system's knowledge of itself.

System unit Piece of hardware housing a computer's CPU and frequently some auxiliary memory as well.

Table A named collection of records of some record type. Each record is composed of one data value for each of the record type's fields. A table is not a file but may exist in one or more operating system files.

Task support system A computer-based system that supports a human or computer in performance of a task (e.g., a knowledge-management task, decision task, communication task).

Team A hierarchically designed organization in which there is one deciding participant and one or more supporting participants. In contrast to a group, there is clear differentiation of decision-making authority, a division of labor into distinctly specialized duties, and a restricted pattern of communication.

Template A piece of presentation knowledge that indicates the visual layout of a report's contents and the sources of values that can appear in particular locations; a piece of procedural knowledge consisting of spreadsheet cell definitions.

Terminal A device for interacting with a computer by entering requests, entering knowledge, and viewing knowledge (e.g., console screen with keyboard).

Terminal emulation A kind of remote communications in which one computer behaves as a terminal of another computer.

Test case A sample problem and solution that can be used to test whether a system (e.g., an expert system) behaves as desired.

Text editing A minimal kind of text management, of primary interest to programmers who are not concerned with narrative text.

Text management A technique of knowledge management in which knowledge is represented and processed as pieces of text.

Text processing The activity of manipulating (creating, altering, viewing) passages of text, usually in the guise of separate documents. In the case of hypertext, processing includes navigation among documents.

Text presentations System responses that appear as passages of text.

Throwaway prototype A prototype developed for exploratory purposes without the intent of modifying it so it could evolve into an operational system.

Time limit A constraint on decision making that requires it to be accomplished in a certain amount of time.

Toggle A means for switching back and forth between two alternatives.

Tool A class of software that operates within a host but is not oriented toward any particular application. A software tool is used by computer professionals to build application systems and by nonprofessionals for do-it-yourself computing.

Top-down design An approach to designing a system in which the major characteristics are specified first. The process is then repeated with respect to each of these until all details are fully specified.

Tracing The activity of following step-by-step through some stated logic (e.g., in a program or rule set) to see whether the results at each step conform to what is intended. When deviations are identified, they indicate where the logic needs to be modified.

Transaction A particular event such as a sale to a customer, receipt of a payment, shipment of a product, paying an employee, etc.

Transaction generation The ability of a data processing system to produce transactions such as checks, bills, shipping labels, etc.

Unilateral decision A decision made by a single individual as opposed to requiring the agreement of multiple participants.

Unknown expression An expression whose value is not known because the value of at least one of the expression's variables is unknown.

Unknown threshold The certainty factor level below which a variable or premise value is considered to be unknown.

Unknown variable A variable whose value is presently unknown.

Unstructured decision The result of rare or novel decision-making processes.

User The person (or machine) that uses a program executing on some computer hardware. The user may be a computer professional or an end user.

User-friendly interface A system's interface that its user judges to be easy to learn, understand, and use; an interface in which the system's LS is a subset of a user's PS and the system's PS is a subset of the user's LS.

User interface The means by which a user is able to interact with an executing program.

User testing A stage in expert system development in which the system's prospective user checks the interface to see whether it is appropriate.

Utility The usefulness (clarity, meaning, relevance, importance) of some body of knowledge.

Validity The accuracy, certainty, and consistency of some body of knowledge.

Variable A named object whose value can change. A variable's present value is referenced via the variable's name.

Variable descriptions That portion of a rule set consisting of descriptions of the natures of variables used in the rule set's rules. Each variable can be described in terms of such characteristics as its find actions and the timing of those actions.

Variable specifications The characterizations of variables involved in a rule set.

Virtual corporation A collection of separate firms that function as integral parts of a greater organization.

Virtual field A field whose values are calculated as needed rather than actually being stored in a database.

Web browser Software on a desktop computer that gives access to the World Wide Web.

Web server A computer that manages a knowledge storehouse at a site on the World Wide Web and handles the distribution of its contents across the Internet.

What-if processing A kind of analysis in which a user examines the impacts of certain potential changes without actually making changes in the knowledge system's basic contents.

Wild-card symbol A symbol that, when encountered in a text string, is considered to match with any other symbol(s).

Window A portion of a console screen for viewing a

desired part of a spreadsheet, piece of text, table, and so on; a portion of a console screen through which a user interacts with an executing program.

Windowing shell A type of host software that allows a user to interact with separate programs through separate windows.

Word processing The most elaborate and extensive variety of text management, of primary interest for heavy-duty document preparation.

Word wrap The ability of text-management software automatically to move the cursor to the next line and place a partially completed word at the beginning of that new line when the right margin is reached.

Work area A portion of main memory devoted to holding knowledge being processed by an executing software package. See *working memory*.

Working memory Short-term memory; a portion of a problem processing system that temporarily stores knowledge representations needed for the current work of the problem processor software.

World Wide Web The Internet's collection of thousands of hyperlinked sites, each with a storehouse of knowledge that can be presented in graphical, multimedia fashion on desktop computers that have access to the Web.

Directory of Publications

To stay abreast of ongoing advances in the decision support system field, it is helpful to monitor a variety of periodicals that publish articles dealing with DSS issues and the proceedings of conferences concerned with DSS research. We identify leading periodicals that should be candidates for monitoring and provide a directory for contacting the publisher of each for sample copies and subscription information. We also provide the table of contents for the proceedings of the most recent conference of the International Society for Decision Support Systems.

LEADING BUSINESS COMPUTING PERIODICALS

A recent study of periodicals relevant to business computing identifies a top tier of 19 publications ("A Citation Analysis of Business Computing Research," *Information and Management* 25, no. 5, 1993). It does so by combining the results of seven studies that rank such periodicals based on various objective and subjective criteria. Alphabetically, the top tier consists of the following journals:

ACM Computing Surveys
ACM Transactions on Database Systems
ACM Transactions on Information Systems
Communications of the ACM
Data Management
Datamation
Decision Sciences
Decision Support Systems
Harvard Business Review
IEEE Transactions on Software Engineering
Information and Management
Information Systems Management
Interfaces
Journal of Computer Information Systems
Journal of Management Information Systems
Journal of Systems Management
Management Science
MIS Quarterly
Sloan Management Review

To these we add a prominent journal that is too new to have been considered in the seven studies:

Information Systems Research

LEADING DECISION SUPPORT SYSTEM PERIODICALS

More specifically, another study focuses on ranking DSS-related periodicals based on more than 7,500 citations in recently published DSS articles ("An Empirical Assessment and Categorization of Journals Relevant to DSS Research," *Decision Support Systems*, 14, No. 3, 1995). It found the top 20 journals influencing the DSS field to be as follows.

Rank		Journal Name
1		*Decision Support Systems*
2		*Management Science*
3		*Communications of the ACM*
4		*MIS Quarterly*
5		*Artificial Intelligence*
6		*Operations Research*
7		*Decision Sciences*
8		*IEEE Transactions on Systems, Man, and Cybernetics*
9		*Journal of Management Information Systems*
10		*European Journal of Operational Research*
11		*IEEE Transactions on Software Engineering*
12	(tie)	*Computer Interfaces*
14		*International Journal of Man-Machine Studies*
15	(tie)	*DATA BASE*
		Harvard Business Review
17		*Journal of the ACM*
18		*ACM Transactions on Database Systems*
19		*ACM Transactions on Information Systems*

20   *Information and Management*

LEADING EXPERT SYSTEMS PERIODICALS

A recent study used about 15,000 citations by expert system articles to identify a top tier of the periodicals that have had the greatest impact on the expert system field ("The Impact of Periodicals on Expert System Research," *IEEE Expert* 9, No. 6, 1994). Ten journals ranked in this top tier are as follows:

Rank	Journal Name
1	*IEEE Expert*
2 (tie)	*Artificial Intelligence*
	AI Magazine
4	*Expert Systems*
5 (tie)	*International Journal of Man-Machine Studies*
	Machine Learning
7	*Communications of the ACM*
8	*Knowledge Acquisition*
9	*AI Expert*
10	*Expert Systems with Applications*

To these we add another journal that is too new to have placed in this study: *Intelligent Systems in Accounting, Finance, and Management*. Also, note that *Knowledge Acquisition* and *International Journal of Man-Machine Studies* have recently merged to form a new journal: *International Journal of Human-Computer Studies*.

LEADING ORGANIZATIONAL COMPUTING PERIODICALS

A substantial segment of the DSS field overlaps with the organizational computing field. Journals that are oriented toward this overlap include the following:

Collaborative Computing
Computer Supported Cooperative Work
Decision Support Systems
Group Decision and Negotiation
The Information Society
International Information Systems
Journal of Global Information Management
Journal of Organizational Computing
Organization Science

PUBLISHER INFORMATION

Information about subscribing to the foregoing periodicals can be obtained from the following sources:

ACM Computing Surveys
Association for Computing Machinery

1515 Broadway
New York, NY 10036-5701

ACM Transactions on Database Systems
Association for Computing Machinery
1515 Broadway
New York, NY 10036-5701

ACM Transactions on Information Systems
Association for Computing Machinery
1515 Broadway
New York, NY 10036-5701

AI Expert
Miller Freeman Inc.
600 Harrison Street
San Francisco, CA 94107

AI Magazine
American Association for Artificial Intelligence
445 Burgess Drive
Menlo Park, CA 94025-3496

Artificial Intelligence
Elsevier Science, Inc.
Journal Information Center
655 Avenue of the Americas
New York, NY 10010

Collaborative Computing
Chapman & Hall
2–6 Boundary Row
London SE1 8HN, UK

Communications of the ACM
Association for Computing Machinery
1515 Broadway
New York, NY 10036-5701

Computer
The Institute of Electrical and Electronics Engineers
345 East 47th St.
New York, NY 10017-2394

Computer Supported Cooperative work
Kluwer Academic Publishers
P.O. Box 358
Accord Station
Hingham, MA 02018-0358

ComputerWorld
P.O. Box 2043
Marion, OH 43305-2403

DATA BASE
Association for Computing Machinery
1515 Broadway
New York, NY 10036-5701

Data Management
Data Processing Management Association

505 Busse Highway
Park Ridge, IL 60068

Datamation
8773 South Ridgeline Blvd.
Highlands Ranch, CO 80126-2329

Decision Sciences
Decision Sciences Institute
College of Business Administration
Georgia State University
Atlanta, GA 30303

Decision Support Systems
Elsevier Science, Inc.
Journal Information Center
655 Avenue of the Americas
New York, NY 10010
        or
International Society for Decision Support Systems
P.O. Box 26595
Austin, TX 78755-0595

European Journal of Operational Research
Elsevier Science, Inc.
Journal Information Center
655 Avenue of the Americas
New York, NY 10010

Expert Systems
Learned Information Ltd.
Woodside, Hinksey Hill
Oxford OX1 5AU, UK

Expert Systems with Applications
Pergamon Press, Inc.
395 Saw Mill River Rd.
Elmsford, NY 10523

Group Decision and Negotiation
Kluwer Academic Publishers
P.O. Box 358
Accord Station
Hingham, MA 02018-0358

Harvard Business Review
Subscription Service
P.O. Box 52623
Boulder, CO 80322-2623

IEEE Expert
The Institute of Electrical and Electronics Engineers
345 East 47th St.
New York, NY 10017-2394

IEEE Transactions on Software Engineering
The Institute of Electrical and Electronics Engineers
345 East 47th St.
New York, NY 10017-2394

IEEE Transactions on Systems, Man, and Cybernetics
The Institute of Electrical and Electronics Engineers
345 East 47th St.
New York, NY 10017-2394

Information and Management
Elsevier Science, Inc.
Journal Information Center
655 Avenue of the Americas
New York, NY 10010

The Information Society
Taylor & Francis, Inc.
1900 Frost Road, Suite 101
Bristol, PA 19007

Information Systems Management
Auerbach Publications
Warren Gorham Lamont
210 South Street
Boston, MA 02111

Information Systems Research
Institute for Operations Research and the
    Management Sciences
940-A Elkridge Landing Road
Linthicum, MD 21090-2909

*Intelligent Systems in Accounting, Finance, and
    Management*
John Wiley & Sons Ltd.
Baffins Lane
Chichester
West Sussex PO19 1UD, UK

Interfaces
Institute for Operations Research and the
    Management Sciences
940-A Elkridge Landing Road
Linthicum, MD 21090-2909

International Information Systems
HBJ Professional Publishing
1250 Sixth Avenue
San Diego, CA 92101-9803

*International Journal of Expert Systems: Research
    and Applications*
JAI Press
55 Old Post Road, No. 2
P.O. Box 1678
Greenwich, CT 06836-1678

International Journal of Human-Computer Studies
Academic Press Limited
24–28 Oval Road
London NW1 7DX, UK

International Journal of Man-Machine Studies
Academic Press Limited

24–28 Oval Road
London NW 7DX, UK

Journal of the ACM
Association for Computing Machinery
1515 Broadway
New York, NY 10036-5701

Journal of Computer Information Systems
International Association for Computer Information
  Systems
217 College of Business
Oklahoma State University
Stillwater, OK 74078

Journal of Global Information Management
Idea Group Publishing
4811 Jonestown Road, no. 230
Harrisburg, PA 17109

Journal of Management Information Systems
M. E. Sharp, Inc.
80 Business Park Drive
Armonk, NY 10504

Journal of Organizational Computing
Ablex Publishing Corporation
355 Chestnut St.
Norwood, NJ 06748

Journal of Systems Management
P.O. Box 38370
Cleveland, OH 44138-0370

Knowledge Acquisition
Academic Press Limited
24–28 Oval Road
London NW 1 7DX, UK

Machine Learning
Kluwer Academic Publishers
P.O. Box 358
Accord Station
Hingham, MA 02108-0358

Management Science
Institute for Operations Research and the
  Management Sciences
940-A Elkridge Landing Road
Linthicum, MD 21090-2909

MIS Quarterly
MIS Research Center
271 19th Avenue South
University of Minnesota
Minneapolis, MN 55455

Operations Research
Institute for Operations Research and the
  Management Sciences

940-A Elkridge Landing Road
Linthicum, MD 21090-2909

Organization Science
Institute for Operations Research and the
  Management Sciences
940-A Elkridge Landing Road
Linthicum, MD 21090-2909

Sloan Management Review
P.O. Box 55255
Boulder, CO 80322-5255

DECISION SUPPORT SYSTEM CONFERENCES

Attending conferences that focus on decision support
system issues is another way to stay current on break-
ing developments in the field. Such conferences are
organized by ISDSS, the International Society for
Decision Support Systems. The contents of the most
recent ISDSS Conference are given here. The next
ISDSS conference is tentatively planned to be in
Europe in the summer of 1997. Information about
ISDSS can be obtained by contacting the International
Society for Decision Support Systems, P.O. Box 26595,
Austin, TX 78755-0595.

THE INTERNATIONAL SOCIETY FOR DECISION SUPPORT SYSTEMS THIRD ANNUAL CONFERENCE: CONFERENCE PROCEEDINGS (JUNE 22–23, 1995)

Preface *The Department of Information and Systems
Management, Hong Kong University of Science and
Technology is proud to host the Third International
Conference on Decision Support Systems (ISDSS'95).
This is the first time that this conference is held in Asia.
Previous conferences were held in Austin, USA and
Ulm, Germany.*

*The purpose of the conference is to promote discus-
sion and interaction among members of the information systems community with research interests in cut-
ting-edge decision support systems. ISDSS'95 seeks
exchange of emerging and innovative research ideas
and results which will not only lay foundation for further research, but also benefit the business community.*

*The Organizing Committee has made every effort to
present the scientific program filled with new ideas and
important discoveries, as well as social events to promote participants' interaction.*

*A total of eighty-four papers have been selected for
the conference. In addition to the opening address and
the plenary session, four parallel sessions are scheduled
over the two-day conference. The two-volume conference include two types of contributions: research papers
and research-in-progress (abstracts). All together, they*

cover a wide range of theoretical and applied DSS-related research. A special effort of this conference is to encourage widespread participation, in particular, participation from the Asia-Pacific region, and to foster links between researchers from four continents.

Our most sincere thanks to all the authors, attendees, chairpersons, reviewers, program committee, conference sponsors, and the administrative support staff to make ISDSS'95 a success.

We hope you find this year conference professionally rewarding and stimulating and these Proceedings a valuable resource for your research.

On behalf of the Organizing Committee

Tung X. Bui

ISDSS '95 RESEARCH PAPERS

A Bibliography of Neural Network Business Applications Research. Wong, Bo K., Youngstown State University, U.S.A.; Bodnovich, Thomas A., Youngstown State University, U.S.A.; Selvi, Yakup, Youngstown State University, U.S.A.

A Graph-based Approach for Rule Based Maintenance. Higa, Kunihiko, Hong Kong University of Science and Technology, Hong Kong; Lee, Ho-Geun, Hong Kong University of Science and Technology, Hong Kong.

Application of Case-based Reasoning System to Public Sector Financial Management. Chim, Lorraine K. H., The Hong Kong Polytechnic University, Hong Kong; Tsang, Eddie W. H., Government Secretariat, Hong Kong.

A Decision Model for a Shanghai Stock Market Investor. Chen, Xinglong, National University of Singapore, Singapore; Poh, Hean Lee, National University of Singapore, Singapore.

A Decision Support System for Equipment Replacement Planning with Capital Rationing. Tan, Yew-Lee, Victoria University of Technology, Australia; Hastings, N. A. J., Queensland University of Technology, Australia.

A Fuzzy Rule-based Decision Support System for Securities Trading. Chan, Tin Man, Bank of China Group, Hong Kong; Bolloju, Narasimha, City University of Hong Kong, Hong Kong.

Decision Support Systems for Strategic Management and Business Reengineering Management—The "Wise" Framework. Probst, Andre R., University of Lausanne, Switzerland; Forrer, Andreas P., Swiss Bank Corporation, U.S.A.

Design and Development of a Medical Decision Support System. Sawar, Mohammad Jamil, National Univ. of Sciences & Technology, Pakistan.

A Model Retrieval Algorithm. Wuwongse, Vilas, Asian Institute of Technology, Thailand; Klumklai, Somsak, Asian Institute of Technology, Thailand.

A Problem Formulation Method for the Joint Problem Formulation Approach to Decision Support Systems Development. Ang, T. S. L., Monash University, Australia; Amott, D. R., Monash University, Australia; O'Donnell, P. A., Monash University, Australia.

Automatic Model Structural Identification for Lagrangian Relaxation: UNIK-RELAX. Kim, Chulsoo, Kyungmin College, Korea; Lee, Jae K., Korea Advanced Institute of Science and Technology, Korea; Kim, Min Yong, Kyung Hee University, Korea.

Integrating Arbitrage Pricing Theory and Artificial Neural Networks to Support Portfolio Management. Hung, Shin-Yuan, National Sun Yat-Sen University, Taiwan; Liang, Ting-Peng, National Sun Yat-Sen University, Taiwan; Liu, Victor Wei-Chi, National Sun Yat-Sen University, Taiwan.

An Issues Identifier for On-line Financial Databases. Yen, J., Hong Kong University of Science and Technology, Hong Kong; Chen, H., University of Arizona, U.S.A.; Ma, P. C., Hong Kong University of Science and Technology, Hong Kong; Bui, T. X., Hong Kong University of Science and Technology, Hong Kong.

Building a Graphical User Interface for Information Visualization. Lai, Wei, Edith Cowan University, Australia; Danaher, Maurice, Edith Cowan University, Australia.

Accessing "Computable" Information Over the WWW: The MMM Project. Krishnan, Ramayya, Carnegie-Mellon University, U.S.A.; Muller, Rudolf, Institut Fur Wirtschaftsinformatik, Germany; Schmidt, Peter, Institut Fur Wirtschaftsinformatik, Germany.

But why should I buy your service? Decision Support for Telecommunications Sales Consultants. Tattersall, Colin, PTT Research, Netherlands; Groote, Jacob, PTT Research, Netherlands; Oudshoff, Sandra, PTT Research, Netherlands.

The Negotiable Alternatives Identifier for Negotiation Support: An Improved Algorithm. Bui, T. X., Hong Kong University of Science and Technology, Hong Kong; Yen, J., Hong Kong University of Science and Technology, Hong Kong.

Developing an "Intelligent" DSS for the Multicriteria

Evaluation of Railway Timetables: Problems and Issues. Pomerol, J.-Ch., Universite Paris VI, France; Roy, Bernard, Universite de Paris IX, France; Rosenthal-Sabroux, C., Universite de Paris IX, France.

Negotiating: A Basic Concept of CSCW. Egger, Edeltraud, University of Technology of Vienna, Austria; Hanappi, Hardy, Austrian Academy of Sciences-Socioeconomics, Austria.

Decision Support by Decomposition of Process Systems. Iijima, Junichi, Tokyo Institute of Technology, Japan.

Knowledge Acquisition for Knowledge-Based Systems. Armoni, A., The College of Management, Israel; Ein-Dor, P., Tel-Aviv University, Israel.

DPS-Linda: A Distributed Problem Solving System Development Environment. Kim, Eun-Gyung, Korea Institute of Technology and Education, Korea.

Designing Representations in Decision Support Systems: A Mental Model Perspective. Kuo, Bob Feng-Yang, University of Colorado at Denver, U.S.A.

User Characteristics as a Basis for DSS Design. Paranagama, Priyanka C., Monash University, Australia; Burstein, Frada V., Monash University, Australia; Arnott, David R., Monash University, Australia.

A Decision Support System for Tactics and Reasoning Final Ranking Based on an Interim Result of a League Match. Sakai, Hiroshi, Kyushu Institute of Technology, Japan; Ishiodori, Atsushi, Kyushu Institute of Technology, Japan.

The Problem of Temporal Aggregation in Judgemental Time Series Forecasting. Hoon, Chae, Hyundai Information Technology Co., Ltd., Korea; O'Connor, Marcus, Hyundai Information Technology Co., Ltd., Korea; Lim, Joa Sang, Hyundai Information Technology Co., Ltd., Korea.

Grading and Prevention Decision Support System of Hydraulic Structure Aging. Ji, Qingyan, Agricultural University of Hebei, China; Zheng, Jinghui, Agricultural University of Hebei, China.

A Task-Oriented Graphical Interface to Federated Databases. Peters, P., Informatik V,RWTH Aachen, Germany; Löb, U., Informatik V,RWTH Aachen, Germany; Rodriguez-Pardo, A., Informatik V.,RWTH Aachen, Germany.

Improving DSS Performance with an "Intelligent Touch". Ajenstat, J., University of Quebec at Montreal, Canada; Hodges, W., University of Quebec at Montreal, Canada; Clermont, P., University of Quebec at Montreal, Canada.

Enterprise Modeling and Object Technology. Dolk, Daniel R., Naval Postgraduate School, U.S.A.; Ackroyd, Michael, Naval Postgraduate School, U.S.A.

Improving User Information Satisfaction in Clinical Decision Support Systems. Lee, Matthew, City University of Hong Kong, Hong Kong; Pow, Jacky, Hong Kong Baptist University, Hong Kong.

Measuring Decision Support Systems in the Development Process. Yau, Chuk, Griffith University, Australia; Cheng, Vincent, Griffith University, Australia.

Automated Decision Rule Discovery from Domains with Joint Decision Outcomes: A Decision Tree Induction Approach. Sheng, Olivia R. Liu, University of Arizona, U.S.A.; Chang, Namsik, University of Arizona, U.S.A.

Machine Learning versus Statistical Methods: Analyzing Questionnaire Data for Marketing Decision Making. Terano, Takao, The University of Tsukuba, Japan; Ishino, Yoko, The University of Tsukuba, Japan.

A DSS to Support the Decision Process and the Creativity in the Context of Mutations. Revaz, Eric, University of Lausanne, Switzerland; Pigneur, Yves, University of Lausanne, Switzerland.

An Architecture for Intelligent Distributed Decision Support Systems. Alwast, Ted, Victoria University of Technology, Australia; Miliszewska, Iwona, Victoria University of Technology, Australia; Leung, Clement, Victoria University of Technology, Australia.

Supporting Model Life Cycle with Traceability. Ramesh, Bala, Naval Postgraduate School, U.S.A.

REVIVAL (Reengineering Vision Visualization): A Support System for Business Process Redesign on the Basis of Process Management. Lu, Hsi-Peng, National Taiwan Institute of Technology, Taiwan; Shen, Cheng-Ching, National Taiwan Institute of Technology, Taiwan.

The Trend of Visual Presentations in Decision Support Systems. Ng Tye, Eugenia M. W., Hong Kong Polytechnic University, Hong Kong.

User Adaptable User Interface Management Systems for Decision Support Systems. Ho, Michael M. T., City University of Hong Kong, Hong Kong.

Supporting Strategic Decisions: Requirements, Approach and Application. Kersten, Gregory E., Hong Kong University of Science and Technology, Hong Kong; Cray, David, Carleton University, Canada; Szpakowicz, Stan, University of Ottawa, Canada.

Defining Business Constraints in Relational Databases

Using a Semantic Data Model. Higa, Kunihiko, Hong Kong University of Science and Technology, Hong Kong; Ma, Pai-Chun, Hong Kong University of Science and Technology, Hong Kong; Smith, Michael A., Georgia Institute of Technology, U.S.A.

Developing Decision Support Systems for Inventory Management in China. Jeganathan, Seger, Victoria University of Technology, Australia; Yeh, Chung-Hsing, Monash University, Australia.

Designing Knowledge Based Systems for Model Building: A Relational Database Approach. Luan, Peter Chung Chang, Arizona State University, U.S.A.; Louis, Robert D. St., Arizona State University, U.S.A.

Executable Documents as the Basis for DSS. Ba, Sulin, The University of Texas at Austin, U.S.A.; Kalakota, Ravi, The University of Texas at Austin, U.S.A.; Whinston, Andrew B., The University of Texas at Austin, U.S.A.

Table-Driven-Tables-Processing for Decision Support System Beyond Spread-Sheet. Toyama, Takayuki, Management Systems Technology Inc., Japan; Endoh, Keiichi, IBM Japan Ltd., Japan.

The Logistic Cooperation: A Model of Decision Making "Through Others". Bodart, Francois, Facultes Universitaires Notre-Dame de la Paix, Belgium; Petitjean, Therese, Facultes Universitaires Notre-Dame de la Paix, Belgium.

Tools and Techniques of Systems Analysis for Decision Support Systems. Atkinson, John, Monash University, Australia; Arnott, David, Monash University, Australia.

Toward DSS Science: A Taxonomic Structure for R & D. Khoong, C. M., Information Technology Institute, Singapore.

Applying Multi-Criteria Group Decision Support to Health Policy Formulation. Bots, Pieter W. G., Delft University of Technology, Netherlands; Hulshof, Josee A. M., General and International Health Policy Department, Netherlands.

Developing Groupware Applications Using Middleware Support. Chen, Nian-Shing, National Sun Yat-Sen University, Taiwan; Hsu, Meng-Hsuang, National Sun Yat-Sen University, Taiwan; Chao, Kuo-Jen, National Sun Yat-Sen University, Taiwan.

Distributed Group Support Systems: A Research Framework. Dase, Mary Ann, California State University, U.S.A.; Tung, Lai-Lai, Nanyang Technological University, Singapore; Turban, Efraim, California State Uni. & Nanyang Technological Univ., U.S.A. & Singapore.

SIPINTAS: an Executive Information System for the University of Indonesia. Abdat, Sjarif, University of Indonesia, Indonesia; Chandra, Berlina, University of Indonesia, Indonesia; Ridwan, Saiful B., University of Indonesia, Indonesia; Savolainen, Vesa, University of Jyvaskyla, Finland.

Storage Planner for Apples and Pears: A Planning Support System. Saedt, Anton P. H., Agrotechnological Research Institute (ATO-DLO), Netherlands; Peters, Rene C. W. M., Agrotechnological Research Institute (ATO-DLO), Netherlands.

Use of ODSS in Strategic Planning. Kivijarvi, Hannu, Helsinki School of Economics, Finland; Tuominen, Markku, Lappeerranic University of Technology, Finland.

DecisionNet: An Architecture for Modeling and Decision Support over the World Wide Web. Bhargava, H. K., Naval Postgraduate School, U.S.A.; King, A. S., Naval Postgraduate School, U.S.A.; McQuay, D. S., Naval Postgraduate School, U.S.A.

On Generalized Access to a WWW-based Network of Decision Support Services. Bhargava, H. K., Naval Postgraduate School, U.S.A.; Krishnan, R., Carnegie Mellon University, U.S.A.; Kaplan, D., Carnegie Mellon University, U.S.A.

Towards a Client/Server Open-DSS Protocol Suite for Automating DSS Deployment on the World Wide Web. Goul, M., Arizona State University, U.S.A.; Philippakis, A., Arizona State University, U.S.A.; Kiang, M., Arizona State University, U.S.A.; Fernandes, D., Arizona State University, U.S.A.; Otondo, B., Arizona State University, U.S.A.

Group Decision Support System for Assessment of Problem-based Learning. Ma, Jian, City University of Hong Kong, Hong Kong.

Logical Foundation of Group Decision Support Systems. Wang, Huaiqing, City University of Hong Kong, Hong Kong.

A Comparative Study of the Use of Executive Information Systems between Korea and the United States. Min, Jungki, Claremont Graduate School, U.S.A.; Park, Hung Kook, Sangmyung Women's University, South Korea.

An Investigation of the Effectiveness of Choice Strategies by Elimination: Some Implications for DSS Design. Chau, Y. K. Patrick, Hong Kong University of Science and Technology, Hong Kong; Bui, Tung X., Hong Kong University of Science and Technology, Hong Kong.

Towards a Comparison of the DSS Evaluation Perspectives of Managers in Hong Kong and U.S.A. Toraskar, Kranti, City University of Hong Kong, Hong Kong.

Idea Support for Planning of Corporate Competitive Strategy and for the Knowledge-acquisition in the Business Domain. Watanabe, Mitsuharu, University Tokyo, Japan; Yosizumi, Hidenori, University Tokyo, Japan; Hori, Koichi, University Tokyo, Japan; Hiromatsu, Takeshi, University Tokyo, Japan; Ohsuga, Setsuo, University Tokyo, Japan.

Implementation of Information Kiosk—The Singapore Scenario. Tan, Juay Hiang, Systems & Computer Organisation, Singapore; Tung, Lai Lai, Nanyang Technological University, Singapore.

Organizational Learning and Decision Support Systems Studies. Ho, Joseph Kim-keung, University of Hong Kong, Hong Kong; Sculli, Domenic, University of Hong Kong, Hong Kong.

Case Based Model Base Management Systems. Chi, Robert T., California State University at Long Beach, U.S.A.; Kiang, Melody Y., Arizona State University, U.S.A.; Sun, Bruce, California State University at Long Beach, U.S.A.

Cased-Based Decision Making for Intelligent Decision Support. Burstein, Frada V., Monash University, Melbourne, Australia; Smith, Helen G., Monash University, Melbourne, Australia.

Methodological and Software Environment for Model Formation Based on Reusable Object Frameworks. Becker, Karin, Pontificia Universidade Catolica de Rio Granda do Sul, Brazil; Bodart, Francois, Facultes Universitaires Notre-Dame de la Paix, Belgium.

On Composition and Process in Group Decision Support Systems. Lockett, Geoff, University of Leeds,

United Kingdom; Naude, Peter, Manchester Business School, United Kingdom.

Supporting Group Decision Processes with Software Agents. Bodendorf, Freimut, University of Erlangen-Nuernberg, Nuernberg; Grebner, Robert, University of Erlangen-Nuernberg, Nuernberg; Seitz, Ralph, University of Erlangen-Nuernberg, Nuernberg.

Handling Risks—Making the Most Valuable Decisions when Managing Projects. Kess, Pekka, University of Oulu, Finland; Palo, J., CCC Software Professionals Oy, Finland; Simila, J., CCC Software Professionals Oy, Finland.

Decision Supporting Systems for Uncertainty Condition. Bae, Kyoung-Yul, Sangmyung Women's University, Korea; Hong, Sung-Chan, Sangmyung Women's University, Korea; Kim, Ha-Kyun, National Fisheries University of Pusan, Korea.

The Idea of Scientific Progress in the Field of DSS. Ho, Joseph Kim-keung, Informated Systems Design Ltd., Hong Kong.

A Decision Support Framework for Scenario Management. Blanning, Robert, Vanderbilt University, U.S.A.

Reengineering Support System for Effective Management of Business Reengineering Project. Suh, Eui-Ho, POSTECH, Korea; Choi, H. A., POSRI, Korea; Jeong, Y. Y., POSTECH, Korea; Hong, S. C., KLB Economic Research Institute, Korea.

Development of an IDSS User-Interface Unit for a Cigarette Company in China. Chen, Xiaohong, Central South University of Technology, China; Ho, Xiaojie, Central South University of Technology, China; Li, Yizhi, Central South University of Technology, China.

Index

Credits and Acknowledgments

CHAPTER 1

DSS Insights, pp. 4–5: Excerpted by permission from R. F. Boykin and R. R. Levary, "An Interactive Decision Support System for Analyzing Ship Voyage Alternatives," *Interfaces,* vol. 15, no. 2 (1985): pp. 81–84. Copyright 1985, Operations Research Society of America and The Institute of Management Sciences (now INFORMS), 290 Westminster Street, Providence, Rhode Island 02903 USA.

Box, p. 7: First part excerpted by permission of the author from Peter F. Drucker, "The Age of Social Transformation," *Atlantic Monthly,* vol. 274, no. 5 (1994): p. 62. Second part excerpted from F. G. Rodgers, *The IBM Way* (New York: Harper & Row, 1986), p. 121.

DSS in the News, p. 8: Excerpted from M. Mehler, "CEO Briefing on Information Technology," *Investor's Business Daily,* December 16, 1993, p. 4. Reprinted by permission of Investor's Business Daily, © 1993.

DSS in the News, p. 10: Excerpted from B. Deagon, "Lack of Staff Expertise Often Dooms Government's Information Systems," *Investor's Business Daily,* October 14, 1992, p. 4. Reprinted by permission of Investor's Business Daily, © 1992.

DSS in the News, p. 15: Excerpted from B. Deagon, "Reengineering Hailed as Holy Grail but, Predictably, Can Lag Projections," *Investor's Business Daily,* March 25, 1993, p. 4. Reprinted by permission of Investor's Business Daily, © 1993.

DSS in the News, p. 16: Excerpted by permission from Joseph Maglitta, "Smarten Up!" *Computerworld,* June 5, 1995, p. 85. Copyright 1995 by Computerworld, Inc., Framingham, MA 01701. Reprinted from Computerworld.

DSS in the News, p. 17: Excerpted from B. Deagon, "How Companies Can Pry Productivity Gains from Investments in Technology," *Investor's Business Daily,* April 22, 1992, p. 4. Reprinted by permission of Investor's Business Daily, © 1992.

Box, p. 18: Excerpted from Daniel Katz and Robert L. Kahn, *The Social Psychology of Organizations,* 2d ed., p. 31. Copyright © 1978 by John Wiley & Sons. Reprinted by permission of John Wiley & Sons.

Box, p. 20: Excerpted from Daniel Katz and Robert L. Kahn, *The Social Psychology of Organizations,* 2d ed. (New York: Wiley, 1978), p. 127. Copyright © 1978 by John Wiley & Sons. Reprinted by permission of John Wiley & Sons.

DSS in the News, p. 20: Excerpted from B. Deagon, "CEO Briefing on Information Technology," *Investor's Business Daily,* April 15, 1993, p. 3. Reprinted by permission of Investor's Business Daily, © 1993.

Box, top of p. 27: Excerpted by permission of the author from Peter F. Drucker, "The Age of Social Transformation," *Atlantic Monthly,* vol. 274, no. 5 (1994): p. 76.

CHAPTER 2

DSS Insights, pp. 33–34: Excerpted by permission from P. W. Shannon and R. P. Minch, "A Decision Support System for Motor Vehicle Taxation Evaluation," *Interfaces,* vol. 22, no. 2 (1992): pp. 52–56, 58–63. Copyright 1992, Operations Research Society of America and The Institute of Management Sciences (now INFORMS), 290 Westminster Street, Providence, Rhode Island 02903 USA.

Box, p. 38: Excerpted by permission from Henry Mintzberg, *The Structuring of Organizations* (Englewood Cliffs, N.J.: Prentice Hall, 1979), p. 58.

Box, p. 43: Excerpted by permission from Henry Mintzberg, *The Structuring of Organizations* (Englewood Cliffs, N.J.: Prentice Hall, 1979), pp. 181, 183, 185.

DSS in the News, p. 50: Excerpted from Mark Mehler, "More Power to the Branches: Wachovia's New Loan System," *Investor's Business Daily,* July 13, 1995, p. A6. Reprinted by permission of Investor's Business Daily, © 1995.

CHAPTER 3

DSS Insights, pp. 57–59: Excerpted by permission of Elsevier Science BV, Amsterdam, The Netherlands, from J. Couillard, "A Decision Support System for Vehicle Fleet Planning," *Decision Support Systems,* vol. 9, no. 2 (1993): pp. 149–152, 157–158.

Text section 3.2, "The Decision Maker," pp. 60–71: Adapted by permission from Clyde W. Holsapple, "Decision Support in Multiparticipant Decision Makers," *Journal of Computer Information Systems,* vol. 31, no. 4 (1991): 37–45.

Box, p. 60: Excerpted by permission from Henry Mintzberg, *The Structuring of Organizations* (Englewood Cliffs, N.J.: Prentice Hall, 1979), p. 61.

Box, p. 63: Excerpted from Daniel Katz and Robert L. Kahn, *The Social Psychology of Organizations,* 2d ed. (New York: Wiley, 1978), pp. 509–513. Copyright © 1978 by John Wiley & Sons. Reprinted by permission of John Wiley & Sons.

DSS in the News, p. 68: Excerpted from M. Mehler, "CEO Briefing on Information Technology," *Investor's Business Daily,* December 16, 1993, p. 4. Reprinted by permission of Investor's Business Daily, © 1993.

DSS in the News, p. 71: Excerpted from T. Bunker, "Why Firms Are 'Reengineering' Information Systems," *Investor's Business Daily,* April 3, 1992, p. 3. Reprinted by permission of Investor's Business Daily, © 1992.

Box, top of p. 74: Excerpted by permission from Henry Mintzberg, *The Structuring of Organizations* (Englewood Cliffs, N.J.: Prentice Hall, 1979), p. 58.

DSS in the News, p. 78: Excerpted from T. Bunker, "How Information Systems Helped Colgate-Palmolive Clean Up Results," *Investor's Business Daily,* June 24, 1993, p. 4. Reprinted by permission of Investor's Business Daily, © 1993.

DSS in the News, p. 79: Excerpted from Y. B. Yanes, "Benefits of Information Technology Hard to Figure," *Investor's Business Daily,* January 31, 1991, p. 8. Reprinted by permission of Investor's Business Daily, © 1991.

DSS in the News, p. 84: Excerpted from B. Deagon, "The Reengineering Revolution: Right Cause for U.S. Business Today?" *Investor's Business Daily,* March 24, 1993, p. 4. Reprinted by permission of Investor's Business Daily, © 1993.

CHAPTER 4

DSS Insights, pp. 93–95: Excerpted by permission of Elsevier Science BV, Amsterdam, The Netherlands, from W. P. A. van der Heyden and J. A. Ottjes, "A Decision Support System for the Planning of the Workload on a Grain Terminal," *Decision Support Systems,* vol. 1, no. 4 (1985): pp. 293–296.

Box, p. 96: First part excerpted by permission of the author from Peter F. Drucker, "The Age of Social Transformation," *Atlantic Monthly,* vol. 274, no. 5 (1994): p. 68. Second part excerpted from R. M. Cyert, "Knowledge and Economic Development," *Operations Research,* vol. 39, no. 1 (1991), p. 5.

Text sections 4.2, 4.3, and 4.4, pp. 97–120: Adapted by permission of Transaction Publishers in whole or in part from Clyde W. Holsapple, "Knowledge Management in Decision Making and Decision Support," *Knowledge and Policy,* vol. 8, no. 1 (1995): 5–22. Copyright © 1995 by Transaction Publishers; all rights reserved.

DSS in the News, p. 97: Excerpted by permission from Joseph Maglitta, "Smarten Up!" *Computerworld,* June 5, 1995, p. 86. Copyright 1995 by Computerworld, Inc., Framingham, MA 01701. Reprinted from Computerworld.

DSS in the News, p. 103: Excerpted from B. Deagon, "Has Your Firm Changed Ways to Compete in a 'Knowledge Economy'?" *Investor's Business Daily,* January 6, 1994, p. 3. Reprinted by permission of Investor's Business Daily, © 1994.

DSS in the News, p. 105: Excerpted from "Perspective: Wealth and Specialization," *Investor's Business Daily,* November 30, 1994, p. B1. Reprinted by permission of Investor's Business Daily, © 1994.

DSS in the News, p. 107: Excerpted from B. Deagon, "Appetite for Information," *Investor's Business Daily,* April 1, 1993, p. 4. Reprinted by permission of Investor's Business Daily, © 1993.

DSS in the News, p. 114: Excerpted by permission from Joseph Maglitta, "Smarten Up!" *Computerworld,* June 5, 1995, p. 85. Copyright 1995 by Computerworld, Inc., Framingham, MA 01701. Reprinted from Computerworld.

CHAPTER 5

DSS Insights, pp. 132–134: Excerpted by permission from R. S. Sullivan and S. C. Secrest, "A Simple Optimization DSS for Production Planning at Dairyman's Cooperative Creamery Association," *Interfaces,* vol. 15, no. 5 (1985): pp. 46–51. Copyright 1985, Operations Research Society of America and The Institute of Management Sciences (now INFORMS), 290 Westminster Street, Providence, Rhode Island 02903 USA.

DSS in the News, p. 137: Excerpted by permission of Hitchcock Publishing Co. from J. Snyders, "Decision Making Made Easier," *Infosystems,* vol. 31, no. 8 (August 1984): p. 54.

DSS in the News, p. 138: Excerpted by permission of Hitchcock Publishing Co. from J. Snyders, "Decision Making Made Easier," *Infosystems,* vol. 31, no. 8 (August 1984): p. 54.

DSS in the News, p. 140: Excerpted by permission of Hitchcock Publishing Co. from J. Snyders, "Decision Making Made Easier," *Infosystems,* vol. 31, no. 8 (August 1984): p. 54.

DSS in the News, p. 143: Excerpted by permission of Hitchcock Publishing Co. from J. Snyders, "Decision Making Made Easier," *Infosystems,* vol. 31, no. 8 (August 1984): p. 54.

DSS in the News, p. 147: Excerpted from T. Bunker, "Blue-Collar Computing Brings New Power to the Masses," *Investor's Business Daily,* April 20, 1992, p. 4. Reprinted by permission of Investor's Business Daily, © 1992.

DSS in the News, p. 149: Excerpted from B. Deagon, "CEO Briefing on Information Technology," *Investor's Business Daily,* June 10, 1993, p. 4. Reprinted by permission of Investor's Business Daily, © 1993.

Section 5.5, pp. 155–161: Adapted by permission from Clyde W. Holsapple, "A Human Metaphor for DSS Research," *Journal of Computer Information Systems,* vol. 34, no. 2 (1994): 16–20.

CHAPTER 6

DSS Insights, pp. 169–171: Excerpted by permission from Douglas A. Gray, "Airworthy: Decision Support for Aircraft Overhaul Maintenance Planning, *OR/MS Today,* December 1992, pp. 24–29.

CHAPTER 7

DSS Insights, pp. 204–205: Excerpted by permission from D. Klingman, N. Phillips, D. Steiger, R. Wirth, and W. Young, "The Challenges and Success Factors in Implementing an Integrated Products Planning System for Citgo," *Interfaces,* vol. 16, no. 3 (1986): pp. 1–16. Copyright 1986, Operations Research Society of America and The Institute of Management Sciences (now INFORMS), 290 Westminster Street, Providence, Rhode Island 02903 USA.

Box, top of p. 213: Excerpted by permission from J. R. Marsden and D. E. Pingry, "Generating an Optimal Information System: PMAX-SDLC and the Redirection of MIS Research (or How to Help Joe Eat Salmon)," *Journal of Management Information Systems,* vol. 3, no. 1 (1986): 32–51.

DSS in the News, p. 213: Excerpted from B. Deagon, "Failed Promise of Automation: Why Computer Projects Often Miss Their Goal," *Investor's Business Daily,* April 21, 1992, p. 4. Reprinted by permission of Investor's Business Daily, © 1992.

Box, p. 216: Adapted from R. W. Blanning, "The Functions of a Decision Support System," *Information and Management,* vol. 2 (September 1979): 87–93.

CHAPTER 8

DSS Insights, pp. 231–233: Excerpted by permission from R. Andreu and A. Corominas, "SUCCES92: A DSS for Scheduling the Olympic Games," *Interfaces,* vol. 19, no. 5 (1989): pp. 1–10. Copyright 1989, Operations Research Society of America and The Institute of Management Sciences (now INFORMS), 290 Westminster Street, Providence, Rhode Island 02903 USA.

Box, p. 235: Excerpted from C. W. Holsapple and A. B. Whinston, *Information Jungle* (Homewood, Ill.: Dow Jones–Irwin, 1988), p. 22.

Box, bottom of p. 237: Excerpted by permission of Elsevier Science BV, Amsterdam, The Netherlands, from N. Ghiaseddin, "An Environment for Development of Decision Support Systems," *Decision Support Systems,* vol. 2, no. 3 (1986): p. 198.

DSS in the News, p. 240: Excerpted from K. Doler, "Graphical Software Creates Style Questions for Corporate Programmers," *Investor's Business Daily,* August 19, 1992, p. 4. Reprinted by permission of Investor's Business Daily, © 1992.

DSS in the News, p. 245: Excerpted from B. Deagon, "What Will Next Five Years Bring for Users of Computer-Related Technology?" *Investor's Business Daily,* March 13, 1992, p. 8. Reprinted by permission of Investor's Business Daily, © 1992.

DSS in the News, p. 248: Excerpted from K. Doler, "New Software Program for Desktops Animates Business Presentations," *Investor's Business Daily,* February 11, 1993, p. 3.

Figure 8.6c, p. 249: Courtesy of Virtus Corporation.

DSS in the News, p. 251: Excerpted from T. Bunker, "Virtual Reality Is Put to Test by Highly Demanding Securities Industry," *Investor's Business Daily,* April 22, 1993, p. 4. Reprinted by permission of Investor's Business Daily, © 1993.

CHAPTER 9

DSS Insights, pp. 278–279: Excerpted by permission from S. O. Kimbrough, C. W. Pritchett, M. P. Bieber, and H. K. Bhargava, "The Coast Guard's KSS Project," *Interfaces,* vol. 20, no. 6 (1990): pp. 5–11, 13–15. Copyright 1990, Operations Research Society of America and The Institute of Management Sciences (now INFORMS), 290 Westminster Street, Providence, Rhode Island 02903 USA.

DSS in the News, p. 280: Excerpted from B. Deagon, "Computer Literacy Is Necessary for Increasing Number of Employees," *Investor's Business Daily,* March 31, 1993, p. 4. Reprinted by permission of Investor's Business Daily, © 1993.

DSS in the News, p. 287: Excerpted from B. Deagon, "Through Image Processing, Vision of the Paperless Office Is Coming into Focus," *Investor's Business Daily,* June 29, 1992, p. 3. Reprinted by permission of Investor's Business Daily, © 1992.

DSS in the News, p. 288: Excerpted by permission from Edward Mendelson, "Word Processors: Documents Take the Center Stage," *PC Magazine,* November 9, 1993, pp. 108, 110. Copyright © 1993 Ziff-Davis Publishing Company.

Figure 9.6, p. 293: Reprinted by permission of Michael P. Bieber, New Jersey Institute of Technology, from Michael P. Bieber, "Automating Hypertext for Decision Support," Hypermedia and Information Reconstruction Conference, University of Houston, Clear Lake, December 1990.

DSS in the News, p. 302: Excerpted from M. Stroud, "Massively Parallel Computer Makers Begin to Target Database Applications," *Investor's Business Daily,* April 23, 1992, p. 4. Reprinted by permission of Investor's Business Daily, © 1992.

CHAPTER 10

DSS Insights, pp. 308–310: Excerpted by permission from C. W. DeWitt, L. S. Lasdon, A. D. Waren, D. A. Brenner, and S. A. Melhem, "OMEGA: An Improved Gasoline Blending System for Texaco," *Interfaces,* vol. 19, no. 1 (1989): pp. 85–98. Copyright 1989, Operations Research Society of America and The Institute of Management Sciences (now INFORMS), 290 Westminster Street, Providence, Rhode Island 02903 USA.

DSS in the News, p. 316: Excerpted by permission from James J. Swain, "Crunching Numbers," *OR/MS Today,* October 1994, p. 48.

DSS in the News, p. 326 Excerpted from K. Doler, "New Software Development Tools Help Move Users into World of Multimedia," *Investor's Business Daily,* May 21, 1992, p. 3. Reprinted by permission of Investor's Business Daily, © 1992.

CHAPTER 11

DSS Insights, pp. 337–338: Excerpted by permission from S. Balardo, P. Duchessi, and J. P. Seagle, "Microcomputer Graphics in Support of Vehicle Fleet Routing," *Interfaces*, vol.15, no. 6 (1985): pp. 84–91. © Copyright 1985, Operations Research Society of America and The Institute of Management Sciences (now INFORMS), 290 Westminster Street, Providence, Rhode Island 02903 USA.

DSS in the News, p. 342: Excerpted with permission of DATAMATION magazine from Lee The, "E-Forms Get Smarter," *Datamation*, December 1, 1994, pp. 67–68. © by Cahners Publishing Company.

DSS in the News, p. 343: Excerpted from K. Doler, "How to Speed Forms Processing, Cut Down Errors with PC Software," *Investor's Business Daily*, March 2, 1993, p. 4. Reprinted by permission of Investor's Business Daily, © 1993.

DSS in the News, p. 350: Excerpted from G. Fuchsberg, "Managing: Tabling the Move to Computer Graphics," *Wall Street Journal*, January 30, 1991, p. B1. Reprinted by permission of the *Wall Street Journal*, © 1991 Dow Jones & Company, Inc. All rights reserved worldwide.

DSS in the News, p. 356: Excerpted from K. Doler, "Pinpointing Network Problems Is Becoming Easier with New Software Products," *Investor's Business Daily*, May 5, 1992, p. 4. Reprinted by permission of Investor's Business Daily, © 1992.

DSS in the News, p. 358: Excerpted by permission of Reuters from "'Personal Communication Era Nears, but Market Remains Ill-Defined," *Investor's Business Daily*, April 21, 1993, p. 4.

DSS in the News, p. 359: Excerpted from K. Doler, "Bulletin Board Systems: An Inexpensive Data Communications Option," *Investor's Business Daily*, February 17, 1994, p. 4. Reprinted by permission of Investor's Business Daily, © 1994.

DSS in the News, p. 360: Excerpted from B. Deagon, "Electronic Mail Advantage," *Investor's Business Daily*, April 22, 1993, p. 4. Reprinted by permission of Investor's Business Daily, © 1993.

DSS in the News, pp. 367–368: Excerpted by permission from Douglas Gray and Nader Kabbani, "Right Tool, Place, Time," *OR/MS Today*, April 1994, pp. 35–36, 40–41.

Part Four opening quotation, p. 385: Excerpted by permission from Herbert Simon, "Foreword," in R. Bonczek, C. Holsapple, and A. Whinston, *Foundations of Decision Support Systems* (New York: Academic Press, 1981), pp. xi-xii.

CHAPTER 12

DSS Insights, pp. 388–389: Excerpted by permission from K. V. Ramani, M. R. Patel, and S. K. Patel, "An Expert System for Drug Preformulation in a Pharmaceutical Company," *Interfaces*, vol. 22, no. 2 (1992): pp. 101–108. Copyright 1992, Operations Research Society of America and The Institute of Management Sciences (now INFORMS), 290 Westminster Street, Providence, Rhode Island 02903 USA.

DSS in the News, p. 393: Excerpted from T. Bunker, "How Artificial Intelligence Can Solve Real Problems in Retail Business," *Investor's Business Daily*, February 3, 1993, p. 4. Reprinted by permission of Investor's Business Daily, © 1993.

DSS in the News, p. 401: Excerpted from M. Stroud, "Are Neural Networks about to Come into Their Own?" *Investor's Business Daily*, June 2, 1992, p. 4. Reprinted by permission of Investor's Business Daily, © 1992.

DSS in the News, p. 402: Excerpted by permission of Associated Press from "Computers Beat Doctors at Diagnosing Heart Attacks," *Lexington (Kentucky) Herald-Leader*, December 1, 1991, p. A22.

CHAPTER 13

DSS Insights, pp. 419–420: Excerpted by permission of Learned Information Ltd. from G. M. Lodge and T. C. Frecker, "LUCVAR: A Computer-Based Consultation System for Selecting Lucerne (Alfalfa) Varieties," *Expert Systems,* vol. 6, no. 3 (1989): pp. 166–176.

DSS in the News, p. 428: Excerpted from T. Bunker, "American Express to Shift Much Processing to 'Knowledge Highway,'" *Investor's Business Daily,* August 24, 1992, p. 3. Reprinted by permission of Investor's Business Daily, © 1992.

CHAPTER 14

DSS Insights, pp. 460–462: Excerpted by permission from Peter Duchessi, Hany Shawky, and John P. Seagle, "A Knowledge-Engineered System for Commercial Loan Decisions," *Financial Management,* Autumn 1988, pp. 57–65.

DSS in the News, p. 490: Excerpted from W. M. Bulkeley, "Expert Systems Are Entering into Mainstream of Computers," *Wall Street Journal,* December 5, 1986, p. 29. Reprinted by permission of the *Wall Street Journal,* © 1986 Dow Jones & Company, Inc. All rights reserved worldwide.

CHAPTER 15

DSS Insights, p. 496: Excerpted with permission from N. D. Clarke, M. D. McLeish, T. J. Vyn, and J. A. Stone, "Using Certainty Factors and Possibility Theory Methods in a Tillage Selection Expert System," *Expert Systems with Applications,* vol. 4, no. 1 (1991): pp. 53–54, by Elsevier Science Ltd., Pergamon Imprint, Oxford, England.

DSS in the News, p. 522: Excerpted from M. Stroud, "Companies Finding Practical Applications for Fuzzy Logic in Products, Factories," *Investor's Business Daily,* May 29, 1992, p. 3. Reprinted by permission of Investor's Business Daily, © 1992.

CHAPTER 16

DSS Insights, pp. 558–559: Excerpted by permission of Online, Inc., from M. E. Bates and K. Allen, "Lotus Notes in Action: Meeting Corporate Information Needs," *Database,* vol. 17, no. 4 (1994): pp. 27–33.

DSS in the News, p. 560: Excerpted by permission from Joseph Maglitta, "Smarten Up!" *Computerworld,* June 5, 1995, p. 86. Copyright 1995 by Computerworld, Inc., Framingham, MA 01701. Reprinted from Computerworld.

DSS in the News, p. 563: Excerpted by permission from Joseph Maglitta, "Smarten Up!" *Computerworld,* June 5, 1995, p. 85. Copyright 1995 by Computerworld, Inc., Framingham, MA 01701. Reprinted from Computerworld.

Figure 16.1, p. 567: Adapted by permission from A. S. Philippakis and G. I Green, "An Architecture for Organization-Wide Decision Support Systems," *Proceedings of the Ninth International Conference on Information Systems,* Minneapolis, November 30–December 3, 1988, p. 260.

DSS in the News, p. 570: Excerpted from K. Doler, "Firms Are Employing 'Groupware' to Manage Projects," *Investor's Business Daily,* November 21, 1991, p. 10. Reprinted by permission of Investor's Business Daily, © 1991.

DSS in the News, p. 572: Excerpted from K. Doler, "How Notes Is Put to Use at Countrywide," *Investor's Business Daily,* December 29, 1993, p. 4. Reprinted by permission of Investor's Business Daily, © 1993.

DSS in the News, p. 573: Excerpted from M. Stroud, "With New Prices and Technology, Videoconferencing Units May Merit a Look," *Investor's Business Daily,* April 2, 1992, p. 4. Reprinted by permission of Investor's Business Daily, © 1992.

DSS in the News, p. 574: Excerpted with permission of DATAMATION magazine from Paul A. Strauss, "Beyond Talking Heads: Videoconferencing Makes Money," *Datamation,* October 1, 1994, pp. 38, 41. © by Cahners Publishing Company.

DSS in the News, p. 575: Excerpted by permission of Reuters from "Videoconferencing Appears to Gain as Alternative to Business Travel," *Investor's Business Daily,* May 4, 1993, p. 4.

DSS in the News, p. 576: Excerpted from B. Deagon, "AT&T, Lotus Seek to Simplify Network Chores while Extending Reach," *Investor's Business Daily,* March 18, 1994, p. 4. Reprinted by permission of Investor's Business Daily, © 1994.

DSS in the News, p. 577: Excerpted by permission from Lynda Radosevich, "KPMG Turns to FirstClass Groupware," *Computerworld,* November 21, 1994, p. 58. Copyright 1994 by Computerworld, Inc., Framingham, MA 01701. Reprinted from Computerworld.

DSS in the News, p. 578: Excerpted from Steve Higgins, "New Generation of Handheld Data Assistants Come Closer to Ideal," *Investor's Business Daily,* September 30, 1994, p. A4. Reprinted by permission of Investor's Business Daily, © 1994.

Box, p. 579: Adapted from J. Grudin, "Groupware and Social Dynamics: Eight Challenges for Developers," *Communications of the ACM,* vol. 37, no. 1 (1994): 97.

Steps in nemawashi-based process, pp. 588–589: Adapted by permission of Elsevier Science BV, Amsterdam, The Netherlands, from K. Watabe, C. W. Holsapple, and A. B. Whinston, "Coordinator Support in a Nemawashi Decision Process," *Decision Support Systems,* vol. 8, no. 2 (1992): 87–88.

Box, p. 590: Adapted by permission of Elsevier Science BV, Amsterdam, The Netherlands, from M. J. Shaw and M. S. Fox, "Distributed Artificial Intelligence for Group Decision Support: Integration of Problem Solving, Coordination, and Learning," *Decision Support Systems,* vol. 9, no. 4 (1993): 354–355.

CHAPTER 17

DSS Insights, pp. 600–602: Excerpted by permission of Elsevier Science BV, Amsterdam, The Netherlands, from A. Dennis, D. Vogel, J. Nunamaker, Jr., and A. Heminger, "Bringing Automated Support to Large Groups: The Burr-Brown Experience," *Information and Management,* vol. 18, no. 3 (1990): 113–117.

Box, p. 609: Excerpted with permission of Ablex Publishing Corporation from R. Johansen, "Groupware: Future Directions and Wild Cards," *Journal of Organizational Computing,* vol. 2, no. 1 (1991): p. 225.

DSS in the News, p. 616: Excerpted from R. J. Maturi, "Computers Can Improve the Efficiency of Meetings," *Investor's Business Daily,* November 2, 1990, p. 6. Reprinted by permission of Investor's Business Daily, © 1990.

List of thirteen decision support processors, pp. 623–625: Adapted by permission from D. R. Vogel, J. F. Nunamaker, Jr., W. B. Martz, Jr., R. Grohowski, and C. McGoff, "Electronic Meeting System Experience at IBM," *Journal of Management Information Systems,* vol. 6, no. 3 (1989): 25–43.

List of eleven GDSS success factors, p. 626: Adapted by permission from R. Grohowski, C. McGoff, D. Vogel, B. Martz, and J. Nunamaker, "Implementing Electronic Meeting Systems at IBM: Lessons Learned and Success Factors," *MIS Quarterly,* vol. 14, no. 4 (1990): 380–381.

Box, p. 627: Excerpted by permission of Elsevier Science BV, Amsterdam, The Netherlands, from J. Nunamaker, Jr., D. Vogel, A. Heminger, B. Martz, R. Grohowski, and C. McGoff,

"Experiences at IBM with Group Support Systems: A Field Study," *Decision Support Systems,* vol. 5, no. 2 (1989): pp. 186–187.

Section 17.5, pp. 634–643: Substantial portions of this section are adapted by permission of Kluwer Academic Publishers from Clyde W. Holsapple, Hsiangchu Lai, and Andrew B. Whinston, "Implications of Negotiation Theory for Research and Development of Negotiation Support Systems," *Group Decision and Negotiation* (in press).

Table 17.6, p. 637: Reprinted by permission from C. W. Holsapple, H. Lai, and A. B. Whinston, "Implications of Negotiation Theory for Research and Development of Negotiation Support Systems," Research Paper No. 69, *Kentucky Initiative for Knowledge Management,* College of Business and Economics, University of Kentucky, Lexington, KY, 1994.

Figure 17.11, p. 641: Adapted by permission from C. W. Holsapple, H. Lai, and A. B. Whinston, "Implications of Negotiation Theory for Research and Development of Negotiation Support Systems," Research Paper No. 69, *Kentucky Initiative for Knowledge Management,* College of Business and Economics, University of Kentucky, Lexington, KY, 1994.

Figure 17.12, p. 642: Adapted by permission from C. W. Holsapple, H. Lai, and A. B. Whinston, "Implications of Negotiation Theory for Research and Development of Negotiation Support Systems," Research Paper No. 69, *Kentucky Initiative for Knowledge Management,* College of Business and Economics, University of Kentucky, Lexington, KY, 1994.

CHAPTER 18

DSS Insights, pp. 653–654: Excerpted by permission from W. C. Burkan, "The New Role for 'Executive' Information Systems," *I/S Analyzer,* vol. 30, no. 1 (1992): pp. 4–5, published by United Communications Group (800/929-4824).

Figure 18.1, p. 658: Courtesy of Comshare, Inc.

Figure 18.2, p. 660: Adapted by permission of Elsevier Science BV, Amsterdam, The Netherlands, from I. Millet and C. H. Mawhinney, "Executive Information Systems: A Critical Perspective," *Information and Management,* vol. 23, no. 1 (1992): 85.

Figure 18.3, p. 661: Courtesy of Comshare, Inc.

DSS in the News, p. 662: Excerpted from Kathleen Doler, "Corporate, Government Users Call Exception Monitor a Useful Tool," *Investor's Business Daily,* August 31, 1994, p. A3. Reprinted by permission of Investor's Business Daily, © 1994.

DSS in the News, p. 663: Excerpted from Kathleen Doler, "New Software Helps Decision Makers Sift through Reams of Data," *Investor's Business Daily,* August 30, 1994, p. A4. Reprinted by permission of Investor's Business Daily, © 1994.

Table 18.1, p. 670: From M. B. Curtis, "The Accountant's Contribution to Executive Information Systems," *Journal of End User Computing,* vol. 6, no. 3 (1994): 3–10. Copyright 1994, Idea Group Publishing (Harrisburg, PA). Reprinted by permission.

CHAPTER 19

DSS Insights, pp. 679–680: Excerpted from M. Mehler, "Boeing Leaves Past Behind with Production Redesign," *Investor's Business Daily,* May 23, 1995, p. A8. Reprinted by permission of Investor's Business Daily, © 1995.

Box, p. 681: Excerpted by permission of Harvard Business School Press from Dorothy Leonard-Barton, *Wellsprings of Knowledge,* p. xiii. Copyright © 1995 by the President and Fellows of Harvard College; all rights reserved.